Insider's Guide to Beijing 2008
在北京生活指南 2008

白康瑞（Adam Pillsbury）等 编

五洲传播出版社
· 北 京 ·

图书在版编目（CIP）数据

北京指南＝Insider's Guide．2008：英文／《城市漫步》北京版英文编辑部编．—北京：五洲传播出版社，2007．9

ISBN 978-7-5085-1172-6

Ⅰ．北… Ⅱ．城… Ⅲ．旅游指南－北京市－英文 Ⅳ．K928.91

中国版本图书馆 CIP 数据核字（2007）第 136417 号

Insider's Guide to Beijing 2008

责任编辑：	樊程旭
特约审稿：	王国振
出版发行：	五洲传播出版社
地　　址：	中国北京　海淀区北小马厂 6 号华天大厦 23-26 层
邮　　编：	100038
电　　话：	58880274
网　　址：	http://www.cicc.org.cn
印　　刷：	北京盛通印刷股份有限公司
开　　本：	889mm×1194mm　1/32
印　　张：	22.5
版　　次：	2007 年 9 月北京第 1 版
印　　次：	2007 年 9 月北京第 1 次印刷
字　　数：	660 千字
图片张数：	600 张
印　　数：	1-14 000 册
书　　号：	ISBN 978-7-5085-1172-6
定　　价：	90.00 元

版权所有，侵权必究，质量问题请联系发行部（86 10 5820 7101）进行调换

Insider's Guide to Beijing
2008

Immersion Guides

General Enquiries:
5820 7100
editor@immersionguides.com
www.immersionguides.com
www.thebeijinger.com

Managing Editor Adam Pillsbury

Editors Reid Barrett, John Brennan, Shelley Jiang, Gabriel Monroe, Jackie Yu

Principal Contributors Eric Abrahamsen, Lee Ambrozy, Jim Boyce, Jon Campbell, Cate Conmy, Alison M. Friedman, Jonathan Haagen, Matt P. Jager, Roy Kesey, Kaiser Kuo, Catherine Lee, Zoe Li, Ann Mah, Eli Marshall, Halla Mohieddeen, Alex Pasternack, Judy Pillsbury, Oliver Robinson, Berwin Song, Alice Wang, Haley Warden, Amy Xue, April Zhang

Photo Editor Simon Lim

Principal Photographers Bai Xu, Tom Carter, Natalie Behring, Mary Dennis, Nick Otto, Janek Zdzarski Jr, Luna Zhang, Judy Zhou

Designers Yuki Jia, Li Xing, Susu Luo, Helen He

Indexer Tammy Liu

Copy Editors Tom Spearman, Lilly Chow

Proofreaders Ian Provan, Iain Shaw

Listings Auditor Jiang Jun

General Enquiries:
5820 7700
Distribution: 5820 7101
sales@immersionguides.com
distribution@immersionguides.com
marketing@immersionguides.com
www.immersionguides.com
www.thebeijinger.com

General Manager Michael Wester

Business Development Toni Ma, Lisa Ji

Sales Manager Claire Tang

Sales Elena Damjanoska, Lynn Cui, Ada Dong, Sally Fang, Kelly Han, Catherine Li, Abby Wu, Cindy Zhang, Sophia Zhou, Emma Zhuang

Distribution Zoe Wang, Victoria Wang

Marketing Fiona Lee, Lynn Lin, Nancy Ding, Kathy Zheng

Finance & Accounting James Li, Teresa Tian, Tracy Ye, Angela Zheng

Office Manager Eileen Huang

Reception Coco Kou, Jenny Wang

Foreword

Right. Let's address the elephant in the room.

Unless you've just arrived from Mars, you've probably heard that Beijing is going to host the Olympic Games. No matter how you feel about the Big O, 2008 will be a watershed year for Beijing. When the Olympic countdown clocks finally hit 00:00:00 on the insanely auspicious date of 08-08-08, four billion pairs of eyes will be watching us on TV. Love the hype or loathe it, the Games will be a historical reference point for many years to come, particularly if they have the lasting impact they had on such former host cities as Seoul and Barcelona.

But that still leaves September 2008 – and the rest of the year, come to think of it. Fortunately, as you'll discover in these pages, Beijing has much more to offer than athletic spectacle. In fact, this city of 15 million is one of the most transfixing, dynamic cities on earth, where confidence in the future is a given and change is the only constant.

Trying to capture such a fast-moving target as Beijing is no easy task, which is why the *Insider's Guide to Beijing* is updated annually. This is also why we drew on the collective knowledge and experiences of more than 40 Beijing "insiders" who contributed articles and photographs, as well as on the questions, comments and critiques we have received about the past three editions.

The result, we believe, is an unparalleled resource for residents and visitors with curiosity to burn. The *Guide* is a trove of useful information on topics like housing, education, medical care and business registration. It also puts the accent on fun and adventure with large sightseeing and excursion chapters, as well as listings of over 130 bars, 200 restaurants and 300 shops. Adding perspective are the *Guide*'s 130 sidebar articles, which gleefully delve into topics weighty and obscure, from what to do after a traffic accident to why Beijing has four bars named "Pure Girl."

Our hope is that this book will help you get the most out of your stay in Beijing, whether it lasts a week, a month, a year or a lifetime.

Please send us your feedback. The *Insider's Guide to Beijing* is a collective endeavor designed to serve a community of readers, of which you are now a member. It's only by letting us know where we erred and what we missed; by asking us any and every Beijing-related question you can imagine; or by pitching story ideas to us, that we can hope to improve the next edition.

We look forward to hearing from you.

Adam Pillsbury
editor@immersionguides.com

About our Contributors

Eric Abrahamsen is a freelance writer and translator. He has so far mercilessly consumed three FLTRP Chinese-English dictionaries in the course of his studies, and wears their battered, bloody covers on a string around his neck. He only comes out for Golden Week holidays, and spotting him swimming beneath Yinding Bridge is said to augur either a bumper year for willow catkins, or hail.

Lee Ambrozy is a writer, translator, and critic of contemporary culture and art in China. She is a regular contributor to *that's Beijing*, *that's Shanghai*, artnet, ARTiT, and other publications, a masters candidate in Chinese Art Theory at Tsinghua University and the curator of sinopop.org, a website devoted to Chinese pop culture and art.

Beijing-born webmaster **Bai Xu** enjoys drinking beer, reading books, traveling and exploring his hometown on foot and bike with his trusty camera at his side. His expensive and time-consuming hobbies could explain his empty bank account and current single lifestyle.

One college summer, **Reid Barrett** took a Chinese class "on a whim." Six years on, he has discovered Beijing's drawl at Beijing Normal University, experimented with a Taiwanese lisp in San Diego and perfected his Russian-accented Chinese at the Xinjiang dive near his apartment. Reid still engages in many whim-related China activities but now they are more apt to be inner-tubing near the Summer Palace and unexpected detours on his commute home. His favorite Friendly is Jingjing.

Natalie Behring, whose portrait of a gymnast is featured in this book's composite cover image, is a freelance photographer based in Beijing, covering stories throughout China and Asia. From a humble beginning in rural America, she arrived in China in 1994 fresh out of university, where she stumbled into photography. Her work includes mostly editorial subjects but also food and architectural images. She is currently working on a project about the modernization of Beijing, which can be seen at www.nataliebehring.com.

It didn[1]t take long for **Jon Campbell** to drum his way into the music scene; pretty soon thereafter he was writing about it for *that's Beijing* and a range of international media. When he's not co-producing the Time Arts Jazz Series, working on the Midi Festival, or promoting any number of shows (ygtwo.com), he rocks with bands Black Cat Bone and RandomK(e). Occasionally he goes to Scandinavia in the company of Chinese punk rockers.

Ithaca New York native **Mary X Dennis** has wanted to come to China ever since Big Bird and Barkley made it look cool in the 80s. Last year she realized her dream and is still here, currently waiting for the ponds to freeze so she can combine her two favorite activities: playing hockey and being outside. She also likes to take pictures.

Photojournalist **Tom Carter** of San Francisco has spent the past two years traveling extensively throughout the 33 provinces of China. He is the author of *CHINA: Portrait of a People*.

When not busy managing communications for an NGO in Beijing, **Jim Boyce** is searching for excellent cocktails, eccentric characters and the latest news in Beijing's drinking scene. This Canuck operates blogs on Beijing's drinking scene (beijingboyce.com) and China's wine scene (grapewallofchina.com).

John Brennan spent a year in China in 1982 teaching English at Beijing Number 2 Foreign Language Institute. Before he returned to China in 2005, he worked in Australia as a policy officer in education and training. In Beijing he gets by as a freelance writer and editor.

Alison M. Friedman has been working in the performing arts in China as a research scholar, choreographer/performer, and consultant since 2002 when she came to Beijing on a Fulbright Fellowship to research the development of modern dance in this country. She escapes Beijing pollution by touring abroad with the Beijing Modern Dance Company as their International Director, and since 2007 she has worked with Ge Hua Cultural Development Group on the Opening Ceremonies of the 2008 Beijing Olympic Games.

Jonathan Haagen is a feature writer for the *Economist Intelligence Unit*, and contributes regularly to the *Far Eastern Economic Review*, *China International Business* and *City Weekend*. His first novel, *Climbing Strange Mountain*, was released by the Liaoning Publishing Group in the fall of 2006. Unsigned copies are considered rare and valuable.

Matt P. Jager's mom told him that he's as cool as he wants to be. After stunted careers in cliff-diving, Stoic dentistry, rock-and-rolling and global loitering, *that's Beijing* rescued him from his aimless misery. Now he is committing suicide by liver cirrhosis for ten grand a month, writing and researching and slaughtering brain cells by the bazillion as nightlife editor for the monthly magazine. He wants to be pretty cool.

Beijing-born **Shelley Jiang** longs to pass for a real Beijinger after 17 years in the US, but to her chagrin, she is generally mistaken for Korean, Vietnamese or – the worst – a *nanfangren*. That doesn't stop her from path-integrating through the city's streets on her bicycle, on an endless search for decent coffee, proper clubbin' and unexpected escapades. Editing and writing for Let's Go helped her fall in love with book-making and overly ambitious travel plans.

Roy Kesey's fiction, nonfiction and poetry have appeared in more than sixty magazines, including *McSweeney's*, *The Georgia Review* and *The Iowa Review*, and in several anthologies including *The Future Dictionary of America*, *New Sudden Fiction*, *The Robert Olen Butler Prize Anthology* and *Best American Short Stories*. He's the author of a novella called *Nothing in the World* and a collection of short stories called *All Over*.

Kaiser Kuo was born in New York, raised in Arizona, and really started living when he moved to Beijing, where he's lived for about 15 years. He's written *that's Beijing*'s back page "Ich Bin Ein Beijinger" column since the magazine launched in October 2001. Between columns he serves as digital strategy director for an ad agency, plays guitar in a Chinese heavy metal band, writes a blog, and tries to be a good husband to his wife Fanfan and a good father to their two young children.

Catherine Lee – "C-Pain" to her colleagues – first fell in love with Beijing during her gap year, but it was only during her summer as an Immersion Guides intern that she discovered her inner fashionista. The theme days she initiated revolutionized office style, making the IG team the best dressed/flashiest/trashiest/clashiest under heaven. When not shopping for sparkly treasure, she enjoys wearing her sunglasses at night and sipping margaritas with *chuan'r*. Back at Stanford, she walks backwards and makes music.

Freelance food writer and translator **Zoe Li** first associated food with power when her mother used chicken mcnugget remunerations and coca cola embargoes to control her children. Zoe is now trying to come to terms with her dark obsession with cheap fried finger foods and fizzy drinks, which she thinks she hides well within *laziji* and champagne, and makes sure to do whatever her mother asks because she loves her mother deeply.

Simon Lim left his native Singapore in 1988 for his first China visit, proceeding to drift from continent to continent, taking photographs all the while. Since floating back in Beijing in 2002, he's published three manuals on the art of charming one's way out of a traffic ticket. When not nursing his passion for making Beijing look beautiful, he follows his muse to Egyptian hookah opium dens and Afghani gun markets as often as he can.

Freelance journalist and food lover **Ann Mah** lived in Beijing for four years. A former Viking Penguin book editor, she has written for the *International Herald Tribune*, *Conde Nast Traveler*, *South China Morning Post* and other publications. Ann is currently researching a self-study project on the regional cuisines of China.

Composer **Eli Marshall** has lived in Beijing since 2003 (first arriving on a Fulbright grant), has taught at the Central Conservatory, and is artistic director of the Beijing New Music Ensemble (www.beijingnewmusic.org). His works have been performed throughout Asia, Europe, and the United States; his recent work, based on Matteo Ricci, premiered in Macau and was awarded the top prize in ASCAP's 2007 young composer awards.

Halla Mohieddeen: "Ah come frae Scotland, ken whit ah mean, pal? I like goan shoappin' and buyin' stuff like trackie bottoms which ah pit in ma soaks. Ah like buying booze an all, and goan fir Buckie seshes wi' ma bezzies. China's guid, 'cos ye can get deep-fried mars bars and cheap bevvies. Ah also ken whit the weather's like the day efter it happens. Aye. Now get oota ma face or ah'll rip yer jaw."

Two years after moving to Beijing from Taipei, Azorean descendant **Gabriel "Lhastravaganza" Monroe** wholeheartedly believes that wearing pajamas in public testifies to spiritual indigenousness. As an Immersion Guides editor, Gabriel bullies talented writers into learning to make a thizz face. When not stirring thick vats of glue, words and whimsy, he makes up vaguely ribald Chinese nicknames for days of the week and regulates his serotonin flow with an ever-present stash of homegrown habaneros.

A self-professed child of the colonies, **Simon Ostheimer** grew up in British Hong Kong, bearing witness to the historical handover in 1997. A magazine editor by profession, this rather young "Old China Hand," is working his way through the publishing houses of China. Formerly a resident of Shanghai, a period which included work for *City Weekend*, *Time Out* and *that's Shanghai*, he is currently Managing Editor of Beijing-based lifestyle monthly, *tbjhome*.

When **Alex Pasternack**, an itinerant New Yorker cum Beijinger, isn't banging his head to some *yaogun*, he's entranced by the heavy metal and the rest of the development transforming the city around him. Before landing in Beijing, Alex lived in Hong Kong and Siberia. He's written for Fodors, Let's Go, *Time*, *Entertainment Weekly*, *The New York Observer* and *that's Beijing*.

Neither his upbringing in Paris nor degree in classics predestined **Adam Pillsbury** to life in Beijing, to which he and wife Judy moved "for two years" in '98. After stints as a teacher and freelance writer, he found his calling editing books and maps with deft and effervescent colleagues. A funk bassist in a post-rock band, Adam is happiest in the company of his wife and crackerjack daughters, Alexandra and Eliza.

Having trained her eye in the markets, boutiques and secondhand stores of Tokyo, Paris and Toronto, artist and Yabaolu expert **Judy Pillsbury** has scoured Beijing for nearly a decade, children in tow, in search of good deals, great finds and amazing tales to share with Immersion Guides and *that's Beijing* readers.

Found asleep on the steps outside the office, **Oliver Robinson** was lured into working full-time for *that's Beijing* with the promise of a warm bowl of milk each morning. Needless to say, the warm milk never materialized, which was lucky since Oliver recently discovered he is dangerously lactose intolerant. "I'm dangerously lactose intolerant," he said recently. Oliver compensates for his inability to attend milk and cheese events with an honest temperament and a keen interest in bespoke costuming.

After **Berwin Song** traded his low-paying freelancer lifestyle and beloved Bay Area hip-hop beat for the full-time, low-paying position as Music (and Stage, and In Print, and finally, Deputy Managing) editor of *that's Beijing*, he got so dangerously immersed in the local music scene, he became a giant man-eating catfish. But because he has dreads instead of whiskers, he was happily accepted into a Chinese reggae band.

Alice Wang has been interested in film since childhood, when she watched movies in the open-air cinema in her seaside hometown in Shandong. Her favorite director is Hou Hsiao-hsien, whose film *A Summer at Grandpa's* (*Dongdong de Jiaqi*) is exactly like her childhood experiences in her grandpa's home. Alice dreams of sating her fixation with the silver-screen at film festivals around the world.

Haley Warden hails from the Middle of Nowhere, Maine, and stumbled into Beijing one day after too many cups of coffee. Currently in her senior year at Yale, Haley capped off several longish stints in China since 2002 with an internship at Immersion Guides, where she excelled at harassing writers and editing listings. She enjoys sparkly things, organizing her desk, and her host family's dumplings.

Despite growing up in suburban Texas, **Amy Xue** is a city girl at heart who has grown fond of squirming through sweaty subways, perching precariously on the back of brake-less bikes, haggling over every *kuai*, and attempting to mask her Shanghai accent with sporadic 'er addendums. This carboholic will miss Beijing's bounty of *bing*, *baozi*, *jiaozi* and noodles, but she is excited about returning to clean air, sunny skies, and palm trees at Stanford University.

Old-school Beijinger and original Insider **Jackie Yu**'s bicycle is broken, and having to find another hobby with which to kill time, he took up traveling. He returns from each trip with dirt-cheap souvenirs and empty pockets, which adds to his panic over how to make his mortgage payments and pay his car bills. His experiences have, however, given him the courage to mishandle the Housing & Hotels and Transportation chapters.

Janek Zdzarski Jr from Poland first came to China in 2001 and… was amazed. More than one year ago he quit his job as a news photographer for a major Polish newspaper and moved to Beijing with his lovely wife, Ola. Janek is a freelance photojournalist for Chinese and European media and sometimes writes stories and articles. China is like a drug for him that makes him alternately feel happy, sad, empowered and ill. His remedy is a camera and a notebook – the effects can be found at: www.zdzarski.com

Once upon a time, **Luna Zhang** worked for a software company and enjoyed dancing, shopping, traveling and watching movies … but it got boring. So in 2005 she picked up a camera and quit her job to become a freelance photographer – a profession which liberated her artistic spirit. Luna loves taking portraits, as well as anything else that communicates the human experience. She hopes to produce works that capture the zeitgeist and stir the soul.

Last but not least, we extend a heartfelt shout out to our editorial colleagues at True Run Media whose wit and wisdom inspired us to soldier on through the dog days of summer. They are giants among humans, really, without whose expertise and assistance this book would not exist. We'd like to single out, in semi-geographical order, Editorial Director **Jerry** "DJ Bootyclap" **Chan**; *tbjHome*-y and ambrosial grinch **Jie Yang**; Staff Writer and Olympic Spirit **April Zhang**; Visual Editor and cartoon master **Joey Guo**; *tbjKids* editors and family funkateers **Cate Conmy** and **Simon Fowler**; the unflappable family of listings editors **Paul Pennay**, **Cecily Huang**, **Venus Lau** and **Michaela Kabat** (our answer to K.C. and the Sunshine Band), and especially our wise, sharp-eyed and forgiving copy editors **Tom Spearman** and **Lilly Chow**, without whom our book would be tragically ridden with misspeelings.

And of course, without the inspiration, hugs, teamwork and support of the entire True Run Media family – especially our rainmakers, Business Development Manager **Toni Ma** and General Manager **Mike Wester** (see Business and Work, p581) – we would most likely be no more than an unknown ecosystem of beautiful, tragically talented germs.

Table of Contents

INTRODUCTION

Merry Go-Round 3
Come home on the Special 8

Frontier Town 6
A brief history of Beijing

Sidebars
Forbidden Fish and Imaginary Ingots 16
Why James Kynge remains bullish on Beijing

HOUSING & HOTELS

Gimme Shelter 21
Finding a billet in boomtime Beijing

E.T. Own Home 33
Buying a home in Beijing

Be Our Guest 44
Hostels and hotels

Hotel Directory 45

Sidebars
There's No Place Like Home 27
Lessons on host family life, straight from the Mouse's mouth

Renter's Rights 30
Locking horns with my landlord in a Beijing court

Four Sides, Six Steps 38
Buying a Beijing courtyard

FOOD

Joy by the Mouthful 53
Beijing's evolving culinary scene

Restaurant Directory 57

A Matter of Taste 97
that's Beijing's 2007 Reader Restaurant Awards

A Taste of Home 104
International and organic groceries … and bakeries!

Bottles Up 110
Buying wine in Beijing

Cha Cha Cha! 114
How to tell your *Longjing* from your *Molihua*

Sidebars
Quack Service 61
A brief history of Beijing's most famous dish

The Long "Capitalist Road" 62
Beijing's first private restaurant

vii

Hutong Hankerings 70
Distinctly Beijing delights nestle in our alleyway warrens

At Your Service 75
An ode to Beijing's distinctive waitresses

A Cauldron for Every Palate 76
Hot pot hot spots

Five Winds of Flavor 84
Dishing delight

Don't Meat Me in Beijing 89
Tips for maintaining a glorious vegetarian lifestyle

The Case for the Street....................................... 90
Why Beijing's *baozi* are still one of life's simple pleasures

A Culinary Tour of China 92
Without ever leaving Beijing

I Eat Alone 96
Yeah, with nobody else

Editor's Picks 103
For a beautiful scarf

The Dread-Free Dinner Party 106
Be the host with the most

Picks of the Bunch 112
A flight of fancy local wines

KIDS

Have Child, Will Travel 119
Raising kids in Khanville

Joy, in a Bundle 124
A primer on adopting children in China

From *Aiyo* to *Ayi* 126
How to cultivate a super *ayi*

School Daze 131
The ABCs (and RMBs) of education

School Directory 138

Sidebars

Bringing Up Baby, Beijing-Style 122

Understanding *Ayi* 129
Why they do the things they do

Taking the Local Route 136
Expat parents choose Chinese schools for their kids

Lord Rabbit of the Moon 147
A Beijing fairytale

A Year of Chinese Culture 158
Fun ways to help them integrate

Duck and Cover.. 172
What (not) to do in an emergency

ART & CULTURE

Happenings at the Hub 177
The arts in Beijing in 2007 and beyond

Unearthing China's Avant-Garde 178
A Short History of Art, 1979-2006

Names You Need to Know 184
Get up to speed on the Beijing art scene

Art Hoods On and
Off the Beaten Path 189
Explore Beijing like an art maven

The Show Will Go On 199
A brief history of modern Chinese theater

Flyin' High 204
Acrobatics shows

Classical Music 207	**Temples** 240
Dancing Outside the Lines 215	**City Walls & Gates** 251
Modern dance in Beijing	**Bring in the Noise** 254
A Journey of Moon and Clouds 217	**Parks** 258
Chinese cinema then and now	**Arts, Architecture & Antiques** 262
The ABCs of CCTV 224	**Museums** 263
Time to turn on the tube	**Other** 265
Sidebars	**Tombs** 268
A View From the Edge 187	**Great Wall** 268
Li Zhenhua on tomorrow's art innovators	
Old Epic, New Journey 193	**Sidebars**
Chi Peng uses digital art to explore a classic of his childhood	It's Lonely at the Top 235
Sage of the Internal Stage 198	The trials and tribulations of being a Chinese emperor
The fiction of Lu Li	Rank Real Estate 232
Theater without Bounds	A stroll through the Legation Quarter
A talk with director Lin Zhaohua 201	Backpedaling 239
Tricks of the Trade 205	Rethinking the pedicab tour
A peek inside the China National Acrobatic Troupe	No *danzi* needed 246
Tan Dun's Musical Alchemy 209	Those old Xicheng neighborhoods
Making Chamber Music Locally 212	Wonderwall...252
The ups and downs of the indie classical scene	An ode to Beijing's vanished city walls
	Roman Holiday..256
SIGHTSEEING	A taste of Tivoli in Rendinghu Park
Spectral Mindset 229	Tranquil Heart 260
The Cubist approach to sightseeing	Rediscovering Beihai's historical treasures
Tian'anmen Square........................... 230	Beijing: The B-Sides 266
Forbidden City 231	An urban explorer wanders the city's underbelly
Lifestyles of the Rich and Famous .. 234	Mythbusting..272
	Great Wall historian David Spindler sets seven things straight

ix

NIGHTLIFE

Now *That* was Fun 277
The good old days … are getting better

Party Zones 283
Meet the clumps

'Til the Break of Dawn 295
Clubbing in Beijing

Bar & Club Directory 296

Toast of the Town 315
that's Beijing 2007 Reader Bar & Club Awards

A Long Strange Trip 324
Beijing rock goes international

Breakout Artists 332
Beijing's hottest bands

Hear Ye, Hear Ye 338
Yaogun classics

Live Alive 342
Beijing's rockinest music venues

Sidebars

Purer by the Dozen 280
The Pure Girls' saga

Evolution of the Peking Man 286
Bar-hopping through the millennia

Proprietors' Picks 293
Busman's holidays

The Yen Recipe 294
Beijing's nomadic party chefs

"China Fury" 301
Hell hath nothin' on her

Death Game! … and More 304
A primer on drinking, Seoul-style

Be Glad! 311
Out of the closet, into the clubs

Frankly Speaking 312
A chat with Beijing nightlife pioneer turned wine shepherd

And Now for Something Completely Different 322
The mainstream – karaoke!

Festive Ideology 329
Midi continues to define the Chinese rock festival

Invested in Beijing Rock 330
A closer look at D-22

Yaogun Meets the World 336
Subs on the road in Nordic Europe

A Family Affair 340
The hottest indie label in town, Tag Team Records

Metal Therapy 346
Don't mind the occasional blood spilling

SHOPPING

Superb Swag 351
Beijing's shopping spoils

Shopping Directory 352

Clothing & Accessories 353

Home 374

Other 385

Sidebars

A Man-Purse for Every Season 354
It's a lifestyle

Branded to Bankruptcy? 358
The freakonomics of face

String Theory 364
A primer on how to buy pearls in Beijing

A Perfect Fit...371
Tips to make your tailoring experience terrific

9 to 5 Glamour....................................372
Princess or pauper, you gotta look good

HEC of a Place....................................376
Beware: equipment nirvana

The Gold and the Dross.......................386
The painful truth about "antiques"

BYOB: Bring Your Own Bamboo 394
Save the pandas!

Lions, Tigers, Bears … and Marc Jacobs! 401
Shopping at the Zoo

Haggling 101 402
Steps to a delightful discount dance

Somebody in Beijing Loves Me… 406
… but all they got me was this lousy shirt?!

Behind Enemy Lines 413
Up close and personal with Yashow's jazziest jeans seller

SPORTS & FITNESS

Olympian Appetites 417
Our thirst for sport in the capital

Sports Directory 418

Olympic Blitz 440
How the capital is reinventing itself for 2008 and beyond

Sidebars

The Peking Pentathlon 425
A modest proposal

The Global Game 426
At home on the pitch

Glide 429
So nice on the ice

Olympic Venues...................................437

Root Root Root 442
The home team

Olympic After-parties 457
Where to pull an Olympian

The Olympic Curse? 458
Listen to the skeptics at your own risk

On Your Marks 454
Olympic warm-up events calendar

Meet Judose..456
One sport that definitely *won't* make the Olympics

Take a Bite Out of the Language Barrier 460
Excerpts from the handbook *Olympic Security English*

HEALTH & BEAUTY

An Apple a Day 465
Still seeing the doctor anyway

Got You Covered............................... 470
Pain relief for health insurance headaches

Special Deliveries............................. 472
Giving birth in Beijing

Medical Directory............................. 476

Lookin' Good and Livin' Easy 490
Beijing beauty

xi

Sidebars

Going Public 468
Embracing the local Chinese hospital

Spotting Roots from Dragon Eyes 474
A few Chinese medicinal foods – and some recipes to boot!

Treat Yourself to Thailand 479
Medical tourism: mixing work and play

Heart and Soul 480
Holistic healing beyond the body

Safer Safe Sex 483
Know thy birth control pills

Is it Magic or is it TCM? 484
The theory and practice behind traditional Chinese medicine

The Cosmetic Surge 488
Mainstream and affordable, *zhengrong* reigns

Bed, Bath, Buffet and Beyond 496
Initiation to a Beijing bathhouse

Real Men Exfoliate 498
Mars can be beautiful too

TRANSPORTATION

Deus Ex Machina 505
Steps to solve Beijing's notorious traffic congestion

Air 506

Taxis and Limos 513

Transportation Smartcards 516

Magic Bus: No Cause for Fuss 516

Subways 518
Trains 519
Cars, Cars, Cars 522
Two and Three Wheels 535

Sidebars

Obi Wan of *Er Huan* 514
Swami Ding and his mysterious oriental wisdom

Emission Statement 517
The steamy bus to a cleaner future

Braving the Iron Rooster 520
Riding the rails from sea to Xizang

Separated at Birth? 524

Driven to the Poor House 527
Average annual car ownership costs

White-Knuckle Motoring 532
One commuter on driving in Beijing – and Shunyi

To My Yongjiu (Forever) 534
Whither has thou gone?

EXCURSIONS

Escape! 541
Spiritual replenishment is close at hand

Daytrips 543

Weekend Excursions 558

Sidebars

The Mystery of Peking Man 545
Hunting for hominids in Zhoukoudian

All Together Now 547
Excursion groups and tour companies

Get Away to Your Getaway 550
Paths to your country home

BUSINESS & WORK

Sky of Blue and Sea of Green 563
Pondering an ocean of opportunity

Welcome to the Wild East 564
So you wanna be an entrepreneur in China?

It's Your Company 568
Business models and registration

Jobs Offered 584
Non-teaching options for plucky foreigners

Hot for Teaching? 588
Instructions for prospective tutors

Sidebars

The Observant Entrepreneur 566
Dominic Johnson-Hill retraces the rise of Plastered T-Shirts

Size Does Matter 572
The inside scoop on expat packages

"Truth Sells" 578
Read all about it in Hu Shuli's *Caijing* Magazine

Healthy Margins 582
How Roberta Lipson tapped the pulse of China's consumption revolution

Wielding a Mighty Pen 586
Advice for aspiring freelance writers

"Hi, I'm Your Weathergirl" 593
The outlook for tomorrow is bright …

ADULT EDUCATION

***Hanyu* Fever** 597
… is here to stay

Chinese Language 599

Non-Chinese Language 617

Non-Language Programs 619

Community Learning Resources 624

Sidebars

The ABCs of KTV 602
Booze cruise to fluency … in a box

Paper or Plastic? 608
Dictionary druthers

The Dude System 615
… for suprasegmental phoneme mastery

Sheets and Giggles 623
Learning to play an instrument in Beijing

L is for Learning 625
And … look out!

USEFUL INFO

For Igor's Sake 629
A useful chapter

Community Directory
Alumni Groups 630

xiii

Chinese Culture Groups	630
Community Groups	631
Foreign Culture Groups	634
GLBTQ Resources	636
Environmental & Humanitarian Groups	637
Religious Services	642
Support Groups	644

Practical Information Directory

Donations	645
Dry Cleaning & Carpet Cleaning	645
Embassies	645
Government Departments	649
Holidays	649
Internet	649
Law Firms	650
Marriage	650
Mail & Couriers	651
Money & Banking	652
Moving & Relocation	654
Music Practice Rooms	657
Pets & Vets	658
Telephones	664
Tickets	667
Visas	668

Sidebars

Eight Books for '08 632
Literary rambles through Beijings old and new

Let's Talk About (Same-Sex) Love 638
A Mandarin-Gaylese phrasebook

The Attack of the 50-Foot Megastar!!! 646
Beijing's ten most ubiquitous personalities

Warrior, Muse and Musician 661
A cricket of many talents

Useful Numbers 663
A handy telephone directory

Beijing 2009 671
Olympic hangover: a sci-fi fable

Back Through the Looking Glass 672
Now what?

INDEX & AREA GUIDES

Index 675
Legend 693
Beijing Municipality Guide 694
CBD Guide 696
Chaoyang-Lido Guide 697
Haidian Guide 698
Houhai Guide 699
Sanlitun Guide 700
Shunyi Guide 701
Beijing Subway Network 702
Beijing City Guide ..... inside front cover
Beijing Central Guide ...inside back cover

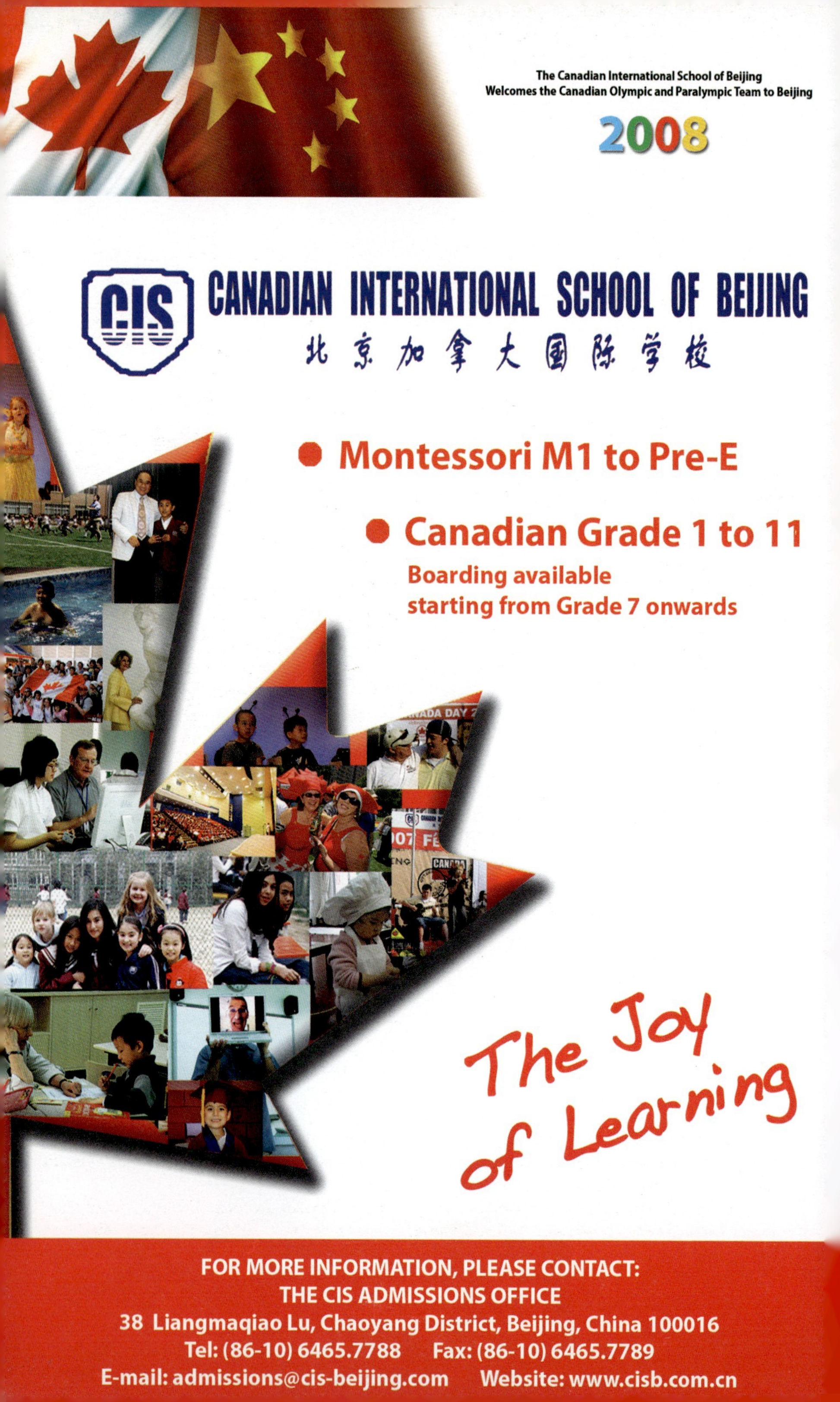

The Canadian International School of Beijing
Welcomes the Canadian Olympic and Paralympic Team to Beijing

2008

CANADIAN INTERNATIONAL SCHOOL OF BEIJING
北京加拿大国际学校

- **Montessori M1 to Pre-E**

- **Canadian Grade 1 to 11**
  Boarding available
  starting from Grade 7 onwards

The Joy of Learning

FOR MORE INFORMATION, PLEASE CONTACT:
THE CIS ADMISSIONS OFFICE
38 Liangmaqiao Lu, Chaoyang District, Beijing, China 100016
Tel: (86-10) 6465.7788   Fax: (86-10) 6465.7789
E-mail: admissions@cis-beijing.com   Website: www.cisb.com.cn

"It's mine, all mine, mwahahaha ..." (Epiphany #37)

Merry Go-Round
Come home on the Special 8
by Eric Abrahamsen

The next time you've got one *kuai* and some time to kill, here's a recommendation: Wait until rush hour's over, then go to the Third Ring Road and catch the Special 8 bus. Either direction is fine: It goes in a circle. Get on the top deck and take the seat directly above the bus driver. Get settled in right behind the window and lean in a little so that you see the road as the driver sees it – as if you were whizzing along out in front of the bus, rather than inside it. Then: go! The Special 8 takes an hour or two to make a complete circuit of the Third Ring Road, depending on traffic, so if you start early you can make a good seven or eight rounds in a day. It's as close to perpetual motion as you're going to get for one *kuai*.

The Third Ring Road is no one's idea of a scenic route – don't expect anything more noteworthy than a shouting match between a cyclist and a driver. After a few rounds, when your mind has wandered as far as it's going to, the footbridges and overpasses will start to become familiar. Familiarity leads to contempt, and how, but if you hold on a bit longer, it leads to another thing.

What you're waiting for is this: the sudden feeling, which goes off like a gong, that the city is yours. As you go, look down into the cars next to you, at the passenger's hands in their laps. Look down the narrow, tree-arched streets in the southern end of town as they blink by. As you ascend the overpasses, look straight into the apartments of the poor bastards who have to live along the roadside. Keep looking.

It might not happen right away (free up some time in your schedule), but at some point as you scan faces at the bus stop your heart will leap and you'll look out over the snarl of traffic and think, "This is mine." Not "mine" like you'd bought it, of course, but "mine" like you belong here. For a moment, all the chaos and curiosity of the city will draw you in, instead of pushing you away, and welcome you home.

That sense of belonging – that the city is yours, and that you are the city's – is something that has to be sought out; it does not come naturally. Some of us have relinquished the search entirely, and retreated behind walls. Others once had vague aspirations of "being a Beijinger," but let them get buried under teaching jobs and visa worries. When it comes, if it comes, it is usually as a thrill which takes us by surprise, and vanishes just as quickly. Beijing has a million ways of reminding you not to get too comfortable. Whether it's a knock on the door from your friendly local *paichusuo*, or someone saying "welcome to China!" 12 years after you emigrated here, every day brings a little something designed to unsettle. The forces that transform the city are beyond the ken of us little people, and the best we can hope for is 100 square meters that we can call our own (at least for the next 70 years). The tacit assumption seems to be that one will never be fully at home in Beijing.

The thing is, there's good reason to believe that no one's got a better handle on the city than you do. Never mind the new arrivals – even the crustiest of the crusty *lao*-Beijingers, with Manchu bannerman blood, is master of little more than his or her ancestral courtyard home. The central metaphor of Beijing is a walled compound, a patch of ground seized and claimed and protected, while the streets outside are abandoned to the winds. That metaphor is more than just architectural – anyone living in a city of 15 million will retain their sanity by carving out a niche for themselves, whether that be a villa in Shunyi, a familiar bar-hopping route, a single karaoke room, or a tight-knit circle of trusted friends.

Outside these enclaves, it seems, the city belongs to no one. That might sound unlikely, because Beijing does a great job of looking like someone's in control. They wouldn't be stuffing blasting-caps under whole city blocks unless there was a deep-laid master plan in place, right? Wrong! They would, and are, and it's anyone's guess what we're going to end up with. The black Audis might drive like they owned the place, but they're really just moving versions of the walled compound, dashing from one safe haven to another. Meanwhile, Beijing itself twists and swells and grows as it will.

So now's your chance. Learn from the taxi drivers – as emblematic of their city as the cabbies of New York or London – who own the open spaces of Beijing, and who are wiser (and crazier and smellier) than any of us. Learn from the old people who dance *yangge'r* under the overpasses – it used to be that any place not zoned for fun was off-limits, but some time during recent years that has quietly changed.

The walls are soon coming down entirely, ladies and gentleman, and once they're down they're likely to stay that way. The days of wary, incremental opening up are drawing to a close; once a certain critical mass is reached, Beijing's development will take on a life of its own. As the grand experiment of 2008 gets underway, the world is rushing in, and if we're not going to be caught with our pants unbuckled and dumb looks on our faces, we need to start making preparations now. When the world pokes its head in and asks, "So, what's happening around here?" someone is going to have to answer, and that someone might as well be you.

Hit the streets, break into conversations, make wild plans, and act like you're supposed to be there, wherever there is. Spend enough time in the midst of the city, and it will welcome you. The first step is to read this book. Don't just read it, absorb it. It's your road map. The next step, of course, is to get on the bus and ride.

Home, where the intersection of old and new is more than architectural

Frontier Town
A brief history of Beijing
by Kaiser Kuo

This aged city has greeted travelers for centuries

Beijing might feel like it spreads endlessly in every direction, but look to the north and west from a tall building on a rare clear day and you'll see mountains not all that far off. It's a reminder that the capital isn't anywhere near the middle of the Middle Kingdom: Rather, it lies on a northern salient of the North China Plain, known to geographers as Beijing Bay, bound by the Yanshan range to the north and the Taihang range to the west.

Northern exposure

Beijing's proximity to the Great Wall has meant, over the centuries, much more than access to good hiking. That the city is located on the periphery of central China goes far towards explaining why this dusty town came to be the capital of three major dynasties and the world's most populous modern state, despite being far from a navigable river and a good trek from the coast.

Throughout its history, Beijing has been a frontier city – strategically located close to the cultural and geographic divide between the world of steppe nomadism beyond the Wall and the world of sedentary agriculture this side of it. Like any frontier city, its character has been shaped by the interplay of cultural forces on either side.

Significantly, Beijing to date has spent more time as the capital of non-Han rulers of China, who held the city facing south, than in the hands of ethnically Han regimes, who held it facing north. As a result, people from beyond the passes in Mongolia and the northeast have given Beijing much of its peculiar character.

Catch sight of the hills girding the North China Plain when the smog clears

Swallows and thistles

A Paleolithic settlement discovered in 1996, during the construction of Wangfujing's Oriental Plaza, indicates that modern man settled in Beijing at least 20,000 years ago. Some 2,000 artifacts unearthed there are displayed in a subterranean museum near the Wangfujing subway station. For most of the first two millennia of recorded Chinese history, Beijing Bay remained a backwater. The first historical mentions of territory within the modern city date to the early Zhou dynasty, which lasted – at least in name – from the 11th to the 3rd century BC. In 1050 BC, Zhou forces swept eastward from their homeland in contemporary Shaanxi province to wrest power from the Shang kings in the Yellow River floodplain – China's ancient heartland. The Zhou parceled out conquered lands to kinsmen and allies, and subjugated Shang lords in a "feudal" system. Two of the original 72 feudal territories were in modern Beijing: Ji, in today's Xuanwu District; and Yan, in Fangshan District. *Ji*, incidentally, is a general word for "thistle," a plant that still grows rampantly in Beijing's uncultivated areas, while *yan* means "swallow," a bird seen in local skies.

E pluribus unum

During the strife-ridden Spring and Autumn period (770-476 BC), Yan conquered its neighbor and made Ji its capital. In the even more tumultuous Warring States period (475-221 BC), the Yan state continued to expand, swallowing up the northern half of modern Hebei province, Beijing and Tianjin municipalities, and parts of Liaoning province. It became one of the seven great powers of the age, but, as the weakest of the seven, Yan relied on intrigue and alliances to survive. When it appeared that the Qin armies might crush all the other states, the King of Yan dispatched an assassin to do in the King of Qin. The assassin's failure made Yan's destruction inevitable: The Qin forces conquered Yan in 226 BC on their way to defeating the remaining Warring States and reuniting China five years later.

During the brutal but short-lived Qin dynasty (221-207 BC), the city of Ji became a regional seat of power. Qin Shihuang, the dynasty's founder, is often credited with creating the Great Wall when he linked various walls his defeated rivals had erected. But the Qin Great Wall was not the masonry construction familiar to us today; rather, it was mostly rammed earth, and has long since vanished.

The more things change …

For the next 1,200 years, Beijing changed names almost as frequently as it changed masters. Through most of the Han dynasty (206 BC-220 AD), Ji was a modestly prosperous frontier garrison and a staging ground for campaigns against the empire's nomadic enemy, the Xiongnu – identified by some historians as the Huns who would later terrorize Europe. Following the collapse of the Han, the region came under the dominion of a sequence of ephemeral kingdoms founded by Turko-Mongolian and proto-Tibetan nomadic tribes. As each successive tribe settled in and became Sinicized, it prized Beijing as a strategic bulwark against other steppelanders eyeing the rich farmlands south of the Great Wall.

100,000 strong

After the Sui unified China in 581, the city served as a base for military operations against the Korean kingdom of Koguryo. Expensive and unpopular adventurism of this sort fuelled dissatisfaction, and the Sui dynasty was toppled in 618 to usher in the glorious Tang dynasty (618-907). During this period, Beijing was named Youzhou ("Deep Town"), and at its height had a population of 100,000 – impressive, but only a tenth of Chang'an, the Tang capital near modern Xi'an.

War – what is it good for?

The peace was shattered in 755 when general An Lushan rebelled against the Tang, proclaiming a new dynasty. The uprising was eventually put down, but new threats materialized on the

Tanzhe Temple, where Kublai Khan's daughter knelt in prayer so often that she wore indentations into a rock

steppes during the interregnum between the Tang and Song dynasties. Chief among these was a Turko-Mongolian tribe called the Qidan in Chinese, who hailed from an area that is now part of Heilongjiang province. The Qidan called themselves "Khitai," and from that name is derived Cathay, Marco Polo's name for China, and Kitai, the Russian word for China. They pushed south of the Wall, which the Sui and others had reinforced and expanded, and destroyed Youzhou in the 940s.

Ganbei!

On its ashes they built a new fortified city, which they called Nanjing ("Southern Capital") or Yanjing ("Capital of Yan") – its name during the Warring States period. (Yanjing remains a moniker for the capital, used in the names of products including Beijing's most widely consumed beer.) From Yanjing, the Khitai ruled over the southern half of their empire – a Chinese-style dynasty called Liao – and threatened China's heartland, which was unified under the Song dynasty in 960. The Song (960-1279) bought them off with hefty tributes of silk and silver, scheming all the while to dislodge the Khitai from the lands south of the Wall.

Wishful thinking

To that end, the Song concluded an alliance in 1120 with the Jürchen, a Tungusic tribe and former Liao vassal that had established an empire called Jin ("golden") centered in modern Harbin. The treaty called for a joint attack on the Khitai, but the Jin did most of the actual fighting. They swiftly overran the Khitai, whose ardor for battle had been softened by sedentary life and the pacifying effects of Buddhism, to which they had converted. The Jin armies took Yanjing in 1122 and destroyed the Liao state entirely three years later. The surviving Khitai fled to modern Xinjiang, where they ruled for a century over many Silk Road oases.

The Song court had badly miscalculated: its armies had been unable to retake much Liao territory and, predictably, its erstwhile Jürchen ally soon turned against it. In the Jin, the Song faced an even more aggressive and powerful foe than the Liao. Indeed, the Jin expanded rapidly into central China, campaigning as far south as Ningbo before the embattled Song bought them off.

The Jin incorporated the ruins of Yanjing into a larger walled city, which they designated as their second capital in 1153 and called Zhongdu ("Middle Capital"). Beijing had now become the capital of a dynasty ruling a significant portion of China. Centered in contemporary Xuanwu and Fengtai districts (in southwestern Beijing), Zhongdu had a population of nearly one million by the late 12th century.

Capital city

In 1215, Zhongdu was flattened, and its population virtually eradicated, for having had the temerity to hold out against the most potent force ever to come off the steppe: the Mongols. Seeking refuge from Chinggis (Genghis) Khan's armies, the Jürchen relocated their capital to Kaifeng in 1214. It was a stay of execution: a second Mongol campaign from 1231 to 1234 finished them off entirely.

Under the reign of Chinggis's grandson Kublai Khan, the Mongols completed their conquest of China and established a dynasty called the Yuan (1279-1368). The Yuan too chose to govern from Beijing, which became the capital of all of China for the first time. They built their capital northeast of Zhongdu, in the north central part of today's city (the Khan's palace stood in Beihai Park). The new city was called Dadu, but was better known in the West as Cambaluc – Marco Polo's transliteration for the Mongolian name Khanbalig, or "City of the Great Khan."

Mongolian masterplan

It was during the Yuan dynasty that the foundations of modern Beijing were laid. Dadu was methodically planned, with the evenly spaced rectilinear streets and symmetrical layout centered on the north-south axis of the palace that still characterize the city today. Additionally, the Yuan bequeathed us Baitasi (White Dagoba) as well as the Tuancheng (Circular City) in Beihai Park. The Mongols left their legacy on language as well: the word hutong, or alleyway, comes from the Mongolian word *hotlog* meaning something like "water well."

The Yuan didn't quite last a century, though, largely because they failed to co-opt the scholarly elites so crucial to administering the empire. As Chinggis Khan's advisor Yelü Chucai had prophetically remarked, "The Empire may be conquered on horseback, but cannot be ruled on horseback."

Ming magnificence

In 1368, Zhu Yuanzhang, an itinerant monk with a checkered past, led his rebel forces to victory over the Mongols and founded the Ming Dynasty (1368-1644). Although he originally intended to rule from Dadu, ministers convinced Zhu otherwise, and he built his capital at Nanjing, in modern Jiangsu province. He renamed the erstwhile Yuan capital Beiping ("Northern Peace").

Zhu Yuanzhang died in 1398, but he was predeceased by his oldest son and original heir Zhu Biao. The throne therefore passed to Zhu Biao's oldest son, Zhu Yunwen, who was still very young. Suspicious of his uncles, he followed the advice of his ministers and began to strip them of their power. One of these uncles, Zhu Di, took up arms. He led his forces from Beiping, usurped the throne from his young nephew in 1403, and almost immediately began construction in Beiping of palaces so grand they could only signal his intention to move the capital north. In this, Zhu Di, known to history as the Yongle Emperor, was vigorously opposed by various ministers, who cited reasons ranging from construction costs to the city's bad feng shui. Yongle executed the most vocal critic and continued building. In 1421 he formally moved the dynastic seat. Nanjing became a secondary capital, and Beijing at last acquired the name Beijing ("Northern Capital.")

Recapture the grandeur of the Yongle Emperor's palace with a nighttime jaunt around the walls

PHOTO: NATALIE BEHRING

Apogee

Yongle's capital was surrounded by a massive city wall, testifying to the ever-present danger of a Mongolian return. Beijing was, after all, an ideal location from which defensive efforts – and the occasional offensive foray onto the steppe – might be coordinated. But it was far more than a garrison town. The palace complex at its heart – the Forbidden City – was built to awe, to overpower and to convey unequivocally the incomparable majesty of the Son of Heaven.

The capital of a mature and robust empire, Beijing was home to the most fully developed civil service the world had yet seen, and scholars flocked to the city seeking high office. This concentration of intellectuals in turn attracted China's most talented literati, painters and artisans who turned Beijing into the empire's cultural center.

Lights out

The Ming dynasty fell into decline during the long reign of Emperor Wanli (r. 1572-1620). In the decades that followed, the confluence of decadent and apathetic rulers, corrupt eunuchs, military reverses, onerous taxation and natural disasters sparked large-scale peasant rebellions. The armies of one rebel leader, Li Zicheng, took Beijing in April 1644, meeting no resistance. Emperor Chongzhen, disgraced and alone, climbed partway up Coal Hill behind the Forbidden City and hanged himself from Crooked-Neck Tree.

The Manchurian candidates

Li Zicheng proclaimed a new dynasty, but it wasn't to last. The Ming general Wu Sangui, who held the strategic pass at Shanhaiguan where the Great Wall meets the sea, faced a dilemma. He could side with the uncouth Li Zicheng, or he could join forces with the new power that had risen in the northeast: the Manchus, a federation of Jürchen tribes led by the charismatic ruler Nurhaci. Wu chose the Manchus and opened the gates at Shanhaiguan to their armies, which in June 1644 drove Li's troops from Beijing and proclaimed a new Chinese-style dynasty, the Qing (1644-1911).

A segregated city

The Manchus were in many ways more Confucian than their Han subjects, but they insisted on maintaining a separate – and by no means equal – ethnic identity. This determination was manifested physically in Beijing, which they re-districted: Its northern half was reserved for Manchu nobles and the banners (hereditary military households), while Chinese families were forcibly relocated to the southern part. The layout and ambiance of the two parts of the city remain different to this day: the hutongs in Xuanwu and Chongwen districts are less rectilinear and teem with more commercial activity than those north of Chang'an Jie.

East meets West

The Qing enlarged the Forbidden City and built enormous imperial pleasure gardens in Beijing's outskirts. The most famous of these was Yuanmingyuan, the Old Summer Palace, constructed on designs drawn up by Jesuit missionaries and razed by British and French troops in 1860. The Western elements in both the origins and demise of the Old Summer Palace illustrate the double-edged nature of Western influence on China during the Qing dynasty: for both their powers of creation and destruction, the "seafaring barbarians" had to be reckoned with. Their military superiority was amply demonstrated in a series of lopsided victories over Chinese troops. Each defeat was followed by concessions. Thus, after the sack of the Old Summer Palace, the Qing court acquiesced in the establishment of foreign legations in Beijing, which introduced an enduring Western influence on the city's architecture.

After '49, it was full steam ahead into the planned-economy promised land (Beijing Railway Station in the '60s)

Get up, stand up

Weakened by foreign encroachment, power struggles and rebellions, the Qing dynasty was unable to stop the Republican Revolution in October 1911. Nominally, Beijing remained the capital of the new Republic of China (1912-1949) until 1928. In fact, after the death of the decidedly non-republican president Yuan Shikai in 1916, power devolved to warlords who fought for control of the capital and the political legitimacy it conferred.

During the turbulent Warlord Period, Beijing emerged as the locus of the May Fourth Movement, named for the demonstration of May 4, 1919 against the attribution to Japan of Germany's concessions in China by the Allied Powers at Versailles. The years that followed witnessed the "New Culture Movement," during which westernized youth denounced China's Confucian heritage and called for gender equality, a new vernacular literature, science and democracy. It was in this heady atmosphere, in 1921, that the Communist Party of China (CPC) was forged; one of its founding members was the Hunanese assistant librarian at Peking University, Mao Zedong.

In 1937, a long-anticipated war broke out between China and Japan. Clashes began at Lugouqiao (Marco Polo Bridge) in southwest Beijing, and soon Japanese troops occupied the city and much of eastern China. At the close of World War II, the civil war between Communist and Nationalist forces resumed. The People's Liberation Army entered Beijing on January 31, 1949, and it was from the rostrum at Tian'anmen Square that Mao Zedong proclaimed the founding of the People's Republic of China on October 1, 1949.

China's opening to the world brought the world (or at least World Park) to Fengtai District

"New Beijing"

In the past half-century, Beijing has changed dramatically. In the 1950s, the Ming-era city wall was torn down to make room for the future Second Ring Road. Tian'anmen Square was expanded and flanked with the Great Hall of the People and the Museum of History and of the Chinese Revolution. Many courtyard homes were subdivided and parceled out to working families. The 1960s saw the construction of enormous apartment blocks, factories and Beijing's first subway line. During the "Great Proletarian Cultural Revolution" (1966-1976), some of Beijing's temples and other architectural treasures were damaged by zealots who saw them as vestiges of the "Old China."

Beijing's physical transformation further accelerated after the reforms initiated by Deng Xiaoping in late 1978. The combination of rapid economic growth, housing market liberalization, and preparations for massive set-piece events – notably the Asian Games of 1990, the 50th anniversary of the founding of the People's Republic in 1999, and the 2008 Olympic Games – has stimulated a massive construction boom. While many ancient hutong neighborhoods have disappeared to make way for apartment towers and multi-lane arteries, the rapidly expanding city has endowed itself with a Central Business District, new subway lines, a futuristic airport terminal, and gee-whiz sports facilities.

However, the real impetus for change – the deeper, more lasting and ultimately more significant change that the city has undergone – is not state-sponsored projects. Rather, it is China's massive social and economic transformation, a phenomenon probably without parallel in history. Fueled by a seemingly inexhaustible stream of rural laborers seeking their fortune in the capital, the economic boom has created new moneyed classes with disposable income to spend on travel, leisure, fashion and entertainment. As the one-child generation has come of age, this has transformed the one-time city of bikes into a city of cars, with attendant consequences for congestion and air quality. Glitzy malls, flashy nightclubs, gated communities, international restaurants – Beijing now boasts most of the trappings of a global metropolis, including a ballooning population of foreign residents and visitors, who provide ever more opportunities for cross-cultural intercourse.

Indeed, nothing on the gargantuan scale of Beijing's transformation could have been imaginable without the opening to the outside world: Foreign investment, technology, markets and ideas have transformed China, and with China's vigorous economy and growing sense of national confidence, interaction with the world – commercial, cultural, technological – will be increasingly reciprocal.

Beijing is more a frontier town today than ever before in its history. It borders, in this age of compressed time and distance, virtually every nation on earth.

From rain-making to flower-arranging, Beijing leaves nothing to chance when it comes to the Olympics

Forbidden Fish and Imaginary Ingots
Why James Kynge remains bullish on Beijing
by Jenny Niven

"You can still get glimpses of what the soul of this place in the past was really like," says Kynge

Talking to someone like James Kynge about the city he lives in is a rare delight. He's knowledgeable and articulate, and his fascination with Beijing is genuine and infectious. An expert witness, as both a journalist and long-term student of Chinese language and culture, he combines the dispassionate, critical stance of a reporter with the perspective of someone whose personal and family life, friendships, memories and experiences are tangled up with the city's own extraordinary recent history.

Kynge first came to China as a student at Shandong University in 1982, and then went on to spend nearly 20 years as a journalist in Asia, first for Reuters, and then as China Bureau Chief for the *Financial Times*. He's lived in Beijing permanently since 1997 and is now head of the mighty Pearson publishing group. In 2006, his book *China Shakes the World* won the Goldman Sachs Business Book of the Year Award. In other words, his credentials as a Beijing Insider are pretty strong.

What seals this impression, however, is his clear enthusiasm for all things *lao* Beijing, whether it's his reverence for the hutong-based oral culture upon which generations of Chinese have been raised, or his confession that nothing makes him happier than listening to *Beijingren* swear: "I have to admit that ten minutes of solid cussing from a Beijing taxi driver puts me in a very good mood indeed."

Today, instead of discussing China's economy or international relations, we're on a verbal tour of Kynge's favourite places in Beijing, and it's surely enough to make even the most jaded of residents dig out a copy of *In Search of Old Peking* and do a bit of exploring.

For Kynge, a vivid sense of history and a fertile imagination are clearly the key to getting under the skin of this city we call home. Block out the neon and screaming Mando-pop, he says, and it's still easy to revel in the imaginative possibilities of the Houhai area of town.

"I can't get over the sense of awe when you stand on the Yinding Qiao – the "Silver Ingot Bridge" – and you think that in the old days that was the end of the grand canal. People came from places as far south as Suzhou and Hangzhou with grain and bolts of silk, and all sorts of other tributary offerings for the emperor, and that's where they would have exchanged them. I have in my mind's eye enormous heaps of silver ingots, piling up on the bridge as people were given money for the magnificent items they brought."

It was at this spot a few years ago that Kynge, on his way up to one of the first rooftop terraces to be built around the lakes, wandered off along a little corridor to the tiny home of the family who ran the bar. There he was greeted with the incredible sight of an enormous altar to Genghis Khan, still worshipped daily by the descendents of a Mongolian princely family who'd been living in the house since Beijing was a Mongol city in the 13th century.

"I love that kind of discovery, and there are still plenty of things like that going on in Beijing." Kynge enthuses. "I think that even though some of the old, physical manifestations of the past have disappeared, if you go hunting for them, it's a fascinating thing to do. You can still get glimpses of what the soul of this place in the past was really like."

Another iconic Beijing location for Kynge is the Confucian Temple, where China's brightest scholars have paid tribute to Confucius since 1302. "I love the Confucian Temple and its wonderful steles because of the incredible sense of grace they have, and of the sense of unbroken history stretching back." Multiple trips to favorite locations, he says, can also yield new discoveries even when you think you've noticed everything about a particular place already.

"The one little thing I discovered the other day there is that as you walk up to the Confucian temple, there is Mongolian, Arabic, and Manchu script on the front of the steles lining the road. I thought 'Why no Chinese?' I looked at the back and the inscription in Chinese says 'Get off your horses here.' I thought that was so beautiful because it's just like when you enter a Chinese university, and it says 'Get off your bike here,' and everyone does that thing where they glide in, pretending to get off the bike … I imagine exactly the same thing used to happen there at the Confucian temple.

"Also, it gives a sense of how international the temple was – the Chinese was on the back! Even though the first 40 years of the era of Communism has been fairly closed, in China's history there were foreigners of all creeds and persuasions coming in."

Inevitably, with the enormously accelerated rate of change and development, many aspects of Beijing's history are harder now to dig out from under the skyscrapers and flyovers. Kynge admits to being saddened by the erosion of landmarks and culture that progress has wrought upon Beijing – "the planners have done this city a great disservice" – and expresses concern that disruption of the old ways of life may be more irreversible than we first imagine. On a personal level too, he says, it's hard to see great swathes of memory lane being dug up. It does, however, help to crystallize little details in the imagination.

"When I was a student, I used to cycle from the uni to the northern gate of the Forbidden City. On the eastern side of the Forbidden City there was a strip of old houses, full of really old Beijingers – really hospitable, fun, interesting people. That place no longer exists, but the greatest thing that happened to me there was once I was invited in to one of these houses and they said, 'Would you like to stay for dinner,' and I said that would be lovely, thank you very much. Just as I said that the husband threw a hook out of his back window into the imperial moat and a few minutes later he'd caught one of the fish living in the imperial moat, and that's what we had for supper. That really kind of blew my mind. Amazing! It was absolutely brilliant. Here we were having the emperor's fish for tea."

With Beijing set to be irrevocably altered by the Olympics (in which Kynge for one predicts that China will sweep the floor with the rest of the world), now seems the best possible time for us to get out and explore this incredible, richly diverse and historically fascinating city. "You quite often need a bit of imagination," warns Kynge, "but perhaps the rewards of finding something that echoes or resonates from the past are actually far greater now that the surroundings are from the 21st century."

Moving your world,
thinking ahead!

**Schenker Relocation Services –
International, domestic and
local removals.**

With more than 1,500 offices in over 120 countries, our multilingual team of removal specialists will design the right solution for all your relocation needs – whether across the street or across the world.

Contact us today!

**Schenker (H.K.) Ltd.,
Beijing Representative Office**
Phone +86 10 8048 0126
Fax +86 10 8048 0115
removal.bjs@schenker.com
www.schenker.com.cn

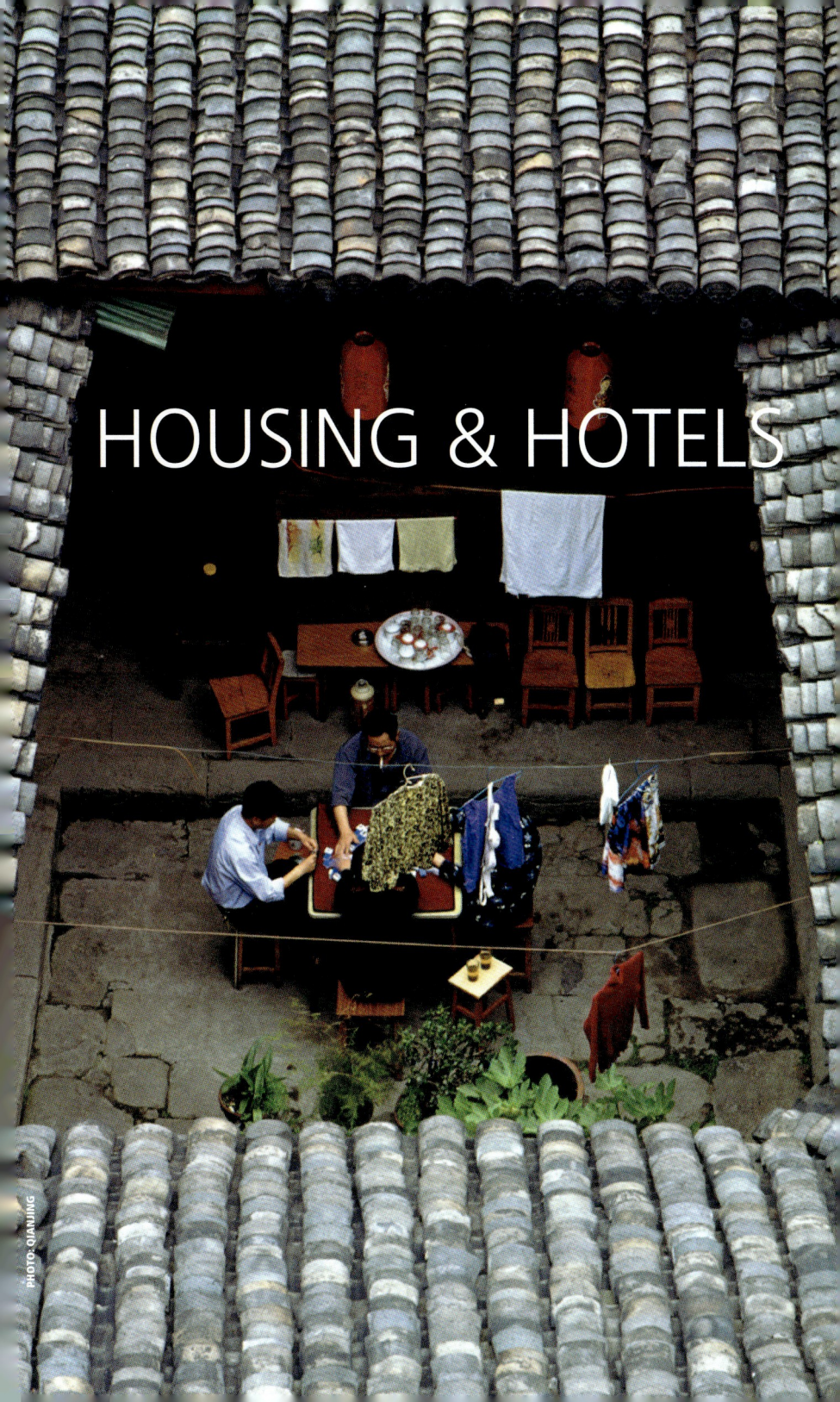
HOUSING & HOTELS

CHENGDU
GUANGZHOU
HONG KONG
BEIJING   WE'RE THERE
SHANGHAI
SHENZHEN

When your Shanghai office is expanding; you need to secure new stores in Beijing; you want to be more energy efficient in your Shenzhen factory; you require your warehouse in Chengdu valued; and you seek the best accommodation for your expatriates in Hong Kong, only one real estate consultancy has the ability to respond.

With more than 12,000 employees in 215 offices throughout 56 countries, Cushman & Wakefield has the expertise and reach to handle any assignment in any corner of the world.

No matter where you are... **WE'RE THERE.**

+ (86 10) 5921 0808
www.cushmanwakefield.com

Build them and they will come...

Gimme Shelter
Finding a billet in boomtime Beijing
by Simon Ostheimer

Following years of uninterrupted construction, Beijing is booming. Nothing is what it once was, and no one knows what it still yet may be. Otherworldly architecture (we mean you, CCTV Tower) rises up over century-old courtyard homes (hello Houhai), the physical embodiment of the capital's identity crisis – old or new, traditional vs. modern, to embrace Chinese values, or the world's?

Some things are already clear. The days of cheap real estate are gone, for one. Prices can always plateau, but don't expect them to come down. Anyone trying to buy property over the last couple of years knows that Beijing is in the grip of a genuine, grown-up real-estate frenzy (no world-class city should be without one). The government is moving actively to cool the market, and changes to laws governing property purchases by foreigners will have their effect on speculation over the next few years. Meanwhile, all this heat affects the rental market, where supply is reasonably tight. It's likely to get tighter in the shadow of the Olympics, though perhaps not in line with the wildest dreams of avarice of some of our local landlords. As for hotel accommodation, the luxury hotel scene is finally coming of age in Beijing, with some real choice at the top end of the market. But, first-class or flophouse, there'll be no room at the inn in August 2008.

In the meantime, whether you're planning to rent a one-bedroom apartment in Dongzhimen, or purchase a four-story villa in Shunyi, read on for our expert guide to the hows and whys (not to mention the whos, whens and whats) of local real estate.

HOUSING & HOTELS

Know Thyself
Picking the home that piques you

To rent or to buy? What kind of place? The strength of your ties to Beijing and the projected length of your stay will be major factors in your decisions. Renting usually makes more sense for people planning to live in Beijing for only a few years, but a growing number of longer-term residents are buying homes in the capital. Conversely, affluent expats whose stay is measured in months, who travel constantly or are disinclined to keep house, may prefer a hotel-style serviced apartment.

The Olympic effect

Whatever kind of accommodation you're looking for, the big question over the next year will be: What effect will the Olympics have on property prices and rents?

Allan Tan of property agency Lihong predicts that the biggest winners in the rental market will be landlords in the serviced apartments sector: they are set up to profitably turn around a short-term lease, and there will be plenty of corporate and provincial visitors. At time of writing, quotes for the two months around the Olympics were three times or more above standard rates. Anyone relying on this sector for accommodation, says Allan Tan, should avoid leases that extend into July and August 2008, or be prepared to pay up.

As for the longer-term rental market, the strongest effect a year before the Games seemed to be in city properties renting for under USD 2500 per month. Quite a few landlords in that bracket were either adding an Olympic premium, or asking for leases terminating in July 2008, hoping for a short-term killing over the Olympic period. Their expectations will probably drop as the Games approach, says Tan, but in many cases, you may have to budget for a 10-15 percent Olympic premium for one-year leases stretching over the Games period. Landlords in the higher ranges don't seem to be as optimistic. This could be because they are more market-savvy, and see the value of steady rental over a short-term windfall. "Consider this," says Tan: "Renting out to Olympic tenants would entail leaving an apartment empty for the month before and the month after the Olympics, equivalent to three months rent. Add in the cost and time of providing bedding & kitchen utensils and it's not looking so profitable."

As for property purchase prices, there is a conventional wisdom that after the Games, things will cool down sharply in the housing market. But Anna Kalifa, head of research at property firm Jones Lang LaSalle, isn't so sure. "Post Olympics, we don't really forecast a decline in prices," she says. Things may slow a little, due to added supply in the city center and an exodus of foreigners and migrant workers just after the Games, but prices won't dip significantly, especially in areas downtown and near the Olympic venues. Beijing's population is set to keep growing, incomes will rise, and the addition of new, world-class infrastructure like metros and malls will help keep up overseas and domestic interest.

So consider it

Whether you rent or buy, the same considerations apply when choosing where to live. Since the range of choices is so wide, it's important to identify your needs in terms of price, size, location, layout and amenities. Consider what you'll need close by: your school or office? A cheese shop? Nightlife within stumbling distance? A gym? Also, consider what amenities you'll require: a backyard? ADSL?

Think further on important details like views, exposure to natural light, and floor level. Consider commuting and its impact on your lifestyle: how many hours of your life do you want to spend in traffic jams? The more clearly you've determined what you want, the more likely you are to find it.

The following are the main types of homes available in Beijing – and the people who inhabit them.

Are you being served?

Fully furnished serviced apartments are equipped with all the mod cons (stoves, washing machines, DVD players, cutlery, bed sheets, etc.) and offer access to fitness and business centers. "Real" serviced apartments offer short-term leases (including weekly and monthly), daily maid service, and hotel-style front desks. Bring piles of dough or your gold card, as prices are steep. Check online, or contact a real estate or travel agent to enquire about discounts, which are frequently available. (Try after the Olympics!) Rates start at about USD 120 per night for a one-bedroom and go sky high from there.

Look for a building with a reliable elevator

To the manor born

Well-to-do foreign and local families looking to (re-)create the Western suburban lifestyle often do so in the gated villa communities (*bieshu*), which are modeled after gated communities in the US. Located for the most part near Capital Airport, these compounds feature spacious homes that often come with backyards and private garages.

Living here, it's possible to momentarily forget the world outside the gates, since amenities include anything from swimming pools to playgrounds, from supermarkets to clubhouses and, in the bigger compounds, primary schools. English-speaking staff can help residents get settled, and private buses ferry the kids to the nearby international schools. All this, combined with generally friendly neighbors and the near absence of crime and poverty, lends a 1950s "Leave it to Beaver" quality to life that appeals to many families. As in suburbs everywhere, however, long commutes, whether by shuttle bus or car, are a fact of life.

At press time, three-bedroom townhouses in Shunyi were being offered at USD 1,500-4,900 per month, while four-bedroom, fully detached villas were being advertised for USD 3,500-9,000. Fully furnished villas were being sold for RMB 11,000-22,000 per square meter.

Absolutely fabulous

The "international-standard" luxury apartment complexes (*gongyu*) that have popped up all over the city – mostly in Chaoyang District – offer an enticing mix of comfort and convenience. They blend proximity to Beijing's clubs, restaurants, shops and cultural attractions with facilities galore, such as gyms, satellite TV and indoor playgrounds. In swish buildings, staff attend to all repairs and help tenants in countless ways, such as arranging deliveries or assisting with translation. What's more, the concentration of expats and super-rich Chinese residing in these buildings means that most are serviced by imported food stores and buses operated by international schools. Some of the larger compounds are self-contained mini-cities replete with supermarkets, schools, cinemas, dance studios and more – you'll never have to leave!

At the time of writing, upscale three-bedroom flats in Chaoyang District ranged from USD 1,700-7,000 per month. Super luxury apartments were being hawked for a cool USD 10,000 per month. Purchasing prices ranged from RMB 11,000-21,000 per square meter in the district.

The good life

If we had the money, home would be a renovated courtyard or *siheyuan* where days

HOUSING & HOTELS

Comfortable living on a budget

are filled with scholarly pursuits and evenings are devoted to gatherings with friends. Consisting of four buildings arranged around a central courtyard – or many buildings around a series of courtyards – these homes are located in the surviving hutongs. Imagine waking up in your opium bed and then taking a brief ride to Beihai to catch the sunrise.

Renting an inexpensive courtyard home will entail boosting your *guanxi*, as choice properties are rare and quickly snatched up by friends of previous residents. If you're buying, start saving: prices are high and these old homes usually require extensive renovations.

Monthly rental prices for courtyards in Xicheng and Dongcheng Districts range from RMB 5,000 for a basic two-bedroom starter to USD 13,000 for a fully renovated aristocrat's mansion. Purchasing prices range from RMB 9,000-33,000 per square meter, and even more for an opulent Ming mansion. Find a local lawyer with ample experience purchasing courtyards. Prospective foreign buyers must first go with the seller to the Beijing National Security Bureau in the Henderson Center (6517 0808) to make sure the property is not in a security sensitive area. It's free, but takes five business days. For more, see "Four Sides, Six Steps: Buying a Beijing courtyard," p38.

Keeping up appearances

If you don't have a fat expat package but still require many creature comforts, check out mid- and upper-tier local apartments (*lou fang*). Popular with young(ish) foreign professionals, well-heeled students and middle-class Chinese, these buildings range from tiny to comfortable and have been built throughout the city – though large clusters of foreigners have settled just inside East Second Ring Road and around Wudaokou, among other areas. Don't expect *laowai*-oriented amenities: if you don't speak Chinese, it's time to learn a few words; if you want spotless stairwells or need to be on an international school bus route, look elsewhere. However, apartments of this type come with nattily-attired guards, internet hookup, Chinese cable TV and parking.

Monthly rental prices for three-bedroom flats in Dongcheng and Chaoyang districts ranged from RMB 4,000-8,000 at the time of writing. Purchase prices ranged from RMB 9,000-17,000 per square meter depending on location and amenities.

Faulty towers

For the impecunious and/or linguistically inclined among us there is another option: cheap apartments. A few steps below and about ten years removed from the places described above, "residential housing" (民宅 *minzhai*) feature limited supplies of hot water, pint-sized kitchens, drafty windows and, when they have them, elevators that shut off at midnight. They're basic but certainly livable. And what these apartments lack in luxuries, they make up for in romance and character. No, seriously. You will get to know your Chinese neighbors very well and, with a little bit of elbow grease and a couple of visits to Golden Five Stars Market (see Shopping p403), you can fix them up nicely in no time.

Monthly rental prices for cheap two-bedroom apartments in Haidian District ranged from RMB 1,500-3,000 per month at the time of writing. Purchase prices ranged from RMB 5,000-10,000 per square meter. There are few buyers.

Homestay

Nothing beats a homestay for an unmediated taste of Beijing. The two avenues for homestay are generally to either become the live-in English teacher for little Xiao Peng, and getting free or very cheap room and board or paying rent (in the range of RMB 1,000-2,500 monthly depending on the location and facilities of the apartment) and getting a language and cultural immersion experience. Unfortunately, in the latter situation, you may still end up being pressured to speak English with the family, so be sure that you're clear with them at the start about your expectations (or choose a family where the parents can't speak any English – old couples are a good bet).

Horror stories about homestay placement companies abound, so if you can, it might be better to post an advertisement or go through a study program or university office to find a host family. If all you want is to live with a native Chinese speaker, it's really easy to get an apartment with a Chinese roommate through websites listed below or by posting flyers around a university campus (see also p27).

Smart Searches

Where to look for a home

There's no shortage of ways to look for a place to live in Beijing – through a friend or through an agent; online or onsite – and the logic holds that the more places you examine, the better your feel for the market and how fair prices will be.

The internet

Local websites replete with rental, home-buying and roommate listings are a great way to quickly find available properties in the areas you want and get a better understanding of the market.

www.thebeijinger.com: Listings in English of all types from low- to high-end as well as classifieds for roommates needed and wanted.

www.wuwoo.com: The best thing about this bilingual website is the interactive map that lists available properties by location. Lots of listings and easy navigation.

beijing.craigslist.org: Same layout and procedure as Craigslist elsewhere. In English.

www.zhantai.com: A knock-off of Craigslist. Good place to find a Chinese roommate.

beijing.kijiji.com.cn: Chinese-language classifieds.

The direct approach

The most direct approach is to knock on doors. A building's management office (物业办公室 *wuye bangongshi*) may have leads for renters or, for buyers, the sales office (售楼处 *shou lou chu*) can give you their pitch. Alternatively, private landlords will post their phone numbers on rentable units. Use this opportunity to quiz current residents about the neighborhood and the compound's management and developer. Be nosy.

The agency

Real estate agents charge a commission based on the rent, but the landlord almost always pays the commission. Although there are exceptions, many agencies will not take on clients unless the expected rent exceeds a certain sum, usually RMB 1,000 for a local agency and around RMB 8,000 or more for an international one. Since the commission is based on rent, it would seem to be in the agent's interest to make you pay as much as possible. With some companies, this is true. Reputable realtors, however, make their living off repeat business and referrals. Therefore, they have an incentive to keep you satisfied, and they may cut their own commissions to close.

Good agents know the market and players inside out, are patient and have a vast portfolio of properties. They can help with everything from assessing your needs and negotiating with the landlord to drafting the agreement and helping you move in and out without incident. Higher end realtors should also provide a higher level of service: Efficiently shuttling you by car between a list of properties and knowledgeably answering your queries are standard. Be forewarned, however, that you will be expected to sign an exclusivity agreement, meaning you won't try to cut them out by going directly to the landlord (more of a guilt trip than a legally binding document) before they show you around.

Shady realtors have been known to pull tricks like charging an upfront fee and then disappearing, publishing artificially low prices to attract clients – if the price looks too good to be true, it probably is – or threatening clients with whom they have disputes.

To distinguish the good apples from the bad, visit the agency and check its license. Find out about its track record: Unhappy customers or no track record at all are both red flags. If your Chinese isn't fluent, make sure your agent is fully bilingual, since most landlords do not speak English. The agent must provide accurate translations of the relevant documents, especially the lease.

Agents should be giving you impartial information on the pros and cons of the properties you're visiting, including information on the developers and management companies. They should also be learning your tastes as you visit properties together, and refining their lists of buildings to show you accordingly. A good agent will stick around after the lease is signed to provide additional services, such as helping make the landlord perform repairs and returning at the end of the lease to make sure you get your deposit back. If you're paying enough, expect a full range of services throughout your lease.

Below are a few agencies – to find more, check out the latest issue of the monthly tbjhome magazine or log onto the real estate classifieds at www.thebeijinger.com.

Local agencies

Golden Keys This large, local agency (330 offices in Beijing) has loads of rental and sales listings posted on the windows of its neighborhood offices. Agents may not be fully bilingual.
S0503 Soho New Town, 88 Jianguo Lu, Chaoyang District. (8589 1006) www.zdhouse.com 中大恒基，朝阳区建国路88号Soho现代城S0503

Wo Ai Wo Jia With over 300 offices around Beijing, this well-regarded property agency services low, mid and high-end listings in almost every neighborhood. It has an English website, but agents may not be fully bilingual. Walk in to arrange a showing. Consult the website to find an agency in your desired neighborhood.
44 Chengfu Lu, Haidian District. (9510 5890) www.5i5j.com 我爱我家，海淀区成府路44号

International agencies

Century 21 Century 21 is a large, worldwide company with 140 branches around town.
1725 Hanwei Plaza, 7 Guanghua Lu, Chaoyang District. (6561 7788) 朝阳区光华路7号汉威大厦东区27A室

Cushman & Wakefield International agency providing service for corporate and high-end clients.
Unit 602-607, Tower 1, China Central Place, 81 Jianguo Lu, Chaoyang District. (5921 0808) www.cushwakeasia.com 高纬环球，朝阳区建国路81号华贸中心1座602-607单元

Knight Frank Product of a merger between Chesterton Petty and Knight Frank. This global agency services high-end corporate and individual clients.
302 E1, Oriental Plaza, 1 Dongchang'an Jie, Dongcheng District. (8518 5758) www.knightfrank.com.cn/home_bj.jsp 莱坊，东城区东长安街1号东方广场东1座302

Lihong Operated by a Danish-Chinese couple, Lihong offers personalized property services to its individual and corporate clients.
2106 Tower 9, Jianwai Soho, 39 Dongsanhuan Zhonglu, Chaoyang District. (8580 2389) www.lihong.biz 利红房产，朝阳区建国路88号建外SOHO 9号楼2106室

Super Sleuth
What to look for

How do you determine the fair value of a property? Whether you plan to rent or buy, do your homework, since the asking price isn't always an indicator of quality. Age is an important factor: as a rule, the older the building, the lower the quality. That said, refurbished buildings can be perfectly good, and established buildings have the advantage of offering fewer surprises: you won't find an unfinished gym, blaring construction noise and spotty water service after you move in.

There's No Place Like Home

Lessons on host family life, straight from the Mouse's mouth
by Haley Warden

With homestay, you're always on display

My Chinese was awful at best, but I gathered that my host family was using their zodiac birth-year animals as nicknames: Mama was "Mouse" and Meimei was "Little Rabbit." But for the life of me, I couldn't figure out what Baba's nickname, *da gongji*, meant, until he proclaimed proudly in English, "I am Big Cock!" This is how my year with a wonderful host family in a tiny but well-furnished apartment near Beijing Normal University began.

The homestay experience is often plugged as the best way to get "real" cultural immersion in China. For some, "cultural immersion" can be more like giving a never-ending English lesson, or worse, weeks of claustrophobia and walking on eggshells, with a curfew on top. At times, the experience is akin to being at a lengthy family reunion as a teenager, stuck hanging out with a younger cousin or listening to a nagging great-aunt – sometimes Little Brother insists on staying in on a Friday to watch ping-pong on TV, or Mama wants to have a long talk about how you should probably lose weight to improve your marriage prospects.

I was particularly lucky – my host mother had no qualms about telling me exactly how Chinese people "normally do things", and so I was able to avoid many of the usual cross-cultural pitfalls that await many a foreign hostee. Here are a few things I learned:
• I am really fat and should lose weight.
• That has nothing to do with the fact that I should definitely eat more (and more, and more), because I can't possibly be full yet.
• Showers lasting longer than four minutes are unnecessary luxuries.
• Phone calls are exclusively for information exchange and grunting affirmations, and should take between five and twenty seconds.
• Bar-hopping is way too expensive. I should just have some *baijiu* at home instead.
• I will catch a cold if I drink water during dinner, shower before bed, don't wear ten layers and a down jacket in the winter, or sleep without a blanket in the summer.

If you're considering staying with a Chinese family, you will definitely have the best experience if you are willing to become 14 years old again for the duration of your stay. Yes, that means seeing less of Sanlitun than of CCTV and being accompanied everywhere you go, at least until your Chinese is impeccable. But if you take it all with a smile, you will leave the experience with better language ability and great memories. And no matter what, you'll have some entertaining stories to tell.

PHOTO: NICK OTTO

Most Beijing buildings are earthquake-proof

Eagle eyes

Find out what you can about the developer and management companies, which are usually two separate companies. It is entirely possible to find a building with shoddy construction and impeccable management, and vice-versa. Check out other properties they have built/managed and speak to current inhabitants. Residents of such buildings are invaluable sources of information about attention to quality – or lack thereof. When visiting a compound, pay attention to the maintenance of the halls and common areas, and check to see if the guards on duty are playing cards or harassing every poor soul who walks by.

In the apartment or home, inspect the level of workmanship. Keep an eye peeled for cracks in the concrete and uneven floors. Homes built in the past ten years have been required to meet Chinese building codes, and you can demand to see the certificate of inspection. Check for double-glazed windows to keep the place warm during the city's brutal winters. Be sure pipes and radiators are well placed and won't negatively affect the layout of a room. Educate yourself about plumbing and ensure your drainpipes have an S-shaped curve to keep odors at bay. Turn on the taps and air conditioners, flush the toilets, open and close doors and drawers ... you get the idea. For mid-level apartments, getting an adequate hot water supply, 24-hour elevator and good shower drainage can be the biggest things to look for. For higher end homes, dead corners, placement of lights and outlets and a dearth of closet space are some common complaints.

Inside scoop

Visit the same unit at several different times of the day. Do not make a decision based on a very short visit. Beijing apartments are generally good about getting enough light, but open the windows (especially if you visit in winter, when they'll be closed) and listen for street noise. If it is a unit near the ground floor, be sure the road and pedestrian noise levels are acceptable.

Finally, find out the occupancy rate, as it will be an excellent indicator of success. The on-site salesperson won't be much help here, but a real estate agent can tell you, or you can get a reasonable idea by looking around – if most of the windows show some sign of life, that's a good sign.

Rental Elementals
Tenant, know your rights!

After you have found the perfect place, it's time to negotiate the terms of the lease. In Beijing

PHOTO: IMAGINE CHINA

INSIDER'S GUIDE TO BEIJING

Found a place? Check out the local eateries

the listed price is almost never the final price. You are expected to bargain and you'll obviously be trying to get the best deal possible, but bear in mind that your relationship with the landlord has only just begun. Use common sense: if the negotiations become acrimonious, it may be difficult later to get the landlord to make prompt, thorough repairs or resolve other problems. Conversely, this is a good time to request improvements to the unit – a paint job, broadband internet connection or a new TV.

The lease

The landlord or the agent will provide the lease and you will usually sign two copies, one for each of you. The contract will be in Chinese, and an English translation may be attached, but only the Chinese version is a legal document, so if your Chinese isn't up to the task, get a Chinese friend to help you (real estate companies should provide translations). Alternatively, some international agencies will provide a free, bilingual lease agreement if you ask.

Rights and responsibilities

The lease will stipulate the rights and responsibilities of each party. The landlord should take care of any standard "wear and tear" repairs for the property, both upon move-in and while you're living there. The document should stipulate the amount of deposit and the penalties for breaking the terms of the lease. Most landlords will ask for a payment of three months' rent at a time with one to two months' rent as deposit, but there are some out there who will insist on six months or a year of rent up front. This is a sign of a potential lemon. Once the landlord has your deposit, she will take care of any renovations, repairs or furnishing needed before you move in. The contract should also contain an inventory of all items provided by the landlord and their condition. If everything's still there and in reasonable shape on move out day, you get your deposit back, so no roughhousing on the furniture, got it? If you and the landlord have an intractable disagreement, you have a couple of options. You should first go to the agent to help mediate. They have a stake in the two of you amicably continuing the relationship. If this doesn't bring relief, you may have to take your complaint to court. Suing a landlord in court is a relatively painless procedure, but requires patience and attention to detail. For more see "Renter's Rights," p30.

Continues on p32

Renter's Rights

Locking horns with my landlord in a Beijing court
by Reid Barrett

"In the end, Judge Wang offered us a negotiated settlement that was pretty much what I asked for"

Nothing hurts like being cheated by your landlord. In fact, probably the only thing more demoralizing than being shaken down is the idea of taking the case to court. Surely your landlord has the keys to the system as well as to your apartment? That's how I felt in October 2005 after my landlord refused to give back my deposit.

I had moved out, paid the last phone bill and arranged to meet the landlord to swap keys for the deposit. Then came the problem. The couch was dirty and she wanted to take some of my deposit to have it cleaned. I wanted to bring in an upholstery-cleaner from the neighborhood for an estimate, but she wouldn't let us in. No swapping the keys, no handing back the deposit.

And that's how I left it for almost a year and a half, this small injustice sitting in the back of my mind and in a folder of papers on a shelf in my new apartment. It wasn't until someone else asked me about how to get a deposit back that I was finally pushed into action. I gathered my courage and all those pieces of paper and decided to brave Beijing's judicial system.

Me v. The System

The System took an early lead. I had marched down to the massive gray Haidian People's Court with determination, but not much preparation. After waiting patiently for my number to come up, I was directed to #4 record taker. Over the course of several weeks and numerous return trips due to incomplete materials, I came to know #4 as so much more than just my record taker. To me, she was Justice Li. All court officials wear streaked gray two-piece unisex suits. On the other justices, they look like court-issued pajamas, but Justice Li was like a svelte Sandra Day O'Connor.

She worked efficiently and with supreme confidence. She could cut through my documents and find the strengths and weaknesses of my case in minutes. Her confidence in my case was invigorating, her skepticism withering. Her close-cropped hair with razor-sharp bangs matched her crisp way of speaking, snapping off words at the ends of sentences like scrawny chicken heads.

I learned in stages that I needed to turn over photocopies of the lease, all rent and deposit receipts, utility bills, my landlord's ID, an official translation of my passport, RMB 50 in court fees and a written statement about the case. I had to make several trips because of small problems, like my middle school Chinese vocab and elementary school handwriting. Justice Li suggested that I type up the statement and get a Chinese friend to proofread it.

A few weeks after my documents were finally accepted, the court date was scheduled. The first thing that struck me about the court was its size: Forget the sweeping oak-paneled rooms of *Law & Order*. Imagine instead holding court in a Mazda 2-door. My landlord, the judge and I could have joined hands and sung "Kumbaya" if the mood had struck us.

The hearing process is pretty commonsensical. The judge tries to establish facts as best she can by getting each side's account. Conflicting evidence is entered and examined. Your best bet is to keep quiet unless called upon. Keep notes about what the other side says and be prepared to dispute inconsistencies when it's your turn. Have your papers in order and make sure you have names, phone numbers, dates, times and facts at your fingertips. And bring a hard-nosed Chinese friend with you to help translate.

Luckily for me, my landlord didn't prepare and she and her boyfriend embarrassed themselves. They made wild claims with no supporting evidence: According to them, I had taken an expensive vase that they had brought from overseas. They also tried to defame me by insinuating that I "brought a different girl back to the apartment every night." To her credit, Judge Wang slapped them down.

In the end, Judge Wang offered us a negotiated settlement that was pretty much everything I asked for – my deposit minus the rent for the seven days I overstayed my lease. My landlord refused the settlement and threatened to counter sue for the cost of the vase, so we had to wait two weeks for the court's decision.

Me + The System = Love

The decision when it came was exactly the same as Justice Wang had offered in the courtroom. It was greeted by a scowl and a mouthed cuss word from the landlord's boyfriend. Unfortunately, getting the money was a more difficult matter. The 15-day appeal period passed, and then the 7-day deadline for handing back the deposit. So, once again, I must go back to the once-scary and esoteric Chinese legal system to ask for justice. But now, The System and I are old acquaintances.

Tips:

The statute of limitations for rental disputes is two years
You must sue in the People's Court of the district where the apartment is located.
Your official passport translation must have the chop of a translation company. See Business & Work p580 for listings of some official companies.

First time lucky

You may get a good deal if you're one of the first renters in a new property: Your landlord may let you choose your own furniture and decor, and may – hopefully, possibly, just maybe – understand the economic advantage of having a tenant paying lower rent immediately than waiting for a sucker to pay sky-high fees at some undetermined point in the future.

What's included

In a furnished apartment, expect large appliances like the refrigerator, washing machine, A/C and TV to be included along with furniture like beds, dressers, tables and couches. Generally, the tenant pays for measured use utilities like electricity, water, gas and phone while regular fees like cable TV bills, club membership dues and management fees are already included in the rent. If a gym membership or parking space isn't included in the rent, expect each to cost about RMB 800 per month. In buildings where the central heating is turned on in the winter, heating bills are generally included in the rent. The landlord is responsible for taxes.

525,600 minutes

Most leases are a one-year affair, though most landlords are happy to lock in a two- or three-year tenancy. Nothing makes a Beijing landlord more nervous than a lease of less than one year, so you may have to pay more for a short lease. If you need to move out before the end of a lease, you'll usually need to give your landlord one to two months' notice, depending on what you've negotiated. In this scenario, you may well have to forfeit most or all of your security deposit. If you're willing to pay a steeper rent, however, it's possible to get a penalty-free break clause in the lease – either diplomatic or contingent on a transfer out of Beijing – which will let you end the lease early without paying extra.

Paper trail

Your landlord *should* give you official receipts (发票 *fapiao*) to acknowledge payment. If she is reluctant to provide a *fapiao* – lest she draw attention from the tax authorities – ask for a discount of 5-20 percent of the initial asking rent. Point out that you need the *fapiao* to reduce your income taxes (which are deducted from your salary, incidentally). If she still refuses, have your landlord sign an informal receipt (收据 *shouju*) acknowledging you paid your rent, just so you both know the matter is settled.

Register with the PSB

On move-in day, bring a copy of your passport so you and your landlord can go to the local office of the Public Security Bureau (PSB) (派出所 *paichusuo*) to register. The process is quick and free, and if you don't register you could face a fine of up to RMB 500 per day. What's more, you won't be able to renew your visa unless you have a registration certificate. You don't have to state how much you pay in rent when registering, so your landlord need not worry about being forced to pay taxes.

Matching wits with the utility companies

Like piles of dishes and stained clothes, overdue utility bills are a reliable indicator of whether your life is spinning dangerously out of control. In Beijing, phone bills are paid monthly at certain banks. You'll need to be able to write the name of the account holder in Chinese for the teller. If they are unpaid, you'll receive a couple of automated reminder calls, then a stern call from a company employee and, if you still can't get it together, discontinuation of service.

Water, gas and electricity bills are paid in one of several ways. Some homes have meters that are periodically read by a utility employee or the building's management – bills are paid at a bank or a management office. In other homes, these utilities operate on a system of prepaid smart cards – you buy a certain number of units at a bank or management office. Be sure to check the meters regularly. Still other apartments use gas canisters (like those seen in restaurants) to power the stove and hot water heater. Keep the local gas supplier's phone number close at hand.

In addition to being able to pay utility bills at various banks including ICBC (Industrial and Commercial Bank of China) and China Agricultural Bank, ATM-like kiosks have been popping up around the city (Chinese only) where you can skip the bank's lines and pay your bills for a RMB 2 fee.

If you're lucky enough to have someone paying the utilities for you, make sure they bring back the receipt.

Ask your landlord to show you where your meters are and make sure the starting numbers are listed in the contract.

E.T. Own Home
Buying a home in Beijing
by Reid Barrett and John Brennan

Next: wallpaper and carpets

Just five years ago, there *was* virtually no Beijing housing market for foreigners. We rented. Then in September 2002, the brakes came off, and, more like a dragster than a juggernaut, the thing shot away, trailing a cloud of consequences – good, bad, intended and otherwise – to cheers from the winners and … well we haven't heard much from the losers yet, but you can bet they're out there.

In 2006, the Government moved to cool the market and control things, particularly large-scale investment by overseas financial institutions. Individual buyers from overseas are now limited to one property per person for private use, and buyers must be resident in China for a minimum of one year. As you might expect, people are looking for ways around the new rules. According to Allan Tan of Lihong, one developer in the city has been offering foreign buyers a pre-purchase deposit arrangement whereby they obtain official rights to purchase after fulfilling the residency requirement, and get usage rights in the interim. Lihong stresses that anyone contemplating an agreement like this should get professional legal advice.

In terms of building styles, most developers are moving away from the Soho-style mixed business/residential construction, which created security and privacy concerns, to single use buildings. Villa construction continues, expanding to suburbs outside Shunyi, despite a ban on "super villas." No one is really sure how big a villa has to be before it becomes "super," but worries about a ban on new supply mean prices are up as people buy before the rule is eventually enforced. And, as the new subway lines open, massive developments (and higher property values) will follow in their tracks, particularly near Yayuncun and East Third Ring Road south of Guomao. New places are also going up in Yizhuang and Tongzhou.

With the right advice, you can find a way through

Risk analysis

Apart from the unfamiliar terrain created by the new laws, there other risks to think about. Construction quality is a major concern. While improving, it generally remains below international standards and horror stories abound even at reputable developments. Worries continue that the housing market could be headed for a sharp correction. There are also scam artists operating in the industry, and there is a need for caution, even though historic legislation in 2007 should help to protect property rights. Be aware also that property owners in Beijing don't own the land on which their homes are built – instead they inherit from the developer or previous owner a Land Use Right Agreement which lasts a maximum of 70 years. Real estate professionals expect that the land use right for residential property will automatically renew at the end of its term, but the term of the extension is unclear, and no one yet knows whether a fee will be involved.

Space cadet

Housing prices in Beijing are usually advertised per square meter of architectural space (*jianzhu mianji*), which is derived from measuring the perimeter of the outer walls with some of the public use space like the stairwells and exterior walkways added in, but standard contracts list the interior space (*taonei mianji*) or useable space (*shiyong mianji*). According to the law, total usable space cannot be less than 70 percent of the architectural space.

Too new

New properties – i.e. skeletal high-rises behind sumptuous showrooms – begin selling the minute the ceiling is on the top floor. This means many will wait months or years before they can open the windows and test the pipes. This requires a lot of trust. Additionally, projects differ as to whether their lots will come as simple concrete shells, semi-finished or fully fitted out. None of the choices is pain-free. Buying a semi- or fully-finished home puts you at the mercy of the developer's interior design tastes and workmanship; buying a concrete shell entails the expense and trouble of fitout.

Rental units

If you are buying a unit that you intend to rent out in the future, think again: Legally, foreigners are only allowed to purchase a single property for "personal use," not for investment. According to Ted Li, Director, Residential Services at Cushman and Wakefield, all foreigners who are looking into buying property as a form of investment technically need to set up investment companies first, as this is the only legal means to invest.

Secondhand roses

When considering a secondhand property, bear in mind that the clock has already been ticking on the 70-year land use rights, and the "automatic" rollover at the end of the period may have hidden costs. Moreover, Ted Li of Cushman and Wakefield has this advice for people thinking of buying into secondhand property: "The current owner must have paid his/her mortgage in full before being able to sell the property unless the seller's bank can transfer the mortgage to the buyer's bank directly. This type of practice is not common in the market, however, and because of restrictions that have been enforced in China's property market, second hand property is financially becoming increasingly difficult to manage. The buyer can normally receive 50-60 percent of the mortgage compared to 60-70 percent previously. The buyer should check with his/her bank first before signing any legal documents with the seller."

You should also bear in mind that if the property has multiple owners – say in the case of a courtyard – all owners must agree to the sale. In addition, historical preservation advocate Hua Xinmin warns that many courtyards are sold without the consent of the real titleholder, which is just asking for trouble down the road. Make sure you are buying from the real owners rather than the tenants. Insist on seeing the original ownership certificate. For more, see "Four Sides, Six Steps: Buying a Beijing courtyard," p38.

The process

Buying a home in Beijing is relatively straightforward, if far from stress-free. For new properties, it generally goes like this: the papers get signed; the developer or owner takes your money; you wait, and wait and wait. Just when you think they've run off with all your hard-earned cash, they collect the final payment and throw you the keys. For secondhand properties you now have the option of getting the owner to sign an escrow agreement, wherein you transfer the money to a third party, who does not release it to the seller until the deed has been transferred to you. A few Beijing law firms and at least one real estate agency (see Wo Ai Wo Jia p26) offer escrow services.

The housing purchase contract

Even if the contract has been translated, only the Chinese version will be valid in court. Make sure there are no blanks left in the contract that could be filled in later without your consent. We highly recommend using the services of a knowledgeable lawyer or an experienced real estate agent to be sure you know exactly what you're signing.

Attorney Harry Du, a partner at King & Wood, explains that you should insist the developer show you the following five key documents before signing the contract:
1) Land Use Right Certificate (*Tudi Shiyongquan Zheng*)
2) Building Work Certificate (*Jianzhu Gongcheng Shigong Zheng*)
3) Project Planning Permit (*Jianzhu Gongcheng Guihua Xuke Zheng*)
4) Land Use Planning Permit (*Jianshe Yongdi Guihua Xuke Zheng*)
5) Commercial Real Estate Presale Permit (*Shangpinfang Yushou Xuke Zheng*)

Be sure to see the original documents, not photocopies. Check if the property has ever been repossessed, used as collateral for another loan, or even already sold to someone else. If any of these things has happened there will be separate chops on the deed, which should be huge red flags to immediately stop any further transactions. Once a deposit has been made on secondhand property, go with the owner (make sure they bring their ID) to the Property Ownership Records Office. Check that the name, ID number and address on the deed matches exactly that of the seller's ID card.

Be aware that the new residency requirements for foreign purchasers mean that you must apply for permission with the PSB to buy and furnish proof of one year or more of residency.

Where do I sign?

Not so fast. Your passport will need to be translated into Chinese and notarized. Each district has an official public notary for foreign documents. The Dongcheng office is Chang An Notary Public on the 7th floor of the Shouchuang Building (首创大厦), 6 Chaoyangmen Beidajie, just south of the Swissotel (6554 4467). If there is more than one name on the deed, a document needs to be produced in Chinese that states the relationship of all the owners and specifies how the property is divided among them.

An "official" chop (or seal) is needed in addition to your signature. This needs to be in simplified characters and can be made on almost any street corner. All signatures must be in Chinese.

Money transfer

Unless you have absolute trust in the developer, wiring money from overseas straight into the developer's bank account is probably not the safest way to proceed. However, some buyers have used this proposition as a bargaining chip to get a bigger discount from the developer. Another option is to wire the money into your own local account and exchange it into RMB before handing it over to the developer. Recently, banks have increased the amount of foreign currency an individual is allowed to exchange into renminbi to USD 50,000 per month. It can be changed all at once, but a month must pass before another USD 50,000 can be exchanged.

Taxes

All properties are subject to a 3 percent sales tax. There is also a stamp duty of 0.05 percent, a one-time contribution to the real estate development's Public Works Fund, which is 2 percent of the total cost, and a "business tax" of 5.5 percent on the sale of any property owned for less than five years applies. All taxes are paid up front.

Agent fees

Real estate agent fees range from 1-3 percent: The fee is negotiable, although agents will deny this initially. The format of the payment is also open to negotiation. Sometimes, buyers and sellers split the cost of an agent. Other times, one party may take over the entire payment.

Lawyers

A lawyer can help you decipher the Chinese documents, conduct due diligence on the developer and project, negotiate the purchase and sales agreement, help obtain a mortgage, draw up and register the contracts, provide escrow services and more.

Note that Beijing's prestigious firms charge "international standard" rates. Billing methods

They come cheaper by the dozen

vary, however: some firms bill by the hour, some charge a percentage of the sale, while others set rates per transaction (i.e. for the entire home purchase). In the end, however, you will probably get what you pay for.

If, after you've bought the place, you find out there's a very grave problem with the quality of the materials used in the building, or if the developer grossly misrepresented something, it may be possible to take legal action. Note, however, that the bulk of unimplemented court judgments in Beijing are real estate related.

Around Beijing, there are many firsthand and eighth-hand stories about homeowners getting concessions from a fast Eddie development company through group pressure and media exposure. So make friends with your neighbors. Be aware though, that there is currently a media barrage of stories from spurned homeowner groups, so you may not get an editor's sympathetic ear.

Mortgages

Obtaining a mortgage for a new property is relatively simple, since the developer typically has a pre-existing arrangement with a bank to provide you with the loan. When no such pre-arrangement exists, or when purchasing a secondhand property, you can apply for a mortgage (and/or home improvement loan) from a handful of Chinese and foreign banks with offices in Beijing.

Continues on p40

HOUSING & HOTELS

Four Sides, Six Steps

Buying a Beijing courtyard
by Tom Luckock

An investment in a Beijing courtyard (*siheyuan*) is not for the risk-averse or fainthearted. The possibility of demolition, title defects and the difficulties of negotiating with five or six vendors make any purchase challenging. In addition, the unique sights and scents of bustling hutong life are not for everyone.

Yet courtyards represent probably the most neglected class of property assets in Beijing and they trade at a significant discount per square meter to similarly located apartments. At the same time they offer exposure to Beijing's booming property sector and an appreciating RMB, they are located in some of the choicest parts of Beijing, there are strict limits on supply and most importantly, behind their drab grey walls lie some of Beijing's richest and most interesting heritage. In this article we trace a six-step process to acquiring a Beijing courtyard.

A timeless view of a courtyard house

Step 1: Is the courtyard in a protected area?

Since 1979 two thirds of Beijing's hutongs and courtyards have been demolished. The vast majority have been sacrificed as part of the city's drive to develop. As a result, compulsory acquisition and demolition remain the greatest threat that any purchaser faces.

To minimize the risk of demolition, buyers should only purchase courtyards in areas designated by the Beijing authorities as cultural protected areas. In addition, some courtyards identified as having unique or historical value have an additional heritage overlay that gives them extra protection from developers. These courtyards can be identified by the blue plaque above the door (see www.beijing.gov.cn/zhuanti/rwbj/lswhbh/shymd/t664428.htm).

Being in a protected area, or having a heritage overlay offers basic protection against demolition. It does not protect an owner from demolition for road widening, subway developments or other public works. A purchaser must still do a little due diligence into local town planning to better understand this risk.

Step 2: Check the title documents

You need to ensure that the property you are interested in has good title. The majority of Beijing's courtyards do not: They are still owned by the state, and in such cases occupants have been granted non-transferable "use rights." These cannot currently be transferred to a foreign purchaser. These courtyards can easily be identified by your lawyer.

Beyond these basic searches a purchaser should also chat with locals to understand whether there may be disputes as to title or squatters living on site (problems which will not show up on title). Many of these disputes stem from the "Cultural Revolution" (1966-76), when large numbers of families were relocated into the courtyards, but never obtained proper title. Evicting these people, many of whom have been living in the courtyard for several decades, is extremely difficult.

Step 3: Check the building footprint

Market practice is to calculate the contract price by reference to the total area of the underlying courtyard land. Notwithstanding this, a purchaser technically only acquires the buildings shown on the title plan and the state owns the courtyard area. In practice, the main significance of this is that a purchaser will not be permitted to extend or build beyond the building footprint shown on the title plan. For example, any renovation plans that involve joining the courtyard buildings together will rarely be approved by the authorities.

Courtyards are filled with antique details

Step 5: Getting finance

Generally, banks will only take a mortgage over a renovated courtyard. This means that purchasers need to obtain offshore bridging financing or tap savings to fund the initial purchase. Purchasers can only look to refinance into RMB once the courtyard has been renovated. Naturally, this involves currency risks and foreign exchange difficulties, but with a flexible bank and a bit of planning these can be overcome.

Step 4: Foreigner approval

Assuming that you have found a place with good title, the local authorities must still approve any purchase of a courtyard by a foreigner. The application process is comparatively simple and only takes one week. Foreigners will generally only be refused approval where the courtyard is located near military areas or high-level government officials. In most parts of Dongcheng and Houhai approval is rarely denied, but the majority of the Tiananmen area remains off limits to foreign purchasers.

Step 5: Signing the contract

Most agents will prefer to have back-to-back purchase contracts, so that the vendors sell the property to the agent who then on-sells to the purchaser. There is little transparency in this process, and unscrupulous agents can on-sell the courtyard at a significant mark-up. Where it is commercially possible, a purchaser should insist on contracting directly with the vendors.

Step 6: Settlement

The settlement process for a courtyard is the same as for the purchase of an apartment. In particular, any foreign investor must get their Chinese name notarized before proceeding to settlement (as the Chinese name will appear on the title certificate).

The process of purchasing a courtyard remains challenging but as more and more of them change hands the market is maturing, the risk of demolition is diminishing and there is increasing transparency in pricing, particularly in the Dongcheng and Houhai areas. The recent restrictions on investment by foreigners in the property sector may take the edge off prices in the short term (although there was little evidence for this at time of writing), but over the longer term, courtyards may still offer some of the best real estate potential in Beijing.

HOUSING & HOTELS

Prices in some areas can be eye-glazing

The institutions that grant mortgages to foreigners include local lenders like Bank of China (BOC), Industrial and Commercial Bank of China (ICBC) and the Bank of Communications, Hong Kong-based banks Wing Hang and Bank of East Asia (BEA), as well as British-based banks Standard Chartered and HSBC. However, Cushman and Wakefield's Director of Residential Services, Ted Li, notes that in his firm's experience, most foreign clients turn to foreign banks for mortgages rather than to local banks. This is largely because of communication issues as well as foreign banks being more familiar and adaptable to their client's needs and practices.

Banks will offer mortgages with lengths of maturity ranging from five to 30 years. To discourage speculation and cool off the market, many banks will now only loan between 50 and 70 percent of the value of the property (though certain banks will not exceed a maximum sum). Some banks only provide loans in RMB, while others, notably BOC, Wing Hang and HSBC can offer loans to foreigners in US dollars and Hong Kong dollars. At the time of writing, however, foreign currency mortgages from BOC had an eight-year repayment limit, while those from HSBC could extend to 30 years.

The interest rate on RMB mortgages provided by Chinese mainland banks is linked to the benchmark lending rate set by The People's Bank of China (PBOC), the nation's central bank. Moreover, the interest rate on such loans is variable: that is, it changes whenever the PBOC raises (or lowers) its benchmark rate.

US dollar loans offered by Hong Kong and foreign banks are typically based on the US Prime Rate. (Some banks offer mortgages below Prime.) Homebuyers who obtain a US dollar mortgage could see their repayment costs decrease relative to those who have Chinese currency loans as the renminbi continues to appreciate against the dollar.

You should contact each bank directly about its specific lending requirements. Many banks – but not all – only provide housing loans to foreigners holding Beijing residence permits. You'll have to fill out forms, show documentation (housing contract, passport, etc.) and provide proof of stable income (i.e. personal income tax return), as well as proof of the statutory one year's residence. Be sure that any English-language documents are translated into Chinese by an officially recognized firm. If you are approved, the bank will draft an offer letter. Once you sign the offer, the bank will prepare and notarize the contract. Your lawyer should review the offer letter and the contract before you sign.

Futures

As with all investments, you should consider your exit strategy when purchasing real estate. Since the *renminbi* is not a fully convertible currency, some potential homebuyers worry about how they will convert the proceeds of the sale of their property into hard currency and wire the funds overseas. But, according to Ted Li of Cushman & Wakefield, if a foreigner has documented evidence that all relevant PRC taxes have been paid, then normally there is no problem to remit the funds through a bank out of China. However, you need approval from the State Administration of Foreign Exchange to convert sums above USD 10,000, says Greg Sy of Lehman, Lee & Xu. Be sure to hold on to the evidence of sale and original receipt of purchase for supporting documentation with the bank and the Administration of Foreign Exchange. In addition, Frank Liew, director of international sales for Sinolink Property, speculates that the 20 percent capital gains levy that is on the books but rarely collected might begin to be enforced soon to discourage short-term overseas investment.

Zhuangxiu
Extreme makeovers for your home

Whether you've just bought a property as a concrete shell and you need to fit it out, or you simply want to give a rental unit a face-lift, interior building work can be either a massive headache or a supremely satisfying experience. Fortunately, for interior design enthusiasts, raw materials for construction are plentiful, affordable, and available at almost every street corner, running the gamut from cheap to luxurious. Services also range from full service design, where a contractor will take care of almost every detail, to complete DIY for weekend warriors. (For listings of decorating firms and stores see Shopping p374).

Design companies

Unless you're extremely confident in your technical and managerial skills, you'll probably want to hire a qualified design firm or architect to help with your project. They can make suggestions and then draw up detailed work plans to submit to the management company and the contractors, plus save you multiple trips to the construction materials market. The contractor will oversee the project from start to finish and call you with questions and regular updates. The standard contract, the Beijing Residential Decoration and Construction Contract, typically requires you to pay 50 to 55

Funny, they said they'd be back after Spring Festival ...

HOUSING & HOTELS

percent of the money upfront, a second tranche midway through the project and between five and 20 percent upon completion.

One disadvantage of hiring a design company, apart from the extra expense, is that their ultimate vision might be horribly different from your own. Another disadvantage is that by not overseeing the whole project yourself, you run the risk of inferior materials being substituted for the classy ones you specified. To be more specific: glue and bond, paint, wire and wire conduit, switch and socket panels, hinges, plywood boards and even heating units can be switched for sub-par stuff behind your back. So beware.

Picking a crew

If you do it yourself, finding a crew and getting an estimate can be relatively easy. However, expect to pay up to 20 percent more than you originally budgeted for: it always ends up that way. Your neighborhood hardware store (五金建材店 wujin jiancai dian) may have some recommendations about crews in your area. You can usually find one main contractor who will then have a group of specialists ranging from electricians and masons to carpenters and plumbers. Alternatively, you may be able to go to different design companies and talk to the crew leader about striking a deal directly with the crew, thus saving the design company fee. Note that workers from Guangdong, Zhejiang, Anhui and Jiangsu usually command higher prices (RMB 70-110 per worker per day) than those from other provinces (RMB 40-60) as they are thought to have more experience. The foreman can be invited over, plans and sketches can be brought out, and estimates made. Then, go and do it again with another crew. Keep going until you get an estimate you are satisfied with, but remember: it's impossible to write thoroughness and attention to detail into the contract. It's vital to get reliable information on the competence and diligence of the crew before you sign them up. If at all possible, go to the site of their last job and inspect the workmanship. Talk to the owner about the crew's performance. Are they hardworking? Punctual? Honest? Most contracts stipulate that if a project is not finished by a certain date, the crew works the extra days for half price or even free. This is your best lever for getting the job finished on time, but it's up to you to ensure that corners aren't cut on the way through.

Watching the clock

Most interior building work in Beijing is done between March and November, when the weather is better for ventilating the workspace, and the radiators are turned off. The only disadvantage is you won't be able to test the radiator to check for any problems with the heat. If you do it yourself, you should visit the site at least once a day to find out what supplies are needed, check on progress and resolve any questions. Power tools are only permitted on weekdays from 9am-noon and 2-5pm. Enforcement is patchy and depends on the building's management company, but it's worth sticking to the rules: If noisy work goes on late or into the weekends, you may earn the enmity of your neighbors. Of course, you can paint and glue tiles to your heart's content until the wee hours of the morning.

Health hazards

Toxic building materials are becoming scarcer on the market thanks to regulations banning noxious chemicals like formaldehyde (甲醛 jia quan) in plywood boards. Nevertheless, you should always ask the vendor if his materials are sufficiently "green" (环保 huan bao) to pass a government inspection. Generally speaking, formaldehyde appears in glue, new furniture, wood composite floor and plywood boards.

Some design companies have been known to boost their profits by buying inferior and even toxic materials. If you're concerned about this but still plan on using a design firm, you could negotiate an arrangement whereby the company buys basic things like fasteners, sand and concrete and you purchase more critical materials like hinges, paints and plywood.

Are you tough enough?

To be honest, fitout and renovation are not for the faint of heart. The entire process is cyclical crisis management. Whether you choose a design company or decide to manage the project yourself, it is still an ordeal. There are many points where things can go wrong and most likely will. Perhaps the best advice is simply to know thyself. If spending all weekend poring over tile designs sounds like a rockin' good time, then going solo is for you. If that scenario sounds like hell on earth, consider hiring a design company to sweat the details.

With the right crew and plenty of patience, your remodeled flat can look something like this

Be Our Guest
Hostels and hotels
by Simon Ostheimer

To quote a famous French proverb, "It is impossible to overdo luxury." Once a barren wasteland when it came to upscale accommodation, Beijing is now bursting at the seams with high-class hotels. With the capital now host to brand-new representatives of all the world's major five star hotels (and plenty of expensive boutique alternatives, see p46), all touting their top of the range amenities (although perhaps at over-the-top prices); *everybody* is cashing in. At time of press, many of these hotels were insisting on 20-night minimum stays over the 2008 Olympics, and quoting prices of over USD 1,000 per night for the duration.

Of course, that's not to say there aren't other choices. Beijing retains a multitude of cheaper options besides the well-known brand names: There are the charms of the many small hostels; the less than charming, but easy on the wallet, local three star hotels; or you can always (as many entrepreneurial Beijingers have realized) rent someone's home – an increasingly popular option for the Games.

No matter where you choose to stay while visiting China's capital city, make sure you ask for a discount, as hotel rack rates are never truly fixed. Also check out popular online travels sites such as www.ctrip.com or www.elong.com for special deals. However, one thing is for sure, if you're looking for the best hotel guide in town, just turn the page to get your search started; and, as the French are wont to say, *bonne chance*.

The face of service at the top end of the market

Getting a good rate

The hotels below have been listed by price category. The tariffs quoted are the hotels' 2007 rack rates -- that is, their maximum published prices. Few guests ever pay rack rates, however, because hotels generally offer discounts, even during the busiest months. (Naturally, however, all bets are off during the Olympics.)

The most direct way to get a discount is simply to ask the hotel – don't be shy about haggling, politely, over the price. A travel agent can obtain a discount on your behalf. Likewise, online travel sites like Elong (www.elong.com), Ctrip (www.ctrip.com) and Beijing Hotels Travel Guide (www.beijing-hotels.net) often offer reductions of more than 50 percent off the rack rate.

Hotel rates are subject to a 15 percent service charge and can be changed without notice.

In addition to the listings below, you can find cheap places to stay by looking for a local travel hotel (*lüguan* 旅馆).

Hotel Directory
Hostels

365 Inn An excellent choice for budget travelers, this lively hostel is the life of the party. The restaurant/bar on the ground floor attracts travelers from several hostels in the area. The rooms are clean and well decorated with new wood furniture. The inn is a ten minutes walk to the Qianmen subway station. Friendly English-speaking staff provide travel planning assistance. Free Internet and laundry services available. Book online in advance – rooms fill up fast, especially during peak season. Dorm beds (RMB 50-60, 4 person rooms), single (RMB 200), doubles (RMB 200-220, 240).
55 Dashilan Xijie, Xuanwu District. (6308 5956) www.365inn.com.cn 安宜之家宾馆，宣武区大栅栏大街55号

Drum Tower Youth Hostel This three-floor hostel boasts a fine location, competitive prices and friendly service. Along with the clean, comfortable rooms, the charming rooftop bar and patio offer pleasant views of the surrounding hutongs and the Drum and Bell towers. Nomadic culinary artists enjoy the self-serve kitchen, while lethargic impulses are enabled by the onsite Internet (RMB 8/hour), basement lounge, board games, chocolate, big screen TV, condoms, beer, etc. Dorm room (RMB 50), double with large TV (RMB 190).
51 Jiugulou Dajie, Xicheng District. (6403 7702/9907) 鼓韵青年酒店，西城区旧鼓楼大街1号

Far East Int'l Youth Hostel Located in an engaging hutong south of Liulichang that retains an essence of the former "Chinese city", Far East has (for now) avoided the wrecking ball, and teems with activity. Slightly insalubrious, this friendly hostel is divided into two compounds. The south building is an ugly, tile-fronted creation, while the north compound is built around a pleasant traditional courtyard. Amenities include on-site dumpling restaurant and nearby bike rental shop and travel agency. Free use of the kitchen. Laundry RMB 20 per load. Dorm beds (RMB 45-60, 70, 4/6/8-person rooms), single (RMB 260), doubles (RMB 368-398, 328).
90 Tieshu Xiejie, Xuanwu District. (5195 8561, 5195 8562) www.fareastyh.com 远东国际青年酒店，宣武区铁树斜街90号

Leo Hostel Great for budget travelers, this lively hostel is located on a bustling market street surrounded by hutongs, ten minutes walk from the Qianmen subway station. Travelers to Tibet can book tours and permits. 12-bed mixed dorm (RMB 45), 4-person room (RMB 70), triple (RMB 270), double (RMB 200), single (RMB 160).
52 Dashilan Xijie, Xuanwu District. (6303 1595, 6303 3318, 139 1192 7715) www.leohostel.com 广聚元宾馆，宣武区大栅栏西街52号

Peking Down Town Backpackers Accommodation Set in one of Beijing's trendiest hutong neighborhoods, this hostel offers standard double rooms and good service. They have an attached cafe/library as well as bicycle rentals for RMB 20 per day. Well situated for partying at Houhai. Doubles (RMB 170), singles (RMB 130), 6-person rooms (RMB 135).
85 Nanluogu Xiang, Dongcheng District. (8400 2429), downtown@backpackingchina.com) 东堂青年旅社，东城区南锣鼓巷85号

Peking Uni International Hostel What might be the slowest elevator in the world brings you to an interior only slightly less institutional than the hostel's facade. Nevertheless, the reasonably clean rooms and bathrooms are the cheapest digs in Haidian, attracting an engaging mix of students and backpackers. With an expansive view, the common room's palatial windows are priceless in an otherwise pane-less facility. Note: Long-term students frequently stay in the 8-bed dorms. Laundry RMB 10 each for wash and dry. Bike rental RMB 20 per day. All rooms have A/C. Free Internet. 8-bed dorms RMB 60, 6-bed RMB 70, 4-bed RMB 80. Singles without bath RMB 180; doubles with bath RMB 228, with bath and windows RMB 248.
150 Chengfu Lu, Haidian District. (6254 9667, pkuhostel@yahoo.com.cn) 北京未名国际青年旅舍，海淀区成府路150号

Qianmen Chang Gong Looking (and sounding) more like a monastery than a youth hostel, Chang Gong's 200-year-old architecture and spacious courtyard help it stand out among the area's many hostels. 6-bed dormitory (RMB 35/bed), 3-4 person dorms, RMB 40/bed), triple (RMB 210), single (RMB 80), double (RMB 160).
11 Yingtao Xiejie, Xuanwu District. (6301 5088, 139 0112 3938, jian_min@yahoo.com) 前门长宫饭店，宣武区前门樱桃斜街11号

Red Lantern House Opened in the winter of 2005, everything here is relatively new and clean, including the shared facilities. Located deep inside Zhengjue hutong, guests enjoy relaxing by the pond. Try Mongolian hot pot (RMB 30) or a cup of Brazilian coffee (RMB 10) in the courtyard restaurant. A 15-minute walk from the Jishuitan subway station. Dormitory (RMB 55/bed in 6-person room, 60/bed in 4-person room), doubles (RMB 160-220, 180-240), single (RMB 180).
5, Zhengjue Hutong, Xicheng District. (6611 5771) www.hostelworld.com 红灯笼客栈，西城区新街口南大街正觉胡同5号

Saga Youth Hostel A pleasant haven for budget travelers, this popular hostel features a large communal kitchen, a common room with a ping-pong table and a rooftop beer garden. The location – several blocks north of Jianguomennei – provides easy access to the train station, subway line 1 and the Dongdan and Jianguomenwai neighborhoods. Bike rental, tour booking and internet access available. Rates are as follows – the lower prices are for International Hostelling card carriers: doubles (RMB 198/180, 218-38), triples (RMB 240/210, 258), 4/5-person dorm bed (RMB 50-65/RMB 40-55).
9 Shijia Hutong, Dongcheng District. (6527 2773, 6524 9098, sagayangguang@yahoo.com.cn) 北京实佳青年旅社，东城区史家胡同9号

Sleepy Inn This youth hostel on the banks of Xihai has much to recommend it: large size, reasonable prices, traveler-friendly amenities, atmospheric location and friendly ambiance. Centered on a courtyard, the three-story building has 27 rooms with 87 beds. The bathrooms are clean and the beds have nice comforters. Guests can surf the Internet (RMB 5 per hour) in the lounge or browse books in the small library. The rooftop deck allows for grand views of the nearby lake and alleys. Rates are RMB 60-80 per bed in dorm rooms and RMB 258 for private rooms. Bicycles are available for rent (RMB 20 per day).
103 Deshengmennei Dajie (on Xihai), Xicheng District. (6406 9954) www.sleepyinn.com.cn 丽舍什刹海国际青年酒店，西城区德胜门内大街103号

HOUSING & HOTELS

Love 40, Guxiang 20

Youyi Youth Hostel Attached to raucous Poachers Inn, this hostel is a favorite of visiting party animals. It has 20 twin rooms and 15 quad dormitory rooms. Although the rooms are a bit stark, you still get TV, phone and A/C and since you're right in the middle of the action, you probably won't be spending too much time inside anyway. Dorm bed RMB 70, double RMB 180.
43 Sanlitun Houjie, Chaoyang District. (6417 2632) www.poachers.com.cn 友谊青年酒店，朝阳区三里屯后街43号

Zhaolong Int'l Youth Hostel The Zhaolong's clean, functional dorm rooms, Sanlitun-area location and friendly service have won plaudits. It has a self-catering dining room, reading room, game room, laundry room, central air conditioning, 24-hour hot water and bike rentals. Singles (RMB 180), doubles RMB 160-300, four-person room RMB 70/bed, six-person room RMB 60/bed. RMB 10 discount for Hostelling Int'l members, who also enjoy priority booking status.
2 Gongti Beilu (behind the Great Dragon Hotel), Chaoyang District. (6597 2299 ext 6111) 兆龙国际青年旅店，朝阳区工体北路2号（兆龙饭店后面）

Mid Range Hotels

Bamboo Garden Hotel A haven from Beijing's bustle, this traditional Chinese courtyard hotel near the Drum Tower has a rich past as the former home of a head eunuch of the Qing dynasty, a Republican era minister and Kang Sheng, one of the architects of the Cultural Revolution. The compound's pavilions, bamboo garden and red lacquered walkways further channel the spirit of "olde Cathay." Some rooms are far better appointed than others, so compare before pulling out your wallet. RMB 760-1360.
24 Xiaoshiqiao Hutong, Jiugulou Dajie, Xicheng District. (5852 0088) www.bbgh.com.cn 竹园宾馆，西城区旧鼓楼大街小石条胡同24号

Home Inn While this budget chain offers nothing fancy, it will meet basic needs and is quite comfortable for the weary traveler. Even though these hotels were built quite recently, their decor is reminiscent of '70s motel chic. Home Inns are typically equipped with a restaurant, a cafe, a KTV, and tennis courts. 16 locations across town. RMB 148-299.
A2 Xinzhongjie, Dongcheng District. (5120 3288, 800 820 3333) www.homeinns.com 如家酒店，东城区新中街甲2号

Hutong Ren Nestled in a small, easily-overlooked side alley north of storied Ju'er Hutong, this charming little hostel offers a quiet, well-lit retreat from the bustle of the surrounding neighborhood while still being right in the middle of everything. A handful of rooms – double for RMB 300 and singles for RMB 200 – surround a stone-floored atrium filled with plants, natural light, books in various languages, wi-fi and a small bar. No full meals here, but you'll not want for good food in this neighborhood, and the relative peace and quiet you'll find here after a long day is worth it.
71 Xiaoju'er Hutong, Nanluogu Xiang. (8402 5238) 北京胡同人文化旅馆，东城区南锣鼓巷小菊儿胡同71号

Super 8 Hotel This large American chain supplies simple quality and inexpensive accommodations to a mainly Chinese business clientele. The staff speaks English, major credit cards are accepted, and the rooms are simple and reminiscent of any 3-star hotel in the United States, with satellite TV, A/C and comfortable beds. Three locations in downtown Beijing. RMB 368-488.
10 Tuanjiehu Beitoutiao, Chaoyang District. (400 810 7822, 6582 1008) www.super8.com.cn 朝阳区团结湖北头条10号

Boutique Hotels

Guxiang 20 Perfect for those wanting to experience the gentrified hutong charms of Nanluogu Xiang from the

comfort of a luxury hotel. Bright-eyed goldfish and posh, high-backed red velvet chairs line the lobby and restaurant, but the place still keeps its siheyuan roots – even if it has an incongruous rooftop tennis court (RMB 100-220 per hour) for guests who refuse to let their game slide while on holiday. A variety of lodging options are available, from standard single rooms (RMB 1280/night, including daily breakfast) to Grand Deluxe rooms (RMB 1,580 with breakfast) and discounts may be available. All rooms boast television, A/C, mini-bar and free Internet.
20 Nanluogu Xiang, Dongcheng District. (6400 5566)
古巷20号商务会所，东城区南锣鼓巷20号

Hotel Cote Cour Situated in one of the city's loveliest old courtyards, Hotel Cote Cour is the perfect place to escape the hustle and bustle of Beijing. Ming Dynasty meets Vogue Living at this 500-year-old hutong residence; the area formerly served as the rehearsal and living quarters for dancers and musicians of the Imperial courts. The 14 rooms, each of a different configuration, are arranged around a central courtyard and connected by intricately painted corridors. Everywhere you turn you'll notice the incredible eye for detail and style displayed by the creator of this cozy hideaway: the rooms are beautifully furnished with handmade Chinese silk beds, the bathrooms with emerald mosaic tiles. The lounge decor is a mix of contemporary chic and traditional Chinese, featuring a stunning room-length mural. RMB 1295-2668.
70, Yanyue Hutong, Dongcheng District. (6512 8020)
www.hotelcotecoursl.com 东城区演乐胡同70号

Kapok Hotel Opened in late 2006, this sleek boutique hotel has been well-received for its hip architecture and personal service. Kapok has set the standard for the kind of boutique hotel that embraces the modern and urban in contrast to the ancient/hutong courtyard look. The rooms are minimalist and tricked out with plasma screen TVs and huge bathtubs with jets. RMB 960-3,180
16 Donghuamen Dajie, Dongcheng District. (6525 9988) 木棉花酒店，东城区东华门大街16号

Lüsongyuan Hotel Short of renting your own courtyard home, nothing beats a stay in the Lüsongyuan for a taste of Beijing's rapidly vanishing architectural past. Centrally located in a hutong north of Ping'an Dadao, and close to Nanluogu Xiang and Houhai, the hotel is built around a series of charming courtyards. The second story suite has a canopy bed and classic views of gray tiled roofs. Bike rentals, Internet access, booking services and more. RMB 780-2,200.
22 Banchang Hutong, Kuanjie, Dongcheng District. (6404 0436, lsyhotel@263.net) 侣淞园宾馆，东城区宽街板厂胡同22号

Red Capital Club Residence A stay in this stylish boutique hotel located in a 200-year-old courtyard home is a memorable experience. There are only five suites, decorated with carefully chosen antiques and furniture used by China's top leaders in the 1950s. Other decorative flourishes include birdcages, porcelain figurines and stained glass ceilings in the bathrooms. A former bomb shelter has been converted into a bar where one can view films from the Cultural Revolution while puffing on a Cuban cigar and sipping on a Mao Tai. Not easy to find: look for the red door with a number "9" on it. USD 150-190.
9 Dongsi Liutiao, Dongcheng District. (8403 5308)
www.redcapitalclub.com.cn 新红资客栈，东城区东四六条9号

Swiss Road Hotel Tucked away among its neighboring hutong dwellings, this charming boutique hotel blends right in on the outside. Its traditional doors conceal a gleaming modern lobby. The six suites are housed in a courtyard house whose exterior has been well preserved. The rooms are simply furnished in contemporary style, with flat screen TVs. The walls of the hotel's restaurant/lounge are covered in beautiful pieces from the owner's personal art collection; the art presented is part of the owner's mission to share Chinese culture with hotel patrons. The hotel is located between the Andingmen and Lama Temple subway stops, within walking distance of Ditan Park. RMB 650-850.
48 Jianchang Hutong, Guozijian Lu, Dongcheng District. (8400 1034) www.swissroad.com.cn 瑞之路酒店，东城区国子监路箭厂胡同48号院

Deluxe Hotels

Beijing Marriott West Corporate travelers with projects in Zhongguancun or meetings on Financial Street make up the bulk of this swanky hotel's clientele. After a day of deal-making and telecommuting via in-room high-speed Internet and dual line phones, guests can unwind in the large indoor pool or 24-hour bowling center. RMB 850-20,000, plus 15% service charge.
98 Xisanhuan Beilu, Haidian District. (6872 6699)
www.marriott.com/bjsmc 北京金域万豪酒店，海淀区西三环北路98号

China World Hotel With bragging rights as the first super luxury hotel in town, the 716-room China World is an oldie but still a goodie thanks to its attentive service, location in the heart of the CBD and quality food outlets – especially Aria Restaurant. The lobby is opulent and marble-laden enough for even the most discriminating Carraran and it leads, via an escalator, to the restaurants, offices and luxury retailers of the China World Trade Center. The affiliated Traders Hotel (Guomao Fandian) just behind the China World Hotel is a less-expensive alternative for business travelers. RMB 2,100-39,000, plus 15% service charge.
1 Jianguomenwai Dajie, Chaoyang District. (6505 2266, cwh@shangri-la.com) 中国大饭店，朝阳区建国门外大街1号

Crowne Plaza Wuzhou This large hotel in Yayuncun is well positioned to profit from the Olympics since it is within a javelin throw both of the Olympic Village and a major conference center. Nine multi-function meeting rooms and a full panoply of amenities and services help guests take care of business. RMB 1198-5355.
Beisihuan Zhonglu, Chaoyang District. (8498 2288) www.parkview.crowneplaza.com 五洲皇冠假日酒店，朝阳区北四环中路8号

Grand Hyatt Though it will always be overshadowed by the more glamorous Grand Hyatt Shanghai (in the Jinmao Tower), this hotel remains one of the most upscale in China – with prices to match. Great for shopping, business and sightseeing, with comfortable, sleekly lit and furnished rooms, in addition to their award-winning Chinese restaurant (Made in China) and indoor pool done up like a tropical grotto. RMB 1,850-32,550, plus 15% service charge.
1 Dong Chang'An Jie, Dongcheng District. (8518 1234) www.beijing.grand.hyatt.com 东方君悦大酒店，东城区东长安街1号

Holiday Inn Lido If you were so inclined, you could live for days cloistered within the suburban Lido compound that is home to a supermarket, Watson's drugstore, ATM, restaurants, Starbucks, hair salon, bowling center,

tennis courts, apartments and corporate offices. Its proximity to the airport makes it an obvious choice for business travelers and airline crews, but it is a bit far from most tourist sites. RMB 1,130-2,030, plus 15% service charge.
6 Jiangtai Lu, Jichang Lu, Chaoyang District. (6437 6688) http://beijing-lido.holiday-inn.com 北京丽都假日酒店，朝阳区机场路将台路

InterContinental Beijing Financial Street Located to the west of the city in Beijing's business and economic district, this is definitely a high-end business stay. The hotel features 330 luxurious guest rooms and suites, 3 restaurants and 1 bar, a Grand ballroom, 5 meeting rooms and venues. Room rates start at RMB 3800.
11 Financial Street, Xicheng District (5852 5888) www.intercontinental.com/icbeijing 北京金融街洲际酒店，西城区金融街11号

Kempinski Hotel Standing in the heart of Beijing's "Teutonic enclave" – an area roughly delimited by the German Embassy School, Lufthansa Center, and German Food Center – the Kempinski is popular with European tourists, airline staff and executives. F&B options include the Kempi Deli and Paulaner Brauhaus. The Kempinski complex is also home to a shopping mall, offices, an international school and the International Medical Center. RMB 2,950-24,950.
Beijing Lufthansa Center, 50 Liangmaqiao Lu, Chaoyang District. (6465 3388) www.kempinski-beijing.com 凯宾斯基饭店，朝阳区亮马桥路50号

Kerry Centre Hotel This CBD-area Shangri-La property is noted for modern design, business-friendly amenities, a kid-friendly restaurant (Horizon) as well as some of the city's best cocktails (at Centro). The Kerry's sports center wins kudos for its big pool, two indoor tennis courts, basketball court and rooftop track. RMB 1,850-28,000. Adjoining the hotel is the Kerry Residences, a luxury serviced apartment complex.
1 Guanghua Lu, Chaoyang District. (6561 8833) www.shangri-la.com/cn/property/beijing/kerrycentre 嘉里中心酒店，朝阳区光华路1号

Peninsula Beijing Located near Wangfujing and Tian'anmen Square, the rooms in this award-winning hotel have hardwood floors, Chinese rugs, elegant furniture and 42-inch plasma TVs. Jing Restaurant, with its fusion cuisine and funky open-plan design has won favorable reviews. The Peninsula's shopping arcade is home to luxury brands like Dior, Chanel and Hermes. The hotel can also arrange hutong tours with a Tsinghua University professor and visits to the Great Wall. RMB 1,650-50,000.
8 Jinyu Hutong, Dongcheng District. (8516 2888) www.peninsula.com 王府饭店，东城区王府井街金鱼胡同8号

Ritz-Carlton Beijing, Financial Street Another top-range hotel on Beijing's "Wall Street." With a striking glass and chrome exterior, the hotel's 253 guest rooms are appointed with flat screen TVs, cordless phones and high speed internet and fax connections. The hotel features three restaurants (including the award-winning Cepe), a lounge and bar serving Chinese, Italian and all-day cuisines. Rates RMB 4000 - 42,500.
1 Jinchengfang Dongjie, Financial Street, Xicheng District (6601 6666) www.ritzcarlton.com 北京丽嘉饭店，西城区金融街金城坊东街1号

Shangri-La Hotel Haidian District's most upscale hotel is distinguished by its gorgeous garden, spacious rooms and arguably the west side's fanciest bar (Cloud 9). Cafe Cha serves a bountiful buffet, with an accent on pan-Asian specialties – wear your stretch pants. RMB 1,150-8,000.
29 Zizhuyuan Lu, at Xisanhuan Lu, Haidian District. (6841 2211) www.shangri-la.com 北京香格里拉饭店，海淀区西三环紫竹院路29号

Sino-Swiss Hotel Convenient access to the airport and a great pool are this hotel's big draws. The attached restaurants serve Swiss, Japanese and Mongolian cuisines among others. Regular shuttle bus service makes getting in and out of the city fairly easy. RMB 1,600-2,600.
Xiaotianzhu, Shunyi District. (6456 5588) www.sino-swisshotel.com 国都大饭店，顺义区小天竺国都大饭店

The St. Regis Beijing With more marble than an Italian quarry and more wood than an old growth forest, the St. Regis is one of the city's most luxurious hotels. At any hour round the clock, guests can summon their personal butler or a professional masseur; to fight jet-lag, there is always the gorgeous pool, spa or putting green. The restaurants, notably the Astor Grill, will satisfy discriminating palates, and the buzz around town is that the bartender whips up a mean tequila Bloody Mary at the Press Club Bar. RMB 1,550-47,950.
21 Jianguomenwai Dajie, Chaoyang District. (6460 6688) www.stregis.com/beijing 北京国际俱乐部酒店，朝阳区建国门外大街21号

Wenjin Hotel Stepping from hot, dusty Chengfu Lu and into the expansive lobby of this five star hotel is like being baptized into luxury. Just opened in May 2007, the hotel features bright rooms, ranging from very comfortable to opulent, all with glass-walled bathrooms and deep bathtubs. Rooms start at RMB 2,049 and Presidential suites top out at RMB 30,000.
Tsinghua Science Park, along Chengfu Lu, Haidian District. (6252 5566 ext 5506) 文津国际酒店，海淀区城府路清华科技园

Westin Beijing Financial Street This new megahotel on Financial Street (West Second Ring Road) appears to have spared no expense in meeting the high expectations of its well-heeled clientele, from its vast lobby and elegantly appointed rooms to its opulent spa and pool. The Westin also boasts seven restaurants and bars – including Senses, which offers what many cognoscenti consider to be Beijing's most decadent Sunday brunch. RMB 2900 to 20900 per night.
9B, Financial Street, XiCheng District. (66068866, westin.com/beijingfinancial) 威斯汀大酒店，西城区金融街乙9号

Zhaolong Hotel Its location near embassies, the CBD and Pacific Century Place has made the five-star Great Dragon – or Zhaolong as it is more commonly referred to – popular with business travelers since it opened in 1985. Recently renovated, it has a swimming pool and five restaurants, including The Tandoor, which serves Indian food. Another perk is that guests can use Nirvana Fitness & Spa. RMB 2,830-28,930.
2 Gongti Beilu, Chaoyang District. (6597 2299) 兆龙饭店，朝阳区工体北路2号

INSIDER'S GUIDE TO BEIJING

The Kapok Hotel is a boutique gem

Kerry Residence - *Luxury, Care and Fine Service with a Personal Touch*

A new episode of lifestyle begins...
your new habitat in Beijing

Professional Management Services

Wireless Internet Access

KTV and Theatre Room

Sports Club

Making living more wholesome with added facilities - the multi-function rooms, conference rooms and study room... we are ready to serve you with even more!

A comprehensive and multi-functional project, Beijing Kerry Centre comprises two Grade A office towers, 195 deluxe serviced apartment units, a shopping mall that provides personal care and convenience, a five-star hotel and a first-class membership sports club.

Enquiry Hotline:
(86-10) 8529 8228 *English / Chinese Service*
(86-10) 8529 8232 *Japanese Service*

1 Guanghua Road, Chaoyang District, Beijing, PRC   Postal Code: 100020
Email: bkcmkt@kerryprops.com   Website: www.beijingkerrycentre.com

北京嘉里中心
BEIJING
KERRY CENTRE

Residence   Office   Mall   Sports Club

FOOD

PHOTO: NATALIE BEHRING

SINCE 1995
北京小王府
XIAO WANG'S HOME RESTAURANT
私家菜・烤鸭

Add: Xiaowang's Home Restaurant at GuangHuaLu.
No.2 Building, GuangHuaDongLi, ChaoYang District.
Tel: 6591 3255/6594 3602/6591 6330/6591 8451

Add: Xiaowang's Home Restaurant RiTan Park,
Inside RiTan Park, ChaoYang District.
Tel: 8561 7859 / 8561 5985

Add: No.15 QianHaiBeiYan Bar & Restaurant Tel: 6613 1118 / 6617 5558

Joy by the Mouthful
Beijing's evolving culinary scene
by Zoe Li

Eating in Beijing is still fun, but a lot has changed since the Great Leap Forward

Welcome to the city that lives to eat.

Beijing's garden of gastronomy continues to blossom, a combination of showy native blooms, exotic hybrids, and a few promising, tightly curled buds.

This vast, fertile taste-scape will only get better from here.

Capital dining

As disposable income continues to rise, restaurant culture becomes ever more entrenched as a core social experience, drawing chefs from all over the country eager to introduce their regional specialties to Beijing's enthusiastic diners. The resulting gourmet mosaic echoes the thriving culinary environment of imperial times. But the local restaurant scene has not always been so *renao* (lit. "hot-noisy," or "raucous"), and memories of leaner times still linger in the collective consciousness.

After 1949, the idea of a "restaurant" jarred sharply with the socialist mode of the era. Dining out was considered a decadent bourgeois indulgence, while politically correct dining meant patronizing dismal communal canteens or cooking inventively at home with meagerly rationed procurements. In 1976 there were only 700 restaurants in Beijing, all of them state- or collectively-run.

Smile! Beijing's universe of eateries dish out everything from simple homestyle favorites to heady flavor blitzes

Deng Xiaoping's economic reforms changed all that. His proclamation, "To get rich is glorious," resonated through society, allowing entrepreneurship to blossom anew. One of the first private restaurants that opened in Beijing was Yuebin, a humble family enterprise opposite the National Museum of Art that served local favorites such as stuffed tofu and fried yellow croaker (see sidebar, p62). Almost three decades later, this gem of a time capsule survives, even as Beijing's culinary landscape has completely changed around it.

The gold rush

Today, a hungry megalopolis with a limitless appetite for culinary adventure has every Chen, Li and Wang grappling for a piece of the pie. Having over 60,000 restaurants in the city to choose from yields delectable benefits, with each eatery striving to furnish a better-tasting, higher-value dining experience.

This boom is only in its infancy. With the Olympics just around the corner, Beijing's restaurateurs are busy beavers, unveiling an unprecedented bounty of quality venues and pushing the bar skyward. Big-time names, such as Jereme Leung, creator of Whampoa Club, and Philippe Starck, design-mastermind behind Lan Club, are flocking to Beijing to make their mark, as they put Beijing on the international culinary map. Of course, the frenzy has also given rise to poorly thought-out restaurants hastily executed with both eyes on the bottom line.

Culinary coming of age

As the city dashes towards cosmopolitanism, and a growing number of locals travel internationally, Beijing's palate for non-Chinese food has become increasingly discriminating. As a result, Western restaurants are experiencing a renaissance, which shows no signs of flagging. No coincidence, perhaps, that such esteemed restaurant guides as Zagat's and the Michelin Guide Gourmand are adding Beijing to their list of reviewed cities.

PHOTO: NICK OTTO

Traditional Beijing cuisine? At Whampoa Club it looks like this

Devotees of gourmet international home cooking also have it easier as Beijing's pantries are better stocked than ever before. A decade ago Beijingers could only desperately dream of clandestine luxuries like cheese and chocolate. Today, rapidly multiplying foreign grocery stores like Jenny Lou's and April Gourmet tend us well, stocking all those essential goodies (see bakery and grocery store listings, p105).

Meanwhile, as the popularity of organic produce burgeons abroad, the movement is gaining steam in China. Though there are still many issues to resolve before local distribution of organic food is dependably regulated, the growing awareness of eating green is undeniable. Stores devoted entirely to organic products are popping slowly but surely, and many restaurants are hopping on the green bandwagon by featuring organic produce on their menus.

Hutong havens

Meanwhile, as our powerful hotels bolster their kitchens with prime-time international chefs, a parallel trend has emerged in the humble honeycomb heart of the ancient city. The labyrinthine hutong passageways bound by the Second Ring Road are narrow enough to keep out cars, and confusing enough to confound the undedicated. Within the past few years, these historical warrens have come to host some of the most unique restaurants in the city, preserving architectural heritage in a most delicious way (see Hutong Hankerings, p70).

Just eat it

With its monolithic landmarks, immense masses of people, and the sheer breadth and depth of its history and culture, Beijing has a knack for overwhelming – we know.

Yet, nibble by nibble, this city nestles its way irrevocably into our hearts.

Eating in Beijing is an experience both private and communal, intrinsically Chinese but culturally unifying – and also the most wholesome fun you ever will have.

FOOD

The Seventh Circle of Hell? Not quite – but Guijie's roast fish will make you feel the burn

Restaurant Directory

The following pages have distilled the hordes of restaurants down to a more manageable selection of Beijing's most notable eateries, bistros and chuck wagons. Some of these dining halls are local institutions, while others reflect our own editorial recommendations. We've also listed the restaurants most popular with the readers of *that's Beijing*, our sister magazine (see p97).

While it's impossible to include every last back alley gem, consider this list encouragement to get out and explore. No matter the craving or the neighborhood, gastronomic satisfaction is just around the corner.

These next three pages are a mini-index for the directory, listing each category, as well as how we have categorized each restaurant.

Categories

American	60
Bakeries & Grocery Stores	104
Beijing	63
Beijing Duck	63
Cafes & Teahouses	64
Cantonese	65
Central & South American	65
Chinese (Other)	66
Delis & Sandwich Shops	68
European	68
French	69
Fusion	72
German	73
Hot Pot	74
Ice Cream	74
Imperial	77
Indian	77
Italian	78
Japanese	80
Korean	81
Middle Eastern/Persian	82
Pizza	82
Russian	82
Shanghai	83
Sichuan	86
Singaporean, Malaysian & Indonesian	87
Thai	88
Vegetarian	88
Vietnamese	94
Xinjiang & Muslim	94
Yunnan	94

Restaurants

1001 Nights – Middle Eastern/Persian
+39 Italian Restaurant and Lounge – Italian
Ai Jiang Shan – Korean
Alameda – Central & South American
Alba – Cafes and Teahouses
Alexander Creek Park – Chinese (Other)
The American Cafe – American
American Steak & Eggs – American
An Die An Niang – Chinese (Other)
Annie's – Italian
Aria – European
Assaggi – Italian
The Astor Grill – American
At Cafe – Cafes and Teahouses
Athena – European
Ba Guo Bu Yi – Sichuan
Bajia Dazhaimen Restaurant – Imperial
Banana Leaf – Thai
Beijing Da Dong Roast Duck Restaurant – Beijing Duck
Bellagio – Chinese (Other)
Bhodi-Sake – Vegetarian
Biteapitta – Middle Eastern/Persian
Brasserie Flo – French
Brazilian Churrascos – Central & South American
Boucherie Michel – Bakeries & Grocery Stores
Cafe Cha - Fusion
Cafe de la Poste – French
Cafe Europa – European
Cafe Sambal – Singaporean, Malaysian & Indonesian
Cai Yunjian – Yunnan
Capone's – Italian
Cepe – Italian
Charcoal Bar – Korean
Ching Pavilion – Fusion
Chongqing Fandian – Sichuan
Chuan Ban – Sichuan
Comptoirs de France – Bakeries & Grocery Stores
The CourtYard – Fusion
Crescent Moon – Xinjiang & Musiim
Crystal Jade Palace Restaurant – Cantonese
Danieli's – Italian
Da Qinghua – Chinese (Other)
The Deluxe Restaurant – Cantonese
Die Kochmützen – German

FOOD

Ding Ding Xiang – Hot Pot
Dini's Kosher Restaurant – Middle Eastern/Persian
Din Tai Fung – Shanghai
Diyi Lou – Chinese (Other)
Dong Lai Shun – Hot Pot
East Ocean Seafood Restaurant – Cantonese
El Fogoncito – Central & South American
Elaine's Vegetarian Restaurant and Bar – Vegetarian
The Elephant – Russian
Family Fu's Teahouse – Cafes and Teahouses
Fangshan Restaurant – Imperial
Feiteng Yuxiang – Sichuan
Fish Nation – European
Fu Jia Lou – Beijing
Fu Ku – Sichuan
Ganges Indian Restaurant – Indian
Gaon Korean Restaurant – Korean
Garden Court - Fusion
Garden of Delights – Central & South American
Gege Fu – Imperial
Gisa – Italian
GL Cafe – Cantonese
Golden Peacock Dai Ethnic Flavor – Yunnan
Grandma's Kitchen – American
Grape Restaurant – Xinjiang & Muslim
Green T. House – Fusion
Gustomenta – Ice Cream
Haidilao Hot Pot – Hot Pot
Haitanghua Pyongyang Cold Noodle Restaurant – Korean
Han Na Shan – Korean
Hatsune – Japanese
Hazara – Indian
The Hot Loft – Hot Pot
Hua'an Feiniu – Hot Pot
Hua Jia Yi Yuan – Beijing
Huang Ting – Cantonese
Hutong Pizza – Pizza
Il Casale – Italian
Indian Kitchen – Indian
Isshin Japanese Restaurant – Japanese
Jaan – French
Jade Garden – Shanghai
Jasmine – Chinese (Other)
Java and Yangon – Singaporean, Malaysian & Indonesian
Jazz-Ya – Japanese
Jia 21 Hao – Yunnan
Jin Ding Xuan – Cantonese

Jing – Fusion
Jiu Yuan – Japanese
Jiumen Xiaochi – Beijing
Junqin Hua – Chinese (Other)
Justine's – French
Kagen – Japanese
Kaorou Ji – Xinjiang & Muslim
Kempi Deli – Delis & Sandwich Shops
King Roast Duck – Beijing Duck
Kiosk – Delis and Sandwich Shops
Kong Yiji – Chinese (Other)
The Kro's Nest – Pizza
Kushinosato – Japanese
La Mansarde – French
Lan Na Thai – Thai
Lao She Teahouse – Cafes and Teahouses
La Paleta – Cantonese
Lau Pa Sak – Singaporean, Malaysian & Indonesian
Le Bistrot Parisien – French
Le Cafe Igosso – Fusion
Le Hugo – Vietnamese
Lei Garden – Cantonese
Lemon Leaf – Thai
Len Len – Japanese
Le Petit Paris – French
Lido Deli– Bakeries & Grocery Stores
Li Jia Cai – Imperial
Liqun Roast Duck Restaurant – Beijing Duck
L'Isola – Italian
Little Italy – Italian
Little Sheep – Hot Pot
Lotus in Moonlight – Vegetarian
Luce Cafe – Italian
Lu Lu – Shanghai
Lynx – American
Made in China – Beijing Duck
Manzo – Japanese
MARE – European
Matsuko – Japanese
The Med – European
Mei Mansion – Shanghai
Meshiya – Japanese
The Mexican Kitchen – Central & South American
Mexican Wave – Central & South American
Miao Ling – Hot Pot
Middle 8th Restaurant – Yunnan
Mima – Cafes and Teahouses
Mirch Masala – Indian
Mondo Gelato Beijing – Ice Cream

Mooi Living – Cafes and Teahouses
Morel's – European
Moscow Restaurant – Russian
Mrs. Shanen's Bagels – Delis and Sandwich Shops
Mughal's Beijing – Indian
Muse Parisian Vietnamese Brasserie – Vietnamese
My Humble House – Fusion
Najia Xiaoguan – Imperial
Nam Nam – Vietnamese
Nishimura – Japanese
Noble Court – Cantonese
No Name Restaurant – Yunnan
Noodle Loft – Chinese (Other)
Nuage – Vietnamese
Nyonya Kitchen – Singaporean, Malaysian & Indonesian
Obelisco – Central & South American
The Olive – European
One East on Third – American
The Orchard – European
Panino Teca – Delis and Sandwich Shops
Paomo Guan – Chinese (Other)
Paper – Cantonese
Paulaner Brauhaus – German
Pazi Hot Pot City – Hot Pot
People 8 – Fusion
Peter's Tex-Mex Grill – American
Phrik Thai – Thai
Piazza Cafe – Fusion
Pink Loft – Thai
Pizza Buona – Pizza
Punjabi Restaurant – Indian
Pure Lotus Vegetarian – Vegetarian
Purple Haze – Thai
Qi – Chinese (Other)
Quan Ju De – Beijing Duck
Qu Na'r – Chinese (Other)
Raj Indian Restaurant and Bar – Indian
Red Capital Club – Imperial
Rumi – Middle Eastern/Persian
Sa Lang Bang – Korean
Sampan Seafood – Cantonese
Saveurs de Corée – Korean
Schiller's – German
Schindler's Anlegestelle (Schindler's Docking Station) – German
Schindler's German Food Center – Bakeries & Grocery Stores
Sculpting in Time – Cafes and Teahouses
Sea of Mercy – Vegetarian

Senses – Fusion
Serve the People – Thai
Si Chou Lu – Cantonese
Sorabol – Korean
Souk – Middle Eastern/Persian
The Source – Sichuan
South Beauty – Sichuan
South German Bakery, Cafe Konstanz and Bodenseestube – Bakeries & Grocery Stores
South Silk Road – Yunnan
Still Thoughts Vegetarian Restaurant – Vegetarian
Sukhothai – Thai
Tafi – Fusion
Tai Bo Tian Fu Shan Zhen – Hot Pot
The Taj Pavilion – Indian
The Tandoor – Indian
Tasty Taste – Cafes and Teahouses
Three Guizhou Men – Chinese (Other)
Tiamo Italia – Ice Cream
Tian Chi – Xinjiang & Muslim
Tianchu Miaoxiang – Vegetarian
Tiandi Yijia – Imperial
Tian Shan Pai – Xinjiang & Muslim
Time Cafe – European
Traders Cafe – Singaporean, Malaysian & Indonesian
Traktirr Pushkin – Russian
The Tree – Pizza
Vanilla Garden – Vegetarian
Victor's Place and Curry House – Indian
Vincent Cafe/Creperie – French
Vineyard Cafe – European
Wawu – Japanese
W Dine & Wine – European
White Nights – Russian
Xiangjiang Mingcheng – Hot Pot
Xiangyang Xiaozhu – Vegetarian
Xiao Shan Cheng – Hot Pot
Xiao Wang Fu – Beijing
Xinjiang Islam Restaurant – Xinjiang & Muslim
Xinjiang Red Rose – Xinjiang & Muslim
Xinjishi – Shanghai
Xu Xiang Zhai Vegetarian Restaurant – Vegetarian
The Yard – Singaporean, Malaysian & Indonesian
Ye Shan Jun Wild Fungus House – Hot Pot
Yotsuba – Japanese
Yuebin Restaurant – Beijing
Yunnan Impression – Yunnan
Yunteng Shifu – Yunnan
Yuxiang Renjia – Sichuan
Yu Xin – Sichuan

FOOD

No glum grumps here: Yankee food and a family-friendly atmosphere earn grins at Grandma's Kitchen

American

At it's best, so-called "American" food can manifest some of the most interesting culinary fusions on earth. However, in most of the restaurants listed below, American food is typified by generous, often beefy portions of comfort food, deep-fried delights, and hot, cheesy mounds of yum.

The American Cafe No-nonsense American-style diner serves up hearty burgers, a selection of Tex-Mex favorites, sizeable salads and breakfast plates in a cozy environment.
Daily 7am-10.30pm. 1/F (behind Evolution Fitness), Blue Castle Apartments, 3 Xi Dawang Lu, Chaoyang District. (8599 7428/29) 博平咖啡，朝阳区西大望路3号蓝堡国际公寓所一层

American Steak & Eggs Chef Paul serves up affordable meals, including classic carb-heavy diner breakfasts and hearty dinner specials. Bottomless cups of coffee and North American style give it a distinctly authentic ilk.
Daily 6.30am-midnight. Xiushui Nanjie, Jianguomenwai (directly north of the Friendship Store, one traffic light west of Silk Market), Chaoyang District. (6592 8088/8788) www.steakeggs.com.cn 喜来中北美西餐，朝阳区建国门外秀水南街（友谊商店北面，秀水西边第一个红绿灯）

The Astor Grill This upscale chop shop with an extensive wine list appeals to visiting CEOs and their bespoke ilk.
Dinner daily, 6-10pm, lunch Mon-Fri 11.30am-2pm. 3/F, St. Regis Hotel Apartments, 21 Jianguomenwai Dajie, Chaoyang District. (6460 6688 ext 2637) 艾斯特扒房，朝阳区建国门外大街21号国际俱乐部饭店公寓三层

Grandma's Kitchen Tuck into hearty Yankee tucker at any of three cozy locations. Enjoy sandwiches, burgers, steaks and shakes (banana variety known to be addictive).
1) Daily 7.30am-11.30pm. 11A Xiushui Nanjie, Jianguomenwai, Chaoyang District. (6503 2893); 2) Daily 7.30am-11pm. 0103, Bldg B, Jianwai Soho, 39 Dongsanhuan Zhonglu, Chaoyang District. (5869 3055/3056); 3) Daily 8am-10pm. 47-2 Nanchizi Dajie, Dongcheng District. (6528 2790) 祖母的厨房，1）朝阳区建国门外秀水街甲11号（友谊商店后面）；2）朝阳区东三环中路39号建外Soho B座0103；3）东城区南池子大街47-2号

Lynx A popular afterschool hangout near ISB in Shunyi, this comfortable and cozy cafe offers favorites such as nachos (RMB 16), hamburgers (RMB 24), shepherd's pie (RMB 28) and lots of pizza. Grownups may be lured by the drink list featuring true Italian coffee as well as fresh juice cocktails. Curl up by the fireplace and browse from a selection of imported English-language magazines.
Daily 8am-8pm. ISB east gate, Anhua Lu, Shunyi District. (8046 4755) 灵思餐厅，顺义区安华路北京顺义国际学校东门

One East on Third Offers modern American cuisine with the largest selection of US wines in Beijing. Set lunch (RMB 120, two courses) consists of delicate dishes that won't send you to sleep when you get back to the office.
Daily 6-10.30pm, Mon-Fri noon-2pm. 2/F, Hilton Beijing, 1 Dongfang Lu, Chaoyang District. (5865 5000 ext 5030) 东方路一号，朝阳区东方路1号希尔顿酒店二层

Peter's Tex-Mex Grill Texas-sized portions at these Lone Star State-inspired restaurants. Enjoy serviceable burritos, fajitas and burgers and wash it all down with a frozen margarita.
Daily 7.30am-11.30pm. 1) Boutique 2, Hairun International Condominium, 2B Jiangtai Lu (southeast

PHOTO: NICK OTTO

Quack Service

A brief history of Beijing's most famous dish
by Ed Lanfranco

One unique aspect of Beijing's culinary culture are the *laozihao* (老字号 literally "old brand names"), veteran vittle-vendors that have endured as a part of the gustatory landscape from dynastic days until now.

One of at least 40 Beijing restaurants that have been around for more than a century, the Bianyifang Kaoyadian is the capital's oldest surviving roast duck restaurant, established in 1416 during the reign of the Ming emperor Yongle (who usurped the throne and moved the seat of power from Nanjing to Beijing). Bianyifang (便宜坊 roughly "convenient to everyone") is credited as the originator of Beijing duck. It began humbly as a takeaway stand on Mishi Hutong (Rice Market Alley) near Caishikou (Vegetable Market Crossroads), in a food district outside the original Ming city walls.

The first Beijing duck was sold from a street stall

The brand caught on – during the Qing dynasty there were eight or nine independent establishments using the Bianyifang name, including several owned by three different Wang families, plus others run by people from Shandong and southern China. Until the current redevelopment of Qianmen/Dazhalan began, a Bianyifang on Xianyukou (Fresh Fish Crossroads) had been at the same location since 1855.

Bianyifang was also at the technological vanguard of Beijing's food service industry in its day. After telephones gained acceptance in the early days of the Republic of China (1912-1949), it was the first restaurant in Beijing where customers could phone in orders for home delivery service by bicycle – the godfather of *waisong*, if you will.

Of course, the modern day standard against which the taste of all Beijing ducks are assayed is Quan Ju De – another *laozihao* – founded by Yang Quanren from Shanxi's Pu County in 1864, the third year of Emperor Tongzhi's reign. He had been a poultry dealer in Qianmen during the reign of the previous emperor (Xianfeng) and brought a noted breed of ducks to Beijing from southern China, perfecting unique methods of preparation and consumption.

The first Quan Ju De (see p64) restaurant was located at 24 Roushi Hutong (Meat Market Lane) off Qianmenwai. Soon Yang operated several other outlets within the nearby entertainment district, noted for fine dining but notorious for its brothels and opium dens. Yang's restaurant name – Quan (all/whole), Ju (friendly gathering), and De (virtuousness) conveyed a sense of morality and safety in a dodgy area catering to baser tastes.

Quan Ju De set itself apart from the well-established Bianyifang by using a recipe dating to the reign of Qianlong (1736-1795), one with a lighter, drier, golden skin, less oily flesh, and the use of fruit tree wood when roasting. Quan Ju De also developed the idea of wrapping the bird flesh in a thin pancake rather than the original way of eating it on a small sesame wheat bun. In addition, Quan Ju De conjured various parts of the duck, either alone or with other ingredients, into 30 cold and 50 hot dishes.

Today Quan Ju De has gentrified and corporatized – it is one of three major stakeholders in the Judehuatian Holding Company, which owns and operates most of the surviving *laozihao* eateries in Beijing. Even their predecessor Bianyifang now deals duck under this Quan Ju De corporate umbrella. While modern-day franchising seems to have gotten the better of the oldest of *lao* Beijing's laozihao, the delicious duck dish they developed shows no signs of losing popularity.

Bianyifang roasts ducks at five locations in the Tiantan area. www.bianyifang.com (Chinese only)

The Long "Capitalist Road"
Beijing's first private restaurant
by Reid Barrett and Zoe Li

Diplomats were among Guo Peiji's first customers

South of the National Art Museum at Wangfujing, tucked away down a narrow hutong, is an unremarkable restaurant serving classic Beijing family food. One fact sets this place apart from a thousand other *jiachangcai*-style restaurants in a thousand other alleyways all over the city – this was the first. In 1980, the Yuebin Restaurant (details opposite) became the first private restaurant to open in Beijing after 1949.

At the time, the idea that a privately run restaurant would be successful was not a forgone conclusion. After many years of experience in the kitchens of The Beijing Hotel, Guo Peiji and his wife Liu Guixian scraped together a few hundred *yuan*, a fortune at the time, and opened Yuebin out of their home, employing family members as chefs and wait staff. "It was tough in the beginning," remembers Guo, "China had just begun to open up, and the system was so rudimentary." Getting fresh meat and vegetables meant cycling outside the city at the crack of dawn in order to trade outside the rationed economy at newly-opened produce markets. Despite Deng Xiaoping's new "get rich" policies, some of Mr. Guo's neighbors were still suspicious of his family's new venture and would mutter about the "capitalist roader" while he walked his children to school. Sometimes, his kids would return home crying because other parents had told their children not to play with them.

Hardest of all was simply the lack of customers with the disposable income to dine out. At first, the restaurant survived on the tiny but growing number of small-time entrepreneurs who, like the Guo family, were setting up their own businesses. It was when staff at the foreign embassies got wind of his restaurant, however, that business really started to take off, Guo recalls. "Diplomats from every country came here to dine," he proudly states. Yuebin's menu is a catalog of Beijing favorites, generously portioned, yet reasonably priced. Since those early days, Guo's restaurant has aspired to prove the Chinese saying: *jiu xiang bu pa xiang zi shen* (酒香不怕巷子深): If the wine (read: food) is fragrant then it doesn't matter how deep you must go to find it.

Now, 27 years on, the restaurant has returned its initial investment a thousand times over. The family now owns several houses, six cars, another restaurant in the same hutong, an antiques store and a furniture factory. Deng Xiaoping would be proud. His policies of risk and reward helped renew both the economy and the culinary landscape of this capital city. Of course, as the times have changed, the restaurant hasn't changed much with them. Yuebin now stands out for its antiquated appearance in a city that has almost completely rebuilt itself in the past six years. Though no longer packed to the rafters, the restaurant still gets by, mostly feeding neighbors from the surrounding hutongs – and once in a while, an old expat who knows that this unremarkable restaurant has quite a remarkable history.

PHOTO: JUDY ZHOU

of Holiday Inn Lido Hotel), Chaoyang District. (5135 8187, 8627 3734); 2) 88A International Club, 21 Jianguomenwai Dajie, Chaoyang District. (8532 2449) 彼德西餐，1）朝阳区将台路乙2号海润国际公寓公建2号（丽都假日酒店东南边）；2）朝阳区建国门外大街21号国际俱乐部88A

Beijing

As the cultural and political capital of China for centuries, Beijing has attracted China's most talented chefs, who in turn have influenced the capital's flavors with their regional flair. As a result, Beijing cuisine is a northern-inflected melting wok of the glories of Chinese cuisine. While wheat-based products like noodles, dumplings, pancakes and steamed breads prevail, simple but fragrant seasonings such as garlic, Chinese chives, vinegar and soy sauce zestfully represent. See also Beijing Duck.

Fu Jia Lou This perennially packed restaurant specializes in old Beijing faves: noodles, soups and cold dishes.
Daily 11am-2.30pm, 5-10pm. 23 Dongsishitiao (200m west of Poly Plaza), Dongcheng District. (8403 7831) 福家楼，东城区东四十条23号，保利大厦西200米

Hua Jia Yi Yuan This Guijie stalwart dishes up dependably delicious Beijing and Sichuan fare in a swanky setting with comfortable private rooms. Popular favorites include the spareribs, *kao mantou* (roasted buns) and *mala xie* (spicy crayfish). Both branches have great food, but the decor at the east location is more modern, while the west branch offers a choice between a large rowdy tarp-topped dining room with nightly acrobatic performances, or intimate courtyard merriment.
1) Daily 10.30am-4am. 235 Dongzhimennei Dajie, Dongcheng District. (6405 1908); 2) Daily 10.30am-3am. 5 Dongzhimennei Dajie, Dongcheng District. (8407 8281/88); 3) Daily 11am-2am. 3 Dangxiao Lu, Jinganli, Dongcheng District. (8451 8809) 花家怡园，1）东城区东直门内大街235号；2）东城区东直门内大街5号；3）朝阳区静安里党校路3号（家乐福对面）

Jiumen Xiaochi Taste some of the best of Beijing's traditional snacks at this collection of *laozihao* snack stalls, most of which were originally located in Qianmen but have been forced to relocate due to most of the area being *chai'd*.
Daily 10am-9pm, 5.30-9pm. 1 Xiaoyou Hutong, Xicheng District. (6402 5858) 九门小吃，西城区孝友胡同1号

Whampoa Club Situated in one of the last *siheyuan* left in the Financial Street district, this beautiful restaurant is a sanctuary from the somber hotels and blocky granite offices. Culinary mastermind Jereme Leung transforms classic Beijing comfort food into something worthy of the sophisticated surroundings. High living comes at a price – expect to pay RMB 700 per person.
Daily 11.30am-10pm. 23A Jinrong Jie, Xicheng District. (8808 8828) 黄浦会，西城区金融街甲23号

Xiao Wang Fu This chain offers down-home Chinese food of consistent good quality in atmospheres ranging from humble (Guanghua Lu) to elegant (Ritan). Also serves crisp-skinned roast duck. *Laowai* appreciate the English menu.
1) Daily 11am-10.30pm. Bldg 2, Guanghua Lu Dongli, Chaoyang District. (6591 3255); 2) Daily 5pm-1am. 15 Qianhai Beiyan, Xicheng District. (6617 5558); 3) Mon-Fri 11am-2pm, 5-10pm; Sat-Sun 11am-10pm.
Inside the North Gate of Ritan Park, Ritan Lu, Chaoyang District. (8561 5985) 北京小王府，1）朝阳区光华路东里2号楼；2）西城区前海北沿15号；3）朝阳区日坛路日坛公园北门内

Yuebin Restaurant Beijing's first privately-owned restaurant post-1949 is also one of its finest. Don't miss the *guota doufu he* (wok tofu boxes) and *ganshao huangyu* (fried yellow croaker).
Daily 11am-2pm, 5-9pm. 43, 31 Cuihua Hutong (opposite the main gates of the National Museum of Art), Dongcheng District. (6524 5322) 悦宾饭馆，东城区翠花胡同43，31号

Beijing Duck

The city that invented *kaoya* still truly creates the best, and options – which range from humble hutong hideouts and train station space bags to posh hotel eateries and the shiny glitz of famous institutions – are numerous. Yes, we're spoiled for choice, but we're also selective. After all, a pancake rolled with crispy roasted skin, moist meat and a swipe of salty-sweet plum sauce is not just a minor habit that hampers our waistline – it's a mouthful of heaven that we'd travel across the Pacific to taste.

Beijing Da Dong Roast Duck Restaurant Swanky duck eatery that does brisk business on prime real estate near Sanlitun and the embassy district. Aside from the excellent duck, they also have a large selection of homestyle standards. Try their unforgettable halibut soup. Expensive, but good for visitors. Reservations recommended.
Daily 11am-10pm. 1) 1-2/F, Nanxincang International Plaza, 22A Dongsishitiao, Dongcheng District. (5169 0329); 2) Bldg 3, Tuanjiehu Beikou, Dongsanhuan Lu, SE corner of Changhong Qiao, Chaoyang District. (6582 2892/4003) 北京大董烤鸭店，1）东城区东四十条甲22号南新仓国际大厦1-2楼（立桥西南角）；2）朝阳区团结湖北口3号楼，东三环长虹桥东南角

King Roast Duck This quality duck chain is quite popular, so you might need reservations. Try the duck liver and minced duck wrapped in iceberg lettuce.
1) Daily 11am-2pm, 5-9.30pm. 1 Minzuyuan Lu, Chaoyang District. (6204 2648); 2) Daily 10am-9.30pm. 24 Jianguomenwai Dajie, west side of Scitech Plaza, Chaoyang District. (6515 6908) 鸭王烤鸭店，1）朝阳区民族园路1号；2）朝阳区建国门外大街24号赛特西边

Liqun Roast Duck Restaurant This tiny family-run eatery is tucked away in a hutong, yet they still get their fair share of business – and publicity. Reservations recommended, as is ordering a duck an hour before you arrive.
Daily 11am-1.30pm, 4.30-10pm. 11 Beixiangfeng, Zhengyi Lu, northeast of Qianmen, Dongcheng District. (6705 5578) 利群烤鸭店，东城区前门东大街正义路南口北翔凤胡同11号

Made in China Don't be fooled by the hotel location. Here, the duck skin is crisp and rich without a trace of hanging fat, the meat succulently tender and the pancakes – which arrive in their own tiny bamboo steamer – are delicate, moist and thin as paper. This swank establishment also serves delicious pork and leek *jiaozi*. Reservations recommended.
Daily 7-10am, 11.30am-2.30pm, 5.30-10.30pm. 1/F Grand Hyatt Hotel, 1A Dongchang'an Jie, Dongcheng District. (6510 9708) 长安一号，东城区长安街1号东方广场北京东方君悦大酒店一层

FOOD

Mima is an oasis of calm nestled deep in Haidian's jungle of scholarship

Quan Ju De If you're looking for the most typical Beijing duck experience, this chain can't be beat. Prices vary according to location, with tourist hotspots invariably pricier.
1) Daily 11am-2pm, 4.30-8.30pm. 9 Shuaifuyuan Hutong, Wangfujing Dajie, Dongcheng District. (6525 3310); 2) Daily 11am-9pm. 6/F, Xiushui Dasha, 8 Dongdaqiao Lu, Chaoyang District. (5169 9058/9); 3) Daily 11am-2pm, 5-9pm. Three traffic lights north of Beichen Shopping Mall, Chaoyang District. (6480 1686); 4) Daily 10am-10pm. 2A Dongsanhuan Beilu, 1/F Jingxin Dasha, Chaoyang District. (8449 2759) 全聚德，1）东城区王府井大街帅府园胡同9号；2）朝阳区东大桥路8号秀水大厦6层；3）朝阳区北辰购物中心向北第三个红绿灯；4）朝阳区东三环北路甲2号京信大厦1层

Cafes & Teahouses

Sip a hot beverage and relax at these soothing spots. Cafes serve European-style coffee and desserts, while classic Chinese teahouses offer a glimpse into a highly refined world that's quickly disappearing.

Alba This cafe offers strong coffee and freshly baked pastries in the morning, pasta and sandwiches during the day, and toothsome desserts in the evening.
Daily noon-2am. 79 Nanluogu Xiang, Dongcheng District. (6407 3730) 日光咖啡，东城区南锣鼓巷79号

At Cafe Perfect resting spot to sip Illy coffee in the company of hipsters and serious art nerds as you rest your feet after 798 gallery hopping. Menu includes sandwiches and pastas.
Daily 10am-midnight. 4 Jiuxianqiao Lu, Dashanzi art district, Chaoyang District. (6438 7264) 爱特咖啡，朝阳区酒仙桥路4号798大山子艺术区

Family Fu's Teahouse Classic teahouse with exquisite Ming/Qing Dynasty furniture on Houhai's south bank.
Daily 10.30am-midnight. Bajiao Ting, Houhai Gongyuan Nei (inside Houhai Park), Deshengmennei Dajie, Xicheng District. (6616 0725, 6616 6343) 茶家傅，西城区德胜门内大街后海公园内八角亭

Lao She Teahouse Check out Lao She's campy Chinese vaudeville show over bottomless cups of tea and traditional snacks.
Daily 10am-10pm. Bldg 3, Qianmen Xidajie, Xuanwu District. (6303 6830) 老舍茶馆，宣武区前门西大街3号楼

Mima This courtyard cafe/bar reconstructs Haidian's old scholarly air, and infuses it with a hip design. Check out the bar made of 5,600 stacked-up books, outdoor seating and the city's most creative bathroom, designed by guru Wang Hui.
Daily 10am-midnight. East gate of Yuanmingyuan (north of the parking lot), Haidian District. (8268 8003) 左右间，海淀区圆明园东门内停车场北侧

Sculpting in Time This Beijing chain is a portal back to US college town coffeeshops. Decorated with old movie posters and furnished with light wood tables and bookshelves, these cafes sell soups, sandwiches, pasta and a variety of drink concoctions that change seasonally. Offers a Western-style breakfast menu until 11am. Great places to lounge with books and/or friends.
1) Daily 7.30am-12.30am. 2B Jiangtai Lu, Hairun International Apartments, Shop 3A (near the Lido Hotel), Chaoyang District. (5135 8108); 2) Daily 9am-12.30am. Bldg 12, 1 Huaqing Jiayuan, Chengfu Lu, Wudaokou, Haidian District. (8286 7026); 3) Daily 8.30am-1am. 7 Weigongcun Lu, south gate of Beijing Institute of Technology, Haidian District. (6894 6825); 4) Daily 9.30am-11.30am. 50 Xiangshan Maimai Jie, Haidian District. (8259 8296) www.sitcafe.com 雕刻时光，1）朝阳区将台路乙2号海润国际公寓商业3A；2）海淀区成府路五道口华清嘉园12号楼1号；3）海淀区魏公村路7号北京理工大学南门；4）海淀区香山买卖街50号

Sequoia Bakery and Cafe Serves up deli-style sandwiches and homemade desserts, as well as good coffee. Also delivers.
1) Daily 10am-6pm. Bldg 15, Nan Sanlitun Lu (north of Sanlitun Houjie), Chaoyang District. (6413 0771); 2) Daily 8am-8pm. 44 Guanghua Lu, Chaoyang

District. (6501 5503) 朝阳区南三里屯路 15楼室；2) 朝阳区光华路44号

Tasty Taste Pleasant, centrally located spot that offers light cheesecake and delicious coffee.
Daily 9am-midnight. Workers' Gymnasium North Gate, Chaoyang District. (6551 1506) 泰笛黛斯，朝阳区工人体育馆北门

Cantonese

The mild flavors of ginger, spring onion and soy sauce characterize this delicate southern cuisine, which is rich with fresh seafood and vegetables. The region is also home to the small dishes, dumplings and sweets that comprise dim sum, China's great brunch treat, which is best enjoyed with noisy clatter on the weekend.

Crystal Jade Palace Restaurant With outlets from Singapore to Seoul, the Crystal Jade group offers high quality Cantonese food, good service, and opulent atmosphere.
1) Daily 11am-4.30pm, 5-10pm. Store BB82, Oriental Plaza, 1 Dongchang'an Jie, Dongcheng District. (8515 0238); 2) Daily 11.30am-2.30pm, 5-10pm. L404A, 4/F, Block A, The Place, 9 Guanghua Lu, Chaoyang District. (6587 1228) 翡翠皇宫酒家，1) 东城区东长安街1号东方广场地铁层BB82店铺；2) 朝阳区光华路甲9号世贸天阶A楼4层

The Deluxe Restaurant Fresh and delicious dim sum attracts hungry families. We miss the carts (which are rare in Beijing), but enjoy the clean, contemporary atmosphere.
Daily 10.30am-3pm, 4.30-11pm. 3/F, Comfort Inn, 6 Gongti Beilu, west of Pacific Century Plaza, Chaoyang District. (8523 6668) 凯悦酒家，朝阳区工体北路6号凯富酒店三楼（东三环长虹桥盈科中心西侧）

East Ocean Seafood Restaurant The numerous Hong Kong natives who flock to this fancy restaurant attest to the authenticity of its dishes. The seafood is swimming in tanks minutes before it's on your table. Fabulous dim sum served daily.
Daily 11am-11pm. 39 Maizidian Jie, Chaoyang District. (6508 3482) 东海海鲜酒家，朝阳区麦子店街39号

GL Cafe Hong Kong fare served in a vast cafeteria; cheap, greasy and always open: perfect for 4am feasts.
Daily 24hrs. 1) 1/F, L134 China World Shopping Mall, Chaoyang District. (6505 6868); 2) 20 Chaoyangmenwai Dajie, Chaoyang District. (6588 9963); 3) 21 Jianguomenwai Dajie, beside St. Regis Hotel, Chaoyang District. (6532 8282) 金湖，1) 朝阳区国贸商城一层L134；2) 朝阳区朝阳门外大街20号；3) 朝阳区建外大街21号（国际俱乐部饭店旁边）

Huang Ting Fancy Cantonese cuisine, including dim sum, amidst Ming and Qing dynasty antiques – for those using the corporate credit card.
Daily 11.30am-2.30pm, 6-10pm. B2/F Peninsula Palace Hotel, 8 Jinyu Hutong, Wangfujing Jie, Dongcheng District. (8516 2888 ext 6707) 凰庭，东城区王府井大街金鱼胡同8号王府饭店地下2层

Jin Ding Xuan Cantonese chain that specializes in just about everything including dim sum.
Daily 24hrs. 1) 77 Hepingli Xijie, Dongcheng District. (6429 6888); 2) 16 Pufang Lu, across from Carrefour, Fengtai District. (6761 7161); 3) 1/F, Entrance B03, north corner of Jinyuan Shopping Mall, 1 Yuanda

Lu, Haidian District.; 4) 15 Anhuixili, Yayuncun, Chaoyang District. (6497 8978); 5) 15 Tuanjiehu Nanlu, Chaoyang District. (8596 8881) 金鼎轩酒楼，1) 东城区和平里西街77号；2) 丰台区方庄蒲芳路16号（家乐福对面）；3) 海淀区远大路1号金源时代购物中心北侧1层B03入口；4) 朝阳区亚运村安慧西里15号；5) 朝阳区团结湖南路15号

La Paleta Sister venue of Bellagio. The menu is light and bears a Cantonese influence, with a large selection of noodles and dim sum and Hong Kong-style iced teas and coffee.
Daily 11am-12am. Bldg 4, Anhuili Erqu (by the Asian Games Village), Chaoyang District. (6481 0887) 彩色盘港式茶餐厅，朝阳区安慧里二区4号楼

Lei Garden Boasting a large menu featuring seafood, steamed dishes, braised/stewed meats, and fresh vegetables, Lei Garden offers a bright, comfortable and contemporary setting for traditional Guangdong cuisine.
Daily 11.30am-3pm, 5.30-10.30pm. 3/F, Jinbao Tower, 89 Jinbao Jie, Dongcheng District. (8522 1212) 利苑，东城区金宝街89号金宝大厦3楼

Noble Court Fine Cantonese cuisine featuring dim sum as well as seafood dishes. Champagne brunch every Saturday and Sunday with open menu and unlimited bubbly.
Mon-Fri 11.30am-2.30pm, 5.30-10pm; Sat-Sun brunch 10.30am-2.30pm. B1/F, Grand Hyatt Beijing Hotel, Oriental Plaza, 1A Dongchang'an Jie, Dongcheng District. (8518 1234 ext 3822) 悦庭，东城区东长安街1号东方广场北京东方君悦大酒店地下一层

Paper A radical change from the low-key, hutong chic decor of Cho Chong Gee's other projects (Bed Bar and Cafe Sambal), this sleek, urban minimalist restaurant serves set menus of contemporary Chinese cuisine, with seafood taking center stage. The portions are small but thoughtfully prepared. By reservation (for dinner only).
Daily 4pm-midnight. 138 Gulou Dongdajie, Dongcheng District. (8401 5080) 东城区鼓楼东大街138号

Sampan Seafood On weekends, this well-appointed hotel restaurant is packed with families chatting in Cantonese, reading Hong Kong newspapers and eating delicious dim sum treats.
Daily 11am-3pm, 5.30-10pm. 1/F Gloria Plaza Hotel, 2 Jianguomenwai Dajie, Chaoyang District. (6515 8855 ext 3155/3166) 船餐厅，朝阳区建国门外大街2号凯莱大酒店一层

Si Chou Lu Dim sum is prepared in the open kitchen of this well-lit Cantonese restaurant. Business lunch set menu RMB 158 per person (+15% service charge).
Daily 11am-2pm, 5.30-10.30pm. Intercontinental Hotel, 11 Jinrong Jie, Xicheng District. (5852 5888 ext 5918/5919) 丝绸路中餐厅，西城区金融街11号金融洲际酒店

Central & South American

Beijing's Mexican food is currently enjoying a modest renaissance, as all-you-can-eat Brazilian BBQ joints sustain popularity with locals and foreigners alike. This category also includes Alameda, the modern Brazilian eatery and *that's Beijing* Reader's Restaurant Awards juggernaut.

Alameda Voted Beijing's best for three years running; this modern Euro-Brazilian eatery recently changed management. Set menus for lunch and dinner (RMB 60/158). Traditional Brazilian dishes also make gratify-

FOOD

ing appearances, such as the black bean and smoked meat stew – feijoada – served every Saturday.
Mon-Sun noon-3pm, 6-10.30pm. Sanlitun Houjie (beside the Nali Mall), Chaoyang District. (6417 8084) 朝阳区三里屯后街

Brazilian Churrascos Latin American diplomats meet up at this carnivore's delight for charcoal-grilled chicken, beef or lamb piled high on metal skewers. Buffet table with unlimited salads and soups to complement the meat feast.
Daily 11.30am-2.30pm, 5.30-10pm. Crowne Plaza Park View Wuzhou, 8 Beisihuan Zhonglu, Chaoyang District. (8498 2288 ext 6178) 巴西烤肉，朝阳区北四环中路8号

El Fogoncito This Mexican chain restaurant's materialization in the CBD is emblematic of how far Beijing's Mexican food options have come. High-value lunch specials (RMB18-48), sweet, gooey platanos, a wide selection of authentic Mex-Mex (not Tex-Mex) and even – gasp – free guacamole are reasons enough to offset the sometimes-spotty service.
Daily 11am-10pm. D01-02, Bldg 19, Wanda Plaza, 93 Jianguo Lu, Chaoyang District. (5820 6551) www.fogoncito.com 福客多，朝阳区建国路93号万达广场19号楼底商D01–02

Garden of Delights Contemporary Latin American cuisine and exciting cocktails. Features unique ceviche bar and fabulous chocolate desserts. Also boasts a good selection of Cuban cigars and two-person RMB 99 lunch special. Lunch, Mon-Fri noon-2.30 pm. Dinner, Sun-Tue 6-10.30pm, Wed-Sat 6-11.30pm.
Daily 6-11pm, Mon-Fri noon-3pm. 53 Donganmen Dajie, across from the Children's Theatre, Dongcheng District. (5138 5688) www.gardenofdelights.com.cn 饕餮源餐厅，东城区东安门大街53号（中国儿童剧场对面）

The Mexican Kitchen This cantina should induce urbanites to run for the Shunyi border. Opened by an American couple, it serves generous portions of flavorful Tex-Mex faves such as burritos, fajitas and tacos. Home delivery available.
Daily 11am-9pm. 705 Pinnacle Plaza, Tianzhu Real Estate Development Zone, Shunyi District. (8046 4558/59) 墨西哥厨房，顺义区天竺开发区荣祥广场705号

Mexican Wave We admire the longevity of this restaurant, founded in '92. The Tex-Mex and Cal-Mex specialties are pretty average.
Daily 11am-midnight. Dongdaqiao Lu, 200m north of Guiyou Dasha (opposite the Silk Market), Chaoyang District. (6506 3961) 墨西哥风味餐厅，朝阳区东大桥路贵友大厦（秀水街正对面）往北200米路东

Obelisco Sophisticated Argentinian eatery with standout steaks and a wine list heavy with New World bottles. A cavernous palace for the carnivorous.
Mon-Thu 11am-2pm, 5-10pm; Fri-Sun 11am-10pm. 1 Laiguangying Donglu (near Lane Bridge – look for the giant obelisk), Chaoyang District. (8470 1666) 阿根廷烤肉，朝阳区来广营东路一号（机场高速4号出口京顺路右边）

Chinese (Other)

Fortunately for all of us, there are far more schools, forms and varieties of Chinese cuisine than one can expediently shake a chopstick at. It sometimes seems that nearly every province, district, village or alley can boast its own delectable specialty nosh. The restaurants in this category are a toothsome retinue of some of the capital's best regional cuisine.

Alexander Creek Park Opened by a Taiwanese nutritionist, Alexander's offers some of the most authentic Taiwanese fare in town, with night market staples, seafood and Japanese influence in evidence. No MSG means delicious and nutritious.
Daily 10am-10pm. 203 Jixiangli, Chaoyangmenwai, Chaoyang District. (6552 5296) 鼎溪园，朝阳区朝阳门外吉祥里203号

An Die An Niang Shandong eatery at Chaoyang Park West Gate serves great down-home *zhou* (rice porridge), small dishes and the biggest *baozi* in town.
Daily 10.30am-3am. Chaoyang Park West Gate, Chaoyang District. (6591 0231) 俺爹俺娘，朝阳区朝阳公园西门

Bellagio See and be seen at these Taiwanese hipster eateries, perfect for late night treats (shaved ice with mango, anyone?). Gongti branch's compelling people-watching offers a tasty respite during a long evening of boogie at the nightclubs nearby. Our favorites include the divine claypot tofu, and the splendidly numbing Chongqing *lazi ji*.
1) Daily 11am-4am. 35 Xiaoyun Lu, beside Kiss Disco, Chaoyang District. (8451 9988); 2) Daily 10am-10pm. 6/F, Shin Kong Place, 87 Jianguo Lu, Chaoyang District. (6530 5658); 3) Daily 11am-5am. 6 Gongti Xilu, south of the Gongti 100 Bowling Alley, Chaoyang District. (6551 3533); 4) Daily 11am-4am. Bldg 4, Area 2 Anhui Beili, Yayuncun, Chaoyang District. (6489 4300) 鹿港小镇，1）朝阳区霄云路35号；2）朝阳区建国路87号新光天地6层；3）朝阳区工体西路6号（工体100南边）；4）朝阳区亚运村安慧北里2区4号楼（炎黄艺术馆斜对面）

Da Qinghua With fancy, Manchu-style decor and a diverse selection of affordable dishes, this is where the homesick Dongbei-ers come for their *jiaozi* fix. Also worth sampling are the donkey ribs and the Dongbei version of *baijiu*: *hujia laojiu*.
1) Daily 10am-11pm. 1-2/F, 8 Baizhifang Xijie, Xuanwu District. (8353 9038/7); 2) Daily 9.30am-11.30pm. 1 Pufang Lu, Fangzhuang, Fangzhuang, Fengtai District. (6768 8275, 6760 7243) 大清花，1）宣武区白纸坊西街8号1–2楼；2）丰台区方庄蒲芳路1号

Diyi Lou Enjoy Henan dishes, including succulent and juicy Kaifeng-style steamed *guantang baozi*, served in an authentic (slightly grubby) dining room. Walk off your meal with a stroll through Qianmen's hutongs.
Daily 10.30am-10pm. 276 Dongsi Beidajie, Dongcheng District. (6401 6563) 第一楼，东城区东四北大街276号

Jasmine This swank Chinese restaurant has its dining halls attached to a vast indoor courtyard containing a three-story wine cabinet, elaborate cast-iron chandeliers, and leather chairs bobbing in a sea of cushy velvet. The food is decent, if not particularly inspiring, but their jasmine white rice can't be beat.
Daily 9am-2am. Gongti Donglu (opposite Gate 9 of Workers' Stadium), Chaoyang District. (6553 8608) 茉莉，朝阳区工体东路（工体东门9号看台对面）

Junqin Hua Bland hutong setting, superb authentic food. Try *zhe'er gen chao larou*. This root is commonly

En fuego! Mexican chain El Fogoncito wins high marks for authenticity

used in the West by avid gardeners as a border or ground cover, but for Guizhou natives it's a delicacy with medicinal properties. Sour soup fish, *suantang yu*, is also highly recommended.
Daily 10am-11pm. 88 Meishuguan Houjie, Dongcheng District. (6404 7600) 君琴花，东城区美术馆后街88号

Kong Yiji Named after the protagonist of a Lu Xun novel, these perennially packed restaurants serves classic Shao-xing dishes such as *zuixia* (drunken shrimp) and *dongpo rou* (stewed pork) amongst a proliferation of calligraphy and antique furniture. Try the surprisingly smooth and palatable *huangjiu*, a yellow rice wine. The stand-alone private room is a perfect spot for a tête-à-tête.
1) Daily 11am-2pm, 5-10pm. 6 Zhushikou Dongdajie, Chongwen District. (6707 5151/5252); 2) Daily 10.30am-10.30pm. Blg 2, Zhonghua Mall, A42 Fuxingmenwai Dajie, Xicheng District. (6856 8801/8796); 3) Daily 10am-2pm, 4.30-10pm. A54, Anli Lu, Chaoyang District. (8480 3966/3977); 4) Daily 10am-2pm, 5-10pm. 1/F, Aviation Science & Technology Plaza, southeast corner of Hangtian Qiao (besides Experimental Primary School), Haidian District. (6876 8776); 5) Daily 11am-3am. South side of No. 8 Apartments on Chaoyang Gongyuan Xilu, Chaoyang District. (6508 2228); 6) Daily 10am-10pm. 322 Dongsi Beidajie, Dongcheng District. (6404 0507); 7) Daily 11am-2pm, 5.30-10pm. South shore of Shichahai, Deshengmennei Dajie, Xicheng District. (6618 4915/17) 孔乙己，1) 崇文区珠市口东大街6号(两广大街与祈年大街口)；2) 西城区复兴门外大街A2号中化大厦附楼2楼；3) 朝阳区安立路甲54号；4) 海淀区航天桥东南角航天科技大厦1层(验小学旁)；5) 朝阳区朝阳公园西门8号公馆内南侧；6) 东城区东四北大街322号；7) 西城区德内大街什刹海后海南岸

Noodle Loft Homestyle Shanxi dishes and noodles in a posh environment. Try the *youmian*, a steamer basket full of shotgun shell-shaped noodles.
Daily 11am-10pm. 1) 3 Heping Xijie, Chaoyang District. (5130 9655); 2) 18 Baiziwan (Soho New Town), Chaoyang District. (6774 9950/ 5372) 面酷，1) 朝阳区和平西街3号；2) 朝阳区百子湾18号Soho现代城

Paomo Guan This oasis of beautiful, authentic Shanxi cuisine offers an assortment of perfect, fluffy noodles with a lively, traditional ambiance. The short stools will make you feel like a giant when you get up to leave, especially if you've had several mugs of mijiu.
Daily 11am-2.30pm, 5-10pm. 53 Chaonei Nanxiaojie, Dongcheng District. (6525 4639) 泡馍馆，东城区朝内南小街53号

Qi Enjoy a culinary journey through China that puts a modern twist on seven regional cuisines including Sichuan, Guangdong and Beijing.
Daily 10am-2.30pm and 5.30-10.30pm. 2/F, The Ritz-Carlton Beijing, 1 Jinchengfang Dongjie, Jinrong Jie, Xicheng District. (6601 6666)，西城区金城坊东街1号北京金融街丽思卡顿酒店二层

PHOTO: JUDY ZHOU

FOOD

Time Cafe: five-star food at two-star prices

Qu Na'r Homestyle Zhejiang chow in a post-modern environment designed and owned by art star Ai Weiwei. Try the plum wine infused with red bayberries, which is delicious when served warm.
Daily 4pm-2am. 16 Dongsanhuan Beilu (in the alley behind the La Popo sign), Chaoyang District. (6508 1597) 去那儿，朝阳区东三环北路16号 (辣婆婆牌子后面巷内)

Three Guizhou Men Artsy dining establishments with very tasty Guizhou Province favorites. Be sure to try the *suantang yu* (sour fish soup) and *xiangban bohe* (fragrant peppermint salad). Adventurous diners will enjoy sampling the region's famously strong pickle, Guizhou *paocai*, which has an unforgettable flavor.
1) Daily 10am-10pm. 6 Guanghua Xili, Jianguomenwai, Chaoyang District. (6502 1733); 2) Daily 11am-10pm. Bldg 7, Jianwai Soho, 39 Dongsanhuan, Chaoyang District. (5869 0598); 3) Daily 9.30am-10.30pm. Bldg 3, Area 2, Fengya Yuan, Huilongguan, Changping District. (8171 5880); 4) Daily 10am-10pm. 58 Beisihuan Xilu (southeast corner of Haidian Book City), Haidian District. (8260 7678); 5) Daily 24 hrs. Inside the West Gate of Workers' Stadium (above Coco Banana), Chaoyang District. (6551 8517) 三个贵州人，1) 朝阳区建国门外光华西里6号；2) 朝阳区东三环中路39建外Soho7楼国贸桥西南角；3) 昌平区回龙观风雅园二区3号楼；4) 海淀区北四环西路58号 (海淀图书城东南角)；5) 朝阳区工体西门内紫云轩

Delis & Sandwich Shops
Sometimes the craving for a great sandwich can be overwhelming. When the itch hits, we recommend the places below, all of which are also great for takeout.

Kempi Deli Tourists and business-types come to the Kempi for filling European-style baguette sandwiches, cookies, great cakes and pies, and Illy coffee.
Daily 7am-10pm. 1/F Kempinski Hotel, Chaoyang District. (6465 3388 ext 5741) 凯宾美食廊，朝阳区凯宾斯基饭店一层

Kiosk Serves up delicious Serbian sandwiches, burgers and sausages from a tiny hut just outside of the Nali Mall.
Tue-Sun 11am-10pm. Nali Mall (in front of Jazz Ya), Sanlitun Beijie, Chaoyang District. (6413 2461) 朝阳区三里屯北街那里秀色服装市场

Mrs Shanen's Bagels Beijing's best bagels, as well as burgers, salads and an extensive breakfast menu. As if you needed an excuse to bring the kids, a large children's playroom is equipped with toys, kid-sized chairs and tables and an entire Chinese kitchen in miniature. Kids love to eat the gingerbread men, limb by limb.
Daily 7.30am-8pm. 5 Kaifa Jie, Xi Baixinzhuang (next to Capital Paradise), Shunyi District. (8046 4301) 单太太贝谷面包房，顺义区西白辛庄开发街5号 (紧邻名都园)

Panino Teca This casual-chic cafe bakes its own bread daily to showcase its exhaustive variety of sandwiches. Outdoor seating is available, but the light streaming through floor-to-ceiling windows ensure that you can enjoy the sun wherever you sit. Delivery is available.
Daily 8.30am-10pm. 1 Sanlitun Beixiaojie, Chaoyang District. (8454 1797) 品味店，朝阳区三里屯北小街1号

European
Consider this the best-of-the-rest of European cuisine, the category that allows us to include all our eclectic favorites like a clandestine brunch paradise and greasy fish & chips. We wouldn't be as happy in Beijing without the following establishments, all of which perfectly illustrate that comfort food comes in many forms.

Aria Elegant restaurant serves inventive European food from monthly changing menus. On many people's short

list of candidates for Beijing's best restaurant. Live jazz adds to the upscale experience. Though the kitchen can be uneven, when they're on, it's bliss.
Daily 11am-midnight. 2/F China World Hotel, 1 Jianguomenwai Dajie, Chaoyang District. (6505 2266 ext 38, 6505 3318) 阿郦雅，朝阳区建国门外大街1号中国大饭店二层

Athena The only Greek restaurant in town. Enjoy everything from tzatziki to baklava in a kitschy "I saw Zorba the Greek" interior.
Daily 11am-11pm. 1 Sanlitun Xiwujie, Chaoyang District. (6464 6036) 雅典娜，朝阳区三里屯西五街1号

Cafe Europa If you're craving authentic Italian or European cuisine, then consider Cafe Europa and expect an evening of fine-dining, cafe-style, with an internationally stocked wine bar. The oxtail is highly recommended.
Daily 10.30am-10.30pm. Rm 1113, Bldg 11, Jianwai Soho, 39 Dongsanhuan Zhonglu, Chaoyang District. (5869 5663) www.cafeeuropa.cn 朝阳区东三环中路39号建外Soho11号楼 1113

Fish Nation Expect hearty servings of chunky chips and the largest piece of boneless fish you may encounter in China. Also has salads, tempura prawns and imported beer and wine. The Nanluogu Xiang location has a nice terrace overlooking the hutong.
1) Daily 11am-2am. Sanlitun Houjie (around the corner from Poachers Inn), Chaoyang District. (6415 0119); 2) 9.30am-1am. 31 Nanluogu Xiang (near Jiaodaokou), Dongcheng District. (6401 3249) 鱼邦，1) 朝阳区三里屯后街（青年酒吧附近）；2) 东城区交道口南锣鼓巷31号

MARE Elegant atmosphere. Fun with a crowd. Selection of tapas is inventive and good for vegetarians and omnivores alike.
Daily noon-midnight. 14 Xindong Lu, Chaoyang District. (6417 1459, 6416 5431) 古老海西餐厅，朝阳区新东路14号

The Med At this hip new eatery, down-to-earth Mediterranean dishes are given gourmet twists by head chef Hector, formerly of The CourtYard. Also turns out crispy, thin crust pizza from the wood-fired oven.
Daily 6pm-11.30. 3/F (above Kong Yiji), south side of No. 8 Apartments on Chaoyang Gongyuan Xilu, Chaoyang District. (6508 8585 ext 206) www.block8.cn 地中海餐厅，朝阳区朝阳公园西门8号公馆内南侧3层

Morel's Appealing Belgian restaurant with a casual, comfortable atmosphere. Steaks are tender and delicious, mussels are fresh and zesty, and the made-to-order waffles are a must, no matter how full you are. Be sure to book ahead, as they get busy.
Tue-Sun 11.30am-2.30pm, 5.30-10.30pm. 1) Gongti Beilu, opposite Workers' Gymnasium North Gate, NW corner of Chunxiu Lu, Chaoyang District. (6416 8802); 2) 1/F East Block, 27 Liangmaqiao Lu, Chaoyang District. (6437 3939) 莫劳龙玺西餐厅，1) 朝阳区工人体育馆北门对面工体北路春秀路西北角；2) 朝阳区亮马桥路27号东座一层

The Olive Serves salads, sandwiches, dinner, health food, juice and desserts without the MSG, as well as a nice brunch on weekends. Pleasant terrace is a great spot on a sunny day.
Daily 10.30am-10pm. 17 Gongti Beilu, Chaoyang District. (6417 9669) 橄榄树西餐厅，朝阳区工人体育馆北路17号

The Orchard A secret garden, tucked away in Shunyi. Difficult to find, but worth the journey for continental cuisine served in a charming country setting.
Tue-Sun noon-2.30pm (lunch, extended to 3pm on Sun), 2.30-6pm (coffee), 6-9pm (dinner). From Jingshun Lu, exit at Sunhe Market (we recommend calling for directions), Shunyi District. (6433 6270) 果园，顺义区路孙河市场出口（建议给餐馆打电话问详细地址）

Time Cafe Five-star food at two-star prices. The menu includes everything from Singapore fried noodles to fish & chips, but the two-course business set lunch (RMB 38) with coffee and dessert helps narrow the choices down – one of the best deals in town.
Daily 9.30am-10pm. 3/F, Bldg 10, Jianwai Soho, 39 Dongsanhuan Zhonglu, Chaoyang District. (5869 3488) 食客满源咖啡厅，朝阳区东三环中路39号建外Soho10号楼3层

Vineyard Cafe This hutong cafe, specializing in comfort food and comfy couches, is both hip and sensible, and their hearty English breakfasts are excellent weekend brunch fare. Good pizza and excellent beer selection.
Daily 11.30am-11.30pm. 31 Wudaoying Hutong (just north of the Confucius temple), Dongcheng District. (6402 7961) www.vineyardcafe.cn 葡萄院儿，东城区五道营胡同31号

W Dine & Wine Belgian chef Geoffrey Weckx – the "W" himself – has created a winner in this trendy restaurant-cum-art gallery. Well-crafted contemporary continental main dishes on offer start from around RMB 48. Plush purple curtains and speakeasy mood lighting create a nightclub-like atmosphere, great to impress a date or friends of discriminating taste.
Daily 11.30am-2.30pm, 6pm-10.30pm. 22-1 Dongzhimenwai Dajie (next to Jingkelong), Dongcheng District. (6416 9538) 万杰福咖啡厅，东城区东直门外大街22-1

French

Beijing's best French food revolves around casual, cozy fare, not haute cuisine. Those seeking a bit of zee French charm can enjoy a range of classics, from bistro dishes like steak frites to Brittany's delicate, buckwheat crepes. And though the Franco-food here may not inspire cries of "ooh la la!" it will definitely stave off Gallic cravings until your next trip to Paris.

Brasserie Flo Owned by the powerful Flo Group, and now a Beijing institution. Faultless French classics include the onion soup, steak au poivre, and profiteroles. Fans hail the sun-soaked terrace, prompt service and classic fare like oysters imported from France and Alsatian choucroute. Delivery available.
Daily 11am-11pm. Rainbow Plaza (Longbo Guangchang), 16 Dongsanhuan Lu (not far from Great Wall Hotel), Chaoyang District. (6595 5135/9) 北京福楼餐厅，朝阳区东三环北路16号隆博广场二层

Cafe de la Poste Art decorates the walls, but it's the simple menu of steak, salads and potatoes, the très casual atmosphere and the friendly, attentive staff that really attract Beijing's French community.
Tue-Sun 9am-2pm, 6pm-late. 58 Yonghegong Dajie, Dongcheng District. (6402 7047) www.cafedelaposte.com.cn 东城区雍和宫大街58号

FOOD

Hutong Hankerings

Distinctly Beijing delights nestle in our alleyway warrens
by Zoe Li

No need to trek out to the country cottage. An English breakfast at the Vineyard is just an amble away

Hong Kong may have its harbor, and Shanghai its Bund, but Beijing has its own unique thang that creates a distinct atmosphere in the city – hutongs. Most of these ancient alleyways have been torn down for redevelopment, but some of those remaining have been snapped up by the enterprising – their dwellings turned into quaint boutiques, mellow bars, and, of course, some of the most characterful restaurants in the city.

One of the earliest and most successful hutong restaurants serving non-Chinese food opened its doors behind the Bell Tower just five years ago. **Cafe Sambal** dishes out classic Malaysian food in a minimalist interior which cleverly utilizes the original structure of the *pingfang* (平房, single-level house). "I like old stuff," says owner Cho Chong Gee, "and I like to contrast it with something new." Cho updates the old space with stylish modern details, bringing out the best in the ancient structure. Out-of-town guests will be wowed by the antique-chic ambience and sense of authenticity about the place. Nearby Italian restaurant, **Luce**, chooses to go in the opposite direction with a complete contemporary remodeling of their *pingfang*. With hardwood floors and strategically dim lighting, it's a snazzy joint for dinner à deux.

However, both of these places are tiny. What happened to the spacious open courtyards and multiple rooms of traditional Chinese houses, a la Raise the Red Lantern? Unfortunately, since 1949, most courtyards have been dissected into smaller, separate households, each occupied by separate families. For a taste of pre-revolutionary luxury – and Yunnan flavor – try the revelatory **Dali Courtyard**, just a kilometer or so east of the Drum Tower, which occupies a complete *siheyuan* (四合院). The owners – he a furniture craftsman, she a jewelry designer – have created an unobtrusive ambience throughout their four-sided courtyard space. The compound's high walls offer protection, while the open courtyard allows for a feeling of spacious isolation from the outside world. The soothing music, the owners' easygoing hospitality and their free-rambling pets, will relax you so completely you'll forget where you are, or what time of day it is.

A short stroll away, nested within the alleys west of Yinding Qiao, past the neon-lit cookie-cut bars, are several more of Beijing's gourmet gems. Admittedly, **No Name Restaurant**'s pairing of Yunnan fare and boho-chic decor is fast becoming endemic to Chinese hutong restaurants. However, here they pull it off with exceptional flair, the quiet rooftop terrace and well-crafted cuisine providing a welcome respite from the lakeside chaos. In an alley just a poke south, hip French wine bar **La Baie des Anges** (see Nightlife, p302) is a beacon to the oenophile community, and also serves quality French nibbles such as crusty baguette sandwiches and pissaladiere. Alternatively, winos who prefer a mass of cheesy, square-shaped nourishment to complement their tipple can dip next door into **Hutong Pizza**.

Further off the beaten track are the hutongs in the Beixinqiao area – best described as intestinal in their geographic complexity. Don't be afraid of getting lost, for you might just end up at the door of **Private Kitchen No. 44**. Deep in a hutong south of Jiaodaokou, PK44 is another converted courtyard residence, serving Guizhou province-style *sifangcai* (私房菜) – that is, dishes from the owners' private recipe collection. Comfy leather love seats, purple hues bathed in the glow of paper lamps and well-worn wooden furnishings are a great setting for a round of addictively tart *suantang yu* (酸汤鱼), the tomato and fish hot pot that is a signature of Guizhou cuisine. For a home-style European meal in another cozy hutong, meander your way to **Vineyard Cafe** for English breakfasts and pizzas in a charming semi-courtyard.

For a taste of old Beijing in a matching setting, check out **Jiumen Xiaochi**. When their original Qianmen location was scheduled for redevelopment, the collection of snack stalls relocated to a courtyard on the idyllic northern bank of Houhai. Though nostalgic locals complain about the over-sanitization of these *laozihao* (for more see Quack Service, p61), they still know this is the place for a comprehensive, one-stop tasting of all of Beijing's traditional treats.

Meanwhile, the **Whampoa Club** from Shanghai's Three on the Bund has opened its Beijing branch in the lone remaining *siheyuan* in the Financial Street district. Mastermind-chef Jereme Leung gives all the classic Beijing dishes a facelift and makes them worthy of the upmarket environs. Restored with meticulous attention to detail, the courtyard's glass ceilings, lotus ponds, and white washed walls create one of the city's best designed spaces.

Whampoa's choice of venue – an old courtyard house – signals the growing appreciation of the capital's traditional architecture, as more and more Beijingers enjoy high-quality dining experiences in unique, ancient surroundings. However, veteran hutong restaurateur Cho is not optimistic: "Most people cannot see the beauty in old things … they will only realize its value when it's all gone; when it's too late." We pray he's wrong.

Dali Courtyard Set meals only: RMB 100/person.
Daily 10am-9.30 pm. 67 Xiaojingchang Hutong, Gulou Dongdajie, Dongcheng District. (8404 1430)
大理，东城区鼓楼东大街小经厂胡同67号

Private Kitchen No. 44 Set meals only: RMB 68/person.
Daily 10am-2.30pm, 4.30pm-10.30pm. 44 Xiguan Hutong, Beixinqiao, Dongcheng District. (6400 1280) www.xiguanhutong44.coku.com 私家厨房，东城区细管胡同44号

See Dining Directory for other restaurant addresses.

FOOD

Jaan This fine dining restaurant presents a modern interpretation of classic French cuisine that is light and innovative. The decor consists of tall, picturesque French windows, elaborate crystal chandeliers and a grand piano resting on the original 1924 dance floor. *Daily noon-2pm, 6.30-10pm. Raffles Beijing Hotel Main Lobby, 33 Dongchang'an Jie, Dongcheng District. (8500 4186, 6526 3388 ext 4186)* 家安, 东城区东长安街33号北京饭店莱佛士一层

Justine's This quality French restaurant is now being managed by the Flo group. *Daily 6.30-9.30am, noon-2pm, 6-10pm. 1/F, Jianguo Hotel, 5 Jianguomenwai Dajie, Chaoyang District. (6500 2233 ext 8039)* 杰斯汀, 朝阳区建外大街5号建国饭店一层

La Mansarde In a cozy, sophisticated attic on Haoyun Jie you'll find the latest effort of Beijing restaurateur Vincent Eve. The atmosphere is quiet, elegant and very French. Devotees of the Vincent Cafe in Dashanzi will not be disappointed, as La Mansarde provides the same Breton crepes and galettes. *Mon-Fri 11.30am-2pm, 6-10.30pm, Sat-Sun 11.30am-10.30pm. 29 Haoyun Jie, Zaoying Lu, Chaoyang District. (5867 0255)* 法兰香西餐厅, 朝阳区枣营路好运街29号

Le Bistrot Parisien Typical Parisian-style brasserie serving classic dishes by a French chef. The menu changes daily and is accompanied by a wine list of over 80 hand-selected French wines. Set menu for lunch (RMB 60) and dinner (RMB 138). Live music every Friday evening. *Daily 11am-11pm. 1/F, Tongli Studio, Sanlitun Houjie, Chaoyang District. (6417 8188)* 巴黎乐事多法餐, 朝阳区三里屯北街43号同里一层 (3.3商业中心旁边)

Le Petit Paris A bar street staple with reasonably priced, decent food, especially sandwiches. The plant-filled outdoor patio is the place to sit in the warmer months, and the back room is a DVD paradise. *Daily 11am-11pm. 29 Sanlitun Lu (opposite the French School), Chaoyang District. (6416 9381)* 小巴黎, 朝阳区三里屯街29号 (北酒吧街)

Vincent Cafe/Creperie With its geranium-filled outdoor patio and brightly painted interior, this charming restaurant is like a breath of sea-fresh Breton air, making it the perfect place to eat a dejeuner of crepes in-between gallery hopping in Dashanzi. *Daily 10am-10pm. 2 Jiuxianqiao Lu (beside China Art Seasons), Dashanzi Art District, Chaoyang District. (8456 4823)* 北京季节咖啡店, 朝阳区酒仙桥路2号院内

Fusion

When done well, fusion fare is truly exciting, incorporating the best of Asian and Western culinary traditions into a remarkable marriage of cutting-edge cuisine. While the fusion cuisine paradigm is increasingly attractive to Beijing's restaurateurs, unfortunately, a "fusion" menu can sometimes mean a mishmash of Asian and Western dishes, thrown together in an attempt to satisfy all palates. That said, the following restaurants are standard-bearers.

Cafe Cha A sumptuous buffet featuring a sushi and sashimi station, pastas, pizzas, Thai laksas and Tandoori specialities. Their dessert section is a show-stopper. *Daily lunch buffet 11.30am-2.30pm, dinner buffet 5.30-9.30pm. Shangri-La Hotel, 29 Zizhuyuan Lu, Haidian District. (6841 2211 ext 2715)* 咖啡Cha, 海淀区紫竹院路29号香格里拉饭店

Ching Pavilion An ambitious three floors of lounge and dining room with a highly designed interior. The menu features Asian flavors and Western presentation. *Daily 9am-11pm. 76 Donghuamen Dajie (at the intersection of Donghuamen Dajie and Nanchizi), Dongcheng District. (6523 8775/76)* 青阁, 东城区东华门大街76号 (东华门大街和南池子的路口)

The CourtYard Still popular after all these years, Handel Lee's modern eatery serves a tourist-friendly blend of East-meets-West cuisine. Some gripe that the food can be mediocre, but it's tough to beat the view – overlooking the Forbidden City. *Daily 6-9.30pm. 95 Donghuamen Dajie (north of Donghuamen parking lot at the Forbidden City), Dongcheng District. (6526 8883)* 四合院, 东城区东华门大街95号 (故宫东华门停车场北面)

Garden Court Brasserie-style buffet featuring an extravagant Champagne brunch on Sundays. *Daily 6am-11pm. St. Regis Hotel, 21 Jianguomenwai Dajie, Chaoyang District. (6460 6688 ext 2340)* 景苑咖啡厅, 朝阳区建国门外大街21号国际俱乐部饭店

Green T. House Like Alice stepping into the Mad Hatter's chinoiserie tea party. Voted "Best to Impress Visitors" in our 2007 Reader Restaurant Awards. Tea-infused fusion cuisine served in a fanciful (and fancifully priced) atmosphere. *Daily 11am-2.30pm, 6pm-midnight. 6 Gongti Xilu, Chaoyang District. (6552 8310, 6552 8311)* 紫云轩, 朝阳区工体西路6号

Jing A funky, minimalist, open-plan restaurant with top-notch cuisine. Watch the chefs in action. *Daily 5.30am-11.30pm. Basement of Peninsula Palace Hotel, 8 Jinyu Hutong, Wangfujing, Dongcheng District. (6559 2888 ext 6714)* 京, 东城区王府井金鱼胡同8号王府饭店地下1层

Le Cafe Igosso A seductive, lush restaurant that's rarely packed – perfect for those occasions that demand privacy. The menu offers an unusual and amusing Japanese interpretation of Italian cuisine. Great for a date. *Daily 11.30am-1am. Dongsanhuan Nanlu (800m south of Guomao bridge on east side of street), Chaoyang District. (8771 7013)* 朝阳区东三环南路 (国贸桥往南走800米路东)

My Humble House With its self-consciously striking decor – including a bamboo grove and reflecting pool covered with floating rose petals – My Humble House seems anything but, well, "humble." Professional, friendly service complements a fusion of Chinese cuisines in an impressively stunning and romantic setting. *Daily 11.30am-2.30pm, 5.30-10.30pm. W307 Oriental Plaza, 1 Dongchang'an Jie, Dongcheng District. (8518 8811)* 寒舍, 东城区东方广场平台层西三办公楼W307

People 8 Shintori's collection of restaurants have long been enjoyed by denizens of Taipei and Shanghai, and now they have finally brought their unique blend of stylish design, immaculate presentation, and elegant cuisine to the capital. The restrooms have to be seen to be believed. *Daily 11.30am-2.30pm, 5.30-11pm. 18 Jianguomenwai Dajie (behind the SciTech Hotel), Chaoyang District. (6515 8585)* 人间玄吧, 朝阳区建国门外大街18号

Gnarled branches and airy latticework shape Green T. House's surreal supper dreamscape

Piazza Cafe If only we had an "everything" category ... Piazza satisfies all cravings with a menu of pizza, western foods, Vietnamese, Thai and Chinese. Cozy cushions and jazz tunes enhance a laid-back atmosphere.
Daily 11am-9.30pm. South gate of Capital Paradise, Shunyi District. (8046 7788/2020) 翰风餐厅，顺义区民族园南门

Senses A contemporary buffet and a la carte restaurant offering a unique combination of Asian and international cuisine. Their brunch is our pick as the best place in town to stuff your face (see p103).
Daily 6am-midnight. 1/F, The Westin Beijing, 9B Jinrong Jie, Xicheng District. (6606 8866) 味，西城区金融大街乙9号北京金融街威斯汀大酒店1层

Tafi Tafi, which stands for "Table and Fellow Indispensable," offers an eclectic mix of Japanese and Italian cuisines. Five-and six-course prix fixe meals make this a worthy Wudaokou destination.
Daily 11am-10.30pm. 8 Zhongguancun Lu, 1/F, Bldg B Dongsheng Dasha (across from the front entrance of Qinghuayuan Hotel), Haidian District. (8252 7433) 海淀区中关村路8号东升大厦B楼1层

German

Achtung! Germans make great sausages! Also, heavy breads and thick noodles, tender, braised roasts and sharp mustard and sauerkraut. This is a filling cuisine that's as hearty and brisk as a vigorous hug from your opa.

Die Kochmützen Appealing German restaurant with a charming, cozy atmosphere serving classically Bavarian food and fresh, unfiltered dark beer.
Daily 11am-11pm. Rm 0718, Bldg 7, Jianwai Soho, 39 Dongsanhuan Zhonglu, Chaoyang District. (5869 3830) www.kochmuetzen.com 德国厨师帽，朝阳区建外Soho7座东三环中路39号建外Soho7座0718室

Paulaner Brauhaus One of Beijing's best choices for authentic, if pricey, German food, the Paulaner brews its own beer.
Daily 11am-1am. 50 Liangmaqiao Lu, Kempinski Hotel, Chaoyang District. (6465 3388 ext 5732) 普拉那啤酒坊餐厅，朝阳区亮马桥路50号凯宾斯基饭店

Schiller's German specialties at affordable prices and a dedicated happy hour crowd.
Daily 10am-1am. 1 Liangmahe Nanlu, south of Capital Mansions, Chaoyang District. (6464 9016) 大明西餐厅，朝阳区亮马河南路1号京城大厦南边

Schindler's Anlegestelle/Tankstelle These two relaxed sister restaurants serve great sausages, grilled meat, pork knuckle, sauerkraut and more, washed down with imported German beer. Really hungry? Try the grilleplatte. Prices are moderate, and the Filling Station's airy outdoor terrace is within Ritan Park. Enormously

satisfying. The Docking Station on north Sanlitun has towering ceilings and a wide-open dining room.
1) *Anlegestelle: Daily 11am-late. 10 Sanlitun Beixiaojie, Chaoyang District. (6463 1108); 2) Tankstelle: Daily 10am-midnight. 15A Guanghua Lu (200m east of Ritan Park South Gate), Chaoyang District. (8562 6439) 1)* 申德勒码头餐厅，朝阳区三里屯北小街10号；2) 申德勒加油站，朝阳区光华路甲15号(日坛南门往东200米)

Hot Pot

Some would argue that hot pot – like hot water – is even better in the summer, when it can help one regulate one's body temperature. Who are you to argue with science? Nevertheless, many people prefer to imbibe from the body and soul-warming – and often nerve-searing – bubbling cauldrons of delight during the bitter winter months. Whatever your philosophy, we've included some of our favorite hot pot places below – they range from swanky eateries with individual burners (perfect for picky eaters), to noisy, cramped and sweaty places that feature a joyous raucousness akin to bedlam.

Ding Ding Xiang Packed throughout the seasons, these popular hot pot "paradises" have a savory sesame dipping sauce to accompany the meat and vegetables. Also offer deliciously fresh *shaobing* (sesame-covered bread). The location opposite East Gate features individual hot pots.
1) *Daily 11am-10pm. Bldg 7, Guoxing Jiayuan, Shouti Nanlu, Haidian District. (8835 7775/7779); 2) Daily 11am-12pm. 1/F, 14 Dongzhong Jie, Dongzhimenwai, Dongcheng District. (6417 2546); 3) Daily 11am-10pm. 2/F, Yuanjia International Apartments, Dongzhimenwai, Dongzhong Jie (opposite East Gate Plaza), Dongcheng District. (6417 9289)* 鼎鼎香，1) 海淀区首体南路国兴家园7号楼1-2层；2) 东城区东直门外东中街14号1层；3) 东城区东直门外东中环广场对面元嘉国际公寓2层

Dong Lai Shun See "A Cauldron for Every Palate," p76.
Daily 11am-9.30pm. 5/F, Xindong'an Plaza, Wangfujing Dajie, Dongcheng District. (6528 0932) 东来顺，东城区王府井大街新东安五层

Haidilao Hot Pot See "A Cauldron for Every Palate," p76.
Daily 11am-midnight. 29 Nanmofang Lu, Chaoyang District. (8779 8677/8911) 海底捞火锅，朝阳区南磨房路29号(近大望路)

The Hot Loft Born again as an upscale buffet-style dining room, this joint serves beautifully presented Asian-inspired fusion cuisine with sushi, shark fin soup and many Chinese favorites. Private rooms for large parties, a glass wine cellar and live pianist add to the hotel-restaurant-like atmosphere.
1) *Daily 11am-12pm. 5/F, 8 Gongti Xilu, Chaoyang District. (6552 7992); 2) Daily 11am-midnight. 4 Gongti Beilu, Chaoyang District. (6501 7501)* 鼎酷，1) 朝阳区工体西路8号；2) 朝阳区工体北路4号院内

Hua'an Feiniu Fresh "Gold Medal" beef in single-serving hot pots. The Qingnianhu Beijie location packs 'em in.
1) *Daily 11am-11pm. 8 Qingnianhu Beijie, Jiangzhaikou, Dongcheng District. (8411 6060); 2) Daily 11am-11pm. 8 Huayuan Dong Lu, Haidian District. (8203 0123)* 华安肥牛，1) 东城区蒋宅口青年湖北街8号；2) 海淀区花园东路8号

Little Sheep Nationwide chain serves mutton hot pot with a twist: a special cumin-based broth. No dipping sauce required.
1) *Daily 10am-10pm. Northwest corner of Caishikou intersection, Xuanwu District. (6316 6668); 2) Daily 24hrs. 209 Dongzhimennei Dajie, Dongcheng District. (8400 1669)* 小肥羊，1) 宣武区菜市口路口西北角；2) 东城区东直门内大街209号

Miao Ling Located on the *renao* Guijie, this perpetually crowded Guizhou-style hot pot restaurant offers *suantang yu*, a sour, tomato-based soup with a whole fish. Some complain that the soup is not spicy enough, yet they keep coming back for more.
Daily 24hrs. 232 Dongzhimenneidajie, Dongcheng District. (6404 9765) 苗岭酸汤鱼，东城区东直门内大街232号

Pazi Hot Pot City Great hot pot served in a lively atmosphere - perfect for a large group. Unless you can truly stand Sichuan's five-alarm spices, order a *yuanyang huoguo*, a pot split into two halves, one containing a mild broth, the other a fiery one.
Daily 10.30am-3am. 13 Xinyuan Jie, Chaoyang District. (8451 0505) 火巴子火锅，朝阳区新源街13号

Tai Bo Tian Fu Shan Zhen Yunnanese and Fujianese-inspired mushroom hot pot.
Daily 11am-11pm. Bldg 9, Erqi Juchang Lu, Xicheng District. (6801 9641) 太伯天府山珍，西城区二七剧场路9号楼

Xiangjiang Mingcheng Spacious and cheerful. Enjoy authentic Canto hotpot in a clean, casually sophisticated environment.
Daily 10.30am-4am. 2/F, Bldg B, Donghuan Guangchang, Dongzhongjie (opposite Ding Ding Xiang), Dongcheng District. (6418 3666/3777) 香江名城，东城区东中街东环广场B座2层

Xiao Shan Cheng Talk about *renao*! The atmosphere at this joint is so authentic your glasses steam up upon entering.
Daily 24hrs. 1) 183 Dongzhimennei, Dongcheng District. (6407 6570); 2) 251 Dongzhimennei, Dongcheng District. (8402 0856) 小山城，1) 东城区东直门内大街183号；2) 东城区东直门内大街253号

Ye Shan Jun Wild Fungus House Mushroom hot pot inspired by Yunnan and Fujian cuisine.
Daily 9.30am-12.30am. 2A Qianmen Dongdajie, Chongwen District. (6512 2708) 野山菌蘑菇宴，崇文区前门东大街甲2号

Ice Cream

A bounty of international brands such as TCBY, Dairy Queen and Häagen Dazs, as well as a handful of smaller operations, help us relieve the summer swelter. From gelato and frozen yogurt to mountains of shaved ice and rich, whole milk iced dairy products, satisfy your cravings and cool your goat.

Gustomenta Enjoy homemade gelato in this stylish Italian cafe. Bring the kids and treat them to a heaped mound of frozen goodness on the patio.
1) *Daily 6.30am-12.30am. 1301, Soho New Town, Chaoyang District. (8580 5111); 2) Daily 9am-midnight. 24 Sanlitun Lu, Chaoyang District. (6417 8890)* 1) 朝阳区Soho现代城1301商铺；2) 朝阳区三里屯路24楼东侧

At Your Service

An ode to Beijing's distinctive waitresses
by Eric Abrahamsen

In the mid 90s, the late author Wang Xiaobo proposed waitresses as the last, best guardians of Beijing's own down-to-earth culture, at a time when a slick flood of money from Hong Kong and Taiwan threatened the capital's beloved crustiness. Wang fondly recalled the no-nonsense waitresses of the early 80s who "don't care who they're serving and won't toady to the rich. Should Rockefeller himself offend them, they would curse him out just the same: 'Don't think just because you've got a bit of stinking cash you can lord it over us! Piss me off and I'll give you the back of my goddamn hand!'" That's pride, that is, and pride cannot be bought.

Later, however, pride wasn't so much sold out as made obsolete by new concepts of professionalism and service – not bad things in themselves, but entailing a certain loss. No one will set foot in a Friendship Store these days but ah, memory *has* grown fond.

Today, local culture is once again threatened, this time by the gentle wash of globalization, which nudges all things towards the paradigmatic state of a San Francisco sushi bar. The roughnecked Beijing style of the 80s is doomed, and the best we can hope for is something a little more genuine than bistros with Chinese characteristics. Our foul-mouthed Amazon protectresses of old may have deserted the field, but they've been replaced by other, possibly more formidable agents – waitresses from the countryside.

Beware her wrath

Consider: The search for The Genuine often leads back to rural roots; in Beijing we're lucky in that the rural comes to us. Busloads of young people seeking work arrive in the capital each day, and a great number of the young women end up in restaurants.

It is here that they begin to serve us, simply by knowing little and caring less about how one "ought" to behave in a modern, cosmopolitan setting. They have been thrust into a strange and baffling new world, in which taking your order and bringing your food are merely two items on a very long list of cosmic puzzles.

So just try being sophisticated and see where it gets you. "I'm vegan," "The chef's recommendation?" "Do you call this a fricassee?" – all the most potent invocations of consumer culture will be rendered powerless by the indifferent stare of a seventeen-year-old girl.

Whenever we need a reminder of where we stand, we can simply duck into the nearest *jiachangcai* joint and order a Kobe beef steak, medium rare, from the waitress. She will peer at us, and blink, and ten minutes later bring out a *tieban niuliu* that sizzles and spatters goo on our shirts. Whereupon those of us for whom salvation is still possible will shake our heads as though awakening from a dream, mutter "Was I being an ass just now?" and eat our beef happily.

All hail waitresses, our unwitting defenders!

A Cauldron for Every Palate

Hot pot hot spots
by Zoe Li

To the uninitiated, a hot pot meal may seem a hassle-heavy eating style. As boil and bubble beget waiting, scrounging and vigilance, the window of perfection for a morsel of meat is elusively delicate. However, we soon realize that the deliberate pace of the meal and the low effort self-service is the perfect set-up for a long night of bacchanalia with friends. Its no surprise that hot pot is something of a national pastime, with many tantalizing interpretations available across the capital. For addresses and details, see Hot Pot listings, p74.

Suantang yu: one of the tastiest ways to eat a fish that you'll ever experience

For traditionalists
Dong Lai Shun Beijingers love to dunk, or *shuan* (涮), their halal mutton here. This *laozihao* (see pXXX) uses traditional copper devices that heat the cooking water with coals. Their lamb is consistently fresh and of high quality, while their *shaobing* (烧饼) will impress even the most finicky of Northern gourmands (see listing on p74 for address).

For health freaks
Alexander Creek Park This health-conscious eatery offers a vegan-friendly soup base that is made from 20 different kinds of fruits and vegetables. Patrons are encouraged to ready their stomachs by first sipping the soup before cooking any of the food. Drink the soup after you've finished your meal, as it takes on the flavors and absorbs the nutrition of the high-quality ingredients (see listing on p66).

For the wealthy Dong on the block
Guolizhuang Nothing could impress your clients more than a night of delicious penis hot pot. Don't agree? Just wait till you see the price tags. The *bian* don't come cheap at this establishment, with prices ranging from RMB 1,288-1,988. And ladies, don't be shy; Management holds that eating penis enhances not only masculine energy, but also female beauty. Just pretend it's fish. 1) Daily 9.30am-2pm, 4.30-9.30pm. 500m west of Dongsishitiao Qiao, south side of the road, Dongcheng District. (6405 5698); 2) Daily 10am-10.30pm. 1A Dongyan, Xihai (south of Deshengmen Qiao), Xicheng District. (6405 5698) 1) 东城区东四十条桥往西500米路南; 2) 西城区德胜门桥南西海东沿甲1号

For late-night cravings
Guijie Most of the hundred or so hot pot joints that line this iconic swath of Dongzhimennei Dajie are open all night, thus earning its colorful name. Whether you're an alcoholic demon for spice or just a hungry insomniac, this block is hot (pot).

For the sourpuss
Miao Ling This perpetually crowded Guijie gem offers Guizhou-style *suantang yu* (酸汤鱼), a whole fish hot pot that features a sour, tomato-based broth. Miao Ling is the city in Guizhou where *suantangyu* was invented, and this restaurant bears the name honorably – this is one of the tastiest ways to eat fish that you will ever experience.

For pampered pique-seekers
Hai Di Lao As famous for its hospitality as it is for its authentic Sichuan cuisine – get your nails done and enjoy a fruit plate while you wait in the long queue. Don't forget to ask for the noodle show – an energetic waiter will pull noodles right in front of your table.

Mondo Gelato Beijing Canadian brand of Italian-style ices and gelatos for your gourmet sweet tooth.
1) Daily 9am-10pm. 5/F Lufthansa Center, 52 Liangmaqiao Lu, Chaoyang District. (6465 1188 ext 536); 2) Daily 9am-9.30pm. 2/F, Henderson Shopping Center, 18 Jianguomennei Dajie, Dongcheng District. (135 0129 3663); 3) Daily 9am-10pm. B1/F, New World Shopping Centre, Phase 2, Chongwen District. (6708 9787) 聚乐多意大利艺术冰淇凌，1) 朝阳区亮马桥路52号燕莎友谊商城5层；2) 东城区建国门内大街18号恒基中心二层；3) 崇文区新世界商场二期青春馆地下一层

Tiamo Italia Smooth and creamy authentic Italian gelato, made fresh on the premises daily. There are currently 13 flavors on offer but this will soon be expanded to 24. Italian espresso and wireless Internet are also available.
Daily 10am-9pm. Grand Constellation, Shop 5-3, Huayuan Lu, Xidan, Xicheng District. (5851 8227) 西城区西单华远街置地星座5-3

Imperial

Many dine like royalty at the traditional restaurants below, which serve dishes once eaten by Qing dynasty monarchs (1644-1911 AD). Though Empress Cixi enjoyed at least 150 dishes at a single meal, you'll have to satisfy yourself on a handful of delicacies (say, ten or twelve) such as camel paw and deer tendon, and delight in the elaborately carved garnishes. Many of the traditional recipes have been lost, but some of the following swanky establishments do boast cooks who are descendents of the chefs of the Forbidden City.

Baijia Dazhaimen Restaurant Haidian's "official cuisine" restaurant features waitstaff clad in traditional Chinese garb and a charmingly secluded garden courtyard. What is "official cuisine"? Essentially it's whatever wasn't good enough for the emperor – his majesty's leftovers – at low-budget prices.
Daily 11am-9.30pm. 15 Suzhou Jie (next to Ba Yi Middle School), Haidian District. (6265 4186) 白家大宅斋门，海淀区苏州街15号(八一中学旁边)

Fangshan Restaurant Unique service and Cixi's favorites, for just less than the price of a marble boat. Come for the experience rather than the food.
Daily 11am-1.30pm, 5-8pm. 1 Wenjin Jie (inside Beihai Park, enter via east gate), Xicheng District. (6401 1889) 仿膳饭庄，西城区文津街1号北海公园东门内

Gege Fu An enclave of the Qing dynasty lives on. Try the great duck hotpot.
Daily 10.30am-2pm, 5.15-9pm (last orders 8.30pm). 9 Daqudeng Hutong, Meishuguan Houjie, Chaoyang District. (6407 8006) 格格府，朝阳区美术馆后街大取灯胡同9号内

Li Jia Cai Mr Li's house restaurant has a devoted following among foreign food columnists and their discerning readers. It serves set meals of Imperial-style food at prices that range RMB 200-2,000 per person. English is spoken and reservations are a must.
Daily 6-8pm. 11 Yangfang Hutong, Deshengmennei Dajie, Xicheng District. (6618 0107) 厉家菜，西城区德胜门内大街羊房胡同11号

Najia Xiaoguan Consistently well-executed Manchu-style imperial cuisine without the pretentious atmosphere. Stylish, understated decor with plenty of flora, and birds trained in the local lingo.
1) Daily 11.30am-10pm. South of the Fragrant Hills Botanical Garden crossroad, Haidian District. (8259 8588); 2) Daily 11.30am-9.45pm. West of 119 Middle School, South of the LG Twin Towers, Yonganli, Jianguomenwai Dajie, Chaoyang District. (6567 3663, 6568 6553) 那家小馆，1) 海淀区香山植物园十字路口南100米路西；2) 朝阳区建国门外大街永安里双子座大厦南侧，119中学西侧

Red Capital Club With lanterns carved out of watermelons and period knickknacks scattered throughout, no aesthetic detail goes unnoticed at this courtyard restaurant. Though the food and service get mixed reviews, if you're longing to immerse yourself in apparat-chic, their rich decor will not disappoint.
Daily 6-12pm. 66 Dongsijiutiao, Dongcheng District. (6402 7150, 8401 8886) 新红资俱乐部，东城区东四九条66号

Tiandi Yijia Aristocratic food, environment and prices – a stone's throw away from the Forbidden City.
Daily 11am-2pm, 5-9.30pm. 140 Nanchizi Dajie, Dongcheng District. (8511 5556) 天地一家，东城区南池子大街140号

Indian

Fragrant with ground spices – including cumin, fenugreek and black mustard seeds – Indian cuisine varies wildly between regions. Northern fare dominates the local subcontinent scene, so look for clay ovens producing succulent kebabs of chicken and flat breads like naan. Southern specialties such as idli (steamed cakes made of rice and gram flour) and dosa (giant crepes that are often filled with a spicy potato mixture) can also be enjoyed at a few locations.

Ganges Indian Restaurant Follow aromas of fresh naan and masala spices into this haven for authentic Tandoori cuisine. Run by two chefs from Delhi, Ganges offers authentic dishes such as lamb tikka (RMB 32), chicken shahi korma (RMB 48) and chana masala (RMB 32).
1) Daily 11am-10.30pm. Sancaitang Xiezi Lou, 160 Chengfu Lu, Haidian District. (6262 7944); 2) Daily 11am-11pm. 138A, B1/F, The Place, 9 Guanghua Lu, Chaoyang District. (6587 2999); 3) Daily 10.30am-midnight. 5/B, Hairun Apartments, 2 Jiangtai Lu, Chaoyang District. (5135 8353) 恒河印度餐厅，1) 海淀区成府路160号三才堂写字楼一层13号；2) 朝阳区光华路9号世贸天阶1号楼；3) 朝阳区将台路2号海润国际公寓底商5号

Hazara While the quality of the food does not quite match the expensive prices, Hazara is intimate and stylish and the service superb. Accepts foreign currencies, Visa and Mastercard.
Daily 5.30-10.30pm. Inside Face Bar, 26 Dongcaoyuan, Gongti Nanlu, Chaoyang District. (6551 6788) 朝阳区工体南路东草园26号

Indian Kitchen The menu is divided into an assortment of spicy subcontinent specialties, but the indecisive can check out the buffet lunch, served weekdays.
Daily 11.30am-2.30pm, 5.30-11pm. 2 Sanlitun Beixiao Jie (opposite the Korean embassy), Chaoyang District. (6462 7255) 北京印度小厨，朝阳区三里屯北小街2号二层

Mirch Masala Tasty, authentic and affordable in a pleasant, well-lit environment. Vegetarian and vegan friendly. Delivery also available.

FOOD

Mon-Sat 11am-2.30pm, 5-10.30pm, Sun 11am-10.30pm. 60-2 Nanluoguxiang, Dongcheng District. (6406 4347) www.mirchmasala.com.cn 马沙拉之香，东城区南锣鼓巷60-2号

Mughal's Beijing Friendly staff serve up Pakistani and Xinjiang cuisine with generous portions which make up for the difficulty of finding the place. While similar to Indian food, the menu favors meat over vegetables.
Daily 11am-11pm. 5188, 5/F, 3.3 Shopping Center, Sanlitun, Chaoyang District. (5136 5575) 新疆卡拉奇餐厅，朝阳区三里屯3.3大厦五层5188室

Punjabi Restaurant The Beijing branch is the seventh store of this nationwide chain and serves up tasty Punjabi cuisine with a focus on tandoor-roasted meats.
Daily 11.30am-11pm. C-8, 2/F, Lucky Street, Chaoyang Gongyuan Lu, Chaoyang District. (5867 0221/23) punjabichina.com/ 本杰比，朝阳区朝阳公园路好运街2楼C-8号

Raj Indian Restaurant and Bar Authentic Indian cuisine at reasonable prices.
Daily 11am-2pm, 5-11pm. 31 Gulou Xidajie (west of the Drum Tower), Xicheng District. (6401 1675) www.raj.com.cn 拉兹印度餐厅，西城区鼓楼西大街31号

The Taj Pavilion Friendly management and some of Beijing's finest Indian food in an authentic setting. Popular and a reliable favorite. Voted "Best Indian" in our 2007 Reader Restaurant Awards.
Daily 11.30am-2.30pm, 6-10.30pm. 1) 3/F Holiday Inn Lido, Jiangtai Lu, Shoudu Jichang Lu, Chaoyang District. (6436 7678, 6437 6688 ext 3811); 2) 1/F West Wing, China World Shopping Mall (next to KFC), Chaoyang District. (6505 5866) 泰姬楼印度餐厅，1) 朝阳区首都机场路将台路丽都假日酒店广场缤纷廊3层；2) 朝阳区国际贸易中心西楼一层，肯德基旁边

The Tandoor Good food, mirror-covered walls and Indian dancers are just enough to distract from the high prices and overly formal service.
Daily 11.30am-2pm, 5.30-10.30pm. 1/F, Great Dragon Hotel, 2 Gongti Beilu, Chaoyang District. (6597 2211, 6597 2299 ext 2112) 天都里印度餐厅，朝阳区工体北路2号兆龙饭店1层

Victor's Place and Curry House This "takeout station" prepares moderately priced Indian and Italian food for home delivery. If the mood strikes, you can eat at one of the few tables.
Daily 10.30am-2.30pm, 4.30-10.30pm. 8 Laiguangying Donglu (near Western Academy Beijing), Chaoyang District. (8470 1306/1308) 天竺阁，朝阳区来广营东路8号（京西学校旁边）

Italian

Cured meat, pasta and cheese, a presto! One of the world's most beloved cuisines, Italian fare is well represented in Beijing, from casual mom-and-pop trattorias to swanky, starched napkin establishments. Of course, it's the ever-popular pizza that's easiest to find (see Pizza p82) – our favorite versions are fired in a wood-burning oven. But it's a delightful surprise to also find fresh ravioli, risotto and even rucola (arugula, or rocket) salads.

+39 Italian Restaurant and Lounge Stands out from the crowd with its catchy moniker, inspired by Italy's country code, and by steering clear of stereotypical Italian fare (no pizza or spaghetti 'n' meatballs here). Patrons can enjoy modern Italian cuisine either in the stylish setting downstairs or surrounded by eclectic artwork upstairs under a glass roof.
Daily 11.30am-2.30pm, 6.30-10pm. 6 Beisihuan Donglu (southeast corner of Wangjing Qiao, directly across from Ikea), Chaoyang District. (8457 2839, reservation@plus-39.it) 朝阳区北四环东路6号（望京桥东南角，IKEA对面）

Annie's Pizzas and unpretentious Italian-American fare served in a family-friendly atmosphere. All locations deliver and have special play areas where, in between creating their own pizzas, kids can romp and shout.
1) Daily 11.30am-11pm. Jiuxianqiao, Jiangtai Lu, Shangye Jie, Chaoyang District. (6436 3735); 2) Daily 11.30am-11pm. West of Soho New Town, 88, Jianguo Lu, Chaoyang District. (8589 8366); 3) Daily 11am-11pm. A1 Nongzhan Nanlu (near the west gate of Chaoyang Park), Chaoyang District. (6591 1931); 4) Daily 10am-11pm. 16 Dongsanhuan Lu (next to CD Jazz Club), Chaoyang District. (6503 3871); 5) Daily 11am-11pm. Across from Western Academy Beijing, 5 Laiguangying Donglu, Chaoyang District. (8470 4768) 安妮，1) 朝阳区酒仙桥将台路商业街；2) 朝阳区建国路88号Soho现代城西；3) 朝阳区农展路甲1号（朝阳公园西门南侧）；4) 朝阳区东三环路16号（农展馆正门南侧）；5) 朝阳区来广营东路5号京西学校对面

Assaggi Charming restaurant with a lovely tree-lined roof garden. Not for the budget diner, though the set lunch menus are a Sanlitun standby.
Daily 11.30am-2.30pm, 6-11pm. 1 Sanlitun Beixiaojie, Chaoyang District. (8454 4508) 尝试，朝阳区三里屯北小街1号

Capone's Swinging London decor, extensive wine list, attentive service, generous servings and quality food all add up to a steep bill.
Sun-Thu noon-midnight, Fri-Sat noon-1am. 4/F Bldg A, The Place, 9 Guanghua Lu, Chaoyang District. (6587 1526) 卡邦意大利西餐厅和酒吧，朝阳区光华路9号世贸天阶A座4层

Cepe Offers authentic northern Italian cuisine in a modern, trendy setting. The low-key atmosphere makes it the perfect place for a romantic dinner. Great food, decor and service mak this one of the best Italian restaurants in town.
Daily 11.30am-2.30pm, 6-10.30pm. Ritz-Carlton Beijing, 1 Jinchengfang Dongjie, Jingrong Jie, Xicheng District. (6601 6666) 意味轩，西城区金城坊东街1号北京金融街丽思卡顿酒店大堂

Danieli's Elegant Italian restaurant in the St. Regis hotel. Arias echo throughout the tastefully decorated dining room, and the menu offers classic, if uneven, Italian fare, including fresh pasta – though it all comes at a price.
Mon-Fri 11.30am-2pm, 6-10pm, Sat-Sun 6pm-10pm. 2/F St. Regis Hotel, 21 Jianguomenwai Dajie, Chaoyang District. (6460 6688 ext 2440-2) 丹尼艾丽意大利餐厅，朝阳区建国门外大街21号国际俱乐部饭店二层

Gisa Authentic Italian cuisine, cooked by Gisa herself. We like the savory antipasti and delicious, thoughtfully prepared pastas. Hearty flavors, though some gripe about the tiny portions.
Daily 11am-2.30pm, 6-11pm. Chaoyang Park west gate, Chaoyang District. (6594 0938) 吉萨餐厅，朝阳区朝阳公园西门北侧

The Taj Pavilion is on the short list of best Indian restaurants in town

Il Casale Homestyle Italian fare in the Lido area. Pizza is recommended.
Daily 10.30-11pm. Jiangtai Xilu at Side Gongyuan (opposite the Japanese International School), Chaoyang District. (6436 8778) 家园意大利餐厅，朝阳区将台西路四得公园（日本人国际学校对面）

L'Isola Consistently good quality home-made pastas and desserts to accompany traditional entrees like Sardinian-style fish. Wine is taken seriously and an extensive selection includes a range of small producers from Italy. Set lunch (RMB 69 for two courses, RMB 96 for three courses) available.

FOOD

Certified sake taster Taka Yamamoto makes sure Manzo's shochu is liquid manna

Daily 11.30am-2.30pm, 6-11pm. 201, 2/F, Pacific Century Place, 2A Gongti Beilu, Chaoyang District. (6539 3773) 益顺客，朝阳区工体北路甲2号盈科中心商场2层201单元

Little Italy Modest family-style Italian restaurant featuring an impressive wine list and a good selection of pastas, pizzas and desserts. Delivery and catering services available.
Daily 11.30am-10pm. 813 Pinnacle Plaza, Tianzhu Real Estate Development Zone, Shunyi District. (8046 4679) 小意大利，顺义区天竺开发区荣祥广场813号

Luce Cafe The fuss-free stylishness of this contemporary Italian restaurant is complemented by the attentive but unobtrusive staff. The menu goes beyond regular Italian favorites, and the Mocha crème brulée is highly recommended.
Mon-Sat 1pm-1am; Sun 11.30am-10.30pm. 138 Jiugulou Dajie, Xicheng District. (8402 4417) 路溪，西城区旧鼓楼大街138号

Japanese

Beijing's Japanese fare runs the gamut from the humble okonomiyaki (Japanese-style pancakes) to sophisticated kaiseki dinners. Almost anything is available – especially if your budget's inexhaustible. Of course, not everything is traditional, but we admit that we've developed a soft spot for American-style sushi rolls. Bring on the wasabi mayonnaise!

Hatsune Reservations recommended at this crowded American-style Japanese joint with a hip, minimalist decor and straight-from-the-sea sushi. Standouts include the transcendent and multi-textured butterfly roll, as well as the popular "Motorola," drizzled with wasabi mayonnaise. Weekday lunch bento box set meals are a fine deal at RMB 65.

Daily 11.30am-2pm, 5.30-10pm. 2/F, Heqiao Bldg C, 8A Guanghua Lu, Chaoyang District. (6581 3939) 隐泉日本料理，朝阳区光华路甲8号和乔大厦C座二层

Isshin Japanese Restaurant Boasts three student-friendly locations in western Beijing, and a fancier new outlet in Jianwai Soho. The sashimi is tasty, as is the remarkable tonkatsu, an enormous plate featuring deep-fried pork cutlet served with lashings of plum sauce, shredded cabbage, rice and miso – all for only RMB 22.
1) Daily 11am-2pm, 5-10pm. Door 3, Bldg B, Ziguang Development Plaza, 11 Huixin Dongjie, Chaoyang District. (6482 3600); 2) Daily 11am-2pm, 5-10pm (stops taking orders at 10pm). 35 Chengfu Lu (30m north of the traffic lights next to Wudaokou subway station), Haidian District. (8261 0136); 3) Daily 11am-1.30pm, 5-9.30pm. 2/F Bldg 1, Oversea Student Dormitory, Beijing Normal University, Haidian District. (5880 9785); 4) Mon-Fri 11.30am-2pm, 5.30-10pm, Sat-Sun 11:30am-3pm, 5.30-10.30pm. Rm 1501, Bldg 15, Jianwai Soho, 39 Dongsanhuan Zhonglu, Chaoyang District. (5869 5769) 一心日本料理，1) 朝阳区惠新东街11号紫光发展大厦B座3单元；2) 海淀区城府路35号院（五道口城铁站旁信号灯往北30米路西院内）；3) 海淀区北京师范大学留学生公寓二层；4) 朝阳区东三环中路39号建外SOHO15号楼1501

Jazz-Ya Stylish, pricey eatery that seems typical of urban Tokyo. Serves a wide range of Japanese and Japanese-inspired foods. Lives up to the name.
Daily 11.30am-2am. 18 Sanlitun Beilu, Chaoyang District. (6415 1227) 爵士，朝阳区三里屯北路18号（北酒吧街）

Jiu Yuan Zhang Ziyi's an investor in this certified organic restaurant featuring a large ice Buddha centerpiece. Delicious farm fresh veggies outshine the wagyu beef and sashimi platters.

Daily 5.30-10pm. 2/F North Bldg, Longbo Guangchang, 16 Dongsanhuan Beilu, Chaoyang District. (6595 1199) 久源，朝阳区东三环北路16号隆博广场北楼二层

Kagen Fiery pot of hot coals at stainless steel tables, black slate floors and cool electronica music to accompany tasty marinated meat grilled fresh at each table.
Daily 11.30am-2pm, 5.30-10pm. 8 Guanghua Donglu, B1/F Heqiao Bldg C, Chaoyang District. (6583 6830) 火源，朝阳区光华东路8号和乔大厦C座B1

Kushinosato Tiny and uncluttered restaurant features Japanese-style chuan'r, called kushiage. Everything comes breaded and deep-fried; chefs keep the kebabs coming until you tell them to stop.
Daily 5-11pm. Xinyuan Jie (200 meters north of Adria near Capital Mansion), Chaoyang District. (6462 1086) 串之乡，朝阳区新源街京城大厦北200米

Len Len Minimalist decor and great lighting highlight the beautiful fare at this Dongcheng delight. One of the best Japanese restaurants in town. Menu changes seasonally.
Daily 6pm-1am. 1/F Ziming Dasha, 12B Xinzhong Jie, Dongcheng District. (6415 6415/6416) 联联，东城区新中街乙12号紫铭大厦1层

Manzo Opened by a qualified sake taster, this diningbar's Panjiayuan location boasts a huge selection of shochu and sake as well as excellent umeshu. The Japanese home-cooking inspired menu features favorites like homemade tofu, deep-fried fish cakes, and innovative salads.
1) Daily 6pm-12.30am, Sat-Sun also 11.30am-2pm. 1/F, Yilongfang, Yilongtai Apt, 28 Panjiayuan Nanli, Chaoyang District. (8770 8767); 2) Daily 11.30am-2pm, 6pm-midnight. 27 Liangmaqiao Lu, Anjialou, Chaoyang District. (6436 1608) 1) 慢走日本烧灼餐厅，朝阳区潘家园南里28号漪龙台公寓伊龙坊1层；2) 慢走日本地酒餐厅，朝阳区安家楼亮马桥路27号

Matsuko Great lunchtime buffet with sushi, sashimi, noodles and more.
Daily 11.30am-2pm, 5-10.30pm. 1) 39 Liangmaqiao Lu (opposite 21st Century hotel), Chaoyang District. (8453 4062); 2) 2/F Jinglong Dasha, 225 Chaoyang Beilu, Chaoyang District. (6509 8999); 3) Baijiazhuang (south east corner of Changhong Qiao), Chaoyang District. (6582 5208) 松子，1）朝阳区亮马桥39号（21世纪饭店对面）；2）朝阳区朝阳北路225号京龙大厦2层；3）朝阳区白家庄乙22号

Meshiya Features an eclectic menu of modern, Kyoto-style cuisine. We relish the dark atmosphere, so reminiscent of our favorite izakaya pubs.
Daily 11.30am-2pm, 4.30-11.30pm. 600m south of the China World Trade Center on the east side of the street, next to the Yanyuan Hotel, Chaoyang District. (6771 0218) 饭屋桥ši，朝阳区国贸大厦往南走600米马路东边燕园宾馆旁边

Nishimura Teppanyaki, robatayaki, sushi and more; great Japanese food in a stylish setting.
Daily 11am-2pm, 6-10pm. Shangri-La Hotel, 29 Zizhuyuan Lu, Haidian District. (6841 2211 ext 2719) 西村餐厅，海淀区紫竹院路29号香格里拉饭店2层

Wawu Those who don't savor pork may find that Wawu is somewhat limited, but for ramen fans, this noodle bar offers fresh ingredients, a vibrant and smart dining room, reasonable prices and fast, friendly service.
Daily 11am-2am. Bldg A, Soho New Town, 88 Jianguo Lu, Chaoyang District. (5446 6584) 瓦屋拉面，朝阳区建国路88号Soho现代城A座

Yotsuba Regulars come here for dishes that are served nowhere else in Beijing and at a fourth of the price of Tokyo. Call ahead several days for reservations – only three tables and very popular, so large parties are not recommended.
Daily 5-11pm. Next to Bldg 2, Xindong Lu, Chaoyang District. (6467 1837) 四叶，朝阳区新东路2号楼旁边

Korean

Spicy, salty and strong, the exciting flavors of Korean food have long been popular in Beijing. As a result, Korean restaurants abound, serving up ruby-red platters of raw meat that sizzle as soon as they hit the barbecue, eggy pancakes filled with seafood and glowing stone bowls of bibimbap, a savory, nourishing mixture of rice, ground meat and spicy pickles, piled into a heated bowl and topped with a fried egg. We love the crusty bits of rice that form on the bottom of the bowl and crunch so satisfyingly between our teeth.

Ai Jiang Shan A gentleman's barbecue, proving that char-grilling and composure can go together.
Daily 10am-10pm. North Gate of Side Gongyuan, Jiangtai West Road, Chaoyang District. (8456 9811) 爱江山，朝阳区将台西路四德公园北门

Charcoal Bar The sleek combination of black furnishings, stone-tiled floors and retractable bamboo partitions sets Charcoal bar apart from the dozen or so other Korean restaurants inside the same complex. Various cuts and preparations of top-grade beef and pork average RMB 30 a plate (including lean and tender pork cheek) while prices for ribs run slightly higher at RMB 45-60.
Daily 3pm-2am. Inside the Jingyu Hotel courtyard, 1 Tsinghua Donglu, Wudaokou, Haidian District. (6234 9997) 炭吧，海淀区五道口清华东路1号京裕宾馆内

Gaon Korean Restaurant The first Chinese mainland outpost of this Seoul-based chain serves posh Korean cuisine in a sophisticated dining room of dark wood, marble and glass – with service and presentation to match. This, along with superior quality meat, organic vegetables and fancy cooking techniques, put Gaon a notch above most Korean restaurants in Beijing, and this is reflected in its prices: main dishes RMB 200-400, lunch sets RMB 50-180/person, supper sets RMB 180-580/person.
Daily 11.30am-2pm, 5.30-9pm. 5/F East Tower, Twin Towers, B-12 Jianguomenwai, Chaoyang District. (5120 8899, 5828 7099) 高恩，朝阳区建国门外大街乙12号双子座大厦东塔5层

Haitanghua Pyongyang Cold Noodle Restaurant Cold War holdover serving North Korean-style eats and atmosphere. Alarmingly talented waitresses delight diners with musical performances.
Daily 11am-2.30pm, 5-10.30pm. 8 Xinyuanxili Zhongjie, Chaoyang District. (6461 6295/6298) 海棠花平壤冷面馆，朝阳区新源西里中街8号

Han Na Shan With more than 20 locations scattered around town, this is one of Beijing's most popular Korean BBQ places. Voted "Best Korean" in our 2007 Reader Restaurant Awards.
Daily 10.30am-11pm. 1) 8 Huayuan Donglu (near the Guo'an Theater), Haidian District. (8203 7888/6886); 2) 11A Chunxiu Lu, Chaoyang District. (6417 8377)

汉拿山 1）海淀区花园东路8号(国安剧院附近)；2）朝阳区春秀路甲11号

Sa Lang Bang With ethnic decor and a pictorial menu, it features classic Korean food at a moderate price. There is the option of sitting cross-legged on straw mats, the traditional Korean way, or in cozy private rooms.
Daily 11am-5am. 3/F Dongyuan Plaza, 35 Chengfu Lu, Haidian District. (8261 8201) 舍廊房，海淀区成府路35号东源大厦3层

Saveurs de Corée Relax on a rooftop seat overlooking the hutongs at this sophisticated Korean bistro, where the set menus are reasonably priced (from RMB 38 for four courses to RMB 78 for six courses) and the dishes are delicate, health-conscious, and intelligently proportioned.
Daily 11.30am-10.40pm. 29 Nanluoguxiang, Dongcheng District. (6401 6083) www.saveursdecoree.com.cn 韩香馆，东城区南锣鼓巷29号

Sorabol High-priced chain of Korean restaurants serves standards like bulgolgi, banfan and delicious raw beef.
1) Daily 11am-9pm. Basement, Lufthansa Centre, Chaoyang District. (6465 3388 ext 5720); 2) Daily 9am-10pm. 2/F, Landmark Towers, 8 Dongsanhuan Beilu, Chaoyang District. (6590 6688 ext 5119) 萨拉伯尔，1）朝阳区燕莎地下一层；2）朝阳区东三环北路8号亮马大厦二层

Middle Eastern/Persian

Time is love for a Middle Eastern chef – a bounty of intricately prepared dishes means your mama loves you, so order away at Beijing's modest selection of Middle Eastern restaurants, where variety is wide – especially among the dips and kebabs.

1001 Nights Sanlitun area restaurant serving some of the best Middle Eastern food in Beijing – falafel, tabouleh, hummus and kebabs. Nightly belly dancing.
Daily 11am-2am. Gongti Beilu, opposite Zhaolong Hotel, Sanlitun, Chaoyang District. (6532 4050) 1001夜，朝阳区三里屯工体北路兆龙饭店对面

Biteapitta Garlic rules at this gem of an Israeli restaurant! Tuck into a home-made falafel sandwich, or dip doughy pitta into a nutty hummus or smoky babaganoush spread – guaranteed to chase away any neighborhood vampires. Worth going out of your way for their reasonable prices and Beijing's best pickles. Try their great pitta burger.
Mon-Thu 9am-11pm, Fri-Sun 9am-12pm. 30 Tianze Lu (near Nüren Jie, turn at the Grape restaurant before the New Get Lucky Bar), Chaoyang District. (6467 2961) 朝阳区天泽路30号（女人街附近，豪运酒吧之前）

Dini's Kosher Restaurant One may be surprised to find few Jewish dishes on Dini's menu – instead, it starts off with sushi and veers towards pastas and burgers. But while Dini's lacks in exotic cuisine, it is true to the laws of Kashrut and everything is kosher.
Mon-Thu 11am-2.30pm, 5.30-10pm Fri, Sun 11am-10pm Sat 8.30pm-12pm. 32 Tianze Lu, Xingba Lu, Nüren Jie, Chaoyang District. (6461 6220) www.kosherbeijing.com 蒂妮犹太餐厅，朝阳区女人街星吧路天泽路32号

Rumi Beijing's only purveyor of Persian cuisine. Its plush, minimalist interior is inviting, but the savory kebabs seal the deal. Don't miss the innovative dessert selection. No alcohol served, but fine to BYOB.
Daily noon-midnight. 1A Gongti Beilu (opposite Zhaolong Hotel to the east of 1001 Nights), Chaoyang District. (8454 3838) 入迷，朝阳区工体北路甲1号兆龙饭店对面

Souk Resembling a North African colonial villa, this stylish eatery serves up a range of Mediterranean and Middle Eastern fare within the quiet environs of Chaoyang Park.
Daily 4pm-2am. West Gate of Chaoyang Park (in the alley behind Annie's), Chaoyang District. (6506 7309) 苏克会馆，朝阳区朝阳公园西门（安妮后面）

Pizza

Originally a Neapolitan specialty, artfully baked flat bread with tomato sauce, cheese and toppings has become the poster pie for gustatory globalization. For more extensive Italian food listings see Italian, p78.

Hutong Pizza Serves surprisingly good, square pizza pies (RMB 45-90), draft beer and wine in a nicely restored traditional home. Local delivery available.
Daily 11am-11pm. 9 Yindingqiao Hutong, Xicheng District. (6617 5916) 胡同比萨，西城区银锭桥胡同9号

The Kro's Nest The original Haidian branch of this haven for Yankee food lovers features high ceilings, stone archways and a lively atmosphere fueled by catchy music. The generously portioned vittles include garlic-covered cheese sticks (RMB 25), tangy barbecue chicken wings (RMB 15) and sumptuous New York-style pizza (RMB 60-90). Delivery available. Look out Chaoyang District, Kro's Gongti roost brings the yum.
1) Tue-Fri 10am-10pm, Sat-Sun 10am-11pm. 1 Fuyuanmen (400 meters north of Beijing University West Gate, on the northwest corner of the intersection), Haidian District. (6252 8057); 2) Tue-Thu noon-midnight, Fri-Sun noon-2am. South door of Vics, Inside the north gate of the Workers' Stadium, Chaoyang District (6553 5253). 乌巢，1）海淀区福缘门1号（从北大西门往北走400米，在路口的西北角）；2）朝阳区工体北门内Vics南门

Pizza Buona Thin crust pies with traditional toppings. Delivery available.
Daily 10.30am-midnight. 7 Gongti Xilu, Chaoyang District. (6551 3518) 百好乐，朝阳区工体西路7号

The Tree Voted "Best Pizza" in our 2007 Reader Restaurant Awards. Enjoy thin crusted pies, and wash everything down with a Belgian beer. See also Bars & Clubs directory p309.
Sun-Thu 11am-1am; Fri-Sat 11am-4am. 43 Sanlitun Beijie (100m west of Sanlitun North Bar street, Youyi Youth Hostel, behind Poachers Inn), Chaoyang District. (6415 1954) www.treebeijing.com 隐蔽的树，朝阳区三里屯北街以西100米，Poachers 后面，三里屯医院旁

Russian

With an emphasis on sour cream, cabbage, potatoes and vodka Russian cuisine packs a caloric wallop that's perfect for those long, bitter Beijing winters. Our favorite local Slavic dishes include borscht – blood red and savory with scraps of tender meat – and succulent chicken Kiev – a breast of chicken, filled with butter, breaded and fried until crisp on the outside, and juicily tender within. Paired with mashed potatoes, this is comfort food at its finest.

Rumi's divine kebabs and Persian elegance will inspire you to lyrical heights

The Elephant Good place to stuff your face and get drunk without the pretension of uppity, hyper-designed restaurants. Good Russian food, especially the appetizers, like stuffed mushroom caps. The floorshow is akin to Eastern Bloc Lakers' girls wriggling out to Shakira.
Daily noon-2am. In a small alley off Yabaolu (50 meters north of Yatai Dasha), Chaoyang District. (8561 4073) 大笨象，朝阳区朝外头条甲93号（雅宝路亚太大厦向北50米）

Moscow Restaurant Virtually the first Western restaurant in Beijing, the Moscow's dining room still serves Russian favorites like borscht, chicken Kiev and vodka by the glass.
Daily 11am-2pm, 5-9pm. 135 Xizhimenwai Dajie, in Beijing Exhibition Center, Xicheng District. (6835 4454) 莫斯科餐厅，西城区西直门外大街135号北展中心内

Traktirr Pushkin Fans of the original Traktirr need not be disappointed by its recent closure, as the managers have taken their menu of affordable Russian favorites over to the Traktirr Pushkin around the corner, which now serves the best of both traditional and contemporary Russian cuisine. Don't miss the pickled cherry tomatoes and RMB 20 Russian beer.
Daily 11am-midnight. 5-15 Dongzhimennei Dajie, Dongcheng District. (8407 8158, 6403 1896) 彼得堡餐厅，东城区东直门内大街5-15号

White Nights The food at White Nights remains true to the spirit of Mother Russia. Get your ruble's worth with succulent peppercorn beef tenderloin accompanied by a working man's serving of creamy mashed potato. The service however, could induce discontent among the masses.
Daily 10.30am-midnight. 13A Beizhong Jie (off Dongzhimennei Dajie), Dongcheng District. (8402 9595) 白夜西餐，东城区东直门内大街北中街甲13号

Shanghai

Food that's sweet as pie, thanks to the cuisine's heavy use of sugar, which is often blended with soy sauce to form a braising sauce. Rich with seafood and wine, this is light and varied fare that includes the famously succulent *xiaolongbao*: pork dumplings filled with a mouthful of soup that are outrageously addictive.

Din Tai Fung We're still scoffing down these airy eateries delicate, succulent *xiaolongbao* as fast as we can. Friendly service and a kid's playroom rounds out the package: It's a dumpling lover's paradise. Also, the soups, fried rice w/ pork and noodles are guaranteed to please.
1) Sun-Thu 11.30am-9.30pm, Fri-Sun 11.30am-10pm. 6/F, Shin Kong Place, China Central Place, 87 Jianguo Lu, Chaoyang District. (6533 1536); 2) Mon-Fri 11.30am-2.30pm, 5-10pm; Sat-Sun 11am-10pm. 24 Xinyuanxili Zhongjie, Chaoyang District. (6462 4502) 鼎泰丰，1）朝阳区建国路87号华贸中心新光天地6层；2）朝阳区新源西里中街24号

Jade Garden Cantonese and Shanghainese cuisine in a sophisticated setting. The place gets particularly convivial on the weekends with Cantonese families gathering for dim sum feasts.

Five Winds of Flavor

Dishing delight
by Zoe Li

Just as Westerners would never say they are going out to eat "Western," Chinese diners are very specific about the type of regional cuisine they hanker after. Chinese food's incredible diversity can be both invigorating and intimidating. These five featured dishes offer an introductory bite of five of China's most important cuisines.

Red-cooked Meat (Zhejiang)
Hongshao Rou 红烧肉

This dish pays homage to the virtue of patience: During the hour in which China's default meat, the fat-lined pork belly, is simmered in Shaoxing rice wine, dark soy sauce and sugar, one's self-restraint is tested by the excruciatingly divine smells released. The resulting meat is lusciously dark, glistening in fat and melt-in-your-mouth tender. The sauce: simply addictive.

Tiger Salad (Dongbei)
Laohu Cai 老虎菜

What would a dish made by a tiger taste like? Probably a lot like this. Large green chili peppers, raw onions, and a tomato or two are finely julienned, then tossed in a simple dressing of sesame oil and salt. Handfuls of cilantro are chucked in for added effect. The resulting salad is so spicy and pungent, anyone who eats it has the courage of a tiger – or at least will end up with breath potent enough to scare them off.

PHOTOS: JUDY ZHOU

Lumpy Soup (Shanxi)
Geda Tang 疙瘩汤

Tuscany may have its bread soup, papa al pomodoro, but here in Beijing, we love our Shanxi-style *geda tang*. Vegetables are first boiled with meat stock to make a nutritious soup base. In a separate bowl, chopsticks are used to mix white flour with cold water until all the flour is gathered into gooey, pea-sized pieces of dough. This is slowly stirred into the soup base so that the resulting thick soup is lumpy from the chunks of dough.

Meat Returned to the Wok (Sichuan)
Huiguo Rou 回锅肉

A dish that illustrates the province's traditional home cooking at its simplest and its best. Fatty pork is first cooked in boiling water flavored with garlic, ginger, scallions and Sichuan peppercorns, then sliced thinly. In a dry wok, sweet bean sauce and fermented beans from Pi County are stir-fried with Sichuan peppercorns to give that distinct numbing-hot kick. Finally, the slices of pork are returned to the wok and fried with the bean sauce to a crispy, curly, golden brown deliciousness.

Squirrel Fish (Jiangsu)
Songshu Yu 松鼠鱼

When it comes to naming dishes, the Chinese people's love for animal imagery knows no bounds. A whole mandarin fish is thoroughly cleansed and de-boned, then butterflied. A crosshatch pattern is meticulously carved into the flesh, such that when the entire fish is deep-fried, the meat naturally curls to resemble the silhouette of a squirrel. Before serving, a sauce is poured on top, producing hisses and squeaks like the cry of a squirrel, further validating the appellation.

FOOD

South Beauty: Sichuan for the Powerbook set

Daily 11am-11pm. 6 Jiqingli, Chaoyangmenwai Dajie, Chaoyang District. (6552 8688) 苏浙汇，朝阳区朝阳门外大街吉庆里6号楼

Lu Lu Restaurant chain serving traditional Shanghai fare in a neo-classical setting.
Daily 11am-2.30pm, 5-10pm. 1A Ciyunsi, Chaoyang District. (6508 0101, 6508 0505) 鹭鹭酒家东方店，朝阳区慈云寺甲1号

Mei Mansion Getting lost on the way here is definitely part of the fun. The dishes prepared in this elegant courtyard restaurant were once served to the great Peking opera star Mei Lanfang. The set-meal menu changes daily and must be ordered in advance. This hidden charm is far from cheap – RMB 300 per person minimum – but the gasps of delight make it all worth it.
Daily 11.30am-2pm, 5-10pm. 24 Daxiangfeng Hutong (south bank of Houhai), Xicheng District. (6612 6847) 梅府家宴，西城区后海南沿大翔凤胡同24号

Xinjishi Specializing in sweet Shanghai dishes, Xinjishi impresses with its tasteful modern decor and attentive wait staff. The Gongti Beilu location has a touch of Shanghai charm.
1) 10.30am-9.30pm. 1-1 Beifengwo Lu, Haidian District. (5184 3938/9999); 2) Daily 11am-2pm, 5.30-10.30pm. 4 Gongti Beilu, Chaoyang District. (6586 8747) 新吉士，1) 海淀区北蜂窝路1-1号；2) 朝阳区工体北路4号

Sichuan

This food is adrenaline out of the wok – not just the slow burn of red peppers, but also the numbing thrill of Sichuan peppercorn. Favorite dishes include *lazi ji* (fried bits of chicken that come hidden in a nest of dried chillies) and *shuizhu yu* (silky chunks of fish, poached in a tingling broth laden with Sichuan peppercorns). The region's humid and wet climate has necessitated a grand tradition of preserved vegetables, which play a large role in the cuisine.

Ba Guo Bu Yi Chengdu import serves authentic Sichuan cuisine. Classy, understated decor looks like a Chinese inn from the movies.
1) Daily 10am-2pm, 5-9.30pm. 89-3 Di'anmen Dongdajie, Dongcheng District. (6400 8888); 2) Daily 11am-2.30pm, 5-9.30pm. 2/F Nanhang Hotel, 10 Dongsanhuan Zhonglu, Guomao, Chaoyang District. (6567 2188); 3) Daily 11am-2.30pm, 5-9.30pm. Xinzhi Dasha, 28 Fucheng Lu, Haidian District. (8819 0088); 4) Daily 11am-2.30pm, 5-9.30pm. 68 Xizhimen Nanxiaojie, Xicheng District. (6615 2230) 巴国布衣，1) 东城区地安门东大街89-3号；2) 朝阳区东三环中路10号南航酒店2层；3) 海淀区阜成路28号新知大厦；4) 西城区西直门南小街68号

Chongqing Fandian Where local Sichuanese go for numbingly spicy prickly ash.
Daily 11am-2pm, 5-9pm. 15 Guangximen Beili, Xibahe, Chaoyang District. (6422 8888) 重庆饭店，朝阳区西坝河光熙门北里15号

Chuan Ban Its location in the first floor of Sichuan province's Beijing rep office fuels its reputation as the most authentic Sichuan cuisine in town. Reasonable prices but often crowded, so expect a wait during peak dinner hours.
Daily 7-9am, 11am-2pm, 5-10pm. 5 Gongyuan Toutiao, Jianguomennei Dajie, Dongcheng District. (6512 2277 ext 6101) 川办餐厅，东城区建国门内贡院头条5号

Feiteng Yuxiang Best *shuizhuyu* in town. Tuck in a bib, and get messy – this chain remains as popular as ever, thanks to its continued attention to what really matters: mouth-watering renderings of Sichuanese favorites. Reservations recommended.

PHOTO: JUDY ZHOU

86 INSIDER'S GUIDE TO BEIJING

Mon-Fri 11am-2.30pm, 4.30-10.30pm, Sat-Sun 11am-10.30pm. 1) 1 Gongti Beilu, 35 Xingfu Yicun 4 Xiang, Chaoyang District. (6415 3764); 2) 17 Zhichun Lu, Haidian District. (8231 1286); 3) Xinyuan Nanlu (opposite Kunlun Fandian), Chaoyang District. (8455 2333); 4) B1/F, Chengming Dasha, 2 Xizhimen Nandajie (north east corner of Xizhimen Qiao), Xicheng District. (5190 1778) www.ftyx.com 沸腾鱼乡，1）朝阳区工体北路1号春秀路，2）海淀区知春路17号，3）朝阳区新源南路佳亿时尚广场旁，4）西城区西直门南大街2号成铭大厦二楼(西直门桥东南角)

Fu Ku One of Houhai's best restaurants, Fu Ku serves delectable Sichuan/fusion in an attractive, modern setting. The *lazi ji* is excellent as are the mashed potatoes with meat sauce and, if you can stand the heat, the cold spinach in mustard sauce (*jiemo bocai*).
Daily 10.30am-10.30pm. 4A Binhe Hutong, Deshengmennei Dajie, Xicheng District. (6405 0706, 6402 4033) www.fukuns.com 福库，西城区德内大街滨河胡同4号

Lan The South Beauty dynasty's newest flagship venue. Voted "Best Decor" in our 2007 Reader Restaurant Awards.
Daily 11-3am. 4/F LG Twin Towers, 12B Jianguomenwai Dajie, Chaoyang District. (5109 6012/13) 兰，朝阳区建国门外大街乙12号LG双子座4层

The Source Sichuan food served in a quaint interior. If the weather is fine, you can eat in the breezy courtyard set beneath an ancient date tree, amid rustling bamboo stalks.
Daily 11am-2pm, 5-11pm. 14 Banchang Hutong (next door to the Lusongyuan Hotel) Nanluoguxiang, Kuanjie, Dongcheng District. (6400 3736) 都江源，东城区宽街南锣鼓巷板厂胡同14号

South Beauty Upscale Sichuan cuisine served in many locations. Fans love the spicy, numbing food and the gorgeous waitstaff. Voted "Best Sichuan" in our 2007 Reader Restaurant Awards.
1) Daily 11am-11pm. 2/F Manhattan CNT Building Beijing (south of Swissotel Hotel), Dongcheng District. (8528 2330); 2) Daily 10am-10pm. 1/F, Henderson Shopping Mall Center, Dongcheng District. (6518 7603); 3) Daily 11am-10pm. 1/F Tower A Raycom Info-Tech Park, 2 Kexue Nanlu, Haidian District. (8286 1698); 4) Daily 11am-11pm. BB88 1/F, Oriental Plaza, 1 Dong Chang'an Dajie, Dongcheng District. (8518 6971); 5) Daily 11am-10pm. 1/F Shuncheng Hotel, 16 Financial Street, Xicheng District. (6622 8989); 6) Daily 11am-10pm. 4/F, Oriental Kenzo Square, 21 Dongzhimenqiao Zhongjie, (southeast corner of Dongzhimenqiao), Dongcheng District. (8447 6171); 7) Daily 11am-10pm. 7-1, 7 Huayuan Lu, Xidan (west of Bank of China Tower), Xicheng District. (5851 8498/9); 8) Daily 10.30am-10.30pm. 68 Anli Lu, Sunshine Plaza, East door, Chaoyang District. (6495 1201); 9) Daily 11am-11pm. 3/F, Pacific Century Place, Gongti Beilu, Chaoyang District. (6539 3502); 10) Daily 11am-2pm. 2/F, West Bldg, China World Shopping Mall, 1 Jianguomenwai Dajie, Chaoyang District. (6505 0809); 11) Daily 11am-11pm. Kerry Centre Mall, North B1, Chaoyang District. (8529 9458) 俏江南，1）东城区首创大厦二层(港澳中心瑞士酒店南侧)，2）东城区恒基中心商场首层西南，3）海淀区中关村融科资讯中心A座北侧(海淀区科学院南路2号)，4）东城区东长安街1号东方广场地下一层BB88，5）西城区金融大街甲16号顺成饭店首层(平安大厦东侧对面处)

成酒店南门)；6）东城区东直门外中街21号东方银座广场4层(东直门桥东南角)；7）西城区西城区华远路7号7-1（西单中国银行总部西侧）；8）朝阳区安立路68号漂亮阳光广场东侧门，9）朝阳区工体北路太平洋百货三层，10）朝阳区建国门外大街1号国贸西楼2层，11）朝阳区嘉里商场B1北侧

Yuxiang Renjia Consistently good Sichuanese food in a pleasant, rustic environment. Reasonable prices ensure constant crowds.
1) Daily 10am-10pm. 6/F Parkson Shopping Center, Fuxingmen, Xicheng District. (6602 3706); 2) Daily 10am-10pm. Hepingli Nankou, across from the Guojia Linye Ju, Chaoyang District. (8422 0807); 3) Daily 10.30am-2pm, 5.30-11pm. 1200m east of the Xisanqi Huandao, Haidian District. (6271 3963); 4) Daily 11am-10.30pm. 5/F Lianhe Dasha, 20 Chaoyang Dajie, Chaoyang District. (6588 3841) 渝乡人家，1）西城区复兴门百盛购物中心6层，2）朝阳区和平里南口国家林业局对面，3）海淀区西三旗环岛向东1200米路南，4）朝阳区朝阳大街20号联合大厦五层

Yu Xin Real Sichuanese recommend this as the most authentic place in town. Each bite of the *shuizhu rou* is flavor rainbow bliss.
1) Daily 11am-10pm. 1/F, Jingtai Bldg, 24 Jianguomenwai Dajie, 100m west of Scitech Shopping Centre, Chaoyang District. (6515 6588); 2) Mon-Fri 11am-2:30pm 5-10pm, Sat-Sun 10am-11pm. 1A Xiyangwei Hutong, Kuanjie, Dongcheng District. (6405 6398); 3) Mon-Fri 11am-2:30pm 5-10pm, Sat-Sun 10am-11pm. 1/F, Chang'an Grand Theatre, 75 Jianguomennei Dajie, Dongcheng District. (6517 1012); 4) Mon-Fri 11am-2pm, 5-10pm. Sat-Sun 11am-10pm. 7/F, Scitech Tower, 111 Xidan Beidajie, Xicheng District. (6618 3918); 5) Daily 11am-10pm. 5A Xingfu Yicun Xili, Chaoyang District. (6415 8168) 渝信，1）朝阳区建国门外大街24号京泰大厦一层，2）东城区宽街扬威胡同甲一号，3）东城区建国门内大街7号长安大戏院首层，4）西城区西单北大街111号西单赛特广场7楼，5）朝阳区幸福一村西里甲5号

Singaporean, Malaysian & Indonesian

Rice and noodles play key roles in these cuisines, which fuse indigenous, Chinese, Thai and Indian flavors. Look for laksa, or rice noodles served in a soup thick with coconut milk, fish and meat, Hainan chicken rice (poached chicken and savory steamed rice) or the mighty beef rendang, a hefty slab of meat, similar to brisket, that's been braised to tender perfection in a spicy curry sauce.

Asian Star Southeast Asian restaurant serves a mishmash of Indian, Thai, Singaporean and Malaysian cuisines.
Daily 11am-2.30pm, 5-10.30pm. 26 Dongsanhuan Beilu, Chaoyang District. (6582 5306) 亚洲之星新马印，朝阳区东三环北路26号

Cafe Sambal Authentic up-market Malay food in a lovely courtyard. Voted "Best Malaysian/Singapore" in our 2007 Reader Restaurant Awards.
Daily 11am-midnight. 43 Doufuchi Hutong (just east of Jiugulou Dajie), Xicheng District. (6400 4875) 西城区豆腐池胡同43号(旧鼓楼大街往东走)

Java and Yangon The cuisines of Indonesia and Myanmar are the focus of this bright, colorful restaurant – the first in Beijing to serve Burmese cuisine.

Daily 11am-2.30pm, 4.30-10.30pm. Sanlitun Xiwujie, Chaoyang District. (8451 7489) 朝阳区三里屯西五街

Lau Pa Sak Bustling Singaporean outlet that serves "hawker" street food indoors. Fans rave about the beef rendang, laksa noodles, spicy nasi goreng fried rice and condensed milk coffee. Oh, and the curry puffs!
Daily 11am-11pm. Xindonglu (opposite the Canadian Embassy), Chaoyang District. (6417 0952) 老吧刹，朝阳区新东路加拿大使馆对面

Nyonya Kitchen Peranakan cuisine at its finest, and if you don't know what that is, no problem. The owners seek to instruct and offer up spices and curry pastes fresh from Malaysia.
Daily 11am-9.30pm. Across from Gaojiayuan Middle School, opposite the Lido Hotel, Chaoyang District. (6433 7377) 娘惹厨房，朝阳区高家园中学丽都饭店对面

Traders Cafe With a typical hotel a la carte menu and a sprawling buffet, what makes Traders stand apart from the rest of the hotel crowd is the quality of the Singaporean and Malaysian cuisine. Standouts include Hainanese chicken rice, laksa, and nasi lemak, but watch out for the high prices.
Daily noon-2pm, 6am-10pm. Traders Hotel, 1 Jianguomenwai Dajie, Chaoyang District. (6505 2277 ext 35) 三江咖啡厅，朝阳区建国门外大街一号国贸饭店内

The Yard This sister restaurant of Nyonya Kitchen oozes colonial elegance and polished charm. Its menu satisfies even the most traditional of Malaysian palates. With service as refined as the setting, this is a truly affordable culinary pleasure.
Daily 11am-10pm. 3 Kaifa Jie, Xi Baixinzhuang, Houshayu, Shunyi District. (8049 9449) 庭院餐厅，顺义区后沙峪西白辛庄开发街3号

Thai

Authentic Thai cuisine blends five fundamental flavors – sweet, spicy, salty, sour and bitter – in each dish, using a combination of ingredients like nam pla (fish sauce), aromatic lemongrass, galangal (a ginger-like root that tastes faintly of soap), fragrant Thai basil, sharply sour kaffir lime leaves and, of course, chillies. Popular dishes include curries rich with coconut milk, pad Thai noodles and sticks of meat satay with peanut sauce.

Banana Leaf Somewhere, amidst a river crawling with fake alligators, harboring long-tail boats and overflowing with exotic fruits, may lurk the answer to your Thai food cravings.
Daily 11am-11pm. 1) 2/F, Finance Center, Zhongguancun Shopping Center, 58 Beisihuan, Haidian District. (5986 3666); 2) 4 Gongti Beilu, Chaoyang District. (6506 8855) 蕉叶，1）海淀区北四环路58号中关村广场金融中心商业2楼；2）朝阳区工体北路4号院内，三里屯南口凯富酒店后

Lan Na Thai A suave Thai eatery decked out with a collection of authentic Southeast Asian artifacts, serving good quality, classic Thai dishes at expensive prices.
Daily noon-2.30pm, 5.30-10.30pm. 26 Dongcaoyuan, Gongti Nanlu, Chaoyang District. (6551 6788) 朝阳区工体南路东草园26号

Lemon Leaf Sleek Thai hot pot eatery with a choice of eight different broths.
Daily 10am-11pm. 15 Xiaoyun Lu, Chaoyang District. (6462 5505) 柠檬叶片，朝阳区霄云路15号

Phrik Thai Cold dishes rule at this refreshing Thai restaurant. We like the papaya salad, which comes rich with cashew nuts and tangy fish sauce, and the chicken larb, a cold salad of ground chicken loaded with chili and cilantro. Though the rest of the menu can be uneven, reasonable prices ensure that adventurous eaters can sample a variety of dishes.
Daily 11am-2.30pm, 5-10.30pm. The Gateway Bldg, 10 Yabao Lu (across from the Bank of China), Chaoyang District. (8561 5236) 泰辣椒餐厅，朝阳区雅宝路10号凯威大厦一楼

Pink Loft Flamboyant setting for average Thai food. In addition to the standard beers and drinks, they have a long wine list and RMB 1,500 bottles of Dom Perignon.
Daily 11am-1am. 6 Nan Sanlitun Lu, Chaoyang District. (6506 8811) 粉酷，朝阳区南三里屯路6号

Purple Haze Thai cuisine served amongst purple hues. Books, coffee and wi-fi create the perfect atmosphere for a lazy afternoon. They've just finished expanding their Gongti branch and plan to open a new branch in Sep 2007. Voted "Best Thai" in our 2007 Reader Restaurant Awards.
Daily 10.30am-1am. Opposite the north gate of the Workers' Stadium, in the small alley behind the ICBC Bank, Chaoyang District. (6413 0899, 8774 6387) 紫苏庭，朝阳区工体北门对面胡同，工商银行后

Serve the People Popular restaurant with a large laowai fan base and pleasant terrace. The tom kha gai (coconut chicken soup) offers the perfect blend of spicy, sour and sweet.
Daily 10.30am-10.30pm. 1 Sanlitun Xiwujie (next to Athena), Chaoyang District. (8454 4580) 为人民服务，朝阳区三里屯西五街1号

Sukhothai Staff in Thai ethnic dress, tables set with golden-tinted plates and a room-dominating altar to a fat, golden Buddha – you get the picture. The English menu offers a variety of curries running RMB 50 and up.
Mon-Fri 10.30am-2.30pm, 5-10.30pm, Sat-Sun 10.30am-10.30pm. 19 Haoyun Jie, Zaoying Lu, Chaoyang District. (5867 0211) 粟库泰泰式餐吧，朝阳区枣营路好运街19号

Vegetarian

Meatless dining is easy at these restaurants, many of which are run by Buddhist monks and have banned not only flesh, but also onions, garlic and leeks. Instead, gluten, agar and soy products are formed into shapes and textures that seem similar to meat – favorites include the "Peking duck." If, however, you're hoping to wash down your meal with a beer or enjoy a postprandial cigarette you may have to go outside: The following establishments enforce a clean, pure lifestyle.

Bhodi-Sake Fluffy rabbits jubilantly hop around the grounds of this Buddhist temple's elegantly converted front courtyard. Large variety of imitation meat dishes, such as Lingering Aftertaste (RMB 26), a vegan version of mala beef jerky, will deliciously flummox your meat radar.
Daily 10am-10pm. 10-16 Heiyao Changjie, Xuanwu District. (6354 2889/ 6155) 菩提缘，宣武区黑窑厂街10–16号

Elaine's Vegetarian Restaurant and Bar Elaine's quaint little garden supplies generous portions of Chinese vegetarian fare. The imitation meat dishes are popular with both vegetarian and non-vegetarian diners.

Don't Meat Me in Beijing
Tips for maintaining a glorious vegetarian lifestyle
by Cate Conmy

Remember when your cunning younger brother used to get his kicks by trying to sneak meat past your vegetarian radar? ("Mmmm, this all-bean taco is sooo good. Oh yeah, nothing in here but pure, bean goodness – have a bite!") Well, Beijing's no match for him. Admittedly, any city that serves live scorpions on sticks is bound to present some vegetarian challenges. That said, while strict vegetarianism may cause your average Beijinger some confusion or bewilderment, rarely will it inspire malice. With a bit of prep, some perseverance, and a good dose of patience, you can definitely stick to your veggie guns in Beijing.

Ready yourself for some very flexible interpretations of the word meat. (Surprise! Pork is still meat no matter how finely it's chopped!) You'll need to be extra-explicit and spell out absolutely everything you don't want showing up in your dinner. Be wary of the invisible *jijing* (aka chicken bouillon powder) – every bit as popular and insidious as MSG – and look out for intruder meat (cooks use the same wok for dish after dish so the occasional piece of beef turns up without invitation). Be specific, be patient, and don't be afraid to pop out a baldfaced lie or two when ordering (e.g. "I'll die if I eat meat!").

No matter your vegetarian vigilance, if you like to hit up your neighborhood *jiachangcai* joint, odds are that something taboo will eventually end up on your plate, or worse, in your mouth. If you're not willing to gamble, don't panic – you're not chained to your rice cooker. A new vegetarian restaurant seems to pop up every month or so (see listings on opposite page), assuring that you can go out and gorge yourself, anxiety-free. Sample veggie versions of classic Chinese meat dishes; if your carnivore vocab is flabby, pack a dictionary so you can fully decipher the menu (and finally fulfill all those cravings for bean-based versions of abalone and chicken feet). If you're lucky, you'll share the dining room with a pair of monks or nuns – up your holy-quotient by buying them a round of mock *chuan'r*.

Most vegetarian restaurants sell packaged foods like veggie instant noodles and fake meat products pre-seasoned for use in Chinese dishes, making cooking at home a little easier. Certain specialty foods like flaxseed, quinoa, and egg replacer are pretty much impossible to find (wise vegans pack vitamins in an extra suitcase), but Carrefour is good for canned beans, pasta and couscous. Jenny Lou's offers the same, plus vegan bread, margarine (Nuttelex brand) and some brands of less beany-tasting soymilk that you might actually be willing to pour into your coffee.

Rejoice, resourceful legume mongers! We may not quite live in the capital of clean veggie living, but valor yields tasty rewards.

V for valorous vegan victory

ILLUSTRATION: LI XING

FOOD

The Case for the Street
Why Beijing's *baozi* are still one of life's simple pleasures
by David Litt

"Sir, fill my bag with baozi"

When I eat my *baozi* I want to sit down on a stoop, unworried about what's happening to the seat of my pants. I want to squirt a dime-sized amount of hand sanitizer onto my left palm, rub my hands together, and rest assured that any residual dirt has, through a process I don't understand, become germ free. I want my buns handed to me piping hot, in a thin plastic bag that defies physics each second it doesn't melt. On its own, the *baozi* is good food. On the street, the *baozi* transcends food.

Baozi don't just taste good, they embody something: simplicity meeting depth. The outside of the *baozi* is basically just flour and water and the filling is surprisingly complex, but the important thing is that neither is worth eating on its own.

Put them together, though, and it's a minor miracle. The filling flavors the bread, the bread gives texture to the filling, and all of a sudden, layers happen. A good *baozi* doesn't have just one taste. Instead, the different elements – and a *baozi* can be salty, sweet, briny, spicy, fatty, juicy and more – each dip and spike around a doughy, meaty baseline. I've heard jazz described as a conversation between instruments – the *baozi* is a conversation between flavors.

And if the *baozi* is like jazz, then the stoop is the perfect club to take it all in, the culinary equivalent of a smoke-filled basement room. Because buns are such a typical Beijing snack, I go from being around people to being among them – there's something about a good *baozi* that makes me feel at home on a foreign sidewalk.

When I first arrived in Beijing, it seemed as if everyone told me I needed to try Din Tai Fung. I understand why – their *xiaolongbao* are delicious, their expensively understated atmosphere is hard to equal. I have no ill-feeling toward the swanky couples and smartly-dressed parties of four to six who pay 38 *kuai* for just ten tiny buns. Like some hometown hero who made it big, the *baozi* has been discovered. Now, the *baozi* is stepping into the limelight, and I'm happy for it – I've certainly wanted to go back to Din Tai Fung since my first visit. But each time, before I could make my reservation, I remembered what made me love *baozi* in the first place, and the choice became clear.

I ended up back on the stoop.

Vegetarian and delicious? Buddha is pleased at Pure Lotus

Daily 11am-11pm. Walk 800m along the banks of Luoma Lake, 100m North of Luoma Roundabout, Houshayu, Shunyi District. (8048 5088) 素心小筑，顺义区后沙峪镇罗马环岛向北100米左转，沿罗马湖畔800米

Lotus in Moonlight A large array of meatless and fishless dishes, made from tofu and related products. You can tell it's the real deal by the number of monks who dine here. Hard to find, but worth the search.
1) Mon-Fri 11am-2pm, 5-10pm, Sat-Sun 11am-10pm. 12 Liufang Nanli, Chaoyang District. (6465 3299); 2) Mon-Fri 11am-2pm, 5-9pm, Sat-Sun 11am-9pm. 3/F, Disanji Creative Space, 66 Beisihuan Xilu, Haidian District. (6268 0848/1318) 荷塘月色素食，1) 朝阳区柳芳南里12号楼；2) 海淀区北四环西路66号第三极3层

Pure Lotus Vegetarian Voted "Best Vegetarian Fare" in our 2007 Reader Restaurant Awards. Run by monks, so their creative dishes will leave you with a full stomach and a clear conscience – and a considerably lightened wallet.
Daily 11am-11pm. 1) Inside Zhongguo Wenlianyuan, 10 Nongzhanguan Nanlu, Chaoyang District. (6592 3627, 8703 6669); 2) 3/F, Holiday Inn Lido, Jiangtai Road, Chaoyang District. (8703 6668, 6437 6288) 净心莲，1) 朝阳区农展馆南路10号 (中国文联院内)；2) 朝阳区丽都假日饭店三层，首都机场将台路

Sea of Mercy The biggest vegetarian restaurant in Beijing features a wide array of mock fish and meat dishes made from mushroom, vegetables and beans.
Daily 10am-11pm. 103 Di'anmen Xidajie, Xicheng District. (6657 1898) 慈海素心，西城区地安门西大街103号

Still Thoughts Vegetarian Restaurant A clean, calm and cozy vegetarian oasis that forgoes the hype for thoughtfully prepared mock meats and other vegetarian dishes.
1) Daily 10.30am-10pm. 30A Gaoliangqiao Lu (inside the Meijuan Hotel), Haidian District. (6225 5792); 2) Daily 10am-10pm. 18A Dafosi Dongjie (in an unmarked hutong one block north of Qianliang Hutong, which is directly north of Sanlian Bookstore on Meishuguan Dongjie), Dongcheng District. (6400 8941) 静思素食坊，1) 海淀区高梁桥路甲30号 (梅苑饭店大院内)；2) 东城区大佛寺东街甲18号 (美术馆东街三联书店北，钱粮胡同北边小区)

Tianchu Miaoxiang Tucked away in Wudaokou, this pleasant place offers mock meat versions of classic and more unusual Chinese fare, as well as select European and Japanese dishes. A large picture menu makes ordering easy.
Daily 11am-10pm. 1/F, Chuangye Bldg, Qinghua Keji Yuan, Haidian District. (6279 7078) www.liaofan.com 天厨妙香素食馆，海淀区清华科技园创业大厦一层

Vanilla Garden More than the sum of its parts, Vanilla Garden is a great place to enjoy vegetarian cuisine, sip imported organic coffees and herbal teas, or just hang out. Also boasts helpful and attentive staff, an English menu, desserts, and wireless Internet access. Location 2 calls itself Lily Vegetarian but it's run by the same people.
1) Daily 10am-2pm, 5-9pm. South of Xinjiankongmen Gate of Summer Palace, Haidian District. (6287 8726); 2) Daily 11am-10pm. 23 Caoyuan Hutong, Beixiaojie, Dongzhimennei, Dongcheng District. (6405 2082) 百合素食香草园，1) 海淀区颐和园新建宫门南；2) 东城区东直门内北小街草园胡同23号

PHOTO: JUDY ZHOU

FOOD 91

A Culinary Tour of China
Without ever leaving Beijing
by Ann Mah

Cheese? Prosciutto? Mint salad? Expand your conception of Chinese cuisine at Yunteng Shifu

The diversity of Chinese cuisine reflects the enormity of the country. From the lamb kebabs of the west to the pan-fried cheese of Yunnan and the searing spices of Sichuan, the provinces' flavors are as unique as they are varied. But in the capital, it is possible to taste China's panoply of regional cuisines without ever leaving the city. Each of the country's 23 provinces and five autonomous areas have representative offices in Beijing, and almost all offer eateries that serve the distinctive dishes of their regions.

Beijing's hunger for regional cuisines has been evident since the 1920s, when no itinerant warlord would establish a household without bringing a chef to recreate his hometown favorites. In recent years, China's capital has attracted migrants from around the country who are nostalgic for a taste of home and who want to sample the complex flavors of far-flung provinces. As a result, interest in regional cuisines has blossomed, making Beijing's gastronomy the most diverse in the country – and these provincial government restaurants the city's best-kept culinary secret.

The popularity of the Sichuan government restaurant, known among regulars as the **Chuan Ban** (short for 四川政府驻北京办事处), is certainly evident on a typical Saturday evening, as crowds fill the dining room and a line of people spill out the door. Some patrons, like Susan Zhao, a human resources manager whose office is near the restaurant, eat there two or three times a week. "It's cheap," she said as she tucked into a plate of *mala liang mian*, a cold noodle dish. "The food is good. It doesn't get much better than this."

The restaurant imports Sichuan spices – including dried chilis, chili sauce and *huajiao*, or Sichuan peppercorn – to create the characteristic numbing burn of the southwestern province's cuisine. These special ingredients are handled by expert hands: All of the restaurant's chefs and servers train at a culinary school in Sichuan. "The flavor is very authentic, very spicy," said Wang Xiaonan, a patron, as his face turned red from the fiery meal. "This is the best Sichuan food in Beijing."

Chuan Ban is but one example of Provincial Office authenticity. At **Xinjiang Islam Restaurant** in the Xinjiang government office, customers stuff kebabs of cumin-scented halal lamb into the region's chewy *nang* flatbread or enjoy savory chicken stews hearty with tomatoes and thick noodles. The far western autonomous region's rough cuisine has been strongly influenced by the Uighur people, as well as by its Central Asian neighbors.

With an emphasis on delicate herbs and vegetables, **Yunteng Shifu**, the Yunnan government restaurant flies in fresh produce three times a week from the southern province. Crowds flock to enjoy salads of mint leaves, bigger and more flavorful than their northern cousins, and seasonal mushrooms, including morels (*yangduzi*, or "sheep's stomach"). Slices of raw-cured Yunnan ham are saltily akin to prosciutto, while shavings of deep-fried cheese, traditionally made by the region's Dai ethnic group, are crisp and light with a milky essence.

Decor takes the spotlight at the restaurant representing Inner Mongolia (**Mengtai Binguan**), an autonomous region not usually celebrated for its cuisine. Here, patrons dine in individual yurts, each adorned with a stuffed sheep's head and a portrait of Genghis Khan. The menu offers roasted lamb rib and salads of wild greens, washed down with salted milk tea. When diners order a flask of airag, a Mongolian spirit, the staff sings a traditional drinking song.

Those seeking to recreate the meals at home can combine a lunch out with a shopping trip. Most government restaurants also have stores that sell hard-to-find ingredients from their regions. Fragrant bags of Sichuan peppercorn, packages of dried five-spice tofu, and jars of Xianglajiang – a renowned chili sauce – are all for sale at the Sichuan government store. "Our chilis and peppercorn are fresher than anything you can find in Beijing shops," said the restaurant's manager, Cheng Lihong, who moved from Sichuan six years ago.

Other government restaurants sell fresh vegetables, tea, cigarettes and liquor from their respective regions.

The flavors of regions outside Beijing are becoming so popular that some fear the city's local cuisine – a wheat-based diet of thick noodles, dumplings and flat breads – is taking a back seat.

And, in spite of the authentic food available, some people find that dining at state-run restaurants has a downside. Service standards and ambiance are often less than endearing. Still, a lack of atmosphere and efficiency has not affected business for the provincial government restaurants, many of which pack the dining room every night.

As he finished his Sichuan meal and swilled the last of his beer, Wang Xiaonan said he was not surprised by the success. "Crowds of people line up here everyday," he said. "If it's run by the Sichuan government, everyone knows it must be good."

Xiangyang Xiaozhu Classic Chinese dishes rendered guilt-free draw us back to this restaurant again and again.
Daily 11am-2.30pm, 5-9.30pm. Beisanhuan (20m west of Dazhong Si), Haidian District. (8211 2104) 香阳小筑，海淀区北三环大钟寺西20米

Xu Xiang Zhai Vegetarian Restaurant Vegetarian gormandizers delight at the glorious all-you-can-eat buffet – wear pants with an elastic band to take full advantage of the offerings, which include veggie twists on Chinese classics, sushi, dumplings, hot pot and more. Monk sightings are common.
Daily 11.30am-9pm. 26 Guozijian Dajie, Dongcheng District. (6404 6568) 叙香斋，东城区国子监大街甲26-1号

Vietnamese

Delicate, fresh cuisine that uses a bounty of herbs, vegetables and spices, as well as copious amounts of fish sauce. Try the summer rolls (pork and shrimp wrapped with cilantro and mint into delicate rice paper) or the famous pho, a steaming, nourishing bowl of noodles and beef.

Le Hugo A self-described Bistro d'Indochine. Vietnamese fare with reasonable business lunches.
Daily 10am-11pm. East side of the Beijing Customs Bldg, 10 Guanghua Lu, Chaoyang District. (6581 5060) 雨果，朝阳区光华路10号，北京海关东侧

Muse Parisian Vietnamese Brasserie A modish Indochine eatery with bowls of pho, spring rolls, soups and coffees of both Vietnamese and French persuasion.
Daily 11am-11.30pm. 1 Chaoyang Gongyuan Xilu, Chaoyang District. (6586 3188) 妙，朝阳区朝阳公园西路一号

Nam Nam Beautifully designed two-story space. Menu is uneven, but the food can be spectacular, even if portions are small.
Daily 10.30am-10.30pm. 7 Sanlitun Lu, next to the Friendship Supermarket, Chaoyang District. (6468 6053) 那么那么，朝阳区三里屯北路7号（小友谊超市旁）

Nuage Worth visiting for its chic, French colonial atmosphere – complete with dim lighting, rickshaws and waitresses in stylish ao dai – and its stunning lakeside location. While the ambiance glistens with charm, the food can fall short of the mark.
Daily 11.30am-2pm, 5.30-10pm. 22 Qianhai Dongyan, Xicheng District. (6401 9581) 庆云楼，西城区前海东沿22号

Xinjiang & Muslim

If you love lamb (or its gamier parent, mutton) you'll adore the food of Xinjiang, which is heavy on roasted skewers of meat – minus lamb, of course – and heady with the liberal use of cumin. *Da pan ji* ("big plate chicken"), an enormous dish of chicken stewed in a soupy, tomato-based sauce with thick, doughy noodles, lives up to its Brobdingnagian name. Other favorites include nang (flat bread) and cold salads. If you see the words *qingzhen* (清真, halal), you've found a Muslim restaurant.

Crescent Moon Muslim Restaurant This clean, atmospheric neighborhood dive is on the short list for the best Xinjiang food in town. From the homemade yogurt (RMB 3) and the all-Uighur staff to the king of mutton *chuan'r* (RMB 5), this courtyard-nestled gem is as authentic as it gets.
Daily 9am-11.30pm. 16 Dongsi Liutiao (alley number six, 100m west of Chaonei Beixiaojie), Dongcheng District. (6400 5281) 弯弯的月亮，东城区东四六条胡同

Grape Restaurant Eat Xinjiang faves like mutton skewers and hand-pulled noodles in its airy and spacious environment. Pleasant but expensive. Requisite singing and dancing happens nightly.
Daily 11am-midnight. Qicai Beilu (next to Laitaihuahui Alley), Chaoyang District. (6465 6565, 6467 6467) 丝路驿站食府，朝阳区七彩北路莱太花卉南侧

Kaorou Ji This *laozihao* has been serving halal cuisine to Beijingers since the Qing dynasty. Try their house speciality: barbecued lamb and steamed sesame buns. Its lakeside location makes Kaorou Ji a fine place to stop for food while boating.
Daily 11am-11pm. 14 Qianhai Dongyan, Xicheng District. (6404 2554) 烤肉季，西城区前海东沿14号

Tian Chi Fresh roasted rack of lamb and exquisitely thin hand-pulled noodles.
Daily 10am-11pm. West gate of the Nationalities University, Haidian District. (6842 4595) 天池，海淀区民族大学西门

Tian Shan Pai This Xinjiang and Muslim eatery does brisk business with its classic and reasonably-priced fare. Try the roast leg of mutton (*kao yangtui* RMB 68), noodle dishes like *chao pian'r* and the spicy *laohu cai* ("tiger" salad). Wash it down with dark Xinjiang beer.
Daily 9.30am-9.30pm. 7 Chunxiu Lu, Dongcheng District. (6416 8831) 天山派食府，东城区春秀路7号

Xinjiang Islam Restaurant Hearty Xinjiang cuisine from the people who know it best in Beijing: the staff of Xinjiang province's Beijing representative office.
Daily 11am-10pm. Xinjiang Provincial Government Office, 7 Sanlihe Road, Xicheng District. (6830 1820) 新疆伊斯兰饭店，西城区三里河路7号

Xinjiang Red Rose The rowdy Red Rose packs 'em in with nightly music and belly dancing performances. Good for kebabs, but no place for the quiet conversationalist. Voted "Best Xinjiang" in our 2007 Reader Restaurant Awards.
Daily 11am-11pm. Inside 7 Xingfu Yicun alley, opposite Workers' Stadium North Gate, Chaoyang District. (6415 5741) 新疆红玫瑰餐厅，朝阳区工人体育场北门对面幸福一村7巷内

Yunnan

Influenced by its Southeast Asian neighbors, Yunnan cuisine balances a mix of sour, spicy and sweet flavors – even the region's soy sauce, which is brewed with brown sugar, has a touch of sweetness. Popular dishes include clay pot chicken (*qiguo ji*), "crossing the bridge" noodles (*guoqiao mixian*), rice noodles that are scooped into a bowl of hot broth, mild goat cheese called *rubing* and raw smoked ham that's akin to prosciutto.

Cai Yunjian This inexpensive restaurant specializes in *qiguo ji*, a delectable chicken dish served in a special double-decker steamer, Dai barbecued fish (*Daishi kaoyu*) and Pineapple Rice (*bolo fan*). But the real test of any Yunnan restaurant is how well they make their *guoqiao mixian* – and to this extent, they take the cake.

Yunnan! Land of exotic ingredients, like ... the potato!

Daily 10.30am-11pm. Lanqiying Chengfu Lu, Haidian District. (6261 0731) 彩云间云南傣族菜馆，海淀区成府路蓝旗营

Golden Peacock Dai Ethnic Flavour Worth traveling across town for. Try the pineapple rice and the spicy lettuce salad, but get there early if you don't want to wait for a table. If there are no free tables try the Dai delicacies of Baoqin Daiwei a couple doors down.
Daily 11am-10pm. 16 Minzu Daxue Beilu, Weigongcun, Haidian District. (6893 2030) 金孔雀傣家风味餐厅，海淀区魏公村民族大学北路16号楼一层

Jia 21 Hao Taiwanese pop star Gao Mingjun has involved some seriously style-conscious buddies in creating his latest venture: a spacious and trendy restaurant for Yunnan minority cuisine, drinks and relaxing.
Daily 11am-10.30pm. 21 Beitucheng Donglu, Chaoyang District. (6489 5066) 甲21号，朝阳区北土城东路甲21号

Middle 8th Restaurant Comfortable and hip Yunnan restaurant. Try the Yunnan-style spare ribs and the dragon beans. There is also a separate and slightly down-market barbecue section diagonally opposite the original store.
Daily 11am-midnight, 5.30pm-midnight. Sanlitun Zhongjie Zhongba Lou, Chaoyang District. (6413 0629) 中八楼，朝阳区三里屯中街中八楼

No Name Restaurant Burrowed within Houhai's hutongs, this stylish Yunnan eatery attracts trendsetters eager to escape Yinding Qiao's neon, noise and tourists. The most compelling reason to visit might be the rooftop terrace.
Daily 11am-midnight. 1 Da Jinsi Hutong, Xicheng District. (6618 6061) 西城区大金丝胡同1号

South Silk Road Opened by a Beijing-based artist, this super hip restaurant's interior is minimalist with down-home Yunnanese specialties and their own brand of rice wine. Voted "Best Yunnan" in our 2007 Reader Restaurant Awards.
1) Daily 11.30am-midnight. 12-13, 19A Shichahai Qianhai Xiyan, Xicheng District. (6615 5515); 2) Daily 10.30am-midnight. 2-3/F, North Bldg 4, Area 2, Anhuili, Chaoyang District. (6481 3261); 3) Daily 11am-10.30pm. 3/F, Bldg D, Soho New Town, 88 Jianguo Lu, Chaoyang District. (8580 4286) 茶马古道，1）西城区什刹海前海西沿甲19号12-13室；2）朝阳区安慧里2区4号北楼3层；3）朝阳区建国路88号Soho现代城D座3层会所

Yunnan Impression Dine on Yunnan specialties in an exotic, rustic atmosphere. The menu features the region's famous cheese and ham, but don't set your heart on a certain dish -- not all menu items are always available.
Daily 10.30am-10.30pm. 16 Dongsanhuan Beilu (in the alley behind the La Popo sign), Chaoyang District. (8595 1277) 云南印象，朝阳区东三环北路16号（辣婆婆牌子后面巷内）

Yunteng Shifu Consistent, fresh Yunnan cuisine. Specialties to try include the mint leaf salad, fried goat's cheese, pine needle salad and the mushroom dishes such as fried mushroom slices and dried mushrooms in spicy oil. Meat dishes galore as well, but quite easy to piece together a vegetarian meal here.
Daily 11am-10pm. Yunnan Provincial Government Office, Bldg 7, Donghuashi Beili Dongqu, Chongwen District. (6711 3322 ext 7105) 云腾宾馆食府，崇文区东花市北里东区7号

I Eat Alone

Yeah, with nobody else
by Ann Mah

A plate of curried Singapore noodles at Cafe Taipan to suit divine solitude

As a freelance journalist, I've eaten a lot of meals alone. Sure, there's the sporadic business lunch, PR feed, interview (eating with one hand and taking notes with the other) or quick bite with a friend. But then there are those days when lunch is the only break from my desk, the sole opportunity to get out of the house and see other people. These occasions, when it's just me and my book, call for a certain type of eatery, casual enough to feel comfortable, yet pleasant enough to be refreshing.

Wawu's Japanese-salary man-style counter is the perfect spot to slurp soupy ramen. Their lunch sets – bowl of noodles and triangle of seaweed-wrapped rice – are carb heaven, anathema to Dr. Atkins, yet oh-so-comforting on a bitter winter day. Their miso ramen is hearty and salty, but it's the complementary salad bar – featuring oh-so-fresh fixings and simple sushi rolls – that keeps me coming back.

In close range of many Jianwai-area media offices, **Sequoia Cafe** is a good spot for sandwiches piled high with freshly sliced deli meat and coffee, with a cafe ambience that encourages lingering. Stronger on drinks than on food (but still good for the solitary) is the **Stone Boat Cafe** (see Bar & Club Directory, p344), where a cool breeze blows across the painted eaves, encouraging productive meditation.

A Serb sandwich at **Kiosk** means you're never really dining on your own, as owner Sasha Unkovic is always available for a friendly chat. **Panino Teca** has its fans – though some may find it too crowded to enjoy alone – try the oversized bowl of mixed greens topped with grilled chicken. If you're eating by yourself you might as well do it healthily. **Biteapitta's** casual dining room and long counter are also ideal for solo noshing; as an added bonus, you won't have to worry about all the garlic they heap into their delicious falafel.

Solitary dining on Chinese food can be a bit trickier. With most dishes designed for sharing, you could find yourself eating leftover *xihongshi chao jidan* for the rest of the week. A better option are the plates of curried Singapore noodles or bowls of wonton soup – available at both **Cafe Taipan** and **GL Cafe** – the latter has a canteen-like atmosphere that's perfect for solitary slurping. For a solo adventure, head over to Houhai's **Jiumen Xiaochi** where twelve of the capital's oldest snack shops have sought refuge from the wrecking ball in an old courtyard home. The food court atmosphere is bustling and fun, the portions manageable, and no one will bat an eye if you're eating alone.

See Restaurant Directory p57 for details.

A Matter of Taste
that's Beijing's 2007 Reader Restaurant Awards

Food, glorious food! It's certainly everybody's favorite topic in this city of 60,000-plus restaurants, cafes, hole-in-the-walls, *chuan'r* stands, and secret family recipes. Every year, our sister publication *that's Beijing* gives readers the chance to weigh in and to heap praise and glory upon their favorites of the bunch. Here are the results. All mentioned restaurants are listed in the restaurant directory.

Alameda's service wins high marks

FOOD

At their best, Hatsune's creatively conceived American-style sushi rolls are something like a bite of heaven

Best Beijing Duck
Da Dong Roast Duck
King of the roost for the second consecutive year, Da Dong continues to impress our readers with its glitzy decor, swish service and of course, fantastic roast duck.

Honorable Mentions
Made in China
Quan Ju De

Best French
Brasserie Flo
With pricey French restaurants opening up every other minute in Beijing, Brasserie Flo has managed to stand out from the crowd with their "generous portions," and readers know that "every time we eat there, we get our money's worth." The swank restaurant specializes in Alsatian dishes, but also offers a selection of classic bistro fare that have stood the test of time.

Honorable Mentions
Cafe de la Poste
Le Bistro Parisien

Best Indian
Taj Pavilion
As one voter notes, "The surroundings are refined and elegant, and service is discreet and professional." Curry fiends enthuse about the "thick, creamy, divine palak paneer."

Honorable Mentions
Ganges
Indian Kitchen

Best Italian
Annie's
On top for yet another year, Annie's service strikes a chord with many readers who love "the warm and family-friendly environment, with staff that have great English skills." As one reader puts it: "Why is Annie's the best Italian? I'm American, so I go for taste over authenticity. I like it sweet and cheesy!"

Honorable Mentions
Assaggi
Cepe

Best Japanese
Hatsune
Morning, noon and night, Hatsune's full house attests to its consistent appeal in this category – no small feat, considering the capital's ample offering of quality Japanese cuisine.

Honorable Mentions
Matsuko
Yotsuba

Best Korean
Han Na Shan
This perennial favorite takes the cake for mass appeal with Beijing's barbecue lovers. With 11-odd individually owned and operated locations around town, it passes the authenticity test with one of our Korean readers: "All of my Korean co-workers go to this restaurant when we want Korean food."

Honorable Mentions
Saveurs de Corée
Sorabol

PHOTO: NICK OTTO

INSIDER'S GUIDE TO BEIJING

Cafe Sambal's Malay morsels keep us coming back

Best Malaysian/Singaporean
Cafe Sambal
Big on style and flavor, with a "low-key hutong location [that] belies the grandeur of its cuisine," including mango and shrimp rolls, spicy prawn, and winged beans. Need another reason to go? "For drinks, the mojitos are the best in town."

Honorable Mentions
Asian Star
Lau Pa Sak
Little Penang

Best Shanghai
Din Tai Fung
The humble dumpling is the quintessential Chinese comfort food, but this international chain from Taiwan takes the concept to a whole new level. As one regular comments, "You will get addicted to this restaurant."

Honorable Mentions
Jade Garden
Lu Lu

Best Sichuan
South Beauty
This popular chain offers spicy Sichuan cuisine served in sleek, upscale settings that are, as one voter remarked, both "elegant and comfortable" – great places to bring the sophisticated out-of-town guest.

Honorable Mentions
Feiteng Yuxiang
Yuxiang Renjia

Best Thai
Purple Haze
The "very nice decor where you can see your life in purple," great location (opposite Workers' Stadium North Gate), efficient service, sociable atmosphere, "quality" and "authenticity" secured Purple Haze's preeminence in the hearts of voters.

Honorable Mentions
Banana Leaf
Pink Loft
Serve the People

Best Xinjiang
Red Rose
Our motto could be theirs as well – ain't nuthin' like mutton! This sensibility, combined with an accessible location and a rowdy performance atmosphere, has won Red Rose the bouquet of *that's Beijing* readers' appreciation.

Honorable Mentions
Afunti
Xinjiang Islam Restaurant

Best Yunnan
South Silk Road
Friendly service, lots of frog on the menu, and "modern, fresh and funky" decor set South Silk road apart for Yunnan-food lovers.

Honorable Mentions
Middle 8th
No Name Restaurant

PHOTO: SIMON LIM

FOOD

The Tree's legendary pies will sate your pizza pique

Best Dim Sum
Din Tai Fung
Din Tai Fung's scrumptious dumplings may not have the range of your typical dim sum joint, but their legendary *xiaolong tang bao* and other assorted dough-wrapped specialties more than compensate.

Honorable Mentions
Crystal Jade Palace
Jin Ding Xuan

Best Hot Pot
Ding Ding Xiang
"Excellent atmosphere," gorgeously sliced meat, fresh veggies, crispy *shaobing* (烧饼 sesame buns) and some of the best *ma jiang* dipping sauce in town earn Ding Ding Xiang another year of championship in this category.

Honorable Mentions
Hot Loft
Lemon Leaf
Little Sheep

Best Pizza
The Tree
Readers rave about the Tree pizza's consistency, ambiance, late night availability, and crust, describing it as "not too heavy … [it's] thin enough so you can really taste the toppings."

Honorable Mentions
Annie's
Hutong Pizza

Best Steak
Morel's
This long-running Belgian restaurant has come out on top of the steak competition by virtue of its "excellent quality, huge pieces of meat and a wide selection of Belgian beers!"

Honorable Mentions
Alameda
Astor Grill
Blockhouse

Best Vegetarian
Pure Lotus
Voted Best Vegetarian for the second year running, Pure Lotus offers some respite in a city where the meat eater is king. "The ambiance is perfect, soothing and relaxed."

Honorable Mentions
Biteapitta
Lotus in Moonlight

Best Brunch
Grandma's Kitchen
"The service, prices and quality of the food is far better than more pretentious places in the embassy area."

Honorable Mentions
The Orchard
The Garden Court

PHOTO: NICK OTTO

Bellagio's clientele are serious about having fun

Best Late Night Dining
Bellagio
The location, people-watching and famous desserts enhance Bellagio's late night magnetism. "The Taiwanese-style fried rice noodles and fried tofu reminds me of home in Taipei."

Honorable Mentions
Jin Ding Xuan
The Tree

Best for a Date
The CourtYard
"I used to date quite a lot and The CourtYard was always my place of choice since its distinct quality always gave my dates the feeling that they are something special – a big step towards sealing the deal."

Honorable Mentions
Alameda
W Dine & Wine

Best Family Meal
Grandma's Kitchen
Nothing goes with a gaggle of tiny tots better than a stack of delicious pancakes, or a genuine root beer float.

Honorable Mentions
Annie's
Xiao Wang Fu

Best to Impress Visitors
Green T. House
"The moment you cross the door, you feel like you've entered a fairytale-land, where everything is oddly elegant and weirdly beautiful." Recently tabbed for Condé Nast's Hot List.

Honorable Mentions
Da Dong Roast Duck
Lan
The CourtYard

Best Business Lunch
Alameda
"Conveniently located on the east side of Beijing, near embassies and multinational companies," Alameda's RMB 60 lunch special is "an oasis between busy working hours" for many.

Honorable Mentions
Aria
Hatsune

Best Wine Selection
Aria
With over 400 labels to choose from, this is the place for oenophiles. Aria's happy hour is popular amongst CBD-ers, and where there is tipple, there must also be tasty treats.

Honorable Mentions
Cafe Europa
The CourtYard

PHOTO: SIMON LIM

FOOD

Lan's outlandish decor makes everyone say "Zowie!"

Best Value for Money
Annie's
"Provides a combination of affordable price with nicely prepared and presented food." Another reader agrees: "With everything hovering around RMB 35-55 for rather authentic Italian food, it truly is the best bang for your buck (or *kuai*)."

Honorable Mentions
Alameda
Steak and Eggs

Best Decor
Lan
Philippe Starck's jumble-sale chic wowed readers into voting it Beijing's most aesthetically pleasing eatery. "I can't remember what I ate at the restaurant and if I can't remember, it means that the place impressed me for its design only!"

Honorable Mentions
Cepe
Green T. House

Best Service
Alameda
One of the secrets of Alameda's popularity, it seems, is the smiling faces behind the tray. Polite, patient and friendly, Alameda's staff consistently impress their clientele.

Honorable Mentions
Cepe
Hatsune

Restaurant of the Year
Alameda
For the third consecutive year, *that's Beijing* readers voted Alameda the cream of the crop. "The service is excellent, they have a great wine selection, and they do the best steak in town."

Honorable Mentions
Cepe
Hatsune

Editor's Picks
For a beautiful scarf

Gloriously over the top, The Westin's Sunday brunch bombards the senses

Best Newcomer
When longing for *ama*'s (阿妈, grandma's) cooking, Beijing's Taiwanese community heads to **Alexander Creek Park**, for homestyle dishes with an accent on health. Their MSG-free classics include *sanbeiji* (三杯鸡, crock-pot chicken) and Taiwan sausage just like the kind you can find in Taipei's famous night markets, plus mountains of shaved ice with generous sweet toppings.

Best Place to Overindulge
Bite-for-bite and sip-for-sip, the Sunday champagne brunch at **Senses** (The Westin) is one of the best deals in town. Arrive early, tackle the spread scientifically, and stay until the staff roll you away in a food coma. Like the staggering range of menu options, the entertainment is completely over-the-top – think short-skirted Bond Girl-types furiously playing air violins and cellos. The brunch is available in a non-alcoholic version, but a mere 50 *kuai* more (RMB 298 +15% tax) nets an unlimited flow of champagne and wine – and eager sommelier service to help you coordinate drinks and vittles. Meanwhile, a clown, a face painter and the kids' clubhouse entertain the young ones.

Best Vegan
Why are the cheese-forsakers flocking to **Hutong Pizza**? The secret is not in the sauce, but inside a bun: The restaurant's huge and hearty veggie burger is 100% vegan. Fortified with a side of thick fries, the burger explodes from its carbo confines in a manner that requires multiple napkins. This behemoth is no Bocaburger – it's an old school, rice-based, gloriously sloppy concoction that harkens back to the days when vegans had to count on ingenuity and a good spice cabinet for a satisfying meal.

Best Student Hangout
Jam-packed with rowdy students devouring gigantic, table-sized pizzas overflow with toppings and stringy cheese, The **Kro's Nest**'s original Haidian branch keeps young scholars coming back for more. A young 'un himself, the 23-year-old owner understands – debating The Analects is best paired with pepperoni and Yanjing.

Restaurant of the Year
Manzo is a sake bar first, and a restaurant second – but the food is hardly an afterthought. On the contrary, their no-nonsense Japanese home cooking adheres to formidably high standards. Handmade tofu is concocted with all-natural nigari (concentrated seawater) and no additives. Their deep-fried fish cakes are ground by a huge mortar and pestle, and their Japanese rice porridge satisfies the soul. Owned and managed by a licensed sake taster, there are some serious distillates in their cabinets, with thoughtful tasting sets for beginners. Unpretentious service adds the finishing touch to this gem of an eatery.

See Dining Directory for addresses.

A Taste of Home
International and organic groceries … and bakeries!
by Ann Mah

Julien Groult of Boucherie Michel picks and cuts the meat sold in his store

If you're craving a taste of home – and mom has shared her recipes – look no further than the stores below, where you'll find *laowai* specialty ingredients like fresh herbs, European cheeses and veal chops. Still, availability is not always reliable so if you're planning a unique dish, it's best to have a backup plan. Many expats tend to stockpile ingredients (to the woman who bought out the entire stock of bucatini pasta at Jenny Lou's: We haven't forgotten you), which means your favorite cereal can be here today, gone tomorrow.

Staples such as canned goods, sliced bread, olive oil and butter can be found at most local grocery stores, while Western cuts of meat such as boneless, skinless chicken breast and beef tenderloin are on offer at Schindler's German Food Center and Boucherie Michel. Remember, good food starts at the market, and with Beijing's variety of ingredients, you have no excuse to stay out of the kitchen.

As for on those days that call for sweet confections, a spate of quality bakeries has popped up around town. Tell your friends you made it yourself …

Grocery Stores

April Gourmet Chain of stores purveying imported cheeses, olives and cold cuts, as well as staples like dried pasta, canned tomatoes (and beans) and cereal. The Shunyi branch offers a small but constant "specials" section, which often features imported cookies and filter coffee.
1) Daily 8am-9pm. Opposite the South Gate of Capital Paradise, Shunyi District. (8046 4132); 2) Daily 8am-midnight. 1/F Jiezuo Mansion, Xingfucun Zhonglu, Sanlitun, Chaoyang District. (6417 7970); 3) Daily 8am-9pm. 1 Sanlitun Beixiaojie, Chaoyang District. (8455 1245) 绿叶子食品店，1）顺义区名都苑南门对面；2）朝阳区三里屯幸福村中路杰作大厦1层；3）朝阳区三里屯北小街1号

Boucherie Michel Opened by a young French butcher of the old school, this artisanal shop and restaurant has gained a wide following with its selection of high-grade beef, veal, lamb, and pork (60-90 RMB per kg). Patrons also recommend the pates, sausages (including merguez) and Parisian-style hams. Freshly roasted chicken, quiches, and frozen dishes such as coq au vin, as well as a range of well-priced French wines, are also for sale. The small French restaurant upstairs delivers the same meat, now cooked, in a cozy checkered-table-cloth setting or, in season, on the curbside patio.
Daily 9am-8.30pm. 1 Jiezuo Bldg, Xingfucun Zhonglu, Chaoyang District. (6417 0489, boucheriemichel@hotmail.com) 米歇尔肉店，朝阳区幸福村中路杰座大厦1段

Carrefour French hypermarket offers a vast selection of imported wine, cheese, coffee, canned goods and much more. Wonderful variety – especially at the Guangqumenwai location – but the crowds can be thick. The Sanyuan Qiao store offers free delivery for purchases over RMB 500 – order by email customer@carrefour.com).
1) Daily 8.30am-10.30pm. 6B Beisanhuan Donglu (beside the International Exhibition Center), Chaoyang District. (8460 1043); 2) Daily 8am-10.30pm. 11 Malian Dao, Xuanwu District. (6332 2155); 3) Daily 8am-10.30pm. 15 Zone 2, Fangchengyuan, Fangzhuang, Fengtai District.(6760 9911); 4) Daily 8.30am-10.30pm. 31 Guangqu Lu, Chaoyang District. (5190 9508); 5) Daily 8am-10.30pm. 56A Zhongguancun Plaza, Haidian District. (5172 1516/7); 6) Daily 8am-10.30pm. 54A Baishiqiao Lu (east of Beijing Zoo), Xicheng District. (8836 2729) www.carrefour.com.cn, e-shop.carrefour.com 家乐福，1）朝阳区北三环东路乙6号(中国国际展览中心正门旁)；2）宣武区马连道11号；3）丰台区方庄芳城园二区15号；4）朝阳区广渠路31号；5）海淀区中关村广场甲56号；6）西城区白石桥路甲54号

Friendship Supermarket Though the decor will take you back to 1982, the prices here are finally on par with Jenny Lou's and April Gourmet. The wine selection is also competitive, while an assortment of DVDs in the back completes your one-stop shopping experience.
Daily 8am-8.30pm. 7 Sanlitun Lu, Chaoyang District. (6532 1871) 友谊超市，朝阳区三里屯路7号

Jenny Lou's We keep coming back to these grocery stores, despite their high prices and occasional lack of fapiao, because, along with the usual staples, they feature fresh meat and cheese, unusual pasta shapes, unsweetened yogurt, fresh herbs, unblemished veggies ... we could go on and on. The Shunyi shop offers the neighborhood's widest variety of alcohol, cheese and bread, as well as services including gardening, ayi'ing, housesitting and cakes to order. What will they think of next?
1) Daily 7.30 am-10pm. Pinnacle Plaza, Shunyi District. (8046 2316 / 3302); 2) Daily 7am-10pm. Opposite Heping Hospital, Laiguangying Donglu, Chaoyang District. (8470 1557); 3) Daily 8am-10pm. West of Soho New Town (next to Annie's), Jianguo Lu, Chaoyang District. (8589 8299); 4) Daily 7am-midnight. 4 Ritan Beilu (opposite to Fancaodi Primary School), Chaoyang District. (8563 0626); 5) Daily 8am-midnight. South of the west gate of Chaoyang Park, Chaoyang District. (6507 5207); 6) Daily 7.30am-10pm. 6 Sanlitun Beixiaojie, Chaoyang District. (6461 6928); 7) Daily 8am-midnight. Hairun International Condominium, 2 Jiangtai Lu, Chaoyang District. (5135 8338); 8) Daily 8am-10pm. Inside East Lake Villa Clubhouse. 捷妮璐，1）顺义区荣祥广场；2）朝阳区来广营东路和平医院对面；3）朝阳区建国路Soho现代城西侧（Annie's餐厅旁边）；4）朝阳区日坛北路4号（芳草地小学对面）；5）朝阳区朝阳公园西门南侧；6）朝阳区三里屯北小街；7）朝阳区将台路2号海润国际公寓底商；8）东湖别墅会所里

Kempi Deli Strong on baked goods, including cookies, breads and some of Beijing's best cake. Sliced meats and other prepared foods also on offer.
Daily 7am-11pm. 1/F Kempinski Hotel, Chaoyang District. (6465 3388 ext 5741) 凯宾美食廊，朝阳区凯宾斯基饭店一层

Lido Deli Wide selection of imported goods at higher-than-average prices. While nearby Jenny Lou's has taken some of their business, this is a reliable, though expensive, standby for Lido-neighborhood denizens.

The Dread-Free Dinner Party
Be the host with the most
by Ann Mah

Brasserie Flo is one of several restaurants that can cater your dinner party

There comes a point in every person's life when enough is enough. You cannot continue blithely accepting invitations. You owe your mates: It is time to throw a dinner party. Though the very words may cause your stomach to clench, there's really nothing to fear. Having friends over in Beijing can involve as little – or as much – effort as you wish to muster. The following tips on gracious entertaining are offered humbly; there's only one Martha Stewart after all, but we could all agree that an evening spent with friends, food and drink is indeed one of life's greatest pleasures.

Know your limits

Yes, yes, the more the merrier – that is, until you consider the amount of effort you'll need to expend. Inviting six people is significantly less work than 12, especially considering the standard Beijing kitchen, which is generally cramped and lacking in every host's greatest asset: the oven. If this is your first dinner party, stick to a smaller group and don't feel too guilty.

Stock up on booze

They say a bottle of wine holds five glasses, which is odd, as I've never managed to squeeze out more than four. The usual suspects – **Jenny Lou's**, **April's**, **Carrefour**, **Schindler's**, **Boucherie Michel** – stock a good selection and their wine salesmen can be helpful, as long as they stick to your budget. For pre-dinner cocktails, stir up a pitcher of something like the lethal Maiden's Prayer, a blend of gin, cointreau, and lemon and orange juices. At the last minute, shake over ice and serve in a martini glass for a festive "house drink." In the summer, homemade lemonade is extremely versatile; teetotalers can abstain from the optional spike of vodka. Check out www.webtender.com for more cocktail recipes.

Don't skimp on the snacks

One of my mothers-in-law (I'm lucky enough to have two) believes that the best parties feature unlimited booze and meager food. That's one school of thought. Though I enjoy drinking on an empty stomach as much as the next person, it's embarrassing when your guests pass out before dinner (ah, Christmas 2004). Pre-dinner snacks can be simple, but they should be plentiful – bowls of grape tomatoes, crisps, and peanuts will suffice. For more elaborate (and pricier) nibbles, order up a few tubs of take-away hummus and babaganoush from **Biteapitta**, along with their signature bread. But don't go overboard – you don't want to ruin anyone's appetite for dinner. Which brings us to …

The main munch

Really, honestly, it doesn't matter what you serve, people will just be grateful for a hot meal. If you're lucky enough to have an oven, head on over to the German butcher for a roast beef and bung it in the old *kaoxiang* at 425 degrees Fahrenheit for 12 minutes per pound. If you don't have an oven, stews and curries are excellent for crowds; you can prepare them ahead of time and stretch them out with loads of fresh vegetables. Check out www.epicurious.com for a treasure trove of recipes.

Feeling flush? Dial up a caterer or chef. Restaurants like **Alameda**, **Brasserie Flo** (Flo Prestige), **Rumi**, **Victor's Place** and **Schindler's German Food Center** – the latter can do an entire barbecue – are just a few options. Chef Li (135 2047 2156) will bring his team to your house to create and serve an elaborate Italian feast (he once worked for the Italian defense attaché). Alternatively, use that old Beijing method and ask your friends if they know a good caterer. Chances are a friend of a friend of a friend knows the perfect person.

Plan ahead

This is key to your enjoyment of the evening; if you're feeling flustered, chances are your guests will too. Don't leave everything to the last minute (or day!). Go booze shopping a few days ahead, set the table in the morning, or make your main dish the day before (stews improve with time, after all). Drink a glass of wine 15 minutes before your guests are due to arrive to ease any pre-party jitters. Then smile, relax and leave the dishes until morning.

Find the contact details of the above named shops and restaurants in this chapter.

Don't forget to have this guy swing by your house the morning before your party: You'll need a lot of booze

The delicate balance between freshness and hygiene: a thrilling puzzle of grocery shopping

Daily 7am-9pm. Lido Hotel, Jichang Lu, Chaoyang District. (6437 6688 ext 1542) 熟食店，朝阳区机场路，丽都假日饭店

Lion Mart If you can tolerate the warehouse ambience, the Shunyi location is good for common frozen products, low-priced produce and fresh flowers. Generally more expensive than April Gourmet with an unimaginative cheese and meat selection. The Somerset location offers a smaller selection.
1) Daily 10am-9pm. 1/F, The Somerset, 46 Liangmaqiao Lu, Chaoyang District. (8440 1143); 2) Daily 8.30am-9pm. Near the south gate of Capital Paradise, Shunyi District. (8046 1868) 新货郎超市，1) 朝阳区亮马桥路46号福景苑1层；2) 顺义区名都园南门附近

Lohao City This organic goods and health food store sources most of its produce from its organic ranch in Miyun County, with the remainder (tropical fruits) imported from Taiwan. Highlights include 100 percent organic homemade soymilk, pickled vegetables and imported dry goods, including muesli, cookies, pasta, as well as organic and dairy free chocolates. Check out the flower and plant shop with cute baby cacti and bonsai, as well as a corner devoted to an assortment of hi-tech Japanese pillows.
Daily 9am-10pm. 1) 52 Jingshun Lu, Chaoyang District (8459 4202/0134); 2) B4 Haoyun Jie, Chaoyang District (5867 0270/0265); 3) 10A, Bldg 5, 76 Nan Er Lu, Baiziwan, Chaoyang District (8772 4132/33) www.lohaocity.com 乐活城，1) 朝阳区京顺路52号；2) 朝阳区好运街乙4号；3) 朝阳区百子湾南二路 76号5号楼10A

Mrs. Shanen's Bagels Bagel schmagel – this quaint and sunny spot, complete with checkered tiles and comfy seating, offers a unique baking selection beyond their cafe menu. Bagels are cheaper by the dozen at RMB 100 on average. Feed your inner artisan with ciabatta and braids of challah. Cakes and pies are made to order, and range from New York cheesecake to sweet potato pie – pricey at RMB 160-280.
Daily 7.30am-8pm. 5 Kaifa Jie, Xi Baixinzhuang (next to Capital Paradise), Shunyi District. (8046 4301) 单太太贝谷面包房，顺义区西白辛庄开发街5号（紧邻名都园）

Schindler's German Food Center Old hands call it the German Butcher, but the sign outside says Schindler's. This spacious and bright shop is a carnivore's paradise. The meat counter features cuts ranging from veal scallopini to pork loin and whole turkeys. The deli section offers sliced ham, salami and other cold cuts, while the bakery whips up fresh, crusty loaves of bread, pretzel rolls, seven grain bread and baguettes. Also sells wine, coffee, chocolate and more. If you can't wait for dinner, order up a doner kebab from the takeout stand.
Daily 9.30am-7pm. 15 Zaoying Beili, Maizidian, (800m east of Nongzhanguan Beilu), Chaoyang District. (6591 9370) 德国食品中心，朝阳区麦子店枣营北里15号（农展馆北路往东800米）

Shuang An Supermarket This is one of the few supermarkets west of Dongzhimen that sells cheese, lunchmeat and peanut butter. The selection of coffee, olive oil, chocolate and other Western imports is comparable to Haidian's Carrefour, minus the mobs.
Daily 9am-10pm. 38 Beisanhuan Xilu, Haidian District. (8214 8000) 双安超市，海淀区北三环西路38号

Sure Save While the name isn't the most flattering, it does ring true in at least two ways – this mini-mart offers the cheapest booze in Shunyi and is a sure save on hunting around other stores for all your imported essentials. An impressive selection of German beers,

108 INSIDER'S GUIDE TO BEIJING

Chocolate Sichuan Pepper (yes, really) and so much more at Comptoirs de France

French vinegars, vegetarian grazing and Korean Nonghyup products. Feast your eyes on the dizzying cookie aisle and fine German treats, including real blueberry jam, Dr. Oetker's and gourmet herring.
Daily 8am-10pm. Pinnacle Plaza, Shunyi District. (8046 4363) 索斯福超市，顺义区日祥广场

Bakeries

21 Cake Incredibly delicious square cakes, with creative presentations and top-notch ingredients. Delivery only. Don't forget that you must order five hours in advance. If you order 24 hours in advance you get a 5% discount. If the location of delivery and payment are in separate locations, be prepared to pay an extra RMB 10. *(6575 2121) www.21cake.com*

Awfully Chocolate Don't let this store's white-walled psychiatric ward decor put you off. Their scrumptious chocolate cakes are to die for – rich in taste yet moist and light, so light that you'll eat a whole cake by yourself and not feel disgusted. Can't go wrong with any item in their classic but limited selection – original chocolate cake (RMB 139), banana chocolate cake (RMB 168), rum and cherry chocolate cake (RMB 178) and dark chocolate ice creams (RMB 20-70).
Daily 10am-9pm. Bldg 2-108, Wanda Plaza, 93 Jianguo Road, Chaoyang District. (5820 5826) 朝阳区建国路93号，万达广场2号楼108

Comptoirs de France This patisserie and bakery is the latest mainland venture of Benjamin Devos, heir to a 150-year family history of producing quality breads, pastries and chocolates. From macaroons (like the chocolate Sichuan pepper and vanilla bourbon, RMB 35 per 100g), chocolate tart (RMB 16 for the large), to a variety of freshly baked rolls, baguettes, and loaves of bread (all within the RMB 10-20 range) Monsieur Devos knows his food … and it shows.
Daily 7am-9pm. 1) Rm 102, 1/F, Bldg 15, China Central Place, 89 Jianguo Lu, Chaoyang District. (6530 5480); 2) 1/F, East Lake Club, 35 Dongzhimenwai Dajie, Dongcheng District. (6461 1525) 法派，1）朝阳区建国路89号华贸中心15号楼102；2）东城区东直门外大街35号东湖俱乐部1层

Exquisite Bakery Probably the only place in town where you can pick up everything you need for a Barbie or SpongeBob SquarePants birthday party, including the cake, of course. Wide selection of cakes and pastries are gratifyingly supplemented by thoughtful extras – some cake purchases include a free bouncy castle rental. DIYers will also find Beijing's most complete collection of cake baking supplies, including simple pie pans, latex cupcake forms and professional-grade icing guns with 100 different nozzles.
Daily 9am-7pm. Shop 7, Riverville Square, Tianzhu, Shunyi District. (6450 9838) 南炉，顺义区天竺温榆广场07店

South German Bakery, Cafe Konstanz and Bodenseestube Provides a variety of German and European rye, wheat and white breads along with tasty homemade cakes and sweets. Upstairs you'll find Cafe Konstanz and the new south German restaurant Bodenseestube, which offers great breakfasts, business lunches and hearty German dinners. Sandwiches and quality coffee also available.
Restaurant, Daily 8am-10pm. Bakery, Daily 7am-9.30pm. 27 Haoyunjie, 29 Zaoying Lu, Chaoyang District. (5867 0201) www.germanbakery.com.cn 朝阳区枣营路29号好运街27号

Bottles Up
Buying wine in Beijing
by Fongyee Walker & Edward Ragg

Be dedicated: The wine you are craving is just an "interweb" surf away

Though hardly thankless, finding the wine you want in this city can be a tisk of a task. Even if you have the patience to endure countless service staff in supermarkets pointing at apparently random bottles and saying "French ... good," selecting wine is still a challenging and sometimes fraught experience. Information on back labels is all too often obscured by a Chinese government sticker that only offers up such informational gems as "This wine is made from 100 percent grape juice." Many of the imported wine brands available here are not, of course, the familiar ones from "back home." It might be a bulk wine bottled here in China, or a wine either past its prime or of dubious quality, shipped off to the nominally "undiscerning" Chinese market. Of course, if you choose a Chinese-made wine, there is no way of telling if it is even made from China-grown grapes.

Fortunately, both the available selection and the quality of wine have been increasing in leaps and bounds in Beijing recently and there are now many good value and tasty bottles to be found. A first step is to find reliable retailers, many of which have their inventories catalogued online. New retailers are popping up with encouraging regularity, but face an increasingly competitive market.

Buying straight from the distributor has a few advantages, including convenient delivery, relatively painless returns (in case of corked wines) and assurance that the wine has been stored properly prior to drinking. Alternatively, supermarkets and the smaller wine stores furnish a more hands-on experience, if you have time for a personal visit. More bijou retail outlets such as **Cellar Le Pinot** in Oriental Plaza (www.lepinot.com) or the various Top Cellar branches. These do not simply cater to the trophy-wine hunters and we were impressed to see a broad price range with various wines imported directly.

As for Chinese wines (see p112), most supermarkets stock reasonable selections. But beware of old stock, particularly as many Chinese wines currently do not survive well much after a year beyond bottling. Get the most recent vintages of the likes of Dragon Seal. Grace Vineyards (from Shanxi) is the exception, as quality is much higher.

ASC Fine Wines China's largest importer and distributor boast an impressive selection of wines from 13 different countries. Order wine through their website (www.asc-wines.com) or over the phone at 6418 1598. Delivery is free on orders over RMB 200 and they guarantee to deliver in less than 24 hours. ASC also offers a free membership program through which you can get a 5% discount.

Bacchus Exclusively distributes French wines, with decent examples from Bordeaux, Burgundy, Alsace and the Rhône. (bacchus-wines.net)

Gelipu With a catalog of boutique Australian producers and avoiding the large brands, Gelipu has some of the most interesting offerings available. (www.ai9.com.cn/eng/index.asp)

Jointek Focus primarily is Bordeaux with some limited selections from the New World. (www.jointekfinewines.com)

Montrose Wines Montrose offers wines from 17 different countries and has an elaborate and informative website through which you can order wines (www.montrosechina.com). You can also order by telephone (5126 7788). In addition to their online and telephone sales, Montrose Wines also has a couple of outlet shops in Chaoyang. Daily 10.30am-7.30pm. 37 Kerry Center Shopping Mall, B1/F, 1 Guanghua Lu, Chaoyang District. (8529 9494); 2) Daily 9.30am-9.30pm. China World Trade Center, 1 Jianguomenwai Dajie, Chaoyang District. (6505 1328) 名特公司，朝阳区光华路1号嘉里中心商场B-37；2) 朝阳区建国门外大街1号国贸商城（华云超市旁边）

Palette Wines Specializes in boutique wineries that produce smaller quantities of wine. While their collection is not as vast as some of the other distributors, what they lack in variety is made up in quality. Their website is designed to look and function as an online wine shop and you can browse through their wines by region, country and variety. (6585 3099) www.palettewines.cn

Palette Vino Suburban sister venue of Palette Wines, the Palette Vino is a wine bar with the comfortable feel of a European villa. They offer a fresh, rustic and wine-friendly menu and an extensive wine selection. Vino offers a yearly membership program whose members receive a 10% discount on all purchases as well as free entrance to the many wine tastings held at the Vino. Daily noon-11pm. Pinnacle Plaza, Shunyi District. (8046 4461) www.palettewines.cn 派乐坊，顺义区荣祥广场

Summergate Wines Summergate hand-selects their producers from 13 countries and offer a phone delivery service (6562 5800) with guaranteed delivery within 48 hours. For a copy of their wine list email Jessie Xiao at jessie.xiao@summergate.com.

Top Cellar Well-laid out, properly temperature-controlled stores offer a compelling selection and knowledgeable service in three locations around Beijing. (topcellar.com.cn)
1) Daily 9am-11pm. Bento & Berries, Kerry Centre, 1 Guanghua Lu, Chaoyang District. (139 1148 6749); 2) Daily 10am-10pm. Central Park, 6 Chaoyangmenwai Dajie, Chaoyang District. (6597 0024); 3) Daily 10am-9pm. B1/F Winland Plaza, 7 Jinrong Jie, Xicheng District. (5181 9969) 1) 朝阳区光华路1号嘉里中心；2) 朝阳区朝阳门外大街6号新城国际；3) 西城区金融街7号英蓝国际中心地下1层

Torres Torres Wines is relatively new to Beijing and feature a growing wine list, which you can get a copy of by emailing info@torreswines.com or calling 5165 5519.

Picks of the Bunch
A flight of fancy local wines
by Jim Boyce

Choose carefully, and you will be rewarded

When it comes to Chinese wines, people generally fall into one of two camps. Many are curious but unsure where to start, while plenty of us are cynical after a bad experience (or two) with low-rent Great Wall, Dynasty, or Changyu. Much local wine *is* bad and makes "two-buck chuck" look like Grand Cru. In fact, much isn't really local – it's more like "wine with Chinese characteristics" as it often includes bulk imported wine.

While unfortunately, the pickings are slim, but there are some drinkable wines to be plucked from the vine, so to speak. Here are some recommendations that would round out the themed tasting: "an optimist's primer to Chinese wine." To keep it somewhat economical – one problem with nicer Chinese wines is their often-extortionate price point – these are seven you can buy in Beijing for less than 700 *kuai* total. Pick up some bread, some cheese, even some tofu, and give them a try.

Note: These wines were picked based on blind tastings bravely organized by myself and/or by friends in the wine industry – in our quest for the truth, no sacrifice is too extreme. Many are available at Jenny Lou's but buying direct from distributors – listed in parentheses – is recommended (for contact info, see p111).

PHOTO: NATALIE BEHRING

1) Grace Chardonnay 2005 or **2006** (RMB 60, Torres)
Grace Vineyard in Shanxi province is considered by many to be making China's best wines, both in terms of quality and value. Well-balanced with nice fruit and a soft finish, this one is served at Beijing's Ritz-Carlton Hotel.

2) Yunnan Red Chateau Chardonnay (RMB 40)
Made from a local grape grown at 1,600 meters in China's southwestern-most province, it smells somewhat like a sweet wine and combines tastes of grape juice, minerals and a slight bitterness. It's worth trying for its uniqueness.

3) Taillan Rosé 2005 (RMB 70, Palette Vino)
Made just outside Beijing by eleven-year China winery veteran Alain Leroux, this wine is appealingly fruity and savory – a good summer drink. If unavailable, try a Grace Rosé.

4) Catai Merlot 2004 (RMB 44, Summergate)
Representing Qingdao, this wine has a strong nose and good initial balance, though it can fall apart quickly; best to drink soon after opening.
Or:
Grace Cabernet Sauvignon 2005 or **2006** (RMB 60, Torres)
If you want to forego the Merlot, this is another Grace wine served at the Ritz-Carlton; it has a light and delicately fruity nose.

5) Grace Tasya's Reserve Cabernet Franc (RMB 198, Torres)
This wine received praise at a bring-your-own-bottle affair at Sequoia Café and one of my blind tastings; it adds yet another variety to your evening.

6) Dragon Seal Huailai Reserve Cabernet Sauvignon 2002 (RMB 220)
Falling in the love-it or hate-it wine, this Hebei wine is worth a try due to its unique aroma and flavors (translation: some people think it smells like pickled vegetables). Tom Stevenson's Wine Report cites the 2005 vintage as an excellent value, making it another option.
Or:
Catai Cabernet Sauvignon Superior 2003 (RMB 238)
Though pricey, this one brings a spicy and somewhat syrupy nose, with hints of toast and a fruity body.

7) Changyu sparkling cider (RMB 26, 7-Eleven)
This 5-percent apple- and peach-scented bottle of fun won't win any awards, but it's quaffable and amazing value at 26 *kuai* – and that's for a magnum (1.5 liters). If you didn't like the previous wines, this one will make you forget all about them. If you did, then it's a nice way to celebrate.

Beyond the magnificent-ish seven, here are more wines to try, though some are hard to find:

Chateau Bolongbao wines
Describing itself as China's only organic winery, this outfit makes wines in the Bordeaux style in down in Fangshan county, Beijing, and garners praise from wine lovers. Unfortunately, while these wines are available in a dozen restaurants in Paris, they are not available for retail distribution in Beijing.

Grace Vineyards Deep Blue (Torres)
Released for sale in August 2007, this is an elegant blend of 60 percent Merlot, 30 percent Cabernet Franc and 10 percent Cabernet Sauvignon; one of China's better wines, though pricey (288 kuai), it tastes as though it'll be even better aged a few years.

Beyond that there are many other Chinese wines worth trying, like ice wines made in Jilin, Gansu and Xinjiang, and the wines of producers such as Xinjiang's Suntime Manas or Shandong's Huadong (particularly the Riesling). This is a big country with an improving wine scene, so venture forth, keep an open mind, and remember that it's all in the name of research.

Cha Cha Cha!
How to tell your *Longjing* from your *Molihua*
by Perri Dong

First, some basics: All tea originates from the same bush (*Camellia sinensis*). Their differences lie in processing. Tea in teabags is usually of inferior grade so be sure to brew loose tea in a teapot with a built-in strainer. Use about four grams of tea for each quarter liter of freshly boiled water. And don't re-boil, as oxygen will disappear, resulting in a flat brew. To avoid "cooking" the volatile oils and flavors out of your tea, brew teas according to this simple guide: white or green tea: 78-85°C; black tea: 99°C; oolong: 85-100°C; Pu'er: 99°C. For some tips on where to buy tea around town, see the Shopping chapter, p412.

Lü cha (green tea) is a non-fermented tea generally produced in Zhejiang, Jiangsu or Anhui. To seal in the essence of the leaf, it is pan-fired, steamed or oven-fired immediately after being picked, resulting in a delicate non-oxidized tea that stays green. *Longjing* (Dragon Well, RMB 80-280/*jin*) is a classic example of a jade-coloured green tea that has a leafy aroma, and roasted nutty taste. It's been famous since the Eighth century and is grown in the hills just west of Hangzhou. Even today, Longjing is still picked and processed completely by hand and is often used as a culinary herb in cooking.

Wulong cha (oolong tea) is semi-fermented and gently rolled after picking to allow the essential oils to slowly oxidize and darken the leaf. *Tie Guanyin* (Iron Goddess, RMB 100-300/*jin*) is a Fujianese *wulong* tea named after the goddess of mercy and labelled "Monkey Picked," a label created for the exclusive enjoyment of the emperor. According to legend, monkeys would collect leaves from wild tea trees off steep mountainsides. Today, "Monkey Picked" denotes the highest quality teas, but monkeys no longer do the picking. Delicate and fragrant, this tea can be steeped up to ten times and is excellent when paired with mildly flavoured items like cookies or cakes.

Hong cha (black tea) is a fully fermented tea resulting from the complete oxidation of the leaf before cooking and drying. If you request *hong cha* you will likely end up with *Qimen* tea (RMB 120-250/*jin*), which is named for an area of Anhui. Cut into thin tight strips, this tea offers a rich amber infusion and an aroma that is distinctive and penetrating without being floral. This medium-bodied tea goes well with just about anything, especially spicy foods.

PHOTOS: LIU JIANFENG

The philosophy behind aging **Pu'er tea** is the same as that of producing a fine Bordeaux wine. The leaves are aged to reduce the harshness and bitterness of tannins present in teas. Green and black teas can all be aged and are highly sought-after. Though rare, some are aged 50 years or more before they are sold and can fetch prices as high as RMB 10,000/jin. *tuo cha* (Bowl-Shaped Tea, RMB 120/jin) is a Pu'er tea compressed into a rounded brick and characterized by aromatic flavor with no bitterness or astringency. This aged tea has very little residual tannic acid, resulting in a very dark, smooth and full-bodied cup of tea.

Infused teas are typically green or black teas that have been perfumed, such as Earl Grey, or flavored with flower blossoms, such as jasmine. The highest quality handmade teas are virtually free of any flower petals: The only contribution flowers make to these teas is the essence of their perfume. A note on Earl Grey: In 1834, England's Prime Minister Charles II, the Earl of Grey, sent a trade delegation to China. During the visit, one of the delegates saved the son of a Chinese official from drowning. As thanks, a package of bergamot-flavored tea was sent to the Earl and the tea was henceforth known as Earl Grey. *Molihua cha* (jasmine tea, RMB 30-140/jin) is a fine example of an infused and cut black tea. The taste ranges from delicate to robust and should produce a nice amber color after steeping. A very popular tea to drink any time, jasmine tea compliments all foods, especially dim sum.

Herbal teas are not technically teas, but the idea behind extracting essential flavors from flowers, grains or herbs is the same. Most herbal teas have no caffeine and the use of herbs in tea is believed to predate traditional tea leaf brewing. *Damai cha* (barley tea, RMB 8 for package of 10 teabags) is a popular herbal tea that uses roasted barley to produce a pale amber nutty-flavored liquid that is soothing to drink. *Babao cha* (Eight-Treasure Tea, RMB 15 for a package of 12 teabags) is another herbal tea that tastes best when steeped a long time and served with large crystal *bingtang* (rock sugar). Probably most well known of herbal teas is *juhua cha* (chrysanthemum tea, RMB 80/jin) which is a very calming brew also served with *bingtang*.

FOOD

Grandma's Kitchen
Breakfast & Lunch / Dinner, Coffee, Desserts

. Breakfast Served All day .
. Best Sandwiches & Burgers in town .
. Fresh Bread Baked Daily.
. Home made Milk shakes & Desserts .

Xiushui Nanjie, Jianguomenwai, Chaoyang District.
朝阳区建国门外秀水南街
Phone: **010 6503 2893**

B/0103 Jianwai SOHO, No.39, 3rd East Ring Road, Chaoyang District
朝阳区东三环39号建外SOHO，B座0103
Phone: **010 5869 3055, 5869 3056**

No.47-2, Nanchizi street, Dongcheng District.
东城区南池子大街47－2号
Phone: **010 6528 2790**

Fifth floor, Wudaokou U-Center, No.36, Chengfu Road, Haidian District
December,2007 Openning Soon
海淀区成府路36号，五道口商业中心五层（2007年12月即将开业）

 **BEIJING CITY INTERNATIONAL SCHOOL**

Community Minded
Culturally Aware
Skilled For Success

Contact our Admissions team to find out more about our innovative educational programs!

- Pre-K to Grade 11
- Central CBD location
- IB Curriculum (Authorized for DP, Candidate school for PYP and MYP)

No.77 Baiziwan Nan Er Road, Chaoyang District. Tel: 8771 7171 Email: admissions@bcis.cn

These are the days of miracle and wonder (boy in a bubble in Chaoyang Park)

Have Child, Will Travel
Raising kids in Khanville
by Cate Conmy

Marco Polo was just 17 when Poppa Polo decided to bring him on his famous voyage to China. As the story goes, when he and his dad finally arrived in Beijing, "Great indeed were the mirth and merry-making with which the Great Khan and all his Court welcomed the arrival of these emissaries. And they were well served and attended to in all their needs." Over seven centuries later, you can pretty much expect the same treatment for your kids.

Benvenuti a Pekino

This giant city offers ample opportunity for merry-making: nearly every park has a playground, and practically every playground has a trampoline (and sometimes go-carts, swings, and shooting games), and in the winter there's ice skating and ice biking (yes, really!) on the frozen lakes. In the spring and fall there are kites to be flown and sections of the wall to be walked. At all times of year there are fun, weird foods to taste or run away from in gleeful disgust. And on top of all that, there's even laser tag.

For older kids and teens, there are markets in which whole new wardrobes can be acquired on a modest allowance and cafes in which afternoons can be whiled away in relative privacy, plus the many freedoms that come from living in a city with cheap taxis and virtually no violent crime. Oh, and laser tag, of course.

You'll find that you and your offspring will be welcomed and very well attended to in the kinds of places that typically greet children with very little mirth back home – fancy restaurants with linen tablecloths and sparkling stemware, for instance, often come equipped with playrooms, and almost all have eager waitstaff looking for any excuse to borrow your kid and take her on a tour of the fish tanks. In fact, if you're looking for service with a smile, you're better off waving your baby than your MasterCard almost anywhere you go in Beijing.

Beijingers are rarely sheepish about family fun

All eyes on them

However, while it has its very definite perks, all the attention the kid-loving locals will lavish on your children can be exhausting and overwhelming. Your kids will frequently find strange hands reaching out to pet them, squeeze them, or even to pluck them out of your arms. And with the physical attention comes running commentary – on the color of your child's skin or eyes, his weight, how good or bad his Chinese is. And expect a very vocal critique of your parenting style as well – how much clothing your daughter is wearing (not enough is the invariable conclusion), whether or not you're holding her the right way, and if she should really be eating what she's eating, will all be popular topics in the park or anywhere else you go with child in tow.

Some children (and parents) warm to all the attention, and the others learn to tolerate or ignore it; in the end, every family develops its own preferred response strategies, and almost everyone learns to take the spotlight for granted. Over time, there are many other things that your kids – flexible, developing creatures that they are – will accept as totally ordinary. You, on the other hand, may never get over the thrill of hearing your 3-year-old answer a taxi driver's curious questions in perfect Beijinghua, of watching your 9-year-old walk into a sea of classmates representing as many countries as your average atlas, or of witnessing your teenager effortlessly haggle for the best price for a DVD. Your children will be too busy living in Beijing's cultural and linguistic melting pot to notice themselves developing into adaptable, urbane and tolerant "global citizens" – which is just as it should be, of course.

Assisted living

Returning to Marco Polo (but fast forwarding a few centuries and relocating to a swimming pool somewhere), there's another analogy to be made: being a parent in Beijing is a bit like being "It" in the children's game that shares his name. Remember it? Everyone else splashes and giggles and swims around you while you flail about with your eyes closed, calling out "Marco," and trying to guide yourself towards one of the voices calling "Polo" in response; in Beijing, you will often find yourself fumbling around blindly, calling out questions – about where to send your kids to school or how to find a doctor or throw a birthday party – trying to guide yourself towards the best answer.

The difference is that (while it can sometimes seem otherwise), the people with the answers in Beijing aren't trying to swim away from you – they're waiting for you to call. You can find them in schools, in playgroups, or at the supermarket; other expats love to show off their expertise and trade stories of their own experiences, and many locals will go out of their way to be of assistance.

Some of the most helpful individuals in Beijing are of the paid variety – live-in or live-out babysitters or housekeepers, aka ayis, aka "aunties," are one of the luxuries of life in Beijing that parents are most thankful for. The availability of affordable help not only frees parents from dish and bathtime duty, it allows them to structure their families in ways parents in other places find harder – to have both parents working, to work from home, or just to have more time to hang out with their kids. For more on *ayis*, see p126.

There's smoke but no fire

Even with help, raising kids in Beijing is still a challenge. It's alarming to live somewhere so polluted that you never have to answer the age-old kid query "Why is the sky blue?" In addition to bronchial infections, sore throats and other pollution-related illnesses, tummy bugs and mild cases of food poisoning are commonplace, and your kids must be up-to-date in all manner of vaccines. Finding a great school with a price tag that doesn't cause heart palpitations is a concern for many familie, and transient friends and classmates can mean a lot of sad goodbyes. And while teenagers everywhere will find ways to get into trouble, they don't have to look quite as hard in Beijing, where access to bars, alcohol, cigarettes and other adult vices is easy.

But don't panic. In the end, most families would agree that the Beijing experience is a good one. There are good Beijing days and bad ones, of course, but even on the bad days, your mini Marco Polos are adventurers, seeing and doing things that their counterparts in other countries can't even imagine. And that can only be a good thing.

Bringing Up Baby, Beijing-Style

by Kaiser Kuo

Chinese people love babies. Push a stroller through downtown Chicago or San Jose, and sure, you'll turn the odd head and get a couple of people going "Awww, she's sooo cute!"True, we haven't taken our kids anywhere but the States yet, so my sample size is limited. But at least in America, babies don't even get the head-turn rates that, say, old guys walking around in the street in pajamas might – something which, go figure, doesn't turn many heads in China.

The flipside of this is that in China, babies also draw a lot of unwanted attention. This comes usually from women over 50, who just can't resist proffering unsolicited advice: he's overdressed, she's underdressed, he's not wearing a hat, she should have thicker socks on. It's maddening. The old biddies mean well, of course. But that doesn't diminish my urge to shout back, as my friend Anne says she's always wanted to, "Look, lady, your kid's genitals are flapping around in the breeze, so shut the hell up."

With my two, we don't do the *kaidangku* thing–the crotchless baby clothes. In fact, despite my wife being a native Beijinger, we don't go in for most of the local customs. My one major concession has been to allow my father-in-law to shave little Johnny's head. "First time you shaved your beard, it grew in thicker, right?"So goes the reasoning from the pro-shaving faction. I used to counter that it was just a function of age, of the passage of time. I first shaved when I was, what, 13? True, I now boast a few more than the half-dozen whiskers I had back then. Anyway, I relented. During the Shaving of Johnny, my 6-month-old boy, I suggested we go for the really traditional Chinese baby boy look – the forelock with the little tufts on the sides. My wife Fanfan shot me a look that said, "Don't cross the line from being a good sport into conscious mockery," and I didn't push it.

Want your Chinese children showered in compliments wherever you go? Bleach their skin. Or, keep them smeared in SPF 40 baby lotion. Both of our kids turned out fair skinned – Fanfan and I both were fair as children, so no surprise – and dozens of times a day, when we take John and 2-and-a-half-year-old Guenevere out for a walk, we hear "Wa! Zhen bai!"from passersby. No matter how much I initially reminded myself of its obvious classist and elitist origins, the aesthetic preference for fair skin in babies starts worming its way into one's thinking once you've spent enough time here. And I'll own up that I've stopped deconstructing it and just smile and say *xiexie*.

Fair hair, on the other hand, is considered a sure sign of malnutrition. Dozens of old biddies have waddled up to us to remark on Guennie's light-colored hair and suggested we feed her more walnuts. Walnuts? Her hair is on the fine side, too, and not super-abundant. They conclude, correctly, that we spared her a shaving and shake their heads sadly. Maybe I should have shaved her, but hey, too late now. She'd be a freak, an outcast in the nursery school where we send her.

Where I'll admit I've screwed up so far in the whole fathering thing is with language. Ostensibly I'm only supposed to speak English with the munchkins, while Fanfan speaks only Chinese. That's no problem for her: she basically speaks only Chinese. I've been rectifying this with Johnny, but with Guenevere, I've already blown it. She started talking early and converses well now in Mandarin, so it's too easy to talk Chinese with her. Okay, I read to her in English still, and I take solace in knowing she understands it well enough. But it doesn't help in conversation: I just don't often find myself coaxing her to eat green eggs and ham in a box, say, or with a fox, or in the rain or on a train. From incessant readings of Robert Munro's classic The Story of Ferdinand, the story of the pacifist bull who just liked to sit quietly and smell the flowers, Guennie now knows all about bull fighting, and the respective roles of the banderilleros, picadores and matadors. Again, not the most useful conversational vocabulary.

Yeah, I have my faults as a father. Somehow I suspect I'm to blame that little Guennie has a good, bilingual command of swear words. It probably isn't good for her neck vertebrae that I've encouraged her to head-bang to Pantera. And I confess that when we do Where is Thumbkin? I probably shouldn't keep adding the "Where is Satan?"verse at the end, with the little heavy metal devil horns.

With that Doc-approved haircut, junior will be hirsute for life

KIDS

Joy, in a Bundle
A primer on adopting children in China
by Catherine Lee

The long and arduous process of adopting a child in China may seem as daunting as a very difficult pregnancy, but the rewards are just as great. Encouragingly, China's adoption process is very streamlined, and there are several people and agencies in China to assist applicants. Once their dossier is submitted, qualified applicants can currently expect the procedure to take at least 13 months if living in China, and up to 24 months if adopting from their home country.

Prospective adopted children are orphans under the age of 14, abandoned children or infants whose biological parents cannot be located or are unable to raise them "due to unusual difficulties" (which usually refers to parents suffering from a serious illness, disability or other hardship).

First steps

The Chinese government agency overseeing adoptions is the China Center of Adoption Affairs (CCAA), part of the Ministry of Civil Affairs. Prospective adoptive families adopting from their home country should contact their embassy in Beijing to find out about their nation's adoption treaty with China and how to initiate the process (see Embassies, p645 for contact details). China-based expat adoptive families will typically submit their dossiers through Bridge of Love, the liaison service for CCAA.

Sixteen countries have treaties with China permitting adoption of Chinese children, but only six of those allow their citizens to adopt while they reside in China: the US, France, Spain, the Netherlands, Australia, and most recently Sweden. Foreigners from the six countries who can adopt while here must reside in China for a year before applying but can start preparing the necessary documentation beforehand. Those from other countries must initiate proceedings from their home country. Note that a Sino-Foreign couple must follow the international adoption process even if one spouse is Chinese and/or both spouses were born in China.

Eligibility requirements

Applying to adopt while living in China can reduce the time needed to review your application, but it will also slow down the process of getting documents from your home country. Your country may require you to return home to apply for a passport on your child's behalf rather than directly though an embassy or consulate in China.

The next step is determining your eligibility. Criteria for potential adopters include age – between 30 and 50 – and complete physical, emotional, and financial fitness. Tightened restrictions instated May 2007 bar morbidly obese, adults on antidepressants, or unmarried individuals from adopting. There are financial requirements regarding assets and income as well. Having biological children is not an impediment to adopting a child, but prospective adopters may not have more than five children living at home, including the adopted child.

Social workers like Karen Friedman conduct home study evaluations that make sure prospective adopters meet the criteria of both their country of citizenship and China. Evaluations include several interviews with individuals and family. (Note that while Friedman can do home studies and dossier preparation for families from many countries, American families must also use the limited services of a stateside adoption agency.)

The paper chase

The next phase involves what Friedman calls "a serious paper chase." When all required documentation is gathered and approved by the passport country, it is submitted to the China Center of Adoption Affairs (CCAA). The documents that applicants must submit to the CCAA include a letter/petition to adopt, a homestudy report, birth certificates, medical reports, a financial statement, letters from their employers, police reports proving lack of criminal history and an approval letter from their home country's adoption or immigration bureau. These materials must be notarized and, when applying from outside China, authenticated by a Chinese consulate or embassy.

Once the dossier is submitted to the CCAA, one must wait to be informed of a Log in Date (LID) – an LID indicates that you have been entered into the CCAA database and will be assigned a child. After getting a referral, you will be well on your way to being the legal parent of a newly adopted child.

When love comes to town

Parents make travel arrangements through an adoption facilitator and receive their child in the capital city of the child's home province. The policies for obtaining a passport for your child are different for every country; for Americans, the child is first given a visa then a passport must be applied for within six months in the US.

One additional place to look for either pre- or post-adoption help is the Families with Chinese Children support group in Beijing and Shanghai, which brings adopted children together in discussion groups that give them the opportunity to see that families are made in different ways. The organizer, Dr. Jane Liedtke, also operates Our Chinese Daughters Foundation (OCDF), which coordinates educational tours for adopted children to come to China to learn about their birth country and study its language.

For more information, contact Karen Friedman (expat_adoption@yahoo.com) or Naomi Kerwin (Naomi@ocdf.org).

Adoption Resources

Beijing United Family Hospital In conjunction with A Helping Hand Adoption Agency, the hospital's Counseling Center provides adoption home studies to assist US expat families seeking to adopt a child in China.
2 Jiangtai Lu, Lido area, Chaoyang District. Contact Rob Blinn (6433 3960) *www.unitedfamilyhospitals.com* 北京和睦家医院，朝阳区将台路2号

Bridge of Love Adoption Service This government-run agency facilitates travel to the adoption site, as well as consulting, document translation and travel arrangements within China. Zhongmin Mansion, 7 Baiguang Lu, Xuanwu District. (6357 5792, 6358 9988 ext 1207) www.china-blas.org 爱之桥收养中心，宣武区白广路7号中民大厦

Oh, little darling of mine: the mother and child reunion

China Center of Adoption Affairs The government agency responsible for adoptions. The CCAA works solely with adoption agencies rather than with individual applicants.
16 Wangjiayuan Hutong, Dongsi Shitiao, Dongcheng District. (6554 8980) www.china-ccaa.org/frames/index_unlogin_en.jsp 中国收养中心，东城区东四十条王家园胡同16号

Families with Children from China - Beijing Chapter Network of foreign families who have adopted or seek to adopt orphans in China. Contact Dr. Jane Liedtke (Jane@ocdf.org) www.fwcc.org

Karen Friedman, MSW Karen Friedman is a licensed social worker who works with expats from around the world to facilitate adoption within China, conducting home study evaluations and assisting families throughout the adoption process.
(5130 3107, 134 3900 9391, expat_adoption@yahoo.com)

OCDF Adoption A division of Our Chinese Daughters Foundation, provides initial consultation, assistance throughout the process and makes travel plans and facilitates at the time of adoption. 137 1887 9311 Naomi@ocdf.org *www.ocdf.org/adoption*

Beijing parents typically rely on the services of an ayi ...

From *Aiyo* to *Ayi*
How to cultivate a super *ayi*
by Katharine Mitchell

If you could choose one person to clean your apartment, cook authentic Chinese and Western dishes, accept your phone calls, and look after your children, all with respect for the health, safety and security of your home and family, who would that person be and why would you entrust that individual with such enormous responsibilities?

Your mother, presumably, isn't in Beijing, and even the most domestic of expats can find it difficult to tend the hearth on top of working or just navigating the language and culture. So ... *zenme ban*? Thank goodness for the readily available domestic goddess of Beijing, aka the *ayi*. Skilled, smart and savvy, the *ayi* is one of the most valuable (and inexpensive) perks of living in Beijing.

What's more, an *ayi* can become a lasting family friend and provide your little ones with endless opportunities for cultural exchange. An ayi can also be an invaluable resource for exposing your children to the Chinese language and way of life. Given the intimacy of the *ayi*-family relationship – she does, after all, have access to your sock drawer or PC – many families develop strong ties with their *ayi*, especially if she's involved in rearing children for a significant amount of time or through a tender age.

Yet how, exactly, does an expat go about entrusting so much responsibility in the hands of a complete stranger, one who might not even speak the same language? While it's rare to hire a Super Ayi off a single interview, it is possible to cultivate a good working relationship – with time. Rebecca Malzacher, a working mom who frequently leads an 'Ayi – Survival Tips' workshop for expats at the International Newcomers' Network (see Community Directory p634), offers a few words of wisdom for finding, and keeping, an *ayi* that matches your family's needs and expectations.

... or call in the grandpappy cavalry

How to find an *ayi*

Word of mouth. Ask other expats for personal recommendations and quiz them about past experiences. Community board postings can also be helpful, especially when leaving families are helping to place their *ayi* in a new home.

Agencies are another option, though Malzacher warns, "Always ask what portion of the payment goes to the *ayi* and agree on how much the agency receives." She also believes in bringing an interpreter to an agency interview-just to make sure the agency isn't answering the questions "for" the *ayi*, as any savvy business owner might do. All in all, agencies are quick, convenient, and they often offer health plans and replacement policies.

What's expected

Set clear expectations. Draw a written agreement that outlines the roles and expectations of both parties, covering items such as:
Designate a work schedule, including breaks and vacation policies
Create a full list of responsibilities so there's no questions about regular tasks
Agree on a fair salary, including holiday bonuses, and the possibility of raises.

Training by demonstration

The number one cause of tension and dissatisfaction in an expat/*ayi* relationship, Malzacher says, is a lack of communication due to either language or cultural barriers. Giving your *ayi* adequate hands-on training is essential to communicating your ideas about proper hygiene, for example. Just because you think it is common sense to wash the cutting board after chopping raw chicken, your *ayi* might find the concept baffling, or even wasteful. Laying out your health and safety standards (both household and occupational) helps you avoid potential mishaps and heartache. To that end, a good phrasebook can be a lifesaver, even for advanced Putonghua speakers.

KIDS

Mother may I?

If children are involved, one-on-one training with the *ayi* is mandatory. The cultural mindset behind raising kids can vary greatly among regions so it's always best to review your child's routine with the *ayi*, even if she's previously worked with foreigners. Take care to discuss hot topics such as discipline and no-no's. Additionally, she should have a list of emergency contacts, in both English and Chinese, and access to petty cash for unforeseen incidents such as taxi rides to the emergency room. Furthermore, if you and the *ayi* don't speak the same language, make sure she has reliable bilingual contacts that are willing to translate for you.

As even the most well-tended kids are prone to mishaps, Malzacher also recommends escorting the *ayi* to your health facility in order to familiarize her with the location, layout and office procedures, including such policies as health coverage and release forms. It's also a good idea to register your *ayi* for a first aid course, such as the ones regularly offered at SOS and Beijing United.

Regardless of whether you expect your *ayi* to mop up after a party or bottle-feed your newborn, it's essential to set expectations, demonstrate safe practices and maintain good communication.

To find out when Malzacher is offering her next 'Ayi – Survival Tips' workshop for expats seeking to learn more about hiring and training *ayis*, contact innbeijing@hotmail.com or visit www.makeiteasybeijing.com.

Ayi Services

The best resource for finding an *ayi* is other parents, especially ones leaving China who may be willing to put you in direct contact with one they know to be responsible, resourceful and kind. If you strike out while asking friends and colleagues for leads, you can try contacting one of the following agencies. They will happily send candidates to your home for interviews.

Beijing Ayi Housekeeping Service
A family membership in this housekeeping service will give you access (with an additional fee) to a large pool of *ayis* who perform services such as babysitting, cooking and cleaning. English-speaking *ayis* available.
Membership: RMB 300; price range: RMB 1,000-3,000 per month. (6434 5647) www.bjayi.com

Beijing Ex-pat Housemaid Service
Serving over 500 families in Beijing, this service offers a supply of English-speaking *ayis* trained to cook, clean, babysit and more.
Price range: RMB 1,600 per month for 8-10 hours per day, 5-6 days per week. (6438 1634) www.expatslife.com

Beijing Merry Home Consulting
Large pool of *ayis* available to perform a multitude of services.
Price range: RMB 15 per hour; RMB 1,500 per month. (8205 0311)

China Youth Union
This service hires out *ayis* for both one-time service as well as regular service. Live-in *ayis* are also available. *Ayis* can all speak simple English. One-time service requires reservations.
Price range: RMB 6-15 per hour; live-in up to RMB 2,000 per month. (6770 2353)

Century Domestic Services
Provides both hourly and live-in *ayis*; different *ayis* can provide different services. English-speaking *ayis* are available, although for a higher price.
Price range: RMB 10-15 per hour (RMB 7-8 per hour with a yearly RMB 120 membership); live-in RMB 500-4,000 per month. (6498 8220)

Good Life Domestic Services
Each *ayi* represented by this firm can speak simple English and perform a variety of services, including childcare, elderly care and house cleaning. Can be hired for live-in or by the hour.
Price range: RMB 8 per hour; live-in RMB 1,000 per month. (6427 1178)

Understanding *Ayi*
Why they do the things they do
by Kim Lee

Ayi may be overprotective for a host of good reasons

Domestic help is inexpensive and widely available in Beijing, so most families hire an *ayi* (or deputize a grandparent) to look after their kids on at least a part-time basis. This is one of the perks of living in the city, but it often leads to misunderstandings, especially when a language barrier separates employer from employee. The communication breakdown can be frustrating, but is generally far easier to overcome than deeply entrenched cultural differences. Every foreign mom has a tale that expresses her incomprehension at something the *ayi* has done. So what is lost in translation? Why do *ayis'* actions seem so peculiar at times? Seeking answers, I held a "playground summit" with some neighborhood *ayis* and grannies and asked them about issues frequently mentioned by foreign mothers.

Afraid of the cold
My first question was why so many *ayis* disapprove of taking babies out on nice winter days – and when they do, pile on enough layers to make baby look like a mini Michelin man. An *ayi* from Jiangsu explained that babies are more susceptible to chills and that in her village pneumonia claims more than one baby every winter. Women like her have seen more direly ill children than we ever will, and explaining that illnesses are caused by viruses and germs won't allay her fears, as long as the health care gap between China's cities and the villages remains vast.

Let me do that for you
The next topic of discussion was over-pampering. I cringe at the sight of a 7-year-old being fed by a woman only slightly taller than he is, or a grandmother loading the heavy schoolbag of an able child onto her stooped shoulders. Why do they do it? Don't they want to foster independence? After baldly asserting that, "It's because we love our children more than Americans," one granny

Continues on next page

Nainai shows her love by bearing an adorable "little empress" into the Forbidden City

went on to explain that, "Chinese children face so much pressure in school as they grow up. They need to concentrate on their studies, not worry about their daily needs. This is how we show our love." According to another *nainai*, letting a child cry is a no-no because, "If you let a little one get frustrated or cry too often, he will grow up to be a nervous and fussy adult." Perhaps the most candid answer came from a young Sichuanese babysitter who offered, "You know, we can only have one baby, we want to do our best to protect him and make his life easy."

No thanks. We are family!

Inevitably, the talk turned to foreigners, and what it's like to work for them. One *ayi* confessed that she found the degree of formality between her and her employer to be downright strange. She could not understand why her employer insisted on thanking her for every task she performed – she wasn't blushing and shaking her head because her boss mispronounced *xiexie*, but rather "because we reserve these words for strangers and find them unnecessary among family members."

Waste not ...

The *ayis* went on to confess that they found their foreign employers extravagantly wasteful. One was marveling at how the mother wanted to change her baby's disposable diapers six or seven times a day! "So expensive! Such a waste! Why not just use split pants?" Another trumped this story with a tale of fresh flowers being replaced twice a week in her household ... and don't even get her started on having to buy bananas at the supermarket for RMB 6 per *jin*, when they are only 2.5 at the wet market! My mother-in-law, who recycles the thread she removes from a hem to re-stitch it, provided a wrap up to this conversation. I sat there red-faced as she entertained the girls with a story of my throwing away three tomatoes because one had a black mold spot. My ears soon stopped burning in embarrassment when the older women commiserated on the difficulty of obtaining fresh vegetables during the Cultural Revolution. When they were young mothers such waste was unimaginable.

I have seen the light

At the risk of sounding like a Hallmark card, my takeaway from this summit was a vow to engage my *ayi* more frequently and never allow myself to attribute her mystifying (to me) actions to stubbornness or backwardness. Good advice, perhaps, for any family who chooses to make an *ayi* a part of theirs?

PHOTO: NICK OTTO

School Daze
The ABCs (and RMBs) of education
by Cate Conmy, Kim Lee and Sharon Ruwart

The trickiest conundrum many parents face in Beijing is finding the right school for their kids. While there are many options – ranging widely in terms of price, language of instruction, methodology, size and amenities – few seem to strike the perfect balance.

Dazed and confused by the complex arithmetic of education

Multiple Intelligences, Montessori, IB, UK Curriculum, etc. – picking the right methodology is not child's play

The international buffet

One end of the spectrum is crowded with pricey international schools, most of which can only enroll foreign passport holders (kindergartens are commonly exempt from this rule). So many international schools have opened, expanded, enhanced or transformed their offerings over the past few years that choosing among them has become pretty complicated.

Trade-offs must be made among location, curriculum, cost, facilities, language of instruction and religious orientation, etc. And as Beijing's foreign community grows, there's increasing competition for spots in the most established international schools – according to some admissions officers, more and more parents are enrolling their kids based solely on website visits, well before arriving in China. (Demand for spots could increase even further if international schools are allowed to enroll Chinese nationals.)

The general consensus is that you should apply as early as possible – six months before the start of the semester isn't too soon – to maximize the chances of snagging a spot in your first-choice school. This is especially the case if you are hoping to enroll more than one child, or if your children will need ESOL (English as a Second Language) support. Many schools have quotas placed on the number of ESOL students they can enroll in a grade or class, so competition for these spaces can be tough, particularly at the most selective schools. Entrance requirements vary, but can include an examination (which can often be taken in the applicant's home country) and an interview in Beijing. Most schools require transcripts, teacher recommendations and, in some cases, standardized test scores.

When you're scouting for schools, you'll want to consider the age of the institution – newer or less popular schools typically have smaller student bodies and larger numbers of ESOL students, which may be a plus or a minus, depending on your situation. Some children may thrive in an environment that affords them more one-on-one attention, while others will struggle socially. This is particularly a concern with teenagers, since many international schools have extremely small high-school classes. And if you're child is a native English-speaker attending school with a large number of ESOL students, she may not be fully challenged academically.

Ka-ching

Private international schools are expensive – one year of tuition can cost well over USD 15,000, even for kindergarten. Some families enjoy company-sponsored education, but everyone else faces steep tuition fees that don't even include special charges for materials, uniforms, bus transportation, meals, after-school activities, tutoring and, in some cases, building levies for infrastructure improvements. If you're paying for school yourself, be careful to get details up front about these fees – they add up.

The financial burden is particularly heavy for parents who do not earn "expat wages" but want an international education for their kids. It is worth noting that most schools offer reduced rates for more than one child. And though they don't advertise it, some schools, especially the newer ones, provide scholarships and off-the-record discounts. One headmaster advises parents to explain their financial situation to the admissions officer and (politely) haggle. "It's like everything else in China, you have to negotiate," he says. Among the more affordably priced international schools are Beanstalk International School, Beijing World Youth Academy, the Indian Embassy School and the Pakistan Embassy College (for details, see School Directory p138).

Wherever you end up sending your child, be sure to check on tuition refund policies. It is always a good idea to have a back-up plan if things don't turn out well.

The wheels on the bus ...

A large number of international schools, including the two with the largest student bodies – the International School of Beijing and the Western Academy of Beijing – are located outside the Fifth Ring Road on the way to Capital Airport. The rest are located primarily in Chaoyang District, within the northeastern quadrant of the city proper. Most schools have bus transportation to take kids to and from the suburban villa compounds as well as major downtown apartment buildings. Note that few, if any, schools provide transportation inside the Second Ring Road, so unless you're prepared to take the kids to school every day, you might need to opt out of that groovy *siheyuan* near Houhai. School websites have information about routes, schedules and costs. Commuting students may face 25 minutes to an hour on the road – one way – every day. With Beijing's traffic getting worse by the month, these times may lengthen – something you'll want to keep in mind when choosing a school.

Choosing a curriculum

Where you're coming from, how long you plan to stay and how old your kids are all affect the school decision. Certain schools, like The British School of Beijing and the Lycée Français de Pékin, to name just two, follow the home country curricula. If you're here for just one or two years, or if your kids are in high school prepping for university, it may make sense to keep them on track to slide seamlessly back into school at home.

Many schools, including several Chinese middle and high schools, now offer the International Baccalaureate (IB) curriculum, which is increasingly popular worldwide and can keep your kids abreast of what their IB classmates at home are learning.

In terms of language, note that some schools offer instruction only in the home language (German, French, Japanese, English). While some English-language schools offer ESOL support for non-native speakers, they may have quotas on the number of kids that they can accept with ESOL needs.

If you're unfamiliar with a prospective school's pedagogical approach, do some research and observe a class in action. Kindergartens typically tout such methodologies as Montessori and Multiple Intelligences, but watch what you're paying for. Some are fully accredited and adhere to the philosophy they promote, while others try to pull the wool over your eyes with a range of pirated Montessori materials displayed on a shelf.

True fluency?

While international schools usually offer some Chinese-language instruction – and some place both English and Chinese native instructors in the classroom – many parents feel that having their kids achieve true bilingual fluency in Beijing's international schools is a huge challenge. Parents of kindergarten and pre-school aged kids enrolled in bilingual programs often see their children developing very strong language skills, particularly if what their kids learn at school is reinforced with lots of time spent with an *ayi*, but things are harder on the fluency front once children reach the elementary school level or above. Difficulties include a lack of support for the language at home, accommodating students with varying ability levels and the special challenges involved in learning to read and write Chinese. While almost all parents praise other aspects of Beijing's international schools, very few seem satisfied with their children's acquisition of Chinese – a weak point you may wish to take into account.

Some schools have a deeper commitment than others to helping foreign students master Chinese. If this is important to you, try to meet with the director of the school's Chinese-language program and find out how many hours of instruction are offered per week, which textbooks are used, what teaching methods are employed, etc. Talking to veteran parents about how much Chinese their kids have learned also gives an insight into a program's effectiveness.

Going native

Parents who can't afford international schools or who simply seek an immersive linguistic and cultural experience for their kids can consider Beijing's public schools. By law, public schools must accept the children of legal foreign residents, but in practice some schools are much less willing than others to enroll international students. Parents report that school officials are often unfamiliar with the law, nervous about their school's ability to support an international student, or worried that a non-native will struggle academically and affect the school's ranking.

Schools that already have international students on their rosters are typically far more welcoming. In light of this, most parents find it easier to target the small number of schools with an established international department or a long tradition of enrolling international students. Schools such as Fangcaodi Primary School and No. 55 Middle School/High School boast foreign populations in the hundreds (although in many instances only a small minority of the foreign students hail from Western nations).

While easier to enroll in, however, schools with a large international student body often charge higher tuition fees for foreign students (RMB 6,000-50,000 on average, not counting fees for buses, books, etc.), making them out of reach for parents for whom cost is a major consideration. Additionally, public schools of all persuasions sometimes demand a non-refundable admission fee or "voluntary donations" that can be costly. To help combat this phenomenon, a new regulation forbidding middle school students from attending schools outside their district of residence has been instituted. However, this rule is unlikely to be applied to foreign applicants.

If you're considering a local school, you'll need to inquire in person about their specific enrollment policies and procedures. Application materials are typically available only in Chinese, and only at the schools themselves. If you're not completely fluent in Chinese, bring an interpreter with you when you visit. As always, there is no substitute for actual observation.

Also note that spaces in public schools typically fill up early. Sarah Peel Li and her husband Li Xiaotian, who placed their daughter in a preschool in Haidian, suggest enrolling your child no later than January for the following academic year. "Schools are full, and there has been a baby boom over the last couple of years," she says, "and it's going to be worse for September 2008-2010." She also points out that the school day for pre-schoolers especially is very long. "Pre-school begins at 7am and pick up is 4.45pm – it's a daycare as much as it's a pre-school," where children get as many as three meals a day plus snacks.

For young children in particular, a Chinese school can provide a dynamic environment in which to learn or improve Chinese. In fact, because the national curriculum allocates about half

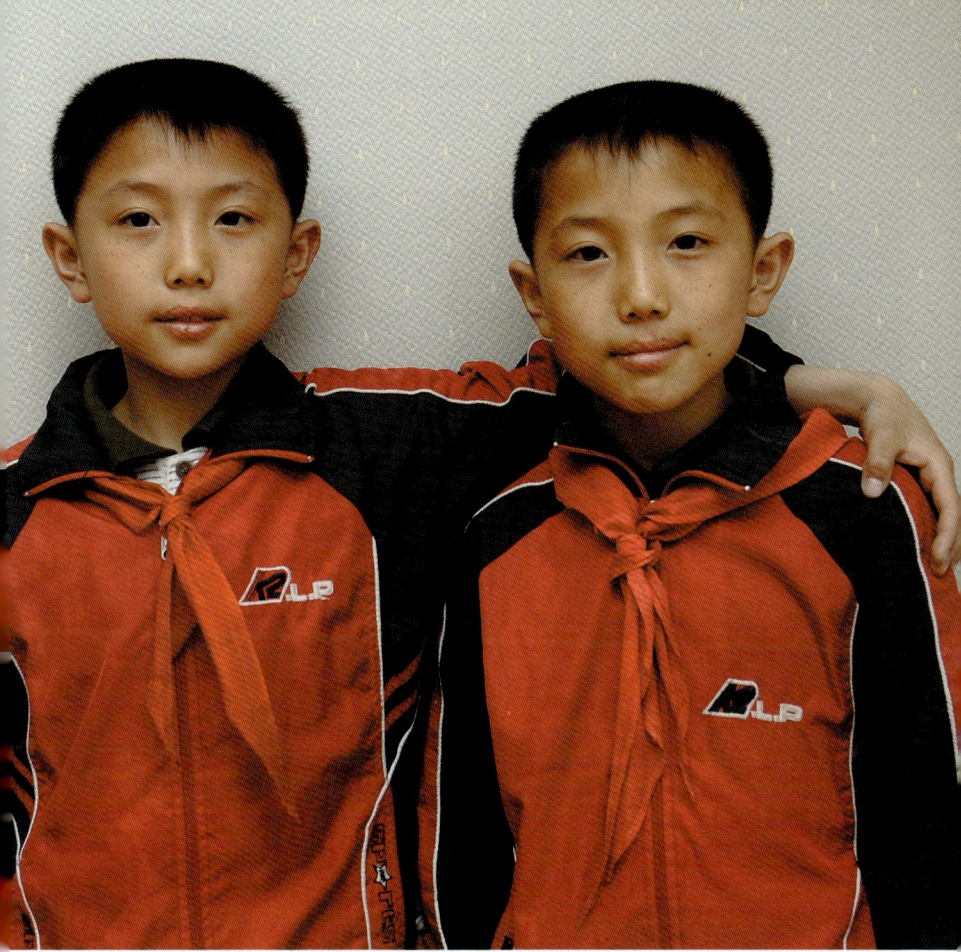

After a few years in a Chinese School, your foreign child will blend right in

the school day to studying Chinese, language acquisition is a big benefit of sending your kid to the neighborhood *xuexiao*. But it's not for everyone. If your child's Chinese skills are weak, she may struggle – and even a well-intentioned teacher can offer little individual support in a class of 35-plus students, the Chinese norm. Often, non-Chinese-speaking foreign children are placed in the first grade, regardless of age, which can deal a big blow to a child's self-esteem and make it hard to find friends his own age.

The Chinese curriculum preps kids for the big, ultra-competitive exams to enter middle school, high school and university, and thus emphasizes reading and writing Chinese, memorizing textbook material and lots of mathematics, to the near exclusion of other topics. English-speaking teachers and administrators are rare. Homework instructions and parent information are in Chinese.

Younger children with at least some Chinese tend to fare much better in Chinese schools than older Western kids who have already experienced schools at home. Unless you intend for your child to take China's middle or high school entrance exams, you may want to consider Chinese schools as a temporary, one- or two-year option before transitioning to a school that will give your child the background they'll need to enter a Western school down the road. (For more on this topic, see "Taking the Local Route," p136)

Taking the Local Route
Expat parents choose Chinese schools for their kids
by Laurie Burkitt

Enjoying well-deserved tanghulu (candied haws) after his ten-hour schoolday

"Many people never even consider Chinese schools for their kids because they get incorrect information from people with no experience ... just generalizations and stereotypes," says Barbara Chen, a Beijing resident who moved back to her native US in the summer of '07. Chen, whose last name came to her by marriage, became something of an expert expat on Chinese education for international students. Her two daughters, Elizabeth (14) and Christie (11), both conducted their school lives here entirely in Chinese. When Chen moved to Beijing in 2000, a relocation counselor told her that Beijing only had two education options for international children: WAB and ISB. But for Chen, those just weren't options. She wanted her girls to grow up outside of the English-speaking community, in the heart of Chinese culture, speaking Chinese socially and learning what she calls, "playground hua."

So how did Chen find schools for her children? She drew a circle with a one-mile radius

Local schools: neither black or white, nor red all over

around her house and knocked on doors. What she found was Yimei, the elementary school affiliated with the Beijing Art University in the northwest corner of the city. With 18 students per class and numerous art classes, Yimei offered the perfect environment for integration. It gave Chen's children, who didn't speak Chinese upon arrival, a chance to learn the language gradually and creatively.

Elizabeth later moved to the Beijing World Youth Academy where she took 12 classes per year, including math, sciences, art, music, history, computer science, English and – of course – Chinese. With all these classes comes a lot of homework. Fourteen-year-old Max Hsu, whose parents hail from Tennessee and Taiwan, goes to Renda Fuzhong, the middle school affiliated with People's University. He is swamped with homework. On a daily basis, he catches the bus at 6.30am in order to make his 7.20am classes, and he doesn't typically leave school until 5pm.

"There is a lot of pressure at the school," admits Wenni Hsu, Max's mother. She chose Renda because of its reputation for high test-scores and standards. But these weren't her only considerations: "We had to be mindful of tuition. We have two kids and had to economize."

Fees for foreign students are rising, unfortunately. Fangcaodi, where Hsu's youngest son Michael goes to school, raised its fees by more than 300 percent (!) during the summer of 2006, from RMB 14,000 to RMB 48,000 per year.

That's still much cheaper than the average international school. "I couldn't justify a USD 15,000 pre-school education," says Su Cheng Harris-Simpson, a Seattle native who has lived in Beijing off and on for the past 11 years. Harris-Simpson is the mother of 5-year-old Cailin, who attends pre-school at the Sanlitun Youeryuan. At age 2, Cailin started daycare at a Montessori school, but for language learning purposes and financial prudence, Harris-Simpson transferred Cailin to the Chinese system. The switch wasn't easy, she says, because the student-teacher ratio in a Chinese school means less personal instruction, and because the Chinese system offers its students less encouragement.

Nevertheless, with companies cutting housing and schooling benefits for expat employees, Chinese schools are becoming the only affordable option. Nationwide, the Ministry of Education has approved 71 academic institutions, including primary, secondary and higher education, fit for foreign instruction. How do you find a Chinese school that will work for your child? "The trick was visiting the neighborhood schools and talking to them," said Harris-Simpson. "Most of them like having foreigners, but because they are typically full, you have to push."

Playground pals

School Directory

3E International Kindergarten Offers a bilingual, bicultural curriculum that fuses Western and Eastern approaches to teaching, and focuses on the development of the whole child, incorporating art, drama, music and science activities. Preschool and kindergarten students spend half the day with American teachers in an English-language environment and half the day with Chinese teachers in a Chinese-language environment. The Nursery Program is a play-based, active learning program and the nursery classroom has both a native Chinese-speaking and a native English-speaking teacher. The learning environment includes a child-sized kitchen, a gym, music rooms and a large outdoor play space. Ages: 1.5 to 6. Price range: RMB 55,000-103,900 (plus RMB 1,500 application fee).
18 Jiangtai Xilu, Chaoyang District. (6437 3344 ext 127) www.3eik.com 3E国际幼儿园，朝阳区将台西路9-1号

Australian International School of Beijing (AISB) Founded in 2004, AISB is the only school in China offering an Australian curriculum. Facilities include a gym, four basketball courts, two tennis courts, a 400m running track, a football field, several language labs, and a "computer barn" housing 200+ computers. While the school currently only enrolls students up to Grade 6, Grades 10, 11 and 12 are offered at AISB's sister school, the National Institute of Technology, which is located on the same campus. Grades: K to 6. Price range: RMB 86,500-115,000 (plus RMB 8,200 refundable deposit, RMB 1,000 uniform fee, RMB 1,640 application fee, RMB 6,000-9,000 bus fee and additional fees for intensive ESL training).
7 Louzizhuang Lu, Chaoyang District. (8439 0878) www.aisb.com.cn 北京澳大利亚国际学校，朝阳区楼梓庄路7号

Beanstalk International Bilingual School (BIBS) and Beijing International Bilingual Kindergarten Its Dongsihuan campus offers an international, bilingual curriculum taught 70 percent in English and 30 percent in Chinese, with the intention of fostering full bilingual fluency as well as cross-cultural understanding. Facilities include a wireless computer lab, English and Chinese libraries, and a gymnasium, soccer field, basketball court and farm garden. Nanshiliju campus opened in August '07. Grades: K to 7. Price range: RMB 50,000-100,000 (plus RMB 1,600 registration fee and RMB 8,000-16,000 capital levy).
1) 38 Nanshiliju, Chaoyang District 2) 6 Dongsihuan Beilu, Chaoyang District. (8456 6019) www.bibs.com. cn 1) 朝阳区南十里居38号 2)青苗国际双语学校和青苗国际双语幼儿园，朝阳区东四环北路6号

Beanstalk International Kindergarten (BIK) This long-running Beanstalk school offers an international curriculum taught entirely in English by qualified native English-speaking teachers. Facilities include a library, piano rooms, and indoor and outdoor playgrounds. Half-day and full-day options are available, as are a range of extracurricular activities including ballet, kung fu and piano. Ages: 2 to 6. Price range: RMB 80,000 (plus RMB 1,600 registration fee and RMB 8,000 capital levy).
1/F, Bldg B, 40 Liangmaqiao Lu (at the 21st Century Hotel), Chaoyang District. (6466 9255) www.bibs. com.cn 青苗国际幼儿园，朝阳区亮马桥路40号21世纪饭店院内B座1层

Beijing BISS International School Founded in 1994, BISS offers the IB program to more than 350 students from over 40 countries. Mandarin classes are compulsory from grades K-6; ESOL support offered when necessary. The campus houses a library, dance studio, visual arts center, design and technology studio, computer and science labs, and sports facilities. Grades: K to 12. Price range: USD 10,500-19,900 (plus USD 500 registration fee, USD 3,000-5,000 refundable deposit and USD 2,000 ESOL fee).
17, Area 4, Anzhen Xili (just off Beisanhuan), Chaoyang District. (6443 3151) www.biss.com.cn 北京BISS国际学校，朝阳区安贞西里四区17号楼

Beijing City International School Founded in 2005, BCIS offers the International Baccalaureate Primary Years Program, Middle Years Program and Diploma Program. All students attend daily Chinese language and culture lessons. BCIS has an inclusive admissions policy and any students with ESOL needs are supported by the ESOL department. The school's 51,000-square-meter campus boasts an indoor swimming pool and rock-climbing wall, a design and technology studio, a 300-seat theater, other facilities for the visual and performing arts, state of the art IT equipment, and over 50 classrooms. Grades: Pre-K to 11. Price range: RMB 96,000-162,000 (plus RMB 1,600 registration fee and RMB 8,000 deposit, discount for third child and above).
77 Baiziwan Nan Er Lu, Chaoyang District. (8771 7171) www.bcis.cn 北京乐成国际学校，朝阳区百子湾南二路77号

Beijing Huijia Kindergarten Run in conjunction with Huijia Private College (see below), Huijia Kindergarten currently has 16 different campuses across Beijing. The school follows a Multiple Intelligences curriculum and instruction is in Chinese. Currently, about one quarter of the students are international students. Ages: 1.5 to 5. Price range: RMB 60,000-80,000.
Head Office: 33C, Bldg B, Huating Jiayuan, 6 Beisihuan Zhonglu, Chaoyang District. (5165 2252 ext 805) www.hjkids.com 北京汇佳幼儿园，朝阳区北四环中路6号华亭嘉园B座33C

Beijing Huijia Private College This combined boarding and day school offers an IB curriculum taught in English and a Chinese curriculum taught in Chinese. Students who wish to follow the Chinese curriculum but don't have the requisite Chinese ability will first be enrolled in an intensive Chinese course. About 200 students from various countries study (and live, if they choose to board) alongside approximately 2,000 Chinese students. Facilities include a swimming pool, gymnasium and science labs. Grades: 1 to 12. Price range: RMB 69,000-75,800.
Zhongguancun Kejiyuan, Changping Yuan, Huijia Kejiaoyuan, Changping District. (6078 5555/1) www.huijia2000.com 北京汇佳私立学校，昌平区中关村科技园昌平园汇佳科教园

Beijing No. 1 Kindergarten Experimental Sister School This bilingual public kindergarten attached to Beijing No. 1 Kindergarten follows a modified form of the Chinese national curriculum. Class size ranges from about 25 to 35 students per class. About half of the students board at the school. Ages: 3 to 6. Price range: RMB 2,500/month.
Bldg 117, Xiaohuangzhuang Xiaoqu, Qingniangou Lu, Dongcheng District. (8428 8913, 8427 5713) http://yiyou.sch.dcjy.net 北京第一幼儿园附属实验校，东城区青年沟路小黄庄小区117号楼

Beijing No. 55 Middle School and High School Unlike other public schools in the city, No. 55 has an international student department specifically tailored for foreign students. High school classes are offered in Chinese (meant for students with no Chinese background) or English, and prepare students for the IB exam or China's college entrance exam. Middle school classes are in Chinese only; a half-year of intensive Chinese training is available if needed. Ages: 11 to 17. Price range: RMB 28,600-32,000.
12 Xinzhong Jie, Dongcheng District. (6416 4252/9531) www.bj55z.net 北京第五十五中学，东城区新中街12号

Beijing World Youth Academy (WYA) This private school is rare in that it enrolls both Chinese and foreign nationals, and offers both English- and Chinese-language curricula. Foreign students can either follow a traditional IB program or the Chinese Foreign Language program, with the latter preparing them for admission to a Chinese university. WYA is also a candidate school for the IB Middle Years Program. More than 400 students from more than 40 nations attend. The school has an indoor pool, and it rents space at a stadium with a track and soccer field. Ages: 10 to 18. Price range: RMB 45,000 (bilingual program), RMB 85,000-95,000 (IB program), RMB 48,000 (Chinese program).
40 Liangmaqiao Lu, Chaoyang District. (6461 7787, admissions@ibwya.net) www.ibwya.net 北京市世青中学，朝阳区亮马桥路40号（燕莎中心附近）

Beijing Xiyi Elementary School One of the first local elementary schools to admit international students, Xiyi continues to enroll non-Chinese. The school's language of instruction is Chinese. In addition to its core curriculum, Xiyi offers computer, art, physical education and Beijing opera classes. A new school building is under construction. Ages: 6-12. Price range: RMB 6,000.
49 Beisanhuan Xilu, Haidian District. (6265 2613) www.hdxyxx.bjedu.cn 北京西颐小学，海淀区北三环西路49号

The British School of Beijing The British School of Beijing offers the English National Curriculum taught by UK qualified teachers, supported by native English-speaking teaching assistants. Approximately two hours of Chinese instruction are provided weekly. The school has strict admission requirements, including entrance exams and a limit on the number of students requiring ESL support to no more than 20% of the total student number in any class. Age-appropriate English speaking and listening skills are required for all children over five. The school's Shunyi campus, which boasts a full-sized football pitch, a 200-seat theater and an indoor pool, enrolls students of foundation stage (pre-primary) to secondary school age, while the Sanlitun campus enrolls foundation stage and primary students. Ages: 2-18. Price range: RMB 70,035-165,540.
1) Linyin Lu, Tianzhu Zhen (on the west side of the National Accounting College), Shunyi District. (6458 0884); 2) 5 Sanlitun Xiliu Jie, Chaoyang District. (8532 3088) www.britishschool.org.cn 北京英国学校，1) 顺义区天竺镇林荫路（国家会计学院西侧）；2) 朝阳区三里屯西六街5号

Canadian International School of Beijing This school, whose campus is said to be the largest of any international school in Beijing, opened its doors last fall. CIS offers a Canadian-style, IB framework curriculum; the curriculum for kindergarten and pre-K is Montessori

KIDS 139

style. Non-native English-speaking students will have their language abilities assessed, and be given ESL support according to their results. Chinese as a second language is offered at three separate proficiency levels. School facilities include 90 classrooms, seven computer labs, a 600-seat theatre, a swimming pool and a dance studio. Grades: Preschool to 11. Price range: RMB 56,000-132,800 (RMB 10,000 deposit, plus RMB 1,600 application fee and RMB 3,200-4,800 ESL fee).
38 Liangmaqiao Lu, Chaoyang District. (6465 7788, admissions@cis-beijing.com) www.cisb.com.cn 北京加拿大国际学校，朝阳区亮马桥路38号

The Children's House Montessori Kindergarten
Established in 1992, The Children's House offers baby group, nursery, preschool and kindergarten programs taught in English by certified Montessori teachers. In addition, the Lufthansa Center campus, and the brand new Yayunxin campus that opened this July, both offer a bilingual program. Activities offered include Chinese, piano, ballet, music and kung fu, and students have access to a gym, tennis courts and an ice skating rink. Mathematics and English Reception Classes, intended to secure the fundamentals of numbers, reading and writing before primary school, are offered to students ages 4 and up. Ages: 0 to 6. Price range: RMB 37,800-107,900 (plus RMB 1,600 registration fee).
1) Rm 102, Bldg 2, Linlanyuan, Xinjiayuan, Yayunxin, 1 Xindian Lu, Chaoyang District. (5202 0293); 2) Yosemite Villas, 4 Yuyang Lu, Houshayu Zhen, Shunyi District. (8041 7083); 3) Unit 114, Lufthansa Center Tower, 50 Liangmaqiao Lu, Chaoyang District. (6465 1305); 4) Level 1, North Lodge, China World Trade Center, 1 Jianguomenwai Dajie, Chaoyang District. (6505 3869) www.montessoribeijing.com 北京巧智博仁国际幼儿园，1）朝阳区辛店路1号亚运新新家园林澜园2号楼1单元102室；2）顺义区后沙峪镇榆杨路4号优山美地别墅区；3）朝阳区亮马桥路50号凯宾斯基写字楼114室；4）朝阳区建国门外大街1号中国世界贸易中心北大公寓1层

Children's Learning Center of Beijing (CLCB)
Established and organized by mothers seeking affordable, quality preschool education for their children, CLCB offers three separate curricula: a bilingual curriculum that alternates between Chinese and English equally, a Chinese curriculum that aims at teaching Chinese in an easy and natural way and a trilingual curriculum (English, German and Chinese). The school's facilities include six study rooms, a playroom, an activity room, a nap room, a garden and a playground. Ages: 1 to 5. Price range: RMB 25,000-61,200.
4059 Gahood Residence Villa, Baixinzhuang, Houshayu, Shunyi District. (80467082, Eng: 135 0120 1368, Chi: 136 1133 4043) www.clcbkids.com 爱嘉励儿童双语培训中心，顺义区后沙峪乡白辛庄嘉浩别墅 4059

Der Kindergarten
This recently founded school offers a German curriculum taught primarily in German, with English and Chinese offered part of the time by native speakers. Facilities include a garden, large indoor gym and a library. Ages: 2 to 6. Price range: EUR 5,200-7,200.
Merlin Champagne Town, 6 Liyuan Lu, Tianzhu, Shunyi District. (6450 8580, Eng: 137 1861 5812, 137 1861 5812) www.derkindergarten.com 德国幼儿园，顺义区天竺镇丽苑街6号美林香槟小镇

Deutsche Botschaftsschule Peking
The German Embassy School offers instruction in German and uses a curriculum and textbooks that adhere to standards set by the German Board of Education. Approximately 90 students are enrolled in the kindergarten class, and 370 in the elementary and upper school. Grades: Kindergarten to Klasse 13. Price range: EUR 5,100-7,800 (plus a EUR 2,600 admission fee, EUR 700 bus fee).
49A Liangmaqiao Lu, Chaoyang District. (6532 2535) www.dspeking.net.cn 北京德国使馆学校，朝阳区亮马桥路甲49号

Dulwich College Beijing
Dulwich has four campuses across Beijing. It offers a Montessori curriculum to students in the Early Years and Key Stage 1 classes, and the English National Curriculum program to older students. Students in Years 10 and 11 follow the IGCSE curriculum; the school intends to offer the IB program for students in Years 12-13. Dulwich students take Chinese classes offered at levels appropriate for native and non-native speakers. School facilities include a recording studio, a theater, science labs and a sports center housing a swimming pool, golf driving range, tennis courts and more. Ages: 1 to 18. Price range: RMB 25,900-168,000.
1) River Garden Villas Kindergarten, Houshayu, Baixinzhuang, Shunyi District. (8046 5132); 2) 7 Sanlitun Beixiao Jie, Chaoyang District. (6532 6713/4518); 3) Legend Garden Villas, 89 Jichang Lu, Shunyi District. (6454 9000); 4) Beijing Riviera, 1 Xiangjiang Beilu, Jingshun Lu, Chaoyang District. (8450 7676) www.dcbeijing.cn 北京德威英国国际学校，1）顺义区后沙峪白辛庄裕京花园别墅；2）朝阳区三里屯北小街7号；3）顺义区机场路89号丽京花园；4）朝阳区京顺路香江北路1号香江花园

Eton International Bilingual Academy
Offers an enriched bilingual Montessori curriculum to both Chinese and international students on three separate campuses. Classes are conducted 70 percent in English, 30 percent in Chinese. Facilities include an art studio, music room and Chinese research room. Ages: 1.5 to 6. Price range: RMB 35,700-55,600 (plus RMB 1,700 application fee and RMB 5,000-8,300 capital levy).
1) C103, Lido Country Club, Lido Place, Jichang Lu, Chaoyang District. (6436 7368); 2) Central Park Campus (opening in August 2007), Central Park, 6 Chaowai Dajie, Chaoyang District. (6533 6566); 3) Palm Springs International Apartments, 8 Chaoyang Gongyuan Nanlu, Chaoyang District. (6539 8967); 4) Pinnacle Plaza, Tianzhu Real Estate Development Zone, Shunyi District. (8046 5338); 5) 3/F, Bldg D, Global Trade Mansion, Guanghua Lu, Chaoyang District. (6506 4805) www.etonkids.com 伊顿国际双语幼儿园，1）朝阳区首都机场路丽都广场俱乐部C103；2）朝阳区朝外大街6号新城国际；3）朝阳区朝阳公园南路8号棕榈泉国际公寓；4）顺义区天竺房地产开发区荣祥广场；5）朝阳区光华路世贸国际公寓D座3层

Eton International School
Eton International School's language of instruction is English. At its three campuses in Beijing, the school employs the Montessori method to bring out children's interests in math, language, culture, arts and sciences. The school provides a community centered American-style education led by Montessori-certified teachers. ESL support is provided free of charge to all students who require it. The school's extracurricular programs take place on soccer fields, in swimming pools and at play areas. Ages: 1.5 to 9. Price range: RMB 62,300-105,000 (plus RMB 1,700 registration fee and RMB 16,600 capital levy).

No horsing around without your safety ("anquan") caps, boys

1) Lido Country Club, Lido Place, Jichang Lu, Chaoyang District. (6436 7368); 2) Pinnacle Plaza, Tianzhu Real Estate Development Zone, Shunyi District. (8046 5338); 3) 3/F, Bldg D, Global Trade Mansion, Guanghua Lu, Chaoyang District. (6506 4805) www.etonkids.com 伊顿国际学校，1）朝阳区北京首都机场路丽都广场俱乐部C103室；2）顺义区天竺房地产开发区荣祥广场；3）朝阳区光华路世贸国际公寓D座3层

The Family Learning House This small, bilingual school integrates a character education program focused on instilling and developing virtues (such as responsibility, service and truthfulness) with a Montessori curriculum. Lead teachers in each classroom speak English with students, while all Chinese staff speak to students in Chinese; older students receive daily Chinese lessons. The school's facilities include a child-sized kitchen, a library, a playground, and a garden with a vegetable patch, rabbit hutch and birdbath. Ages: 1.5 to 6. Price range: USD 6,000-10,500.
B7 Liyuan Xiaoqu, Xiangjiang Beilu (directly across from Cathay View Residences), Chaoyang District. (8430 2547) www.thefamilylearninghouse.com 家育苑，朝阳区香江北路丽苑小区B7

Fangcaodi Primary School Fangcaodi is a state-run primary school that has been accepting foreign students for over 40 years. Classes are in Chinese, with the exception of English language classes. The school uses the same textbooks as other Chinese schools in the municipality and places a strong emphasis on math and Chinese. Fee-based after-school activities include badminton, arts and crafts, wushu and rollerblading. Grades: 1 to 6. Price range: RMB 48,000.
1 Ritan Beilu, Chaoyang District. (8563 5120 ext 2005) www.fcd.com.cn 芳草地小学，朝阳区日坛北路1号

Harrow International School Beijing Opened in August 2005, Harrow provides a British-style education to secondary school students. Offering qualifications at GCSE, AS and A level, it aims to provide progression routes into British and international universities. Individual programs of study and tutorials are available, and ESOL support is provided for those who need it, including a "Sheltered Curriculum" program for students who require more intensive language support. Chinese is included in the curriculum at all levels and is a GSCE and A-level subject choice. Ages: 11 to 18. Price range: RMB 149,970-169,530 (plus RMB 3,000 application fee and RMB 4,000 uniform fee).
5 Anzhenxili, Block 4, Chaoyang District. (6444 8900) www.harrowbeijing.cn 北京哈罗英国学校，朝阳区安贞西里四区5号

Indian Embassy School Located in and operated by the Indian Embassy, this school offers an Indian-style curriculum to 100 students from 36 different countries. Instruction is in English. Chinese classes are part of the curriculum, and extracurricular activities such as music, tennis, and tai chi are offered. Ages: 4 to 11. Price range: available upon inquiry.
1 Ritan Donglu (inside the Indian Embassy), Chaoyang District. (6532 1827, indianembassyschoolbeijing@yahoo.com) 印度使馆学校，朝阳区日坛东路1号（在印度大使馆内）

"Watch out world, here we come" (Western Academy of Beijing, Class of '07)

International Academy of Beijing IAB offers a Christian-infused US-style curriculum and is accredited by the Association of Christian Schools International (ACSI). In addition to their regular classes, IAB students take subjects like computers, art, music appreciation and sports. Chinese instruction is provided at all levels, and non-ESL students attend Chinese classes daily. ESL support is offered up to the Grade 6 level, with ESL students generally permitted to occupy no more than 40 percent of any class. The school's first high school class opened last fall, and will follow an American college-prep curriculum. Grade 10 is scheduled to open in August 2007, with the remaining high school grades to follow. Grades: K to nine Price range: RMB 74,520-109,350 (plus RMB 18,630-28,350 annual capital levy, RMB 1,620 application/registration fee and RMB 12,150 for the ESL program).
Lido Office Tower 3, Lido Place, Jichang Lu, Jiangtai Lu, Chaoyang District. (6430 1600/1142) www.iabchina.net IAB国际学校，朝阳区将台路机场路丽都广场丽都写字楼3座

The International Montessori School of Beijing (MSB) This well-established school, founded in 1990, is operating on its own again with a new campus across from River Garden Villas, and two additional campuses scheduled to open before September 2007. It offers a child-centered, individualized Montessori curriculum taught by certified, native-English speaking teachers. Intensive Chinese language study is an additional option available. Ages: 1-9. Price range: RMB 74,100-136,900.
1) Near River Garden Villas, Houshayu, Baixinzhuang, Shunyi District. (8046 3935); 2) Champagne Cove Campus, 1 Shunfu Road, Shunyi District; 3) Cherry Tree Lane Campus, 18 Maquanying Lu, Chaoyang District. (8046 3935) www.msb.edu.cn 北京蒙台梭利国际学校，1)顺义区后沙峪白辛庄裕京花园附近；2) 顺义区顺福路1号；3) 朝阳区马泉营路18号

The International School of Beijing (ISB) Beijing's largest English-language school has more than 1,800 students from 55 nations and a history of more than 25 years. It teaches an international curriculum and also offers both the IB diploma program and select Advanced Placement (AP) classes. The school's Chinese program offers more than 80 language classes at both the "academic" and "neo-native" level. ESOL students are limited to a percentage of the total student number in each grade, with that percentage depending on the grade level. The large campus boasts a 600-seat high-tech theater, swimming pool, indoor rock climbing wall, large art department, computer facilities and well-equipped science labs as well as a big "Outdoor Learning Environment." Grades: Early Childhood (ages 3 to 4) to 12. Price range: USD 7,500-18,970 (plus USD 200 application fee and USD 1,330-3,840 capital fee).
10 Anhua Jie (near Capital Paradise), Shunyi District. (8149 2345) www.isb.bj.edu.cn 北京顺义国际学校，顺义区安华街10号（名都园附近）

The International School of Collaborative Learning ISCL is a small, progressive school that follows a university laboratory-school approach to education. Its curriculum, originally based on one formulated by the Sidwell Friends School in Washington, D.C., combines both US and Chinese content. It's distinguished by small class sizes, an English and Chinese dual language academic program and a strong China focus designed to help students profit as much as possible from their Beijing experience. Newly arrived foreign students are put into intensive Chinese classes. Children in the primary school are grouped in multi-age classrooms (grades K-2, 3-4 and 5-6), while middle and high school students are grouped by Chinese and English ability. The school's facilities include a media center/library, theater, computer lab and athletic fields. Grades: K to 12. Price range: USD 10,500-15,500.

Naidong Gongyequ, Shunbai Lu (inside the white building), Chaoyang District. (6433 7366/9557) www.iscl-beijing.org 北京协力国际学校, 朝阳区顺白路奶东工业区（在白楼内）

Ivy Academy Ivy Academy boasts a team of foreign teachers trained at the world's top universities, who teach a curriculum based on the Multiple Intelligences theory developed at Harvard. The student-to-teacher ratio is 1:5. Classes are conducted in English and only children with previous exposure to English are admitted after the age of 4. Chinese classes are taught daily, and Chinese is also offered in afterschool sessions. School facilities include a kids' kitchen, a playground and sports courts. Ages: 2 to 6. Price range: RMB 78,000-116,000 (plus RMB 200 registration fee).
Suite C101, East Lake Villas, 35 Dongzhimenwai Dajie, Dongcheng District. (8451 1380/1381) www.ivyacademy.cn 艾毅幼儿园，东城区东直门外大街35号，东湖别墅C101室

Ivy Bilingual School Ivy Bilingual School teaches a curriculum informed by the Multiple Intelligences theory. Both Chinese- and English-speaking teachers are present in the classroom at the same time in order to offer a truly bilingual environment. Students are expected to understand, speak, read and write basic characters by the time they graduate from the program; about 60% of the children enrolled at Ivy Bilingual graduate into local elementary schools, while about 40% move on to international schools. Ages: 1 to 6. Price range: RMB 46,000-54,000 (plus RMB 200 registration fee).
1) Ocean Express, Bldg E, 2 Dongsanhuan Lu (north of the Kempinski Hotel), Chaoyang District. (8446 7287); 2) Orchid Garden, Laiguangying Donglu (east of Jingshun Lu), Chaoyang District. (8439 7080); 3) Seasons Park, 36B Dongzhimenwai Dajie, Dongcheng District. (8453 0366) www.ivybilingual.com 艾毅双语幼儿园，1) 朝阳区东三环北路丙2号远洋新干线E座（凯宾斯基饭店往北）; 2) 卓锦万代，朝阳区来广营东路, 京顺路与机场高速之间; 3) 东城区东直门外大街36B号海晟名苑

KinStar Bilingual School In addition to a bilingual kindergarten, KinStar also runs a bilingual elementary school. The school follows curriculum guidelines issued by the Chinese Ministry of Education for instruction in Chinese and a US-style curriculum for instruction in English. Both ESOL and Chinese support classes are available. Facilities at the elementary school building include music, art and dance studios, a spacious library, a running track, a tennis court and a basketball field, and the campus is equipped to accommodate handicapped children. Grades: Pre-K to 7. Price range: RMB 31,500-68,000 (plus RMB 1,500 uniform fee).
1) Elementary School: 5 Yumin Road, Houshayu, Shunyi District. (8041 0390/1/2); 2) Kindergarten: Merlin Champagne Town Clubhouse, 6 Liyuan Jie, Tianzhu Zhen, Shunyi District. (6450 8259) www.kinstarschool.com 海嘉双语国际学校，1) 顺义区后沙峪裕民大街5号; 2) 顺义区天竺镇丽园路6号美林香槟小镇会所

The Learning Center of Beijing LCB is an extracurricular community center that offers a wide variety of small group academic classes (maximum eight students per class) and one-on-one tutoring sessions after school and on weekends. Subjects include ESL, math, science, history and creative writing, as well as private tutorial programs. Ages: 6 to 18. Price range: RMB 350/hr (math or science tutoring, RMB 300/hr (tutoring in all other subjects), RMB 1,400-1,800 (group classes). Mon-Fri 10am-8pm, Sat 10am-4.30pm.
2108 Gahood Villa, Houshayu, Xibaixinzhuang, Shunyi District. (8046 3886) www.learningcenter.com.cn 顺义区后沙峪西白辛庄嘉洁别墅2108号

Lycée Français de Pékin (The French School) The LFP is administered in accordance with the guidelines established by the French Ministry of Education. Classes are taught in French, but non-French-speaking children are admitted into the kindergarten (which is on a separate campus), and the elementary school. This school has full sports and extracurricular programs. Ages: 2 to 18. Price range: EUR 4,490-7,820 (French children), EUR 5,130-8,980 (non-French children).
1) Primary and Secondary School: 13 Sanlitun Dongsijie, Chaoyang District. (6532 3498); 2) Kindergarten: 4 Sanlitun Lu, Chaoyang District. (6532 7881) www.lfp.com.cn 1) 朝阳区三里屯东四街13号; 2) 朝阳区三里屯路4号

Mammolina Children's Home A bilingual kindergarten that opened its doors in August 2005, Mammolina offers a Montessori curriculum covering practical life, language, math, cultural studies, art and music, and more. The school boasts a huge classroom, limited enrollment of 30 children, a kitchen area, a spacious garden/playground area, as well as a library for parents. Ages: 2.5 to 6. Price range: USD 9,850-13,850 (plus USD 600 lunch fee, USD 800-1,000 bus fee and USD 2,000 capital levy).
36 Maquanying Siqu (Liyuan Xiaoqu), Xiangjiang Beilu, Chaoyang District. (8470 5128) www.montessori.ws 三为园幼儿园，朝阳区江北路马泉营四区（丽苑小区）36号

Oxford Baby Bilingual Kindergarten This long-standing Chinese kindergarten offers a Chinese-style bilingual curriculum at four separate locations. Much of the instruction is in Chinese, with native-English teaching staff responsible for English instruction. A significant number of children board at the school. Age range: 1.5 to 6. Price range: RMB 30,000-40,000.
1) 88 Jianguo Lu, Soho New Town, Chaoyang District. (8589 7363); 2) 308 Huizhongli, Yayuncun, Chaoyang District. (6493 6626); 3) 10 Anhuili, Section 4, Yayuncun, Chaoyang District. (6489 5533); 4) 6 Nanxinyuan, Chaoyang District. (8731 1098) www.oxfordbaby.org.cn 北京小牛津双语幼儿园，1) 朝阳区建国路88号Soho现代城; 2) 朝阳区亚运村慧忠里308号楼; 3) 朝阳区亚运村安慧里4区10号; 4) 朝阳区南新园6号楼

Pakistan Embassy College This embassy-run school offers two types of curricula: the Pakistan national curriculum, and an English curriculum associated with London University that offers GCSE and A-level qualifications. Both curricula are taught in English, but a number of ESOL students are accepted, and remedial English classes are provided. Chinese language classes are mandatory for all except senior-level students. An enrollment of 400 students from more than 40 different countries makes for an excellent student-teacher ratio and a diverse student body. School facilities include science, computer and language laboratories, and a gymnasium and indoor basketball court. Ages: 4 to 18. Price range: USD 250-600/month.
1 Dongzhimenwai Dajie, Sanlitun, Chaoyang District. (6532 1905) www.embassyofpakistan-beijing.org.cn/en/college.htm 朝阳区三里屯东直门外大街1号

KIDS

Renda Middle School and High School The combined middle school and high school attached to Renmin University, *Renda Fuzhong* is known in Chinese circles for its high standards and *gaokao* results. The school's language of instruction is Chinese, and it offers A-level qualifications. International students take a Chinese assessment exam that determines whether they are placed directly into regular classes with Chinese students or into an intensive Chinese program. A total of 4,000 students attend this large school, of which approximately 180 are international students. Ages: 12 to 16. Price range: RMB 50,000 (standard program), RMB 43,600 (intensive Chinese program).
37 Zhonguancun Dajie, Haidian District. (6251 3962/2094) www.rdfz.cn/english 人大附中，海淀区中关村大街37号

Ritan School This public school has four separate divisions open to international students: an elementary school, two middle schools and a high school. A bilingual program is offered at the elementary school, but the middle and high school divisions follow the Chinese national curriculum and instruction is in Chinese only. In addition to academics, students participate in a range of electives and extracurricular activities, including the celebrated school band. Grades: 1 to 12. Price range: RMB 17,000-36,800.
1) Elementary and Middle School: 38 Nanshiliju (south of Jiuxian Qiao), Chaoyang District. (6438 2945); 2) High School (senior year only): 36 Dongsanhuan Beilu (south of Tsinghua University's Central Academy of Fine Arts), Chaoyang District. (6506 2605); 3) Middle School: Inside Baijiazhuang No. 80 Middle School, 2 Baijiazhuang Xili, Chaoyang District. (6500 4609); 4) High School: A7 Daojiayuan, west of Honglingjin Qiao, Chaoyang District. (6591 2920) http://rtzx.bjchyedu.cn 北京日坛中学，1）朝阳区南十里居38号(酒仙桥南)；2）朝阳区东三环北路36号清华大学美术学院南；3）朝阳区白家庄中学里面白家庄西里2号；4）朝阳区道家园甲7号红领巾桥西

Sanlitun Kindergarten This local kindergarten enrolls international students. Instruction is in Chinese and the school places a strong focus on physical exercise. Special classes for children ages 2.5 and accompanied by a parent are offered every week; the standard kindergarten program runs daily. Ages: 1 to 5. Price Range: RMB 500-800/month (children under 2.5), RMB 10,000 (plus RMB 380/month childcare fee) (children ages 2.5-5).
3 Jiqingli, Chaoyangmenwai Dajie, Chaoyang District. (6551 0877) 三里屯幼儿园，朝阳区朝阳门外大街吉庆里3号

Sino Bright School (Beijing No. 25 Middle School) Located on the grounds of Beijing No. 25 Middle School, SBS offers a curriculum taken from British Columbia, Canada, and taught by British Columbia-certified teachers, with the aim of preparing students for higher education in Canada or other Western countries. Founded in 2005, the school previously focused on Chinese students but is now enrolling international students. The school's language of instruction is English, but Chinese language classes are offered. Grades: 10-12. Price range: RMB 49,800-56,000 (RMB 4,000-plus for boarding students).
55 Dengshikou Dajie (at Beijing No. 25 Middle School), Dongcheng District. (6527 8189/8180) www.schoolbj.com 中加高中学校，东城区灯市口大街55号（在北京第二十五中学内）

Sunshine Learning Center This is the only special-needs school in Beijing that has an English program. The curriculum fosters a variety of academic, social and vocational skills, and includes physical education, music and arts classes. Physical, occupational and sensory integration therapies are all offered. School facilities include one-on-one therapy rooms, a sensory integration room, and the use of a swimming pool. Current enrollment is ten students, and the student to teacher ratio is 1:2. Ages: 6 to 19. Price range: USD 20,000 (plus USD 100 registration fee).
2066 Gahood Villa, Houshayu, Baixinzhuang, Shunyi District. (8046 1606) www.sunshine.org.cn 北京顺义阳光康复培训中心，顺义区后沙峪白辛庄嘉浩别墅城2066

Swedish School Beijing This school's language of instruction is Swedish, but the curriculum encompasses broader Scandinavian culture. To be admitted, either the child or one parent must be fluent in a Scandinavian language. Ages: 2 to 12. Price: RMB 65,000 (for ages 3-12).
Legend Garden Villas, 89 Jichang Lu, Chaoyang District. (6456 0826) 瑞典小学，朝阳区机场路89号丽京花园别墅

Western Academy of Beijing WAB students follow the International Baccalaureate Curriculum programs (PYP, MYP, DP) in a nurturing atmosphere that fosters a strong sense of community among its 1,400 students from over 58 countries. Children learn Chinese culture in nursery and pre-kindergarten; in kindergarten, students also learn Chinese language. From Grade 1 onwards, students who are not participating in ESOL or other English language support programs have the option of joining one of five different levels of Chinese. ESOL students are limited to 25 percent of the total number of students in any class (average ESOL enrollment throughout the school is 15 percent). Resources and facilities are extensive and include three libraries, computer labs, gymnasiums, sports fields, dance and art studios and a swimming pool, climbing wall, fitness center and outdoor experiential education center. The school provides a wireless, technology-focused learning environment with a 1:1 laptop ratio for Grade 5-12 students. Grades: nursery (age 3) to 12. Price range: RMB 67,520-136,855 (plus RMB 9,960-37,350 capital levy).
10 Laiguangying Donglu (off the Airport Expressway), Chaoyang District. (8456 4155) www.wab.edu 北京京西学校，朝阳区来广营东路10号

Yew Chung International School Part of the 75-year-old Yew Chung Education Foundation of Hong Kong, YCIS offers the National Curriculum of England and Wales, including IGCSE, and is also a certified provider of the IB Diploma Program. From K2 to Year 1, classes are taught half in English and half in Chinese. From Year 2 to Year 6, each subject is taught 70% in English and 30% in Chinese. High school classes are in English, with compulsory daily Chinese classes. Through its curriculum, Yew Chung aspires to help its students become capable of moving between Western and Eastern cultures. Facilities include two computer labs, three libraries, and a new multipurpose auditorium and performing arts center. Grades: K2 to Year 13. Price range: RMB 52,290-138,000 (plus RMB 1,660 application fee, RMB 9,300-10,960 bus fee and approx. RMB 5,800 optional lunch fee).
Honglingjin Gongyuan Dongmen, 5 Houbali Zhuang (near Dongsihuan), Chaoyang District. (8583 3731) www.ycef.com 北京耀中国际学校，朝阳区后八里庄5号红领巾公园东门

Hutong Cuisine imparts lessons they can sink their teeth into

Extracurriculars

Many international schools offer after school programs with classes devoted to arts, dance, music, science and sports. Turn to the Sports Directory on p418 for swimming pools, skating rinks and more that offer instruction for kids. Kids can also go on hikes organized by Beijing Hikers and Beijing Amblers.

Kids' Sports Leagues

Sports Beijing A community based, non-profit organization dedicated to providing quality sports and recreational programs for the youth of Beijing. Offerings include soccer, baseball, cheerleading, tennis, ice hockey, golf, gymnastics, judo, rugby and girl's softball. Mon-Fri 9.30am-5.30pm.
2/F, Lido Country Club, Holiday Inn Lido, Jichang Lu, Chaoyang District. (6430 1412) www.sportsbj.com 朝阳区北京首都机场路丽都乡村俱乐部2层

Dance

DanZ Centre Offering a range of classes in English for kids and teenagers, in styles such as ballet, jazz, tap, hip-hop and Latin. RMB 1,200 for 20 lessons. The school has both Shunyi and downtown campuses.
1) 2/F, Children's Clubhouse, Yosemite Villas, 4 Yuyang Lu (West Gate of ISB), Shunyi District. (8046 2286/2287); 2) EA2/EA3, B1/F, Bldg B, East Gate Plaza, 9 Dongzhong Jie, Dongcheng District. (6418 5525/5535) www.danzcentre.com 安斯舞蹈培训中心，1) 顺义区优榆阳路4号山美地别墅儿童俱乐部2层； 2) 东城区东环广场东中街9号B座地下EA2/EA3

J-Ballet School Formerly the Western Ballet School, J-Ballet offers instruction in Chinese, Japanese or English to children and adults. Courses are divided into fall (Sept-Dec), spring (Feb- July) and summer (July-Aug) terms. Children's lessons are in six levels (RMB 50-70 per class). Adult classes are RMB 70 each, with packages of 10 lessons for RMB 600 and 20 lessons for RMB 1000. Students get 10% discount on adult classes.
1) Pulse Health Club, Kempinski Hotel, 50 Liangmaqiao Lu, Chaoyang District. (8453 3003); 2) 1/F Bldg D, Jingxiu Yuan, Xingfucun Zhonglu, Chaoyang District. (138 0103 6364) www.j-ballet.com 1) 朝阳区亮马桥路50号 凯宾斯基饭店 脉搏健身俱乐部；2) 朝阳区幸福村中路 景绣园D座一层西侧

Western Ballet School Ballet instruction in English and Chinese available for children ages 4 to 14 years. Classes for different levels/ages are offered on different days. Classes are offered at two separate locations. RMB 1,500/semester (Kempinsk branch), RMB 1,300/semester (Shunyi branch).
1) Kempinski Hotel, 50 Liangmaqiao Lu, Chaoyang District.; 2) River Garden Villas, Houshayu, Baixinzhuang, Shunyi District. 西方芭蕾学校，1) 朝阳区亮马桥路50号凯宾斯基饭店；2) 顺义区后沙峪白辛庄 裕京花园别墅

Football (Soccer)

ClubFootball This outfit runs several soccer coaching programs for foreign and local kids ages 4 to 18. Held after school, on weekends and during holidays, at various locations around Beijing, courses are designed and delivered by ClubFootball's English Football Association-qualified coaching staff. An eight-week course costs RMB 725-850 and includes kit, beverages, certificate and team photo.
Jingdu Hotel Suite A10, 26 Jiuxianqiao Road, Chaoyang District. (5130 6893) www.clubfootball.com.cn 万国群星足球俱乐部，朝阳区酒仙桥路26号京都酒店甲10,号

Golf

SGA Junior Golf Coaching Offers one-on-one golf coaching for children ages 5 and up, from SGA-qualified, Australian PGA-certified golf coaches. Lessons can

KIDS 145

be designed for children at beginner or intermediate levels. Instruction covers everything from the full grip and swing technique to golf etiquette and handicap calculation. Clubs are provided for the duration of a purchased package. RMB 7,500 (10 lessons), RMB 13,400 (20 lessons) (does not include ball and green fees). Coaching Center is located at Chaoyang Kosaido Golf Club.
Shangsilu Cun, Tuanjiehu Xiaoqu, Chaoyang District. (6507 7389, 400 650 5169) www.SGA-China.com 朝阳广济堂高尔夫俱乐部，朝阳区团结湖小区上四路村

Martial Arts

Beijing Black Tiger Academy Get your kick on! Internationally certified instructors provide Muay Thai kickboxing and Brazilian jiujitsu programs for both adults and kids. The kids Black Belt Program offers weekly classes taught in English for children ages 6-16. Kids can work up to reaching the awe-inspiring black belt level. A flat rate fee of RMB 750/month for unlimited training. Mon-Fri (evenings), Sat-Sun (afternoons).
Rm 906, Jianwai Soho, Bldg 9, 39 Dongsanhuan, Chaoyang District. (5879 3459, 136 8140 2122, chet@graciechina.com) www.blacktigerclub.com 朝阳区东三环中路39号建外Soho9号楼906室

Jinghua Wushu Association Traditional, combat-style Chinese *wushu* for kids ages 5 and up, taught in English by teachers from Shaolin. The youngest aspiring masters start off with moves based on different animals; older, more experienced learners study traditional Shaolin forms. Classes are held Saturdays and Thursdays at the Chaoyang location listed below, and on Mondays at the Western Academy of Beijing. Classes are also scheduled to open at Dulwich. RMB 650/10 classes.
B1/F, Kempinski Hotel, 50 Liangma Qiao, Chaoyang District. (Chinese 131 4107 2677, English 135 2228 3751) 精华武术，朝阳区亮马桥路50号凯宾斯基饭店里面写字楼地下1层俱乐部

Music

Ao Yue Piano Center Offers all kinds of pianos for sale and rent, lessons, and practice space. For RMB 180/month you can rent a locally made piano; an import can temporarily grace your living room for RMB 500/month. The center's tutors, all hailing from the prestigious Central Conservatory of Music, can schedule lessons onsite (RMB 100/hour) or at your home. Practice rooms can be rented by the hour (RMB 10), or buy a monthly card (RMB 300/month for two hours of practice a day, RMB 450/month for three hours of practice a day).
Daily 9am-9pm. Northeast corner of Jianxiang Qiao, Beisihuan Lu (300m east of Zhongguo Yinyue Xueyuan), Chaoyang District. (6492 4835) 奥乐钢琴中心，北四环路健翔桥东北角中国音乐学院往东300米

Beijing Yilun Piano Center Pianos for sale and rent. Rental rates range from RMB 500-800/month. In-house lessons are available for children ages 4 and up for RMB 60/30 min, RMB 80/45 min.
Daily 9am-8pm. 48-1 Zhongguancun Nandajie, Haidian District. (6218 3582) 北京艺伦钢琴中心，海淀区中关村南大街48—1号

Kindermusik with Sarah Offers fun, innovative music and movement curricula that support children's development. CBD area studio classes begin in late August for all age groups. *Suite 1501, Huaqing Jiayuan, Huaqing Shangwu Huiguan, Chengfu Lu,, Haidian District. (8772 3419, 136 9354 1489, kmwithsarah@yahoo.com.cn) www.kmwithsarah.com* 海淀区成府路华清嘉园华清商务会馆1501室

Music Home With a small but growing staff of highly skilled instructors, Music Home offers instruction and practice space for students of classical Chinese music. Lessons are taught in either English or Chinese and the staff seem willing to work around their students.
Daily 10am-6pm. 505 Pinnacle Plaza, Tianzhu Real Estate Development Zone, Shunyi District. (138 1009 8962) 天颂音乐艺术之家，顺义区嘉浩别墅4层

Tom Lee Music Four floors of quality musical instruments make this a must-see for young musicians (and their parents). The store offers professional, age appropriate instruction for every instrument it sells. And if the lessons pay off, there's also a multifunction hall for performance and recording.
Daily 9.30am-8.30pm. 57 Tiantan Lu, Chongwen District. (6702 0099) 通利琴行，崇文区天坛路57号

Other

Hutong Cuisine Trained chef Zhou Chunyi can adapt her lessons in traditional Guangdong and Sichuan cooking for families or kids.
Courtyard 3, West Bldg, Shajing Hutong, Nanluoguxiang, Dongcheng District. (8401 4788, 134 2631 7097) www.hutongcuisine.com 东城区南锣鼓巷沙井胡同3号楼西房

SinoScuba Offers PADI Open Water and advanced scuba courses, with trips to the Blue Zoo Aquarium arranged for ages 10 and up. All courses in English. *(steven@sinoscuba.com, 136 9302 8913)*

Super Moverz "Movement training for little heroes." Kids ages 3-4 and 5-7 don their favorite superhero costume and gather for a session of fantasy fitness and fun involving obstacle courses, tumbling, leaping and more. *(135 2110 0261) www.supermoverz.com*

Swimming

Dragon Fire Swim Team Nearly 130 international students receive training in competitive swimming under the tutelage of founder and head coach Kevin Hua. Instruction is offered in the pools of Beijing international schools for kids ages 4-18 at the beginning (able to swim 10m), intermediate and advanced levels. The team has competed in races in Singapore and Hong Kong, and also competes with local Chinese teams. Fees RMB 1,400-5,800/season, plus RMB 200 registration fee. Training is offered at various times and locations, seven days a week. To register, contact Coach Hua.
(136 0106 4534, dragonfireswimming@gmail.com)

Tennis

Potter's Wheel International Sports Center Offers junior tennis education program for kids ages 5 and up. Instruction is by international coaches following the LTA curriculum. Group classes RMB 160/90 min (ages 5-8), RMB 210/2 hours (ages 9-14); tailored classes RMB 190/hr.
1 Chajia Donglu, Langxinzhuang, Chaoyang District. (8538 2803, mail@potters-wheel.cn) 匠心之轮国际学校，朝阳区郎辛庄茶家东路1号

Lord Rabbit of the Moon

A Beijing fairytale
by Lee Ambrozy

Once upon a time, many years ago, a terrible plague swept through Beijing. No family was spared and no medicine could halt the spread of the disease. The Goddess of the Moon (*Chang'e*), one of only three inhabitants of the lonely Moon Palace (*Guanghan Gong*), saw the people of Beijing in their misery, begging for a cure with hearts full of fear. Taking pity on them, she told the Jade Rabbit (*Yutu*), a lunar palace resident who concocts elixirs of immortality with a mortar and pestle, to descend to Beijing and save its people.

The Jade Rabbit donned a disguise and traveled to earth. He initially appeared as a young woman and traveled from household to household curing countless Beijingers. He accepted no payment for his cures, but only asked to borrow some clothes from the commoners. This way, the Jade Rabbit could wander through the city incognito, appearing sometimes as a man, sometimes as a woman, sometimes as a farmer, and sometimes as a merchant. Riding a menagerie of animals – including snails, horses, tigers and panthers – he beat a path around the capital, spreading his and the other animals' footprints along with his remedies.

The plague was eradicated and the Jade Rabbit returned to the Moon Palace, but his image remained in local folklore. Thus, beginning early in the Ming dynasty (1368-1644), Beijingers made clay images and toys of the "Grandpa Rabbit" (*Tu Ye*) and "Granny Rabbit" (*Tu Nainai*) in various shapes and sizes depicting the Rabbit's numerous loveable and cute incarnations. Every Mid-Autumn Festival (15th day, 8th lunar month), when the "harvest moon" lingers close to earth, the Jade Rabbit was memorialized in various games and Beijing households would make offerings to the Jade Rabbit, thanking him for having sympathy and bringing auspiciousness.

Home of the long-eared alchemist

The most prominent of Beijing's local gods, *Tuye* is probably the only one still familiar to local children, young and old. At the Mid-Autumn Festival, Chinese families eat mooncakes filled with bean paste, egg yolks and, yes, Häagen-Dazs ice cream, and venture to marvel at the splendorous moon and see on its surface not the man on the moon but the silhouette of the Jade Rabbit pounding elixirs with his mortar and pestle.

Today you can find *Tu Ye* and *Tu Nainai* in all shapes and sizes at the Bannerman Traditional Toy Shop in Guozijian. See Shengtangxuan, p157.

PHOTO: QUANJING

Summer Camps

Not only does summer bring in the sultry, smelly weather, but it seems to make your apartment shrink. Throw bored kids into the mix and you have a potentially combustible situation. The solution may be to send them to a summer camp. As the programs below indicate, Beijing offers a variety of enriching activities. Unfortunately, the list of camps and programs changes every year. Here are some of the camps that were held in the summer of 2007. To find out if they will be held again in 2008 and 2009 – and to inquire about fees – please contact the organizers or pick up the June issue of tbjKids.

3e Summer Camp 3e Kindergarten offers a Chinese-focused camp for nursery age kids (ages 2-3) and a bilingual camp for older kids (ages 3-5 and 5-8). Both camps will offer weekly field trips along with a range of art, music and outdoor activities. Ages: 2-8.
3E International School, Chaoyang District. (6437 3344 ext 127)

ABC Music & Me Day Camps This bilingual camp offers week-long sessions combining different themes. Music and cookery come together in the Jazz Kitchen session, Irish music is the theme of the Under the Rainbow session, and good old-fashioned humor and games are the driving forces of the Giggles themed week. A 45-minute Kindermusik class is included every day. Lots of movement based learning, sports, and arts and crafts ensure this will be a lively camp for the little ones. Ages: 4-7.
Children's Learning Center of Beijing, Shunyi District. (8046 1840)

Beanstalk International Kindergarten Summer Camp A chance for kids from different cultures to come together to learn and play in a fun, English-language atmosphere. The fun quotient gets upped with weekly field trips and cooking lessons, with a goodbye party thrown in for good measure. Ages: 2-6.
Beanstalk International Kindergarten, 21st Century Hotel Campus, Chaoyang District. (6466 9255)

Camp Adventure 2007 A camp for the adventurous ones in your bunch. The American Employee's Association of the US Embassy has administered this Beijing camp for over 10 years. Run in conjunction with the University of Iowa, Camp Adventure offers a full range of educational and recreational activities and aims to help its participants make new friends and learn about Chinese culture. Ages: 5-13.
Dulwich College, Legend Garden Campus, Shunyi District. (6532 3831)

The Children's House Olympic Summer Camp With 2008 just around the corner, it's about time your kid got clued into the Olympics theme! This camp will explore the history and culture of the Olympics and the different sports and nations that will make up the monumental event. Ages: 1.5-6.
The Children's House Montessori Kindergarten, China World (Chaoyang District), Kempinski (Chaoyang District) and Yosemite (Shunyi District) campuses. (6505 3869)

ClubFootball Junior Summer Coaching Courses The soccer season may be officially over, but young soccer fans need not despair: ClubFootball offers courses at a number of locations and times throughout the summer. ClubFootball's coaches are all English Football Association qualified and instruction focuses on the development of ball skills for younger children, and tactics and match play for older ones. Ages: 4-18.
Various locations around Beijing. (6416 7786) www.clubfootball.com.cn

Dulwich Community Programmes (DCP) Summer Sports Camps These one-week day camps focus on sports but also offer arts and crafts and time to splash about in the pool. Choose from golf, football or tennis. Group sizes are kept small and instruction comes from qualified coaches. Early bird discount fees (registration and payment before June 16) are available. Ages: 5-14.
Dulwich College, Legend Garden Campus, Shunyi District. (6454 9126)

Eton Camp Eton's week-long English Immersion programs aim to bolster your child's language ability in a playful and low stress environment. The courses are spread throughout the summer to suit your particular needs. The Globetrotter Team program will see young adventurers whisked off on a different field trip every day to experience and learn about the different cultures of the world. Ages: 3-6.
Eton Academy, Palm Springs campus, Chaoyang District. (6539 7171 ext 1020) www.etonkids.com

Kindermusik Summer Camp Separate morning and afternoon classes, each with a heavy emphasis on art and storytelling to encourage awareness of movement and rhythm. Tell Me A Tale (mornings) will let the kids hear some of the great stories from around the world, while the afternoon On The Road session will cover music and art as your children take a journey using their imagination. Ages: 4-7.
40 Dongsi Liutiao, Dongcheng District. (8772 3419) www.kmwithsarah.com.cn

Ivy Chinese Culture Summer Program Immerse your little ones in Chinese culture with Ivy Bilingual Preschool's A Festival a Day program. Each day, kids will celebrate a different Chinese festival, be it by munching on mooncakes, making dragon boats or receiving lucky red envelopes. It's a great chance to learn a little more about the traditions of these festivals. The language of instruction is Chinese, so this will definitely appeal to the little language learners in your posse. Ages: 2-6.
Ivy Bilingual Preschool, Seasons Park campus, Dongcheng District, and Oceans Express campus, Chaoyang District. (8453 0366 Seasons Park, 8446 7287 Oceans Express) www.ivyacademy.cn

Kids' Gallery Summer Program Covering the junior end of the age spectrum, CreativePlay (ages 2-4) and the Summer Workshop (4-6) at the Kids' Gallery are perfect for piccolo Picassos who want to use the summer heat to help get their creative juices flowing. The courses focus mainly on arts and crafts (calligraphy, painting, fine arts), but have healthy doses of sports (swimming, kung fu, ping-pong) thrown in. Ages: 2-6.
Kids' Gallery, Capital Paradise Club House, Shunyi District. (8046 1454)

The Learning Center Summer Enrichment Programs For those looking to catch up (or get ahead) in their studies this summer, the Learning Center is offering a wide variety of academic programs to suit kids of all ages. Elementary age students can choose from science, history, language arts and language immersion classes, while middle school students have the options of language and literature. Independent study programs and private classes are also available. Ages: 6-14.

Summer's hopping at Potter's Wheel Tennis Camp

Learning Center of Beijing, Shunyi District. (8046 3886) www.learningcenter.com.cn/summercamps

Me To We Volunteer and Leadership Trips Choose from two adventurous trips (to Hebei, Gansu and Henan, or Hebei, Guangzhou and Hainan). All trips start off in Beijing and then participants head off to start teaching English and volunteering with local schools in the areas they visit. Truly for the adventurous. Ages: 10-25.
(136 8143 3140) www.metowe.com.cn

MIkids' Multiple-Intelligence Summer Camp Focusing heavily on the development of your child's intelligence through playful methods, this course is broken up into two sessions with eight mini workshops, as well as indoor and outdoor activities. Sports activities are conducted by professional coaches every afternoon and both Chinese and English will be spoken. Ages: 3-9.
The International Montessori School of Beijing, River Garden Campus, Shunyi District. (8049 9496)

Neighborhood Chinese Happy Children Summer Camp Returning for its fifth year, this camp is all about advancing your child's Chinese language ability. The usual Chinese reading, writing and listening classes are combined with fun activities like field trips, sports and chances to interact with local Chinese children. Each term lasts two weeks so you can choose the one that best suits your summer plans. Ages: 5-12.
Riviera Clubhouse, Shunyi, Eton International School, Chaoyang District. (8450 1789) www.chineseneighbor.com

Potter's Wheel International Sports Center Tennis Camp Primarily focused on tennis instruction, this summer-long program also includes other sports and weekend tours around Beijing to mix things up. The kids in attendance form an extremely international bunch, with 16 countries represented in the summer of '07. The length of the program is flexible, according to your needs, and residential places are also offered. Ages: 4-16.
Potter's Wheel Tennis Academy, Chaoyang District. (8538 3269) www.potters-wheel.cn

Sports Beijing Morning Tennis Camp Suitable for beginners and Roger Federer wannabes alike, with classes offered at beginner, intermediate and competitive levels. Beginner and intermediate levels will be a reinforcement of the basic skills with fun drills thrown in. The competitive level is suitable for players who can already serve and volley consistently, and will provide coaching on match play. Three or six day a week programs are available. Ages: 12-17.
British School of Beijing, Shunyi Campus (6430 1412) www.sportsbj.com

Sports Beijing Sports & Soccer Summer Camp The major objective of this series of five-day courses is to develop kid's soccer skills and help them obtain FA SoccerStar Challenge Certificates. The focus will be on learning the basic skills and tactics of the sport and how to apply these in competitive matches. Training in basketball and volleyball will also be included. Younger kids will also enjoy lots of fun games. Ages: 12-17
BISS International School, Chaoyang District. (6430 1412) www.sportsbj.com

YCIS Summer Experience in China Available in either two-week or three-week form, the Yew Chung International School summer experience offers your kids a chance to learn more about Chinese culture while polishing their Chinese language skills. Exciting trips around the city are also planned and for three-week campers a six day excursion to the grasslands of Inner Mongolia is also planned. Ages: 8-18.
Yew Chung International School, Chaoyang District. (8583 3731) www.ycef.com/summerschool

Kids' Essentials
Books

Beijing Star Kids Children's Bookstore This English children's bookstore sells a range of soft- and hardcover books from big-name publishers in the US, Canada, Australia, Italy and England. Kids up to age 16 should be able to find something that tickles their fancy here. Francophiles may be interested in the store's small selection of French language study materials.
Mon-Fri 9am-6pm, Sat-Sun 10am-5pm. 1205, Block D, Xingyuan International Apartments, 222 Wangjing Xiyuan, Chaoyang District. (8472 7131, 136 9114 3572) 北京市佳星趣儿童书店，朝阳区望京西园222号星源国际公寓D座1205室

The BookMark The BookMark offers a wide range of books for the whole family, in English and other languages, including a sizable selection of children's literature. Children can enjoy regular book club gatherings and a weekly thematic story hour with integrated art activities. A family membership (RMB 500) gets you and your crew the chance to borrow five books for up to two weeks at a time.
Wed-Sun 10am-6pm. 1 Kaifa Jie (near The Yard restaurant), Xi Baixinzhuang, Houshayu, Shunyi District. (8049 9175) www.bookmarkbeijing.com 顺义区后沙峪西白辛庄开发街1号

The Bookworm English language books to borrow or buy. Book larvae can graze in the library's Kiddies' Corner, which houses child-size chairs and toys in addition to books. A family library membership (RMB 500) allows your family to borrow up to six books for two weeks at a time. A growing selection of for-sale books includes favorites like Wicked Chickens and The Gruffalo's Child. In addition, The Bookworm's Kids Club offers both young children and teens opportunities to share books with their peers.
Daily 9am-2am. Bldg 4, Nansanlitun Lu, Chaoyang District. (6586 9507, Kids Club: 138 1163 7831) www.beijingbookworm.com 书虫书吧，朝阳区南三里屯路4号楼

Chaterhouse Booktrader The kids' book selection is fabulous and includes a vast number of Dr Seuss books as well as Maisie, Thomas & Friends, Dora the Explorer, Clifford, the Judy Blume series, the Chronicles of Narnia, Tintin, many kids' encyclopedias, Madlibs and even Kaplan review books for older kids preparing to take the SATs or GREs.
Daily 10am-10pm. Shop B107, The Place, 9 Guanghua Lu (Dongdaqiao Lu), Chaoyang District. (6587 1328) www.chaterhouse.com.cn 朝阳区光华路9号世贸天阶中心地库B107

Foreign Language Bookstore – Lufthansa Center This branch of the Foreign Language Bookstore features a good selection of classic children's tomes in English like the Random House Step Reader series, the novels of Roald Dahl, the Chronicles of Narnia, the Berenstain Bears, creative activity books, sticker books and shelves of encyclopedias. The store's stock has recently grown a little, and books for kids up to middle school age are on offer.
Daily 9am-10pm. 4/F, Youyi Shopping City, 52 Liangmaqiao Lu, Chaoyang District. (6465 1188 ext 675) 燕莎购物中心，朝阳区亮马桥路52号

Friendship Store Slim hit-or-miss selection of English-language books – you can usually find a few choices for each age group, and the selections vary widely from month to month. If your kid likes comics but you want to sneak in some culture, check out the softbound comic books based on Chinese stories like The Water Margin, Empress Wu Zetian, and even Sun Tzu's Art of War.
Daily 9.30am-8.30pm. 17 Jianguomenwai Dajie, Chaoyang District. (6500 3311) 北京友谊商店，朝阳区建国门外大街17号

Ivy Kids Book Club This Ivy School-affiliated club offers over 1,400 titles for children ages 0-6 (including books written by Ivy's own staff). RMB 400/year buys an individual membership with basic book borrowing privileges and a family membership goes for RMB 600/year. The library offers a cozy reading environment and guided reading lessons for a range of reading abilities. The book club is open to the general public, although students of Ivy Academy and Ivy Bilingual have priority in joining.
Tue-Sat 10am-12.30pm, 1.30-6pm. Bldg E, Ocean Express, 2 Dongsanhuan Beilu (behind Silver Tower), Chaoyang District. (8446 7286, info@ivybookclub.cn) www.ivybookclub.cn 朝阳区东三环北路2号远洋新干线E座（南银大厦后面）

Peekabook House Home to a range of classic English picture books and popular novels for younger readers, as well as a variety of Chinese children's books. Both branches offer bilingual story times, arts and crafts programs, and birthday party options.
Tue-Sun 9.30am-8.30pm. 1) 2/F, Wanliu Shequ Shenghuo Guan, 15 Wanliu Zhonglu, Haidian District. (8256 7276, 8256 6324); 2) 2/F, Huatengyuan Club, Jinsong Qiao, 54 Dongsanhuan Nanlu, Chaoyang District. (8773 8382) www.peekabook.com.cn 皮卡书屋，1) 海淀区万柳中路15号万柳社区生活馆二层；2) 朝阳区东三环南路54号花藤园俱乐部二层（劲松桥）

Poplar Kids Republic Bookstore One of China's first and most extensive children's bookstores. More than 3,000 illustrated storybooks from Europe, America, Japan and China are on sale, including favorites such as The Very Hungry Caterpillar, The Giving Tree, and Badger's Painting Gifts. The store encourages children and their parents to stop by, read together and enjoy the in-store facilities, which include a comfortable play area. On weekends, a free storytelling hour is offered and often followed up with arts and crafts activities.
Daily 10am-7pm. Rm 1362, Bldg 13, Jianwai Soho, 39 Dongsanhuan Zhonglu, Chaoyang District. (5869 3032) www.poplar.com.cn 蒲蒲兰绘本馆，朝阳区东三环中路39号建外Soho13号楼1362室

Wangfujing Foreign Languages Bookstore The mother lode for kids' books in English, the store has classic picture books by Dr. Seuss, plus many series like Junie B. Jones, The Famous Five, Arthur and more. Older kids will find a slew of must-read books as well. Also offers books on tape and loads of photo-illustrated, hardbound series on science, nature and animals. The selection keeps getting better, but prices remain Western.
Daily 9am-9pm. 235 Wangfujing Dajie, Dongcheng District. (6512 6903) www.bpiec.com.cn 外文书店，东城区王府井大街235号

Poplar Kids Republic Bookstore is well-stocked and enchantingly designed

Wangfujing Xinhua Bookstore Fabulous Chinese-language selection of kids' books, including lavishly illustrated kids' encyclopedias, tons of easy-readers and brightly illustrated books for kids just learning Chinese, plus posters, fun interactive books and myriad learning aids. The English selection is slim, but a budget-stretching option is to pick up the super cheap, green-bound, China published softcover editions of classics like Kidnapped and Tom Sawyer.
Mon-Fri 9am-9.30pm, Sat-Sun 8.30am-9.30pm. 218 Wangfujing Dajie, Dongcheng District. (6525 2592) 王府井新华书店，东城区王府井大街218号

Clothing

Benetton Colorful wool and linen clothes for style savvy kids and teens. RMB 400 and up.
Daily 10am-9pm. NB139, China World Shopping Mall, 1 Jianguomenwai Dajie, Chaoyang District. (6505 6810) 贝纳通，朝阳区建国门外大街1号国贸商城NB139

Bixiulan Skip past the schlock and head for this Yaxiu market stall offering exquisite British- and French-style children's wear (like Jacadi brand) in sizes ranging from newborn to 6x. If you see something you like, buy it, or someone else will snatch it while you deliberate.
Daily 9.30am-9pm. Stall 3083, 3/F, Yaxiu Market, 58 Gongti Beilu, Chaoyang District. (133 1153 8720) 毕秀兰，朝阳区工体北路58号雅秀服装市场3楼3083室

Chicco Chicco sells adorable clothes and shoes for infants and toddlers, as well as toys, infant gyms and more. The store has more than 15 branches around town; just a few are listed below.
1) Daily 9am-9pm. NB136, China World Shopping Mall, 1 Jianguomenwai Dajie, Chaoyang District. (6405 6721); 2) Daily 9am-10pm. Lufthansa Shopping Center, 6/F, 52 Liangmaqiao Lu, Chaoyang District. (6465 1188 ext 675); *3) Daily 10am-10pm. Pacific Century Place, 5/F, A2 Gongti Beilu, Chaoyang District. (6539 3888)* 智高儿童用品，1）朝阳区建国门外大街1号国贸商城NB136；2）朝阳区亮马桥路52号燕莎购物中心6楼；3）朝阳区工体北路甲2号太平洋百货5楼

Embroidered Shoes Exquisitely embroidered with floral motifs, the pink, hot red and pure white slippers sold here will have your daughter feeling like Cinderella. Moms with small feet can join in the fun: sizes go up to woman's 39 (starting at RMB 50).
Daily 10am-8pm. Jinjie, Laitai Flower Market, Nuren Jie, Chaoyang District. 女人街绣花鞋，朝阳区莱太花卉市场女人街金街

Jacadi If you feel like splurging on baby shoes or an outfit for a special occasion, nothing beats this French store. Prices are sky high, but who's counting when the clothes are so stylish? If your credit card can take more punishment, visit the other kid's clothing stores in the China World Shopping Mall.
Daily 10am-9pm. NB135-137, China World Shopping Mall, 1 Jianguomenwai Dajie, Chaoyang District. (6505 0766) 亚卡迪，朝阳区建国门外大街1号国贸商城NB135–137

Jiayi Vogue Square Patrolled by diva moms on a budget, Jiayi offers a more upscale and relaxing shopping experience than Yaxiu but with similar bargains on designer brands. Don't forget to haggle.
Daily 10am-9pm. 3A Xinyuan Nanlu, Chaoyang District. (8451 1810) 佳艺时尚广场，朝阳区新源南路3号

Kingkow Kingkow sells well-tailored, attractive (think Norwegian Benetton) shirts, pants and outfits. Guomao prices.
Daily 9am-9pm. NB129, China World Shopping Mall, 1 Jianguomenwai Dajie, Chaoyang District. (6505 9369) 小笑牛童装，朝阳区建国门外大街1号国贸商城 NB129

If baby doesn't need brand names, get a whale of a deal at Whale Baby

Kong De Cai Great selection of kids' pants, shirts, skirts and more from toddler up to size 14, with "brand names" such as Gap, Barbie, OshKosh, Polo, Nike and Burberry. Please help to fight inflation by refusing to pay over RMB 70 for any item (unless it's a cashmere coat with solid gold buttons!).
Daily 9.30am-9pm. Stall B7057, 2/F, Yaxiu Market, 58 Gongti Beilu, Chaoyang District. (136 0129 4508) 孔德才，朝阳区工体北路58号雅秀服装市场2楼B7057室

Little Felicio Beautiful children's clothes and shoes at extremely painful prices.
Daily 10am-8.30pm. NB138, China World Shopping Mall, 1 Jianguomenwai Dajie, Chaoyang District. (6505 5818) 宝宝波特欧洲童装店，朝阳区建国门外大街1号国贸商城 NB258

Lufthansa Center In addition to the brands individually listed in this section (like Kingkow and Chicco), Lufthansa carries threads and footwear by Lawlandee, Montagut Paris, Nike Kids and Mashi Maro. A pricey, but convenient, one-stop shopping destination.
Daily 9am-10pm. 52 Liangmaqiao Lu, Chaoyang District. (6465 1188 ext 675) 燕莎购物中心，朝阳区亮马桥路52号

Mikihouse Okay, the preppy outfits and footwear made by this Japanese firm are durable and adorable, but such cuteness comes at an outrageous price: a pair of simple sneakers costs RMB 700. Yikes. Plus, the service can be very moody.
Daily 10am-9pm. NB133, China World Shopping Mall, 1 Jianguomenwai Dajie, Chaoyang District. (6505 9652) 朝阳区建国门外大街1号国贸商城 NB133

Naturino From pretty sandals to gumboots, this unpretentious kids' store is all about quality. Prices start at RMB 300.
1) Tue-Sun 10.30am-6pm. Pinnacle Plaza, Tianzhu Real Estate Development Zone, Shunyi District. (8046 1788); 2) Daily 9.30am-10pm. 5/F Scitech Shopping Center, Chaoyang District. (8512 0141) 自然之子／那都乐，1）顺义区天竺房地产开发区荣祥广场；2）朝阳区赛特购物中心5层

Okaïdi It may come from Paris, but this kids' clothing shop is more Gap Kids than Bonpoint, with jeans, cargo pants and other casual clothes for trendy tots and teens, ages 0 to 14.
Daily 10am-10pm. 4/F, The Place, 9 Guanghua Lu, Chaoyang District. (6587 1515) 朝阳区光华路9号世贸天阶4层

Plastered T-shirts This hip shop sells its own line of comfortable cotton T-shirts for kids featuring acrobats, space kids, retro buses and other colorful, Beijing-inspired designs. For address and times see Shopping, p363.

Sunny Baby Kids' Clothing With its collection of inexpensively priced dresses, pants, sweaters, shirts, shorts and socks, Sunny will brighten your infant-to-4-year-old's day.
1) Daily 10am-9pm. Xinyuan Nanlu 562 Jiayi Vogue Square, 3A, Chaoyang District. (6466 3028); 2) Daily 10am-8pm. J2-17, Jinjie, Nuren Jie, Chaoyang District. (6462 8111). 阳光宝贝童装，1）朝阳区新源南路甲3号佳艺广场562号；2）朝阳区女人街金街J2-17号

Tot to Teen Moderately priced children's clothing, including a quality selection of infant layette, toddler pajamas and preteen everyday wear.
1) Daily 9am-7pm. 703 Pinnacle Plaza, Tianzhu Real Estate Development Zone, Shunyi District. (8046 4419, tot-to-teen@hotmail.com); 2) Daily 10am-7pm. Store 102, 30 Sanlitun Beijie, Chaoyang District. (6417 9640, tot-to-teen@hotmail.com) 红马车儿童用品商店。1) 顺义区天竺房地产开发区荣祥广场703房。2) 朝阳区三里屯北街30号102商店

Whale Baby Clothing These shops have not a single garment for young cetaceous mammals, but they do a brisk trade in toddler-to-preteen quilted coats with embroidered flowers, sparkly jeans and shoes decorated with soccer balls on the side.
1) Daily 9am-9pm. 7 Gongti Nanlu, Chaoyang District. (6551 4622); 2) Daily 9am-9pm. 1/F, Gold Peacock Art Center,13 Dongtucheng Lu, Chaoyang District. (6428 5745); 3) Daily 9am-9pm. 2A Dongzhimen Nanjie, Dongcheng District. (6413 1550) 鲸鱼宝宝童装。1) 朝阳区工体南路7号；2) 朝阳区东土城路13号，金孔雀艺术中心1层；3) 东城区东直门南大街甲2号

Xiao Fu Xing The Chinese-French couple that runs this pint-sized boutique use cotton fabrics bought from the countryside to make lovely traditional Chinese garments for kids aged 1-5, including mian'ao and mian'ku (padded jacket and pants, starting at RMB 100), padded tiger shoes and boots (RMB 50 and up) and tiger hats (RMB 60). Other good buys include bright pink A-line dresses and flowery baby blankets.
Daily 10am-7pm. 43 Zhonglouwan Hutong (between the Bell and Drum towers), Dongcheng District. (8403 4740) 小福星。东城区鼓楼湾胡同43号 （钟鼓楼附近）

Xiushui Fuzhuang Shichang (Silk Market) Rows upon rows of toddler and baby-sized clothing stalls can be found on the fourth floor. Choose from bibs, parkas, warm-ups, T-shirts, hats and more.
Daily 9am-9pm. 8 Jianwai Xiushui Dongjie, Chaoyang District. (5169 8800) 秀水服装市场。朝阳区建外秀水东街8号

Yaxiu Market The stall owners here are spoiled by the gaggles of free-spending tourists who come for bargain shopping, and so are less amenable to offering deep discounts to residents than their counterparts in other markets. Nevertheless, teen after teen told us they enjoy shopping here for copies of recent fashionable clothes: low-slung jeans, branded T-shirts, baggy pants, oversized athletic kids.
Daily 9.30am-9pm. 58 Gongti Beilu, Chaoyang District. (6415 0063) 雅秀市场。朝阳区工体北路58号

Gear

Beijing United Family Hospital & Clinics Gift Shop Sells useful stuff like cold packs, baby toothbrushes, safety scissors, breast pumps and first aid kits.
Daily 24hrs. 2 Jiangtai Lu (near Lido Hotel), Chaoyang District. (6433 3960 ext 262) www.unitedfamilyhospitals.com 北京和睦家医院。朝阳区将台路2号（丽都酒店附近）

Carrefour Drawn by the low prices, the crowds in these stores can be thick and fierce. Try coming on a weekday morning to stock up on diapers, creams, breast pads, sipping cups, pacifiers, wet wipes, baby shampoos, soaps and powdered milk. You'll also find cribs, high chairs, potties and pink Cinderella bikes.
1) Daily 8.30am-10.30pm. 6B Beisanhuan Donglu (beside the International Exhibition Center), Chaoyang District. (8460 1043); 2) Daily 8am-10pm. 11 Malian Dao, Xuanwu District.; 3) Daily 8am-10pm. 15, 2 Zone, Fangchengyuan, Fangzhuang, Fengtai District.; 4) Daily 8.30am-10.30pm. 31 Guangqu Lu, Chaoyang District. (5190 9508); 5) Daily 8.30am-10.30pm. 56A Zhongguancun Plaza, Haidian District. (5172 1516/7); 6) Daily 8am-10pm. 54A Baishiqiao Lu (east of Beijing Zoo), Xicheng District. (8836 2729) www.carrefour.com.cn, e-shop.carrefour.com 家乐福。1) 朝阳区北三环东路乙6号（中国国际展览中心正门旁）；2) 宣武区马连道11号；3) 丰台区方庄芳城园二区15号；4) 朝阳区广渠路31号；5) 海淀区中关村广场甲56号；6) 西城区白石桥路甲54号

Chicco Chicco comes from Italy, where mamas know how to care for their bambini. So durable it will last right through your seventh child, the equipment includes high chairs, baby carriers, car seats, bottles, thermometers, cribs and prams. The store has more than 15 branches around town; just a few are listed below. For addresses and hours see listing on p151

Ikea Stocks a wide range of children's gear, including extendable beds, high chairs, changing tables, cupboard units and Patrull safety equipment (cabinet/door locks, safety gates, corner bumpers, window catches, etc.). Save your skin by paying to have Ikea technicians assemble your purchases at home.
Daily 10am-10pm. 1 Taiyang Gonglu, Dongbahe (northwest corner of Siyuan Qiao), Chaoyang District. (800 810 5679) www.ikea.com.cn 宜家家居。朝阳区东坝河太阳宫路1号（四元桥西北角）

Jacadi Jacadi's fashionable French equipment will yank at both your heartstrings and purse strings. A crib costs RMB 7,000, plus an additional RMB 890 for the mattress and RMB 2,000 for covers and sheets. The changing table with a built-in bathtub retails for RMB 3,500, while a wardrobe goes for a cool RMB 6,520. Jacadi also sells children's clothes. For address and hours see listing on p151

Leyou Leyou sells all the essentials, like thermometers, breast pumps, breast pads, diapers, spoons, bottles, formula, baby food and cribs. Prices are competitive and you can order online.
1) Daily 9am-8pm. 111 Jiaodaokou Dajie, Dongcheng District. (6405 6406); 2) Daily 9am-8pm. 143, Beituchen Xilu, Haidian District. (6201 7536); 3) Daily 9am-8pm. East gate of Sanyuanli Community, opposite Silver Tower (between Sanyuan Qiao and Sanyuan Dongqiao), Chaoyang District. (6463 8880); 4) Daily 9.30am-9pm. 203-204 Section A, 9 Wangjing Jie, Chaoyang District. (5920 3191) www.leyou.com 乐友儿童用品。1) 东城区交道口大街111号；2) 海淀区北土城西路143号；3) 朝阳区南银大厦对面三源里社区东门（三元桥和三元东桥之间）；4) 朝阳区望京街9号A座203-204

Lijia Baby This chain of baby supply stores sells competitively priced diapers, formula, baby cereal, as well as thermometers, breast pads, bottles and other baby essentials. Most of its 20-plus stores in Beijing are small, but the Maliandao and Fanzhuang superstores carry a vast selection of cribs, bassinets, strollers, potties and much, much more. Visit the Chinese-only website to order online or find for the store nearest you.
1) Daily 8.30am-8.30pm. 2/F Jiezuo Dasha (go through the pharmacy), 55 Xingfucun Zhonglu,

KIDS

Chaoyang District. (6417 5297); 2 Daily 9am-8pm. 10 Malian Dao (across from Carrefour), Xuanwu District. (6328 8715); 3) Daily 9am-8.30pm. 1-3 Store, Sifang Jingyuan, Chengchousi, Fengtai District. (8764 6704) www.lijiababy.com.cn 丽嘉玉，朝阳区幸福村中路55号杰座大厦嘉事堂药店内；2）宣武区马连道10号（马连道家乐福对面，百安居三层0；3）丰台区左安门成寿寺四方景园1-3号商铺

Lufthansa Center Stocks well-made if pricey car seats, high chairs and strollers by the likes of Aprica, Iglesina, Combi, Evenflo, Chicco and Baby Bjorn. Also stocks Nuk bottles, Advent breast pump kits, pacifiers and, in the supermarket in the basement, baby detergent, formula, diapers, and plenty of wine for mom and dad. A larger selection and fewer shoppers can be found at its sister store in the Yansha Golden Resources Shopping Mall.
Daily 9am-10pm. 52 Liangmaqiao Lu, Chaoyang District. (6465 1188 ext 675); 2) Mon-Thu 10am-9pm, Fri-Sun 10am-10pm. 1 Yuanda Lu (300m north of Changchun Bridge), Haidian District. (8887 5888) www.newyanshamall.com 燕莎购物中心，朝阳区亮马桥路52号；2）金源新燕莎商城，海淀区远大路1号（长春桥北300米）

New China Children's Store Offers some good deals on China-made gear: Angel strollers, Geoby wood cribs with a bassinet and mosquito net, and Angel travel cots with changing mats and colorful plastic four-drawer dressers. Head up to the second floor for essentials like diapers, basins and thermometers. Also features various play possibilities.
Mon-Fri 9am-9pm, Sat-Sun 9am-9.30pm. 168 Wangfujing Street, Dongcheng District. (6528 1774) 新中国儿童用品商店，东城区王府井大街168号

NU2YU Baby Shop This unique store specializes in "gently-used" imported items for babies and children under 12. Offload or stock up on quality brand name cribs, strollers, bassinets, car seats, booster seats, changing tables, children's bicycles, toys, books and more. All items on sale have to pass a rigorous quality examination. Got a grandkid coming to visit and nowhere to put her? Cribs, high chairs and other items can also be rented on a short-term (RMB 30/day) or long-term (RMB 20/day) basis. They also organize monthly inventory intake drives, call Karen on the mobile number below for more information.
Sun-Thu 11am-5pm or by scheduled appointment. Rm 101, Bldg 18, Huayang Jiayuan, Yaojiayuan Lu, Liulitun Beili (directly across from the Beijing Obstetrics and Gynecology Hospital), Chaoyang District. (6500 5332 Chinese, 136 7129 5154 English) www.nu2yubabyshop.com 朝阳区六里屯北里姚家园路华阳家园18号楼101室（北京妇产医院附近）

Pacific Century Place Go to the basement of this upscale mall for extra-large diapers, sterilizing equipment, Braun hand blenders (great for pureeing food) as well as a pharmacy with baby cough syrup.
Daily 10am-10pm. 2A, Gongti Beilu, Chaoyang District. (6539 3888) 太平洋百货，朝阳区工体北路甲2号

Qiseguang Baby Store Located in Jing'anli, the straightforwardly named Qiseguang 0-3 Baby Articles Monopoly Store (Qiseguang 0-3 Ying'er Yongpin Zhuanmai) sells formula and baby food with prices ranging from a few kuai for the simple stuff, to a few hundred for gourmet goodies. They also stock feeding bottles, clothing, toys, books, cribs and strollers.

Daily 9am-7.30pm. B1/F, International Exhibition Center, Jing'an Xijie, Chaoyang District. (6462 5797) 七色光0-3婴儿用品专卖，朝阳区静安西街国展地下1层

Sogo Department Store The Japanese outlet sells countless necessities like breast pads, pumps, rubber cot sheets, nail clippers, junior cups, teethers, bottlebrushes, sterilizing kits and more.
Daily 10am-10pm. 8 Xuanwumen Dajie, Xuanwu District. (6310 3388) 庄胜崇光百货，宣武区宣武门大街8号

Xingfu Mama (Happy Mother) Devoted entirely to the needs of mothers and their little bundles of joy, Xingfu Mama boasts a wide range of maternity wear, baby products and toys. Chinese brand names are stocked alongside imported ones like Nuk (Germany), Pigeon (Japan) and Piyo Piyo (Singapore). Member's cards offer a 20% discount.
Daily 9am-8.30pm. 112 Xinjiekou Nandajie, Xicheng District. (6615 9808) www.xingfumama.com 幸福妈妈孕婴专卖，西城区新街口南大街112号

Services

Bounceabout Bounceabout rents out inflatable bouncy castles of many different designs, from Spongebob Squarepants to Spiderman. Great for birthday parties, these castles are also available in different sizes, from those small enough to fit in your living room to bigger ones for the backyard.
Rental RMB 3,000 per day. (133 1139 1468)

Dkids Photography Studio A professional photography studio specializing in family portraits and high quality shots of your wee ones.
Daily 9.30am-6pm. Rm 707, Bldg B, Jianwai Soho, 39 Dongsanhuan Zhonglu, Chaoyang District. (5869 1527) www.Dkidsphoto.com 守望者儿童摄影空间，朝阳区东三环中路39号建外Soho B座707室

Mr. Magic A Mr. Magic Party includes one hour with a clown, magician or superhero and face painting, an interactive magic show, a treasure hunt, circle games, crazy dances and more (RMB 2,000, RMB 1,600 (kids), discount rates for schools and charities). Prize bags, balloon art and a DVD of the event are also available for additional charges.
(139 1062 6059, parsons59@yahoo.com)

Piñatas by Mr. Zhang Piñata maker Mr. Zhang learned his craft at the Mexican embassy. It costs RMB 300 for piñatas of any shape, and you purchase the piñata's contents separately and fill it on your own. Order at least two weeks in advance. (137 0103 9306)

Toys

Alien Street Market The building is occupied by individual stall owners who sell all kinds of toys for indoor and outdoor use, including kiddie pools. Quality is uneven, so inspect toys carefully before buying and be sure to haggle.
Laofanjie Shichang, Yabao Lu (south of Fulllink Plaza), Chaoyang District. 老番街市场，朝阳区雅宝路

Beijing Comic City Got a manga maniac on your hands? Drop him off here and he'll spend hours drooling over the selection of comic book, cartoon and video game paraphernalia (but keep your eyes peeled because some of the goods are definitely not rated PG!).

Handmade, hand-painted high flyers at San Shi Zai Kite Store

Mon-Thu 10am-9pm, Fri-Sun 10am-9.30pm. 6/F, Soxiu Mall, 40 Chongwenmenwai Dajie, Chongwen District. (5167 1263) 北京动漫城．崇文区崇文门外大街40号搜秀商城6层

BigDog Balloon Party Shop Balloons galore, plus streamers, silly hats and all kinds of party products. Go for one of the balloon sculptures or bouquets for some extra fun at your kid's next birthday bash.
Daily 10am-10pm. Rm 0102, Unit 4, Bldg 3, District C1, Upper East Side, 6 Dongsihuan Beilu, Chaoyang District. (5130 7088) www.bigdogparty.cn 朝阳区东四环北路6号阳光上东C1–3–4–0102

Carrefour The Gallic emporium carries foreign brands like Fisher Price, Disney and Lego and their domestic counterparts. For addresses and hours see listing on p153.

Chicco Colorful mobiles, infant gyms, activity tables, baby phones and toy cars that are purportedly designed to foster your child's mental development. The store has more than 15 branches around town; just a few are listed below. For addresses and hours see listing on p151.

Haba Toys Well-made, all-wood European toys like building blocks, animals on wheels, train sets, tricycles, a Noah's ark, plus a playhouse for the kids to unwind in.
Daily 10am-9pm. NS2, China World Shopping Mall, 1 Jianguomenwai Dajie, Chaoyang District. 哈芭玩具．朝阳区建国门外大街1号国贸商城NS2

Hongqiao Market One entire floor is filled with cheap toys, from stuffed animals to Barbie sets, kites and remote controlled cars.
Daily 8.30am-7pm. 36 Hongqiao Lu, Chongwen District. (6713 3354) 红桥市场．崇文区红桥路36号

Ikea Intelligently designed, competitively priced and unusually named toys and accessories await your kids here, including mobiles, stuffed animals, easels and play tents. For address and hours see listing on p153.

Jack Toys Located inside Jenny Lou's, beyond the bedding, flowers, DVDs, clothing and cosmetics, Jack Toys boasts a medium-sized selection of moderately priced but often cheaply made toys. These include Pokemon cards, rubber snakes, Game Boy cartridges and rainy day activities (paint the dinosaur, foam art, etc.). Also provides balloon delivery service for birthday parties (RMB 3 per balloon).
Daily 9am-8pm. Inside Jenny Lou's Supermarket, Pinnacle Plaza, Tianzhu Real Estate Development Zone, Shunyi District. (136 8330 0568) 顺义区天竺房地产开发区荣祥广场Jenny Lou's超市内

Kids Plus Is your child looking for something to go with her magic wand? Many a Beijing parent has made an emergency trip to this Shunyi toy store to pick up a fairy or Batman costume (RMB 190) to reward junior for staying dry all night. Wide selection for a small shop but toys can be a bit pricey. If you are looking for Little Tikes gear, Kids Plus can order from an extensive catalogue with a turnaround of a few weeks.
Daily 9am-7pm. 701 Pinnacle Plaza, Tianzhu Real Estate Development Zone, Shunyi District. (8046 4572) 顺义区天竺房地产开发区荣祥广场701号

Lego Enthusiasts can buy classic sets of 30 to 1,000 pieces, while those with less imagination can purchase themed Lego sets, such as Star Wars, Harry Potter, Alpha Team and Jack Stone.
*1) Daily 9am-9pm. NB134A, China World Shopping Mall, 1 Jianguomenwai Dajie, Chaoyang District.;
2) Daily 9am-10pm. Lufthansa Shopping Center, 52*

Dashing duds at Kids Plus

Liangmaqiao Lu, Chaoyang District.; 3) Daily 10am-10pm. 5/F Pacific Century Place, A2 Gongti Beilu, Chaoyang District. 乐高。1）朝阳区建国门外大街1号国贸商城NB134A；2）朝阳区亮马桥路52号燕莎购物中心；3）朝阳区工体北路甲2号太平洋百货5楼

Leyou Sells toys from brands like Chicco, Koochie, Play Doh, Playwell and Ravensburger. Prices are competitive and you can order online. For addresses and hours see listing on p153.

Longmen Children's Educational Toys Sells socially progressive Lego-style construction toys. Build a contraption that demonstrates how hydro-electricity works or make a solar-powered tractor and a solar-powered car. All sets come with instructions in English. Mon-Thu 10am-9pm, Fri-Sun 10am-9.30pm. 4072, 4/F, Yansha Golden Resources Shopping Mall, Yuanda Lu, 300m north of Changchun Bridge, Haidian District. (8887 5764) 龙门少儿。海淀区金源燕莎购物中心4层4072店

Lufthansa Center Kids World on the sixth floor has genuine toys from Lego, Chicco, Barbie, Playwell and Fisher-Price. Foster a culinary appetite with the cooking sets that come in Korean, Western (magimix, coffee maker, oven) and Japanese (velcro fish, hibachi) versions. Other gift ideas include electric cars and motocycles, bouncing indoor trampolines, kids' computers and more. A larger selection and fewer shoppers can be found at its sister store in the Yansha Golden Resources Shopping Mall. For addresses and hours see listing on p154.

New China Children's Store This store is bursting with all manner of toys, including outdoor gear and bikes. For address and hours see listing on p154.

Pacific Century Place Brands include Fisher-Price, Hot Wheels, Barbie, Chicco, Lego and Playwell. For address and hours see listing on p154.

Park Classic Toys The real life Mini Cooper in the window hints at this store's wares. Owned by an archetypal car freak, Classic Toys stocks unique models of antique cars, many of them handmade. Also on offer is a range of novelty toys and collectibles: old-school metal robots, 3D puzzles, plastic models of movie characters, even a set of Backstreet Boys puppets. The goods don't come cheap, and won't appeal to every kid, but the store's a great bet if you're looking for something one-of-a-kind. Mon-Fri 9am-9pm, Sat-Sun 10am-8pm. 1/F, Huixin Bldg, 6 Xiangjun Beili (Bldg of Dongsanhuan, opposite Tuanjiehu Park west gate), Chaoyang District. (6506 8952, 139 0102 7915) www.toysclub.org 爬客。朝阳区向军北里6号汇鑫写字楼1层（东三环团结湖公园西门对面）

San Shi Zhai Kite Store Ninety-year-old Liu Huiren began making kites after retiring and passed on his skill to his grandson Liu Bin, who is now the owner of the San Shi Zhai kite store, located on Di'anmen, east of Houhai. Each of the store's kites is handmade out of bamboo, silk or paper, and painted by the owners themselves. Choose from a variety of goldfish, butterfly or eagle kites - all available in different sizes - and different types, including "hard wing" (which can fly 1,000 meters high) and "soft wing" kites (that fly up to 500 meters), as well as dragon or centipede kites, which

have long bodies composed of dozens of segments connected by strands of twine. Even the smallest and simplest kites take three days to make, hence the steep prices ranging from RMB 100-800 (factory printed kites usually cost only RMB 20 each). The store guarantees quality and offer repair service. Daily 9am-9pm. 25 Di'anmen Xidajie, east of Lotus Lane, Xicheng District. (8404 4505, 6403 0393) 三石斋风筝店。西城区地安门西大街25号

Shelcore Toys Shelcore caters mainly to toddlers under 3 (and their parents, who appreciate the in-store play spaces). As with rival Fisher-Price, design novelty and educational value are draw factors for the brand. Spending RMB 1,000 (doesn't have to be all at once!) gets you a discount of 20 percent off regular prices. Sun-Thu 9am-9pm, Fri-Sat 9am-10pm. Rm 402, Sun Dong An Plaza, 138 Wangfujing Dajie, Dongcheng District. (6528 2410) 世高玩具。东城区王府井大街138号新东安商场402室

Shengtangxuan Shengtangxuan's owner Tang Qiliang, an ethnic Manchurian in his 80s, started crafting toys 70 years ago and a number of his toys are part of collections in the China Art Gallery and the Capital Museum. In 2003 he and his daughter opened this shop in Guozijian to preserve his time-honored handicrafts. Made from wood, paper and clay, many of Tang's toys take their influence from classic tales and include figurines from Journey to the West and the legend of The Eight Immortals Crossing the Sea. The store also sells wooden spinning tops (RMB 15), toy drums (RMB 8), paper windmills (RMB 7-10) and Peking Opera masks (RMB 35). Daily 9am-7pm. 38 Guozijian Jie, Dongcheng District. (8404 7179) 盛唐轩。东城区国子监街38号

Steiff This Steiff store, the first of its kind in China, stocks an assortment of the classic mohair teddy bears and animals, famous worldwide for being firm childhood favorites. Adults will be enchanted by the adorable limited edition bears, including one playing violin in a purple dress (RMB 3,980), a bear in a pilot's outfit (RMB 3,880), and one in full bridal attire (RMB 1,480) Daily 9am-9pm. EB 106, China World Trade Center Shopping Mall, 1 Jianguomenwai Dajie, Chaoyang District. (6505 9875) 泰迪熊。朝阳区建国门外大街1号国贸EB 106室

Tianyu Market Toys of all manner at prices that won't make you blush. Daily 9am-6pm. 10 Tuanjiehu Dongli, Chaoyang District. (8598 9422) 天宇市场。朝阳区团结湖东里10号

T.O.T.S. This is the place to visit for "intelligent" wooden toys from abroad like building blocks, rocking horses, boats, playhouses and seagull mobiles. T.O.T.S. also stocks items like Teletubbies dolls, wax crayons and xylophones. Daily 9am-9.30pm. NB138A, B1/F, China World Shopping Mall (near Le Cool ice rink), 1 Jianguomenwai Dajie, Chaoyang District. (6505 4548) www.tots.com.cn 头大原创玩具房。朝阳区建国门外大街1号国贸商城地下1层NB138A

Tot to Teen This clothing store also stocks a small selection of games like Shrek Monopoly and Uno (RMB 45-70), art supplies, wands, butterfly wings and temporary tattoos (RMB 48). For addresses and hours see listing on p153.

KIDS 157

A Year of Chinese Culture
Fun ways to help them integrate
by Cate Conmy and Kim Lee

Here are some suggestions for fun activities that will help your kids learn about China throughout the year.

January/February
Spring Festival is here
1) Hit the Laitai Flower Market in Nüren Jie (p381) for symbols of good fortune such as miniature orange trees, narcissus bulbs and fresh flowers.
2) Get busy making *jiaozi*. Be sure to hide a coin in one for luck in the coming year.
3) Get in the giving spirit by preparing *hongbao* for all your short friends. (It's not the amount of cash inside but the gesture that counts – or at least that's what parents say.)
4) Adorn your door with some festive couplets and your windows with pretty papercuts. If you're feeling poetic, create your own couplets – indulge in a nice calligraphy set and you can show off your brushwork.
5) Give your teenagers a safety lecture (and maybe a pair of goggles) and then let them scare away evil spirits with some noisy firecrackers.
6) Lantern Festival falls 15 days after Spring Festival. Larger local supermarkets sell crepe paper and other lantern-making supplies. They also have a large drum used to make perfectly round *tangyuan* or *yuanxiao* (sweet sticky rice dumplings).
7) Visit a lantern display. All of the major parks have them, but the one at Chaoyang Park is particularly kitschy and therefore photogenic.

March
Herald all things green
1) On March 12, celebrate Chinese Arbor Day and head to the park for some tree hugging. Or better yet, plant a sapling of your own. Try the Goose 'n' Duck Ranch (contract Goose 'n' Duck Pub on p300) for an organized tree planting activity.
2) How can you tell that spring has sprung? Look for the "welcome spring flowers" (aka *yingchunhua*, aka forsythia). This little yellow flower is the first to blossom when spring arrives, and spotting one is said to be good luck. Scout for a bush at the Beijing Botanical Gardens.

April/May
Kit up with a kite
1) Go fly a kite. It's windy and there's no faster way to befriend an older gentleman than to ask for advice on hoisting a kite!
2) Go make a kite: the Chinese Culture Club usually holds a kite-making workshop in the spring. Did you know that kites were used to send messages in imperial times?
3) Go buy a kite: the owners of San Shi Zhai Kite Store (see p157) handcraft every one of the many classic kites packed into their small, colorful shop.

June/July
Ships ahoy: it's Dragon Boat season
1) Brush up on the festival's history by picking up a history of the festival at the Foreign Language Bookstore.
2) Go see Beijing's own dragon boat team in action on Houhai (see p446).
3) Enlist an *ayi* or neighbor to show you how to make *zongzi* (sticky rice dumplings wrapped in reed leaves). Be forewarned that these are far more difficult to make than you might imagine, but most kids enjoy anything that involves getting sticky.

Expose 'em to the mirth and pageantry of Spring Festival Temple Fairs

4) If you can take the heat, summer afternoons are a great time to visit tourist sights as crowds are thin.

August/September
Prep for Ghost Festival, Mid-Autumn Festival and Teacher's Day
1) Get some spirit money at Dongjiao Market and burn it to keep a deceased relative satiated during the Hungry Ghost Festival.
2) Buy or make mooncakes to give to your child's instructor on September 10, Teacher's Day.
3) Read up on the legend behind Mid-Autumn Festival, then visit the Kempinski Hotel Lobby and enjoy the marvelous display of Chang'e and her lost love.

October/November
Take a hike with your *tongzhimen*
1) The National Day holiday (Oct 1-7) is a fine time to visit one of the city's museums and reflect on the changes China has undergone since 1949.
2) On Chongjiu (or Double-Nine day, the ninth day of the ninth month of the lunar year), it's traditional to head to the hills. Gather up your fellow citizens for a hike, and don't forget to pack a thermos of chrysanthemum tea.

December
Eat yourselves warm
1) Things are chilly during the Winter Solstice, the shortest day of the year. Tradition has it that a meal of dumplings on Dongzhi day will keep your ears warm for the rest of the season.
2) Head out for hotpot: This warming meal is a favorite for families when the mercury drops. Try Ding Ding Xiang (p74) on a weekday evening.

KIDS

Child-Proof Restaurants

Beijing may pose child-rearing challenges, but bringing kids to local restaurants isn't one of them. Very few Maitre D's frown on young patrons, and Chinese restaurants are particularly welcoming. Thus, what follows is but a short list of parent-endorsed establishments that have play facilities for kids or have staff who, workload permitting, will be happy to lead your toddlers on a long tour of the restaurant, allowing you to enjoy your meal in peace. Bon appetit!

Agrilandia A farm, a rustic restaurant, an agri-tourism destination – Agrilandia is many things to many people. On a warm spring day, your kids will run around its green lawn, pet small furry creatures, go swimming and eat hearty Italian dishes made from locally grown ingredients. Dogs are also welcome.
Daily 9am-11pm. Baigezhuangcun, Mapozhen, Shunyi District. (6940 7650, 130 0127 1094) www.agrilandia.cn 意大利农场，顺义区马坡镇白各庄村

The American Cafe No-nonsense American-style diner serves up hearty burgers, pizza, sizeable salads and breakfast plates in a cozy environment next door to Evolution Fitness at Blue Castle Apartments. The small kids' corner makes it a good bet for CBD-area families.
Daily 7am-11pm. 1/F (behind Evolution Fitness), Blue Castle Apartments, 3 Xi Dawang Lu, Chaoyang District. (8599 7428/29) 博平咖啡，朝阳区西大望路3号蓝堡国际公寓所一层

American Steak & Eggs Affordable meals, from classic American diner breakfasts to fancier dinner specials. They have a kids' menu, books, toys and patience.
Mon-Fri 6.30am-midnight, Sat-Sun 5.30am-midnight. Xiushui Nanjie, Jianguomenwai (directly north of the Friendship Store, one traffic light west of Silk Market), Chaoyang District. (6592 8088/8788) www.steakeggs.com.cn 喜来中北美西餐，朝阳区建国门外秀水南街（友谊商店北面，秀水西边第一个红绿灯）

Annie's Serves trattoria favorites like antipasto, soups, pastas and pizza. Parents give the restaurant gold stars for its numerous high chairs, while kids enjoy making their own small pizzas and playing in the well-stocked toy corners.
1) *Daily 11.30am-11pm. Across from Western Academy Beijing, 5 Laiguangying Donglu, Chaoyang District. (8470 4768);* 2) *Daily 11am-11pm. Jiuxianqiao, Jiangtai Lu, Shangye Jie, Chaoyang District. (6436 3735);* 3) *Daily 11am-11pm. 16 Dongsanhuan Lu (next to CD Jazz Club), Chaoyang District. (6503 3871);* 4) *Daily 11am-11pm. A1 Nongzhan Nanlu (near the west gate of Chaoyang Park), Chaoyang District. (6591 1931);* 5) *Daily 11am-11pm. West of Soho New Town, 88, Jianguo Lu, Chaoyang District. (8589 8366)* 安妮，1）朝阳区来广营东路5号京西学校对面；2）朝阳区酒仙桥将台路商业街；3）朝阳区东三环路16号（农展馆正门南侧）；4）朝阳区农展南路甲1号（朝阳公园西门南侧）；5）朝阳区建国路88号Soho现代城

Biteapitta No forks required for the tasty and cheap Middle Eastern fare on offer at this bright, laid-back joint. The falafel sandwiches and small, seasoned breads are a good bet for kids of all ages, and the staff will whip out a highchair if needed.
Sun-Thu 10am-10pm, Fri-Sat 10am-11pm. 30 Tianze Lu (near Nuren Jie, turn at the Grape restaurant before the New Get Lucky Bar), Chaoyang District. (6467 2961) 朝阳区天泽路30号（女人街附近）

Brasserie Flo Superb, if pricey, French cuisine (the chateaubriand, in particular, is outstanding, and the wine list is good). This restaurant also has a pleasant playroom for children, complete with toys, arts-and-crafts, and, on weekends, an *ayi* keeping things real.
Daily 11am-11pm. Rainbow Plaza (Longbo Guangchang), 16 Dongsanhuan Lu (not far from Great Wall Hotel), Chaoyang District. (6595 5135/9) 北京福楼餐厅，朝阳区东三环北路16号隆博广场二层

Ding Ding Xiang You'd be nuts to bring a toddler to a hot pot joint, but Ding Ding Xiang's individual hot pots make it easy even for picky eaters to satisfy their own tastes. And who doesn't like playing with fire? Let the flames begin!
1) *Daily 11am-10pm. 1/F, 14 Dongzhong Jie, Dongzhimenwai, Dongcheng District. (6417 2546);* 2) *Daily 11am-10pm. Bldg 7, Guoxing Jiayuan, Shouti Nanlu, Haidian District. (8835 7775/7779);* 3) *Daily 11am-10pm. 2/F, Yuanjia International Apartments, Dongzhimenwai, Dongzhong Jie (opposite East Gate Plaza), Dongcheng District. (6417 9289)* 鼎鼎香，1）东城区东直门外东中街14号1层；2）海淀区首体南路国兴家园7号楼1-2层；3）东城区东直门外东中环广场对面元嘉国际公寓2层

Din Tai Fung The internationally renowned chain has a home in Beijing – taste just one hand-rolled dumpling and you'll know why they're famous around the world (and a big hit with the kids). Roll your own little dumplings into the newly opened playroom and let them veg out with a movie under an *ayi*'s watchful eye.
Mon-Fri 11.30am-2.30pm, 5-10pm; Sat-Sun 11.30am-10pm. 1) *24 Xinyuanxili Zhongjie, Chaoyang District. (6462 4502);* 2) *Mon-Fri 11.30am-9.30pm, Sat-Sun 11.30am-10pm. 6/F, Shin Kong Place, China Central Place, 87 Jianguo Lu, Chaoyang District. (6533 1536)* 鼎泰丰，1）朝阳区新源西里中街24号；2）朝阳区建国路87号华贸中心新光天地6层

Donghuamen Night Market Every evening, a block of Donghuamen is occupied by an army of food carts manned by cheerful chefs serving myriad Chinese snacks. Good fun can be had by filling your child's plate with some of the more exotic offerings (scorpions, deep-fried silk worms, sparrows on a stick) and telling them that unless they finish everything it's no TV for the rest of the month!
Donghuamen Dajie (west of Wangfujing's Sun Dong An Plaza, by the Forbidden City), Dongcheng District. 东华门夜市，东城区东华门大街（王府井新东安商场与故宫）

East Ocean Seafood Restaurant Upon arrival, the staff plies younger patrons with small stuffed animals and, at the meal's end, will take them on a tour of the voluminous, well-stocked fish tanks while mom and dad polish off some of Beijing's best dim sum.
Daily 11am-11pm. 39 Maizidian Jie, Chaoyang District. (6508 3482) 东海海鲜酒家，朝阳区麦子店街39号

Eudora Station Bar and Restaurant This Lido area spot gets points for quality and service, and its large verandah is a great place to park with the kids on a sunny day. There are two highchairs for especially wee ones.
Daily 9am-2am. 6 Fangyuan Xilu, Chaoyang District. (6437 8331) 朝阳区芳园西路6号

INSIDER'S GUIDE TO BEIJING

Rice and tea soup: more nutritious than mudpie

Exquisite Bakery Probably the only place in town where you can pick up everything you need for a Barbie or SpongeBob SquarePants birthday party, including the cake, of course. Some cake purchases even include a free bouncy castle rental. D-I-Y-ers will also find Beijing's most complete collection of cake baking supplies, including simple pie pans, latex cupcake forms and professional-grade icing guns with 100 different nozzles. If there's no birthday on the horizon, stop by just for the baked goods.
Daily 9am-7pm. Shop 7, Riverville Square, Tianzhu, Shunyi District. (6450 9838) 南炉，顺义区天竺温榆广场07店

Fish Nation Pizza, french fries and fried fish served with ketchup and tartar sauce – we can debate the nutritional benefits of the food served here – and to be fair they also have carrot sticks – but who would question their appeal to kids? With its comfortable couches and gorgeous rooftop deck, Fish Nation's Nanluogu Xiang outlet is an excellent dining option for families visiting Houhai.
1) Daily 9.30am-1.30am. 31 Nanluogu Xiang (near Jiaodaokou), Dongcheng District. (6401 3249); 2) Daily 11am-2am. Sanlitun Houjie (around the corner from Poachers Inn), Chaoyang District. (6415 0119) 鱼邦，1）东城区交道口南锣鼓巷31号；2）朝阳区三里屯后街（青年酒吧附近）

Fu Ku Serves Sichuan cuisine with a modern twist and such easy-to-sell dishes as mashed potatoes with gravy. The friendly staff and the presence of other broods make is a good option on the northwest bank of Houhai.
Daily 10.30am-10.30pm. 4A Binhe Hutong, Deshengmennei Dajie, Xicheng District. (6405 0706, 6402 4033) 福库，西城区德内大街滨河胡同甲4号

Grandma's Kitchen Sandwiches, gravy-based dinners and high-powered desserts from middle America. A critical mass of families, grandma's hospitality, and a stash of markers for budding artistes make it a safe bet for a weekend brunch with the kids.
1) Daily 7.30am-11.30pm. 11A Xiushui Nanjie, Jianguomenwai, Chaoyang District. (6503 2893); 2) Daily 7.30am-11pm. 0103, Bldg B, Jianwai Soho, 39 Dongsanhuan Zhonglu, Chaoyang District. (5869 3055/3056) 祖母的厨房，1）朝阳区建国门外秀水南街甲11号（友谊商店后面）；2）朝阳区东三环中路39号建外Soho B座0103

Gustomenta Enjoy homemade gelato in this stylish Italian cafe. Bring the kids and treat them to a heaped mound of frozen goodness on the patio on breezy evenings.
Daily 7am-midnight. 1) 24 Sanlitun Lu, Chaoyang District. (6417 8890); 2) 1301, Soho New Town, Chaoyang District. (8580 5111) 1）朝阳区三里屯路24楼东侧；2）朝阳区Soho现代城1301商铺

Helen Sun Bakery and Cake Shop In addition to its French pastries, cookies and pralines, the shop also bakes custom-made cakes in any flavor or shape imaginable (electric guitar perhaps?) and can top them with your kid's favorite cartoon character and some amazing icing art.
Daily 6am-9pm. 806 Pinnacle Plaza, Tianzhu Real Estate Development Zone, Shunyi District. (8046 1190) www.helensun.com.cn 阳光海伦蛋糕店，顺义区天竺开发区日祥广场806号

Horizon If your kids are like ours, their appetite for chashaobao (steamed bbq pork buns) is insatiable, so

KIDS 161

"I'm like omigod, like, totally ..." (after-school exchange at Lynx)

ordering them by the plate is a budget buster. This is why Horizon's all-you-can-eat dim sum buffet, which is free for kids under 6 and half-price for kids under 12, is a real deal. It even includes a big fruit bar and a toddler corner with plastic toys on weekends.
Daily 11.30am-2.30pm, 5.30-10pm. 1/F, Kerry Centre Hotel, 1 Guanghua Lu, Chaoyang District. (6561 8833 ext 41) 海天阁，朝阳区光华路1号嘉里中心饭店1层

Lau Pa Sak On weekdays, this Singaporean joint is packed with diplomats and professionals, but at lunch on weekends it's taken over by kid-toting *huaqiao* feasting on nasi goreng, curry puffs and Hainan chicken. Surprisingly, they serve a pretty satisfying hamburger. The forgiving staff are happy to let your kids check out the fish tank.
Daily 11am-11pm. Xindonglu (opposite the Canadian Embassy), Chaoyang District. (6417 0952) 老巴刹，朝阳区新东路加拿大使馆对面

Little Italy This Shunyi standby has come under new management who take your kids (and their lung capacities) very seriously – so seriously, in fact, that they've enclosed the children's play area in soundproof glass originally installed at the gorilla cages at the Beijing zoo! Now grownups can indulge in quiet conversation over pizza and salad while their cheeky monkeys shout and screech with abandon. The children's menu includes pasta, chicken nuggets and milkshakes served in colorful kid-sized dishes.
Daily 11.30am-10pm. 813 Pinnacle Plaza, Tianzhu Real Estate Development Zone, Shunyi District. (8046 4679) 小意大利，顺义区天竺开发区荣祥广场813号

Lynx A popular afterschool hangout near ISB, this comfortable and cozy cafe serves many kid-friendly choices (nachos, hamburgers, pizza) in a sunny environment. Catered birthday parties (in the small garden) can be organized if your apartment is too small (or clean!) to accommodate the young masses.

Mon-Thu 8am-7.30pm, Fri-Sun 8am-9pm. ISB east gate, Anhua Lu, Shunyi District. (8046 4755) 灵思餐厅，顺义区安华路北京顺义国际学校东门

The Mexican Kitchen Mexican food for Beijing's gringos, the smaller of which will be kept happy with the tasty treats on the kids' menu. The restaurant provides a convenient baby-changing table in its bathroom, and is also happy to host your kid's next birthday party.
Daily 11am-9pm. 705 Pinnacle Plaza, Tianzhu Real Estate Zone, Shunyi District. (8046 4558/59) 墨西哥厨房，顺义区天竺开发区荣祥广场705号

Mrs Shanen's Bagels Beijing's best bagels, as well as burgers, salads and an extensive breakfast menu. As if you needed an excuse to bring the kids, a large children's playroom is equipped with toys, kid-sized chairs and tables and an entire Chinese kitchen in miniature. Kids love to eat the gingerbread men, limb by limb.
Mon-Fri 7.30am-8pm, Sat-Sun 7.30am-8.30pm. 5 Kaifa Jie, Xi Baixinzhuang (next to Capital Paradise), Shunyi District. (8046 4301) 单太太贝谷面包房，顺义区西白辛庄开发街5号（紧邻名都园）

The Orchard Set on bucolic property, this elegantly renovated compound houses an upscale shop and a Continental restaurant. The Sunday buffet is popular with families since children can enjoy their own buffet while watching cartoons in comfy little armchairs. One caveat: kids should be discouraged from running wild in the garden or around the lake. Call for directions.
Tue-Sun noon-2.30pm (lunch, extended to 3pm on Sun), 2.30-6pm (coffee), 6-9pm (dinner). From Jingshun Lu, exit at Sunhe Market (we recommend calling for directions), Shunyi District. (6433 6270) 果园，顺义区路孙河市场出口（建议给餐馆打电话问详细地址）

OurLounge Haidian families can save their taxi money for another day. This newly opened family club and restaurant aims to be an all-in-one food and fun location

for kids and parents in the far-flung west. RMB 25/child buys access to the club and its play areas and activities, along with the opportunity to sit down and order a meal or snack from the extensive menu.
Daily 9.30am-midnight. 1/F, Bldg 3, Shidai Zhiguang Xiaoqu, 45 Xizhimen Beidajie, Haidian District. (6227 9800) www.ourlounge.com.cn 玩吧, 海淀区西直门北大街45号时代之光小区3号楼1层

Papa John's Featuring pizzas, pastas and salads at reasonable prices, Papa John's is exactly what you would expect from the American chain. Locations scattered around Beijing and a kid-friendly atmosphere make for a good destination for the family. Little Papa pizza-making course available for kids' parties, call your nearest store for details and to book an English speaking instructor.
1) Daily 11am-10pm. B1/F, Kerry Centre, 1 Guanghua Lu, Chaoyang District. (5165 9299); 2) Mon-Fri 11am-10pm, Sat-Sun 10.30am-10pm. 1/F, Fuli Cheng, Guangqu Menwai Lu, Chaoyang District. (5165 9733); 3) Daily 10.30am-10pm. Yansha Mall, 1 Yuanda Lu (near McDonald's), Haidian District. (5165 9939); 4) Daily 11am-10pm. Fl1 (North Side), Zi Changhe Plaza, 3 Suzhou Jie, Haidian District. (5165 9581) www.papajohnsbeijing.com 棒约翰, 1)朝阳区光华路1号嘉里中心地下1层西侧; 2)朝阳区广渠门外大街1号(双井桥西北侧); 富力城; 3)海淀区远大路一号金源时代购物中心后门附近(麦当劳相邻); 4)海淀区苏州街3号紫金长河大厦1层北侧

Peter's Tex-Mex Grill The mighty Lone Star State rises again! With a menu offering burritos, fajitas and enchiladas, this eatery pays tribute to Texas's enduring popularity. The portions are Texas-sized, but the kids will love it.
Daily 7.30am-11pm. 1) 88A International Club, 21 Jianguomenwai Dajie, Chaoyang District. (8532 2449); 2) Boutique 2, Hairun International Condominium, 2B Jiangtai Lu (southeast of Holiday Inn Lido Hotel), Chaoyang District. (5135 8187, 8627 3734) 彼德西餐, 1)建国门外大街21号国际俱乐部88A; 2)朝阳区将台路2号海润国际公寓2号建2号(丽都假日酒店东南角)

Piazza Cafe An airy space, relaxed atmosphere and a plethora of kids' chairs make for comfortable dining. The menu is enormous and includes mini pizzas for the munchkins.
Daily 11am-9.30pm. South gate of Capital Paradise, Shunyi District. (8046 7788/2020) 翰风餐厅, 顺义区民族园南门

Rumi This excellent Persian place – Beijing's only – has moved to stylish new digs in Sanlitun. The owners' 7-year-old helped design and outfit the small playroom. Let your kids judge her interior design choices while you chow down on the city's best hummus. Children can pick from the children's menu and park themselves in high chairs.
Daily noon-midnight. 1A Gongti Beilu (opposite Zhaolong Hotel to the east of 1001 Nights), Chaoyang District. (8454 3838) 入迷, 朝阳区工体北路1号兆龙饭店对面

Sculpting in Time A perfect spot to fuel up after romping on the nearby Fragrant Hills, Sculpting in Time's Xiangshan location serves yummy pizza, pasta, muffins and hot chocolate on its vast plant-filled patio that is home to lots of friendly cats. The restaurant also has board games, comic books and very kind staff.

Daily 9.30am-midnight. 50 Xiangshan Maimai Jie (in the Village at the foot of the Fragrant Hills), Haidian District. (8259 8296) 雕刻时光, 海淀区香山买卖街50号

Senses While ma and pa indulge in one of Beijing's most decadent champagne brunches, a talented clown, face painter, the ayi-supervised TV corner/play area and the kids' clubhouse entertains the young'uns. The spread is so extensive that even the most fickle of short diners will find something to chomp on – and boy will they drool before the dessert selection.
Daily 6am-midnight. 1/F, The Westin Beijing, 9B Jinrong Jie, Xicheng District. (6606 8866) 味, 西城区金融大街乙9号北京金融街威斯汀大酒店1层

Smallville This cafe invokes the name of that hallowed Midwestern town where Superman was raised on wholesome food and family values – two things Smallville offers in abundance. Young comic book fans will get a kick out of the jumbo comic book posters and dishes named "The Avenger" and "The Hulk." A kids' menu offers child-friendly versions of North American comfort food, but we bet the biggest lure will be the Oreo milkshake.
Daily 8am-8pm. 3 Kaifa Jie, Xi Baixinzhuang, Houshayu, Shunyi District. (8046 5448) 顺义区后沙峪西白辛庄开发街3号

TGI Friday's Yes, it's bedecked in "wacky" curios, but the youth (including teens from international schools) can't seem to get enough of this place. The booths provide great cover for naughty behavior, and the nattily attired wait staff bring placemats for the kiddies to color in. When all else fails, there's always the cathode ray ayi (i.e. the TV playing cartoons – at the Friendship Hotel location, at least). Burgers are good, but expensive.
1) Daily 11am-11.30pm. Beijing Friendship Hotel, 1 Zhongguancun Nandajie, Haidian District. (6849 8738); 2) Daily 11am-midnight. 9-2 Jinchengfang Jie, Xicheng District. (6622 0880); 3) Daily 11.30am-midnight. Bldg C, Beijing International Plaza, 19 Jianguomenwai Dajie, Chaoyang District. (8526 3388) 星期五餐厅, 1)海淀区中关村南大街1号北京友谊宾馆; 2)西城区金城坊街9-2号; 3)朝阳区建国门外大街19号国际大厦C座

Traktirr Pushkin Pick the right time (lunch, early dinner) and you'll understand why so many Russian families are loyal patrons. Who can argue with hearty portions of well-priced kid-friendly fare like chicken Kiev, steaks, pork schnitzel and mashed potatoes? Thanks to the heavy mayo application, even the salads make it down most kids' throats.
Daily 11am-midnight. 5-15 Dongzhimennei Dajie, Dongcheng District. (8407 8158, 6403 1896) 彼得堡, 东城区东直门内大街5-15号

Vincent Cafe/Creperie Madeleines are overrated; French children fill up on crepes. What's not to like about a thin pancake wrapped around a favorite filling? And get this: You can expose your kid to art in one of the neighboring galleries before or after your meal. How's that for a combo?
Daily 10am-10pm. 2 Jiuxianqiao Lu (beside China Art Seasons), Dashanzi Art District, Chaoyang District. (8456 4823) 北京季节咖啡店, 朝阳区酒仙桥路2号院内

Xiao Wang Fu Chinese homestyle is comfort food for your family, and this bustling place is great to initiate

the younger members of your crew into the tradition of delicious Beijing duck. While swankier, the Ritan Park venue is especially family friendly since the kids can, after excusing themselves from the table, run around outside while the mamas and the papas chat on the terrace. Steep prices.
1) Daily 11am-10.30pm. Building 2 Guanghua Lu Dongli, Chaoyang District. (6591 3255); 2) Daily 11am-2pm, 5-10pm. Inside the North Gate of Ritan Park, Ritan Lu, Chaoyang District. (8561 5985); 3) Daily 5pm-1am. 15 Qianhai Beiyan, Xicheng District. (6617 5558) 北京小王府，1）朝阳区光华路东里2号楼；2）朝阳区日坛路日坛公园北门内；3）西城区前海北沿15号

Xihe Yaju This pleasant compound is a fine place to enjoy an al fresco meal on a nice spring day. Parents love it because it has many highchairs, patient staff, and, since it attracts lots of families, children don't draw angry stares when they start screaming.
Daily 11am-2pm, 5-10pm. Northeast corner of Ritan Park, Chaoyang District. (8561 7643) 羲和雅居，朝阳区日坛公园东北角

Fun Places

In many respects, taking your kids out for public amusement in Beijing is less tension-fraught than it is elsewhere, due mainly to the fact that crime and violence against children are rare. For most of the facilities listed below, children's entrance rates are set by height rather than age, with those under 1.2m often allowed in for free. You can thus save a good deal of money by encouraging bad posture and forcing your children to walk barefoot.

A-Z Kids A cleaner, pricier version of Fundazzle, A-Z features a multitude of play equipment including a maze, an art corner, a play supermarket as well as bilingual staff and entertainers to ensure your kids are never bored. Best suited for kids ages 2-8, it also features a restaurant where parents can keep a watchful eye on their little ones. A-Z is nice on a rainy day, but the lack of visitors on a recent visit could spell trouble.
Daily 10am-9pm. 4/F, Shang Jie Plaza (corner of Chaoyang Lu and Qingnian Lu), Chaoyang District. (8559 2883) 英伦创意园，朝阳区青年路尚街4层

Badaling Wild Park Wolves, lions, tigers, bears and assorted other large animals roam (not quite) free here, but certainly with a great deal more liberty than you'll see elsewhere in China. Neither the carnivores nor the elements will threaten your well-being as you tour the park, as the animals can be seen and heard from the comfort of a vehicle (your own or one of the buses available at the park). RMB 70, RMB 45 (students), free (kids under 1.2m).
Daily 8am-5pm (summer), daily 9am-5pm (winter). South across the highway from Badaling Great Wall Center, Yanqing County. (6912 1842) www.bdlsw. com.cn 八达岭野生动物园，延庆县八达岭长城南

Beijing Amusement Park This underrated park is no Hong Kong Disneyland, but it's within the Second Ring Road and offers an abundance of thrills thanks to its looping roller coaster, water slide, giant Ferris wheel, 3-D cinema, E-motion cinema and go-carts. Your admission ticket provides access to all the rides except for the carting circuit. RMB 120, RMB 80 (kids 1.2-1.4m), free (kids under 1.2m). Go-carts RMB 25/2 laps.
Daily 9am-9pm. 19 Zuo'anmennei Dajie, Chongwen District. (6711 1155) www.bap.com.cn 北京游乐园，崇文区左安门内大街19号

Beijing Aquarium Modern, well equipped and recently restocked, the aquarium features thousands of freshwater and saltwater fish from around the world, including huge Amazonian arapaima, giant sturgeon and many sharks. The piece de resistance may be the enormous tank containing an entire coral reef – with sea turtles, manta rays and garoupa. There are also several Sea World-style shows every day, featuring seals and dolphins. RMB 100 (includes zoo), RMB 50 (kids, includes zoo), free (kids under 1.2m).
Daily 9am-5pm (Aug-May), 7am-10pm (Jun-Jul). 18B Gaoliangqiao Xiejie, Haidian District. (6217 6655) www.bj-sea.com 北京海洋馆，海淀区高粱桥斜街乙18号

Beijing Museum of Natural History The largest natural history museum in China has displays that are old hat, a bit scary, but educational nonetheless. Exhibits include animatronic dinosaurs, fossils, a rusting aquarium and an enormous taxidermy collection. The human anatomy display was evidently a little too traumatic and has now been banished to a separate building away from the dinosaur skeletons, fossils and stuffed animals. RMB 30, RMB 15 (students).
Tue-Sun 8.30am-5pm (last ticket 4pm). 126 Tianqiao Nandajie (near the west gate of Temple of Heaven), Chongwen District. (6702 4431, 6702 1155) www. bmnh.org.cn 北京自然博物馆，崇文区天桥南大街126号

Beijing Planetarium The once retro planetarium now boasts state of the art facilities, including the SGI Digital Universe Theater which takes patrons on a tour of the cosmos with six Carl Zeiss laser projectors that simulate the movement of stars and constellations. You can also travel through time in the 4-D theater, where you strap on a pair of goggles and watch a multidimensional film about the creation of the solar system and evolution of life on earth, replete with snarling T-Rexes and saber-toothed tigers. Where does the fourth dimension come from? We don't want to spoil the surprise but the experience terrified our three-year olds. Other draws include the 3D space shuttle simulator and a cool exhibit about the sun. GI Digital Universe Theater: RMB 45, RMB 35 (students); 4-D Theater: RMB 30, RMB 20 (students); 3D Space Shuttle Simulator: RMB 30, RMB 20 (students).
Wed-Fri 9.30am-3.30pm, Sat-Sun 9.30am-4pm. 138 Xizhimenwai Dajie, Xicheng District. (6835 2453, 6831 2517) www.bjp.org.cn 北京天文馆新馆，西城区西直门外大街138号

Beijing Zoo The conditions for the animals in the zoo and the behavior of some local patrons (who have been known to give chips and soda to the polar bears) will upset animal lovers. However, conditions are improving, as the new chimpanzee and panda houses testify, and most kids will be oblivious to the zoo's shortcomings and enjoy the vast collection of animals and the leafy compound, which was the former private garden of a Qing dynasty aristocrat. Apr-Oct: RMB 15, RMB 8 (students), Nov-Mar: RMB 10, RMB 5 (students), free (kids under 1.2m). RMB 5 for Panda House. RMB 100 combined zoo/aquarium ticket.
Daily 7.30am-5pm (winter), 7.30am-6pm (summer). 137 Baishiqiao Lu, Xizhimenwai Dajie, Haidian District.

Cheap fun: In local parks, the shorter you are, the lower the admission price

(6831 4411) www.bjzoo.com.cn 北京动物园，海淀区西外大街白石桥路137号

Blue Zoo Beijing Not to be confused with either the Beijing Aquarium or the Beijing Zoo, the Blue Zoo is actually an aquarium with an enormous coral reef tank containing eels, tuna, shark, stingrays and (we swear we're not making this up) the occasional underwater marriage ceremony. Sinoscuba (see sports p391) arranges scuba dives here for qualified divers aged 10 and up. RMB 75, RMB 50 (kids under 12 years old), free (kids under 1m).
Daily 8am-8pm (summer), daily 8.30am-6.30pm (winter). Workers' Stadium South Gate, Chaoyang District. (6591 3397) 富国海底世界，朝阳区工人体育场南门

Chaoyang Park Kitschy but fun. Kids can kick or throw a ball on the big grass field near the entrance, and the concrete podiums beyond are tree-free kite flying zones. There's lots of room to stroll, a range of boating options, a handsome merry-go-round and many rides including a roller coaster, flying dinosaurs, bumper cars, sky swings and several large inflatable castles. On top of all this, Sony ExploraScience has moved into the park. The outdoor pool is a great place to while away a summer afternoon and winters see a makeshift ski slope go up near the west gate – thrill seekers can rent skis and inter tubes onsite. The delightful northwestern section of the park includes a lake, flower beds and grassy expanses where families can enjoy a picnic. RMB 5, RMB 2.5 (students).
Daily 6.30am-9pm (winter), 6am-9.30pm (summer). 1 Nongzhan Nanlu, Chaoyang District. (6506 5409) 朝阳公园，朝阳区农展馆南路1号

China Puppet Theater The theater puts on shows every Saturday and Sunday at 10.30am. RMB 220/show.
1A Anhua Xili, Beisanhuan Lu, Chaoyang District. (6425 4798) www.puppetchina.com 中国木偶剧院，朝阳区北三环路安华西里甲1号

China Science and Technology Museum A hands-on oasis of educational fun. Featuring hands-on exhibits, robots, optical illusions, IMAX films (in Chinese only) and more, this museum is popular with school-age kids, but is not as cutting edge as the planetarium or ExploraScience. There's a vast, well-equipped indoor play area on the third and fourth floors of Building B, which can be mobbed by rugrats, so exercise common sense about when to visit. RMB 30, RMB 15 (students), free (kids under 1.2m); Building B: RMB 30, RMB 20 (students), free (kids under 1.2m).
Tue-Sun 9am-4.30pm, extended hours for special events (last ticket 3.30pm). 1 Beisanhuan Zhonglu (Beisanhuan at Anhua Qiao – look for the geodesic dome), Xicheng District. (6237 1177 ext 3216) www.cstm.org.cn 中国科技馆，西城区北三环中路1号

China Aviation Museum Asia's biggest aviation museum has over 200 different airplanes on display, over 1,000 types of aerial weapons including aerial bombs and missiles, plus radars, aerial cameras and rare aeronautical gifts the leaders received from foreign countries. RMB 50, RMB 25 (students), free (kids under 1.2m).
Daily 8am-5pm. Xiaotangshan (9km east of the Xiaotangshan Exit on the Badaling Expressway), Changping District. (6178 4882) 中国航空博物馆，昌平区小汤山镇西侧（八达岭高速公路小汤山出口东9公里）

PHOTO: COLIN PHILIPS

KIDS 165

"Oooh. I shouldn't have eaten that shuizhu yu ..." (tummy-churning fun at Happy Valley)

PHOTO: SIMON LIM

Chinese Military History Museum Tired of jungle gyms? Try tanks! Tykes can clamber over an array of sturdy metal military gear or take turns sitting on an anti-aircraft gun or in the pilot's seat of a combat aircraft (RMB 2). To board the Chinese 024 Missile-Equipped Boat (RMB 5) you don't even need to enter the museum – it's docked in the front courtyard. Parents and older kids can marvel at the socialist realist artwork. RMB 20, RMB 10 (students).
Daily 8am-5.30pm (Apr-Oct), 8am-5pm (Nov-Mar). 9 Fuxing Lu, Haidian District. (6686 6244) 中国军事博物馆，海淀区复兴路9号

Commune by The Great Wall Kempinski With a swimming pool, mini kitchen, meadow, TV room and arts and crafts center, the Commune of the Children at this nouveau kibbutz is all about play. If your kids aren't up to a serious hike, drop them off here to be entertained with storytelling, games, cooking, painting and more. RMB 290 (kids, full-day package), RMB 150 (kids, half-day package), RMB 240 (kids, family package), RMB 150 (adult, family package).
Daily 9am-5pm. The Shuiguan Great Wall exit on the Badaling Expressway, Yanqing County. (8118 1888 ext 5706) 长城脚下的公社，延庆县北京市八达岭高速路水关长城出口

Crab Island It's no Ibiza, but it's closer than Qingdao and the substantial fake beach boasts real, well-maintained sand and comes dotted with free sun umbrellas and chairs. When the wave pool gets turned on, families charge into the huge pool – the docile waves are best enjoyed while perched on an inner tube (RMB 10, RMB 50 deposit). When your kids get tired of the wave pool there are two sets of waterslides, an extremely lazy river, and a human-powered waterwheel that dumps buckets of water on eager heads. A shallow water play area draws in families with little kids. All in all, a pretty good day at the "beach."
Daily 8am-1am. 1 Xiedao Lu (take the Weigou exit off the Airport Expressway and follow the signs), Chaoyang District. (8433 5566/5588) www.xiedao.com 蟹岛绿色生态度假村，朝阳区蟹岛路1号

Ditan Park When it's not being used as an exhibition space, the park's centenarian cypresses provide nice shade in summer, making it a pleasant destination for an urban picnic. The children's activities are concentrated in the north end and include a go-cart track, bouncy castle, merry-go-round and abrasively loud electronic games. There's also a fishing stream with magnetic fish for toddlers and a goldfish pond. Note that the Ditan Ice Arena is just east of the park's north gate. If they aren't claustrophobic, bring your troops to Ditan during the wonderful Spring Festival fair. The area outside the south gate is popular with kite masters. RMB 2, RMB 1 (students).
Daily 6am-9.30pm. A2, Andingmenwai Dajie, Dongcheng District. (6421 4657) 地坛公园，东城区安定门外大街甲2号

Fundazzle Fundazzle makes young kids squeal with delight, while it makes their parents wince (because it smells of feet), then gasp (at the size of the plastic-ball-filled pool) and finally sigh (as they realize that for a few precious hours, the furniture in their home is safe). This cavernous, indoor playground has a huge two-story jungle gym, trampolines and a toddler area with small cars, swings, seesaws, toy houses and so on. On weekends, counselors put on shows, lead the kids in song and dance, and teach arts and crafts. RMB 30 (kids), adults free, except on weekends when entry costs RMB 15.
Mon-Fri 9am-5.30pm, Sat-Sun and public holidays 9am-7pm. Gongti Nanlu, Chaoyang District. (6593 6208) 翻斗乐，朝阳区工体南路

Goose 'n' Duck Ranch Easy to visit, the "ranch" is unevenly maintained but hyperactively landscaped and is better suited for younger kids than teens. Activities include swimming, archery, horseback riding, fishing, soccer, basketball, badminton, softball and paintball. You can stay for a day or spend the entire weekend in one of the cabins. Shuttle buses depart from Goose 'n' Duck Pub. Single day packages (RMB 200, RMB 100 kids 4-12) include food, beverages and round-trip transportation; two-day packages (RMB 500, RMB 250 kids ages 4-12) include the above plus accommodation. Reservations are required.
Huairou Beizhai, Huairou District. (6067 1097) www.gdclub.net.cn 鹅和鸭，怀柔区北寨

Gymboree Beijing Gymboree offers music, play and art classes in English. Held in a clean, cheery room painted with primary colors, the music class offers kids a chance to play instruments, sing songs, and try out a Mr. Microphone contraption to practice saying basic words. After class, participants are welcome to play on the extensive gym equipment in the room where the play class is held. The play class emphasizes concepts like in and out, and up and down. In the rock and roll class, kids practice rolling balls and rocking the gym equipment back and forth. Classes are in English and all children must be accompanied by an adult. RMB 3,120/12 classes or RMB 14,976/96 classes.
Daily 9am-6pm. 1) Rm 2, 1/F, Lead International Building, 2 Wangjing Zhonghuan Nanlu, Chaoyang District. (5166 0516); 2) 5/F, Bldg B, Jianwai Soho 39 Dongsanhuan Zhonglu, Chaoyang District. (5869 4087) 金宝贝，1) 朝阳区望京中环南路甲2号佳境天城一层02号；2) 朝阳区东三环中路39号建外Soho B座5层

Haidian Park If you're not feeling imperial, this large park just south of the Summer Palace is a good bet. It's stocked with a lake, a fishing canal, a large kite-flying field, and a modest kids' amusement area with two moonwalks, a trampoline, an inflatable climbing wall, a labyrinth, and more. RMB 2.
Daily 8am- 9.30pm. 2 Xinjiangongmen Lu, Haidian District. (6285 0282) www.haidianpark.com 海淀公园，海淀区新建宫门路2号

Happy Land Arts and Crafts Center Let your children discover their inner Picasso. Happy Land offers pottery, painting, paper folding, jewelry making and much more. Kids and parents love this spot, especially in the dead of winter. The staff is patient, knowledgeable and able to speak functional English. Birthday parties can also be arranged. RMB 50/hr, RMB 60/hr for home tutoring.
Daily 9am-5pm (winter), 9am-6pm (summer). Xibaixinzhuang (near Capital Paradise), Houshayu, Shunyi District. (8046 4055, 136 6104 5892) 乐土工艺坊，顺义区后沙峪白辛庄村东（名都园的附近）

Happy Valley Amusement Park Beijing's best amusement park sprawls out across a square kilometer of land outside the East Fourth Ring Road and offers 40 rides, an IMAX theater, more than 100 games and seven cinemas. The park is divided into a number of themed areas inspired by such civilizations as Mayan Central America, Minoan Greece and Shangri-la – the little kid-

KIDS

dies play in Ant Kingdom. The roller coasters are world class, the park is well maintained, and the lines for rides are fairly reasonable. RMB 160, RMB 80 (kids 1.2-1.4m), free (kids under 1.2m).
Mon-Fri 9am-7.30pm, Sat-Sun 8.30am-7.30pm. Wuji Beilu, Dongsihuan Lu, Chaoyang District. (6738 9898 ext 0, 6205 0088) http://bj.happyvalley.com.cn/park/ 北京欢乐谷，朝阳区东四环路小武基北路

Honglingjin Park Has ample indoor and outdoor playgrounds, several rides, boats, a duck feeding area, and a popular mini-car driving course. Also look out for the much-coveted adult-sized swings strewn around the grounds. Free.
Daily 6.30am-9pm (winter), 6am-9.30pm (summer). 5 Houbalizhuang (on Dongsihuan Lu, East of Honglingjin Bridge), Chaoyang District. (8581 9548) 红领巾公园，朝阳区后八里庄5号（东四环路红领巾桥东）

Houhai Okay, so it isn't a park. And we've taken the liberty of referring to two lakes (Qianhai and Houhai) with the name of the latter. These provisos aside, Houhai merits inclusion because of its family-friendly atmosphere, especially in winter, when the frozen lake looks like a scene by some modern-day Brueghel, with families and couples skating, playing ice hockey, and jubilantly riding on ice chairs and other phantasmagoric contraptions. There's an old school amusement area with trampolines, electric cars and a dragon train on the southwest bank near Kong Yiji.
Dianmenwai Dajie (aka Ping'an Dadao), across from the north gate of Beihai Park, Xicheng District. 后海地区，西城区地安门外大街（北海公园北门对面）

Kids' Gallery Kids' Gallery after-school "interest classes" for 5- to 12-year-olds include speech and drama, Chinese painting, Chinese sketching, art, French and creative writing classes. Prices range from RMB 65-125.
Mon-Fri 9am-6pm, Sat 9am-noon. 2/F, Capital Paradise Clubhouse, Baixinzhuang, Houshayu, Shunyi District. (8046 1454) www.kidsgallery.com 儿童艺廊，顺义区后沙峪白辛庄村名都园会所2楼

KindyROO International Early Childhood Development Centre KindyROO offers music, dance and play classes designed to encourage spatial awareness, balance and coordination. Its facilities are clean and bright but nowhere near as grand as Gymboree's and this is reflected in the price. Most of the instructors go through a corporate training program to learn the organization's teaching philosophy, and they speak English. Free trial class. RMB 2,400 (12 sessions), RMB 3,600 (24 sessions), RMB 6,024 (36 sessions), RMB 9,400 (96 sessions).
1) 8.30am-5.30pm. Inside the Drive-in Cinema (1500m east of Yansha Qiao), Chaoyang District. (8457 4793, bj1@kindyroo.com); 2) 9.30am-6.30pm. B17 Huating Jiayuan, East of Jianxiang Qiao on North Fourth Ring Road, Chaoyang District. (5166 8078, bj1@kindyroo.com) www.kindyroo.com 菁童启育咨询中心，1）朝阳区汽车电影院内（燕莎桥往东1500米）；2）朝阳区北四环健翔桥东华亭家园B17

Kishow Kids Club Children can sign up for the Mad Science course and learn how to make water rockets or build marshmallow molecules. Also hosts birthday parties in the wacky experiment room complete with real scientists (well, science majors) in white coats and

lots of bubbling beakers. Non-scientists can sign up for classes in Chinese calligraphy, Chinese traditional painting, pottery, drama and other subjects. Bilingual staff, though the majority of classes are taught in Mandarin. Suitable for children between 4 and 12 years old. RMB 4,500 (four-month membership or 40 hours), RMB 7,000 (nine-month membership or 80 hours), RMB 12,000 (18-month membership or 160 hours).
1) Mon-Sat 8.30am-6pm, Sun 8am-6pm. 2/F, Yulin Plaza Building, 5 Xiangjunnali (west of the Jingguang Building), Chaoyang District. (5131 1001 ext 17); 2) Fri 4-8pm, Sat-Sun 8am-9pm. Stall 4024-4028, 4/F, Jinyuan Xinyansha Mall, 1 Yuandalu, Haidian District. (8886 1300) 疯狂家族，1）朝阳区向军南里5号雨霖大厦2层（京广大厦西）；2）海淀区远大路1号金源新燕莎大厦4层4024—4028商铺

Liuyin Park Liuyin is one of Beijing's most picturesque parks, with a duck- and lotus-filled lake surrounded by reeds, weeping willows and pavilions. Kids will prefer the play area with the usual kit (electric cars, trampoline, arts & crafts stand, playground with Little Tikes gear, shoot-the-duck-with-water-cannons arcade game) as well as bumper cars and paddleboats. Visit the charming outdoor tea garden on the island, which serves beer, soft drinks and snacks as well as tea. RMB 1.
Daily 6am-9pm. Jiangzhaikou, Andingmenwai, Dongcheng District. (8411 3699) 柳荫公园，东城区安定门外蒋宅口

Longtanhu Park The park boasts a popular outdoor playground with many slides and swings, as well as a trampoline, an indoor playground and several rides including hovercraft-type bumper cars. There's a roller skating area on the island, lots of gym equipment, badminton courts and boats in which you can explore the lake. Older kids may enjoy the climbing wall in the park's southwest corner. Other things to discover include an old MiG fighter jet. Fun to visit during Chinese New Year, when the park becomes a giant fairground. RMB 2 for park entry, additional fees for rides.
Daily 6am-9pm. 8 Longtanhu Lu, Chongwen District. (6714 4336) 龙潭湖公园，崇文区龙潭湖路8号

Merry Water World Itching for a dip? This indoor pool emporium located in the Tulip Hot Spring Garden Resort allows for year-round swimming fun. Adventurous swimmers will rush for one of the six tall waterslides, while the less energetic family members can stick to the lazy river. There's also a large wave pool, a children's area, a lap pool and several hot tubs. Weekdays: RMB 98, RMB 60 (kids under 1.4m), free (kids under 1.1m). Weekends: RMB 138, RMB 60 (kids under 1.4m), free (kids under 1.1m).
Daily 9.30am-10.30pm. Jinzhan, Dongweilu (Take the Airport Expressway to the Weigou exit. Turn left at the first stoplight, right at the second, and then go straight.), Chaoyang District. (8433 0606 ext 5104) www.yujinxiang.com.cn 郁金香花园，朝阳区东苇路金盏

New China Children's Store Features various play possibilities with prices varying according to the activity. RMB 10 for 20 minutes with the goldfish, but they look a little depressed. Give them a miss in favor of the huge sandpit (RMB 20) – bigger than your living room.
Sun-Thu 9am-9.30pm, Fri-Sat 9am-10pm. 168 Wangfujing Street, Dongcheng District. (6528 1774) 新中国儿童用品商店，东城区王府井大街168号

A budding engineer creates shadow animals at Sony ExploraScience

New Trend Rollerskating World Groovy, cheap fun that may remind parents of the halcyon days of the 1970s. Rental sizes start at 35 so smaller kids should bring their own skates. At night, the dancers come out in force and the indoor rink is then more appropriate for teens than young kids. Don't worry: the foot smell evaporates as you start to have fun. RMB 10 (10am-5pm), RMB 15 (5pm-midnight). No time limit.
Daily 10am-midnight. 54 Zhongguancun Nanlu, Haidian District. (6218 4225) 新潮流滚轴溜冰大世界．海淀区中关村南路54号

OurLounge Haidian gets a welcome dose of family fun with this newly opened family club that boasts a well-stocked kiddies corner, pingpong and pool tables, a library and even a squash court. English and Chinese story times are held daily; weekends are for puppet shows. There's also an onsite restaurant in case you work up a post-play appetite. RMB 10/hr, RMB 30/day (weekdays); RMB 20/hr, RMB 50/day (weekends), 12% discount for members.
Daily 10am-midnight. Bldg 3, Shidai Zhiguang Xiaoqu, 45 Xizhimen Beidajie, Haidian District. (6227 9800, welcome@ourlounge.com.cn) www.ourlounge.com.cn 玩吧．海淀区西直门北大街45号时代之光小区3号楼1层

Playground The brainchild of two Beijing parents who wanted a fun space where working parents could bring their children, Playground has an inbuilt fishpond, a library, and an open area that doubles as a mini basketball court. The real draw of Playground is its hands-on science, art and computer courses for children ages 4-12. Entrance free, drop-off service: RMB 50/hr. Courses: RMB 400/4 hour-long sessions.
Mon-Fri noon-8pm, Sat-Sun 10am-8pm. 40 Dongsi Liutiao (between Pingan Dajie and Chaoyangmennei Dajie), Dongcheng District. (6407 6889) www.myplayground.cn 东城区东四六条40号（平安大道朝内大街之间）

Qingnianhu Park This pleasant park contains a hard-top basketball court, a croquet area, electric boats, paddleboats and an amusement zone with a trampoline, cheesy rides and bumper cars. Your budding Tiger Woods might enjoy the split-level golf driving range. If you're not deterred by the "Station for Red Eye Disease Testing" at the entrance to Water World, you'll find a huge pool filled with families in floaties, with a couple of waterslides. Park entrance: RMB 1.
Park: Daily 6am-10pm (summer), 6am-9pm (winter). Andingmenwai Dajie, Dongcheng District. (8411 6321; Beijing Youth Lake Intl. Golf Club: 8411 6911; Water World: 8411 6321 ext 8032) 青年湖公园．东城区安定门外大街

Ritan Park The CBD's "lungs," Ritan Park packs a surprising amount of child-friendly stuff into a limited space: the playground area includes an inflatable playhouse, large trampolines, a mechanical bull, a merry-go-round with Technicolor unicorns and an infrequently washed indoor playhouse. Other attractions include the fishing pond, climbing wall and mini-golf – the latter attracts few customers, so don't worry about triple-bogeying each hole. The altar is a great place to watch weathered gentlemen fly kites. If you need a snack, Schindler's Filling Station, the Stone Boat Bar and Xiheyaju all have terraces opening onto the park.
Daily 6am-9pm (summer), daily 6.30am-8pm (winter). 6 Ritan Beilu, Chaoyang District. (8561 6301) 日坛公园．朝阳区日坛北路6号

The School House at Mutianyu This renovated elementary school proves there is more to Mutianyu than just

the Great Wall. Located 90mins northeast of Beijing (via Jingcheng expressway) and offering a restaurant with fresh local ingredients, art glass studio and art room and is a creative way for the family to escape the city.
Thu-Tue 10am-6pm. Mutianyu Village (for detailed directions see website), Huairou District. (6162 6506) www.theschoolhouseatmutianyu.com 慕田峪小园餐厅，怀柔区慕田峪（具体路线请查看网站信息）

Shijingshan Amusement Park Accessible by subway, this large amusement park features a water slide, roller coaster, paintball area, water park for younger kids, racecar circuit, bumper cars and bumper boats. Heck, you can even experience the joys of international travel thanks to the park's Gothic Cinderella Castle (which owes absolutely nothing to Disney), Arab-style restaurant and European-style blue bridge. RMB 10 per ride, RMB 5 per ride (kids), RMB 100/all access ticket.
Daily 9am-4.30pm (winter), 8.30am-6pm (summer). 25 Shijingshan Lu, Shijingshan District. (6886 2547) www.bs-amusement-park.com 石景山游乐园，石景山区石景山路25号

Side Park This Lido-area park boasts plenty that will keep the young'uns amused, including an inflated castle, indoor funhouse, outdoor playground, merry-go-round, football pitches, a rollerblading rink, and fishing pond. A circular walking track is popular with morning walkers – if you can get the crew out the door early enough, have fun watching the tai chi practitioners. Free.
Daily 6am-9pm. Jiangtai xilu, Chaoyang District. (6438 6093) 四得公园，朝阳区将台西路

Sony ExploraScience The most technologically sophisticated museum in the city has a range of interactive displays appealing to kids of all ages, including musical sculptures, sound and light distortion machines, soap bubble rings and much more. The staff offer fun hands-on demonstrations and host live science shows in Chinese and English. Makes for great fun on a cold or wet day. RMB 30, RMB 20 (students), free (kids under 1.2m) – buy your tickets at the museum booth outside the park's south or east gates and you won't have to purchase park entry tickets.
Mon-Fri 9.30am-6pm, Sat-Sun 9.30am-7.30pm, closed on second Mon and Tue of each month. Inside Chaoyang Park (near the south gate), Chaoyang District. (6501 8800) www.explorascience.com.cn 索尼探梦，朝阳区朝阳公园里（南门）

Splash Recreation Club Boasts a large outdoor/indoor pool, a sand volleyball court, a playground, a gym, pingpong tables, a poolside bar and restaurant. The hotel also has squash and tennis courts as well as a sauna. RMB 100, RMB 50 (children), free (children under 4).
Daily 6am-10pm. Sino-Swiss Hotel, 9 Xiao Tianzhu Nanlu, Shunyi District. (6456 5588 ext 1217) www.sino-swisshotel.com 浪花俱乐部，顺义区小天竺南路9号国都大饭店

Summer Palace and Ruins of Yuanmingyuan Park (Old Summer Palace) The crowds that cluster predictably around the buildings and ruins in these two imperial abodes may dissuade you from visiting with the kids, especially on a spring day in cherry blossom season. The key to a happy family outing is to explore the little known corners in these vast parks: Walk around the far lakes, rent a boat and then sit in the shade of a weeping willow and enjoy a picnic. For addresses and times see Sightseeing p234 and p237.

Taoranting Park Why schlep the kids all the way down to Taoranting? Here are six reasons: 1) Its intelligently designed, clean playground, with padding on the ground, tall covered slides, swings, trampolines and more; 2) Water Land, an enormous water park; 3) Peacock Park, a weird, Yunnan-themed retreat with Dai-style buildings, the eponymous birds, monkeys and rabbits; 4) The symphony of colors that is the rose garden; 5) Car-shaped paddleboats; 6) Priceless signage: "No hunting animals in park," "Transparent swimming suits are not allowed," "Those swimming while drunk will be fined RMB 10-50." RMB 2, RMB 1 (students).
Daily 6am-9pm. 19 Taiping Jie (near National Ballet of China), Xuanwu District. (6353 2385) 陶然亭公园，宣武区太平街19号

Tiantan Park Although Tiantan has no rides, it offers ample room to run around, throw a frisbee and get away from the crowds. The rose garden is worth a look when in season. And there's superior people-watching to be had in the covered galleries east of the Altar of Heaven. Get a kick out of visiting the park at dawn, when practitioners of arcane and mystifying forms of exercise come out in force. Combine a stroll through Tiantan with a visit to the Beijing Museum of Natural History. For Tiantan address, see Temple of Heaven p240.

Tuanjiehu Park Did you know that there's a beach with a wave pool less than 15-minutes walking distance from Pacific Century Place? Tuanjiehu is home to downtown Beijing's best and most hygiene conscious water park, which is great fun on summer weekdays – less so on weekends when it teems with masses seeking relief from the heat. Tuanjiehu also features a roller-skating park, several rides and boats. Budding ornithologists may enjoy the pigeon house. Beach: RMB 20, RMB 15 (kids). Pleasure boats: RMB 30-40/hr, RMB 50-100 (deposit). Roller-skating: RMB 5 (entrance), RMB 10 (skate rental).
Daily 6.30am-9pm. 16 Tuanjiehu Nanli, Chaoyang District. (8597 3603) 团结湖公园，朝阳区团结湖南里16号

Wanfangting Park Wanfangting Park boasts the only equestrian club (with over 50 horses) inside the Third Ring Road (albeit the South Third Ring) as well as a huge water park, an air castle and a trampoline area. RMB 1 (entrance ticket), separate fee for each ride. Equestrian Club: RMB 120/hr (horse rental), RMB 50/hr (tutor), RMB 12,000 (membership conferring unlimited usage).
Daily 6am-9pm. A2, Yangqiao Xili, You'anmenwai, Fengtai District. (6721 5333); Equestrian Club: Daily 9am-6.30pm. (6722 7339) 万芳亭公园，丰台区右安门外洋桥西里2号

World Park 100 shrunken versions of world famous landmarks and attractions. Visit 50 countries, all just a 30-minute drive from downtown. RMB 65, RMB 35 (students), free (kids under 1.2m).
Daily 8am-6pm. 158 Fengbao Lu, Huaxiang, Fengtai District. (8361 3344) 世界公园，丰台区花乡丰葆路158号

Yuyuantan Park Enormous Yuyuantan Park attracts families and student groups on full-day outings. They bring tents, hammocks and blow-up mattresses and kick back with sausages, tea, eggs and sunflower seeds. Kids ride bikes, blow soap bubbles (check out the Toucan Sam-shaped bubble "guns") and fill the two large, well-stocked playgrounds. There's plenty of room here to fly kites, and a big aquatic park with many slides and

Beijing's park oases: Savor the springtime of youth

an area for younger children. You can catch the boat to the Summer Palace near the park's south gate. In winter, it's a fine place to skate and ride ice chairs. RMB 2, RMB 1 (students).
Daily 6.30am-9.30pm (summer), daily 6.30am-8.30pm (winter). Xisanhuan Lu, across from CCTV Tower, Haidian District. East entrance on Sanlihe Lu (just south of Diaoyutai), south entrance (with parking lot) behind China Millenium Monument, Haidian District. (8865 3804/6) 玉渊潭公园，海淀区西三环中央电视塔对面（东门在三里河路，南门在世纪坛后面）

Zhongshan Park Elegantly formal, with a Sun Yat-Sen statue, rockery, ancient cypresses, bamboo groves, cherry trees and covered walkways, Zhongshan Park offers a poetic escape from the crowds in Tian'anmen Square. Take in some of Beijing's best views by renting a boat and paddling along the Forbidden City's moat. If old buildings leave your offspring cold, there's always the bumper cars (festooned with the Statue of Liberty) and Merry Land, the park's indoor playground, with its sea of balls, slides and funny mirrors. Entrance: RMB 3, RMB 1.5 (students), free (kids under 1.2m).
Daily 6.30am-8pm (winter), 6am-9pm (summer). Carnio of Children: 8.30am-5pm. West of Tian'anmen Gate, Dongcheng District. (6605 5431 ext 270) 中山公园，东城区天安门西侧

Zizhuyuan Park Purple Bamboo Park in Haidian District has a network of lakes and canals to explore by boat or ice chair, as well as a spacious playground with a sea of balls, slides, rocking horses and more. You could make it an enriching educational day by asking your children to pick out the ten-plus different species of bamboo found on site. Free.
Daily 6am-8pm (winter), 6am-9pm (summer). 45 Baishiqiao Lu, Haidian District. (6842 5851) 紫竹院公园，海淀区白石桥路45号

KIDS

Duck and Cover
What (not) to do in an emergency
by Roy Kesey

"Keep cool, Daddy-o"

Every parent knows the importance of making one's house safe for young children – outlets filled, door-handles baffled, knife-drawers rigged, DVD players toast-proofed – but it's the kind of activity that is easily postponed in the rush of work, school and other day-to-day activities. And every parent knows the importance of keeping emergency medical information close to hand, but that safe place you chose, where was it exactly? On top of the refrigerator? Taped to the back cover of your appointment book? Inside the knife-drawer you can no longer open?

Please take the time to childproof your house and organize your medical information today, because believe me, if you don't, tomorrow (which will be a Sunday, it's always a Sunday, and most likely at six o'clock in the morning) your child will be practicing gymnastics in the living room, and will double-flip-half-twist-triple-salchow into the corner of the coffee table. He or she will neatly open his or her left eyebrow. Now two of your walls will be more sort of burgundy than the handsome off-white they used to be.

(Insert your favorite non-child-appropriate word here)

And that exact moment, with your child screaming and your spouse screaming and you screaming at everyone to stop screaming, is not a good moment to be fiddling around trying to find the business card with the name and address of the hospital you decided on months ago when you first arrived here. By now there will be blood all over you and your child and your spouse and your floor, so instead of continuing the search you will head out, and despite your best efforts at remembering the four tones, the cabbie will not quite understand what you're trying to say, but that doesn't matter, because of course you know how to get to the hospital, right?

Well, under normal circumstances you do, but now, with all the blood and screaming and whatnot, what happens if you accidentally miss a turn? And end up, say, on the (insert your favorite non-child-appropriate word here) Second Ring Road? Say, going the wrong direction? And by the time you get off it, you're in the middle a swarm of hutongs you've never seen before, and now you have no idea which direction to go, and of course you have your cell phone and could just call someone like you should have done in the first place, except you forgot to check it before you left and now you see that the (insert that word again) battery is dead?

Not that I have any personal experience with any of this, of course. I'm just saying, what if?

Well, chances are that by now it will be clear that your child is not going to bleed out, though his or her modeling career is pretty much doomed. At some point you will start to recognize landmarks, and sooner or later you will somehow arrive at the emergency bay of the hospital, where you will see one very pregnant woman and one man with an eye-patch. Ten minutes after that, the doctor will have found the right office key, and the good news is, your child doesn't even need stitches, just tangerine-colored disinfectant, and a couple of butterfly bandages, and gauze, and tape, and a lollipop. So you'll take care of business, and now everything's cool so you'll all take a walk around, and your child, with his or her huge bulge of eyebrow gauze, will be a big hit with everyone, and people will take his or her picture as he or she stands with his or her feet in that sort of sidewalk sculpture consisting of huge bronze shoes.

So everything will work out.

But what about next time?

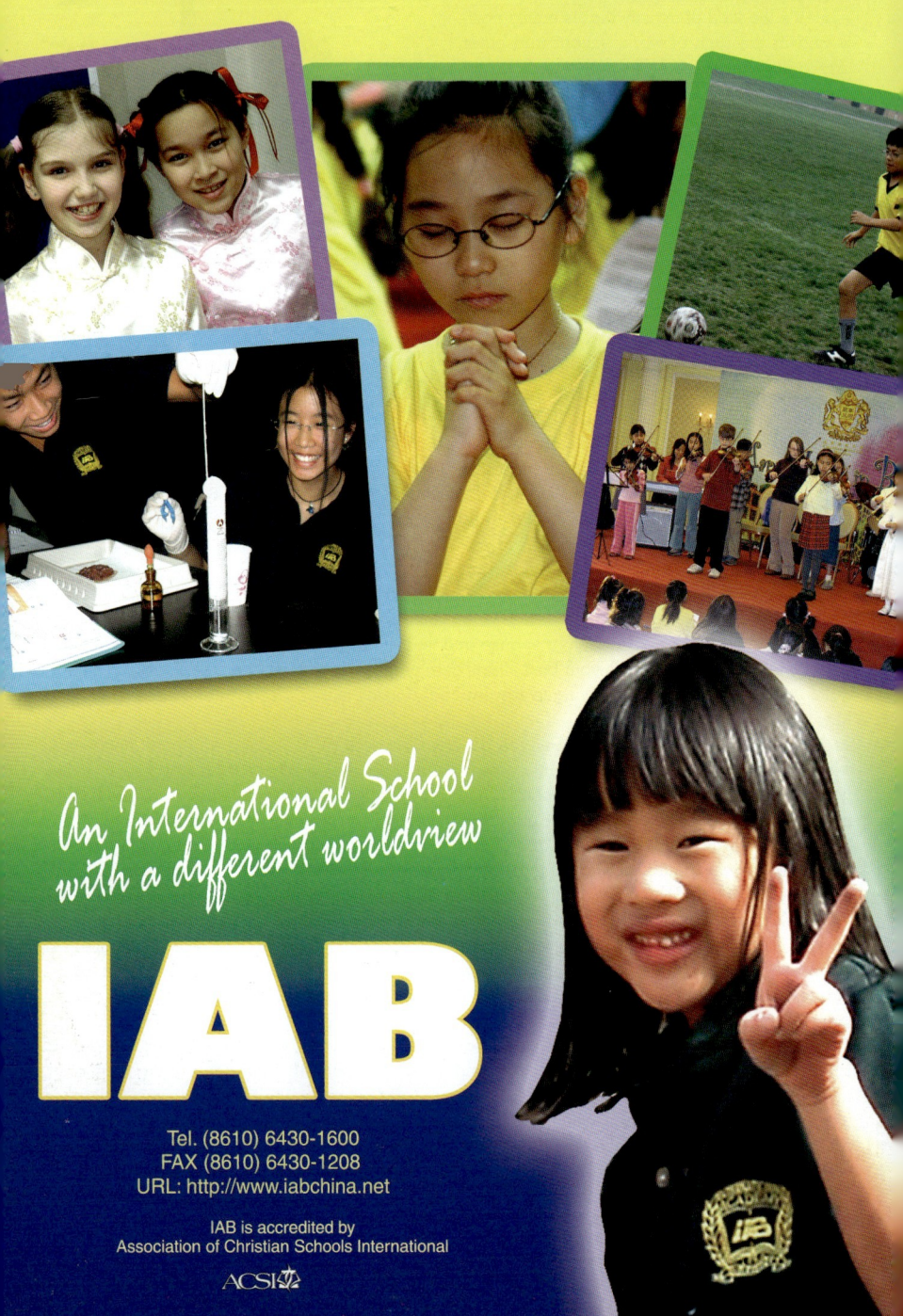

ART & CULTURE

Immersion Guides

One year before the Beijing Olympics begin ...

One year before the biggest debut party the world has ever seen. *One Night in Beijing.*

Capturing the heartbeat of a city and its people, **One Night in Beijing** presents a portrait of the capital from dusk to dawn on a historic night. With 200 pages of dramatic photographs by 30 photographers, covering every inch of the city from the official party in Tian'anmen Square to breakfast in a Buddhist nunnery, this lavish book is a remarkable document of China's capital in anticipation.

For more information about *One Night in Beijing* and the Immersion Guides line, please visit our website at www.immersionguides.com

One Night in Beijing
Fall 2007

Happenings at the Hub
The arts in Beijing in 2007 and beyond
by Michael Hatch and Reid Barrett

If 2006 was the year contemporary Chinese art exploded onto the international scene, 2007 was the year it proved it could hold its own. Chinese modern and contemporary art is setting auction house records in Beijing and Hong Kong, with Chinese buyers ready and willing to compete with foreigners for the choicest works. Despite talk of a massively overvalued contemporary art market, prices steadily increase, supporting both a large range of talented (and mediocre) artists as well as a young emerging generation.

Diversified gallery zones expanded their presence as well. Aside from the 798 district, capital art aficionados have been flocking to alternative areas such as the Liquor Factory (Jiuchang), Caochangdi, Songzhuang and East End Arts District (see Art Hoods, p189).

The year 2007 also brought the best of classic international masterpieces to the capital. Traveling shows from the National Museum of India, the Prado Museum in Spain, and a combined collection of more than 50 American museums, including the Guggenheim, signaled the focus of an international arts eye on the Chinese capital as well as the power of art as a cultural ambassador.

But not every field of art is as fertile as the visual arts. Contemporary theater continues to be relatively quiet despite the injection of

Jue-Aware *by Beijing Modern Dance Company*

talented international touring shows such as *Mamma Mia* and Broadway Asia Theater Group's *putonghua* adaptations of overseas hits, such as *I Love You, You're Perfect, Now Change*.

In cinema as well, the big shots Zhang Yimou, Feng Xiaogang and Chen Kaige are still smarting from last year's disappointing reception of their big-budget historical dramas *Curse of the Golden Flower*, *The Banquet* and *The Promise*. But this has pushed them in new directions, with some hoping to delve into innovative genres and others looking to return to the art house cinema that launched their careers and made Chinese directors regulars on the international film festival scene (See A Journey of Moon and Clouds p217).

In classical music and modern dance, Beijing is finally reaping the rewards of the state planning that established the leading schools and best conservatories here in the capital. With continuing modernization, internationalization and privatization of orchestras and dance studios, innovation has flowered and performances are becoming more audience-oriented (See Classical Music and Dancing Outside the Lines, pages 207 and 215).

In recent years Beijing has indeed become an international arts hub as both a prolific producer and a consumer of international exhibits and shows. Yes, it's a great time to see art in Beijing. But don't just take our word for it – get out there and see for yourself.

Unearthing China's Avant-Garde
A short history of art, 1979-2006
by Lee Ambrozy

Luo Zhongli's "Father" (1979)

The history of the Chinese avant-garde is closely intertwined with social change, economic reform and Chinese art history. Another important part of the story is the development of Beijing art zones like 798, Caochangdi and the Liquor Factory.

The long, bumpy road to "success" has at last paid off for some of the earliest members of the avant-garde, and the incredible sums they now command at auction seem like compensation for their previous marginalization and exclusion from both city limits and institutional art systems. What was once underground has been unearthed and now holds a prominent position in the arts world and popular media, even gaining attention among average folk. The face of the new artistic vanguard – like everything in modern China – is changing, and quickly. We can only guess where things will go next. After all, 15 years ago, who could have foreseen the art districts of 2007?

1979-1984
Scars and Stars

Even after the bans on individualist perspectives and themes had been lifted, "Cultural Revolution" (1966-1976) themes had still not completely disappeared. Realism still reigned on the canvas, though there was a visible rejection of the socialist art of the extreme left. Abstract forms, nudity and personal themes, although not forbidden, were still taboo in the mainstream. Emotionally charged personal subjects and themes were creeping back into the milieu with **"Scar Art"** (*shanghen yishu*), perhaps best represented by the oil painting "Father," completed in 1979 by **Luo Zhongli**. The work featured the sweaty face of a sun-withered peasant executed in photo-realist style.

Wu Guanzhong (see p185) emerged at the forefront of a movement of traditionally trained painters who struggled to integrate Western expressionist aesthetics with Chinese mediums such as ink and wash. In this politically relaxed and emotionally charged atmosphere, a group of radicals known as **the Stars** (among them **Ai Weiwei** – see p184) was busy acting on bottled-up experimental impulses after years of having no public voice. In the autumn of 1979, the Stars reveled in a renegade exhibition on the fence outside the National Art Gallery before the police closed it down.

1985-1989
Too far too fast

As young artists branched out in different creative directions, they chafed at what they saw as the overregulation of the art scene. Artists' groups like the Stars sprang up around China as an

PHOTO: COURTESY NATIONAL ART MUSEUM OF CHINA

Ai Weiwei, an original member of the radical Stars group, drops a piece of history

alternative to "official" channels, and there was an explosion of new publications. The first steps in rejecting the realist status quo involved playing with and paying homage to Western masters.

"Alternative" art forms leapt directly into postmodernism; **Xu Bing** first exhibited his landmark installation work "Book of Heaven" (see p185) at the National Art Gallery of China (now the National Art Museum of China) in 1988. Its secret meaning was apparently encoded in thousands of Chinese characters, but none of these could be pronounced or interpreted, as each had been invented by the artist himself. The work sparked a heated debate in the arts community.

Ink artists experimented with abstract forms, but seldom made it into exhibitions or attracted critical attention. The challenge of translating traditional art techniques into avant-garde forms of expression continues to perplex artists.

In this fertile intellectual atmosphere, the watershed moment came in 1989 in the form of the long-awaited "**China Avant-Garde**" exhibition. The show was to reflect emerging trends in art around the entire nation, and artists were abuzz at the prospect of official acknowledgement. However, it was all too much too soon, and the show was closed twice in two weeks. The first ban came when artist **Xiao Lu** fired two pistol shots into her piece "Dialogue." The work featured life-sized photographs of a man and a woman talking on the phone in two booths placed a meter apart with a glass mirror in between. Firing her pistol into the mirror, the artist hoped to produce a long crack, but the only results were two round holes and police closure. Just a few days later a bomb threat was phoned in, and that was the end of "China Avant-Garde." The hopes of many artists for public recognition were broken along with the mirror.

1990-1999
Avant-garde redux

In the two years after the "China Avant-Garde" incident, artistic development went into the deep freeze. This was partly because of a debate about the direction of the avant-garde which played out in a series of critical articles in the popular print media.

In 1992, Deng Xiaoping publicly set the course of economic reform during his "Southern Tour" to special economic zones, and the pace of change quickened. At all levels of society, there was a sense that there was no going back. Amid a national debate about spiritual values, art turned to sociological themes, an interest in reality and the "true" state of existence.

In the early 1990s, the Chinese avant-garde opened a dialogue with the wider world and entered the international art circuit. The year 1992 saw **Lü Shengzhong**, **Li Shan**, **Cai Guoqiang** and others at the Kassel Documenta, an important exhibition of modern and contemporary art. In 1993 **Yu Hong**, **Fang Lijun** (p185), and **Geng Jianyi** participated in the 45th Venice Biennale – the next year, they exhibited at the 1994 Sao Paolo Biennale.

Artist communities began to form across the nation, experimenting with performance, video and installation. In Beijing's distant northwest corner, an artists' commune born in the late '80s – known as "**Yuanmingyuan Village**" – was at full throttle. Artists from across the nation migrated here

Zhang Xiaogang's "Pink Boy" (detail) – yours for a cool squillion

to soak up the creative atmosphere and anti-establishment lifestyle. Important names emerged, including graffiti-man **Zhang Dali** (p186), **Yang Shaobin** and **Zhang Xiaogang** (p186). By the mid-'90s the group had caught the attention of national and overseas media. When city development swallowed up Yuanmingyuan Village, artists scattered to other areas, including the **East Village**, **Songzhuang** and **Huajiadi**.

In 1994, under the direction of eminent curator **Feng Boyi**, the "**Black Skin Book**" (*heipi shu*) was published. Recording the most important avant-garde works of the era and including all the significant forms, it is essential reading for understanding the art of this time. The following are some of the forms and trends it recorded.

Oil painting was more mature and had greater influence than other forms. Paintings stressed the role of the individual within society, blended art with everyday experience, and began to borrow more from popular culture and everyday life. Personal narratives and individuality were key topics. Soviet Realism, once fundamental to academic training, evolved into new forms through which artists expressed their personal experiences and began to criticize their perceived "reality."

Artists mastered techniques and ideology to create works in homage to Western styles. When the Chinese avant-garde met Western pop art, the result was **Political Pop,** associated with **Wang Guangyi** (p185). **Cynical Realism** emerged with its dark, alternative reality, evidenced in the works of **Fang Lijun** (p185) and **Yue Minjun**. **Liu Xiaodong** (p185) led a similar group of artists dubbed **New Generation Painting**, whose works were subtle reflections and representations of social change.

Liu Xiaodong's "Co-operation" (detail)

Performance or Behavior Art was rampant in the '90s, and distinguished itself as the most uniquely Chinese art form. In the absence of serious collectors or commercial spaces, individuals' homes became the exhibition space and friends became the audience. Fondly dubbed "apartment art," this new form of expression became the vibrant alternative to official art channels. Performance and Behavior Art was snubbed by critics and institutional exhibition spaces alike, and many viewed it as an opportunistic excuse for nudity and violence. These artists were brave, markedly direct and proactive communicators. Behavior Art sparked endless debate and its fair share of police intervention. Examples include **Ma Liuming** and his transsexual persona, or the tenacious sit-in by **Zhang Huan** at the stinkiest public toilet in the **East Village** artist commune. These notorious acts of self-determination and stamina were perhaps most effective in catching the eye of the international world. In contrast to overwhelming local disinterest, word spread overseas like wildfire.

With the rise of experimental video and photography in the mid-'90s, **Photography and Video Art** took an important place in the art world. **Zhao Bandi**, a gifted member of the "New Generation" painters, switched to conceptual photography. His posed photographs with a signature stuffed panda signalled the first appearance of "advertising language" in art. Although pure photography remained, altered digital photography established a major presence on the photographic scene, with the word "photoshop" becoming a verb in artists' circles. Conceptual artists the **Gao Brothers** began to move away from installation art to photography in both unaltered and photoshopped form, choosing the latter for its direct visual communication and ease of interpretation when portraying the human state in modern China.

ART & CULTURE

Painter Yue Minjun is THE Cynical Realist

With the historical marginalization of women in the arts, it is no surprise that a majority of the most prominent female artists explored feminist themes. Artists borrowed from their own bodies and used symbols of womanhood embedded in Chinese culture. Works ranged from the subtle – as in **Yu Hong**'s personal perspective in oil paintings – to the extreme, such as **Chen Lingyang**'s close-up photographs of her twelve-month cycle, juxtaposed with flowers, fans and chinoiserie. **Cui Xiuwen**'s "Washroom" hid video cameras in a public washroom and captured women at their most candid. She later went on to make shockingly uncomfortable, digitally altered photographs of women and young girls (p184).

2000-2007
Factory of the avant-garde

Around 2000, artist studios which had concentrated in the 798 factory space began to draw tourists. At the same time, a boom in the international art market led to a "bubble" in the prices of Chinese contemporary art. Finally the world, including locals, was taking notice of the avant-garde. A flurry of new gallery openings and commercial art fairs followed.

A new, younger generation of artists such as **Song Kun**, **Qiu Xiaofei** and **Cao Fei** (see p185) began to show in galleries for the first time. Their life experiences were radically different from those of their elders. Single-child upbringings and consumer pleasures, not politically charged memories, have launched them into the mind-frame of the globalized world. First they branded themselves as the **Post-'70s** generation, followed quickly by a so-called **Post-'80s** generation, but their art is unified by the "logo-fication" of the modern age – be it pandas or big-eyed, big-headed Japanese-style cartoon characters. Their work has left behind idealism for the heady new promise of capitalism, spurred by the "get rich quick" success of their avant-garde predecessors. Meanwhile, the creative cycle continues: Poor artists have now moved even further away, to cheap rents in places like Huilongguan, beyond the northwest city limits. They are the avant-unknown, the Stars of an era yet to come.

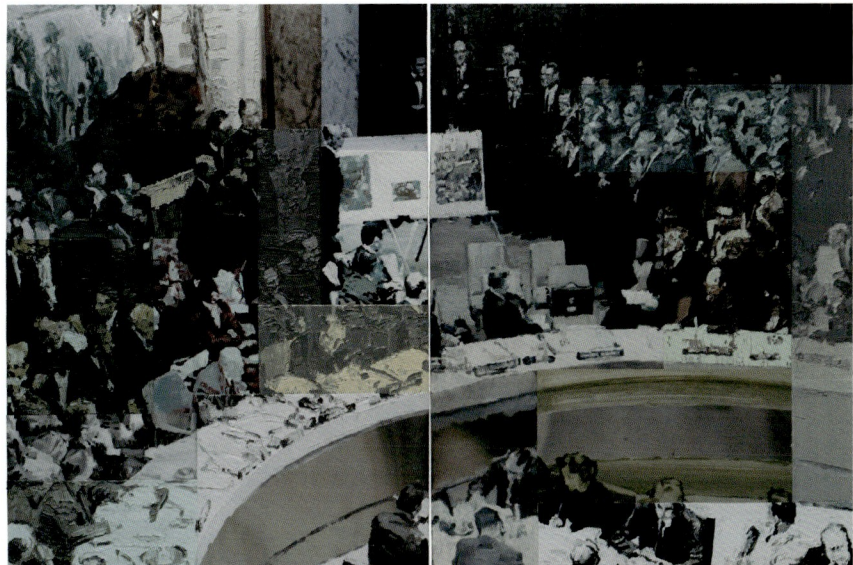

Li Songsong's "Cuban Sugar" recalls the Missile Crisis of 1962

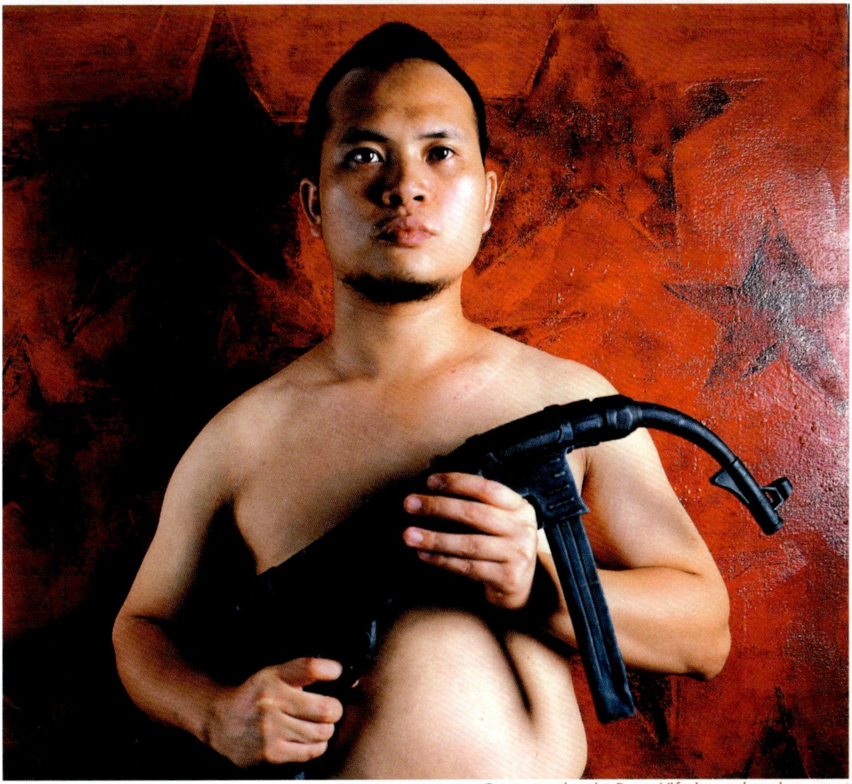

Conceptual artist Deng Yifu in a relaxed moment

PHOTOS: COURTESY URS MEILE GALLERY / RED GATE GALLERY

Names You Need to Know
Get up to speed on the Beijing art scene
by Lee Ambrozy

The girl in the white dress is Cui Xiuwen's signature image

Artists come and go with trends and market ups and downs, and now with over 150 galleries, Beijing is the ideal lookout post to watch the creative winds roll in. However, visitors can sometimes find it hard to find their footing in the art scene or to reference what they see in galleries. The following artists are all strongly representative of particular trends in Chinese art. You can't afford most of them, but you should get to know all of them. The order is alphabetical, by the way.

Ai Weiwei

The true renaissance man of the art world, from the early Stars group (see p178) to conceptual art, architecture and design, then again to restaurants and publishing, Ai Weiwei has the social calendar of a political heavyweight. He is the Beijing-born son of poet Ai Qing and also spent a decade in New York; his art has rollicking non sequitur elements and recently has become more "hands-off" than ever. The artist relies on a group of workers or participants to carry out his designs or performances. Last year he realized an art "experience" that took 1,001 Chinese to Kassel, Germany for an exhibition. He is the single most important figure on the contemporary art scene, the godfather of Beijing's avant-garde art.

Cao Fei

Video artist Cao Fei (b. 1978) has emerged as perhaps the most visible Post-'70s artist, or artist of the "young" generation. She works mostly in photographic and video mediums to produce edgy, colorful, often dryly humorous works that lie somewhere between visual art and social commentary. Her "Cosplayers" series of Guangzhou teenagers who dress up as their favorite manga characters was well-received internationally. Her later work, "Hip-Hop," was a parody capturing regular people in China, New York and Japan showing off their mock hip-hop style.

Cui Xiuwen

She has been a fixture on the art scene since her controversial 1998 work, "Washroom," that filmed prostitutes in a KTV restroom. Working primarily in video and digitally altered art, Cui Xiuwen has stuck close to her feminist inclinations. Her latest series of photos show a young girl, multiplied infinitely, against nondescript – yet unmistakably Beijing – backgrounds. Either wounded at a young age, or pregnant as a pre-teen, these girls make the viewer exceptionally uncomfortable, and are a not-so-subtle critique of the condition of young women today.

Fang Lijun

A heavy hitter in the annals of Chinese contemporary art history, Fang Lijun is central to Cynical Realism (玩世现实主义 *wanshi xianshi zhuyi*). As one of the artists most widely exhibited internationally, he has proved exceptionally important as a mascot for the success of the avant-garde in China. His early works are characterized by orange, balding heads against surrealist backdrops of desolate sands or underwater scenery; they are often interpreted as disillusionment or displeasure with social conditions. These days Fang has proven himself a more successful restaurateur than avant-garde artist: While his works monotonously riff on the same themes, he is making himself a pop culture legend with successful auction prices and a chain of Yunnanese restaurants, South Silk Road.

Liu Xiaodong

A figurative painter influenced equally by academia and bohemia, Liu made history last year as one of the highest-selling living painters with the USD 2.75 million sale of the "Three Gorges Dam" project. Although his realistic style is slightly understated, his choice of subjects illuminates underrepresented social elements such as displaced populations, prostitutes and transvestites. Liu is also a professor of oil painting at Beijing's Central Academy of Fine Arts and is prone to playing cameos in the films of famous Sixth Generation filmmakers.

Wang Guangyi

Blending Pop Art of the '60s with propaganda art, Wang Guangyi found the formula for success and notoriety in the canon of contemporary art: Political Pop (政治波普 *zhengzhi bopu*). Most people will have seen his "Great Criticism" series, where the chiseled profiles of revolutionaries are painted in red and yellow, but instead of slogans praising socialist ethics, the canvases blend in capitalist logos like Coca Cola and VISA. His juxtaposition of capitalist and socialist themes was the first of its kind. These days, Wang Guangyi is out of the limelight, as he hasn't exhibited new works for many years now.

Wu Guanzhong

Wu Guanzhong is one of the most remarkable and well-known painters in Chinese modern art. Born in 1919, he has won acclaim for successfully blending Western aesthetics with traditional Chinese watercolor techniques. In the 1940s he spent four years studying at the Ecole des Beaux Arts in Paris. When the impressionist painting style he was bent on introducing to his students was deemed too bourgeois during the "Cultural Revolution" (1966-1976), he was banned from painting, teaching and writing. Bouncing back with fervor, he went on to pioneer "aesthetic beauty" (形式美 *xingshi mei*) in his works. In the manner of two of his idols, Van Gogh and Cezanne, he often paints from nature.

Xu Bing

Xu Bing's "Book of Heaven" (天书 *tian shu*) is one of the most remarkable works in Chinese contemporary art history. The fruit of three years' labor, it consists of scores of books and scrolls printed with complex traditional techniques, but all the characters are unintelligible, as the artist himself invented them. He even made an unreadable dictionary to explain the characters. He now lives in New York and has continued to use language in his art.

A detail from "Montmartre" by modern master Wu Guanzhong

Yue Minjun

Starkly resembling the artist, Yue's laughing heads are an important characteristic of his early paintings. Toothed and guffawing in infinite jest, this early body of work is of definitive importance to Cynical Realism. Their surreal landscapes trapped everyone, and the mocking smiles also reflect the precarious position of a population whose future was hanging in the balance.

Zhang Dali

Zhang wanted his iconic graffiti to create testimonies of what Beijing was before momentous changes forever altered the city: The profile of a head, and tags "AK-47" and "18K" were everywhere on soon-to-be-demolished buildings around Beijing circa 1997. The effects were profound and later his name was immortalized in galleries through photography of his graffiti in situ; "tagging" – Beijing's first political graffiti – was born. Recently, Zhang has been less active.

Zhang Xiaogang

Zhang's famous "Bloodlines" series of oil paintings, begun in the 1990s, have come to symbolise the recent Chinese art market boom. Every collector across Asia is itching to get their hands on one of these black-and-white muted portraits of cartoonish Chinese families that mournfully stare back at the viewer. This series has made Zhang millions although his current auction record was for a piece depicting Tiananmen Square, which sold for USD 2.3 million in the spring of 2006.

A View From the Edge
Li Zhenhua on tomorrow's art innovators
Lee Ambrozy

Visitors to Beijing's trendy art districts today are just as likely to see Olympic "Friendlies" as they are to encounter fine art. In an era of soaring prices and production-line studios, where do you get a glimpse of tomorrow's avant-garde iconoclasts?

Well, you can stay away from most art galleries, says Li Zhenhua, a long-time luminary of China's alternative art scene: "Painters today think they should become millionaires first and then establish their art." And galleries are part of the problem, signing young artists even before graduation and buying a year's work at a time. "The artists are locked in their studios, they've become art slaves," Li laughs.

Few people are better qualified to comment on the avant-garde than Li Zhenhua. Multimedia artist, photographer, designer, and curator, he plunged into new media before the term had been invented: In 1996 he set up the Mustard Seed Garden, an online portal to Beijing's art, music, film and design. He has curated shows at the Walker Art Center in Minneapolis, and for festivals across Europe and Japan – not to mention increasingly high-profile work in China.

He is typical of the new breed of multi-tasking, cross-disciplinary types who move comfortably between the avant-garde and the "official" art establishment. In Li's view, the future belongs to artists who won't stay in their pigeonholes. He cites the example of Ou Ning,

Multimedia artist Li Zhenhua

a graphic designer, curator, critic and urban researcher, who is every bit the new media renaissance man. "You can find lots of young designers [like him] who are working on their own stuff on the side," he says.

Sitting comfortably at an outdoor cafe, he reflects on how technology drives change in the art world, shifting the leading edge away from the bricks-and-mortar gallery. While a tour of the gallery scene might suggest that the avant-garde has disappeared, Li promises that the revolution isn't over, it has just shifted locus. The old artist communes have had their day, he thinks. In a wi-fi urban jungle, communities can flourish in cyberspace.

As an example of a new "borderless" art community, Li cites we-need-money-not-art.com, a China-based web portal that brings artists, programmers, critics and the public together in one "space" to create and discuss art. "What's great about forums like this is the communication," he says, bringing the site up on his laptop through the cafe's wi-fi connection.

What is ironic about our discussion is its location: Our cafe is in the heart of the trendy 798 art district, which a few short years ago was gritty pioneer territory. Now the commercial present has caught up with it, and the future floats just out of reach on Li Zhenhua's computer screen.

PHOTO: JUDY ZHOU

ART & CULTURE

Liu Ren's "Paradise" (detail) is typical of her imaginative digital landscapes

PHOTO: COURTESY THE ARTIST

Art Hoods On and Off the Beaten Path

Explore Beijing like an art maven
by Lee Ambrozy

Men at work? Dashanzi art district

ART & CULTURE

Factory 798 – Dashanzi

This is it: the creamy caramel center of Beijing's art buzz. But the experience may be a little soft for real crunchy nougat art lovers. Factory 798 is the 20,000-square meter district where galleries, studios and trendy eateries collide. It is the much talked-about child of the international art scene – CNN even rated it one of the top five tourist sites in Beijing.

A self-guided tour is a fine way to pass any weekend afternoon. Open gallery doors encourage browsing, new exhibits often rotate in, and classy cafes provide welcome rest stops. Be prepared for cultural pilgrims photographing themselves in various poses amidst the unique blend of factory-chic and art.

To check out what's new and prolific in the Chinese art world, the best galleries are Beijing Commune, Marella Gallery, Beijing Tokyo Art Projects, Chinese Contemporary, Star Gallery and White Space.

Getting There
Bus: From the Dongzhimen Long-Distance Station, take bus 915, 918 or 934 to Dashanzi (and then walk, following directions below).
Car: Go to the Dashanzi Roundabout (Dashanzi Huandao), and head north on Jiuxianqiao Lu. Approaching from the south, stop at the second pedestrian overpass, and look for two orange-pink high-rise apartments on the east side of the road. The entrance is marked by a large 798 sign on the east side of Jiuxianqiao Lu. As you walk in, signs mark the prominent galleries.

Caochangdi

A satellite of Dashanzi, Caochangdi is a mere five kilometers north of Factory 798. Art takes a conceptual turn in this small community, and the atmosphere has less of the commercial sheen than 798. Many resident artists fled here as the rents rose in Dashanzi.

The China Art Archives and Warehouse was the first gallery in the Caochangdi area, paving the way for the larger "East End Arts" community-style development, which now hosts various activities such as intimate outdoor concerts. It tends to show installation art and is anchored by the cutting-edge Platform Gallery. Look also for the F2 gallery and the CourtYard Annex. Recently the Galerie Urs Meile established itself amidst the noodle steamers and three-wheeled bicycles prominent in the area – worth a visit for hardcore art fans.

The journey to find Caochangdi can be a form of performance art in itself, occasionally resulting in a darkly humorous cab fare – so arm yourself with directions, spare time or some keen language skills.

Getting There
Bus: From the Dongzhimen Long-Distance Station take bus 418, or pick up a 402 from anywhere on the East Third Ring Road – get off at Caochangdi.
Car: Head north on the Airport Service Road (Jichang Fulu), go through the underpass for the Fifth Ring Road and continue north, then head east onto Nangao Lu, and turn left (north) at the Chang Jian Driving School. Look for signs for the F2 gallery.

Liquor Factory (Jiuchang)

The third art district to arise in Beijing's booming art economy. This one sets itself apart with its location in what used to be a liquor factory. Unlike 798's charming worker-bourgeoisie juxtaposition, you won't find any booze flowing here, unless you're attending an opening.

Jiuchang's star occupant is the Korean Arario Gallery, a massive international collection of contemporary art weighted towards Chinese artists. There are also plenty of artist studios around, and new galleries open every month.

The area around Jiuchang might just make you wish you knocked back a couple of drinks, as it is located in distant Beihuqu – most cabs don't know it, it's surrounded by dusty roads, and it's literally located "across the tracks."

Getting There:
Bus: If you live in the western part of Beijing, take the light rail to Wudaokou station and change to the 630 bus. Get off at Beihuqu. If you live in the eastern part of the city, take the subway to Dawang Lu station and change to bus 976, which goes directly to Beihuqu.
Car: Take Jingcheng Expressway to Wangjing Kejiyuan Exit, turn west and get on Lize Xijie, and proceed some 10km to Beihuqu.

Songzhuang Artists Village

Living on the fringe is still a phenomenon for artists in China – maybe it's their need for creative open spaces? Or maybe it's the inexpensive property to be found in the surrounding county of Tongzhou? Regardless of what brings them here, they come from all over the nation.

They come to 798 from far, far away

Some great talent can be found in Songzhuang – just ask "Lao Li," the art critic and curator Li Xianting, a presence in the area who is something akin to the "Godfather" of Beijing's bohemian world. Alumni of Songzhuang include the cynical realists Fang Lijun and Yue Minjun as well as photographer Wang Qingsong and painter Yang Shaobin. These and other artists have built impressive estates in the area, and hey, who knows what else lies behind the unassuming gates of countless courtyards ...

The local mainstay is the Artist's Village Gallery, which hosts summer festivals and regular shows. Be aware that returning home late from Songzhuang will be a challenge, since buses stop running and taxis are a rarity.

Getting There

Bus/subway: Take the Line 1 subway to Dawang Lu station, the origin of bus 930. Take 930 区间 (Qu Jian) (there are multiple 930 lines) to Ren Zhuang. This is nothing but a gas station, but don't worry, you've arrived in the village! From here, negotiate with local drivers to take you to one of the local sites – a few kuai should do the trick.

Car: Take the Jingtong Expressway east to the Xima Zhuang exit, drive to the Beiguan Roundabout, and get onto the Jingha Expressway heading to Ren Zhuang. After passing three traffic lights, look for the gas station, and you're in artist utopia. Contact individual galleries for specific directions.

The Artist Village Gallery in Songzhuang arranges day tours that include transportation and a meal for RMB 100 per person. Call for information (6959 8343).

Commune by the Great Wall

If your visiting friends aren't convinced that Beijing has any class, take them to the "Commune," an architecture installation just outside the city. Designed by 12 of Asia's most prominent architects, these homes were the first modern Chinese buildings to be recognized abroad as "art."

The 11 original villas, with names like Cantilever House, are rented out as boutique hotel residences – there are also 31 cheaper Phase 2 buildings. With diverse materials, from glass and steel to authentic stones from the Great Wall, each of the original villas showcases the distinctive style of its designer in innovative structures, portraying both harmony and dynamism. For more information, see Excursion chapter p553 or visit www.commune.com.cn.

Getting There

Bus: Catch a tourist bus to the Badaling Great Wall (see Sightseeing p269). From the Great Wall entrance, hire a minibus or a cab to the Shuiguan section of the Wall, and keep your eyes peeled for contemporary architecture.

Car: Take Badaling Expressway to the Shuiguan exit. Follow clearly marked signs to the Commune, 2km after the exit.

ART & CULTURE

The horror, the horror ... a detail from Chi Peng's "Fight Against the White Bone Demon #1"

Old Epic, New Journey
Chi Peng uses digital art to explore a classic of his childhood
As told to Leon Lee

Chi Peng is a 26-year-old new media artist who is a master of digital manipulation. In May 2007 he exhibited a series of photographic works based on Journey to the West.

"If you do a survey of youth my age and you ask us the one thing that was burned into our memories, it's *Journey to the West*. When I was maybe five, there wasn't much going on in our lives until television. So the thing that a kid my age can recall most clearly is *Journey to the West*.

The story spoke to us because a child can distinguish clearly between good and evil. And as I became older, I started to see stories within the epic like pages from my life. They have to do with memories, experiences, the process of growing up, and the twists of circumstance that make me who I am today.

This character is called Hong Hai'er. Hong is of aristocratic stock and has had a charmed life. In my childhood there were kids like Hong who came from good family backgrounds with fathers who were officials. For kids like me, watching the doting and coddling and being the disadvantaged was pretty depressing. Now Hong was always beating up on the Monkey King even though he didn't deserve it. This series expresses those childlike emotions like when you took a beating for nothing – those little childhood injustices that have a great effect on as an adult.

Or look at this one, "White Bone Demon #1." When you're a kid, who are the scariest people in the world? Parents! If a teacher reprimands you, it sucks but it's no big deal. But when your mom and dad reprimand you, it's serious. Parents are your sky and if parents don't hold you up, then you're left hanging and things really get frightening.

The White Bone Demon is an evil character that looks horrific so I've superimposed the face of horror to represent the kinds experienced as children. I think being reprimanded is worse than being spanked because that's when horror rears its frightening face – the horror of knowing you did something wrong and being demeaned and scolded for it. So the look on my dad's face when he's angry with me, yelling at me – this is kind of like the horror of being forced into a corner by a monster."

Chi Peng: "Five Elements Mountain"

ART & CULTURE

... or forever hold your peace

Gallery Directory

3/4 Gallery China's first gallery devoted to female artists seeks to foster a sense of community among them.
Tue-Sun 10am-7pm. B-102, Landmark Crystal, 9 Jiuxianqiao Nanlu, Chaoyang District. (6433 7401) 四分之三画廊，朝阳区酒仙桥南路9号亮马水晶 B-102

3818 Cool Gallery Showing mainly contemporary oils, this converted warehouse gallery shares its roof with several other galleries and a coffee shop.
Tue-Sun 10.30am-6.30pm. Dashanzi art district, 3818 Warehouse, 2 Jiuxianqiao Lu, Chaoyang District. (8688 2525) www.3818coolgallery.cn 3818 库，朝阳区酒仙桥路2号798大山子艺术区（706厂对面）

798 Photo Gallery The best place in Beijing to find a wide selection of ethnographic and artistic photographic editions. Monthly rotating shows of Chinese and international photographers.
Daily 10am-6pm. Dashanzi art district, 4 Jiuxianqiao Lu, Chaoyang District. (6438 1784, 6437 5284) www.798photogallery.cn 百年印象摄影画廊，朝阳区酒仙桥路4号798大山子艺术区

798/Red Gate Gallery The eminent Red Gate Gallery's tiny project and exhibition space in the 798 area.
Tue-Sun 11am-6pm. Dashanzi art district, 2 Jiuxianqiao Lu (across from White Space Beijing), Chaoyang District. (6525 1005) www.redgategallery.com 798/红门画廊，朝阳区酒仙桥路2号（空白空间对面）

798 Space The namesake of the 798 area, this converted weapon factory now exhibits interesting, general shows in between high couture product launches that draw crowds.
Daily 10am-11pm. Dashanzi art district, 4 Jiuxianqiao Lu, Chaoyang District. (6438 4862, 6437 6248) www.798space.com 798 时态空间，朝阳区酒仙桥路4号798大山子艺术区

Arario Beijing Korean-owned gallery exhibiting its vast collection of international powerhouses, such as Jorg Immendorf, paired alongside local artists.
Tue-Sun 11am-7pm. Inside the Liquor Factory, Beihuqu, Anwaibeiyuan, Chaoyang District. (5202 3800) www.arariobeijing.com 阿拉里奥画廊，朝阳区北苑北湖渠朝阳酒厂艺术园

Artists Village Gallery In the dusty eastern village of Songzhuang live many bohemian painters and a few big names too – find their art and lots of *chuan'r*.
Daily 9am-9pm. 1 Renzhuangcun Bei, Songzhuang, Tongzhou District. (6959 8343, sally-liu@263.net) www.artistsvillagegallery.com 画家村画廊，通州区宋庄任庄村北1号

PHOTO: TOM CARTER

Beijing Art Now Gallery (BANG) Located inside the Workers' Stadium, BANG aims to keep Chinese art within national borders. They carry out their mission with a steady stream of exhibitions of quality contemporary artists.
Daily noon-7pm. Workers' Stadium, opposite Gate 12, Chaoyang District. (6551 1632) www.artnow.cn 现在画廊，朝阳区工人体育场12号看台对面

Beijing Central Art Gallery & Cultural Venue In this somewhat more traditional gallery you can find high-quality original watercolors, oil paintings and sculptures, as well as some contemporary pieces. Conveniently located for the Shunyi crowd.
Mon-Sat 9am-7pm, Sun noon-7pm. 2 Riverville Square, 1 District 1, Tianzhu Development Zone (take the Yang Lin exit from the Airport Expressway), Shunyi District. (6450 8483/8646) www.bjcagallery.com 硕华画廊，顺义区天竺丽来花园一区1号温榆广场2号 (机场高速杨林大道出口)

Beijing Commune Run by international curator Leng Lin, a mainstay on the arts scene, this is a space to watch for progressive shows of the avant-garde in all mediums.
Tue-Sun 11am-7pm. Dashanzi art district, 4 Jiuxianqiao Lu, Chaoyang District. (8654 9428, lenglin@yahoo.com) www.beijingcommune.com 北京公社，朝阳区酒仙桥路4号大山子798艺术区

Beijing Cubic Art Center Bare-bones concrete space devoted to experimental new media projects. Regularly hosts digital sound projects and high-tech art. Call for hours.
Tue-Sun 11am-6pm. Dashanzi art district (southern section), 4 Jiuxianqiao Lu, Chaoyang District. (6437 9853) www.11-art.com 北京立方艺术中心，朝阳区酒仙桥路4号798大山子艺术区南边

Beijing MoCa BJ MoCa elevates "factory-chic" to a new level of rawness. It is buried in the distant hamlet Huan Tie ("steel ring," inside old railroad tracks), northwest of the Fifth Ring Road. Originally intended as warehouse space, MoCa has become an unexpected non-profit haven for contemporary art.
Mon-Fri by appointment, Sat-Sun 1-6pm. Rm 301, 798 Hong Yuan Apartments, Chaoyang District. (8457 4759) 朝艺堂，朝阳区798宏源公寓301室

Beijing New Art Projects This studio maintained by the Gao Brothers hosts politically charged shows and serves as a meeting space for artists from around the nation.
Tue-Sun 11am-7pm. Dashanzi art district, 4 Jiuxianqiao Lu, Chaoyang District. (8456 6660) www.gaobrothers.com 北京新锐艺术计划，朝阳区酒仙桥路4号798大山子艺术区

Beijing Tokyo Art Projects As one of the first international galleries in 798, BTAP continuously hosts a stream of great exhibitions, including artists from Japan and beyond.
Tue-Sun 10.30am-6.30pm. Dashanzi art district, 4 Jiuxianqiao Lu, Chaoyang District. (8457 3245) www.tokyo-gallery.com 北京东京艺术工程，朝阳区酒仙桥路4号大山子艺术区

C5 Art A new gallery on the scene for emerging and new media artists with great potential, C5 is nestled beside the International SOS clinic in Sanlitun.
Tue-Sun 10am-7pm. 5 Sanlitun Xiwujie, Chaoyang District. (6460 3950) 西五画廊，朝阳区三里屯西五街5号院内

China Art Archives and Warehouse Focusing on conceptual and experimental fine arts from China, the CAAW was one of the first galleries in Beijing and a key shaper of the fine arts scene. With Ai Weiwei as arts director, it already has the curatorial touch of gold.
Wed-Sun 1-6pm, or by appointment. Opposite the Nangao Police Station, Caochangdi (take the Airport Service Road one exit past Fifth Ring Road, then the first right past the Chang Jian Driving School), Chaoyang District. (8456 5152/3) www.archivesandwarehouse.com 艺术文化仓库，朝阳区机场辅路草场地村南皋派出所对面(机场辅路北五环外第一个路口)

China Art Seasons Exhibits of young academy and emerging artists, along with an occasional cameo by one of the Chinese art luminaries.
Tue-Sun 11am-7pm. Dashanzi art district, 2 Jiuxianqiao Lu, Chaoyang District. (6431 1900) www.artseasons.com.sg 北京季节，朝阳区酒仙桥路2号798大山子艺术区

China Blue Gallery Gallery deals in a variety of mediums including photography, painting, sculpture and installation work. One of the few home-grown galleries to be making inroads into the international art scene.
Daily 9.30am- 6pm. 2-3/F, Bldg 7, Ego Center, 16A Baiziwan Lu (south of Dawang Lu subway station), Chaoyang District. (8774 6332/6339) www.chinabluegallery.com 环碧堂画廊，朝阳区百子湾路甲16号易构空间7号楼2－3层

China Millennium Monument Art Museum Large, relatively central space hosting shows with distinct approval from the Central Government.
Apr 15-Oct 7: Mon-Thu 8am-6pm, Fri-Sun 8am-9pm. Oct 8-Apr 14: Daily 9am-5.30pm. 9A Fuxing Lu, Haidian District. (5980 2222) www.bj2000.org.cn 中华世纪坛艺术馆，海淀区复兴路甲9号

Chinese Contemporary Beijing Sister to the London gallery specializing in art from the mainland, CC regularly shows the provocative avant-garde, with a focus for foreign buyers.
Daily 11am-7pm. Dashanzi art district, 4 Jiuxianqiao Lu, Chaoyang District. (8456 2421) www.chinesecontemporary.com 中国当代，朝阳区酒仙桥路4号798大山子艺术区

CourtYard Annex The "project space" of megalith CourtYard Gallery located in Caochangdi – more experimental and installation shows found here.
Tue-Sun noon-7pm. 155 Caochangdi Village, Nangao Xiang, Chaoyang District. www.courtyard-gallery.com 四合苑艺术空间，朝阳区南皋乡草场地村155号

CourtYard Gallery China's homegrown answer to an international gallery, but primarily featuring mainland artistic talent. The CourtYard opened in 1996 underneath the restaurant of the same name and basks in the glory of the Forbidden City's eastern moat.
Tue-Sun 11am-6pm. B1/F, 95 Donghuamen Dajie, Dongcheng District. (6526 8882) www.courtyard-gallery.com 四合苑，东城区东华门大街95号地下一层

Creation Gallery Tourist-friendly exhibitions of oils, acrylics and traditional materials; a good place to find something nice for your home that doesn't scream "contemporary Chinese art" in an offensive way.
Daily 10am-7pm. North end of Ritan Donglu, Chaoyang District. (8561 7570) www.creationgallery.com.cn 可创艺苑，朝阳区日坛东路北口

Dimensions Art Center Taiwanese-owned and operated, Dimensions Art Center shows pan-Asian, hip digital art.
Tue-Sun 11am-7pm. Dashanzi art district (southern section), 4 Jiuxianqiao Lu, Chaoyang District. (6435 9665) www.dimensions-art.com 帝门艺术中心，朝阳区酒仙桥路4号798大山子艺术区南边

F2 A foreign-owned gallery representing a handful of Chinese contemporary artists, as well as occasional shows of overseas artists such as Julian Schnabel and Keith Haring.
Tue-Sun 10am-6pm. Guanghantang Nangao, East Dashanzi Lu, Chaoyang District. (134 8870 9596) www.f2gallery.com F2画廊，朝阳区大山子路东机场辅路南皋广汉堂院内

Galerie Urs Meile, Lucerne-Beijing This stunning grey brick structure, designed by Ai Weiwei, is the partner gallery to CAAW. Consistently shows high-quality contemporary art while working in tandem with its Lucerne gallery.
Tue-Sun 11am-6.30pm. 104 Caochangdi Village (take the Airport Service Road north past the 5th Ring Road, turn right at the "China Film Museum" billboard and continue to the traffic light. At the light veer right onto a slanted road and continue heading right. The gallery is the two-story gray building on the left), Chaoyang District. (6333 3393) www.galerieursmeile.com 麦勒画廊，朝阳区草场地村104号

Galleria Continua This giant three-story structure in the center of 798 exhibits fine contemporary art from Italy and the world.
Tue-Sun 11am-6pm. Dashanzi art district, 4 Jiuxianqiao Lu, Chaoyang District. (6436 1005) www.galleriacontinua.com 常青画廊，朝阳区酒仙桥路4号798大山子艺术区

Hart Center of Arts The Hart Center of Arts can be a good place to catch an art film, hear some ethnic music, see modern dance or see an exhibition – which have lately been spotty in quality. But don't worry, it's always a good place to nosh on a bagel sandwich. Open for functions, call to confirm.
Dashanzi art district, 4 Jiuxianqiao Lu, Chaoyang District. (6435 3570) www.hart.com.cn 哈特沙龙，朝阳区酒仙桥路4号798大山子艺术区

NOON A Korean-funded non-profit arts center promoting Asian cultural exchange. They show an interesting selection of artists from Korea alongside some of China's young and established talent.
Tue-Sun 10am-6pm. Dashanzi art district, 4 Jiuxianqiao Lu, Chaoyang District. (6438 3551) www.ieshu.com 交流空间，朝阳区朝阳区酒仙桥路4号大山子798艺术区

Imagine Gallery Located in far-off Feijiacun, the Imagine Gallery regularly hosts interesting shows, featuring the international artists who participate in their dynamic residency program.
Tue-Sun 10.30am-5.30pm. 8 Feijiacun Donglu, Cuigezhuang, Laiguangying Donglu, Chaoyang District. (6438 5747) www.imagine-gallery.com 想象画廊，朝阳区来广营东路崔各庄费家村东路8号香格里拉附近同达饭店对面

Long March Committed to the promotion of Chinese arts abroad, the Long March has been one of the most influential players on the arts scene. It consistently manages to show an interesting cross-section of new artists working in diverse media.
Tue-Sun 11am-7pm. Dashanzi art district, 4 Jiuxianqiao Lu, Chaoyang District. (6438 7107) www.longmarchspace.com 长征空间，朝阳区酒仙桥路4号大山子艺术区

Marella Gallery Italian-run gallery showing mainly Chinese artists. Shows range from provocative to sweet to humorous, but they are always memorable.
Tue-Sun 11am-7pm. Dashanzi art district, 4 Jiuxianqiao Lu, Chaoyang District. (6433 4055) www.marellart.com 朝阳区酒仙桥路4号798大山子艺术区

National Art Museum Well-designed rotating shows from their collection and traveling exhibitions. A must-visit for anyone interested in 20th century socialist and traditional medium art, the museum is less stodgy than its name would suggest, and has recently turned its eye to more and more contemporary pieces.
Daily 9am-5pm, last ticket 4pm. RMB 20, students RMB 10. Audio guide RMB 10 with RMB 100 deposit. 1 Wusi Dajie, Dongcheng District. (8403 3500) www.namoc.org 中国美术馆，东城区五四大街1号

Onemoon Nestled in a traditional courtyard inside shady Ditan Park, onemoon shows fine art from Chinese artists of different media and directions, all with an elegant feel.
Tue-Sun 10am-6pm. Inside Ditan Gongyuan, enter from the south gate, Dongcheng District. (6427 7748) www.onemoonart.com 一月当代，东城区安定门外地坛公园内

Pekin Fine Arts Pekin Fine Arts prepares exhibitions of contemporary Chinese artists to display and send to galleries and museums around the world.
Wed-Sun 10am-6pm. 241 Caochangdi, Jichang Fulu, Chaoyang District. (5127 3220) www.pekinfinearts.com 艺门画廊，朝阳区机场辅路草场地241号

Platform China A dynamic and experimental art space exhibiting video and installation art in a fresh, non-commercial setting. They also have a residency program for international artists.
1) Tue-Sun 11am-6pm. Dashanzi art district, 4 Jiuxianqiao Lu, Chaoyang District. (6438 8451); 2) Daily 10am-6pm. 319-1 East End Art (Zone A), Caochangdi Village (take the Airport Service Road one exit past Fifth Ring Road, take the first right and turn north on the road opposite the Chang Jian Driving School), Chaoyang District. (6432 0169/0091) www.platformchina.org 站台中国当代艺术机构，1）朝阳区酒仙桥路4号大山子艺术区；2）朝阳区草场地村319-1 艺术东区A区内（机场辅路由南往北五环外第一个路口路东，长进驾校对面路口）

Qin Gallery Qin specializes in professional exhibitions of non-confrontational artists from around China, many featuring folk themes.
Tue-Sun 9.30am-6pm. Rm 1E, Bldg 1, Enjoy Paradise, Huaweili (north of Beijing Curio City), Chaoyang District. (8779 0461) www.qingallery.com 秦昊画廊，朝阳区华威里翌景嘉园1座1E室(北京古玩城北)

Red Gate Gallery One of the major shapers of Chinese contemporary art internationally and locally, the magnificent Red Gate Gallery is located in an ancient Ming Dynasty watchtower. Red Gate still delivers punchy Chinese artists and supports the arts community with a strong international residency program.
Daily 9am-5pm. Levels 1 and 4, Dongbianmen Watchtower, Chongwenmen, Chongwen District.

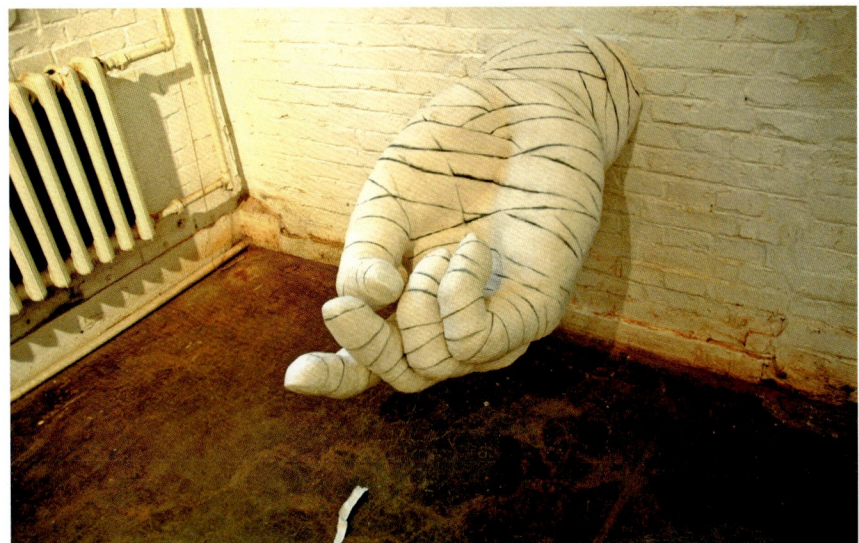

A Polanski moment in a Beijing gallery

(6525 1005) www.redgategallery.com 红门画廊，崇文区东便门角楼

Soka Art Centre/ Soka Modern Soka holds an unsurpassed collection of modern masters from throughout Asia and recently expanded to include a China-focused department.
Tue-Sun 10am-7pm. Rm 101, Bldg B, Tianhai Shangwu Dasha, 107 Dongsi Beidajie, Dongcheng District. (8401 2377) www.soka-art.com 索卡(北京)艺术中心，东城区东四北大街107号天海商务大厦B座101房

Star Gallery Devoted to artists of the "Post '70s" generation, Star Gallery delivers shows devoid of political machinations but still hyper cutting-edge.
Tue-Sun 10am-6pm. Dashanzi art district, 2 Jiuxianqiao Lu (inside 3818 Cool Gallery warehouse), Chaoyang District. (8456 0591) www.stargallery.cn 星空间艺术中心，朝阳区酒仙桥路2号院内，3818库

Tang Contemporary Gallery This Beijing branch of a Bangkok-based gallery is committed to high-concept curated shows of Chinese contemporary art. A visit here is never boring.
Tue-Sun 10.30am-6.30pm. Dashanzi Art District, 2 Jiuxianqiao Road, Chaoyang District. (6436 3518/3658) 当代唐人艺术中心，朝阳区酒仙桥路2号。大山自艺术区

Thinking Hands Primarily the curatorial offices of the DIAF and other international projects in 798, this is also an exhibition space with unusual installation projects and a place to buy T-shirts or collectable exhibition posters).
Daily 10.30am-6.30pm. Dashanzi art district, 4 Jiuxianqiao Lu, Chaoyang District. (6437 9737) 思想手，朝阳区酒仙桥路4号798大山子艺术区

Today Art Museum One of a few privately owned art "museums" in Beijing, Today Art focuses on high-quality contemporary art, as well as calligraphy and other traditional media. Expanded into a huge new space.
Daily 10am-5pm. Pingguo Space: 32 Baiziwan Lu, Chaoyang District. (5862 1100) www.artnow.com.cn 今日美术馆，朝阳区百子湾路32号

Universal Studios Beijing's first non-profit art space is funded by a Dutch foundation and run by curator Pi Li. Get your fill of Northern European artists and off-the-beaten-path art you won't find in more commercial spaces.
Tue-Sat 10am-6.30pm. Compound 8A, Airport Service Road, Caochangdi, Chaoyang District. (6432 2620) www.universalstudios.org.cn U空间，朝阳区机场辅路草场地甲8号院

White Space This German-owned cavernous gallery of eminent importance in 798 provides excellent shows, featuring Chinese as well as European artists.
Tue-Sun 11am-7pm. Dashanzi art district, 4 Jiuxianqiao Lu, Chaoyang District. (8456 2054) www.alexanderochs-galleries.de 空白空间，朝阳区酒仙桥路4号798大山子艺术区

Xin Dong Cheng Space For Contemporary Art The French-educated Chinese curator/owner has made quite an impact on the exhibition scene in Beijing.
1) Tue-Sun 10am-6pm. Chaoyang Liquor Factory, Beihuqu Jie, Anwaibeiyuan, Chaoyang District. (5202 3868); 2) Tue-Sun 10.30am-6.30pm. Dashanzi district, 4 Jiuxianqiao Lu, Chaoyang District. (6433 4579) www.chengxindong.com 程昕东国际当代艺术空间，1）朝阳区安外北苑北湖渠朝阳区酿酒厂内；2）朝阳区酒仙桥路4号798大山子艺术区

Yan Club Art Centre By day, enjoy a range of media by different big-name or emerging artists; by night, trance and jungle parties entreat clubbers to zone out to funky video art.
Daily 10.30am-6pm. Dashanzi art district, 4 Jiuxianqiao Lu, Chaoyang District. (8457 3506) www.yanclub.com 仁画廊，朝阳区酒仙桥路4号798大山子艺术区

Sage of the Internal Stage
The fiction of Lu Li
by Eric Abrahamsen

Chinese cultural commentators never seem to be happy unless they're putting things in boxes. There's no phenomenon so obscure that it can't be lumped in with others of its age cohort – 1980s this, Fourth Generation that – and criticism all too often stops at classification.

Luckily for Chinese writers, however, literature (usually) isn't sexy enough to merit much press, and most authors are left to pursue their idiosyncrasies unmolested. Lu Li (陆离), for instance: Born in the mid '70s, she is too old for the high-school fantasies of Chun Shu or Han Han, but too young for the rural themes of Mo Yan or Yan Lianke. She belongs to the first generation of modern Chinese writers who have led relatively undisturbed, middle-class lives, and thus have new leeway when it comes to choosing fictional subjects.

Lu Li didn't start writing until 2000, when she was studying in Canada and needed something to distract her from dull computer science courses. "It wasn't until someone later called me a 'writer'," she says, "that I realized how serious the situation had become."

The cover of Lu Li's first collection of stories

Lu Li's earliest stories described life in Shanghai, her birthplace. After making a name for herself online, she published a story collection called *Now It Starts, When Will It End* (现在开始，什么时候结束?) in 2002, and is currently in discussions to publish a novel. As her writing progressed, it strayed farther and farther from realism – her current stories are eerie re-imaginings of familiar urban scenes, sometimes dreamlike, sometimes terrifying. A girl's boyfriend makes her a pair of wings which may or may not function; a neighbor who seems at first merely lonely is gradually revealed to be in the grip of some inhabiting madness.

In a literary scene marked by deep insecurity and frenetic trends, Lu Li displays a curious self-possession. She has learned to disassociate herself from criticism of her work, and to observe public reaction "not so I can adjust my writing, but as a way of examining people, understanding people. The better I understand myself and others, the less I'm swayed by other people's judgments."

Discussing freedom of the imagination, Lu Li employs the metaphor of an internal stage – a space where stories play out without outside interference. When Chinese readers find her work simultaneously familiar and unsettling, that may be a measure of her success. "The important thing isn't whether you're describing real life or creating something new, it's whether you can expand your field of vision, and stop writing from your self. So many of us are constrained by the limits of the age, unable to pull ourselves free." Worse, those who try often try too hard, struggle to get outside of the box, to the detriment of their writing. But Lu Li is smiling – she's taught herself to forget that the box is there.

The Show Will Go On
A brief history of modern Chinese theater
by Eric Abrahamsen

Moving beyond ritualized makeup, and skirting altogether the pitfalls of mimes, musicals and Dadaism, China has developed a tradition of theater as we know it in the West: men and women on stage, wearing more or less normal clothes, speaking in more or less normal voices, and portraying scenes that speak to the lives of regular people. It has been about one hundred years since exchange students – both foreigners coming to China and Chinese students studying abroad – introduced Western-style theater to the mainland, and during that time the art form has developed, struggled and ultimately produced something unique to China.

Not quite "Made In China"

Like many other "new" ideas in the early 20th century, modern theater was a Western concept that Chinese students encountered in Japan and brought back with them to China. Plays like Henrik Ibsen's *A Doll's House*, in which the character Nora wakes up from an unexamined life of domesticity to question the foundation of everything she believes in, were enormously influential to the young intellectuals of the May Fourth Movement.

The Chunliushe, a student drama society, gave birth to several of China's proto-dramatists, such as Ding Xilin and Ouyang Yuqian. They wrote, directed and acted in their own semi-improvised works – works that were primarily political, directed towards the improvement of Chinese government and society. The great theatrical age might be said to begin with Cao Yu, a 23-year-old student at Tsinghua University, who, in 1932, holed himself up in his school library and wrote the play *Thunderstorm* (*Leiyu*), a tragic drama which follows the decline and disintegration of a traditional family and its servants. The plays of Cao Yu are still performed to great applause today, and purists regularly grumble that modern works don't even come close.

Propaganda machine

During the chaotic years before the establishment of the PRC in 1949, theater came out into the streets as an instrument of propaganda, helping to stir up patriotic, anti-Japanese sentiment and galvanize the people into armed resistance. Plays were mostly just roadside skits, and at a time when literacy was scant and communications technologically spotty, *huabaoju*, as it was known, did much to coordinate public sentiment and action.

Following the establishment of the PRC, theater took a nose-dive, along with the rest of the arts. The prevailing opinion was that art's proper function was to propagate correct political ideas and action, not to entertain or to explore. Limited by political conformity, the theater

Ge You in Looking West to Chang'an *by Lao She*

PHOTO: CHINA NATIONAL WORKERS UNION CULTURAL TROUPE

ART & CULTURE   199

I Love You, You're Perfect ... the Chinese production

of the time entailed lots of smiling, singing and exhortations to ... Work Harder!

Things got even stranger during the "Cultural Revolution," when theater as we know it essentially died out. In its place came the Model Operas, a limited repertoire of "politically correct" plays, which crossbred Peking Opera singing styles with simple plotlines and characters: The villains were slinking and cowardly, the heroes doughty and mascara'ed, everyone wore military uniforms or peasant outfits, the pancake makeup was applied liberally, and so on.

One step back, two steps forward

The period following the "Cultural Revolution" was marked by heartfelt efforts in many disciplines to restore and improve the country, and reviving the field of theater was no exception. The 1980s were reminiscent of the 1920s and 1930s, in that theater concerned itself deeply with the plight of the common citizen and social improvement. The plays of Ma Zhongjun and Gao Xingjian ushered in a new social awareness and launched dialogue about theater as an art form – Gao's play Bus Stop (Chezhan) is not only a commentary on contemporary society, but also on the nature of theater itself.

A small theatrical renaissance began, and gave rise to such eclectics as Mou Sen – whose plays included scriptless scenes of people crawling across floors or cooking complete meals onstage – and Meng Jinghui, who was avantgarde yet still watchable, and whose influence dominated the theater scene until the late 1990s, when DVDs nearly destroyed it altogether.

Has video killed the theatrical star?

The rise of film and television has done great harm to the popularity of theater (as has happened in many countries), and led to distraught examinations of the purpose and necessity of Chinese theater. Truth be told, these questions have not been satisfactorily answered, and while the theater has bounced back slightly in the past four or five years, it is still waiting, like so many other Chinese art forms, for the wind to pick up once again and fill its sails.

As things stand today, Beijing is home to several excellent theaters. Capital residents frequently – and rightly – claim their city as the vanguard of Chinese theater, where a few well-established troupes play regularly. The best-known troupe is probably the National Theater of China (Zhongguo Guojia Huajuyuan), which typically plays at the Capital Theater and is neck and neck with the Beijing People's Art Theater (Beijing Renmin Yishu Juyuan) in terms of quality. There are a handful of other, smaller troupes that play regularly around the city, but the scene is still far from being vibrant.

The market to the rescue

No Beijing university has a theater department yet – although one is in the works at Peking University. And while students often form drama clubs, Beijing's professional actors still come from one place only: the Central Academy of Drama. Entrants are chosen primarily for their comeliness, as a quick stroll around the campus will confirm. But the consequences of having only one school of acting, where dramatic ability ranks far down on the list of entrance qualifications, are clear.

If anything is going to save Chinese theater, inasmuch as it needs saving, it is likely to be the same gentle pressure which is being applied to all aspects of Chinese culture and media: commercialism. For all the distaste Westerners may feel for the influence of commercialism on art, there are few forces which act more swiftly to sweep aside crusty tradition and ossified authority.

No, it won't be an overnight transformation when it comes, partly because audiences have come to expect what they've been getting, and will have to gradually accustom themselves to headier mixtures. But as they do, China's thespians – the young ones, the irreverent ones – will be ready.

PHOTO: COURTESY BROADWAY ASIA

Theater without Bounds
A talk with director Lin Zhaohua

by Alison M. Friedman

If actions speak louder than words, director Lin Zhaohua needs no translator. Known as "the father of experimental theater in China," Lin has persisted in creating work that pushes boundaries while many of his contemporaries have either pursued more commercial careers or have been exiled from China.

In 1989, Lin was vice president of the Beijing People's Art Theatre, the preeminent government-run theater company in China, where he still directs today. "At that time," recalls the stoop-shouldered septuagenarian, "I felt an urge to have my own 'space' so that my artistic ideas could be implemented, or experimented with, freely. Working in the most prestigious theater company in China has its advantage, of course, for there are so many resources. But there is also a bureaucracy that limits artistic creation and puts obstacles before ideas that are considered too unconventional."

Lin therefore created an independent company, Linzhaohua Theatre Studios. Until 2004, however, laws in China did not allow independent theater companies to exist, so the studio

Lin Zhaohua – independent and an innovator

produced work by engaging in partnerships with other government-recognized organizations. According to Lin, these kinds of practical actions are essential: "The theater artist is in his essence a social artist – he needs an audience – so he has to find ways of creating and communicating under all kinds of conditions. He has to be innovative not only onstage but also offstage. An artist's freedom has to be created, not given."

"Lin Dao" (Director Lin), as most people respectfully refer to him, has directed works ranging from Chekhov and Ibsen to Peking Opera classics and Lao She's *Teahouse*, but for a new twist, he often incorporates modern dancers and an electronic music DJ in his pieces. He insists each piece is an absolute original: "There is no Lin Zhaohua style. And there is no Lin Zhaohua method. Every theater work has its own unique style to be discovered, and created."

Even after more than 40 years in "the biz," Lin Dao continues to innovate. His recent projects include the Theatre Research Institute at Peking University as well as China's first Masters of Fine Arts program in acting and directing. He explains, "Realism borrowed from Russia [the Stanislavsky method] has been assigned a holy status in Chinese theater schools. This is very limiting. Theater training, styles of acting and other creative works have to change, adapt, improve, and move ahead." With the Theatre Research Institute he hopes to provide alternative theater training in China: "One that is contemporary, open and experimental – in which methods and techniques from both East and West, traditional and modern, will be used to explore the art of the stage. Art should have no boundaries, and theater needs freedom to be alive."

Lin Zhaohua Drama Studio Peking University Theatre Research Institute, Haidian District. (6275 3253); www.linzhaohua.com (Chinese only); www.pku-theatre.com (English and Chinese)

A scene from I Heart Beijing

Theater Directory

Beijing Conference Center *88 Laiguangying Xilu, Chaoyang District. (8490 1199)* 北京会议中心，朝阳区来广营西路88号

Beijing Exhibition Theater *135 Xizhimenwai Dajie, Xicheng District. (6835 4455)* 北京展览馆剧场，西城区西直门外大街135号

Beijing Modern Dance Company Theater *7 Xichang'an Dajie, Xicheng District. (6601 5928, 6758 7161, info@bmdc.com.cn)* 北京现代舞团，西城区西长安大街7号

Beijing North Theater *Beibingmasi Hutong, 67 Jiaodaokou Nandajie, Dongcheng District. (6406 0175)* 北兵马司剧场，东城区交道口南大街67号北兵马司胡同

Beijing Peking Opera Theatre *30 Haihu Xili, Fengtai District. (6724 8222)* 北京京戏院，丰台区海户西里30号

Beijing Seven-Color Light Children's Theater *14A, Ju'er Hutong, Jiaodaokou, Dongcheng District. (8401 6487)* 北京七色光儿童剧院，东城区交道口菊儿胡同甲14号

Beijing Traditional Opera Theater *8 Majiapu Dongli, Fengtai District. (6757 2221 ext 2155)* 北京戏校排演剧场，丰台区马家堡东里8号

Beijing Youth Palace *68 Xizhimen Nanxiaojie, Xicheng District. (6615 2211) www.bjqng.com.cn* 北京青年宫，西城区西直门南小街68号

Capital Theater *22 Wangfujing Dajie, Dongcheng District. (6524 9847)* 首都剧场，东城区王府井大街22号

Central Academy of Drama Theater *39 Dongmianhua Hutong, Dongcheng District. (6407 4406)* 中央戏剧学院实验小剧场，东城区东棉花胡同39号

Central Conservatory of Music *43 Baojia Jie, Xicheng District. (6642 5657) www.ccom.edu.cn* 中央音乐院，西城区鲍家街43号

Central Experimental Drama Theater *45A Mao'er Hutong, Di'anmenwai Dajie, Dongcheng District. (6403 1099) www.ntcc.com.cn* 国家话剧院，东城区地安门外大街帽儿胡同甲45号

Century Theater *21st Century Hotel, 40 Liangmaqiao Lu, Chaoyang District. (6466 4805, 6468 3311 ext 3126)* 世纪剧院，朝阳区亮马桥路40号（21世纪饭店）

Chang'an Grand Theater *7 Jianguomennei Dajie, Dongcheng District. (6510 1309/1310)* 长安大戏院，东城区建内大街7号

Chaoyang Theater *Shows daily 7.15pm (call for additional show times). 36 Dongsanhuan Beilu, Chaoyang District. (6507 2421/1818)* 朝阳剧场，朝阳区东三环北路36号

China Children's Art Theater *64 Dong'anmen Dajie, west of Wangfujing, Dongcheng District. (6521 1425)* 中国儿童剧场，东城区东安门大街64号

China Grand Theater *27A Wanshou Temple, Xisanhuan Lu, Haidian District. (6841 9381) www.chinatheater.com.cn* 中国剧院，海淀区西三环路万寿寺甲27号

China Ping Opera Theater *19, Block 4, Xi Luoyuan, Yangqiao, Fengtai District. (8726 6331)* 中国评剧大剧院，丰台区洋桥西罗园四区19号

China Puppet Theater *1A Anhua Xili, Beisanhuan Lu, Chaoyang District. (6425 4798) www.puppetchina.com* 中国木偶剧院，朝阳区北三环路安华西里甲1号

Chongwen Workers' Palace *44 Xingfu Dajie, Chongwen District. (6711 6135)* 崇文工人文化宫，崇文区幸福大街44号

PHOTO: COURTESY OF CHEEKY MONKEY PRODUCTIONS

Edward Lam's Production of Madame Bovary is Me

Dongyuan Theater *In the garden of Changpu He, Dongcheng District. (8511 5372)* 东苑戏楼，东城区菖蒲河公园内

East Pioneer Theater *8-2 Dongdan Santiao (east of Oriental Plaza), Dongcheng District. (6559 7394)* 东方先锋剧场，东城区东单三条8-2号

Ethnic Cultural Palace Theater *49 Fuxingmennei Dajie, Xicheng District. (6605 2404)* 民族文化宫大剧院，西城区复兴门内大街49号

Grand View Garden *Daily 8.30am-5pm. 12 Nancaiyuan Jie, Xuanwu District.* 大观园，宣武区南菜园街12号

Guo'an Theater *16A Huayuan Donglu, Haidian District. (6202 6328)* 国安剧院，海淀区花园东路甲16号

Haidian Theater *28 Zhongguancun Dajie, Haidian District. (6255 8026)* 海淀剧院，海淀区中关村大街28号

Huguang Guild Hall *3 Hufang Lu, Xuanwu District. (6351 8284, 6352 9134)* 湖广会馆，宣武区虎坊路3号

Lao She Teahouse *Daily 10am-10pm. Bldg 3, Qianmen Xidajie, Xuanwu District. (6303 6830)* 老舍茶馆，宣武区前门西大街3号楼

Li Yuan Theater *1/F, Qianmen Hotel, 175 Yong'an Lu, Xuanwu District. (6301 6688 ext 8860 or 8864)* 梨园剧场，宣武区永安路175号前门饭店一层

Peking University Hall *Inside Peking University, 75 Haidian Lu, Haidian District. (6275 1278) www.pku-hall.com* 北大百年纪念礼堂，海淀区海淀路75号北京大学内

People's Art Experimental Theater *3/F, Capital Theater, 22 Wangfujing Dajie, Dongcheng District. (6525 0996)* 人艺实验剧场，东城区首都剧场3层，王府井大街22号

People's Art Theater *22 Wangfujing Dajie (behind Capital Theater), Dongcheng District. (6525 0123)* 人艺小剧场，东城区王府井大街22号，首都剧院后面

People's Theater *74 Huguosi Dajie, Xicheng District. (6618 1634)* 人民剧场，西城区护国寺大街74号

PLA Song and Dance Theater *60 Deshengmennei Dajie, southeast corner of Jishuitan Qiao, Xicheng District.* 解放军歌舞剧院，西城区德胜门内大街60号积水潭桥东南角

Poly Theatre *Poly Plaza, 14 Dongzhimen Nandajie, Dongcheng District. (6500 1188 ext 5126/5127) www.polytheatre.com* 保利剧院，东城区东直门南大街14号保利大厦1层

South Gate Space *South gate, Dashanzi art district, 4 Jiuxianqiao Lu, Chaoyang District. (6437 9737)* 南门空间，朝阳区酒仙桥4号798大山子艺术区南门

Tianqiao Acrobatics Theater *Shows daily 7.15pm. 95 Tianqiao Shichang Lu, east end of Beiwei Lu, Xuanwu District. (6303 7449)* 天桥杂技剧场，宣武区北纬路东口天桥市场街95号

Tianqiao Theater *30 Beiwei Lu, Xuanwu District. (8315 6337)* 天桥剧场，宣武区北纬路30号

Universal Theater (aka Heaven and Earth Theater) *Shows daily 7.15pm. 10 Dongzhimen Nandajie, Dongcheng District. (6416 9893)* 天地剧场，东城区东直门南大街10号

Workers' Stadium *Gongti Beilu, Chaoyang District. (6501 6655 ext 5033)* 工人体育场，朝阳区工体北路

Xin Rong Theater *16 Baizhifang Xijie, Xuanwu District. (8355 9285)* 鑫融剧院，宣武区白纸坊西街16号

Zhengyici Theater *220 Xiheyan Dajie, Xuanwu District. (8315 1649)* 正乙祠戏楼，宣武区西河沿大街220号

Flyin' High
Acrobatics shows
by Dixie Ching and Annie Jonas

Normal gravity service will resume shortly ...

Ok, so maybe an acrobatics show isn't what you'd consider "high culture" entertainment – unless you're clambering off the tour bus after a long day of following around a yellow flag-toting guide at the Forbidden City. Many of us living in Beijing might consider ourselves past that stage already. But think back to the days when you first got here, when every little taste of Beijing culture was fascinating and intriguing, and acrobats were still a novelty. Whether taking the kids out for a night on the town, or giving your friends and relatives some ooh's and ahh's when they come to visit, these acrobatics shows might be just what you need to put a little bounce back into the Beijing experience.

Chaoyang Theater Featuring lasers, smoke machines and thumping music, this is not your grandfather's acrobat show! The standard plate-spinning, hoop-jumping and bicycle tricks are augmented by impressive feats of strength, balance, contortion and derring-do. Your kids will be wiggling in their seats in a happy, adrenaline-induced frenzy. Tickets RMB 180, 280, 380 (half-price for kids under 1.1m).
36 Dongsanhuan Beilu. (6507 2421/1818) www.acrobatics.com.cn 朝阳剧场，朝阳区东三环北路36号

Tianqiao Acrobatics This century-old theater is your chance to avoid kitsch-overload. It is small and rarely packed, so you can get super-close to the action. (We recommend you get the cheap seats, since you can probably move forward once you get inside.) The troupe compensates for the modest-sized stage by emphasizing spare demonstrations of their strength and agility: young boys tumble while balancing towering beams and lope up and down poles. While the costumes are a little threadbare and the sound system has seen better years, these acrobats don't need glitz or glitter to impress. During the intermission, make sure to check out the photo of the "Pyramid of Bowels" on display in the lobby – it's not a trick that you're likely to see performed live (we hope). Tickets are RMB 100, 150, 200. Student tickets are RMB 80.
Daily 7.15pm. 95 Tianqiao Shichang Lu (east end of Beiwei Lu, next to Tianqiao Le Tea House), Xuanwu District. (6303 7449) 天桥杂技剧场，宣武区北纬路东口天桥市场街95号

Universal Theater The China Acrobatic Troupe performs nightly at the Universal Theater (also called Heaven and Earth Theater). The tumbling, juggling and contorting will keep you on your toes, but the highlight is the bicycle act – about 20 girls pile themselves on a single moving bike! Best of all, you can buy a cone of fresh, hot popcorn in the lobby and make like you're at the movies. Tickets are RMB 100, 150, 200, 300.
Daily 7.15pm. 10 Dongzhimen Nandajie (about 50m north of the Poly Theatre), Dongcheng District. (6416 9893) 天地剧场，东城区东直门南大街10号

PHOTO: SIMON LIM

Tricks of the Trade
A peek inside the China National Acrobatic Troupe
by Alison M. Friedman

Whether you've been in Beijing for six years or six days, chances are you've seen an acrobatics performance. While the plethora of troupes in this town may try to distinguish themselves from each other with one or two signature tricks, most acts like plate spinning or balancing dozens of people on a bike are pretty standard fare. So how do they do it? Do invisible wires hold up these performers who defy laws of gravity (and child labor)? Or are these masters of athleticism really as incredible as they seem?

After spending more than a week backstage with the China National Acrobatic Troupe, I learned that the answer to both questions is a qualified yes. Yes, these performers are really as phenomenally skilled and daring as it seems from the audience; and yes, every now and then they need a little help. Here are a few of the tricks of the trade I observed.

Let's stick together

For the plate-spinning act, the bottoms of the plastic plates have little runners that snap onto the tops of the metal sticks. Although it does require skill to keep the plates spinning while contorting and balancing, the performers nevertheless can rely on the runners to prevent the plates from flying off into the audience or dropping onto the floor.

During the glass-balancing act, all glasses in the towering pyramid are securely glued to each other. When I questioned the prowess needed to balance glued glasses, artistic director Sun Lili argued, "Well the tricks aren't about the props – they are about what their bodies can do!" And yes, their bodies really can bend in all those mind-boggling directions.

Training wheels

They use harnesses and safety lines only for training and occasionally for rehearsals. But in performance, boys and girls, there are no strings attached!

Sun says most students enter their training school at age nine. "But we don't want them if they haven't already been training before that."

She's an intern, so she starts with just one

Career lengths vary, but Sun performed until she was 46.

Elbow grease

One of the troupe's signature acts involves two vertical poles rising from floor to ceiling. The male performers flip and pounce from pole to pole like monkeys, catching themselves with their legs or the crook of an elbow, sliding down the poles headfirst and stopping only when their noses are a hair's breadth from the floor.

While the precision, timing and strength required for this act are undeniable, the trick does involve the help of a strange concoction they cook up before each show. Each pole is coated with a toxic-smelling, viscous fluid made from boiling together motor oil and rosin (a brittle substance derived from tree sap, used to make varnishes). This noxious stuff – which is hard to remove even with paint thinner – creates traction to facilitate climbing and grabbing the poles. When asked what injuries are most common for the acrobats, Sun politely declined to answer.

Beijing's new National Grand Theater will house three music performance spaces

Conductor Tan Lihua in action with the Beijing Symphony Orchestra

Classical Music
by Eli Marshall

Sounding off on Beijing

For years, Beijing has enjoyed a reputation as a prime exporter of raw talent and an important destination on the international touring circuit. Now in its reclaimed cosmopolitan identity, it is making motions toward becoming a homegrown musical powerhouse in its own right. Concertgoers in the city seem to be just beginning to catch on to this burgeoning scene. At the same time, people abroad are sitting up to note the swift rise of Chinese instrumentalists around the world.

Silk Road instruments

Classical music is nothing new to China – the Shanghai Symphony, for instance, has a history as long as the New York Philharmonic's. Looking to earlier dynasties, a telling example of China's porous musical borders lies in the fact that almost all of today's traditional folk instruments have origins in Central Asia. Through established trade routes, European traffic would follow, too. As a result, China was witness to every major period of European classical music history, later transmitted through colonial concessions.

Beijing's own flirtations with late-Renaissance European music started during the Ming Dynasty, through the Jesuits. Matteo Ricci personally delivered four clavichords from Macau in the first decade of the 17th century as an offering to Emperor Wanli, teaching court eunuchs to play while singing Italian parlor songs in Chinese. Such experiments remind us that the very idea of "crossover" music is nothing new. As time passed and the Qing Dynasty waned, Beijing received its largest Western musical influences secondhand from the foreign concessions, which boasted the first orchestras in the country.

A national sound

Upon the Communist Party's rise to power, the reestablishment of Beijing as the nation's center meant a need to establish a modern, national musical agenda. Orchestras were viewed as Western in origin, but also a vital component of any developed culture, going hand in hand with media, film, and a social realist outlook modeled closely after the Soviet system.

Further models were found closer to home. Musical activities previously centered in the concession areas became templates for groups built on national identity. The Central Conservatory of Music was officially founded in Beijing in 1955, though it had actually been established earlier in concessionist Tianjin. Over the next few decades, the conservatory would engage in exchange between schools in Russia; much of its library collection until even a few years ago consisted of scores and recordings from Moscow schools. In 1956, the Central Philharmonic was established, drawing from trained musicians all around the nation and even Chinese musicians educated and living abroad.

ART & CULTURE

The narrower doctrines of the late sixties led to repertoire like the Model Operas and the Yellow River Cantata – the best output of a rather one-sided musical language. But a few years later, training in music hit a standstill altogether, as would-be students headed to the provinces and the Central Conservatory closed its doors for over a decade. (During this period, conductor Li Delun is said to have narrowly saved the trombone from Jiang Qing's wrath in the "revolutionary opera orchestra"; she worried it was a "non-Socialist instrument.") Suffering even more than Western classical music – and with more permanent repercussions – were living folk music traditions in Beijing.

Retuning

The end of the "Cultural Revolution" in 1976 led to a more open environment for music. From the international perspective, the documentary *From Mao to Mozart* chronicling violinist Isaac Stern's visit in 1979 remains an illuminating portrait of this time period and its mix of backward inertia with newfound vibrancy and hunger for international exchange.

The Central Conservatory reopened in 1978. What followed was by all accounts a fertile, even fervent, artistic period. By the late '80s, there was a general feeling of reestablished momentum; many conservatory-trained artists (yes, including Cui Jian and his cronies) hopped effortlessly between classical and popular genres and began to fill the ranks of the old and new musical organizations. Many influential musicians now on the world stage, such as composers Chen Yi, Chen Xigang, Guo Wenjing, Liu Sola, Qu Xiaosong, Tan Dun, Tang Jianping, Ye Xiaogang and Zhou Long, hail from the classes entering that year or in the few years following.

Of course, many of them left for foreign pastures, feeling either constrained by a still-provincial system or pulled by career opportunities elsewhere. But economic reforms followed the loosening of social control, and musicians here started smelling the money, too. More families, achieving middle-class status and bourgeois values, began to purchase pianos and seek music lessons. Newly designed concert halls opened their doors and began to actively invite foreign performers and promote local musicians. Many students from the late '70s (those who hadn't left) became professors. Orchestras pushed for higher quality and made small steps toward independent functioning. This era saw the beginning of the Beijing Symphony Orchestra (formerly the Song and Dance Troupe) and the China National Symphony (formerly the Central Philharmonic). It also saw the launch of the China Philharmonic (formerly the Central Broadcasting Symphony) in 2000, the first orchestra to employ a significant amount of foreign funding. In 1998, the first annual Beijing Music Festival was held, bringing many top-list classical names to Beijing for the first time.

Ready to play

Musical Beijing, like everyone else, has been acutely aware of the pre-Olympic global spotlight directed at the city. With a doubly laden sense of something to gain and something to prove, groups from the conservatories and the primary orchestras in the city have been frequently embarking on tours overseas. Chinese ensembles and performers living in the country are signing contracts with major international labels. Significant numbers of musicians who had made a life abroad are beginning to return to China, some after decades, to take up positions as professors. The lasting impact of these voluntary participants is likely to mean good things for the next generation – and their increased numbers will hopefully translate into good things for audiences today.

Big organizatons still dominate the scene, but bureaucracy just can't write a good tune on its own. Those of us lucky to be in the city now are catching the first taste of a more zesty and locally oriented concert scene which has nothing if not potential to grow. When concert presenters realize that the audience is right here, and not a TV audience in Berlin, they're usually rewarded with a flood at the ticket office. Examples aren't always obvious; yes, piano stars like Lang Lang are an easy sell, but mere mention of the 2005 *kunqu* opera performance *Palace of Eternal Youth*, which packed the Poly Theatre to the gills, is still enough to make the college professor crowd salivate. Already seen as a major player on the world stage, especially for its exporting of talent, Beijing is now drawing rapt listeners around the world to hear the fledgling tones of what may become known as the "Beijing sound." And even those of us on the ground are beginning to catch on that this is one of the few places in the world where you can watch classical music grow even bigger.

Tan Dun's Musical Alchemy

by Alison M. Friedman

Tan Dun has composed music for stones, paper, for basins full of water and the odd ceramic jug. The world-renowned composer-conductor does not allow convention to impair creativity. Not even the rules of arithmetic get in the way.

"According to my formula, one plus one equals one," says Tan, who won the Academy Award in 2001 for the score to *Crouching Tiger, Hidden Dragon*, and whose most recent opera, *The First Emperor*, played to packed houses at New York City's Metropolitan Opera in January 2007.

"You combine different elements like a classical and a pop melody, with aboriginal rhythms, and bring it together into one cohesive whole," he explains. "In this way, one and one combine to become another unique 'one.'" An example of his creative philosophy in action includes

Composer Tan Dun

"Organic Music Series," which consists of works like *Paper Concerto for Paper Percussion and Orchestra* (2003), in which musicians rip and flutter rolls of paper in addition to playing traditional Western instruments. His goal is something synthesized and whole, in which the disparate parts are no longer perceptible.

However subversive his math might be, Tan's music and reputation have earned him the position of head musical curator for the Opening Ceremony of the 2008 Beijing Olympics. His 2002 opera *Tea: A Mirror of Soul* had its US premiere in Santa Fe, New Mexico last July, after which Tan flew to Beijing to present his musical bid for the Torch Lighting ceremony to the Beijing Olympic Committee. Two days later, he conducted a retrospective of three of his major works at the Beijing Hotel for a VIP gala marking the one-year countdown to the Olympics.

Tan Dun doesn't take his Olympic role lightly. "Olympic music isn't just pop music, this is a misconception. It is a duty entrusted to us [the creative team] by our culture. This is different from other music I've composed. This is music for television, music for media, music for a mass audience. This is music for *history*."

Tan will once again call on his tried-and-true mathematical formula to combine multicultural elements for this international event – yet with a strong nod to ancient Chinese civilization. He says he will use ancient metal bells and jade chimes to achieve what he calls *jin yu qi sheng*, or, "the music of gold and jade." But this is Chinese culture with Olympian characteristics: "You have the Olympic medals – gold, silver and bronze – so I [will] transpose the metal of these medals into the design, the timbre, the structure of my music."

In addition to the Olympics, he's currently working on an opera called *The Forbidden City of Marco Polo*, which will have its world premiere in Amsterdam in 2008 and will be performed in Beijing's Forbidden City in 2009. This project will also follow his cultural formula of combination. "It's a dialogue between Kublai Khan and Marco Polo, between Peking Opera and Western Opera," says Tan.

You can catch Tan Dun's large-scale, open-air Zen Musical Ceremony, which incorporates over 1,000 monks performing martial arts and traditional chants at the 1,510-year-old Shaolin Temple on Songshan Mountain in Henan Province.

ART & CULTURE

Beijing offers a feast of live classical music

Musical Resources
Orchestras
Beijing Symphony Orchestra Music director Tan Lihua slowly built this orchestra from a gewutuan (song-and-dance troupe) into a prominent local player over the last 15 years. In recent years, they have toured Europe twice and in 2007 ventured to Taiwan. In 2007 the BSO also released two CDs on the EMI label. www.bjso.cn

China National Symphony Orchestra and Chorus This ensemble is the oldest orchestra in Beijing, the traditional flagship orchestra of the Ministry of Culture. Recent years have been turbulent, but with the new appointment of international-caliber music director En Shao last year, things are looking up. www.ccno.net

China Philharmonic Orchestra The "China Phil" was founded after a split with China Central Television's Broadcasting Symphony in 2000, using a combination of foreign and local support and political savvy. Raising the bar on salaries, it remains by a hair the best orchestra in town and today is still the best-funded, with continued high-profile tours, guest soloists and recordings on the Deutsche Grammophon label.

The founder, Yu Long, is a phenomenon in and of himself and is probably the most powerful purveyor of classical music in the country, operating his projects with unquestionable business savvy. In addition to this ensemble, he directs the Beijing Music Festival (see below). www.chinaphilharmonic.org

Concert Halls
Beijing has three primary halls that devote themselves primarily to classical or concert music: the **Beijing Concert Hall,** the **Forbidden City Concert Hall**, and **Poly Theatre.** Poly Theatre is the only one of these boasting staged opera capabilities. Acoustically, none is "world-class." This is expected to change with the imminent opening of the **National Grand Theater**, known to locals as "the Egg." This enormous structure, seated centrally next to Tiananmen Square and a stone's throw from both the Forbidden City Concert Hall and the Beijing Concert Hall, will house three state-of-the-art halls under one roof, suited for grand opera, orchestra or chamber music. Once its management is fixed, it will no doubt receive significant national and world media coverage in its first few seasons.

Universities
Beijing's conservatories are large venues for professional education servicing all ages, from toddlers to doctoral students. Beijing municipality's **China Conservatory**, traditionally a center for Chinese *minyue* (folk music) instru-

The Asian Youth Orchestra in performance

ment instruction as well as voice and piano, has recently started a Western orchestral program to go up against the **Central Conservatory**, the central government's choice music school. Both are also outfitted for public performances. The **Peking University Hall** hosts scores of musical performances. They have a large hall, as well as a recently opened, state-of-the art recital hall. Other university venues of note include small halls at **Capital Normal University** and at **Renmin University**.

See page 607 for addresses and listings.

Festivals

Of all the annual festivals hosting classical or concert-oriented music, the **Beijing Music Festival** probably draws the most international attention. With a strong funding base, the festival has brought a whirlwind five weeks of activity every fall since 1998, importing A-list foreign soloists and orchestras and a whole host of programming. In 2007 and 2008, concerts run from late September to late October.

The Central Conservatory of Music hosts a number of annual festivals: the international **Beijing Modern Music Festival** (May), the more internally focused **Conservatory Festival** (December), and **Musicacoustica** (October), a festival dedicated to electro-acoustic music. In addition, the conservatory hosts an ever-growing multiplicity of single-focus events, conferences and guest performances. Other festivals with music include the **Dangdai International Arts Festival** in the fall and a new festival at **Renmin University** scheduled for November. The **Great Wall Music Festival and School**, founded in 2004, is a summer academy dedicated to young string players from China and abroad, with some name-brand faculty from the United States in residence who usually perform on midsummer weekends.

Beijing Music Festival: www.bmf.org.cn
Musicacoustica: cemc.ccom.edu.cn
Great Wall Academy: www.greatwallacademy.org
Central Conservatory (Beijing Modern, Musicacoustica, Conservatory Festival): www.ccom.edu.cn

Media

Websites that list live events include www.piao.com.cn and www.piao.com (they're different) – the former has an English-language section, though it's not always updated as often as the Chinese. The **CCTV Music Channel** (音乐频道) often broadcasts live classical music concerts, with a host of other programming ranging from glitz and glitter to educational highbrow. **CCTV 3, 4** and **9** occasionally hold in-depth interviews with local and international musical figures.

Making Chamber Music Locally

The ups and downs of the indie classical scene
by Eric Mendel

Four members of the Beijing New Music Ensemble

PHOTO: LUNA ZHANG

So far, Beijing's more successful developments in classical music have been limited to the blockbuster phenomenon: big, expensive and international. But musicians are beginning to stand up and say that if Beijing is going to really cut it as a musical superpower, it will need to have a vibrant scene on the ground – which means thinking small, too.

In the mind of Yang C. Lin, chamber music is one of the highest priorities for the concert scene. He studied in Shanghai and abroad at the Moscow Conservatory, coming back to China in 1997 at age 28 to teach at the Central Conservatory, where he founded the now-defunct Beijing String Quartet. He also has a small-scale production company, Linzarts (www.linzarts.org), specializing in supporting recitals and similar endeavors.

Expat clarinetist Keith Lipson combines his musical training with a more recent background in Sinology. A graduate of the Curtis Institute of Music, he co-founded the Beijing New Music Ensemble (www.beijingnewmusic.org), one of the few independent chamber music ensembles in the country and the only one dedicated to promoting contemporary music.

IG: Could you sum up the current state of chamber music here?
Yang C. Lin: In this society we like soloists too much. The biggest soloist is the emperor; this is our tradition. But as China is opening, a lot of Chinese performers are accepting chamber music now, at least those who have been around the world, so I think the cultural movement will inevitably have more of this kind of activity.
Keith Lipson: So many of the problems have to do with too much competition in the field. On top of that, musicians are nervous about their financial status. But there are exceptions. I admire those who put a more purely musical career first, but they encounter so much apathy. They need to be supported more.

IG: How did you each come to be doing music in Beijing?
Lipson: I was fascinated with China and came to study, and also to escape from the classical music scene. Only after coming in contact with like-minded people did I start to play concerts. It's a real fulfillment to be able to choose the people I work with. Now I'm able to do that in the context of China, a place I love.
Lin: In my case, while living in Europe I made a decision: I must work in my homeland. It's open and it's empty – a very simple reason. We needed at least one group really working on a strong musical foundation. Personally, I think the Beijing String Quartet was, in the last ten years, one of the more interesting projects. With three years' work we reached a very high level, and engaged in exchange programs. We ended only because we did not have enough financial support ... The string quartet is a very special group which needs a lot of spirit put into it, and you cannot work one month and rebuild a quartet. And people don't have many three-year slots they can devote to rebuilding.

IG: Are there people who really want to listen to this kind of music – not only chamber music, but cutting-edge contemporary music on top of that?
Lipson: I think the audience is already there and pretty hungry. We [the Beijing New Music Ensemble] make a point of performing to different kinds of audiences. We play regularly for the D-22 crowd, for instance, even while we do our more formal concerts in other venues. We performed at a wonderful small recital hall at Peking University last year. I was shocked at the level of concentration – we were doing some pretty avant-garde repertoire, and the audience was really into us.

Student musicians, though, have little exposure to chamber music, even less than in America where there's also not enough. It's a drawback, but in some ways it opens up lots of new opportunities and in some cases it means people are more receptive to trying new things. But there's so much societal pressure. I wish the most promising students could be given a platform of financial support and also have more opportunities to experiment as artists instead of worrying about testing and about their future careers.
Lin: Yes, there have been educational changes, but from an old, traditional system to a mechanical system. Like everywhere else, we had a tradition, but that has changed along more international lines, not always for the best.

IG: Can we talk more about education?
Lin: Right now, all talented young musicians, all of them, have gone abroad. Nobody stays in China; they are done here after high school.

IG: All of them?
Lin: All of them, unless they can't afford it. Around the world, investment in basic education and the support of classical music is never enough. But the contrast in China between the support, the investment, and the production, is very sharp. We have a powerful classical market, but we "sell" more than "grow." I think we already have some kind of upper class which would be interested in offering a different kind of support, but they need the [right direction]. It would become a great help and a symbol for more musical changes.

Twice I obtained the opportunity to work in Japan with Isaac Stern, and the Japanes classical music foundations did a really good job, supporting Chinese, Korean and Italian musicians. Something strange, something very beautiful happened there. Classical music is not native to Japan, but they did it. This makes me feel optimistic.

25-year-old piano virtuoso Li Yundi

Concert Hall Directory

Beijing Concert Hall *1 Beixinhua Jie, Xicheng District. (6605 7006/5812)* 北京音乐厅，西城区北新华街1号

Capital Gymnasium *54 Baishiqiao Lu, Haidian District.* 首都体育馆，海淀区白石桥路54号

Central Conservatory of Music *43 Baojia Jie, Xicheng District. (6642 5746) www.ccom.edu.cn* 中央音乐学院，西城区鲍家街43号

Forbidden City Concert Hall *Inside Zhongshan Park, Xi Chang'an Jie, Xicheng District. (6559 8285)* 中山公园音乐堂，西城区西长安街中山公园内

Goldsail Concert Hall *24 Wangfujing Dajie, Dongcheng District. (6525 0615)* 金帆音乐厅，东城区王府井大街24号

Great Hall of the People *West side of Tian'anmen Square, Dongcheng District. (6309 6156)* 人民大会堂，东城区天安门广场西侧

Instituto Cervantes *1A Gongti Nanlu, Chaoyang District. (5879 9666)* 北京塞万提斯学院，朝阳区工体南路甲1号

National Library Concert Hall *33 Zhongguancun Nandajie, Haidian District. (6848 5462)* 国家图书馆音乐厅，海淀区中关村南大街33号

Peking University Hall *Inside Peking University, 75 Haidian Lu, Haidian District. (6275 1278) www.pku-hall.com* 北大百年纪念礼堂，海淀区海淀路75号北京大学内

Poly Theatre *Poly Plaza, 14 Dongzhimen Nandajie, Dongcheng District. (6500 1188 ext 5126/5127) www.polytheatre.com* 保利剧院，东城区东直门南大街14号保利大厦1层

South Gate Space *South gate, Dashanzi art district, 4 Jiuxianqiao Lu, Chaoyang District. (6437 9737)* 南门空间，朝阳区酒仙桥4号798大山子艺术区南门

Stadium of Beijing Olympic Sports Center *1 Anli Lu, Haidian District. (6491 2233)* 国家奥林匹克中心体育场，海淀区安立路1号

Tianqiao Theater *30 Beiwei Lu, Xuanwu District. (8315 6300)* 天桥剧场，宣武区北纬路30号

Workers' Gymnasium *Gongti Beilu, Chaoyang District. (6501 6300)* 工人体育馆，朝阳区工体北路

Workers' Stadium *Gongti Beilu, Chaoyang District. (6501 6655 ext 5033)* 工人体育场，朝阳区工体北路

Dancing Outside the Lines
Modern dance in Beijing
by Alison M. Friedman

China's dancers execute gravity-defying leaps and dizzying spins with superhuman precision and flexibility. They are known the world over as being some of the best-trained technicians in dance. And now, pioneers of modern dance in China are pushing beyond traditional limits in choreography to express their own individual voices. It will be only a matter of time before the Martha Grahams of the Middle Kingdom emerge to redefine this art form.

Modern dance reared its rebellious, creative head in China as early as the 1920s, but the art's development was squelched during the "Cultural Revolution" when it was deemed a foreign import associated with American imperialism. Its practice was prohibited until the 1980s.

In 1987, Yang Meiqi, then-principal of the Guangdong Dance Academy in southeast China, set up a four-year modern dance training program with support from the province and foreign benefactors. In 1992, some of the graduates formed the Guangdong Experimental Modern Dance Company, China's first official such company. Ms. Yang now splits her time between Guangdong, Shanghai and international festivals to continue promoting modern dance education in China.

Over the past few years, Beijing has seen a surge of modern dance classes, performances and festivals, perhaps as the handful of modern dance companies try to keep up with each other. Or perhaps they are responding to the audience's increased demand for more diverse, innovative performances. Whatever the reason, Beijing audiences are the beneficiaries.

A member of The Beijing Modern Dance Company

The Beijing Modern Dance Company

Founded in 1995, BMDC is still the most prestigious modern dance company in China, boasting such accomplishments as commissioned world premieres at the Venice Biennale, the Berlin Arts Festival and the Singapore Arts Festival, among others. In 2006 Italy's *Danza & Danza* magazine honored BMDC with the award for "Best Performance in Italy in 2006." After a decade of lobbying, in 2005 BMDC successfully convinced the government to change a law so that they could be an artistic non-profit, the first in China.

Performances: Thanks to an extensive schedule abroad – BMDC spends almost six months of the year at international festivals and on tour – the company has become better known overseas than in China. To develop modern dance audiences at home, BMDC performs at least once a month at the Chaoyang Culture Center/TNT Theater and other venues throughout Beijing. Student and group ticket prices are always available.

Classes: BMDC hosts regular classes for all skill levels at their Training Centre (schedules on website) in addition to monthly open master classes taught by BMDC members or invited international artists. Visitors may watch rehearsals or attend company class (if they can keep up!).

Festival: BMDC organized an annual Modern Dance Week in 1999 that lasted until SARS interrupted in 2003. In fall of 2007, they revived the festival on a larger scale: The Beijing International Modern Dance Festival, with performances, workshops, lectures and screenings all over the city. This festival will become the Beijing Dance Biennale in 2009.

Beijing Modern Dance Company 7 Chang'an Xijie, Xicheng District (inside Beijing Ministry of Culture Compound, east of Xidan subway exit C) (6601 6107) www.bmdc.com.cn

The Living Dance Studio / Caochangdi Arts Workstation

Founded in 1994 by choreographer Wen Hui and documentary filmmaker Wu Wenguang, the Living Dance Studio is China's first underground dance-theatre company. Their multimedia shows, more performance art than pure dance, address issues in contemporary Chinese society. In 2005, Wen and Wu opened Caochangdi Arts Workstation "to provide space and information resources, free of charge, to performance and video-media artists who wish to create new works." The Workstation includes studio space as well as a video library (and cafeteria!).

Festivals: If you are in Beijing in May, you might catch the **Young Choreographers Project**. Since 2006, the YCP has chosen around ten individuals and groups from applicants throughout China to showcase each May. Of those, three are then selected to further develop their work under the guidance of local and international artists, and perform in the fall at the **Crossing Festival**. A contemporary performance festival in its fourth year, the Crossing Festival includes performances, lectures and workshops by groups from throughout China and abroad.

Classes: Workstation invites artists from overseas to give lectures, present screenings and teach master classes, in addition to hosting workshops by the Living Dance Studio. All are free of charge and open to the public. Some focus on film as well as dance.

Performances: Aside from their two festivals, Living Dance Studio rarely performs in Beijing, as the artists spend a substantial amount of time performing and teaching abroad.

Workstation Arts Center 105 Caochangdi, Chaoyang District (6533 7243, 6433 6143) www.ccdworkstation.com (bilingual)

Beijing LDTX Modern Dance Company

The new kid on the block, LDTX was founded at the end of 2005 by Willy Tsao, former artistic director of the Beijing Modern Dance Company. LDTX stands for *Lei Dong Tian Xia*, which means, "Thunder shakes everything under heaven." Tsao also holds the reins of the Guangdong Modern Dance Company and Hong Kong's City Contemporary Dance Company.

Festival: LDTX doesn't hold a festival in Beijing yet, but each May their Guangdong Modern Dance Festival presents Tsao's three companies as well as companies invited from abroad.

Classes: LDTX holds regular classes in Beijing for beginners and advanced students in various dance styles at their studios. Check the website for updated schedules.

Performances: In addition to their own performances, LDTX also produces Beijing performances by Hong Kong dance companies and other domestic and international groups. Check their website for the latest information.

Beijing LDTX Modern Dance Company Studios *Dongcheng Cultural Center, 111 Jiaodaokou Donglu, Dongcheng District. (6405 4842, 6405 4292) www.beijingldtx.com (bilingual)*

The Beijing Dance Academy

Touted as China's most prestigious professional dance-training academy, this government-run institution is slowly opening up to the outside world. After finishing the four-year training program at the Guangdong Dance Academy, choreographer Wang Mei returned to BDA and helped establish its modern dance program under the choreography department. The teachers here work the system to create innovative modern dance that blends foreign techniques with Chinese content. Teachers like Wang Mei, Wan Su, Zeng Huanxing and Zhang Yuanchun treat their students like professional company members and create elaborate evening-length works each semester. The arts communication department, led by Zhang Zhaoxia, trains students in dance or film techniques and often holds mini-showcases of student films.

Although the Dance Academy is involved with many national and international dance competitions, it does not host its own festival. Foreigners can enroll as full-time students, but the Academy does not offer drop-in classes. Call the foreign affairs office to watch a class or rehearsals, or to find out if there is a *hui bao ke* (final class performance) scheduled.

Beijing Dance Academy *19 Minzu Xueyuan Nanlu, Haidian District. (Foreign Affairs Office:6893 5859) www.bda.edu.cn (Chinese only)*

A Journey of Moon and Clouds
Chinese cinema then and now
by Alice Wang

Fan Bingbing looking winsome in Lost in Beijing

Blood Brothers – *bad guys and Brylcreem in 1930s Shanghai ...*

Today, you can walk down the restored section of Dashilar in the Qianmen area, and begin to imagine what it must have been like over a century ago when the first Chinese film ever made, a recording of the Peking Opera *The Battle of Dingjunshan* (a story from the *Romance of the Three Kingdoms*), was screened in the sweltering Daguanlou cinema on this very street. Although the area has been almost completely rebuilt, the old cinema was preserved as a testimony to the journey of Chinese movies over the past hundred years.

In 1913, eight years after that first screening, a worker at a foreign bank, Zhang Shichuan, partnered with the drama critic Zheng Zhengqiu to start the Xinmin Film Company in Shanghai, which produced China's first feature film, *The Difficult Couple* (难夫难妻 *Nanfu Nanqi*), a critical piece about forced feudal marriage. In the late 1910s, China began to import American-made film stock. In the 1920s and '30s, with its access to fresh cultural trends as an international city, Shanghai became China's first oasis of cinema. It was a gathering place for filmmakers and stars and was the scene of a golden period of Chinese cinema.

During wartime, film was used to inspire nationalist sentiment. *Spring River Flows East* (*Yijiang Chunshui Xiangdong Liu*) and *Eight Thousand Miles of Cloud and Moon* (*Baqian Lilu Yunheyue*) are both classics from that period. In Chinese film history, the period from 1949 until the start of the "Cultural Revolution" in 1966 is called the "Seventeen Years." Despite political constraints, a variety of strong films emerged at that time. During the social upheaval of the 1960s and 1970s, even though most films were formulaic "model operas" (*Yangbanxi*), movies became an emotional release for many, including the intellectual youth who were sent down to the countryside. For them, watching a film in the open air with friends was a way of forgetting the hard physical labor of country life for a while.

The '80s and after

After the reforms of the 1980s, TV sets entered the lives of ordinary families, but movies still took up a large part of people's leisure life. Film magazines and star calendars are testament to the popularity of films at that time. In the 1990s, Chinese society changed rapidly, which is reflected in social and cultural ideas imported from Hong Kong, Taiwan, Japan and South Korea. The torrent of culture from abroad swept through the lives of young people. Teenagers would skip classes to watch a Chow Yun-Fat

PHOTO: COURTESY HUAYI BROS PICTURES/CMC ENTERTAINMENT/LION ROCK

... yep, 1930s Shanghai again, but this time it's ghosts, not gangsters in The Matrimony

action movie in a video parlor, rather than go on a school excursion to the cinema to see a mainstream film for free. Jia Zhangke, the director of the 2000 independent film *Platform*, confesses that most of his youth was spent in video parlors watching Hong Kong movies.

Recently, the Chinese movie industry has been experiencing hard times. TV is taking the place of film in people's leisure time. Crowded open-air cinemas, once a part of so many people's youth, have all but disappeared. State-owned film factories have had to reform or face bankruptcy. For example, Xi'an Film Factory, once an industry leader that produced films like Zhang Yimou's *Red Sorghum* and Wu Tianming's *Old Well*, declined in the 1990s. Because of the outdated organization of these "factories," many talented people like Wu Tianming left to work abroad.

At the beginning of the 21st century, Chinese people have access to more choice in culture and entertainment than ever before. Students play computer games adapted from Japanese cartoons, young professionals watch South Korean and American TV dramas, and people of all ages enjoy DVDs on their sofa at home, or go to movie theaters to watch Hollywood blockbusters. All this dilutes interest in local film. A lot of private film companies have been set up; some, like the Huayi Brothers, producers of *Big Shot's Funeral*, *Cell Phone* and *A World Without Thieves*, have been very successful in little more than a decade. There's no shortage of young talented directors, most of whom started as independent filmmakers. No matter how fast things change in China, film still entertains and delights a moviegoing population that has grown in taste and sophistication just as quickly, if not more quickly, than the film industry itself.

The hard journey of Chinese film over the past hundred years is like the old poem about "traveling with the moon and clouds for eight thousand li." Where has the journey taken us? Let's take a close look at Chinese film in the past year, 2007.

Chinese Film in 2007

Chinese film spans the range from epic blockbusters to mainstream movies to art house cinema.

2006 was the year for costume blockbusters with Chinese characteristics: Think *The Banquet* (夜宴 *Ye Yan*) by Feng Xiaogang, *The Promise* (无极 *Wu Ji*) by Chen Kaige and *Curse of the Golden Flower* (满城尽带黄金甲 *Mancheng Jindai Huangjinjia*) by Zhang Yimou. In 2007, however, the fever for historical dramas has cooled. After finishing his USD 45 million budget-busting *Curse*, Zhang Yimou is taking a break from films and transferring his attention to directing the opening ceremony of the 2008 Olympic Games.

Chen Kaige, after the failure of *The Promise* at home and abroad, returned to the familiar field of art movies. His new project is a biopic about Mei Lanfang, China's great Peking Opera star. The production has called up some heavy star power, including Hong Kong pop singer Leon Lai and China's most famous leading lady, Zhang Ziyi.

This year it seems Hong Kong directors are more interested in costume films than their mainland peers. John Woo's *Red Cliff*, a historical drama about a battle during the Three Kingdoms period, is the most expensive Chinese movie ever, with a budget of nearly USD 75 million. The four-hour epic is in two parts, the first to be released before the Olympics. Peter Chan (*Comrades: Almost a Love Story*), a director with a talent for urban romances, presents his first action movie, *Warlords* (刺马 *Ci Ma*). Action king Jet Li and pop star Andy Lau star in this story about the struggle of three brothers during the Qing dynasty. Chinese cinema is beginning to follow the tried and tested Hollywood formula of high production values and big stars.

At the end of 2006, *The Knot* (云水谣 *Yunshuiyao*) stood out among other mainstream movies. Spanning a 50-year period from the 1940s to the present, it tells the tragic love story of a couple kept apart by the separation of the Chinese mainland, Hong Kong and Taiwan. A Chinese mainland-Taiwan-Hong Kong co-production, it has earned RMB 37 million. While this number pales in comparison to the USD 70 million earned worldwide by *Curse of the Golden Flower*, there was no 2007 mainstream domestic film that could match the box office success of *The Knot*.

The success of *Crazy Stone* (疯狂的石头 *Fengkuang de Shitou*), a multi-dialect spoof-comedy about thieves trying to steal a precious piece of jade, shows that some genres can still be successful in China. Similarly, *Big Movie* (大电影之数百亿 *Dadianying zhi Shubaiyi*), a collaboration between thriller director Ah Gan and popular internet writer Ning Caishen, is a spoof of classic Chinese and Hollywood blockbusters. Another movie belonging to this popular comedy trend is *Calling in Love* (爱情呼叫转移 *Aiqing Hujiao Zhuanyi*). Despite the varied quality of these movies, they represent the most successful examples of uniquely Chinese cinema in the domestic market at this time.

Chinese art house movies, while critically acclaimed on the international festival circuit, are rarely popular at home. At the 2006 Venice Film Festival, Jia Zhangke won the Golden Lion for Best Film for *Still Life* (三峡好人 *Sanxia Haoren*). In 2007, Jia returned to Venice with his documentary *Useless* (无用 *Wu Yong*), which tells the story of how the young Chinese fashion designer Ma Ke started her "Wu Yong" brand and took it to the fall/winter 2007 Ready-to-Wear Fashion Show in Paris. The documentary was shown in the Horizons Documentary Section, along with another Chinese documentary, *Umbrella* (伞 *San*) by Du Haibin.

Tuya's Marriage (图雅的婚事 *Tuya de Hunshi*) took the Golden Bear for Best Film at the 2007 Berlin Film Festival. This prestigious award helped the film get preferential screening times at theaters, but the producers of *The Go Master* (吴清源 *Wu Qingyuan*) by Tian Zhuangzhuang, are not so confident that festival success will translate into good box office. The movie won a Special Award at the 2007 Shanghai Film Festival, but its release has been repeatedly postponed because of concerns about its appeal to a general audience.

Investment funds in the art movie sector are scarce, and the entertainment media are more interested in star trivia than in substantial stories about new films and emerging directors. And ticket prices don't make economic sense for most people: If a film doesn't have a name director or a famous star, it is hard to persuade audiences to pay RMB 80 when they can see the same movie later on DVD for RMB 8.

However, there are still signs of progress on the local scene. For example, there are now more women directors in the industry than ever before. Li Shaohong, China's most prolific female director, released her thriller, *The Door* (门 *Men*) in January 2007. Ann Hui, the veteran female Hong Kong director, moved audiences in 2007 with *The Postmodern Life of My Aunt* (姨妈的后现代生活 *Yima de Houxiandai Shenghuo*), a comedy-drama starring Siqing Gaowa and Chow Yun-Fat.

Whatever the future holds for China's film industry, Beijing's pulsating cultural scene and vibrant nightlife will ensure that local cinemagoers will have a ringside seat.

Feng Xiaogang's The Banquet *was Hamlet with Chinese characteristics*

Cinema Directory
Major Multiplexes

APM The comfy chairs at the back are big enough, and hidden enough, for two to get cozy. The selection is solid: Sun Dong An runs the newest flicks in town and tickets on Tuesdays are half price. Word to the hungry: the theater staff won't let you in with food and beverages from outside the theater. Tickets: Chinese movies RMB 30, foreign movies RMB 40-50.
Daily 9am-10pm. 138 Wangfujing Dajie, Dongcheng District. (8511 4393) 新东安商场，东城区王府井大街138号

East Gate Cinema It may be small and expensive, but with four well-equipped halls showing the newest in foreign and Chinese celluloid, East Gate is one of Beijing's best. Tickets are half price before noon every day, and it's also the only cinema in town to offer double-seats (RMB 140, 150 and 160 – the highest price lands you in the "VIP Hall"), which are ideal for cuddling couples or those inclined to get into armrest fights. Head to the nearby Subway shop, bakery or cafes to stave off hunger pangs.
B1/F, Bldg B, East Gate Plaza (behind the Poly Theatre), Dongzhong Jie, Dongcheng District. (6418 5931) www.dhyc.cn 东环影院，东城区保利大厦北侧东环广场B座地下一层

Star City This theater has the best snacks in town, making it an excellent place to take a date. No wonder Star City attracts in droves the pining pairs who favor Oriental Plaza as the launch site for puppy lovin'. Besides showing the latest commercial releases, the theater often hosts small-scale foreign movie festivals – your best bet for catching less mainstream foreign flicks. Tickets from RMB 20.
B1/F Oriental Plaza, Wangfujing Dajie, Dongcheng District. (8518 6778) www.xfilmcity.com 新世纪影城，东城区东方广场地下一层

Stellar International Cineplex Beijing's most extravagant movie theater, where top-end digital projectors fill the screens with the latest in Chinese and foreign flicks. Hit the screens early in the week to take advantage of various promotions: a free Coke on Monday, half-price tickets on Tuesday, free popcorn on Wednesday. Or get there any day of the week before noon to watch for half-price. On holidays, they screen films all night long. Tickets: RMB 50 and 60.
1) 4/F Bldg A, Wangjing International Business Center, 9 Wangjing Jie, Chaoyang District. (5920 3788); 2) 5/F, Golden Resources Shopping Center, 1 Yuanda Lu, Haidian District. (8887 2743) www.bjxingmei.com 星美国际影城，1) 朝阳区望京9号望京国际商业中心A座4层；2) 海淀区远大路1号金源购买物中心5层

UME International Cineplex The five-floor building is famed for its state-of-the-art equipment, clean environment and screening of recent foreign movies. It's open all day, but half-price tickets can be snagged before 8.30pm. Nosh on the standard array of popcorn flavors or head to the nearby Pizza Hut, Subway or Haagen-Dazs to fuel up pre-show. The Cineplex's biggest claim to fame – literally – is a 430-square-meter screen. Tickets RMB 50 and 60.
44 Kexueyuan Nanlu, Shuangyushu, Haidian District. (8211 5566) www.bjume.com 华星影院，海淀区双榆树科学院南路44号

Wanda Cinema Built and then abandoned by Warner Bros, this sleek, modern theater shows the latest Chinese hits and undubbed movies from Hollywood. The seating is comfortable, but traditionalists be forewarned: There's no salty popcorn, and the picture quality is occasionally grainy. Nonetheless, the large, adjacent arcade (with whack-a-mole!) is a draw in itself. Tickets are RMB 60-70. Tuesdays are half-price for everybody, while students pay half-price every day. RMB 150 VIP seats allow CBD swanksters to enhance their cinema-viewing experience with ultra-comfy seats, snacks and beverages including up to three glasses of wine.

Popcorn working its magic in Wudaokou

Daily 9am-10pm. 3/F, Bldg B, Wanda Plaza, 93 Jianguo Lu. (5960 3399) www.wandafilm.com 万达国际电影城，建国路93号万达广场B座3层

Alternative Fare

Cherry Lane Movies Located in an unattractive yard, Cherry Lane holds regular screenings of new and classic domestic films with English subtitles. The screens are large and they sell cookies and drinks. Cherry Lane shows low-profile, local documentaries once a month – often with the directors on hand to answer questions. Tickets RMB 50.
Anjia Lou, inside the Kent Center (turn north at Gaolan Dasha traffic light, off Liangmaqiao Lu, 70m ahead), Chaoyang District. (139 0113 4745) www.cherrylanemovies.com.cn 北京友厅公司，朝阳区高澜大厦红绿灯向北70米路东安家楼肯特中心院内

China Film Archives Founded in 1995, the cinema screens various Chinese and foreign classics at 6.30pm every Thursday. It also regularly hosts film festivals. Good sound and image quality, but snacking options are only so-so. If you can't stomach cinema without hot popcorn, walk on. Tickets RMB 25.
3 Wenhuiyuan Lu, Xiaoxitian, Haidian District. (6225 4422 ext 1214) 中国电影资料馆，海淀区小西天文慧园路3号1213室

French Cultural Centre Each week this cinema shows films of the classic French ilk. The clean and comfortable theater seats 80. Don't miss a chance to hang out in the cafe or bookstore next to the theater. Service is kind and informative. Tickets RMB 20.
16 Gongti Xilu, Chaoyang District. (6553 2627) www.ccfpekin.org 法国文化中心，朝阳区工体西路16号

Hart Centre of Arts Run by an artist couple, the center shows original Chinese art movies and new foreign documentaries every Saturday. The directors themselves often show up for Q&A sessions post-screening. One of the best places to catch Chinese art films. Lounge on the long, wooden bleachers padded with soft cushions. Tickets RMB 30. Open for functions, call to confirm.

Dashanzi art district, 4 Jiuxianqiao Lu, Chaoyang District. (6435 3570) www.hart.com.cn 哈特沙龙，朝阳区酒仙桥路4号798大山子艺术区

Soho New Town Cinema This fancy new picture house sits opposite South Silk Road restaurant and occasionally runs some of the city's more interesting film festivals. For example, Soho Cinema has housed Finnish and Turkish film festivals, as well as a screening of Asian shorts. Because it is little known, it's never crowded, even during the festivals. Still, there are no snacks and few drinks from which to choose. Tickets RMB 20.
3/F, Soho Club, Bldg D, Soho New Town, 88 Jianguo Lu, Chaoyang District. (8589 8990/92) www.startimes.cc Soho 电影放映厅，朝阳区建国路88号Soho现代城D座三层电影院

Other Cinemas

Beijing Theater Area 3, 10 Anhui Beili, Yayuncun, Chaoyang District. (6491 1228) bj-show.51.net 北京剧院，朝阳区亚运村安慧北里三区10号

Beijing Youth Palace Cinema 68 Xizhimen Nanxiaojie, Xicheng District. (6615 2241) www.ntcc.com.cn 北京青年宫影城，西城区西直门南小街68号

Changhong Cinema 75 Longfusi Jie, Dongcheng District. (6404 2159/1160) www.chfilm.cn 长虹电影院，东城区隆福寺街75号

China Cinema 25 Xinjiekouwai Dajie, Haidian District. (6223 0207) www.cfc.com.cn 中影影院，海淀区新街口外大街25号

China National Film Museum Tue-Sun 9am-4.30pm. 9 Nanying Lu, Chaoyang District. (6431 9548) www.cnfm.org.cn 中国电影博物馆，朝阳区南影路9号

Chonggong Cinema 44 Xingfu Dajie, Chongwen District. (6712 0697) 崇工电影院，崇文区幸福大街44号

Daguanlou Cinema 36 Dashilan, Qianmen, Xuanwu District. (6303 0878) 大观楼电影院，宣武区前门大栅栏36号

PHOTO: NICK OTTO

Where's Dr. No when you need him?

Dahua Cinema 82 Dongdan Beidajie, Dongcheng District. (6527 4420) 大华电影院，东城区东单北大街82号

Dizhi Cinema 30 Yangrou Hutong, Xisi, Xicheng District. (6616 8376) 地质电影院，西城区西四羊肉胡同30号

Dongchuang Cinema 3 Xinzhongjie, Dongzhimen, Dongcheng District. (6415 7332) 东创影院，东城区东直门新中街3号

Dongsi Workers' Culture Theater 47 Longfusi Jie, Dongcheng District. (6403 1596) 东四工人文化宫，东城区隆福寺街47号

Dongtu Cinema 85 Jiaodaokou Dongdajie, Dongcheng District. (6404 2764) 东图影剧院，东城区交道口东大街85号

Drive-in Cinema 100 Daliangmaqiao (1,500m east of Yanshaqiao), Chaoyang District. (6431 9595, 5165 2832) 汽车影院，朝阳区燕莎桥东1500米路北，大亮马桥100号

Goethe Institute 17/F, Bldg B, Cyber Tower, 2 Zhongguancun Nandajie, Haidian District. (8251 2909) www.goethe.de/peking 歌德学院北京分院，海淀区中关村南大街2号数码大厦B座17层

Guang'anmen Cinema 8 Baiguanglu, Xuanwu District. (6352 1766/2713) 广安门电影院，宣武区白广路8号

Hongxia Cinema 13 Hongxia Lu (opposite Jiuxianqiao Market), Chaoyang District. (6437 1383) 红霞影剧院，朝阳区红霞路13号酒仙桥商场对面

Hujialou Cinema Xinjie Dayuan, Chaowai Xiaozhuang, Chaoyang District. (6593 1765, 6593 1720) 呼家楼电影院，朝阳区朝外小庄新街大院

Instituto Cervantes 1A Gongti Nanlu, Chaoyang District. (5879 9666) 北京塞万提斯学院，朝阳区工体南路甲1号

Italian Embassy Cultural Office 2 Sanlitun Dong'erjie, Chaoyang District. (6532 5015) 意大利大使馆文化处，朝阳区三里屯东二街2号

Jinsong Cinema Bldg 404, Area 4, Jinsong Zhongjie, Chaoyang District. (6778 2727) 劲松电影院，朝阳区劲松中街4区404

Mexican Embassy Cultural Office 5 Sanlitun Dongwujie, Chaoyang District. (6532 2574) 墨西哥大使馆文化处，朝阳区三里屯东五街5号

Sam Cinema 42 Shijingshan Lu, Shijingshan District. (6687 9104) 山姆电影院，石景山区石景山路42号

Shengli Cinema 55 Xisi Dongdajie, Xicheng District. (6617 5091) 胜利电影院，西城区西四大街55号

Shoudu Shidai Cinema B1/F, Capital Times Square, Xidan, Xicheng District. (8391 3644/5) 首都时代影城，西城区西单时代广场地下一层

Wudaokou Workers' Club Cinema 23 Chengfu Lu, Haidian District. (6231 3624) www.wdkclub.com.cn 五道口工人俱乐部电影院，海淀区成府路23号

Xicheng Workers' Culture Cinema 24 Yuetan Nanjie, Sanlihe Dongkou, Xicheng District. (6852 7788 ext 6302) 西城工人文化宫电影院，西城区三里河东口月坛南街24号

Xinjiekou Cinema 69 Xizhimennei Dajie, Xicheng District. (6225 6713) 新街口电影院，西城区西直门内大街69号

Yingxie Cinema 22 Beisanhuan Donglu, Chaoyang District. (6420 7759) 影协电影院，朝阳区北三环东路22号

Ziguang Cinema 5-6/F, west section of Landao, 168 Chaowai Dajie, Chaoyang District. (6599 2228/2229) 紫光电影院，朝阳区朝阳门外大街168号蓝岛大厦西区5层6层

ART & CULTURE

The ABCs of CCTV
Time to turn on the tube
by Lee Ambrozy

Every province, autonomous region and big city has at least one local television station, and Beijing is far in the lead with a whopping ten. But if you want to tune in to the national mood, there is nothing like plugging into the nearly 20 channels of China Central Television, the country's national public broadcaster. To help you surf with ease, we've compiled the following guide to CCTV channels. For specific show information, get programming schedules online at www.cctv.com or pick up a copy of the very comprehensive *China TV News* (*Zhongguo Dianshi Bao*) for RMB 0.80.

CCTV's new headquarters will turn heads. But will it change channels?

CCTV 1 综合频道
Channel 1 is the omnibus of CCTV, which speaks with the authority of the central organs. All-inclusive programming via the nation's strongest signal also ensures nearly all citizens can access its orthodox content.

CCTV 2 经济频道
Economic Channel
News and reports ranging from microeconomics to macroeconomics, complete with streaming ticker-tape news bites and nearly up-to-the minute international exchange rates.

CCTV 3 综艺频道
Entertainment Channel
If you are mesmerized by variety shows featuring coiffed hosts in glittery evening wear, you will be entertained. Other programming includes news, music and televised music or theater performances.

CCTV 4 国际频道
International Channel
View the nation from an international perspective: talk shows, documentaries and news examine politics, economics and "Eastern Civilization" on a global scale. Viewers can also learn English or watch experts discuss international affairs.

CCTV 5 体育频道
Sports Channel
Fans rejoice for the ESPN of CCTV, featuring all the perks including national and international matches, games and tournaments, with occasional live coverage. Lots of volleyball and table tennis.

CCTV 6 电影频道
Movie Channel
Short films, old films, international films and tons of stuff from the Hollywood back lots. Mandatory dubbing into Chinese.

CCTV 7 儿童，军事和农业频道
Children's, Military and Agricultural Channel
Cartoons are shoved between daily reports on military affairs (even occasional mess hall cooking shows) and relevant news for farmers.

CCTV 8 电视剧频道
Soap Opera and Serial Channel
A station exclusively devoted to serial dramas and soap operas – some internationally syndicated as well. These emotional cliffhangers come interspersed with healthy doses of dish.

CCTV 9 英语频道
English Channel
All-English programming. News "from a Chinese perspective," programs such as Culture Express, Biz China and much more. Also home to beloved news anchor James Chau.

CCTV 10 科教频道
Science and Educational Channel
Meet artists and filmmakers through daily profiles, learn about nature and the environment through various programs, and see documentaries on a broad spectrum of smart topics.

CCTV 11 戏曲频道
Traditional Opera Channel
Screeching long-sleeved performers and revolutionary folk operas keep elders sated with traditional entertainment. Excellent background noise for the illiterate or uninitiated.

CCTV 12 社会与法频道
Society and Law Channel
See the legal system in action with reports from across the nation, exposés and other law-related talk shows and news.

CCTV News 新闻频道
On-the-hour news coverage, talk shows, survey programs and forums with experts, experts and more experts.

CCTV Kids 少儿频道
Cartoons rule daytime programming, and look out for some great kid-oriented soaps! In the evening, movies from the '50s through the '70s "instruct" children in soon-to-be forgotten morals.

CCTV Music 音乐频道
MTV? Not quite. This is a mix of classical and symphonic concerts alongside glitzy and extravagant patriotic, minority and folk music videos.

CCTV E&F 西班牙语和法语频道
Programming en Español and en Français
This mysterious new channel is a near-replica of its English brother, CCTV 9. Unfortunately, it is currently only available in Europe and parts of Africa by satellite. Eventually, news from the Chinese perspective will be available in the four corners of the world.

Top Cellar

The finest wine collection

Great Wine Selection

Professional Wine Accessories

Wine & Gift Suggestions

Wine Party Organisation

Free Delivery
Minimum Order RMB600

Visit us in:

CBD
Central Park Shop 103   Tel: (86 10) 6597 0024
Kerry Centre Hotel   Tel: (86) 13911 486 749

Financial Street
Winland Plaza B109   Tel: (86 10) 5181 9968

marketing@topcellar.com.cn
www.topcellar.com.cn

Immersion Guides

Beijing getting you down?

Get out of town with our **Excursion** and **Lhasa** guides!

Beyond the sights of China's ancient capital, there is another Beijing. The **Beijing Excursion Guide** takes you on day and weekend trips to the wonders that lie beyond the Fifth Ring Road. Find the wildest sections of the Great Wall, camp among the cypresses of Yunmengshan Mountain, or get in touch with your inner Mongol on the Kangxi grasslands. Maps, reviews, directions and transportation tips on over 70 destinations give you the perfect cure to cabin fever.

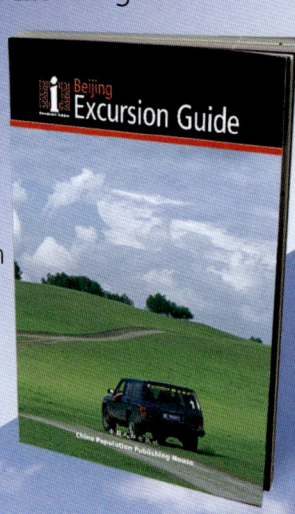

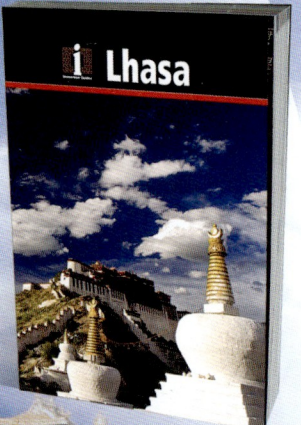

Lhasa, one of the great religious and artistic centers of Asia, fascinates visitors as much today as it ever has. Written with insight and passion by Tibet insiders and scholars, **Lhasa** combines cultural knowledge, practical travel advice and stunning photography in an indispensable guide to this ancient capital embracing its 21st century future.

Find the **Excursion** and **Lhasa** guides in bookstores around Beijing or to order a copy, please e-mail distribution@immersionguides.com

www.immersionguides.com

Spectral Mindset
The Cubist approach to sightseeing
by John Brennan

My first memory of Beijing sightseeing takes me back an alarming number of years into the past. I am completely alone in the Forbidden City, pawing with wind-numbed fingers at the pages of the only guidebook I could scrounge: a 1979 French-language Nagel.

Today, Beijing and I are still going strong, even though it wasn't easy then, and it isn't now. Let's face it, Beijing has always been advanced sightseeing. You have to know how to conserve your energy, your humor and your sense of wonder. If you do, the rewards are matchless. So whether you're a Beijing tenderfoot or a veteran of a score of spring sandstorms, the following fragments of advice may help.

A portal into the past at Dongbianmen Watchtower

Think small. By all means think big, too (see below), but remember that Beijing is full of tiny nuggets and side tracks that can rescue an afternoon that you thought was lost. You may find yourself transfixed by an ink painting of birds in a storm by the modern master Xu Beihong at his memorial museum in Xinjiekou. Or surreptitiously twisting your neck to see if a particularly bizarre wood carving is the right way up in the Song Tang Zhai Museum in Liulichang. Or watching a lone figure skater swooping across a corner of the Palace moat to "The Sound of Silence." One of these little detours can do your relationship with Beijing more good than a dinner of oysters and champagne.

Think big. Specifically, don't lose sight of the template that the Yongle emperor laid out in 1421. True, much of it has gone, but you can still find its traces in the modern metropolis. For the best view of how things once looked, try the Museum of Ancient Architecture (p262). You can gaze at the patch of ground where the emperor used to plough ceremonial furrows at the spring equinox (it's now a basketball court). But what really resonates is an astonishing 9m x 9m scale model of Beijing in 1949, when the city was little changed from Yongle's capital. No map, photo or painting can capture its scale like this model. It is all there: the encircling walls, mighty and yet dwarfed by the great city they girdled; the imperial geometry of the Tartar city in the north, the hectic bird's nest of the Chinese quarter south of Qianmen and the huge sweep of sacred ground in the south.

Even though the old walls are gone, their prosaic replacements – the Second Ring, the subway circle line – tell you whether you're inside the old city or have passed through one of its spectral gates. Most of Beijing's ancient monuments were aligned to the symmetry of the city's master plan, and you'll enjoy them more if you recall the whole of which they were once a part.

Go back. Most of Beijing's best attractions reward return visits. It's February and too cold to go out? It's not too cold for the magnolias in Jingshan Park. If it's May, the pomegranates will be flowering in the courtyards of the Lama Temple, and you can fall in love with the place all over again. Keep an eye on the Forbidden City website: some of the temporary exhibitions there are gems, and as you walk through the Palace again, some roofline or doorway is sure to stop you in your tracks as if you've never seen it before.

Finally, remember: More and more sites will emerge this year from their renovation cocoons. With the Olympics ahead, Beijing's sights are going to be looking better than they have in a long time. Carpe diem.

As the winds of change buffet China, the Great Helmsman stares on

Tian'anmen Square

It's the world's biggest square – three times the size of Moscow's Red Square and designed to hold one million people. Looking at the crowds that pack it today, it's hard to imagine that during the Qing dynasty it was merely a corridor, running southward between ministry buildings. These structures were swept away after 1911, but it wasn't until the late 1950s that Tian'anmen Square acquired its present size and was flanked with massive Sino-Soviet-style buildings as part of an architectural program to mark the 10th anniversary of the People's Republic. The next big change occurred in 1977, when the Chairman Mao Memorial Hall went up less than a year after his death.

The square has been a political focal point since the May Fourth Movement in 1919, but these days most activities are of the photo-snapping and kite-flying varieties. Held daily at sunrise and sunset with plenty of pomp, the flag raising and lowering ceremonies draw patriotic tourists from all over China, but relatively few foreigners.

The best place to view the square is from Tian'anmen Gate, which is the super-famous one with Mao Zedong's portrait.

Tian'anmen Gate
Daily 8.30am-4.30pm. RMB 15. North end of Tian'anmen Square, Chang'an Jie, Dongcheng District. (6524 3322) 天安门，东城区长安街天安门广场北侧

Great Hall of the People

The home of China's parliament (National People's Congress) was built in only ten months in 1959. Owing to a breakdown in Sino-Soviet relations, the Russian engineers who designed the massive meeting hall went home before the roof was finished, and the planned traditional Russian cupolas were scrapped in favor of flat Chinese eaves. The "10,000-seat theater" has nearly that many seats and features an illuminated red star on the ceiling. The tour guide describing the five-pointed light fixture pronounces the word "Plexi-glass" *(youji boli)* as if it were a rare valuable metal. It's worth a visit to experience the austere socialist realist design templates' attempt to contain the Chinese tendency toward baroque. Held regularly (except during parliamentary sessions), tours include bonus plastic socks to slip over your shoes. Concerts, performances and film premieres are occasionally held here, but the Hall is better constructed for politics than acoustics.

Daily 8am-4pm, but closed during government meetings. RMB 30, children RMB 15. West side of Tian'anmen Square, Dongcheng District. (6309 6156) 人民大会堂，东城区天安门广场西侧

National Museum

Like just about everything else in Beijing, the National Museum of China has plans to become the largest of its kind in the world. A massive expansion effort will close the museum from

PHOTO: LUNA ZHANG

2007 to 2010 and add 28 new exhibition halls, bringing its total area of 65,000 square meters to a mind-boggling 192,000. All this extra space means that historical and quirky treasures like Mao Zedong's "eight-cornered hat," Han dynasty jade suits and wine vessels will get state-of-the-art display and storage facilities. Fans of socialist grandeur need not fret: Originally commissioned for the 10th anniversary of the PRC, the building will keep its 1959 façade, which fronted the museum's previous incarnation as the dual Museum of the Chinese Revolution and Museum of Chinese History.

During the renovation, the collection's 620,000 pieces will be lent out to other museums in China and around the world, and the Capital Museum will host a major exhibition of Beijing-related artifacts during the Olympics. But until the dust settles, the only reason to visit will be the giant Olympic countdown clock facing the east side of Tian'anmen Square.

East side of Tian'anmen Square, Dongcheng District. (8447 4902) www.nationalmuseum.cn 中国国家博物馆，东城区天安门广场东侧

Chairman Mao Memorial Hall

The hall houses the embalmed body of Mao Zedong. The room is dimly lit, and guards shuttle patrons through quickly, so you'll only get a brief peek at the Great Helmsman, but it's still a worthy experience.

Tue-Sun 8-11.30am. Free. Middle of Tian'anmen Square, Dongcheng District. (6513 2277) 毛主席纪念堂，东城区天安门广场南侧

Monument to the People's Heroes

Erected in 1958, this 10,000-ton marble and granite obelisk has bas-reliefs that depict a people in revolt against their oppressors, starting with the burning of 20,000 chests of British opium in 1839 during the Opium War and culminating, inevitably, with the liberation of 1949.

Tian'anmen Square, Dongcheng District. 人民英雄纪念碑，东城区天安门广场中央

Forbidden City

This Ming dynasty masterpiece was built as the political and cosmic centerpiece of the Celestial Empire. The high walls surrounding its grandiose courtyards and ceremonial halls dwarf all who enter. At the northern end, where the imperial family lived and relaxed, the imposing grandeur dissolves into intimate private palaces and gardens. The entire complex is 900 meters long, 750 meters wide and contains more than 8,700 rooms (though a poetic legend puts the number at 9,999.5). It was built by tens of thousands of people, and took 12 years and 32 million bricks to complete.

As part of a Manchu shamanistic ritual during the Qing dynasty (1644-1911), four pigs were sacrificed daily to the gods in the Palace of Earthly Tranquility – 39 on holy days. Nine altars, placed around the city according to *fengshui* principles, were used by the emperor during holy rites, and many can still be seen today.

After the fall of the Qing in 1911, the imperial collections were relentlessly pillaged and pilfered. Most of the Qianmen antique shops in the 1920s were set up by sticky-fingered eunuchs who had left imperial service, and Emperor Pu Yi himself, perhaps confused about where his own property ended and China's began, spirited many items out of the palace. The remaining artifacts had to be moved out of Beijing when the Japanese invaded, and the Kuomintang (Nationalists) took 4,000 crates of treasure to Taiwan after the civil war that followed. Today, while the Forbidden City has one of the world's largest collections of Chinese art, hundreds of crates remain gathering dust in Nanjing.

During the "Cultural Revolution" (1966-1976), the Palace Museum had another big scare. In 1966, Red Guards prepared to march on the museum, the very citadel of the "Four Olds." Premier Zhou Enlai immediately closed the gates, however, and troops of the Beijing Garrison Command defended the perimeter. The Red Guards covered what they could with revolutionary slogans, and for the next five years the Museum remained closed, to be quietly reopened in 1971 ahead of Richard Nixon's historic visit the following year.

Today, the palace's main challenge is finding enough space to fit its entire collection. In recent years, they've already opened up an extra 50,000 square meters of exhibition space. The new exhibitions are in a series of rooms along the colonnade that begins on the western side of the courtyard immediately north of the Wumen Gate and extends past the western side of the Hall of Supreme Harmony. They include: Qing-era banners and insignia; imperial weaponry, firearms and riding gear;

Continues on p234

Rank Real Estate
A stroll through the Legation Quarter
by Eric Abrahamsen

Tunnel vision: this shady stretch of Zhengyi Lu once channeled sewage, not strollers.

One of the most alluring detours in all of Beijing is Zhengyi Lu, which leads south from Chang'an Jie just a hair west of Wangfujing. When you're stuck on the Parking Lot of Eternal Peace, on the verge of the broiling expanse of Tian'anmen, the tree-lined tunnel of Zhengyi Lu looks like the place you'd rather be.

Standing at the top of the street one hundred years ago, however, the view would have been far less idyllic. The fragrant sewage outflow of the Forbidden City would have been at your feet, and before you a wide swath of open land, cleared for the defense of the Foreign Legation Quarter – a 200-acre, heavily fortified city within a city.

Foreign diplomats had been living and working on this spot since the early 1860s, after the invasion of the Eight Allied Armies "convinced" the Qing government to yield land to foreign representatives. By the end of the 19th century, 11 countries had established missions here, and the foreign population was around 500. The legation buildings were mixed in with the regular Chinese dwellings, though there was little love lost between the two populations.

The remnants that can be seen today, however, date from the very early 20th century – the original Legation Quarter was very nearly razed in the Boxer Rebellion of 1900. Following the rebellion, the outraged and vindictive foreign representatives demanded the right to build and govern as they saw fit. Solid walls were erected, a defensive glacis raised on three sides, and eight iron gates built, through which Chinese citizens were not allowed to pass.

A stroll down Zhengyi Lu would have taken you straight into the heart of the foreign enclave. On the right, the vast British Legation, its grand gate now opening into a Public Security Bureau compound. On the left, the former Japanese Legation, which now houses Beijing's mayor. When you reach Dongjiaomin Xiang – once Legation Street, the heart of the Quarter – turn right.

On the north side of the street is the Supreme People's Court, once the location of the Russian Legation. Some of the earliest foreign residents once lived here – following a 17th-century clash between Russia and China, some Russian prisoners settled in Beijing, and their descendants were allowed an Orthodox mission on this site. Some of the original buildings survived up until 1991.

Going further in the direction of Tian'anmen Square, the former US Legation is on the left. At press time, the whole area was being rebuilt and remodeled – a Handel Lee project that will house swanky restaurants like Enoteca Pinchiorri and should open before the end of 2007 (or early 2008, or …).

Turn back around and head east on Dongjiaomin Xiang. As you pass the intersection with Zhengyi Lu, you'll see the former Yokohama Specie Bank on the northeast corner – one of the best-preserved legation-era buildings in the area. Further on are the former German Legation on the right and the French Legation on the left (the former French post office is now a Sichuan restaurant). The exiled King Sihanouk of Cambodia used to stay here, behind the gate flanked by two snow-white stone lions, left over from the days of the French.

A little farther, past the intersection with Taijichang Lu, St. Michael's Cathedral is on the left. This beautiful church was built by the French in 1902, narrowly survived destruction in the '60s (though its pipe organ is no more) and reopened for services in 1989. Tap on the gate and you can go in and wander around.

Across the street from St. Michael's was the Zijin Guesthouse, which is no more – though you wouldn't know it since all the signs are still up. This underlines one of the unfortunate things about the Legation Quarter: You can't actually see any of the legation buildings. Until the US embassy fine-dining complex is complete, there isn't a single former legation building that you can stick your head into without drawing a sharp bark from an armed guard.

Back up to Taijichang Lu (once known as Rue Marco Polo) and head north. The former French barracks on the left now house the Chinese Worker's Union, and further north the old Peking Club – once the heart of diplomatic society, with an extensive wine cellar and luxurious gaming facilities – is now the Beijing People's Congress. As you pass the mouth of Taijichang Toutiao, peer closely at the wall. A street sign reading Rue Hart, after Sir Robert Hart, the head of the Imperial Customs Service, is still visible under layers of paint.

Farther north, Taijichang Lu opens out again onto Chang'an Jie and the bustling southern end of Wangfujing. Out from under the trees, and into the crowds of the present day.

Suggested reading: *Foreigners Within the Gates: The Legations at Peking*, by Michael Moser and Yeone Wei-Chih Moser. Serindia Publications, 2006.

St. Michael has staved off more than a century of change

The Forbidden City: the original gated community

imperial music; precious ceramics and other outstanding donations to the Palace Museum; painting and calligraphy by the Kangxi and Qianlong emperors and the Empress Dowager Cixi; medical and scientific instruments of the Qing court; tribute items, including gifts from the Panchen Lama and Dalai Lama; exquisite artifacts from the imperial workshops, including ceramics, jade and carved ivory; and Chinese antiquities from the Han, Qin, Zhou and Shang dynasties, collected by the Qing emperors. By the time of the Beijing Olympics, a total of 400,000 square meters of exhibition space will be on display – a 60 percent increase since 2001, but still barely half the total area that was in use during imperial times.

When you visit, be strategic: The site has always been too big for a single pass, and it's worth targeting an area or a theme. If you can't afford to spend more than one day there, the classic four-hour south-north trek remains the best bet, and the audio tour, while no longer narrated by Roger Moore, is very well done. Certain exhibits like the Hall of Clocks and Hall of Jewelry require an additional RMB 10.
Daily 8.30am-5pm (Apr-Oct); 8.30am-4.30pm (Nov-Mar). RMB 60 (Apr-Oct), RMB 40 (Nov-Mar), free (children under 1.2m). Audio tour RMB 40 plus RMB 100 deposit. North of Tian'anmen Square. (8511 7311) 故宫，天安门广场北侧

Lifestyles of the Rich and Famous

Few buildings in Beijing offer glimpses of the lives of commoners in the past, but you can discover how the other 1/1000th of the population lived by visiting the following palaces, mansions and residences. As always, crowds are thinner during the low season, early morning or late afternoon.

Summer Palace

This area has served as a royal summer home since the Jin dynasty, but not until Emperor Qianlong remodeled it for his mother did it become the Summer Palace we know and love today. Twice sacked by foreign armies – in 1860 and 1900 – the palace was twice rebuilt by the indefatigable Empress Dowager Cixi. Nearby Yuanmingyuan, the Old Summer Palace, was also razed in 1860, but it wasn't so lucky – it was left fallow as a symbol of foreign aggression against China.

Continues on p236

It's Lonely at the Top
The trials and tribulations of being a Chinese emperor
by David Litt

It's good to be the king, right? You get a nice house, lots of servants, no commute – what's not to love? If you could go back in time and become a Ming or Qing dynasty emperor, you'd probably jump at the chance. But it turns out being the Son of Heaven isn't all fun and games and executing people – absolute power can get a little frustrating.

After waking up and putting on your nine-dragon robes, you probably want to get a bite to eat, but chances are you're out of luck. As emperor, you only get two meals a day, at 6.30 in the morning and 12.30 in the afternoon – after that, there's only tea and snacks available. The palace doesn't have any dining rooms, so your eunuchs bring the food to you, but you don't get to order for yourself – the Office of Household Affairs is in charge of deciding every meal because knowing your food preferences might help a potential assassin. You also have to go through the Office of Household Affairs if you want to eat with an empress or concubine, so if you're like most emperors you'll eat alone, except for the eunuch who scolds you if you eat more than two bites of any dish (food preferences again). In case you're still worried about poisoning, each dish gets tasted twice before it reaches you, and has a strip of silver placed on the bottom of the bowl – the strip's supposed to turn black if it touches poison. You'll be impressed by the size of the meals themselves – they sometimes each have more than 100 dishes. The downside is that most of those dishes are ceremonial, and they'll keep coming back at every meal until they spoil.

Emperor Qianlong liked to get out of the house

When nature calls the Son of Heaven, you may be surprised to discover that your 8,700-room house doesn't have any bathrooms. Instead, those ubiquitous eunuchs show up with your platinum chamber pot and a few squares of imperial tribute toilet paper, transported 1130 kilometers from Hangzhou. Don't worry about smells – all the charcoal burned in the palace creates lots of smothering ash to go in the pots, and low-ranking eunuchs are in charge of emptying them each day.

After a busy day of governing the Middle Kingdom, you might want to enjoy the company of one of your many, many palace ladies, but even this will prove difficult. Astrologers are in charge of determining which women are acceptable for an amorous rendezvous, and once your Ms. Right has been okayed, she's wrapped in a blanket and carried (yes, carried) by eunuchs, who deposit her in your chambers. Sadly, there's no mood music – but there are a few more of those eunuchs, standing on the other side of a screen and urging you to take it easy ("Preserve your imperial body, sire!") as you do your thing.

So the next time you're feeling down, just order off a menu, spend a little quality time in your own bathroom, and put on some Marvin Gaye: You'd make even an emperor jealous.

Paddle to Kunming Lake's southern shore after the tour buses chug off

The Summer Palace's signature piece is Kunming Lake, sprawling over three-quarters of the park. Originally a reservoir in the Yuan dynasty, it was modeled after Hangzhou's West Lake, and around its south and west shores are several gracefully arching footbridges. Also don't miss the north shore's marble boat, which Cixi ordered refurbished and decorated as a tribute to the Chinese navy. The navy, however, probably would have preferred real ships to marble ones – the fleet was decimated in 1894 by the Japanese – and today the sculpture is a reminder of Cixi's shortsighted extravagance. Other sights include the Hall of Jade Ripples, where Cixi had her nephew Emperor Guangxu placed under house arrest after discovering a plot to undermine her power. The Garden of Harmonious Virtue houses the original multiplex: a three-level Peking Opera theater designed for Cixi's amusement. Her birthdays were celebrated there with multi-day extravaganzas involving as many as 380 performers (some of these parties were also funded with the naval budget – suffice to say that the Summer Palace isn't a good place for the Cixi fan club's annual meeting). The theater requires a separate RMB 10 ticket, but it's worth it. The Long Corridor, with its 10,000 different painted scenes, is another classic Summer Palace attraction, and while the corridor is usually crowded with tourists and vendors, it shouldn't be missed.

For a whole different way to enjoy the Summer Palace, do as the locals do and forget the big halls and Kodak moments. Instead, just buy the most basic entry ticket and stroll the parks and grounds like Cixi herself (minus the sedan chair and eunuch porters), especially on a crisp autumn day. If the crowds become oppressive, you can find a bit of tranquility by renting a boat, walking to the north side of Longevity Hill, or strolling around to the west side of the lake. Unless you're into overpaying for stuff, avoid the crowds and kitschy souvenir shops of "Little Suzhou Water Town."

If you want to travel to the Summer Palace in true imperial style, come by boat via canal. Boats depart from Yuyuantan Park (9.30am, noon, 2.30pm; RMB 60, round-trip RMB 80) and from behind the Beijing Exhibition Center (every hour 10am-3pm; RMB 40, round-trip RMB 70). Call Jingcheng Shui Shang You (京城水上游) for more information (6852 9428).

Daily 6.30am-8pm (last ticket 6pm). RMB 30 (Apr-Oct), RMB 20 (Nov-Mar); students half price. Yiheyuan Lu, Haidian District. (6288 1144) 颐和园，海淀区颐和园路

PHOTO: BAI XU

236 INSIDER'S GUIDE TO BEIJING

Old Summer Palace (Yuanmingyuan)

"Unfortunately," reads a sign at the Old Summer Palace, "this 'wonder of civilization' was sacked, looted, and razed to the ground by Anglo-French forces in 1860." The Old Summer Palace, designed by Jesuit missionaries, was known as the "Versailles of the East," and until it was destroyed, it was the best combination of western and Chinese palace designs in the world. Today, we can only imagine.

It's best to ignore the "palace" label, and treat Yuanmingyuan as a park. For RMB 10, you can wander the day away among the lakes, hills and small bits of ruin. Bring a picnic and go to the lakes at the north end of the park, or sit on a bench and shoot the breeze. Because Yuanmingyuan doesn't get as many tourists as the well-preserved Summer Palace, quiet moments are easy to come by. Of the tourists who do come, the lion's share are Chinese, so it's actually a great place to make friends from across the country. For an extra RMB 15, you can walk through some "restored" ruins, which have been carefully arranged to be at once majestic and dilapidated.

Among the objects that were plundered from here are 12 bronze statues of animal heads representing the signs of the Chinese zodiac. Symbols of national humiliation for many years, these statues have come to represent China's emerging power now that four of them have been purchased in auctions by patriotic Chinese businesses (for a combined RMB 39 million) and brought back to China. These four statues – the ox, tiger, monkey and pig – are now proudly displayed at the Poly Museum (see p262).

Beijing-based animator Wang Lifeng has spent ten years creating a virtual reality model of the baroque palace, which will eventually appear as a virtual tour and perhaps a video game.

Daily 7am-7pm. RMB 10, plus RMB 15 (ruins and labyrinth), students RMB 5 (but they don't accept foreign students, even with Chinese IDs). 28 Qinghua Xilu, Haidian District. (6262 8501) 圆明园，海淀区清华西路28号

Prince Gong's Mansion

Built in 1777 by He Shen, one of the most corrupt officials of the Qianlong period, this compound later became home to Prince Gong, Emperor Xianfeng's younger brother. Gong helped negotiate the Treaty of Peking after the Opium War, and promoted western-style reforms in the late 19th century. This willingness to embrace western customs made him reviled by many mid-century Chinese historians, but he has since been rehabilitated. Today he is considered a model statesman, and his compound is a textbook example of a noble's mansion during the Qing dynasty.

The strange rock garden and massive lily pond have none of the delicate subtleties of the gardens in Hangzhou or Suzhou. Peking Opera performances in the theater, with requisite tea sipping and seed cracking, are part of the guided RMB 60 package tour, though the regular RMB 20 entrance ticket allows for strolling at your own pace. Not so popular with foreign tourists, this site is packed with domestic travelers and may be very crowded. For companies with VIPs in town, group lunches and dinners may be hosted at the mansion. The common folk can eat in the Zhou Enlai-established Sichuan Restaurant on Liuyin Jie, which overlooks the compound.

Daily 8am-5pm. RMB 20, RMB 60 (with guide). 14A Liuyin Jie, Xicheng District. (6616 8149) 恭王府，西城区柳荫街甲14号

Sichuan Restaurant *Daily 11am-2pm, 5-9pm. 14A Liuyin Jie, Xicheng District. (6615 6924, 6615 7061)* 四川饭店，西城区柳荫街甲14号

Soong Ching Ling's Former Residence

The Former Residence of Soong Ching Ling (a.k.a. Song Qingling) is more interesting as a garden than a museum, but the displays inside this grand estate open a fascinating window into the life of a Communist Party "aristocrat" in the early days of the People's Republic. Educated in the US, Song defied her parents to marry Dr. Sun Yat-sen, the founder of the Republic of China, and she herself became vice-president of the People's Republic of China. Her sister May-ling married Jiang Jieshi, better known in the West as Chiang Kai-shek. The displays include the pistol Sun gave her as a wedding present. Kids will enjoy clambering on the rocks, looking at the pigeons and playing on the swings.

Daily 9am-5pm. RMB 20, college students RMB 10, middle & primary school students RMB 5. 46 Houhai Beiyan, Xicheng District. (6404 4205 ext 815) 宋庆龄故居，西城区后海北沿46号

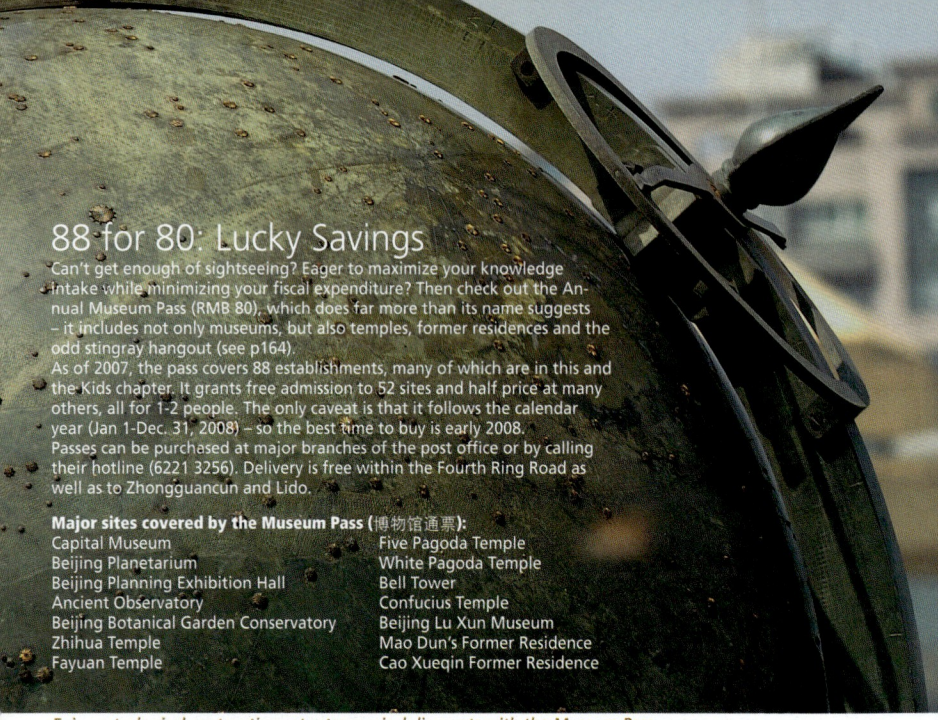

88 for 80: Lucky Savings

Can't get enough of sightseeing? Eager to maximize your knowledge intake while minimizing your fiscal expenditure? Then check out the Annual Museum Pass (RMB 80), which does far more than its name suggests – it includes not only museums, but also temples, former residences and the odd stingray hangout (see p164).

As of 2007, the pass covers 88 establishments, many of which are in this and the Kids chapter. It grants free admission to 52 sites and half price at many others, all for 1-2 people. The only caveat is that it follows the calendar year (Jan 1-Dec. 31, 2008) – so the best time to buy is early 2008.

Passes can be purchased at major branches of the post office or by calling their hotline (6221 3256). Delivery is free within the Fourth Ring Road as well as to Zhongguancun and Lido.

Major sites covered by the Museum Pass (博物馆通票):

Capital Museum	Five Pagoda Temple
Beijing Planetarium	White Pagoda Temple
Beijing Planning Exhibition Hall	Bell Tower
Ancient Observatory	Confucius Temple
Beijing Botanical Garden Conservatory	Beijing Lu Xun Museum
Zhihua Temple	Mao Dun's Former Residence
Fayuan Temple	Cao Xueqin Former Residence

Enjoy astrological contraptions at astronomical discounts with the Museum Pass

Mei Lanfang's Residence

The most accomplished Peking Opera star of modern times, Mei Lanfang (1894-1961) became a household name in China for his mastery of female roles, smooth, poised performance style (now known as the "Mei Lanfang School"), and his comprehensive blending of acting, singing and dancing. He broke the previously rigid distinction between two traditional female roles in Peking Opera, the virtuous *qingyi* and the flirtatious *huadan* (trust us, it's a bigger deal than it sounds). He also revolutionized stage make-up and costumes, wrote many original plays, and choreographed new dances. During his 50-year career he played over 100 different roles and served as a "cultural ambassador," spreading Peking Opera throughout the world on trips to the USA, Japan and the former Soviet Union. The story of his life was the basis for the acclaimed 1993 film Farewell My Concubine. Mei's Beijing residence was converted into a museum in 1986, displaying his furniture, costumes and other opera paraphernalia. A full Mei Lanfang pilgrimage should include a walk through the surrounding hutongs to Mei Mansion, the elegant restaurant near Houhai that specializes in the opera star's favorite dishes (see p86).

Tue-Sun 9am-4pm. RMB 10. 9 Huguosi Lu, Xicheng District. (6618 0351) www.meilanfang.com.cn 梅兰芳纪念馆，西城区护国寺路9号

Mao Dun's Former Residence

Tucked away in a quiet hutong lies the former residence of Chinese writer Mao Dun. Born Shen Dehong in 1896 in Zhejiang province, he took his pen name ("contradiction") as a response to the conflicting revolutionary ideologies of the 1920s. His friend Ye Shengtao changed the "*mao*" character from 矛 (spear) to 茅 (straw) so that the name kept the same pronunciation without making him vulnerable to political prosecution. In 1921 he became the first writer to join the CPC. In 1930 he joined the League of Left-Wing Writers, and in 1933 published his most important work, *Midnight*, a critical and realistic look at business in Shanghai. After the founding of the People's Republic in 1949, he became Minister of Culture and secretary to Mao Zedong himself. During the "Cultural Revolution," Mao Dun was dismissed and mistreated, and until his death in 1981 he went into self-imposed confinement: The last seven years of his life were spent here.

Continues on p240

Backpedaling
Rethinking the pedicab tour
by John Brennan

Cultural ambassador or tourist trap?

Until recently, I avoided the pedicab hutong tour experience. After all, where would it take me that a bike or my own two feet wouldn't? Besides, sometimes, as I watched a sweating driver laboring past, I fancied I saw the ghost of Lao She palely glaring from the lakeside.

This second objection – that it all looked uncomfortably feudal – disappeared when I saw the price list. These guys must earn in a month what the eponymous hero of *Rickshaw Boy* made in a lifetime. So in the interests of research, I signed up for the two-hour tour. This middle way seemed best. The one-hour tour was hardly worth it, while the half-day monster, with its school visit and *jiaozi*-making lesson, was not me. The published price for two hours was RMB 180 per person: a hefty, but fortunately elastic number.

We had hardly got going when we pulled into a little shop selling *gongbi* art (finely detailed folk watercolors), including a line in mild erotica. Back on the road after a tasteful purchase (a cat picture, OK?), we spent another fifteen minutes weaving through impressively narrow alleys, then pulled up at a *siheyuan*. Our driver kicked back in the shade while we paid the RMB 20 entry fee, to find ourselves in a pretty courtyard shaded by a huge phoenix tree. The daughter of the house explained that the place, over 400 years old, was once a palace official's residence. She then imparted bits of *siheyuan* lore, such as the significance of the goldfish (good fortune), the potted pomegranate (good fortune), the phoenix tree (fertility and good fortune), and bumping your head on the hanging gourd (good fortune).

Back in the cab, our driver offered us a second *siheyuan* experience, but we elected to watch the scenery spin by for a while. We passed Prince Gong's mansion (closed for renovation except for a fragment of garden) and two other sites that are obviously making the transition from government office back to their glory days as noble residences. After skirting Houhai's western shore, we crossed over to the former residence of Soong Ching Ling (a.k.a. Song Qingling). This was pretty much a compulsory stop, and after wandering the quiet gardens for a while, it was on to the Drum Tower, after which it took every ounce of polite diplomacy to turn down a visit to the Jingdezhen porcelain emporium. Disappointed, our driver pedaled moodily down the east shore of Qianhai and delivered us back at our starting point on Di'anmen Dajie ten minutes early.

The verdict? Be prepared for lots of stops and predictable pressure to buy. That said, it's a pleasant and reasonably practical way to cover the main sights around the Qianhai and Houhai hutongs.

SIGHTSEEING

Caretakers preserved this traditional courtyard home much as the writer left it, with personal belongings and simple, socialist-style furniture in their original state. The desk calendar even remains open to February 19, 1981, the last page the writer personally turned. The small exhibit includes some 400 mementos, including original manuscripts, letters and family photos (unfortunately, English translations are not available). Although not the most overwhelmingly impressive exhibit in Beijing, it is certainly worth a stop on a leisurely stroll through the neighboring hutongs, and an important site for anyone interested in contemporary Chinese literature.

Tue-Sun 9am-4pm. RMB 5, students RMB 2.5. 13 Yuanensi Hutong (behind Jiaodaokou Nanjie), Dongcheng District. (6404 4089) 茅盾故居，东城区原恩寺胡同13号（交道口南街后面）

Cao Xueqin Former Residence

Think of it as the Stratford-upon-Avon of China. Cao Xueqin wrote the last of China's four classic novels, *Dream of the Red Chamber* (also translated as *A Dream of Red Mansions* or *Story of the Stone*). The story narrates the downfall of a wealthy noble family at the height of their power, focusing on the young heir, Jia Baoyu, and his many talented and beautiful female cousins.

Cao's family underwent a similar decline; this residence is thought to be where he lived and wrote in poverty. Surrounding the courtyard are 18 rooms in the Qing architectural style. Inside you will find his reconstructed living quarters and study, including exhibits on his life, on his family history back to his great-grandfather, and on the influences of *Dream of the Red Chamber*. The exhibits tend to be text and photograph heavy, with few actual artifacts save for one – the highlight of the residence – the novel's first hand-written manuscripts.

The residence is small and can be browsed through in half an hour. Only diehard enthusiasts should make a dedicated trip, but a literary respite may not be a bad idea if you're already wandering the botanical garden.

Daily 8.30am-4.30pm (summer); 9am-4pm (winter). RMB 10, students RMB 5, plus RMB 5 to enter Beijing Botanical Garden. 39 Zhengbaiqi (inside Beijing Botanical Garden), Xiangshan, Haidian District. (6259 1561 ext 2028) 曹雪芹故居，海淀区香山正白旗39号 （北京植物园内）

Guo Moruo's Former Residence

In his day, Guo Moruo was an influential author, philosopher, dramatist and intellectual, but his work doesn't resonate with today's generation the way that some of his contemporaries' books still do. The real attraction of visiting his former home is the well-preserved courtyard, which gives you an excellent sense of how spacious and luxurious hutong life was before the overpopulation and crowding that began in the 1950s.

Tue-Sun 9am-4.30pm. RMB 20, students RMB 10. 18 Qianhai Xijie, Xicheng District. (6612 5392) 郭沫若故居，西城区前海西街18号

Temples

Often, to the unenlightened, a temple is a temple is a temple – seen one, you've seen 'em all. Have faith: Each of these places of worship is distinctive to the eye and embodies a particular school of religion, from folk customs and Taoism to Buddhism and Islam.

Temple of Heaven

Too many Tiantan visits are blighted by the clamor of Chongwenmen Dajie. Instead, approach the Temple of Heaven as the emperors did: slowly, quietly, through the west gate. Work your way down Qianmen Dajie, along the imperial pathway that once stretched from the Forbidden City to Yongdingmen. Forget the boarded-up shops and imagine the emperor's procession through the hushed city – the great gates of Qianmen rolled open, the sound of the cavalcade muffled by new-laid sand, and blue cloth draped across side streets to shield the ruler from the common gaze.

The emperor's passage was as menacing as it was grand. Residents were warned that he was on the move with a palace notice bearing the ominous coda: "Let there be no carelessness." In Imperial China, carelessness was broadly defined and a very bad career move. When lightning destroyed the Hall of Prayer for Good Harvests in 1889, no fewer than 30 officials were held responsible, and they paid the ultimate penalty.

The emperor's ceremonies at Tiantan fulfilled his most solemn spiritual duty. As the Son of Heaven, only he could seek the blessing of his progenitor, the Ruler of the Universe. Poor harvests, strife and disaster were all signs that

Knockin' on heaven's door

the emperor had lost the favor of Heaven, and the twice-yearly rituals maintained stability and prosperity. On the tenth day of the first lunar month, the emperor would seek the blessing for a fruitful year. His second visit was at the winter solstice, when he would burn sacrifices to the supreme deity and report to him on the previous year's events.

The west entrance of Tiantan Park has an old Beijing charm that the tourists' turnstile to the north lost years ago. The graceful Ming-era gate looms over a *jianbing* stall and a little knot of hawkers, while the occasional cyclist wobbles past down a hutong. About a quarter of a mile east is the West Celestial Gate, immediately to the right of which is the Hall of Abstinence, where the emperor would spend the night before the winter solstice. Like most of the park, the hall has suffered various indignities over the past century, but it's been restored, and has regained some of the seclusion that its double moat and gentle cypresses were meant to provide.

To the east lies the great causeway that runs north-south through the complex. At the north end is the recently restored Hall of Prayer for Good Harvest, its famous triple roof tiled in cobalt blue as a symbol of heaven. This was where the emperor came on the tenth day of the first lunar month. You can lose yourself in the soaring lines, the hallucinatory roof carpentry and the intricate numerology of the design. Not a single nail or screw was used, and the walls bear no weight: the roof load passes through interlocking brackets to the columns. The Hall has four inner, 12 middle and 12 outer columns, representing the four seasons, 12 months and 12 traditional Chinese hours respectively. The 28 columns match the 28 Chinese constellations, and the circumference of the uppermost roof is 30 *zhang* (an ancient unit of measurement), the number of days in the lunar month.

To the south lies the Imperial Vault of Heaven, which was a storehouse for ancestor tablets. Surrounding it is the Echo Wall. They say that you can stand at any point around the circular wall and speak in a normal tone, and you can be clearly heard at any other point – that is, if you can first make it across the surrounding fence and project your voice above those of hundreds of other tourists trying to do the same.

Further south lies the Round Altar, its three marble terraces open to the sky, ringed by two walls: one circular, representing Heaven, the broader one a perfect square symbolizing earth. Emperor Qianlong had the altar enlarged and rebuilt as a symphony of the heavenly numbers

SIGHTSEEING

Studying sutras at Yonghegong, one of Beijing's few active monasteries

one, three, five, seven and nine. Most in evidence are nine and its multiples: Count the altar steps, the balustrade panels, the platform paving stones. More numbers are hidden in the proportions: the diameter of the first terrace is precisely nine *zhang*, the second is 15 *zhang* (3x5), and the third measures 21 *zhang* (3x7).

It was here that the emperor communicated with heaven at the winter solstice in an intricate ritual divided into nine passages, each with its assigned choreography and music. It began at midnight with the lighting of the lamps, and culminated a day later at dawn with the emperor's prayers to heaven at the Round Altar, and the burnt offering of a whole bullock. A diagram from the Qing dynasty specifies 46 places on the altar for shrines, vessels and ancestor tablets, for musicians, dancers and singers, for officials such as the keepers of incense and placers of kneeling cushions, and, of course, for the Son of Heaven himself.

Seen from the edge of the outer courtyard, the inner wall mirrored three times in a gentle ascent toward the sky, the altar is the most beautiful expression, in its understated way, of the celestial purpose of Tiantan.

Arriving early is always advised. Between 6am and 8am it seems like you can meet every south Beijing resident over 50 doing *wushu*, playing shuttlecock or even cracking whips. At 8am the key monuments are open, but half-deserted for a magical hour until the tour buses roll in. At any time, though, Tiantan is worth a visit. Some of the best views are surprises – the famous Hall seen through a stand of cypress, or the heart-catching roofscape looking north from the top of the round altar.

Daily 6am-9pm (park), 8am-6pm (sites). RMB 15 (park), RMB 35 (all access). Yongdingmennei Dajie (West Gate), Chongwen District. (6702 8866) 天坛，崇文区永定门内大街

Lama Temple (Yonghegong)

The spectacular Lama Temple was originally the home of Qing dynasty Prince Yong before he became the Emperor Yongzheng, which is why you'll see the golden roof tiles of an imperial residence. After his elevation in 1723 he kept with tradition by making a portion of the grounds into a lamasery for Tibetan monks, and another part became the headquarters for his terror posse and secret intelligence agency.

The temple is invariably filled with equal parts monks, worshippers and tourists. At Spring Festival it teems with the devout praying for luck in the coming year. On the last day of the first lunar month, monks perform "Devil Dances" wearing fantastic masks of huge animal heads. The incense burners are authentic cultural treasures – the one in the second courtyard dates to 1746.

Impossible to miss, the 18-meter high Maitreya statue in the last building was made from a single piece of sandalwood given by the Dalai Lama to Emperor Qianlong in 1750. It took three years to ship from Nepal to Beijing, and they had to construct the surrounding hall around the finished statue. If Maitreya looks shorter than 18 meters, it's because part of the statue is underground, lest it topple over: Beijing's subway system rattles right underneath the temple.

Daily 9am-4.30pm. RMB 25, audio tour RMB 20 plus RMB 200 deposit. 12 Yonghegong Dajie, Dongcheng District. (6404 4499 ext 251) 雍和宫，东城区雍和宫大街12号

Confucius Temple and Guozijian

Honoring a philosopher who has been elevated to divine status over the past 2,500 years, the Confucius Temple is a quiet refuge from the "New, Great" Beijing being built up around it. The 198 stone tablets in the front courtyard are carved with the names of all the *jinshi* scholars who passed the imperial exam during the Qing, Ming and Yuan dynasties. Another 189 stone tablets in the northwest of the courtyard have all 13 Confucian classics carved into them. The main hall has stimulating exhibits of musical and ritual instruments. In warmer months, art students sketch buildings, trees and scenes in the main court. Since it receives relatively few visitors, the Confucius Temple is one of the rare tourist spots in Beijing where one can spend the day reading in peace, and it's not uncommon to see locals sitting on the courtyard benches, shooting the breeze. When visiting, spare a thought for the students of Beijing 321 Middle School across the street – imagine the endless lectures they must hear from educators and parents about China's greatest teacher.

If you can wait until the end of 2007 to visit, however, you should. Renovation work is supposed to be completed by then, and right now the temple's atmosphere leans more toward "largely off-limits" than "peaceful."

The Guozijian Imperial College just west of the Confucius Temple educated China's best students in Confucianism and was a cram school for the imperial exam. By 1462 the college had 13,000 students who lived in dorms south of the entrance. Graduates of Guozijian could immediately receive government postings without taking the imperial exams, but their positions would be relatively low – besides, who wouldn't want to see his name carved on one of the stone tablets next door?

Serene and shaded by trees, Guozijian Street has a true scholarly air and makes for a pleasant stroll from Lama Temple to Andingmennei Dajie.

Daily 8.30am-5pm (4.30pm last ticket). RMB 10, students RMB 3. 13 Guozijian Jie (near the Lama Temple's main gate), Dongcheng District. (8402 7224) 孔庙和国子监，东城区国子监街13号

Niujie Mosque

The oldest and largest of the 40-odd mosques in Beijing, Niujie is a central religious and social gathering place for Beijing's 250,000 Muslims. The mosque was built in 996 AD, during the Liao dynasty, and was originally designed by the son of an imam, Nazruddin. After Genghis Khan's armies destroyed it in 1215, the mosque was rebuilt and later significantly expanded in 1442. By the Qing dynasty, the neighboring markets were well known for halal beef and mutton, and today the Muslim presence is still quite strong, with Muslim grocery stores lining the road and Arabic script on most of the signs.

Of the 42 rooms in the complex, the most important is the 600 square-meter prayer hall, which can hold more than 1,000 worshippers and is a striking blend of Islamic and Chinese design. Imams used the Tower for Observing the Moon to determine the start of Ramadan each year. Both the tower and the interior of the main prayer hall are off-limits to non-believers, and women are restricted to certain areas. The front gate of the mosque is only open during Ramadan and Corban, two important Muslim festivals. The son of the founding Arab imam is buried in the courtyard garden, along with two sheikhs from Central Asia who came to China along the Silk Road. The mosque complex also contains several stone tablets, including epitaphs for the two sheikhs and a stele by Emperor Kangxi (1654-1722) absolving the Hui Muslim minority of a conspiracy to overthrow the Qing dynasty. Other artifacts housed in the mosque include ancient porcelain and classical Islamic texts.

Recently, the mosque has been given an RMB 20 million facelift, which has drastically increased the complex's square footage and also allowed the mosque to reclaim two buildings in the area, one of which serves as a separate place of worship for women. Friday prayers have been known to draw upwards of 700 worshippers, so a great time to visit is around 1pm on Fridays. Visitors must dress conservatively: long trousers or skirts and shirts with sleeves.
Daily 6am-7pm. Locals RMB 2, foreigners RMB 10. 88 Niu Jie, Xuanwu District. (6353 2564) 牛街礼拜寺, 宣武区牛街88号

White Cloud Temple (Baiyun Guan)

Established in 793 AD during the Tang dynasty, this is one of Beijing's few Taoist temples, replete with long-haired monks. Unless you're claustrophobic, visit during the Spring Festival when good-natured worshippers throng the grounds to burn incense and leave prayer tags to the deities. The home of the Chinese Taoist Association and a Taoist clinic with three medically licensed priests and ten herbalists, White Cloud Temple is peaceful the rest of the year. For those with an astrological bent, plaster statues depict the 60 combinations of the heavenly branches and earthly stems as guardian deities.

Early religious Taoism evolved from an interest in alchemy and the search for the elixir of life. Distinct from Taoist philosophy, it provided a sense of spirituality that Confucianism lacked. Pantheons of deities, including manifestations of philosopher Laozi, are worshipped. Because of Taoism's tendency toward mysticism, its temples became breeding grounds for secret societies.
Daily 8.30am-4.30pm. RMB 10. 6 Baiyunguan Jie, Xibianmenwai, Xuanwu District. (6346 3531) 白云观, 宣武区西便门外白云观街6号

White Pagoda Temple (Baita Si)

The oldest presence of Tibetan Buddhism in Beijing, Baita Si often goes by the English name of White Pagoda Temple, though its iconic structure is actually a stupa (or *chorten*) and its official name is Miaoying Temple. Built by a Nepalese architect, the graceful stupa towering over the surrounding gray hutongs has a distinctly foreign look. The original monastery used to be much larger: legend has it that Kublai Khan had arrows shot in the four cardinal directions to determine its bounds. Unfortunately, a fire destroyed the original during the fall of the Yuan dynasty. Ming emperor Tianshun rebuilt the temple in 1457 and renamed it Miaoying (Marvelous Powers of Manifestation). Recently restored, the temple houses a fascinating collection of Tibetan Buddhist sculptures and other artwork.
Daily 9am-5pm. RMB 20, free on Wed (for the first 200 visitors). 171 Fuchengmennei Dajie, Xicheng District. (6613 3317, 6617 6164) 白塔寺, 西城区阜成门内大街171号

Temple of the Origin of the Dharma (Fayuan Si)

Beijing's oldest Buddhist temple, Fayuan retains both an air of antiquity and the feel of a genuine active monastery. Built in memory of troops killed in Sui dynasty (581-618 AD) expeditions against Korean "rebels," the original structure was commissioned in 645 AD by Emperor Tang Taizong. Over the years, it was destroyed by fire, water and earthquake several times; the current structures are from the Qing dynasty. Fayuan was also notorious as the prison of two important political leaders, Emperor Qinzong (reigned 1125-1127) of the Northern Song and Xie Fangde, an official who starved to death rather than surrender to the Yuan army.

Today the temple houses the China Buddhist Institute and the China Buddhist Literature and Cultural Relics Museum. Highlights include the central wooden Buddha, Beijing's biggest reclining Buddha statue at 7.4 meters, and Ming dynasty bronze statues of lions and the Four Heavenly Kings. The grounds themselves are lovely, with several extremely old trees and famous lilac gardens. During the Qing dynasty, emperors and famous poets were inspired by the temple's legendary flowers and came to write calligraphy and poetry within its walls.

What makes this temple truly fascinating, though, is getting a glimpse of monastic life. Saffron-robed monks go about their business in earnest, and while visitors are asked to "not interfere with religious activities," you are free to observe. Some of them will strike up conversations with visitors. The ancient hutongs immediately surrounding the temple are also worth a wander.
Mon-Tue, Thu-Sat 8.30am-4pm. RMB 5. Jiaozi Hutong, 7 Fayuansi Qianjie, Xuanwu District. (6353 3966) 法源寺, 宣武区法源寺前街7号

Five Pagoda Temple (Wuta Si)

Not so long ago Wuta Si, or Five Pagoda Temple, was surrounded by the fields of Beijing's

In Beijing did Kublai Khan a White Pagoda Temple decree

northwestern suburbs, and until the early 20th century families would go there to picnic and enjoy the view. Today it's surrounded by tall buildings and the views have disappeared, but this under-appreciated Tibetan temple is still worth a visit.

The first thing you'll notice about Wuta Si is its five namesake towers, the trademark of the "diamond throne style" of temple design. China has only six examples of this style, which places five pagodas on top of one large square foundation (the "throne"), with just two others in Beijing. This one dates to 1473, but the only original feature you'll be able to see is the foundation – Wuta Si was renovated under Emperor Qianlong and looted during the Boxer Rebellion of 1900. That orange tint you'll notice on the pagodas comes from iron oxidization in their white marble exteriors.

When you get up close to the towers themselves, you'll see that they're covered with some of the best relief carving in Beijing – take special notice of the carving of the Buddha's feet under the central pagoda. The temple also houses the Beijing Stone Carving Museum, with some particularly interesting tombstones of Jesuit missionaries. The altar is less special – it's been turned into a bomb shelter.

When you've had your fill of stone carvings, enjoy the temple grounds – with ancient trees, more exhibition halls and even a teahouse, you'll find a relaxing atmosphere that's missing from many of Beijing's more crowded destinations. *Tue-Sun 9am-4pm. RMB 15 (plus RMB 5 for pagodas), free on Wed. 500m west of the National Library, Baishiqiao, Haidian District. (6217 3543)* 五塔寺，海淀区白石桥国家图书馆西侧500米

Zhihua Temple

Hugged by hutongs on all sides, Zhihua Temple is an oasis of quiet courtyards and exquisite Buddhist artwork undiscovered by busy tour groups. Wang Zhen, a corrupt eunuch, built the complex in 1443 as his personal ancestral hall, but later it was converted to a temple. Today it's one of Beijing's finest examples of Ming Buddhist architecture, though some of the captions read more like absentee lists: many of the statues were carried off, as were two ornate caisson ceilings (now in museums in the USA).

Still, Zhihua has enough to awe even the most jaded of visitors. Aside from the main statues, whose serene features and faded colors are wonderfully free from modern touch-ups, Zhihua is also home to performances of Ming-era court

Continues on p248

No *danzi* needed
Those old Xicheng neighborhoods
by Shelley Jiang

Most hutong hunters head for Dongsi and Houhai, but you're slightly west of Beihai, on Xi'anmen Dajie, contemplating the corner of a red wall. You just walked its length down Fuyou Jie, from Chang'an Jie, and you're reluctant to leave its calm. But a glimpse into hutong life awaits, as well as serene temples, tree-shaded lanes and bustling markets.

Head west down Xi'anmen until it dead-ends. Wedding photo studios flaunt their displays, unlikely dresses with too many ruffles. But take a right on Xisi Nandajie and soon you'll see a dusty little store called Dazhong Arts & Accessories, at No. 8 (大众工艺百货商店, 6616 5047). Walk in, and the owner shuffles out of his back room and invites you to look around – knick-knacks, antiques, cloisonné and seal stones, even housewares, all at fair prices.

This is no tourist trap: Customers come looking for rooster-feather dusters, and Mr. Fu will talk about Old Beijing's best makers of rooster-feather dusters, their decline after '49, and how the bride's family should always give her a duster (*danzi*) as a wedding present to give her courage (*danzi*, pronounced identically) in her new home. Another woman will duck in for a quick consultation on character selection for an engraving. In between all this activity, you'll learn from Mr. Fu that his family has owned Dazhong since 1943, with a hiatus in the 1960s, and that the government wants him to tear down and rebuild everything.

Emerging, you return again to the T-intersection and cross Xisi Nandajie. It takes some head-craning to find what you're looking for, almost hidden by the dense foliage (and yes, we're still in Beijing).

It's an octagonal brick pagoda, not particularly tall but surprisingly delicate. What is amazing, though, is the simple fact of its survival. For over 600 years it has slumbered here in nondescript anonymity, since it was built to house the remains of the Elder of Ten Thousand Pines (Wansong Laoren), a Buddhist monk. Qianlong, the emperor who couldn't keep his hands off anything, added an outer pagoda in 1753; they discovered the Yuan-era original intact inside in 1986.

The pagoda isn't on most maps, and in fact, only the hutong it's on recalls its existence – Zhuanta, or "brick tower." But try as you might, you can't find a way in. Ramshackle houses have replaced the surrounding monastery, and every entrance leads into a home. Still, in their recent mood of historical consciousness, Beijing authorities are reportedly fixing up the pagoda, with the goal of opening it by 2008.

From the sleepy residential courtyards, you'd never know that Zhuanta Hutong hummed with musicians, opera singers and stageplayers in the Yuan dynasty. In fact, this was a red light district in the Qing dynasty. Years later, Lu Xun lived here briefly. Today you can only walk past the *siheyuans*, admiring their carved beams or gate stones. Locals sit around chatting and drinking tea, whiling away the afternoon.

Continue down Zhuanta for the straight way to White Pagoda Temple, but you can also turn left onto Jingsheng Hutong. Here, old men play chess on folding tables, and melon vendors drowse in the shadows of their trucks. Peek into nameless courtyards and into an ordinary, quintessentially Beijing way of life on the verge of disappearing: bright fluttery clotheslines, a rusting bike, old cloth shoes, the doorway crammed with dangling mops and chipped basins and other forgotten things.

Follow the hutongs' twists, always turning south (left) and west (right), onto Sidaowan Zhalan Hutong and finally Bingmasi Hutong. You'll have to skirt a construction site just before reaching Taiping Jie, a newly widened behemoth of a street. (This is also where Zhuanta Hutong leads.) South stand the mastiffs of the Financial District, and to the north, the white stupa of Baita Si rises from the treetops. It's slightly squat, but there are no competing skyscrapers here.

After the obligatory temple (p244) visit, don't forget the warren of hutongs behind Baita. Qingfeng Hutong is particularly shady, but to reach Guanyuan Fish & Bird Market, stay on Anping Hutong

Look, but you can't touch: the leaning tower of Xisi

and take a right on Fusuijing Hutong, which runs past idle shops, fruit sellers and scrabbling children. Until, that is, you suddenly hit a gleaming all-glass structure: the sales office for an international apartment.

Take a left in front of this glass box and head down the unmarked street (Xi Gongjiang Hutong) until you reach Guanyuan Market (p660). It's a curious sight, but not for the soft-hearted, who may well be tempted to purchase the entire market. At the stalls are pets of almost all imaginable sorts, from kittens and hamsters to scorpions to strange aquatic creatures. This is also, apparently, *the* place to jumpstart your collection of walnut shells.

After exiting the market, turn left on Fuchengmen Beidajie, which runs to the Fuchengmen subway station. Or, avoid the throbbing traffic a little longer and detour left on Gongmenkou Ertiao: you'll find the Beijing Lu Xun Museum (p265) and endless wandering potential.

SIGHTSEEING

247

A stilted view of the Dongyue Temple Spring Festival fair

and Buddhist music (see p254). The finely carved revolving sutra cabinet is the only one of its kind in Beijing. A reported 9,999 Buddha statuettes decorate the Tathagata Hall, though we wonder who's actually counted. Brave the steep staircase to see the Vairocana Buddha atop an elaborate pedestal, which has individually carved lotus petals – no small feat, considering that there are hundreds – and playful guardian sprites. The balcony offers a good view of changing Beijing: battered hutong rooftops crowd up right to the very edge of the temple's distinctive black-glazed tiles, while in the distance construction cranes toss up the newest additions to the city.

Daily 7.30am-5pm. RMB 20, students RMB 10. 5 Lumicang Hutong, Chaoyangmen Nanxiaojie,

Dongcheng District. (6525 0072) 智化寺，东城区朝阳门南小街禄米仓胡同5号

Dongyue Temple

Perhaps better known as "that temple over there by FullLink Plaza," this complex receives few visitors despite being in the heart of the CBD. Hundreds of amazing life-size plaster figures make up the 73 Chiefs of Departments and 18 Layers of Hell at this Temple of the God of Taishan Mountain (in Shandong Province). Offerings can be given to deities responsible for anything from the Department of Resurrection to the Department of Fish and Animals. Note the overwhelming number of prayer tags left at the Department of Morality for Officials. The temple is Taoist, but the "departments" are influenced by traditional folk beliefs. The Beijing Folk Arts Museum in the back of the temple features a collection reminiscent of the Panjiayuan Antique market. The wedding certificates and children's toys from the Republic era are lovely, as is a small bronze cow's head from the Song dynasty.

Daily 8.30am-4.30pm. RMB 10. 141 Chaowai Dajie, Chaoyang District. (6551 0151) 东岳庙，朝阳区朝外大街141号

Baoguo Temple (Compensate the Country Temple)

Founded in 1103, this temple is perhaps notable only for its history, though antique collectors may fancy the onsite market as a welcome change from busy Panjiayuan. Poets and picnickers once flocked to Baoguo for its high pavilion and crab apple orchard, neither of which are accessible today. Nor are the inner halls open to visitors, but the exteriors and an original archway have been preserved. The China Collector's Association sponsors the outer halls and sells coins, porcelain and other collectibles, while vendors sell cheaper goods in the courtyard. Particularly interesting are the *lianhuanhua*, small picture books that had their heyday in pre-1949 Shanghai but were later co-opted by the Communists. From Baoguo, one can wander to nearby Fayuan Temple, Niujie Mosque and dozens of shops selling classic Beijing street food.

Daily 7am-4pm. Free. Baoguosi Qianjie, Guang'anmennei Dajie, Xuanwu District. (6317 3169) 报国寺，宣武区广安门内大街报国寺胡同1号

Tongjiao Temple

Marooned in a sea of new high-rise blocks in Beixinqiao area, this nunnery is very active and has a peaceful, luxurious garden to relax in when the temple is open. It was built for eunuchs in the Ming dynasty and converted to a convent during the Qing. In 1942 two nuns from Fujian persuaded warlords, bureaucrats and capitalists to fund its renovation, and until the mid 1960s there were over 70 nuns in the temple, supporting themselves by spinning hemp and sewing. During the Cultural Revolution, the temple became Beixinqiao police station. It was repaired and reopened in 1981.

Open 1st and 15th of each lunar month, 8am-noon. Free. 19 Zhenxian Hutong, Dongzhimen Beixiaojie, Dongcheng District. (6405 5918) 通教寺，东城区东直门北小街针线胡同19号

Guanghua Temple

Constructed during the Yuan dynasty, this active temple and monastery is only open to the public on the 1st and 15th of each lunar month, when devout capitalists come to burn incense and pray for profits. China's last known eunuch, Sun Yaoting, was the temple's caretaker for 20 years until he died in 1996. Though he had the poor timing to be emasculated in 1911, he served the last emperor, Pu Yi, inside the Forbidden City even after the fall of the Qing dynasty. His life is documented in *The Secrets of the Last Eunuch*, a biography by Jia Yinghua.

Open 1st and 15th of each lunar month, 7am-5pm. 31 Ya'er Hutong, Xicheng District. (6403 5032) 广化寺，西城区后海鸦儿胡同31号

Lidai Diwang Temple

Monumental in scale and quite stark, the temple was constructed in 1530 to legitimize the power of conquering emperors. By making sacrifices to past emperors and key historical figures, rulers showed that they were part of the civilized tradition, and the 188 memorial tablets show that it was a long tradition indeed. From 1925 onwards the temple was used for other purposes, including a memorial service to mark the death of Sun Yat-Sen; after 1931 it became a school. The temple reopened to the public in 2004 after ten years of renovation, the biggest repair since Qianlong's time.

Daily 9am-4pm. RMB 20. Fuchengmennei Dajie, Xicheng District. (6616 1141) 历代帝王庙，西城区阜成门内大街

SIGHTSEEING

This goodwill gift from the Jesuits to the Ming now observes traffic patterns at Jianguomen

City Walls & Gates

"Nine inside, seven outside, seven imperial and four in the Forbidden City" – for hundreds of years, this handy phrase helped people keep track of the gates in Beijing's mighty city wall. Built at the beginning of the Ming dynasty in 1435, the wall ran in a 23.5km circle around the city. It was 20m thick at the base and 15m tall (that's six and a half Yao Mings!). Eight imposing watchtowers surveyed the surrounding area, symbols of imperial might and strength.

Sadly, starting in the 1950s, the Ming dynasty wall went the way of the Liao, Yuan, and Jin walls before it. Most of the gates and towers were torn down to make way for the Second Ring Road. The Imperial City's Zhonghuamen was torn down to expand Tian'anmen Square, and the construction of the number two subway line in the 1960s destroyed most of what was left. Today only a few sections of the old wall remain or have been rebuilt. But the "men" in place names like Deshengmen, Andingmen, Dongzhimen, Chaoyangmen etc., remind us that, not too long ago, each of these roundabouts and bridges was a giant stone portal into a walled-off world.

Ancient Observatory

Observatories have stood on this spot since the Yuan dynasty. Located in a former watchtower at Jianguomen, this one houses stargazing instruments like armillary spheres and a quadrant altazimuth as well as a reproduction of a Ming dynasty star map. These instruments were designed in the 17th and 18th centuries by Jesuit missionaries who sought to use their knowledge of astronomy to win the court's trust and admiration, with the ultimate goal of converting the emperor and his subjects to Catholicism. The Jesuits also sought to advance their cause by teaching the Ming how to make cannons. The juxtaposition of baroque astronomical instruments on the observatory's deck and the sea of modern highrises beyond creates a quintessentially Beijing vista, especially picturesque after a snowstorm. Try to imagine what the night sky would have looked like from the observatory before pollution. Special programs are arranged here to mark celestial events like the appearance of comets.
Daily 9am-4pm. RMB 10, students RMB 5. 2 Dongbiaobei Hutong (southwest corner of Jianguomen Bridge), Dongcheng District. (6524 2202) 古观象台，东城区建国门东裱褙胡同2号 （建国门桥西南）

Qianmen

Originally named Zhengyangmen ("Facing the Sun Gate"), Qianmen was used exclusively by the emperor on his way to perform rituals during the winter solstice and first lunar month at the Temple of Heaven. These days, plebeians can not only enter the gate, but can also view its compelling exhibits of old photographs, scale models of the Ming city gates and old playing cards. The Arrow Tower just south of Qianmen is also an impressive structure, but it's not open to the public.
Daily 8.30am-4pm. RMB 20. Qianmen Gate (South end of Tian'anmen Square), Chongwen District. (6522 9384) 前门和箭楼，崇文区天安门广场南侧

Deshengmen

The highways, byways and bus depot surrounding this ancient gate scare off amateur pedestrians and tour groups, while the Ancient Coin Museum inside only thrills hardcore fans of numismatics. So why visit? The gate is unusually elegant and the jumble of architecture visible from the rooftop snack bar is highly photogenic. Kick back with a beer and boiled peanuts and imagine scenes of victorious troops returning from battle.
Tue-Sun 9am-4pm. RMB 10. Deshengmen Jianlou, Bei'erhuan Lu, Xicheng District. (6201 8073 ext 0) 德胜门箭楼，西城区北二环德胜门箭楼

Ming Dynasty City Wall Ruins Park

This awkwardly named wall section was refurbished using traditional lime and plaster. It also contains many of the original bricks, returned by residents who were using them in homes, air-raid shelters and toilets. The eastern end is Dongbianmen Watchtower, a former gate to the Inner City that now houses the hip Red Gate Gallery. From here, it's possible to walk to another remnant of the wall, the Ancient Observatory.
Park: Daily 24 hours, free. Tower: Daily 8am-5pm. RMB 10. Along Chongwenmen Dongdajie, Chongwen District. (6527 0574) 明城墙遗址公园，崇文区崇文门东大街沿线

Continues on p254

SIGHTSEEING

Wonderwall
An ode to Beijing's vanished city walls
by Roy Kesey

There is no longer any *here* here, or at least not much. Of the myriad archways and watchtowers and barbicans, the sluice gates and sighting towers, the nested walls themselves – Palace, Imperial, Inner, and Outer, the latter 15 meters high, 20 meters thick at the base and 12 at the top, with a circumference of nearly 40 kilometers – all that remains are a short stretch between Chongwenmen and Dongbianmen, the Inner City's southeast corner, a bit of barbican at Xibianmen, and five scattered towers. Instead of walls as such we now have stacked arteries: the Second Ring Road above and the subway loop line below.

"They obtained sight of a very large and magnificent city entirely built of stone, but as the outer walls were still being built, a hundred thousand scaffoldings concealed them…" According to Ghiassudin Nakkash, this is how things were when Shah Rukh's envoy arrived to pay homage to Emperor Yongle in 1420, though of course they'd been begun long before, the Yuan walls built around what was then called Khanbaliq in the mid-thirteenth century. And yes, I have a thing for city walls, for what they try to keep in or out and the ways they fail and succeed.

Long after Yongle, more Ming work thickened the walls, and many more towers were built; wooden bridges were reconstructed in stone, and revetments laid in stone and brick. In 1553 the outer wall was extended to enclose the southern part of the city, and lasted three and a half centuries, though in the end it failed, as did the other elements of the city's defense. Domingo Navarrete noted that there were seven thousand cannons on the walls as the Manchu army drew near, and not a single one fired – the Ming troops had long since fled to the south, and the Peasant King who routed them had run west at the approach of Shunzhi.

The Qing government saw no need for greater extension, concerning itself only with occasional repairs. The Beijing City Archive contains hundreds of thousands of documents from the Manchu Ministry of Public Works, discussing the need to fix a given gate or stretch of wall, listing needed materials, and determining the best region from which to bring them. At times the calculus became more complicated: At the First National Archives there is a splendid mid-19th century file regarding the imperial treasure room inside Donghuamen; the ceiling beams needed urgent repairs, but the government minister in charge couldn't judge the extent of the damage, as he wasn't allowed to see the room's contents.

Whom to keep in, whom to keep out, and when – these questions were asked and answered not only in terms of treasure vaults, but in terms of the city itself. At the end of each excursion beyond the wall, there was invariably a race to make it back in through the outside gates before they closed for the night: "Clouds of dust surrounded each cart, through which one saw dimly only the barrel glimpse ahead, nothing but the darkening waste and the endless, endless walls […] [J]ust when every joint seemed racked loose, mules turned in the great arch […] streaming through the tunnel as the bells' slower clang and the pipes' shrill whistle proclaimed the last moments of grace. Then mules and muleteers and dust-laden passengers stopped to breathe, and caracoling knights called into cart interiors their thanksgivings at such a fortunate escape…"

That was E.A. Scidmore writing in 1900. The wall began to fall in earnest that very year: the Boxer Rebellion brought the guns of the Russians and Japanese, the torches of the Righteous Harmony Society, and the cannons of the British, over and over, gate after gate knocked down. However, for the next few years, most of the wall was still intact. From B.L Putnam Weale in 1905: "As you swung round the great keep, you would see to your left […] the Tartar wall, mighty and massive, stretching away mile after mile, and capped and crowned at regular intervals with great *lou* or storied towers. Below the wall was a vast sand-stretch, furrowed by countless cartwheels and often encumbered with thousands of camels coming or going, where you might gallop and

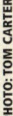

"Below the wall was a vast sand-stretch...often encumbered with thousands of camels"

gallop until you were fairly pumped." What he meant by "fairly pumped" I haven't the faintest idea, and it is not easy for me, imagining Beijing full of camels.

    The damage continued: half a century of incursion and neglect. The Republican and warlord governments punched holes for railways, broke barbicans to ease traffic, tumbled most of the Imperial City wall. The Outer City wall came down in the Fifties, the Inner City wall in the Sixties, all gone to make room for the subway, the bricks stripped and sent wherever bricks were needed. Gone are the Imperial Equipage elephant stables at Xuanwumen, the glazed yellow roof of Chengtianzhimen, the iron pagoda at Dongzhimen, all the moats but the innermost. And you can argue that there was no other way for Beijing to modernize, that in fact the city is better off without her wall.

    But you'd be wrong.

Bring in the Noise

In the old days, it was the yelling of street hawkers, not mobile phone owners, that filled the air in Beijing. That seemingly off-key singing came from Peking Opera actors, not the KTV junkies down the hall. And at night, a smaller, walled Beijing was so quiet that time was marked simply by the beat of a drum. Here are a few places to explore Beijing's antique sounds.

Drum & Bell Towers

Although the current structure dates to 1800, buildings similar to the Drum Tower have stood in this vicinity for over 700 years. During the Song dynasty, an intricate system of bronze clepsydras (water clocks) mechanically sounded out the hours on a gong. Later, the hours were beaten on 24 drums, but apparently only one was used at any one time. Today, the tower houses 25 drums that are beaten for visitors every half-hour between 9-11.30am and 2-5pm.

Qing dynasty timekeeping was a convoluted affair. A drum would sound 13 times at 7pm, then once every two hours thereafter – the watchman also struck a bamboo clapper to help locals distinguish between, say, the hours of 11pm and 3am. This was important, as many high-ranking civil and military servants awoke at 1am, assembled outside the Forbidden City's Wumen gate at 3am, and entered the palace en masse at 5am to receive the emperor's instructions.

Just north of the Drum Tower is the Bell Tower, not to be confused with the Big Bell Temple. Also a copy of a Yuan predecessor, the current structure is a sprightly 300 years old. The bell that gives the tower its name is a 500-year-old bronze beast with 10cm thick walls. Legend has it that after the bronze master had several casting mishaps, his daughter threw herself into the pot of molten metal to secure a good casting. While her methods may have been slightly unorthodox, they apparently worked, and the emperor was so moved by her display of filial piety that he established a temple near the bell foundry in her honor. During the Spring Festival, RMB 100 will buy visitors a chance to ring the bell.

On clear days, the Drum and Bell towers offer splendid views of the leafy neighboring hutongs and the modern concrete jungle in the distance. In the evening, after the pedicab operators and tour buses have left, the plaza between the towers has a neighborhood flavor from days past. Known by the combined name of the two towers, the Zhonggulou neighborhood is one of the best areas to explore old Beijing on foot and was commemorated in punker He Yong's eponymous acoustic song from his 1991 album *Garbage Dump*.

Daily 9am-5pm. Drum tower: RMB 20, students RMB 10. Bell tower: RMB 15, students RMB 8. Di'anmen Dajie, Dongcheng District. (6401 2674) 钟鼓楼，东城区地安门大街

Big Bell Temple

No hyperbole here: this temple is home to the biggest bell in China. The bronze giant is six meters tall, weighs 46.5 tons and is adorned with 230,000 characters of Buddhist scripture. It is rung for prosperity on New Year's Eve and during the Spring Festival. The temple also features a complete set of Ming-style chimes and, in the museum to the rear, well-preserved Song and Yuan dynasty bells.

For RMB 100, musicians will perform on command. Don't feel limited to classical Ming compositions, which the attendant described as "a little depressing": They will play anything from Beethoven's "Für Elise" to "Happy Birthday." CDs are available to enjoy the good vibrations at home.

Daily 8.30am-4pm. RMB 10. 31A Beisanhuan Xilu, Haidian District. (6255 0819) 大钟寺，海淀区北三环西路甲31号

Ancient Music Center

The Ancient Music Center is located in Zhihua Temple (p245), which was once the family home of a powerful eunuch responsible for imperial rites and ceremonies. Regular musical performances take place each day, even for audiences of one. Using period instruments like the *yunluo*, a set of tuned gongs, the musicians play Ming dynasty ritual music and Buddhist pieces designed to help monks memorize scriptures. Zhihua monks passed down their music from generation to generation; today's lay performers learned from the last living monk of the 28th generation, who is over 80 and still teaching this 500-year-old tradition. In the last courtyard, the Hall of Great Mercy holds a display on this ancient art form. Don't miss the rest of the serene temple, either: Its woodcarvings and statues are intricate and lovely.

500-year-old beats brought to life at the Ancient Music Center

Daily 7am-5pm. 15-minute performances at 9, 10, 11am and 3pm. RMB 20, students RMB 10. Zhihua Temple, 5 Lumicang Hutong, Dongcheng District. (6528 6691) 文博交流馆，东城区禄米仓胡同5号智化寺内

Huguang Huiguan

Designed as guesthouses for scholars taking the imperial exams, the provincially-based guild halls, or *huiguans*, evolved into entertainment centers after nightfall, with lively restaurants and theater performances. Arguably the most popular *huiguan* was that of Huguang province – today's Hubei. Restored in 1994 to its Qing-era glory, the Huguang Huiguan does a brisk trade with contemporary tourists – keep this in mind the next time you have guests. One of its rooms serves as the Peking Opera Museum and features handwritten scripts, books and vintage photos of Chinese opera star Mei Lanfang, who often performed here. Snippets of famous operas are performed nightly in the ornate 300-seat theater. Watch the stage antics, sip tea and snack on roasted sunflower seeds. To show fellow patrons how well you've assimilated, shout "*Hao!*" at the top of your lungs after particularly acrobatic moves or high notes. Watch the performance intensely for a few moments and then go back to chatting with your friends. Do this repeatedly. The attached restaurant, Chuwanyuan, is superb and specializes in creative Hubei and Beijing dishes; snag the sumptuous Furongyuan private room if you really want to impress.

Daily 9am-7.30pm. RMB 10 (museum), RMB 150-580 (performance). 3 Hufang Lu, Xuanwu District. (6351 8284) 湖广会馆，宣武区虎坊路3号

Roman Holiday

A taste of Tivoli in Rendinghu Park
by Roy Kesey

Even the gods of Olympus vacation in Beijing

I have a thing for parks. The old men walking their caged birds around the Temple of Heaven, the young couples noodling on shaded benches in Ritan, the kids wading through the fountains at Chaoyang – green spaces where people like these feel free to do things like this, holding their ground against the urban crush, make the prospect of slogging through acre after acre of cement and asphalt and brick day after day seem not quite so unbearable.

I also have a thing for arboreal variety. And for statues of attractive naked people. And for inexplicable weirdness. And for Rome. In other words: Bury my heart at Rendinghu.

It's one of Beijing's smaller parks, tucked away down a series of sun-dappled lanes a bit north of the Second Ring. It isn't particularly well-known, which means that it's rarely crowded. At the moment there's still a bit of small-scale construction going on, but not to worry: The noise of the one backhoe at work is more than drowned out by the steady song of cicadas in the trees.

Entering at the east gate, take a quick counterclockwise loop around the north end of the small but stylishly sculpted lake. You can skip the ugly round yellow stucco buildings labeled "Colour Baby" and focus instead on the large grassy areas, the willows and pines and ginkgos, the sycamores and ornamental cherry trees and massive firs. Also worth skipping is the large blue sculpture in the center of the park, which appears to have been inspired by fungi. But on the far side of the lake, near the park's west gate, there are people playing cards and mahjong and chess in the shade.

Continuing your circle and now headed south, you'll pass through an extremely well-tended, multicolored rose garden. And here is where things get interesting. First there is a complex of curved, elevated stone walkways. It is not entirely clear why they are curved, or for that matter why they are elevated; push on nonetheless past the massive bronze globe, past the stylized tile mosaics, and you will soon be looking down upon a large terraced garden of flowers and fountains and statuary.

I have heard it said that the view from here looks something like that of Hadrian's villa at Tivoli: This is perhaps true, if you squint, and have been drinking. Regardless, there is nothing for it now but to enjoy: the columns and colonnade, the naked gods and goddesses in marble and (in one case, way up in the air) bronze. To either side of the main sward are beautiful sub-gardens designed by someone with a splendid eye for hue. It is without a doubt the most peaceful and pleasant inexplicably weird Rome-inspired corner in all of Beijing.

Daily 6am-9pm. 11 Liupukangjie, Dewaiande Lu, Xicheng District. (6202 3200)
人定湖公园，西城区德外安德路六铺坑街11号

Sino-Roman statuary afflicts Beijing's public parks with flair

Re-acquaint yourself with the color green (and bubblegum pink, and lifesaver orange ...) in city parks

Parks

Some days it seems like every Beijinger must own stock in a concrete company. On these days, consider escaping to one of Beijing's many parks and get some time away from claustrophobic city life. Even the bigger parks here aren't just tourist attractions – early in the mornings, you'll see senior citizens doing all manners of exercise, and in the late afternoon and evenings, young and old alike come to relax and stretch their legs. So if you're looking to do as the locals do, here are some great places to re-acquaint yourself with the color green. Also see the Fun Places Directory in Kids (p164).

Coal Hill (Jingshan)

The dirt from the moat around the Forbidden City had to go somewhere – why not just dump it in the backyard? Created in 1420 using earth from the moat and the expansion of Beihai's lakes, this hill is, in fact, far from a Ming dynasty dumping ground. *Fengshui* principles ordered a sheltering hill to protect the Imperial palace from chilling northern winds. Politically, since it occupied the former site of the Yuan dynasty palace, the hill symbolically squashed the Yuan and buried its emperor. Ironically, the last emperor of the Ming also ended his reign at Coal Hill: He hanged himself from a tree as Manchu troops stormed Beijing. (Another version of the story has him committing suicide in the Forbidden City's gardens.) This hill is known by two names in Chinese: "Coal Hill" (Meishan), as coal was often piled at its foot, and "Prospect Hill" (Jingshan), its Qing-era name. A climb to the top is rewarded with beautiful views of the Forbidden City, Tian'anmen Square and Beijing's ancient symmetry. Go early in the morning for the best photo opportunities of the world's largest palace complex.

Daily 6am-9pm. RMB 2. 1 Wenjin Jie, Xicheng District. (6404 4071) 景山公园，西城区文津街1号

Botanical Garden and Wofo Si Temple

With a state-of-the-art greenhouse and the largest plant collection in China, the Beijing Botanical Garden has a whole day's worth of flora. There are over 2,000 varieties of orchids,

PHOTO: SIMON LIM

100-year-old bonsai and peach and pear blossoms that provide a visual feast in spring. The highlight is the artificial jungle inside the greenhouse, with orchids, tropical trees and cacti. The sprawling grounds also contain Wofo Si, the Reclining Buddha Temple. The big shoes on display are offerings to the temple's namesake sculpture, which weighs 54 tons and took 7,400 slaves to build. It's unlikely the giant reclining Buddha would be worried about footwear, however – he's actually supposed to be dying, not sleeping. Cao Xueqin, the author of *Dream of the Red Chamber*, wrote much of his manuscript in the grassy areas behind the temple (see p241). See also China Honey Bee Museum (p265). *Daily 7am-5pm (garden), 8am-4.30pm (Wofo Si and greenhouse). RMB 50 greenhouse, RMB 5 Wofo Si Temple. Wofo Si Lu, Xiangshan, Haidian District. (6259 1283)* 北京植物园和卧佛寺，海淀区香山卧佛寺路

Fragrant Hills Park (Xiangshan) and Azure Clouds Temple (Biyun Si)

Everyone recommends going to the Fragrant Hills to see the leaves turn in autumn, but no one mentions that the city's entire population will be there with you. At off-peak times, this park, carved from imperial hunting grounds, is a civilized jumble of smoke trees, small pagodas and scenic pools culminating in a view of Beijing from Incense Burner Peak (Xianglu Feng). A chairlift is available for those not up to the hour-long hike (read: stair-climb) to the top. Trails lead from the peak further into the Western Hills.

Near the park's north entrance, Azure Cloud Temple is worth exploring. It was built in 1331 and refurbished by two powerful eunuchs who wanted a stunning tomb. In lieu of their mausoleum, which was never completed, you'll find the Hall of Arhats, featuring 508 life-size figures of holy men, and the marble Diamond Throne Pagoda, surrounded by stupas. The grounds also serve as a memorial to the founder of the Republic of China, Sun Yat-sen. He lay in state here from 1925 to 1929 before his remains were moved to Nanjing. His crystal coffin, a gift from the Soviet government, was left behind.

A stroll through the Fragrant Hills Hotel can also start or end the visit. The understated building successfully blends traditional Chinese design with modern architecture and was designed by famed architect I.M. Pei, whose works include the Louvre Pyramid and the Hong Kong Bank of China Building.

Fragrant Hills Park *Daily 6am-6.30pm (summer), 6am-6.30pm (winter). RMB 10, RMB 5 (students). Xiangshan, Haidian District. (6259 1155)* 香山公园，海淀区香山

Azure Clouds Temple *Daily 8am-5pm (summer), 8.30am-4.30pm (winter). RMB 10. Inside Fragrant Hills Park, Haidian District. (6259 1155 ext 470)* 碧云寺，海淀区香山

Fragrant Hills Hotel *Inside Fragrant Hills Park, Haidian District. (6259 1155)* 香山宾馆，海淀区香山公园内

Beihai Park – Circular City

Descriptions of Beihai often claim that this body of water is entirely man-made. In fact, Beihai and the other "seas" (*hai*) to the west and north of the Forbidden City are built-up expansions of naturally occurring small lakes that were imperial summer playgrounds from the Jin dynasty (1115-1234) onwards – their existence is reflected in the name Haidian or "Sea District." The central and southern lakes, Zhongnanhai, abut the Chinese leadership complex of the same name west of the Forbidden City and are off-limits to the public. The Yuan dynasty built its imperial palace on the eastern shore of Beihai, the sole remnant of which is the Circular City and the green jade jar housed within.

Atop Qionghua Island is Beihai's centerpiece, the White Dagoba. Shunzhi, the first emperor of the Qing dynasty to reign from Beijing, ordered this Tibetan *chorten* in 1651 to honor the visit of the Fifth Dalai Lama. Don't bother with the imperial-style banquet at Fangshan, also on the island – either the royals had wooden palates or the restaurant has altered the recipes. The Qing emperors didn't lack taste in pleasure gardens, though: Just check out the park's stunning views and sculpted shores. Famous for its seas of lotuses that bloom in June and July, Beihai is particularly popular as a boating destination, though a stroll around the lake offers another perspective into the park (see p260).
Daily 6am-8.30pm. RMB 10 (park), RMB 20 (all access), students half price. 1 Wenjin Jie, Xicheng District. (6403 1102) 北海公园-团城，西城区文津街1号

Tranquil Heart
Rediscovering Beihai's historical treasures
by John Brennan

We all know Beihai Park for its tree-lined paths, pedal boats and gorgeous water vistas. Less celebrated are the architectural treasures dotted throughout the park. You can connect these dots in three or four hours of car-free wandering and surprising discoveries. As with most Beijing sites, go early to avoid the worst of the tour groups.

Begin at the graceful Jade Rainbow Bridge that divides the lakes of Beihai in the north from Zhonghai in the south. (You're now near the southeast gate of the park.) Yuan Shikai once built a large red wall along the length of the bridge to stop the hoi polloi from peeking at his presidential mansion. And they were surprised when he made himself emperor.

Sunset views await from the White Dagoba

Just east of the bridge is the entrance to the Tuancheng (Round City). Go in and climb the stairs to a peaceful courtyard with a pavilion known as Cheng Guang Hall, built in 1690. Inside is an image of the Sakyamuni Buddha (flawless white jade or Italian alabaster, depending on who you believe). Foreign soldiers attacked it with a sword in 1900: the gash on its left arm is believed to be a defense wound. In the courtyard is the only relic of the Yuan dynasty palace that once stood here: a magnificent carved nephrite bowl that used to belong to Kublai Khan.

Now head to the north side of the pavilion, enter Beihai Park and cross the bridge to Qionghua Dao (Jade Island), which is crowned by the White Dagoba. You first pass through two temples, then a steep flight of 70 steps takes you to the Dagoba and fine 360-degree views. To the south, the new National Grand Theater (a.k.a. "the Egg") dominates the skyline: You can decide if it is a masterpiece or the greatest eyesore in Beijing's history. Behind the Dagoba, make your way down to the lakeside pavilion, avoiding the seriously weird cave (RMB 3: Don't say I didn't warn you).

From the covered walkway by the lake you could catch a ferry to the Five Dragon Pavilions on the western shore. But you won't. This is a walk – what are you *thinking*? Head around the north of the island and through the gate tower. Cross the bridge, turn left and follow the path past a lovely grove of willows and scholar trees. Walk north and try not to let the drop-dead lake views distract you: You need to keep your eyes peeled for a hidden gem. See a small building on your right with a covered staircase to the left of it going up the slope? Good. Follow the staircase up till you reach a lotus pool surrounded by greenery, in the middle of which stands a little pavilion joined to the shore by a zigzag stone bridge. You are in the Haopu Jian (dubiously translated as "Carefree Compound"), which was built in 1757.

Back on the lake path, you'll pass an intriguing enclosure with curvy white walls, where the Dowager Empress used to retire to smoke opium. However, you can't do the same thing, because it's not open to the public. Keep going north, cross the bridge and turn left. Not far along, you'll

INSIDER'S GUIDE TO BEIJING

This azure sea of Buddhas complements Beihai's placid waters

come to an unforgettable example of the Chinese genius for the garden within a garden. Originally built in the Ming Dynasty and later remodeled by Qianlong, it was a favorite retreat of Cixi, who made her own additions to it. You can drink tea in a pavilion by a miniature stone bridge above a tiny hidden waterfall and count yourself king of infinite space: just one of a hundred delights and surprises in this, the Jing Xin Zhai – the Studio of the Tranquil Heart.

Drag yourself away and head along the lakeshore to a series of architectural gems. First is the Hall of the Kings of Heaven (Tianwang Dian), a superb Ming-era wooden structure. Move on to the celebrated Nine Dragon Screen, which depicts dragons as huge writhing animals covered in scales, then make your way to the lakeside Five Dragon Pavilions (Wu Long Ting), which are said to resemble dragons, although they are square and have no scales at all. Next door is the entrance to a botanical garden, worth a visit for its gingko-shaded paths and for the Pavilion of Wonderful Images (Miao Xiang Ting) featuring 16 Qing-era copies of 10th-century carvings. Finally there is the Little Western Heaven (Xiao Xi Tian), a fine building erected in 1770, flanked by four small pavilions and four stone *pailou*. The interior features many statues of the Goddess of Mercy and a dazzling coffered ceiling.

Finally, enjoy the 700m walk south to the park exit, a few hundred meters west of your starting point, at the other end of the Jade Rainbow Bridge.

Arts, Architecture & Antiques

Xu Beihong Museum

Xu Beihong is considered the father of modern Chinese painting, and you can find poor imitations of his work for outrageous prices in souvenir shops across town, but we'd rather go here and see over 100 of his actual works. Xu lived from 1895-1953 and studied Western painting techniques in France. He was one of the first painters to merge western and Chinese techniques, but he remains most famous for his pictures of forceful galloping stallions painted in traditional Chinese style. Xu founded the Central Academy of Fine Arts in 1950 and was chairman of the Chinese Artists Association from 1949 until his death.
Tue-Sun 9am-4pm. RMB 5, RMB 2 (students). 53 Xinjiekou Beidajie, Xicheng District. (6225 2042) 徐悲鸿纪念馆，西城区新街口北大街53号

China Red Sandalwood Museum

A wonderland for wood enthusiasts, this museum displays a tantalizing range of the possibilities of Burmese ebony, tropical mahogany, Indian sandalwood and other precious timbers. Most of the 1,000 handcrafted pieces are modern creations and not antiques, but that doesn't dimish the extravagance of Forbidden City scale models or exquisitely carved furniture. If the majestic birdcages and thrones don't impress you, then perhaps the knowledge that everything was built without a single nail or screw will. The museum also doubles as a shrine to its founder, Madame Chen Lihua, one of the richest women in China, who pals around with Jackie Chan and Eastern European heads of state.
Tue-Sun 9am-4.30pm. RMB 50. 23 Jianguo Lu, Chaoyang District. (8575 2818) www.redsandalwood.com 紫檀博物馆，朝阳区建国路23号

Arthur M. Sackler Museum

(for description and address, see p264)

Song Tang Zhai Museum of Traditional Chinese Folk Carving

If there's a "hidden" museum in Beijing, then this is it. Located behind a trinket vendor on the eastern end of Liulichang arts and crafts street, it looks just like any of the other stores lining the block. Inside, however, the museum has two small floors full of old fashioned doors, wood blocks, furniture, and a variety of other wood and stone carvings from all over China. Some of the pieces are really extraordinary, and just as extraordinary is the atmosphere, which feels like you are walking through a collector's home. On-site guides will give you a free tour in Chinese, and there's no admission fee, though donations are gladly accepted as you leave. The whole building can be browsed through in 30 minutes (maybe a little longer, if you take the tour or read the Chinese captions), so it isn't worth going out of your way to visit, but if you're in the area it shouldn't be missed.
Daily 9am-6pm. Free (donations accepted). 14 Liulichang Dongjie, Xuanwu District. (8316 4662) 松堂斋民间雕刻博物馆，宣武区琉璃厂东街14号

Museum of Ancient Architecture

Sure, visiting all the old buildings is nice, but at some point, everyone has that urge to contrast and compare, and that's where the Museum of Ancient Architecture comes in. It lies on the site of the Xiannong Altar, where Qing dynasty emperors performed tilling ceremonies during the spring equinox. The emperor made offerings to the mythical first farmer, Shen, then pushed a plow for a few meters before returning to his sedan chair to watch underlings finish the rest. These days it contains a large model of Beijing's old city and exhibits on the capital's traditional architecture.
Daily 9am-4pm. RMB 15. 21 Dongjing Lu, Xuanwu District. (6301 7620) 古代建筑博物馆，宣武区东经路21号

The Poly Museum

Yes, it's RMB 50 for a museum only one-tenth the size of the Capital Museum (see p263), and yes, it's tucked away in a hard-to-find section of Poly Plaza, but this is still one of the nicest little museums in Beijing, and it's definitely worth a visit. The Poly Group is a well-funded semi-private organization dedicated to buying Chinese artifacts abroad and bringing them home, and their two main collections here, ancient bronzes and Buddha statues from throughout Chinese history, are each well-lit and well presented. Stroll through them and notice the differences between periods and regions, and appreciate the subtle expressions on the faces of the Buddhas. You can also find four of the 12 bronze animal heads that were looted from the waterworks of the Old Summer Palace – when

Laduzi and learning go hand in hand at the Capital Museum

the Poly Group brought them back to China it was considered a national triumph.
Mon-Sat 9am-4pm. RMB 30. 14 Dongzhimen Nandajie, Dongcheng District. (6500 8117) 保利博物馆，东城区东直门南大街14号

Museums

Beijing has museums of all shapes and sizes, many of which will be upgraded in the next few years as part of the capital's RMB 615 million program to enhance historical and cultural attractions. If you plan on taking in many of these within one year, the museum pass (p238) is eminently worthwhile.

Beijing Museum of Natural History
(For description, opening times and address, see Kids, p164).

Beijing Planetarium
(For description, opening times and address, see Kids, p164).

Capital Museum
Beijing finally has a museum it can be proud of. Formerly housed in the Confucius Temple, the new Capital Museum now holds sway in a undeniably cool modernist building, complete with state-of-the-art technology, thoughtfully curated exhibits and mostly coherent English captions. Nostalgic about vanishing hutongs? The Capital Museum features reconstructions of old hutong homes as part of its permanent exhibits on Beijing history, culture, folk customs and urban development. Don't miss the ancient bronzes, jade, porcelain, paintings and everything else you'd hope to find in a Chinese art and antiques collection. Temporary exhibitions run a gamut of subjects and often feature traveling exhibitions from foreign museums.
Tue-Sun 9am-4pm, RMB 50, students RMB 25. 16 Fuxingmenwai Dajie, Xicheng District. (6337 0491) www.capitalmuseum.org.cn 首都博物馆，西城区复兴门外大街16号

Peking University: where brains and beauty blossom

Beijing Planning Exhibition Hall

If you need a little more weirdness in your life, head to this surreal showcase of Beijing's city layout. The highlight is a massive scale model of the city, which takes up an entire floor and is best viewed with binoculars from above. Elsewhere, the first floor has nice old photographs of hutongs and traditional homes, and the second through fourth floors are simply strange, with 3D movies, booths showcasing the best of Beijing's municipal districts and a model for a "future house." Don't ask.
Tue-Sun 9am-4pm. RMB 30. 20 Qianmen Dongdajie (just east of the old railroad station), Chongwen District. (6702 4559) 北京规划博物馆，崇文区前门东大街20号（老火车站东边）

Arthur M. Sackler Museum

A highlight of Peking University's verdant campus, the Arthur M. Sackler Museum of Art and Archaeology offers not only a wealth of treasures but also well-curated exhibits. With over 10,000 objects, it presents many collections as they were excavated.

Highlights include a 280,000 year-old pre-human skeleton, Shang dynasty polished bronze pots, red jade jewelry from the Jin dynasty, Tang-era terracotta figures and intricately carved tomb guardians: spirits armed with stegosaurus spikes, hooves and the occasional horn, meant to scare off grave robbers – like archaeologists, perhaps.

As befitting its past life as an imperial garden, the surrounding campus is home to ponds pink with summer lotuses, shady woods, pavilions, the willow-lined Weiming "Yet Unnamed" Lake, and reflected in its waters, the classical Boya Pagoda.
Daily 9am-5pm, last entrance 4.30pm. RMB 5. Inside the Peking University West Gate, Haidian District. (6275 1667) 北大赛克勒博物馆，海淀区北京大学大西门内

PHOTO: NICK OTTO

National Museum of Modern Chinese Literature

This institution offers a one-stop "shopping experience" for fans of 20th century Chinese literature. Exhibits include reproductions of writers' homes, complete with mannequins of their likenesses, original manuscripts and personal effects. If you prefer real homes to model homes, many of the featured writers' houses have been preserved and turned into museums of their own.

Tue-Sun 9am-4pm. RMB 20. 45 Wenxueguan Lu, Shaoyaoju, Chaoyang District. (8461 9060) 中国现代文学馆，朝阳区芍药居文学馆路45号

Beijing Lu Xun Museum

Although he was born in Zhejiang and did some of his best work in Shanghai in the early 20th century, Lu Xun, the "father of modern Chinese literature," also lived in Beijing from 1912-1926, where he was a key figure in the May Fourth Movement in 1919. The museum features some of Lu's personal effects, first editions of some of his works and copies of his writings for various literary magazines. The museum also sells copies of Lu's works in Chinese and other languages, including his classic and biting satire, *The True Story of Ah Q*.

Tue-Sun 9am-4pm. RMB 5. 19 Gongmenkou Ertiao, Fuchengmennei, Xicheng District. (6616 5654) 北京鲁迅纪念馆，西城区阜成门内宫门口二条19号

The Chinese Military History Museum

With 5,000 years worth of war paraphernalia, this museum will curl the toes of any military buff. The collection includes AK-47s, flame throwers, US tanks captured during the Korean War, U-2 spyplane wreckage, ancient weaponry and uniforms, as well as exhibits on the "War of Resistance against Japanese Aggression" and the war against the "Eight Power Allied Forces." If your revolutionary fervor is still not ignited, then maybe the display of socialist realist artwork will do the trick. Good place to pick up military gewgaws and army souvenirs. Kids dig the place.

Daily 8am-5pm. RMB 20, students RMB 10. 9 Fuxing Lu, Haidian District. (6686 6244) 中国军事博物馆，海淀区复兴路9号

Other
Underground City

Little did you know, but Beijing is mostly hollow underneath. The city sits on a warren of tunnels, air-raid shelters and escape routes, rumored to lead as far out as the Summer Palace. Most of the 85 square kilometers worth of tunnels were dug out manually, by a combined force of the army, citizen "volunteers", and schoolchildren. Ordered by Mao after "big brother" USSR ceased to be so brotherly, the extensive network was designed to hold 40 percent of Beijing's population and had everything from arsenals to infirmaries to a mushroom cultivation farm (not even chemical attacks can overcome the Chinese passion for fungi). Today the ghost of the tunnels can still be seen as part of the subway lines and the Xidan underground mall, but a more direct experience is at the Beijing Underground City. Just opened in 2000, this section of the subterranean behemoth is decked out in obligatory Mao statues, posters and photos of old tanks, planes, top cadres and sexy soldiers, and even a Buddhist shrine. A guide, appropriately wearing camo, leads you through the tunnels, tantalizingly pointing out the passages that lead deeper and farther in all directions.

Daily 8.30am-6pm. RMB 20, students RMB 10. 62 Xidamochang Hutong, Qianmen, Chongwen District. (6702 2657) 前门地下城。崇文区前门西打磨厂胡同62号

China Honey Bee Museum

Located on the west side of the Botanical Garden in the Fragrant Hills, this quaint little museum is devoted to all things apian. Sample different varieties of honey, see bee keeping accoutrements and spend your afternoon engrossed in apicultural studies.

Daily Mar-Oct 8.30am-4.30pm. Free. Fragrant Hills Botanical Garden, Haidian District. (8259 4910) 中国蜜蜂博物馆，海淀区香山北京植物园内

Beijing Tap Water Museum

Includes a map of Beijing's underground water system and models of the city's main water purifying systems and water towers. Free guides on hand will clarify the finer points of water flow for you.

Continues on p268

Beijing: The B-Sides

An urban explorer wanders the city's underbelly
by Eric Abrahamsen

"You know, I'm a little afraid of heights." Chen Chu has waited until we're 80 meters off the ground to mention this. We're both inching our way up a spiral staircase inside an unfinished concrete tower, easing around nubs of rebar in the gloom. The open stairwell gapes to our right – no railing.

We're in Wonderland, or as much of Wonderland as was ever built. Construction began on this grand amusement park in 1996, stopped a year later, and the skeleton of Wonderland has squatted outside Changping ever since, looking like an alien rocket facility.

Chen Chu is one of the capital's few bona fide Urban Explorers – a very rare breed of Beijinger who shuns the malls and bright lights in favor of underground ruins and abandoned buildings. While you trod the city's byways, Chen Chu may be beneath your feet, or sliding along on the other side of a concrete wall.

Chen Chu's hobby began in 2005, when he and some friends were telling idle ghost stories. Someone mentioned a supposed suicide in the old colonial ruin at 81 Chaonei Dajie, one of Beijing's more atmospheric wrecks. Chen Chu made a boastful noise, his manhood was impugned, girls were present – in short, he found himself in the building at night, with a flashlight, on a dare. "I was absolutely terrified," he admits. But also, after the experience, increasingly intrigued. He returned to the building on Chaonei. He wondered what other empty places laid in wait. He began to explore.

Chen Chu knows where the skeletons are

In many ways, Chen Chu is a typical twenty something Chinese guy. Rail-thin, a chain-smoker, single, he chose a career in IT primarily so he could spend more time on the Internet. He talks readily on all subjects, including his country – about which he's both dubious and defensive – and gently complains about how easy it is for foreign guys to pick up Chinese girls.

On the other hand, he's very clearly not like other guys. There are at most two or three other people in Beijing interested in urban exploration. For whatever reason, peering underneath Beijing's belly is an activity with very limited appeal. According to reports in the Chinese media, Chen Chu is a rebel, and likes breaking rules – he goes exploring out of some latent desire to stick it to The Man. After meeting him in person, however, this theory seems highly unlikely, and he himself dismisses it with a wave of his hand. "Actually, I'm very traditional," he says, before assuming a faraway look and quoting a Buddhist proverb to prove it: "A world in a grain of sand; all of heaven in a flower."

Later he comes up with a slightly more modern simile to explain his hobby: "Cities are like records. Each one has an A side, and it also has a B side." The A side is bright and perpetually crowded; only the B side can ever belong to you. "I can go into a half-finished building and imagine it any way I please – no one can say anything. I can go into a place that's been abandoned for decades, and feel that I've entered another time." To Chen Chu, every door is a portal between worlds, and he likes nothing more than to slip out of this one from time to time.

Seen this way, it's a wonder more people aren't interested in urban exploration. Who hasn't felt worn out by the constant public exposure of living in Beijing? Who wouldn't like to feel that they are the secret master of a piece of the city, if only briefly? And yet Chen Chu is generally alone in his explorations. At most, a reporter goes with him ("But they don't like to go anywhere dangerous or scary"). People like to know he's out there, though they're reluctant to follow suit.

Beijing's changes are affecting Chen Chu as much as anyone. "There aren't so many places inside the city where you can go exploring anymore." The house at 81 Chaonei Dajie has been put under more rigorous guard, and there are hardly any unlocked entrances to the underground city. Other sites are being renovated after decades of disuse – as Beijing strains and swells, it consumes even its smallest unused spaces.

As a result Chen Chu's explorations are becoming less and less urban – he's visiting sites like Wonderland outside Beijing, ancient tombs in the hills around the city ("*not* tomb-robbing!"), and even old Ming and Qing battlegrounds, where ancient armor and weapons can sometimes be found.

But these can be decidedly less satisfying than a hidden corner inside the city. After what seems like hours on the stairs, we finally see a platform above us, only to discover that the last leg of stairway was never built. We're caught in a dark little concrete box, high in the air but sealed off from the view. "This is why I like underground sites better," grumbles Chen Chu, and we head back down the stairs.

Wonderland, where profligacy ended in broken dreams, is an El Dorado for urban explorers

SIGHTSEEING

Wed-Sun 9am-4pm. RMB 5, students RMB 2. 6A Dongzhimenwai Beidajie (inside Qingshui Yuan), Dongcheng District. (6465 0787) 北京自来水博物馆，东城区东直门外北大街甲6号（清水苑社区内）

Beijing Police Museum

Start at the fourth floor, where you get to shoot laser pistols at moving targets, and work your way down through a collection of over 8,000 police tools and weapons from the Han Dynasty through to the present. The exhibit on fingerprint forensics is a highlight, as is the gruesome second-floor display of old-fashioned torture devices and photos (families with kids would be advised to skip it). On the first floor there's an exhibit detailing the police force's origins and history – don't miss the section on Kuomintang reactionary agents and the signed, fingerprinted confessions from failed "subversion schemes." Tue-Sun 9am-4pm. RMB 5. 36 Dongjiaomin Xiang, Dongcheng District. (8522 5018) 北京警察博物馆，东城区东交民巷36号

Beijing Ancient Coins Exhibition Hall

Four thousand years of China's numismatic history jampacked into three rooms; includes a permanent exhibition of, you guessed it – coins! With experts available for free coin appraisal, this is a hang out for collectors, traders and sellers.
Tue-Sun 9am-4pm. RMB 10. Deshengmen Jianlou, Beierhuan Zhonglu, Xicheng District. (6201 8073 ext 0) 北京古代钱币博物馆，西城区北二环中路德胜门箭楼

Tombs

Steeped in ancestor worship, the ancient Chinese took as much, if not more, care with the tombs of the dead as they did with the houses of the living. To ensure a comfortable afterlife, emperors and nobles were entombed with objects, pets, spouses and attendants – but unlike their Egyptian counterparts, they used ceramic statues to replace actual human sacrifices from the Zhou dynasty onward. Regular folk simply had to hope that their forebears had made it to heaven and would use their *guanxi* to affect any decision-making there. When Buddhist ideas of reincarnation were introduced, things got complicated, as one's ancestor might – to the family's horror – be reincarnated as someone else. To accommodate, Buddhist monks in China altered their teachings so that enlightenment could be achieved in one lifetime, allowing for direct ascension into heaven. For the Qing Tombs, see the Excursions chapter (p557).

Ming Tombs

Thirteen of the 16 Ming emperors are buried in this picturesque valley of rolling hills and orchards. Adhering to fengshui principles, each tomb is backed by a hill to the north. King Tut's Tomb they ain't – the interiors of the tombs are surprisingly plain. The tombs all have the same basic layout and share a single marble archway and statue-lined Spirit Way. Only three of the mausoleums – Changling, Dingling and Zhaoling – are open to the public, but you can poke around the others to escape the tour-bussed masses. The three Ming emperors not buried here are the dynasty's founder Zhu Yuanzhang, buried in Nanjing; the second emperor, who was deposed by his uncle and never had a tomb built; and the seventh emperor, Jingtai, who was buried in a prince's tomb west of Beijing. Jingtai seized power when Mongols captured his brother Yingzong. After Yingzong was eventually freed, he executed his brother as punishment for disloyalty.

During spring and autumn, the area is great for picnics. The nearby Shisanling Reservoir is the remnant of a public works project started in the 1950s. It was built in record time, but engineers soon discovered that the lakebed absorbed water, rendering it useless.

Changling Tomb

Daily 8am-5pm. RMB 45 (Apr 1-Oct 31), RMB 30 (Nov 1-Mar 31), students half price. (6076 1334) 长陵，昌平区

Dingling Tomb

Daily 8am-5.30pm. RMB 65 (Apr 1-Oct 31), RMB 40 (Nov 1-Mar 31), students half price. (6076 1424) 定陵，昌平区

Zhaoling Tomb

Daily 8am-5pm. RMB 30 (Apr 1-Oct 31), RMB 20 (Nov 1-Mar 31), students half price. (6076 3104) 昭陵，昌平区

The Great Wall

Zig zagging its way from east to west across the northern edge of the ancient Chinese Empire,

Only hapless tourists, thieves and ladder-toting dudes may leave the Ming mausoleums

the Great Wall is an unfathomable exercise in large-scale construction – even if it's not really visible from the moon. Although the emperor Qin Shihuang is credited with laying the cornerstone in 221 BC, his wall of tamped earth actually linked a series of pre-existing structures into a 5,000km barrier. Every dynasty since the Qin built, fortified and extended the mammoth fortification, but most structures visible today near Beijing date from the Ming dynasty.

The exact length of the wall is unclear, since new sections continue to be discovered – an 80km stretch was found in Ningxia in 2002. Officially, it snakes across 6,200km of territory and, if stretched out end-to-end, would measure 15,000km.

Years of tourist encroachment have taken a toll on the wall. In an attempt to protect this historical site, the Beijing government has banned hiking on sections of the so-called "wild wall". The ban is not always enforced, but bear in mind that some sections of the wall are over 700 years old, poorly maintained and can crumble under even the most delicate steps. In addition, while the 2008 Great Wall Marathon will be run on May 17th, the once-annual Great Wall Rave has been cancelled.

Many Beijing residents have visited the wall so many times they've become blasé about the "glorified fence" in their backyard. If you fall into that category, you should consider rediscovering it with William Lindesay, a British researcher who was the first foreigner to traverse the wall's length

from desert to ocean. Lindesay works with the Beijing Administrative Bureau for Cultural Relics and leads legal, multi-day treks to wild parts of the wall. He also organizes wall conservation efforts such as clean-up days, short videos about modern threats to the wall, and a "pilot ranger program" which employs local farmers to help collect trash. Information on these hikes and conservation activities is available at www.wildwall.com

If you're not hiring a private car or joining a hotel/hostel tour, most sections of the Great Wall are accessible via public transportation. Beijing tourist buses depart from various locations around town bright and early in the morning (between 6.30am and 9 or 10am) when full, but only the routes to Badaling and Juyongguan run year-round. Call 8729 9990 to make sure the tourist bus to your particular destination is running.

Badaling Great Wall

Oh, the humanity! This, the mother of all tourist sites, will give an empirical sense of what it means to be in a country of 1.4 billion people. One hour's drive from Beijing.

Daily 7am-7pm. RMB 45, students RMB 25. Yanqing County. (6912 1737) 八达岭长城，延庆县
Car: Take Badaling Expressway to Badaling Exit.
Bus: Take bus 919 from Deshengmen, tourist bus 1 from Qianmen, or tourist bus 2 from Beijing Railway Station.

PHOTO: SIMON LIM

SIGHTSEEING

No hordes in sight – neither tourist nor Mongol – at Huanghuacheng

Train: Train 6427 runs from Beijing North Station (8.06am) to Juyongguan (10.04am) and Badaling (10.49am). Train 6428 leaves Badaling at 2.32pm and Juyongguan at 3.20pm, arriving back at Beijing at 5.07pm.

Juyongguan Great Wall

This fortress served as a gate to the wilds beyond the Wall during the Ming dynasty. Less crowded, but more recently restored than Badaling. One hour's drive from Beijing.
Daily 8am-5pm. RMB 45, seniors, students RMB 25, children below 1.2 m free. South of Badaling. (6977 1665) 居庸关长城，八达岭南边
Car: Take Badaling Expressway to Juyongguan Exit.
Bus: Take tourist bus 1 from Qianmen or tourist bus 2 from Beijing Railway Station.

Mutianyu Great Wall

Like Badaling, it's a modern, crowded section of Wall – the chairlift or gondola can ferry visitors up, and a colorful slide can bring them down. Still, it's a great view that gets even better as the amusement park is left behind, and if you get there before 8am, you can even find some peace and quiet. Ninety minutes' drive from Beijing.
Daily 6.30am-6.30pm. RMB 40 (students half price), RMB 35 (chair lift), RMB 50 (gondola). Mutianyu Town, Huairou District. (6162 6505, 6162 6022) 慕田峪长城，怀柔区慕田峪镇
Car: From Sanyuan Qiao on Third Ring Road, take Jingshun Lu (which becomes National Road 101) to Huairou Qiao and turn toward Huairou, follow signs to Qingchunlu Roundabout (青春路环岛) and turn to Huaisha Lu (怀沙路), keep driving to Mutianyu Roundabout and follow signs to the Great Wall.
Bus: Tourist bus 6 leaves from Xuanwumen on weekends and national holidays from Apr 5 to Oct 15. Or take bus 916/936 from Dongzhimen long-distance bus station to Huairou International Conference Center (怀柔国际会议中心) and change to minibus to Mutianyu (RMB 25-30).

Huanghuacheng Great Wall

Once overrun by peasants extracting a few *kuai* at every tower for passage, the local government has now put a stop to this extortion and started refurbishing the Wall into an official tourist site. Ninety minutes' drive from Beijing.
Daily 8am-5.30pm. RMB 25. Chengguan Town,

Huairou District. 黄花长城，怀柔区城关镇
Car: Take Badaling Expressway and exit at Changping Xiguan. Follow signs toward the Ming Tombs, then turn right when you reach Changling Tomb toward Jiuduhe (九渡河), turn left at the Jiuduhe intersection, and continue to the Huanghuazhen (黄花镇) intersection, then turn left. Once you reach the Y intersection, bear right and continue for a few more km to the Wall.

Simatai Great Wall

It's less of a circus than Badaling or Mutianyu, and the four-hour hike from Simatai to Jinshanling is one of the most spectacular ways to experience the Wall, but it is very steep in parts. The less physically fit can ride the Simatai cable car. Visitors can also take a zipline (i.e. cable-suspended pulley) from the halfway point to the parking lot.
Daily 8am-5pm. RMB 40, students RMB 20, zipline RMB 35. Gubeikou, Miyun County. (6903 1051) 司马台长城，密云县古北口镇
Car: From Sanyuan Qiao on Third Ring Road, take Jingcheng Lu past Miyun. At Tanghe Daqiao (Tanghe Bridge 汤河大桥) before the bridge, turn right, then follow signs to Simatai Great Wall for the next 10km to get there. About 2.5 hrs.
Bus: On weekends take the 8.30am luxury tour bus (RMB 95) from Qianmen. The bus leaves Simatai around 3-4pm. Or, from Dongzhimen long-distance bus station, take 980 to Miyun station (RMB 15, 1.5 hrs) then switch to a Simatai bound bus (RMB 15, 1 hr). Tourist bus 12 leaves from in front of the Xuanwumen Cathedral on weekends from Apr 5 to Oct 15 (RMB 60).

Jinshanling Great Wall

Jinshanling is on the other end of the Simatai-Jinshanling trek. It's one of the only sections of Wall where it's legal to camp overnight.
Daily sunrise-sunset. RMB 50. Gubeikou, border between Miyun County and Hebei's Luanping County. (0314 883 0222) 金山岭长城，北京密云县与河北滦平县交界
Car: From Sanyuan Qiao on Third Ring Road, take Jingshun Lu all the way past Miyun. At Gubeikou follow signs toward Chengde and then follow signs to Jinshanling Great Wall.
Bus: From Dongzhimen long-distance bus station, take a Chengde-bound bus and get off at Jinshanling. Then take a cab to the entrance for RMB 10.

SIGHTSEEING

Mythbusting

Great Wall historian David Spindler sets seven things straight
by Eric Abrahamsen

Myth 1: The wall is a single, continuous entity

"Even within China," says Spindler, "people often believe the wall is or was continuous." But in fact, the wall sections are laid out like strips of ribbon along a broad swath of territory. By the Warring States period (475-221 BC), several of China's kingdoms had built walls to protect themselves from other kingdoms, or from nomadic raiders from the north. As dynasties emerged, some built new walls on the ruins of old – some of the Ming wall around Beijing overlaid that of the Northern Qi, from around 550 AD – and others built parallel to existing wall, either outside or inside the old borders.

A dynasty's wall also wasn't always continuous – typically it was built across vulnerable territory such as valleys or lowlands, while naturally defensible terrain such as steep mountainside was often left un-walled. Further confusing the question, many sections of "wall" were nothing more than rows of watchtowers with nothing in between.

Myth 2: Rice was used in the wall mortar

"There's just no proof for this," says Spindler. Admittedly, the city walls of Xi'an, built in the Ming dynasty, were mortared with a compound which included sticky rice, but until chemical analysis has been done on the Great Wall itself, we just don't know.

Early pre-Ming wall wasn't built of bricks and mortar at all, but of rammed earth, piled stone, or earth with layers of straw matting – most of the wall in western China is of this latter type. The Ming probably began to use small quantities of brick and mortar in their walls in the first half of the 16th century. Starting in the middle of the 16th century, large-scale building with local stone and mortar began, and late in the 16th century and early in the 17th century, some key sections of wall were reinforced with brick, mortar, and quarried stone. Ming bricks were fired in local kilns, and mortared using a mixture of water and cured lime.

Myth 3: Dead laborers were buried in the wall

The builders of the Great Wall were no fools – a dead body would rot and leave a hole, weakening the entire structure. This myth is tied to another general misconception – that huge slave-labor forces were worked to death on the wall. Spindler says that in truth little is known about early wall-builders, though we do know that some wall-building campaigns used hundreds of thousands to over a million workers.

The Ming wall was built primarily by soldiers, with the help of civilian laborers and artisans and craftsmen – these soldiers were specialized workers, and most likely spent their entire careers building. Ming construction projects were generally more incremental, many smaller projects accomplished over longer periods of time.

Myth 4: The wall was used as a highway

"It's possible this myth was started by a Jesuit priest named Father Ripa, who was in Beijing during the reign of Kangxi (1662-1722)," says Spindler. Ripa's memoirs read: "Such is its breadth ... that carriages can drive along the top with ease." Perhaps the term "carriage-width" was simply used to illustrate the wall's dimensions in some spots – clearly no horse and carriage could squeeze through the guard-towers, and carriage-driving on the wall's steeper passages would be suicidal.

If the wall wasn't used as a highway, how did such a complex defensive system keep itself supplied? "Supplies and men were actually gotten to the wall using a hub-and-spoke system," explains Spindler. Many valleys had a small fort behind the wall (the modern-day village of Simatai is located in what was once a Ming fort of the same name), from which men could be sent to various sections of the wall. Even farther back were larger forts (located in places such as modern-day Miyun) where soldiers were garrisoned and granaries built.

Fortified with the corpses of deceased workers? Nope

This system meant that the wall developed its own little economy. The average soldier would be stationed on the wall for life, with reinforcements brought from other provinces to bolster key regions, including Beijing, during the peak defense seasons in spring and fall. Satellite businesses – including alcohol, gambling, and prostitution–grew up around the wall.

Myth 5: Signals were mainly sent using smoke and fire

While watch signal towers at times used smoke and fire to communicate, the most common method of warning against attacks was gunpowder blasts which, along with flares and flags, could indicate the location under attack. These signals would alert local forts, which would send reinforcements, and the reinforcements would often send runners back to convey more detailed information.

Gunpowder, which was invented before the Yuan dynasty and in widespread use during the Ming, was much in evidence on the wall – small-bore cannons were used for defense, as were musket-type firearms, and "grenades" made from hollowed-out stones packed with powder and sealed. The Mongols, for their part, were mostly using bows and hand-weapons. "Not many people died from arrow wounds," notes Spindler, explaining that the Mongolians' purpose was mainly to raid and loot, not to kill.

Myth 6: Shanhaiguan is the easternmost end of the Ming wall

This myth may have started because Shanhaiguan was the place where the invading Manchu crossed the wall, flooding south towards Beijing and establishing the Qing dynasty. In truth, the Ming wall once extended all the way across present-day Liaoning Province, marking off the Liaodong Peninsula as Ming territory, and terminating at the Yalu river, near modern-day Dandong on the North Korean border. By the time the Manchus were prepared to make their assault on the capital, the section of the wall east of Shanhaiguan had been under their control for so long, they may no longer have thought of it as belonging to the Ming.

Myth 7: The wall "didn't work"

Though the wall did prove porous at various points throughout history, it still accomplished the Ming goal of territorial sovereignty for hundreds of years. Spindler cites two major instances when Mongol armies numbering in the tens of thousands were successfully held off: in 1554 at Jinshanling, and later in 1561, at Badaling – whether you re-enact these battles the next time you visit is entirely up to you.

SIGHTSEEING

Beijing Ayi Housekeeping Service

- Our company is specialized in providing housekeeping services and child care service for foreign families in Beijing.
- Our experienced Ayis are specially trained in housekeeping and child services.
- Our Ayis have regular physical checkups every year.
- With our Ayi's insurance against personal acciden injuries, you can rest assured our Ayis are covered for any on-the-job accidents.

Tel: 6434 5647/48   E-mail: Service@bjayi.com   Website: www.bjayi.com

Sublet.cn

Cheap than hotel, Comfort, Private, Flexible, Convenient
Reserve Short Term Apartment Now
& Beijing Olympic 2008!

www.sublet.cn

Service Apartment, Villa for Daily Rent, Short Term Lease
Beijing, Shanghai, Hainan, Yunnan, Tibet, Hangzhou, Guangzhou, Shenzhen etc. around China

NIGHTLIFE

As long as there's cheap meat and beer, the Nanjie spirit will live on

Now *That* was Fun
The good old days … are getting better
by Oliver Robinson

"Well, I thought I might hang around until the Olympics." A splendid idea. Why didn't I, and the other 600,000 expats in the city, think of that? Oh, wait, we did. Or at least we say this, but really, who cares about a bunch of muscled blokes running as fast as they can in a straight line? Not me. Not many of us, I'm sure, but it's a more believable justification than "I really get off on the pollution and commuter etiquette," and sounds better than the truth: The booze is cheap. Granted, I'm a little bit drunk right now, but in a roundabout way I think I might be onto something here: We stick around because we have a great time here. Beijing is a fun and interesting place during the day and continues to be so when night falls.

NIGHTLIFE

You think *this* is fun?

It's worth knowing that no matter how good a time you're having in a Beijing bar, you're officially *not* having as good a time as you would be on the old South Street. "Now *that* was fun." At least it was according to the Old China Hands who hang around bars to tell us young'uns we don't know what we're missing: "On the first day, there was South Street, and all that was on South Street was good and everyone was happy because the beer (or crazy juice, as we called it back then) cost little more than a kilo of rock salt, which was good value at the time, considering …"

Just stop them before they start an impromptu rendition of the jitterbug.

They'll doubtless also reminisce about the original Frank's Place, or Jam House, or a slew of other über-fun bars, which met their fate at the wrong end of the wrecking ball. What perhaps grates these old boozehounds the most is that nothing has been built in place of the old South Street, which, to this day, remains a weed-infested memorial to the glory days. But, as much as it pains me to admit it, the ramblings of these Grandpa Simpson equivalents do shed some light on just how far Beijing's bar scene has come – for better and for worse.

For worse

The developers (that's what they call the people who knock stuff down in Beijing) who smashed South Street didn't do so without realizing that alcohol + people = money, and before you could say "ka-ching!" a number of "designated" bar streets had been hastily erected across the city. It soon became apparent, however, that the "If you build it, they will come" catchphrase is more applicable to baseball diamonds in cornfields than to places like Yuan Dynasty Bar Street. The emergence of such heavy-handed, heavily invested, supply-side attempts to create a teeming nightlife zone out of thin air seem to have amounted to a hard-learned lesson. To have a "designated" bar street is tantamount to having an area designated for fun, which all but guarantees that none will be had.

A recent fad to afflict Beijing nightlife is the word "bar-club-lounge," slapped onto the side of the kind of venues that populate the aforementioned bar streets (or those in, on, above, or underneath a shiny new shopping plaza). Take for example Nice: Bar, Club, Lounge. We wouldn't have as much of a problem with it if it simply called itself Nice Club (well, except as it's not nice at all, it's rubbish, and it's most likely closed by now), but instead it, and other "lounges" like it, represent an aspect of the Beijing scene which is more about feigning class than actually delivering it. Perhaps if such places didn't bother lying and adopted a more truthful mantle (Nice: Noisy, Neon, Nightmare) they might get a few more customers. The "bar-club-lounge" handle also belies a jack-of-all-trades attitude to business – *we don't quite know what we're doing so we'll cover all our bases, just to be sure* – like a boastful brat, flashing his cash to impress the in-crowd.

For better

The garishness of these clubs is also due in part to a misconceived impression of what makes Beijing an international city. Contrary to this, some of the best bars take advantage of their unique location in Beijing, seamlessly integrating wine and cocktails into the heart of the old city. Bed Bar has become a Beijing favorite by utilizing the dimensions of a courtyard in Zhangwang hutong, just off Jiugulou Dajie, while Luna Lounge is another example of minimal cool contrasted with *lao* Beijing, boasting a tranquil roof terrace where guests can soak in views of the Bell Tower. The Drum and Bell Bar has a cluttered yet cozy feel to it (as does Candy Floss Cafe), not forgetting a beautiful roof terrace, while La Baie Des Anges has transported a little bit of the south of France (and its fine wines) into another former courtyard residence.

These bars capture the essence of modern Beijing, just like those that have been relocated by the kiss of the wrecking ball. Like the resilient residents of the city, many Beijing bars have learnt through years of trial and tribulation that to succeed on this often-volatile scene is just a matter of doing the simple things right. Take Nanjie, which in reality is little more than a room, a bar, cheap drinks, and good music (well, pop-rock, but that's a winner in my book). There are no pretensions about the kind of place it is, which is evident from the slogan "Shut Up, Just Drink" (diligently obeyed by patrons ... at least the second part, anyway). The success of live music venues like D-22 and Yugong Yishan can also be attributed to this no-frills attitude: Their dedication to music is evidenced by an enthusiastically loyal clientele, and of course, great shows.

Future sexy

It would be a disservice to attribute all of the scene's positive aspects solely to cheerful speakeasies and hutong bars. After all, the times they are a-changing and the capital's fast-growing contingent of well-traveled, increasingly cosmopolitan citizens is demanding more from the high-end scene. Long confined to the transient atmosphere of hotels, Beijing's new classy nightspots have moved out into the wider world, endowing the city with an increasing number of choices for that post-work cocktail or late night schmooze session. Face, the Indonesian chain, has quietly established itself as a favorite of the city's more affluent expatriate and local drinking population. Managing Director Haidhi Angkawijana and Chief Designer Francis Drake (a pox on all ye carousers who be thinkin' this be not his real name!) deserve credit for beautifully converting a dilapidated schoolhouse into one of the city's most tasteful venues – a valuable lesson for Beijing's over-eager developers (but it's doubtful they were paying attention).

Beijing's high-end scene has a new Face

Likewise, entrepreneur Alan Wong (the man behind popular eateries Hatsune and Kagen – see Restaurant Directory, p80 and p81) and hospitality guru Sebastian Noat pushed standards skyward with the opening of i-Ultra Lounge. Boasting a unique aesthetic appeal and efficient service, i-Ultra should become the city's new see-and-be-seen destination, a crown long held by Noat's first Beijing project, Centro. Though somewhat dated now, Centro was arguably Beijing's first true lounge destination and has maintained its immense popularity with the power-suit set.

But it's not just the white-collar ballers who are raising the bar, so to speak. Suzie Wong's and newcomer China Doll have established remarkable popularity as vaguely tasteful alternatives to the usual clubs, with a certain oriental mystique-appeal and good service. Meanwhile, smartly made beverages and a spacious roof terrace put Q Bar first on many a professional's list for an after-work cocktail. During Beijing's sweltering summers, the pleasant breeziness of venues with such rooftop terraces can be a welcome draw: Kokomo and Bar Blu's respective rooftops provide great views of Sanlitun's metamorphic skyline, as well as elevating one above the sweaty hedonism of Shooters, Kai and the string of not-so-innocent Pure Girls (see Sidebar, p280).

And so?

Well, perhaps the Pure Girl saga is somehow emblematic of our town's nightlife charms. I mean, any town that has four bars called Pure Girl, all next to one another, has got to be worthy of our love, right? Beijing certainly doesn't have one of the most developed or diverse scenes in the world, but its unique eccentricities and its vibrancy combine for a memorable night on the town if ever there was one. Plus the beer's cheap. Really cheap.

Purer by the Dozen

The Pure Girls' saga
by Matt P. Jager

Statistically speaking, Pure Girl is four times easier to find than any other bar in Sanlitun

Once upon a time, a convenience store shaped like a beer mug stood at the corner of Gongti Beilu and Sanlitun Jie. Half a block away an alley snaked south towards Gongti Nanlu. We called it South Street, and three years after its tragic destruction, Sanlitun Nanjie has been canonized in the Gospel of Beijing Nightlife.

By day, schoolchildren skipped down tranquil South Street, swinging lunchboxes and singing songs in matching jumpsuits. By night, it degenerated into an anarchic, lawless arena of combative drinking. The huddled masses and wretched refuse assembled every weekend for a massive street party, leaving the swankier swine to hunt for classy hide-outs on the periphery of the chaos. Along the main drag of South Street, a row of one-room, closet-sized bars provided beer, shots and cocktails at rock-bottom prices, fueling the revelry until sunrise.

In the summer of 2004, the bar owners were notified that the local government was buying back all the land around Sanlitun Nanjie. The owners were tossed a pittance for their property, and by the end of the year South Street was a ruined lot with the half-demolished husks of our favorite drinking-holes. South Street became a memory. The day of the dive had passed.

One intrepid bar-owner and former tender, Jackie Chen, wasn't worried that his target market – cheapskates and poor alcoholics – had dissolved along with South Street. His bar was Pure Girl, and it was destined to be one of the few South Street dives to emerge victorious from the rubbled wrath of the wrecking ball. Jackie had managed Pure Girl since 2003. The founding owner was a dance teacher who wanted to dedicate his bar to his 8-year-old daughter. "Zhenzhen is a bad name for a bar – so instead he called it Pure Girl," Jackie explained. Zhenzhen's father, however, didn't know how to follow the market. He was selling Tsingtao for 20 *kuai* a bottle. Jackie and an old friend bought out the bar, and transformed it into the dive that still lives today – ten *kuai* beers and five *kuai* shots.

PHOTO: SIMON LIM

After the devastation of South Street, Jackie and his partner re-immaculated Pure Girl in the spring of 2005, a block north of the other landmark Sanlitun dive, Bus Bar, on Chunxiu Lu. The new Pure Girl was bigger, had better deals and a pool table, but only embassy rats and determined regulars from the old days made the hike up Chunxiu. It had closed by the end of the summer, with lessons learned.

The next and current Pure Girl incarnation came at the end of the summer in 2006. The failure of the Chunxiu Pure Girl strained the relationship between Jackie and his old South Street partner. This time, Jackie resolved, he would go solo. "Two people are twice the trouble," he told me later. "In every aspect, it is a headache." Jackie opened in the Sanlitun ghetto on Houjie, beside Poachers. He borrowed money from friends and took a loan from the bank, using his RMB 30,000 car as collateral. "It felt so much like gambling," he said. "If this one failed too, I wouldn't have a bar or a car."

This time, Jackie struck gold. He recreated the original atmosphere of the South Street dive that made him famous. He was understandably startled, then, when his rebuffed partner opened a bar two doors down – a bar called Pure Girl. And in the crowning absurdity worthy of South Street itself, Jackie bought the room between the two Pure Girls and turned it into a new bar he named – can you guess? – Pure Girl. As of print date, yet another Pure Girl has joined the ranks, leaving a veritable strip mall of dives, all sharing the same niche, same closet-sized layout, and same drinks. Although they share the same English translation, Jackie's Pure Girls – like the ancestral South Street Pure Girl – are virginal, simple and innocent lasses (*qingchun nühai*), while the other two Pure Girls are devoted and beloved, one-man little ladies (*chunqing nühai*). These days, there is no bad blood between the former partners. "More bars around here means more business," says Jackie. "I wish there were even more Pure Girls. This is a good brand." We the people can only thank God and Adam Smith for competition, keeping the Pure Girls cheap and close to their South Street roots.

Those who once beheld the belligerent glory of the South Street dives will be happy to know that the current location should survive the Olympics. The four neighboring Pure Girls and their patrons are like historical interpreters — a little slice of transplanted Nanjie. There are no plans currently to redevelop the Sanlitun ghetto until 2009. And what will happen to the Pure Girls after that? Jackie shrugs. "Wait and see. I want to do something bigger – maybe open a Pure Girl Disco. But who knows the future? We can only wait and see."

Pure fun with less-than-pure alcohol awaits at Pure Girl

Wu vision: A Haidian bar crawl may leave you seeing double.

PHOTO: NICK OTT

Party Zones
Meet the clumps
by Eric Abrahamsen, Jim Boyce, Adam Pillsbury, Haley Warden and Matt P. Jager

The governing principle of Beijing's bar scene has traditionally been "The Clumping Effect." The template for this phenomenon is, of course, Sanlitun, the original *jiuba jie*. Dozens of embassies in the area spurred business for the first bars, and the rest is history. Time and time again, Beijing's aspiring bar barons have followed the pattern – find a successful bar, often one unusual in concept or execution, and open another one right next to it, with brighter lights, louder music, and a more obnoxious staff to whistle and clap at passersby. The result of this herd mentality is that Beijing's taverns and clubs are disproportionately concentrated in a few bar districts. Increasing pockets of nightlife are arising and expanding in obvious spots, such as student stronghold Wudaokou and the lakeshores of the Houhai area, as well as in more fabricated areas such as Ladies' Street (Nüren Jie) and Yuan Dynasty Wall Bar Street.

Trumping the clumping effect are the bars scattered across Beijing's sprawl of white-collar Lego land – the CBD ("Central Business District"). Catering to the professional crowd's need for a wind-down martini (and so on, e.g. Maggie's) at the end of a busy day, the emerging business-oriented debauchery venues peppering Chaoyang District's glass and concrete heartland aspire to cosmopolitanism rather than cozy clustering.

Sanlitun

This neighborhood is a major draw for tourists, newcomers and long-term residents alike, but more than a few people gave it up for dead when the popular South Street was razed for re-development in late 2004, followed by some North Street establishments meeting the same fate months later. In hindsight, these events seem to have been the one step backward preceding the two steps forward in the process of creative destruction, and Sanlitun has emerged more diverse than ever. The phrase, "Whatever doesn't kill you, makes you stronger" seems appropriate here.

True, Sanlitun's main northern strip features far too many sub-par copycat bars and the requisite promoters, beggars, DVD sellers and lady bar touts that come with them. There have even been some disturbing reports of bouncers attacking patrons. In spite of that, there has been a wave of bars (and restaurants) targeting new niches, particularly in the Sanlitun Houjie / Tongli Studio area (which parallels the strip). This trend has kept Sanlitun on top in terms of diversity and allows it to offer some of the city's "best of the best." Consider that the area has venues offering high-end cocktails (Q Bar), great pub grub and sports (Rickshaw), a wide range of imported beers (Beer Mania, The Tree) and cheap drinks (Phil's Pub, Shooters, Kai Club), as well as dancing options that include Latin (Salsa Caribe) and drunken club-grooving (China Doll).

Sanlitun Area

Aperitivo 296	Phil's Pub 306
Bar Blu 297	Poachers Inn 306
Beer Mania 297	Pure Girl(s) 307
Cheers 298	Q Bar 307
China Doll 298	The Rickshaw 308
Jazz-Ya 302	Salsa Caribe 308
Kai Club 302	Sanlitun Bar Strip 308
Kokomo 302	Shooters 308
Nanjie 305	The Tree 309

Ain't no thing if you've got that bling: the philosophy behind the Gongti West megaclub strip

Workers' Stadium

Once considered a puddle of Sanlitun spillage, the area surrounding Workers' Stadium (or "Gongti") is now a party hotspot in its own right. Clubbers have ventured here since the late '90s, when now-defunct Havana Cafe started playing salsas and rumbas. Today they head to the stadium's north gate, to shake and shimmy at Mix, Vics, across the street at Alfa, or to its west gate for the cluster of glittering mega-clubs, including Angel, Babyface, Cargo, and Coco Banana (see p295).

The loud success of these mega-clubs has helped sustain a flush of other interesting venues in the area; from branches of some of Beijing's flagship/showcase restaurants (Bellagio, Three Guizhou Men, Green T. House) to high-end venues like the Pavillion and Face that cater to an older and more expat-oriented crowd. As the Workers' Stadium itself prepares to reopen for the Olympics, the east gate and south gate sections of the compound are filling in with ever more upscale entertainment tubs – the neighborhood seems to have been earmarked as a revelry-based money factory.

Workers' Stadium Area

Alfa 296	Destination 300
Angel 296	Face 300
Babyface 297	Mix 303
The Bank 297	Pavillion 306
Cargo Club 298	Pipe's 306
Coco Banana 299	Sunset Grill 308
Cosmo 299	Tango 323
The Den 299	Vics 309

PHOTO: NATALIE BEHRING

Chaoyang Park

Despite undergoing some serious demolition in recent years, this area still brings in the crowds. The first branch of veteran sports bar Goose 'n' Duck is still kicking, and Souk (see Food, p82), at Chaoyang West Gate, exudes a serene atmosphere with its Middle Eastern flair and hookahs. The music, drinks, and foosball table at Black Sun Bar provide excellent value for the budget-minded.

Yet Chaoyang Park's biggest draw remains Suzie Wong's, which easily ranks among the city's most famous (or infamous) nightspots. Its swish, pink-hued decor, reputation as a pick-up joint and spacious deck attract the city's "glitterati" who groove until the wee hours of the morning (or whenever the cologne runs out). Nearby, i-Ultra Lounge and Pepper round out the club quota.

Chaoyang West Gate

Black Sun Bar	297
Goose 'n' Duck	300
i-Ultra Lounge	302
Pepper	306
Souk	308
The World of Suzie Wong Club	310

Where in the world? Suzie Wong's

Nüren Jie (Ladies' Street) / Xingba Lu (Super Bar Street)

Concrete lovers and Mad Max fans will rejoice in this desolate spot, where the world's campaign against grass seems to be headquartered. Located north of Chaoyang Park west gate, this soulless strip includes recently refurbished African bar Pili Pili, the New Get Lucky bar (with some of the city's better live music), Tim's Texas Roadhouse, and numerous dark-windowed, neon-festooned establishments, such as Gunman Bar. It's also home to the only Kosher restaurant in town (the Israeli Embassy is across the way), as well as Biteapitta. A short bike ride back toward Chaoyang Park's west gate is Lucky Street (Haoyun Jie), home to several restaurants and bars.

Bar and restaurant owners in this area might be hoping for a big boom in business once the US Embassy opens nearby, but given that employees there, like everyone else, have access to taxis, they'll need to be more than just handy to draw patrons.

Nüren Jie/Super Bar Street

New Get Lucky	344
Pili Pili	306
Tim's Texas Roadhouse	309

Lucky Street

Coco Zen	322
Nashville	305
Sangria	308

Nüren Jie: not so hot, but fishy

Continues on p288

Evolution of the Peking Man
Bar-hopping through the millennia
by Oliver Robinson

i ii iii iv

i. Nanjie
Simple, undeveloped, yet as good a place to start as any, Nanjie is the primeval soup of Beijing's drinking scene – a mixing pot of promise – enjoyed by all ages, cultures, professions or lack thereof.

ii. The Rickshaw
Omnivorous packs of hunter-gatherers (expat sports teams) emigrate to The Rickshaw, a feeding ground abundant with burritos, chicken wings and burgers. The Peking Men have fashioned tools for recreational activities (pool cues).

iii. Bar Blu
Breaking away from the pack, the Peking Man now exhibits individualist tendencies. With a desire to engage in horizontal gene exchange, the species has now developed individual mating rituals, such as the bump 'n' grind technique (also known as the pant ram) common to the Bar Blu dance floor.

iv. The World of Suzie Wong Club
Natural Selection has rendered pant ramming an ineffective means by which to attract a mate. The Peking Man must resort to decorating himself with ridiculous trucker hats and now displays an insufferably annoying penchant for wearing sunglasses inside.

v. Q Bar
The savage landscape of Suzie Wong's and lack of intellectual stimuli, such as conversation, forced this more sensitive breed to return south, to the altitudinous environs atop the Eastern Inn. The Peking Man now displays appreciation of taste and etiquette.

vi. Centro
Having over-developed his hierarchical sensibilities, the Peking Man distances himself from lesser breeds found on Nansanlitun, communing at a choice watering hole to exchange capital for goods and services. Having no natural predators, the significant muscle loss renders a physical appearance best described as … pudgy.

vii. Maggie's
Rendered physically or emotionally incapable of attracting mates on his own merit, hold conversation or maintain good physical hygiene, The Peking Man retreats to the comfortable confines of Ritan Park South Gate where he farms mating partners. The species resorts to wielding wooden implements (pool cues) as its only form of exercise.

viii. Nanjie
When all else fails, Nanjie is still there.

Houhai

Once upon a time, Houhai was a picturesque neighborhood filled with quiet breezes, lapping waters, and (presumably) happy residents, most of them charmingly elderly. Now it is a beer-soaked, neon-lit circus where bar owners resort to increasingly desperate ploys to reel in customers, and the charming old people are slowly getting pushed out.

Would the area have been better off undiscovered, pristine but "underutilized?" Or is a bit of commercialization a fair price to pay so that more people may experience Houhai's charms? Where people stand on this question often depends on when they themselves discovered the area, with particular bitterness coming from the elite minority who once lounged in the window of No Name Bar in 2000, when it was still the only watering hole in the area.

Greater Houhai is comprised of several areas. Starting from the southernmost end, Lotus Lane is a swish row of bars and restaurants, heavily designed and intentionally reminiscent of Shanghai. Moving up the bank one comes to Yinding Bridge, which is a charming little spot by itself but is generally clogged with strollers, drunks, vendors and motorists who insist that their vehicles could make it over the bridge if only the pedestrians would all just get out of the way right now. Bars on the banks near the bridge are packed together more tightly than the luggage of an Uzbek shuttle trader.

Just off the bridge is Yandai Xiejie, or "Tobacco-pouch Diagonal Street," a Ming-era relic which, if you come at the right time of day and squint your eyes in a certain way, does look like a touch of the distant past. Some of the buildings are mock-ancient, but the triple-arched stone entryway of the Guangfuguan Daoist Temple is the real deal (though, predictably, it now houses a bar).

Houhai does have its gems, but they're generally well-hidden, tucked away from the glare that surrounds Yinding Qiao – one notable exception is No Name Bar, which is steps away from the bridge. The East Shore Live Jazz Cafe (opened by legendary sax man Liu Yuan) keeps the groove right in the pocket, while neighboring Houhai Zoo is a larger and more relaxed version of Huxley's – think cheap drinks and friendly service. Best of all may be to strike away from the lakes, heading west to the quiet bars of Xihai or north to the hutong haven near the Drum and Bell towers.

Houhai

15 Qianhai Beiyan	296
Buddha Bar	298
East Shore Live Jazz Cafe	343
Eye on the Lake	300
Gogo	300
Goldfish Home	300
Hai Bar	300
Herrenhauser	300
Hope Bar	300
Houhai Zoo	302
Hutong Bar	302
Huxley's	302
Iron & Fish	302
Ji Xian Tang	302
La Baie des Anges	302
No Name Bar	305
Obiwan	305
Touch	309

Drum and Bell Tower

Ball House	297
Bed	297
Drum and Bell	300
Jiangjinjiu Bar	343
Luna Lounge	303
Xin Bar	310

Elderly couples still waltz at Houhai, despite the neon

PHOTO: HAN JUNWEI

Nanluogu Xiang

To long-term area residents, the transformation of this once somnolent hutong into a full-fledged "entertainment zone" in 2005-06 engendered a mix of delight and trepidation: the delight came from having many more groovy restaurant and bar choices within strolling distance; the trepidation was inspired by the negative precedent set by Houhai, where unchecked development blighted the once calm lakeshore (see above). Ironically for the traditionalists among them, it was the neighborhood's foreigners – notably Ju'er Hutong residents and Lusongyuan Hotel guests – who inspired the changes by flocking to the street's first cafe/bar, the Pass By Bar. Local entrepreneurs noted their free-spending ways, and the hutong's fate was sealed.

Fortunately, the Pass By Bar was a good model to copy: Occupying a tastefully redone courtyard complex with outdoor seating in summer, and decorated with Tibetan masks and travel photographs, it serves coffee, wine and decent food (pastas, salads and "hutong pizza") in the mellowest atmosphere this side of Lijiang. This relaxed vibe also permeates Xiao Xin's Cafe, another Nanluogu Xiang landmark, which was opened in 2004 by the eponymous cheesecake master.

Establishments that opened later – including the offbeat Candy Floss with its delightfully green courtyard, and fish-and-chip purveyor Fish Nation (see Food, p69) with its fine terrace – maintain a tasteful, reserved mood quite lacking in most of the Houhai area. During the daytime, these Wi-Fi spots attract freelance writers and the under-employed. At night, the scribblers are joined by hepcats and clued-in tourists seeking to have a quiet drink in a historic neighborhood that retains some of its unique Beijing flavor. Despite its potential for perilous overdevelopment, there are no touts or drunken louts on Nanluogu Xiang – for the moment. Let's try to keep it that way.

Greens are good for your health. So is Candy (Floss)

Nanluogu Xiang

Candy Floss Cafe 298	MAO Livehouse 343
Desert Oasis Bar 300	Pass By Bar 306
Long Long Ago Courtyard 303	Salud 308

Hot young thangs, drinks-a-plenty and raging hormones keep the party pumping at Propaganda

Wudaokou

The Wudaokou hotspots aren't flashy or fashionable. They are, with few exceptions, cheap and welcoming, playing host to hipsters and hippies, pop-and-lockers and hip-hoppers, rockers and ballers, and the jocks and the nerds all at once. Over the past few years, the student crowd and their drinking holes have developed a unique style and neighborhood snobbery. Old cornerstones near the light-rail station like Lush – with its weekly Sunday open-mic night and sinfully scrumptious hangover breakfast – and Propaganda – with its grinding meat market – still flourish. We tip our hats to live music purveyors D-22 (see "Invested in Beijing Rock," p330) and Club 13. Although Club Taku, just east of the Chengfu Lu and Xueyuan Lu intersection, isn't new, its RMB 50 all-you-can-drink deal every Thursday, Friday and Saturday night has infused its original Korean patron base with an increasingly international crowd.

Beginning in May, beer gardens take some business from Bla Bla – a renowned BLCU college bar. The biggest, International Beer Town (Guoji Pijiu Cheng) opposite Lush, is packed by ten on summer nights. Skewers and noodles and spicy *nang* are delivered by a line of kiosks, while uniformed waiters bring *zhapis* by the armful for a measly four *kuai* each. Even outside the beer gardens, the summertime Wudaokou 'hood channels a street-party vibe reminiscent of the Kai/Poachers corner on the other side of town.

Perhaps the boisterous, drunken parties are a hard sell for east side professionals, but even those pushing the upper limits of the demographic might benefit from loosening a tie, losing a blazer, and letting the darn kids and their music teach them a thing or two about tossing 'em back.

Wudaokou

13 Club	296
Bla Bla Bar	297
Club Taku	299
D-22	343
International Beer Town	302
Loco	303
Lush	303
Pepper	306

Propaganda	307
Red Rock Bar	308
Reggio	308

Haidian (Other)

180°	296
Cloud Nine Bar	299
Magic Rock	303
SLD (Sulede)	308

PHOTO: SEAN GALLAGHER

CBD and Jianguomenwai

Beijing professionals convene in the CBD from nine to five (or eight, or nine, or ten…), and it doesn't shut down after dark. The conglomeration of upscale business hotels in this area play home to many of the city's poshest eateries and bars; meanwhile, Ritan Park-area embassies fuel a bustling restaurant and bar scene, notable nightspots being Stone Boat Cafe and the infamous Maggie's. The Place, a colossal shopping center north of Silk Street Market, is home to a few more luxury locales.

CBD and Jianguomenwai

Aria	297
Banana	297
Casa Habana	298
Centro	298
Charlie's Bar	298
KISS	302
Lan	302
Maggie's	303
Mexican Wave	303
Press Club Bar	307
Stone Boat Cafe	344
Together	309
Xuancaotang	310

The Place

Arena	297
Capone's	298
CJW	299

Whether they seek to work hard or play hard, deal-makers of all shades cozy up at Centro

NIGHTLIFE

Beijing's bars come in all shapes and colors: There must be one that's right for you

Going it alone

Of course, some bars stand ruggedly alone in Beijing's harsh drinking landscape, like the Marlboro man smoking a butt defiantly on a, um, butte. Only time can tell whether they'll eventually become the next paradigm for a row of copycat neighbors.

Notably, the gentrified suburbs northeast of the city center are showing signs of nightlife. The reincarnation of Beijing's original bar, Frank's Place, opposite the Rosedale Hotel is hoped by many, not least its 16 investors, to bring pub-goers to the Lido area. Further out, the cavernous factory-cum-galleries of the 798 Dashanzi art district have proven to be superb places to throw a party (see Yen, p294), as wine-soaked openings and trendy cafe-restaurants set the scene. Finally, the expat heartland better known as Shunyi has witnessed the opening of sports bar The Pomegranate, and Palette Vino, a wine outlet in the Pinnacle Plaza strip mall – darn decent venues for their demographic.

Dongcheng

Latinos	Nanxincang, 302
Palace View Bar	Dongchang'anjie, 305
Redmoon	Oriental Plaza, 308
Sino-Chu Tayuan Diplomatic Compound, 309	
The Star Live	Ditan Park, 344
Tango	Ditan Park, 309
Writers Bar	Oriental Plaza, 310
Yugong Yishan	Ping'an Dadao, 344

Xicheng

West Wing Bar	Deshengmen, 309
What? Bar	Xicheng, 344
X'Change Bar	Financial Street, 310

Chaoyang (Other)

2 Kolegas	Liangmahe (Drive-in), 343
Area	Lido, 297
Beijing Okhotsk Beer	Sanyuanqiao, 297
Cave Cafe	798, 298
CD Jazz Club	Nongzhanqiao, 343
The Cellar	Lido, 299
Durty Nellies	Liangmahe, 300
Frank's Place	Lido, 300
Goose 'n' Duck 2	Chaoyang East, 300
Obelisk	Laiguangying, 66
Zeta Bar	Northeast Third Ring Road, 310

Shunyi

Palette Vino	Pinnacle Plaza, 305
The Pomegranate	Xi Baixinzhuang, 306

Proprietors' Picks

Busman's holidays
by Oliver Robinson

When they're not pulling pints, mopping up vomit or throwing antisocial rascals through saloon doors, where do bar managers go to wet their whistles?

Chad Lager
Rickshaw "I hardly get any time to leave The Rickshaw," says the affable Yank. "But when I do, I head down to Nanjie. Huxley's places will never be as cool as mine, so I have to support him in any way I can."

Lu Bin
Luna Lounge "I'd say my favorite bars are Q Bar and Centro – for the drinks. But my favorite kind of bars are bars like Nanjie, because the drinks are cheap so you can get wasted without feeling bad for your wallet. To quote Sia: 'I don't know why I smoke, but I drink to get drunk.'" Who's Sia?

Rich Akers
Lush "I like unpretentious, rowdy places, where you can get up to malarkey," says busy-handed Rich Akers, the self-styled aficionado of all things bonkers. "I like real places – flip-flops, tattoos and inappropriately dressed college girls doing shots off of each other … messy."

Olivier Six
La Baie des Anges Frenchman Olivier shattered any illusions we had that he was a smooth customer with the shocking admission: "If I had to pick one, I'd have to say Angel." Zounds! Or, rather, sacre bleu! "Seriously," he continues (digging), "when I finish work, it's open and it's where I met all my Chinese friends. The music isn't great, but it's still fun."

Michael Pettis
D-22 "I try to get to 2 Kolegas on as many Tuesdays as I can, since Yan Jun's are shows you can't miss. I also try not to miss some of the shows Rockforchina and Spli-t put on at The Star Live," says the D-22 honcho. "Finally, when I need to get away from the noise, however, I usually end up at [Houhai's] No Name – I've been going there for nearly six years and I'm too lazy to change."

The Yen Recipe
Beijing's nomadic party chefs
by Oliver Robinson

Today's bar scene isn't half as tumultuous as it used to be. A bar would open, reopen, close and be bulldozed to make way for another bar that would inevitably suffer a similar sequence of events. "Clubs were opening and closing so quickly," says Kiko Su. "We [grew tired] of just waiting around for a new place to party, so we decided to [throw one] ourselves."

True to his word, in May 2004 Kiko hired out an empty space near Sanlitun South Street, promoted it with posters, flyers and, most importantly, word of mouth. The party gave revelers a chance to convene at a neutral location, without the stigma often attached to a bar, and to listen to Beijing's DJ talent spin into the small hours.

The capital moves to the beat of Yen's roving parties

"We organized everything, the drinks, security, the music," says Kiko. "Seven hundred people came – businessmen, punks, everyone. This was very new ... very fresh entertainment."

The party was an instant hit and has since become a Beijing institution. Three years on, Yen has hit various locales in and around the city – including the Dashanzi art district, the Great Wall, and the MIDI Festival – continually changing its venue according to season and situation, keeping one step ahead of the city's remorseless development. This nomadic nature also ensures that the organizers can avoid the *mafan* that usually accompanies holding an event in a club. Beijing's club owners notoriously prefer the sound of cash tills to that of a good DJ and don't object to hiking up door prices through the course of the night.

"Yeah, it's certainly nice that we don't have the trouble of dealing with local club owners," agrees Yen associate Dan Stephenson. "Artists have total creative freedom and that's one thing we're very proud of: giving a platform for local DJs to make themselves known."

Yen makes just enough money to cover its own costs, but for now, Kiko is happy just to be able to throw the parties and promote local Beijing talent. While China isn't renowned for its DJing exports, it's telling that the DJs to have toured internationally so far have all been featured at Yen. Gao Hu toured Norway (2005), Youdai spun at the Berlin Love Parade (2004), Wordy went to Jamaica with Upstepper in 2006, and Mickey Zhang played WIRE07 in Japan.

Kiko concedes that the pool of talent in Beijing isn't as big as that in Japan, Europe or the States, but he is encouraged by what he's seen over the years. "Ten years ago, there was no one. Five years ago, it was better. Now we have enough DJs to play for two days at the MIDI Festival. China's opening up, people are more open-minded."

China's openness and its people's attitude are one thing, but the fact is that people are getting richer, and, if they're so inclined, have time and resources to dedicate to a costly hobby such as DJing. "It's a natural progression. It'll take time," says Kiko.

And when it does?

"We'll take Yen to other cities. Then, who knows?"

Until then, Beijingers can continue to enjoy Yen as the party brand that defines their city – ever changing, unstoppable and irreplaceable.

Yen holds quarterly themed parties – Yen Countdown (Jan 31), Yen Fetish (Halloween), Yen White (Last weekend of March/beginning of April), Yen Out (July) – as well as having dance tents at Beijing MIDI and Beijing Pop Festival. For more information see www.o2culture.com.

'Til the Break of Dawn
Clubbing in Beijing
by Matt P. Jager

Shake your booty 'til the wrecking ball swings

Beijing's best clubs are truly hilarious at first sight. Rich, ugly frogs from the provinces with square-top haircuts and shiny belt buckles sway with beautiful young women. Hips swing back and forth like off-beat pendulums. Hands brace on knees to support a vigorous and constant shaking of the head as if trying to dump an earful of water. This is called "getting a groove on." Be careful though, the laughter doesn't last long. After a few nights on the town, you will find yourself digging the free-wheeling, anything-goes Chinese dancing. After a few more, you will check out someone with '80s disco hands and sharp pelvic jabs. You will nudge your friends and say, "Damn, that girl can move."

Each 'hood has its hit dance spots. Ensconced in its new Naxincang digs, Latinos is bringing sabor to Dongsishitiao. Taku and Propaganda pull in the foreign students with cheap drinks and Billboard music in Wudaokou. The Shanghai export Babyface opened a second Beijing location in Xizhimen in the summer of 2006. But these pale before the masses of neon lights, convulsive lasers flashing off bunches of disco-balls, and the polished shiny decor of the Workers' Stadium West Gate ("Gongti Xilu") strip.

In the past couple of years, the scene at Gongti Xilu has exploded, adding more superstar discos to Babyface's original Beijing location. Cargo and Coco Banana filled in the twin towers of Babyface and Angel to create the biggest clump of discos in the city. Beautiful girls on the payroll decorate the clubs every night, but on weekends traffic on Gongti Xilu literally stops. BMWs and Mercedes fill the parking lots. This is where movie stars, models, and Mafiosi come to play. Everyone else is along for the ride, with affordable covers that don't rise above RMB 50 (unless there is a foreign DJ around).

Although early in the night the music is often remixed pop, all the clubs at the West Gate boast first-class electronic DJs, and continue to mix up their weekly lineups. Now it is possible, and even normal, to hear legitimately good house and drum 'n' bass from the regular DJs, and the best foreign DJs tend to end up here as well. The effect of the new West Gate scene on clubbing cannot be understated. Lone rangers like Banana at Jianguomen or Hiway on Chaoyangmenwai have been totally eclipsed.

But the wrecking ball is ubiquitous in this transforming town, so get up to get down while the party's still hearty – just make sure to throw any preconceptions about discos, China, or luxury out the window before you go.

PHOTO: LUNA ZHANG

A Bloody Mary adds a splash of color to Jianwai Soho's KISS (but where's Gene Simmons when you need him?)

Bar & Club Directory

For live music venues, see p342.
For karaoke bars, see p322.

13 Club For description and address, see "Live Music Venues," p343

15 Qianhai Beiyan With indoor and outdoor seating areas sheltered from the neighborhood's pedestrian and vehicular traffic, this upscale establishment is a fine place to contemplate the Qianhai waters and Lotus Lane over a cocktail or glass of wine.
Daily 5.30pm-late. 15 Qianhai Beiyan, Xicheng District. (6617 5558) 前海北沿15号，西城区前海北沿15号

180° Looming between neon pillars along Zhongguancun Beidajie is 180°, Haidian's biggest club. Its biggest asset is space and even with several hundred clubrats dancing to the standard hip hop/techno mix it doesn't feel too crowded. No cover charge, and beer and snacks are only RMB 10.
Daily 8pm-3am. 18 Zhongguancun Beidajie, opposite east gate of Yuanmingyuan (Old Summer Palace), Haidian District. (8261 3366 ext 702). 海淀区中关村北大街18号，圆明园东门对面

2 Kolegas For description and address, see "Live Music Venues" p343

Alfa Alfa's theme nights are jam-packed without fail, especially their award-winning '80s party every Friday. Newly renovated with an intimate upstairs, bamboo lawn chairs, semi-private bed-style alcoves, this is a great place to chill with friends or spot hotties. Daytime alter-ego Cafe St. Laurent is fast becoming one of the best brunch spots in town.
Daily 11am-2am. 6 Xingfu Yicun (in the alley opposite the north gate of Workers' Stadium), Chaoyang District. (6413 0086) 阿尔法，朝阳区幸福一村6号（工体北门对面的胡同里）

Angel Explicitly modeled after Babyface and located on the other side of Gongti 100 bowling alley, Angel does its neighbor one better on several counts: more seating, more lights, more staff and more space. Larger private rooms have their own DJ decks; otherwise, you can lounge in the main area and just be cool. A narrow corridor leads to sister joint Queen Club, which features fashionable creatures reclining on sofas or moving in time to progressive house music.
Daily 8.30pm-4am. 6 Gongti Xilu (between Gongti 100 Bowling and Bellagio), Chaoyang District. (6552 8888) 唐会，朝阳区工体西路6号（工体一百和鹿港小镇之间）

Aperitivo This bar boasts a faithful Europhile crowd, thanks to its shrub-lined patio, continental atmosphere and Italian-themed drinks menu. Grab a glass of wine or the infamous "Aperitivo cocktail" (white wine, tonic

and flavoring, RMB 38). A satisfying dose of class on Sanlitun Houjie, Aperitivo was voted "Outstanding Place to Start the Night" in the 2007 *that's Beijing* Reader's Choice Bar & Club Awards.
Daily 10am-late. Next to Tongli Studio, 43 Sanlitun Houjie, Chaoyang District. (6417 7793) 意式餐吧，朝阳区三里屯后街43号（同里旁边）

Area Opened by a pair of artists, Area provides the perfect setting for Lido's stylish set. Filled with white sofa beds surrounding a central dance floor, it exudes a modern, sleek, and upscale ambience. Parties every weekend featuring DJs from all over the world but don't forget your purse, as most of the club's cocktails are RMB 50-60.
Daily 8pm-2am. Behind Pascucci restaurant, 500m east of Xiaoyun Qiao, Fangyuan Xilu, Chaoyang District. (6437 6158) 空间俱乐部，朝阳区芳园西路霄云桥往东500米，帕斯古奇餐厅后面

Arena Located in the expansive basement of The Place, this aesthetically and acoustically appealing club has a touch of Taipei about it, courtesy of Taiwanese owner Patrick Lee and resident DJ Edmund Huang. Plays lots of hip-hop and hosts kickin' parties.
Daily 8pm-4am. B133, B1/F, The Place, 9 Guanghua Lu, Chaoyang District. (6587 2888/2666) arena.mosh.cn 北京小巨蛋，朝阳区光华路9号世贸天阶地下一层B133

Aria With its muted jazz combos, intelligent wine list and cocktails prepared by award-winning bartender Bruce Li, the lobby-level bar section of this China World Hotel establishment has long been popular with well-heeled CBD types and couples seeking a subtle and intimate alternative to Centro. Patrons who don't venture upstairs to the restaurant can order from a selection of tapas and finger foods. Voted "Outstanding Business Networking" in *that's Beijing's* 2007 Bar & Club Awards, and "Best Wine Selection" in the 2007 Reader Restaurant Awards.
Daily 11.30am-2.30pm, 6-10pm; bar 11am-midnight. 2/F China World Hotel, 1 Jianguomenwai Dajie, Chaoyang District. (6505 2266 ext 38, 6505 3318) 阿郦雅，朝阳区建国门外大街1号中国大饭店二层

Babyface A hip, moneyed feel pervades this mega-club, which is part of a nationwide chain based in Guangzhou. It is well-designed and filled with big spenders.
Daily 8pm-4am. 1) 6 Gongti Xilu (next to the Gongti 100 Bowling Lanes), Chaoyang District. (6551 9081); 2) Babyface West, Triumph Plaza, A143 Xizhimenwai Dajie (west of Beijing Zoo), Xicheng District. (8801 6848) www.babyface.com.cn 1）朝阳区工体西路6号（工体100保龄球旁边）；2）西城区西直门大街甲143号凯族大厦

Ball House Understated, intimate and elegant, Ball House is the perfect place to take a pool-playing date or a small group of friends. The upstairs loft spaces and the areas around the three pool tables (RMB 30/hr) are separated with furniture and curtains, fostering relaxed conversation and unhurried play over well-made drinks.
Daily 3pm-late. In a small alley directly east of Zhonglou, behind and to the left of the Hosanna Cafe, Dongcheng District. (6407 4051) 波楼，东城区钟楼湾40号，钟楼东边的小胡同里（大熊165咖啡左后）

Banana Throngs of people pulsing to beats on the bouncy dance floor, dancers in cages and a whole lot more ... if that scares you, hide away in the Spicy Lounge upstairs where world-class DJs play when they come to town. Cover charge is from RMB 20-30 when there are no special guests.
Weekdays 8.30pm-4.30am, weekends 8.30pm-5am. Scitech Hotel, 22 Jianguomenwai Dajie, Chaoyang District. (6528 3636) 巴那那，朝阳区建国门外大街22号赛特饭店一层

The Bank This velvet-draped, chandelier-lit nightclub-cum-restaurant-cum-KTV lounge boasts an altar-like DJ booth surrounded by gargantuan video screens, all of which underscore The Bank's stated mission to fly in big-name spinners. A lounge on the second floor overlooks the dance floor, with VIP rooms on the third floor with a roof-top garden. Expect drink prices in line with the expensive decor.
Sun-Thu 9pm-4am, Fri-Sat 9pm-7am. Gongti Donglu (opposite Gate 9 of Workers' Stadium), Chaoyang District. (6553 1998) 湖岸俱乐部，朝阳区工体东路（工体东门9号看台对面）

Bar Blu A drinking hotspot with a pool table, Western food, nightly DJs and one of the best terraces in town, Bar Blu has become a staple of the Sanlitun bar hopper. In the happy hour game, held nightly before 9pm and all night Tuesdays, the price of your beverage depends on a combo of luck and trigger finger speed. It also hosts a popular Wednesday-night pub quiz.
Sun-Thu 4pm-2am, Fri-Sat 4pm-4am. 4/F, Tongli Studio, Sanlitun Houjie, Chaoyang District. (6417 7567, info@barblu.cn) 蓝巴，朝阳区三里屯后街同里4层

Bed Its quiet hutong location and brilliant design, which updates the courtyard compound concept for the 21st century, have helped Bed establish itself as one of the city's most distinctive bars. Other draws include its spacious nook-filled layout (great for a date), efficient service and selection of tapas and Asian finger foods.
Daily 3pm-2am. 17 Zhangwang Hutong, Xicheng District. (8400 1554) 床吧，西城区旧鼓楼大街张旺胡同17号

Beer Mania Spacious it ain't, but this simply and solidly furnished place has a great glistening refrigerator packed with dozens of Belgian beers and a few from other countries, as well as Belgian beer on tap.
Daily 2pm-late. 1/F, Taiyue Haoting, Nansanlitun Lu, Chaoyang District. (6585 0786) 麦霓啤酒吧，朝阳区南三里屯路（泰悦豪庭一层）

Beijing Okhotsk Beer The three sizeable copper vats behind the bar of this microbrewery help to create one of Beijing's most unique drinking experiences.
Daily 5.30pm-2am. 7 Shangye Jie, Phoenix City, 5 Shuguang Xili, Chaoyang District. (5866 8552) 北京欧可啤酒，朝阳区曙光西里甲5号凤凰城凤凰新天商业街7号

Bla Bla Bar Long a favorite hangout of the huge international student body at Beijing Language and Culture University, this bar offers budget booze and unbridled fun in the heart of campus.
Daily 3pm-2am. Inside Beijing Language and Culture University, Chengfu Lu, Haidian District. (6239 7033) 海淀区成府路语言学院内

Black Sun Bar Not to be confused with the old Black Sun Bar in the largely *chai*'d south street of Sanlitun, the original owner has moved his sunshine to this location, featuring bargain-basement drinks, pool tables,

darts, foosball, the original caipirinha recipe and a patio.
Daily 5.30pm-2am. West gate of Chaoyang Park, Chaoyang District. (6593 6909) 黑太阳 2，朝阳区朝阳公园西门

Buddha Bar Popular with visiting and resident French people, Lao Qi's lounge – one of the first on Houhai – not only plays better music than most of its competitors (with a focus on Latin, house, funk and r&b), but also offers one of the area's most generous happy hours (50% off from 2-7pm).
Daily 2pm-2am. 16 Yinding Qiao, Shichahai, Xicheng District. (6617 5746) 不大，西城区什刹海银锭桥16号

Bus Bar This invincible stalwart of the Beijing scene has moved again and sports a classy new makeover. As ever, two busses gutted out and welded together house the evening's entertainment. Cheap drinks and a convivial atmosphere attract a loyal clientele of bus boarders. Next stop: detox!
Daily 6pm-late. Inside Longbo Guangchang, northeast corner of Changhong Qiao, Chaoyang District. (no tel) 车吧，朝阳区长虹桥东北角隆博广场内

Candy Floss Cafe Tucked away around the corner from the main strip of cafes along Nanluogu Xiang, directly behind the Central Academy of Drama, Candy Floss sets itself apart with an amazingly pretty courtyard. Also hosts a tango milonga every Sunday evening.
Daily 6.30pm-midnight. 35 Dongmianhua Hutong, Dongcheng District. (6405 5775) 棉花塘咖啡馆，东城区交道口南大街东棉花胡同35号

Capone's With a large selection of wines from around the world, Capone's offers chic decor and swinging jazz after 9pm. They also have a daily 5-8pm happy hour. Also see Restaurant Directory under "Italian."
Sun-Thu noon-midnight, Fri-Sat noon-1am. 4/F, Bldg A, The Place, 9 Guanghua Lu, Chaoyang District. (6587 1526) 卡彭意大利西餐厅和酒吧，朝阳区光华路9号世贸天阶A座4层

Cargo Club An '80s-inspired dance floor with a massive LED wall display that flashes in time to the overpowering sound system and neon lighting. KTV rooms and lounge areas are available for those partial to singalongs and civilized conversation, respectively. Cargo books super DJ line-ups in the hope of winning over the fashionable crowd spilling over from neighbors Babyface and Angel.
Daily 8pm-late. 6 Gongti Xilu, Chaoyang District. (6551 6898/78) 朝阳区工体西路6号

Casa Habana Cuba grows the world's finest tobacco and Casa Habana offers some of Beijing's best Cuban cigars. This comfortable lounge sports Cuban-themed decoration, an on-site humidor and private lockers where customers can leave their stogies for future contemplative puffs. Cigars run from RMB 60 to 2,000.
Daily 10am-midnight. 1/F, Jinglun Hotel, 3 Jianguomenwai Dajie, Chaoyang District. (6595 0888) 哈瓦那之家，朝阳区建国门外大街3号京伦饭店1层

Cave Cafe Befitting the arty-industrial labyrinth that is the 798 arts district, Cave Cafe is a hip, inviting hangout. The decor is minimalist: exposed brick walls, unvarnished wood floors, and black and white tables and couches. Jazz is played at the perfect volume, while the proprietors' funny little dog Yeahbee struts around like he's the real owner of the joint.

Daily 11am-midnight. Next to 798 Space, Dashanzi art district, 4 Jiuxianqiao Lu, Chaoyang District. (8456 5520) 洞房咖啡，朝阳区酒仙桥4号798大山子艺术区时态空间旁边

CD Jazz Club For description and address, see "Live Music Venues" p343

The Cellar Located in the basement of the Trio complex and decked out medieval style, The Cellar houses some of the finest wines to be found in Beijing. Those interested in compiling a wine collection of their own can join Club 88, The Cellar's very own wine club (lifetime membership fee: RMB 12,000; annual fee: RMB 3,888), and enjoy the benefit of temperature-controlled personal wine lockers.
Daily 5pm-3am. B1/F, Trio, Jiangtai Xilu, west of Rosedale Hotel, Lido area, Chaoyang District. (6437 8399) 朝阳区丽都将台西路

Centro A giant bar, spacious lounge areas, a stage, a private room, an excellent wine and cigar selection ... the Kerry Centre's bar is designed and branded right down to the carpets. Though far from overdone, Centro is a very comfortable spot to down drinks from bottled beers to blue cheese martinis, while doing your best Cary Grant impression. Happy hour (2-for-1 specials, 5pm to 8pm), and live jazz performances held every night.
Daily 24 hours. 1/F, Kerry Centre Hotel, 1 Guanghua Lu, Chaoyang District. (6561 8833, ask for Centro) 炫酷，朝阳区光华路1号嘉里中心饭店1层

Charlie's Bar Once upon a time, maybe there was a Charlie. What's there now is a newly renovated, quiet lounge bar set beside the Jianguo Hotel's graceful garden courtyard. The prices (Tsingtao RMB 40) remind us of the tavern's pre-1990 history when it was the only game in town and you had to pay in Foreign Exchange Certificates, but despite the arm and leg, Charlie's is still a great place in the heart of the CBD to grab a beer.
Daily 9am-2.30am. 1/F, Jianguo Hotel, 5 Jianguomenwai Dajie, Chaoyang District. (6500-2233 ext 8038) 查理酒吧，建国门外大街5号建国饭店1层 朝阳区

Cheers Given the rousing live music, flamenco-Uighur jam band, paintings of naked women on the wall and a pool table in the back, RMB 20 for a Tiger beer is pretty reasonable. You will come for the paintings but become a regular for the house band, which is arguably one of the best in Beijing. Live shows every Friday and Saturday night.
Daily 6pm-late. 2/F, Tongli Studio, Sanlitun Houjie, (next to Aperitivo), Chaoyang District. (135 2044 6062) 朝阳区三里屯后街同里二楼

China Doll This sleek dance club and lounge, spread over three floors and decked out in a titillating subaquatic theme, features yummy signature cocktails and music spun by DJ Youdai. The Suzie Wong's of Sanlitun, China Doll is equally popular with Chinese and foreigners, and the club has attracted many international DJs since it opened in late 2006. Two-for-one deals before 11pm Sun-Thu, and ladies get free mixed drinks all night Wednesdays.
Daily 8pm-late. 2/F, Tongli Studios, Sanlitun Beilu, Chaoyang District. (6417 4699) 中国娃娃，朝阳区三里屯北路同里2楼

Chun Yu Ting Your friendly neighborhood lesbian bar. Less popular than other lesbian hangouts, but Chun Yu Ting has been around for a while now, so they must be doing something right.

Boozy bliss at China Doll

Liren Jie East, Xuanwu District. (6356-1320) 春雨亭，宣武区里仁街东口

CJW Top-level prices are complemented by the bar's nouveau riche decor – a dark, smoky, neon-accented lovechild of a cinema, hotel and nightclub, with a double helping of a Bond villain's lair. The talented Las Vegas house band plays a wide range of classic jazz and Motown, making for an enjoyable night despite the lightened wallet.
Daily 11am-2am. L-137, The Place, 9 Guanghua Lu, Chaoyang District. (6587 1222) 雪茄爵士酒吧，世贸天阶 L−137 光华路9号 朝阳区

Cloud Nine Bar This upscale bar in the Shangri-La Hotel has it all – swanky interior, an incredible drink list, and regular live music – with prices to match.
Daily 8am-2am. Shangri-La Hotel Beijing, 29 Zizhuyuan Lu, Haidian District. (6841 2211 ext 2723) 九霄云外，海淀区紫竹院路29号，香格里拉饭店内

Club Taku Student-oriented (what else could a Wudaokou bar be?), Club Taku is cavernous but comfortable, a little shoddy, but ultimately a fine place to hang out. Big draws begin and end with all-you-can-drink nights. A good place to stay up late, get a little toasty and dance.
Daily 8.30pm-late. 16 Zhixin Lu (just west of the intersection between Zhixin Lu and Zhixin Donglu), Haidian District. (no tel) 海淀区志新路16号（志新路和志新东路的路口往西）

Coco Banana Smaller than Banana, Coco Banana features a square bar and lounge areas around the dance floor. With its modern and shining decor and go-go dancers, Coco Banana clearly draws on Banana's style, although high rents on Gongti Xilu means higher drink prices (Corona is the cheapest beer on the menu at RMB 35).
Daily 9pm-late. Gongti Xilu, Chaoyang District. (8599 9999) 朝阳区工体西路8号

Coco Zen For description and address, see And Now for Something Completely Different p322

Cosmo Opened in summer 2007, Cosmo brought Beijing's gay community a long-awaited alternative to Destination. Friendly to both men and women (and straight people), this stylish and sexy refuge boasts not only a healthy-sized dance-floor but also a charming bar amidst the distressed concrete and exposed brickwork. Don't miss the lip-smacking house special, the Cosmo-BJ (RMB 40).
Daily 8pm-late. Grand Rock Plaza, Gongti Beilu (opposite Asia Hotel), Chaoyang District. (5190 8918) 朝阳区工体北路（新中街路口）巨石大厦

D-22 For description and address, see "Live Music Venues" p343

The Den The ground floor offers a bar, booths and tables, while upstairs a dark and sweaty dance floor dominates. DJs play a mix of R&B and pop for an enthusiastic, booty-shaking international crowd. Voted

NIGHTLIFE

"Outstanding Sports Bar" by *that's Beijing* readers in 2007, The Den serves a decent menu of Western and Asian food, including brunch on weekends, and is a good place for late-night refueling. Happy hour 5-10pm daily.
Daily 24 hours. 4 Gongti Donglu (next to City Hotel's main entrance), Chaoyang District. (6592 6290) 敦煌, 朝阳区工体东路4号城市宾馆主门旁边

Destination Beijing's most well-known gay club features spare concrete walls, de rigueur plush sofas and now an attached restaurant. Absolutely packed on the weekends, Destination is clearly doing something right.
Daily 8pm-late. 7 Gongti Xilu, Chaoyang District. (6551 5138) 目的地, 朝阳区工体西路7号

Desert Oasis Bar (Shanmulan) Set within the charm of the Nanluogu Xiang-area hutongs, this cozy three-floor bar aims to evoke the ambiance of exotic locales. Offers specialty beverages such as refreshingly tart Mongolian raspberry juice (RMB 20/cup, 40/pitcher), Xinjiang iced yogurt (RMB 15), and Lhasa Beer (RMB 15), as well as a range of western food such as pizza and pasta. Also has a roof terrace and numerous comfortable nooks, and is popular with Chinese lesbians who come on weekends to shoot the breeze with the owner.
Daily 11am-2am. 3 Shajing Hutong, Nanluogu Xiang, Dongcheng District. (6403 7856) 山木蓝, 东城区南锣鼓巷沙井胡同3号

Drum and Bell Overlooking the courtyard between the Drum and the Bell towers, this cafe is infused with the history of Beijing. Coal-burning stoves inside the quadrangle garden create warmth during the winter, while during the summer the rooftop patio is a great place to catch some sunshine.
Daily 1pm-2am. 41 Zhonglouwan Hutong, Dongcheng District. (8403 3600) 鼓钟咖啡馆, 东城区钟楼湾胡同41号

Durty Nellie's Straight outta Dublin … well almost. Guinness on tap, Irish stew, Michael Collins portraits, occasional live music (sometimes Irish, but mainly local cover bands), pool tables and dartboards.
Daily 10am-1.30am. B1/F and 1/F, Liangmaqiao Flower Market, Chaoyang District. (6593 5050) 爱尔兰酒吧, 朝阳区亮马桥花卉市场1/B 燕莎商场南岸

East Shore Live Jazz Cafe For description and address, see "Live Music Venues" p343

Emperor's Treasure Bar Flamboyant decor and drag shows on weekends.
2/F, building adjacent to west side of Jintai Lante Hotel, 20m north of Jinsong Xikou, 9 Guanghe Nanli Ertiao, Chaoyang District. (no tel.) 至尊宝雄吧, 朝阳区广和南里二条9号, 金泰蓝特宾馆西侧, 劲松西口北20米

Eye on the Lake Catering to an upscale, pan-continental market, Guan Tang (as it is also known) offers a cozy bar area, three private rooms and an outdoor courtyard terrace. All the spaces are immaculately designed with a blend of *lao* Beijing and Western-style luxury.
Daily 7.30pm-2am. 13 Dongming Hutong, Houhai, Xicheng District. (135 0111 9555) 观塘, 西城区后海东明胡同13号

Face Sister to the popular Shanghai bar, Face features an upscale bar tastefully decorated with artifacts from China, Indonesia and India. Prices are high, but it's

the only place in Beijing where you can find a pint of Tetley's.
Daily 10am-late. 26 Dongcaoyuan, Gongti Nanlu, Chaoyang District. (6551 6738) 妃思, 朝阳区工体南路东草园26号

Frank's Place This legend of the Beijing nightlife scene has been reincarnated as part of a three-floor establishment called Trio. Arguably the best sports bar in Beijing, Frank's has multiple screens and all the essentials for enjoying the game: decent pub grub like pizzas, burgers and snacks, quality draft lagers, and a pool table for the ad breaks. Also has plentiful seating and a nice leafy terrace out back.
Daily 9am-2am. Jiangtai Xilu, west of Rosedale Hotel, Lido area, Chaoyang District. (6437 8399) 朝阳区丽都将台西路

Gogo An unremarkable courtyard from the outside, the interior of Gogo is encased in glass, and transparent from end to end. This little architectural trick sets the place off nicely, showcasing the fishpond, rock garden and dark wooden furniture. Emphasizing wines, fusion foods and exotic cocktails, Gogo is definitely a change for the neighborhood.
Daily 10am-2am. 13 Beixiang Lu (100m from Changqiao), Xicheng District. (8403 6253) 印甜, 西城区北巷路13号（离厂桥100米）

Goldfish Home Bringing a touch of class to a street otherwise ruled by Carlsberg girls, Goldfish boasts three floors decked out in a decadent 1920s style similar to that of Suzie Wong's. The third floor-cum-roof terrace elevates you above the Houhai bustle and provides a great view of the lake. Beers start from RMB 35.
Daily noon-late. 5 Lotus Lane, Houhai, Dongcheng District. (6615 8966) 金鱼私房吧, 东城区什刹海前海荷花市场天荷坊5号店

Goose 'n' Duck Pub This massive sports bar has two pool tables, a shuffleboard set, darts and TVs galore showing sports at all hours. Take your frustration out on heavy foam baseballs in their batting cage (no charge) if your team loses; or celebrate a win by playing big-screen video archery or video golf, where you hit real balls against a screen. Two-for-one drinks 4-8pm, or order any time from their comprehensive menu of burgers, pizza, pasta and more. Great sloppy joes.
Daily 24 hours. 1) 1 Bihuju, Chaoyang Park West Gate. (6538 1691); 2) S1, Green Lake International Tower (east of Chaoyang Park East Gate). (5928 3045) 鹅和鸭, 1) 朝阳区朝阳公园西门西侧碧湖居1号; 2) 朝阳公园桥东侧路北观湖国际大厦1号写字楼首层

Hai Bar Great terrace with views of Houhai on one side and the Drum and Bell towers on the other. Secure the table in the turret to drink in the scenery.
Daily 1pm-2am. 36 Yandai Xiejie, Xicheng District. (6403 4913) 海吧, 西城区烟袋斜街36号

Herrenhauser Named after a German biergarten, this upmarket cafe on Houhai's western shore is surprisingly polished, with a rose on every table, plants in the corners and an excellent roof deck.
Daily 11am-late. 22 Deshengmennei Dajie, Houhai West Bank, Xicheng District. (6404 2059) 温森主题会所, 西城区德内后海西沿22号

Hope Bar Tropical plants, large rattan chairs and a standard-issue chill out soundtrack make you feel like

"China Fury"
Hell hath nothin' on her
by Matt P. Jager

They said it was "Chinese white wine." My first gulp unveiled the cruelty of the mistranslation. My tongue tingled, my lips puckered and burnt, my tonsils convulsed, my neck kinked, my cheeks filled with spit, I felt a thickness where mouth becomes throat, and then I gargled some Coke to wash away the horror. As my sinuses began to drain, I felt her in my belly, a warm evil puddle.

Erguotou, a sorghum spirit made from a two-pot distilling process, is the most apocalyptic of liquors. A drummer I know calls her "China Power." A martial arts acolyte told me, "Drunken boxing is powerful kung fu. No one feels pain after a bottle of this stuff." I refer to her as "devil juice," but the most accurate euphemism is China Fury.

China Fury makes you scream the things that common courtesy locks in the subconscious creases of your brain. She makes you act on the impulses that legal disincentives and social inhibitions usually harness. She is the devil on your shoulder banishing the angel to the harsh light of sobriety. She is a cruel mistress.

Sumptuous networking dinners and business negotiation feasts are lubricated with her sickly-sweet, high-class southern cousin *maotai*. Devil

A cruel mistress indeed

juice doesn't belong there. *Erguotou* is the pin on the blue-collar lapel. Her place is on a fold-out table beside a steaming plate of *chuan'r*.

Baijiu is an umbrella term for all Chinese "white wine," but *erguotou* is a liquor (characterized by its distilling process), not a brand. The most well-known and accessible variety is produced by Hong Xing (Red Star), available at every cheap restaurant and *xiaomaibu* in the city. For only three *kuai*, she will accompany you on your travels in a flask-sized bottle which research suggests shatters upon meeting asphalt at high velocities. Beware the screw-cap that does not pop off at first twist – it heralds fake booze and an eyeball-pounding hangover. The first three-hundred-ton batch of Red Star hit the market in September 1949, paving the way for the formal proclamation of the People's Republic of China. The 50-plus years of mass production that followed were a testament to her mind-melting fury and proletarian price tag. Now the Red Star distillery churns out upwards of a hundred thousand tons a year.

Some have tried to tame *erguotou* with Sprite or green tea. Others have acquired the taste by mixing small doses into their beer. *Laobaixing* are disgusted by such sissy tactics. They will say knowingly, "*Laowai* can't drink our China's badass booze." To earn the admiration of your local bike-repairman, the street-side chess masters, and the neighborhood convenience store boss, you must overpower *erguotou* with sheer strength of will. Drink respectfully and powerfully. Have no fear. But be warned – if someone offers you a clear cup of "Chinese white wine," take a whiff or two before guzzling it down.

PHOTO: MARY DENNIS

NIGHTLIFE

you've landed in Ibiza or French colonial Vietnam, with the exception of the decidedly affordable drinks.
Daily 4pm-2am. 20 Houhai Nan (50m west of Yinding Qiao), Xicheng District. (6613 6209) 后海吧，西城区后海南20号银锭桥往西50米

Houhai Zoo Perched on the east shore of Houhai and with a relatively stylish design. The prices (RMB 10 for almost everything: beer, shooters, mixers) are about the only thing this venue has in common with its sister bars Nanjie and Huxley's. They've also got a micro-brewery (drafts RMB 15) and have been known to host parties.
Daily 3pm-2am. Bldg 2, Qianhai (next to East Shore Live Jazz), Xicheng District. (6404 6690) 后海卒，西城区前海南沿2号小楼一层

Hutong Bar A small but airy courtyard house on Houhai with open-concept rooms – one of the few bars in the 'hood that has paid more attention to the space between its walls than outside beside the lake. There's another Hutong Bar on Nanluogu Xiang.
Daily 2pm-2am. 8 Houhai Nanyan, Xicheng District. (6615 8691) 胡同写意，西城区后海南沿8号

Huxley's Though Sanlitun's South Street is long gone, Huxley's keeps its flame alive in gentrifying Houhai with cheap booze, friendly bartenders and an unpretentious attitude. Rock on.
Daily 6pm-late. Yandai Xiejie (the street running diagonally between the Drum Tower and Yinding Bridge), Xicheng District. (6402 7825) 德彼酒吧，西城区烟袋斜街16号

International Beer Town Just when you thought that Wudaokou was getting classy, summer came and the beer garden appeared. Despite the name, there's no yodeling here, only a wide selection of food kiosks, a rain roof and a ton of plastic tables. Some of them have umbrellas, too. Pints of beer for RMB 4. Good for chats, snacks, and getting rowdy later in the night.
Daily 6pm-late. West of the Wudaokou light rail station. (No phone.) 国际啤酒城，五道口城铁站西侧

i-Ultra Lounge This sleek, modern lounge, under the same ownership as restaurants Hatsune and Kagen, is aesthetically pleasing, but its real strength lies behind the bar, where a friendly and efficient staff brings the ever-evolving drinks selection to life. Try the Japanese fusion cocktails (averaging RMB 60), mixed with Nigori – unfiltered, exceptionally tasty sake, which is near impossible to find in Beijing. The roof terrace, "The Beach," offers spa treatments and a view of Chaoyang Park.
Daily 6pm-midnight. Block 8, Apartment 8 Complex, Chaoyang Gongyuan Xilu, Chaoyang District. (6508 8585) 朝阳区朝阳公园西路八号公馆

Iron & Fish The name has us flummoxed and the rash of string lights is unfortunate, but this place is a cut above most other Houhai spots as it is set back among the trees and furnished with plush red sofas. Get there early to secure the swing seats.
Daily 1pm-3am. Behind 8 Ya'er Hutong. (6401 6835) 铁和鱼，西城区鸦儿胡同8号后门

Jazz-Ya This comfortable bar and restaurant maintains the look and feel of a Japanese diner, with the clientele and music (J-Pop and jazz) you would expect. The cocktails – particularly the Long Islands – are better than average.
Daily 11.30am-2am. 18 Sanlitun Beilu (North Bar Street), Chaoyang District. (6415 1227) 爵士，朝阳区三里屯北路18号（北酒吧街）

Jiangjinjiu Bar For description and address, see "Live Music Venues" p343

Ji Xian Tang What looks like a traditional teahouse has a hidden secret: its own private terrace that may well offer the best view over Houhai.
Daily noon-late. Opposite 36 Houhai Nanyan, Houhai Nanyan. (6618 3502) 集贤堂，西城区后海南沿（36号对面）

Kai Club This mainstay of the Sanlitun weekend scene draws a young party crowd with cheap drinks and a diverse music set. House, indie rock, break beats and old school are played for a packed dance floor downstairs and lounge upstairs.
Mon-Fri 6pm-2am, Sat-Sun 6pm-4am. Sanlitun Beijie (around the corner from Poachers Inn), Chaoyang District. (6416 6254) 开，朝阳区三里屯北街（从友谊青年酒店馆拐弯）

KISS is a laidback lounge bar, geared towards Beijing yuppies looking to kick back and relax. Tall windows open out onto the business district, and wine-red velvet seating adds warmth to the otherwise minimalist interior. The spiral staircase by which guests reach Kiss Club from the restaurant and sandwich store below also provides access to the fourth-floor roof terrace.
Daily 24 hours. Rm 112, 3/F, Bldg 6, Jianwai Soho, Dongsanhuan Lu, Chaoyang District. (5869 4820/3/5) 朝阳区东三环路建外Soho6号别墅3层112号

Kokomo Kokomo has a fresh beachy look and with the focus on Caribbean food and quality cocktails, it's a pleasant place to enjoy the heat of a Beijing summer. Hosts award-winning Sundays On Top event on their lovely terrace, and free Wi-Fi is available.
Sun-Thu 11am-2am, Fri-Sat 11am-4am. 4/F, Tongli Studios, Sanlitun Houjie (above China Doll), Chaoyang District. (6413 1019) 朝阳区三里屯后街同里4层

La Baie des Anges The bright, breezy decor of this courtyard wine bar and the extensive ever-evolving wine list admirably reflect the ideals of the three French managers who "love wine and want to provide a comfortable place to enjoy it."
Daily 6pm-2am. 5 Nanguanfang Hutong (just south of Hutong Pizza), Houhai, Xicheng District. (6657 1605) 西城区后海南官房胡同5号（胡同批萨南边）

Lan The opulence of this huge luxury venue is matched by the attention to detail behind the bar, which is stocked with a vast array of European and New World wines. Guests can choose between a restaurant, a lounge that features live entertainment and DJs most nights, an oyster bar, a cocktail bar, a cigar room and 45 private VIP Rooms. Voted "Best Decor" in *that's Beijing's* 2007 Reader Bar & Club Awards and Restaurant Awards.
Daily 11.30am-2am. 4/F LG Twin Towers, 12B Jianguomen Waidajie, Chaoyang District. (5109 6012/13) 兰，朝阳区建国门外大街乙12号LG双子座4层

Latinos Latinos brings much needed salsa-dancing sauciness to Beijing. Evening croons come courtesy of resident Venezuelan-Colombian band Makore, and guest dancers from across the globe and reggeton-spinning DJs are expected to visit.
Daily 9pm-late. A12 Historical Complex, Nanxincang, Dongsi Shitiao, Dongcheng District. (6409 6997) www.latinosclubchina.com 东城区东四十条南新仓甲12号

High-rollers and high-rises at i-Ultra Lounge's rooftop "Beach"

Loco A stylish blend of purple walls, mahogany tables and red everything-else creates the mellow mood you need to shoot the breeze, smoke a hookah or play boardgames. Strawberry soju available.
Daily 10.30am-2.30am. 1/F, Bldg 4, Xijiao Hotel, 18 Wangzhuang Lu, Wudaokou, Haidian District. (6232 2288 ext 4989) 海淀区五道口18号王庄路西郊宾馆4号楼1层

Long Long Ago Courtyard Part of the Nanluogu Xiang bar scene, the Long Long Ago Courtyard is a slightly excessive mix of East and West, but nevertheless is a quiet, intimate place to take a date and relax. Try the Western menu by a former Kunlun Hotel chef.
Daily noon-3am. 111 Nanluogu Xiang, Dongcheng District. (6851 1489) 红人坊，东城区南锣鼓巷111号

Love Island Frequented mostly by Chinese men, this drag bar is on a touristy art-street hutong and has shows Wednesdays, Fridays and Saturdays.
6 Liulichang Dongjie, Xuanwu District. (8316-1284) 都市情岛，宣武区琉璃厂东街6号

Luna Lounge Following in the footsteps of Bed, Luna Lounge, which shares the sleek design of attached Italian restaurant Luce, is the latest Jiugulou Dajie venue to capitalize on its unique hutong location. The roof terrace gives nice views of the nearby neighborhood, and the section of glass floor at its center provides nice views for those eating downstairs – so wear pants, ladies.
Daily 1pm-1am. 138 Jiugulou Dajie, Xicheng District. (8402 4417) 潞娜，西城区旧鼓楼大街138号

Lush A Wudaokou institution, Lush provides foreign students with a caffeinated study spot by day and place to cut loose by night. The breakfasts are highly-rated, as are the homemade foccacia sandwiches and special desserts, or show up for events packed with foreign students. On Sunday nights Lush puts on the most vital and eclectic open-mic night in town. 2-for-1 happy hour 8-10pm every night.
Daily 24 hours. 2/F, Bldg 1, Huaqing Jiayuan, Chengfu Lu (across from the Wudaokou light rail station), Haidian District. (8286 3566) 海淀区成府路，华清嘉园1号楼二层（五道口城铁站对面）

Maggie's One of Beijing's oldest nightspots, and the target of more polemics than any in the city. Some see it as a "misunderstood" bar, with "excellent music and people-watching opportunities." Others view it as a dreary place where middle-aged expat men come to engage the company of younger Mongolian women.
Daily 9pm-late. South Gate of Ritan Park, Chaoyang District. (8562 8142/8143) www.maggiesbar.com 美琪，朝阳区日坛公园南门

Magic Rock This bar caters to the West Side climbing crew and organizes climbing trips around Beijing. Mountaineering gear and camping equipment are the bar's equivalent of wallpaper, along with posters of beefy studs flexing their pecs as they ascend boulders.
Daily noon-2am. 3 Weigongcun Lu, Haidian District. (6845 1142) 魔岩酒吧，海淀区魏公村路3号

MAO Livehouse For description and address, see "Live Music Venues" p343

Mexican Wave See Restaurant Directory under Central/South American.
Daily 11am-midnight. Dongdaqiao Lu, 200m north of Guiyou Dasha (opposite the Silk Market), Chaoyang District. (6506 3961) 墨西哥风味餐厅，朝阳区东大桥路贵友大厦（秀水街正对面）往北200米路东

Mix Now bigger than ever, Mix hosts numerous foreign DJs to the delight of Beijing's hordes of hip hop clubbers.

NIGHTLIFE

Death Game! ... and More

A primer on drinking, Seoul-style
by Matt P. Jager

Korean student haunts are some of the rowdiest around, typified by tables of tipsy victims of uproarious drinking games. To join in on the fun, enlist a South Korean buddy to bring you to a restaurant in the cul-de-sac behind Jingyu Hotel on Qinghua Donglu in Wudaokou; or the short alley a hundred meters east of the light rail station, beneath a Blue KTV sign, which also hosts a cluster of BBQ joints and bars.

South Koreans have formalized drinking etiquette – pour with two hands, accept a drink with two hands, for example. Friends and foreigners can ignore these guidelines – but if you really want to crash a party, you must learn the drinking games.

Three – six – nine

The game begins with everyone bouncing both fists on the table, chanting, "Three, six, three-six-nine! Three, six, three-six-nine!" Then, in a circular progression, the players count in consecutive order starting from one. A player who says a multiple of three or any number with the digit three must clap. It gets tough at thirty (thirty-three gets two claps). If you screw up, you drink and begin anew at the chant.

Friendship game

Pour a shot for every player and pick two captains. The captains play rock-paper-scissors, and the winning captain gets to choose one teammate. The chant in Korean goes, "Gawee – bawee – boh!" Repeat until everyone is picked. The teams may be unequal. The last player picked will then challenge the last player of the opposing team to a game of rock-paper-scissors. The losing player is eliminated and the winner advances, until an entire team is defeated. By the end, the losers must finish all the shots on the table. The losing captain, who goes last, must drink all the remaining booze – so to show friendship to the captain, drink as much as you can. Unlike Western-style rock-paper-scissors, no fist pumping is necessary. Korean scissors look like Chinese eights, the thumb and index finger in the shape of a pistol.

Death game

This is a game of chance and suspense. First count the people around the table. Beginning from one, the goal is to consecutively count up to the number of players. There is no order. Each person can speak only once, but if you say a number at the same time as another player, you both drink. If you are the last person to say a number, you must drink. The key is to gauge when everyone else around the table will be silent, and then shout your number out. Do not forget the introductory chant – "Jugeumae (death) ... game!" Fist-pumping is optional.

"Gawee – bawee – boh!"

PHOTO: MARY DENNIS

No Name, no shame: The bar that launched the Houhai craze is still a damn fine place for a lakeside tipple

Daily 8pm-late. Inside the north gate of Workers' Stadium, Chaoyang District. (6530 2889) 密克斯，朝阳区工体北门内

Nanjie Opened and designed by a friend of Huxley's (a close enough friend to use the slogan "Shut Up, Just Drink"), it is a little cleaner than the old South Street holes, and maybe that's a good thing. The clientele is young and lubricated. To get into the spirit of things, order a "rack" of shots: RMB 100 for 12.
Daily 2pm-3am. Sanlitun Nanjie (east side of The Bookworm, west of Hot Loft), Chaoyang District. (6586 7757) 南街，朝阳区三里屯南街（Bookworm东侧，藏酷西侧）

Nashville Bar & Restaurant Nashville's two-story venue provides live music seven nights a week, with 80 percent country and 80 percent classic rock. In addition to wine, whisky and cocktails, this long-lived bar offers a wide selection of draft and bottled beer, (RMB 25 to RMB 50), and reasonably priced snacks. Nashville is also open for lunch.
Daily 11am-3am. Haoyun Jie, 29 Zaoying Lu, Chaoyang District. (5867 0298) www.nashville.com.cn 乡谣，朝阳区枣营路29号好运街

New Get Lucky For description and address, see "Live Music Venues" p344

No Name Bar The first bar on Houhai is still among the best. Featuring rattan furnishings, tropical plants, tasteful art and colorful fabric swathes, the bar's design combines with the groovy soundtrack, lake views, and moderately priced coffees and drinks to induce a mood of languid contemplation. A legend.

Daily noon-2am. 3 Qianhai Dongyan (next to Kaorou Ji restaurant), Xicheng District. (6401 8541) 无名酒吧，西城区前海东沿3号烤肉季隔壁

Obelisco For description and address, see Restaurant Directory under Central and South American, p66

Obiwan With a large roof terrace overlooking placid Xihai (Houhai's sleepier cousin), Obiwan is our favorite little bar in which to unravel away an afternoon and make a night of it with their great parties. The bar is expansive but not expensive and the selection is varied, from Tsingtao (RMB 10) to a cheeky Campari and soda (RMB 35).
Weekdays 11am-2am, weekends 1pm-late. 4 Xihai Xiyan (300m from Jishuitan subway station), Xicheng District. (6617 3231) 西城区西海西沿4号

Palace View Bar Enjoy a bird's eye view of the Forbidden City and Tian'anmen Square with a drink and service worthy of an emperor.
Daily 5pm-9.30pm. 10/F Grand Hotel Beijing, 35 Dongchang'an Dajie, Dongcheng District. (6513 7788 ext 458) 观景酒吧，东城区北京贵宾楼饭店10层东长安街35号

Palette Vino Oenophiles will delight in this Shunyi-area wine shop and bar which offers a wide selection of bottles divided by grape variety, including vintages imported directly by the owners, and a pleasant lounge in which to sample purchases. Palette Vino has opened a kitchen to provide some food to go along with your good drop.
Daily 11am-11pm. Pinnacle Plaza, Shunyi District. (8046 4461) 派乐坊，顺义区荣祥广场

NIGHTLIFE

Fine vintages and satellite sports meet at Pavillion, in the spirit of its progenitor, Frank's Place

Pass By Bar A favorite for foreigners and tourists residing in the neighborhood, this pleasant courtyard bar and restaurant is an ideal place to fuel up and enjoy a conversation or surf the net on your laptop. Tibetan prints and wooden masks adorn the walls and there's a selection of reading material to browse and borrow (if you donate three books).
Daily 9am-2am. 108 Nanluogu Xiang, Dongcheng District. (8403 8004, 130 0102 3334) www.passbybar.com 过客，东城区南锣鼓巷108号

Pavillion Started by a former Frank's Place owner, Pavillion is a sports bar with five-star hotel leanings and notably good food. The focal points: a square-shaped bar, a glass-walled wine room, and a spacious deck.
Daily 10am-2am. Gongti Xilu (opposite west gate of Workers' Stadium), Chaoyang District. (6507 2617) www.pavillionbeijing.com 万龙腾飞，朝阳区工体西路（工人体育场西门对面）

Pepper Pepper offers nightly mixological entertainment, where bartenders take turns tossing bottles around and pouring elaborate cocktails. Drinks are far from cheap, but there are a few deals to be had – a six-pack of Beck's costs a reasonable RMB 100, an order that includes a serving of popcorn.
1) Daily 7pm-late. North of Xijiao Hotel, Wangzhuang Lu, Wudaokou, Haidian District. (8237 2963); 2) Daily 7.30pm-late. 2 Chaoyang Xilu, West Gate of Chaoyang Park (30m east of the West Gate), Chaoyang District. (6592 0788/6506 9588) 辣椒，1) 海淀区五道口王庄路西郊宾馆北边；2) 朝阳区朝阳西路2号朝阳公园西门（西门往东30米）

Phil's Pub Once on the verge of obscurity, this old Sanlitun south bar street hangout has turned it around with a spiffy renovation and crowd-pleasing tunes. Drinks are cheap (Erdinger RMB 30) and the Playstation 2 is a good update to the usual bar games. Weekends sometimes draw big crowds of cheap expats drifting between Phil's and the old Black Sun Bar across the street.
Daily 7.30pm-late. 15 Dongdaqiao Xiejie, Chaoyang District. (6503 3811) 大菲酒馆，朝阳区东大桥斜街15号

Pili Pili Perhaps Beijing's first African-themed restaurant and bar (the managers once owned an African import business), Pili Pili draws a boisterous international crowd. Make an alliterative night of it by visiting Pula Pula (no joke) across the street.
Daily 10am-1.30am (bar remains open after 10pm). In Oriental Qicai World, near Nüren Jie, Chaoyang District. (8448 3372, 8448 4332) 比利比利，朝阳区莱泰花街星吧路

Pipe's Six days a week, this bar is a quiet, unexceptional spot to smoke a pipe or cigar, but on Saturday nights, it transforms into Feng Bar, a hopping dance party frequented by Chinese lesbians in their late teens and early 20s.
Daily 6pm-2am. South gate of Workers' Stadium, Chaoyang District. (6593 7756) 烟斗，朝阳区工体南门（富国海底世界东100米）

Poachers Inn Thanks to cheap drinks and a soundtrack of pop and disco anthems, Poachers is often packed with young things flirting and dancing on the tables. Not the place to discuss Kierkegaard.
Daily 8pm-late. 43 Bei Sanlitun Lu, Chaoyang District. (6417 2632 ext 8506) 友谊青年酒店，朝阳区北三里屯路43号

The Pomegranate The courtyard setting (with actual pomegranate tree) might suggest that a meditative ex-

Q Bar: love at first sip

perience awaits, but this place is all about carb-loading with draft beer and the sports channel. 1980s grooves and sharp service accompany an extensive drinks list, including Carlsberg drafts (RMB 25) and classic cocktails (RMB 30). The refreshingly brief menu includes quesadillas, steak and mushroom baguette, and fabulous french fries. There's open mic every Thursday, and a music festival each spring.
Daily 11am-midnight. 19 Kaifa Lu, Xi baixinzhuang, Hou Sha Yu, Shunyi District. (8046 2558) 石榴园，顺义区后沙裕西白辛庄开发路19号

Press Club Bar This classy bar was founded on hallowed ground – the very spot where journalists chronicling US President Richard Nixon's groundbreaking 1972 visit to Beijing would knock back a few. Nowadays, tasteful live music frequently complements the soft lighting, warm brass rails, and soft leather chairs that imbue a hush-hush ambiance.
Daily 4.30pm-1.30am. 1/F, St. Regis Hotel Beijing, 21 Jianguomenwai Dajie, Dongcheng District. (6466 2288) 记者吧，东城区建国门外大街21号北京国际俱乐部饭店1层

Propaganda This longstanding nightclub is frequented by an army of loyal patrons, most of them students, and most of them looking for booty, or to shake some. Expect to hear Tupac's "California Love" at least three times on always-crowded weekends.
Mon-Fri 8pm-4.30am, Sat-Sun 8pm-5am. 100m north of the east gate of Huaqing Jiayuan, Wudaokou, Haidian District. (8286 3991) 海淀区五道口华清嘉园东门往北100米

Pure Girl Pure is probably the last adjective you'd use to describe this place: The clientele are anything but, and the pricing of the RMB 5 shooters is proportional to the amount of real alcohol used. However, for those on a shoestring budget and anyone who is resigned to cirrhosis, Pure Girl is a worthy launch pad for an evening on the tiles. This, the original Pure Girl, is the northernmost one. (See Sidebar p280)
Daily 6pm-late. Sanlitun Houjie (opposite Tongli Studio), Chaoyang District. (no tel) 清纯女孩酒吧，朝阳区三里屯后街同里对面

Pure Girl, Pure Girl and Pure Girl 2 Adjust your eyes, citizen, to the future of Beijing's bar scene. Where every bar is named Pure Girl. This dream will only become a reality if you ignore their obviously knockoff liquor and drink, drink, DRINK!
Daily 6pm-late. Sanlitun Houjie (opposite Tongli Studio). (no tel) 清纯女孩酒吧和清纯女孩2号酒吧，三里屯后街同里对面

Q Bar The latest home of popular bartenders George and Echo, this classy and well-decorated establishment is set atop the incongruously mediocre Eastern Inn on South Sanlitun Street. Q Bar offers quality nu-jazz tunes, top-notch cocktails (ask for a George Special) and a spacious, well-treed rooftop patio. Voted "Best Cocktails" in *that's Beijing*'s 2007 Reader Bar & Club Awards.
Daily 6pm-2am. On the top floor of Eastern Inn Hotel, 100m south of Beer Mania, Nansanlitun Lu, Chaoyang District. (6595 9239) www.qbarbeijing. com 朝阳区南三里屯路逸羽酒店顶层（Beer Mania 南100米）

The Red Club Cabaret shows most nights, karaoke, and ample space to stretch out.
Daily 8pm-2am. 2/F, 4 Dongzhimen Nandajie, Dongcheng. (6534 0986) 红调酒吧，东城区东直门南大街4号，东方银座西门向南200米

NIGHTLIFE

Red Rock Bar It isn't so much the place but the clientele that give this shady bar its nickname "Rock Bottom." Come in the wee hours and witness Wudaokou's drunkards pouring in for the cheapest fried chicken this side of the track.
Daily 5pm-2am. North of the east gate of Huaqing Jiayuan, Wudaokou, Haidian District. (8286 3665) 来则来，海淀区五道口华清嘉园东门以北

Redmoon This classy Grand Hyatt spot includes a wine bar, sushi bar, cigar lounge and live music, all sleekly tailored to the executive set.
Sun-Thu 5pm-1am, Fri-Sat 5pm-2am. 1/F, Grand Hyatt Hotel, Beijing Oriental Plaza, 1 Dong Chang'an Dajie, Dongcheng District. (6510 9366) 东方亮，东城区东长安街1号东方君悦酒店大厅

Reggio Hey, did you know this is a lesbian bar? That's why there are no boys here! With comfy red couches and a mellow vibe, this is a great spot to come even midweek and surf the web while chatting over a beer. Want to have your wedding here? You wouldn't be the first.
Daily 2pm-2am. 300m south of the Wudaokou light rail station, Haidian District. (8262-1516) 五道口城铁站南300米

The Rickshaw The Rickshaw brings us something that most of over-produced Sanlitun doesn't: a comfortable, cheerful place to kick back with friends and a cold beer. This welcome addition to Kris Ryan's Sanlitun empire takes the yummy fare offered at Saddle and adds pizza, all-day breakfast, and best of all, fried Snickers. Upstairs you can find a balcony, a pool table, a number of flat screen televisions. Downstairs provides a cozy area with wireless to enjoy coffee on plush sofas, and a garden terrace with beer-pong.
Daily 24 hrs. Nansanlitun Lu (north of the turn-off to The Bookworm), Chaoyang District. (6500 4330) 朝阳区南三里屯路

Salsa Caribe A Latin dance club with a pirate theme, Salsa Caribe is a raucous house of sweat, sin and extremely tight pants. Facilities are excellent, with a central dance floor, high-tech DJ booth, and house band.
Daily 7.30pm-late. Area 4, Gongti Beilu, (across from The Loft), Chaoyang District. (6507 7821) www.caribechina.com 卡利宾拉丁舞俱乐部，朝阳区工体北路4号院（藏酷对面）

Salud Beloved Salud, one of Nanluogu Xiang's worthiest restaurant/bars, serves tapas, excellent sangria (only RMB 15 per glass) and a selection of homemade infused rums in such flavors as coconut, apple cinnamon, and orange (RMB 20 per glass). Its kind staff, tasteful decor, and live music events round out its appeal.
Daily 3pm-2am. 66 Nanluogu Xiang, Dongcheng District. (6402 5086) 老伍，东城区南锣鼓巷66号

Sangria Bar Having started life as a tavern with a vaguely Iberian ambiance, Sangria has transformed itself into arguably the best sports bar in Beijing. They show a wide range of sports on multiple screens, as well as offering decent food, German ales and, indeed, a fine glass of Sangria.
Daily 4pm-late. Haoyun Jie (next to Elisa's Italian Restaurant), 29 Zaoying Lu, Chaoyang District. (5867 0248) 桑格丽雅酒吧，朝阳区枣营路29号好运街

Sanlitun Bar Strip Since the dawn of time (late '90s) the Sanlitun Bar Strip (a.k.a. "The Gauntlet") has attracted credulous tourists and callow locals to its neon peep show. We'd name all the bars on this strip (we've done it before), but this year, gentle readers, in the event of a discretion digression, we invite you to explore at your own risk.
Daily noon-late. Sanlitun Lu. "酒吧街" 三里屯路

Seven Colors A mostly local crowd, with karaoke and drag show nightly. Look for a neon sign reading "Happy Together" behind the hotel entrance.
Daily 7pm-6am. Huatai Hotel, 200m south of Jinsong Qiao, Jinsong Dongkou, Chaoyang District. (8772-0166, 6773-5632) www.7sebar.com 七色，朝阳区劲松东口北京华泰饭店，劲松桥往南路西200米

Shooters A slightly classier alternative to the other budget Sanlitun favorites like Poachers, Kai and Pure Girl. As the name suggests, Shooters boasts a variety of, well, shooters for RMB 10 each, plus decent mixed drinks and cocktails. "Outstanding for Cheap Drinks" in the 2007 Bars and Clubs Awards.
Sun-Thu 6pm-2am, Fri-Sat 6pm-4am. Bldg 40, 5 Sanlitun Houjie (opposite Fish Nation), Chaoyang District. (6416 3726) 朝阳区三里屯后街5号40号楼（鱼邦对面）

Sino-Chu Offering decent, well-priced European fare, this cozy bar comes alive on Sunday nights with Beijing Tango's weekly milongas.
Daily 24hrs. 18 Liangmahe Nanlu (behind the Australian Embassy), Dongcheng District. (8532 2418) 亮马河红酒屋，东城区东直门外大街亮马河南路18号

SLD (Sulede) You wouldn't come to this Mongolian bar south of the ethnic minorities college for the atmosphere; it's about the size of a large newspaper stand. And you wouldn't go for the mixology; a whiskey-coke can sometimes net you a whiskey-sprite. You come to this bar to hear the nightly, mighty Mongolian folk-rock band, whose throat-singing and horse-head fiddle take you right out of Beijing and into the wide, starlit grasslands.
Daily 6pm-2am. 66 Minzu Daxue Xilu, Haidian District. (6893 8903) 苏勒德音乐酒吧，海淀区民族大学西路66号

Souk For description and address, see Restaurant Directory under Middle Eastern, p82

The Star Live For description and address, see "Live Music Venues," p344

Stone Boat Cafe For description and address, see "Live Music Venues" p344

Sunset Grill Alternatively known as Sunset Cafe, Sunset Bar, and Sunset Grill Bar, this is, as they say, all 4 the Beer Lovers. Opened by Sammy, the man who brought you Bus Bar, Sunset Grill has the cheapest draft beer in the city. Starting at RMB 2 in the afternoon when daytime boozers bring their own music, rising to RMB 5 in evenings, and climbing to RMB 10 for early morning, the beers are Tsingtao and fresh. Do not expect a grill.
Daily 2.30pm-late. Xingfucun Zhonglu (across from Chaoyang Experimental Elementary School), Chaoyang District. (131 4133 3018) 凤凰咖啡，朝阳区幸福村中路（朝阳实验小学对面）

Tango The original, larger Yonghegong location boasts a vast dance floor, a chillout lounge called Mango on the second floor and KTV suites in the basement, but it is best known for bringing some of Beijing's most highly-rated DJs to Beijing. The third floor of the building is home to live music venue Star Live (see Live Music Venues,

Kriek, Kwak, Delirium Tremens – when it comes to Belgian beer, your cup overfloweth at The Tree

p344). The second venue at Gongti Xilu is a behemoth underground KTV city (See Karaoke Joints, p322).
Daily 24 hours. South Gate of Ditan Park (next to Jindingxuan restaurant), Dongcheng District. (6428 2288) www.tanguo.com 糖果，东城区地坛公园南门

Tim's Texas Roadhouse From Texaco signs to steer skulls, Lone Star State memorabilia cover every corner of this sequel to Tim's Texas BBQ (located at Silk Street 2). The stuffed jalapeños (RMB 25) with pungent flavors and oozing with warm cream cheese hit the bulls-eye, as do their margaritas (RMB 45). They also have a pool table, dartboards, and a stage for some good ol' country singing. Hosts Texas Hold'em nights.
Sun-Wed 11am-11pm, Thu-Sat 11am-2am. 2 Tianze Lu, Xingba Lu, Chaoyang District. (6461 1141) 西部牛仔餐吧，朝阳区星吧路天泽路27号

Together Coffee shop by day and pleasantly scruffy bar by night, Beijing's sole reggae bar reaches out to folks in search of beer and classic Wailers tunes. The brick fireplace keeps customers feeling irie all winter.
Daily 5pm-1am. 500m south of China World Trade Center, east side of Dongsanhuan, Chaoyang District. (8771 4865) 朝阳区国贸向南500米，东三环外侧

Touch Touch occupies most of an old-style courtyard home off the hind-end of Lotus Lane, and has done a good thing with it. The main building sports a little rooftop deck, and the interior yard is glassed in greenhouse-style, including an old tree and a fishbowl worthy of the word "placid."
Daily 2pm-6am. 8 Qianhai Beiyan, Xicheng District. (6618 0809) 接触，西城区前海北沿8号

The Tree This South Street transplant with decade-old roots in Sanlitun has stood strong through the changing winds of fashion. Its consistent popularity with a diverse clientele is attributable to its good service, thin-crust pizza and impressive selection of imported Belgian beer, including Hoegaarden and De Konick on tap. The muted lighting and wood tables make it a convivial place to catch up with friends, except in the back room when the earnest band performs amateurish covers of "Brown Eyed Girl" or "Every Breath You Take." "Best Place to Start the Night" in the *that's Beijing* 2007 Reader Bar & Club Awards.
Mon-Sat 11am-late; Sun 1pm-late. 43 Sanlitun Beijie (100m west of Sanlitun North Bar street, Youyi Youth Hostel, behind Poachers Inn), Chaoyang District. (6415 1954) www.treebeijing.com 隐蔽的树，朝阳区三里屯北街以西100米，Poachers 后面，三里屯医院旁

Vics This dance behemoth has expanded underneath Outback Steakhouse and back up on the other side. DJs play a mix of R&B, pop, soul, reggae and hip hop. Now featuring a "relaxation zone" where minimalist decor combines with trance music. Hosts a popular ladies night, and is a perennial winner of Best Dance Club in the *that's Beijing* Reader Bar & Club Awards.
Daily 8.30pm-late. Inside the north gate of the Workers' Stadium, Chaoyang District. (5293 0333) 威克斯，朝阳区工体北门内

West Wing Bar The West Wing teahouse/bar is a comfortable lesbian-friendly lounge with a bright ground floor filled with tables and a basement room made cozier with sofas, DVD stations and … er … a punching bag.
Daily 2pm-2am. Inside the west end of the Deshengmen Tower, Xicheng District. (8208 2836) 西厢房，西城区德胜门城楼的西边

What? Bar For description and address, see "Live Music Venues" p344

Steps away from the Forbidden City, What? Bar is gloriously unadorned

The World of Suzie Wong Club Suzie's is part 1930s Shanghai opium den and part postmodern lounge. Show up early to ensure a spot on one of the Ming dynasty beds before the ravenous crowds arrive. Ample mixed drinks (featuring daiquiris and the "pineapplicious" Lights of Havana) are RMB 35, and beers go from RMB 25 up. The second-floor dance area is a den of bodies and sweat on weekend nights – find relief on the outdoor patio. Recipient of seven *that's Beijing Reader Bar & Club Awards* in 2007, including "Best After-hours Club" and "Best for People Watching."
Daily 8pm-late. 1A Nongzhanguan Lu (west gate of Chaoyang Park), Chaoyang District. (6500 3377) 苏西黄，朝阳区农展馆路甲1号朝阳公园西门

Writers Bar Aspires to honor the literary luminaries who have stayed at Raffles. Caviar and oysters complement the wide selection of cocktails and cigars.
Daily noon-midnight. Raffles Beijing Hotel, Main Lobby, 33 Dongchang'an Jie, Dongcheng District. (6526 3388 ext 4181) 作家酒吧，东城区东长安街33号，北京饭店莱佛士一层

X'Change Bar A chic bar and lounge with a double volume glass video wall, offering the perfect setting to linger, whether it be for a daytime soiree or for late evening high-energy entertainment with a live band, contemporary DJ sounds and cool, imaginative selections of new and old world wines, spirits and cocktails.
Daily 10.30am-1am. 5/F, InterContinental Hotel, 11 Financial Street, Xicheng District. (5852 5888 ext 5920/5921) 幻吧，西城区金融街11号，金融街洲际酒店

Xin Bar Tucked away just off the main road, near the Drum and Bell towers, this tiny little gem is a cozy place to kick back and relax on a hot summer's night. The jumble of colorful Yunnan decorations complement the bar's distinctly old Beijing feel.
Daily noon-late. 152 Jiugulou Dajie, Xicheng District. (6400 7571) 润心阁，西城区旧鼓楼大街152号

Xuancaotang This little location is placed and designed to be an after-work haven for CBD white-collar workers. Highly trained waiters, separate business rooms, and set lunch menus are perfect for relaxing or conducting business.
Daily 11.30am-4am. Next to the Tianfuyuan Gongyu, Shenlu Jie, Chaoyangmenwai Dajie, Chaoyang District. (8562 2614) 炫草堂，朝阳区朝阳门外大街神路街天福园公寓内

Yuan Dynasty Bar Street A ready-made bar street in the style of Houhai's Lotus Lane, the Yuan Dynasty Bar Street is heavily invested, heavily designed, and more or less devoid of soul. Crowded along the north bank of the Tucheng river is a series of bars with names like Liky, Nest and Climax, adorned with lights and kitsch. The south bank provides a nicely manicured walk past willows and stone balustrades, but as for the north – you have been warned.
North bank of the Tucheng River, immediately north of the Yuan Dynasty Earth Wall Park, north of Beisanhuan Lu, Chaoyang District. 元朝酒吧街，朝阳区往南，元大都土城遗址公园北边，土城河北岸

Yugong Yishan For description and address, see "Live Music Venues" p344

Zeta Bar This lounge and dance club offers eye candy galore, with sherbet oranges and antifreeze blues, groovy chairs and a twisty bar, and a lofty roof zig-zagged by funky spotlights and festooned with enough shiny stuff to keep chrome fetishists in bliss. The default music is house and the drinks focus is on champagne, wine and cocktails, though other beverages are available. At the time of writing, Promen, a professional gay men's group, had its regular Thursday night socials here.
Mon-Thurs 5pm-2am, Fri-Sun 5pm-3am. 2/F, Hilton Beijing, Dongfang Lu, Dongsanhuan Beilu, Chaoyang District. (5865 5050) 颐达吧，朝阳区东三环北路，东方1路，希尔顿饭店2层

PHOTO: JUDY ZHOU

Be Glad!
Out of the closet, into the clubs
by Haley Warden

Rainbow over Beijing

As Beijing becomes a global city, it has begun to recognize the payoffs of being gay-friendly. With greater public acceptance, bars and clubs have moved above-ground and away from a shady past as pick-up joints and money-boy lairs. Destination's undeniable success has led the way for other "alternative" bars in town, a notable addition being Cosmo, Beijing's second largish gay dance venue, which opened in summer 2007. Though the patrons at Cosmo and Destination predominantly carry Y-chromosomes, women (and straight folks) are always welcome to join the rowdy revelry. Love Island, Emperor's Treasure Bar, The Red Club and Seven Colors are great bets for live shows.

Many of Beijing's queer ladies take the party to smaller bars around town: West Wing Bar, located inside the magnificent old city gate at Deshengmen, is a long-standing favorite of Beijing's laid-back lesbians, while "Feng Bar," the Saturday night dance party at Pipe's Cafe, is always hopping with young *lala*s. Numerous lesbian-friendly bars have sprung up in town, including Reggio Cafe, a smoky but comfy joint south of the Wudaokou light rail station, Desert Oasis in Nanluoguxiang, and Chun Yu Ting in Xuanwu. (See directory, p296, for details and addresses of the aforementioned bars.)

For info on LGBTQ social groups and the current scene in China, see Useful Info, p636.

NIGHTLIFE

Frankly Speaking
A chat with Beijing nightlife pioneer turned wine shepherd
by Jim Boyce

Frank Siegel in action: nurturing Beijing's wine community with a smile

Frank and Jennifer Siegel opened Beijing's first non-hotel joint venture bar – **Frank's Place** – in 1990, selling it in the late 1990s, and ran the **John Bull Pub** for a decade, closing it in 2006. They now run two branches of **Sequoia Cafe** (see p64 for details), where Frank organizes Friday night wine tastings.

Insider's Guide to Beijing: What were some of the biggest challenges with opening Frank's?
Frank Siegel: We had problems with the neighbors – they stopped our construction because they wanted a free apartment. We went to the landlord and local government to get it solved, and the landlord basically ended up giving them a place.

In terms of staff, there weren't many bars around and locals wanted to practise English [with customers], so it was relatively easy to find employees. The regulations were easier then than now. They weren't really fixed so you could get things done easily.

IG: Who were your customers?
FS: We only accepted foreign exchange certificates at that time and Chinese didn't have them, so we basically had a lot of Westerners and people from Hong Kong.

IG: What did you have on tap in 1990?
FS: We started with bottles of Beijing draft. The [tap beer] came later and we were the first to have it - I think Mexican Wave was second. San Miguel, out of Hong Kong, was actually the first draft in Beijing. There was no Tsingdao draft then. We didn't have a problem with spirits.

IG: How did John Bull Pub differ from Frank's Place?
FS: That was a bigger project. We were pretty comfortable in China then, but the bureaucracy involved in a joint venture with a big multinational (Allied Domecq) was something we weren't used to.
The main reason we opened was that I wanted to expand and go upscale a bit. The location was relatively close to the British Embassy, so we thought John Bull Pub would be a good fit, though we pulled in a general expatriate crowd.

IG: What's the difference between running a bar then and now?
FS: There is more competition. Back in 1990, we knew everyone, but now the population is more diffused and a lot of that client base lives in Shunyi and outside the city center.

IG: Why did you go into cafes instead of continuing with restaurants/pubs such as Frank's Place and John Bull Pub?
FS: A few reasons – I've been in the bar business a long time and at this point of my life the cafe business has better hours and a better lifestyle. Also, it's a scalable business. Instead of a 200-square-meter bar, you can have cafes of 20 square meters and up, and have numerous branches.

IG: How did you get interested in wine?
FS: Through Beef and Burgundy (a Beijing social group) – I started enjoying wine there and my interest accelerated. I went back to the States (in 1999) for a couple of years, to Seattle, and the major tasting rooms in Washington State were 20 minutes from my house.
The thing I like about wine as opposed to the bar industry is that many women enjoy it and it attracts people from all sorts of cultures – it's really a nice-cross section of people.

IG: What's the scene at your Friday night tastings?
FS: What sets our tastings apart is the casual setting. We have people who know a lot about wine, such as Taillan winemaker Alain Leroux, and they talk to people who don't know as much. People aren't intimidated or afraid to express opinions.

IG: Why haven't you gone into distribution?
FS: Chinese aren't sitting on docks waiting to buy wine. It's a lot of work to sell this stuff. Everyone talks about big companies like ASC and Summergate, but you have a second wave of younger kids coming in and handpicking wines from smaller producers. There are young French or German guys who are passionate about wine, close to the producer, and putting in a lot of effort to knock on doors.

IG: Your wine tastings cover makers from six continents. What are your favorite themes?
FS: The offbeat ones like the Canadian wine and cheese tasting or the Livermore, California tasting – that last one was fun because I'm familiar with the area. I liked the Cabernet Franc tasting because it's an unusual variety for Beijing – my tasting was probably the first one in the city. And the blind tasting of Argentinean Malbec, since that grape is off of the beaten path.

IG: When you've had a bit too much vino, what's your cure for a hangover?
FS: Drink Gatorade or Pocari Sweat and then go to the gym. It's painful, but it works.

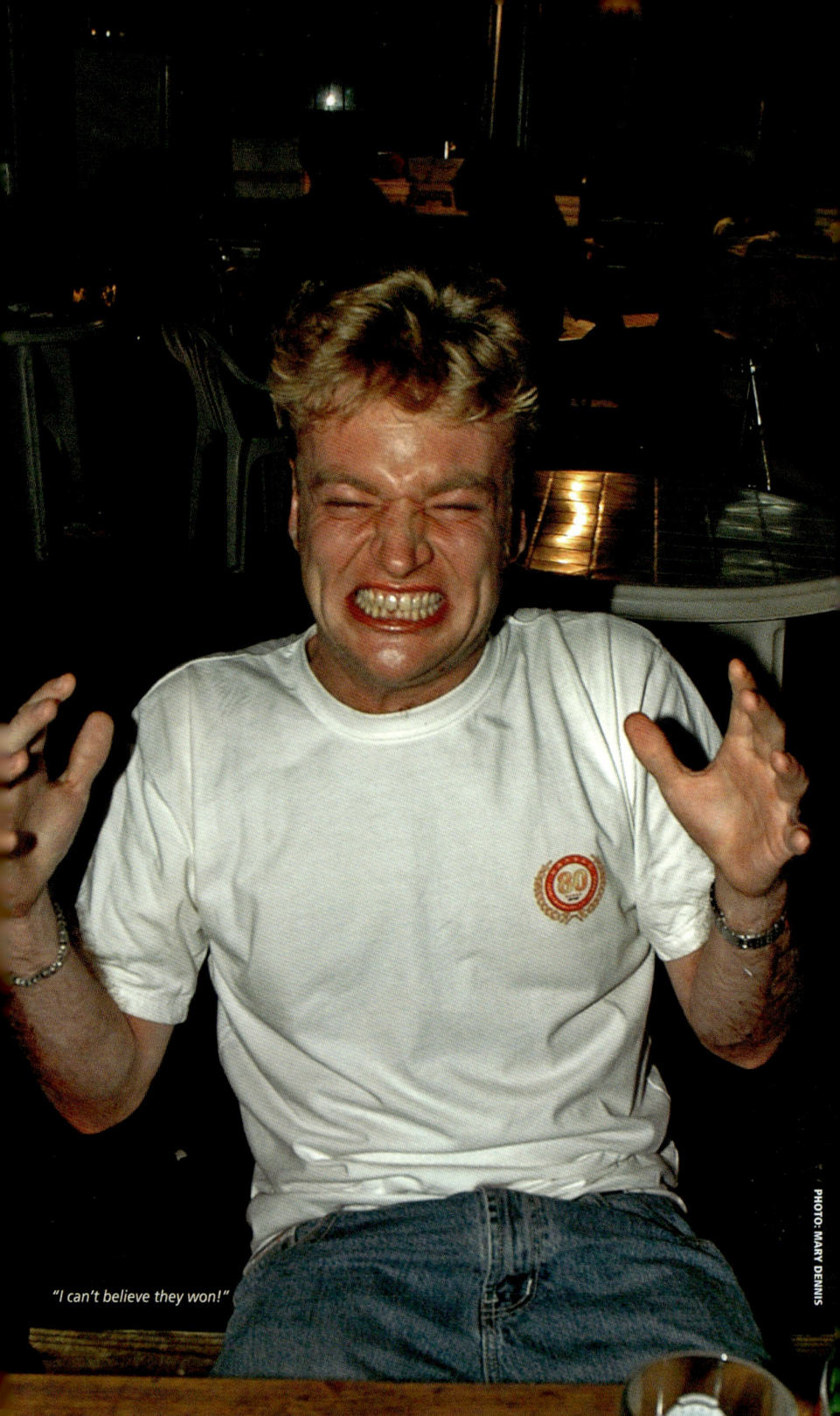

"I can't believe they won!"

Toast of the Town
that's Beijing 2007 Reader Bar & Club Awards

Every year, *that's Beijing*, our sister publication, gives readers the chance to cast votes and shower praise and happy thoughts upon the best-of-the-best nighttime haunts in town. Over 2,500 *that's Beijing* readers were suitably motivated to vote in the 2007 Reader Bar & Club Awards (that's a whopping 1,000 more than in 2006), testament, perhaps, to just how important pubs, clubs, discos and dives are to us here in Beijing. Or we're just a bunch of incurable alcoholics. I'll drink to that.

So, without further ado, let's raise a glass to Beijing's best boozers. Note: All venues mentioned are listed in this chapter's Bar & Club Directory.

Up-and-coming bands like Hedgehog have helped make D-22 a rockin' yaogun *clubhouse*

The gong-banging guys of China Doll are the new kids on the block

Best New Bar
China Doll
Bursting onto the scene late last year, China Doll brought a little extra class to Sanlitun. Readers appreciate its signature cocktails and sexy decor (courtesy of Epic Design), but China Doll's real strength lies in its ability to attract expat and Chinese clientele in equal measure, embodying the values of the modern Beijing club scene.

Runners-Up
MAO Livehouse
The Rickshaw

Best Place to Start the Night
The Tree
The perfect precursor to a night out, this leafy sanctuary tucked away from the rest of the bustle of Sanlitun is acclaimed for two things: great pizza and Belgian beer. When you do decide to move on from The Tree, you'll find yourself contentedly bloated and perfectly placed to go off in search of whatever the rest of the night holds for you.

Runners-Up
Aperitivo
The Rickshaw

Best Happy Hour
Bar Blu
What's more fun than happy hour? Happy hour with a remote control! Press the button and drinks are 2 for 1, press it again and you've won a free drink. You can't lose with Bar Blu's happy hour, especially with their generously-sized mixed drinks and couches long enough to lie down on if you've overplayed your hand.

Runners-Up
Centro
The Rickshaw

Best Outdoor Terrace
Kokomo
Kokomo has enjoyed a resurgence of popularity since its makeover last year, which saw it adopt an inclination for all things Cajun. The tropical feel certainly complements Beijing's hot summer months, when bar-goers flock to enjoy Beijing's developing skyline with a well-made cocktail in their clammy grasp.

Runners-Up
Bar Blu
The World of Suzie Wong Club

PHOTO: LUNA ZHANG

INSIDER'S GUIDE TO BEIJING

Not ready for slumber? Head to Bed!

Best Business Networking
Centro
Located a stone's throw from the CBD, our readers cite Centro as the perfect place for rubbing elbows and clinching deals, the third time they've done so in as many years. With wine, cigars and cocktails on hand, work has never been so much fun.

Runners-Up
Aria
The Bookworm

Best Place to Find a Date
The World of Suzie Wong Club
Renowned for attracting a diverse crowd of different nationalities, professions and mental histories, chances are you'll bump into your dreamboat at Suzie's. From the chattalicious rooftop terrace to the sweaty dance floor to the nookie lounge – Suzie provides multitudinous options for you and your new friend get to know each other.

Runners-Up
China Doll
Vics

Best Place to Bring a Date
Bed
Lounging in Bed takes dating to a whole different level. Tucked inside a traditional courtyard house, with its comfy *kang*-style beds and great mojitos, this peaceful bar is the perfect spot for deep conversations while light techno plays in the background.

Runners-Up
Face
Stone Boat Cafe

Best Bathrooms
Lan
An odd category really, since few of us decide where we're going to go on the strength of a bar's toilets. If we did, we probably wouldn't have come to China in the first place. However, if you're really the kind who judges a place by where you lay a cable, then check out the porcelain beauties at Lan.

Runners-Up
The World of Suzie Wong Club
Zeta

PHOTO: SIMON LIM

NIGHTLIFE

A fourth-quarter touchdown at the Goose 'n' Duck. But will he get the Heisman?

Best Regular Event/Party
'80s Night at Alfa
So what if the DJs take a broad interpretation of the '80s? It's hard to complain when you're busy doing the running man to "I Got the Power." This is one place where your power dance moves will be appreciated, not just tolerated.

Runners-Up
Sundays On Top: Kokomo
Ladies' Night: Suzie Wong's

Best Live Music
Yugong Yishan
Yugong Yishan took the live music crown in August 2007 for the fourth year in a row. It was a bittersweet win, as the same month saw the demolition of the original venue and all the shared memories of drunken rock & roll nights. But don't worry – the music ain't over yet; here's to year number five in a new guise.

Runners-Up
D-22
MAO Livehouse
Stone Boat Cafe

Best Service
Centro
Beijing's service industry is still lagging behind London, New York, Shanghai, Vancouver, Queenstown, Jakarta, Rio de Janeiro, Los Angeles, Mexico City, Kathmandu, Kinshasa and Baghdad. But according to our readers, Centro manages to maintain happily high standards when it comes to bringing us our tipple on time.

Runners-Up
Lan
Press Club Bar
The Tree

Best Sports Bar
Goose 'n' Duck
The original venue by Chaoyang Park west still packs 'em in, sports fans can now wander over to Green Lake International Tower east of Chaoyang Park's East Gate, where two floors of pool, darts and the long-awaited games center (batting cage!) makes the G'n'D a strong contender for next year's honors.

Runners-Up
Browns (closed)
The Den

PHOTO: SIMON LIM

INSIDER'S GUIDE TO BEIJING

Steamy Suzie's: an ogler's delight

Best Dance Club
Vics
Those who like their clubs hot and heavy have collectively voted that Vics is the best place to head for some good ol' hormone-charged, body-rubbin' fun. With a mix of hip-hop, R&B, pop, reggae and soul, the DJs have got everyone in the house shaking it like a Polaroid picture.

Runners-Up
China Doll
Latinos

Best Decor
Lan
The popularity of Philippe Starck's 54,000 square-foot Beijing interior design masterpiece shows no signs of waning. The hyper-ornate space is brimming with Starck originals, such as the infinitely long tables and sofas and the signature eagle-headed throne. Dress your best when you show up to mingle with A-listers at this glamorous bar.

Runners-Up
Bed
China Doll

Best Night Away from the Kids
The Tree
Leave the kids with the *ayi*, or pack them off to Nanjie, and head for the coziest watering hole in town. A great place to wind down with a Belgian draft after work, or simply to have a tête-à-tête with your significant other.

Runners-Up
Centro
Face
Latinos

Best for People Watching
The World of Suzie Wong Club
Just for the record, to watch someone you must spend over 7.5 seconds looking at them. Any less and you're just glancing at them or, even worse, you're spotting them. But in the cozy *kang* cubbies or under the mesmerizing lights of the dance floor at Suzie Wong's, you'll have plenty of time to feast your eyes.

Runners-Up
Centro
China Doll
Vics

PHOTO: MARY DENNIS

NIGHTLIFE

Eskimo kisses aren't on the Lush menu, but Mud Pie is

Best Cocktails
Q Bar

Q Bar remains one of the city's most valuable refuges – from the noise and smog of street-side life, and from inadequate drinks. You'll snort at paying RMB 15 for a Tsingtao or 20 for a cheap martini elsewhere, but as you chill on the terrace at Q, you won't resent a single *fen* spent on that icy-cold RMB 55 lychee daiquiri. Bargain.

Runners-Up
Centro
Kokomo

Best Wine Selection
Centro

Centro has a plethora of tasty vintages, as well as an impressive champagne selection – in fact, Centro is the top seller of champagne in Beijing, and is second only to Shanghai's Bar Rouge in all of China.

Runners-Up
Aria
La Baie des Anges

Best for Cheap Drinks
Nanjie

With beers at RMB 10 a pop, and racks of shooters barely making a dent in patrons' weekly pocket money allowance, Nanjie remains the people's choice as best for getting smashed on the equivalent of your bus fare home.

Runners-Up
Kai Club
Shooters

Best Student Hangout
Lush

It's impossible to make it through a weekend night at Lush without hearing a Sublime cover. Then again, who doesn't love a Sublime cover, coupled with hookah and good eats? We don't hear anyone complaining, especially not the masses of Wudaokou students to whom Lush consistently delivers on its promise of good, relaxed divey fun.

Runners-Up
D-22
Nanjie

Best After-Hours Club
The World of Suzie Wong Club

It's the turning point of many an eventful night in Beijing. Approaching the wee hours, someone lays down the gauntlet: "Let's head over to Susie Wang!"
"You mean, Suzie Wong's?"
"Yeah, whatever."
At this moment, the truly dedicated party animals are distinguished from the Beijing nightlife tourists. Suzie likes to party late. She has a make-out room.

Runners-Up
Bed
China Doll

Bar of the Year
D-22

Hot damn! In a contest that rarely reveals any surprises, this was the biggest one of all. Upsetting the typically upscale, frilly favorite watering holes of Beijing, D-22 is the new punk kid on the block that everyone's got their eye on, proving that keeping it real and doing it for the love matters far more than clean bathrooms, fancy drinks, and the rest – thanks in no small part, of course, to the blossoming of the excellent local bands they've supported and nurtured since before their doors even opened.

Runners-Up
China Doll
The World of Suzie Wong Club

PHOTO: COURTESY OF LUSH

320 INSIDER'S GUIDE TO BEIJING

Live stars perform regularly at Star Live

Editor's Picks
Our penny's worth
Even all 22 categories don't do justice to Beijing's increasingly diverse scene, so the *that's Beijing* and Immersion Guides editors put their heads together and picked a few of their favorites.

Best Place to Shoot Pool
Ball House
Shoot pool and chill out in this beautifully restored *pingfang*. For armchair pool sharks, enjoy a bird's eye view of the game from the open loft space, with a cold beer in hand. Don't be put off if pool's not your thing – a foosball table is on hand to keep your busy hands occupied.

Best Beer
Schindler's
You can go there just to drink, you know. If you do, have the dark draft (*hei zhapi*). 22 *kuai*. 33cl. Nice thin glass. Near beer heaven.

Best Strip of Real Estate that Should be Made Into a Bar District
The wrecking ball looms over the row of warehouses north of the Kerry Centre on Guandongdian, but their distinctively pink exteriors and vaulted ceilings seem to cry out for some creative real estate developers to transform them into an oh-so-hip strip of bars and restaurants, a la New York's Meat Packing District. If and when that happens, we expect royalty checks in the mail.

Best Hormone Bath
Propaganda
Some days, sweaty grinding in a packed house of raunchy students is just what the doctor ordered. Luckily, no matter what day the feeling sneaks up on you – Monday, Tuesday … or the "mainstream" weekend – Propaganda is always there.

Best Unlisted Bar
Gezou
We hesitate to introduce this well-kept secret to you: Gezou, the tiny Japanese bar hidden in Sunshine 100 off Guanghua Lu is our choice for taking the edge off a hard day's night. Not only are the staff hospitable in a way only the Japanese can be, but the bar's handful of homemade snacks will carry you through the limbo between work and your dinner date. The Japanese beer is served in chilled clay mugs.

Best Bar for Dinner
La Baie Des Anges
This low-key wine bar tucked away in the hutongs has personable owners, quality wines, and, best of all, incredible food. The menu barely fills a page, but the crusty baguettes are served warm, the tartines are authentic and the salads fresh and generously proportioned – hardly your average bowl of peanuts.

Club of the Year
The Star Live
You know we couldn't have slept on this place – there might have been a few bumps early in the game, but c'mon: from Ziggy Marley to Sonic Youth, or even XTX to Ziyo (to name just a few) – this is the venue that has truly taken Beijing's scene to the next level.

And Now for Something Completely Different
The mainstream – karaoke!

"O sole mio! ..." Giving Placido Domingo a run for his money

It is joyous human nature. Diva dreams are always lurking below the surface, and combine nicely with the pleasures of drinking, dancing and carrying on. That's why sometimes there's nothing quite like renting a little box of a room with a flock of your best friends or acquaintances – to unleash the Wang Fei or Axl within.

Below are some of our favorite karaoke venues around town. Fortunately, these several holler halls barely scratch the surface of KTV possibilities in Beijing. When you've got a song in your heart, but can't bear to let it out in public without reverb, keep your eyes open. Your neighbor down the hall or the restaurant next door is almost certain to have the equipment you require.

17 Miles KTV A slick choice for Haidian-sequestered soul singers, 17 Miles is cheap and natty.
Daily 11am-6am. Daheng Keji Dasha, 3 Suzhou Jie, Haidian District. (8282 8988) 17英里KTV，海淀区苏州街3号大恒科技大厦

Coco Zen This karaoke joint lurks on basement level one, while a pleasant cocktail bar attends below, and both places are quietly trendy. Japanese through and through, with many a CZ patron working for large electrical and automobile giants.
Daily 7pm-2am. 21 Haoyun Jie, Zaoying Lu, Chaoyang District. (5867 0261) 朝阳区枣营路好运街21号

Go West How could those Xidan hipsters be so hip without a place to let loose their musical passions? Well, of course, they couldn't. Luckily they have Go West. With a Chinese name that's kind of like "gold vault," imagine yourself bathing in a lake of riches and gold a la Scrooge McDuck – the lake of your own golden harmony. Prices per hour range from RMB 49 (for two people in the morning) to RMB 389 for a 20-plus person room in primetime.
Daily 9am-2am. 8-10/F Xidan Xinyidai Shangchang. (6605 1199) www.kingcoo.com 金库，西城区西单新一代商场8至10层

Laser 8000 Reputedly the one place in town where melodists can elaborate their interpretations of Helloween, Megadeth and Dr. Dre. Cozy environs and tasteful color blob decorations gonna get you wailin'. Other amenities include cheap rates, cheap snacks and alcohol and location a few blocks away from Sanlitun. "Accompanied" singing on the third floor. RMB 400 for a small room and RMB 600-800 for a large room the entire night.
Daily 7pm-2am. 18 Xinyuan Jie, Chaoyang District. (8454 2289) 白马江雷射8000，朝阳区新源街18号楼

Melody A brand name you can trust. This popular chain makes up for its higher prices with an above average selection of English songs and the ultimate waiting-for-my-song-to-come time-burner – tambourines.

PHOTO: IMAGINE CHINA

INSIDER'S GUIDE TO BEIJING

Remember to make a reservation, especially in the evenings on weekends, because they're often booked. Otherwise you'll be cooling your heels to the Philippine cover band croonin in the mezzanine – could be worse, I guess ... Small room: RMB 35/hour before 8pm, RMB 109/hour after 8pm.
1) *Daily 8am-2am. A-77 Chaoyangmenwai Dajie (northwest of Landao Dasha), Chaoyang District. (6551 0808)*; 2) *24 Zhongguancun Nandajie (Across from Renmin University), Haidian District. (6218 9088)* 麦乐迪．1）朝阳区朝阳门外大街乙77号(蓝岛大厦西北)．2）海淀区中关村南大街24号(民族大学对面)

Nightman No matter how many times you say "*lai te man*" it just never stops being funny. Dirt-cheap wailin'! Known to have fight club in the parking lot occasionally. Cheapest rates are RMB 8 for a small room and RMB 12 for a large room.
Daily 2pm-6am. 2 Xibahe Nanli, Chaoyang District. (6466 2562) 莱特曼迪斯科广场．朝阳区西坝河南里2号

Partyworld The hottest KTV destination around, also where the city's mando-pop groupies stop in at least once each weekend to sing the latest hits and finish off a few bottles of Chivas and green tea. Rooms start at RMB 49/hour (Mon-Thu 7am-11am) but rise to as much as to RMB 385 (deluxe large room for 15-20 people at peak hour).
1) *Daily 8am-2am. 1/F Fanli Dasha, 22 Chaowai Dajie, Chaoyang District. (6588 3333)*; 2) *Daily 8am-2am. Qunlou, Shengda Dasha, Xizhimenwai Dajie, Xicheng District. (8857 6588)* 3) *Daily 8am-2am. No.1 East Building, Yonghe Dasha, Andingmen Dongdajie, Dongcheng District. (8857 6566)* 钱柜．1）朝阳区朝阳门外大街22号泛利大厦1楼；2）西城区西直门外大街腾达大厦裙楼；3）东城区安定门东大街28号雍和大厦东楼1楼

Tango For a break from your Gongti Xilu bump and grind, dip down into this banshee bin. While most of its mega-club neighbors have KTV-enabled private rooms, many of us prefer not to drop 20 grand every night. This underground KTV city (formerly "Big Echo") is an economical haven by comparison with 39 swanky private rooms and a free buffet from midnight to 2am. Mediocre song selection, but its location – right under the bowling alley – can make for a classy nightlife biathlon.
Daily 24 hours. Worker's Stadium West Gate, 6 Gongti Xi Lu. www.tanguo.com 糖果．朝阳区工体西路6号

Youth Palace The choice of Beijing's teen punk rock set, Youth Palace is both cost effective and looks like Shaft's living room. Fill up on irony here, while you croon to some great authentic videos: Michael Jackson's "Thriller" in its entirety, and The Animals' "House of the Rising Sun." Rooms start at an affordable RMB 15/hour (before 8pm), but can cost as much as RMB 150/hour (deluxe room for 20-30 people at peak hour).
Daily 1pm-6am. 68 Xizhimennei Nanxiaojie, Xicheng District (6618 3593) 青年宫．西城区西直门内南小街68号

"Ahhhhhh love karaoke!"

NIGHTLIFE

The vanguard of the yaogun revolution, Subs, rocked an audience of thousands at the 2006 Oya Festival in Oslo

A Long Strange Trip
Beijing rock goes international
by Berwin Song

Wow, would you believe there are Chinese punks? With mohawks? And they play their own music? Well, it might be a never-ending surprise to *Time* magazine, which, ever since Cui Jian belted out "Nothing To My Name" (*yi wu suoyou*) at Capital Gymnasium 21 years ago, never seems to tire of "breaking" stories about discord and – gasp – rock & roll leaking through the seams of China's tight-fisted culture.

But if you're hip to the scene, you'll know that local music magazines like *Painkiller* and international publications like *The Fader* or *Global Rhythm* run stories concentrating on the strength of the music played by Beijing bands rather than the "novelty" of torn jeans and spiked collars. For in the year 2007, *yaogun* in Beijing is a many-headed hydra, easy to generalize about, but constantly shifting shape right before our eyes – like China itself.

INSIDER'S GUIDE TO BEIJING

In the beginning

Of course, it wasn't always this way. Not so long ago (within most of our lifetimes), music options in Beijing were limited to Peking Opera, the *Yellow River Oratorio*, party hymns, or the guy in the park with the *erhu* – there weren't even *yaogun*-appropriate venues. And while the neat, mythologized version pegs the day China started to rock at May 9, 1986 – the date of Cui Jian's performance – it didn't exactly come out of nowhere. The truth is, it came out of the west.

Yes, the birth of *yaogun* in China would have been impossible without those pesky "foreign devils" (*yangguizi*) – the journalists, early expatriates, foreign diplomats and students whose musical tastes – and cassette tapes – trickled down to China's sheltered youth. In late spring of 1985, Beijing got its first taste of a full-scale Western pop concert in the form of Wham, the Brit pop-cheese duo of George Michael and Andrew Ridgeley, at the Capital Gymnasium. Many local musicians, Lao Cui included, were in attendance, and the experience, to say the least, was formative.

Looking back on those days, Cui Jian says, "I started playing trumpet when I was 14, so actually, I started from Western classical music. But the first time I listened to rock music, I felt, oh this was the kind of music I want to play." Soon enough, impromptu bands were formed, playing everything from bad Beatles covers to their own fledgling tunes. The years that followed saw the emergence of some of *yaogun*'s most seminal rock acts, including Cui Jian's first band Fuyou Shengwu (Plankton). Though the band was short-lived, members of Plankton would go on to form other historical bands: Singer Gao Qi led Overload, the late bassist Zhang Ju became a member of the metal group Tang Dynasty, and guitarist Cao Jun formed Huxi (Breathing). These bands are known today as *lao yaogun* (old rock & roll), a term that, according to Lao Cui, came when he heard the Beatles sing [a version of Chuck Berry's] "Roll Over Beethoven" – which inspired [him] to write a song about the Long March entitled "*Xinchangzheng Lushang de Yaogun*" (Rock & Roll and the New Long March).

"For me," explains Cui, "that is the meaning of rock & roll. The first time I played rock & roll music, I felt I could say no to everybody. 'No, I don't like anything. I'm not like that. I don't agree with you' – it was the start of being a person, to show certain people that I'm different, I'm special. It was a good feeling, because everyone said 'yes' – to traditions, to the politicians, to teachers. I think we were the first generation to say 'no'."

The middle path

By the 1990 Asian Games, the rock scene was rolling, and more bands were garnering serious attention, leading Beijing to its first large-scale Chinese rock concert, featuring Tang Dynasty, pop-rockers Black Panther, and the all-girl punk collective Cobra. The result was incendiary: Tang Dynasty was immediately signed by Rock Records in Taiwan, while Black Panther was picked up by JVC in Japan, both big labels which helped broadcast the mainland sound to the rest of Asia. At the height of this "golden age" of *yaogun*, Black Panther frontman Dou Wei became a fixture of glossy magazines after his high-profile marriage to Mando-pop diva Faye Wong, and his erstwhile celebrity status was proof of a kind that Chinese rock & roll had hit the big time.

Yaogun, of course, was just another byproduct of China's opening to the outside world, and the following years saw an explosion of even more rock genres – there was grunge rock, nu-metal and punk (in flavors ranging from skate to gutter). Elaborately coiffed, hard-charging punk bands such as Brain Failure and Reflector established themselves on the scene, while Hang on the Box took Cobra's riot-grrl lead and started making so much noise that even Marilyn Manson noticed (they also landed on the cover of *Newsweek* in 1999, not necessarily for their music, but more to illustrate a "Wow, China has punks?" piece). Cold Blooded Animal's Xie Tianxiao started Beijing's grunge movement, channeling Kurt Cobain and smashing guitars – a few years behind the rest of the world, of course. Invited to London in 1999, Wild Children emerged as the standard for alt-rock folk types. They turned their base at the South Sanlitun hippie bar River into a folk utopia, which gave rise to bands such as Glamorous Pharmacy and IZ, solo artists such as Wan Xiaoli, Zhao Laoda, and Zhou Yunpeng, and a series of highly coveted *Live at the River Bar* bootlegs.

It was twenty years ago today when Cui Jian (center) taught the kids to play

Boom, boom, boom

In a modern Beijing, with development on overdrive, the music scene reflected the frantically changing times. In the early part of this decade, plenty of bands, musicians and venues came and went – many of the latter fell victim to the wrecking ball (R.I.P. River). But this ferment also produced riotous growth in the number of bands and styles, with everything from pampered middle-schoolers playing death metal, Xinjiang cowboys channeling flamenco, MCs flashing more bling than mic skills, and heaps of Filipino groups playing covers.

If many of these bands were forgettable, several ensuing albums (see Hear Ye, Hear Ye, p338) were produced by newly-emerging Beijing-based labels such as Modern Sky, Scream and Taihe Rye Music (Taihe Maitian). Bands from Beijing also began taking small steps outside of China: in 2001 Cold Blooded Animal (led by Xie Tianxiao) became the first China representatives at South By Southwest in the US, while bands like FM3, PK14, SUBS and Brain Failure toured Europe and North America.

The rock scene has also been galvanized by a number of music festivals. The most prominent, with a reputation throughout China as the highlight of the *yaogun* calendar, is the Midi festival now entering its ninth year. Midi's success has inspired emulators to hold rock pageants in distant provinces, all invariably billed as "China's Woodstock," with uneven results (sometimes the journey is more interesting than the music). While none of these festivals have had the impact that the "three days of peace and music" had on Nixon's America, the best of them, such as 2002's Snow Mountain Music Festival in Yunnan and the "What if Another Twenty Years?" festival in Shenyang in 2006 – to mark the anniversary of Cui Jian's breakout performance – have allowed fans and bands to party, trade musical ideas and bear witness to their growing numbers and clout.

Another (D-)22 years?

High-profile anniversary celebrations aside, 2006 may have been better marked by a series of important developments in the local Beijing scene – most notably, the emergence of the music venue D-22 in Wudaokou (see sidebar, p330). A "hardcore music dive," as described by proprietor Michael Pettis – an economics professor at Beida by day – D-22 became the locus of the new underground, giving a solid, focused front to several movements.

The band that would become known as the first of D-22's many "house bands" was Carsick Cars. It had been at the forefront of a collective of rising young bands, dubbed the "No Beijing" movement by prominent music maven Yan Jun (the tireless organizer of the weekly Waterland Kwanyin experimental music showcases at 2 Kolegas). Among the bands involved in No Beijing were Nezha, the Houhai Sharks and Snapline, each of which began building its reputation at the tiny hole-in-the-wall known as What Bar. The movement culminated in a full tour around China, which ended in defining performances for each band at (the original) Yugong Yishan.

The raw explosiveness and potential of these bands began to reach the ears of the outside world, thanks largely to Pettis' connections. Part-time Beijing resident Blixa Bargeld (of Einstürzende Neubauten fame) took Carsick Cars frontman Jeffray Zhang under his wing, tempering his already abstract sonic experimentation in the direction of controlled noise rock, leading to the formation of White. Several incarnations of the group (which at one point featured a nine-person ensemble, including members of Arrows Made of Desire) eventually gave way to a duo with Shen Jing (aka Shenggy, the drummer of Hang on the Box). A series of fearless performances throughout the year were the talk of Beijing audiences, some of whom saw pure genius in the abstract noise of the duo and others who simply didn't get it. But regardless, White emerged as one of the most important new bands of the year, kicking off Yan Jun's 1+ showcase at D-22, performing a series of noise-driven recitals featuring traditional instruments (the most acclaimed being their *guzheng* performance), and collaborating with every avant-gardist whom Pettis managed to bring through town, including Elliott Sharp, John Myers, and Alvin Curran.

Reality check

All this *yanggui* interest culminated in the arrival in late 2006 of Martin Atkins, the drummer of Public Image Limited and producer of the Chicago-based Invisible Records. Atkins strode onto this burgeoning scene looking for gems in the rough. Practically every young punk band in town with overseas aspirations lined up to strut their stuff for the man, and Atkins left town with hours of live recordings and at least eight Beijing bands signed to Invisible, leaving in his wake disgruntled groups, jealous producers, bickering managers and probably many delusions of grandeur.

What Atkins' ultimate intentions are, and what he will be able to achieve, are still unclear, but his visit reflects the music world's dawning interest in Chinese rock. Prior to leaving Beijing, Atkins had this to say: "Somebody was asking me about the Beijing scene and Chinese bands and blah blah blah, and I was like, fuck off. The bands here are great. And that's it." As for the business end, he confirms, "We signed eight, nine bands [including Snapline and Subs]; we recorded 16 bands in a live situation, eight bands in the studio. So I think I'm able to say that something will happen." And yet Atkins is far from starry-eyed when it comes to the commercial viability of *yaogun* outside China. "Looking at the music business here," Atkins offers, "it's different. Bands are treated differently; but bless 'em, they still want more than maybe they're entitled to. Yeah, I paid a bunch of bands for a live recording. And then you get into 'well, that's not much for a live album.' Right, I'm going to take a live album [from a Chinese band nobody knows] back to the States and ... what? Sell ten? Come on! I don't mean to be insulting, but this is reality."

And yet some local labels are proving – through thoughtful, measured actions, rather than frenzied signing and recording – that Chinese bands can indeed sell overseas. The two-year-old Tag Team Records enjoyed plenty of international success in 2007 (see "A Family Affair," p340), while continuing to invest in Beijing bands along with local stalwarts such as Modern Sky. Meanwhile, an international debut Snapline album seems to be on the horizon, while other local groups are beginning to think of the larger picture. Previously unrecorded bands such as Carsick Cars and Houhai Sharks are planning debut releases, while an official, much-hyped White album is finally ready for release.

Welcome you to Beijing

The recent opening of two new musician-friendly venues has also benefited the scene. Backed by Japanese label Bad News Records, MAO Livehouse boasts a large stage, an excellent sound system, an even better sound engineer and good stage views. More newsworthy still was the launch of The Star Live, which filled the void in Beijing for a mid-sized venue accommodating 1,500 people. True, there were cancellations and promoter complaints in year one. That said, The Star Live attracted foreign acts that never would have come in the past. And when local bands take the stage – and almost every notable local act has – there's no doubt that this venue's slickness and professional feeling inspire genuine performances: while D-22 is the city's neighborhood CBGB hangout space, The Star Live is its Bowery Ballroom.

Thanks to the availability of a suitable space to perform, well-known foreign performers (as opposed to the obscure, but earnest – and usually Scandinavian – acts Beijing hosted when limited to Yugong Yishan) are beginning to include a Beijing date on their Asian tours. Perhaps more importantly, they are being granted performance permits. While it's still a long way from the regular event schedule typical of most international hubs, 2007 certainly marked a huge increase in the quality – and regularity – of acts crossing into the mainland. In quick succession, Ziggy Marley, NOFX, the Roots and Sonic Youth all performed for Beijing during the spring; summer brought younger, hipper acts such as The Infadels, the Go! Team and Yndi Halda – all hosted at The Star Live.

It's also worth noting that even old-time traditions such as Midi have been gradually upping their star power: the 2007 edition of the Midi Festival included a performance by Sweden's Soundtrack of Our Lives – granted, not necessarily a household name in Peoria or Adelaide. And perhaps the clearest sign of Beijing's newfound openness can be found in the 2007 Beijing Pop Festival, whose third edition included Nine Inch Nails, Public Enemy and even Cui Jian, who was finally approved to perform at an outdoor festival in Beijing – in this city's equivalent of Central Park, Chaoyang Park, no less – for the first time in his career.

Ch-ch-changes

Certainly, much of this change has been the product of the shifting attitudes towards *yaogun*. While obtaining permits in the early years involved jumping through many hoops, Midi Festival organizer Zhang Fan reports that "Haidian District has been very good to us" for the past few festivals, even going as far as "renovating [Haidian] park (where the festival is now held) and planting new trees to make the lawn 30 percent bigger." Likewise, the Beijing Pop Festival's brand also carries a certain amount of *guanxi*. "The government definitely recognizes the event as a crucial cultural addition to the events calendar," says festival organizer Jason Magnus. "They understand that it has developed a reputation in and out of China and is now one of Asia's main music festivals. Even the Olympic Committee was involved [in 2007] in supporting us in a variety of ways." Magnus also maintains that securing his often controversial lineups has always been about "giving the correct presentation and focusing on the music and importance of the band."

As for finally getting Cui Jian on stage in an outdoor venue for the first time ever, Magnus acknowledges the power of his international *guanxi*. "I honestly don't know if Cui Jian would have gotten a permit without the Beijing Pop Festival," admits Magnus, "All I can say is that after this gig I hope it will show that there's absolutely no reason to deny him an outdoor permit [in Beijing] in the future." As for Lao Cui himself, he's content to say that his presence at the festival is simply "meant to be," which, given his crazy history throughout *yaogun*'s ups and downs, is probably a pretty good way of looking at things.

Meant to be … ?

In the end, for all the steps Beijing's *yaogun* has taken, there's still a realness and innocence to it all that even the greenest of music followers can experience. Walk into any one of Beijing's venues (see "Live Alive," p342): At Jiangjinjiu Bar, you'll find yourself five feet away from the stage; or, you might catch laughing, smiling Kang Mao of Subs having a pre-show drink at MAO Livehouse before ripping into the scariest, sexiest performance you've seen since the 1970s punk scene. Even the great Cui Jian is easily approachable – you might catch him cooling out at the East Shore Live Jazz Cafe on the weekend, listening to his bandmate Liu Yuan playing some light jazz. On the other side of town at D-22, there's bound to be plenty of musicians in the house on any given night. One by one, they'll trickle into the upstairs ready room, affectionately (or rather, haphazardly) dubbed "Henry's Room," even if they're not performing that night. And when they look up and see you, and invite you to share a smoke or have a beer, you'll realize, hey, maybe you're in the middle of something pretty special.

Festive Ideology
Midi continues to define the Chinese rock festival
by Berwin Song

Eight years ago, the Midi music school held a student showcase, and started a tradition that would turn into the longest-running rock festival in China. "The first festival was just for fun," the director, Zhang Fan, says. "I remember it like it was yesterday – there was free entry, free beer, about 800 people [on each of the two days], all in the school concert hall … it was like a crazy college house party!" Two years later, Midi moved outside, claiming the title of the first outdoor rock festival in China, and by 2003, the crowds had expanded beyond the capacity of the campus. Even though the 2003 event was postponed until October because of SARS, 43 bands played, and 4,000 people showed up each day.

Midi is the keynote event of the musical calendar

Zhang remembers the 2003 festival fondly: "The happiest moment for me was when the audience rushed the stages and started shaking their booties with the band. We called it a Utopian party – in the evenings, people could camp out at the school." In 2005, the festival expanded yet again, to Haidian Park. Two more stages were added and the crowd swelled to 7,000 per day. As the festival's fame and popularity continues to burgeon year after year, Zhang Fan has been looking towards the Olympic Park as a suitable future site for when the festival outgrows Haidian Park. That day may come soon – the 2007 festival saw about 20,000 visitors each day for four days.

The Midi Modern Music Festival is huge news for youth culture from Xinjiang to Hong Kong. Fans come from the most remote corners of China to attend. "Midi is special because of the young people," Zhang says with conviction. "This festival is about freedom. That's why we keep it cheap, why we try to minimize the police presence. I always talk first with the police bureau and tell them about the festival. I explain what the festival is, why people are there … why it's okay to let kids up in front of the stage, why it's better not to have chairs, why it's even okay for them to drink." According to Zhang, the Haidian government is supportive of the festival: "Haidian is beginning to be seen as the arts and culture district and Midi is an important part of that."

Aside from its significance in China's cultural scene, Midi also makes an effort to spread environmental awareness: A connection with Greenpeace in 2007 followed in the tradition of past Midi themes, like 2003's Protection of Animals and 2005's Protect China's Rivers and Lakes. "Greenpeace's message is something that we must spread to all of our countrymen," Zhang says.

The 2007 festival featured over 70 Chinese acts and 20 overseas bands on five stages, as well as the festival's famous flea market, which has become as much of a headliner as any band on the bill. At the market, enthusiastic concert-goers buy, sell, trade or craft anything from homemade graphic T-shirts and burned CDs to imported vinyl. Though the government may close down the informal flea market, Zhang Fan insists that the festival will never "go commercial." In line with this ideology, Zhang usually can't provide artist fees for the international bands. "There are plenty of good bands who aren't famous," Zhang says. "Midi is just about good music."

Preparations for the Olympics could mean that the next Midi will have to wait until 2009, but *yaogun* addicts can still get a dose of the good medicine at a number of live music clubs around town (see "Live Alive," p342).

Invested in Beijing Rock
A closer look at D-22
by Alex Pasternack and Lindsey Newhall

Professor Pettis and Charles Saliba are instrumental in fomenting Beijing's vibrant rock scene, onstage and off

CBGB, The Kitchen, Danceteria ... Michael Pettis, the 50-year old owner of Beijing's punky art-rock club D-22, remembers those hallowed New York venues not as music clubs so much as bohemian foundries, messy delivery rooms for entire musical genres.

Mr. Pettis wouldn't say that his Wudaokou bar D-22 is Beijing's answer to those New York venues. He's too precise and understated to do that. But listen to the way he raves about the up-and-coming acts that are now synonymous with D-22 – Hedgehog, Carsick Cars, PK14, The Scoff, Joyside, and newcomers like IC Girlband, The Gar, The K and Guai Li – and it's clear that for the bands' sake, he's hoping D-22 can be all of those legendary clubs at once.

"We look back at that period in awe now," says Pettis, naming great NY experimenters like Sonic Youth, Swans and Elliott Sharp that he remembers from earlier days in the East Village. "Beijing's not that different now in terms of quality." But Pettis, a 15-year veteran of Wall Street who holds a professorship in finance at Peking University, says crucial backing is harder to find in Beijing. "This isn't a city like New York, where there's so much money available to support the arts. That's what we're trying to do."

Not many people blow their cash on music the way Pettis does. Born and raised in southern Spain to music-fanatic parents, he spouts off his musical loves – Mahler, de la Isla, Coltrane, Johnson, Reich, Reed – as if flying around a record store, grabbing albums at random. After graduating from Columbia University with degrees in finance and development economics (and an unofficial minor in bebop, postbop and rock), a good record collection wasn't enough.

"I wanted to be able to meet and hang out with guys like Arto Lindsay, Alan Vega and Lee Renaldo, who were extraordinary and slightly intimidating people to me," he says. "In New York, respected artists are gods, even long before they become famous, and you can't just meet them by buying them a drink like in Beijing," Pettis says. In 1983, he decided to open a music joint on New York's Avenue C, named SIN Club. During its one-year run, it drew junkies, criminals and New York's post-punk luminaries. Thurston Moore of Sonic Youth was an occasional doorman. "I figured that if I ran a club that programmed nothing but great music, I would be able to meet these guys finally."

Over a decade spent in East Village undergrounds and Wall Street corner offices convinced Pettis he would never leave New York – until he visited the Chinese capital on a week-long vacation in 2001. He flew home, quit his job and, following a narrative familiar to many Westerners half his age, relocated to Beijing to teach at a university. "There's no way you could have the kind of influence in the US or Europe that you can have here," he says. The sheer talent and eagerness he found in his students he also saw in the city's ragtag rock crowd. In 2005, Pettis enlisted Charles Saliba, a friend and fellow Columbia alumnus, to help open a bar smack in the middle of the city's college town. If his New York venture was all about getting close to the scene, D-22 would be more about helping to build it.

"There's going to be a major scene, it's just a question of when it will happen," says Pettis. Clearly he's eager for it to happen soon. A punk entrepreneur, Pettis speaks of nurturing *yaogun* with a focus and zeal borrowed from Wall Street, where he ran the division at Bear Sterns responsible, fittingly enough, for emerging markets. His growth plan for Beijing *yaogun* is simple: resist borrowed international tastes, develop a sense of self-confidence and attract Chinese students, at any cost. "We're doing whatever we can to get our artists out there," adds Saliba, who manages the club. "We're total prostitutes."

That has meant not just publicity campaigns but setting up recording sessions, paying for bands' travel expenses, hiring a handful of young artists as staff, and more. Soon after spotting a young man in a Velvet Underground shirt a few years ago, Pettis taught him guitar chords. Shao Wang, aka Jeffray Zhang, would come to found one of Beijing's best indie acts, the shoegazer Carsick Cars, and still uses Pettis' brother's Gibson SG. "It took him six months to do what I did in six years," says Pettis.

Prioritizing music above all else, the D-22 formula cares as little for mainstream tastes as it does for the bottom line – financially, the club relies on Pettis, who still runs a New York-based hedge fund, and anonymous donations. "If you want the nicest version of a show, this is not really the place to come," the owner says. "But [it is] if you really want to know what Chinese musicians are thinking and doing."

People want to know. Full-throated, beer-and-sweat-soaked rock and punk nights headlined by bands like Joyside and Carsick Cars draw ever larger crowds ripped from across Beijing: foreign and local, young and old, hip and square. Certain head-spinning experimental electronic and jazz nights have been known to match visiting luminaries like Elliott Sharp, Alvin Curran, and Glenn Braca with local musicians; and the place occasionally fills up for acoustic punk shows, one-of-a-kind punk KTV extravaganzas and a thoughtfully themed film series. But the biggest regulars, Pettis and company say, are the artists themselves, the musicians, filmmakers and painters who congregate at D-22 after hours – even after shows at other clubs – to wash beer mugs, hang out, or jam. "Some of those sessions are terrible, as you can imagine," he says. "Some are great."

Either way, the impact on the scene has been tangible. "Self-confidence, that has shot up. The young bands don't just want to sound like their favorite [western] bands. They want their own sound." Though Pettis is adamant that the rock scene needs to break away from its foreign pedigree, foreign recognition is crucial to building confidence. In the summer of 2007, Joyside sold out shows in Germany, while Jeffray Zhang's avant-garde side project White received standing ovations at the Sonar festival in Barcelona. D-22 was on people's lips, Pettis says incredulously.

While this may be the club's glorious moment, Pettis and company are more concerned about the history being written on stage. "The other night we had a punk band here doing crazy stuff with a guitar that I've never heard before," Pettis says. "We hope they reach a point where they can't play here any more."

For more see the *that's Beijing Reader Bar & Club Awards, p315*.

"The bands here are great," says US producer Martin Atkins of groups such as Snapline (above)

Breakout Artists
Beijing's hottest bands
by Berwin Song

The Beijing music scene has come a long way since Cui Jian picked up a guitar. For the generation of bands that emerged in this century, 2007 was indeed "the year Beijing broke," as Michael Pettis put it. They attracted international attention, toured widely, and finally recorded albums and signed contracts. The music being made in Beijing ranges from sweetly mimicked Britpop to extreme black metal, but it's the following bands that define Beijing as China's rock capital and make it a place (and time) about which we might one day gravely say, "I was there." In the meantime, catch these bands live and check out their albums. They're good, the shows are fun, and the scene is ebullient.

Arrows Made of Desire

Led by Dutch-Chinese boy wonder Joewi Verhoeven, who has played in Glen Branca's guitar army, this Tag Team Records' (see "A Family Affair," p340) signee bops around town, offering pure lo-fi alternative rock. the Beck of Beijing. Check out their 2006 debut, *Songs That Sell Fish*, and prepare for the upcoming (tentatively titled) *Songs That Sell Out*, produced by BBC dub-daddy Steve Barker.

Brain Failure 脑浊

The quintessential Beijing gutter punk band, led by frontman Xiao Rong – he of the leopard-print hair. Originally signed to Japan's Bad News Records (the label backing MAO Livehouse), and as a result, breaking internationally – even opening for the Dropkick Murphys during their 2006 US tour – Brain Failure finally offered a domestic release this year on Modern Sky, entitled *Welcome to Beijing*, a remastered version of their Bad News debut.

Carsick Cars

Led by sonic axeman Jeffray Zhang, this was the original band championed by D-22 (see sidebar p330), a power trio that keeps the feedback and squeals within the tight melodies of pop-punk. Though they missed out on one chance to open for Sonic Youth, they're just too good to forget: They've been personally asked to open for SY's upcoming European tour. Sharing two members with Snapline, they've finally released their official debut, featuring the single "Rock and Roll Hero."

Hedgehog 刺猬

The hottest band in town right now plays bright poppy sounds driven by the tiniest, cutest lil' button of a drummer, Atom, while ZO and BoX play perfect pop melodies, some of the catchiest you'll hear anywhere in the world. It's all captured on their forthcoming Modern Sky debut, *Noise Hit World*.

Joyside

It's no secret that these boys like to drink: their bad-boy antics were captured in the award-winning film documentary *Wasted Orient*. Lead singer Bian Yuan stumbles around and slurs his words onstage like he couldn't care less, but the band has tightened up considerably. Full of rich melodies, their latest album, *Booze on Neptune's Dawn*, is by far their finest work, having garnered many accolades in Europe, where it was first released during their 2007 German tour.

Lonely China Day 寂寞.夏.日

Their live show applauded by the *New York Times* and their album voted number two on *Global Rhythm*'s summer '07 list, Tag Team Records' marquee band has been making huge international waves, thanks to frontman Deng Pei's eclectic – yet localized – taste in guitar/computer-driven soundscapes. Check out their distinctive brand of Chinese indie rock on their full-length debut, *Sorrow*, which is perfect for getting washed away in a set of headphones.

PK14

White Paper was one of the best albums of 2005 – and 2007 saw the band through a successful European tour, arriving home to excited fans at all their performances. Led by bespectacled singer Yang Haisong, who sings exclusively in *putonghua* and throws his body around onstage, PK14 is one of those bands that's turning heads in the west – "damn, the Chinese rock like *that*?"

Re-TROS 重塑雕像的权利

This is another rock outfit that gives 110% at every show. Hua Dong performs with a wild rawness that offsets his nonsensical words, and the killer basslines from Liu Min (a cute little girl with a big scary bass) and monster beats will make you forget that you can't understand what Hua is saying. Their not-to-be-missed 2005 release *Cut Off!* captures their accomplished, equally dark and sparse post-punk sound, and it's selling out even in the States, thanks to Re-TROS' 2007 SXSW appearance and first US tour.

Snapline

The first band snapped up by producer Martin Atkins, this tight-knit trio plays drum machine-driven, darkly-poppy dance-rock. They appear destined to break onto the international market in a big way. Fortunately for Beijingers, they haven't forgotten their beloved home crowds, offering a locally-produced CD with the studio-clean versions of all their live favorites honed right here in Beijing.

Subs

The hardest-rocking, loudest-screaming band on the block – seeing this band live is a quintessential Beijing experience. Lead screamer Kang Mao writhes and rants with a sexual rawness you won't find in most bands overseas. Check out their 2006 effort *Down*, which attempts to stuff their live intensity onto a CD ... but of course, doesn't really compare.

Members of Carsick Cars, PK14, Arrows Made of Desire, Joyside and Hedgehog at their group home (aka D-22)

Su Yang 苏阳

The Bob Dylan of Ningxia, Su Yang takes music back to basic folk-singing roots. With an aim to preserve the songs and stories he gathered throughout his native land, he channels songs of the folk, made into his own unique compositions, with a guitar and a powerful voice, captured perfectly on his excellent 13th Month debut, *Able and Virtuous*.

Wan Xiaoli 万晓利

The best example of modern folk, Wan Xiaoli's powerful voice goes from husky melodies to rumbling throat-singing. Hear studio-polished renditions on his 13th Month release, *Everything is Always Okay*, or witness his vocal range on his Modern Sky live disc, *Walk Here, Walk There*.

Xiao He 小河 **/Glamorous Pharmacy** 美好药店

The lead singer of Glamorous Pharmacy has branched off on his own in a big way, taking his experimental yowls and howls on the solo circuit. Now that Nameless Highland is gone (where he performed solo weekly), chances have improved that he will devote more time to his reformed group, now signed to 13th Month Records. Take a listen to Xiao He's Modern Sky solo debut, as well as Glamorous Pharmacy's 2005 effort *Please Blow-Up A Picture of My Little Cousin For Me*.

Other Notable Acts

Hanggai 杭盖

Playing traditional horsehead lap-fiddles and various other strings, these guys perform straight-up Mongolian folk tunes, augmented with throat-singing. Lots of throat-singing. Their 2007 effort is lamely titled *Mongolian Folk Music*.

Houhai Sharks 后海大鲨鱼

We refuse to use their Chinglish moniker Queen Sea Big Shark – c'mon, with a name like that, how are you ever going to break out? – but nevertheless, this upbeat pop-punk quartet is

PHOTO: JUDY ZHOU

INSIDER'S GUIDE TO BEIJING

Carsick Cars' Jeffray Zhang's unorthdox approach to the guitar recalls that of Sonic Youth's Thurston Moore

ready with a new album from Modern Sky and a tight sound, led by an oh-so-cute frontwoman.

IZ
Improvising music based on traditional Kazakh music and instruments, singer Mamer is one of the most respected folk musicians in town, though he's been scarce as of late …

New Pants 新裤子
One of Modern Sky's most popular acts, these guys went through a hipster-disco rock-pop makeover with their latest album, *Dragon Tiger Panacea*, a video of which was run on Beijing buses.

Nogabe
Why this band isn't playing to packed houses around the world is a mystery. Frontman Nogabe Randriaharmala, a Beijing resident since the early 80s, was one of the prime movers on the local *yaogun* scene, though his music harkens back to the traditions of his Madagascar home. Run, don't walk, to the band's gigs.

Recycle 再循环
Not to be confused with that other, older, R-starting skate punk band, these guys have been making their voices heard on the scene, even landing an opening slot at NOFX's 2007 Beijing gig.

Reflector
Together for over a decade, this skate-punk outfit remains one of the city's tightest and hardest rocking.

Ruins 废墟
A band that can blow the roof off a room, Ruins plays a captivating brand of spacey rock that has been likened to Radiohead, Pink Floyd and Mogwai.

Ziyo 自游
Now fully recovered and fully signed to Warner, this female-led rock outfit is back, playing their accomplished pop-rock on the local circuit. When the album will be ready, though, is anyone's guess …

Yaogun Meets the World
Subs on the road in Nordic Europe
by Jon Campbell

Guitarist Wu Hao and his band Subs sank Scandinavia with their rock torpedo

I think I was sitting at a table on a medieval farm somewhere in very western Norway in August, 2006, when I first thought that maybe Chinese rock is, in fact, the way to go. The Subs and I were being served a farm-fresh breakfast by a woman in Viking-farmer period costume, some of us picking berries that we soon added to homemade vanilla sauce. We'd been on the road for 35 days or so, and had 25 more to go. It had been a long and hard road, full of car trouble, fast food, and the floors of far too many Nordic crash pads. Oh yeah, and some great gigs with audiences across Nordic Europe discovering that Subs – and, by extension, China – could, in fact, rock.

Long one of Beijing's favorite rock acts, Subs are known for their high-energy punk- and garage-tinged rock and inspiring live shows. Formed in 2002 and comprised of Kang Mao on vocals, Wu Hao on guitar, Zhang Shun on drums and Zhu Lei on bass, the band got their first overseas opportunity in the summer of 2005 at Oslo's Oya Festival (followed by a small tour of Norway and Finland). In October, 2005, an invitation to an Amsterdam festival netted a few gigs in Germany as well. The summer of 2006 was the Big One: eight weeks, four countries, twenty-seven cities, thirty-two gigs.

It wasn't all antique Viking farmhouses, though; nor was it all waterskiing (Swedish punk festival), boat trips (Helsinki and Oslo), and fishing (Karlsoy and Bygstad). There were also the rigors of the road: fatigue, long drives, roadside fast food, and – to the supreme concern of the band that'd loaded up most of a suitcase with *fangbianmian* – a diminishing stock of instant noodles. And as the one non-punk member of the crew, I didn't relish, as did the band, the gigs in dilapidated squat-venues like the abandoned fire station outside Helsinki, where punks came from miles around to show their support for Anarchist Action.

Though we loved our van, an early-90s beast of a VW we named Xiao Bai, you put any five people together in close quarters and there are bound to be Problems. But *yaogun* is larger than any interpersonal rock rifts, and Subs were on a mission, whether or not they realized it. Guys like me and the members of the *yaogun* delegations I've been a part of can talk about it all we want, but until a band like Subs hits the stage, it's hard for anyone to conceive of China, let alone Chinese rock music. Subs' mission: letting people know that *yaogun* looks a lot like rock.

The nice thing about the general lack of knowledge about China is that curiosity brings people out. The flipside, though, is that since nobody really knows much about China, much of the band's offstage time was spent explaining it. Interview topics included the perceived oppression that every Chinese citizen *must* face on a daily basis, and even, in one case, the one-child policy. "Japan" and "China" were often used interchangeably.

It's one thing for a local paper not to delve too deep, but Kang Mao's frustrations over having to answer China questions came to a head when these were posed by a semi-legendary punk-rock interviewer. "That's it?!" Kang Mao asked. "You could've asked any Chinese person those questions. You didn't need to ask us."

But Subs know that they're not just a China band: Their tour poster in 2006 featured an exasperated panda trying to throw off traditional clothing and the question: "Why must we say we are made in China?"

They must, for now. Changing from a China band to a rock band is a slow process, but there's good news: "We felt that the audience, when they were jumping around … they didn't see us as Chinese, or Japanese or whatever," recalled Kang Mao. "They saw us as a punk band. And even more, they liked us."

People across the region were moved by the rawness of the performances, saying how it'd been years since they'd seen a band that was so truly "rock," that brought back the spirit of the old days of punk, of rock, of live music in general. One guy in Tampere, Finland, was at a loss for words: "These guys … I felt it. They had … *something*. It brought me back. They came all the way from China! And they had *it*." One Norwegian paper said that the band was playing music "so real, it might seem fake to the typical audience, but music snobs will probably recognize them as the real deal." In every city we were told that the local audiences never reacted to anyone like they reacted to Subs. A chance to see The Exotic up close may have brought them in the door in the first place, but the music kept them there. Mission accomplished? It's a start.

Visit Subs online (Subs.blogcn.com, www.myspace.com/Subsband) or relive the '06 tour on Jon Campbell's blog (http://ygtwo.com/Subsnordictour06/Subsnordictour06.html)

Hear Ye, Hear Ye
Yaogun classics
by Berwin Song

Cui Jian 崔健: *Rock & Roll on the New Long March* 新长征路上的摇滚 **(1986)**
The recording that captured the birth of *yaogun*.

Tang Dynasty 唐朝: *Tang Dynasty* 唐朝 **(1992)**
Combines old school heavy metal riffs with elements of traditional Chinese opera, including poetic lyrics. The title track is a bona fide Chinese metal classic.

Cobra 眼镜蛇: *Hypocrisy* **(1994)**
The album that proved women could rock as much as men – paving the way for a new generation of Chinese riot-grrrls.

Dou Wei 窦唯: *Black Dream* 黑梦 **(1994)**
Better than any metal-derived effort of his band Black Panther, this album established singer Dou Wei as Beijing's erstwhile rock figurehead.

Zhang Chu 张楚: *Shameful Being Left Alone* 孤独的人是可耻的 **(1994)**
A quiet and contemplative alternative to the anger and the noise of Dou Wei and He Yong, Zhang Chu's Rock Record labelmates from Tang Dynasty.

Overload 超载: *Overload* 超载 **(1996)**
China's first and finest thrash metal release was made in a time before singer Gao Qi sold out, pursuing a sideline career in soap operas.

Wild Children 野孩子: *Yellow River Ballad* 黄河谣 **(1997)**
An album of central plains-style folk classics from Beijing's most influential folk band, re-released in 2006, two years after the tragic passing of lead singer Xiao Suo.

Zi Yue 子曰: *The First Chapter* 第一册 **(1997)**
Produced by Cui Jian, *Diyi Ban* introduced the wildest band to ever come out of Tianjin, featuring their brand of crazy, cross-talking prog-rock.

V/A: *Wuliao Contingent* 聊 **(1998)**
A classic collection from Scream Records, featuring sounds from the bored punk underground of Wudaokou in the late '90s: Reflector, Brain Failure, Hang on the Box and more.

Ma Music 麻音乐: *The Insulted Pose* 被侮辱的姿势 **(1999)**
The first offering from Glamorous Pharmacy, Ruins and Wood Pushing Melon, this collection documents some of Beijing's finest early experimental rock.

Cold Blooded Animal 冷血动物: *Cold Blooded Animal* 冷血动物 **(2000)**
Grunge lives on in Beijing through this album by this defunct collective, lead by frontman Xie Tianxiao, now known as XTX.

IZ: *Live at the River Bar* **(2003)**
One of the final recordings from River Music, capturing an excellent set of improvised traditional Kazakh music from folk-genius Mamer.

Muma 木马: *Yellow Star* **(2003)**
This album established Muma's alternative rock firmly in the mainstream and made the band a staple of the Beijing Pop Festival.

Second Hand Rose 二手玫瑰: *Second Hand Rose* 二手玫瑰 **(2003)**
Faithfully captures the Dongbei crosstalk-meets-acidic-folk-rock outfit at its creative peak, though you'll have to imagine cross-dressing front, er, man Liang Long's visage in your head.

Ruins 废墟: *Glide Like a Leaf* 像叶子一样飞 **(2004)**
An album of gorgeously layered space-rock that instantly placed this band among the top acts in the Beijing scene.

FM3: *The Buddha Box* **(2005)**
Has there been anything more famous to come out of Beijing? Putting China's experimental noise scene on the map … and into a little, perfect stocking-stuffer-sized box with nine sound loops.

New Pants 新裤子: *New Dragon Panacea* 龙虎人丹 **(2006)**
A mainstream transformation, which just happened to produce some of the catchiest dance-rock tunes of 2006.

Nogabe: *Afatra* **(2006)**
A musician sharing his Madagascan guitar skills with Beijing since the first days of *yaogun* – the Ali Farka Toure of China.

Their album Yellow Star won Muma many new fans and invitations to play the Beijing Pop Festival

A Family Affair
The hottest indie label in town, Tag Team Records
by Berwin Song

Lonely China Day's critically acclaimed 2007 US tour was a highlight for Tag Team Records' Matt Kagler

Operating out of a small converted apartment in cozy Ju'er Hutong since 2005, Tag Team Records is Beijing's little label that could. Run by a team of eight, comprised of friends and family, the label represents three of Beijing's most excellent acts: Lonely China Day, Arrows Made of Desire, and Re-TROS. For if 2007 was the year that Beijing music broke, it was also the year that Tag Team Records completely exploded.

Label honcho Matt Kagler, who started Tag Team with his wife, explains. "Initially, Heike (the muscle behind the label) and I wanted Tag Team to be something quite regional, release a few limited edition records on a local level, consign everything ourselves, etc." Then came 2007, and well, "things are pretty cramped at the moment," he says, signaling that their lil' household project label may soon outgrow its hutong hominess – though not quite just yet. "We're looking at a slightly larger hutong office a couple of alleys over."

Certainly, they deserve a bigger office and more, given their list of accomplishments and accolades from around the world. Performance slots at Austin City's world-famous festival, South By Southwest, expanded into a full-blown US tour for LCD and Re-TROS, something Kagler considers one of this year's highlights: "Successfully tour-managing a 7,000 mile jaunt through the US ... certainly up there." The bands turned plenty of heads along the way. Re-TROS was prominently featured in *The Fader* magazine and interviewed on ABC News, while LCD received major props from *New York Times*' critic Jon Pareles. "I think all of us were pretty blown away with the amount of coverage the bands got Stateside," Kagler chuckles. Indeed, the accolades continue to pour in: in recent months, LCD's full-length debut, *Sorrow*, was named in *Global Rhythm* magazine's summer Top Ten albums.

"We have four releases scheduled for the next six months," Kagler reports, which will double the label's catalog. And despite growing at such a rapid rate, he says, "we're trying to keep everything as home-spun/indie as possible. At the same time, we don't necessarily discourage corporate affiliations. We're open to all sorts of opportunities, provided they don't compromise the core of what we (or the bands we represent) hold near and dear." For Kagler, it's all for the love of the music. "We now have eight bands officially on our roster," he explains. "We don't sign anyone we don't have personal relationships with and are extremely selective with regard to who we work with in general. We take a lot of pride in only releasing music we strongly believe in and we are very serious about not working with people we don't feel comfortable with. In other words, our relationships with the bands we represent are not simply 'business'-oriented."

And certainly, Tag Team has been proving it plenty on the home front, constantly organizing local gigs and collaborations. Their second annual CH+INDIE Festival (dubbed "The Wrath of Khan"), a co-production with local mega-label Modern Sky, for example, was easily one of the most critically successful events of the year, putting the emphasis on everything and anything local: from venues (the neighborhood favorite 2 Kolegas), to bands (featuring Subs, Brain Failure, Hedgehog, New Pants and more), to local nonprofits and clubs (veggie societies to independent CD stores).

And while the label has recently made moves in the US market – distributing international versions of LCD's *Sorrow* and Re-TROS's *Cut Off!*, as well as signing indie-rock darlings EVERYBODY (based in Indiana) and Venice is Sinking (of Athens, Georgia) – they continue to orient themselves to the local market. In a surprise move, undaunted by the obstacles that keep plenty of labels hesitant about local releases (rampant piracy and the low cost of CDs to name a few), they're flipping the script on the Chinese market, putting out a few China-only releases from the US-based signees.

"Every time we release a record, it gets more and more exciting," Kagler says. "A lot of work goes into those little plastic boxes with CDs inside of them, and I'm jazzed about all of them. There's actually so much going on right now, it's making all of our heads spin." For future plans, he promises a special Christmas party involving all their recent signees, as well as "a CH+INDIE Fest III: The Search for Spock," and, most immediately, the new Arrows Made of Desire album, featuring production by longtime BBC DJ Steve Barker. "We're all just trying to keep up with this monster we built," he says, "but mostly, it's just great to be a part of a collective which involves all my close friends and family."

Live Alive
Beijing's rockinest music venues
by Berwin Song

Here are Beijing's top live music venues, but be advised that music clubs tend to lead short, brutish lives – even by Beijing standards. To find out about upcoming shows, consult the print or web editions of magazines like *that's Beijing* and *Time Out Beijing*. Of course, musicians and club managers lead complex lives, and shows are sometimes cancelled at the last minute.

The Clarence Clemmons to Cui Jian's Bruce Springsteen, Liu Yuan plays often in his East Shore Live Jazz Cafe

2 Kolegas Now two years old and going strong, this cozy music joint is true to its name in that it is owned and managed by "two good friends," Liu Miao and Gao Feng. Though it's not the flashiest of places, 2 Kolegas is an integral part of the Beijing scene hosting a wide variety of musical genres, from blues and folk to punk and experimental (the celebrated Kwanyin Waterland series is hosted here on Tuesdays). Improbably located in a sylvan drive-in movie complex, 2 Kolegas sets up tables on the grassy patch adjoining the bar in season where patrons can enjoy beer and *chuan'r* under the star(s).
Daily 7pm-late. 21 Liangmaqiao Lu (inside the drive-in movie theater park) north of Chaoyang Park, Chaoyang District. (8196 4820) 两个好朋友，朝阳区亮马桥路21号（燕莎桥往东1500米路北汽车电影院内）

13 Club With better surroundings, but worse music than D-22 just next door, this comfortable joint has persevered by doing what they do best: metal. Owner Liu Lixin, lead guitarist of the thrasher band Ordnance, doesn't seem to care that the music isn't on a par with D-22's – in fact, his club has debuted and nurtured many a young headbanger, many of whom don't play a repeat date. But hey, that's what being loud and not giving a fuck is all about, right?
Daily 6pm-late. 161 Chengfu Lu (Lanqiying Bus Stop, doorway is recessed in a small alley next to Waguan Restaurant), Haidian District. (8261 9213) 13俱乐部，海淀区成府路161号（蓝旗营车站下车，马路南边即是，瓦罐饭馆的西边）

CD Jazz Club Once the city's jazz hotspot, this club has fallen behind the field since Liu Yuan's departure for the East Shore Live Jazz Cafe in '06. Still, you can catch regular performances on the weekend.
Daily 4pm-late. South of the Agricultural Exhibition Hall main gate, Dongsanhuan Lu, Chaoyang District. (6506 8288) CD爵士俱乐部，朝阳区东三环路农展馆大门往南300米

D-22 This cramped, two-story musician's haunt in Wudaokou is making history as the CBGB of Beijing – in less than two years, it has asserted itself as one of the premier live music venues in Beijing and, somewhat surprisingly, been named the city's Bar of the Year by the readers of *that's Beijing*. Benefiting from the munificence and encouragement of owner Michael Pettis, bands flock to the bar even on nights they aren't performing – in fact, between ten and 20 of Beijing's best bands are considered D-22 "house bands," performing at least twice a month, with some musicians even taking regular weekday gigs. The bar's "Punks on Wood" concerts are a chance to hear some of Beijing's most distortion-friendly bands unplugged. (Also see "Invested in Beijing Rock," p330.)
Wed-Sun 7pm-2am. 242 Chengfu Lu (two doors west of 13 Club), Haidian District. (6265 3177) www.d22beijing.com 海淀区成府路242号

East Shore Live Jazz Cafe Appropriately smoky and dark, this cool, lakeside jazz haunt opened by saxophone maestro and Cui Jian bandmate Liu Yuan hosts shows every night of the week. Though the music rarely strays beyond jazz-lite, the musicians are proficient, the drink prices are standard and there's no cover charge. Reservations often required.
Daily 4.30pm-late. 2/F, 2 Qianhai Nanyanlu (just to the west of the post office on Dianmenwai Dajie), Xicheng District. (8403 2131) 东岸咖啡，西城区地安门外大街前海南沿2号楼2层

Jiangjinjiu Bar Every weekend, for the price of a drink, this bar hosts acoustic performances, often by ethnic minority bands. Old timers say Jinajinjiu comes close to recapturing the halcyon days of River, the legendary (and defunct) Beijing folk club.
Daily 11am-2am. 2 Zhongku Hutong, (between Drum and Bell towers on the west side, a few doors south of The Drum and Bell cafe), Dongcheng District. (8405 0124) 疆进酒吧，东城区钟库胡同2号（鼓楼北门）

MAO Livehouse Managed by the folks of Bad News Records from Japan, MAO Livehouse boasts the most massive sound system in town, a knowledgeable sound engineer, and an excellent line-up of acts, both local and international. The stage is sectioned off from the bar and lounge while the large concert floor (i.e. gutted movie theater) slants towards the stage, offering the choice between the pit and a high view.
Daily 4pm-late. 111 Gulou Dongdajie, Dongcheng District. (6402 5080) www.maolive.com 光芒，东城区鼓楼东大街111号

New Get Lucky It's no longer new, and it sure ain't all that lucky: Floundering over on Nüren Jie for over three years now, but with a change in management, the potential of New Get Lucky's ample space may finally be utilized. Our suggestions? A new sound system and focused programming that avoids, say, televised sports events, pop karaoke and death metal on a single night.
Daily 11am-2am. A1 Xingba Lu, Nüren Jie, Chaoyang District. (8448 3335) 新豪运，朝阳区女人街星吧路甲1号

The Star Live Beijing's oh-so-needed mid-sized venue came of age in '07, hosting Ziggy Marley, Sonic Youth, Maximo Park and The Roots. This is the place that's bringing Beijing's music scene to the next level – let's hope it stays there.
Daily 7pm-late. 3/F, Tango, 79 Heping Xijie (50m north of Yonghegong subway station), Dongcheng District. (6425 5677) www.thestar-live.com 星光现场，东城区和平西街79号糖果三层（雍和宫桥路北50米）

Stone Boat Cafe Perched on the edge of a lake, and surrounded by scholars' rocks and willow trees, the Stone Boat may seem a delightfully improbable *yaogun* venue. Though there aren't any gigs in the winter (what, you want to sit outside in January?), a new tent and upgraded PA system allows the Boat's excellent summer performance series to roll on even in the rain. Expect plenty of acoustic acts – from bossa nova to blues – as well as ethnic minority folk music.
10am-late. Lakeside, southwest corner of Ritan Park, Chaoyang District. (6501 9986)
石舫，朝阳区日坛公园里，湖边

What? Bar Where all the D-22 bands used to play before D-22 came around, it's still representing … and it's still possibly the smallest bar in the world. A new branch on Yuan Dynasty Bar Street was short lived, but at the Forbidden City location, a regular rotation of small and tiny local acts ensures that there is almost always music of some kind on the stamp-sized stage. It is absolutely no-frills, but hey, every seat is in the front row.
Daily 3pm-late. 72 Beichang Jie (just north of the west gate of the Forbidden City), Xicheng District. (133 4112 2757) 什么酒吧，西城区北长街72号（故宫西门往北）

Yugong Yishan
After its beloved, original haunt in a Gongti-area parking lot was *chai*'d, Beijing's Best Live Music club (as voted by *that's Beijing* readers for four years straight) reopened as this book went to print in larger digs formerly occupied by Rui Fu. YGYS built its devoted following thanks to its investment in quality equipment, common-sense, friendly management, and memorable concerts, featuring established local bands, visiting foreign bands and raucous DJ parties.
6pm-2am. 3 Zhang Zizhong Lu, (former Duan Qirui government building, on Ping'an Dadao just west of Dongsi), Dongcheng District. (6404 2711) 愚公移山，东城区平安大街张自忠路3号（段祺瑞执政府旧址大门左侧）

Hang on the Box's Wang Yue at The Star Live

PHOTO: SIMON LIM

Xiao Rong of Brain Failure channels Pete Townsend at Midi

Metal Therapy
Don't mind the occasional blood spilling
by Alex Pasternack and Lindsey Newhall

"Hear our paean, oh gods of heavy metal"

It's hard to make out what the lead singer of Hades is growling about, but it sounds like it has something to do with overcoming pain, or perhaps coping with the numbing tedium of the earthly realm. Or maybe he's just kvetching about how hard it is to maintain that long silky hair.

And then he unleashes it. With some intense head-banging, the mane begins to swirl like a mace; the black-clad devotees in the front row bow down to resume their prostrations; a tangle of young men, whose own hair tends toward extremes, hurdle their bodies at each other in a slow-motion trance; amidst a rush of guitars, the lead singer returns to the edge and spreads his arms, summoning the heavy metal (*jinshu*) gods.

Welcome to Beijing's most intense underground therapy session.

"I'll work hard for a whole week but here, I don't have to think about my future, my job, feeding myself," says Wang Bin, 25, a fresh-faced marketing specialist, outside of a seven-band bender at Mao Livehouse. "I just…" He launches into some street-side head-banging.

Like punk, heavy metal's appeal, when it arrived in Beijing in the early 1980s, was its sound and fury. "I was feeling very lonely then," says Cai Hua, the editor of *Painkiller* magazine, the bible of China's metal scene, of his high school days. Then he discovered a Van Halen tape. "This was what we all needed."

Even as the music has grown darker and more hardcore (for once, the influence of Scandinavia is largely to blame), time or maturity have kept Beijing's metal, well, kind of innocent.

"I think [metal] still taps into this *wu xia* mentality, a martial arts ethos," says Kaiser Kuo, founder of China's first-ever metal band, Tang Dynasty; schools, masters and styles are also a staple of the metal scene. "It gets your chops in shape – a drummer or guitarist who comes up playing metal is going to be able to break out and do other forms of music." Kuo's bands and a few others, like the outlandish Mongolian-tinged black metal outfit Voodoo Kungfu, have embraced the sound of folk instrumentation and classical arrangements to produce a kind of "metal with Chinese characteristics." "The music is about the empowerment of the individual," says Kuo, who is also a director at an ad agency. "[It] doesn't have to be distinctly Chinese," he says, "but it has to be distinct."

It matters little that the lyrics are hard to decipher. "If they growl"– Liu Yiming musters his deepest Satanic bass –"'URRRRRR, WEEEE WILLL KILL YOUUU,' we can't understand," says the 19 year-old fan, at a recent concert. "But we can understand their feelings."

"These people know what happiness means," says Cai Hua after a six-band show at MAO Livehouse. He is wearing a black band shirt, the obligatory shiny metal font spelling out the words "Slayer" in a not unintimidating way. But there is little intimidating about Cai; his nickname, "Dirty F," only adds to his charm. "They're very passionate for this music. It's full of romance."

That may not be the word that comes to mind after a no-holds-barred metal fest at 13 Club or New Get Lucky, some of the hold-outs from the rock underground's earlier days. But look past the spilled blood, the corpse paint, the eerie death metal growls, the gruesome gothic T-shirt imagery, and those sinister *yin tu ling* – devil's horns – lingering in the air, and there's something nobler there, swear devotees: at its heart, metal is friendly, positive music.

Just don't confuse metal with its bastard brother, punk rock. "Punk is a bit too simple. And in metal there is way more camaraderie than in punk," said Du Shuiyao, a young fan from Beijing. He might be onto something. If the punk mosh pit often looks like the anarchy the music wears on its sleeve, moshing at a metal concert is more akin to an elegant tribal dance. "Everyone here is each other's *gemen'r*," he says.

"People who come to metal shows don't fight," a sturdy, shirtless fan called Pogo Pangzi, chimes in. "It's the punks who fight all the time." But Kuo remembers an olive branch moment with Beijing punks Brain Failure: "Our bands were sitting on either side of this van, and one of the guitarists finally leaned over and was like, 'do you like Marshall amps?' They admitted they secretly love a lot of metal and they were totally familiar with my old band's stuff," he laughs. "But they said not to tell anyone."

Yaogun Secret Revealed! Punk and metal are not such strange bedfellows after all

propaganda

Mon-Fri 8pm-4.30am, Sat-Sun 8pm-5am.
Tel: 8286 3991
Add: 100m north of the east gate
of Huaqing jiayuan, Wudaokou, Haidian District.

raj
INDIAN RESTAURANT
拉兹印度音乐餐厅
www.raj.com.cn

Indian Restaurant @ Drum Tower

Located in a 200-year old wooden house close to the Drum Tower, Raj offers a wide variety of authentic Indian dishes with very reasonable price. In this warm and cosy environment you can enjoy a breath-taking view of the Beijing hutongs from Raj's large rooftop.

Live Indian music and dance performance every weekend
Family Brunch Buffet every Sat.& Sun.,RMB 68/person
Free Home delivery within 3 KM
Outdoor catering with perfection
Parties and Meetings facilities on order

Tel: 8610-8403 7462, 6401 1675
Open Hour: 10:30 - 14:00, 16:30 - 23:30
No.31 Gulou Xi Street, XiCheng District, Beijing, China
E-mail: info@raj.com.cn

LOTUS ROOT THAI
Restaurant & Bar

Absolute in Love
with our delicious food

No.32 Yandai Xiejie, Houhai, Xicheng District
Tel: **8401 5544**

RADIANCE

An Experience Like No Other....

for

Fine Furniture, Porcelains, Lamps, Carpets, Gift Items and more...

2nd Location Dan Shui Area

New Shop Tel: (86-10) 8459 5510
Add: A No118, Shunhuang Road, Sunhe Village, Chaoyang District

Old Shop Tel: (86-10) 8049 6400
Add: 9 Kaifa Jie, Xibai Xinzhuang, Shunyi District

www.radiancechina.com

Colorful treasures are tucked away on the shelves of Qiancaohua

Superb Swag
Beijing's shopping spoils
by Halla Mohieddeen

London, Paris, New York … Beijing? It doesn't quite trip off the tongue, but Beijing remains one of the world's best-kept shopping secrets.

Of course, this city's commercial side has its eccentricities. Yes, it's frustrating having to wade through piles of be-sequinned tat in order to find something vaguely presentable, not to mention the eternal quest for garments and shoes in sizes other than miniscule. Running the gauntlet of market stalls can be another potential passion killer. Fending off physical grappling and the repeated aggressive cries of "Bag you want? I have many color" is wearying for even the most superhuman shopper.

So why do we bother? What on earth makes the Beijing shopping experience so bloody amazing? Well, quite simply, it's not necessarily the journey, it's the final result – and the swag you can get for your troubles is superb.

A fructiferous bargaining sesh can lift the spirits immeasurably. Getting sackloads of goodies (be they Kuchi or Plada) at rock-bottom prices – barking banter all the while – bestows a buzz that every true shopaholic thrives on. Granted, bargaining isn't always easy, but as mother always said, you appreciate things so much more when you've had to work hard for them!

There's also the thrill of discovering that tiny overlooked boutique, and picking up the funkiest threads in town for less than the price of your cab fare home. Beijing is full of these hidden gems – and unearthing them is one of life's great pleasures.

And if you just can't find the specific item you have your heart set on, simply go out and get it tailored to your exact specifications (see "A Perfect Fit," p371). Quality tailoring work in Beijing can be gratifyingly easy on your wallet and exemplifies one of the city's biggest shopping boons: Whatever you want, you can find someone to make it for you – on the cheap.

But the true lure of the Beijing shopping experience is the sheer wealth of objects available. The selection of goodies on offer is truly astounding: From bargain basement threads to luxury branded luggage, this city's got it all. It can be a minefield, but this chapter aims to help you navigate the eccentricities. Search past the lace and pearls, and you can find the most unique, and stylish, garments on the planet. There's no better feeling than being asked where you got X, Y or Z, and replying, "Oh this? It's just a little something I picked up in Beijing."

PHOTO: NATALIE BEHRING

Leave plenty of time to leaf through

Shopping Directory

Clothing & Accessories

Big & Tall	353
Boutiques & Clothing Stores	353
Children's Clothes	151
Designer Clothes	356
Glasses	360
Handbags & Wallets	361
High Street Fashion	361
Jewelry	363
Lingerie	366
Secondhand Clothing	366
Shoe Repair	367
Shoes	368
Tailors	369
Wedding & Formalwear	370

Home

Carpets	374
Decorating Companies & Materials	374
Electronics & Home Appliances	377
Framing	378
Furniture	378
Home Essentials	381
Lighting	385

Other

Antiques & "Antiques"	385
Art	194
Art Supplies	389
Bicycles & Motorcycles	389
Bookstores	390
Cameras & Photo Equipment	392
Computers & Software	392
Cosmetics & Beauty Supplies	393
Department Stores & Shopping Centers	396
DVDs & CDs	398
Fabrics & Threads	399
Flowers & Plants	400
Markets	400
Mobile Phones	405
Musical Instruments	405
Online Shopping	408
Pharmacies & Medical Supplies	409
Silk	409
Sports Equipment	409
Tattoos	494
Tea	412
Tibetan Trends	412
Tobacco Products	412

PHOTO: SIMON LIM

Clothing & Accessories

(See also Markets p400 and Department Stores & Shopping Centers p396)

Big & Tall

Shoes: see Big Shoes p368, Long.com p368, Huacheng Shoe Store p368, Link Step p367, Lisheng Sports Store p410, Nine West p368, Qingqing's Stall p368, Yashow Market p368

Clothes: Alien Street Market p400, Decathlon p410, Flower's Secret p366, Hejia Clothing p362, Jimmy and Tommy Foreign Trade Fashion Club p353, Lang Ken p353

Boutiques & Clothing Stores

Aigle This famous French store specializes in outdoor wear. Watch out for their signature handmade Wellington boots.
Daily 9am-9.30pm. Rm 140, Sun Dong An Plaza, 138 Wangfujing Dajie, Dongcheng District. (6512 6797) 东城区王府井大街138号新东安商场140

A You Fashion Country-style Chinese jackets, pants, shirts, bags and accessories made with fabrics (linen, cotton) dyed in nature's most brilliant hues (haw red, wheat gold, alfalfa green). Expect to pay RMB 200 per non-sale item.
1) Daily 9am-9.30pm. 100m north of northwest exit of Andingmen subway station, Dongcheng District. (8412 8606); 2) Daily 10am-10pm. 1/F, Gate 2, Tower 12, Leisure Garden, Wudaokou, Haidian District. (8286 4391) 阿尤服装。1）东城区地安门外大街安定门地铁西北出口向北100米；2）海淀区华清嘉园12号楼02户1层

Bameede Shop here for cheap, market-style "name brands" without the market attitude. The selection of pants, shirts, skirts and shoes changes according to local trends. Most items cost around RMB 100.
Daily 10am-9.30pm. EC-2, B1/F, East Gate Plaza, Dongcheng District. (6418 3690) 百媚，东城区东环广场地下1层EC-2号

Botao Haute Couture Botao is one of China's most prominent brand names for high-end, fashionable clothing for professional women. Features dresses tailored by local designers.
18 Dongzhimenwai Dajie (at Xindong Lu), Chaoyang District. (6417 2472) 薄涛高级时装社，朝阳区东直门外大街18号

Copa Fashion Fashion is a passion at the Copa, which offers elegant day and evening wear for the stylish modern woman. The cuts are smart, the fabrics are handsome, prices are reasonable (RMB 150 and up) but sizes only go to 38. Six locations in Beijing.
Daily 11am-9pm. 001, Nali Mall, Sanlitun Beilu, Chaoyang District. (6413 0254) 朝阳区三里屯北路那里服装市场1号

Feng Ling High fashion dresses and jackets featuring Mao portraits and propaganda slogans. All designs are one of a kind and individually made. This is the best of "Mao chic."
Daily 9am-6pm. 798 Dashanzi, 4 Jiuxianqiao Lu, Chaoyang District. (6436 3926) 枫灵，朝阳区酒仙桥路4号大山子798艺术区

Five Colours Earth A popular secret among expats in Beijing, local fashion designer He Hongyu's earthy jackets, shirts, and more – many of which incorporate embroidered pieces sourced from Guizhou – have a one-of-a-kind style not yet seen in many of Beijing's boutiques, and cost up to three times as much if you purchase them abroad. She recently launched a second line called 5 Colours, a funkier, dressier collection aimed at a younger clientele.
Mon-Sat 9am-6pm. 1505, 15/F, Bldg 5, Jianwai Soho, 39 Dongsanhuan Zhonglu, Chaoyang District. (5869 2923) www.fivecoloursearth.com 五色土，朝阳区东三环中路39建外Soho 5号楼15层1505

French Connection Simple but oh so stylish, the popular UK brand now has a store in The Place connected to an outlet of www.izzue.com. The relatively small store stocks dresses and shirts as well as accessories.
Daily 10am-10pm. The Place, 9A Guanghua Lu, Chaoyang District. (6587 1455) 朝阳区光华路甲9号世贸天阶

In One of Houhai's best shops sells gorgeous, justifiably pricey silk dresses and women's accessories as well as funky stationery.
Mon-Fri noon-midnight, Sat-Sun 10am-midnight. 11 Yandai Xiejie, Xicheng District. (131 4632 6697) 印，西城区烟袋斜街11号

Jimmy and Tommy Foreign Trade Fashion Club Search no longer, my tall and strong friend: this outlet shop carries a wide selection of attractive clothes for large-boned men and women (pants up to size 46). The selection includes pants, sports coats and jackets, jean jackets, skirts, dresses, shorts, shirts, sweaters, golf wear, shoes, bags, and some kids wear, with prices starting around RMB 70. Brands include Polo, CK, DKNY, Tommy, Hugo Boss, Zegna, A/X, and Burberry. If you can't find what you're looking for, they'll try to source it for you.
1) Daily 10am-9.30pm. 14 Dongdaqiao Lu, Chaoyang District. (6591 1286); 2) Daily 10am-9.30pm. A102 Winterless Center. Xidawang Lu, Chaoyang District. (6538 8165) 天润外贸服装店，1）朝阳区东大桥路14号；2）朝阳区西大望路温特莱中心A102室

Lang Ken Features plus-size waistline pants from 100-135cm.
1) 10am-10pm. 4/F, Sogo Department Store, 8 Xuanwumenwai Dajie, Xuanwu District. (6310 3388); 2) 9.30am-10pm. 3/F, Scitech Plaza, Chaoyang District. (6512 4488); 3) 9am-10pm. 2/F, Youyi Shopping City (Lufthansa Center), Chaoyang District. (6465 1188) 浪肯特大腰围裤装专柜。1）宣武区宣武门外大街8号庄胜崇光百货4层；2）朝阳区赛特中心三层；3）朝阳区燕莎友谊商城2层

Levi's It's all about a tiny, red label that wrote jeans history. Levi's sells stylish and authentic outfits for men and women, including embroidered miniskirts and pants "rugged as the men who wore them." Jeans (from the legendary 501 to the latest cuts) start at RMB 799, jackets from RMB 1,099 and belts from RMB 189.
1) Daily 10am-9.20pm. Bldg 9, Jianwai Soho, 39 Dongsanhuan Zhonglu, Chaoyang District. (5869 1948); 2) Daily 9.30am-10pm. Ginza Mall, 48 Dongzhimenwai Dajie, Dongcheng District. (6616 4610) 1) 朝阳区东三环中路39号建外Soho9号别墅；2）东城区东直门外大街48号东方银座大厦

Continues on p356

A Man-Purse for Every Season
It's a lifestyle
by Ann Mah

It walks the line between casual and formal: the man bag

Like many newly prosperous men across the globe, Andy Zhou accessorized to match the improvement in his status.

After Zhou, 29, made the leap from graduate student to doctoral candidate and freelance journalist, he cast aside his backpack for a sleek leather bag, a cross between a small attaché case and, well, a purse.

It's the *shou bao*, or men's handbag.

"People take it as a symbol of your identity," Zhou said, adding that for many men the bag signifies professional success. Many European brands have sold the bags here for some time — Gucci, Furla, Loewe, Zegna, Louis Vuitton and Burberry, among others. For Dunhill, the English menswear brand with 70 locations around the country, it is their best-selling item in China and retails for about RMB 4,000 each.

Annie Shi, Dunhill's regional sales manager, noted that the handbags have special appeal for men aged 30 to 50 who want to show that they are moving up in the world. "They have money and they want luxury goods," she said. "It's a status symbol." In fact, Shi said, some men do not consider one bag to be enough. "They buy a new bag for every season."

"It's perfect for when I'm not carrying too much stuff," said Ning Zhou, 25, a construction manager. "I have a lot of bags, but this one is the most convenient. You don't have to dig around — just open it up and everything is right there."

"You don't have to dig around"

The earliest form of the style dates to the 1980s, when government cadres carried important papers in slim cases called *gongwen bao*, or public document bags. Later, Hong Kong kung fu films from the 1980s and '90s fed the look, with bad guys carrying under-the-arm or clutch styles.

But it is the increased affluence of the average urban guy that has provoked the recent popularity. "Today, you have so many things to carry — your driver's license, laptop, car keys, PDA," said Zhou, now an assistant professor at Tsinghua University. "In the 1980s, no one had these things."

Whether tucked under the arm, or swinging jauntily from the wrist or shoulder, the handbags embody not only status, but a certain style. "Beijing is very casual," said Shi, noting that many of the capital's men forgo suits and ties in favor of relaxed outerwear like sweaters or cotton or wool jackets. "A briefcase doesn't fit in with local style — it's too formal," she said. "The handbag is between casual and formal."

Though younger men often favor over-the-shoulder satchels, the handbag is "a special look embraced by businessmen, or government officials," said Maggie Ma, the associate publisher of *Men's Uno*, one of China's leading men's fashion magazines. "It's the sign of a successful, traditional, stable man. Someone to take seriously." However, Ma added, "They're not elegant, they have no style, they don't express any kind of individuality."

"We would never feature these bags in the pages of our magazine," she said.

Nicole Chen, a Beijing-based fashion stylist, believes that the bag's small size contributes to its lack of fashion appeal. "A bigger business bag is fine, but a smaller handbag looks like something women use. Frankly, I don't understand why men carry that type of bag," she said.

Such criticism not withstanding, the *shou bao* has clearly earned a place in the hearts of certain Chinese men, like Shu Jienan, 55: "I think it makes me look more successful."

MNG Viva España! This Iberian fashion house sells extremely sexy clothes and must-have accessories, including pants (RMB 300 plus), leather belts (RMB 300 plus), cigarette bags (RMB 350) and leather coats (RMB 900 and up). The Oriental Plaza outlet seems to have a better selection than the China World one. Many locations, including:
Daily 9.30am-10pm. 1) BB53, B1/F, Oriental Plaza, 1 Dongchang'an Jie, Dongcheng District. (8518 7870); 2) EB104, B1/F, China World Trade Center, 1 Jianguomenwai Dajie, Chaoyang District. (6505 1608) 芒果，1) 东城区东长安街东方新天地地下1层BB53；2) 朝阳区建国门外大街1号国贸商城地下1层EB104

Qian Cao Hua The owner imports from Japan new and old fabrics like silk, embroidery and quilting which she uses to make super chic and affordable threads, accessories, and home decorations. Custom orders can be made. She also manufactures the delightful Vietnamstyle curtains that are hanging in Nuage.
Daily 11am-9pm. Nali Mall, Sanlitun Lu, Chaoyang District. (6417 7366) 千草花，朝阳区三里屯北路（北酒吧街）那里服装市场

Quiksilver Purveyor of surf and snowboard style, Quiksilver seems to have reinvented itself for China, selling its über-cool image through street clothes (puffy blue vest RMB 477, Roxy miniskirt RMB 550). Sadly, none of the label's signature swimwear is available, though you will find a good selection of accessories.
Daily 10am-10pm. 2/F, Ginza Mall, 48 Dongzhimenwai Dajie, Dongcheng District. (8447 6447) www.quiksilver.com.cn 旭日，东城区东直门外大街48号东方银座大厦二层

Red Hero This Beijing designer's clothes combine hippy-chic with *qipao* resulting in A-line peasant skirts, Mandarin-collar tops and wide-leg trousers that are simple, feminine and devoid of sparkles, Chinglish slogans or strange dangly bits. Nearly all the clothes and bags are 100% cotton, good quality and very affordable (shirts start at RMB 80, skirts at RMB 150 and sweaters and pants at RMB 200).
Daily 9.30am-9.30pm. 191 Haidian Lu, Haidian District. (6256 1148) 红英，海淀区海淀路191号

Surface Surface offers unique, stylish clothing and accessories for both men and women. Items are mainly understated – colors are earthy and subdued – and are made with high quality material. Prices vary from bargain to ludicrously overpriced; spend time browsing the racks for good finds.
Daily 9.30am-9.30pm. Bldg 6, Jianwai Soho, Dongsanhuan Zhonglu, Chaoyang District. (5869 0392) 表面，朝阳区东三环中路建外Soho6号别墅

Vivienne Lee Designer Vivienne Lee has opened a new cashmere venture that should leave both you and your grandmother very happy. That's not to say that you should retire before buying one of Lee's cable-knit sweaters, but rather that the shop boasts bold colors and styles for all ages (though a senior citizen's discount wouldn't hurt for these pricey pullovers, ranging from RMB 900 to 3,000).
Stall 2125, 3.3 Shopping Center, Sanlitun Beijie, Chaoyang District. (5136 5125) 朝阳区三里屯北路3.3大厦2125

Wayne's This little second floor shop is Wudaokou's new gold nugget for men who long to be stylish but don't want to singe their savings. Wayne's primarily stocks big names for reasonable prices. Button-down, collared shirts from brands like Esprit are available for RMB 88, and Diesel jeans are a steal at RMB 198. Don't want to exchange all your money for Armani Xchange? You know where to go. The store is small but the selection is not.
Daily 9.30am-10.30pm. 5 Huaqing Jiayuan, Chengfu Lu, Haidian District. (8286 4815) 海淀区成府路华清嘉园5号

Xinde Chinese Clothing Shop Sells reproductions of *qipaos* from the Qing dynasty, old Shanghai styles from the 1920s and some modern fashions to boot.
Daily 9am-1pm, 2-7pm. 198 Gulou Dongdajie, Dongcheng District. (6402 6769) 北京鑫德露华衣商行，东城区鼓楼东大街198号

Yu Chen Hand Painting Store Unique hand-painted T-shirts, as well as ties, underwear, masks, sneakers, bags and socks.
Daily 9am-8pm. 72, 7/F, Huawei Department Store, 180 Xidan Beidajie, Xicheng District. (136 2137 7003) 雨辰手绘，西城区西单北大街180号西单华威商场7层72号

Yunshuige This lovely shop has beautiful handmade clothing in Chinese and Western styles and an impressive jewelry selection.
Daily 9am-midnight. 22 Yandai Xiejie, Houhai, Xicheng District. (8402 5572) 云水阁，西城区后海烟袋斜街22号

Zara It seems half of the foreign women in Beijing have visited Zara since its opening. What's the draw? The first floor of this popular Spanish chain store is stocked with plenty of women's clothing and also boasts a vast shoe selection. The casual line for ladies, Trafaluc, is located on the second floor and carries mostly jeans and oversized jersey T-shirts. They also have a small children's and men's section.
Daily 10am-10pm. The Place, 9A Guanghua Lu, Chaoyang District. www.zara.com 朝阳区光华路甲9号世贸天阶中心

Children's Clothes
(See Kids chapter, p151)

Designer Clothes
Blanc de Chine Honey, if you have the money for high fashion, join the Hong Kong and New York buyers who flock here for elegant, simple Indochine-style garments such as linen suits for men and women, *qipao* dresses, Sun Zhongshan jackets, silks and more.
Mon-Sat 10am-8.30pm, Sun noon-7pm. Suite 116, Kerry Centre Mall, 1 Guanghua Lu, Chaoyang District. (8529 9450) 源，朝阳区光华路1号嘉里中心商场116

Chanel The original in classy, elegant haute couture. Accept no substitute.
Daily 11am-9.30pm. B1/F, Peninsula Palace, 8 Jinyu Hutong, Wangfujing, Dongcheng District. (6512 8899 ext 3590) 香奈儿，东城区王府井金鱼胡同8号王府饭店地下1层

Christian Dior Couture J'adore Dior. Need we say more?
Daily 11am-9.30pm. GF-7, Peninsula Palace Beijing Shopping Arcade, 8 Jinyu Hutong, Wangfujing, Dongcheng District. (6510 6000) 东城区王府井金鱼胡同8号王府饭店1层

HUGO BOSS Hip new threads, fabulous accessories and great shoes. Many locations, including:
1) Daily 9.30am-9pm. 1/F, Oriental Plaza, 1 Dongchang'an Jie, Dongcheng District. (8518 0686); 2) 2/F, Shin Kong Place, 87 Jianguo Lu, Chaoyang District. 1）东城区东长安街1号东方广场1层； 2）朝阳区建国路87号新光天地2层

Jean-Paul Gaultier French haute couture designer Jean-Paul Gaultier is famous for his shirts, jackets, handbags, purses and a range of other fashion accessories.
Daily 11am-9.30pm. L12-13, B2, Peninsula Palace Beijing Shopping Arcade, 8 Jinyu Hutong, Wangfujing, Dongcheng District. (6522 1009) 东城区王府井金鱼胡同8号王府饭店地下二层L12–13店

Louis Vuitton The French luxury brand attracts two types of shoppers: those of limited means who come to drool over the real McCoy, and those who don't need to look at price tags, who come to buy LV-branded trunks, valises, bags and fashions that scream (ostentatious) wealth.
1) Daily 10am-9pm. Rm 201, China World Shopping Mall, 1 Jianguomenwai Dajie, Chaoyang District. (6505 6213); 2) Daily 11am-9.30pm. 1/F, Peninsula Palace, 8 Jinyu Hutong, Wangfujing, Dongcheng District. (6523 4220) 路易．威登. 1）朝阳区建国门外大街1号国贸购物中心201室； 2）东城区王府井金鱼胡同8号王府饭店1层

Marc Jacobs The recently opened Marc Jacobs boutique is the epitome of stylish, yet fun clothing, with plenty of colorful bags, flirty styles, playful patterns and more.
Daily 10am-10pm. 1/F, Shin Kong Place, 87 Jianguo Lu, Chaoyang District. (6533 1697) 朝阳区建国路87号新光天地1层

Marc by Marc Jacobs A longtime favorite of serious fashionistas, the funky clothing line (mainly stocked in small sizes in the Beijing stores) is the perfect casual wear. But, like most big name brands, the tags carry big prices.
1) Daily 10am-9pm. SB118, China World Shopping Mall, 1 Jianguomenwai Dajie, Chaoyang District. (6505 9885); 2) Daily 10am-10pm. 2/F, Shin Kong Place, 87 Jianguo Lu, Chaoyang District. (6533 1638) 1）朝阳区建国门外大街1号国贸商城SB118店； 2）朝阳区建国路87号新光天地2层

Marni This young Italian label features a great collection of eclectic, beautiful silk and cotton dresses. But be prepared to drop some serious *kuai* in here – any of the above items will set you back at least several thousand.
Daily 10am-10pm. 1) SB109, China World Shopping Mall, 1 Jianguomenwai Dajie, Chaoyang District. (6505 0708); 2) Shop M2021, 2F, Shin Kong Place, 87 Jianguo Road, Beijing. (6533 1091) 1）朝阳区建国门外大街1号国贸商城SB109； 2）新光天地，朝阳区建国路87号2层

Mushi Beijing-based French designer Caroline Deleens uses Chinese silk to create European-style couture and has managed to navigate the dangers of East-meets-West fashion with aplomb.
Mon-Sat 10.30am-8pm, Sun 1-6pm. L107, 1/F, LG Twin Towers, B12 Jianguomenwai Dajie, Chaoyang District. (8529 9420)
模西，朝阳区建国门外大街乙12号双子座大厦1层

Continues on p360

Mirror, mirror at my feet, designer clothing can't be beat

Branded to Bankruptcy?
The freakonomics of face
by Ann Mah

I'm too sexy for these boys. But not too sexy for my Gucci dress

Amber Li earns what she describes as a modest salary, but that does not stop her from indulging in her favorite activity: shopping for designer clothes.

On a recent visit to Guomao, Li, 30, a publisher's assistant at an interior design magazine, could not resist the lure of Chloé, dropping RMB 7,000 on a pair of trousers.

"When I was growing up, my parents didn't even have a fridge or TV," the Beijing native said. "I can't afford these pants, but I bought them because I've never had anything like them before." She says jobs like hers pay RMB 5,000 a month, a salary that is squarely in the middle of urban white-collar compensations.

Beijingers' thirst for brand-name products is no secret, with Chinese consumers already accounting for 10 percent of global luxury sales. But what fuels the mania for logo-splashed products?

For Nicole Chen, a Beijing-based fashion stylist, current luxury consumers fall into two categories. "Some people simply love beautiful things," she said. "They appreciate the quality and history of the brand. But I think 90 percent of the people who buy luxury goods have no idea why. They just want to show off."

Sometimes the flaunting comes at the expense of couture continuity, or plain good taste.

"Women mix and match luxury products regardless of style," said Audrey Ma, the editorial director at *Madame Figaro*, one of China's leading fashion magazines. "Chinese people like symbols. Logos and brand names are symbols that people can understand."

Radha Chadha, co-author with Paul Husband of *The Cult of the Luxury Brand: Inside Asia's Love Affair with Luxury*, agrees. "Luxury brands with their loud logos and unmistakable sign language provide a handy tool to let the world know your financial power," she says.

Wearing expensive products also gives one *mianzi* ("face"). "*Mianzi* is about being successful and displaying success through ostentation," says Chadha, a Hong-Kong based marketing expert. "Chinese still save a lot compared to Western countries, but luxury brands are a social investment. They help the Chinese define their position in society."

The prestige of brand-name goods has also made them popular as presents: According to Chadha, 50 percent of all luxury sales in China are for gifts. "The single biggest factor that has spurred the growth of luxury in China is the gifting-for-*guanxi* practice," Chadha said, referring to the traditional practice of bestowing presents to build personal connections.

Recent government campaigns against corruption have made envelopes of hard cash too risky. "Luxury brand gifts are seen as a lot safer," she said. "It's another instance of the rule book being rewritten."

In the past most luxury consumers were older businessmen and their wives or mistresses, but the desire for brand-name products is filtering down to a younger audience. "With the 80s generation, it doesn't matter how little they make. They spend it all on clothes," said Chen, the fashion stylist. "They don't worry about money because they know they can always ask their parents for help."

The improved economy and one-child policy mean that many parents have more expendable income to share, she noted. "These young people are more sophisticated than older shoppers. By the time they reach their 30s most of them will be buying luxury regularly."

According to Chadha, this new group, which the book dubs "the nouveau cool," will demand an even greater variety of brands and products to help them express and differentiate themselves.

This growing compulsion to buttress one's identity with material goods must be good news indeed for luxury brands, and it certainly helps to explain Beijing's rash of high-end malls.

LV LV LV LV LV LV LV. Okay, we get the point

SHOPPING

NC. Style From women's silk skirts to sexy underwear, and knee-high boots to sandals, the shop sells all genuine imported fashions: A.P.C., Paul & Joe, Zara, Burberry Blue, Prada, Miu Miu and Marc Jacobs. Of course, authenticity isn't cheap: Gucci sandals go for RMB 1,650, D&G Jeans range from RMB 1,000-2,000, and a huge Hermes leather bag runs a whopping USD 4,000.
Daily 10am-6.30pm. 7B1, Xiangxieshe Apartment, 6 Xinyuan Xilu, Chaoyang District. (8732 4145) www. fashion555.com 朝阳区南新园西路6号香榭舍7B1

Ports Elegance and simplicity lie at the heart of stylishly designed women's and men's wear, handbags, shoes and accessories from the luxury brand. Many outlets, including China World Shopping Mall.
Daily 10am-9pm. SB 110 (ladieswear), 1/F, China World Shopping Mall, 1 Jianguomenwai Dajie. (6505 5279, 6505 3830) 宝姿，建国门外大街1号国贸商城1层SB109(女装)

Prada Fabulously overpriced Italian bags, shoes, clothes and accessories await you in these two upscale shopping locations.
1) Daily 10.30am-9.30pm. Peninsula Palace, 8 Jinyu Hutong, Wangfujing, Dongcheng District. (6559 2888 ext 3648); 2) Daily 10am-10pm. 2/F, Shin Kong Place, 87 Jianguo Lu, Chaoyang District. (6530 7528) 1) 东城区王府井金鱼胡同8号王府饭店; 2) 朝阳区建国路87号新光天地2层

The Red Phoenix Gui Lin is a self-taught designer whose boutique attracts a prestigious clientele of film stars, musicians and business leaders. A true artisan, she creates her own fabrics by using traditional techniques like blowing smoke on silk. Prices range from RMB 200 for simple tops to well into the thousands. No one said style comes cheap.
Mon-Sat 9-11am, 1-6.30pm. 1/F, Bldg 30, Sanlitun Beijie, Chaoyang District. (6416 4423) 红凤凰，朝阳区三里屯北街30号楼1层

SFI Luxury Boutique Pitching itself firmly at the city's luxury market, you can find Prada, Gucci, Fendi, Emporio Armani, D&G and other top-name Italian brands here. SFI also offers many limited editions, some of which aren't even available in the brands' own specialty stores.
Daily 10.30am-9pm. Store 0662, Bldg 6, Jianwai Soho, 39 Dongsanhuan Zhonglu, Chaoyang District. (5869 1329) SFI，朝阳区建外大街建外Soho6号楼0662商铺

Shanghai Tang Stylish Hong Kong-based brand name specializing in custom-made Shanghai-style tailored clothing. The place to purchase China chic gifts. You will find the main boutique on the UG Level.
Daily 10am-10pm. B1/F, Grand Hyatt Beijing, Oriental Plaza, 1 Dongchang'an Dajie, Dongcheng District. (8518 0898) 东城区东长安街1号东方广场东君悦大酒店UG层

Vivienne Tam Hong Kong-born, New York-based designer Vivienne Tam's beautiful designs are now available in Beijing.
1) Daily 9.30am-9.30pm. WB101, China World Shopping Mall, 1 Jianguomenwai Dajie. Chaoyang District. (6505 0767); 2) Daily 9.30am-10pm. BB50, Oriental Plaza, Dongcheng District. (8518 0871) 1) 朝阳区建国门外大街1号国贸商城WB101; 2) 东城区东方新天地BB50

Zemo Elysée Run by Elysée Yang, who studied fashion in Paris, this small boutique in the Nali shopping area carries some gorgeous, brightly colorful dresses. Prices range widely from affordable (RMB 380) to extravagant (RMB 28,000!).
Daily 11am-9pm. Nali Mall, Sanlitun Lu, Chaoyang District. (6413 2187) 朝阳区三里屯路那里服装市场内

Fabrics & Threads
(See Fabrics & Threads, p399)

Glasses
Baodao Optical This reliable operation can craft lenses in about 24 hours and has a large selection of frames, starting at RMB 180 (not including lenses). Tons of branches all over the city, including:
1) Daily 9am-9pm. Rm 107, Bldg A, 1 Xidawang Lu, Chaoyang District. (6538 8651); 2) Daily 9am-9pm. 1/F, Tianlun Dynasty Hotel, 50 Wangfujing Dajie, Dongcheng District. (6528 6198); 3) Daily 9am-9.30pm. 105 Bldg 3, Jianwai Soho, 39 Dongsanhuan Zhonglu, Chaoyang District. (5869 2608) www. baodao.com.cn 宝岛眼镜店，1) 朝阳区西大望路1号温特莱中心A座107号; 2) 东城区王府井大街50号天伦王朝饭店1楼; 3) 朝阳区东三环中路39号建外Soho3号楼105室

Beijing Glasses City A four-story building with more than 200 stalls, Glasses City features wholesale and retail spectacles at very reasonable prices. Retail frames and lenses start at RMB 150 and RMB 50, respectively. Prescription glasses also include a free eye exam. A box of one-month-disposable Renu contact lenses costs RMB 70 – cheaper than anywhere else in town.
Daily 8am-7pm. 64 Dongsanhuan Nanlu (north of Beijing Curio City), Chaoyang District. (6731 2024) 北京眼镜城，朝阳区东三环南路64号（北京古玩城对面）

Chaoyang Eye Hospital Store A reliable supplier of prescription lenses attached to the well-known eye hospital, this shop boasts an extensive selection, honest prices and dependable quality. Frames and lenses start at around RMB 100 and RMB 70 respectively, and the eye test is free.
Daily 8am-6.30pm. 8 Baijiazhuang Lu (near the hospital's west gate), Chaoyang District. (6593 1238) 朝阳配镜中心，朝阳区白家庄路8号（医院西门附近）

Happy Eye Glasses, contact lenses, Korean eye care products and frame repairs are available here.
Tue-Sun 10am-7pm. 510 Pinnacle Plaza, Shunyi District. (8046 3558) 快乐眼镜，顺义区荣祥广场510

Lenscrafters Premium retail brand offers eyecare, service and fashion advice to the high-end customer. Lenscrafters carries luxury eyewear brands including Bulgari, Chanel, Dolce & Gabbana, Prada, Versace, and Burberry. You can also find Ray-Bans here. Many outlets including:
The Place, 9A Guanghua Lu, Chaoyang District. 朝阳区光华路甲9号世贸天阶

Vision Infinity Hidden in the Jianwai Soho Office Building, Vision Infinity is an eyewear salon featuring optical frames, sunglasses and a prescription glasses service. You'll find frames from Burberry, Gucci, and Prada, among others. Expect to drop around RMB 3,000. Prescription specs are usually ready in two days, and free cleaning and repairs are also available.

Faites attention! Mushi's fabulous designs are on the cutting edge of fashion

Rm 2105, Bldg 9, Jianwai Soho, 39 Dongsanhuan Zhonglu, Chaoyang District. (5869 8323) 朝阳区东三环中路39号建外Soho9号楼2105室

Yishikang Eyeglass Company Superfly frames and fast service are the hallmarks of this store, where prescription glasses can be whipped up to order in about half an hour for just RMB 300.
Daily 9am-9pm. 66 Dongsi Nandajie, Dongcheng District. (6528 2195) 益视康眼镜，东城区东四南大街66号

Handbags & Wallets

Furla It's all about bags here, from dinky pastel totes to fancy purses. Show your brand loyalty with a matching wallet and key chain. Prices start at RMB 800.
Daily 10am-9pm. Rm 115-116, B1/F, China World Shopping Mall, 1 Jianguomenwai Dajie, Chaoyang District. (6505 5978) 朝阳区国贸商城地下一层115–116室

Loewe Founded in 1846 by Enrique Loewe Roesseberg, this Spanish brand features luxury leather products including clothing, keychains, belts, shoes and handbags. Materials also include twill and silk crepe, suede and fur.
Daily 10am-9.30pm. L120, China World Shopping Mall, 1 Jianguomenwai Dajie, Chaoyang District. (6505 6866) 罗意威，朝阳区建国门外大街1号国贸城一层L120

Milan Station This excellent purveyor of leather handbags and wallets sells the AAA-quality goods at a fraction of the price one would pay in Italia. Forza!
Daily 10am-9pm. 809 Jiayi Market, A3 Xinyuan Nanlu (opposite Kunlun Hotel), Chaoyang District. (8448 5607) 米兰站，朝阳区新源南路甲3号佳亿市场809

Yi Bag Busy bag maker Xiao X describes her work as "art on fabrics." Made from cloth, the bags are classified as either modern or classic.
Tue, Thu-Sun 11am-9pm. 230-3 Gulou Dongdajie, Xicheng District. (8404 5308) 意bag，西城区鼓楼东大街230–3号

High Street Fashion

33 T Shirt Choose any motif to print on your T-shirt.
Daily 10am-9pm. B2-C-33, 77th Street, Xidan Culture Plaza, Xicheng District. (6601 9996) 三拾三，西城区西单文化广场77街B2–C–33

Decay Decay specializes in today's street fashions such as tight jeans, sexy clubbing apparel, D&G and Versace knockoffs. Prices vary, with shirts starting at RMB 90. A good sales bin. Slim sizes only.
Daily 9am-10pm. 1) Nansanhuan Lu (across from Silver Tower, near a Dongbeihu Restaurant), Chaoyang District. (6467 7178); 2) 24 Xinyuan Jie (opposite KFC), Chaoyang District. (6463 2617) 蜕变，1) 朝阳区东三环北路南银大厦对面（东北虎餐厅附近） 2) 朝阳区新源街肯德基（新源街24号）对面

Giordano The Hong Kong equivalent of Gap is deservedly praised for its well-made, affordable basics for men and women like T-shirts, khaki pants and drawstring trousers. Many other branches in Beijing.
Daily 9am-11pm. 1) 17 Wangfujing Dajie, Dongcheng District. (6512 8191); 2) Daily 9am-10.30pm. 176 Xidan Beidajie, Xicheng District. (6606 6025) 佐丹奴，1) 东城区王府井大街17号；2) 西城区西单北大街176号

Gobi Gear Stocks quirky slogan T-shirts ranging from "Asian Slim" to "Big Foreigner" size. T-shirts retail from RMB 90.

SHOPPING

Branch out and spice up your wardrobe with funky jewelry

Tue-Sun 11am-7pm. Unit 15, Bldg 11, Central Park Apartment Complex, Guandongdian Nanjie, Chaoyang District. (6533 6559) 朝阳区关东店南街新城国际11号楼15号

Hejia Clothing A real fashion find, Hejia has an excellent selection of men's and women's "market" clothes in US sizes, carrying brand names like Polo, DKNY, Gap, Morgan, Abercrombie & Fitch and Jack & Jones. Prices are lower than in the hectic markets, but no haggling.
Daily 10am-9pm. 1) Xinyuanli (opposite Jinkelong, north of Capital Mansion), Chaoyang District. (6467 2607); 2) 38 Fuxing Lu, Haidian District. (8820 3166) 简单和家，1）朝阳区新源里（京客隆对面，京城大厦北侧）；2）海淀区复兴路38号

Hot Station Hot Station sells men's and women's skateboard gear, hip hop threads, DJ wear, jeans, sneakers, sweaters, jackets and accessories at mid-level prices (e.g. men's jeans RMB 300).
Daily 9am-10pm. C-168, 1/F, COFCO Center (near Starbucks), Jianguomennei Dajie, Dongcheng District. (6513 8692) 热门驿站，东城区建国门内大街中粮广场1层C-168（星巴克旁边）

Jack & Jones This Danish chain has slick duds for sleek dudes that are perfect for a casual day out or a late night at the jazz joint. A gray summer linen shirt is RMB 150 and cut-off denim trousers are RMB 200. Many outlets around town including China World and Oriental Kenzo.
Daily 9.30am-10pm. B1/F, Oriental Plaza, 1 Dongchang'an Jie, Dongcheng District. (8518 6364) 杰克琼斯，东城区东长安街1号东方广场地下一层

Kookai All you need to feed your French fix, from denim-trimmed pink boucle jackets (RMB 980) to pais-

ley tea dresses (from RMB 789). The shop assistants have perfected the Parisian-style helpful service, too.
Daily 9.30am-10pm. BB36 Oriental Plaza, 1 Dongchang'an Jie, Dongcheng District. (8518 2933) 酷凯，东城区东长安街1号东方新天地BB36

Longfusi Dajie Browse through the stores and minimalls along this pedestrian street, and you'll find tons of trendy light dresses, shirts, decorated jeans, and accessories. While a bit overpriced (RMB 200-900 for a summery dress), you can bargain things down a lot. At the other end of the block are some outdoor stalls, with more forceful shopkeepers selling shirts, lingerie, and accessories. Also fun to just walk around and check out the scene.
Longfusi Dajie (north of Dongsi Xidajie, the block between Dongsi Beidajie and Meishuguan Houjie), Dongcheng District. 隆福寺大街，东城区隆福寺大街（东四西大街北边，东四北大街和美术馆后街之间的街区）

Made in China Outlet Teens congregate here after school to browse through jeans (from RMB 200), sweatshirts, funky T-shirts and other hip fashions – including angel wings (and they're always in style!).
Daily 10am-6pm. 302 Pinnacle Plaza, Shunyi District. (no tel) 顺义区荣祥广场302号

Meirenji Handmade, roughly sewn clothes – the Sichuanese punk-peasant look – in neon greens and pinks. Spicy! Beauty's Bar is upstairs – tiny, cozy, and inexpensive, with a balcony overlooking Yandai Xiejie.
Daily 11am-midnight. 38 Yandai Xiejie, Xicheng District. (8402 2892) 美人记，西城区后海烟袋斜街38号

Noise Trendy, funky and fresh, the T-shirts on sale in Noise are set to bring a breath of fresh air to the Bei-

jing hipster's wardrobe. Their range features products from US brand Vintagevantage.com and the UK's Junk Shop, brands which are firm favorites among trendsetters in the USA and Europe.
Tue-Sun 1-10pm. Unit 7, Bldg 42, South Bldg, Sanlitun Beijie (opposite Tongli Studios), Chaoyang District. (6417 5451) 朝阳区三里屯北街南楼42号楼7单元（同里对面）

Only The sister store to Jack & Jones, Only offers a wide selection of au courant fashions for the ladies. The jeans (around RMB 300 per pair) are especially worth recommending, as they look good, fit well and don't fall apart after the first wash.
Many locations, including Oriental Plaza, Pacific Century Place and Sogo. 东方新天地，太平洋百货，庄胜崇光百货

Plastered T-shirts This shop sells its own line of comfortable cotton T-shirts whose eye-catching designs are inspired by, and celebrate, such classic local icons as the 1.20 *kuai* Xiali sign, the Beijing subway ticket and the "I climbed the Great Wall" shirt (with a blonde vixen preening in front of the rampart). A fun place to source gifts, Plastered also carries retro toy robots, *danwei*-style tea mugs and posters of raffishly-hued boxy Beijing buildings from the 70s and 80s.
Mon-Fri 1-10pm, Sat-Sun 10am-10pm. 61 Nanluogu Xiang, Dongcheng District. (134 8884 8855) www.plastered.com.cn 东城区南锣鼓巷61号

Shuangyushu Fashion Street This street includes stores for women's fashion, shoes, leather goods, and children's clothes. Most boutiques feature twentysomething fashions. For linens with an ethnic flair, try A Tree ("Yike Shu"). Varying hours. *Shuangyushu Hutong (north of UME International Cineplex), Haidian District. (8708 2095)* 双榆树时尚一条街，海淀区双榆树胡同（华星国际影城往北）

Yandai Xiejie In this Houhai pedestrian area, you can find some diamonds in the rough. Look in Qiao Zhi for hand-knitted clothes, You Yu for imaginative clothes and shoes, Subdivision for handmade traditional garments, Shu Sheng Hang for funky clothes, Ga Rong Mi Jing for Tibetan items, and Wen Feng Tang for tasteful souvenirs. Varying hours.
Yandai Xiejie, Houhai, Xicheng District. 烟袋斜街，西城区烟袋斜街

Jewelry

Agatha French-style jewelry boutique featuring handbags, earrings, pendants, hair clips, cuff links, etc. Most items display the cute image of a Scottie dog. All of their products are designed and handmade in Europe, using gold, silver and crystal. Prices are reasonable: A silver necklace with crystal Scottie dog pendants costs RMB 620; a black dog-shaped handbag goes for RMB 490; colorful Scottie hair clips cost RMB 190.
Daily 9.30am-10pm. A107, The Malls at Oriental Plaza, 1 Dongchang'an Jie, Dongcheng District. (8518 6503) 东城区东长安街1号东方新天地A107铺

Athena Xu Stocks accessories, hats and home furnishings, most hand-crafted from leather, silk, chiffon and ribbon and adorned with glass beads, crystal and pearls. Jewelry can also be designed to order.
10.30am-9pm. 100m in from the road west of Yashow Market, Chaoyang District. (6415 5025) 朝阳区三里屯雅秀西侧路口北100米

Beijing Fine Jewelers An enormous selection of stones to bedazzle even the most jaded viewer. Custom-made gold, silver and gem-encrusted pieces are in the back viewing rooms. Bring a photo of your favorite jewel and the store's craftsmen can replicate it, usually in less than two weeks.
1) Daily 9.30am-7pm. A6 Gongti Donglu (opposite East Gate of Workers' Stadium), Chaoyang District. (6592 7118, 139 0114 6739); 2) Inside Friendship Supermarket, 7 Sanlitun Beilu, Chaoyang District. (6468 6881) 北京大方元珠宝行，1）朝阳区工体东路甲6号工人体育场东门对面；2）朝阳区三里屯北路7号友谊超市内

Beijing Mengda Accessories Jewelers Silver and pearl jewelry shop will custom-make pieces of your own design. Also has a jeweler on site for jewelry repair.
Daily 9.30am-7pm. 509 Pinnacle Plaza, Shunyi District. (8046 7029) 梦达美饰珠宝行，顺义区荣祥广场509号

Cartier Famous international jeweler.
Daily 10am-9pm. L103-104, China World Shopping Mall, 1 Jianguomenwai Dajie, Chaoyang District. (6505 6660) 卡地亚，建国门外大街1号国贸购物中心L103-104室

Cool Jade Jewelry Studio Truly worth visiting, this shop sells beautiful jewelry produced by the talented owner – who holds a Master's degree in the art and accepts custom orders – as well as second-hand pearls, handbags and hip home wares (plates, glasses, etc). Appointments recommended.
Fri-Tue 1-8pm. 2 Dashibei Hutong (near Yandai Xiejie), Xicheng District. (132 4198 9177) 翡冷翠，西城区大石碑胡同2号（烟袋斜街附近）

Dragon House Jewelry Find a wide selection of beautifully designed, handcrafted gold and silver pieces at this expat favorite. Repairs and custom orders are available, prices are fair and service is attentive and polite.
Daily 9.30am-8pm. Yashow Market (attached to the east side of the building), 58 Gongti Beilu, Chaoyang District. (6413 2927) 朝阳区工体北路58号雅秀市场

Hiersun Hiersun's 10,000-watt displays attract well-heeled shoppers and slack-jawed gawkers. This large store has everything from glitzy modern pieces to renovated antique watches, plus excellent service.
Daily 9am-10pm. AA29, Oriental Plaza, 1 Dongchang'an Jie, Dongcheng District. (8518 5120) 恒信钻石，东城区东长安街1号东方新天地AA29

Kavenna Diamond Sells high-class diamonds and classic engagement and wedding rings.
Mon-Sat 11am-8pm. 112, 1/F, Kerry Centre Shopping Mall, 1 Guanghua Lu, Chaoyang District. (8529 9696) 卡文那钻石，朝阳区光华路1号嘉里中心商场112号

Pearl Market Hongqiao sells loose precious stones and more pearls than the South Seas. Come here for fun accessories, notably chunky turquoise and coral. The quality of the pearls – most of them cultured – is uneven, so be careful about spending too much money. Single pearls are as cheap as RMB 10. Big strands cost far more. Go upstairs with the big spenders for classier stores and higher quality jewels, as well as salespeople who are likely to speak decent English.
Daily 9am-7pm. 3/F, Hongqiao Market, Tiantan Donglu, Chongwen District. (6713 3354) 红桥珍珠市场，崇文区天坛东路红桥市场3层

Continues on p366

String Theory

A primer on how to buy pearls in Beijing
by K. L. Murphy

Don't let the pearl vendor string you along – do your homework

Most people buying pearls at the markets ask just two questions: "How much?" and "Are they real?" But you'll get better pearls and a better deal – instead of just getting overwhelmed – if you prepare yourself with a little bit of knowledge.

Spotting the Real Deal

Natural pearls, rare in Beijing markets, occur when an oh-so-sensitive mollusk soothes the irritation of a foreign object by coating it with a substance called nacre. Cultured pearls – what you are most likely to find here – are just as lovely and "real" as natural pearls, but have been created through a sort of artificial insemination and raised in a controlled environment. (And which culture was the first to experiment with cultured pearls? The Chinese, of course!)

Then there are the dreaded fakes: imitation pearls, which are glass or plastic beads coated with a pearly substance; and reconstituted pearls, which are basically made of pearl powder and glue. There are several different ways to test whether you're dealing with fake pearls. One way, according to expert Lise Lepa of Pearls Only, is to rub the pearls together. Lepa says two real pearls will feel a bit gritty, like fine sand paper, whereas fakes will usually feel smooth. Beijing-based gemologist Keturah Mason suggests that you hold the suspicious pearls against one cheek and authentic cultured pearls against the other – the fakes will not be as cool to the touch. Finally, you can examine the surface of the pearls (ideally under 10x magnification), focusing especially on the drill hole. Most likely, the fake pearls will appear bumpy, and the drill holes will be rough or ragged.

Quality Characteristics of Cultured Pearls

Size: All else being equal, the larger the pearl, the more valuable it is. But size ranges vary depending on the type of pearl. For instance, the average size of an Akoya pearl is 7 to 7.5mm, whereas Tahitian and South Sea pearls are somewhat larger.

Shape: Ranges from "round" (usually considered more desirable and thus more valuable) to off-round to "baroque," or irregularly shaped.

Color: The major classifications include white, cream, rose, gold, and black (but most black pearls found in the markets have been either irradiated or dyed with silver nitrate, post-harvest). A pearl will also have a certain "overtone" – usually pink, green, or silver – that will affect both its value and how it looks with your skin tone.

Luster: Often considered the most important of the quality characteristics, luster refers to the pearl's surface brilliance and glow, and ranges from bright to dull (or "low luster") – low quality pearls will appear chalky or dull. According to Mason, it's important to place strands of pearls side by side to compare them.

Surface: As you might expect, the fewer imperfections – such as scratches, spots and pits – the better. And if you really want to see what you're buying, you should examine the pearls through a jeweler's loupe, which will reveal surface flaws invisible to the naked eye.

Buying Tips

Knowing what you want is the best way to keep from getting overwhelmed by the seemingly infinite options. Mason recommends that you consider who will be wearing them: black baroque pearls are fine for a recent college grad, but grandma might prefer larger-than-average round pearls in a more conservative color. If you'll be wearing them, check how they look against your skin (by draping the pearls over your arm rather than just holding them up around your neck). Lepa suggests you also give some thought to where you plan to wear your pearls, because the type of pearl and length of strand may depend on whether you're wearing them to, say, the office or a formal ball.

It's important that pearls on a strand "match," and it may be worth buying several strands of compatible pearls in order to create one very special strand using only the best pearls. When dealing with a seller, handle the pearls with confidence and demonstrate that you know a thing or two. And before you take home a finished strand, check the clasp and length of the strand, and make sure that the pearls are well-matched and well-strung.

Caring for Your Pearls

Pearls are vulnerable: their hardness is around 4 on Mohs' scale (diamonds, the hardest, are 10), so they can easily be scratched. Pearls dislike cosmetics and perfume, which can discolor or dull them, so always put your pearls on last. Protect them from acids such as wine and vinegar; in the event of contact, pat them with a damp cloth and then pat them dry, and, ideally, have them restrung. Speaking of which, when you buy a strand from the market, they will be strung on nylon – have them restrung on silk if possible. If you wear your pearls a lot, take them occasionally to a jeweler for a check-up. And finally, when you're not wearing them, keep them separate from other jewelry in non-airtight containers. However, as Victoria Finlay writes in *Buried Treasure: Travels Through the Jewel Box*, "Pearls need people to remain beautiful: if they are left in a bank vault they turn dry and yellow. Placed next to human skin, they become luminescent." In other words, wear your pearls!

Shard Box Who can resist the pretty jewelry boxes available at this store? The craftsmen take porcelain fragments – many from vases smashed during the Cultural Revolution – and make them the centerpieces of wooden, silver and ivory boxes ranging in price from RMB 20 for a ring-sized container, to large chests for RMB 2,000.
Daily 9am-7pm. 1) 2 Jiangtai Lu, Chaoyang District. (5135 7638); 2) 1 Ritan Beilu, Chaoyang District. (8561 3712) 慎德阁，1) 朝阳区将台路2号海润国际公寓商务4A座；2) 朝阳区日坛北路1号

Silver Jewelry The fa-bu-lous stall stocks beautiful bling including well-made silver copies of pieces by Cartier, Tiffany, and Bulgari. Enjoy rooting through this treasure chest – and tell the staff that Judy sent you!
Daily 9.30am-9pm. 4117, Yashow Market, 58 Gongti Beilu, Chaoyang District. (135 2093 7004) 银饰，朝阳区工体北路58号雅秀市场4117

Swarovski Everybody seems to love their high-quality crystal jewelry, as well as their arts and crafts, including colorful crystal animals and flowers.
Daily 9.30am-9.30pm. AA57, Oriental Plaza, 1 Dongchang'an Jie, Dongcheng District. (8518 6790) 施华洛世奇，东城区东长安街1号东方新天地AA57

Things of the Jing Tired of variations on a gaudy theme? Then check out the innovative and stylish jewelry designed by Gabrielle Harris. Her mainly silver pieces are so reasonably priced, it's hard to leave the store without carrying off something small and pretty.
Tue-Sun 10am-5pm. Kaifa Jie (next to Radiance), Xi Baixinzhuang, Houshayu, Shunyi District. (136 9151 3985) 西京之东西，顺义区后沙峪西白辛庄开发街（瑞氏东方家居装饰旁边）

Tiffany & Co. Because diamonds (and rubies, sapphires, emeralds and gold) are still a girl's best friend.
1) Daily 9.30am-9.30pm. A401, 1/F, The Malls at Oriental Plaza, 1 Dongchang'an Jie, Dongcheng District. (8515 1314); 2) Daily 11am-9.30pm. GF10, Peninsula Palace, 8 Jinyu Hutong, Wangfujing, Dongcheng District. (6512 9048) 蒂芙尼，1) 东城区东长安街1号东方新天地1层A401; 2) 东城区王府井金鱼胡同8号王府饭店GF10

Treasure House The loot here includes jewelry made of gold, silver, pearls and various gems. Original pieces, custom designs and reproductions available.
Daily 10am-7pm. 5 Sanlitun Xiwujie, Chaoyang District. (8451 6096, 139 1055 5372) 宝月斋珠宝店，朝阳区三里屯西五街5号

Yangrou Hutong If jade's your thing, you're in luck – almost every jewelry store on the eastern half of this hutong specializes in jade – both carvings and set jewels – that are distinctly Chinese and very well-crafted. False jade is tough to spot, so if you want to be absolutely, positively sure, poke around the gift shop in the Chinese Geological Museum at the east end of the street, where certificates of authentication can be provided.
Yangrou Hutong, Xicheng District. 羊肉胡同，西城区羊肉胡同

Yinshu Jewelry Studio Boldly distinctive designs incorporate silver, semi-precious stones, shells and even plastic.
Tue-Sun 10.30am-6.30pm. 4 Jiuxianqiao Road (next to the Hart Art Salon), Chaoyang District. (6437 3432) 银珠首饰，朝阳区酒仙桥路4号，哈特艺术沙龙旁边

Zhejiang Pearl Shop Paupers and princesses alike will find that this is THE place in Yashow to purchase pearls. Owner Cindy and her English-speaking staff offer cheerful, professional service and do excellent repairs. She sells all sorts of pearls from freshwater to sea (RMB 10 and up per strand), as well as semi-precious gems including corals, jade, turquoise and onyx. She's also happy to search for items for her customers, especially rare saltwater pearls. Free delivery for big orders. Tell them that Judy sent you, and remember to bargain.
Daily 9.30am-9pm. 4014-4164, Yashow Market, 58 Gongti Beilu, Chaoyang District. (139 0115 3404) 珍珠坊，朝阳区工体北路58号雅秀市场4014-4164

Lingerie

6ixty 8ight French lingerie brand 6ixty 8ight has a wide selection of styles from girlish to a more mature look.
3/F, Pacific Century Place, Chaoyang District. 朝阳区太平洋百货3层

Eve's Temptation Eve's Temptation purveys super-sexy bras, panties, bikinis and pajamas. Bras here are not functional and supportive, but made from thin material like silk, satin and lace – a good choice for summer. Set the mood with a variety of frilly bed gowns, or spice things up with a set of exotic leopard print bras (RMB 328) and skirts (RMB 238).
Daily 9.30am-9.30pm. S102, Blue Castle Apartments, 3 Xidawang Lu, Chaoyang District. (8599 9266) 夏娃诱惑，朝阳区大大望路3号蓝堡公寓S102

Flower's Secret Designs inspired by Victoria's Secret and Lormar. Bra sizes range from 70B to 110E, so a good choice for women with curves. Best buys include sexy lace tops (RMB 120-160) and thongs (RMB 25).
Daily 10am-8pm. Rm 3002, Ritan Office Bldg, 15A Guanghua Lu, Chaoyang District. (8563 1708) 天雅丽，朝阳区光华路甲15号日坛商务楼3002房间

La Senza In the sleepwear stakes, there's something for everyone at La Senza, from cutesy pajamas to cozy robes to sexier gauzy lingerie and even a selection of sportswear. For the basics, La Senza also has much to offer with an incredible range of bras and panties.
Daily 10am-10pm. 3/F, Ginza Mall, Dongzhimenwai Dajie, Dongcheng District. (8454 9663) 娜圣莎，东城区东直门外大街48号东方银座大厦

The Sex Store It's not the size that matters, right? Although small, The Sex Store has some lingerie and aphrodisiacs as well as an extensive collection of toys, both of the mechanical and leather varieties. They set themselves apart with their (relatively) tasteful spread of libidinal luxury.
Daily 10.30am-10.30pm. 23 Dongdaqiao Lu, Chaoyang District. (8562 4853) 成人店，朝阳区东大桥路23号

Super Bra Offering products from 6ixty 8ight, Victoria's Secret, Jockey and Roxy with sizes ranging from 65A to 110E. A selection of jewelry is also on offer.
Daily 2-11pm. 60 Nanluogu Xiang, Dongcheng District. (6402 5058) 世花殊，东城区南锣鼓巷60号

Secondhand Clothing

Chaina This Tokyo-style vintage shop sells cool, previously loved gear including jeans, '80s Nike hightops, Doc Marten's boots and 3-D Bruce Lee cards. Note the slack business hours.
24 hours. 16 Beiwutiao, Xisi, Xicheng District. (130 0109 0247) 拆那，西城区西四北四条16号

Pretty in pink: La Senza's collection covers more variety than skin

Discover Secondhand fashion boutique that, despite its limited space, stocks an alluring array of designer labels and styles from the stars' wardrobes. Customers are welcome to trade in their luxury goods for either barter or sale, with a 10% commission applied to listed price.
San Kong Jian, Dongsihuan Beilu (next to Ito Yakato Shopping Mall), Chaoyang District. (131 6428 8125) 朝阳区北四环东路三空间小区商业街

Hui Owner Liu Bin, famous for starring in the TV show *Da Zhai Men* (Life Show), sells his celebrity friends' clothes and accessories, donating three percent of the store's profits to the Beijing Hope Project.
Mon-Fri 1-11pm, Sat-Sun 11am-11pm. 3/F, 3.3 Shopping Center, Sanlitun Beijie, Chaoyang District. (5136 5507) 东西会，朝阳区三里屯北街3.3大厦3层

V2 Allows customers to trade in previously-owned items for goods that are nearly new.
Mon-Fri 11am-6pm, Sat-Sun 11am-8pm. Rm 4302, 3/F, Bldg 4, Jianwai Soho, 39 Dongsanhuan Zhonglu, Chaoyang District. (5166 0088) 二手奢侈品交流店，东三环中路39号建外Soho4号楼商铺3层4302

Shoe Repair

Lai Si Te Shoe Beauty Salon For waxing (RMB 10) and custom cobbling (RMB 780-1,350), go directly to the Lai Si Te in the basement of Sogo Shopping Mall. They also sell good quality shoe lifters (RMB 210) and offer cleaning (RMB 30) and dyeing (RMB 70) services for suede shoes. Many other locations across the city.
Daily 10am-9pm. B1/F, SOGO Shopping Mall, 8 Xuanwumennei Dajie, Xicheng District. (6507 8875) 莱斯特，西城区宣武门内大街8号庄胜崇光商场地下1层

Link Step Bust your boot? Cursing the dud zip on that genuine Italian handbag? This quick-fix counter gets the job done, smiles 'n all. Men's and ladies' leather footwear – small selection, but big sizes. With kids leather sneakers and sandals at RMB 30-60, it's Yashow prices in the countryside.
Daily 10am-8pm. Daily 10am-8pm. Pinnacle Plaza (in the Tianzhu Real Estate Development Zone), Shunyi District. 顺义区荣祥广场（天竺房地产开发区内）

TOPS Shoe Beauty Salon TOPS deals with the care, repair and alteration of leather shoes. Shoes can be dyed just about any color (RMB 60-180), resoled (RMB 35-65), patched (RMB 30-80), cleaned and restored (RMB 30-90), and the uppers can even be refinished (RMB 30). TOPS also sells some imported shoe care products.
2/F, Parkson Shopping Mall, 101 Fuxingmennei Dajie, Xicheng District. 西城区复兴门内大街101号百盛购物中心2层南北楼交界处

Zhengren Shoe Shop Zhengren in Zhongyou Shopping Mall is another good spot for shoe care and clamper work. Gum velours (RMB 55) and sponges (RMB 50) are also available, both of which are essential for suede cleaning.
Mon-Fri 10am-10pm, Sat-Sun 9am-10pm. B2/F, Zhongyou Department Store, 130 Xidan Beidajie, Xicheng District. (6601 4488) 郑人鞋艺，西城区西单北大街130号中友百货地下2层

Shoes

An De Li Si A store selling beautiful handmade shoes made to your specifications. Choose between more than 100 sample designs or bring your own. Expect to pay RMB 1,500-3,000 for a pair, depending on the design.
Daily 11am-11pm. Rm 4075, 4IF, 3.3 Shopping Center, 33 Sanlitun Beijie, Chaoyang District. (138 0132 8747) 安德利斯，朝阳区三里屯北街33号3.3购物中心4层4075号

Aldo Canadian shoe retailer carries quality shoes with unique, edgy designs. Prices from RMB 400. There are also outlets at Shin Kong Place, Wangjing Department Store, and Grand Pacific mall in Xidan.
Daily 10am-10pm. The Place, 9A Guanghua Lu, Chaoyang District. (6587 1578) 朝阳区光华路9号世贸天阶2层

Big Shoes Big feet are a big headache in Beijing, but that's still no reason to settle for ugly footwear. Instead, head here for a great selection of ample-sized work shoes, heels, pumps, sandals, loafers, flats, cowboy boots, high heels – for just about any occasion. They usually only have one pair per size, so if the pretty shoe fits, buy it!
Daily 9.30am-9pm. 064, B1/F, Yashow Market, 58 Gongti Beilu, Chaoyang District. (137 0113 9838) 朝阳区工体北路58号雅秀市场地下1层064

Crocs Purveyors of unique, slip-resistant, lightweight and comfortable footwear, Crocs are those colorful shoes you've been seeing everywhere. The original Beach shoe retails here for RMB 249. Many locations, including:
Daily 10am-10pm. B1/F, South Tower, The Place, 9A Guanghua Lu, Chaoyang District. (6587 1503) 卡洛驰，朝阳区光华路9号世贸天阶南楼

Forget stilettos: At Crocs chunky plastic is the new sexy

Easy Spirit Shoes Fashion meets comfort in Easy Spirit Shoes. Stocks a wide range of styles from sporty to formal.
Daily 9.30am-10pm. BB70, The Malls at Oriental Plaza, 1 Dongchang'an Jie, Dongcheng District. (8518 8987) 东城区东长安街东方新天地BB70

Huacheng Shoe Store The shelves of this cozy store are bursting with Western brand name footwear in sizes 40 and up. They have sexy pumps for summer (RMB 100-150) and great suede and leather knee-high boots for winter. The store caters mainly to women but does offer a small men's selection.
Daily 9am-7pm. 25-5 Zhangzizhong Lu, Kuanjie, Dongcheng District. (6405 2448) 花城鞋店，东城区宽街张自忠路25-5

Long.com Don't be fooled by the ".com" – this is a real-life shoe store. Tucked away at the end of Nali Mall, it has rows upon rows of men's and women's shoes. The emphasis is on youthful fashions, with a good selection of flip-flops and strappy sandals (RMB 400). Sizes for ladies' shoes range from RMB 35-43, and mens' shoes range between RMB 39-50.
Daily 10.30am-9.30pm. Nali Mall, Sanlitun Lu, Chaoyang District. (8643 2880) 龙.com，朝阳区三里屯酒吧街那里市场内

Nine West When you want fashionable and slick, Nine West comes to the rescue. High-heeled sandals start at RMB 730 but are guaranteed to be the height of fashion. Large sizes are available. There are also outlets in China World, Xidan, and Sogo.
Daily 9am-10pm. 133, APM (formerly Sun Dong An Plaza), Wangfujing, Dongcheng District. (6528 0091) 玖熙，东城区王府井新东安商场133号

Pi'erman Maoyi This cobbler works wonders with leather. Using a photo that you bring in, he'll manufacture a comfortable and sturdy pair of shoes or boots in about three weeks. Prices for shoes and boots start at RMB 360 and RMB 800, respectively.
Daily 9.30am-9pm. 37 Gulou Dongdajie (just west of Jiaodaokou), Dongcheng District. (6404 1406, 136 6100 2780) 皮尔曼贸易公司，东城区鼓楼东大街37号（交道口路口往西）

Qingqing's Stall Catering to a clientele of ample-footed Slavic ladies, this shop offers flats, heels, boots and more in sizes above 40. The stock changes frequently. You should be able to bargain shoe prices down to around RMB 100 per pair unless you're a size 44 or barefoot. Many neighboring stalls also sell large shoes.
Daily 9.30am-6.30pm. Stall 1263, 1/F, Alien Street Market, Chaoyang District. (8561 6813, 135 1103 3533) 朝阳区老番街市场1层1263号

Scholl Moving away from its stodgy image, Scholl now stocks comfortable *and* cute shoes, including suede boots (RMB 1,598) and metallic pumps (RMB 598).
Daily 10am-10pm. 2/F, Ginza Mall, Dongzhimenwai Dajie, Dongcheng District. (8454 9234) 爽见，东城区东直门外大街48号东方银座大厦2层

Yashow Market The basement of this Sanlitun market offers several good "brand name" shoe stalls with an extensive selection in larger sizes.
Daily 9.30am-9pm. 58 Gongti Beilu, Chaoyang District. (6415 1726) 雅秀市场，朝阳区工体北路58号

Tailors

Dave's Custom Tailoring Perpetuating the Shanghainese tradition of handmade suits. Savile Row quality. *Daily 10am-7pm. 104 Kerry Centre Shopping Mall, 1 Guanghua Lu, Chaoyang District. (8529 9433)* 朝阳区光华路1号嘉里中心商场104单元

Dunhill Classy and sophisticated men's suits – with a matching price tag (starting at RMB 20,000 per suit). Many locations, including: *Daily 10am-9pm. China World Shopping Mall, 1 Jianguomenwai Dajie, Chaoyang District. (6505 4148)* 登喜路，朝阳区建国门外大街1号国贸商城内

Fabric Store The sister establishment of the tailor shop in Sanlitun's Friendship Supermarket, this tailor offers good, friendly service in English at reasonable prices. They produce both Western and Chinese style garments and sell a smattering of fabrics, though prices are higher than at the markets. Expect to pay RMB 80-120 for a blouse and RMB 450 for a *qipao* – fabric not included. *Daily 11.30am-7.30pm. 317-318, Pinnacle Plaza (in the Tianzhu Real Estate Development Zone), Shunyi District. (8046 4517)* 裁缝店，顺义区荣祥广场317-318号（天竺房地产开发区内）

Family Tailor Sews and alters Chinese dresses, men's and women's clothing, and children's wear. Free pick up and delivery. *Daily 8am-8pm. Kaifa Jie, Shunyi District. (8049 4940)* 家庭裁缝，顺义区开发街

Fei Fei Locals swear by this tailor for everything from dress shirts to linen suits. Labor-only around RMB 500. *Daily 8.30am-9pm. 35-1-103, Xinyuanli Compound (opposite Jingkelong Supermarket), Chaoyang District. (8455 1939, 133 6627 5682)* 朝阳区新源里35号楼1门103（京客隆超市斜对面）

Huang Yue Studio Fashion designer Huang Yue produces gorgeous, hand-tailored men's and women's suits out of luscious fabrics (RMB 2,000-plus). Styles range from streamlined "Armani" cuts to more traditional scholars' jackets in lime green with ebony-hued accents. Yes, prices are high, but justified, given the quality of the workmanship. *Mon-Sat 9am-7.30pm. Sanlitun Beijie (Opposite Tongli), Chaoyang District. (6417 1093)* 黄跃工作室，朝阳区二里屯北街（同里对面）

Hujingyuan Tailors *Daily 10am-10pm. 4 Yandai Xiejie, Xicheng District. (6400 3744)* 湖景源裁缝店，西城区后海烟袋斜街4号

Jeannie Fei Hong Kong native Jeannie Fei is China's exclusive distributor of a line of German fabrics called Elegance, used in the collections of top designers like Armani and Valentino. Her ultra-customized, handmade garments will cost you a bundle (USD 400-700 for a silk business suit), but you'll get compliments every day and wear it forever. *Daily 10am-8pm. 1/F, Kerry Centre Shopping Mall, 1 Guanghua Lu, Chaoyang District. (8529 9489, 139 0136 5969)* 费亮珠，光华路1号嘉里中心商场1层

Lily's Boutique Located in Sanlitun, Lily's specializes in stylish tailoring and designer ready-to-wear clothing. Prices start from RMB 400 for a jacket to RMB 8,000 for

Fit for royalty

an embroidered evening gown. Also offers a shoe tailoring service. Besides tailoring, Lily's also has her own ready-to-wear collection available (RMB 300 to RMB 5,000). Designer pieces are showcased as well. *Daily 9am-10pm. 8, Bldg 39, Xindong Lu, Chaoyang District. (6416 6701)* 朝阳区新东路北三里屯南39楼8号

Paul Rousseau Bespoke suits, shirts, sports jackets and tuxedos made with exclusively imported fabrics from Italy and England. *Daily 11am-8pm. 206, Fortune Plaza, 7 Dongsanhuan Zhonglu, Chaoyang District. (6530 9182)* 朝阳区东三环中路7号财富大厦206号店

Rong Xin Tailor and Boutique Friendly English-speaking tailor Toby Shao makes handcrafted Western and Chinese clothes and shoes. Bring your own fabric or choose from his wide selection. Expect to pay around RMB 700 for a woman's tea jacket. *Daily 9.30am-8.30pm. 2/F, Friendship Supermarket, 7 Sanlitun Lu, Chaoyang District. (6532 7913)* 荣鑫裁缝店，朝阳区三里屯路7号友谊超市2层

PHOTO: NATALIE BEHRING

The dress is just for the day, but the memories will last forever

Senli & Mae Beijing's premier tailoring experience for stylish men and women, Senli & Mae leads in both service and craftsmanship. Whether you favor traditional Saville Row or avant-garde Dior Homme, they make your vision a reality. Offers a large selection of imported English fabrics and native English-speaking service. Prices start from RMB 1,500 for women, RMB 1,800 for men. Call to schedule an appointment.
Yaxing Bldg, 46A Liangmaqiao Lu, Chaoyang District. (139 1009 2419) 亮马桥路甲46号亚星大厦一层

Tangyun Tailor Tangyun specializes in high-end, tailor-made *qipao* and *tangzhuang* (traditional men's robes), along with some stunning East-meets-West and "with it" styles. A quick and painless fitting appointment takes care of your sizing needs. There is also an off-the-rack collection – but be prepared to shell out the big bucks.
Daily 9.30am-8.30pm. 5-3 Jinbao Jie, Dongdan (200m north of Xiehe Hospital, diagonally across from Paris Weddings, next to the KTV), Dongcheng District. (6524 9057) 唐韵，东城区东单金宝街5–3号

Tom's Tailor Shop Specializing in tailor-made suits for men and women and traditional *qipao*. Custom orders can be ready in 24 hours.
Daily 9.30am-9.30pm. B218 Lidu Yangguang Jinjie, 2 Fangyuan Xilu (across the street from Chateau Regency), Chaoyang District. (5135 7768, 1380 133 3256) 欧曼洋服设计制作中心，朝阳区芳园西路2号丽都阳光金街B218（和乔丽晶马路对面）

Yashow 3066 Sunny kits out suits for visiting bigwigs like Condoleeza Rice (with a photo to prove it). Fast friendly service, fair prices and a wide selection of fabrics. From a user-friendly catalog, choose from Chinese apparel, men's suits, women's dresses, tuxedos, and evening gowns. Remember to select your linings carefully and inspect the fabric for flaws. Door-to-door service by appointment. Most items can be made in three to seven days, and rush orders are available. Expect to pay RMB 80 and up for a shirt and RMB 800 and up for a suit.
Daily 9.30am-9pm. Stall 3066, Yashow Market, 58 Gongti Beilu, Chaoyang District. (6413 2432, 137 0132 0756) 雅时裁缝店，朝阳区雅秀市场3066

Yashow Market Tailors The entire third floor is a trove of decent tailors - and not a bad selection of fabrics, if you don't have time to buy your own elsewhere. "My Tailor" comes highly recommended, though you'll need to bargain a bit for the best price on their wide selection of fabrics and services.
Daily 9.30am-9pm. 58 Gongti Beilu, Chaoyang District. (6415 1726) 雅秀市场，朝阳区工体北路58号

Wedding & Formalwear
(Formalwear can also be found in Ritan Office Building, p404, and at the back of Jiayi Vogue Square, p403)

Galatea Bridal One-stop shop for all things a bride might need. Choose from over 100 simple and elegant dress samples; the store custom tailors your chosen design. Tailoring takes 45-60 days, so orders should be placed early.
Daily 10am-8pm. Rm 1230, 3/F, Bldg 12, Jianwai Soho, 39 Dongsanhuan Zhonglu, Chaoyang District. (5869 7887) 葛澜婚纱，朝阳区东三环中路39号建外Soho12号楼3层1230室

La Vincci Specializes in name-brand wedding dresses.
Daily 11am-7pm. 303, Bldg 5, Soho New Town, 88 Jianguo Lu, Chaoyang District. (8776 0680) 薇安嫁衣工房，朝阳区建国路88号Soho现代城5号楼303

A Perfect Fit

Tips to make your tailoring experience terrific
by Betsy Lowther and Catherine Lee

Custom-made clothing, cheap as chips – one of the perks of life in Beijing. Going to the tailor can be intimidating for the inexperienced, and it can be difficult to find someone who can consistently create exactly what you want, but that gorgeous, perfectly fitting dress will make the experience well worth it. Try these tips to make your tailoring experience more stylish than scary.

Ask questions

Make an appointment for a less busy time of the day to get measurements and explain the job. Ask about the tailor's specific services and specializations to make sure these are in line with what you're looking for. Examine samples of their past work to get a sense of whether they're up to snuff.

Start small

The best way to break in a tailor is one piece at a time. As tempting as it is to order a load of clothes at once, you need to rein yourself in until the tailor has proven himself. This goes for different types of clothes – your tailor may be terrific at corduroys and terrible at silks. Don't assume that one great piece means they're all going to be good.

Copy what you can

Your best bet in getting something that fits well is to bring clothing you already have and let them copy it. Not only will they match the style of the old piece, they can also copy the stitching, buttons and other important details. Don't want an exact copy? Bring a similar piece and explain what you want changed – they'll still have something to start with. Don't have anything close to what you want? Bring a picture from a magazine and review it with them thoroughly.

Bring your own fabric

While the actual tailoring tends to be cheap in China, you can get overcharged if you buy from the tailor's own fabric selection. Fabrics are almost always cheaper at local markets, and buying your own fabric guarantees that it'll

Will it be an apron or a ballgown? Only Fei Fei knows

be exactly what you're looking for; the selection will be much larger than what's available at your local tailor.

Tweak, tweak, tweak

Never be afraid to ask your tailor to re-do any ill-fitting clothing – even if it means sending it back four or five times. "I used to be hesitant to ask them to keep altering it," says one local tailor-lover. "But I ended up with a closet of clothes that weren't quite right. Finally, I just took it all back to the tailor shop and had them tweak everything that was wrong. Now, I always speak up right away if I don't quite like it."

Be nice

Want the coveted frequent customer discount? Befriend your tailor, let them know you've recommended them to others (and make sure the others mention you), and above all, be genteel. Discounts are arbitrary, and they certainly don't hand them out to people who boss or bully.

So how to find a great tailor? The best way is word of mouth: After all, experience speaks for itself. Ask around to find a good fit, or try our suggestions (see Tailors p369) to help you get started.

9 to 5 Glamour

Princess or pauper, you gotta look good
by Halla Mohieddeen

You've got the job, hurrah! Now it's time to look the part. Landing the corporate job in Beijing is seen as the Holy Grail for many, but once that switch has been made, it's important to look like you mean business, to avoid slipping back down into the realms of backpacker layabout. The tricky part, however, is revamping the wardrobe on a limited budget. Thankfully there are options aplenty around town, to suit whatever budget you may have. The fun part is getting out there and finding it.

OUTFIT 1:
Dress – RMB 100, Dongwuyuan Wholesale Market

OUTFIT 2:
Dress: RMB 45
Jacket: RMB 120

¥ (RMB 300 and under)

For options under 200 *kuai*, the best places to start tend to be the various markets Beijing is famous for. There is a wealth of options to choose from: **Hongqiao** market north of Tiantan East Gate, **Yashow** in Sanlitun, **Yueshow** in Chaoyangmen, and even the Beijing stalwart, the **Silk Market**. However, you get more bang for your buck up at the **Dongwuyuan Wholesale Market** near the Zoo, where it's possible to pick up a suit for RMB 100 if you're prepared to bargain hard.

You don't need to restrict your buying options to market haggling though. Surprisingly funky threads are also available at little boutiques and factory outlets around town. Our favorites include the tiny stores along Dongsishitiao and Andingmen. You'll need to rummage around a bit to find something stylish, but your efforts will be well rewarded when you walk off with dresses for RMB 30, trousers for RMB 20 and other thrilling purchases at thrifty prices.

¥¥ - ¥¥¥ (RMB 1000 and under)

For those with a bit more money to spend, consider getting something tailored (see "A Perfect Fit" p371). Depending on what fabrics you choose and your bargaining skills, a tailor-made suit can be had for around RMB 500. Mid-range options are plentiful in the larger malls around town. High street favorites **Zara, Kookai, Esprit** and **MNG** all provide chic, fashionable outfits. Don't be afraid to be adventurous though - working in an office doesn't have to mean black and boring. Spice up your wardrobe by combining a dress with a jacket or pairing a fun skirt with a more conservative blazer. If you're looking for an Asian infusion for your wardrobe, try the handmade Japanese silk pieces at **Qiancaohua** boutique in Nali Mall.

OUTFIT 3:
Dress – RMB 670, Qiancaohua

OUTFIT 4:
Shirt, RMB 2,410 – Shanghai Tang
Pants, from a selection

OUTFIT 5:
Silk dress, RMB 4,460 – Shanghai Tang
Blue Jacket, RMB 5,730 – Shanghai Tang

¥¥¥ - ¥¥¥¥ (over RMB 1000)

Once you've hit the big time though, you'll want to get that exceptional edge with your office wear. Yes, the big-name designers are out in force here, especially at malls like **Shin Kong Place** (Gucci, Chanel, Prada etc.) and **China World Shopping Mall** (Dunhill, Moschino, Hugo Boss, Kenzo), but for something a little more unique, try brands such as **Shanghai Tang** or **Vivienne Tam**. For an experience to die for, try the high-end tailors **Red Phoenix** in Sanlitun or **Jeannie Fei** in the Kerry Centre.

(The stores and markets in bold are listed in this chapter)

Home
Carpets

Jia Na Ma Ni Tibetan Carpets This Lido-area store stands out for its hip and modish designs. Choose from piles of bright, colorful rugs of varying sizes, designs and prices flown in from far-off lands, such as Pakistan and Tibet (prices range from a paltry RMB 160 to a princely RMB 80,140). Also, check out an assortment of traditional knick-knacks and home accessories. Try your luck rubbing one of the lamps that are scattered about the shop.
Daily 10am-10pm. 6 Fangyuan Xilu, Chaoyang District. (6437 8812) 嘉纳玛尼藏饰中心，朝阳区芳园西路6号

Qianmen Carpet Co. One of the city's most reputable rug merchants sells antique carpets from Tibet, Qinghai, Xinjiang and Inner Mongolia, as well as reproductions and contemporary creations.
Daily 9.30am-5.30pm. 1/F, Bldg 3, Tiantan Mansion, 59 Xingfu Dajie, Chongwen District. (6715 1687) www.carpetrealm.com 前门地毯厂，崇文区幸福大街59号天坛公寓3号楼1层

Samling/Tufenkian What looks like the lobby of an internet startup is actually the showroom for the large carpet design company, Tufenkian. Designed in America, these hefty, handmade rugs are made from Tibetan wool in Nepal. The company boasts of its fair trade conditions in Nepal and lower prices than you will find in their North American stores. The carpets aren't cheap though, with an 8' x 10' traditional pattern design carpet going for RMB 22,587 and a 2.45m x 3.42m floral design carpet for RMB 38,140.
Daily 9.30am-7pm. 58 Fuqian Yijie, Tianzhu Town, Shunyi District. (5810 1226/7) 山林心，顺义区天竺镇府前一街58号水木阑亭一层

Torana Gallery This justifiably popular carpet shop deals exclusively in beautiful carpets made of wool from Tibetan highland sheep and decorated with traditional regional motifs. Prices range from RMB 2,200 (60cm x 90cm) to RMB 15,800 (180cm x 270 cm). Friendly owner Chris Buckley insists that these carpets will last a lifetime and not fade after being washed.
1) Daily 10am-10pm. 1/F, Kempinski Hotel, Chaoyang District. (6465 3388 ext 5542); 2) Daily 11am-7pm 2) Danshui Town, 3A Shunhuang Lu, Chaoyang District. (8459 0785) 1）康晨手工地毯，朝阳区凯宾斯基饭店1层；2）朝阳区顺黄路甲3号淡水小镇

Wu Xin Zhai Carpet Store This place stocks superb antique Chinese, Persian and needlepoint rugs, as well as Aubusson carpets and tapestries and vegetable-dyed rugs. Prices are competitive, starting at RMB 300 for a 1.5m rug, and shopping here beats 6am-haggling at Panjiayuan.
1) Daily 10am-6pm. 106, 2/F, Beijing Curio City, Chaoyang District. (5760 9372, 137 0121 9378); 2) Daily 10am-5.30pm. A501, Liangma Antique Market, Chaoyang District. (6432 1831) 悟心斋地毯店，1）朝阳区北京古玩城2层106；2）朝阳区亮马古玩市场A501

Xu's Antique Carpets Does custom reproductions of genuine antique carpet patterns.
Daily 8am-6pm. 404 Lujiaying Village, Shibalidian, Chaoyang District. (8769 3331) 徐氏地毯，朝阳区十八里店吕家营404号

Zang Han Zhai Carpet Gallery Vast selection of carpets costing an average of RMB 5,000 from Inner Mongolia, Tibet and Qinghai, as well as antique furniture and jewelry. They also provide free repair, cleaning, and packing.
Daily 10am-6pm. 6A Gongti Donglu. (6501 8258) 藏汉斋，工体东路甲6号

Decorating Companies & Materials

Aika The radio commercial has been pounded into your head in countless taxi rides. So what will you find at – repeat twice after me – "Ai Jia Jia Ju?" Cheap, modern-ish furniture of every make and model, as well as construction materials and interior decoration companies.
1) Mon-Fri 9am-6.30pm, Sat-Sun 9am-7pm. Nansanhuan outlet, 75 Chengshousi Lu, Fengtai District. (6765 7187); 2) Mon-Fri 9am-6.30pm, Sat-Sun 9am-7pm. Yansha outlet, 36A Liangmaqiao Lu, Chaoyang District. (6432 1125); 3) Daily 9am-9pm. Xisihuan outlet, 119 Xisihuan Beilu (200m south of Sijiqing Qiao), Haidian District. (8845 7900/2); 4) Mon-Fri 9.30am-6.30pm, Sat-Sun 9.30am-7pm. Wangjing outlet, 66 Beixiangbin Lu, Guangshun Qiao, Guangshun Beidajie, Chaoyang District. (8490 4695) www.china-ajjj.com 爱家家居，1）丰台区南三环店，成寿寺路75号；2）朝阳区燕莎店，亮马桥路甲36号；3）海淀区西四环路店，西四环北路119号（四季青桥南200米）；4）朝阳区望京店，广顺北大街香宾路66号

American Standard & Moen Specialty Store Sells American Standard and Moen brand low-flush model toilets and bathroom accessories.
Daily 9am-5.30pm. Inside Huansanhuan Discount Store (northwest corner of Yuquanying Qiao), Fengtai District. (5107 2282) 美标摩恩专卖店，丰台区玉泉营桥西北角环三家居名品折扣店内

Beijing Jiancai Jingmao Dasha Need a deluxe toilet? This upscale mall carries a good selection of mid- to high-end bathroom fixtures and other furnishings, with showrooms dedicated to Kohler, Toto, Giesseldorf and other world-class brands.
Daily 9.30am-6pm. 14 Dongtucheng Lu, Chaoyang District. (8527 1688) 北京建材经贸大厦，朝阳区东土城路14号

Beijing YWT Interior Design Specializes in interior design, construction, decoration and furniture design for apartments, villas, lofts, retail, dining and office spaces. Contact Phoebe Yeo *(130 1114 1563, ywtdesign@gmail.com)* 北京青年万通装饰工程公司

Boloni Home Decor (Beijing) Co. Ltd. Lifestyle Museum This store displays more than 60 integrated Italian-designed kitchens and stocks cabinets, tables, doors, gas cookers, flooring materials, sinks, faucets, ovens, refrigerators and plants. In-house designers can design and measure kitchens free of charge, and all decoration projects are guaranteed to be finished within 40 days.
Daily 9am-7.30pm. 9 Dingcheng Road, Beisihuan (100m north of Easy Home), Chaoyang District. (8489 9001) 博洛尼家居用品(北京)有限公司，朝阳区博洛尼生活方式馆，北四环鼎成路9号(北四环居然之家往北100米)

B&Q These superstores stock around 40,000 different products including flooring, bathroom and kitchen materials, doors, windows, paints, hardware, tools, curtains, fabrics, furniture and a fabulous drill section. The paint and latex selections are extensive. Wood flooring in oak, teak and walnut are available from RMB 58 to

Even when the stove is off, this kitchen is red-hot

200 per square meter. The staff is knowledgeable and eager. Has an English website.
Daily 9am-9pm. 1) Laiguangying Store, 66 Xiangbin Lu, Chaoyang District. (8490 4848); 2) Nine Dragons Store, 1km east of Shuangjingqiao, Chaoyang District. (8776 8811); 3) Jianxiang Store, 200m south of Jianxiangqiao on eastern side of the street, Chaoyang District. (6235 6611); 4) Golden Season Store, 117 Xisihuan Beilu, Haidian District. (8846 6611); 5) Maliandao Store, 10 Maliandaolu, Xuanwu District. (6331 6611) www.bnq.com.cn 百安居，1) 朝阳区来广营店，香宾路66号；2) 朝阳区九龙店，双井桥往东1公里；3) 朝阳区健翔桥往南200米路东；4) 海淀区金四季店，西四环北路117号；5) 宣武区马连道店，马连道路10号

Castle Interiors Home If your villa needs the royal treatment, visit Castle Interiors for home furnishings, upholstery, curtains, shades, etc. made to order. Wide selection of fabrics.
Daily 10am-6.30pm. 1) 506, Pinnacle Plaza (in the Tian Zhu Real Estate Development Zone), Shunyi District. (8046 4244, 138 1024 9652); 2) 1/F, 13 Jiuxianqiao Lu (intersection of Jiangtai Lu and Jichang Fulu), Chaoyang District. (6433 4858) 悦烨布艺，1) 顺义区天竺房地产开发区荣祥广场506；2) 朝阳区酒仙桥路（将台路和机场辅路十字路口）13号1层

DC Design Features over 1,500 bathroom products, including sanitary, tapware, tiles and accessories from a variety of European brands including Flaminia, Fantini, Cosmic and Caroma.
Daily 8.30am-6.30pm. 1/F, 30 Dongzhong Jie, Dongzhimen, Dongcheng District (6416 1385) www.dcdesign.com.cn 东城区东直门大街30号一层

Dragon Decoration & Engineering Co. Ltd This highly professional and agreeable decorating company can do custom paint jobs at your request.
Daily 9am-6pm. Bldg 1, Donghuashi Beili, Chongwen District. (6718 6972) 北京有龙金胜装饰工程有限责任公司，崇文区东花市北里东区1号楼1层

Easy Home Enormous selection of things like paint, tiles, doors, windows, false ceilings, wallpaper, stone slabs, tiles, wood flooring, carpeting, light fixtures and more. It also sells tons of furniture. Interior decorating companies have offices in these shops.
1) Mon-Fri 9.30am-7.30pm, Sat-Sun 9.30am-8.30pm. Shilihe Outlet, 106 Dayangfang Lu, Shibali Dian, Chaoyang District. (6730 5322); 2) Mon-Fri 9.30am-7.30pm, Sat-Sun 9.30am-8.30pm. Yuquanying outlet, 58 Nansanhuan Xilu, Fengtai District. (8367 9622); 3) Daily 10am-9pm. Golden Resources Outlet, Yuanda Lu, Haidian District. (8887 3558); 4) Mon-Fri 9.30am-7.30pm, Sat-Sun 9.30am-8.30pm. Beisihuan Outlet, 65 Beisihuan Donglu, Chaoyang District. (8463 9988) www.juran.com.cn 居然之家，1) 朝阳区十里河店，十八里店大羊坊路106号；2) 丰台区玉泉营店，南三环西路58号；3) 海淀区金源店，远大路1号；4) 朝阳区北四环店，北四环东路65号

Ferranini Kitchen Furniture Shop This Italian chain features a variety of cutting boards in different shapes, elaborate crystal and glassware (including martini, wine and champagne glasses) and sells top quality integrated kitchens, though prices are steep (RMB 80,000 and up).
Daily 9.30am-6.30pm. 1/F, China International Culture Exchange Center, B9 Dongtucheng Lu, Chaoyang District. (6448 1888) 法尼尼厨卫家居中心，朝阳区和平里东土城路乙9号，中国国际文化交流中心1层

HEC of a Place

Beware: equipment nirvana

by Roy Kesey

HEC is, as its name (kind of) implies, a very dangerous place. By this I mean that it would serve as an excellent setting for "Die Hard 9: John McClane Kicks Ass Without Ever Leaving His Wheelchair". There is an entire aisle devoted to cleavers of various weights and sizes, and don't get me started on what the man could accomplish with an industrial meat-slicer.

An explanation: HEC is the Hotel Equipment Corporation – the mother lode of food-service supplies and furnishings and fittings. If you are looking to equip your kitchen, or to start a restaurant or bar or hotel, or just want to make your friends or enemies think that you're going to start one, this massive three-story box-shaped building is the place to begin.

The first floor is perhaps the most interesting, as it opens with a spectacular selection of knives, then Turkish coffee makers, then toasters that can make twelve pieces of toast at once. Ten steps further in and you're looking at their display of … well … you know how some restaurants have a goofy-looking chef statue out front, holding a blackboard on which are written the Specials of the Day? This place has eight full-size models to choose from, plus five small ones that appear to be more in the condiment family, plus one who's just kind of hanging out.

"Ho ho ho! Bon appétit!"

After that, the list gets very long. Food-warmers and dishware, straw dispensers and ashtrays, an aisle of chopsticks and another of ice-cream scoopers, all sorts of silverware and dishware, plastic serving trays, staff uniforms (including bow ties in assorted colors), menu covers and bread baskets, bedclothes and round glass tabletops, and an astoundingly large number of other things.

Again, that's just the first floor. Non-professionals needn't rise to the third floor – that's where the walk-in freezers, wash stations and monstrous drink dispensers are displayed. But the second floor is a mixture of the small- and the big-time: display cases and oven mitts, pastry molds and kebab racks, scales and meat-hooks and strainers and baking utensils I don't understand at all. Also here is small writ large: cutting boards, for example, that measure three inches thick, three feet wide and eight feet long. There are pots big enough to boil entire families. Vacuum cleaners and brooms and detergent and huge … Huge …

My apologies. My notes get a little hard to read at this point. Apparently this was the moment when I lost control, gave up all pretense at journalism and just started throwing shit in my cart. I left with bags full of cocktail umbrellas, frying pans, tasseled toothpicks and Tupperware. When I got home I found that HEC had already delivered a portable hot dog stand, which I can't remember buying and can't imagine wanting. I don't even like hot dogs. Like I said: a dangerous, dangerous place.

Helen's Interiors For the past four years, Helen has been arranging custom furniture, upholstery, drapery and more for Shunyi residents. Her quaint shop is filled with swatches, fabric and wallpaper books.
Daily 8am-7pm. 6 Tianzhu Huayuan Xilu, Tianzhu Development Zone, Shunyi District.
(6458 6211) 海伦布艺，顺义区天竺开发区天竺花园西路6号

Leroy Merlin Aside from the usual hardware and tools, Leroy Merlin carries kitchen and bathroom materials, flooring, lighting, paint, plumbing, storage units, doors and windows, building materials, electricity, gardening tools and fabrics. The store offers a low-price guarantee: if you find a lower price for the same product at any other DIY chain store in town within 14 days of purchase, Leroy Merlin promises a 200% price difference reimbursement. They also provide a range of services, including interior design consulting, custom ordering, installation, free paint mixing and timber cutting. Free parking and complimentary shuttle bus service to and from Wukesong subway station.
Daily 9am-9pm. 1 Linfeng Lu, (head south on Xisihuan, take the service road and turn left at Fufeng Lu), Fengtai District. (6373 8393) www.leroymerlin.com 乐市梅兰，丰台区科兴桥林枫路1号（东南四环）

Lu Xin Jiayuan A market that features a host of independent retailers. The first floor has wood and stone textured, ceramic and marble wall tiles, as well as colorful glass mosaics for bathroom walls. Some stalls sell the same paint and wallpaper products as those at B&Q, but prices can be bargained down.
Mon-Fri 9am-5.30pm, Sat-Sun 9am-6pm. 1 Xingshikou Lu (north of B&Q's Golden Season chain), Haidian District. (8844 6374) 绿馨家园建材城，海淀区杏石口路1号（百安居金四季店北边）

Orient Home The home furnishings sold here include paint, doors, hot water heaters, toilets, bathroom and kitchen appliances from local and foreign brands, including Bosch, American Standard, Moen and Nippon Paint. Furniture also available. Interior decorating companies have outlets in these stores.
Daily 9am-9pm. 1) Laiguangying outlet, 55 Laiguangying Xilu, Chaoyang District. (8495 0800); 2) Luying outlet, 1 Nansihuan Donglu, Chaoyang District. (8769 9771); 3) Guanzhuang outlet, 28 Chaoyang Lu, Chaoyang District. (6547 6880); 4) Lize outlet, 55 Xisanhuan Nanlu, Fengtai District. (8366 6611); 5) Xisanqi outlet, west of Badaling Expressway (300m south of Xisanqi Qiao), Haidian District. (8271 3311); 6) Bajiao outlet, 168 Fushi Lu, Shijingshan District. (6886 2886) www.orienthome.com.cn 东方家园，1）朝阳区来广营店，来广营西路55号；2）朝阳区吕营店，南四环东路1号；3）朝阳区管庄店，朝阳路28号；4）丰台区丽泽店，西三环南路55号；5）海淀区西三旗店，西三旗桥南300米八达岭高速西侧；6）石景山区八角店，阜石路168号

Roca Sells bathtubs, whirlpools, faucets and accessories for the bathroom.
Daily 9am-6.30pm. 1) 1/F, Tianheng Mansion, 46 Dongzhimenwai Dajie, Dongcheng District. (8460 8586) 2) Rm 003, 1/F, Bldg 3, Easy Home Shilihe Store, 106 Dayangfang Lu, Shibalidian, Chaoyang District. (6730 1741) 3) Rm 1-023, 1/F, Easy Home Yuquanying Store, 58 Nansanhuan Xilu, Fengtai District. (6371 2098) 4) Rm J-1032, Easy Home Jinyuan Store, 1 Yuandalu, Haidian District. (8887 2879) 乐家洁具，1）东城区东直门外大街46号，天恒大厦1层 2）朝阳区十八里店大羊坊路106号，居然之家十里河店3号楼1层003厅 3）丰台区南三环西路58号，居然之家玉泉营店1层1－023厅 4）海淀区远大路1号，居然之家金源店J－1032厅

Sihui Jiancai Cheng A massive market filled with shops selling different kinds of doors, tiles, paints, massive slabs of stone, kitchen counters, electrical wires and anything else you could need for remodeling.
Daily 8am-5.30pm. Southeast corner of Sihui Qiao (directly east of Soho), Chaoyang District. (6774 5216) 四惠建材城，朝阳区四惠桥东南角（Soho正东面）

Sureline Design and Construction This Australian-owned company provides renovations and interior decoration services for homes, offices, shops and nightclubs. English spoken. Ask for Chi or Ryan.
Daily 9am-5.30pm. 25P New York Building, Duhui Huating Compound, Shilipu, Chaoyang District. (6557 0729, 139 117 35922) 顺兴堂，朝阳区十里堡都会华庭纽约阁25P

Ye Zhi Feng One of Beijing's largest decorating companies.
Daily 9am-5.30pm. Headquarters at 10/F, Tower A, Chengjian Building, Beitai Pingzhuang, Haidian District. (8225 5866) www.yzf.com.cn 业之峰装饰，海淀区北太平庄城建大厦A座10层

Electronics & Home Appliances

Bang & Olufsen Fashionable and expensive retailer of boutique electronic goods sells products ranging from home theater systems to wireless phone systems.
1) Daily 10 am-10 pm. 2/F, Shin Kong Place, 87 Jianguo Lu, Chaoyang District. (6553 1041); 2) Daily 10.30am-10pm. AA63, Oriental Plaza, 1 Dongchang'an Jie, Dongcheng District. (8518 6808) 波士，1）朝阳区建国路87号新光天地2层；2）东城区东长安街1号东方广场AA63

Bose Bose's new store at Oriental Plaza sells home theater systems, stereo speakers, headphones and headsets, outdoor and marine speakers as well as accessories. Prices are reasonable relative to quality, and the store offers home delivery service.
Daily 9am-10pm. AA52A Oriental Plaza, 1 Dongchang'an Jie, Dongcheng District. (8518 6885) 博士音响，东城区东长安街1号东方新天地AA52A

Bower & Wilkins B & W speakers are legendary in the audiophile world and range in price from affordable to extremely costly. Their award-winning 705 series speakers are priced at RMB 14,650, but you can try to bargain.
Daily 9.30am-10pm. BB90 Oriental Plaza, 1 Dongchang'an Jie, Dongcheng District. (8518 6834) B&W音响，东城区东长安街1号东方新天地地铁层

Dazhong With 41 stores across Beijing, it's easy to find a branch of this chain, which stocks domestic and foreign brands of household appliances, TVs, DVD players, PCs and more. Just don't expect helpful service here.
www.dzelec.com 大中电器连锁店

Digao Audio Digao sells high performance audio equipment, so you can transform your living room into a hi-fi arena. Choose from over a dozen types of speakers from RMB 4,000 to RMB 10,000, and a range of CD players, DVD players, amplifiers and high-quality cables.

SHOPPING 377

Daily 10am-6.30pm. 2/F, Golden Resources Mall, 1 Yuanda Lu, Haidian District. (8887 0088) 迪高音响，海淀区远大路1号金源燕莎购物中心2层

Dongfang Qicai Dashijie A secondhand electronics store offering TVs, stereos, DVD players, refrigerators and more. Prices are cheap, but sometimes you get what you pay for. Test out everything carefully on-site.
Daily 9am-6pm. Dongfang Qicai Dashijie, Laitai Huajie, Chaoyang District. (8448 4336) 东方七彩大世界二手家电市场，朝阳区莱太花街东方七彩大世界

Gome In its 14 stores across the city, Gome stocks a wide range of home appliances as well as PCs and DVD players from the cheap to the mind-blowingly expensive. The sales assistants are very capable. If taking your player to another country, ask if it has encoding restrictions. See www.gome.com.cn/upload/2005/8/18/20050818053557142.jpg for all addresses.
Daily 9am-9pm. 76 Beisanhuan Zhonglu, Haidian District. (5857 2628, toll free 400 811 3333) 国美电器商城，海淀区北三环中路76号

Top Electronics City This five-story electronics super mall is well known for its stock of PDAs, DV cameras, MP3 players, mobile hard drives, Bluetooth accessories and smart phones. There are also computer parts and laptops at reasonable prices.
Daily 9am-9pm. Southwest corner of Zhongguancun Dajie and Beisihuan Lu, Haidian District. (800 810 7168, 8269 8269) 鼎好数码商城，海淀区中关村大街和北四环路十字路口西南角

Xinxingguang Audio Shop Xinxingguang in Xinjiekou sells high performance audio equipment. With a collection of international brands ranging from Elac loudspeaker to Arcam power amplifier, their prices range from RMB 2,000 to 30,000 and beyond. Customers are encouraged to try the products in the audition room before taking them home.
Daily 9.30am-6pm. 118 Xinjiekou Nandajie, Xicheng District. (6611 2141) 鑫星光，西城区新街口南大街118号

Framing

Beijing Golden Light Exhibition Services For the best prices, reliable service and guaranteed quality, go to this frame shop opposite the National Art Museum. They stock all the frames you can find in Sanlitun - for about half the price. Look next door too.
Daily 9am-6.30pm. 18A Wusi Dajie, Dongcheng District. (6528 4940) 金辉画框，东城区五四大街甲18号

Red Passion Folks Arts Gallery This family-owned and operated framing shop offers polite, prompt and exact service. It carries a wide range of frames at all prices and all colors, and can frame anything. Best of all, Red Passion uses identical materials to Wins and charges half the price, with free delivery and polite service thrown in. Healthy competition is indeed a good thing.
Daily 9.30am-7pm. Sanlitun Beilu (opposite Unicef), Chaoyang District. (6413 0885) 朝阳区三里屯北路

Tammy's Framing Shop Not easy to find, this small shop in the Shunyi area sells quality frames at reasonable prices (4 x 6 for RMB 5, 8 x 10 frames for RMB 30).
Daily 9am-6.30pm. House 15-4-8 (behind Beijing Riviera, turn north at Li Yuan Garden and continue for 50m), Shunyi District. (6438 2998, 136 4135 0949) 顺义区香江花園街，丽苑小区往北50米，15-4-8号楼

Wins Arts and Framing A quality but very pricey operation staffed by knowledgeable pros, Wins has a large selection of good frames.
1) Daily 10am-7pm. 702, Pinnacle Plaza (in the Tianzhu Real Estate Development Zone), Shunyi District. (8046 5266); 2) Daily 9.30am-7pm. A6 Gongti Donglu, Chaoyang District. (6508 0876) 文饰画框，1）顺义区荣祥广场702号（天竺房地产开发区内）；2）朝阳区工体东路甲6号

Furniture

Beijing Xinbiaozhi Furniture Center You will find cheap, basic furniture here, such as a queen-sized bed for RMB 1,000, a foam pad for RMB 100, or a bookshelf for RMB 400. You can have things made to order for only a little more; make sure to bargain their ticketed prices down at least 10-30%.
Daily 8am-8pm. 187 Dongsi Beidajie, Dongcheng District. (8402 8684) 北京鑫标志家具中心，东城区东四北大街187号

Beking The designs look Scandinavian but the slogan is "Really as good as German." Whatever the label, Beking stocks contemporary wood furniture similar in appearance to, but cheaper than, the pieces available at QM.
Mon-Fri 9am-6.30pm, Sat-Sun 9am-7.30pm. Inside Aika (see Decorating Companies & Materials), A36 Liangmaqiao Lu, Chaoyang District. (6432 1159) www.baiqiang.com.cn 北京世纪百强家具，朝阳区亮马桥路甲36号爱家家居内

Bo Concept Denmark's Bo Concept offers, at reasonably affordable prices, understated designer furniture and accessories made of wood (oak, maple and cherry), steel and leather. An ultra-modern, low-lying Lino-3500 bed is yours for RMB 8,999.
Daily 9am-8pm. 1) B2/F, Cofco Plaza, 8 Jianguomennei Dajie, Dongcheng District. (6526 3847); 2) Daily 9am-10pm. 4/F, North Bldg, Parkson Center, Fuxingmen, Xicheng District. (6607 3644) 北欧风情，1）东城区建国门内大街8号中粮广场地下2层；2）西城区复兴门百盛北楼4层

Chengwaicheng Furniture Mall This massive barn could be called "Cheap Furniture 'R' Us." Avoid coming on weekends, when it seems all of Beijing's new homeowners meet here.
Mon-Fri 9am-6pm, Sat-Sun 9am-7pm. 308 Chengshousi Lu (northeast of Xiaocun Qiao on Nansihuan), Fengtai District. (6765 1234) 城外城家居文化广场，丰台区成寿寺路308号（南四环肖村桥东北）

Colombini One of the largest furniture groups in Italy, specializing in bedroom furniture. Their products have a distinctive Italian design and are characterized by a high level of functionality.
Daily 9.30am-7.30pm. 1) North Easy Home, 65 Beisihuan Donglu, Chaoyang District. (8463 8705); 2) Daily 10am-9pm. West Easy Home, 1 Yuanda Lu, Haidian District. (8887 3380) www.colombinigroup.com 哥伦比尼，1）朝阳区北四环东路65号居然之家 2）海淀区远大路1号西居然之家

Dadizheyang Outdoor Garden Furniture This store is a real find with its showroom chock-full of garden furniture including durable, attractive outdoor tables & chairs, umbrellas, and chaises. On either side of this shop along Jingshun Lu are many plant shops carrying all manner of indoor and outdoor plants so you can

Rain or shine, these rainbow-hued chairs from Sunstyle will brighen up any patio

deck out your patio or garden like a tropical paradise.
Daily 7:30am-7.30pm. Jingshun Lu, Chaoyang District. (8459 3665, 8167 7425) www.zheyang.com.cn
大地遮阳，朝阳区京顺路

Dara Featuring Asian and European designs, this trendy expat favorite sells furniture, antique accessories, dishware, cushions, lamps, lush fabrics, mirrors, pottery and more. Dara's Dashanzi outlet houses a small gallery showing contemporary art. Paintings do not come cheap, starting at around RMB 8,000. Custom design service available.
1) Show room: Daily 10am-6pm. Zone D, 798 Xijie, 798 Art District, 2 Jiuxianqiao Lu, Chaoyang District. (6434 5382); 2) Daily 10am-6pm. 1A south of Huantie Qiao, Dong Wuhuan Lu, Chaoyang District. (6431 6366); 3) Daily 9am-6pm. 1/F, Central Park, 6 Chaowai Dajie, Chaoyang District. (6597 0650); 4) Daily 10am-7pm. 17 Gongti Beilu (opposite north gate of Workers' Stadium), Chaoyang District. (6417 9365) 家大家业，1）朝阳区酒 仙桥2号798艺术新区798西街D区；2）朝阳区东五环铁桥南甲1号；3）朝阳区朝外大街6号新城国际公寓1层；4）朝阳区工体北路17号（工体北门正对面）

Do Link Come here for unique, quality furniture, puppets or collectable pandas in Chinese outfits. Made-to-order pillows, cushions and more.
Tue-Sun 10am-6pm. 508, Pinnacle Plaza (in the Tianzhu Real Estate Development Zone), Shunyi District. (8046 5643, 139 1135 4272) 东篱阁，顺义区荣祥广场508号（天竺房地产开发区内）

Ethan Allen (Markor Furnishings) Solid, handsome and unabashedly retro, the pieces range from heavy black leather sofas and beach tables to Victorian four-poster beds, dining room sets, chests of drawers and chaises. You can call toll free (800 818 6337).
Daily 10am-9pm. 1) 1-3/F, Bldg A, Markorhome Mansion, 57 Xisanhuan Nanlu, Fengtai District. (6386 2727); 2) 108 Beisihuan Donglu, Chaoyang District. (8483 1330); 3) Bldg 2, Greenlake Place, northeast corner of Chaoyanggongyuan Qiao, Chaoyang District. (5928 2211) www.markorhome.com 美克美家，1）丰台区西三环南路57号美克美家大厦；2）朝阳区北四环东路108号；3）朝阳区朝阳公园桥东北角观湖国际2号楼

Exquisite Chinese Classical Furniture Stocks a wide variety of classic styles and custom-made pieces. English-speaking staff.
Daily 8.30am-7.30pm. Baixinzhuang Village, Houshayu Town, Shunyi District. (8046 3323, 136 0118 3786). 中式古典家具，顺义区后沙峪镇白辛庄村

Flexa Flexa sells durable, wooden kids' furniture such as beds, desks, shelves, wardrobes, cribs and all the attendant accessories like mattresses, playpens, tunnels, linen, bean bags, changing mats and much, much more. Best of all, the items "grow" with your kids: for example, the Flexa (RMB 4,743) can be turned into an extendable trainer bed (from 120cm-200cm). Want your kids to think you're the best parents ever? Get a bunk bed with a slide.
1) Daily 9.30am-8pm. B2/F, Cofco Plaza, 8 Jianguomennei Dajie, Dongcheng District. (6524 2726); 2) Mon-Fri 9.30am-8pm, Sat-Sun 9.30am-8.30pm. 2/F, Easy Home, 65 Beisihuan Donglu, Chaoyang District. (8462 9029); 3) Mon-Fri 9.30am-8pm, Sat-Sun 9am-9pm. 1/F, Lanjinglijia, Dazhongsi, Haidian District. (8211 7233); 4) Mon-Fri 9am-6.30pm, Sat-Sun 9am-7pm. 3/F, Red Star Macalline, 193 Dajiaoting Qiao,

SHOPPING

Oh deer! This chair could use a few cushions

Chaoyang District. (8795 1515); 5) Mon-Fri 10am-9pm, Sat-Sun 9.30am-9pm. 1/F, Easy Home, Golden Resouces Mall, 1 Yuanda Lu, Haidian District. (8887 3379) www.flexa.dk 芙莱莎，1）东城区建国门内大街8号中粮广场地下1层；2）朝阳区北四环东路65号居然之家2层；3）海淀区大钟寺蓝景丽家1层；4）朝阳区大郊亭桥193号东四环红星美凯龙3层；5）海淀区远大路1号世纪金源居然之家1层

Fulite This discount furniture city offers beds ranging from RMB 900 to 4,000 – mattress included. A good place to kit out an unfurnished flat at minimum cost. *Mon-Fri 9am-6pm, Sat-Sun 9am-6.30pm. Beisanhuan Zhonglu, Xicheng District. (6204 3196)* 福利特家具商场，西城区北三环中路

Homexcel Haidian area furniture dealer specializes in Stanley furniture, Uttermost lights and Flexsteel sofas. *Daily 10am-6.30pm. A103, Jiahao International Center, 116 Zizhuyuan Lu, Haidian District (5893 1156)* www.homexcel.com.cn 北京非常家家具，海淀区紫竹院路116号嘉豪国际中心A103

Ikea Yes, we poke fun at the names of its products, but, truth be told, we've ventured here several times for affordable, quality home furnishings. In addition to an enormous selection, its draws include an indoor playground and a canteen that serves Swedish meatballs and decadent chocolate cookies. The store will, for a fee, send a technician to your house to assemble your purchases. Delivery available. *Daily 10am-10pm. 1 Taiyang Gonglu, Dongbahe (northwest corner of Siyuan Qiao), Chaoyang District. (800 810 5679)* www.ikea.com.cn 宜家家居，朝阳区东坝河太阳宫路1号（四元桥西北角）

Illinois Home Illinois is a funkier, pricier version of Ikea that sells wall-sized mirrors (RMB 2000 and up), tangerine sofas (RMB 8,880) a martini glass-shaped chair (3,600 RMB) and home essentials like candy-colored bathmats (RMB 117), pots and pans, groovy lanterns, juice-makers and stainless steel salt and pepper shakers (RMB 60). *Daily 9am-7.30pm. 1 Jingang Dadao, inside Goldenport (look for the big pink building), Chaoyang District. (8433 4969, 8433 4902)* 伊力诺依，朝阳区金港大道1号金港公园内

Jingetiema Ma Baoju, the friendly owner of this custom metalworking shop, works out of his colorful courtyard home. He can make bedframes, tables, chairs, and pretty much anything else you want out of metal – the emphasis is definitely on practicality over style. Prices vary, but a raised, loft-style metal cot frame costs around RMB 1200. If you want to be absolutely sure about what you're getting, be sure to print out a picture beforehand, especially if you don't speak Chinese. *Daily 9am-6pm. 16 Hucang Hutong, Ping'an Dajie, Xicheng District. (6618 1375, 135 2040 7569)* 金戈铁马，西城区平安大街护仓胡同16号

Kang Deco Features modernized reinventions of Ming dynasty furniture. Full-height, louvered panels (RMB 800 each) partition the window display area from the rest of the shop, which has a selection of stylish living room, dining and bedroom pieces, to make that ideal "contemporary Asian" home. Exquisite birdcage-shaped, beaded table lamps (RMB 1,450) are among a collection of classy accessories that could solve the dilemma for housewarming gift-givers. Customizing services are available.

Daily 10am-8.30pm. Rm 9104, Holiday Inn Lido, Jiangtai Lu, Chaoyang District. (6437 6330) 东喜々福。朝阳区将台路丽都公寓9104室

Laitai Flower Market Basement Here you'll find many stalls selling traditional Chinese-style lamps including reading lamps with porcelain bases. Prices range from RMB 400-700, though natural jade lampshades are considerably more (from RMB 2,000-4,000).
Mon-Thu 9am-6pm, Fri-Sun 9am-6.30pm. 9 Maizidian Xilu, Chaoyang District. (6463 5588) 莱太花卉市场。朝阳区麦子店西路9号

Ligne Roset Home of modern French furniture at its finest. Made of steel, leather and fancy wood, the award-winning sofas, chairs, beds and tables are flawlessly designed. "Look at me," they command, "I am French! I am stylish!" Or something to that effect.
Daily 9am-8pm. C7, B2/F, Cofco Plaza, 8 Jianguomennei Dajie, Dongcheng District. (6526 3965) www.ligne-roset.com.cn 写意空间。东城区建国门内大街8号。中粮广场地下2层C7

Modern European Design Sparse, contemporary home and office furniture from Europe that is not devoid of humor. Favorites include a steel and milk-cow leather chair from Porado (RMB 19,656) and a green lip-shaped chair by Dema (RMB 24,156). The bulbous lights from IQLight are far freakin' out, man.
Daily 9.30am-9pm. C1, B2/F, Cofco Plaza, 8 Jianguomennei Dajie, Dongcheng District. (6526 3965) www.eurohome.com.cn 欧罗巴。东城区建国门内大街8号中粮广场地下2层C1

Nature's Secret This furniture showroom is filled with Australian-designed chairs, tables, consoles, etc. which are crafted from a variety of beautiful woods, imported from Oz, including Tasmanian Oak, Tiger wood, Blackwood, and Redgum. They also carry a selection of hard-to-find plush mattresses with three different levels of softness.
Daily 9am-9pm. 38 Fuqian Yijie Tianzhu Town, Shunyi District. (6457 8736/6038) www.natures-secret.com.cn 自然风格。顺义区天竺镇府前一街38号

QM Furniture European design at Chinese prices! This local firm hires Danish designers to turn out sleek furniture.
Mon-Fri 8.30am-8pm, Sat-Sun 8.30am-8.30pm. 29 Xiaoyun Lu, Chaoyang District. (6464 6301) 曲美家具城。朝阳区霄云路29号

Royal Furniture Modern Hong Kong-designed furniture, beds, bookshelves and soft pillows. Also sells glassware and home decor items.
Daily 10am-9pm 1) 10 Langjiayuan, Dongchang'an Jie, Chaoyang District. (8580 4270); 2) 2/F, Bldg 4, Easy Home Shilihe Store, 106 Dayangfang Lu, Shibalidian, Chaoyang District. (8736 6919); 3) Rm 14, 3/F, Easy Home Yuquanying Store, 58 Nansanhuan Xilu, Fengtai District. (8367 9343) www.hkroyal.com 皇朝家私 1) 朝阳区东长安街郎家园10号 2) 朝阳区十八里店大羊坊路106号居然之家十里河店4号楼2层 3) 丰台区南三环西路58号家玉泉营店3层14号

Shang Gu City Classical Furniture and Arts Center This two-story emporium sells high but there is room for bargaining. There's also a carpet shop on the ground floor and, on the first floor, a boutique with reasonably priced home decor items like table runners, Thai-style triangle pillows and placemats. A good spot to source holiday gifts.

Daily 10am-8pm. 5 Laiguangying Donglu, Chaoyang District. (8470 3996) www.antiquefurniture.com.cn 尚古城古典家具艺术中心。朝阳区来广营东路5号

Sunstyle Specializes in upscale outdoor furniture, featuring such brands as Dedon (Germany) and Gloster (UK). The showroom has a swimming pool and bar area available for corporate events.
Daily 9am-6pm. 1 Nangao Donglu, Chaoyang District. (6431 0020) www.sunstyle.com 圣诗得。朝阳区南皋路东1号

Vita If you have all the money in the world but don't know where to blow it, this is the place. A purveyor of Italian chic, Vita sells high-priced furniture and accessories by designers like Alessi, B&B Italia, Flou, Ultramobile, Magis and Matteograssi. Customers can also search through Vita's many catalogues for European goods that can be imported.
Daily 10am-7pm. 2-2 Jinbao Jie, Dongcheng District. (8511 8880) www.vita-furniture.com 丰意德。东城区金宝街2-2号

Yue Fu Zhai High-end Ming-style furniture made with rare hard woods like scented rosewood and May Dou wood. Not for paupers, as prices are on par with the quality - a side table starts at RMB 22,000; a pair of chairs sells for RMB 50,000.
Daily 9am-5pm. A25 Mananli, Laiguangying Donglu, Chaoyang District. (8470 1107) www.huanghuali.com.cn 阅甫斋。朝阳区来广营东路马南里甲25号

Zizaoshe Design Possibly the most interesting store in Cofco Plaza, Zizaoshe sells elegant Chinese furniture that mixes traditional and contemporary elements: carved chairs with backs made of untreated wood, old Shanghai-style screens, handmade pottery, lamps, fabulous prints and gallery-caliber art.
Daily 9.30am-8pm. D2, B3/F, Cofco Plaza, 8 Jianguomennei Dajie, Dongcheng District. (8511 8611) www.zizaoshe.com 自造社。东城区建国门内大街8号中粮广场地下3层D2

Home Essentials

Alessi Created in 1921, this leading Italian brand has made a reputable name in designer household items including tableware, kitchen, bathroom products and everyday knick-knacks. Interesting items include the "Girotondo" Ice Cube Mould (RMB 400), which makes 14 "little person-shaped" ice cubes, the "Big Bubble" soap dish (RMB 330), a companion toothpaste holder (RMB 330), and plenty of polished stainless steel Cactus utensils.
Sun-Thu 9.30am-9pm, Fri-Sat 9.30am-9.30pm. NB142, China World Shopping Mall, 1 Jianguomenwai Dajie, Chaoyang District. (6505 1689) 朝阳区建国门外大街1号国贸商城NB142

Aussino Good quality, no-nonsense linens and towels. Double-bed sheet sets cost RMB 159-179.
1) Daily 8.30am-9.30pm. 2/F, Piaoliang Shopping Center, Changping District. (6498 9482); 2) Daily 8.30am-9.30pm. B1/F, Bldg D, Sunshine 100, 2 Guanghua Lu, Chaoyang District. (6508 4232); 3) Daily 10am-10pm. 4/F, Wangjing Mall, 13 Guangshui Beidajie, Chaoyang District. (8472 9297); 4) 8.30am-10pm. 1/F, Shuangjing Carrefour, 31 Guangqu Lu, Chaoyang District. (5190 9459); 5) Daily 9.30am-9.30pm. 54 Dongsi Nandajie, Dongcheng District. (6512 8161); 6) Daily 8am-10.30pm. B1/F, Zhongguancun Carrefour, Haidian District. (5172 1231); 7) Daily 9.30am-9.30pm.

55 Xinjiekou Nandajie, Xicheng District. (6618 7224); 8) Daily 8.30am-9.30pm. 2/F, Carrefour, 15 Maliandao, Xuanwu District. (6331 3605) 澳西奴，1）昌平区飘亮购物中心2楼；2）朝阳区光华路2号阳光100公寓D座地下1层；3）朝阳区广顺北大街13号嘉贸购物中心4层；4）朝阳区广渠路31号双井家乐福一层；5）东城区东四环大街54号；6）海淀区中关村家乐福超市地下一层；7）西城区新街口南大街55号；8）宣武区马连道家乐福2层

Bed Top the Thing Tonny Xu sells the same quilts you find at Yashow market without the attitude and for less than a third the price (RMB 180 vs RMB 600 for a double). Sweet dreams.
Daily 10am-7pm. Stall 128B, 2/F, MEN Shopping Center, Yabao Lu, Chaoyang District. (139 0130 6084) 朝阳区雅宝路朝外MEN市场2层128B

Beijing Binfen Gardening & Landscaping A toast to this shop which specializes in stylish, inexpensive drinking vessels, including champagne flutes (RMB 10) and large Bordeaux wine glasses (RMB 10), as well as blood-red square dinner plates (RMB 10) and candles. Cheers.
Daily 8.30am-6pm. 2/F, Liangma Flower Market, 8B Dongsanhuan Beilu, Chaoyang District. (6504 4070) www.binfen.com.cn 北京缤纷玻璃器皿，朝阳区东三环北路乙8号亮马花卉市场2层

Blissliving Blissliving features European-style sheets, pillowcases and fine quilts. It also offers custom-tailor services to cater to your unique taste.
Daily 10am-10pm. 1043-1045, 3.3 Shopping Center, 33 Sanlitun Lu, Chaoyang District. (5136 5296) www.blissliving.com.cn 布莉丝，朝阳区三里屯路3.3服饰大厦1043－1045

Cat Shop It's as though your sister returned from her backpacking trip and decided to sell all her souvenirs. Thai silver jewellery, Thai textiles, bags and Balinese cat figurines (RMB 15) seem to be the main focus. A miniature biplane (RMB 498) graces the shelves beside wooden CD holders (RMB 168), Thai cow-bone rice spoons (RMB 85) and coffee mugs (RMB 35).
Daily 11.30am-9pm. 22 Dongzhi Jie (facing East Gate Plaza Bldg A), Dongcheng District. (6416 7585) 时光杂货铺，东城区东中街22号（东环广场A座对面）

Chang and Biörck Chang and Biörck take a dash of Scandinavian sensitivity and add Chinese flair to their designer enamelware, fabrics, cushions, lanterns and other tableware – a perfect fusion of East and West. Products are sold by appointment only in their office showroom. Visit the website to book an appointment.
Rm 511, Bldg A, Sky & Sea Business Plaza, 107 Dongsi Beidajie, Dongcheng District. (8400 2296) www.changbiorck.com 东城区东四北大街107号天海商务大厦A座511室

Chief Chop Deals in Bentuzi vases, off-kilter bottle holders, Alessi juicers and fancy wine racks – cool gear for your home bar.
B058, 3.3 Shopping Center, 33 Sanlitun Lu, Chaoyang District. (139 0119 3605) 朝阳区三里屯路33号3.3服装大厦B058

emo+ This store is purveyor to some of the world's most famous houseware and accessory designers. The store also sells Twemco's "flipping digit" style clocks (RMB 858), colorful fridge magnets that double as bottle openers (RMB 385), and Alessi's well-known "Dr. Skud" fly swatters, which stands on its own three feet and sports the face of Dr. Skud on it. Photo buffs will find a selection of interesting cameras.
Daily 1pm-8.30pm. 1) Opposite the south gate of the Great Wall Sheraton Hotel, Liangmaqiao, Dongsanhuan, Chaoyang District. (8587 4805); 2) Mon-Fri 10am-9pm, Sat-Sun 1pm-8.30pm. Rm 103, Bldg 4, Soho New Town, 88 Jianguo Lu, Chaoyang District. (8589 2787) emo+生活概念店，1）朝阳区东三环亮马桥长城饭店南门对面（农展北路路口）；2）朝阳区建国路88号Soho现代城4号桔色公寓103

Emperor Gorgeous placemats, napkins, runners and other decorative items that incorporate traditional Chinese silk. Find great housewarming gifts ... or keep them for yourself.
1) Daily 9.30am-9.30pm. Store NB148, B1/F, China World Shopping Mall, 1 Jianguomenwai Dajie, Chaoyang District. (6505 6146); 2) Daily 9.30am-10pm. AA12 Oriental Plaza, 1 Dongchang'an Jie, Dongcheng District. (8518 6148) 皇锦，1）朝阳区建国门外大街1号国贸商城地下1层NB148店；2）东城区东长安街1号东方新天地AA12

Esprit Home Sells stylish sheets and linens.
F7, Zhongyou Shopping Center, 176 Xidan Beidajie, Xicheng District (6601 8899) 西城区西单北大街176号中友大厦7层

Exquisite Chinese Classical Furniture Yes, it lives up to its name. A wide variety of classic styles and custom-made pieces. The adjoining workshop repairs pieces and re-creates furniture from diagrams or photographs. Average prices, convenient location, English-speaking manager.
Daily 8am-7pm. Baixinzhuang Village, Houshayu Town, Shunyi District. (8046 3323, 136 0118 3786) 中式古典家具，顺义区后沙峪镇白辛庄村

Felissimo Felissimo is a Japanese chain stocking a variety of lifestyle knick-knacks like ceramic utensils, green-tea-filled pillows and many other smart ideas for home decor. Felissimo also has a casual but stylish clothing line.
1) Daily 10am-9pm. WB117, China World Shopping Mall, 1 Jianguomenwai Dajie, Chaoyang District. (6505 3077); 2) Daily 10.30am-9.30pm. 2/F, Fulllink Plaza, Chaoyangmenwai Dajie, Chaoyang District. (6588 0848); 3) Daily 9.30am-9pm. 3/F, Xidan Juntai Shopping Mall, Xicheng District. (6615 6487); 4) Daily 9am-10pm. 1/F, Yulin Bldg, 5A Er Xiang, Xiangjun Nanli, Chaoyang District. (5131 1127) 芬理希梦，1）朝阳区建外大街1号国贸商场WB117；2）朝阳区朝外大街丰联广场二层；3）西城区西单君太百货3层；4）朝阳区向军南里二巷甲5号雨霖大厦一层

Flora Homeware Flora boasts an extensive selection of interior decor accessories and upholstery fabrics. The shop's artisans can custom design everything from bamboo shades to curtains.
Daily 9.30am-8pm. 8 Laiguangying Donglu (near WAB), Chaoyang district. (8470 1547, 1352 0874 820) 曲院风荷，朝阳区来广营东路8号，京西学校旁边

Gaojingzhong Kitchen Supplies For the professional cook within: industrial mixing machines, metal pastry cases, woks, cute bronze hotpots and even a selection of chef's whites.
Daily 8.30am-5pm. 23 Di'anmenwai Dajie, Xicheng District. (6404 0749) 高精中厨具，西城区地安门外大街23号

Doughn't try baking without cookie sheets

Gogo Fish This sophisticated shop sells ceiling lanterns in funky colors like ash brown, brushed rose, tangerine and lime; their organic shapes recall Gaudi or a dipped cone at Dairy Queen. Gogo Fish also stocks hand-painted china, embroidered pillows, Buddha statues, folk art, jade jewelry and lots of fish designs, of course.
Daily 10am-10pm. South of Luoma Lake, Shunyi District. (8049 8699/4566) www.gogofish.cn 鱼乐居, 顺义区裕京花园罗马湖边

Home and Beyond If the candle craze is still waxing at your pad, or if power failures are frequent, you'll adore Home and Beyond's candles and candleholders of every shape, color and purpose (e.g. romance-inducing). Who can resist the apple-scented tea candles (six for RMB 6)?
Mon-Thu 9am-6pm, Fri-Sun 9am-6.30pm. B1/F, Laitai Flower Market, 9 Maizidian Xilu, Chaoyang District. (6463 5588 ext 8123) 东京蜡烛, 朝阳区莱太花卉市场地下1层

Hotel Equipment Corporation It's three huge stories of everything you would ever need in the way of dishware, silverware, glassware, tableware, cooking utensils, cooking appliances and kitchen gear. It's the only place you need to know if you are opening a bar or restaurant or just kitting out your own kitchen. You'll find a martini shaker for RMB 40, set of 6 wine glasses for RMB 22-40, and a US/Metric measuring cup for RMB 15.
Daily 9am-5.30pm. 1 Kaiyangli Yijie, You'anmenwai, Fengtai District. (8355 2598) www.hec.com.cn/english/index.asp HEC 酒店设备, 丰台区右安门外开阳里一街1号

Ifugao Inexpensive bed linens: RMB 99 for a set of double bed sheets (150cm x 200cm) and four pillows. Or how about RMB 2 for a colorful 45cm x 45cm pillowcase? That's cheaper than a sundae at McDonalds!

Daily 10am-9pm. 4/F, Golden Resources Mall, 1 Yuanda Lu, Haidian District. (8887 5385) 依富高, 海淀区远大路1号金源新燕莎Mall4层

Karolina Lehman Fans of traditional Chinese porcelain will delight in the store's lovely tea sets, which are decorated with floral patterns, birds, fish and even hippos. You'll also find lamps, bowls, candleholders, decorative ducks and lions and wallpaper at decent prices.
Mon-Fri 9am-6pm, Sat-Sun 9am-6.30pm. B1/F, Laitai 49 Flower Market, Chaoyang District. (8454 0387, 139 1139 7922) 卡罗丽娜雷门, 朝阳区莱太花卉市场地下1层

Laitai Xinda Ceramics The ceramics sold here include plates and bowls (RMB 15 and up) in different sizes and colors, teapots (starting at RMB 10) and coffee sets. Their hand-drawn ceramic series is a bit more expensive: a Qing-style painted plate costs RMB 240.
Daily 9am-6pm. B1/F, North Hall, Laitai Flower Market, 9 Maizidian Xilu, Chaoyang District. (6463 5588 ext 8107) 莱太鑫达陶瓷公司, 朝阳区麦子店西路9号莱太花卉地下1层北厅

Life Shop High-end antique reproduction accessories such as Buddha heads and Vietnamese scarves.
1) Mon-Sat 10am-5pm. 2 Jiuxianqiao Lu, Chaoyang District. (8456 7780); 2) Daily 10am-9.30pm. 111 Lido Hotel, Jiangtai Lu, Chaoyang District. (6430 1245) 乐福行, 1) 朝阳区酒仙桥路2号; 2) 朝阳区将台路丽都酒店111

Piv: style This small shop specializes in funky home accessories, including lamps, designer rugs, kitchenware, ashtrays and more.
Daily 10am-9pm. WB120, B1/F, China World Shopping Mall, 1 Jianguomenwai Dajie, Chaoyang District.

A square disco ball!? Potato & Co's inventive chandeliers are the ultimate razzle-dazzle

(6505 0375) www.pivstyle.com 朝阳区建外大街1号国贸商城地下一层WB120

Potato & Co Features a wide array of modern, inventively designed goods for the home, such as chandeliers, photo frames, clocks and novelty items, from around RMB 100-300.
1) Daily 10am-9.30pm. NB 144, B1/F, China World Shopping Mall, 1 Jianguomenwai Dajie. (6505 1469);
2) Daily 10am-10pm. L331, 3/F, The Place, 9A Guanghua Lu, Chaoyang District. (6587 1301) 图逗，1) 建国门外大街1号中国国际贸易中心国贸商城地下1层NB144号； 2) 光华路9号世贸天阶3层L331

Pyramid Glassware Stocks martini glasses and an assortment of tasteful glass items for your kitchen and dining area.
Shop 4178, 4/F, Yashow Market, Gongti Beilu, Chaoyang District. 朝阳区工体北路雅秀市场4层4178

Radiance Shunyi-area purveyor of Chinese and Western-style lamps, antique furniture and unique home accessory gifts.
Daily 10am-6.30pm. 1) 9 Kaifa Jie, Xibai Xinzhuang, Shunyi District. (8049 6400); 2) A118, Shunhuang Lu, Sunhe Xiang, Chaoyang District. (8459 5510, huang518@hotmail.com) 瑞氏东方，1) 顺义区西白辛庄开发街9号； 2) 朝阳区孙河乡顺黄路甲118号

Rouge Baiser Enter the striking white shopfront and discover Rouge Baiser, which specializes in applying traditional French embroidered art to their linen bedsheets, napkins, tablecloths, pajamas, and kids' clothing. They can also tailor-make curtains, tablecloths and bed sheets.
Mon-Sat 10am-7pm, Sun 11am-5pm. Sanlitun Xiwujie, Chaoyang District. (6464 3530) www.rougebaiser-elise.com 红色之吻，朝阳区三里屯西六街

The Singing Dragon Small gallery/home furnishing shop carries the works of two local artists (from RMB 800) as well as a selection of fluffy towels, Chinese furniture and other knick-knacks for your home.
Daily 10am to 6pm. Rm 509 Pinnacle Plaza, Tianzhu Real Estate Development Zone, Shunyi District. (138 0138 2146, 138 0104 9078, nou-paul@hotmail.com) 顺义区天竺房地产开发区荣祥广场509

Spin Ceramics Gary Wang, chief designer of Spin, combines his innovative, modern style with traditional Chinese handicraft and applies it to ceramic products such as cups, plates, jugs, pillar candles, as well as around 150 limited-edition tableware items.
Daily 11am-9.30pm. 6 Fangyuan Xilu (in Lido area), Chaoyang District. (6437 8649) 旋，朝阳区芳园西路6号

Villa Lifestyle Their stainless steel barbecue grill, which has four main burners and a side burner, costs RMB 5,750;

smaller grills go for RMB 2,950. Delivery and set-up are free and grills come with a one-year warranty. Also sells hot tubs and other outdoor gear.
Daily 10am-6pm. W-8, Tianyun Plaza, Tianzhu Garden (next to Bank of China), Shunyi District. (6457 1922, 139 1187 9236, 139 1187 9326) 别墅生活方式，顺义区天竺花园天韵广场W-8号（中国银行旁边）

Wal-Mart The big box retailer you know and love (or know and hate). In its cavernous aisles, you'll find a huge spectrum of products ranging from fresh fruit and vegetables, beverages and ready meals, to housewares, sporting goods, electronics, clothing and cosmetics.
Daily 7.30am-10pm. 1) B1-2/F, A48 Zhichun Lu, Haidian District. (5873 3666) 2) B1/F, Wanda Plaza, 93 Jianguo Lu, Chaoyang District. (5960 3566) 沃尔玛超市，1）海淀区知春路甲48号地下1-2层；2）朝阳区建国路93号万达广场地下1层

Yves Delorme Sells Egyptian cotton, high thread count and luxury linen sheets and bathrobes.
Daily 8.30am-9pm. B1, China World Shopping Mall (near the ice rink), 1 Jianguomenwai Dajie, Chaoyang District. (6505 6293) www.yvesdelorme.com 伊芙德伦，建国门外大街1号国贸商城B1（溜冰场附近）

Xing Mu Handcraft This shop specializes in classic, stylish goods made from natural materials, such as leather, wood, and paper, using authentic handcraft techniques to challenge the culture of mass production. Sells everything from paper purses (RMB 20) to wooden clocks (RMB 120), all with embellishments featuring calligraphy and other items from Chinese traditional culture. A great place for finding gifts.
Daily 11am-midnight. 99 Nanluogu Xiang, Dongcheng District (8404 3217) 兴穆手工，东城区南锣鼓巷99号

Lighting

Beijing Lizhi Gardening Despite its name, this shop specializes in lamps, ranging from brass elephant-shaped ones (perfect for kids' rooms) and Buddha-shaped offerings to streamlined, six-foot "wall-of-light" lanterns. The owner is very gentle, so bargain politely. Delivery available.
Daily 9am-6pm. 12 Luzhi Hall, Liangma Flower Market, Chaoyang District. (6586 8551, 130 4125 0134) 北京励智艺之公司，朝阳区亮马花卉市场绿植厅12号

Beisihuan Lighting Market Beijing's largest lighting retailer houses over 200 international and domestic brands offering more than 100,000 types of lights.
Mon-Fri 9am-6pm, Sat-Sun 9am-6.30pm. Nanhu Liugongzhucun, Laiguangying Xiang, Chaoyang District. (6439 5581) 北四环灯具市场，朝阳区来广营乡南湖六公主村北四环灯具市场

Boyu Lighting Specializes in arty paper shades that create soft mood lighting, with wall sconces and ceiling, bedside, floor and table lamp shades made out of rice paper and bamboo ribs. Prices range from several hundred to ten thousand *kuai*.
Daily 10am-6pm. 46 Laitai Flower Market, Chaoyang District. (6463 5588 ext 2831) 博钰灯艺，朝阳区莱太花卉市场46号

Legend of the Wooden Lamp Designs and produces handmade wooden lamps incorporating traditional styles, with themes inspired by ancient Chinese official caps, Qing dynasty copper coins, and more. Prices range from RMB 69-250. Made-to-order lamps are also available, although prices are slightly higher.
Daily 10.30am-9pm. 108 Gulou Dongdajie, Dongcheng District (6406 1036, 133 9197 7530) 木灯传说，东城区鼓楼东大街108号

Lizhi Stocks an excellent assortment of porcelain lamps and silk palace lanterns (RMB 150 and up).
Daily 9am-6pm. 15 Liangma Flower Market, Chaoyang District. (6586 8551) 励智灯具，朝阳区亮马花卉市场15号

Loushiming Lamp Studio Customized lamps in any shape, color or fabric made to order in about a week.
Daily 9.30am-9.30pm. 41 Huahuijie, Chaoyang District. (6466 8562) www.loushiming.com 陋室铭，朝阳区花卉街41号

Shilihe Lighting Market 160 storefronts of lighting manufactures offering the most trendy home lights as well as more simple items.
East side of Shilihe Qiao, Dongsanhuan Nanlu, Chaoyang District. (6735 1778) 十里河灯具市场，朝阳区东三环南路十里河桥东

Other

Antiques & "Antiques"

Beijing Curio City With four floors of jewelry, porcelain, teapots, furniture, Buddhist statues and more, this is a good spot to buy chinoiserie for the folks back home. You'll have more fun if you arrive early in the day, before the tour buses, and assume that the pieces are not genuine antiques.
Daily 9.30am-6.30pm. 21 Dongsanhuan Nanlu, Chaoyang District. (6774 7711) 北京古玩城，朝阳区东三环南路21号

Chaowai Furniture Warehouse Chaowai's four floors are crammed wall-to-wall with stalls selling furniture, carpets and decorative items like vases, statues and birdcages – most are reproductions. The merchants are low pressure and will come down by at least 15%. They also offer help with overseas export.
Mon-Fri 10am-5.30pm, Sat-Sun 9am-5.30pm. 43 Huawei Beili, Chaoyang District. (6770 6402, 6770 6410) 兆佳古典家具市场，朝阳区华威北里43号

C.L. Ma Furniture This highly respected antique dealer sells antique and reproduced trunks, tables, chairs, shelves, screens etc. to an enthusiastically loyal customer base from here to Hong Kong.
Daily 10am-9.30pm. 109-110, Bldg 4, Park Avenue, Chaoyang District. (6466 7040) 可乐马家具，朝阳区朝阳公园南门公园大道4号楼109-110室

Dynasty Antique Furniture Hard to beat if you want a custom-built item. From reproductions of Ming and Qing furnishings and cushions to ultra-modern couches and tables, Dynasty can do it all – at slightly higher prices than average.
Mon-Fri 10am-5.30pm, Sat-Sun 9am-5.30pm. 58, Chaowai Furniture Market, Chaoyang District. (6770 3525) 王民工艺古典家具，朝阳区兆古典家具市场58号

Continues on p388

The Gold and the Dross
The painful truth about "antiques"
by Eric Abrahamsen

Am I real? Or fake? Hmm ... existential crisis

You've finally bought a home in Beijing, and at last you can say that you legitimately belong here. Now that you belong in China, you've got a license to look the part, right? You could start wearing a PLA overcoat and pin a red star to your cap, as so many have before, or you could go the more understated route and simply furnish your apartment with antique Chinese furniture. May we recommend the latter?

Every homeowner gets the antique bug eventually, and why not? Chinese furniture is classy, plentiful and beats the heck out of a certain Swedish blight which shall remain nameless. You probably already know what you like, but do you know how to get it? How to keep from getting cheated? Where's the "good stuff"?

Furniture hunters have a couple of options. One is to visit the many antique shops in Beijing proper; another is to head out to a suburban place like Gaobeidian and try your hand at picking the wheat from the chaff yourself. Both options have their advantages and disadvantages.

Siri Dyal Khalsa, who runs a furniture export company called China Onsite, makes Gaobedian his second home. What does he think of the antique furniture for sale in Beijing? His advice can be boiled down to two words: It's fake.

"It's hard to say exactly, but probably 95 per cent of the furniture that is marketed as 'antique' was made in the past 20 years. The older stuff might be 40-80 years old, the very oldest 100 years," says Khalsa. But take note: this doesn't necessarily mean it's poor quality, just that your lovely *hongmu* chair is unlikely ever to have been graced by a Qing dynasty rear.

"Antiques" can be had at several markets around town, including Gaobeidian, Panjiayuan, Liulichang and Hongqiao. Word on the street is that, while good pieces can occasionally be found at Panjiayuan or Liulichang, the chances of being misled or overcharged are considerably higher there. If you're determined to scour the market, by all means make the complete rounds – but if your time is limited, Gaobeidian is the spot.

Here's how it works: Old furniture is constantly being gathered in from the countryside (mostly from the north) and sold by wholesalers located far to the rear of the Gaobeidian area. Furniture retailers buy from these wholesalers and restore the pieces in their workshops. Many stores will also employ carpenters to copy the genuine pieces and either pawn them off as antiques or sell them honestly as *fanggu* (antique reproductions).

When negotiating with store owners, Khalsa recommends assuming that the piece is *fanggu* and hinting as much to the shopkeeper – avoid accusing them outright of selling fakes. Above all, keep in mind that a good piece of *fanggu* furniture can be of excellent quality and, if you keep it in your family, may someday be an antique in its own right ...

Another class of furniture is known as *laomu xinzuo* (old wood, newly-made), which uses salvaged wood from old house beams to make new pieces. It's already difficult enough to distinguish *fanggu* from a real antique – "carbon date it," jokes Khalsa – but in the case of *laomu xinzuo*, it's nearly impossible.

Other things to keep in mind: beware of Tibetan anything. A 300-year-old, two-meter-tall Tibetan wardrobe is necessarily fake – Tibetans simply didn't make that sort of thing. Real Tibetan furniture consists of low tables, seats and small boxes, painted with an extremely fine brush. Big, blotchy red flowers are a sign of a recent vintage (also watch out for "antiques" decorated with simplified characters or paintings of airplanes).

Types of wood commonly found in Chinese furniture include poplar (*yangmu*) or elm (*yumu*) on the cheaper end (identifiable by their whitish hues); more expensive hardwoods are rosewood (*hongmu*), red sandalwood (*zitan*) and yellow flowering pear (*huanghuali*). These woods have a yellow, red or even purple cast; they are harder, more expensive and likely to increase in value as they age.

If spending weeks tromping around Gaobeidian and other distant markets seems like more effort than it's worth, Beijing is also home to a host of high-quality furniture and decoration stores. These stores have several advantages: they provide a better guarantee of quality, better customer service and one-stop shopping – it's often possible to get matching furniture, pillows, lamps and carpets at one store. The main disadvantages, of course, are higher prices and a smaller selection. In general, the more time you spend exploring, the finer the treasures you'll uncover. The true antique-hound leaves no stone unturned.

You might be in for a ride to the poorhouse on the American Express if you're a gullible buyer

Find a new home for your flowers at Liulichang

Gaobeidian Furniture Street The main road of this dusty hamlet is lined with warehouses and showrooms that overflow with reproductions of Ming and Qing tables, opium beds, chairs, benches, stools, drums – you name it. What's more, the merchants can custom-build whatever you can't find in stock. While the sheer selection makes Gaobeidian worth visiting, prices here are rising, thanks to free-spending overseas furniture exporters.
Outside Dongsihuan (turn right at the Gaobeidian exit of the Jingtong expressway, then drive south), Chaoyang District. 高碑店家具一条街，朝阳区东四环外，京通快速路高碑店出口处出来右转往南走

Ho Ho Hang Antique Furniture Ho Ho Hang offers beautiful and very competitively priced antique reproductions (imposing armoires, delicate chairs, dining room sets, screens and the like).
Daily 10am-6pm. 1) B1/F, Chaowai Furniture Market, Chaoyang District. (8771 2484, 139 1028 5919) 2) B39 Liangma Collection Market, 27 Liangmaqiao Lu, Chaoyang District. (139 1028 5919) 和合行，1) 朝阳区兆佳白典家具市场地下1层，2) 朝阳区亮马桥路27号，亮马收 藏品市场B39号

Liangma Antique Market Less crowded than other markets, Liangma attracts savvy, budget-conscious antique aficionados. You'll find bird cages, screens, silver mirrors, scroll paintings, jewelry and porcelain, as well as an extensive carpet selection. Great spot to order custom-made furniture: select from their photos or bring your own. Furniture repair and rug cleaning available. Our favorite shops include Stall 11 (contact Shang Xuemei, 8125 7910) and Chinese Carpet Store (A602, Lisa Liu, 6542 9140).
Daily 9.30am-7pm. 27 Liangmaqiao Lu, Chaoyang District. (6467 9664, 6462 1625) 亮马古玩市场，朝阳区亮马桥路27号

Life Shop High-end antique reproduction accessories such as Buddha heads and Vietnamese woven scarves.
1) Daily 9.30am-5.30pm. 2 Jiuxianqiao Lu, Chaoyang District. (8456 7780); 2) Daily 10am-9.30pm. 111 Lido Hotel, Jiangtai Lu, Chaoyang District. (6430 1245) 乐福行，1) 朝阳区酒仙桥路2号；2) 朝阳区将台路丽都酒店111

Lily's Antiques Offers a photo-enhanced catalogue that makes choosing easy – or more difficult for the indecisive. The lowest quoted price for a traditional Chinese pharmacy cabinet with DVD-sized drawers is RMB 1,200.
1) Daily 9.30am-6pm. 1-60, Beijing Curio City (west of Huawei Bridge), Chaoyang District. (6773 5923/6087); 2) Daily 10am-5.30 pm. Stall 32, 2/F, Chaowai Furniture Market, Chaoyang District. (6770 3703); 3) Daily

8.30am-6.30 pm. Gaobeidian Showroom, Chaoyang District. (8579 2458) Contact Lily Quan (6572 9746, 138 0139 6309, 8579 2458)
华伦古典家具1）朝阳区华威桥西北京古玩城 1–60；2）朝阳区华威北里43号兆佳古典家具市场2楼32号；3）高碑店家俱一条街

Min Jie Classical Furniture Art Offers striking sets of wooden doors taken from now-demolished courtyard homes, many from Shanxi province.
Daily 9am-6.30pm. Inside Lujiaying Antique Furniture Market, Shibalidian area (first exit off Jingtang Expressway, drive 500m), Chaoyang District. (8769 6693, 136 4120 5506) 民洁古典家具，朝阳区吕家营古典家具市场内

Na Mu Zhuo Ma Sells tapestries and hanging lanterns and a variety of embroidery fabrics from Pakistan or India. They can be tailored for your sofa or used as tablecloths.
Daily 9.30am-midnight. Yandai Xiejie, Xicheng District. (8403 3115) 娜姆卓玛，西城区烟袋斜街

Naxi Popo Sells hand-carved wooden wall hangings painted in the distinctive and extraordinarily vivid Naxi style. Along with an intricate Bai belt mounted in a frame, the store also sells Naxi puppets from between RMB 80 and 120 depending on size.
Daily 10am-midnight. 14 Yandai Xiejie, Xicheng District. (8404 1300) 纳西婆婆，西城区烟袋斜街14号

Panjiayuan Antique Market The mother of all "antique" markets is home to over 3,000 dealers who scour the countryside in search of antiques, family heirlooms and curios. This is the place to go for life-size terracotta warriors, vintage photographs, porcelain vases and figurines, Qing-style furniture and much, much more. The best bargains are offered early on weekend mornings, between 6 and 8.30am.
Daily 4.30am-6pm. West of Panjiayuan Qiao, Chaoyang District. (6775 2405) 潘家园旧货市场，朝阳区潘家园桥西边

Tanghouse Gallery Formerly Lee & Lee Antiques, this purveyor of elegant antique furniture and reproductions aims to bridge the gap between contemporary and classic styles. Its enormous warehouse is filled with screens, armoires, desks, opium beds, and myriad other furniture as well as buddha sculptures and decorative pieces.
Daily 9.30am-6pm. 4/F, Antique Furniture Market, 519 Fenzhongsi, Nansanhuan Donglu, Chaoyang District. (6764 2214) 现代禅风古典家具，朝阳区南三环东路分钟寺519号，古玩城古典家具市场4层

Tibet Shop Has colorful Tibetan hanging lanterns (RMB 50-150), beautiful tapestries, and "singing bowls" – metal bowls (RMB 30-300, depending on size) that you place in the palm of your hand and rub with sticks.
37 South Building, Sanlitun Beilu, Chaoyang District. (6417 5963) 爱尔屋，朝阳区北三里屯南37楼

Wanyou Antique Furniture Consistently reliable, this antiques purveyor stands out for its traditional decorative items – including fabulous masks, bronze statues and wooden sculptures – and excellent prices. The warehouse in Tongzhou is massive.
1) Mon-Fri 10am-6pm, Sat-Sun 9am-6pm. 3/F, Chaowai Furniture Market, Chaoyang District. (6771 0087); 2) Daily 9am-6pm. South of Nanliuhuan Lu (1.5km south of Dongtianyang Village), Majuqiao Town,

Tongzhou District. (6158 6826) 万有古典家具行，1）朝阳区朝外兆佳古典家俱市场3层；2）通州区马驹桥镇东田阳村南1.5公里（南六环路南边）

Art
(See Galleries, Art & Culture p194)

Art Supplies
Beijing Gehua Baihua After deriving some inspiration from the China Art Museum, cross the street and get the fixin's to make your own masterpiece. With a huge selection of art supplies for drawing and painting – paint (RMB 25), easels (starting at RMB 25), canvas (RMB 8 to 72) – this store is more organized and more spacious than others nearby (although you should look through those too). It sells some international brands like Prismacolor.
Daily 9am-6.30pm. 10 Wusi Dajie, Dongcheng District. (6522 2511) www.baihuaart.cn 北京歌华百花艺术用品，东城区五四大街10号

Central Academy of Arts and Design The art supply store on the campus of Beijing's second most prestigious art school is very well stocked.
Daily 7.30am-10pm. 34 Dongsanhuan Zhonglu, Chaoyang District. (6561 9594) 中央工艺美术院美术用品部，朝阳区东三环中路34号

Gongyi Meishu Fuwubu
Daily 9am-9pm. 200 Wangfujing Dajie, Dongcheng District. (6528 8866) 工艺美术服务部，东城区王府井大街200号

Bicycles & Motorcycles
Beijing Windspeed Bike Shop Favored by Beijing's serious riders, this shop has a wide selection of bikes, helmets, shorts, tools, high-tech components and cyclist fashions. It can order parts from abroad. Another reason to come is the Shimano-trained repairmen. Be sure to bargain. For directions to the shop see http://themob.404.com.au/index.php?page=windspeed
Daily 9am-7pm. 1/F, 10 Ritan Jinghua (behind the North Korean Embassy and southeast of the Chaoyang Government building), Chaoyang District. (8562 2509) 行如风自行车专卖店，朝阳区日坛晶华10号1层

Feng Huo Lun Motorcycle Sells imported and local motorcycles and scooters, including Hondas with 50cc engines and above. They also carry an extensive selection of helmets and parts. A Honda Xindazhou 50cc scooter costs RMB 7,000, and the store can help you acquire a motorcycle license plate, which costs an extra fee of RMB 1,000 (for '京' plates) to 8,000 (for '京A' plates).
Daily 9am-6pm. W3 (above Harley Davidson), Dongrun Fengjing, 28 Nanshiliju, Chaoyang District. (6222 3456) 风火轮摩托车，朝阳区南十里居28号东润风景W3

Forever Bicycle Store (Min Lu Bicycle Store) Sells Yongjiu (Forever) electric bikes priced at RMB 2,000-2,500, with speeds reaching 30-35 km/hr. Batteries for these bikes (which do not require a license to operate) need to be charged after every 50km and usually have a two-year lifespan. Other accessories and repair services are available at the store.
Daily 8.30am-9.30pm. 4 Di'anmen, Ping'an Dajie, Xicheng District. (6402 0396) 闵鹿车行，西城区平安大街地安门大街4号

Giant Bicycles Be sure to buy a sturdy lock if you purchase one of the bicycles on offer at Giant's flagship store. Inside the cavernous shop is a wide range of mountain and racing bikes, components, accessories and frames including the TCR Team Alu series (RMB 12,800-21,000). Their Chinese-only website lists other branches, including one on Jiaodaokou Dongdajie.
Daily 9am-7pm. Rm 101, Bldg E, Guoheng Jiye Mansion, 7 Beitucheng Xilu, Chaoyang District. (8227 5718) www.giant-bicycle.com 捷安特自行车专卖店, 朝阳区北土城西路7号国衡基业大厦E座101室

Harley Davidson The 1,500-square-meter store features Harley bike assembly parts, "Beijing Harley-Davidson" T-shirts, jewelry, hats, gloves, and a variety of Harley's classic black leather jackets (around RMB 6,000). The store's select range of motorbikes are all built in compliance with Chinese regulations. Prices range from RMB 100,000-300,000. The store organizes training sessions and regular outings for their customers. Keep in mind that motorbikes are banned inside the Third Ring Road, unless you have an A plate.
Daily 9am-7pm. W3 (above Feng Huo Lun Motorcycle), Dongrun Fengjing, 28 Nanshiliju, Chaoyang District. (8450 2900, 5165 9800) 哈雷戴维森, 朝阳区南十里居28号东润风景W3

Jindian Xintuo Shop Evidence that it's quite possible to get quality used bikes without breaking the law, Jindian sells second-hand bicycles that all have permits and *fapiaos*. RMB 250 for a Giant woman's bike and RMB 360 for a man's bike. Classic black steel Forever (Yongjiu) bikes cost around RMB 150.
Daily 9am-5.30pm. Dongsi Beidajie, Dongcheng District. (8402 1939) 金典信托商行, 东城区东四北大街

Trek The same line that helped propel Lance Armstrong to seven Tour de France championships has opened China's first branch at Di'anmen. Inside this spacious two-story shop is a wide range of high-end road bikes, mountain bikes (starting from RMB 2,000) and bikes for tykes (RMB 920). They also stock a full line of accessories including wheels, chains, brakes, helmets, lights, locks and jerseys. Guaranteed free repair service for the bike's lifespan. Organized cycling trips to Mang Shan and racing events take place every weekend.
Daily 9am-7pm. 66 Di'anmen Dongdajie (100m west of Nanluogu Xiang on the south side of Ping'an Dadao), Dongcheng District. (8403 6967) 崔克, 东城区地安门东大街66号 (南锣鼓巷往西100米平安大街路南)

Bookstores
(see also Kids' Bookstores p150, and Libraries, under Adult Education p624)

All Sages Bookstore Although it doesn't have many English language titles, the range and quality of All Sages' Chinese titles and the stylish cafe on the second floor make it one of the best bookstores in Beijing. It has a great selection of Chinese translations of the latest academic releases as well as a large range of social and political science texts.
Daily 10am-10pm. 1) Bldg 10, Fangcaodi Xijie, Chaoyang District. (8561 4331, 8563 1710); 2) 123 Lanqiying, Chengfu Lu, Haidian District. (6276 8748) www.allsagesbooks.com 北京万圣书园, 1) 朝阳区芳草地西街10号楼; 2) 海淀区蓝旗营成府路123号

Amazon.com The website that never lets you down – they will even deliver to your door. *www.amazon.com*

Blue Goat Books & Cafe The walls of this tiny, wonderful bookstore are plastered with movie posters and the shelves are filled with quality books about cinema – though the majority are Chinese-language editions. They also have a good range of hard-to-find Chinese movies. After browsing the aisles, head upstairs to the cafe to curl up with a cup of coffee and read away the afternoon.
Daily 12.30am-12.30pm. 3 Shuimo Xinqu (200m north of west gate of Tsinghua University), Haidian District. (6265 5069) 蓝羊书坊, 海淀区水磨新区3号 (清华西门向北200米)

The Bookworm This sleek lending library and bookshop has the best selection of English language books and magazines in town and is often cheaper than Amazon et al. The bibliophile manager arranges a fabulous lecture series that features both local and international authors. Other drawcards include the rooftop terrace, comfy couches and a kitchen that serves European fare.
Daily 9am-2am. Bldg 4, Nansanlitun Lu, Chaoyang District. (6586 9507, books@beijingbookworm. com; Kids Club: 138 1163 7831, kidsclub@beijingbookworm.com) www.beijingbookworm.com 书虫书吧, 朝阳区南三里屯路4号楼

Chaterhouse Booktrader Prices are generally a bit higher than those at the Foreign Language Bookstore but they do stock a good range of travel, kids', health, and coffee table books.
Daily 10am-10pm. 1) Shop B107, The Place, 9A Guanghua Lu, Chaoyang District. (6587 1328, customer@chaterhouse.com.cn); 2) River Garden Clubhouse, No. 7 Yuyang Road, Houshayu Xiang, Shunyi District. (8046 6211) 1) 朝阳区光华路9号世贸天阶中心地库B107; 2) 顺义区后沙峪乡榆阳路7号

China Arts Bookstore Sandwiched among Dongsi's hipster boutiques, this 1,300sqm store sells books on sketching, Western oil painting, traditional Chinese painting, design magazines, software – you name it – in three stories of space decorated with scrolls of Chinese calligraphy and traditional paintings.
Daily 9.30am-6pm. 390 Dongsi Beidajie, Dongcheng District. (6403 6880) 中美联艺术书店, 东城区东四北大街390号

Cuckoo Bookstore Nestled in the basement of Guo Mao, the Cuckoo Bookstore hosts an abundance of big arty books on design and architecture. Also carries glossy imported magazines and a few shelves of English language novels and non-fiction.
Daily 9.30am-8pm. B1/F, Bldg 2, China World Shopping Mall, 1 Jianguomenwai Dajie, Chaoyang District. (6505 9286) 布谷鸟书店, 朝阳区建外大街1号国贸商城2座地下一层

Disanji Bookstore This gigantic store is billed as the biggest Chinese language bookstore in the world and offers a great selection of original editions from Taiwan and Hong Kong.
Daily 9am-9pm. 66 Beisihuan Lu (opposite the south gate of Peking University), Haidian District. (5128 2300) www.d3j.com.cn 第三极书局, 海淀区北四环西路66号

Foreign Languages Bookstore For foreign language books, the aptly-named Foreign Languages Bookstore is far and away the largest and most diverse bookstore in town. Here, you'll find locally published foreign language books on the first floor, sheet music books on the fifth floor, and on the recently-opened sixth floor, a tea shop and clearance books.

INSIDER'S GUIDE TO BEIJING

You don't say! Learn something new with every book you read at The Bookworm

1) Daily 9am-9pm. 235 Wangfujing Dajie, Dongcheng District. (6512 6911/6838); 2) Daily 9am-10pm. 4/F, Lufthansa Center, 52 Liangmaqiao Lu, Chaoyang District. (6465 1188 ext 421) 外文书店，1）东城区王府井大街235号；2）朝阳区亮马桥路52号燕莎中心4层

Friendship Store Why shop here? The goods are viciously overpriced, it's overrun by tourists and service is snooty. Its only redeeming feature is the foreign language books section, where the previous day's editions of the South China Morning Post, the IHT and other foreign publications, including an extensive selection of travel books, are available.
Daily 9.30am-8.30pm. 17 Jianguomenwai Dajie, Chaoyang District. (6500 3311) 北京友谊商店，朝阳区建国门外大街17号

Haidian Book City This bookstore gets props for its enormous size alone - its four stories house nearly 200 shops that sell the biggest and most up-to-date collection of publications you can find in the city. Books available cover a range of topics, including literature, sociology, economics, science and technology, plus a limited selection of English fiction in the basement.
Daily 9am-6pm. 36 Haidian Xidajie, Haidian District. (6257 3167) 海淀图书城，海淀区海淀西大街36号

Le Petit Gourmand A lending library/French bar and restaurant that has a great selection of secondhand English and other foreign language books. Membership, RMB 150 for 6 months or RMB 300/yr, entitles you to borrow two books at a time.
Daily 9.30am-midnight. 3/F, Tongli Studios, Sanlitun Houjie, Chaoyang District. (6417 6095) www.lepetitigourmand.com.cn 小美食派，朝阳区三里屯后街同里3层

O2SUN Bookstore This Macanese chain store's Beijing flagship attracts the student crowds in Wudaokou with its wide selection of Chinese language learning books. It also houses a few shelves of English language books, a wide array of magazines and a great cafe on the second floor. The second branch also stocks some classic English-language works.
1) Daily 24 hours (1/F), 9am-midnight (2/F). Bldg 1, Huaqing Jiayuan, Chengfu Lu (across from Wudaokou light-rail station), Haidian District. (8286 3032/33); 2) Daily 9am-midnight. S3001, Bldg B, Soho New Town, 88 Jianguo Lu, Chaoyang District. (8580 2786/2789) www.o2sun.com 光合作用，1）海淀区五道口华清嘉园1号楼；2）朝阳区建国路88号Soho现代城B座S3001

Sanlian Taofen Bookstore Filled with quality philosophy and art books. Head up to the second floor to find a large range of English language editions and a small cafe. The store also organizes occasional lectures and has a good magazine selection.
Daily 9am-9pm. Meishuguan Dongjie (east of the National Art Museum of China), Dongcheng District. (6407 1664) 北京三联韬奋图书中心，东城区北京美术馆东街（中国美术馆东侧）

San Wei Bookstore A bookstore downstairs and a teahouse with live music upstairs. Friday nights have jazz performances and Saturday nights feature live traditional music with *guzheng* and *pipa* performances. Tickets RMB 50. Reservations recommended.
Daily 11am-10pm. 60 Fuxingmennei Dajie, Xicheng District. (6601 3204) 三味书屋，西城区复兴门内大街60号

Timezone 8 Bookstore The shop sells an amazing selection of fashion and art books from both local and foreign publishers.

Daily 10am-8pm. Dashanzi art district, 4 Jiuxianqiao Lu, Chaoyang District. (8456 0336) 现代书店北京艺术书屋，朝阳区798大山子艺术区酒仙桥路4号

Wangfujing Bookstore One of Beijing's biggest bookstores has travel guides and maps on the first floor, English-language novels, self-help/business tomes and kids' books as well as a good range of Chinese language learning materials on the third floor, and art books and sheet music on the sixth floor, where lectures are held on weekends, usually in Chinese.
Daily 9am-9.30pm. 218 Wangfujing Dajie, Dongcheng District. (6513 2842, 6525 2592) www.wfjsd.com 王府井书店，东城区王府井大街218号

Xidan Books Building In the cavernous basement of Xidan Books Building, you'll find a boatload of English language classics and a broad, eclectic selection of new-ish paperbacks (usually many copies of each, which might be helpful to book club members), cookbooks, a big business/management section, and an excellent selection of oversized books on art, architecture, and design. There's even a bit of seating, and the English-speaking staff is usually friendly and helpful.
Daily 8.30am-9pm. C17 Xichang'an Jie, Xicheng District. (6607 8477) www.bjbb.com 西单图书大厦，西城区西长安街丙17号

Yesasia.com The amazon.com of Asia.

Zhongguancun Bookstore Located in the university district, this store is up there with Xidan and Wangfujing in terms of the range of English language titles, which can be found on the third floor alongside a broad selection of textbooks for Chinese-language study.
Daily 9am-9pm. 68 Beisihuan Xilu, Haidian District. (8267 6696/7/8) www.zgcbb.com 中关村图书大厦，海淀区北四环西路68号

Business Supplies
(See Business & Work, p576)

Cameras & Photo Equipment

22 Film Studio Along with housing a comprehensive selection of digital camcorders and accessories, 22 Film Studio says that most of the camcorders it sells are RMB 400-3,000 cheaper than their real market value. Accessories include camera lenses, professional lighting equipment, DV batteries, tapes and a lot more. If you plan to use a camcorder on a more occasional basis, equipment is available to rent.
Daily 9am-6pm. Unit 2, Bldg 32, west area of Guanyingyuan Compound (north end of Zhaodengyu Lu), Xicheng District. (5126 0201) 行影浪潮，西城区赵登禹路北口冠英园西区32号楼2门

Beijing Photographic Equipment City Favored by serious shutterbugs, this mall groups numerous individual vendors selling everything from simple digital cameras to high-end film cameras with telescopic lenses, as well as film, tripods and other gear.
Daily 9am-6pm. 4 Wukesonglu (southeast corner of Dinghui Qiao), Haidian District. (8811 9797) 北京摄影器材城，海淀区五棵松路4号（定惠桥东南角）

Golden Lens Photography Handily placed, this group sells a good range of name-brand cameras, together with film, ancillary equipment and accessories, including lenses, filters, tripods etc. There is also a camera repair service for most brands.
Daily 9am-6.30pm. 12 Xichang'an Jie (first intersection west of Tian'anmen West subway station), Xicheng District. (6605 6386) 北京摄贸金广角贸易有限公司，西城区西长街12号

Lomography This artsy camera company has long been a favorite with artists and photographers due to the amazing colors and effects that can be produced using their cameras. Cameras start from RMB 320 for a multi-lens pop 9, while the super sampler cameras retail between RMB 400-500. Top of the line cameras include the Horizon 120 (RMB 1,920) and the original L-CA (RMB 1,980). The helpful, laid-back staff are knowledgeable and enthusiastic.
Tue-Sun 10am-9pm. 9 Loutongjing Jie (next to the Gongwangfu Carpark), Xicheng District. 西城区龙头井街9号（恭王府停车场西南侧）

Wande Photo Equipment This store impresses with its wide selection of photographic equipment (including underwater gear and aerial cameras), black and white film and processing and enlarging services. Enlarging ranges from RMB 280-490, and developing costs RMB 25-45 for an individual transparency.
Daily 9am-6pm. Cuifujiadao (east along the alley at the San Lian Bookstore), Dongcheng District. (8401 1883) 北京万得摄影器材行，东城区崔府夹道35号（三联书店小巷往东走）

Computers & Software

Apple Centre Get any Apple products – iPods, laptops, etc. – fixed up with these friendly Apple-certified repairmen.
1) Daily 9am-6pm. Rai Se Plaza, 126 Jianguo Lu, Chaoyang District. (6566 2068); 2) Daily 9am-5.30pm. 10 Laiguanying Donglu (inside Western Academy of Beijing Campus, Property Building), Chaoyang District. (8456 4155 ext 4090) 苹果维修中心，1）朝阳区建国路126号瑞嘉大厦；2）朝阳区来广营东路10号（京西学校内物业楼）

Apple Experience Centre Sells groovy Apple computers, laptops and iPods as well as software, accessories and printers.
Daily 10am-9pm. 106A, 1/F, Oriental Plaza, 1 Dongchang'an Jie, Dongcheng District. (8518 0002) 苹果体验中心，东城区东方新天地106A

Bainaohui Computer Shopping Mall If you don't feel like trekking out to Zhongguancun, this mall is a good place to pick up computers, printers, hard drives, wi-fi equipment, gaming equipment, software, blank CDs and more – both foreign and domestic brands. Prices might be a bit higher than Zhongguancun, but warranties are more reliable.
Daily 9am-8pm. 10 Chaoyangmenwai Dajie, Chaoyang District. (6599 5912) 百脑汇电脑商场，朝阳区朝阳门外大街10号

Hailong Shopping Mall This five-story shopping mall has prestigious tenants like Samsung, Sony and Lenovo selling fully assembled PCs, as well as dealers selling motherboards, hard drives, power supply systems and other parts. You can also find other digital products like CD, DVD and MP3 players. This area is rich with electronics mega-malls, so browse around the new E-Plaza Zhongguancun and Top Electronics City while you're there.
Daily 9am-9pm. 1 Zhongguancun Dajie, Haidian District. (8266 3838/3939) 海龙大厦，海淀区中关村大街1号

Strutting around with a giant chip on your shoulder won't stop the sun

Johnson Computer Connections Your one-stop shop for IT products and services: Johnson's sells computers, printers, cables, cartridges, software, upgrades – the list is endless and items can be custom ordered. Their friendly, English-speaking repairmen have saved the day (and data) more than once and can make house calls (RMB 50).
Daily 9am-7.30pm. 312 Pinnacle Plaza (in the Tianzhu Real Estate Development Zone), Shunyi District. (8046 3358, 139 1156 7529) www.johnson.net.cn 同舟联达科技有限公司，顺义区荣祥广场312号(天竺房地产开发区内)

Silicon Valley Computer City Though a little far from the main shopping area in Zhongguancun, Silicon Valley still draws in the crowds. Opened in 1999, this is an ideal place for assembling a computer, because the prices here are a little bit lower than on "The Strip".
Daily 9am-5.30pm. 1 Xicaochang, Haidian District. (8285 2635) 硅谷电脑城，海淀区西草场1号

Wonderful Electronic Shopping Mall A good one-stop shopping location near Bainaohui, this mall houses outlets selling brand-name electronics and countless computer peripherals. An ultra-atmospheric Internet cafe, 520, resides on the top floor.
Daily 8.30am-10pm. 12 Chaoyangmenwai Dajie, Chaoyang District. (6599 3308) 旺东百利数码商城，朝阳区朝阳门外大街12号

Zhonghai Computer Market This second-hand market is a great spot to pick up cheap used laptops from IBM, Compaq and Dell. Neophytes beware: there are many fakes so bring along a computer-savvy friend. Super low prices.
Daily 9am-5.30pm. 27 Haidian Lu, Haidian District. 中海电子市场，海淀区海淀路27号

Cosmetics & Beauty Supplies
Also sold at any major department store (see Department Stores & Shopping Centers, p396).

Fruits & Passion Well-known international personal care brand, specializing in body care, face care, hand care, eau de toilette, ambiance and aromatherapy products.
1) Daily 9.30am-10pm. 1/F, Zhongyou Shopping Mall, 176 Bei Dajie, Xidan, Xicheng District. (6425 9757, 6615 9225); 2) Daily 10am-9pm. NB 146, China World Shopping Mall, 1 Jianguomenwai Dajie, Chaoyang District. (6505 1538) 嘉贝诗，1) 西城区西单北大街176号君太百货商场一层；2) 朝阳区建国门外大街1号国贸商城NB146商铺

M.A.C. The flagship store of this well-known brand is sleek and modern, and boasts a vast range of products (lipstick from RMB 150, eye shadow from RMB 140, brushes from RMB 110). Also offers make-up masterclasses.
Daily 10am-10pm. L120, 1/F, Bldg C, The Place, 9A Guanghua Lu, Chaoyang District. (6587 1598) 魅可，朝阳区光华路9号世贸天阶C座L120

Sephora The new branch of this international chain is already a hit, as it offers free makeovers and fragrance consultations. Brightly lit aisles are filled with upscale makeup and skincare products from lines such as L'Occitane, Anna Sui and Dior. Men can fulfill their skin care, shaving, and cologne needs. The makeup products are all imported, so prices are steep. Tubes of Lancome lipstick range from RMB 220 to 270, and Clinique's moisturizing lotion costs RMB 460.
1) Daily 8am-10pm. Store 28, 29, Zhongguancun Carrefour Shopping Center, Haidian District. (5172 1136); 2) Daily 9am-10pm. 1/F, Wangjing Capital Mall, Guangshun Beilu, Chaoyang District. (8472 9388);

Continues on p396

BYOB: Bring Your Own Bamboo

Save the pandas!
by Catherine Lee

According to the World Bank, China is the world's second-largest producer of greenhouse gases. Do your part to help China achieve its green dreams with these simple shopping habits.

Chopsticks

With China's disposable chopsticks gobbling up an estimated 25 million trees a year, bringing your own pair of chopsticks is not only healthy and sanitary (reducing the chances of a case of *la duzi*) but also environmentally friendly. What's more, carrying your own *kuaizi* is a great way to spread awareness and guilt your friends and acquaintances into joining you in reducing waste.

Here are a few of our favorite pairs, from trendy collapsible silver to simple no-frills wood.

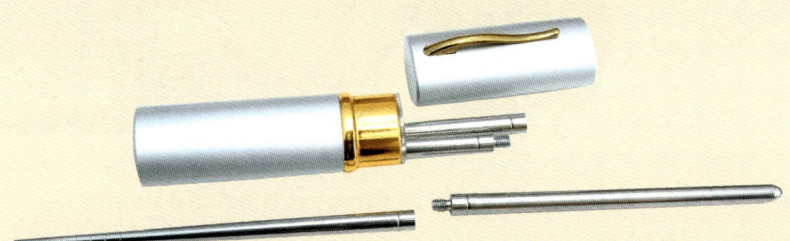

Collapsible silver chopsticks (RMB 20)

Wooden chopsticks (RMB 5 each)

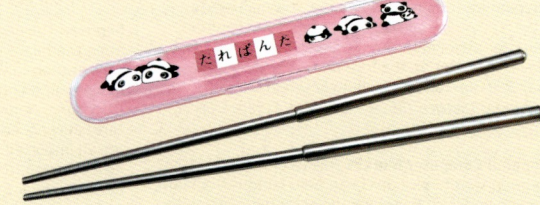

Panda bear kids' set (RMB 15)

Zou Wei, Stall 4055, 4/F, Yashow Market. (6701 6469)

Bookworm tote (free with purchase of books, see The Bookworm, p390)

"I'm Not a Plastic Bag" tote (USD 15, www.anyahindmarch.com)

Tote bags

An average shopping spree at any Chinese market tends to yield about twenty miniscule plastic bags stuffed into four medium plastic bags all stuffed into one giant black plastic bag. Beijing consumes an estimated 10 billion plastic bags annually, equivalent to around 27 million bags per day. Save yourself the *mafan* (who wants to dig through ten bags just to find that Hello Kitty purse) and invest in a tote bag – from free (with purchase of books from The Bookworm) to cheap (RMB 20 at Dongjiao Market) to designer (Anya Hindmarch's "I'm Not A Plastic Bag" bag).

Water bottles

Bottled water, the world's fastest growing beverage category, carries a heavy environmental cost. Research suggests that more water is consumed in the production of a plastic bottle than what it actually holds. To reduce the waste, order a *tong* of water to be delivered to your home and fill up your own reusable water container.

When buying water bottles, bigger is better. Bigger bottles contain larger amounts of water relative to the plastic used.

See Grocery Stores, p104, for organic food shopping. Sign up for the green consumption mailing list of the Beijing Organic Consumers Association at health.groups.yahoo.com/group/Beijing_organic_consumers

For more information on organic food and green living in China, visit www.chinagreentravel.com, www.greenchoice.cn. and www.20to20.org.

SHOPPING

3) Daily 10am-10pm. NB 128, B1/F, China World Shopping Mall, 1 Jianguomenwai Dajie, Chaoyang District. (6505 6726) www.sephora.cn 丝芙兰，1）海淀区中关村广场地下28&29；2）朝阳区广顺北大街望京华联商厦一层；3）朝阳区建外大街1号国贸城地下一层NB128

Watson's This Western-style drugstore sells health and beauty products, diapers, confectionery, stationery, condoms, over-the-counter medications and more. Several other outlets in Beijing including Ginza Mall, China World and Full Link Plaza.
Daily 9.30am-9.30pm. CC17, Oriental Plaza, 1 Dongchang'an Jie, Dongcheng District. (8518 6426) 屈臣氏，东城区东方新天地CC17

Department Stores & Shopping Centers

3.3 Shopping Center This five-floor shopping center has more than 300 shops, mostly boutiques. The clothes (and shoppers) are super trendy, and the prices are high – the kind of place where they rearrange the racks after you look through. Though well-decorated, clean and air-conditioned, the atmosphere is somewhat spoiled by the noise pollution of pop music and TV ads. A good place for guys too – the shoes on the third floor can go up to size 48!
Daily 11am-11pm. 33 Sanlitun Beijie, Chaoyang District. (6417 8886) www.3d3.cn 3.3服饰大厦，朝阳区三里屯北街33号

77th Street A mall infused with soul, and a boundless outburst of zany creativity and energy. Check out the trendy clothing shops and stalls of accessories, as well as the funky customers.
Mon-Thu 10am-9.30pm, Fri-Sun 9.10am-10pm. B2-3/F (the former Xidan Cultural Plaza), 180 Xidan Beidajie, Xicheng District. (6608 7177/7877) 77街，西城区西单北大街180号原西单文化广场地下二三层

APM Formerly known as Sun Dong An Plaza, this commodious Wangfujing mall has mid-range tenants like Nine West, Esprit and U, Tony Jeans for men, plus a big cinema on the top floor and a children's jungle gym in the basement.
Daily 9am-10pm. 138 Wangfujing Dajie, Dongcheng District. (5817 6688) 新东安商场，东城区王府井大街138号

CAT Lifestyle Mall Dashanzi's first shopping mall aims to be "Creative, Artistic, and Trendy," pushing many local and more obscure brands and designers. More Western-friendly stores include Doright on the second floor, which sells great men's summer shirts, shoe retailers Angel Infantes, Vancini, and Honghe on the first floor, and accessories store Anna on third floor.
Daily 9.30am-9pm. Star City, 10 Jiuxianqiao Lu, Chaoyang District. (5838 5555) 妙典时尚广场，朝阳区酒仙桥路甲10号星城国际

China World Trade Shopping Mall Guomao, as it is universally called, offers a yummy array of choice brand names like Moschino, Celine, Loewe, Louis Vuitton, Prada and Burberry. More affordable offerings are found in such shops as Max & Co., Ports, BCBG, Esprit, L'Occitane and Red Earth makeup. It also houses home decorating and appliance boutiques.
Daily 9.30am-10pm. 1 Jianguomenwai Dajie, Chaoyang District. (6505 2288) 国贸商城，朝阳区建国门外大街1号

Friendship Store Quite an easy target for trash-talk – only starry-eyed tourists browse through these almost laughably overpriced goods. Currently, the store's only redeeming feature seems to be its foreign language books section. However, with its plans for a whopping RMB 4 billion renovation over the next few years, the first store open to foreigners in Beijing may just have hope for a new heyday.
Daily 9.30am-8.30pm. 17 Jianguomenwai Dajie, Chaoyang District. (6500 3311) 北京友谊商店，朝阳区建国门外大街17号

Golden Resources New Yansha Mall Until recently the world's largest mall, Golden Resources has over 500 stores sporting everything from toys and clothes (Ports, Ecco and Esprit), to restaurants, to car showrooms, and there is also an onsite movie theater and ice-skating rink. Great kids' area. Parking for 10,000 (!) cars.
Mon-Thu 10am-9pm, Fri-Sun 10am-10pm. 1 Yuanda Lu, (300m north of Changchun Bridge), Haidian District. (8887 5888) www.newyanshamall.com 金源新燕莎商城，海淀区远大路1号（长春桥北300米）

Kerry Mall Connected to the Kerry Residences and the Beijing Kerry Centre Hotel (and its bars and restaurants), this swish mall's tenants include a number of clothiers tailors (e.g. Blanc de Chine, Shanghai Xu, Leaves Fashion, Ho's Fashion, Jeannie Fei, Dave's Tailor), a hair salon (Eric Paris), restaurants (Bento & Berries, Horizon, Nihonbashi, Subway, and Papa John's), a CRC/Ole Supermarket, Montrose Wine Shop, a Starbucks, several golf shops (Honma Golf Shop, Mizuno Golf Shop, S-Yard Golf Shop) and Beijing Vista Clinic.
Daily 10am-8pm. 1 Guanghua Lu, Chaoyang District. (8529 8418) www.beijingkerrycentre.com 嘉里商场，朝阳区光华路一号

LCX Building This Xidan area mall is currently undergoing a facelift with many new stores being added and a revamped food court downstairs. The first floor houses designer stores including Gucci, Coach, Ferragamo, Trussardi, and Versace. You'll find less expensive shopping upstairs at Esprit and Hush Puppies.
Daily 9.30am-9.30pm. 88 Xichang'an Dajie, Xicheng District. (8391 3311) 时代广场，西城区西长安大街88号

Lufthansa Center The very first Western-style department store built in Beijing, the Lufthansa Center carries many international designers. Find (genuine) Tumi luggage, cosmetics like Clinique and Estee Lauder, Hugo Boss men's clothing, Balenciaga bags, Calvin Klein lingerie, Wedgwood dishes, Rolex watches, and Sony TVs. Browse the Sport store for Speedo swimsuits and Wilson tennis rackets, and check out the supermarket below for a decent selection of international products. Excellent children's section – see Kids p152. High-priced, international grocery store in the basement. Friendly salespeople, but be prepared for steep prices.
Daily 9am-10pm. 52 Liangmaqiao Lu, Chaoyang District. (6465 1188 ext 675) 燕莎购物中心，朝阳区亮马桥路52号

The Malls at Oriental Plaza Oriental Plaza has proved an unmitigated hit, with shoppers drawn to brands like Burberry, Givenchy, Sisley, H2O, Soda, TSE, Max Mara, Bally, Valentino and Esprit. If you're looking for a flamboyant striped tie and a vintage edition of the Ramones' *Rocket to Russia*, then you should pop by the Paul Smith shop. Don't forget to drop by Watson's pharmacy and the mega CRC supermarket. Enter the

Shop 'til you drop ... into one of the luxurious purple couches at Shin Kong Place

attached Grand Hyatt hotel to find the Shanghai Tang boutique.
Daily 9.30am-10pm. 1 Dongchang'an Jie, Dongcheng District. (8518 6363) 东方新天地，东城区东长安街1号

NOVA Zhongguancun NOVA claims to be the biggest IT shopping mall in the world – altogether 75,000 square meters. Their main concept is one-stop-shopping. NOVA has a good product channel from Taiwanese manufacturers, which makes for reasonable prices.
Daily 9am-7pm. 18 Zhongguancun Dajie, Haidian District. (8253 6688) 中关村科贸电子城，海淀区中关村大街18号

Pacific Century Place The Pacific Department Store is filled with premium brand goods and relatively unencumbered by shoppers. The first floor includes a Mercedes showroom and Nine West shoes. Go upstairs for clothing, DVDs, electronics, sporting goods, toys and prams. Recently added pharmacy and shoe repair services available.
Daily 10am-10pm. 2A Gongti Beilu, Chaoyang District. (6539 3888) 太平洋百货，朝阳区工体北路甲2号

The Peninsula Palace Beijing Shopping Arcade This Versailles of fashion is home to such royalty as Dior, Chanel, Gucci, Hermes and Versace. And if shoes, clothes and handbags don't sate your appetite for luxury, the hotel's Cartier and Tiffany outlets can drape you in gold and diamonds. Price tags should not be read by the faint of heart.
Daily 11am-9.30pm. 8 Jinyu Hutong, Wangfujing, Dongcheng District. (6559 2888) 王府半岛酒店，东城区王府井金鱼胡同8号

The Place This new Beijing landmark, with its striking outdoor video screen, houses Spanish fashion chain Zara and Canadian shoe retailer Aldo's flagship store. Other outlets include Potato & Co., Folli Follie, Miss Sixty, Energie, Adidas, MAC makeup, Promod, Jessica, Chaterhouse Booktrader and the Swiss Perfumery Shop. A good kids' selection can be found on the fourth floor. Those looking for a refueling can head downstairs to the giant food court.
Daily 10am-10pm. 9A Guanghua Lu, Chaoyang District. (8595 1755/6) 世贸天阶，朝阳区光华路甲9号

Sogo The Japanese have found the perfect shopping recipe: take a funky selection of Japanese and European boutiques, mix in an excellent food court with uncommonly good sushi and sprinkle an espresso bar on each floor. You can even deposit the kids at Sega World on the sixth floor for an uninterrupted schlep.
Daily 10am-10pm. 8 Xuanwumen Dajie, Xuanwu District. (6310 3388) 庄胜崇光百货，宣武区宣武门大街8号

Shin Kong Place Walk into Shin Kong Place and you feel you've stepped into a glossy Hong Kong shopping mall. Part shopping mall, part department store, Shin Kong Place distinguishes itself from the competition not only due to its sheer size but also due to the caliber of stores within. Having successfully attracted 938 international class brands, including Chanel, Marc Jacobs, and Prada, they also boast the largest Gucci flagship store in Asia, and more than 20 brands make their debut appearance on the Chinese mainland. Also a great place for children.
Daily 10am-10pm. 87 Jianguo Lu (beside China Central Place), Chaoyang District. (6530 5888)

www.shinkong-place.com 新光天地，朝阳区建国路87号（华贸中心旁边）

Sun Dong An Plaza (See APM)

Wangfujing Department Store The store – a Beijing landmark – was the city's answer to the New York flagship Macy's. Now all spruced up, it offers floor after shiny floor of local and foreign clothing, cosmetics and more.
Sun-Thu 9am-10pm, Fri-Sat 9am-10.30pm. 255 Wangfujing Dajie, Dongcheng District. (6512 6677) 王府井百货大楼，东城区王府井大街255号

Xidan Shopping Center Pass by the costume-wearing candy sellers on the first floor and take the escalators to the top. The top floors of this local favorite are stocked with stalls selling everything from sparkly ballet slippers to retro T-shirts and fake bling. Weekends are outrageously packed (weekday mornings are best). Expect to spend several hours navigating the entire selection.
Sun-Thu 9am-9.30pm, Fri-Sat 9am-10pm. 132 Xidan Beidajie, Xicheng District. (6602-5016) 西单购物中心，西城区西单北大街132号

Zhongguancun Mall Normally known as the electronics epicenter of Beijing, Zhongguancun has been transformed into Haidian's newest one-stop shopping center. Lacoste, Only and Sephora are amongst the bigger brand names in the basement level. Above, however, are boutique-style stores with rarer finds: Yunnan honey in the Honey Workshop, modern lamps and clocks at Chief Chop, an esoteric collection of Italian imports at Huasen, and personalized pens at the Parker Pen Shop.
12 Zhongguancun Nandajie, Haidian District. 中关村购物广场，海淀区中关村南大街12号

DVDs & CDs

A Life as Film Just off the hutong tour track is this small shop that's funky in more ways than one: that smell is Lu Hua, the house dog. But don't mind him: hold your breath and hit the small but eclectic collection of CDs, DVDs and memorabilia.
Daily noon-11.30pm. 9 Yinding Qiao Hutong, Xicheng District. (6657 0234) 九阁，西城区银锭桥胡同9号

DVD Shop This shop stocks good quality copies of recent movies, TV series, concert films and classic films from Japan, Europe and the USA. You can preview some DVDs before buying.
Daily 10am-9pm. West of Yashow Market, Chaoyang District. (6415 7182) DVD店，朝阳区雅秀市场西ící

Fusheng Record Shop This little shop's selection of local rock, whether indie or DIY, is tops, and their foreign collection ain't too shabby either. The knowledgeable staff are eager to offer suggestions. Prices average around RMB 30, but may go as high as RMB 80-100. Fusheng is the exclusive sales agent for the Midi Festival DVD and also maintains a great website (www.fmusic.cn).
Daily 10am-10pm, 5m east of the Ping'anli intersection (where Xinjiekou meets Ping'an Dadao, on the south side of the street), Xicheng District. (6613 6182) 福声唱片店，西城区平安里路口往东50米路南

Hongyun A musician's paradise, with a vast catalogue of imported jazz, indie rock and other esoteric stuff (RMB 150-250 'cause they are the real deal). The selection of local music is equally extensive.
Daily 10am-10pm. 62 Xinjiekou Beidajie, Xicheng District. (6651 1363) 鸿运音像，西城区新街口北大街62号

Music Centre With two locations within two blocks, the small shops supply the 'hood with a bumpin' soundtrack that ranges from NWA to Dennis Chambers to the techno that is favoured by the boss, an old-school member of the local DJ massive. The shops, in operation since 1999, host great rock and jazz collections, many of which are imports priced sky-high (at the overseas standard of RMB 85) or not even for sale (Quoth the manager: "That one's mine!").
Daily 10am-10pm. 101 Dongsi Nandajie, Dongcheng District. (6523 2460) 音乐中心，东城区东四南大街101号

Rockland From David Bowie to Joan Jett to Infectious Grooves and Dio, you can find it all here in Rockland. There are also respectable jazz, blues, classical, hip hop, pop and techno selections (even an entire rack devoted to weird J-pop), but Rockland's specialty is, surprise... rock. This is any rockaholic's paradise.
Daily 1.30pm-midnight. 2 Nanguanfang Hutong, Houhai, Xicheng District. (138 1036 7674) 摇篮，西城区后海南官房胡同2号

Sound of Universe A popular little shop where you can find a wide selection of DVDs, including full boxed sets of almost every TV show (RMB 10 per disc).
Daily 1.30pm-2am. Bei Sanlitun Lu (across from Tongli Studio), Chaoyang District. (6417 7805) 小胡音像，朝阳区北三里屯路（同里对面）

Sugar Jar The coolest little music shop in town finally found digs worthy of its status as the top purveyor of local underground music. The shop's miniscule size belies the depth of even their international collection. Lao Yang is the best source of information on both the up-and-coming and already-gone, and often hauls part of his collection to rock shows and big events. Also has a location at the 798 Dashanzi Art District.
1) Tue-Sun 12.30pm-7.30pm. Dashanzi Studio, 2 Jiuxianqiao Lu (opposite Galleria Continua), Chaoyang District. (6433 1449); 2) Daily 1-9pm. 3 Shuimo Xinqu (300m north of Tsinghua University west gate), Haidian District. (6257 3351) www.sugarjar.cn 白糖罐，1）朝阳区大山子酒仙桥路2号（常青画廊对面）；2）海淀区水木新区域号（清华大学西门往北300米路东）

Tom's DVD Shop This chain of well-organized video stores stocks a wide selection of classic films, TV series and recent releases (starting at RMB 10 each), as well as countless boxed sets. Patrons must walk down the stairs at the back of the street-level framing shop to reach the cavernous DVD-lined basement at this outlet.
Daily 9.30am-11.30pm. 2A, Hairun International Bldg, 2 Jiangtai Lu, Chaoyang District. (5135 7487) 朝阳区将台路海润国际公寓商业2号

Xinhua Post DVD Shop This DVD store has a good selection of American, Chinese and Korean movies and TV series. Also rents VCDs for as little as RMB1 and DVDs for RMB3 (with a RMB 99 deposit). Because who wants to shell out a whopping RMB 6 for a new DVD?
Daily 10am-11pm. Rm 103, Bldg 19, Huaqing Jiayuan, Haidian District. (6745 9995) 新华驿站，海淀区华清嘉园19号楼103

Don't let substandard shops pull the wool over your eyes – head to Torana Gallery (see p374) for the real deal

Fabrics & Threads

Beixin Jingfeng Fabric This store is packed with different types of fabric, including fashionable cottons, minority fabrics, silk embroidery and African cloth, with prices starting around RMB 13 per meter. Best buys here are custom-made quilts (RMB 200 for double) and pillows (RMB 30). The layout is more straightforward than Muxiyuan, and the service is friendlier, but they don't have as big a selection. If you're looking for Western-style suit material, you'll find yourself out of luck.
Daily 8.30am-6.30pm. 4-23 Jiaodaokou Dongdajie (west of Guijie), Dongcheng District. (6404 2658) 北新京丰纺织品，东城区交道口东大街4—23号

Daxin Textiles Co. This mini-emporium sells cotton, wool, linen, silk, minority fabrics, etc. There's a huge variety here, though the store's claim that it has nearly 10,000 styles probably should be taken with a grain of salt. A number of on-site tailors will make custom clothes in 24 hours, with delivery available. Prices are higher than at Muxiyuan, but it's easier to navigate, quality is higher, and the staff is friendlier (not to mention more open to bargaining).
Daily 8.30am-8pm. Northeast corner of Dongsi crossing, Dongcheng District. (8602 3919) 大新纺织，东城区东四十字路口东北角

Iidea Calling all grannies and other knitting fiends. This store carries more than a hundred kinds of fine imported woolen threads from Italy's Filatura Di Crosa brand.
Daily 10am-9pm. NB 110A, B1/F, China World Shopping Mall, 1 Jianguomenwai Dajie, Chaoyang District. (6505 6350) 蝴蝶毛线，朝阳区建国门外大街1号国贸城地下1层NB110A

Jingjusishi Fabric Market Luxurious fancy cloth for curtains, bed sheets, tablecloths etc. is to be found in this market. They also offer a custom-tailor service.
Mon-Fri 9.30am-5.30pm, Sat-Sun 9.30am-6pm. Section 1, B1/F, Jiancai Jingmao Mansion, 14 Dongtucheng Lu, Chaoyang District. (6427 4730) 金启泰布艺公司，朝阳区东土城路14号建材经贸大厦地下北一厅

Linfuxiang Fabric Sells pure cottons, blends, traditional Chinese fabrics and stuffing for pillows. On-site tailors will make pillowcases with inner casing for RMB 30 and a double quilt with a thin layer of cotton stuffing for RMB 180. Expect commissioned pieces to take seven days.
Daily 9am-8pm. 324 Andingmennei Dajie, Dongcheng District. (6404 5747) 琳福祥纺织品，东城区安定门内大街324号

Muxiyuan Fabric Market It is easy to get lost – happily – in this enormous and crowded fabric and accessory "city." Divided into sections devoted to a specific product, Muxiyuan sells a galaxy of fabrics (silk, cashmere, lace, cotton, embroidery) as well as fake and real fur, zippers, brass buttons, and so much more. Finding the nicer material may take some effort, though the east side of the street is a good place to start. Prices are very, very low, especially if you haggle. But watch your purse and don't bring young kids here.
Haihutun Area, Nansanhuan Lu (south of Muxiyuan Qiao), Fengtai District. 木樨园纺织品市场，丰台区南三环路木樨园桥往南海户屯

Qianxiangyi (Beijing Silk Store) Established in 1840, this huge silk shop has tailors on site ready to whip

up a high quality outfit. The ground floor has a huge selection of silk bolts (RMB 40-120 per meter), and the second floor has pret-a-porter shirts, pajamas and tapestries.
Daily 8.30am-7.30pm. 50 Dazhalan Xijie, Qianmen, Xuanwu District. (6301 6658) 北京谦祥益丝绸商店，宣武区前门大栅栏西街50号

Ruifuxiang This emporium has been selling silk in Dazhalan since 1893. Respect.
1) Mon-Fri 9am-8pm, Sat-Sun 9am-8.30pm. 5 Qianmen Dazhalan, Xuanwu District. (6303 5313); 2) Daily 9am-10pm. 190 Wangfujing Dajie, Dongcheng District. (6525 0764, 6523 2807) 瑞蚨祥绸布店，1) 宣武区前门大栅栏5号; 2) 东城区王府井大街190号

Shantung Silk This place is a real find. It deals in all types of silk – including Thai brush silk – for as little as RMB 45 per meter. The store also sells finished products like lanterns (RMB 48 and up) and cushions, and is happy to accept custom orders. Don't forget to negotiate.
Daily 9am-5pm. 357 Chaoyangmennei Xiaojie, Dongcheng District. (6523 2440, 139 0100 5583) 山东丝绸，东城区朝内小街357号

Wansha Cashmere Store Nothing staves off the cold like fine wool, and the Wansha Cashmere Store is full of basic and unique yarns at cheap prices. Choose from a range of sumptuous colors and textures, including cashmere, wool, mohair, rabbit fur and many other artistic threads imported from Korea. Knitting enthusiasts will be especially interested in the knitting and crochet needles, pattern books and plastic buttons (all the staff are expert knitters). Wansha also offers custom-made (albeit machine-woven) services starting at RMB 35.
Daily 8.30am-7.30pm. 14-2 Dengshidongkou Dajie, Dongcheng District. (6512 7090, 6527 0450) 万纱经典毛纺织品，东城区灯市口东大街14-2

Flowers & Plants

Dushi Fangqun Gardening & Flower Market Covering an area of over 6,000sqm, Dushi Qunfang is the largest flower market in the south of Beijing. Large variety of breeds, including Dutch tulips and flowers shipped from Yunnan.
Daily 9am-5.30pm. 27 Chengshousi Lu Zhongjie, Fengtai District. (8762 8630) 都市芳群园林花卉市场，丰台区成寿寺路中街27号

Laitai Flower Market The cut bunches and potted plants in the basement will brighten anyone's day. Expect to pay around RMB 40 for a trailing ivy and RMB 50 for a small bonsai tree. You can also pick up some tropical fish on the first floor.
Mon-Thu 9am-6pm, Fri 9am-6.30 pm, Sat-Sun 9am-7pm. 9 Maizidian Xilu, Chaoyang District. (6463 6145) 莱太花卉市场，朝阳区麦子店西路9号

Liangma Flower Market This store sells almost every variety of cut flower or potted plant you could want at very reasonable prices. There are loads of individual vendors, so variety is good and bargaining is the norm. Delivery by flatbed bicycle costs between RMB 10-30, depending on the distance and your haggling skills.
Daily 8.30am-6pm. South bank of Liangma River, Dongsanhuan Beilu, Chaoyang District. (6504 2446) 亮马花卉市场，朝阳区东三环北路，燕莎商城南，亮马河南岸

Sureline Design & Construction With professional experience in landscape design and gardening, they work with you to create green space and enhance the beauty of your home.
Daily 9am-6pm. Suite 25P, New York Tower, 3A Shilipu, Chaoyang District. (6657 0729, 139 1173 5922) 顺兴堂，朝阳区十里堡甲3号都会华庭纽约阁25P

Yuquanying Flower Market Looking for Dutch tulips? The Yuquanying Flower Market sells said posies for only RMB 6, and stocks a wide selection of flowers and plants, including a good number of rare breeds. Flowers can be ordered for delivery online or over the phone.
Daily 8.30am-5.30pm. 71 Nansanhuan Xilu, Fengtai District. (6330 3946) www.bjfzj.com 玉泉营花卉市场，丰台区南三环西路71号

Zhongshu Grand Forest Flower Trade Market Tucked into the campus of Beijing's Agricultural University, this market is divided into three sections: the first sells potted plants, cut flowers and bonsai trees; the second section deals in traditional Chinese crafts and teashops; while in the third part, stands sell fish, turtles and aquarium supplies.
Daily 8.30am-6pm. 200m south of Lianxiang Qiao, Beisanhuan (near east gate of Chinese Academy of Agricultural Science), Haidian District. (6211 9255) 中蔬大森林花卉市场 海淀区北三环联想桥南200米(中国农科院东门)

Markets

Alien Street Market One of Beijing's most pleasant markets: Sellers are polite, prices are fair, and the selection defies our powers of description. Since they cater to Russian shuttle traders, the stalls here generally carry more ample sizes – notably for bras, stockings and pants. Particularly worthy of attention are the coats, pants, and belts. They also have accessories galore, and random stuff like toilet fixtures or swords. You'll also find tea, shoes, toys, camping gear, spy equipment and electronics. Definitely haggle.
Laofanjie Shichang, Yabao Lu (south of Fulllink Plaza), Chaoyang District. 老番街市场，朝阳区雅宝路

Beijing Sunhe Ethical Goods Market If you want to shop where the locals do, visit this huge indoor/outdoor market which offers a little bit of everything, including clothing, shoes, kitchen sundries, baby items, furniture and all types of food. Not at all touristy, but beware of the "*laowai tax*": one wily merchant tried to charge more for a basketball than what was printed on the price tag.
Daily 10am-9pm. Jingshun Lu, Chaoyang District. (136 8312 5376) 北京孙河市场，朝阳区京顺路

Dongjiao Market This incredible market is a maze of shops and stalls with wonderfully inexpensive treasures. Dongjiao redefines "one-stop-shopping", selling everything from hammers to dishes to fire extinguishers. A favorite of the locals, the shopping experience here is hectic but exciting, and with such low prices it's hard not to walk away with a little something … or two.
Daily 8am-5.30pm. Xidawang Lu (south of Soho New Town), Chaoyang District. (6774 7864) 东郊市场，朝阳区西大望路 (Soho现代城边)

Dongwuyuan Wholesale Market (See "Lions, Tigers, Bears… and Marc Jacobs!" p401) This vast market an

Lions, Tigers, Bears ... and Marc Jacobs!

Shopping at the Zoo
by Catherine Lee

"Beijing Zoo." The words conjure up images of miserable animals imprisoned in depressing cement "habitats." After an unpleasant visit that left me haunted by nightmares of crying monkeys, I was rather wary of returning to any place with the word "zoo" in the name. However, to my Chinese roommate those two words were a shopping mantra. After persistent admonition, I decided to leave my Silk Street elbow pads at home and move on to the real shopping – at the zoo. For the zoo area is not only home to dirty pandas, but also mazes of treasure-filled shops and stalls – at the Dongwuyuan Wholesale Market.

You won't find smiles this big at the panda prison...

Our cab driver pointed out several of the large, adjacent buildings that comprised the market. Already feeling overwhelmed, we randomly chose to start with the faded brick red building. Upon entering we found ourselves immersed in a chaotic, noisy realm – a zoo, of sorts. Instead of cages, there were stalls. Instead of melancholy beasts, there were piles of clothes, shoes and bags. As for the visitors ... well, let's just say the predominantly female crowd was far more excited to be ogling Chloé jackets and Gucci flats than a glum zebra.

Six aisles of stalls crammed with goods stretched for what seemed like forever. We, self-proclaimed shopping queens, were reduced to stuporous wandering for several minutes – before our instincts kicked into gear. A dress I'd fallen in love with at Yashow was being sold here for a tenth of the price! Evidently Dongwuyuan is still off the tourist radar (zero *laowai* spotted in six hours), a blessing that has kept prices low. In welcome contrast to most markets around town, the low prices are wholesale and thus non-negotiable. With lower starting quotes than the final, painstakingly negotiated price anywhere else, minimal bartering sessions are necessary – which means more energy to buy, buy, buy!

Racing from stall to stall, we soon slipped into shopping-beast mode, buying with total abandon. We squealed over H&M lookalike dresses for a quarter of the price, Marc Jacobs shorts for RMB 100, adorable summer camis for RMB 25, American Eagle flip-flops for RMB 20. With prices this good for clothes this cute, we were filled with the uncontrollable urge to refit our entire wardrobes, buying outfits that looked as if they'd come straight off the runways and pages of *Vogue*, indulging dreams of looks that we would ordinarily never dare to attempt.

Our love for all things tacky and sparkly was well sated by the offerings next door – glittering caps, plastic purple sunglasses, gold braided belts – all for under RMB 20. And, of course, the day's prize purchase – an "iPod girl is my co-pilot" shirt for RMB 40.

We emerged only as the last vendor was pulling their curtain closed. Weighed down like sherpas with bundles of goodies, with sore feet and empty wallets, we stood with dazed smiles stretched across our faces. Going to the zoo has never been more fun.

PHOTO: MARY DENNIS

Haggling 101
Steps to a delightful discount dance
by EP Williams

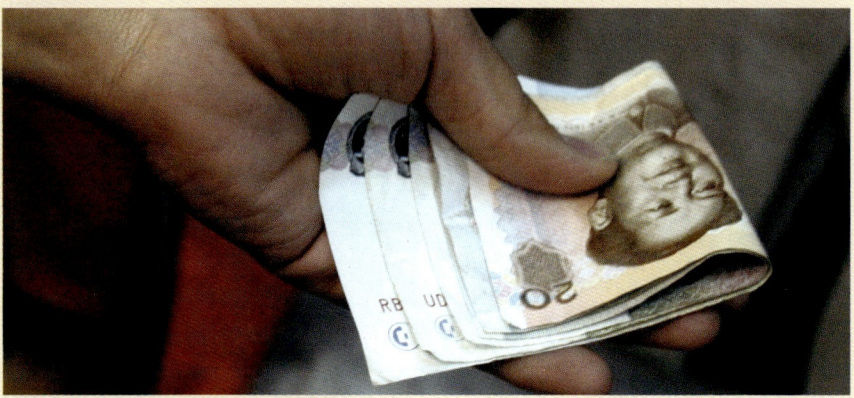

I can't afford that Rolex, I have only fifty kuai

The first rule of haggling is that if there's no price tag on an item, haggle. The second rule of haggling is that if there's a price tag, still try to haggle. The third rule of haggling, and the key to an increased lifespan, is to approach the whole discount dance with a sense of fun. Nobody wins if you berate the seller and their goods while whipping yourself into a frenzy over being taken.

The haggling Holy Grail is the ultimate counter-offer. Some swear by the "offer 50 per cent and accept 25 per cent off" strategy, while others refuse to pay more than the humidity index multiplied by the square root of the lunar month. In the end, it is an art, not a science. You have to use your sixth sense, but the following methods can save you multiple *mao*.

The all-time classic is the fake walk-away. When properly executed it can bring a tear to the eye. Simply put, when you aren't getting the price you want, pretend to walk away hoping that the merchant, facing the loss of the sale, will call you back and cave in on the price. Utter failure is assured when you shout out repeatedly, "Right, that's it. I am now leaving. OK, on my way out. Going now," as you back away slowly caressing the item. The walk-away works best in less touristy areas, having lost much of its effectiveness at Hongqiao and Yashow.

The "this is a piece of crap, so it must be cheap" gambit is a bit nebulous and makes vendors inwardly chuckle, as you are in fact indicating that you want this piece of crap, and the longer you spend denigrating it the more you reveal how much you desire it. To make this one work you have to think hard and fast. Then throw in the fake walk-away to seal the deal.

A more devious, somewhat evil method is the "I plan to buy in bulk" maneuver. Essentially, it involves lying, or seriously massaging the truth: You indicate a desire to buy multiples of a selected item, thereby planting visions of the "Big Sale" in the merchant's mind. You then attempt to buy one piece at "volume price" to "make sure it is ok" before coming back to buy the rest, wink, wink. This one is morally dubious and only works once in a shop. Odds improve if you can put on a Russian accent.

If you're wearing your oldest clothes and can master a pained and hungry look, try the "I love it, but I don't have enough money" approach. You need to stress that you really like that bright pink Tods bag, and then mournfully explain that you don't have much money because you're a student / unemployed / raising 12 children. Only serious actors should try this one since the tale of woe must be accompanied by an unusually pitiful demeanor.

So, get your game face on. Treat your opponent fairly by first trotting out a "Can you go cheaper (*neng zai pianyi yidian'r*)?" If you don't like the price, act a bit shocked, chuckle sadly, then make the counteroffer and kick off the haggling hoedown.

PHOTO: ROB PATTERSON

"When you have only two pennies, spend one on bread and the other on a flower." - Chinese proverb

the similarly laid out buildings around it (Jinkaili and Tianqi) consist of mazes of shops and stalls selling "brand name" clothes and tons of non-branded trendy Chinese styles and accessories.
Daily 6am-4pm. Xizhimenwai Dajie (south of Beijing Zoo), Xicheng District. (8837 8056) 动物园服装批发市场，西城区西直门外大街（北京动物园路南）

Golden Five Stars Market This vast market sells every imaginable made-in-China manufactured item. The vendor stands start with shoes and jewelry, progress to clothes, blankets, electronics, pottery and sporting goods and end with school and art supplies at the rear. This market is a cheap, one-stop-spot for souvenir shopping or an Ikea-alternative for customizing a pre-furnished apartment. Bargaining is necessary.
Daily 8.15am-6.30pm. Xueyuan Nanlu (north of Mingguang Market), Haidian District. (6222 6827) 金五星百货城，海淀区学院南路（明光市场北边）

Hongqiao Market Here you'll find T-shirts, silk pajamas, Chinese tchotchkes, beads, shoes, and some electronics, as well as a great fish market in the basement. But under daily siege from foreigners eager to share their wealth, this landmark market is seriously overpriced – for everything. Don't say we didn't warn you. If you nevertheless find yourself there with your camera, head up to the fifth floor balcony for an amazing view of the Temple of Heaven.
Daily 8.30am-7pm. 36 Hongqiao Lu, Chongwen District. (6713 3354) 红桥市场，崇文区红桥路36号

Jiayi Vogue Square Swarming with style-conscious babes and their bag-toting boyfriends, this market is lined with stalls selling clothes for every occasion (from underwear to evening wear, and from T-shirts to ties), as well as towels, accessories, handbags, eyewear, toys,

silver jewelry and much more besides. For some reason, prices are better on the left side of the market than on the right. Most items are only available in smaller sizes. There's also a cafeteria and an ATM in the back.
Daily 10am-9pm. 3A Xinyuan Nanlu, Chaoyang District. (8451 1810) 佳艺时尚广场，朝阳区新源南路3号

MEN Shopping Center One of Beijing's newest markets, MEN is clean, air-conditioned, and staffed by polite stall-holders. In the basement, find knockoff handbags, luggage, wallets and shoes (RMB 60) as well as a clean cafeteria. The first floor has Chinese handicrafts, eyewear, DVDs, toys, electronics as well as Liumeng Beautiful Nail Salon and a wine wholesaler. Children's, men's and women's clothes are on the second floor.
Daily 11.30am-8pm. Sanlitun Beijie, Chaoyang District. (6413 2663) 朝外MEN购物中心，朝阳区三里屯北街

Nali Mall This clean, cul-de-sac market channels the spirit of the former Sanlitun clothing street. It incorporates stores selling underwear, funky-colored stockings, fashionable clothes, cute accessories, and large-sized shoes (at the store Long.com) for the big-footed foreigner. Men can check out the Sophia Men store. In between purchases, have a manicure or pedicure at Jiali and grab a meal at Kiosk, Alameda or Tapas. Prices range from reasonable to way over the odds.
Sanlitun Lu, Chaoyang District. 那里服装市场，朝阳区三里屯路

Panjiayuan Antique Market (See directory p389 under Antiques & "Antiques")

Ritan Hotel South Building Don't be afraid to peek past the sheets covering every doorway in this five-story market, because inside you'll find great deals on puffy jackets of every size and color, denim (jeans, vests,

Worlds collide at Panjiayuan Antique Market.

jackets, you name it), sweaters, kids' wear, and athletic clothes. Not a huge variety, but cheap.
Daily 9am-7pm. Ritan Hotel, South Bldg, 1 Ritan Lu, Chaoyang District. (8563 5588) 朝阳区日坛路1号日坛宾馆南楼

Ritan Office Building If you wish you were on *Sex and the City*, come to this warren of boutiques to find glam threads like Marc Jacobs jackets (RMB 360), D&G jeans (RMB 300), and dresses by harder-to-find designers like Laundry, Anna Sui, and Catherine Malandrino. Yes, they're copies, but they're more fashionable and better made than the market knock-offs. Unfortunately, the prices have risen thanks to hordes of haggling-averse foreigners.
Daily 10am-7pm. 15A Guanghua Lu, Chaoyang District. (6502 1528) 日坛商务楼，朝阳区光华路甲15号

Silk Market Although this six-story market is overwhelmingly touristy (and therefore overpriced, even with bargaining), it is filled with everything imaginable – clothing, souvenirs, jewelry, electronics, and fabrics – each with its own section. Be prepared for loud and pushy sellers who are accustomed to dealing with foreigners.
Daily 9am-9pm. 8 Xiushui Dongjie, Jianwai Dajie, Chaoyang District. (5169 8800) 秀水市场，朝阳区建外大街秀水东街8号

Sunny Gold Street Market This two-story building which caters to tourists and airline staff ain't too shabby for B-grade reproductions of name brand bags, wallets, luggage, shoes, sportswear, jeans, shirts,

dresses, sunglasses, children's wear, nightwear, hats, belts, bathing suits, accessories, Chinese silk, DVDs and more. Expect to see names like Nike, Puma, Barbie, Jamboree, Hermes, Chanel, Gap and more. The shop owners are polite and enjoy a good haggle.
Daily 9am-11pm. 2 Fangyuan Xilu (near the Holiday Inn Lido hotel), Chaoyang District. (136 8127 8856) 阳光金街，朝阳区芳园西路2号（丽都假日酒店附近）

Wudaokou Clothing Market With two floors of small shops, you might have to wade through seas of cheese before you find something you really like, but there are great finds here such as imitation Diesel jeans, sport and hip hop wear, shoes and trainers, some fantastically funky t-shirts and temporary tattoos (RMB 10-25). Be sure to bargain hard.
Daily 9am-7.30pm. Northeast corner of Xueyuan Lu and Beisihuan Lu, Haidian District. (6239 6347) 五道口服装市场，海淀区学院路和北四环路十字路口的东北角

Xidan Outdoor Market This semi-outdoor market has a maze of stalls and a variety of selections. Prices here tend to be dirt cheap (after bargaining), though the merchandise can be hit-or-miss. Still, we've walked away with funky RMB 15 newsboy caps and RMB 10 oversized sunglasses – which, when we're going for something supertrendy, are prices we're prepared to pay.
North of the grassy hub of Xidan Square (between 77th Street Plaza and Xidan Shopping Center), Xicheng District. 西单户外市场，西城区西单广场绿地北侧（77街和西单购物中心之间）

Xiushui 2 (east) Most of the items on sale in this sister market of the original Xiushui are chic dresses, sandals, blazers, shorts and accessories that are hard to find in other markets. Prices are higher then the original Xiushui.
Daily 10am-8.30pm. 14 Dongdaqiao Lu, Chaoyang District. (6501 8811) 秀水2号，朝阳区东大桥路14号，贵友大厦正北200米

Xiushui 2 (west) The four-floor building has more than 50 fancily decorated boutiques. Though you can still spot some "designer" items here, most items are trendy chic threads and accessories. Check out the Cashmere Shop on the second floor. Sadly, there's not much for the guys, except some jeans.
Daily 10am-8.30pm. 2 Xiushui Jie, Jianwai Dajie (west of St. Regis Hotel), Chaoyang District. (6506 2326) 秀水2号，朝阳区建外秀水1号院国际俱乐部西上岛咖啡旁

Yabaolu Fur Street If your name is Ivanka, you'll probably feel at home at this winter headquarters in the Russian-heavy Yabaolu neighborhood, which features a long strip of stores that sell only thick fur coats – long, short, and even multi-colored. "Palace Peeress Furs" is the biggest, but you should compare prices and walk in the various shops. Short coats start around RMB 1,000, and long coats can hit RMB 12,800.
Daily 9am-7pm. Ritan Lu (south of Alien Street Market), Chaoyang District. (8563 8216) 雅宝路皮草市场，朝阳区日坛路（老番街市场南面）

Yansha Outlets Sells real brand names ranging from Armani to Adidas and Nautica to DKNY.
Daily 10am-9pm. 9 Dongsihuan Lu, Chaoyang District. (6739 5678) 燕莎奥特莱斯购物中心，朝阳区东四环路9

Yashow Market Yes, it's overrun by free-spending tourists, but Yashow is an unavoidable fixture in the life of a serious shopper. It has a good selection of "brand-name" underwear, jeans, jackets, shoes, sports equipment, bags and souvenirs. Don't forget to bargain ruthlessly. Some of the tailors on the third floor have a large following, as does the Creative Nail Beauty Salon on the fourth floor.
Daily 9.30am-9pm. 58 Gongti Beilu, Chaoyang District. (6415 1726) 雅秀市场，朝阳区工体北路58号

Yueshow Clothing Market Tell only your good friends about this spot, which has a selection to rival Yashow and no crowds. The best buys here include Japanese and Korean kids' wear and heaps of Western "brand name" clothes. There's also an Olympic souvenir shop, a kids' play area, and a good manicurist.
Daily 9.30am-9pm. 99 Chaoyangmenwai Dajie, Chaoyang District. (6416 8945) 岳秀市场，朝阳区朝阳门外大街99号

Mobile Phones

Grand World Secondhand Electrical Market Wonder where your mobile phone ends up when you leave it in a taxi? Expect to pay about two-thirds of what the phone would cost new. Inspect everything carefully and make sure to get a receipt in case it breaks down on the second day. Aside from handsets, there are three floors packed with used TVs, CD players, turntables and more.
Daily 9am-6pm. Laitai Flower Market, Nuren Jie, Chaoyang District. (8448 4336) 七彩大世界二手电器市场，朝阳区女人街莱太花卉市场

Xidan Science & Technology Shopping Mall This mobile mall has more than 20 cell phone stores including Siemens, Nokia, Sony Ericsson, Samsung and Motorola. The biggest advantage of shopping here is the security: Authenticity and repair service are guaranteed. They also sell accessories including batteries, chargers, earphone and cell phone ornaments. Best of all, you can bargain.
Mon 10am-9pm, Tues-Sun 9.30am-7pm. 131 Xidan Beidajie (north of Juntai Shopping Market), Xicheng District. (6651 9639) 西单科技广场，西城区西单北大街131号（君太百货北边）

Zoomflight This mobile phone chain with 58 outlets in Beijing has all the latest models, good prices and long warranties. Visit the website to find the location nearest you.
Daily 8.30am-8.30pm. A18 Gongti Donglu, Chaoyang District. (6585 2322/2555) www.zoomflight.com.cn 中复电讯，朝阳区工体东路甲18号

Musical Instruments

Ao Yue Piano Center Ao Yue Piano rents a selection of new and secondhand pianos in addition to its wholesale and tuning services. Choose from Yamaha, Kawai, and local brands Xinghai and Zhujiang. The rental fee for local pianos starts from RMB 180/mth, imported ones cost RMB 500/mth and renting a grand piano costs RMB 1800/day. For each rental, customers get free tuning and delivery. Piano lessons are also available. There are three on-site practice rooms, which charge RMB 10/hr.
Daily 9am-9pm. Northeast corner of Jianxiang Qiao, Beisihuan Lu (300m east of Zhongguo Yinyue Xueyuan), Chaoyang District. (6492 4835) 奥乐钢琴中心，朝阳区北四环路健翔桥东北角中国音乐学院往东300米

Beijing Yilun Piano Center The Yilun Piano Center sells refurbished pianos at a fraction of the usual prices: A Yamaha grand piano costs half the price of a new one. The used pianos are mostly under 10 years old. In addition to selling pianos, the center offers piano classes (RMB 100/hr).
Daily 9am-8pm. 48-1 Zhongguancun Nandajie, Haidian District. (6218 3582) 北京艺伦钢琴中心，海淀区中关村南大街48-1号

Fierce The shop's small size belies its influence, in terms of gear sold and major concerts outfitted (Norah Jones, Deep Purple, Beyond, Wang Fei, the Lijiang Snow Mountain Music Festival and more) – not to mention practice space. A drum (Pearl, Slingerland), percussion (LP) and cymbal (Sabian, Paiste, Meinl) section sets it apart from most other Xinjiekou shops, and its staff is the best on the block.
Daily 9am-7pm. 64 Xinjiekou Nandajie, Xicheng District. (6304 2708) www.bjfierce.com 菲尔斯，西城区新街口南大街64号

Fuda Like most shops on the strip, its size is misleading. The Behringer sign in the front window is your hint that it's a good spot for effect pedals, but they've got decent drum-related stuff (skins, sticks) as well as a good selection of instruments. A small recording studio down a dark alley next door is another bonus.
Daily 10am-6.30pm. 57 Gulou Dongdajie, Dongcheng District. (6402 9720, 139 1117 0825) www.fuda123.com 福达，东城区鼓楼东大街57号

Continues on p408

Somebody in Beijing Loves Me...

...but all they got me was this lousy shirt?!
by Catherine Lee

Dreading the cries of "What did you get me?!" when you return home? Fear not, intrepid shopper. Souvenir shopping for so many family members and friends can be a daunting task, and it may sometimes seem like it would be easier to just give up and dole out cash in red envelopes. But with a few pointers on where to start, you can actually enjoy the treasure hunt. Try some of these time-tested gift ideas, for everyone from Grandma to your newborn cousin.

▼ **1. Tiger shoes** Baby's feet will be roaringly cute in these slippers. Irresistibly odd, the combination of textures and prints on these guys are practically hypnotic. [RMB 30, Shengtangxuan, p157]

▼ **2. Kite** Mary Poppins couldn't have dreamed up a cooler kite, and kids and adults alike will enjoy this handmade piece. [RMB 10, San Shi Shan Zhai, p157]

▼ **3. Art book** So you want to be a culture vulture? Let someone else write about it and you can reap the face points. [RMB 300, Timezone 8 Bookstore, p392]

▼ **4. T-Shirt** Too cool for tourist scrub? For a good dose of snarky fun, head to Plastered for tees that charmingly capture the essence of Beijing. [RMB 90, Plastered T-Shirts, see p363]

PHOTOS: JUDY ZHOU, SIMON LIM AND COURTESY OF PLASTERED T-SHIRTS

▼ **5. Clock** Nothing like waking up to the sound of revolution. [RMB 20, Yashow Market, p405]

▼ **6. Doll** Guaranteed to dream deeper than Barbie. [RMB 150, Shanghai Tang, p360]

▼ **7. Snake liquor** I'm gonna buy you a drank ... of this delicious (-ish) booze. The snake at the bottom is real; eating it may enhance the medicinal benefits. [RMB 40, try the Russian grocery stores around Dongzhimen and Yabao Lu]

▼ **8. Shard box** Bring back a piece of China – literally. These gorgeous jewelry boxes are made from fragments of porcelain vessels smashed during the Cultural Revolution. [RMB 20-250, Shard Box, p366]

▶ **9. Business cards** Your dream identity: Read it, touch it, savor it ... and make sure everybody else does too. Whether you want to be the California Beef Noodle King or a Court-Appointed Genius: impress. [RMB 30-40/box (100 cards), most neighborhood print shops, or anywhere fine identities are sold]

SHOPPING 407

Hengyun/Henry Music The staff has been known to be of the too-cool-for-school school, but probably because they know how *niu* their store is. Equipment rental can be arranged. Stocks mid-range guitars like Ibanez and Jackson (RMB 5000) and American ESP guitars (up to RMB 16,000). Talk to Wang Wei from the now-defunct speed metal band Bloodbath (Shalu) for a good deal.
Daily 10am-6.30pm. 105 Xinjiekou Nandajie, Xicheng District. (6618 8745) 恒韵琴行，西城区新街口南大街105号

Lanyao Their locally-produced Vorson guitars play quite nicely and come with Floyd Rose tremolo systems and Seymour Duncan pickups. Higher end gear includes Paul Reed Smiths, Fender Telecasters and a few high-end Warwick basses. They also have Master Man *pipas* (RMB 1,200-8,000) and a selection of upright pianos (RMB 12,000 and up).
Daily 9.30am-7.30pm. 248 Beisihuan Zhonglu (50m east of North gate of Beihang University), Haidian District. (8232 8407) 蓝摇，海淀区北四环中路248号（北航北门往东50米）

Nan Mu Xiu Come for a glimpse of the Joe Satriani Y2K Limited Edition Crystal Planet axe hanging on the back wall, stick around to try your hand at all kinds of guitars, Ibanez (Joe's weapon of choice) and otherwise: Fender, Gibson, Musicman, et al. Owner Liu Chunyang is intimate with many guitar gods, goddesses and company execs, as evidenced by the pictures lining the walls.
Daily 9.30am-7.30pm. 132 Xinjiekou Nandajie, Xicheng District. (6618 2516, 6446 6803) www.guitarchina.com/ liuchunyang 楠木秀，西城区新街口南大街132号

Parson's Music This chain store, found in almost every province in China, sells world-class brands like Schimmel, Siler, Toyama and Casio. Instruments include pianos, wind, stringed, percussion, electroacoustical and classic Chinese. Their 1,500sqm flagship store at Golden Resources Mall is open later, until 9.30pm.
Daily 9am-6pm. 1) 54-3 Xisanhuan Beilu, Haidian District. (6873 2880); 2) 4006-4011, Golden Resources Mall, 1 Yuanda Lu, Haidian District. (8887 4340); 3) 4/F, Wanjiao Plaza, Nanhu Beilu, Wangjing area, Chaoyang District. (8471 3688); 4) A404-405, 4/F, Metro City, 189 Dongsihuan Zhonglu, Chaoyang District. (6772 8100) www.parsonsmusic.com
柏斯琴行，1）海淀区西三环北路54-3号；2）海淀区远大路1号金源新燕莎时代购物中心4006-4011号；3）朝阳区望京南湖北路旺角广场4楼；4）朝阳区东四环中路189号美罗城4楼

Steinway and Sons Why settle for anything less than the best? The piano maker to the stars has models ranging in price from RMB 25,000 to 736,800 – suitable for Elton John or Lang Lang wannabes with deep pockets.
Daily 9.30am-5.30pm. 88 Guangqumennei Dajie, Chongwen District. (6716 4658) 北京星德威钢琴行，崇文区广渠门内大街88号

Tom Lee Music The most famous emporium in town is divided into various areas, for keyboard and midi systems, brass instruments, guitars, pianos, percussion and professional audio gear. The four-floor shop offers a multitude of fancy brand-name instruments, many of which have been unavailable in China until now, especially the electric guitars and pianos. Highlights include a Petrof Concert Grand Piano (RMB 770,000) and a high-tech Freehand Music Pad (RMB 14,500) – an easy-to-use digital music notebook that takes the place of printed sheet music. Tom Lee also offers a range of music classes for both kids and adults.
Daily 9.30am-8.30pm. 57 Tiantan Lu, Chongwen District. (6702 0099) 通利琴行，崇文区天坛路57号

Wangfujing Musical Instrument City A succession of stalls with a large number of traditional Chinese instruments like the *erhu* as well as more flutes, violins and recorders than you can shake a tambourine at.
Sun-Thur 9am-9pm, Fri-Sat 9am-10pm. Lisheng Sports Shopping Mall, 201 Wangfujing Dajie, Dongcheng District. (6525 6255) 王府井乐器城，东城区王府井大街201号利生体育用品大厦内

Xuan Zhuan A tiny shop run by drummer Li Ming (of Brit-pop act No Fish) with a great selection of new and used effects pedals, snare drums, Mapex drum kits, a smattering of guitars and basses and a rehearsal space in the back closet/room.
Daily 1.30-7pm. 28A Gulou Dongdajie, Dongcheng District. (8404 3614) 旋转七天乐器，东城区鼓楼东大街甲28号

Zhiyin Wanli Instruments The store specializes in Ibanez guitars and basses (RMB 1,000 – 30,000) and also carries some amps and effects pedals (RMB 500 plus).
Daily 9.30am-6pm. Southeast corner of Jiaodaokou intersection, Dongcheng District. (8403 7683) 知音万里琴行，东城区交道口十字路口东南角

Online Shopping

Dangdang.com Originally an online book store, this site has expanded to include music, movies, home appliances, and more. It is pretty Chinese text-heavy, but has some pictures. The real zinger? They can deliver anything to you within just four hours if you are inside the Fourth Ring Road (RMB 20 per item). *www.dangdang.com*

EasyExpats.com This site is all in English and can tell you prices in USD, Euros, pounds, or RMB. They sell international cosmetics, books, computers and electronics, iPods, and flowers. They deliver anywhere within the Fifth Ring Road (with free deliveries on purchases over RMB 100). *www.easyexpats.com/catalog/*

eBay.com The Chinese version is just like the one you're used to except that, well, it's mostly in Chinese. You can still search for items in English, since some of the descriptions are in both languages. It has great pictures, and tons of categories to browse through – by type of object or by price (including a fun RMB 1 section). *www.ebay.com.cn*

GladBuy.com Specializing in gifts such as wine and chocolate, this website has an all-English version and features free (or cheap, depending on where you live) delivery, but with a pretty limited selection of merchandise. *www.gladbuy.com/en/index.asp*

Joyo.com As the Chinese branch of Amazon, this site has an extensive "Foreign Language Bookstore" section, but also has tons of other categories, like movies, music, toys, home appliances, jewelry, and electronics. It's in Chinese but has good pictures, and has free delivery within the Fourth Ring Road. *www.joyo.com*

Taobao.com Similar to eBay, this site allows you to bid on other people's unwanted items, but unlike eBay, you can sometimes negotiate with the seller, directly bypassing the whole bidding process. They deliver anywhere

If music be the food of love, you'll swoon over this buffet of guitars.

in China, and have a huge selection of items. In Chinese, but searches in English will bring up plenty of options too, and it has good pictures. www.taobao.com

Pharmacies & Medical Supplies

Beijing Kailong Medical supplies such as wheelchairs, blood pressure meters, hospital beds, and x-ray machines.
Daily 9am-8pm. 274 Dongsi Beidajie, Dongcheng District. (6404 3688) 北京凯隆医疗器械，东城区东四北大街274号

Golden Elephant Medicine This chain of pharmacies sells a wide range of over-the-counter Western and Chinese medicine. Check their website to find the nearest location.
Daily 24 hours. 114 Xidan Beidajie, Xicheng District. (6607 7021, 6606 4935) www.jxdyf.com.cn/address/map.php 西单金象大药房，西城区西单北大街114号

Wangfujing Pharmaceutical Store While the first floor stocks imported medicines alongside traditional Chinese medicines like "antler nourishment," the second floor contains products such as wheelchairs (regular RMB 700, electric RMB 9500) and crutches (90).
Daily 8.30am-9.30pm. 267 Wangfujing Dajie, Dongcheng District. (6525 2322) 北京王府井医药商店，东城区王府井大街267号

Watson's This Western-style drugstore sells health and beauty products, diapers, confectionery, stationery, condoms, over-the-counter medications and more.

Several other outlets in Beijing including Ginza Mall, China World and FullLink Plaza.
Daily 9.30am-9.30pm. Holiday Inn Lido, 6 Jiangtai Lu, Chaoyang District. (6436 7651) 屈臣氏，朝阳区将台路（丽都内）

Silk
(See Fabrics & Threads p399, Tailors p369, The Red Phoenix p360, and Emperor p382. Silk can also be purchased at markets with tailors. See Markets p400)

Sports Equipment

Beijing Honma Golf Service Store This shop stocks prestigious, authentic Japanese Honma clubs. Bring piles of cash, since a set of top-of-the-line clubs costs RMB 350,000.
Daily 10.30am-8pm. Stall 5, B1/F Kerry Centre Mall, 1 Guanghua Lu, Chaoyang District. (8529 9448) 北京本间高尔夫用品专卖店，朝阳区光华路1号嘉里中心商场地下1层B05

Beijing Longteng Athletics Thing Gotta love the name and very cheap prices for a wide range of "brand name" athletic gear including tennis rackets. Don't forget to bargain.
Stall 1290, Alien Street Market, Chaoyang District. (139 1042 4388) 朝阳区老番街市场2层（电梯附近）1290室

Bibo A paradise for fishing enthusiasts, Bibo sells high-end fishing gear brands from Japan, Korea and Taiwan,

including rods, lines, hooks, bait, nets, containers and any other fishing accessory you can think of. There's a more complete collection of products on their website, which offers delivery services.
Daily 10am-6.30pm. 3100, 3/F, Golden Resources Mall, 1 Yuanda Lu (west of Suzhou Bridge), Haidian District. (8886 1286) 天龙碧波渔具，海淀区金源时代购物中心三层3100室

Decathlon French sporting goods chain combines quality products with bargain prices. The huge warehouse store sells everything from tents to wetsuits, climbing gear to bike shorts, golf clubs to riding boots, as well as localized favorites like table tennis paddles and badminton rackets. Shuttle departs from Jianwai Soho every 15 minutes.
Daily 9am-9pm. 3 Wenhuayuan Xilu, Economic-Technological Development Area (Dongnan Wuhuan, Yizhuang exit, close to B&Q), Chaoyang District. (6782 6100) 迪卡侬体育用品，朝阳区东四环北路6号阳光上东中环广场A区8号

Demokratic Snowboard Skate Surf Shop In the process of relocation at time of writing, this purveyor of snowboarding, skateboarding, and surfing apparel, plans to reopen a store in Beijing in Spring 2008. They also organize regular trips and offers lessons to beginners and advanced level riders.
www.demokratic.com

DIY Club Come here for snowboards (RMB 2,000-5,000), boots (RMB 500-3,000) and snow pants (RMB 400-1,500) from Flow, Burton, K2, Head and Rossignol.
312 Daduhui Shopping Mall, Ciqikou, Chongwen District. (1331 102 1256) www.snowboard.com.cn DIY单板滑雪俱乐部，崇文区磁器口大都会312号

Dolomite The place to go for specialist outdoor clothing and gear. The storied Italian brand is famous for its top quality goods, in particular its climbing gear. And it's not merely the quality which will draw fans – being an Italian brand, style is naturally of the essence.
Mon-Thu 9am-9pm, Fri-Sun 10am-10pm. 3078, 3/F, Golden Resources Mall, 1 Yuanda Lu, Haidian District. (8889 2642) 多洛迈特，海淀区远大路1号金源新燕莎购物中心3层3078号商铺

Explorer This conveniently located adventure gear outlet supplies a bevy of high quality and international name brand equipment for hiking, camping, climbing and outdoor reconnaissance.
Daily 9.30am-9.30pm. B1/F, Bldg A, East Gate Plaza, 9 Dongzhong Jie, Dongcheng District. (6418 5696) www.cnexplorer.com 探索者，东城区东中街9号东环广场A座地下1层

Extreme Beyond A reliable camping and mountaineering store with classic gear (boots, jackets, backpacks, tents, sleeping bags) as well as more unusual imports (snakebite kits, biodegradable soap and freeze dried beef stroganoff). Prices are reasonable and discounts are available – just ask.
Daily 10am-7.30pm. A6 Gongti Donglu, Chaoyang District. (6506 5121) www.8853.com 中双野营探险登山装备店，朝阳区工体东路甲6号

Golf Town A golf widow's worst nightmare: a massive floor dedicated to the game that inspires obsession. They stock Callaway, Cleveland and Titleist, among others, and there is even a small green to try out your putters before you buy.

Daily 10am-7.45pm. 3/F, Laitai Flower Market, Nuren Jie, Chaoyang District. (6462 2552) 迈达康高尔夫，朝阳区女人街莱太花卉市场3层

KNS Pick up Head skis and snowboards here. Expect to fork over at least RMB 2,000 for the board alone, or RMB 10,000 for a snowboard, boots and bindings package. Become a member (RMB 15 or free with RMB 600 worth of purchases) and enjoy discounts and the chance to join their weekly ski trips.
Daily 9am-8.30pm. 149 Beitucheng Xilu, Haidian District. (8202 3765) KNS滑雪俱乐部，海淀区北土城西路149号

Lisheng Sports Store A mall whose four floors are filled with odd-shaped balls, large shoe sizes and esoteric athletic gadgets. True, more than half of the floor space is dedicated to run-of-the-mill athletic wear and trainers, but these include sizes unavailable elsewhere (up to USA 16/EU 49). Lisheng also stocks items like ice skates, inflatable boats, starter pistols and prescription swimming goggles.
Sun-Thur 9am-9pm, Fri-Sat 9am-10pm. 201 Wangfujing Dajie, Dongcheng District. (6525 2746) 利生体育用品商厦，东城区王府井大街201号

Nike Store They've got a wide variety of expensive athletic shoes (RMB 800) – up to men's size 45, women's size 40 – as well as sportswear, and a small selection of gear. What were you expecting, pet food?
1) Daily 9.30am-9pm. Guiyou Store, Chaoyang District. (6562 9312); 2) Daily 8am-10pm. B2/F, Zhongguancun Carrefour, Haidian District. 耐克专卖店，1) 朝阳区贵友商场，2) 海淀区中关村家乐福地下2层

Nirvana Yoga Center Carries a full range of mats (RMB 260), bags, clothes and blocks.
Daily 9am-9.30pm. 2A, Unit 5, Shijicheng, Yuanda Lu (100m south of the Golden Resources Mall), Haidian District. (5198 0591) 青鸟瑜伽，海淀区远大路世纪城5单元2A（世纪金源购物中心南100米）

Red Rain Dance Supplies Located near the Beijing Dance Academy, this place satisfies all your needs for gym shoes, dance skirts (including tutus!), gym pants and tops, alluring leg warmers and more. Another hint of Red Rain's target market is baggy pants made of air tight cloth, which can purportedly help the wearer lose weight. Online catalogue available.
Daily 9am-8pm. 29 Zhongguancun Nandajie, Haidian District. (6842 1815) www.redrain.com.cn 红雨舞蹈用品，海淀区中关村南大街29号

Sanfo This chain has a great selection of international brand shoes, ropes, harnesses and other climbing accessories, as well as a load of camping gear for rental or purchase. Want to try the gear before you buy it? The Madian store has a climbing wall. Great places to meet outdoor enthusiasts and seek advice. Sanfo also organizes weekend and week-long hiking, camping and horseback riding trips (with rock-bottom prices). Info about upcoming trips is available on their website (Chinese only).
1) Daily 10am-8pm. 1/F, Jinzhiqiao Dasha (northwest of China World), Jianguomenwai Dajie, Chaoyang District. (6507 9298); 2) Daily 10am-9pm. Bldg 5, 4 Madian Nancun, Beisanhuan Zhonglu, Chaoyang District. (6201 5550/5559 ext 11) www.sanfo.com 三夫户外，1）朝阳区建国门外大街金之桥大厦1层，2）朝阳区北三环中路马甸南村4号楼5号

INSIDER'S GUIDE TO BEIJING

These shoes were made for walking ... and running too!

Sky Outdoors A great selection of high quality name brand camping and outdoor gear.
Daily 10am-9pm. 1/F, Lotus Supermarket, Wudaokou, Haidian District. (8252 7523) www.skyoutdoors.com.cn 长天户外，海淀区五道口易初莲花超市1层

Snow Favor Carries K2, Briko and Rossignol skis and snowboards – you'll pay RMB 5,000-10,000 for a snowboard, pair of boots and bindings. Enroll online to join their club and enjoy weekly ski trips.
Daily 9am-5pm. South Bldg 1, Dadushi Shangyejie, Ciqikou, Changping District. (6707 1085) www.snowfavor.com 雪上飞专卖店，昌平区磁器口大都市商业街1号楼南侧

Sports 100 Got game? This mega sports store sells athletic shoes, sports equipment, hiking gear and attitude from Nike, Adidas, Puma, Fila and Converse. The shop assistants know their sports and offer impartial advice. Good for teens rather than younger children.
Daily 9.30am-10pm. Oriental Kenzo (aka Ginza Mall), 48 Dongzhimenwai Dajie, Dongcheng District. (8447 7117) www.sports100.com 运动100，东城区东直门外大街48号东方银座内

Sports Street East of the Temple of Heaven, a whole series of sporting goods stores line the streets. Although part of the area was recently *chai*'ed, tons of shops still remain. These mom and pop operations stock a random assortment of sports equipment, gear, clothes, shoes and accessories for cheap. Bargaining is necessary, but no need to get too rough. Recommended stores are Fuxinquan Sports at 66 Xilu (6715 8508), Donggan Paodao at 80 Xilu (6712 3926) and #1 Sports Equipment Store at 1 Xilu (6718 3668).
Daily 9am-7pm. Tiyuguan Xilu, Chongwen District. 崇文区体育馆路

Sunwind Outdoor This camping store carries backpacks, rock- and ice-climbing equipment, tents and smaller supplies. Brands include Camper, Garmont (mostly boots), Sigg Bottles and North Face (the real stuff).
Daily 9.30am-9.30pm. 6A Xiangjun Beili, Dongsanhuan Beilu, Chaoyang District. (6585 8278) 桑温特户外，朝阳区东三环北路向军北里甲6号

Tiger Sports Market-quality sporting goods, mostly for kids, including American footballs, soccer balls, roller blades, baseball gloves. You can also buy bigger items here – a trampoline (RMB 500), a made-to-order soccer net and blow-up swimming pools in all sizes. They also string tennis racquets here for RMB 30 (strings not included).
Daily 10am-8pm. 504, Pinnacle Plaza (in the Tianzhu Real Estate Development Zone), Shunyi District. (6645 8463, 136 0101 9210) 飞虎体育，顺义区荣祥广场504号（天竺房地产开发区内）

Tigerway Golf & Fashion Store Chains A huge variety of golf equipment is on sale here, including brands like Honma, Titleist and Taylormade. The stores also have wide selections of cheaper equipment. Most importantly, they offer one- and two-year warranties on most products. Other locations.

PHOTO: SIMON LIM

Daily 10am-8pm. WB117, B1/F, China World Shopping Mall, 1 Jianguomenwai Dajie, Chaoyang District. (6505 5250) 虎路威高尔夫用品连锁专营店，朝阳区建国门外大街国贸商城地下1层WB117

Trek Bicycle This small shop packs in a surprising amount of cycling gear including Trek mountain and road bikes for adults and children, parts, bike racks, helmets and shoes (up to size 45) as well as massive chain locks. Repairs available.
Daily 9am-8pm. 805, Pinnacle Plaza (in the Tianzhu Real Estate Development Zone), Shunyi District. (8046 5538) 崔克自行车，顺义区荣祥广场805号

Yingxiong Here martial artists will find excellent – though pricey – swords, and a limited selection of other weapons, martial arts uniforms and great pads and bags.
Daily 8.30am-8pm. A2 Tiyuan Xilu, Haidian District. (6297 6380, 131 4699 5675) www.yxwushu.cn 中武英雄，海淀区体院西路甲2号

Yoga Yard Yoga Yard sells English yoga books, bags, blocks and sticky mats available in various colors.
Fri-Sun 9am-8pm, Mon-Thu 7am-9.15pm. 6/F, 17 Gongti Beilu (across from the north gate of Workers' Stadium), Chaoyang District. (6413 0774) www.yogayard.com 朝阳区工体北路17号6层（工人体育场北门对面）

Zhong Wu Martial artists will find a good selection of weapons and some clothes at this small store. Quality varies, but prices are quite reasonable. You can also order from their comprehensive catalog.
Daily 9.30am-5pm. 48, 2/F, Huamu Shopping Center, 55 Tiantan Lu (east of Tiantan Qianmen), Chongwen District. (6701 5880) www.zhongwu.net 北京中武体育用品，崇文区天坛路55号天隆昌工艺品花木批发市场2层48号

Tattoos
(See Health and Beauty, p494)

Tea
Jia Xiang Tea Shop Offers a large assortment of teas from Fujian and free delivery with every purchase.
Daily 9am-midnight. 44 Yandai Xiejie, Xicheng District. (6407 1946) 嘉香茶庄，西城区后海烟袋斜街44号

Tea Street Actually called "Iris Street" in Chinese, this thoroughfare contains eight wholesale tea markets and more than 600 teashops selling over 500 kinds of fresh tea. Average tea prices, which are around 30-50% cheaper than in other locales, hover around RMB 30 per *jin* (half kilo). Top teas, like Longjing from Hangzhou, cost RMB 200 per *jin*. Ceramic and cloisonné teapot-and-cup sets average RMB 60.
Daily, with most shops open 8.30am-6pm. Maliandao Chayecheng, Xuanwu District. 宣武区马连道茶叶城

Ten Fu's Tea This is the largest branch of the Taiwanese chain (other stores are in Oriental Plaza, Dazhalan and Liulichang).
Daily 9am-11pm. Danyao Dasha, Dongcheng District. (6524 0958) 天福茗茶，东城区王府井大街丹耀大厦

Tibetan Trends
Ga Rong Mi Jing Doesn't stock as much gaudy Indian/Tibetan hippie gear as its Yandai Xiejie neighbors. Their little evil-repelling Tibetan paper-hanging lamp (asking price RMB 18) is sure to dress up any empty corner.
Mon 12.30pm-midnight, Tue-Sun 10.30 am-midnight. 12 Yandai Xiejie, Xicheng District. (6402 8988) 嘎绒密境，西城区烟袋斜街12号

Tibet Shop Owned by Tibetan artist You Tao, the shop features reproductions of antique Tibetan carpets ranging in price from RMB 700-1,500. Other items include wooden Buddhist wall hangings, paper lamps printed with Tibetan script (RMB 20), flags printed with scriptures, and Thangka paintings with images of Sakyamuni allegedly dating to the Ming Dynasty and valued at RMB 8,000 or up.
Daily 11am-9pm. 2, Unit 1, South Bldg 37 (on the road behind Yashow Market near Xindong Lu), North Sanlitun, Chaoyang District. (6417 5963) 爱尔屋，朝阳区北三里屯南37楼1单元2号（雅秀服装市场后边）

Torana Gallery (For description and address see listing on p374).

Tobacco Products
Acanta Cigar Shop Fine selection of cigars, pipes, and smoking paraphernalia.
Daily 10am-10pm. 1) 1/F, Shangri-La Hotel, 29 Zizhuyuan Lu, Haidian District. (6841 2211 ext 2885); 2) 1/F, Kempinski Hotel, 50 Liangmaqiao Lu, Chaoyang District. (6465 3388 ext 5735) 爱康娜雪茄店，1）海淀区紫竹院路29号香格里拉酒店1层；2）朝阳区亮马桥路50号凯宾斯基酒店1层

Brother Pipe Stocks rolling tobacco sold by the gram as well as many pipes.
Daily 9.30am-midnight. 52 Yandai Xiejie, Xicheng District. (6402 3396) 兄弟烟斗，烟袋斜街52号

La Casa Del Habano Habano serves as both a retailer of fine Cuban cigars and cigar lounge. An onsite humidor stores a range of fine stogies, including classic Cohibas (RMB 180-278 each) and Fonsecas (RMB 63 each). Also sells stylish humidors, jet flame lighters, cigar cutters, ceramic ashtrays and leather cigar cases.
Daily 10.30am-10pm. 163, 1/F, St. Regis Hotel, 21 Jianguomenwai Dajie, Chaoyang District. (8532 1288) 哈瓦那雪茄店，朝阳区建国门外大街21号国际俱乐部饭店F1163号

Leon's Pipes Store A large selection of different brand pipes like Dunhill and Savinelli, with prices ranging from RMB 200 to 3,000. Also sells cut tobacco and lighters. Pipe-fixing service available (RMB 200 per pipe).
Daily 11am-9pm. A36 Xingfucun Zhonglu, Chaoyang District. (6417 0102) 伍佰烟斗俱乐部，朝阳区幸福村中路甲36号

Pipe's Cafe Come to smoke: 60 blends of pipe tobacco and 20 cigar brands are for sale. Fire up in one of the free house pipes – the more hygienically conscious can buy their own on the spot.
Daily 6pm-2am. South gate of Workers' Stadium, Chaoyang District. (6593 7756) 啤酒屋，朝阳区工体南门（富国海底世界东100米）

Behind Enemy Lines
Up close and personal with Yashow's jazziest jeans seller
by Catherine Lee

Our interactions with the people we buy from are often limited to adversarial mutterings of numbers and a few choice phrases: "How much?" "Too expensive!" But what's it like on the other side of that negotiation? To truly master the art of shopping, we need to go beyond bargain-speak and learn the ways of the seller.

So I set out to probe the dark secrets of Beijing thing-sellers. But from the Tibetan seller to the *xiaomaibu* dude, most people I met were none too keen to answer questions. Fortunately, my quest was not completely fruitless, thanks to the wonderful, the amazing … jeans lady!

Within the first minute of my conversation with Zhang Zhuan, we had bypassed friendship for sisterhood. This new little sister didn't hesitate to share her true feelings on everything from Yashow bosses to karaoke, all with a sweet smile spread across her cherub face.

How scary can you get with sellers this sweet?

Most Yashow sellers are around Zhang Zhuan's age (18) and hail from Zhejiang or Anhui province. As we bonded over our small town upbringings, I almost forgot why I was there. Luckily, the conversation naturally turned to selling. "I don't really like my job," Zhang Zhuan stated simply. Casting a withering look at an angry man yelling in a stall nearby, she leaned in conspiratorially: "Sometimes I see people coming in to our store who look very scary, and then I run to the other side of the stall and pretend to be looking through the jeans so my co-worker has to help them." I felt a pang of pity as I glanced at Zhang Zhuan's tiny, gloomy-looking co-worker a few feet away.

So what constitutes "scary"? Could one intimidate the seller into giving the buyer a better price? She explained that Europeans tended to be harder bargainers than Americans who were "friendlier but less intelligent." But ultimately, who wins – the mean or the nice? "I don't want to give a good price to the mean person. But sometimes they scare me a little so they get a good price," admitted Zhang Zhuan. So is the only way to avoid getting ripped off to buy a Halloween mask and practice roaring at the mirror? No, "You can get the same price without yelling." There is always the post-purchase worry that you could have gotten an even lower price, but according to Zhang Zhuan, "If they're too difficult, sometimes it isn't worth it, and we just tell them to go. I have to make a profit, I can't sell it for too low."

So there is a limit to how low you can go. But what kind of pitfalls should buyers look out for? Would Zhang Zhuan care to share a few selling strategies? "Don't tell, but we always say they look so good and tell them their butt looks so nice in the jeans. People like to hear nice things." As memories of many a seller's compliments washed over me, I could feel my ego deflate like a balloon. "So even when it isn't true, you still say these things? How do you think I look in my jeans?" I sputtered. "You are so beautiful, of course you'd look good in anything!" came the reply. "But *meimei*, now I know you are lying," I sighed, trying to believe. "We are friends now, I can't lie to you," finished Zhang Zhuan with an innocent smile.

The truth hurts, my friend. So take the lies; your butt *does* look nice in those jeans. How much for another pair, Zhang Zhuan?

PHOTO: SIMON LIM

413
SHOPPING

Health & Beauty
美容塑身

Golf
高尔夫

Custom Tailoring
量身定制

Chic and Elegance... All In Style
精致优雅 生活品味

THE KERRY MALL
嘉里商场

1 Guanghua Road Chaoyang District Beijing 100020
北京市朝阳区光华路一号 ☎ (86 10) 8529 8533 www.beijingkerrycentre.com

SPORTS & FITNESS

What will *your* child discover?

International School of Beijing is a world leader in education, but we go beyond the classroom. We offer your children countless ways to develop their talents and strengths in the Arts, Sports, and Community Projects. Our world-class faculty and state-of-the-art campus provide unmatched advantages for your children.

Explore the spectrum of opportunities at ISB

北京顺义国际学校
INTERNATIONAL SCHOOL OF BEIJING

中国北京顺义安华街10号 邮编: 101318
No. 10, An Hua Street, Shunyi District, Beijing 101318, P.R.China
Telephone: 86 10 8149 2345
Facsimile: 86 10 8046 2003
www.isb.bj.edu.cn

Olympian Appetites
Our thirst for sport in the capital
by Oliver Robinson

At first glance, Beijing doesn't appear to be a city conducive to sporting activities – the grey housing complexes, clogged roads, bitter winters and suffocating summers do little to tempt the sportingly inclined outside. Of course, there's the "small matter" of the Olympics coming to Beijing in 2008, but it takes more than hype to make people love to exercise and be fit.

The reality is that Beijing has always been a city on the move. Millions of commuters cycle to work everyday, while parks blossom with elderly folk engaging in early-morning exercise – tai chi, wu shu, ballroom dancing and, erm, walking backwards and clapping their hands. Though Beijing's cramped urban anatomy allows little room for expansive athletic fields, the national sporting pastime of badminton can be played just about anywhere – a car park, a shop front, the middle of the street – and most neighborhoods find a way to furnish a few ping pong tables to keep the paddle-handed happy.

Then, of course, there's the requisite Beijing exercise regime. Anyone who has lived in the city's oldest tower blocks may have experienced that Cinderella moment – the elevators lock up at midnight, forcing residents to blast their quads up the stairs. Meanwhile, those of us brave enough to take on the subway during rush hour are in for an unparalleled anaerobic workout: scrumming on and off the train against thousands of sharp-elbowed commuters.

Beijing spawns a brave breed of urban athlete

For those looking for more structured forms of exercise, Beijing contains a rich variety of athletic ecosystems. Options range from global standards (namely basketball and football, which both boast extensive leagues, to niche sports like rugby, Gaelic football and ultimate frisbee.

Those not taken by the team thing can enjoy a plop in the pool or pumping up with one of the relatively cheap gym memberships available around town, as well as abundant martial arts and dance courses. Yoga and Pilates are also increasingly popular options for those seeking recess from Beijing's grimy grind. Many find the breathing and meditative techniques of yoga to be perfect ways of dealing with some unfortunate dividends of Beijing life, such as stress and air pollution.

Of course, plenty of Beijing's sporting organizations take a more literal escapist approach. The Hash House Harriers run (and drink) around scenic areas well outside the Fifth Ring Road, while the Mountain Bikers of Beijing (MOB) take on tough terrain around Beijing, as well as the grasslands of Inner Mongolia.

Indoor or outdoor, ego-repping alone or whooping it up with a team, Beijing's fitness options run the gamut of ways to turn on your adrenaline and keep your glutes cute. Hustling to prepare for the Olympics (see p440), our personally designed daily Olympiad maintains our strength and serenity.

Sports Directory

Aussie Rules Football
Beijing Football Club Learn how to get your hands on the "pill," take a "speccie" and boot a "sausage." Confused? Enlighten yourself by coming out to play Aussie rules football. Anyone is welcome, no fee necessary. Basic skills training followed by regular 9-a-side scratch matches for this fast, free-flowing, ultra-skillful game. Contact Tom Luckock (tom.luckock@nortonrose.com)
Training at the Beijing International School on Sat 4pm. Boxing training (fitness) on Tue 8pm and Sat 9am at the Evolution Gym, opposite Jianwai Soho.

Badminton
Note: Many universities allow badminton enthusiasts to reserve courts by the hour.

Beijing International Badminton Club This multinational expat group of more than 60 members welcomes any player with at least one year of experience. Contact John Ho (johnsk_ho@hotmail.com)
Every Wed 7-10pm and Sun 10am-noon. Si'de Gongyuan Badminton Center near Lido (across the street from the Rosedale Hotel). 北京国际羽球俱乐部

Shichahai Sports School Jet Li learned his nasty kung fu styles at this high-class, centrally located athletics school. Their badminton courts run RMB 30-60/hr, depending on the surface and time of day. Unlike most badminton facilities around town, the sports school is open until midnight – perfect for after supper 'cock thwacking.
57 Di'anmen Xidajie, Xicheng District. (6618 4748/3671) http://sch.bjedu.gov.cn 什刹海体育学校，西城区地安门大街57号

Baseball
Bad News Bears Baseball Club Bringing the real game to Beijing. Regular weekend meets against college and semi-pro teams. Must pay for own uniform and split field costs. Contact Eric (8557 4961, 139 1140 6745, baseballchina@yahoo.com).
Chaoyang Sports Center, 77 Yaojiayuan Lu, Chaoyang District. (8557 4961) 朝阳体育健身休闲公园，朝阳区姚家园路77号

Basketball
Beijing Overseas Students Basketball League Run by a BLCU PE teacher. Start your own team or walk on. Must split court fees. Contact Chris (137 0137 1063, rocarecl@yahoo.com).
Spring/fall weekend games mostly at BLCU; indoor winter games at Haidian Tiyuguan. 北京留学生篮球联盟

Dongdan PE Center You and the rest of the crew can rent indoor full courts for RMB 500/hr and half courts for RMB 300/hr. Outdoor court prices vary.
Daily 8am-10pm. 108 Chongwenmennei Nandajie, Dongcheng District. (6512 9255) 东单体育中心，东城区崇文门内大街108号

East Gate Plaza Fitness Center RMB 50 will get you an hour on a half court and one basketball (to be returned!). Book in advance.
Daily 7am-10pm. B1/F, Bldg A, 9 Dongzhong Jie, Dongcheng District. (6417 1188 ext 5070) 东环广场健身中心，东城区东中街9号A座地下1层

Biking
Cycle China This Beijing-based tour group organizes cycling tours, and hiking trips to the Great Wall. Bike hire available from RMB 60/day. You can also get helpful information about accommodations, sights, and tour-booking through their tourist information centre & Cycle China booking office.
Opposite the East Gate of Jingshan Park, Dongcheng District. (8402 4147, 139 1188 6524) www.cyclechina.com 东城区景山公园东门对面

Kingdom Bike Rental Provides a large selection of bikes, including mountain bikes and collapsible bikes. Bikes can be booked online and delivered to hotels or subway stations across the city.
B428 North Garden Office, Oriental Plaza, Wangfujing, Dongcheng District. (133 0100 0738, 6522 9478) www.bicyclekingdom.com 康多自行车租赁，东城区王府井东方广场北办公楼B428

Mountain Bikers of Beijing (The MOB) Every Saturday, the MOBsters organize challenging 60-120km mountain bike rides on paved, dirt and non-existent roads. Although sometimes they offer an easier "Mushie" route, it's not for lazy pedallers. Helmets are a must!
http://themob.404.com.au

Billiards and Pool
Note: Many bars such as Ball House, Bar Blu, Face Bar and Rickshaw have pool tables. See Bar & Club Directory on p296 for listings.

East Forever Billiard tables RMB 20/hr (members pay RMB 16/hr Mon-Thu).
Daily 24 hours. 2/F, Tower B, Zhongding Mansion (300m west of Jimen Qiao on the south side of the street), Haidian District. (6216 8000/9000) 东恒，海淀区中鼎大厦B座2层（蓟门桥南侧往西300米）

Xuanlong Pool Hall Snooker tables RMB 32/hr, billiards tables RMB 20/hr.
Daily 24 hours. 79B Hepingli Xijie, Dongcheng District. (8425 5566) 旋龙台球厅，东城区和平里西街乙79号

Boating, Sailing and Windsurfing
Beijing International Dragon Boat Team Hard-core paddlers and curious dabblers are welcome to join this multinational team in the ultimate team sport. The crew competes in races across China. Practices held from April to October on Houhai Lake.
bjdragonboatfans@yahoo.com 北京国际龙舟队

Beijing Fubang'emin Waterski Club From May to September, this club organizes waterskiing for RMB 1,800/hr at the Xiangtan Reservoir out in Changping District – a stone's throw from the Great Wall. Also offers flywheel and "banana boating."
Nankou Town, Changping District. (8019 1920, 130 1118 7913) 北京富邦敏滑水俱乐部，昌平区南口镇

DIY Club Organizes weekend trips to Miyun Reservoir at RMB 200/day for windsurfing enthusiasts.
(136 5120 8107, 133 1102 1256) www.snowboarding.com.cn 北京DIY俱乐部

Gold Sailing Rent sailboards (RMB 120/hr), kayaks (RMB 60-80/hr), a sculling shell or a dragon boat (RMB 50/hr/person). This spot also doubles as a bar that was remarkably cheap a few years ago and is now as pricey

From mountain biking to Yongjiu, and from Flying Pigeon to BMX, if you've got a wheel, you've got fun

as its neighbors – at least the view is still pretty. Members enjoy discounts.
Daily 10am-10pm. 81A Houhai Xiyan, Xicheng District. (6401 2664) 北京金帆运动俱乐部，西城区后海西沿甲81号

Ziran Dongli Wind/Kite Surfing School The closest professional seaside wind/kite surfing venue to Beijing, this school boasts an 800m long private beach in Nandaihe, where their members can go windsurfing, kite boarding, canoeing and sail boarding. Prices vary.
Bihai Lantian Country Resort, Nandaihe, Qinhuangdao, Hebei province. (Beijing office 8406 4481, 137 0133 8855; Nandaihe base 136 4336 9091/2) www.a2.com.cn 自然动力风帆学校，河北省秦皇岛市南戴河碧海蓝天度假村内

Getting there: Take Jingshen Expressway to the Beidaihe/Nandaihe Exit and follow the Nandaihe direction. At the BTV Training Center sign, turn right, past Daihe Bridge, and continue past Yanghe Bridge. The resort is 3km away, on the left side of the road.

Bowling

Gongti 100 When he's in town, Andy Lau apparently bowls at Gongti 100, which is named for the number of lanes. The complex also has a plethora of video games along with snooker and pool tables and KTV 100, whose wide selection of current hits makes it the place for younger warblers. Bowling costs RMB 30/game/person, plus RMB 5 for shoe rental.
Daily 8am-2am. 6 Gongti Xilu, Chaoyang District. (6552 2688) 工体100，朝阳区工体西路6号

Jade Palace Hotel Bowling Center Expect higher standards here than at your regular ten-pin dive, with eight immaculately maintained lanes and an army of helpful and friendly staff. RMB 30/game.
Daily 10am-11pm. B1/F, Jade Palace Hotel, 76 Zhichun Lu, Haidian District. (6262 8888 ext 55080) 翠宫宾馆保龄球中心，海淀区知春路76号

Jing'an Entertainment Center Bowling RMB 5-15/game depending on the time of day. Cold outside? Make a day of it by shooting snooker or pumping up your bowling muscles in the adjacent weight room, going for a dip in the pool or sweating your worries away in the sauna (RMB 35/activity, RMB 65 for swim/pump/sweat).
Daily 7am-1am. 8 Beisanhuan Donglu, Chaoyang District. (8455 2288 ext 8032) 静安娱乐中心，朝阳区北三环东路8号

Jinlandao Bowling Club Mid-quality balls and scoring equipment. Games cost RMB 6-15, depending on time of day. Bonus: They don't mind if you bring your own drinks.
Daily 6am-midnight. 10 Tuanjiehu Dongli (south of 20ft bowling pin southeast of the Tuanjiehu Tianyu Market), Chaoyang District. (8596 5149) 金兰道保龄球馆，朝阳区团结湖东里10号（团结湖天宇市场东南侧，大保龄球雕塑南侧）

Bungee Jumping

Longqing Gorge Bungee Along with hiking, horseback riding and boating, this scenic area boasts a 50-odd-meter bungee jump for RMB 150. There is a weight limit – call ahead to ask if you exceed it. Closed in winter. Tourist bus 8 departs from the Qianmen and Andingmen subway stations on weekends at 8am, and returns between 4-5pm. For a non air-conditioned option, take Bus 919慢 (be careful ther are several 919s!) from Deshengmen, which depart regularly between 6am-6pm.
(6919 1020) 龙庆峡蹦极，延庆县龙庆峡

Shidu Ju Ma Fun Park This organization offers a decent 55m tandem or solo plunge (RMB 175) above the Ju Ma

Ritan Park's climbing wall

River in the touristy but pleasant Shidu Reserve, about 90km southwest of Beijing.
Daily 8am-6pm. Shidu, Fangshan District. (6134 0841) Bus 917 leaves Tianqiao for Shidu hourly from 6am; last bus from Shidu returns at 5pm. Trains connect Beijing South Railway station with Shidu. 十渡拒马游乐园，房山区十渡

Wangfujing Slingshot Propel yourself and two friends above the masses in Wangfujing on this reverse-bungee contraption. If you survive, watch yourself screaming on video afterwards. RMB 120 (one person), RMB 300 (three people).
Daily noon-10pm. Wangfujing Dajie (in front of the Li Sheng sports store), Dongcheng District. (6559 5259) 王府井空中弹射，东城区王府井大街利生体育商店门口

Climbing

Longtanhu Climbing Center Beijing's largest outdoor climbing wall, Longtanhu has hairy overhangs and massive routes. RMB 20/climb.
Daily 9am-5pm. Dongerhuan Nanlu (inside Longtanhu Park), Chongwen District. (6718 6358 ext 9031) 龙潭湖攀岩中心，崇文区东二环南路（龙潭湖公园内）

Extreme Experience Though not as spectacular and massive as their old location, which used to be just 100m up the road, it's still the home for indoor bouldering in Beijing, especially in the winter months. A challenging wall that doesn't leave much room for beginners. RMB 20-30/person; shoe rental available.
Daily 10.30am-10pm. B1-12 Pingod Community, 32 Baiziwan Lu, Chaoyang District. (5876 0008 ext 516) www.exbear.com 极度体验，朝阳区百子湾路32号苹果社区12号楼地下1层

Fengyuxue Ritan Park Climbing Wall The home of Beijing's climber community. Ritan Park's convenient location and late hours make this outdoor wall a popular destination for experienced alpinists. RMB 10/climb, RMB 30/day.
Daily 10am-10pm. 6 Ritan Beilu (inside Ritan Park), Chaoyang District. (8563 5038) 风雨雪日坛公园攀岩墙，朝阳区日坛北路6号（日坛公园内）

University Rock Climbing Hall Outdoor man-made rock. Open every Sunday from the end of March to the middle of November. Make sure you reserve a spot in advance. RMB 15 or RMB 35 with equipment rental.
29 Xueyuan Lu (inside Uni. of Geoscience), Haidian District. (8231 8655) 大学抱石馆，海淀区学院路29号

Cricket

Beijing Cricket This active team competes in Shanghai and Hong Kong and plays matches each Sunday at Dulwich College in Shunyi District on the only grass cricket pitch in northern China.
Contact Ian (135 5274 7032, belgianking@gmail.com), http://sports.groups.yahoo.com/group/beijing-cricket-club

Dancing

Beijing Ballroom Friendly teacher Ken Wiland offers group and private lessons and will show you some new moves at the casual, free ballroom dance party each Saturday. No partner necessary.
Sat 8pm. Sino-Chu Wine Bar. 18 Liangmahe Nanlu (behind the Australian embassy), Dongcheng District. (131 2102 5208) www.beijingballroom.com

Beijing Swing Monday night classes at CD Jazz. Classes are RMB 200 for four hours, students RMB 120. Intermediate class runs 7-8pm, beginner class 8-9pm, free dance from 9pm-onwards. No partner required.

Contact Adam Lee (136 7105 1491) www.chinaswing.com
See p343 for CD Jazz Club

Casa De David Designated by the Cuban embassy has the official site for Latin dance instruction. Founder and coach David Huo teaches merengue, conga, samba, rumba, cha-cha and, of course, salsa. No partner or previous experience required. Free trial class 8.30pm daily. RMB 150 per session, RMB 500 per four sessions.
5/F, Yaxing Dasha, 46A Liangmaqiao Lu, Chaoyang District. (6466 1606) www.salsafly.com 飞舞拉丁俱乐部，朝阳区亮马桥路甲46号亚星大厦5层

DanZ Centre Offers kids and adults a range of classes including ballet, jazz, tap, hip-hop, Latin styles, ballroom and flamenco. Also has yoga to keep you limber. The 15-week Latin American course costs RMB 80 per class.
1) C/F, Bldg 46, Oriental Kenzo, Dongzhimenwai Dajie, Dongcheng District. (8041 7745/6); 2) 2/F, Yosemite Children's Clubhouse, 4 Yuyang Lu, Shunyi District. (8046 2287) www.danzcentre.com 黛安斯舞蹈培训中心，1）东城区东方银座48号楼C层；2）顺义区优山美地别墅儿童会所2层

Golden Dancing Academy Founded by American-trained teachers, the academy teaches ballroom, swing, Latin, ballet, jazz, hip-hop and their special "Golden Dance." Classes are taught in both Chinese and English to encourage participants to practice their language skills while they're cutting a rug. Over 100 dance classes each week starting at RMB 60 per class (RMB 40 for students). Group oral Chinese lessons start at RMB 100 per class. Other discounts available.
Mon-Fri 11am-9pm, Sat-Sun 11am-7pm. 10/F, Chongwen Culture Center, 7 Chongwenmenwai Dajie, Chongwen District. Contact Mary (6708 0167/9567/3267) www.goldendancing.com 金池舞蹈学院，崇文区崇文门外大街7号崇文文化馆10层

Ignition Dance and Art Center Seeking to light up your life, Ignition offers a wide variety of dance and art lessons. All adult dance classes last 90 minutes and cost RMB 50. Student and long-term discounts available.
53 Maizidian Zhongjie (behind Beijing World Youth Academy, near Chaoyang Park Northwest Gate), Chaoyang District. (6508 3314/4774) 点燃舞蹈文化艺术中心，朝阳区麦子店中街53号（世青学校后面，朝阳公园西北门附近）

J-Ballet School English and Chinese instruction (RMB 1,100/3 months) is available for children aged 4-14 years. Different levels/ages of instruction on different days.
1) 1/F, Bldg D, Jingxiu Yuan, Xingfucun Zhonglu, Chaoyang District; 2) Pulse Health Club, Kempinski Hotel, 50 Liangmaqiao Lu, Chaoyang District. (138 0103 6364) www.j-ballet.com 1）朝阳区幸福村中路景绣园D座一层西侧；2）朝阳区亮马桥路50号凯宾斯基饭店

Sunny Ray Dance Company Specializes in salsa, but also teaches cha-cha and bachata. Classes are held on weekday evenings and weekend afternoons. Beginner classes start at RMB 300 for 12 sessions. Membership cards provide discounts.
Rm 601-2, Bldg 1, Wanda Plaza, 93 Jianguo Lu, Chaoyang District. (5820 3177/6) www.china-salsa.cn, www.sunnyray.cn 朝阳区建国路93号万达广场1号楼601-2室

TangoRen Meets every Thursday and Sunday at the Sino-Chu Wine Bar for a free milonga (9pm-1am). Thursday 8-9pm Practica is RMB 30 (RMB 10 for members).
*Sino-Chu Wine Bar. 18 Liangmahe Nanlu (behind the Australian embassy), Dongcheng District.
http://groups.yahoo.com/group/TangoRen*

YSO Dance Studio Offering private lessons and over 30 dance classes every week ranging from jazz to ballet and even belly dancing. Taught by professional teachers, the small classes (maximum 6 students) are run on a casual basis. No enrollment is necessary and you can join a class at anytime. A single 90min class costs RMB 100 and a 1hr private lesson costs RMB 250, payable in cash only.
Suite 15B1, Champs Hotel Apartment, 6 Nanxinyuan Xilu, Chaoyang District. Contact Polly (8732 5133, 130 5130 7528) www.ysodance.com YSO舞蹈工作室，朝阳区南新园西路6号香榭舍公寓15B1室

Driving & Motor Sports

Beijing CJ750 Sidecar Club Ride out with a group of CJ750 riders for a weekend escape: overnight camping, wild Great Wall visits, BBQ, horse riding, etc. All levels of riders welcome, no bike left stranded. Affiliated with the largest sidecar dealer in Beijing.
37 Xiaoyun Lu (about 100m west of the Fourth Ring Road), Chaoyang District. (130 3119 5542) www.cj750.org 朝阳区霄云路37号（四环路西约100米）

Beijing Motorsports Your source for everything fuel-injected. Run by a Trans-Am-driving car fanatic, this website has all the info for local racing fans.
www.beijingmotorsports.com

Goldenport Motor Park Heaven for car-owning motorheads. Located a few miles from Beijing Capital Airport, Goldenport Race Track hosts a variety of car and motorcycle club races. Bring your own car and race for RMB 200/hr or join others in watching the fast-paced competition. Smaller dirt track available for kids and smaller motorcycles (RMB 130/hr with RMB 200 annual membership fee). Their new track can take Champ Car series and A1 Grand Prix races. Goldenport also has a bar, cafe, auto-mall and hotel for post-race celebrations. Call in advance to make sure the track is available.
Daily 9am-5pm. 1 Jingang Dajie, Jinzhan Xiang (follow signs off the Airport Expressway), Chaoyang District. (8433 3497) www.goldenport.com.cn 金港汽车公园，朝阳区金盏乡金港大街1号

Offroader 4x4 Club Those with a 4x4 can join these cowboys for twice-monthly one- or two-day weekend adventures around Beijing. Rallies are likewise organized in more far-flung places like Xinjiang, Tibet and Yunnan. Membership is free, with members responsible for their own excursion expenses.
1 Siyuanqiao, Jingshun Lu, Chaoyang District. (6474 5595/7877) www.offroader.com.cn 越野者俱乐部，朝阳区京顺路四元桥1号

Sunniwell City Karting Club Sunniwell has little cars for those with none of their own. Enjoy 5 minutes of thrills on the 800m track in a standard kart or the high-performance model for a slightly higher fee. RMB 48 (RMB 35 for students) each time, or RMB 900 for 30 times. Insurance recommended.
Mon-Fri 10am-9pm, Sat-Sun 9am-10pm. Inside Xinglong Park, Gaobeidian, Chaoyang District. (8575 1433) 北京四惠卡丁车俱乐部，朝阳区高碑店兴隆公园内

SPORTS & FITNESS

Fencing

Beijing Sport University If you are just beginning to learn the art of the sword, Sports University is the best place to pick up your first weapon. Fencing is taught to students and community members as young as 12 years old. Classes are taught in Chinese and are RMB 50 per hour for any weapon. Contact Mr. Tao Jinhan (6298 9028).
Zhongguancun Beidajie, Haidian District. 北京体育大学，海淀区中关村北大街

Fenxing Fencing Club Regular club meetings at the Olympic Stadium inside the Asian Games Complex. Mon-Fri 10am-last class, Sat-Sun 10am-11pm. East gate of the Olympic Sports Centre, Yayuncun, Chaoyang District. (6492 9041) www.fenxing.com 奋兴击剑俱乐部，朝阳区亚运村奥体东门

Fishing

The rule banning fishing in most park lakes is not enforced with much vigor, and it is not uncommon to see wizened anglers pass pleasurable hours fishing there anyway. The real mystery, though, is what they do with their catch afterwards.

Bibo A fishing equipment store that organizes fishing events and competitions, including deep-sea fishing in the summer.
For listing see Shopping p410.

Flying

Beijing Flying-man Club
Flying-man specializes in various airborne activities, including paragliding, paramotor and microlighting. The only flying club that owns a field and has champion instructors from China and abroad. The paragliding course costs RMB 2,600. Pray for wind.
8A Huizhongan, Taiyanggong Lu, Chaoyang District. (135 2023 0772 for English) www.flying-man.com 北京飞人俱乐部，朝阳区太阳宫路惠忠庵甲8号

Rainbow RC Hobby Club Specializes in any kind of radio control modeling, especially planes, helicopters, jets, cars and boats. The only club coached by China F3A champions. Flies every weekend from its own small civil airport.
73 Xueyuan Nanlu, Haidian District. (6221 5655) www.hobbybj.com 飞彩虹遥控模型，海淀区学院南路73号

Superwing Paragliding Club Organizes seven-day paragliding courses for RMB 2,200 and tandem flights for RMB 300 in Changping District. Also arranges flying excursions to Inner Mongolia and Shanxi Province.
B2/F, Yingdong Swimming Hall North Gate, Olympic Sports Centre, Chaoyang District. (6491 2233 ext 201, 136 0124 1119) 超级翅膀滑翔伞运动俱乐部，朝阳区奥体中心英东游泳馆B02(北门)

Tianlang Hot Air Balloon Club Established in 2003, their airspace and training base is near Taoyukou Reservoir. The price for a basic training course (including license and at least 16 hours of flying) is RMB 18,000, and a made-in-China hot air balloon set costs RMB 65,000.
Near Taoyukou Reservoir, Xingshou Town, Changping District. (6170 0750, 138 0123 7203) www.reqiqiu.com 天狼热气球俱乐部，昌平区兴寿镇桃屿口水库岸

Football (Soccer)

ClubFootball Everything footy: They organize amateur men's and kids' leagues. Their men's five-a-side league has 32 teams and plays all year round. Their popular kids' courses are held in a number of international schools and led by FA-qualified coaches.
Unit 10A, Jingdu Hotel, 26 Jiuxianqiao Lu, Chaoyang District. (5130 6893/4/5/6) www.clubfootball.com. cn 万国群星足球俱乐部，朝阳区酒仙桥路26号京都饭店甲10

French L' Equipe Also known as "French Le," this multinational team was created in Beijing in 1994 and has played in the first division since 2000. They play five-a-side games on Thursdays starting at 8pm and 11-a-side games from noon-6pm on weekends. Both take place at Si'de Park, near the Lido, opposite the Rosedale Hotel. Contact coach Mickael Perpoil (135 0102 4447) or captain Thomas Marechal (139 1026 3962) www.frenchlequipe.com

International Friendship Football Club With over 800 members from 70 countries playing on 30 established men's and women's amateur adult and youth teams, the IFFC has been devoted to the "world game" in Beijing since 1994. It now consists of 30 amateur men's teams divided into three divisions of ten, as well as junior and women's teams, making it one of the largest weekly intercultural events in China. You can join an existing team or create your own. Matches are held on good fields in various locations. The match fees (RMB 100 for expats, RMB 50 for students) help pay for referees. RMB 300 (membership). RMB 1,000 (team fee), RMB 500 (student team fee).
Contact Robert (6234 7106) www.iffc1994.com 国际友谊足球俱乐部

Inter United Football Team Kick some balls with friendly locals and expats in five-a-side league games from spring to autumn. Pitch-hire fees are shared.
Contact Jimmy Zhang (135 0113 4827, 6737 9466, interunitedsc@hotmail.com) 国合足球队

Red Ball Football Club & Bar Half playground, half watering hole. At press time this bar/football club was in the process of relocation.
(137 0116 8132) www.redball.com.cn 热球俱乐部

Odds and Ends (7788) Women's Team The Odds and Ends (7788) is Beijing's only amateur team for adult women. Players of all skill levels are welcome, although some experience is preferable. They have two seasons each year (spring and fall) and play 10-13 games each season. You can join the team at any time. They play or practice each Saturday from 3-5pm at Beijing Geosciences University.
Contact Liao Liao (wf7788@yahoo.com), www.wf7788.blog.sohu.com 7788女足俱乐部

Gaelic Rules Football

Beijing Gaelic Football Club Gaelic football for men and women, catering to all skill levels. New players always welcome. For updates on training, competitions and social events email beijinggaa@yahoo.com or join their Facebook group.
www.beijinggaa.com 北京盖尔人运动家协会

Golf Courses

Beijing Country Golf Club After playing one of their three 7,000yd courses, which weave around a man-made lake and an orchard, how about a sauna in the

Learn to really stick it to people the way you always wanted to

clubhouse? RMB 568 on weekdays and RMB 888 on weekends. Membership is RMB 22,000/yr.
Daily sunrise-sunset. West bank of Chaobai River, Mapo Xiang, Shunyi District. (6940 1111) www.bccgolf.com 北京乡村高尔夫会、顺义区马坡乡潮白河西岸

Beijing Daxing Capital Golf Club This course snakes around a long goldfish-filled lake. Reservations required. RMB 800 on weekdays, RMB 1,100 on weekends, plus a caddie fee of RMB 150.
Daily 6.30am-7pm. West end of Xingzheng Jie, Huangcun Town, Daxing District. (6121 6000) www.bdcgolf.com 北京大兴京城高尔夫俱乐部，大兴区黄村镇兴政街最西头

Beijing Golf Club Opened in 1987, the Beijing Golf Club hosts the annual Helong Cup, China's premier amateur golf invitational tournament. Facilities include a driving range, 4-hole practice course, professional instructors, restaurant and Japanese-style bathhouse. Membership costs RMB 7,000/yr. Members pay RMB 350 on weekdays, RMB 600 on weekends; non-members RMB 800 on weekdays, RMB 1,200 on weekends.
Daily sunrise-sunset. East bank of Chaobai River (1km east of Beijing Country Golf Club), Shunyi District. (8947 0245/0005) 北京高尔夫俱乐部，顺义区潮白河东岸（北京乡村高尔夫俱乐部东1公里）

Beijing International Golf Club Beijing's first golf club has a highly rated Japanese-designed course offering great views of forested hills and the Ming Tombs river and reservoir. Membership is RMB 23,000/yr, with compulsory RMB 200/round caddy fees. Non-members: RMB 1,400 (Sat-Sun), RMB 480 (women, Mon-Fri), RMB 800 (men, Mon-Fri).
Daily 7am-7pm, last tee time 3pm. Northwest of Ming Tombs Reservoir, Changping District. (6076 2288) 北京国际高尔夫俱乐部，昌平区十三陵水库西北

Beijing Links Golf Club This 18-hole, 72-par, 7,040yd course has a 6,000 sqm clubhouse that includes VIP hotel rooms, pro shop, cafe, bar, indoor swimming pool, gym, billiard room, sauna and locker room. Non-members pay RMB 720/round. RMB 300/hr for instruction, RMB 20/club, RMB 200/set, discount cards available. Reservations required. Also has a 60-lane, 200yd driving range. Non-members pay RMB 30 for the entrance fee and RMB 1/ball. Membership cards cost RMB 398,000.
Daily 6am-9pm. 88 Jiangzhuanghu, Huixin Donglu, Beisihuan Lu, Chaoyang District. (8463 8888) 北京北辰高尔夫球会，朝阳区北四环惠新东路姜庄湖88号

Beijing Pine Valley International Golf Club One of Beijing's premier courses, Pine Valley's gorgeous 7,300yd course was designed by Jack Nicklaus. The club also has a driving range, swimming pool, tennis court, badminton court, sauna, business center, stables and villas. The golf course is only open to members, who pay a steep admission fee of USD 180,000 and annual dues of USD 1,500.
Daily 11am-4.30pm (winter), 7am-sunset (summer). Pine Valley Resort, Nankou Town, Changping District. (8528 8038) www.pinevalley.com.cn 北京华彬国际高尔夫俱乐部，昌平区南口镇华彬庄园

Beijing Yaoshang Golf Club Located in southwest Beijing, this club once hosted the Volvo Masters Amateur. Features an 18-hole, 72-par course. Also has 10 driving ranges where members pay RMB 15 for 50 balls. Non-members pay RMB 30 for 50 balls. Green fees cost RMB 550 on weekdays, RMB 800 on weekends. A membership card costs RMB 108,000, plus RMB 1,000 annual fee. Reservations required on weekends.
Daily 6.30am-6pm. Yaoshang Cun, Liulihe Zhen, Fangshan District (8032 1678) 北京窑上高尔夫球会，房山区琉璃河镇窑上村

SPORTS & FITNESS

Chaoyang Kosaido Golf Club While this club only has a short, nine-hole course (par 30, 300yd), its low greens fees and great location – about 500m east of the Zhaolong Hotel – make it the ideal place to sneak in a quick round during work hours. Driving range on site. RMB 230 on weekdays, RMB 290 on weekends. Three- and six-month discount packages available.
Daily 6.30am-9.30pm (closed in winter). 9A Nongzhan Nanlu, Chaoyang District. (6501 8584) 朝阳广济堂高尔夫俱乐部，朝阳区农展南路甲9号

Longxi Wenquan Golf Club Mon-Fri RMB 690/round; Sat-Sun RMB 1,100/round.
Daily 6am-11pm. Guaxiang Lu, Panggezhuang Town, Daxing District. (8928 2288) 龙熙温泉高尔夫俱乐部，大兴区庞各庄镇瓜乡路

Golf Driving Ranges

Beijing Legend Holiday Golf Club RMB 25/basket of balls or RMB 80/hr on weekdays; RMB 30/basket or 100/hr on weekends.
Daily 9am-9pm. 89 Jichang Lu, Chaoyang District. (6456 0111) 北京丽晶假日高尔夫俱乐部，朝阳区机场路89号

Beijing Meisong Golf Club One of the largest driving ranges in town, Meisong has 124 tees on two levels. Non-members pay RMB 30-75 for 50 balls (includes entrance fee). Club rental RMB 20-40. Offering unlimited use of balls, annual membership is RMB 8,000 – whilst RMB 1,600 will get you 4,000 balls.
Daily 7am-midnight. 10 Xinglong Xijie, Gaobeidian, Chaoyang District. (8575 3959) 北京美松高尔夫俱乐部，朝阳区高碑店兴隆西街10号

Moon River Country Club Golf Club Hum Henry Mancini's "Moon River" as you take advantage of this establishment's reasonable prices: RMB 1/ball, or RMB 2,980 for 10,000 balls.
Daily 7.30am-11pm. Moon River Country Club, Tongzhou District. (8952 3737 ext 6820) 月亮河乡村俱乐部高尔夫俱乐部，通州区月亮河乡村俱乐部

Yuanlin Golf Club RMB 50/hr, RMB 70/2hr.
Daily 6am-11pm. Nanhuqu, Huajiadi (Wangjing Qiao, Airport Expressway), Chaoyang District. (6479 1951) 园林高尔夫俱乐部，朝阳区花家地南湖渠（机场高速望京桥）

Golf Groups & Training Schools

Beijing Golfer's Club The group meets every Sunday for a 10am tee-off at various courses around Beijing. Membership is RMB 900, which includes annual fees, handicap cards, invitations to over 40 golf events a year and discounted greens fees. Games are RMB 900 for non-members and RMB 200-500 for members.
www.beijing-golfers-club.org 北京高尔夫爱好者俱乐部

Beijing Ladies Golf Club This group is comprised of women of various nationalities who share a love for golf. They organize events throughout the season such as games, luncheons, dinners, clinics and workshops. All lady golf enthusiasts are welcome to play every Thu. Membership dues for the BLG are RMB 300/year. Members enjoy discounted weekday greens' fees of RMB 260 at the BCC.
beijingladiesgolf@yahoo.com

Beijing Rivers and Resort Golf Training Academy This academy offers serious training to mid-level and advanced players by pro golfers, sports psychologists and American PGA-sanctioned coaches. A membership (RMB 108,000) allows unlimited visits, while RMB 20,000 will provide 240 hours of instruction and RMB 1,680 will get you 8 hours.
1A, west of Sunhe Beidian, Chaoyang District. (8046 5566, 135 2162 3597) 北京金色河畔高尔夫学校，朝阳区孙河北甸西甲1号

Beijing Yiquan Golf Club Located near the Summer Palace, the Yiquan Golf Club claims to be the largest, most prestigious golf-training center in northern China. Pay RMB 1,200-2,800 for 10 lessons, depending on the caliber of coach and class size. Not very suitable for non-Chinese speakers.
South of Yuquanshan Middle School, Haidian District. (6287 5990) 北京颐泉高尔夫俱乐部，海淀区玉泉山中学南边

Shenghua Universal Golf Advisors (SGA) SGA-China offers golf coaching for all levels and age groups by professional Australian PGA golf coaches (English and Chinese language classes available). Coaching plan is designed according to individual level and needs.
1) SGA – China Advisors Office. A-3105 Sunshine 100, 2 Guanghua Lu, Chaoyang District. (5100 0758/759);
2) SGA – China Coaching Center. Beijing Chaoyang Kosaido Golf Club, 9A Nongzhanguan Nanlu, Chaoyang District. (6507 7389) *www.SGA-China.com*
环宇升华高尔夫，1）朝阳区光华路2号阳光100公寓A座3105；2）朝阳区农展馆南路甲9号北京朝阳广济堂高尔夫俱乐部

TeeTime Golf Social golfing club that plays various courses around Beijing on Saturday mornings and some Friday afternoons. Membership fee RMB 100. Handicap system available after 5 games. Can help arrange transportation to courses.
Contact Chad (139 0113 6379) www.teetimechina.com

Gyms & Fitness Centers

Note: Gyms often offer promotional discounts on their listed membership prices.

Amrita Fitness Running machines, weights, fitness classes, traditional Chinese massage and one of Beijing's nicest indoor pools. RMB 1,000 (1 mo), RMB 2,400 (3 mo), RMB 4,200 (6 mo), RMB 7,200 (1 yr).
Daily 6am-10.30pm. Swissotel Beijing, 2 Chaoyangmen Beidajie, Dongcheng District. (6553 2288 ext 2305) 瑞士酒店健身中心，东城区朝阳门北大街2号港澳中心瑞士酒店

Beijing YMCA Fitness Center Indoor swimming pools with lap lanes and children's pools, a fully equipped fitness center and dance aerobics rooms. Fitness programs include contemporary Chinese and Latin dance, yoga, Pilates, karate, aerobics, graded swim and water aerobics.
Daily 10am-9pm. Bldg 13, Nolita Center, Guangqumennei Dajie, Chongwen District. (6719 5151) www.ymcabj.org 北京青年会健身中心，崇文区广渠门内大街Nolita那里13号楼

China World Fitness Centre Scores points for the most sumptuous changing rooms in Beijing. Besides that, it boasts a 20m pool, steam bath, jacuzzi, squash courts and a range of classes. RMB 200/visit, RMB 8,000/6 mo, or RMB 15,000/yr.
Daily 6am-11pm. 1 Jianguomenwai Dajie, Chaoyang District. (6505 2266 ext 33) 中国大饭店健身中心，朝阳区建国门外大街1号

The Peking Pentathlon

A modest proposal
by Gabriel Monroe

First introduced to the Olympic Games in 1912, Modern Pentathlon's moniker draws attention to itself on the 2008 event roster. In fact, upon reaching the realization that the five events are comprised of swimming, fencing, shooting, running and riding, it starts to sound much like a casting call for the Elite Guard of the Austro-Hungarian Empire.

If the event were to be revised after a century, these are some of the events that we hope might make it into the Beijing Modern. The five components are competed consecutively, similar to a triathlon, and the starting gun would be fired at Tiantan Park at 5.15pm on the first Friday afternoon of the Games:

1) Chain-smoking*
This would be the first event in order to add further difficulty to following events. Each athlete smokes one full pack of .8 Zhongnanhais as fast as they can, one at a time. The current world record for chain-smoking a regulation pack of cigarettes is believed to be 16:19.09.

2) Cycle through rush hour traffic
Each athlete is provided with a 1976 vintage steel frame 28-inch wheel Yongjiu one-speed. The finish line is just outside the Water Cube on North Fourth Ring Road. Distance 10.4km as the crow flies.

3) 800-meter ice swim
This event is decided in the specially designed Ice Cube patio area adjacent to the Water Cube. A 200m trench is cut through the cube on the afternoon of the competition.

4) Five-liter Yanjing beer swallow
The "yan" (燕) in Yanjing is an ancient name for the Beijing area, as well as the Chinese pictograph for the tiny, graceful swallow bird.

5) Distance spit
Unconfirmed accounts credit the local/world record distance of 32.76m to Madam Zhao Xiaomei, 81.

*Alternatively, for a sort of "shoot the moon" gold medal, an athlete may legally attempt to smoke one pack of Zhongnanhais during all four of the other events. This gold medal is awarded as that of a separate event (牛B四项, or "badass quadrathlon" in English).

Training for the "badass quadrathlon"

The Global Game
At home on the pitch
by Oliver Robinson

Make friends, and get to know yourself, booter

Football both exacerbates and transcends nationalism: We cheer parochially for the home side but share our passion for the beautiful game and its extraordinary players with the world. In Beijing, football definitely brings people together – whether it's an animated discussion with a cab driver about the form of Beike Hanmu [Beckham] and Luonaerdiniao [Ronaldinho], or game day at one of Beijing's amateur leagues, where week in and week out, hundreds of people from every corner of the globe play together. Indeed, joining a squad is a great way for newcomers to integrate themselves into Beijing life, and a hallowed ritual for many old hands.

The two best-established leagues are those run by the IFFC and ClubFootball, which draw players of all nationalities, ages and standards. ClubFootball runs a five-a-side league that has around 600 players and over 50 teams, while IFFC's 11-a-side divisions number around 800 members in 30 teams. As team names such as Eagles Korea FC, Russia United and Azzuri FC indicate, both leagues have country- or language-specific squads, which offer players the simple luxury of speaking in their native tongue for an evening. Other teams are gloriously, proudly multinational, like the Barbarians, the self-styled "United Nations of Football," or Afrika United FC, the IFFC's perennial powerhouse, which includes players from all corners of that continent and beyond (from Canada to Papua New Guinea).

Of course, these leagues are also deeply local. David Niven of Club Football estimates that the ratio of foreign to Chinese players in his leagues is 60:40, with the latter figure on the rise. The league's diversity presents good learning opportunities, argues Dong Yu, a former professional player with Beijing Guo'An who makes a living by renting out football pitches. "It's good for Chinese and foreign players to play together," says Dong, "because Chinese players need to learn the spirit of Western players and … Western players need to learn Chinese!"

Played on quality pitches and arbitrated by strict, sometimes whistle-happy, referees, the games are spirited and competitive. Industrial language, petty squabbles, occasional red cards and football that is sometimes painful, but occasionally glorious, to watch (by the obligatory friends, wives/girlfriends, stray pets, etc.) – the leagues have all the ingredients of classic amateur sports. And a lot more to boot. "Football unites a wealth of nationalities," notes British Embassy employee and Spitfire FC player Daniel Lotinga, "and affords participants the rare opportunity in China to understand and be understood while the language of free kicks and yellow cards prevails."

CSI – Bally Total Fitness Highly recommended for the sheer volume of gym equipment and group classes on offer at its Dongcheng location. The posh Jianwai Soho location includes a pool and a tennis court. Access to all ten locations around town: RMB 4,850/yr, RMB 6,499 (pool access). Jianwai Soho location: RMB 4,299/yr, RMB 5,188 (pool access). District-inclusive memberships available.
1) Daily 7am-10.30pm. B/F Bright China Chang'an Bldg, 7 Jianguomennei Dajie, Dongcheng District. (6518 1666); 2) Daily 6am-10pm. 1/F, Bldg 2, Jianwai Soho, 4 Jianguomenwai Dajie, Chaoyang District. (5869 0666) 中体倍力健身俱乐部，1) 东城区建国门内大街7号光华长安大厦内地下；2) 朝阳区建国门外大街4号建外Soho现代城2号楼1层

Evolution Fitness Center This smart outfit has two locations offering cardio, weights, 25m pools, group exercise classes (including yoga, Pilates, spinning) and juice bars. Dabeiyao Center location: RMB 100/visit, RMB 1,700/3mo, or RMB 4,000/yr. Blue Castle Center location: RMB 3,775/6mo, RMB 6,295/yr.
1) Mon-Fri 6.30am-10.30pm, Sat-Sun 8am-9pm. Dabeiyao Center, 2 Dongsanhuan Nanlu, Chaoyang District. (6567 0266); 2) Mon-Fri 6.30am-10.30pm, Sat-Sun 8am-10.30pm. Blue Castle Center, 3 Xidawang Lu (300m north of Soho New Town), Chaoyang District. (8599 7650) www.evolution-fitness.com 进步健身中心，1) 朝阳区东三环南路2号大北物业中心；2) 朝阳区西大望路3号

Fusion Fitness Center This small gym has weightlifting equipment along with lots of running, stepping and cycling machines. Not exactly state-of-the-art, but they do the trick. RMB 30/visit, RMB 298/mth, RMB 1,598/yr. 2/F, Sports Lab Fitness Bldg, 15 Xueyuan Lu (inside BLCU), Haidian District. (8237 2979) 凝酷健身中心，海淀区学院路15号北体逸夫体育馆2层

Haosha Fitness Center This clean gym has running machines, free weights, bench presses, an aerobics room, dance classes and more. Membership costs under RMB 400/mth, RMB 2,500/yr. Frequent specials and lots of locations around town.
Daily 9am-9.30pm. B1/F, Bldg B, East Gate Plaza, 9 Dongzhong Jie, Dongcheng District. (6418 1088) 浩沙健身中心，东城区东中街9号东环广场健身中心B座地下1层

HA-Sports Fitness Center HA attracts stressed-out office workers with its state-of-the-art fitness equipment and a 25m swimming pool. Also holds regular aerobics classes with well-qualified instructors.
Mon-Fri 8am-10pm, Sat-Sun 9am-9pm. B2/F, Bldg 7, Wanda Plaza, 93 Jianguo Lu, Chaoyang District. (5820 7788) HA Sports 健身俱乐部，朝阳区建国路93号万达广场7号楼地下2层

Hong Kong Boss Fitness Club This upscale fitness center is a great location for students in Haidian as it is right across from the Friendship Hotel on Zhongguancun. Although the service is sometimes lacking, the gym is perched on the top floor of a tall office building so you can gaze at the cityscape while you swim. RMB 100/visit, RMB 6,800/yr.
Daily 7am-10pm. 18/F, Cyber Tower, 2 Zhongguancun Nandajie, Haidian District. (5162 6060 ext 111) 香江堡狮健身会，中关村南大街2号数码大厦银座18层

IntelliFitness Worthy competition to Nirvana Fitness and Spa, IntelliFitness is one of Haidian's elite gyms.

A month of unlimited use runs RMB 600, but student discounts and long-term commitment lower prices significantly.
Mon-Fri 8am-10pm, Sat-Sun 10am-10pm. 3/F, Bldg B, Caizhi Bldg, 18 Zhongguancun Donglu, Haidian District. (8260 1166) 财智健身，海淀区中关村东路18号财智国际大厦B座3层

Kerry Sports This fitness mecca includes a celebrated 35m pool, tennis courts, basketball courts, snooker classes, excellent equipment and a price tag to match. RMB 10,500/6 mth or RMB 16,000/yr, off-peak discounts available.
Daily 6am-11pm. Kerry Centre Hotel, 1 Guanghua Lu, Chaoyang District. (6561 8833 ext 6465) 嘉里健身，朝阳区光华路1号嘉里中心酒店

Mani's Body Combing Not really a gym, but not easy to categorize. Offering "body combing," a new age melange of ballet, gymnastics, Chinese dance and even acupuncture, it promises to improve practitioners' health and wellbeing. Call to make a booking.
1) Daily 8.30am-8.30pm. 3/F, Yiduge Shopping Centre, 1A Xizhimen Beidajie, Haidian District. (5129 5066); 2) Mon-Fri 9am-8pm, Sat-Sun 10am-6pm. 3/F, Cultural Center, 111 Jiaodaokou Dajie, Dongcheng District. (6400 4986, 6402 5090) www.mani.com.cn 马妮形体梳理，1) 海淀区西直门北大街甲一号"依都阁"商业楼三层；2) 东城区交道口东大街111号东城区文化馆三层

Nirvana Fitness Center Classes galore and A-grade equipment bring the beautiful people to this fitness center. Annual membership ranges from RMB 4,500 to 10,000, with off-peak discounts available. Membership valid at any of the eight locations around town.
Daily 7am-11pm. Zhaolong Hotel West Suite, 2 Gongti Beilu, Chaoyang District. (6597 2008) www.nirvana.com.cn 青鸟健身中心，朝阳区工体北路2号兆龙饭店西翼

Pacific Century Club Pacific Century is one of the few places in Beijing that offers a comprehensive core-strengthening program with a full range of Pilates equipment. Three one-hour group classes offered per week (RMB 100 for non-members, free for members). One-hour private lessons: RMB 240/lesson, RMB 2,000/10 lessons.
Daily 6am-10pm. 2A Gongti Beilu, Chaoyang District. (6539 3434, pacificcenturyclub@gmail.com) 科会所，朝阳区工体北路2号

Powerhouse Gym Has every type of equipment you could want, with more than enough for everybody – even during busy hours. Personal trainers are happy to help. Classes include aerobics, Pilates, yoga and hot yoga, salsa, kickboxing, tae bo, belly dancing, and hip hop. RMB 680/mo, RMB 1,500/3mo, or RMB 4,900/yr.
Mon-Fri 7am-10pm, Sat-Sun 10am-10pm. 5/F, Shouchuang Dasha, 6 Chaoyangmen Beidajie, Chaoyang District. (8528 2008) www.powerhousegym.com.cn 宝力豪健身，朝阳区朝阳门北大街6号首创大厦5层

St. Regis Spa & Club An amazing pool, top-of-the-line machines, squash courts and bowling. RMB 500/visit, RMB 21,000/yr or RMB 33,000 for a 2-person family plus RMB 500/child.
Daily 6am-11pm. 1/F, St. Regis Hotel, 21 Jianguomenwai Dajie, Chaoyang District. (6460 6688 ext 2759) 北京国际俱乐部温泉健身中心，朝阳区建国门外大街21号国际俱乐部饭店1层

SPORTS & FITNESS

Verve Wellness Art Fitness and personal training studio specializes in weight loss, functional training, sport-specific conditioning and pre/post natal programs. The first class is free.
Mon-Fri 9am-10pm, Sat-Sun 10am-8pm. 6 Dongsihuan Beilu, Upper East Side, Chaoyang District. (5130 7001/7008) www.bjverve.com 非梵健康艺术工作室，朝阳区东四环北路6号阳光上东底商

World Health Store Located inside a gym, this foreign-owned and managed store offers a complete selection of Western-style health supplements, including organic foods, vitamins, minerals and herbs from around the world.
1/F, Bldg 8, Julong Huayuan, 68 Xinzhong Jie, Dongcheng District. (134 2613 1535) www.worldhealthstore.com.cn 东城区东四十条新中街68号聚龙花园8号楼1层

Hiking & Camping

Note: See also Excursions on p547 for groups that organize hikes around Beijing.

Beijing Amblers The hyperactive stepchild of the Chinese Culture Club. The Amblers head out almost every weekend, usually to locations with historical or cultural significance as well as natural beauty. Prices range from RMB 150 to 400 for day trips, more for overnight excursions. Online registration usually required. Contact Feng Cheng *(6432 9341) www.chinesecultureclub.org*

Beijing Hikers Hikes of varying difficulty in villages near Beijing. Open to everyone. Prices vary for overnight hikes; regular hikes are RMB 200/adult, RMB 150/child under 12, including round-trip transport, post-hike snacks and beverages, detailed map and professional guidance. Advance reservations necessary. Call for info on hikes and what to bring.
Contact Huijie *(139 1002 5516) www.beijinghikers.com*

Hockey

(For rinks, see Ice Skating below. For kids' hockey, see Sports Beijing p145)

Beijing Street Hockey Bring a pair of running shoes and an attitude.
Sat 3-5pm. Ta Yuan Diplomatic Compound (north of the Canadian Embassy), Xindong Lu, Chaoyang District. Contact Darren (139 1039 3077) 北京街道曲棍球队，朝阳区新东路塔园外交公寓(加拿大使馆北侧)

Beijing International Ice Hockey For fans of physical punishment, this well-organized outfit plays weekly and tours annually to other Chinese cities, Mongolia and Bangkok. A four-team league in Beijing plays on Sunday evenings at Century Star Arena (see Ice Skating, below), from September through April/May. Equipment is very limited in China – be sure to bring what you need. Full face-masks recommended. Season registration fee RMB 3,000.
(peking_puck@yahoo.com), www.beijinghockey.com

Horseback Riding

Beijing Green Equestrian Club RMB 380/hr, RMB 29,000 for yearly membership (incl. lessons).
Loutai Village, Tianzhu Town, Jichang Fulu, Chaoyang District. (6457 7166) 格林马会俱乐部，朝阳区机场辅路天竺镇楼台村

Equidorf Carries everything you need for horse and rider. They offer a nice selection of riding boots and breeches (including Pikeur breeches for RMB 1,980), horse blankets, saddles (and saddle bags for RMB 320), grooming supplies, imported nutritional supplements and more.
Daily 9am-6pm. 89 Beimafang Dongwei Lu, Chaoyang District. (8431 0600) www.saddlery.cc 艾奇达马术用品，朝阳区东苇路北马房89号

Equuleus International Riding Club Prices range from RMB 2,400 for 10 lessons over the course of 3 months to RMB 19,200 for 80 lessons over 15 months (with 30 free lessons).
Summer: Tue-Sun 7-11am, 3-7pm; other seasons: Tue-Sun 8am-noon, 2-6pm. 91 Shunbai Lu, Sunhe Town, Chaoyang District. (6438 4936) www.equriding.com 北京天星调良国际马术俱乐部，朝阳区孙河镇顺白路91号

Han Ci Horse Club Stable your horse here (RMB 1,500/mth) or use theirs: Mon-Fri RMB 120, Sat-Sun RMB 160. Classic and western lessons (RMB 30-80/45min) for all ages.
Daily 8am-7pm. Tianlongyuan Spa, Xiguan Roundabout, Changping District. (136 7139 7716, biansl@126.com) 汉慈马术俱乐部，昌平区西关环岛天龙源温泉

Sheerwood Beijing Equestrian Country Club This 33,350-acre club has a stable of 110 horses, two racetracks, one indoor and four outdoor equestrian arenas.
Summer: Tue-Sun 7am-6.30pm; winter: Tue-Sun 8am-5pm. Picun Village, Jinzhanxiang, Chaoyang District. (5188 4137) 西坞北京马术俱乐部，朝阳区金盏乡皮村

Ice Skating

Note: from late December until early February, many Beijingers gleefully skate outdoors on Peking University's Weiming Hu, Tsinghua University's Hetang Lake, Houhai Lake, Zizhuyuan Park and Lianhua Shan in Shunyi. Entrepreneurs set up shop on the shores and rent figure and speed skates as well as ice chairs, ice bikes and other speedy contraptions.

Century Star Skating Club Offers ice-skating lessons in a slightly smaller than regulation-size rink. Private lessons are priced at RMB 120-150/45min, and group lessons start at RMB 120-150/90min. Hours vary each day; call or check online for open times.
1) B/F, Capital Gymnasium, 54 Zhongguancun Nandajie, Haidian District. (6834 8684, 6786 7028); 2) 5 Tianhua Beijie, Yizhuang, Daxing District. (6786 7028, 6788 0194) www.centurystar.com.cn 世纪星滑冰俱乐部，1)海淀区中关村南大街54号首都体育馆 2）大兴区亦庄开发区天华北街5号

Champion Rink Due to its low patronage, it's a good option for skaters who wish to go fast or practice triple salchows. Offers basic private lessons for RMB 120 and up. Advanced classes RMB 60/90min. Entry-level group lessons are RMB 350 for five 90min classes, but group sizes vary.
Daily 10am-9.30pm. Golden Resources Mall, 1 Yuanda Lu, Haidian District. (8887 4899) 冠军溜冰场，海淀区远大路1号金源新燕莎内

Ditan Ice Arena Open year-round, this "rink" is more like an ice track, but is the only rink in Beijing where you can practice the fine sport of curling! Please note that this rink is kept at very low temperatures year

Glide
So nice on the ice
by Adam Pillsbury

A sliding star, that's who you are

In the dark depths of winter, when the Siberian winds blow, the urge to hibernate is hard to resist. But hunkering down with the remote and a cup of hot cocoa would be to miss out on some of the best experiences Beijing has to offer. Instead, learn from those who know a thing or two about winter – the Russians and Canucks. Don an *ushanka* or *touque* and go skating.

Indoors

Besides smooth ice and all-season skating (a tantalizing prospect on a hot summer's day), rinks like Le Cool and New World Champion have professional instructors, some of them English speakers, and monitors who discourage speedy skating – perfect conditions for novices and kids. Le Cool can even provide a private room and a Spider Man on skates for birthday parties. For all that, these rinks tend to be miniature, and can be jammed with ice princesses and coaches on weekends.

Experienced skaters will feel less constricted and enjoy a better workout at the Ditan Ice Arena, which is one of the most fantastical spots in the city. Located in a former bomb shelter at the end of a tunnel mysteriously lined with photos of tropical isles, and kept at an ambient temperature of about –20 degrees Celsius, it's not so much an ice rink as it is an oval speed-skating track – a long neon-lit green-and-gray concrete tunnel with the best ice in Beijing that draws only a handful of initiates.

Outdoors

Rink skating pales by almost any measure to lake skating, especially in Beijing. The short outdoor season lasts from about late December to early February. Ice conditions range from hard black to dangerously mushy, but the atmosphere is always friendly. Many lakes offer dramatic vistas, notably Yuyuantan, the pond south of the Workers' Stadium and Peking University's Weiming Hu.

Skating on Houhai under a rising moon within sight of the Bell and Drum towers is quintessential Beijing enchantment. It's worth paying RMB 10-15 to skate in the enclosed section near Lotus Lane since it's flooded every night to maintain a smooth ice surface (lake ice is often bumpy). This vast area allows plenty of room for skaters of all levels and persuasions, from gleeful youngsters to graceful seniors and from speed skaters in bodysuits to hockey players in NHL jerseys – the latter playing marathon matches of shinny.

Speaking of pick-up hockey, Beijing International Ice Hockey captain Ray Plummer recommends the section of the Forbidden City moat north of Zhongshan Park, which doesn't always freeze over. "In '98 we played a touring team from New Jersey [there] on Chinese New Year's Eve," he recalls. "The wall was lit up and fireworks were crackling around us as we played until 11pm! It was magical!"

For rink addresses and hours, see Ice Skating p428. Skate rentals are available at all of the spots listed above. Quality ranges from so-so to rancid and larger sizes are hard to find. Skates, Russian-brands mainly, are sold at the Alien Street Market, Lisheng Sports Store and at some rinks.

round, so bring a sweater, hat and gloves. Skating with rental costs RMB 26/hr (RMB 16/hr for students); curling costs RMB 400/hr (call ahead to reserve the "sheet").
Tue-Fri 1.30-9pm, Sat-Sun 9am-9pm. 14A Hepingli Zhongjie (east of Ditan Park north gate), Dongcheng District. (6429 1619) 地坛滑冰场，东城区和平里中街甲14号

Hosa Skating Center RMB 30/90 mins, plus RMB 10 for skate rental.
Daily noon-8pm. Gaojing, Chaoyang Lu (east of Civil Aviation Hospital), Chaoyang District. (8576 8918) 浩沙冰上运动中心，朝阳区朝阳路高井（民航医院往东）

Le Cool If you want to squeeze in a skating lesson between shopping jags, head to the China World Shopping Center's indoor rink. Le Cool's 14 coaches run lessons following Ice Skating Institute (ISI) training courses. RMB 50/90min (skate rental included), RMB 100/40min private lesson.
Mon-Sat 10am-10pm, Sun 10am-7.30pm. B2/F, China World Trade Center, 1 Jianguomenwai Dajie, Chaoyang District. (6505 5776) Le Cool 国贸商城地下溜冰场，朝阳区建国门外大街1号国贸商城地下2层

New World Champion Skating Rink With its many coaches, this smallish mall rink draws many student skaters. All fees include 90min of ice time and skate rentals. Weekdays: RMB 25 (9.30-11.30am), RMB 35 (11.30am-5pm), RMB 40 (5-9.30pm). Weekends: RMB 45.
Daily 9.30am-9.30pm. B1/F, New World Shopping Mall, Chongwen District. (6708 9523) 新世界冠军溜冰场，崇文区新世界商城地下1层

Shangmei Ice Skating This indoor facility spans a modest 1,000 square meters. 90min of ice time costs RMB 35 (weekdays) or RMB 45 (nights and weekends).
Daily 10am-9.30pm. Xidan Cultural Centre (in 77th Street), Xicheng District. (6603 0050) 尚美溜冰场，西城区西单文化广场77街

Lacrosse

Men's and Women's Lacrosse Looking for players with experience for spring practices and tournaments; current roster includes Beijing Sport University students and graduates and expat lawyers. No cost involved, but bring your own equipment.
Saturdays 9am. Beijing Sport University. Contact Mike (mchao98@hotmail.com)

Martial Arts

Beijing Black Tiger Academy This Martial Arts and Fitness training facility offers Muay Thai, Brazilian Jiu-jitsu, Mixed Martial Arts, Combat Conditioning training, Brazilian Capoeira and Filipino Escrima programs for different ages, from beginner to professional advanced students. Experienced instructors include China's only Brazilian jiu-jitsu black belt and the former Muay Thai kickboxing world champion. Classes are RMB 750/month for unlimited training in both arts. Free introductory class. Mon-Fri (evenings), Sat-Sun (afternoons). All classes conducted in English.
Rm 906, Bldg 9, Jianwai Soho, 39 Dongsanhuan, Chaoyang District. (139 1079 8122, 136 8140 2122, 131 2042 9724) www.blacktigerclub.com

Beijing Jiu-Jitsu Academy The Academy focuses on the relatively new discipline of Brazilian jiu-jitsu but also teaches "mixed martial arts" including wrestling, Thai boxing, boxing, judo and *wushu*. Children aged 14 and up are welcome. RMB 500 (registration fee), RMB 80 (one class, members), RMB 100 (1 class, non-members); private lessons available. Free introductory class. Classes daily.
309 Olympic Sports Centre, Yayuncun, Chaoyang District (5129 5028, 138 0137 8214) www.baxiroushu.com 北京安迪柔术馆，朝阳区亚运村奥体中心309

Beijing Kendo Club Call for schedule.
3-1 Liangmaqiao Lu, Chaoyang District. (139 1177 1871) 北京剑道同好会，朝阳区亮马桥路3-1号

Beijing Milun School of Traditional Kung Fu A wide range of styles including *baguazhang*, tai chi, *sanda*, Shaolin and *qigong* taught in a courtyard in Wangfujing. RMB 60/class or RMB 500/month. One-on-one lessons held in Ritan Park cost RMB 150/90min. Also hosts free Chinese language lessons every Sunday.
(139 1072 4987) www.kungfuinchina.com 北京弥纶传统武术学校。

Beijing Sport University BSU offers degree and non-degree *wushu* courses, including dozens of forms of tai chi, boxing, swordplay and plenty of other intimidating weapons.
Call for schedule. Zhonguancun Beidajie, Haidian District. (6298 9341, 6298 9391) 北京体育大学，海淀区中关村北大街

Chinese Culture Club CCC's Martial Arts Club holds regular Monday night *qigong* classes and Thursday night tai chi classes, with movements and breathing methods taught according to the lunar calendar. RMB 100/class.
29 Anjialou, Liangmaqiao Lu, Chaoyang District. (6432 9341) www.chinesecultureclub.org 中国文化社，朝阳区亮马桥安家楼29号

Jinghua Wushu Association English instruction of tai chi forms, barehand and weapons *wu shu*, *qigong* and *chan* meditation from teachers who have trained since childhood in traditional Shaolin forms. RMB 90 (per class), RMB 600 (ten classes).
Liangma Qiao, near Nuren Jie, Chaoyang District. (135 2228 3751) 京华武术协会，朝阳区亮马桥女人街附近

Sunplace Sports & Fitness This palatial fitness center in the northwest offers routine martial arts (including *changquan* and tai chi) along with more damaging Chinese wrestling (*shuaijiao*), "arresting" and taekwondo classes. RMB 80/class, with discounts for multiple classes.
Call for schedule. 26 Laiguangying Xilu, Wangjing North, Chaoyang District. (8491 6789) 东方全红体育健身中心，朝阳区望京北来广营西路26号

Tai Chi Workshop Traditional tai chi, weapon play and push-hands are taught at the CTS Plaza Health Club. RMB 50/hr. Translation provided.
Wed, Fri 6.30-7.30pm. 1/F, CTS Hotel, Sanyuanqiao, Chaoyang District. (130 0103 9563) 太极拳工坊，朝阳区三元桥中旅大厦1层

Tianyi Kung Fu Club Specializes in Shaolin kung fu, Xingyi kung fu and self-defense techniques. RMB 500 (1 month), RMB 1,200 (3 months).
Tue, Thu, Sun 3.30-5pm, 7.30-9pm. (8776 6058, 130 5113 8804) www.tianyiculture.com 天一武术俱乐部

Wing Chun Kung Fu Class Wing Chun kung fu is the Chinese martial art system made famous by Bruce Lee. Simple, direct and practical, this form of self-defense is good

Another tender jiu-jitsu moment

for both men and women. Group, private and in-house classes available in and around Chaoyang District. Lessons can be taught in English, Chinese, German or Italian.
Contact Lee Kwan Wah (131 2655 3900, wingchun. china@gmail.com) 咏春功夫培训

Pilates
(see Gyms and Fitness Centers, p424)

Squash
Squash Ladder Club For all squash addicts from beginners to advanced experts. Free.
(bsll.coo@uss-squash.cn)

Rugby
Aardvarks Rugby Club Student-based foreign team that loves to play rugby… and drink. Join the team for regular games, training and drinking sessions. The Aardvarks are sponsored by the Rickshaw (see p308). *Inside the Beijing Language and Culture University campus. Contact Dave (135 2224 8133) www.geocities.com/aardvarksrfcl*

Beijing Devils Rugby Club Join the senior, mixed touch or women's rugby teams for weekly training (see website for schedules) and drinks at their headquarters, The Den. Annual membership fees RMB 600, (students and locals RMB 300), social members RMB 100.
4 Gongti Donglu (next to City Hotel, inside The Den), Chaoyang District. (6592 6290) www.beijingdevils.com
北京鬼子橄榄球俱乐部，朝阳区工体东路4号（城市宾馆旁边，敦煌酒吧内）

Running & Training
Beijing Hash House Harriers "The drinking club with a running problem" organizes hour-long 8-10km runs around Beijing every Sunday afternoon followed by more beer than you could possibly drink, lots of noise and a meal. Occasional out-of-town trips. RMB 20 for the run. RMB 60 for the run and meal.
Contact Dave "Minime" White (139 1131 6130) www.hash.cn

TRIBEIJING Formerly known as BUTT (Beijing United Triathlon Team), this multinational group of ambitious triathletes meets at Pinnacle Plaza in Shunyi early Saturday and Sunday to train together. Both males and females are welcome to join, but make sure you bring your own equipment.
Contact Patrik Li (135 0113 3504, tribeijing@gmail.com) http://tribeijing.org

Scuba Diving
SinoScuba Offers PADI open water and advanced scuba courses, with trips to the Blue Zoo Aquarium arranged for ages 10 and up. All courses in English.
Contact Steven Schwankert (136 9302 8913, steven@sinoscuba.com) 中国潜水

Ocean Image Dive Club Organizes aquarium dives as well as domestic and international dive trips, rents/sells gear and offers PADI courses held at Evolution Fitness Center pool.
(6568 5768, 6566 3036) www.oceanimage.com.cn 北京海洋印象潜水

PHOTO: SIMON LIM

Shooting & Archery

Oriental Dragon Archery Club Idle employees at this bowling alley-esque archery range mean lots of personal attention if you want it. RMB 100/hr. RMB 200 membership gets you 60% off.
Daily 2pm-1am. West hall, North Gate of Workers' Stadium, Gongti Beilu, Chaoyang District. (6501 6655) 东方巨龙射箭俱乐部，朝阳区工体北路工体北门西厅

Olympic Sports Centre Paintball Strike Range Warmongers take note: This 10,000 square meter course provides two-hour paintball games for RMB 80. Guns and protective gear are included, but after the first 30, paintballs are RMB 1.5-1.7 each. Or you can rent the whole course for RMB 128/person/hr and bring your own gear and balls.
Daily 8am-5pm. 1 Anding Lu, Chaoyang District. (6492 1603) 奥体中心匹特博运动场，朝阳区安定路1号

Star Trooper Laser Tag Indulge your trigger-happy inner child in a very tripped-out atmosphere. Each game lasts 15 minutes. Kids must be taller than 1.3m. RMB 40 (first game), RMB 30 (second game), RMB 30 (third game). Groups of six or more can hire the entire venue for RMB 1,000.
Tue-Fri 2-8pm, Sat-Sun 9am-8pm. 316 Wangjing Xincheng Xiyuan Sanqu, Chaoyang District. (6475 8329) www.startrooper.net 激光搏击，朝阳区望京新城西园三区316楼

Skateboarding, In-line Skating, Roller Skating & Trick-Biking

66Show.net Group of young, mostly local in-line skaters who take to the city streets a couple of times a month for all-night monster trips around the city.
http://bbs.66show.net/

Honglingjin Park Honglingjin is home to both an oval roller skating area and a modest skate park.
Daily 6am-8.30pm. 5 Hou Balizhuang, Chaoyang District. (8581 9548) 红领巾公园，朝阳区后八里庄5号

Longtanhu Park There's a popular roller skating area on this park's island.
Daily 6am-10pm. 8 Longtanhu Lu, Chongwen District. (6714 4336) 龙潭湖公园，崇文区龙潭路8号

New Trend Roller Skating World Let's all head down to the roller rink! Pop music pumped in while you skate till the cows come home (no time limit). RMB 10, RMB 15 (after 6pm).
Daily 10am-midnight. Capital Gymnasium, 54 Zhongguancun Nandajie, Haidian District. (6218 4225) 新潮流滚轴溜冰大世界，海淀区中关村南大街54号首都体育馆内

Tuanjiehu Park There's a roller skating park near the pool.
Daily 6.30am-9.30pm. 16 Tuanjiehu Nanli, Chaoyang District. (8597 3603) 团结湖公园，朝阳区团结湖南里16号

Skiing

Badaling Ski Resort Badaling has two 800m long ski runs and a 2,300m snowmobile run. It also has sledding runs and a ski lodge with accommodation, food and drinks, stores and a gym. Entrance fee RMB 20, weekend price RMB 70 (1 hour), RMB 140 (2 hours), RMB 190 (4 hours), RMB 340 (8 hours).
Daily 8.30am-6.30pm. Badaling Town, Yanqing County. (6501 0335) 八达岭滑雪场，延庆县八达岭镇

Cuiyunshan Ski Resort Carved out from a white birch forest, this ski resort features three runs, one each for beginner, intermediate and advanced skiers. Covers a total of 122,100 acres and is accessible by train. Sauna (RMB 20) and lodging (RMB 200-400) available. Entrance RMB 30. 1 hour RMB 60 (Mon-Fri), RMB 80 (Sat-Sun); 6 hours RMB 300 (Mon-Fri), RMB 420 (Sat-Sun). Snowsuit rental RMB 50.
Daily 9am-9.30pm. Chongli County, Zhangjiakou, Hebei Province. (6400 9569) 翠云山滑雪场，河北省张家口市崇礼县

Hebei Saibei Ski Resort This unique scenic environment with a backdrop of snow-covered mountains and forest has an 800m ski run and a 2,800m beginner slope. Lodgings include the No. 1 "Show" hotel (RMB 680-1,880/night), four villas (standard room RMB 150-200), and the "white birch" (*baihua*) style villa (RMB 100 a bed or RMB 60/person in farmhouse). The trip from the city takes about 2.5hr on the newly-built Beijing-Zhangjiakou highway. There is a shuttle bus to the resort on the weekends (RMB 120/person).
Daily 8am-9pm. North of Xiqueliang, Chongli County, Zhangjiakou, Hebei Province. (6710 3778) 河北塞北滑雪场，河北省张家口市崇礼县喜鹊梁北

Huaibei International Ski Resort Located in Jiugukou, Huaibei boasts one advanced, two intermediate, three beginner trails and a 1,200-meter long cable car ride. Other features include a grass run (for summer) and night skiing. Free shuttle bus from Dongzhimen. Entrance RMB 20. 1 hour RMB 60 (Mon-Fri), RMB 80 (Sat-Sun); half day RMB 140 (Mon-Fri), RMB 200 (Sat-Sun); full day RMB 220 (Mon-Fri) RMB 360 (Sat-Sun); night (6-9pm) RMB 50 (Mon-Fri), RMB 100 (Sat-Sun).
Daily 8.30am-9.30pm. 548 Hefangkou Village, Huaibei Town, Huairou District. (8969 6677) www.hbski.com 北京怀北国际滑雪场，怀柔区怀北镇河防口村548号

Jindinghu Ski Resort Proximity to the city (89km) is one of Jindinghu's biggest draws. On arrival, you'll find intermediate and novice runs as well as a beginner's slope. Those wishing to extend their stay can spend the night at one of 20 villas built along the Jinding Lake. Entrance RMB 20. 2 hours RMB 100 (Mon-Fri), RMB 140 (Sat-Sun); full day RMB 220 (Mon-Fri), RMB 340 (Sat-Sun). Sledding RMB 50/30min, snowmobile RMB 8/min.
Daily 8am-9.30pm. Northeast of Jugezhuang Town, Miyun County. (6808 7910) 北京金鼎湖滑雪场，密云县巨各庄镇东北

Jundushan Ski Resort Jundushan features seven ski trails (one advanced, two intermediate, three beginners, one exclusive ski-school run and one slalom run) serviced by a two-person chairlift and a T-bar lift. It is located 34km from the city and covers an area of nearly 330 acres. Jundushan's southern exposure means the snow can get slushy. Sleds, inner tubes and snowmobiles are available for rent. Accommodation options include "Russian-style" villas and Mongolian tents. One hour RMB 60 (Mon-Fri), RMB 80 (Sat Sun); full day RMB 240 (Mon-Fri), RMB 380 (Sat-Sun). Night skiing RMB 100 (Mon-Sat).
Daily 8am-10pm. 588 Zhenshun Village, Cuicun Town, Changping District. (6072 5888) www.bjski.com.cn 北京军都山滑雪场，昌平区崔村镇真顺村588号

Marco Huang flies high at Nanshan Mellow Park

Lianhuashan Ski Resort Lianhuashan offers two advanced runs, three intermediate runs and two beginner trails. Entrance RMB 20. 2 hours RMB 100 (Mon-Fri), RMB 140 (Sat-Sun); 4 hours RMB 140 (Mon-Fri), RMB 190 (Sat-Sun); full day RMB 400 (Mon-Fri), RMB 340 (Sat-Sun). Snowmobile RMB 8/min. Inner tube RMB 50/30min. Snowsuit RMB 30/day.
Daily 8.30am-5pm, 6-10pm. Zhangzhen, Shunyi District. (6148 8333) 莲花山滑雪场，顺义区张镇

Longfengshan Ski Resort Only 26km from Tian'anmen Square and a 10min ride from Pingguoyuan subway station, this hill features six ski runs: two for beginners, two for intermediates and two for advanced, as well as hiking year-round. Entrance RMB 20. Half day RMB 60, full day RMB 100.
Daily 8am-4pm. Wanfotang Village, Yongding Town, Mentougou District. (6980 4549) 龙凤山滑雪场，门头沟区永定镇万佛堂村

Nanshan Ski Village One of the area's top ski resorts, Nanshan has ten well-groomed trails for skiers of all levels and a snowboard park (Nanshan Mellow Park) with a halfpipe, four kickers and six rails – all served by a quadruple chairlift, a double chairlift and nine T-bars. You'll also discover a 1,318m long toboggan run and even a snow football pitch ("he slips, he slides, he scores"). Nanshan has many ski and snowboard instructors – some trained by the Austria Snowboard Association – and it is also home to snowboarding camps. Visit this all-season facility in summer for water skiing, grass skiing and paragliding. Nanshan is 108km from Siyuan Qiao. Entrance RMB 20. 2 hours RMB 100 (Mon-Fri), RMB 150 (Sat-Sun); 4 hours RMB 140 (Mon-Fri), RMB 200 (Sat-Sun); full day RMB 220 (Mon-Fri), RMB 360 (Sat-Sun). Sledding RMB 50 per 30 min. Lodging available (RMB 320-360).
Daily 8.30am-5.30pm. Shengshuitou Village, Henanzhai Town, Miyun County. (6445 0991) www.nanshanski.com 北京南山滑雪场，密云县河南寨镇圣水头村

Qiaobo Ice and Snow World The first and only indoor ski resort in Beijing, Qiaobo has a 150m bunny slope and a 260m long slope. Great place to cool off from the summer heat. Experienced skiers should keep their expectations low. No entrance fee, 2 hours RMB 180 (Mon-Fri), RMB 230 (Sat-Sun); 4 hours RMB 230 (Mon-Fri) RMB 320 (Sat-Sun). 30% off for skiers with their own equipment.

PHOTO: MARY DENNIS

SPORTS & FITNESS

Daily 8.30am-9pm. Inside Chaobai River National Forest Park, Mapo, Shunyi District. (Drive along Jingshun Lu to Mapo Roundabout in Shunyi, turn right and drive 1km east to the first intersection, then turn left and drive another 3km north; it's on the right (east) side of the road.) (8497 2568) www.qbski.com 乔波冰雪世界，顺义区马坡潮白河国家森林公园内

Shijinglong Ski Resort With Beijing's longest trails, a snowboard park and a good snowboard shop, Shijinglong is one of the area's most popular resorts. Recent additions include a new intermediate run, two new lifts and a widened advanced run as well as a beginner trail. The wind can be bracing, especially when you're on a slow-moving chairlift. Located near the donkey-pulled sleighs and snowmobile circuit, the lukewarm hot springs are a mixed pleasure. Entrance RMB 20. Two hours RMB 100 (Mon-Fri), RMB 150 (Sat-Sun); 4 hours RMB 140 (Mon-Fri), RMB 200 (Sat-Sun); full day RMB 220 (Mon-Fri) RMB 360 (Sat-Sun). Snowmobiles RMB 20 per loop. Hot springs RMB 50.
Daily 8am-6pm. Zhongyangfang Village, Zhangshanying Town, Yanqing County. (6919 1617) www.sjlski.com 石京龙滑雪场，延庆县张山营镇中羊坊村

Snow World Ski Park The grandly named Snow World, located near the Ming Tombs, is a mere 30 minutes by car from downtown Beijing. It has only two ski runs – one advanced and one intermediate. Entrance RMB 20. Skiing: 1 hour RMB 50 (Mon-Fri), RMB 70 (Sat-Sun); 4 hours RMB 120 (Mon-Fri), RMB 190 (Sat-Sun); full day RMB 200 (Mon-Fri), RMB 340 (Sat-Sun). Snowboarding: 1 hour RMB 70, 4 hours RMB 180, full day RMB 320. Sledding RMB 20 per round.
Daily 8.30am-5pm. Xiaogongmen, Shisanling, Changping District. (8976 1886/1899) 雪世界滑雪场，昌平区十三陵小宫门

Wanlong Ski Resort Wanlong is located 249km from Beijing – a three-hour drive. The resort has five ski runs for beginner to advanced skiers, two lifts, snowmobiles and sledding. Two hours RMB 120, half day RMB 160, full day RMB 260.
Daily 8.30am-4.30pm. Honghualiang, Chongli County, Zhangjiakou, Hebei Province. (0313 461 6784/7676 or 6553 6830/1) www.wlski.com 万龙滑雪场，河北省张家口市崇礼县红花梁

Yunfoshan Ski Resort Surrounded by mountains in three directions, Yunfoshan has two advanced runs, three intermediate runs, four beginner runs and a 1,500m cross-country route for snowmobiles. It also offers horse and dogsled rides (RMB 20). Has earned mixed reviews. Entrance RMB 20. One hour RMB 60 (Mon-Fri), RMB 80 (Sat-Sun); 4 hours RMB 180 (Mon-Fri), RMB 260 (Sat-Sun); 8 hours RMB 300 (Mon-Fri), RMB 400 (Sat-Sun). Snowsuit rental RMB 20. Snowmobiles RMB 8 per minute.
Daily 8am-5pm. Xiwengzhuang Town, Miyun County. (6901 6896/7086) 北京云佛山滑雪场，密云县溪翁庄镇

Ski Clubs

KNS KNS not only stocks Head skis and Smith goggles but also runs a club for serious skiers. Membership cards cost RMB 15 or are free with purchases over RMB 600. Members get 15-25% discounts on stock and can join their weekly ski trips.
Daily 9am-8.30pm. 149 Beitucheng Xilu, Haidian District. (8202 3765) KNS滑雪俱乐部，海淀区北土城西路149号

Snow Favor This club for white powder addicts stocks Rossignol, K2 and Briko gear. Members can join online and enjoy weekly ski trips taught by members of the French Ski Association. Also offers free ski lessons for members.
Daily 9am-5pm. South Bldg 1, Dadushi Shangyejie, Ciqikou, Chongwen District. (6707 1085) www.snowfavor.com 雪上飞专卖店，崇文区磁器口大都市商业街1号楼南侧

Softball

Beijing Softball League – "United Beijing" Spring and fall seasons. All are welcome.
Sat-Sun 1-5pm. Chaoyang Sports Center. Contact Monti (8557 4959) www.beijingsoftball.com

Spectator Sports

Note: In the run-up to the Olympics, many teams' sporting venues are being juggled around. See Tickets (p667) for info on how to buy tickets to sporting events.

Beijing Jockey Club Three international standard racetracks host nearly 10 races every Saturday from March to November. Members enjoy free entrance on race day, priority in booking, VIP rooms and horse leasing and buying.
Neijunzhuang Village, Xuxinzhuang Town, Tongzhou District. (6518 2312/3) www.mawwww.com 北京通顺赛马场，通州区徐辛庄镇内军庄村

Beijing Shougang Basketball Center Beijing's CBA-level basketball team, Capital Steel, plays here from late October to March/April. Go, Capital Steel, Go!
159 Fushi Lu, Shijingshan District. (8829 6158) 北京首钢篮球中心，石景山区阜石路159号

Capital Gymnasium Hosts events like figure skating, sumo wrestling and concerts.
54 Zhongguancun Nandajie, Haidian District. (tickets 6835 4055, 6831 7646) 首都体育馆，海淀区中关村南大街54号

Fengtai Sports Center Home to the city's premier football team, Beijing Guo'an, who play from mid-March to mid-October.
55 Xisihuan Nanlu, Yuegezhuang Qiao, Fengtai District. (6381 1576) 丰台体育中心，丰台区岳各庄桥西四环南路55号

Lucheng Sports School Temporary home of the Beijing Tigers baseball team.
South of Lucheng, Huangcun Town, Daxing District. (6123 9856) 芦城体育学校，大兴区黄村镇芦城南

Goldenport Motor Park Located a few miles from Beijing Capital Airport, Goldenport Race Track hosts a variety of car and motorcycle club races. Their new track can take Champ Car series and A1 Grand Prix races.
Daily 9am-5pm. 1 Goldenport Dajie, Jinzhanxiang (follow signs off the Airport Expressway), Chaoyang District. (8433 3497) www.goldenport.com.cn 金港汽车公园，朝阳区金盏乡金港大街1号

Olympic Sports Centre Stadium The Olympic Stadium is being groomed for Olympic football matches.
Daily 10am-10pm (summer), 1-9pm (winter). 1 Anding Lu, Chaoyang District. (6491 0468, 6491 2233 ext 315) 奥体中心体育场，朝阳区亚运村安定路1号

Workers' Gymnasium Slated to hold Olympic boxing, the Workers' Gymnasium hosts boxing and international basketball matches, among others.

China's first super motorbike race at Goldenport Motor Park

Gongti Beilu, Chaoyang District. (6502 5757) 工人体育馆，朝阳区工体北路

Workers' Stadium With an estimated seating capacity of 72,000, the Workers' Stadium is the first choice for spectator-busting events like Manchester United-Guo'An exhibition matches. It was undergoing pre-Olympic renovations at the time of publication.
Gongti Beilu, Chaoyang District. (6501 2372) 工人体育场，朝阳区工体北路

Swimming

Note: Pools generally require bathing caps, which – conveniently – can usually be purchased on site for those that forget.

Beijing Winter Swim Club Members can attend their seasonal activities that include (surprise!) swimming in ridiculously cold water. Performances and competitions in Beijing and further afield. Dues: RMB 5/yr.
(8278 0313) www.china-ws.org (Chinese only) 北京冬泳俱乐部

China World Hotel Ride the wake of the rich and famous. RMB 200 for adults and RMB 80 for kids (under 12) to use the pool and all other facilities (such as spa, sauna, gym, etc.).
Daily 6am-11pm. 1 Jianguomenwai Dajie, Chaoyang District. (6505 2266) 中国大饭店，朝阳区建国门外大街1号

Crab Island (aka City Seaview) Inside this resort is a substantial fake beach with parasols overlooking a large pool. After a swim and a game of beach volleyball on one of the local courts, visit the concession stand to pick up beers and *chuan'r* (lamb, chicken, squid, etc.), which you barbecue on the onsite grills. RMB 60 per day (RMB 40 for children under 1.4m).
Daily 9am-8pm (till 10pm in Jul and Aug, closed in winter). Xiedao Dujiacun (take the Weigou exit off the Airport Expressway and follow the signs), Jichang Lu, Chaoyang District. (8432 5188) www.cityseaview.net 城市海景，朝阳区机场路蟹岛度假村

DHY Conveniently located, DHY is a swimming training center catering to adults.
Fri-Sun 7-8.30pm. B1/F, Bldg 1, 9 Nongzhanguan Nanlu, Chaoyang District. (135 2126 4441) 博雅员会所，朝阳区农展馆南路9号博雅园B1层会所（天安豪园北侧）

Ditan Swimming Pool RMB 30 for unlimited pool use.
Mon-Fri 8.30am-3.30pm, 6.30-9.30pm, Sat-Sun 8.30am-10pm. 18 Hepingli Zhongjie, Andingmenwai, Dongcheng District. (6426 4483) 地坛游泳池，东城区安外和平里中街18号

Dongdan Indoor Swimming Pool This centrally located public pool offers swim classes (12 lessons cost RMB 420 for adults, RMB 380 for children) between 3-4.30pm and 6-7pm. RMB 30 (adults), RMB 20 (students).

Continues on p438

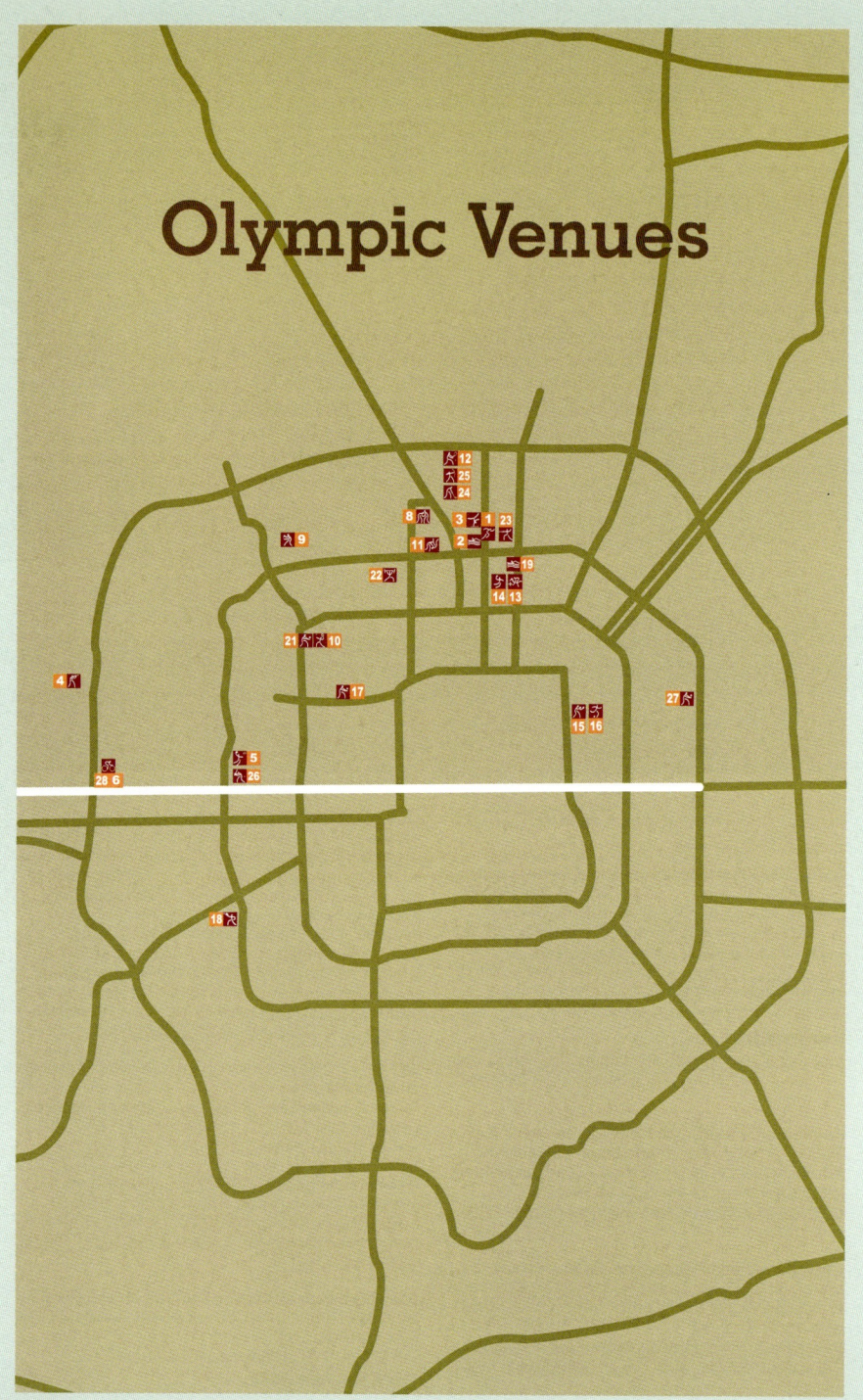

Olympic Venues

by Alex Pasternack

1) National Stadium ("Bird's Nest") – Athletics, Football

The 42,000 tons of steel that bend around and even support the futuristic National Stadium, designed by Swiss architects (and recent recipients of the UK's Royal Gold Medal) Jacques Herzog and Pierre de Meuron, evoke more a Martian-mother-ship than a sports arena.

While government officials were initially keen on a groundbreaking design being broadcast around the world, concerns about safety and cost (the original price tag was USD 360 million, compared with its current meager price tag – RMB 270 million) seemed to endanger the project early on. But with the encouragement of Beijing artist Ai Weiwei and with the clock ticking, the government gave the green light – on the condition that a costly retractable roof be removed. While the building's open shell fosters natural air circulation, it also covers gaps in the lattice with a translucent membrane like that used on the Aquatics Center; even if it rains on the opening ceremony, the shell will protect the stadium's 91,000 spectators, and in futuristic style. What happens to the stadium after the Olympics flies the coop, a concern for any Games host, will be up to Beijing's imagination.

2) National Aquatics Center ("Water Cube") – Swimming, Diving, Synchronized Swimming

Like the nearby National Stadium, the National Aquatics Center draws inspiration from nature, but on a microscopic scale. The "Water Cube," as it's become known, is clad with 3,000 air pockets made of a recyclable Teflon-like plastic in a pattern evocative of nature's most common shapes: the arrangement of organic cells, or the formation of soap bubbles. Such a design mimics nature's most efficient way of filling three-dimensional space: "We realized that a structure based on this unique geometry would be highly repetitive and buildable whilst appearing very organic and random," says engineer Tristram Carfrae, whose firm Arup assisted Australian architects PTW and the CSCEC in their design.

Ingeniously, the matrix of thin steel pipes that crisscross between the bubbles will also keep it standing through an earthquake, without the help of concrete or structural beams. And the translucent envelope lets in more light and heat than glass, helping to warm the building's five pools and slashing energy costs by 30 percent.

3) National Indoor Stadium – Artistic Gymnastics, Trampolines, and Handball
4) Beijing Shooting Range Hall
5) Wukesong Indoor Stadium – Basketball
6) Laoshan Velodrome – Cycling (Track, Mountain)
7) Shunyi Olympic Rowing-Canoeing Park – Rowing, Canoe/Kayak (Flat-water and Slalom)
8) China Agriculture University Gymnasium – Wrestling
9) Peking University Gymnasium – Table Tennis
10) Beijing University of Technology Gymnasium – Badminton, Rhythmic Gymnastics
11) University of Science and Technology Beijing Gymnasium – Judo and Taekwondo
12) Olympic Green Tennis Center – Tennis

Existing venues in Beijing

13) Olympic Sports Centre Stadium – Modern Pentathlon (running and equestrian)
14) Olympic Sports Centre Gymnasium – Handball
15) Workers' Stadium – Football
16) Workers' Indoor Arena – Boxing
17) Capital Indoor Stadium – Volleyball
18) Fengtai Softball Field – Softball
19) Ying Tung Natatorium – Water Polo, Modern Pentathlon (swimming)
21) Beijing Shooting Range
22) Beijing Institute of Technology Gymnasium – Volleyball
23) Beijing University of Aeronautics & Astronautics Gymnasium – Weightlifting

Temporary venues in Beijing

24) Fencing Hall – Fencing, Modern Pentathlon (fencing and shooting)
25) Olympic Green Hockey Field
26) Olympic Green Archery Field
27) Wukesong Baseball Field
28) Chaoyang Park Beach Volleyball Ground
29) Laoshan Bicycle Moto Cross (BMX) Venue

Daily 9am-10pm. 2A Dahua Lu, Dongcheng District. (6523 1241) 东单室内游泳池，东城区大华路甲2号

Friendship Hotel Swimming Pool Legs were added to the snake when this beloved Olympic-sized pool was roofed over. The throngs that used to swarm here on weekends have dwindled. Good for those who don't remember this pool's former glory. RMB 100 plus RMB 500 deposit.
Daily 10am-11pm. Friendship Hotel, 1 Zhongguancun Nandajie. (6849 8888 ext 32) 友谊宾馆康体中心，海淀区中关村南大街1号

Huaqing Jiayuan Pool/Gym Although it isn't nearly as glamorous as neighboring gyms, the price is low – RMB 250 per 20 hrs – and it gets the job done. Choose between the swimming pool, treadmills, stationary bike, weights or jump rope. Come early in the day to avoid lining up for the treadmill.
Mon-Thu 2-10pm, Fri 2-11pm, Sat-Sun 10am-11pm. Inside clubhouse of Huaqing Jiayuan (next to Bldg 5), Haidian District. (8286 5800) 华清嘉园游泳池，海淀区华清嘉园会所内（5号楼旁边）

Lido Hotel Pool Jacuzzi, pool, sauna, gym included in fee. Located inside the hotel. RMB 600 (ten visits).
Daily 6am-11pm. 6 Jiangtai Lu, Jichang Lu, Chaoyang District. (6437 6688 ext 1871) 北京丽都假日酒店，朝阳区机场路将台路6号

Olympic Sports Centre Train to be the next Ian Thorpe at this indoor pool. RMB 40 per visit or RMB 130 card for 10 visits.
Daily 9.30am-9.30pm. 1 Anding Lu, Yayuncun, Chaoyang District. (6491 2233) 奥体中心，朝阳区亚运村安定路1号

Sino-Japanese Youth Center This 50m pool is located in the 21st Century Hotel. RMB 50 per visit.
Daily noon-9.30pm. 40 Liangmaqiao Lu, Chaoyang District. (6468 3311) 中日友好青年中心，朝阳区亮马桥路40号

Splash Recreation Club The Sino-Swiss Hotel's Splash boasts a large outdoor-indoor pool, a sand volleyball court, a playground, a gym, ping pong tables, a poolside bar and a restaurant. The hotel also has squash and tennis courts as well as a sauna. RMB 100 per day (adults), RMB 50 per day (children over 4), free (children under 4).
Daily 6am-11pm; outdoor pool closed Oct-Mar. Sino-Swiss Hotel, Xiaotianzhu, Shunyi District. (6456 5588 ext 1428) www.sino-swisshotel.com 浪花俱乐部，顺义区小天竺国都大饭店

St. Regis Spa & Club Swim in this gorgeous pool for a cool RMB 500 per day – includes access to gym and spa facilities.
Daily 24hrs. 21 Jianguomenwai Dajie, Chaoyang District. (6460 6688 ext 2757) 国际俱乐部温泉健身中心，朝阳区建国门外大街21号

Tsinghua University Outdoor Swimming Pool The budget option for those looking to escape the summer heat. Facilities are basic and the shallow wading pool fills up with staff and students on a hot day, but it is a fun place to splash around for RMB 8 (RMB 3 for Tsinghua students who register for a swimming card). Entry to the Olympic-size lap pool requires a special permit.
Daily 1.30-3pm, 3.30-5pm and 5.30-7pm (June-Sept). West gate of Tsinghua University (100m east of the gate, the pool is on the left at the first intersection), Haidian District. 清华大学游泳池，海淀区清华大学西门（门内向东100米，第一个路口的左侧）

Tuanjiehu Pool Fans of kitsch will dig this big, clean wave pool that also has a "beach" (small and muddy), food stations and water slides. The pool entry fee of RMB 25 provides unlimited use on weekdays and three hours on weekends.
Daily 6am-9.30pm (summer). Inside Tuanjiehu Park, 16 Tuanjiehu Nanlu, Chaoyang District. (8597 4677) 团结湖游泳池，朝阳区团结湖公园内

Workers' Stadium Swimming Pool This slightly murky but very cheap outdoor pool will let you cool off before a night on the town. Great people-watching. RMB 15 (free for kids under 1m).
Daily noon-6pm (Jun-Aug). Gongti Beilu, Chaoyang District. (6593 6221) 工人体育场游泳池，朝阳区工体北路

Tennis

Beijing International Tennis Centre This complex for fat cats has five courts. RMB 300/hr (non-members), RMB 100/hr (members), annual membership (RMB 8,000).
Mon-Fri 10am-10pm, Sat-Sun 8am-8pm. 50 Tiantan Donglu, Chongwen District. (6715 2532) 北京国际网球中心，崇文区天坛东路50号

Beijing Tennis Center 1 Guangcai Lu, Fengtai District. 光彩体育中心网球场，丰台区光彩路1号

Beijing Tennis Club Organized tennis ladder for all levels. All nationalities, gender or ages welcome.
Contact Daniel (135 0105 9590) www.tennisrank.com

Capital Gymnasium This grim architectural statement contains three indoor tennis courts, several badminton courts and ping pong tables. RMB 150-200/hr (tennis court), RMB 35/hr (badminton), RMB 35/hr (ping pong).
Daily 8am-10pm. 54 Zhongguancun Nandajie, Haidian District. (8836 5536) 首都体育馆，海淀区中关村南大街54号

Chaoyang Tennis Club RMB 200/hr; after 4pm and weekends RMB 240/hr.
Daily 8am-10pm. 1A Nongzhanguan Nanlu, Chaoyang District. (6501 0953/0959) 朝阳网球俱乐部，朝阳区农展馆南路甲1号

Kerry Sports Offering Peter Burwash International Tennis Clinics and Programs. Tennis courts available – members RMB 150-200/hr, non-members RMB 400/hr. The Kerry Centre Hotel, 1 Guanghua Lu, Chaoyang District. (6561 8833 ext 6465) 嘉里体育，朝阳区光华路1号嘉里中心酒店

Tennis Fans Club Play tennis every week. Meet great tennis players and more. A NTRP tennis level of 3.0+ is required. Members share court fees.
(box4queen@yahoo.com)

Ultimate Frisbee

Beijing Ultimate Frisbee Fast and friendly, mostly expat team plays pickup and tournaments throughout the year. All skill levels welcome.
Contact Michelle (136 0103 6430)
www.beijingultimate.com

Yoga

Note: Many gyms offer yoga and hot yoga classes.

Alona Studio Offers hatha, ashtanga, power and bikram (hot) yoga for all levels, as well as Pilates mat classes. Private lessons available. Now offering personal training and rehabilitation sessions. Yoga mats and other wellness products available for purchase.
Rm 802, Bldg 6, Wanda Plaza, 93 Jianguo Lu, Chaoyang District. (5820 6920, alonayoga@gmail.com) 朝阳区建国路93号万达广场6-802

Beijing Yoga Offers traditional ashtanga yoga for all levels, with experienced instructors. They also offer hot yoga, kids' yoga, hatha yoga and prenatal yoga. Classes offered throughout the day and evening.
Mon-Fri 6-9pm, Sat-Sun 9am-6pm. 2610, Tower D, Soho New Town, Chaoyang District. (8589 3102, 139 1176 7521) www.beijingyoga.com 朝阳区Soho现代城D座2610

Bikram Hot Yoga Bikram China representative Huiping Mo and Bikram-certified instructor John Williams conduct 90min classes (RMB 140) in their heated studio. All classes in English.
(6539 3434, 139 1051 3285) 5/F, Bldg E, Pacific Century Club, 2A Gongti Beilu, Chaoyang District. http://bikramyogabeijing.googlepages.com 莫慧萍比克拉姆热瑜珈，朝阳区工体北路甲2号盈科中心会所E座5层

Mountain Yoga Organizes and hosts yoga retreats in the mountain areas northwest of Beijing. Weekend workshops sometimes feature special guest teachers and themes such as art, photography, cooking and Bollywood dancing. Also offers yoga travel packages such as yoga on the Great Wall.
6 Gongzhufen Cun, Fragrant Hills, Haidian District. (6259 6702, 139 0102 1322) www.mountainyoga.cn 海淀区香山公主坟村6号

Nirvana Yoga Global Trade Mansion Yoga Club Hatha yoga, ashtanga yoga, bikram hot yoga and iyengar yoga.
B1/F, Bldg D, Global Trade Mansion, 9 Guanghua Lu, Chaoyang District. (6593 7509/10) 青鸟瑜伽，朝阳区光华路9号时髦国际公寓D座地下1层

OM Yoga 42° Specializes in hot yoga, wqhere the studio temperature is kept at 42-48°C. Classes available in English, Chinese or both. Prices start at RMB 150 per class with monthly (RMB 2,200) and yearly (RMB 9,800) memberships available.
Rm 9102/9103, Lido Apartment Bldg, Chaoyang District. (6437 8810) www.omyoga42.com 朝阳区丽都公寓9102/9103

Sunplace Sports & Fitness Indian teacher teaches traditional hatha yoga and regular yoga classes (in English).
Daily 10am-10pm. 26 Laiguanying Xilu, Wangjing Beiqu, Chaoyang District. Contact Jane Zhao (8491 8999, 136 0106 0802) 东方全红体育健身中心，朝阳区望京北区来广营西路26号

Yoga Club Mon, Sat 6.30-8pm. RMB 60 (75min class), RMB 440 (8 classes).
C&M Center, 53 Maizidian Zhengjie, Chaoyang District. 2) Citichamp (northwest of Maidian Qiao), Haidian District. (6200 0127) www.I-yoga.com.cn 1) 朝阳区麦子店正街53号；2) 海淀区冠城园（马甸桥西北角）

Yoga Yard This friendly center offers hatha yoga classes daily in the morning and evening at various levels. Includes both post- and pre-natal yoga. Yoga mats, bags and wellness products available for sale. RMB 90 per 90min lesson, RMB 700 for unlimited one-month pass. Discounts available for new students.
6/F, 17 Gongti Beilu, Chaoyang District. (136 1126 6962) www.yogayard.com 瑜伽苑，朝阳区工体北路17号6层

Yogi Yoga Indian master Mohan teaches a blend of yoga forms at serene Ritan Park, with a heavy focus on stress management and meditation. Private lessons available (RMB 300). RMB 8,500 (annual membership).
North Gate of Ritan Park, Chaoyang District. (8561 5506/07) www.yogiyogacenter.com 悠季瑜伽，朝阳区日坛公园北门

Alona knows how to tone ya

2008 Olympic Blitz

Olympic Blitz
How the capital is reinventing itself for 2008 and beyond
by Alex Pasternack

Our goal: NEW. Our deadline: NOW

"Not bad." A fresh-faced young man from Hebei province was talking about his job – cleanup around the Olympic Park during an eight-hour workday – as the hulking steel girders of the remarkable National Stadium rose in the distance behind him. He wore a slight grin that seemed completely unrehearsed, an unconcerned model of the municipality's ongoing "smile" campaign intended to spread Olympic spirit to the world.

As the days tick off before the Games, traces of that spirit are everywhere in Beijing – on lips, on billboards, on the city's massive construction sites. Clearly though, it's a buzz that has little to do with athletics.

"This is a once-in-a-lifetime opportunity for China," says Sun Weide, deputy director of the Beijing Organizing Committee for the Games (BOCOG). Despite perpetual concerns about a post-Olympics

Olympic Blitz

bubble-burst, the Games, he says, will be nothing short of a great leap forward. Sun's ability to rattle off statistics is almost as impressive as the numbers themselves: 12 percent annual GDP growth, a USD 8 billion Olympics budget, and half a million visitors – but also 241 "blue sky days" last year, 198km of new subway track, one million cars off the roads, and 11 new world-class athletic venues.

But what will those statistics mean when the torch finally arrives – and after it leaves?

All signs point to two weeks of a different Beijing than we've ever known before, where up is down, all English is immaculate and "green" is green. This magical, temporary Beijing, reconceived as a nirvana of hospitality and sports fanaticism, will leave a transformative legacy. Just how big that transformation is remains to be seen.

Congestion Question

The officials are predictably (if not dementedly) optimistic: "Traffic," says Liu Xiaoming, deputy director of the Beijing Municipal Communications Commission, "will not be a headache at all, but rather will become an enjoyable experience by 2008."

Beijing has said that during the games only "Olympic-related" traffic will be allowed to park near the venues; for the rest of us, the best options will be an upgraded public transit system, which will be free to all Games ticket-holders and Olympics staff.

Breathing Easier

As the city ramps up its USD 13 billion efforts to prepare for the "Green" Olympics, the "fog" is getting harder to scrub. Though 2006's 241 "blue sky days" – days with an air pollutant index of under 100 – exceeded the government's target by three days, the target of 245 blue skies for 2007 is one that officials admit will be "very difficult" to achieve.

Strategies to improve air quality during the Games include attempts to clean up coal plants and factories in nearby provinces, efforts to tackle heavily polluting companies, and a temporary citywide cessation and slow down of construction projects. Sustainable? Perhaps not, but stashing away a couple of canisters of Olympic Beijing air might one day be worth a pretty penny.

Reaching Out

When the lights go up on the opening ceremony on August 8, 2008, the occasion will be significant not just for what's seen, but how. Beijing's will not only be the first Olympics to be broadcast in high definition TV, but also across digital channels and the Internet – allowing a Beijinger, for instance, to choose to watch the ceremony on a so-called "3G" mobile phone, a screen in the back of a cab or the city's new TV-equipped subway lines.

The Olympics "changes the entire communication infrastructure in China," says Hu Bo, who produced the promotional films for Beijing's two Olympic bids. A host of new "hardware" isn't the only thing Beijing gains from the Games, he says, but a chance to push forward the "software" – the technical skills and creative content – crucial to shaping the country's cultural realm and, come the lighting of the flame in Beijing, its international image.

Public Works and a Charm Offensive

Creating a good impression for the hundreds of thousands set to land in Beijing in 2008 is an Olympian challenge that Beijing is not leaving up to chance. On an aesthetic level, the city government's plans include traditional renovations of popular streets, such as Yonghegong Dajie, and the expansion of green spaces. In addition to the sprawling Olympic Forest Park in the north, Beijing is doing what it can to spruce up the city's canals and has promised 30 more parks will be added to the outskirts of the city by 2008. One of the ten most polluted cities on earth has promised the world a green Olympics, and we are the beneficiaries.

So while we prepare to soak up these gains begat by the Games, it's hard to do enough homework. The following pages are a primer on several of the most prominent Chinese athletes vying for Olympic glory, as well as a roving spotlight on several of the more idiosyncratic aspects of the Olympic Blitz that is our city.

SPORTS & FITNESS

2008 Olympic Blitz

Root Root Root
The home team
by Jackie Yu, April Zhang, Jerry Chan and Gabriel Monroe

These are some of China's best hopes for striking gold at the 2008 Games. Plucked from the chaff as children due to their athletic gifts and relentlessly trained into adulthood, these super athletes all have the same goal in mind: winning Olympic gold on home turf.

Come August, the hometown fans will be out in force

Olympic Blitz

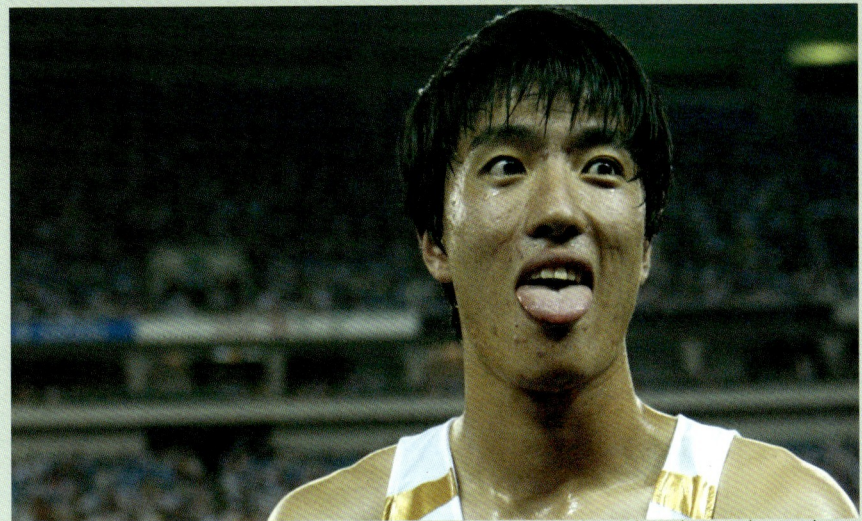
Liu Xiang is an Olympic hero that people can relate to

Leaps and bounds

Born in Shanghai in 1983, **Liu Xiang** is the perfect embodiment of China's post-reform child-of-the-80s generation – healthy, energetic and brimming with confidence. At 10 years of age he was selected to be a long jumper by a coach at the Putuo District Junior Sports School. However, doubts were cast on his future athletic prospects after a bone scan revealed that he might never grow tall enough to succeed in sports.

But Liu persisted and, of course, it paid off: In 1998 Sun Haiping, a track and field coach from the Shanghai Athletics Team, recognized Liu Xiang's jumping talents and began training him. By then the 18-year-old had already defied his bone scan by growing to a solid 1.88m.

Under Coach Sun's tutelage, Liu's talents extended beyond jumping to sprinting – prompting a switch to hurdling. It was the right move: Liu quickly excelled in the event, breaking both the World Youth and Asian 110m hurdles records with a time of 13.12 seconds in the 2001 IAAF Grand Prix in Lausanne. He also went on to win titles at the Asian Championships, the World University Games and the Asian Games. Just a few months before the 2004 Athens Olympics, he broke the Asian record with a time of 13.06 seconds at the IAAF Grand Prix in Osaka, Japan, by defeating the great American hurdler Allen Johnson.

Then, of course, came the 2004 Olympic Games in Athens, where Liu stunned the world by winning the 110m hurdle gold medal in a time of 12.91 seconds, becoming the first Asian male Olympian to win gold in a track and field event. Liu's fame skyrocketed, and his is now arguably the most ubiquitous mug in China – an advertising empire relentlessly striding across buses, billboards and credit cards. (For more about his and some of the other visages that haunt you everywhere you go in Beijing, see Attack of the 50ft Megastar, p646).

All hype aside, Liu has done his damnedest to shun the money bin, and maintain his focus on competing. He is a star in his prime. At the IAAF Grand Prix in Lausanne in July of 2006, he set a new world record for the 110m hurdles with a time of 12.88 seconds. Then, after being out of commission for two months with an ankle injury, he won the 110m hurdles in 13.23 seconds at the Prefontaine Classic Grand Prix. In June 2007, he clocked a 12.92 in New York and told reporters that he is fully confident that he will break his own world record. Beijing, and all of China are counting on Liu Xiang to maintain his excellence when it counts most, on the evening of August 24th, 2008, when he runs for his second Olympic gold.

PHOTO: IMAGINE CHINA

SPORTS & FITNESS

2008 Olympic Blitz

Cheng Fei: smaller than you, but famous

Tiny twister

Try to imagine this gymnastics move: a Yurchenko half into a layout front with a one-and-a half twist. Sound too professional? Let's make it a bit easier to understand – a round-off, half-turn onto the vault, then a 540-degree twist in the "lay-out" position. Now do you get it? Well, neither do we. But this vault, now commonly dubbed "The Cheng" in honor of blossoming gymnast **Cheng Fei**, is perhaps one of the most difficult ever attempted by a female gymnast.

In fact, Cheng is the only gymnast in the world who can execute two vaults at the highest difficulty rating (10.0). The power and athleticism of her vaults is all the more striking in such a petite package: Cheng measures 1.41m and weighs a mere 38kg. Her strength, technique and poise have helped her collect a bag full of championship hardware, including a gold medal for the vault in the 2005 World Gymnastics Championships – a first for a Chinese woman. In 2006, she picked up where she left off by claiming gold medals for the vault and floor exercise at World Cup tournaments in both France and China.

Cheng, who says her idol is Zhuge Liang, the legendary Three Kingdoms strategist, will likely approach the Beijing Games like a military tactician, disciplined and perfectly conditioned in body and mind to thrash the competition. As long as she can avoid physical injury, she will be a favorite to win gold in her top events. By then, Cheng will be 20, "the golden age for winning gold medals," according to her coach. Of course, like Liu Xiang, she can count on the intense pressure and scrutiny of her countrymen, who expect nothing short of victory from her.

INSIDER'S GUIDE TO BEIJING

Olympic Blitz

Warming up for the "Li Xiaopeng Jump 2"?

Hanging tough

Born in 1981 in Changsha (Hunan Province), **Li Xiaopeng** is one of China's best male gymnasts. Earning comparisons to the legendary Li Ning (no relation), he has won 14 gold medals in international competition to date, starting with his first at the World Artistic Gymnastics Championships at just 16 years of age.

Li's marquee events are the vault and parallel bars, and he has perfected moves on both – the "Li Xiaopeng Jump" and the "Li Xiaopeng Hang" are both named after him. In 1999, at the age of 18, he won the gold medal in the vault competition at the World Gymnastics Championships in Tianjin, thus ending an 11-year gold medal drought for Chinese gymnasts in that event, and four years later he won his third gold medal in the vault at the same competition. He was also named the 2003 World Gymnast of the Year for winning three individual gold medals to help China win the men's team gold at the World Championships.

Yet despite his precociousness, Li was something of a bust at Athens in 2004, where – hampered by a chronic ankle injury – he managed only a bronze medal in the vault. He was sidelined by surgery for most of 2006, but recovered to win gold in the parallel bars at the 2006 São Paulo World Cup Series Final.

Currently nursing a foot injury suffered in March 2007, Li has scaled back on training, but is rumored to be working on a new secret weapon for the vault. The "Li Xiaopeng Jump 2" is said to be even more difficult than the original Li Xiaopeng Jump. While his coach, Chen Xiong, is still unsure if Li will regain his best form in time for the Beijing Games, all bets are on that he will still compete.

SPORTS & FITNESS

2008 Olympic Blitz

Guo Jingjing: born to dive, born for fame

Diving diva

Guo Jingjing, China's reigning diving diva, was born for the water. Her precocious talent in aquatic sports earned her a spot on the National Diving Team at the age of 12, and three years later, she took fifth place in the three-meter springboard at the 1996 Atlanta Olympics.

Placing so high at such a young age surprised many people, not least Guo herself: She had been told that she would never make a perfect dive because her kneecaps were "misshapen" – they bulged too far out. But she found her own unconventional therapy to overcome this handicap: Guo asked her father, who weighs 90kg, to flatten her kneecaps by sitting on them every night.

Knobby kneecaps were not the only challenge Guo had to overcome. For years, she was overshadowed by her glamorous teammate Fu Mingxia, a world champion known as China's "Diving Queen" throughout the '90s. Indeed, Fu edged out Guo to claim gold in the 2000 Sydney Olympics.

But Guo has done much to gain ground since then by winning the World Diving Championship, the Diving World Cup, the FINA Diving Grand Prix and most notably, the gold medal in the 2004 Athens Olympics – achievements that brought her wealth and fame, not to mention endorsement deals worth an estimated RMB 5 million.

As with her former rival's much discussed love life, Guo's private affairs have been fodder for the paparazzi, most notably her relationship with Huo Qigang – a wealthy Hong Kong socialite – and her glamorous lifestyle has incited a minor backlash, with some wagging tongues criticizing her for succumbing to financial temptation.

The gossip, however, has not interfered with Guo's preparations for the 2008 Olympics. Dismissing talk that she is motivated by financial incentives, Guo has instead wrapped herself in the flag, claiming that her principal desire is to win honor for China – a move that might finally move her out of the shadow of her former rival and firmly onto the throne as the undisputed Diving Queen of China.

Olympic Blitz

From dark horse to champion

At 1.83m **Chen Zhong** seems much more suited for the basketball court than martial arts, but this towering tae kwon do champ has helped put China on the international competition map.

Chen Zhong was discovered by coach Chen Liren in her home province of Henan, where she underwent rigorous training under his watchful eye – so much so that she has affectionately nicknamed him the "Coach from Hell." The hard work quickly paid off: just two years after she started training in tae kwon do, Chen joined the national team and quickly made her mark by winning the bronze medal in the 67kg weight class at the 1997 East Asia Games. Three years later, 18-year-old Chen Zhong grabbed the gold medal as the dark horse competitor at the 2000 Sydney Olympics and went on to repeat her success at the 2004 Athens Olympics, despite a painful thigh injury that almost knocked her out of contention.

If Chen can win gold again in 2008 (by which time she will be 26), she will become the only Chinese athlete aside from retired diving champion Fu Mingxia to win gold in three successive Olympics.

Mess with two-time Olympic gold medalist Chen Zhong at your own peril

2008 Olympic Blitz

Three-time singles world champion Wang Liqin: due for Olympic gold?

Towering ambition

1.86 meters may not seem unusually tall for a star athlete, but for table tennis it makes a big difference. **Wang Liqin**'s stature makes him appear all the more daunting across the net, but since table tennis is all about deftness, dexterity and precision, height is not always an advantage. Nevertheless, Wang's skills – most notably his powerful forehand – are among the best in the sport.

Born in 1978 in Jiangsu Province, Wang was selected for the national team at the age of 15, and he improved quickly as a result of his solid-steel work ethic. During a match in 1995, he even snapped a tendon in his right arm but played on despite excruciating pain – a sacrifice that unfortunately cost him full use of that arm, but incredibly enough, did not prevent him from winning Olympic gold in doubles play at the 2000 Games in Sydney.

Solid skills aside, Wang is incredibly emotional both on and off the table – rumors have flown in the past about how his rumored relationship with bombshell actress Zhao Wei distracted him into losing four key international matches.

In fact, Wang's propensity for mental distraction is widely noted to be his greatest weakness. Despite competing in two Olympic Games to date, the three-time individual world champion Wang has yet to claim a singles title on his sport's brightest stage. Will he seize his opportunity in Beijing to finally put it all together?

Olympic Blitz

Zhang Yining aims to be a hometown hero

Paddle power

Ping-pong queen **Zhang Yining**'s humble roots belie her current status. Born in a small Beijing hutong near Taoranting Park in 1982, she spent her early childhood as a mischievous tomboy who liked playing with toy swords. Recognizing their daughter's athletic prowess, Zhang's parents enrolled her in a variety of sports activities ranging from dancing and swimming to martial arts and table tennis – none of which, save for the latter, appealed to her.

And what an appeal it was: At the age of nine, Zhang joined the prestigious Shichahai Sports School, where the tough training took a heavy toll on her nerves. But the hard work (and butterflies) paid off: At 16 she made it onto the roster of the Beijing table tennis team, and just two years later, she was selected for the national team.

Since then, Zhang has won 13 world championships in singles and doubles competitions – including double gold in Athens – establishing herself as a major force in international women's table tennis. Unfortunately, she has struggled somewhat of late, and she'll have her work cut out for her to become a repeat Olympic champion in 2008. Former teammate Jiang Huajun – now playing for Hong Kong – has defeated Zhang four times since 2005.

Other formidable opponents like Spain's Zhu Fang and Singapore's Li Jiawei and Yang Zi (all originally played for the Chinese mainland) look to present a serious challenge. Zhang's situation is sure to stir the passion of the crowd – she'll most likely have to fight her way through a talent diaspora to become the champion in her hometown.

SPORTS & FITNESS

2008 Olympic Blitz

Shi Zhiyong (L) and Zhang Guozheng (R) are set to square off for a high stakes heft-off

Clash of the titans

Thirty-three-year-old **Zhang Guozheng** is a nine-year veteran of the Chinese National Weightlifting Team, and the 2008 Olympics will be his third.

He placed fourth in his Olympics debut in the 2000 Sydney Games (69kg), but just three years later he broke the world record in "Clean and Jerk" for the weight class with a lift of 197.5kg at the 2003 Asian Weightlifting Championships. Then, at the Athens Games in 2004, Zhang achieved ultimate victory, taking home Olympic gold.

Despite some nagging injuries, Zhang has his sights set on the upcoming World Weightlifting Championships in September and has been training harder than ever to compete. However, another intriguing obstacle stands in his way: 27-year-old **Shi Zhiyong**, who won the gold medal in the 62kg class in the 2004 Athens Olympics, will be moving up a weight class to the 69kg class to compete in the next Games.

China's chances of winning gold in men's weightlifting in 2008 are strong, and though both Zhang and Shi insist that so long as one of them wins it won't matter who takes the gold in 2008, watching these two titans battle it out will truly be a sight to behold.

PHOTOS: IMAGINE CHINA

Olympic Blitz 2008

Bad pair

Men's badminton star **Lin Dan** is a charmed golden boy. The 24-year-old Fujian native is handsome, talented, and successful, and has an equally gorgeous and successful girlfriend, Xie Xingfang – one of the best female badminton players in China. Both are favored to challenge for singles gold medals in 2008.

Super Dan (Chaoji Dan, 超级丹), as the media and his fans have dubbed him, has won more than 20 singles gold medals in international competition and – except for a short two-month period in 2006 – he has been ranked number one by the International Badminton Federation since 2004.

Unfortunately, at the 2004 Athens Olympics, Lin lost the men's singles gold medal to Indonesia's Hidayat Taufik, the biggest blow to his career up to that point. Since then, he has lost to Taufik twice in major competitions. Will his golden dreams be dashed again in 2008 by his Indonesian nemesis?

To whip him into shape, team coach Li Yongbo is whipping up the psychological froth, letting Lin play and train more than his teammates and even publicly chiding Lin's "lack of resolve" – ostensibly to goad him into being more aggressive.

Meanwhile, Lin's better half, **Xie Xingfang**, seems wedged between two generations of Chinese women's badminton greats. As Xie attempts to follow in the footsteps of 32-year-old Zhang Ning (gold medallist in Athens), 17-year-old prodigy Wang Lin – singles gold medalist at the 2006 China Masters Badminton Championships – is nipping at her heels.

Though yet to win Olympic gold, Xie has won a host of international competitions, including the 2007 Yonex All England Open Championships and the 2006 Hong Kong Badminton Open. Unfortunately she did not fare as well at the recent Sudirman Cup, and lost her number one position in the International Badminton Federation rankings to Zhang Ning. However, despite the slip in rankings, Xie's age and experience still make her one of the favorites to win gold in 2008.

Though both halves of this athletic romance face significant challenges, the possibility that they could deliver matching championships in Beijing is tantalizing. It would mark only the second time (!?) a romantically involved couple have taken the two top singles spots in Olympic badminton (Indonesian players Alan Budikusuma and Susi Susanti both won singles gold medals at the 1992 Barcelona Olympics while the two were an item).

Will we see a double happiness moment in Beijing from this golden couple? It happened at the 2007 Yonex All England Super Series – and the victory was so sweet that Lin could not help but smooch Xie at the awards ceremony after the competition. As a couple, what could beat that? Perhaps a honeymoon at the PRC Olympic Athlete Breeding Factory Spa and Resort in Inner Mongolia – a fitting epilogue.

Li (L) and Xie (R) hope to match each other swat for swat and smooch for smooch

SPORTS & FITNESS

2008 Olympic Blitz

The sincerest form of flattery: borrowing an Iron Hammer

Following the gold medal triumph of the **China National Women's Volleyball Team** in Athens, women's volleyball will likely be one of the most highly publicized and enthusiastically followed events of the Beijing Games.

The home team are heirs to a powerful tradition: With seven world Championships since 1980 and two Olympic gold medals, China is an established powerhouse. Even the USA – perennial all-sport heavyweight – currently looks to China for volleyball expertise, as they strive to join the PRC in the ranks of the world's elite. Since 2005, former Chinese national team star player and coach Lang Ping (aka "Jenny" or "the Iron Hammer") has assumed the head coaching reins of the US women's national team.

In spite of Lang's formidable status as the best player on China's best team (winning five straight world championships from 1981-1985), she'll need more than a clever volleyball mind to defeat her home country in Beijing. China's current team is stacked with a daunting roster of young, strong, skilled athletes – inspired since their youth to continue the tradition of triumph that Lang Fang pioneered during their infancy.

Coach Chen Zhonghe has complained to the media that his relatively untested players are still "technically raw" and need more work in the countdown to 2008. The plan: five months of intensive winter training, followed by a series of international competitions in the run-up to the big throw down.

China's volleyball bashers are pumped up to defend their Olympic title

Olympic Blitz

Sandy dandy Xue packs a killer punch

Xue set to storm

Meanwhile, as China's female volleyball talents gel in the gymnasium, recent years have seen the emergence of a parallel power in a younger sister sport – beach volleyball. In the sand pits of Chaoyang Park, where competition will be held for the Beijing Games, things are looking good for the athletes and spectators alike.

At the time of publication, Chinese pairs accounted for two out of the world's top three female beach volleyball duos, despite the sport's traditional dominance by Brazil and the USA.

China's prize beach volleyball prodigy is the towering **Xue Chen**, barely 18, with a model's physique and a lethal kill. Xue's take on her chosen discipline: "Blue sky, sandy beach, sunshine, toned bodies, dark skin, famous personalities, these are the unique charms of beach volleyball."

Groomed for the national team since the age of 14, Xue Chen sheepishly recalls her early memories of the sport. "Three years ago, when I'd just started competing, I was like a bashful ugly duckling. I felt strange wearing a swimsuit [to compete], as we usually wear short sleeves and shorts to train. Back then, my mind was very conservative," she laughs.

These days, towering at 1.9 meters, Xue is a pillar of hope to achieve golden sand glory for the motherland in 2008. True, a Chinese duo has never won an Olympic medal or world championship, but results have been consistently improving. While the defending Olympic champions (Kerri Walsh and Misty May from the USA) have to be considered the favorites in Beijing, China's "Beach Baby" is one to watch with hopes of coming up big for the crowd.

2008 Olympic Blitz

On Your Marks
Olympic warm-up events calendar

Nov 16-18
2007 Beijing Judo Open
USTB (University of Science and Technology Beijing) Gymnasium

Nov 17-22
International Boxing Invitational Tournament
Worker's Indoor Arena

Nov 28-Dec 3
2007 Artistic Gymnastics Invitational Tournament
National Indoor Stadium

Nov 30-Dec 3
2007 Trampoline Gymnastics International Invitational Tournament
National Indoor Stadium

Jan 5-12
2008 International Handball Tournament
Olympic Sports Centre Gymnasium; National Indoor Stadium

Jan 20-24
China Weightlifting Open
BUAA (Beijing University of Aeronautics & Astronautics) Gymnasium
The women's event gives new meaning to the Chinese Super Girl phenomenon. Watch Yang Lian show the rest of the world what she can do.

Jan 20-26
2008 Wheelchair Basketball International Invitational Tournament
National Indoor Stadium

Mar 18-23
2008 Water Polo China Open
Ying Tung Natatorium

| Nov | Dec | Jan | Feb | Mar |

Dec 5-7
2007 Rhythmic Gymnastics International Invitational Tournament
Beijing University of Technology Gymnasium

Dec 7-9
07-08 UCI Track Cycling World Cup Classic
Laoshan Velodrome

Dec 13-19
ITTF Pro-Tour Table Tennis Grand Finals
Peking University Gymnasium

Feb 1-5
China National Swimming Open / 2008 Swimming China Open
National Aquatics Center
The long-awaited opening of the Water Cube will see China's new generation of Olympic hopefuls take to the water.

Feb 19-24
The 16th FINA Diving World Cup 2008
National Aquatics Center

Feb 26-29
2008 International Taekwondo Invitational Tournament
USTB Gymnasium

PHOTOS: IMAGINE CHINA

INSIDER'S GUIDE TO BEIJING

Olympic Blitz

Aug 8-24
Beijing 2008 Olympic Summer Games

May 22-25
China Athletics Open
National Stadium

May 31-Jun 1
Marathon Swimming Olympic Qualification
Shunyi Olympic Rowing-Canoeing Park

| Apr | May | Jun | Jul | Aug |

Apr 16-20
Synchronized Swimming – Olympic Qualifiers
National Aquatics Center

Apr 16-21
2008 China Club Volleyball Tournament
Beijing Institute of Technology Gymnasium; Capital Indoor Stadium

Apr 18-19
2008 IAAF Race Walking Challenge
National Stadium / Olympic Green
Catch slow-speed action at the first event to grace Beijing's flagship Olympic venue. Who said competitive walking was boring?

Apr 18-20
FIE World Fencing Championship
Fencing Hall

Apr 20
2008 China Marathon
National Stadium / Beijing

Apr 19-25
2008 Women's Basketball International Invitational Tournament
Wukesong Indoor Stadium

SPORTS & FITNESS

2008 Olympic Blitz

Meet Judose

One sport that definitely *won't* make the Olympics …
by David Drakeford

Foot warriors in action

It is said the reason Chinese martial arts failed to become an official Olympic event is because they are not visually interesting enough for spectators and too complex. One sport seeking to redress the problem – and perhaps add a sure gold medal to the Chinese National Team's haul – is "Judose," a mangled transliteration of the Chinese term *jiaodoushi* (脚斗士 or "foot fighter"). Originally a scrappy children's contest, it is also affectionately known as "cockfighting," as it aspires to reproduce all the fun of the pit.

Like prized birds earning their spurs, each contestant carefully crosses one leg in front of their body – a threatening knee raised to attack. The other leg then has the tricky problem of keeping the knee-pummelled player upright for as long as possible. To lose balance or stray from the ring is to admit defeat.

Judose is a trademark of Dedao Media, the company behind the creation of the modern sport. Each bout lasts for a minute – longer than it sounds for spectators of this bizarre display. Victory requires simple tactics and bloody-mindedness – and Judose is being marketed in the same vein. After coming across the confounding headline "Cripple Knocking Takes its Place in Cultured Circles" on the official website, I decided to join the cultural elite at a press conference and cockfight held at the State Administration of Sport.

Arriving at the reception hall, we collected our press packs: branded stationery, a DVD and the *hongbao* ("red envelope") – disappointingly white – containing RMB 300. The Chinese slang for hyping an event is "stirfry" (*chao re* 炒热) and things were hotting up nicely in the Judose press-wok. Nine TV cameras were trained on the stage, including one manned by reporters from a Tokyo news channel (most likely stashing a much thicker envelope than mine).

There were some foreign representatives from a local sports university hanging around – would they be roped into some farcical stunt? The compere worked the crowd skillfully as he herded in the lambs: "One foreigner! Is it enough?" "No!" whooped the mob. "Two foreigners – enough?" "Not likely!" "Three foreigners! ..." Three students were to face the Judose King – a handsome, stocky young lad with a dauntingly low centre of gravity.

Amazingly, even *three* foreigners were insufficient to knock the King off his perch.

As for Judose's Olympic dream, the King's coach admitted it would be difficult for the sport to become an official event. However, he was pleased to announce that it will be a fixture in the Chinese Minority Sports Games in 2008. Looking at the planned events – stilt racing, top whipping and competitive swinging – I have circled the date in my diary with anticipation.

PHOTO: JAMES WASSERMAN

Olympic Blitz 2008

Olympic After-parties
Where to pull an Olympian
by Michael Donohue

Synchronous boozy movements: priceless

No one's going to be busier preparing for the Olympics than the athletes themselves, who'll be competing for 302 gold medals in 28 different sports. The gold medalists will definitely want to celebrate.

Since it's bad form to be flipping through the Bars & Clubs Directory (see p296) while up on the medals podium weeping through your national anthem, we're offering a few insider tips to a few teams likely to be celebrating victories. Non-athletes take note: You may not bring home a gold medal, but that doesn't mean you can't go home with a gold medalist …

Russian Synchronized Swimming
This synchro squad hung its competition out to dry in Athens. When they do it again at the Water Cube, it'll be time to ditch the nose clips and head to Elephant (see p83) for some synchronized smoked-salmon eating and enough vodka to swim in. Happily, the synchro medal ceremony falls on a Friday, the night the Russian restaurant has scantily-clad women dancing to techno arrangements of Beethoven.

United States Softball
This team was so dominant in the last Games that the IOC banned the whole sport from future Olympic Games. (Okay, that's exaggerating. But not by much.) This is softball's swan song and these hard-throwing ladies are going to slide into Suzie Wong's (see p310) like a bachelorette party on Ritalin. Expect hugs, expect tears, expect RoboPound. Then it's to the backup shortstop's room where ten cases of Pabst Blue Ribbon will be floating in icy bathtub water (invitation only).

Romanian Women's Gymnastics
Only one question for these princesses of the mat: Pure Girl 1, 2, 3 or 4? (see p280)

German Canoeing/Mongolian Judo
If Andreas Dittmer and the rest of the flotilla can fend off Slovakia and Hungary to repeat their nine-medal run in Athens, you should see them late-night at The Stone Boat (see p344), where they'll doubtless have convinced the staff to let them blast David Hasselhoff's 1989 album *Looking for Freedom*. Watch for a late night beer-chug challenge from the Mongolian judo team walking over from Maggie's (see p303), all riled up on hot dogs.

Dutch Women's Field Hockey
Their party might be the place to be on the late-night Olympics scene. Carrying sticks but not speaking softly, the ladies from the nether regions are looking to avenge a 2-1 loss to Germany in the '04 final, and if they do, they'll turn Poachers (see p306) into a Dutch oven.

ILLUSTRATION: JOEY GUO

SPORTS & FITNESS

2008 Olympic Blitz

The Sydney model: dreams come true

The Olympic Curse?
Listen to the skeptics at your own risk
by John Brennan

"When the Opening Ceremony starts, Nigel and I will be in a Paris café. You can have the traffic jams and the tourists." It was June 2000, and my colleague Sally, the office cynic, was riding a certain mood in Sydney: The coming Olympics was a frightful bore, a sure-fire flop, or both.

The closer the big day came, the worse the Games were going to be. The main Stadium was whispered to be on a chemical waste dump. Long-range weather forecasters saw floods. Olympic politics turned toxic, with a fiasco over ticketing, and the "revelation" that popular events would be expensive.

But the doomsayers' favorite riff was trains. Sydney's ramshackle train system is regularly paralyzed by anything from a hot day to a dead possum in a signal box. When it was announced that rail would be the only way to the stadium, Sydney convulsed. By the day before the Games, the sense of doom was intense. Near Central Station, a bus driver had a heart attack and hit a pedestrian. The media saw it as an omen of the transport Armageddon to come.

Then we watched the Opening Ceremony. Through that magic looking-glass, Sydney entered an enchanted world. In the morning, strangers chatted on sun-drenched streets. Around the city, parks were given over to video screens, where thousands sat companionably into the evening, discussing obscure games to which they didn't know the rules. In Sydney's dingy train stations, an army of

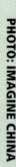

Olympic Blitz 2008

Soon it will be our turn. Don't run off to Paris and miss it!

volunteers, brightly clad, funny and resourceful, waved us to the right platform. There, incredibly, trains waited to trundle patiently and punctually to their destinations. A long red line appeared on the roadway, snaking through the city's streets and across the Harbor Bridge. It was, we learned excitedly, the marathon line – it would guide runners through the Games' final iconic event.

By the Closing Ceremony, we were sure that things would never be the same again. Nothing this good could just … end. But it did. As the video screens came down, so did the rain, and the trains muddled to a stop. Volunteers wore their uniforms for a day or two, then quietly folded them away. Couldn't we keep the marathon line, we asked, as a … national monument or something? The workaday traffic scrubbed it away as we spoke.

Here in Beijing with the Games looming, it all seems familiar. The Olympics are a drag: everything's closed for renovations. Look at the traffic jams – how will we cope? And of course, there's air quality – China's answer to Sydney's trains. The runners will choke to death.

Relax. The 2008 Olympics will be a huge success. The Olympics always are, because governments can't let them fail. Behind the scenes, the Sydney authorities used brute force to make things happen. Need 100 more buses? They were ripped out of suburban routes and handed to the all-powerful SOCOG. Worried about the trains? The Government spent a fortune, putting backups on backups and crunching problems out of existence. If Australia's politicians can corral the resources they need to get a result, do you *really* think China's can't?

Traffic? There won't *be* any traffic where it counts. And clean air *will* happen. Beijing's skies will be bluer than they've been in 200 years. Of course, some things won't come to pass. No one will get rich renting their apartment to BOCOG. There will be no cheap outbound plane tickets during the fortnight. But when the Games come, you'll love them. And when they're gone? Well, there'll be the new subway lines … and I guarantee you some great memories.

PHOTO: SIMON LIM

2008 Olympic Blitz

Take a Bite Out of the Language Barrier

Excerpts from the handbook *Olympic Security English*
by David Litt

There's nothing like the Olympics to improve communication between policeman and, well, criminals. That's why in 2002, the Police University published *Olympic Security English* as a way to make sure that Beijing's finest can talk their way through any legal situation with an English-speaking foreigner. Hopefully you won't have to hear any of these dialogues or pattern drills in real life – but if you do, you heard it here first.

Dialogue: Stopping a Stolen Car

Policeman: I'm afraid we can't let you go until we clear up this matter.

Foreigner: You're violating my human right. I protest!

P: No tricks! Don't move!

F: What lousy luck!

P: We've no determined that there's no such man as Jiangwei in Qianmen Hotel. The owner of this car is a man from Beijing, who's just found his car stolen and reported the case to the police.

F: How absurd! This is not a stolen car!

P: Come along with us to the Administration Division of Aliens for further questioning.

Pattern Drills

Police: Are you carrying any (dangerous articles / weapons / contraband / illegal drugs)?

Foreigner: Of course not.

P: But this (looks like a bomb / looks like an explosive / looks like cocaine / smells like marijuana).

Dialogue: Fighting

Foreigner: It's unfair! Why are you only questioning me?

Police: We'll question him when he comes to. For now I'm going to question you. If you don't want to answer my questions, there is no need to answer. That is your legal right.

F: I know. But I'll tell you the truth.

P: Good. First, please tell me your name, date of birth, nationality, occupation and your present address.

F: Michael Davis, born on March 15, 1981, a South African, now a second year overseas student of Beijing Foreign Languages University. My present address is Room 307, Dormitory Building No. 5 for Overseas Students, Beijing Foreign Languages Unversity.

P: How did you come to fight with him?

F: I couldn't bear his insult!

P: Did you know him?

F: No, I didn't.

P: Did you ever see him at the bar?

F: I saw him each time I went to the bar.

P: Why did you fight with him this time?

F: Because he took too many liberties with my girl friend.

Olympic Blitz

P: Did you try to keep away from him?
F: Yes. At first, we kept away from him, but not very far.
P: Why didn't you leave the bar?
F: Who could tell that he was so impudent? Not long afterwards, he came close to my girl friend and held her in his arms!
P: Did you girl friend resist him?
F: Of course she did. She tried hard to push him away. But he was very rude to her. He even kissed her by force. What a rascal!
P: Did you try to stop him?
F: Yes, I did. I tried to push him aside.
P: Did you succeed?
F: No. On the contrary, he hit me in the face with his fist.

Pattern Drills
Foreigner: He (punched me on the chin / struck me hard in the face / hit me on the head / clubbed me on the arm / stabbed me in the back).
Police: Did you (fight back with anything / use any weapon)?
Foreigner: Yes. I used a (bottle / knife / dagger / club / rod / stick).
Police: You (injured him badly / caused a bad injury to him / inflicted a bad injury on him / seriously damaged the public facilities / undermined the public order).
Foreigner: So what?

Dialogue: At the Lost and Found Office
Police: Here is your wallet. Please sign your name of the Report on Lost Article.
Foreigner: All right. It's really incredible! A lost wallet can be recovered. Only in Beijing can this be possible!

SPORTS & FITNESS

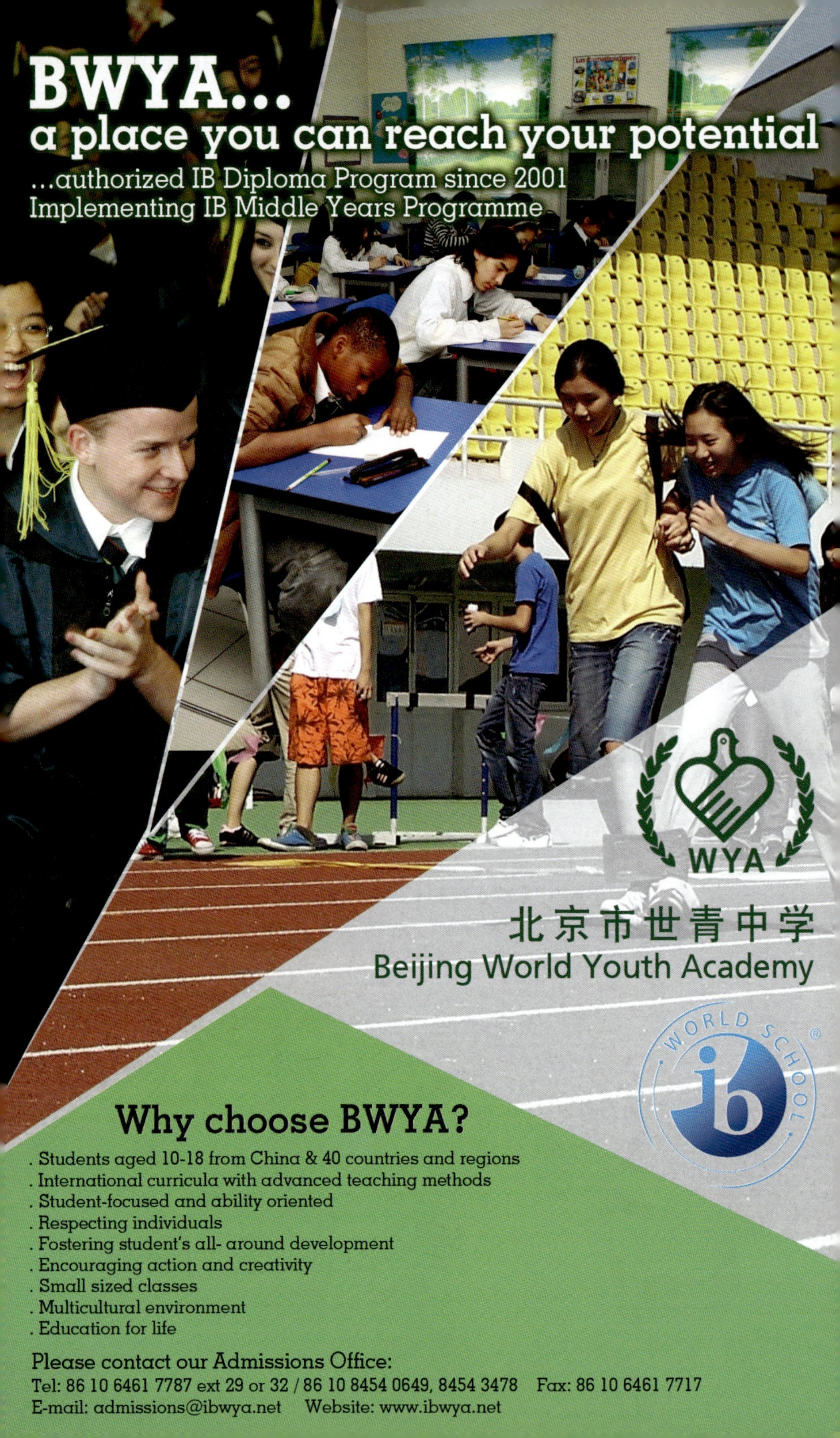

BWYA...
a place you can reach your potential
...authorized IB Diploma Program since 2001
Implementing IB Middle Years Programme

北京市世青中学
Beijing World Youth Academy

Why choose BWYA?

. Students aged 10-18 from China & 40 countries and regions
. International curricula with advanced teaching methods
. Student-focused and ability oriented
. Respecting individuals
. Fostering student's all- around development
. Encouraging action and creativity
. Small sized classes
. Multicultural environment
. Education for life

Please contact our Admissions Office:
Tel: 86 10 6461 7787 ext 29 or 32 / 86 10 8454 0649, 8454 3478   Fax: 86 10 6461 7717
E-mail: admissions@ibwya.net   Website: www.ibwya.net

HEALTH & BEAUTY

PHOTO: JANEK ZDZARSKI JR

(Promotion)

Emergency Medical Services Available in Beijing

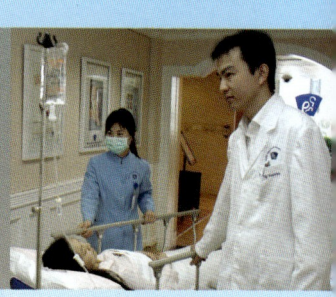

Whether at home, on the street, or in a restaurant, an emergency can happen when you least expect it. Knowing how to respond and being familiar with locally available emergency services and how to access them has been proven to greatly improve the outcome of an emergency situation.

Access to Care

As an expatriate in China, the emergency response network here may differ from that of your home country. Beijing United Family Hospital and Clinics (BJU), an international standard facility accredited by the Joint Commission International, offers emergency medical services that are available 24 hours a day, 7 days a week.

BJU has partnerships with the national 120 and local 999 ambulance services. If called directly, operators at these numbers may speak only Chinese. By calling BJU's emergency hotline, you are put directly in touch with trained emergency medical staff who speak fluent English. They can give you emergency advice and if you need, dispatch an ambulance to you.

When you arrive at the Emergency Room (ER) at BJU, you will be treated by experienced emergency physicians and nurses who speak fluent English and who offer the most up-to-date, international standard level of care available. A 24-hour translation service is available for patients needing assistance beyond English and Chinese.

Since BJU is a full-service hospital, patients coming to the ER can be admitted directly into the hospital for further treatment if necessary. In-house specialists, including a pediatrician, obstetrician, and surgeon are available 24 hours a day. Imaging, laboratory, and pharmacy services as well as hospital operating rooms, an Intensive Care Unit, and a supply of triple-tested blood are also available 24 hours a day.

An Ounce of Prevention

It is said that an ounce of prevention is worth a pound of cure. While living and traveling in China, you may be exposed to preventable diseases or encounter new health challenges. To avoid emergencies, it is recommended to follow a routine of regular health check ups and to keep your vaccinations current. BJU offers routine medical services as well as vaccination and travel medicine counseling.

Being Prepared

Since you never know when an emergency may arise, it's always good to be prepared. The minutes before trained help takes over can be crucial. To teach your family and those close to you how to better react in an emergency, BJU offers First Aid and CPR training courses for you, your driver, and your ayi. These courses, given in Chinese and English, teach how to respond in an emergency and how to start emergency care for infants, children, and adults.

BJU Emergency Hotline:
+86 (10) 6433 2345

For appointments:
+86 (10) 6433 3960

An Apple a Day
Still seeing the doctor anyway
by Eileen Ho and Amy Xue

The list of potential health hazards in Beijing can run as long as the lines in the city's busiest emergency rooms. From sanitation to smoking, the anxiety over health alone might be enough to send you running for the doctor. Whether it's polluted air, a case of the sniffles, or the general stresses of urban living, you can only handle so much on your own before it's time for professional help.

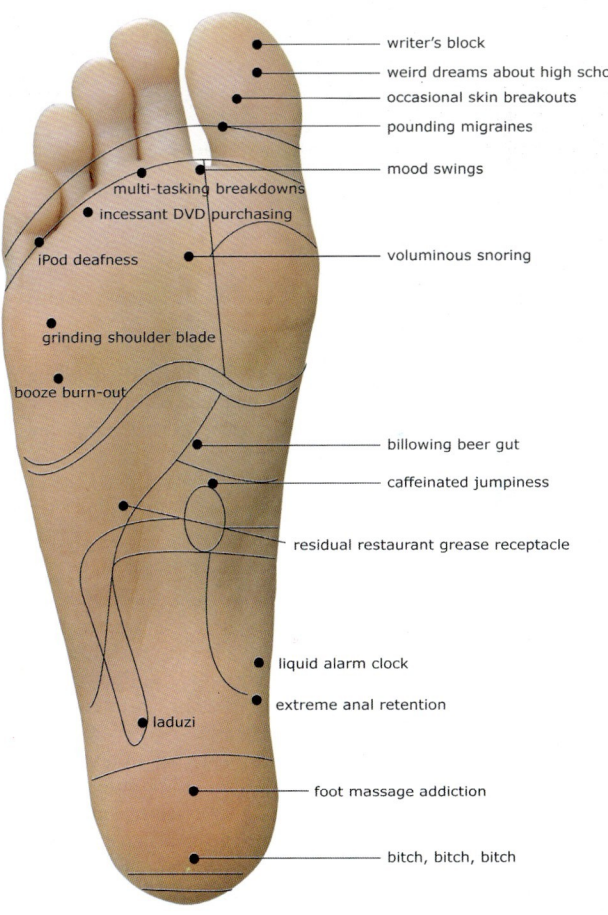

Pressure points: an illustrated diagram

Dealing with Beijing's health hazards can be frustrating, but it doesn't have to be painful

Luckily, medical services in Beijing are constantly improving and expanding, and many clinics and hospitals have been providing an international standard of care for years now. Furthermore, between Western and traditional Chinese medical practitioners, public and private hospitals, you have a wide range of options.

Armed and ready

Getting caught unprepared might make the emergency room seem like a war zone, but you don't have to stumble blindly into the ambush. The first step to protecting your physical (and financial) health here is to take preemptive measures. Scout out and secure a good health insurance plan, because it won't be cheap to get healthcare in Beijing at a standard that you would be used to back home (see "Got You Covered" p470). Preparedness for medical emergencies is critical. Despite a new law banning the practice, some international clinics and hospitals may be unwilling to treat a patient until they have assurance that the patient can afford treatment. Therefore, make sure to have your insurance card on you at all times and/or a valid credit card or access to an emergency cash supply. Make a detailed study of your insurance plan to see what it covers, because a night's stay in a private medical facility can cost upwards of RMB 10,000 – if you're not insured, you might wake up the next morning to an enormous bill. Keep all medical records in a safe and easy-to-reach place. If you have complicated medical needs, consider having special requirements or information translated into Chinese. We've compiled an emergency card (p487) for you to photocopy and fill out in both English and Chinese. Carry the card and a copy of your passport at all times, and stand alert, soldier!

Public or private?

To select your primary healthcare center, look through the list of international standard hospitals and clinics in this chapter's Medical Directory (p476). Both Beijing's top public and private

PHOTO: JANEK ZDZARSKI JR

A spoonful of sugar makes the medicine go down

hospitals offer Western-standard care, but these luxuries also come with Western prices. The VIP wings at public hospitals, with many foreign-trained doctors and cheaper fees, can sometimes rival private hospitals. In fact, the same doctors sometimes work at both a pricey private hospital and a major public one. However, you can expect to pay in more waiting time, inconvenience and language difficulties at the public hospitals. Still, some have specialists who are the best in their fields, and you may be referred to one of them anyway for conditions that cannot be treated in a private hospital or even for ongoing hospitalization or operations.

Relax!

Blood supply in Beijing is now up to international standards, and cases of tainted blood are virtually unheard of. However, because most Chinese genetically do not have Rhesus negative blood, these blood types may not be found in the blood bank, while about 15% of Caucasians have Rh-negative blood. If you have a negative Rh factor, contact your hospital to ensure that you can get blood when you need it.

Though this section focuses on maintaining your physical health, don't forget to take care of your mental health, too. Newcomers often find it stressful to adjust to a city like Beijing, which can cause problems that are best alleviated when out in the open. Instead of suffering alone, seek out a professional (p480) or check out the variety of support groups available (p644). They're here for you!

For a quick cure to a less serious bout of depression, ease away the stress (and its tell-tale signs) at Beijing's bountiful beauty parlors, spas and massage salons (pp490-501). You can get pampered and prettified on any budget here. And should an urgent situation arise – whether it's a dodgy post-*chuan'r* stomach or an emergency pre-date leg waxing – be sure to keep your Insider's Guide handy.

HEALTH & BEAUTY

Going Public
Embracing the local Chinese hospital
by Lee Ambrozy

Major public hospitals offer "VIP" wings, but don't expect them to roll out the red carpet

The crowded, bleak lobby of local hospitals can be downright scary when you're ill or injured. But the Chinese medical system, for all its flaws, is still relatively effective in providing low-cost medical care to enormous numbers of people. And the system can serve you, too, if you know how to approach it.

Choosing a hospital

Beijing's most reputable public hospitals, China-Japan Friendship Hospital and Peking Union Medical College Hospital (PUMCH), offer the most qualified physicians and most user-friendly organization. Here you can take advantage of "International VIP" departments, where you find cleaner, more "Western" facilities, English-speaking staff and guides to walk you through the steps. Most importantly, you avoid the grueling hours of queuing and over crowded waiting rooms. Even though the basic doctor's fees here are 20 times higher than those of the general ward (compare RMB 100-300 at Peking Union's VIP department to RMB 5), it's still less than half the price of a consultation in a Western hospital. But beware of "VIP" prices at smaller hospitals where the advantages are less obvious or even non-existent.

Getting care

When seeing a doctor at any hospital, VIP or otherwise, you'll first line up to get a number (*guahao*), indicating what department and level of doctor you wish to see. Physicians at Chinese hospitals are divided into three categories: doctors (*daifu*), professors (*jiaoshou*) and department heads (*zhuren*). Rest assured that almost every zhuren at major Beijing hospitals will have overseas training and an extensive vocabulary of English medical terms.

The first hospital experience can seem like a carnivalesque series of ticket windows: after lining up to take your number, waiting to see your doctor and then receiving your diagnosis scribbled on various slips of thin white paper, you'll proceed to the "price your treatment" (*huajia*) window to pay the total cost of blood tests, prescriptions, x-rays and other treatments. Then you'll take your little white slips, now adorned with red stamps indicating "paid in full," to a separate window to pick up your medicine (*quyao*), or to other departments for further testing or treatment. Sometimes even the results will need to be picked up personally before your next consultation. Treatments and medicines are generally on par with Western standards, and there are many imported pharmaceuticals available, especially at the larger hospitals. But be aware that your doctor might prescribe inexpensive medicines that could be less effective; always ask if you are suspicious. Most Chinese hospitals currently do not have direct billing with foreign insurance providers, but they will help fill out reimbursement forms. Upfront payment is the status quo, and major credit cards are accepted at most hospitals.

Seeing a doctor

The general approach to healing here is DIY, from prevention through lifestyle and nutrition (influenced by Chinese medicine) to the complicated process of seeing a doctor. You will find a different bedside manner: whereas Western doctors are expected to give detailed explanations of an illness and treatment options to a patient, Chinese doctors prescribe treatment like heavenly decrees and rarely offer you a choice of treatment plans. Options like psychiatric therapy, anti-depressants or anti-anxiety drugs won't be proactively offered, but they won't be denied either if you inquire. Despite the rise of psychological care services in China (see p480), mental disorders are still not institutionally considered as critical as physical ailments. Your doctor would be more likely to recommend you go home and get more "rest."

Your doctor may also seem more brusque, clinical and unconcerned. Doctors in China have seen plenty of cases much worse than yours, so don't expect a lot of sympathy. On the bright side, since Chinese physicians have ample practical experience treating enormous numbers of patients, they can quickly identify symptoms and have thoroughly tested various therapies. Nurses and other medical technicians are also highly practiced and skilled in their fields, able to administer injections, IVs, etc., quickly and painlessly.

Integrating Chinese medicine

An integrated Western-Chinese approach to healing is found in most hospitals, and while some exclusively dedicated to Chinese medicine, all hospitals will have a Chinese medicine (*zhongyi*) department or at least a few certified traditional healers on hand. Doctors here might refer you to alternative healers in acupuncture and herbs, and even physicians practicing Western medicine will often use prefabricated medicines derived from Chinese herbology. Treating the body as a complete organism with the use of slow and non-invasive treatments is a basic theory of *zhongyi* that has made a lasting impression on the modern medical system, as is a general "seven parts maintenance, three parts cure" approach to lifestyle and disease. Although facets of Western and Eastern medicine may sometimes appear conflicting, the complementary combination of the two has become increasingly recognized.

Whether trying the local medical system is an option or a necessity, becoming informed is the first step to a successful experience. With experienced physicians and the resources of both Western and Chinese medicine, they just might have what you need, whether you were expecting it or not.

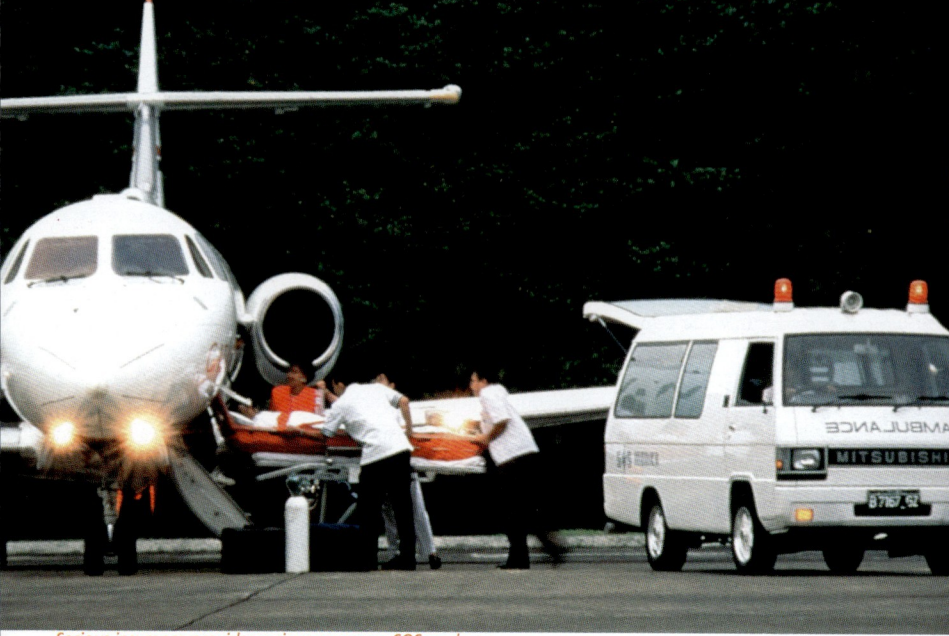

Serious insurance provides serious coverage: SOS medevac

Got You Covered
Pain relief for health insurance headaches
by Eric Abrahamsen and Amy Xue

Health insurance in Beijing is a tricky compromise between cost and coverage. Though it might seem like a gamble deciding if it's worth shelling out the money now to avoid hefty health expenses later, you can usually expect to get what you pay for. An international plan in hard currency (USD, GBP or EUR) with a USD 1.5 million overall annual lifetime limit is the recommended minimum, but it won't come cheap.

To keep your premiums (yearly fees) low, you might have to accept a high deductible. A USD 1,000 deductible means that you pay the first thousand dollars, and your insurance pays for everything beyond that for the rest of the year (deductibles "reset" every calendar year). If you don't go to the hospital that often, you can also save money in premiums with a higher co-pay – the percentage of every medical expense that you pay out of your own pocket. However, you shouldn't settle for a plan that puts low limits on nightly room rates or doctor consultation fees, as it's usually the inpatient bills at Western-style medical facilities that'll leave you bankrupt. For example, each night at Beijing United Family Hospital will cost you USD 825.

Other factors affecting insurance policy prices are coverage of regular check-ups, dental care, maternity and terrifying-sounding things like "repatriation of remains" (would you like to be buried in a Chinese cemetery?). No matter how much you spend on an individual healthcare policy, chances are it still won't reimburse teeth whitening, orthodontics, bone marrow transplants, dialysis and cosmetic surgery. The more bells and whistles you have in your policy (dental, vision, outpatient, etc.), the more administrative costs your insurance company will incur and inevitably pass on to you in ever-rising prices. Another reason behind those suspiciously increasing premiums is that they're weighted on age. Still, you shouldn't delay in getting insured. Most insurance companies refuse to cover pre-existing conditions (note that pregnancy counts as a pre-existing condition), so get your insurance before you get sick (or pregnant). Post-pregnancy, babies will need their own insurance after the first 30 or 40 days.

PHOTO: COURTESY OF INTERNATIONAL SOS

If you're from North America, additional coverage in your home country will cost a lot more. Consider obtaining limited geographical coverage if you only spend a few days at home each year. Those who are just visiting Beijing should purchase short-term travel insurance beforehand. If you sign up here, you'll automatically be stuck with a year of regular insurance. Students especially should take advantage of travel plans tailored to students' needs and budgets before leaving for China. Be careful with plans set up by regional offices in Asian countries where medical costs are cheaper, as they may not take into account the higher cost of Beijing joint-venture facilities. If you travel a lot, consider purchasing a medical evacuation package, just in case you get stuck in a remote part of China. International SOS, among others, provides this membership service for USD 187-385 per year. Other services, such as GlobalDoctor and MedEx, can be purchased back home through your insurance agents. These services have alarm centers in various cities throughout the world, and can answer your medical questions remotely, even patching you to doctors in other parts of the world if necessary.

If you do need to get insurance in Beijing, where do you go? Paige Mushinsky, an experienced healthcare consultant, says there's no master directory of insurance providers. "The best thing to do is to contact a health care institution in Beijing, and ask them for the names of some insurance brokers." Find out how long they've been in China and if they have financial security – you don't want to be the victim of a fly-by-night outfit that exists only long enough to snap up your first year's premiums. Don't be afraid to ask questions, and don't you dare skip the fine print!

A final reminder: Insurance companies are for-profit businesses. If you file a lot of claims, you won't win in the long run, since rates are adjusted annually. Pay for cheap TCM treatments or visits to your local clinics with cash, as the time and energy taken to process your claims will be more than it's worth for both you and the insurance provider. A plan that includes direct billing options with local hospitals and clinics will save you a lot of time and hassle, but be vigilant about claims made to your insurance company by the hospital to avoid possible overbilling. Should you have any suspicions or concerns, don't hesitate to communicate with your agent. For the price you're paying for health insurance, they'd better listen to you!

Benefits consultant Paige Mushinsky contributed to this article. Send her an email for more information: info@expatsolutions.com

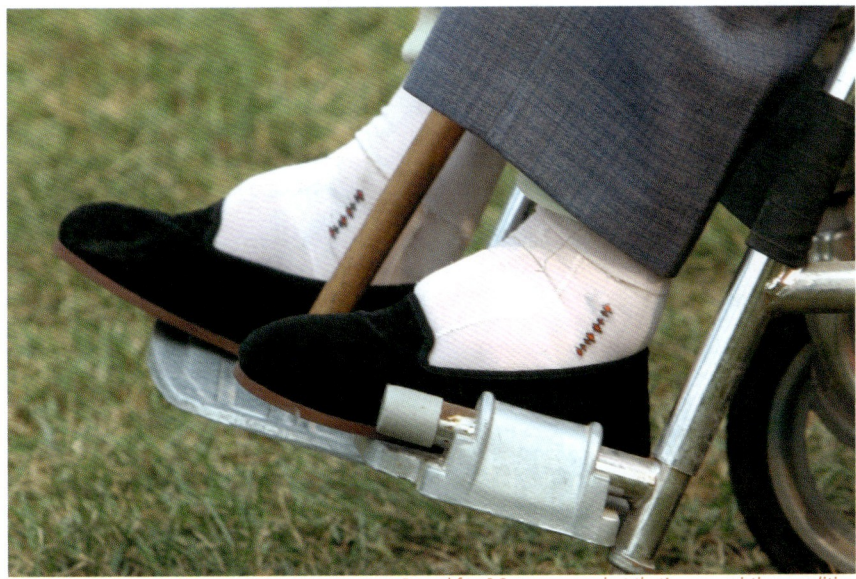

Bound feet? Sorry granny, but that's a pre-existing condition

HEALTH & BEAUTY

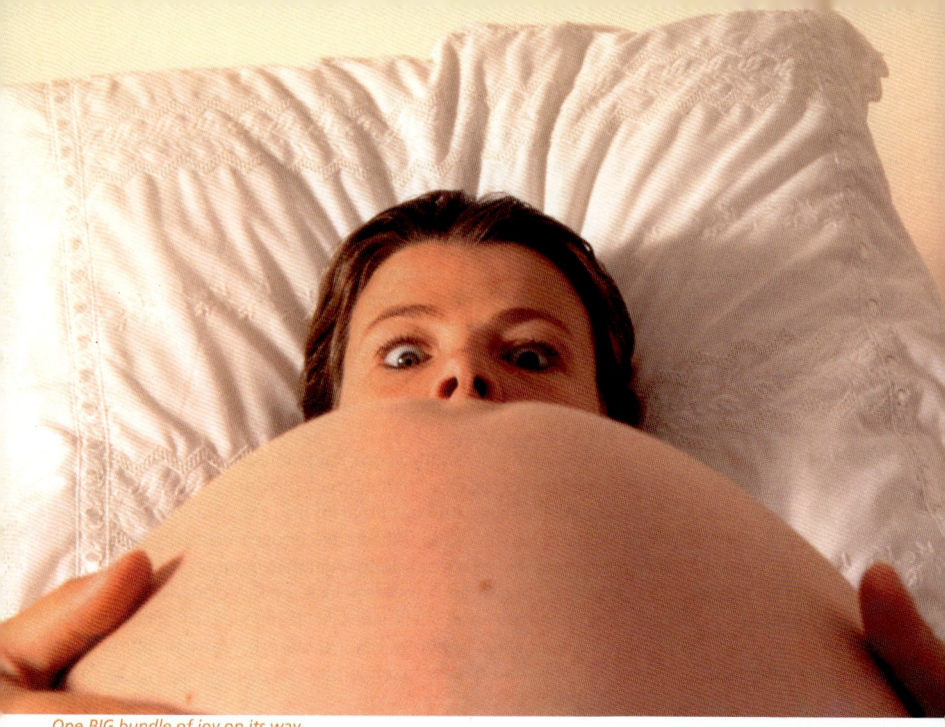

One BIG bundle of joy on its way

Special Deliveries
Giving birth in Beijing
by Eileen Ho

The question many expectant mothers ask themselves is: Should I stay or should I go? In many respects, having a baby in Beijing is just like having one at home. There is an array of hospitals that you can choose from, and the difference may just be your comfort level. When it comes to giving birth, the two hospitals preferred by expat and wealthy local expectant parents are the Beijing United Family Hospital & Clinics (BJU) and the Peking Union Medical College Hospital (PUMCH). American-Sino OB/GYN Service (ASOG) and China-Japan Friendship Hospital also have birthing units that match Western standards of care.

On the safety of having kids in Beijing, Dr. Evelyn Fang of BJU reassures us, "Giving birth in China at a reliable hospital is a safe thing to do, although some women still choose to go home because they feel safer there. Besides the healthcare issue, some women choose to go home because they have better support from their parents, in-laws and friends. Insurance is also a factor, since some expats do not have good enough insurance coverage here to afford higher quality hospital care." Some women decide to stay in Beijing during the prenatal period and go home for the actual delivery and postnatal recovery, but expectant mothers should note that airlines may not allow women over 36 weeks pregnant aboard their aircraft, and a physician's note may be required.

Cost is another factor to consider when deciding whether to give birth in Beijing. A birthing package at BJU can cost more than RMB 60,000 for a vaginal delivery and RMB 100,000 for a Caesarean. At PUMCH, births cost between RMB 10,000 and 20,000 depending on the type of delivery. In between these two popular options is ASOG, where a vaginal birth costs RMB 25,000 and a Caesarean costs RMB 45,000. If you have the money, Beijing's top hospitals have great post-delivery amenities. You can get clean private rooms with hotel-like service and plenty of

Postnatal yoga practitioners demonstrate the bridge and fist-in-mouth poses

recovery time (up to four days after a C-section). Staff will even teach you how to properly clean your baby's belly button to prevent infection.

If you think you might be at risk of a complicated pregnancy, the best option for peace of mind is probably going to either Hong Kong or home. Although Beijing hospitals are fine for normal births, they may not have neonatal intensive care units (NICU) that meet Western standards. A Beijing doctor points out, "One big issue all women should be aware of is that if a baby is born with problems and needs to be moved out of China, this is a very difficult issue – their insurance may not cover this. There is only one NICU retrieval team in the region in Singapore and they are not always available. The baby also needs a passport and visa in order to leave the country, which there may not be time to do." However, that is not to say that all complicated births are impossible for Beijing hospitals to handle. Lisa Liu, who had planned to have her baby out of the country and then was forced to stay due to complications, stated, "I later had all the medical records from this time checked out by a well-known pediatrician in the US, who told me that it seemed that my baby got the same level of care as she would have received back in my home country."

Beijing does have extensive options for prenatal and postnatal care if you plan to stay here. From midwife home visits to breastfeeding support groups like La Leche (see p644), there are plenty of ways to stave away the postpartum blues. Beijing Vista Clinic offers intensive postnatal care services, including advice and counseling. Many hospitals and clinics organize prenatal and postnatal yoga classes for moms and babies, as do groups like Yoga Yard (see p439). BJU also runs weekly seminars to educate parents-to-be on how to take care of their newborns.

If you have an *ayi* or are planning to employ one after your child's birth, make sure she is aware of how you'd like your child to be taken care of in the event of an emergency. From experience, Rebecca Malzacher of International SOS recommends, "Take your *ayi* to the clinic or hospital of your choice to show her where exactly you want your kid to be taken in case you're not around." Several private clinics offer *ayi* emergency training courses, which may put your mind at ease while you're gone during the day. For more information on raising kids in Beijing, check out the Kids chapter (p117).

HEALTH & BEAUTY

Spotting Roots from Dragon Eyes

A few Chinese medicinal foods — and recipes to boot!
by Lee Ambrozy

Is this edible?!

What's floating in those steaming pots of porridge at the 24 hour *zhou* restaurant? What makes them "blood cleansing" or "liver nourishing"? Perhaps you've been eyeing the section of your Chinese grocery store where unseen bagged goodies lie in clumps. Maybe you just want to know what the eight treasures in "Eight Treasures tea" are …

Whether you think it's all hogwash or a great pride of the East, Chinese medicinal foods crush McDonald's record of "more than 70 billion served" with countless served for more than 5,000 years. Regardless of their efficacy, the recipes for tea below are simple to prepare and enjoyable!

Jujubes (红枣) *hongzao*: "Chinese dates" are effective in treating symptoms of anemia, insomnia, and acid stomach. Useful for treating coughs, increasing urination, and improving stomach and spleen function. An added plus: jujubes make your cheeks red, smooth, and bright.

Lotus seeds (莲子) *lianzi*: These are white and oval shaped, and improve circulation, overall kidney and spleen health and are very useful in preventing signs of aging.

Lotus hearts (莲心) *lianxin*: Suppress liver inflammation, cure acne, soothe the nerves, increase urination and suppress thirst.

Lotus leaf (荷叶) *heye*: Relieves internal heat and diarrhea, and eliminates grease and fats in your digestive system. Common ingredient in diet teas.

Silver ear (白木耳, 银耳) *bai mu'er, yin'er*: This jelly fungus is used to prevent excessive bleeding, aid in hormone secretion and to prevent wrinkles. Legend has it, eating them will bring you eternal youth.

Chinese angelica (当归) *danggui*: Improves blood quality, regulates menses, coats the intestines, eases pain, stimulates urination, and soothes fetuses. Effectively a female "miracle" herb – especially effective in females with poor blood quality.

Dried orange peel (陈皮) *chenpi*: Aids in digestion, encourages the production of digestive fluids and eliminates fats in body.

Black sesame (芝麻) *zhima*: Good for treating constipation, brings a natural glow to the skin, and can prevent hair from turning white while giving it a healthy sheen.

Milk vetch root (黄芪) *huangqi*: Improves blood circulation, immune function, and replenishes low blood protein, often used in foods to give you rosy cheeks, and enrich the blood and nutrients in females.

Chinese wolfberry (枸杞) *gouqi*: A precious food for those seeking longevity, improves liver function, as well as coloration, and prevents kidney fatigue.

Angelica plant root (白芷) *baizhi*: Used for pain and swelling reduction, pus elimination, and stress headache alleviation.

Hangzhou chrysanthemum (杭菊) *hangju*: Reduces inflammation, improves clarity, lowers blood pressure, helps purge fats, eases diarrhea and improves abdominal functions.

Sweet licorice root (甘草) *gancao*: Improves the body's "essential *qi*," stops coughing, expels internal heat, clears toxins and clears up pimples. Low appetite or diarrhea can be treated with licorice root and ginseng.

Lily bulbs (百合) *baihe*: The warming lilium are high in nutrients, help stop coughs, improve the blood *qi*, urination, and soothe nerves.

Cassia seeds (决明子) *juemingzi*: Also known as "sickle senna seeds," they help eliminate black circles around the eyes. Drinking cassia seed tea will help regulate digestive problems and dispel accumulated toxins.

Longan (桂圆) *guiyuan*: Also known as "dragon eyes" (*longyan*), this fruit unique to China nourishes the blood and prevents aging. Improves circulation and prevents cold extremities. Women with painful menstrual cycles can use it to prevent cramps and promote metabolism. Longan fruit, while tasty, is not easily digestible, so do not eat too much at once.

Safflower (红花) *hong hua*: Aids in the treatment of extravasated blood, stops pain, and regulates the female cycle. Useful in blood purification, it can relieve menstrual cramps due to stasis. Women with heavy periods or who are pregnant should consult their doctors before ingesting.

Hibiscus flower (洛神花) *luoshenhua*: Used as a tea for cooling, dispelling heat, increasing urination, and lowering the internal fires. Will calm internal heat and fire from eating oily and fried foods, improve your color, dispel fats and eliminate blemishes in the skin.

Chinese yam (山药) *shanyao*: Aids digestion, lowers blood pressure and slows artery hardening.

Slimming Tea
Hibiscus flower, 100g
Dried hawthorn, 25g
Licorice root, 5g
Rock sugar, to taste
Plunge all (except sugar) into 600mL of boiling water then simmer, covered, for 15 min. Add the rock sugar to taste. Also excellent as a cold tea.

Lemon Cassia Seed Tea
Cassia seeds, 15g
½ Lemon, dried or fresh
Put the washed lemon and seeds into 600mL of boiling water, cover and simmer for 5 minutes. Good for calming nerves, clarity, constipation and dispelling inner heat. Loaded with vitamin C.

Wolfberry and Ginseng Tea
Hangzhou chrysanthemum, 15g
Wolfberries, 15g
Ginseng beard, three strands
Wash everything in warm water first, then plunge in 600ml boiling water for ten minutes. Helps to replenish the "inner qi."

Nighttime Tea
Lotus heart, 2g
Licorice root, 3g
Boil in 600ml of water for 5 minutes and drink if you have a hard time falling asleep, or suffer from frazzled nerves.

Longan and Date Tea
Plunge equal parts of longan fruits and dates (about 8-10 of each) into 500ml boiling water and simmer for 15 min. Good for poor blood quality, and has beautifying qualities!

Huangqi and Wolfberry Tea
Boil about 10 *huangqi* chips and 10g wolfberries together for 20 minutes in 600ml water. This tea prevents aging, improves color and boosts the immune system.

"Silver Ear" Soup
Silver ears, 1 big handful, presoaked for 30min and hard edges cut away
Wolfberries, 8g
Milk vetch root, about 10 dried chips
Dates, 8-10
Ginger, 1-2 slices, fresh or dried
Rock sugar, to taste
Plunge all into boiling water and let simmer for 30 minutes, until the silver ears are slightly crispy. Add rock sugar and let dissolve. Served hot or cold, this is a low-fat and satisfyingly sweet "soup."

A good laugh is sometimes the best medicine

Medical Directory
Public Medical Services

Most major hospitals will have some English-speaking staff members and on-site pharmacies with Western as well as Chinese medicine. Registration fees in the general hospitals are low, but the wait might make it worth paying more for the VIP wings. You might also find scalpers in the normal wards selling registration numbers for RMB 100-800 more than the original price, especially for popular departments.

Amcare Women's and Children's Hospital This hospital near the Lido provides services in obstetrics, gynecology, pediatrics, childhood development, family planning, ultrasound and radiology. Also offers out-call, evening outpatient and car services. Houses 36 home-style private suites, several operation and delivery rooms, recreation center and gym. 18 doctors on staff, 7 full-time. No registration fee. Consultation fee depends on level of doctor: RMB 100 (physicians), 200 (specialists), 300 (professors). Doctors do not speak fluent English, but an accompanying Portuguese nurse provides language support. Accepts cash, check or credit card and has direct billing with some international health care insurers. *Clinic hours Mon-Sat 8-11.30am, 1-4.30pm. 9 Fangyuan Xilu, Chaoyang District. (6434 2399, English 6434 2388 ext 8157, 24-hour consultation and appointment hotline 800 610 6200) www.amcare.com.cn* 美中宜和妇儿医院，朝阳区芳园西路9号

Beijing Children's Hospital Has some English-speaking doctors with overseas training. Registration fee range: RMB 2-300. No direct billing, but cash and credit cards are accepted for regular check-ups and medicine. Checks accepted only from inpatients. *Clinic hours daily 8am-4.30pm. 56 Nanlishi Lu, Xicheng District. (6802 8401)* 北京儿童医院，西城区南礼士路56号

Beijing Friendship Hospital This general hospital specializes in infection first aid and organ transplantation and includes a VIP wing and a recently added building. Registration fee RMB 5-14; RMB 70-200 for VIP. Accepts cash and credit card, with direct billing from some insurers. *Clinic hours Mon-Fri 8am-noon and 1-4pm, Sat-Sun 8am-noon. 24-hour emergency care. 95 Yong'an Lu, Xuanwu District. (6301 4411) 6313 8325* 北京友谊医院，宣武区永安路95号

China-Japan Friendship Hospital A state-run hospital with a pleasant foreigners' wing. Medical staff speak

476 INSIDER'S GUIDE TO BEIJING

English, but don't always have overseas training. Services include general check-ups, internal medicine, pediatric, orthopedics and ENT. Specialist services, such as TCM and dental, may require an appointment. Registration RMB 100; pay by cash or credit card. Inpatient services require a minimum RMB 10,000 deposit. 80 beds set aside for foreigners. Blood comes directly from China Central Blood Bank. Direct billing with over 40 foreign insurance companies.
Clinic hours Mon-Fri 8am-11.30am and 1-4pm, Sat 8am-11.30am, 24-hour emergency care. Yinghua Dongjie, Hepingli, Hepingjie Beikou, Chaoyang District. (6422 2952 or 6422 3209) www.zryhyy.com.cn 中日友好医院, 朝阳区和平里北口和平里樱花东街

Haidian Hospital Cheap and conveniently located for university students, this general hospital specializes in internal medicine and neurosurgery. Registration fee RMB 2.5-13; cash only.
Clinic hours Mon-Fri 7.30-11.30am and 1-4.30pm, Sat-Sun 7.30-11.30am, 24-hour emergency care. 29 Guancun Dajie, Haidian District. (6258 3042, emergency 6258 3093) www.hdhospital.com 北京市海淀区中关村大街29号

New Century International Children's Hospital This joint-venture institution affiliated with the Beijing Children's Hospital features an English-speaking medical staff (some from the U.S. and Europe), 15-minute minimum clinic visits, playgrounds, and daily entertainment with clowns and musicians. Also has pediatric eye care and dental programs. Consultation fee depends on child's age and condition (on average RMB 800), payable by cash or credit card. Deductible and co-insurance waived for members of the Panda Club, available for patients with insurance companies that have a direct billing relationship.
Clinic hours Mon-Fri 8am-5pm, daily 24-hour pediatric emergency care. 56 Nanlishi Lu, Xicheng District. (6802 5588) www.ncich.com.cn 新世纪国际儿童医院, 西城区南礼士路56号

Peking Union Medical College Hospital This state-run hospital has a reputable foreigners' wing (50-bed capacity) with departments including ENT, internal medicine, pediatrics, surgery, dental, ophthalmology and OBGYN. Most doctors are trained overseas and speak good English. Services and medicine are much cheaper than in private clinics, but expect longer waiting times. The birthing unit is considered to be the best among Beijing's Chinese hospitals and is popular among expats. TCM specialists in massage and acupuncture available daily. Blood is supplied from an in-house bank stocked with blood donated by volunteers and hospital staff members. The cost of registration is RMB 100, 200, or 300, depending on the status of the doctor: physician, assistant professor or university professor. Cash or credit card, with direct billing available with some insurance companies. Private rooms cost RMB 800-1,500 per day.
Clinic hours Mon-Fri 8am-4.30pm, 24-hour emergency care. 1 Shuaifuyuan, Wangfujing (the foreigners' wing is located south of the in-patient building), Dongcheng District. (6529 5284) www.pumch.ac.cn 北京协和医院, 东城区王府井帅府园1号（外国人就诊楼在门诊楼的南侧）

Peking University Third Hospital Hospital affiliated with Peking University includes 22 clinical departments and 945 beds. Specialty departments include gynecology and obstetrics, sports medicine, cardiovascular, orthopedic, in-vitro fertilization and reconstructive surgery. Also includes departments such as ENT, eye care, dentistry and TCM. On-site blood bank. Consultation with medical experts and professors, from RMB 5-200. Cash only.
Clinic hours Mon-Fri 8-noon and 1.30-5pm, Sat 8-11am, 24-hour emergency care. 49 Huayuan Beilu, Haidian District. (6201 7691, 6209 1230) 北医三院, 海淀区花园北路49号

Tongren Hospital Comprehensive state-run hospital with one of China's best optical departments, a popular place to get lenses. Also specializes in diabetes and psychology and has TCM, ENT, orthopedic, cardiovascular and cosmetic surgery departments. Some doctors speak English. Registration fee RMB 220, cash only.
Clinic hours Mon-Fri 8am-noon and 1-5pm, Sat-Sun 8am-noon. 24-hour emergency care. 2 Chongwenmennei Dajie, Dongcheng District. (5826 9911) www.trhos.com 同仁医院, 东城区崇文门内大街2号

Xuanwu Hospital Pain Treatment Center High-quality imported imaging and electrophysiology technology. English-speaking doctors treat every kind of pain. Specializes in neurology, general surgery, and blood and medical imaging, but also has 24 clinical departments of traditional Chinese and Western medicine. Registration fee RMB 4.5-14.
Clinic hours Mon-Fri 8am-noon and 1-5pm, Sat-Sun 8am-noon. 45 Changchun Jie, Xuanwu District. (8319 8899) www.xwhosp.com.cn 宣武医院疼痛诊疗中心, 宣武区长椿街45号

Private Medical Services

American-Sino OB/GYN Service This US-based hospital provides a range of gynecological services and OB care packages, as well as prenatal classes, including prenatal yoga in Chinese only (RMB 400 per class). Auxiliary services provided by the hospital include fertility consultation and treatment, and counseling for pre-teens and adolescents. No registration fee. Consultation fee RMB 500, second time RMB 300 for gynecologist. RMB 25,000 for a natural delivery with 2 nights and 3 days, RMB 45,000 for a C-section with 3 nights and 4 days. Additional nights cost RMB 2,500 each. VIP membership available. Make prior arrangements for direct billing.
Daily 24 hours. 218 Xiaoguan Beili, Andingmenwai, Chaoyang District. (6496 8888/5151) www.asog-beijing.com 美华妇产, 朝阳区安定门外小关北里218号

Bayley & Jackson Medical Center Located in a Chinese courtyard by Ritan Park, Bayley & Jackson provides comprehensive medical and dental healthcare services with experienced international clinicians. Services cover: family medicine, internal medicine, OB/GYN, dentistry, orthodontics, ophthalmology, optometry, psychological counseling, nutrition and dietary advice, general surgery and specialist clinics. Includes on-site laboratory, pharmacy and digitized imaging facilities. Direct billing available with major worldwide insurance providers. No registration fee. Consultation fee RMB 500 for GP, RMB 1000 for specialists, RMB 456 for dental.
Clinic and dental hours Mon-Fri 8am-6pm, Sat 8am-4pm, doctor on 24-hour call. 7 Ritan Donglu, Chaoyang District. (8562 9998, emergency 8562 9990, dental 8561 9296) www.bjhealthcare.com 庇利积臣医疗中心, 朝阳区日坛东路7号

Beijing International SOS Clinic International-standard clinic providing a full spectrum of medical services

HEALTH & BEAUTY

including 24-hour emergency ward, ambulance, family medicine, pediatrics, dentistry, orthodontics, OB/GYN, prenatal care, ENT, optometry, orthopedics, vaccinations, counseling, TCM and occupational and physical therapy. Expatriate and internationally trained doctors. On-site X-ray and laboratory services. Pharmacy stocks international-standard medications, including over-the-counter drugs. Languages spoken include English, Mandarin, Cantonese, French, German, Japanese, Italian, Spanish, Mongolian, Dutch, and Korean. House or hotel calls available. First-aid training and health screening services for ayis and drivers. Direct billing with all major insurers. No registration fee. Consultations cost RMB 1,010 for non-members and RMB 768 for members. Student price is RMB 606 for non-members and RMB 525 for members. Membership packages include additional services and benefits.
Daily 24 hours. Bldg C, BITIC Jingyi Building, 5 Sanlitun Xiwujie, Chaoyang District. (6462 9112, 24 hours 6462 9100). www.internationalsos.com 北京国际SOS诊所，朝阳区三里屯西五街5号北信京谊大厦C座

Beijing United Family Hospital and Clinics The only hospital in Beijing accredited as an international-standard medical provider by the JCI (Joint Commission International). Focuses on providing comprehensive and integrated quality medical services for both expatriate and local communities. Staffed by a team of over 60 internationally trained and certified physicians, surgeons and dentists, and supported by a multilingual team of nurses, technicians and support staff. Telephone translation service in over 40 additional languages. 24-hour emergency room and ICU are staffed by international emergency specialists. Clinics include pediatrics, OB/GYN, dental, ophthalmology, family counseling, ENT, physiotherapy, TCM, chiropractics and dermatology. The first choice for many expatriates giving birth in China and referral choice for other hospitals without in-house birthing units. Well-stocked pharmacy and on-site independent blood bank. Offers lectures on physical and mental health, first aid training for ayis and drivers, prenatal classes and more. Consultations cost around RMB 900, emergency service around RMB 1,500. Direct billing available with a range of insurance companies.
Clinic hours Daily 8.30am-5.30pm, 24-hour emergency care. 2 Jiangtai Lu, Lido area, Chaoyang District. (For appointment 6433 3960, emergency 6433 2345) www.unitedfamilyhospitals.com 北京和睦家医院，朝阳区将台路2号

Beijing United Family Clinic - Shunyi This satellite clinic of BUFH has been a vital part of the Shunyi community for over five years. It provides easily accessible, high-quality medical services and wellness promotion. Services include family medicine, family counseling, a pediatric clinic, and travel medicine.
Clinic hours Mon-Thu 7.30am-7.30pm, Fri 9.30am-4.30pm, Sat 9am-4pm. Unit 818, Pinnacle Plaza, Tianzhu Real Estate Development Zone, Shunyi District. (8046 5432, emergency 6433 2345) www.unitedfamilyhospitals.com 北京和睦家诊所，顺义区天竺房地产开发区荣祥广场818号

Beijing United Family Health & Wellness Center - Jianguomen Offers family medicine, counseling services, stress management, radiology, health screening (official immigration check-ups for many embassies), dental and laboratory services.
Clinic hours Mon-Fri 8.30am-5pm. B1/F, St. Regis Hotel, 21 Jianguomenwai Dajie, Chaoyang District.

(8532 1221, emergency 6433 2345) www.unitedfamilyhospitals.com 北京和睦家建国门保健中心，朝阳区建国门外大街21号国际俱乐部饭店地下一层

Beijing Vista Clinic – Kerry Center Multilingual doctors in family medicine, OB/GYN, pediatrics, dentistry, orthodontics, psychology, psychiatry, TCM, acupuncture, and sports medicine. On-site pharmacy, laboratory, and imaging. Specialist services include cardiology, dermatology, ENT, gastroenterology, hematology, immunology, neurology, ophthalmology and orthopedics. Observation rooms available for people with acute problems who don't need to be hospitalized (stays for up to three days). Prenatal services and intensive postnatal care with infant health check-ups and counseling/support services for new parents. House calls available. Japanese, Korean and English-speaking staff on site and available via phone 24 hours. Community work includes first-aid training, health checks and educational activities in kindergartens and schools. Direct billing with some international insurers. Free telephone consultation. Consultation fee RMB 660.
Daily 7.30am-6pm. 24-hour emergency care. B29, Kerry Center, 1 Guanghua Lu, Chaoyang District. (8529 6618) www.vista-china.net 北京维士达嘉里中心诊所，朝阳区光华路1号嘉里中心B29号

Hong Kong International Medical Clinic This joint-venture clinic offers a range of high-standard medical services including general medicine, OB/GYN, pediatrics, ENT, dermatology, dentistry, ophthalmology and physical exams for immigration. The pharmacy stocks Western and TCM medicine. House and hotel visits available. The 24-hour helpline provides support in English, Chinese and Japanese. Other languages available on request. Direct billing with 20 international insurance companies and 31 Japanese insurance companies. Basic consultation (including registration) fee is RMB 400. An additional RMB 300 if a specialist is called in.
Clinic hours daily 9am-9pm. 24-hour emergency care. 9/F, Office tower of the Swissotel, 2 Chaoyangmen Beidajie, Chaoyang District. (6501 4260, 6553 2288 ext 2346) www.hkclinic.com 香港国际医疗诊所，朝阳区朝阳门北大街2号港澳中心办公楼9层

International Medical Center (IMC) Foreign doctors on-site 24 hours daily, offering a wide range of services, including family medicine, dentistry, pediatrics, TCM, internal medicine, dermatology, psychological counseling, OB/GYN and minor surgery. All medical, nursing and administrative staff generally conduct services in English, but Chinese, Japanese and Arabic are also spoken. Drop-in service for travelers. On-site pharmacy, full laboratory, ultrasound, cardiac examination and dental surgery rooms. Additional benefits with paid membership plan. Direct billing available with credit card guarantee. Offers assistance with reimbursement forms. No registration fee. Consultation fee USD 60-120.
Daily 24 hours. S106, 1/F, Lufthansa Center, 50 Liangmaqiao Lu, Chaoyang District. (6465 1561/2/3, dental 6465 1384/94/28) www.imcclinics.com 国际医疗中心，朝阳区亮马桥路50号燕莎中心1层S106

Pharmacies & Medical Supplies
(See Shopping p408)

Treat Yourself to Thailand
Medical tourism: mixing work and play
by Eileen Ho and Amy Xue

Medical tourism may have originated thousands of years ago with Mediterranean pilgrims, but it is now an increasingly popular industry in developing areas such as Southeast Asia. Cheap, speedy medical services bundled with tourist attractions in exotic locales offer an appealing package to many who are frustrated with high costs, long waits, inadequate insurance coverage or lack of health care options. Although Beijing's public hospitals reputedly have China's best doctors (richly experienced from the sheer number of patients they treat), language barriers and waiting time could be deterrents to undergoing a major operation here. The high prices of Beijing's private hospitals and clinics might also be enough to send patients flying out of the country.

In fact, some expats are choosing to fly to Hong Kong or Thailand to get either routine check-ups or major work done. Hong Kong is closer, but Thailand is cheaper, and what better place for a relaxing recovery than a tropical

Tropical tree-tment in Thailand

beach? English is widely spoken there, and lower labor costs translate into significantly cheaper yet more personalized health care. An executive health check could be up to 75 percent cheaper than one you would get here. Popular expat hospitals in Bangkok include Bumrungrad International and the oddly named Bangkok Nursing Home. Bumrungrad boasts over 200 US board-certified Thai doctors and was the first Asian hospital to receive accreditation from the Joint Commission International (JCI), a branch of the US non-profit that reviews American hospitals and certifies Medicare and Medicaid centers. All 12 of Hong Kong's private hospitals are accredited by the UK equivalent, the Trent International Accreditation Scheme, and some have obtained dual international accreditation. When asked whether or not the trip is worth it, Dr. Evelyn Fang of Beijing United Family Hospital warned, "If your goal is simply to get a lot of tests done, those destinations are as good as any. However, since most doctors who see you for such 'check-ups' may never see you again, they will not tell you about your preventive healthcare needs. Also, any time you do tests you do not need, you are risking having false-positive tests and having to do even more tests to make sure that the previous test result was just a false alarm." Furthermore, should anything go seriously wrong, patients may not be able to seek compensation through malpractice lawsuits.

So it might be safer to stick with a primary care doctor here who knows your medical history. Still, going to Hong Kong or Thailand can save you major moola even after the additional travel expenses. So check out a travel agency offering medical tourism deals if you really want it all – sun, sand, surf and surgery.

Bangkok Nursing Home Hospital www.bnhhospital.com +662 686 2700
Beijing representative office: 6/F, W2, Oriental Plaza, 1 Dongchang'an Jie, Dong Cheng District. (8520 0442)

Bumrungrad International www.bumrungrad.com +66 (0) 2667 1000

HEALTH & BEAUTY

Heart and Soul
Holistic healing beyond the body
by Ashleigh Braggs

Seek help if you see signs of danger

Whether it's the waiter who can't understand your tones or the business meeting that just won't cut to the point – at some point, all of us have questioned the mental soundness of our decision to continue living here. Thankfully, the understanding and sympathy of friends or family can lend us the emotional fortitude to plunge ahead.

However, we can't always expect our traditional support network to shoulder all our burdens, which may include depression, anxiety, adjustment issues, marital discord, or child behavior problems. But at what point does one seek out a professional? "When it starts to interfere with functioning at work or school relationships," says Rob Blinn, a clinical psychologist at Beijing United Family Hospital. "If you're angry all the time, crying, anxious or can't settle down, then it's probably time to come in." Vista Clinic psychiatrist Mickie Xu adds that emotional problems can also manifest themselves through physical ailments, such as fatigue or headaches. If a physician can't diagnose the problem, it may be time to seek out psychological counseling.

Finding a therapist who speaks the same language you do – both literally and figuratively – is the first step. Services in English and other foreign languages are available throughout the city. Mickie Xu, who speaks English, Chinese, and Japanese, is also skilled in counseling mixed nationality couples. Another area where counselor and patient might need to find common ground is spiritual belief. The members of Beijing International Christian Fellowship (BICF) Counseling Center are all Christians (and foreign passport holders), which can be beneficial for those also dealing with religious identity issues. However, the BICF Counseling Center feels that its role is to help all people, not just believers. "We're professionals," says clinical psychologist Stephen-Claude Hyatt. "We respect the relationship between theology and psychology. If clients want to combine the two, then great; but if they don't … we help any person needing support." While expatriate hospitals charge well over USD 100 per hour, the center emphasizes that finances should not be a barrier to getting help. Their counselors' fees are reasonable and take individual situations into consideration. In addition to the 10 professionals on staff, the center also has about 12 trained peer counselors who take cases on a voluntary basis.

Although confidentiality should be a given, some counselors make additional efforts to ensure their patients' privacy. Xu accommodates patients who ask her not to take notes, and Hyatt uses alternate venues to meet patients who do not want to be seen at the BICF Counseling Center. While these extra measures can make patients feel more secure about confiding their personal issues, it may take a couple of sessions to get comfortable. On finding the right therapist for you, counselors agree that it all boils down to personal rapport. Hyatt says not to be afraid of hurting the therapist's feelings if you eventually want to switch and try someone else: "The most important thing is to go."

Doctor knows (and smells) best

Specialist Services

Beijing Emergency Medical Center With a modern medical aid command center, 75 first-aid stations, hundreds of ambulances and an interactive system of professional medical staff, Beijing EMC switched in 2005 from in-hospital medical treatment to out-hospital first-aid, assuming the command of emergency phone number 120. Provides medical guarantee services for major political, cultural and sports events in Beijing, including the 2008 Olympic and Paralympic Games. *103 Qianmen Xidajie, Xuanwu District. (6609 8114) www.beijing120.com* 北京市急救中心，宣武区前门西大街103号

BICF Counseling Center A service provided by the Beijing International Christian Fellowship (BICF). Professional or peer counseling is available to any person with a need in their life. Services available in English, Mandarin and Cantonese. Also offers regular counseling skills training, as well as courses and seminars focusing on relational, psychological, emotional or spiritual issues. *Golden Land Building, Rm 32, 13/F, Liangmaqiao Lu, Chaoyang District. (6467 2362 ext 12) www.bicf. org/counsellingcenter.cfm* 朝阳区亮马桥路32号高澜大厦1325室

Beijing Suicide Research and Prevention Center Specializes in suicide prevention and in treating depression. Only Chinese spoken. *1) Mon-Fri 8.30-11.30am, 12.30-4pm. Inside Huilongguan Hospital, Changping District. (6271 6497, 6271 2221, 24-hour crisis hotline in Chinese 800 810 1117); 2) Mon-Sat 8am-4pm. 1 Yuetan Nanjie (opposite the Children's Hospital), Xicheng District. (6804 9865) www.crisis.org.cn* 北京心理危机研究与干预中心，西城区月坛南街1号（儿童医院对面）

Dentists

In addition to the dental listings below, major medical providers also have special dental care facilities.

Arrail Dental Clinic Offers the full spectrum of non-surgical dentistry with about 200 professionals. All dentists speak English, and some have overseas training. The CITIC branch specializes in cosmetic dentistry and the Exchange branch specializes in implants. First time registration fee (including check-up and consultation) RMB 100. *1) Mon-Thu 9am-8pm, Fri-Sun 9am-5pm. Rm 208, CITIC Bldg, 19 Jianguomenwai Dajie, Chaoyang District. (6500 6473); 2) Mon-Thu 9am-6pm, Fri-Sun 9am-5pm. Rm 201,The Exchange-Beijing, B118 Jianguo Lu, Chaoyang District. (6567 5670); 3) Mon-Thu 9am-6pm, Fri-Sun 9am-5pm. 1/F, Somerset Fortune Garden, 46 Liangmaqiao Lu, Chaoyang District. (8440 1926/7/8); 4) Mon-Thu 9am-6pm, Fri-Sun 9am-5pm. Rm 308, Tower A, Raycom Infotech Park, 2 Kexueyuan Nanlu, Haidian District. (8286 1956, 24 hours 139 1100 1367) www. arrail-dental.com* 瑞尔齿科，1）朝阳区建国门外大街19号国际大厦208室；2）朝阳区建国路乙118号京汇大厦201室；3）朝阳区亮马桥路46号福景苑1层；4）海淀区科学院南路2号融科信息园A座308室

Beijing United Family Dental Orthodontics & Implant Center Provides comprehensive dental services for whole family including cleaning, crowns, bridges, dental implants, fillings, tooth whitening and more. *Daily 8:30am-5:30pm. 2 Jiangtai Lu, Lido area, Chaoyang District. (6433 3960 or 8532 1221)* 中国北京朝阳区将台路2号

Elite Dental Clinic Has a top-level dental implant and prosthetics team, with German-standard equipment and quality control. Dr. Arnulf-Reimar Metzmacher specializes in dental aesthetic restoration and implant

prosthetics. Multilingual service includes English, German, and French. Basic consultation RMB 100. No first-time registration fee.
Mon-Sat 9am-5pm. Rm 206, Bldg 2, New Start Garden, 5 Changchunqiao Lu, Haidian District. (8256 2566, 136 9149 0559) www.bjelitedental.com 北京精质牙科诊所, 海淀区长春桥路5号新起点家园2号楼206室

Joinway Dental Clinic Western-style services include preventive dental care, restorative treatments, cleaning, whitening, and orthodontics. Membership discounts and benefits. Free registration and consultation.
Daily 8am-6pm. 11D, Bldg D, Oriental Kenzo Plaza, 48 Dongzhimenwai Dajie, Dongcheng District. (8447 6092/93, English 132 6181 6708) www.dentalcn.com 久汇齿科, 东城区东直门外大街48号银座大厦D座11D

King's Dental Offers general, laser, cosmetic and pediatric dentistry, including crowns for baby teeth. Also has orthodontics and full mouth rehabilitation. Well-trained, experienced international medical team works with German equipment. First-time registration fee RMB 200.
Daily 9am-9pm. Shop 118, 1/F, Beijing Towercrest Plaza, 3 Maizidian Xilu, Chaoyang District. (8458 0388) www.kingsdental.com 京典口腔, 朝阳区麦子店西路3号北京新恒基国际大厦1层118号

SDM Dental Offers teeth cleaning, fillings, root canal treatment, tooth replacement, dental implants, orthodontics, cosmetic dentistry (whitening, bonding, veneers), pediatric dentistry and gum disease treatment. English-speaking staff and visiting renowned dental experts from Hong Kong and Canada throughout the year. All nurses have received comprehensive training from foreign experts. Basic consultation RMB 50. First-time registration fee RMB 50. Credit cards accepted.
1) Daily 9am-8pm. NB 210, China World Trade Shopping Mall (beside skating rink), 1 Jianguomenwai Dajie, Chaoyang District. (6505 9439/31); 2) FC 222, 21st Century Hotel, 40 Liangmaqiao Lu, Chaoyang District. (6466 4814, 6461 2745); 3) F-0186B, Sunshine Plaza, 68 Anli Lu, Chaoyang District. (6497 2173, 6498 2173); 4) Rm 106, Bldg 11, 22 Yuanda Xilu (near Golden Resources Mall), Haidian District. (8859 6912/13) www. sdmdental.com 固瑞齿科, 1)朝阳区建国门外大街1号国贸商城NB210（溜冰场旁边）; 2) 朝阳区亮马桥路40号二十一世纪饭店FC222; 3) 朝阳区安立路68号阳光广场F-0186B; 4) 海淀区远大路22号11号楼106室（金源新燕莎附近）

Smart Health Medical & Dental Center English-speaking staff provides services in family dentistry, orthodontics, implant dentistry, teeth whitening, and family medicine. Direct billing available with some insurers. Consultation (including registration) fee RMB 300.
Mon-Fri 9am-8pm, Sat-Sun 9am-6pm. Rm 102 & 215, Holiday Inn Lido, 6 Jiangtai Lu, Chaoyang District. (6437 6898) www.smarthealth.cn 维健医疗中心, 朝阳区将台路6号丽都广场102及215室

Sunny Dental Care Offers professional surgical dentistry and specializes in orthodontics, extractions and wisdom tooth removal, dental implants, root canal treatment and cosmetic dentistry. Dentists and staff speak fluent English, and some have overseas training. First-time registration (includes check up and consultation) costs RMB 120.
Mon-Sun 9am-6pm (Close Thu & Sat). Rm 606, Times Fortune Bldg A, Shuguang Xili, Chaoyang District. (5867 7705/6/8, emergency 139 1196 9907) 赛德齿科, 朝阳区曙光西里国际A座6层606室

Eye Care
(also see Glasses in Shopping p360)

Beijing Intech Eye Hospital Leading eye center in terms of scale, quality, and quantity, as well as a referral center for international medical evacuation assistance companies. Quality professional team with overseas and domestic training. Eye care, including emergency treatment, telephone consultations and preventive care. Popular place to get laser corrective surgery. On-site shop sells frames and lenses. VIP clinic has English speaking staff and choice of family ophthalmologists. Registration RMB 400. Basic consultation RMB 280.
Daily 8.30am-4.30pm. 5IF, Panjiayuan Plaza, 12 Panjiayuan Nanli, Chaoyang District. (6771 5558) www. intecheye.com 北京英智眼科, 朝阳区潘家园南里12号潘家园大厦5层

Daming Optical Offers optometry and lens-fitting services. Consultation fee RMB 5-15. Glasses start at RMB 158 for frames and RMB 40 for lenses.
1) Daily 9am-9pm. 176 Wangfujing Dajie, Dongcheng District. (6513 1327); 2) Daily 10am-9pm. Rm 1026, Golden Resources Mall, 1 Yuanda Lu, Haidian District. (8887 5633) 大明眼镜, 1) 东城区王府井大街176号; 2) 海淀区远大路1号金源燕莎店1026商铺

Perfect Vision Optometry Australian optometrist James Charles provides highly professional optometry service to adults and children. First expatriate optometrist to be registered in China and to operate a private practice. Registration fee USD 45. Frames start at USD 70.
Mon-Sat 9am-6pm. International SOS Clinic, Bldg C, BITIC Jingyi Building, 5 Sanlitun Xiwujie, Chaoyang District. (6410 5850, 130 0111 1829) www.perfectvision.com.cn 博凡特视力, 朝阳区三里屯西五街北信京谊大厦C座国际SOS诊所内

Cosmetic

Bioscor Beijing Clinic International clinic specializing in cosmetic surgery, skincare, hair regrowth, cosmetic dentistry and anti-aging techniques. English-speaking Chinese doctors. Appointments with an Australian surgeon and physician available.
Daily 9.30am-6pm. Rm 1008, E Bldg, 12 Guanghua Lu, Chaoyang District. (6503 5707) www.bioscor.com. cn 朝阳区光华路12号数码01大厦1008室

Confidant Medical Services Provides bilingual and discreet American medical care for expatriates and Chinese nationals. Services include family medicine (with pharmacy, lab, and imaging services), pediatrics, gynecology, dermatology, anti-aging therapeutics, teeth whitening, cosmetic laser treatment and plastic surgery.
Daily 10am-7pm. 701, Chang'an Club (Beijing Tower), 10 Dongchang'an Jie, Dongcheng District. (6559 6769) www.confidantmedical.com 纽曼德诊所, 东城区东长安街10号长安俱乐部701

Viv International Medical Beauty Clinic Offers plastic surgery, IPL skin refining and hair removal, LPG body reshaping, and Chinese health and beauty treatments. All attending doctors have medical college education, some with professional training overseas. Combines international standards with Chinese prices.
Daily 9.30am-6.30pm. 2/F, Tower D, Global Trade Mansion, A9 Guanghua Lu, Chaoyang District. (6530 2348) www.vivbeauty.com 明色红国际医疗美容机构, 朝阳区光华路甲9号世贸国际公寓D座2层

Safer Safe Sex
Know thy birth control pills
by Laurie Burkitt

Avoiding unplanned parenthood while living in Beijing should be rather easy considering that China has become a world leader in contraceptive use. In 2003, the United Nations Population Fund published a study indicating that a lofty 83 percent of China's sexually active are using contraception. Population prevention is practically at your fingertips. A slew of products – from condoms to sponges to birth control pills – can be purchased over the counter at walk-in pharmacies like Watsons and your neighborhood *yao dian*.

While there's no harm in buying condoms at these street-side vendors, purchasing oral contraceptives is a different story. "There are dangers involved in buying walk-in pharmacy medications. The biggest question is quality control," says Shirley McCulloch, former senior midwife advisor at Beijing United Hospital. McCulloch says that although smaller pharmacies stock brand-name oral contraceptives, there's no guarantee that these are not imitations. With something as serious as pregnancy, you may not want to take that risk.

Both McCulloch and Beijing Vista Clinic's Dr. Qin Li advise women to consult a physician prior to purchasing oral contraceptives. "Birth

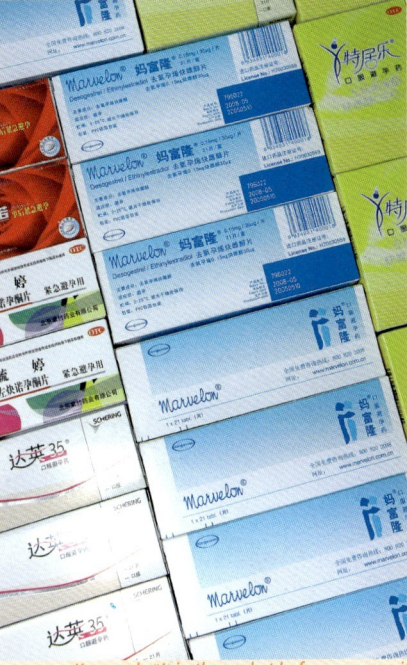

Know what's in the packet before you pop it

control pills increase the risk of blood clots," says Qin. "Women should have their blood pressure taken first to make sure that everything is normal, and then they can safely take the pill." Qin also warns that pills vary in hormone levels. "Local pharmacies may offer high levels of estrogen only," she says, whereas a physician would prescribe an appropriate estrogen level based on a patient's age and health. But buyers should resign themselves to the fact that assured quality control comes with a higher price tag. Vista charges a RMB 660 consultation fee and around RMB 200 for a month's worth of prescription pills. Meanwhile, local pharmacies offer birth control pills from RMB 30 to RMB 69.

"There are more and more students in Beijing," says McCulloch, "and many who don't have health insurance." For such people, lower-priced contraceptives are seemingly a better option. But again, when opting for the cheap, keep in mind that most oral contraceptives contain at least 30 micrograms of estrogen. McCulloch also warns that using cheaper medication available at Chinese pharmacies may be more dangerous, if only because the instructions will be in Chinese. If you haven't quite reached the Da Shan level of fluency, the section on "what to do if you've missed a pill" may be easier to read in English.

Aside from Beijing United and Beijing Vista pharmacies, regulated birth control pills are available in the pharmacies of AEA International (6462 9112), the Bayley & Jackson Medical Center (8562 9998), and the International Medical Center (6465 1561). Birth control pills (*biyun yao*) can typically be found next to condoms and pregnancy tests in any local Chinese pharmacy.

Is it Magic or is it TCM?
The theory and practice behind Traditional Chinese Medicine
by Eileen Ho

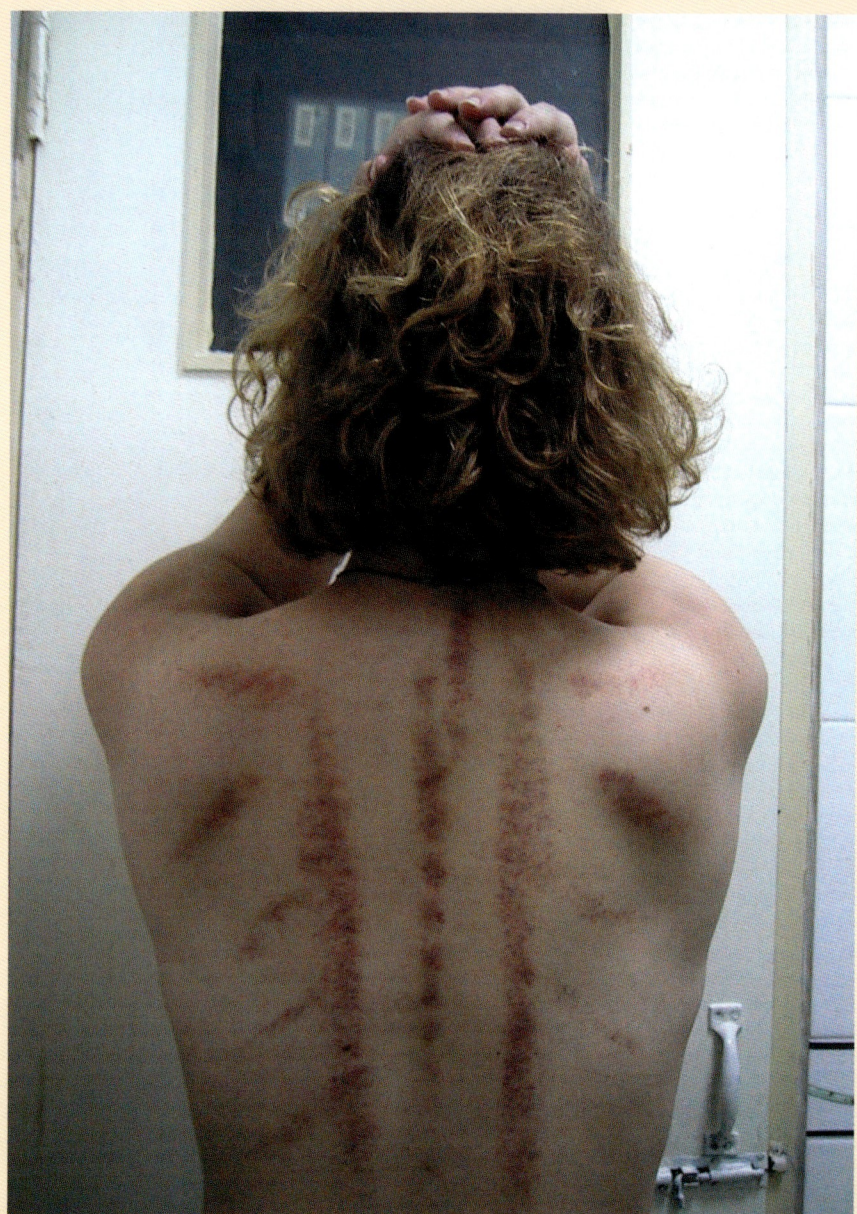

It might be traditional, but those aren't tribal markings. They're the result of gua sha.

Traditional Chinese Medicine (TCM) has its mysteries – we don't always know why or how it works, but its treatments can sometimes be surprisingly more effective than Western medicine, particularly when practiced regularly for a long period of time. Curious about the practice of TCM and its longstanding tradition in China, Insider's Guide to Beijing called on Ping Xin Tang, one's of Beijing's most famous TCM clinics (see p486), to ask Dr. Xu Wenbing a few questions.

IG: What is the general theory behind TCM?
XWB: TCM comes from Taoism, a Chinese belief that started more than 5,000 years ago. The principle behind Taoism is that since we cannot change natural things, we should embrace them. Your own body has the innate ability to cure itself without medicine. We believe in the "tiny god," which is the spirit inside each individual's body that gives him/her the instinct to protect him/herself. In TCM, the doctor can only help you - your body must cure itself. We abide by the doctrine that everyone is the same, and that as a doctor, you must treat even your enemies.

IG: What kinds of medicines are used in TCM and where are they obtained?
XWB: Seventy percent of TCM medicines are natural herbs, such as leaves, flowers, bark and roots. A smaller percentage is comprised of animal parts, and the last category is minerals. They are either collected on mountains or grown on herbal medicine farms. Nowadays, 99 percent of herbs are grown on farms, because it keeps the costs down. TCM clinics usually get their ingredients from these growers.

IG: What is *ba guan* (cupping) and *gua sha* (scraping), and how do they work?
XWB: We use *ba guan* medicinally to cure colds, fevers and coughs. The point is to use hot air to suck out the cold air that has invaded your body. People do ba guan for fun at massage parlors, but this is ineffective and has no purpose other than temporary relief. *Gua sha* is used to promote blood flow. The small blood vessels slow and clog, and we scrape to improve circulation on special meridians.

IG: How is TCM integrated with Western medicine in Beijing?
XWB: Probably 85 percent of medical centers in Beijing are Western. The law doesn't protect TCM doctors as much, so more and more doctors are choosing to study Western medicine instead. You'll find many doctors who claim to also be TCM specialists at hospitals and clinics, but they typically combine Western medicine treatments with TCM, which isn't necessarily good for the body. It's like getting treated twice for the same problem. Some of these doctors haven't had enough real TCM training, and can't really be called either modern medicine doctors or TCM doctors. However, TCM is attracting more and more foreign students. We treat a lot of embassy staff, who also recommend us to foreign diplomats – TCM can really influence the world.

IG: What kinds of sicknesses are best treated with TCM? How long does it take?
XWB: A lot of Europeans and Americans come to see us because of problems that cannot be treated with Western medicine. Examples include depression, infertility, pain, chronic fatigue and mental retardation. Many times, when people lose hope in their home countries, they come to China to seek alternative treatments. The amount of time it takes to cure really depends on what the circumstances are. Depression usually takes 10 to 20 treatments. Infertility takes from half a year to about a year. Pain usually takes five to ten treatments to cure. TCM is also effective in aiding weight loss.

IG: How much schooling and training do TCM doctors go through?
XWB: You'd be surprised. We spend six years in medical school, 60 percent studying Chinese medicine and 40 percent studying Western medicine. Then we spend a year working at a hospital before we're qualified to become doctors.

IG: What is the future of TCM?
XWB: Though TCM is called "traditional Chinese medicine," in actuality, it is a worldwide phenomenon. For example, the US grants licenses to TCM doctors, so many of the best TCM doctors currently practice there. Obviously, people prefer to go to Western doctors if they feel that it can cure them faster or better, but I think a lot of our patients are realizing that there are some things TCM does better than Western medicine.

HEALTH & BEAUTY

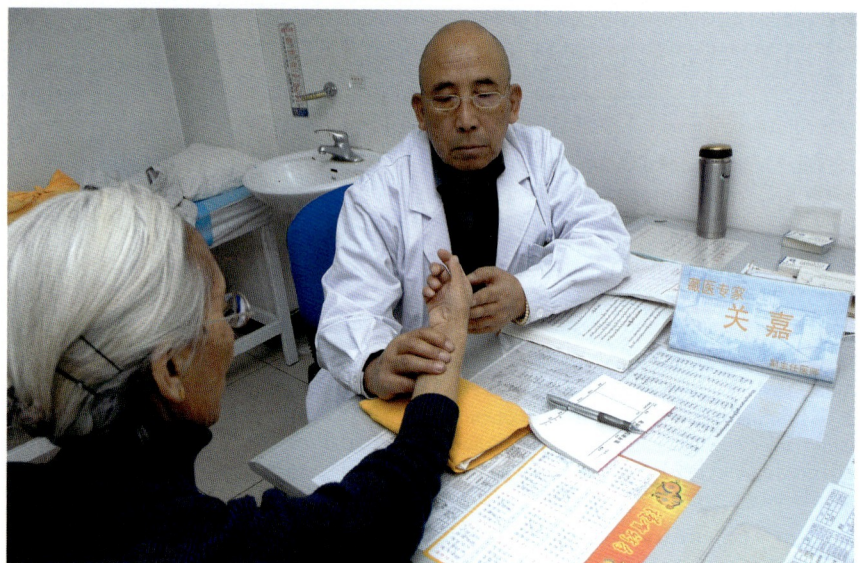
TCM: a traditional approach to everything in medicine, including pulse-taking

TCM (Traditional Chinese Medicine)

Beijing Massage Hospital More than half of the 80 massage doctors are blind at this clinic, which specializes in *tuina* therapy for neck, shoulders, back and arthritis. Forty years experience in traditional Chinese massage technique and combining TCM with Western medicine. Also performs acupuncture, cupping, scraping, moxibustion, physiotherapy and X-rays. Consultation fee RMB 1-3, registration fee RMB 3-50.
Daily 7.30-11.30am, 1.30-10pm. 7 Baochan Hutong, Xinjiekou, Xicheng District. (6616 1064, 6616 8880) www.massage-hospital.com 北京按摩医院，西城区新街口宝铲胡同7号

Beijing Tongrentang Traditional Chinese Medicine Clinic Founded in 1669 during the Qing dynasty, Tongrentang is one of the most renowned TCM clinics in China. Services offered include internal medicine, dermatology, and of course, acupuncture. They also specialize in treating diabetes, obesity, and high blood pressure. Stocks a wide range of TCM remedies as well as Western medicines such as antacids, vitamins and Viagra. Reservations required. Registration fee RMB 12.5-100.
Daily 8.30am-noon, 2-5pm.15, Block 7, Jianwai Soho, 39 Sanhuan Zhonglu, Chaoyang District. (5869 1171/2, 135 2287 3781); 2) Daily 8:30am-8pm. Next to River Garden entrance, Shunyi District. (8046 1907); 3) Daily 8-11.30am, 1-5pm. 20 Nansanhuan Zhonglu, Fengtai District. (6766 8793) 北京同仁堂中医馆，1)朝阳区三环中路39号建外Soho7座15号同仁堂药店；顺义区裕京花园旁边；2) 同仁堂药店，顺义区裕京花园旁边；3)北京同仁堂中医馆，丰台区南三环中路20号

Liuzheng Massage Clinic Liuzheng's fingerpressing massage, based on TCM, activates the endocrine system to secrete substances that increase immunity, prevent and treat diseases, slow aging, and beautify the skin and face. 1 hr massage options RMB 88, 120, 320.
Daily 10am-midnight. 1/F, Bldg 7, Jiqingli, Chaoyangmenwai Dajie (opposite the Industrial and Commercial Bank at the west gate of Julong Garden), Chaoyang District. (6552 9282) 刘正诊疗所，朝阳区朝外吉庆里七号楼一层

Middle Way Chinese Medicine Clinic Offers traditional Chinese medicine consultation and treatment. Specializes in treating diabetes and high blood pressure. Consultation fee RMB 50.
Daily 9am-5pm. A23 Yangfang Hutong (by Houhai Lake), Xicheng District. (6613 8885) 中道堂中医诊所，西城区羊坊胡同甲23号（后海旁边）

Ping Xin Tang Clinic One of Beijing's best TCM clinics in terms of quality of medicine and service. Specializes in a range of chronic problems, including cancer, brain tumors, insomnia, depression, hypertension, skin problems, diabetes and neck problems. Dental services are also available. A consultation costs RMB 110, with RMB 100-200 registration fee.
Mon-Sat 8-11.30am, 2-5.30pm, Sun 8am-11.30am. 3, 4/F, 218-2 Wangfujing Dajie, Dongcheng District. (6523 5566) 平心堂诊所，东城区王府井大街218-2号3—4层

Yanhuang TCM Clinic Highly qualified TCM doctors specializing in a range of areas including pediatrics, gynecology and disease. Registration fee RMB 50-200.
Daily 8.30am-6pm. 1 Dayabao Hutong, Dongcheng District. (8542 4635) 炎黄国医馆，东城区大雅宝胡同1号

Support Groups

(see Useful Info p644)

Emergency Card
(Please photocopy and fill out as needed)

Name _____ City of residence _____
姓名 _____ 城市 _____

Home Address _____
家庭地址 _____

Company Address _____
公司地址 _____

Home phone number _____ Mobile _____
家庭电话 _____ 手机 _____

Blood type _____ Known Allergies _____
血型 _____ 过敏症 _____

Current medications _____
目前用药 _____

Insurance Provider _____
承保商 _____

Policy Number _____ 24/7 Emergency Number _____
保险号码 _____ 紧急电话号码 _____

Country of Citizenship _____ Passport Number _____
国籍 _____ 护照号 _____

In case of emergency, please contact 紧急事件联系人

Name 姓名 _____ Mobile 手机 _____
Name 姓名 _____ Mobile 手机 _____
Name 姓名 _____ Mobile 手机 _____
Name 姓名 _____ Mobile 手机 _____

Useful Numbers 重要电话号码

Police/ (警察): 110   Fire Department/ (火警): 119   Ambulance/ (救护车): 999/120

HEALTH & BEAUTY

The Cosmetic Surge
Mainstream and affordable, *zhengrong* reigns
by Gabriel Monroe

Money might not be able to buy happiness, but it can buy beauty and a whole new you

Commonly referred to in Chinese as *zhengrong*, an innocuous abbreviation of "corrective beautification" (*zhengxing meirong* 整形美容), cosmetic surgery is certifiably entrenched in China's mainstream culture. With chic-seeking cities like Beijing and Shanghai leading the way, China has become the world's second biggest market for plastic surgery (after the USA). Following years of positive publicity engineered by clinics and the national media, cosmetic surgery is now widely accepted as a pragmatic means for personal improvement. More than a million Chinese people a year are sauntering up to the operating table for cosmetic enhancement. According to Xinhua, "*Zhengrong* has broken through the ancient and absolute opposition between beauty and hideousness."

In Beijing's highly populated, highly competitive urban environment, adjusting one's appearance can mean a distinguished rise above perpetually snubbed limbo. Local cosmetic surgeon-in-training Ma Yiyuan theorizes: "Chinese people often have roundish faces and indistinctive features, so it's widely accepted that surgery to make a Chinese person's face more angular, more pronounced, more Western-looking, will make that person's face more striking." Job hunt-oriented cosmetic operations during the summer after convocation have become an increasingly popular strategy for Chinese university graduates.

In a job market flooded with talented and qualified people, applicants are routinely submitted to strict screening based on height, age, gender and physical appearance. In many cases, skill and experience alone may not be enough to land the job. Various operations that enjoy particular popularity – such as leg stretching surgery and wrinkle removal – seem like practical tactics to outmaneuver these potential professional prejudices. And the newly enhanced patient might even nab a bonus in the bargain: a wealthier, more attractive or otherwise upgraded mate.

PHOTO: IMAGINE CHINA

While nose and bosom enhancements, facial and calf liposuction, chin adjustment, eye circle removal, and buttock lifts are all prevalent cosmetic operations, one procedure is particularly emblematic of the zhengrong phenomenon in China: double eyelid (shuangyanpi 双眼皮) surgery. This operation involves surgically folding an additional crease of skin into the eyelid, causing the patient's eyes to appear less squinty and supposedly more "Western." The allure of possessing the irresistible glamour enveloped within that coveted extra fold has made shuangyanpi surgery by far the most popular cosmetic operation in China, particularly among women.

As with other modern cultural trends (TV, music, fashion) in China, the blaming finger is pointed squarely at South Korea. Outrageous statistics claim that more than half of women over 20 in the Republic of Korea have undergone cosmetic surgery.

In China, the majority of zhengrong patients are women from 25 to 45, but recent years have seen increasing numbers of people outside this range angling to get onto the beautification operating table. The desire for nose jobs, lip enhancements and John Travolta chins have Chinese men clambering into the hospital in increasing numbers.

Yet despite the ubiquity and popularity of cosmetic surgery procedures, unsuccessful operations are quite common, and patients are routinely asked to sign waivers before medical procedures are performed. At best, a failed surgery can leave patients back where they started, but disfigurement is a perilous possible risk in altering one's physical architecture. And there's little chance of getting a refund after signing a waiver, even if the patient ends up looking like Quasimodo instead of J-Lo. "Doing plastic surgery is always gamble," says Ma, "It's just a gamble with pretty high chances of success."

According to Xinhua, statistics suggest at least 200,000 annual cases of cosmetic surgery-related malpractice complaints nationwide, accounting for roughly 10-20 percent of all patients. While failure rates for plastic surgery are under researched worldwide, a 10 percent failure rate is generally accepted as the nature of the beast in the United States. As such, China's failure rates may range anywhere from normal to double the international average.

Despite the risks, enthusiasm towards the pragmatic gains of cosmetic surgery is not going to wane in Beijing any time soon. Flaunt your double-skin eyelids if you've got 'em, and if yours is a single, cherish it. It might soon become a relic of an enlightened age.

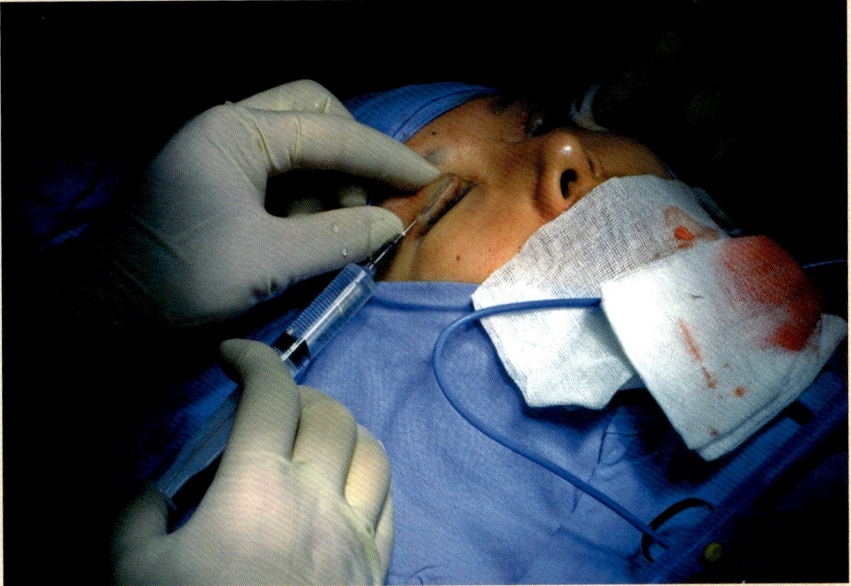

Better keep your eyes closed ... surgery can get scary

HEALTH & BEAUTY

You don't have to be a princess bride to get the royal treatment at Beijing's salons and spas

Lookin' Good and Livin' Easy
Beijing beauty
by Halla Mohieddeen and Amy Xue

Make no mistake – city living is tough. The everyday stresses that make Beijing the place it is (late nights, early starts, not to mention the perma-fog and dry air) wreak havoc on your hair, skin, nails, muscles and general frame of mind. Thankfully, the other thing we have in abundance here is a wealth of beauty parlors and spas to help us look and feel better on any budget.

From the RMB 10 *xi toufa* (hair wash) and massage, to the luxury five-star treatments and packages in some of the world's top resorts and hotels, Beijing has every base covered. It's all available here: massage, waxing, threading, facials, UV-therapy, hydro-therapy, tanning, whitening, whatever it takes to make you look and feel like a million *kuai*.

Even within our slightly narrowed-down list, the vast selection can often seem confusing and overwhelming. But exploring is also part of the fun. Remember, there's no such thing as too much pampering. So get out there and take it easy!

PHOTO: JANEK ZDZARSKI JR

490 INSIDER'S GUIDE TO BEIJING

Beauty Salons

While some hair salons also do nails, some nail salons also do massages, and some spas also do hair, these multi-taskers really defy labels. The point is, they're here to make you beautiful, whether it's removing dead skin or unsightly hair.

Daisy's Beauty Salon Specialties include waxing (upper lip RMB 60, full face RMB 320, and full body around RMB 1,000), permanent IPL laser hair removal, and weight loss (3-10kg). Also offers facials (RMB 218), manicures (RMB 80), and pedicures (RMB 150). Uses quality products from Paris.
Daily 10am-8.30pm. Rm 301, Bldg B, Sunshine 100, Guanghua Donglu, Chaoyang District. (5100 0557, 139 0108 2549) 黛丝美容沙龙，朝阳区光华路阳光100 B座301室

ES Lifestyle Lasers, they claim, are the way to remove hair and rejuvenate the skin. Also offers slimming and skin treatments and aromatic body massages.
Daily 9.30am-10pm. Rm C, 2/F, Estoril Court, 9 Gongti Beilu, Chaoyang District. (6415 5230) 纤姿坊，朝阳区工体北路9号爱德公寓2楼C室

Massage Salon Expect moderate prices and limited frills in this salon which offers shampoo & cut (RMB 30-80), perms (RMB 200 and up), manicures, pedicures, facials (RMB 150 for 90min). Home service available for nearby locations.
Daily 10am-midnight. Pinnacle Plaza, Shunyi District. (8046 2395) 顺义区荣祥广场

Natural Beauty This beauty salon chain offers massage, facials and slimming in a pleasant environment. For best value, prepay a few months at a time. Those spending in the RMB 1,000-2,000 range can get discounts up to 50%. Sells Chitlina brand beauty care products.
Daily 10am-10pm. 109, Bldg A15, Huaqing Jiayuan, Chengfu Lu, Haidian District. (8286 5511) 自然美，海淀区华清嘉园15A号

Hair Salons

Entrusting your locks to a total stranger can be a scary prospect, especially when the stranger in question doesn't speak your language. However, this doesn't mean you should suffer split ends and outgrown roots for the sake of avoiding the hairdresser. The results are often as good, if not better, than those you'd get from salons back home, for a much better price too. Local salons offer cuts as cheap as RMB 10 and equally inexpensive hair washing combined with a head massage. However, these places usually don't have much experience with Western hair. If you're not confident in your ability to effectively communicate and procure your desired 'do, it may be worth forking out extra for one of the pricier salons.

Asakura A fashionable hair salon with stylists flown in from Tokyo, targeting expat Japanese and nouveau riche Chinese clientele. Cuts begin at RMB 450.
Mon-Tue 11am-8pm, Wed-Thu and Sat 10am-9pm, Fri noon-9pm, Sun 9am-8pm. 4 Gongti Beilu (near the Loft), Chaoyang District. (6506 7455/6) www.asakura.com.cn 朝仓时尚，朝阳区工体北路4号（藏酷旁边）

C. de France Using French products (L'Oreal and Phytomer), the regularly trained staff offers haircuts ranging RMB 150-420 for women, manicures, facials, waxing and more. VIP programs and discounts also available.
Tue-Sun 10am-8pm. Nali Mall, Sanlitun Lu, Chaoyang District (6417 3029) 朝阳区三里屯北街那里

Come & Surprise Hair Studio
With cuts going from RMB 80-200, this classy red-and-gold Chinese-themed salon features wall-to-wall mirrors and a relaxation room complete with flat screen TVs. Features TIGI & Bedhead products.
Daily 11am-10pm. West of Yashow Market, Chaoyang District. (6415 1953) 红簌美场，朝阳区雅秀市场西边

Eric Paris Salon & Hair Club
High-quality hair salon staffed by foreign stylists who know their stuff. A range of beauty treatments are also available in this swanky upscale salon, including waxing, facial, and, lo and behold, a sun bed. A basic cut ranges from RMB 215-385.
Daily 10am-8pm. 1) 43 Nanlu, Sanlitun Beijie, Chaoyang District. (135 0137 2971); 2) Inside Lido Hotel, 112 Jichang Lu, Chaoyang District. (135 0107 5843); 3) Shop 123, Kerry Centre, 1 Guanghua Lu, Chaoyang District. (139 1179 8376); 4) G4-G5, Palm Springs Lifestyle Plaza, 8 Chaoyang Gongyuan Nanlu, Chaoyang District. (139 1007 5974); 5) 5/F, The Westin Beijing, 9B Jinrong Jie, Xicheng District. (139 1162 6051) 爱丽克美容美发，1）朝阳区三里屯北街南路43号；2）朝阳区机场路112号丽都宾馆内；3）朝阳区光华路1号嘉里中心123号商铺；4）朝阳区朝阳公园南路8号棕榈泉生活广场G4—G5；5）西城区金融街乙9号威斯汀大酒店5层

ERIC Paris/Kérastase Institute Sectioned off from the main salon itself, the Kérastase Institute plays up the "science" and technology appeal. A technician proposes individually tailored treatments after a computerized hair analysis, using a magnifying camera to diagnose scalp and hair condition (from root to tip). Treatments cost RMB 200-350 for short hair and RMB 300-600 for longer styles. A full range of Kérastase products is also available in store to complement your at-home hair care regime. Shampoos start from RMB 155.
Daily 10am-8pm. 1/F, Hilton Hotel, 1 Dongfang Lu, Dongsanhuan Beilu, Chaoyang District. (137 0118 3307) 朝阳区东三环北路东方路1号希尔顿饭店1层

Gary Lewis Salon This beauty parlor offers the full range of hair care services, including cuts (starting at RMB 200 for short hair), permanent color (RMB 350-500) and perms (RMB 450) as well as skin care (facials start at RMB 140), waxing and pricey manicures (RMB 95) and pedicures (RMB 135).
Daily 10am-7pm. 704, Pinnacle Plaza, Shunyi District. (8046 4410, 1360 1078 963) 嘉笠美容美发中心，顺义区荣祥广场704

Hair Plus Hong Kong-run hair salon provides a salon experience in a comfortable atmosphere. Offers haircuts from RMB 150-280.
Daily 10.30am-9.30pm. Centennial Heights, Oriental Plaza, 1 Dongchang'an Jie, Dongcheng District. (8515 0700) www.hairplusconcept.com 东城区东长安街1号东方广场

Hair and Beauty These salons provide haircuts and skincare at reasonable prices (ladies' cut RMB 30, up-do RMB 80, facials RMB 100 and up). They also offer massages, manicures and pedicures that can be enjoyed in

HEALTH & BEAUTY

the comfort of your own home. Full body massage RMB 70/hr, aromatherapy massage RMB 150/hr, foot massage RMB 80/hr.
1) Daily 9am-11pm. Fresh Hair and Beauty, Laiguangying Donglu (near WAB), Chaoyang District. (8470 3110); 2) Daily 9am-midnight. Flower River Beauty Salon (south gate of Beijing Capital Paradise, opposite Lion Mart), Shunyi District. (8046 6112);
3) Flower River Beauty Salon, 12 Riverville Square, Shunyi District. (6450 8868) 4) Daily 9am-midnight. Qi Qi Beauty Salon, Capital Paradise Clubhouse, Shunyi District. (8046 1403) 1) 清新美丽美容院，朝阳区来广营东路（京西学校附近）；2) 花溪美容院，顺义区名都园南门，新货郎超市对面；3) 顺义区温榆广场12号；4) 琦琦美容院，顺义区名都园会所

Hair Rodeo This Korean-run salon is home to Wudaokou's premier hairstylists and very popular with Korean and Japanese students. Asian hair perms are their strong suit; coloring is popular with Westerners. Hair extensions deserve an honorable mention for both flair and precision. Haircuts run a modest RMB 50. Little English spoken.
1) Daily 9.30am-9pm. Chengfu Lu (across from Wudaokou Hotel), Haidian District. (8238 7066); 2) Rm 301, Bldg 7, Huaqing Jiayuan, Haidian District. (8286 7811) 发新社，1) 海淀区成府路（五道口宾馆对面）；2) 海淀区华清嘉园7号楼301室

Hair Show The full range of hair and skin care is offered at competitive prices (ladies' & men's cuts RMB 50, facials RMB 220 and up). The DVD players and car-shaped kid's chair make this a good spot to bring your wriggly ones for haircuts (RMB 40) or have them accompany you to the hairdresser on ayi's day off! They even get a lollipop afterwards.
Daily 10am-10pm. Pinnacle Plaza (next to Jenny Lou's), Shunyi District. (8046 3168, 1360 1282 388) 轻丝秀坊，顺义区荣祥广场Jenny Lou's超市旁边

Image Momentum Featuring deluxe cuts by Hong Kong stylists from RMB 60-150.
Daily 11am-8pm. 15, 1/F, Bldg 12, Wanda Plaza, 93 Jianguo Lu, Chaoyang District. (5820 4500) 木棉藤形象工作室，朝阳区建国路93号万达广场12号楼1层

Punk Has a decent reputation for wave perms. Foreigners beware: contemporary Chinese hairstyles do not always convert well to laowai locks. Haircuts RMB 38-68.
Daily 9am-11pm. Chengfu Lu (300m south of Tsinghua University east gate), Haidian District. (8286 7393) 海淀区成府路清华大学东门往南300米

Silk Hair Studio
A sleek Italian-designed salon with haircuts starting at RMB 120 and perms at RMB 380.
Daily 10-am-10pm. Rm S-234, 2/F, Bldg 2, south area, Blue Castle Apartments, 3 Xidawang Lu, Chaoyang District. (8599 9938) 朝阳区西大望路3号蓝堡公寓南区2号楼2层S-234室

Simba International Hair Dressing Salon A hair salon especially for people of African descent and those who love to mimic their hairstyles. Braiding ranges from RMB 200-RMB 2,000, and relaxing starts at RMB 80. Also does beard trims for RMB 20 and haircuts starting at RMB 100 for adults and RMB 80 for children. Stocks a range of Afro hair and body care products.
Mon-Sat 9am-8.30pm. 601, Bldg 2, Jianwai Soho, Chaoyang District. (5869 6459) www.simbasalon.com 朝阳区建外Soho 2号楼601

Toni & Guy British international hair salon offers haircuts for RMB 80-380. Perms and colorings cost about RMB 400-700. Surprisingly little English spoken. You can get a free haircut from a stylist-in-training next door at the Toni & Guy Academy if you're willing to accept the risk and some waiting.
Daily 10am-10pm. 1) 105, Bldg F, Sunshine 100, 2 Guanghua Lu, Chaoyang District. (6585 9288); 2) Daily 10am-9pm. Oriental Plaza, 1 Dongchang'an Jie, Dongcheng District (8518 2646) www.toniandguy.co.uk 托尼英盖，1) 朝阳区光华路2号阳光100 F座105；2) 东城区东长安街1号东方广场内

Tony Studio Tony Studio is on many a celebrity's speed-dial, and is responsible for makeup duties on several local magazines' photo shoots. Flagship store in Jianwai Soho features four floors of facial spa facilities, hair stylists, a cafe and a professional photo studio. Haircuts cost RMB 180-280, and perms around RMB 730.
1) Daily 10am-9pm. 919, 9/F, Bldg 2, Sun Dong An Plaza, Wangfujing, Dongcheng District. (6528 1568); 2) Daily 10am-10pm. V-0117, Villa 9, Jianwai Soho, Dongsanhuan Zhonglu, Chaoyang District. (5869 0050) 东田造型，1) 东城区王府井新东安市场2号楼9层919；2) 朝阳区东三环中路建外Soho 9号别墅V-0117。

Vajra Innovations include a dye-mixing laboratory and a training center, where guests can learn hairstyling from the pros. Comfy couches and big screen TVs give the downstairs a lounge-y feel – an ideal place to grab a cup of coffee while you ruminate on art. Haircut/styling runs RMB 400-1,500.
Daily 10am-8pm. S106, 18 Gongti Xilu, Glory World Apartments, Chaoyang District. (6551 6461/3) 画间沙龙，朝阳区工体西路18号光彩国际公寓S106商铺

Nails

Beijing's manicure options run from hole-in-the-wall joints to high-end savvy salons. You can also find manicurists in your local hair salon and nail bars in markets such as Chaowai Yuexiu and 3.3. Make sure you check the tools before getting a manicure or a pedicure, and if they look dodgy, ask the staff to sterilize them. Alternatively, you can always bring your own tools and sterilize them at home. Another note: if you want those calluses smoothed away, you might have to pay extra for a scrub in addition to the pedicure.

Frangipani
This modern, clean and relaxed nail bar is great for meeting a few friends for a chat and a drink, while being pampered by the skilled staff. Their beauty oil smells subtly of lemons and keeps skin moist for hours after application. Other beauty products, thongs, make-up bags and nail kits for sale. Manicure RMB 98, pedicure RMB 168.
Daily 9am-9pm. Shop 6, 30 Sanlitun Beijie, Chaoyang District. (6417 0889) 美甲时尚坊，朝阳区三里屯北街30号6门

Frost Nails Choose from manicures (RMB 30 and up), pedicures (RMB 50 and up), dead skin removal (RMB 60) and other services. Usage of OPI products costs an extra RMB 20-40. Rest assured: The boutique has a sterilizer that cleans all the tools before treatments. Manicure tools and stylish nail jewelry also for sale. High-tech waxing and eyelash curling also available.

At the open air salon, it's two for RMB 10

Daily noon-midnight. 2/F, Jiezuo Dasha (above O Sole Mio), Xinfucun Zhonglu, Chaoyang District. (6417 9148) 小瑞美甲，朝阳区幸福村中路杰座大厦底商2层

Jiali Manicure Brightly decorated place for manicures (RMB 25) and pedicures (RMB 50). They have fat yellow couches for you to sit on and enjoy a foot massage after a long day of shopping.
Daily 10am-10pm. 004-005, Nali Mall, Sanlitun Lu, Chaoyang District. (6417 8565) 佳丽美甲，朝阳区三里屯路那里市场004-005

Lovely Nails Rather stylish joint with professional uniformed staff offering manicures (RMB 90), pedicures (RMB 130) and other services. The Taiyue Heights location is slightly cheaper, with manicures for RMB 70 and pedicures for RMB 100.
1) Tue-Sun 10am-9pm. W06 Skyplace Market, Tianzhu Garden, Shunyi District. (6458 0603); 2) Daily 11am-11pm. Taiyue Heights, Sanlitun Nanjie, Chaoyang District. (6502 5989); 3) Mon-Tue noon-10.30pm, Wed-Sun 9.30am-10.30pm. 1/F, Tongli Studios, Sanlitun Houjie, Chaoyang District. (6417 5813) 1）顺义区天竺花园；2）朝阳区三里屯南街泰悦豪庭；3）朝阳区三里屯后街同里1层

Nail Plus Get manicures (RMB 98), pedicures (RMB 150), or both (RMB 230). Also offers crystal nails, gel nails and nail art.
Daily 10.30am-8.30pm. B23, Kerry Centre Mall, 1 Guanghua Lu, Chaoyang District. (8529 9078) 诺亚专业美甲，朝阳区光华路1号嘉里商场B23号

Nan Nan Nails Manicures start at RMB 80. Nail art costs anywhere between RMB 100-1,000 – choose from a wide selection of designs.
Daily 10am-10pm. 2/F, Shutterbox Accessory Shop (south of Lido Hotel, opposite the Heqiaolijing Gongyu), Chaoyang District. (5135 7477) 楠楠美甲，朝阳区丽都酒店南边（和乔丽晶公寓对面）Shutterbox商店2楼）

Qiu Ran Nail Salon All OPI products for your nails. Offers manicures (RMB 48) and pedicures (RMB 68) and also serves coffee. Nail polishing costs RMB 30 extra.
Daily noon-midnight. Store 2049, 3.3 Plaza, Sanlitun Beilu, Chaoyang District. (134 2603 5565) 秋然美甲，朝阳区三里屯北路3.3服饰大厦2049商铺

Sandy Nailspa From the impeccable decor to its range of quality products, Sandy Nailspa distinguishes itself as a high-end establishment. Salon services include manicures (RMB 88) and nourishing hand and foot care treatments (RMB 228 and 558).
Daily 10am-10pm. 302, Tower B, Jianwai Soho, 39 Dongsanhuan, Chaoyang District. (5869 7560) 仙蒂美甲沙龙，朝阳区东三环中路39号建外soho B座302号

Sunshine Nails The friendliest of an ever-increasing number of nail salons on Yashow's fourth floor. Take a well-earned shopping break and enjoy a manicure (RMB 20), pedicure (RMB 40), foot or head and shoulder massage (RMB 30 for 30min, RMB 50 for 1hr). Full skin treatment, including waxing, costs RMB 120 for arms and RMB 160 for legs. Selection of nail designs, colors and styles. No extra charge for OPI nail polish.
Daily 9.30am-9pm. 4/F, Yashow Market, 58 Gongti Beilu, Chaoyang District. (6413 2426) 晴雨表美甲，朝阳区工体北路58号雅秀市场4层（茶店对面）

Tanning
(Also see Eric Paris in Sanlitun, p491)

Bronze Bodies Tanning Club Beijing's first professional indoor tanning club offers UV tanning, spray tanning,

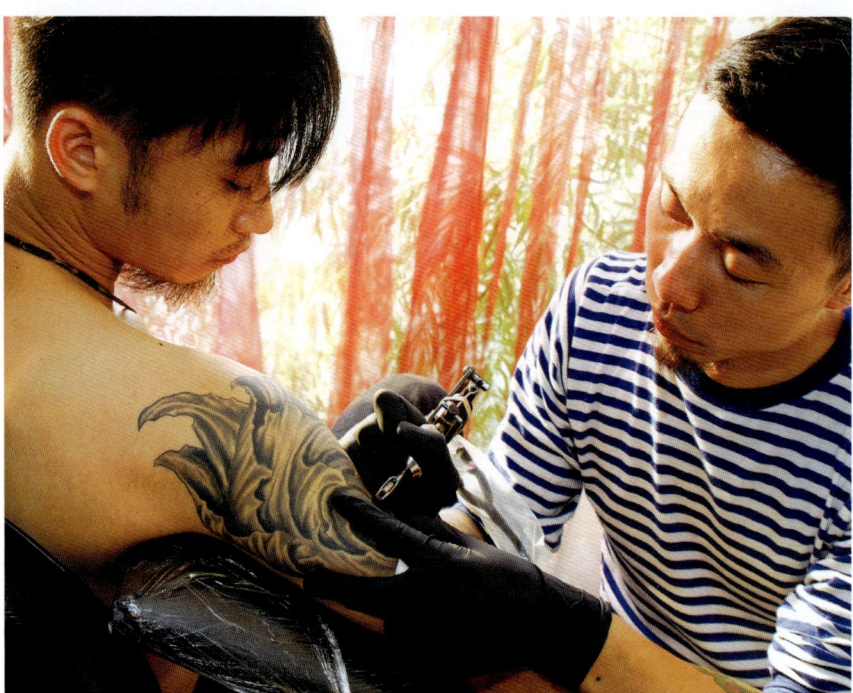

It's permanent, so think before you ink

body bronzing treatments and a selection of self-tanning products (RMB 300-800). Facilities include an elliptically shaped sun bed, a standing tanning cabin, and a shower room. Each 12min session costs RMB 90. You can also purchase 100min for RMB 650 or 240min for RMB 1,200. The staff speaks English.
Daily 11am-9pm. 6/F, Bodhi Therapeutic Retreat, 17 Gongti Beilu, Chaoyang District. (6413 1180) 朝阳区工体北路17号菩提会所6层

Solaris Tanning Studio Has two sun beds and English-speaking staff. RMB 90 per session. Range of VIP packages, including 100min for RMB 600.
Daily 11am-9pm. Sanlitun Lu, Nali Mall (next to Jazz-Ya), Chaoyang District. (6417 0398) 朝阳区三里屯路那里服装市场

Sole Tanning Studio This elegant studio has several private rooms with either a standing tanning cabin or a sun bed, RMB 120 for each 10min session, or RMB 900 for 100min. The VIP room includes a private bathroom, for RMB 160 each session or RMB 1300 for 100min.
Daily 10am-9pm. 1032, Bldg 10, Jianwai Soho, 39 Dongsanhuan Zhonglu, Chaoyang District. (8783 9696) 朝阳区东三环中路39号建外Soho 10座1032号

Tattoos

If you're looking to get some cool "tats," you can also check out the many parlors in the Tongli Studio-area Jiu Ba Street, which might as well be called Tattoo Street.

Jipin Tihui Edward Zhang has started a chain of tattoo shops catering to a white-collar clientele – there are now franchises in Shanghai, Guangzhou and Qingdao. The parlor uses disposable needles, sterilized equipment and inks from the US. Ever-popular Chinese characters are RMB 300 each, and red rose armbands are RMB 400.
Daily 10am-9pm. 466 Dongsi Beidajie, Dongcheng District. (8404 4558) 吉品体绘，东城区东四北大街466号

Tattoo Among the Gui Jie restaurants lies this tattoo parlor and clothes store. The clothes are funky and punky, and the shop is open all night for those booze-fuelled urges to decorate your body.
Daily 4pm-1am. Rm202, Bldg 14, Houxiandaicheng, Chaoyang District. (138 1021 4298) 纹身，朝阳区后现代城14号楼202室

Tattoo Artist Alliance Five qualified tattoo artists offer personal and reassuring service every stage of the process. Tattoos start at RMB 500, depending on the size and degree of difficulty.
Daily 11am-late. 10 Super Bar Street, Chaoyang District. (6463 2063, 133 6686 5698, 139 1073 761) 纹身艺术家联盟，朝阳区星吧路10号

Yicitang Get branded with an indelible reminder of Beijing for as little as RMB 300 in this clean-looking tattoo parlor. The kind staff will calm your nerves, but they don't speak English, so be sure you know what you're requesting!
Daily noon-midnight. 1 Dashibei Hutong, Xicheng District. (6400 2808) 艺刺堂，西城区大石碑胡同1号

Massage

Massages in Beijing can be very gratifying, and definitely worth a trip if you're feeling a bit stressed or under the weather. Like everything else in Beijing, they run from high-rolling luxury to bare bones minimalism. Although the expensive ones may promise you respite from city life and much more, sometimes the cheaper ones may actually be more effective.

99 Massage and Spa Center Body (RMB 150), foot (RMB 100) and aromatic oil massage (RMB 200-380), with free food, fruit and drinks. Single and double rooms. Membership guarantees great discounts.
Daily 24 hours. Rm 703, e-Tower C12, Guanghua Lu, Chaoyang District. (6501 0799) 99按摩中心，朝阳区光华路丙12号数码01大厦703室（嘉里中心与国贸之间）

Aibosen Blindman Massage Foot, body and oil massages employing the much-famed special powers of blind masseurs and masseuses. Staff receive high standards of TCM training; expect to pay extra for a "master." RMB 88 for 70min.
Daily 10am-1am. 11 Liufang Beili, Chaoyang District. (6465 2044, 6466 1247) 爱博森盲人按摩院，朝阳区柳芳北里11号

Bodhi Therapeutic Retreat A range of luxurious massage options available in stylish, minimalist surroundings. Thai traditional massage, aromatherapy massage, Thai herbal treatments and Ayurvedic massage are available. Bodhi's Chinese therapist is trained in TCM and offers services such as *tuina* (body massage) and foot reflexology. Enjoy discount rates (RMB 78) before 5pm from Monday through Thursday; prices begin at RMB 138 otherwise.
Daily 11am-12.30am. 17 Gongti Beilu, Chaoyang District. (6417 9595) www.bodhi.com.cn 菩提会所，朝阳区工体北路17号

Club Les Fleurs Offers a tailored menu of massage and aromatherapy treatments, as well as luxurious spa packages. Prices start at RMB 60 for a 30min back and shoulder massage. The most popular massage is the 90min Oriental Foot Massage (RMB 138). Great discounts for members.
Daily 11am-1am. 6/F, Bldg 7, Central Park, 6 Chaowai Dajie, Chaoyang District. (6533 6288) www.clubles-fleurs.com 青花会馆，朝阳区朝外大街6号新城国际7号楼6层（嘉里中心往北）

Comfortable Blind Massage Blind masseurs and services ranging from back rubs (RMB 25 per 30 min) to traditional treatments like scraping (RMB 30) or cupping (RMB 20). They'll come to your house for an extra RMB 40 plus cab fare.
Daily 9.30am-midnight. 18 Zhongfangli, Sanlitun Nanlu, Chaoyang District. (6507 0036) 康福特保盲人保健按摩，朝阳区三里屯南路中纺里18楼前面

Dongfang Massage This parlor specializes in foot and oil massages. Featuring single, double and group rooms with private bathrooms. Foot massages RMB 30 for 40min or RMB 60 for 70min. Full body massages cost RMB 80 (Chinese style) to RMB 200 (oil massages). 20% discount for cardholders.
1) Daily 8am-2am. Gongti Nanlu (opposite Chaoyang Hospital), Chaoyang District. (6508 3328); 2) Daily 24 hours. 4/F, Nanhang Hotel, 10 Dongsanhuan (southeast of Guomao Bridge), Chaoyang District. (6567 6688 ext 6699); *3) Daily 11am-2am. Downstairs from Cross Bar, 78 Sanlitun Nanlu, Chaoyang District.* (6586 9789, 136 9101 3328) 东方足道，1）朝阳区工体南路（朝阳医院对面）；2）朝阳区东三环10号南航酒店4层（国贸桥东南角）；3）朝阳区三里屯南路78号法雨酒吧楼下

Dragon Foot Club Thai and oil massages in a relaxing environment. RMB 198 for 60min, plus 60min complimentary Chinese Medical Bath.
Daily 24 hours. 15 Jianguomennei (east annex of All China Women's Federation), Dongcheng District. (6559 6957) 龙足健身俱乐部，东城区建国门内15号（中国妇联东配楼）

Dragonfly Therapeutic Retreat This extremely popular boutique avoids rowdy groups, leaving ample room for relaxation and solace. Chinese, Shiatsu and foot massages start at RMB 135 per hour. An exhaustive menu of spa packages include the 2hr Hang over Relief Massage and the Ultimate Indulgence (an hour each of full-body and foot massage), both RMB 270. Other services include manicures, pedicures, waxing and more. Candles, statues, jewelry and aroma oils for sale. Discounts for members.
Daily 10am-1am. 1) 60 Donghuamen Dajie, Dongcheng District. (6527 9368); 2) Daily 11am-1am. 1/F, Eastern Hotel, Sanlitun Nanlu, Chaoyang District. (6593 6066); 3) Daily 9am-midnight. 888, Pinnacle Plaza, Shunyi District. (8046 6682) www.dragonfly.net.cn 悠庭保健会所，1）东城区东华门大街60号；2）朝阳区三里屯南路逸羽连锁酒店1层；3）顺义区荣祥广场888号

Foot to Foot Reflexology Utilizes TCM techniques in various foot massages (RMB 108-188/hr). Also offers oil and hot stone massages.
Daily 11am-2am. 14A Guanghua Lu (inside the Nuo'an Bldg, southwest of the Kerry Centre), Chaoyang District. (5130 9718) 朝阳区光华路甲14号（嘉里中心西侧诺安大厦3A）

Heping Massage Center Specializes in TCM massage (RMB 150/hr, RMB 80 for cardholders) and foot massage (RMB 120/hr), which includes a free 15min herbal medicine foot bath. TCM treatments such as scraping and cupping also available. Appointments recommended, especially on the weekend.
Daily 9.30am-1am. Commercial Bldg 1, Hairun International Bldg, A2, Jiangtai Lu, Chaoyang District. (6436 7370) 和平盲人保健按摩中心，朝阳区将台路甲2号海润国际公寓商业1座

Hezi Leisure and Health This massage parlor caters to Wudaokou's pampered but price-savvy overseas students who just need a good rest at the end of their four-hour day, damn it! Full body massages cost RMB 80/hr, and the 80min "foot" massage (including a bucket of herbal tea and much more) costs RMB 38 before 5pm and RMB 55 after. Prices are reasonable, services are reliable, and someone else has to deal with your feet.
Daily 24 hours (massage), 9am-11pm (beauty salon). Bldg 1, Huaqing Jiayuan, Chengfu Lu, Haidian District. (8286 3988) 和子休闲健身，海淀区华清嘉园1号楼

Liangzi Sports and Fitness Chinese massage, acupuncture and vibrating foot treatment. Spend RMB 200 and you'll receive a membership card valid in 300 + Liangzi Fitness Centers nationwide. Full body massage costs RMB 158 for non-members, RMB 98 (or 78 matinee) for members.

HEALTH & BEAUTY

Bed, Bath, Buffet and Beyond
Initiation to a Beijing bathhouse
by Aamir Wyne

Rubber ducky not included

A critical part of getting to know Beijing well is being able to make bad decisions with little or no hesitation. So when my friend suggested that we try at one of Beijing's swankiest bathhouses, I readily agreed.

Aesthetically, I found the upscale bathhouse to be a living testament to Beijing's love of all that is tacky and Roman. Each room greeted my eyes with a celebration of faux marble columns and statues. If a surface could be made to look gilded, it was – if not, it was painted pastel or covered with a tasteful still life painting.

For reasons of hygiene, the staff made us change into pajamas and provided us with complementary underwear. The house underwear strived to be unisex but erred on the side of "people with no genitals whatsoever," a design flaw that would come back to haunt me several hours later in the steam room. Word to the wise: BYOU.

The clientele were Beijing's nouveau riche; a collection of yuppies and politicos gathered together over a shared love of cleanliness mixed with sweaty nudity. Apparently, the bathhouse, much like the *baijiu* dinner, serves as a nexus for cementing business relationships.

We were the only Westerners in the entire establishment, and the manager, mistaking us for high rollers from out of town, decided to give us the grand tour. The first floor was reserved for single-sex bathing, sauna and steaming. The second floor boasted a 24-hour buffet and three obscenely hot saunas with walls of semi-precious stones. The third floor was one huge dark room filled with recliners and televisions. The fourth floor featured massage rooms, party rooms with plasma screen TVs and electric mahjong tables, and a VIP suite featuring leather furniture, a heart-shaped bed, and jacuzzis. Apparently, at this bathhouse, morality and elevation were inversely proportional.

The highlight of the evening occurred on the first floor, where we were treated to a complimentary full-body exfoliation. While I will spare my more delicate readers from the details of the scrub itself, I will say this – it was just like going to the doctor – that is, if your doctor is a 65-year-old man from Lanzhou who takes an abrasive cloth to your nether bits.

Several hours and a few layers of skin later, we emerged cleaner and wiser men.

Daily 10.30am-1.30am. 2/F, Just Make Mansion. 57 Xingfu Zhonglu Sanlitun, Chaoyang District. (6417 2272) 良子健身，朝阳区三里屯幸福村中路57号杰作大厦2层

Long Island Massage & Spa This large establishment offers Chinese and Thai-style massage and reflexology, as well as facials and other beauty treatments. It distinguishes itself from the pack by boasting several licensed medical masseuses on staff, and a drink and food menu that emphasizes healthy southern-style specialties. 90min foot massages and 1hr full body massages cost RMB 88 during the day, RMB 108 at night.
Daily 11am-1am. B/F, Jiahui Center, 6 Jiqingli, Chaoyang District. (6551 6112/13) 长岛健身，朝阳区吉庆里6号佳汇中心地下

Lotus Spa Has foot massage (RMB 60 for 75min), wooden tubs for soaking, and private rooms for massage (oil massage RMB 168 for 90min). The attached men's and women's hair salon does basic cuts (RMB 30-70).
Daily 10am-10pm. W-02, Tianzhu Huayuan, Fuqian Yijie, Shunyi District. (6457 4822) 顺义区府前一街天竺花园W-02

Miao Feng Zhou Full body massage RMB 88/hr (with oil RMB 180/hr), foot massage RMB 68/hr. Those who exceed 90min of oil massage will get a free 60min foot massage.
Daily 10am-1am. 2/F, Bldg 34, Zaoying Beili, Maizidian Jie, Chaoyang District. (6591 2791, 133 9187 2003) 妙凤洲，朝阳区麦子店街枣营北里34号楼

Oriental Taipan Massage and Spa The perfect place to invigorate tired muscles and leave the stresses of the day behind. Helpful, friendly staff. Private rooms are available; bring your favorite tunes or DVDs and feel those serotonin levels rise. 90min of fabulous foot massage, with healthy fruit juices and snacks included, cost RMB 138 or RMB 97 before 6pm. VIP cards provide considerable discounts.
1) *Daily 11am-1am. B1/F, Xindong Lu, Chaoyang District. (8532 2177);* 2) *Daily 11am-1am. 2/F, Block 9, Holiday Inn Lido, 2A Fangyuan Xilu, Chaoyang District. (6437 6299);* 3) *Daily 11am-3am. Sunjoy Mansion, 6 Ritan Lu, Chaoyang District. (6502 5722);* 4) *Daily 11am-1am. 101, Block B, Winterless Center, 1 Xidawang Lu, Chaoyang District. (6538 8086) www.taipan.com.cn* 东方大班保健休闲会所，1) 朝阳区新东路1号沈记靓汤地库；2) 朝阳区芳园西路甲2号丽都广场9号公寓2层；3) 朝阳区日坛路6号新族大厦院内；4) 朝阳区西大望路1号温特莱中心B座101号

Tianhe Liangzi Highly recommended chain of foot massage establishments. A relaxing herbal foot soak is followed by thorough foot and ankle massages (RMB 139 for 90min), with TCM health tips if your Chinese is up to scratch. Full body massages RMB 120 for 50 min.
Daily noon-2am. 1) *China Wenlian Hotel, 10 Nongzhan Nanli, Chaoyang District. (6506 2697);* 2) *1/F, Bldg A, Qingzhu Hotel, 1 Chedaogou, Haidian District. (6871 6903);* 3) *Jinzhiqiao Daxia, 1A Jianguomenwai Dajie, Dongcheng District. (6507 9285)* 天河良子健身，1) 朝阳区农展南里10号中国文联宾馆；2) 海淀区车道沟1号青竹宾馆A座1F；3) 东城区建国门外大街甲1号金之桥大厦

Top Club – Yang Yuan Tang Foot Massage Offers royal, aromatic, and Chinese foot massages. Japanese/Thai massage, cupping, scrubbing, pedicure, callus and corn removal, and ear-cleaning are also available. Free movies, food and fresh fruit.

Daily 10am-2am. 1/F, Longge Apartment, 15 Chaoyang Gongyuan Xilu, Chaoyang District. (5867 0158/0156) 北京养元堂高级足疗会馆，朝阳区朝阳公园西路15号龙阁公寓首层

Qing Song Blind Doctor Massage Rough and ready surroundings, but excellent massage at a fraction of Western prices. Staff are also experts in diagnostics and offer health advice on everything from diet to desk ergonomics.
Daily 10am-11.30pm. 21 Chunxiu Lu, Chaoyang District. (6417 6047) 真轻松盲人保健按摩中心，朝阳区春秀路21号

Xin Yue Xing Cheng Massage Center Body or foot massage RMB 180 for 2hr, Korean or oil massage RMB 300 for 2hr, spa/kidney massage RMB 150. House calls available 24hr.
Daily 11am-1am. Rm 2510, Bldg B, Sunshine 100, 2 Guanghua Lu, Chaoyang District. (5100 0299) www.xingchengmassage.com 心悦星城，朝阳区光华路2号阳光100国际公寓B座2510室

Spas

Going beyond basic massages, these spas and resorts offer an extensive spectrum of facials, scrubs, light therapy, and other indulgent beauty treatments.

Anantara Spa This luxuriously calm yet simply decorated spa has 15 treatment rooms, all with private showering and changing facilities. Massages start at RMB 480 for 60min, and facials from RMB 520. The 2.5hr signature treatment "Culture of Anantara" incorporates a body polish, massage and floral bath for RMB 1,380.
Daily 10am-8pm. The Commune by the Great Wall, Shuiguan Great Wall, Badaling Highway. (8118 1888 ext 5100/01) anantaraspa@commune.com.cn 延庆县八达岭高速公路水关长城脚下公社

CHI, The Spa Based on Asian healing philosophies and Himalayan mystique, this 1,000sqm spa features 11 suites, each with its own herbal steam room and infinity bath with color light therapy. Choose from 35 massage, facial, water and body therapies based on the five elements (metal, water, wood, fire and earth). Signatures include the 1hr soft mountain tsampa rub (RMB 680), and the 2.5hr Empress Imperial Jade Journey (RMB 1,480), inspired by Empress Cixi's regal beauty regimen.
Daily 10am-2am. Shangri-La Beijing, 29 Zizhuyuan Lu, at Xisanhuan Lu, Haidian District. (6841 2211) www.shangri-la.com 北京香格里拉饭店，海淀区西三环紫竹院路29号

Chun Hui Yuan Warm Springs Resort Popular spot with jacuzzis, hot springs and a range of massage treatments. RMB 128 entrance fee.
Daily 9am-midnight. Gaoliying Yuzhuang, Shunyi District. (6945 4433) 春晖园温泉度假村，顺义区高丽营于庄

Essence Vale Spa The Beijing branch of the Singapore-based spa draws hot water directly from a natural hot spring 3,000m beneath the Yosemite compound and features dark oak wood Asian décor, personal balconies and large bathtubs in some VIP suites. A 60min Thai herbal massage will set you back RMB 480, a 30min *guasha* (scraping) RMB 200, and bikini line waxing RMB 220. The masseuses, who hail from the Philippines and Thailand, all speak English.

Real Men Exfoliate

Mars can be beautiful too

by Jenny Niven

To fully become a "Beijing man," it seems that rolling your T-shirt up over your *baijiu* belly and setting one jaunty trouser leg at calf height is no longer enough. Alpha males across the city are reaping the benefits of a flourishing industry in health treatments, beauty products and good ol' fashioned luxury. Beautification has become so popular with Chinese men that new terminology has appeared to describe those who indulge: *aimei nanren*, or "love-beauty men."

John Chiu, a fan of organic beauty products, laments the current dearth of salons in Beijing, but sees the market growing. He advises others to throw aside their preconceptions and to spend some serious time grooming. "You don't have to look fancy. But to be a gentleman, you should do this." Although many men profess to be beautifying themselves for business, or for their own personal comfort, other influential factors are discernible fairly near the surface. Explains Peter Keim, "Women look at three things. Your face, your hands…and then your butt."

In recent years, the market for men's beautification appears to have skyrocketed, with Botox, liposuction and teeth whitening amongst the regular treatments Beijingers – expat and Chinese alike – are willing to splash their cash on. Joshua Granson, consultant at *Beyond: Dental & Health* sees an increasing number of Chinese men paying attention to dental cosmetics. "Studies show that 80% of American men have spent money on teeth whitening products. We're still a little bit off that in Beijing at the moment, but it's definitely a growing concern."

In the name of scientific research, we commissioned an informal survey of attitudes towards grooming amongst expatriate men, diligently conducting our research amid the rose-scented water and soft lighting of Mei's Lounge. "It's a question of affordability," explains James West, a journalist from Sydney. "If I could be as indulgent as this elsewhere I most certainly would."

"There's the anonymity factor too," says Mike Hatch as his feet are freed of their rough skin. "I'm certainly more cavalier about this knowing it's unlikely I'll bump into anyone I know." For every hardheaded Botoxer however, it seems there are still just as many men who find pampering to be a vaguely emasculating process. One nameless virgin manicuree expresses his belief that many men are still more comfortable with the less salubrious services available at some Beijing salons than the "intrusive" process of having their cuticles trimmed.

Whatever your personal preferences, there is no doubt that Beijing's trained professionals are now equally as comfortable providing grooming services for men as for women. Beijing man, it may be high time for that lone, gigantic pinkie-nail to be given the snip.

The "love-beauty man" loves a pretty pedi

Mei's Lounge Professional Manicure and Pedicure
Daily 11.30am-midnight. Unit H, 1/F, Jiezuo Dasha (next to April Gourmet), Xingfucun Zhonglu, Chaoyang District. (6417 1798) 朝阳区幸福村中路杰作大厦1层H单元

The hands-on treatment at Anantara Spa is so soothing, it's sleep-inducing

Daily 10am-10.30pm. Yosemite Club, 4 Yuyang Lu, Houshayu, Shunyi District. (8041 7588 ext 6316) www.yosemiteclub.com 顺义区后沙峪渔阳路4号优山美地俱乐部

Fengshan Hot Spring Resort Located in the mountains of Changping east of the Ming Tombs Reservoir, Fengshan Hot Springs is equipped with 200 standard guest rooms, hot springs, sauna, swimming pool, karaoke and exercise facilities. Entrance fee RMB 198.
Daily 24 hours. East side of Changping Reservoir, Changping District. (6071 1188) www.fsdj.com.cn 朝阳区昌平水库东侧

Flora Spa Specializes in treatments using French Ceeture products and organic products by Australian brand Jurlique. Emphasizes friendly service to a more relaxed clientele and a community environment with frequent customer parties. A 150min full body treatment package costs RMB 988 for Jurlique, RMB 420 for French Ceeture. Jurlique Facials cost RMB 480, Ceeture RMB 298. Package discounts and regular promotions.
Daily 10am-9pm. 313 Tower E, Sunshine 100, Guanghua Lu, Chaoyang District. (5100 2004, 133 9198 1379) www.floraspa.cn 朝阳区光华路阳光100 E座 313

Golden Corolla Oft-recommended day spa offering aromatic facial treatments (RMB 560), herbal body scrubs, and milk and oil body massages. Full body massages range RMB 360-700. Specialist services such as cellulite removal are also available. Discounts available for regulars.
Daily 10am-9pm. 1/F, Bldg 7, Julong Garden, 68 Xinzhong Jie, Dongcheng District. (6551 8091) 金可丽雅，东城区新中街68号聚龙花园7号楼1层

Herbal Spring Offers professional skin care, aromatherapy, tub baths, haircuts (RMB 200) and all-natural oil massages (RMB 580-1000).
Daily 9.30am-9.30pm. Rm 102, Block C, Hairun Guoji Gongyu, B2 Jiangtai Lu (near Holiday Inn Lido), Chaoyang District. (5135 7971/73) 草本山泉，朝阳区将台路乙2号海润国际公寓C座102室

Huaqing Hot Springs Hotel Sink into a traditional Chinese medicinal herbal bath surrounded by natural hot spring pools, steam it up in the sauna, or bake away your stresses on a hot stone *kang*. A range of massage options is also available.
Daily 9am-2am. North of the Lishuiqiao Station on Line 13 (200m south of Tiantongyuan Residential Area), Changping District. (8482 6665) 华清温泉宾馆，昌平区立水桥城铁站北，天通苑南200米

I-Spa Located in the InterContinental Hotel, this spa combines the Western practice of soothing oil massages with traditional Chinese massage that focuses on healing muscles. Treatments include facials, tanning, foot reflexology, body massages and Vichy shower. Massages start at RMB 200 for a 30min neck and shoulder massage, but the main attraction is the InterContinental Massage (RMB 980 for 105min). Add a 15% service fee.
Daily 10:30am-midnight (last appointment 11pm). 6/F, InterContinental Financial Street, 11 Jinrong Jie, Xicheng District. (5852 5888 ext 5601) 西城区金融街11号洲际酒店6层

I Spa Resonates Thai harmony in both its décor and its services. Choose from a luxurious selection including facials (RMB 438 for 60min), body wraps (RMB 498 for 60min), aroma baths (RMB 280), Thai herbal scrubs (RMB 298 for 30min) and their signature head-to-toe massages with specially blended oil (RMB 558 for 90min). For those who prefer stronger palm strokes, the traditional Thai massage (RMB 498 for 90min) includes stretching and concentrates on the body's pressure points. The second location offers an escape from the city and a soak in a natural hot spring.
Daily 11am-11pm. 1) 5/F, Block B, Taiyue Suites, 16 Sanlitun Nanlu, Chaoyang District. (6507 1517); 2) Daily noon-11pm. Inside Napa Valley Club, 68 Shashun Lu, Xiaotangshan, Changping District. (6178 7795) www.ispa.cn 泰美好，1) 朝阳区三里屯南路16号泰悦豪庭B座5层; 2) 昌平区小汤山沙顺路68号纳帕溪谷内

Jiuhua Spa and Resort
Formerly a royal retreat, Jiuhua Resort features courtyard accommodation, private villas and a string of restaurants. All kinds of spa treatments are offered, using naturally sourced springs. Their medicinal hot mud spas are reputed to cure back and leg pain, improve skin tone and detoxify the body. Holistic health checks and dietary advice also available on request.
Daily 9am-2am. Xiaotangshan Zhen, Changping District. (6178 2288) 九华山庄温泉，昌平区小汤山镇

My Spa This stylish Malaysian-inspired spa offers more than 30 treatments, presenting a fusion of ancient traditional techniques (for example, the Sabai Stone Therapy treatment, RMB 750 for 90min), and state-of-the-art technology and equipment (Bio-Light Facial Therapy, RMB 450 for 60min). Chinese full body massages start at RMB 300/hr, and oil massages at RMB 550/hr. Waxing services (from RMB 90 for upper lip) also available.
Daily 10am-11pm. 9/F, South Wing, Loong Palace Hotel & Resort, Huilongguan, Changping District. (8077 8515/8151) www.loongpalace.com 昌平区回龙观龙城丽宫国际酒店南楼9层

Palm Springs Spa Lavishly designed Asian, Persian, and European-style rooms reflect a journey along the Silk Road. Services include foot massage (RMB 260 for 60min), stress relief back massage (RMB 450), full body massage (RMB 760 for 90min), whitening facial (RMB 680), and men's deep cleansing facial (RMB 780). Appointments by reservation only.
Daily 10am-midnight. Palm Springs International Club, 8 Chaoyang Gongyuan Nanlu, Chaoyang District. (6539 8888 ext 8080/8081) www.palmsprings.cn 棕榈泉国际俱乐部，朝阳区朝阳公园南路8号

Pattaya Pleasures Features a series of elementally themed rooms where you can enjoy Thai style massage therapy (around RMB 500, RMB 200 for club members), a foot massage (RMB 86), body treatment or facial (RMB 180-780).
Daily 11am-11pm. Seasons Club, Chunxiu Lu, B36 Dongzhimenwai Dajie. (8453 0399, 8453 0398) 芭堤雅养生，东城区东直门外大街乙36号春秀路海晟国际俱乐部

Renewal Spa Club After the consultation, the friendly and knowledgeable staff will show you to a color-themed treatment room specially suited to your mood and treatment aims. Services include facials starting at RMB 480 and massages at RMB 380. All products are organic and culture-specific treatments feature products imported from the country of origin. The traditional Javanese massage (RMB 600 for 90min) is followed by a delightful organic Indonesian ginger tea.
Daily 10am-10pm. Area C1, Upper East Side Central Plaza, Dongsihuan Beilu, Chaoyang District. (5139 5555) 朝阳区东四环北路阳光上东商业广场C1区

Ritz-Carlton Spa Occupying the entire basement floor of the hotel, this spa is elegant, understated and stylish. Staff is friendly and helpful, without being overbearing. There is a pool and fitness suite for members and hotel residents, but most people visiting will be drawn to the spa treatments, such as facials starting at RMB 300 for 30min, and other beauty services (like a haircut, shampoo and blow dry for RMB 290 and a 60min spa manicure for RMB 280). On the pricier end, these are massages from RMB 350 for 30min to the signature Imperial Treasures at RMB 980 for 90min, but as the saying goes, you get what you pay for. All rates subject to a 15% service charge.
Daily 6am-11pm. B/1F, 1 Jinchengfang Dongjie, Financial Street, Xicheng District. (6601 6666, 6629 6907) www.ritzcarlton.com 西城区金融街金城坊街1号地下1层

Serenity Spa Features 7 single and 5 double treatment suites, steam rooms, a Vichy shower room, foot massage suite, and hair & beauty salon. Wide range of pampering treatments from China, Thailand, and

At the Ritz, it's "no grain, no gain" if you want petal-soft hands

Europe include massages (RMB 350-1280), facials (RMB 650-950), 45min body scrubs (RMB 380), manicures (RMB 230-280) and pedicures (RMB 250-320).
Daily 10am-2am. The Regent Beijing, 97 Jinbao Jie, Dongcheng District. (8522 1888) 东城区金宝街97号丽晶酒店

Spa de Feng for Men Only "Exclusively for men," they're out to prove that there's nothing as manly as flower petals, facials and mood music. The spa features French products, Eastern-inspired treatments and an English-speaking manager to help you decide which is right for you. A sauna and tearoom give the finishing touches to an indulgent, guys-only experience – with prices to match. Full body massage costs RMB 360/hr.
Daily noon-midnight. C306, Sunshine 100, 2 Guanghua Lu, Chaoyang District. (5100 1330) www.linfeng-spa.com 临枫，朝阳区光华路2号阳光100 C306号

St. Regis Spa Center The last word in luxury, the St. Regis Spa represents self-indulgence in the extreme, offering treatments such as deep tissue and traditional Chinese massages, aromatherapy, facials, body wraps, antioxidant treatments and many more. Prices start from RMB 125 for a 15min hand massage, RMB 250 for a head and neck massage, RMB 500 for spa treatments, and RMB 350 for an express 30min facial.
Daily 24hrs. St. Regis Hotel, 21 Jianguomenwai Dajie, Chaoyang District. (6460 6688 ext 2759) 国际俱乐部Spa中心，朝阳区建国门外大街21号国际俱乐部酒店

Touch Spa With 11 tastefully decorated single and double spa rooms (each with their own shower), steam room, restroom, couches and massage tables, it's all soothing stillness. The impeccable attention to service and luxury comes with a price tag (from RMB 200 for a 45min foot massage to full body massages at RMB 680 for 60min and spa packages up to RMB 2250 for 5hr), but we all deserve a touch of luxury, don't we?
Daily 10am-2am. 6 Jiangtai Lu, Holiday Inn Lido, Chaoyang District. (6430 1072) 怡婷水疗，朝阳区将台路6号丽都假日酒店（健身房旁边）

Westcoast Bathing Centre While spartan – one sauna, one steam room, two tubs and a row of showers – these baths are clean, rarely crowded and convenient. The wooden sauna comes close to a Scandinavian original, using heated rocks atop an oven and a thermostat set to around 90 degrees Celsius. Entry RMB 38, tub use RMB 28, scrub-downs RMB 28.
Daily 24 hours. B1/F, Dongyuan Dasha, 35 Chengfu Lu, Haidian District. (6252 0953) 西海岸洗浴中心，海淀区成府路35号东源大厦地下1层

Zen Spa Located in a Chinese-style courtyard filled with traditional furniture, Zen Spa offers a tranquil retreat. Services include floral bath, sugar and ginger bath, herbal and salt scrub, detoxification seaweed mask, traditional Thai massage, deep-cleaning facial, Thai herbal heat treatment, ear-wax treatment and more. Also enjoy complimentary rose tea, watermelon juice and sandwiches.
Daily 11am-11pm. House 1, 8A Xiaowuji Lu, Chaoyang District. (8731 2530) www.zenspa.com.cn 朝阳区小武基路甲8号1号院（东四环南路15号出口）

HEALTH & BEAUTY

Medical Services for the Whole Family

Our family practice clinics and emergency services are run by a professional team of foreign family physicians and specialists, who are highly trained to ensure you and your family receive quality, comprehensive medical care and peace of mind whilst in China.

A full spectrum of medical care services including:

- Family Medicine
- Obstetrics & Gynaecology
- ENT
- Physiotherapy
- Counselling
- Orthopeadics
- Paediatrics
- Dentistry
- Orthodontics
- Traditional Chinese Medicine
- Optometry
- Health Screening Services

Emergency Medical Services include: House calls, Ambulance Service, 24 hour Emergency Department, Medical Evacuation and/ or Repatriation by Beijing Based Air Ambulance.

Open 24 hours/ 365 days per year, operating in over 70 countries.

Clinic Appointments: 6462 9112
24-Hour Alarm Center: 6462 9100

Bldg C, BITIC Jing Yi Building, 5 Sanlitun Xiwujie, Chaoyang District
朝阳区三里屯西五街5号北信京谊大厦C座

www.internationalsos.com

An AEA Company

TRANSPORTATION

At your favourite local Chinese joint and don't know what to order besides *gong bao ji ding*? Try something new with our **Spicy Chinese Cuisine** and **Healthy Chinese Cuisine** guides! Whether you're in the mood to set your mouth on fire or start on a diet (again), our guides will introduce you to delicious dishes you've never tried before!

Our guides come with colorful photographs, names and ingredients in Chinese, English, French, and Russian, all packaged conveniently in a pocket-sized book. Just point and order with **Spicy Chinese Cuisine** and **Healthy Chinese Cuisine**!

Available at bookstores around Beijing or to order a copy, please e-mail distribution@immersionguides.com

www.immersionguides.com

Deus Ex Machina
Steps to solve Beijing's notorious traffic congestion
by Jackie Yu

Blues skies and clear roads ahead? That would be nice

Whether you're jammed in a winding dragon of other cars, crushed between other bodies on a subway or bus, or dodging cars on your bike while choking on the air, Beijing presents challenges for any commuter.

The situation beneath our gray skies, however, is far from static. As the big O approaches, transportation in Beijing is simultaneously hurtling in two very opposite directions. With pledges for a "Green Olympic Games," the government has budgeted RMB 250 billion to enhance the city's public transportation infrastructure. In the year leading up to the Games, we can look forward to the opening of three spiffy new subway lines and the high-speed airport rail line, the introduction of 5,000 natural gas buses, and the unveiling of a new Norman Foster-designed airport terminal. Along with such carrots to take commuters off the roads will be a few sticks. City authorities vow to limit vehicular traffic for the Olympics by nearly halving the number of cars on the roads for the two months preceding the Games, and further limiting the number of cars to less than one million during the Olympics themselves. How exactly this will be accomplished has yet to be revealed, but there is talk of drastic measures such as encouraging public servants to work from home or take mandatory vacations. Liu Xiaoming, deputy director of the Beijing Municipal Communication Commision, says, "Traffic will not be a headache at all, but rather will become an enjoyable experience by 2008." A stunning prospect.

Beijing residents, especially those without cars, would be amazed and delighted if the government simply made traffic disappear during the Games. Anything beyond that is hard to envision, given that Beijingers are buying over 1,100 new cars every single day. The city is already home to over 3 million cars – three times more than in 1997 and a million more than in 2003 – with the number expected to climb to 3.5 million in 2008. According to the most recent survey, theoretically nearly one of every five Beijingers owns a car. Beijing seems fated to lose its reputation as the capital of the "kingdom of bicycles."

At the time of writing, average speed on the roads stood at a snail-like 12km/h, down from 45km/h in 1994. While the traffic becomes worse and the pollution gets thicker by the day, Beijing's automotive appetite remains insatiable, driven by status as much as by convenience. As the government pushes for alternatives, Beijing's transportation system will reach equilibrium – or total stasis. In time, Beijing must learn to curb its appetite and find – we hope – some healthier alternatives, or else face mounting health, pollution and productivity costs. Until then, here are some tips to help you get there and back again.

Air

The Airport

To keep up with a surge in demand, the airport is in the midst of a massive expansion project to nearly double its current handling capacity to 60 million passengers by 2008. At present, the airport consists of two terminals: most domestic and all international flights arrive and depart from Terminal 2, while Terminal 1 (a.k.a. Nanhangzhanlou) is only used by China Southern Airlines and Xiamen Airlines for domestic flights. Terminal 2 has been spruced up and is more user-friendly than ever. True, the newsstands have disappointingly thin selections, but the expanded duty-free section offers cheaper prices than do most airlines, and the selection includes more toy pandas and Olympic tchotchkes than you can shake a stick at.

Restaurant prices have been lowered to mildly extortionate, and the selection now includes several Starbucks, a Subway and a KFC – welcome to China! The banking options have expanded too, with several bureaux de change, money-changing machines, and ATMs that accept foreign cards (notably in arrivals). For its part, Terminal 1 attempts to tempt your tummy with a KFC, a UBC and a Le Jazz (the chicken joint once known as Kenny Rogers' Roasters). Note that the departure tax is now included in the price of your ticket, so you no longer have to pay the tax at the airport. Further note that the red-capped porters are prohibited from charging for their service, but will gladly accept a tip.

Cheers, Sir Norman

When it opens in February 2008, Terminal 3 will become home to flagship carrier Air China and most international airlines. Its star designer, Sir Norman Foster, says the new terminal will be "the world's largest and most advanced airport building." Its triangular forms – designed to evoke the shape of a dragon (what else?) – maximize the perimeter, allowing for a "record" number of aircraft parking spaces, while minimizing walking distances. Conveyor belts will be present throughout and a high-speed automated train called APM (Auto People Mover System) – the thin torso of the dragon's body – will ferry passengers across the open-air green space that connects the third Terminal's three buildings. Sounds fab.

Getting into town

Unless you like being overcharged, do not accept a ride from a tout. Legitimate taxis line up in well-marked ranks outside the arrivals level of each of the terminals. Since cab drivers typically line up for hours to get a fare into the city, they occasionally grumble when passengers "only" wish to travel to nearby Shunyi. To avoid this, some savvy Shunyi residents head up to the departures level and flag a taxi that is dropping someone off. Since that driver has been spared the long wait, s/he is happy to take the fare. A taxi to the heart of the city should cost RMB 75-100 including the RMB 10 for the toll.

You can also take the shuttle bus (see below for details). The highly anticipated airport express train from the Dongzhimen transportation hub is slated to commence operation in June 2008, which will blast across the 27.3km at a top speed of 110 km/h, arriving in only 18 minutes. Reminiscent of Hong Kong's widely-hailed Airport Express, passengers will be able to check in and get their boarding pass at Dongzhimen Station. The one-way ticket price is tentatively set at RMB 20.

Beijing Capital International Airport *Airport Road, Chaoyang District. (6454 1100, lost luggage 6459 9523/4, customer complaint hotline 6457 1666) www.bcia.com.cn/en/index.jsp* 北京国际机场，朝阳区机场路

Airport Bus

At the moment, the cheapest way into town is to take CAAC's comfortable airport shuttle bus. Tickets cost RMB 16 and the ride takes between 40-90 minutes, depending on traffic and origin/destination. The buses have much more luggage room than taxis. Look for a white bus stop sign at the pickup location (see below). The shuttles leave the airport from outside gates 11-13 in the arrivals level of Terminal 2. Buses depart every 15-30 minutes. Call 6459 4375/6 for information (Chinese only).

A map representation of the following information is available online: www.bcia.com.cn/en/photo/bashi_map.html

Connecting bus, subway and light rail, Xizhimen's intermodal station is a reflection of things to come

Thank you, Sir (Norman Foster): Terminal 3 will double the airport's handling capacity to 60 million passengers

From the airport to downtown:

Line 1: Capital Airport, Liangmaqiao, Hujialou, Dabeiyao (World Trade Center), Panjiayuan, Shilihe (King Wing Hot Spring International Hotel), Fangzhuang (Guiyou Shopping Mall). Daily 7.30am-10.30pm.

Line 2: Capital Airport, Sanyuanqiao, Dongzhimen, Dongsishitiao, Xidan (Civil Aviation Building). Daily 7am-last domestic arrival.

Line 3: Capital Airport, Yuyang Hotel, Dongdaqiao (bypassed after 10.30pm), Chaoyangmen, Yabaolu, Beijing Railway Station. Daily 7.30am-last domestic arrival.

Line 4: Capital Airport, China Intl Exhibition Center, Xibahe, Anzhen Qiao, Madian Qiao, Beitaipingzhuang, Jimen Qiao, Friendship Hotel, Beijing TV Station, Zizhu Qiao, Hangtian Qiao, Gongzhufen (Xinxing Hotel). Daily 7am-11pm.

Line 5: Airport, Wangjing (Huajiadi), Xiaoying, Yayuncun (Anhui Qiao), Xueyuan Qiao, Zhongguancun (No.4 bridge). Daily 8.30am-9.30pm.

Capital Airport-Tianjin Line: Buses leave Capital Airport every 30 minutes from outside gate 15 in the arrival level of Terminal 2. Ticket price is RMB 70. Will arrive in Tianjin at the intersection of Nanjing Lu and Shanxi Lu, which is also the departure point of Tianjin-Capital Airport line (see below). Daily 7am-11pm.

From downtown to the airport:

Line 1: Fangzhuang (Guiyou Shopping Mall), Dabeiyao (South China Aviation Hotel), Capital Airport. Daily 6am-7.30pm.

Line 2: Xidan (Civil Aviation Building), Dongzhimen (50m from the east of the bridge), Jingxin Building (West Entry), Capital Airport. Daily 5.40am-9pm.

Line 3: Beijing Railway Station, International Hotel (West Entry), Dongzhimen (50m from the east of the bridge), Jingxin Building (West Entry), Capital Airport. Daily 6am-7.30pm.

Line 4: Gongzhufen (Xinxing Hotel), Friendship Hotel (North Entry Air Ticket Office), Beitaipingzhuang (50m from the east of the crossroad), Anzhen Building, Capital Airport. Daily 5.40am-9pm.

Line 5: Zhongguancun (No.4 Bridge), Beihang University (North Entry), Huixin Xijie (Anhui Building), Huixin Dongjie (SINOPEC), Capital Airport. Daily 7am-7.30pm.

Tianjin-Capital Airport Line: Daily 4am-6pm. (022 2311 0782). Ticket price is RMB 70.

To confirm this information, visit the Beijing Capital International Airport site: www.bcia.com.cn/en/passengers_Land_airport_page.html

The Other Airport

Thirteen km south of Tian'anmen, deep in Fengtai District, is the purgatory of Beijing air travel – Nanyuan Airport. Only travelers with frightening karmic debt end up here – and all clients of China United Airlines, formerly a military carrier, which bases its operations at Nanyuan. The entire airport is exclusively reserved for CUA planes, serving 15 different destinations, including hot spots like Qingdao and Sanya. Free Nanyuan Airport shuttle bus for passengers runs to and from Xidan Aviation Building. *Ticket hotline: (800 810 0099, 400 610 0099) www.cu-air.com*

Nanyuan Airport *Nanyuan Lu, Fengtai District (6797 8899)* 南苑机场，丰台区南苑路

Airlines

The airport's expansion means more international airlines are obtaining coveted landing slots in Beijing (e.g. Continental Airlines and American Airlines). New transpolar routes are also being pioneered that shave hours off the journey to North America, such as Air Canada's direct Beijing-Toronto flight – which avoids the Vancouver layover – and Continental's Beijing-Newark connection. Domestic travelers tired of paying high prices may be heartened by the launch of China's first low-cost airlines, Okay Airways, which flies out of Tianjin's Binhai International Airport, about ... er ... 200 kilometers from the capital.

If you need to get airborne, call one of the following carriers or a travel agent (see p509-510)

Aeroflot *Apartment Building, Swissotel, 2 Chaoyangmen Beidajie, Chaoyang District. (6500 2412) www.aeroflot.com* 俄罗斯航空，朝阳区朝阳门北大街2号港澳中心瑞士酒店公寓楼

Air Canada *Rm C201, Lufthansa Center, 50 Liangmaqiao Lu, Chaoyang District. (6468 2001) www.aircanada.com* 加拿大航空，朝阳区亮马桥路50号燕莎中心C201

Air China *Xidan Minhang Building, 15 Xi Chang'an Jie, Xicheng District. (800 810 1111) www.airchina.com.cn* 中国国际航空，西城区西长安街15号西单民航大厦

Air France *Rm 1606-1611, Bldg 1 Kuntai Intl. Mansion, 12A Chaowai Dajie, Chaoyang District. (4008 808 808) www.airfrance.com.cn* 法国航空，朝阳区朝阳门外大街甲12号昆泰国际大厦1号楼1606 – 1611

All Nippon Airways *N200, Fazhan Dasha, 5 Dongsanhuan Beilu, Chaoyang District. (800 820 1122, 6590 9191) www.anaskyweb.com/cn/c/index.html* 全日空，朝阳区东三环北路5号发展大厦N200

Asiana Airlines *12/F Building A, Jiacheng Plaza, 18 Xiaguangli, Dongsanhuan Beilu, Chaoyang District. (400 650 8000) http://cn.flyasiana.com/* 韩亚航空，朝阳区东三环北路霞光里18号佳程广场A座12层

Austrian Airlines *Rm 603-604, Lufthansa Center, 50 Liangmaqiao Lu, Chaoyang District. (6464 5999) www.aua.com* 奥地利航空，朝阳区亮马桥路50号燕莎中心603-604号

British Airways *Scitech Tower Rm 210, 22 Jianguomenwai Dajie, Chaoyang District. (400 650 0073) www.britishairways.com* 英国航空，朝阳区建国门外大街22号赛特大厦210

China Southern Airlines *Building A, AVIC Building, 2 Dongsanhuan Nanlu, Dongcheng District. (95539) www.cs-air.com* 中国南方航空，东城区东三环南路2号艾维克大厦A座

Continental Airlines *500 Sunflower Tower, 37 Maizidian Jie, Chaoyang District. (8527 6686) www.continental.com* 美国大陆航空，朝阳区麦子店街37号盛福大厦500号

Dragon Air *28/F, East Tower, Twins Tower, 12B Jianguomenwai Dajie, Chaoyang District. (400 811 0288) www.dragonair.com* 港龙航空，朝阳区建国门外大街乙12号双子座大厦东塔28楼

Japan Airlines *1/F, Changfugong Office Building, 26 Jianguomenwai Dajie, Chaoyang District. (400 888 0808) www.jal.com.hk/zhcn* 日本航空，朝阳区建外大街26号长富宫1层

KLM Royal Dutch Airlines *1609-1611 Kuntai International Building, Chaoyangmenwai Dajie, Chaoyang District. (400 880 8222) www.klm.com/travel/cn_cn* 荷兰皇家航空，朝阳区朝阳门外大街乙12号昆泰国际大厦1609-1611

Korean Air *1602, Hyundai Motor Building, 38 Xiaoyun Lu, Chaoyang District. (400 658 8888, 8453 8137) www.koreanair.com.cn* 大韩航空，朝阳区三元东桥霄云路38号现代汽车大厦901-903

TRANSPORTATION

Lufthansa Airlines Unit S101 & C202, Lufthansa Centre Office Building, 50 Liangmaqiao Lu, Chaoyang District. (6468 8338) www.lufthansa.com.cn 汉莎航空，朝阳区亮马桥路50号燕莎中心S101和C202

Northwest Airlines 501B, West Wing, China World Trade Centre, 1 Jianguomenwai Dajie, Chaoyang District. (400 814 0081) www.nwa.com/cn 美国西北航空，朝阳区建国门外大街1号国贸中心西楼501B

Qantas Airlines B7-8, 10/F West Tower, LG Twin Tower, B12 Jianguomenwai Dajie, Chaoyang District. (400 888 0209) www.qantas.com.au/international/cn/index 澳洲航空，朝阳区建国门外大街乙12号双子座大厦西塔10层7–8单元

SAS Rm 430, Beijing Sunflower Tower, 37 Maizidian Street, Chaoyang District. (8527 6100) www.flysas.com 北欧航空，朝阳区麦子店街37号盛福大厦430

Shanghai Airlines Nanzhuyuan Yiqu, Building 3, Beijing Capital International Airport, Chaoyang District. (800 820 1018, 6456 9019) www.shanghai-air.com 上海航空，朝阳区首都机场3号航站楼南竹园1区

Singapore Airlines Rm 801, Tower 2, China World Trade Centre, 1 Jianguomenwai Dajie, Chaoyang District. (6505 2233) www.singaporeair.com 新加坡航空，朝阳区建国门外大街1号国贸中心2座801

Swiss Air 101 Lufthansa Center, 50 Liangmaqiao Lu, Chaoyang District. (8454 0180) www.swiss.com 瑞士航空，朝阳区亮马桥路50号燕莎写字楼101

Thai International Rm 303, W3 Tower, Oriental Plaza, Dongcheng District. (8515 0088) www.thaiair.com 泰国国际航空，东城区东方广场西三座303

United Airlines C/D1 Unit, 15/F Tower A, GATEWAY, 18 Xiaguangli, Dongsanhuan Beilu, Chaoyang District. (800 810 8282, 6463 1111) www.cn.united.com 美国联合航空，朝阳区东三环东三环北路霞光里18号佳程广场A座15层C/D1单元

Vietnam Airlines S121 Lufthansa Center, 50 Liangmaqiao Lu, Chaoyang District. (6463 8448) www.vietnamair.com.vn 越南航空，朝阳区亮马桥50号燕莎中心写字楼S121

Travel Agents

Besides booking air tickets, the following English-speaking agencies can arrange everything from Great Wall tours or seats on the Trans-Siberian to tailored adventure packages in Yunnan. Compare prices and be wary of "come hither" promotional deals that look too good to be true. They usually are.

Banner Travel Service Offers international tours and domestic trips for individuals and groups. Frequent packages to places like Paris, London, Frankfurt, San Francisco, Los Angeles and Hong Kong.
9B-010-8, Pingod, 32 Baiziwan Lu (300m south of Guomao, east side of the Third Ring Road), Chaoyang District. (133 6602 1791) 中国太和旅行社，东城区滨河路甲1号大象投资大厦5层

BTG International Travel & Tour Has experience with city, domestic and international tours. Offers holiday packages in cooperation with Singapore Airlines and Thai Airways. Also organizes frequent Beijing sightseeing tours – let them take those pesky guests to Badaling.
206 Beijing Tourism Building, 27 Jianguomenwai, Chaoyang District. (9609 6798) www.btgtravel.cn 北京神州国旅，朝阳区建国门外27号北京旅游大厦206

China Swan International Tours Many years of experience have resulted in a full palette of services, including custom tours and packaged holiday specials.
4/F, Longhui Building, 1 Nongguang Nanli, Dongsanhuan Lu, Chaoyang District. (6731 6393) www.china-swan.com 中国天鹅国际旅游公司，朝阳区东三环路农光南里1号龙辉大厦4层

CnAdventure Organizes hiking treks to the Great Wall, as well as trips to destinations like Pingyao, Datong, Chengde. The company also sets up expeditions to Yunnan, Tibet, Guizhou and the Silk Road.
5/F, Daxiang Investment Building, A1, Dongbinhe Lu, Dongcheng District. (5126 8494) www.cnadventure.com 太和旅行社，东城区滨河路甲1号大象投资大厦5层

Koryo Group Tours In business for over a decade, Koryo Group Tours offers tours to North Korea leaving from Beijing. Strives to introduce travelers to the "true" North Korea. British tour guides lead each trip. Note that Americans are

Filmmaker, gallery owner and Koryo Group Tours founder Nick Bonner has been to the DPRK over 100 times

not permitted to travel to North Korea, except once a year during the Arirang Mass Games. *West of Yashow Market (inside a hutong next to the DVD shop), Gongti Beilu, Chaoyang District. (6416 7544) www.koryogroup.com 朝阳区工体北路雅秀市场西侧DVD店旁边的胡同内*

Mercury International Travel Full-service, English-speaking travel resource.
Mon-Fri 9am-6pm. 25A, Tower B, Oriental Kenzo Plaza, 48 Dongzhimenwai Dajie, Dongcheng District. (8454 9420) www.mercurytravel.com.cn 东城区东直门外大街48号东方银座B座25A

Monkey Business Arranges Trans-Siberian train trips, with stopovers in Mongolia and Russia.
Rm 201, Youyi Youth Hostel, South 43, Sanlitun Beijie, Chaoyang District. (6591 6519) www.monkeyshrine.com 朝阳区三里屯北街南43号友谊青年酒店201

Kingdom Travel Beijing This bilingual outfit arranges domestic and business air tickets, family vacation packages and weekend escapes.
1815 Shangdu International Center, 8 Dongdaqiao Lu, Chaoyang District. (5870 3388) 中侨国旅，朝阳区东大桥路8号尚都国际中心1815

TUI China Travel Co. Ltd. With its extensive international network, this German-Chinese joint venture can arrange personalized tours to destinations all over the world, including China.
Unit 921-926, Bright China Chang'An Building, Tower 2, 7 Jianguomennei Dajie, Dongcheng District. (6517 1370) www.tui.cn 中旅途易，东城区建国门内大街7号光华长安大厦2座921–926

WildChina From treks in "Shangri-la" to village homestays in ethnically diverse Guizhou, WildChina offers a range of cultural and activity-oriented excursions. Trips closer to Beijing include birding in Shandong, weekend trips to Pingyao, and tours of the Great Wall led by Great Wall historian and author David Spindler (see p272).
Rm 801, Oriental Place, 9 Dongfang Donglu, Dongsanhuan Beilu, Chaoyang District. (6465 6602) www.wildchina.com 朝阳区东三环北路东方东路9号东方国际大厦801室

Online agencies

Try your luck online with one of these travel websites. Note that fare searches in Chinese sometimes yield lower prices than in English.
Ctrip (http://english.ctrip.com) This site has a simple and well-designed English site. It offers hotel and flight deals.
Elong (www.elong.net) Elong has hotel, flight and car rental deals, but is best known for offering fantastic last-minute bargains.
Golden Holiday (www.goldenholiday.com) The site is available in Chinese and English and sells plane tickets with free delivery within the Fourth Ring Road (usually within two hours). It also lists discounted plane ticket information and budget travel trips and allows you to book hotel reservations.

Many visitors – like this fella outside the train station – will form their first Beijing impressions in the city's colorful taxis

PHOTO: JANEK ZDZARSKI JR

Taxis and Limos

Taxis are the default mode of transportation for most foreigners in Beijing. Piloted in shifts by 130,000 generally honest, friendly and opinionated drivers, taxis are relatively convenient and agreeable, if not always swift, conveyances. There are some 67,000 cabs in Beijing, which makes the 12,000 taxis in New York City look like chump change. The flagfall rate is RMB 10 for the first three kilometers, RMB 2 for each subsequent kilometer. A long-distance surcharge applies once the ride exceeds 15km, subsequent kilometers are charged at one and a half times the normal rate. There's also a night rate: after 11pm, the fare begins at RMB 11 and increases by RMB 3 per kilometer after the first three kilometers.

Cabs are also where many visitors form their first impressions of Beijing, and as such have become the objects of several pre-Olympic image enhancement campaigns. A few years ago, Beijing's municipal government decreed that all drivers ought to study English before the Games, and while you may come across an occasional enthusiast, most drivers still draw a blank at the English words "Forbidden City." In the spring of 2007, the authorities unveiled new regulations governing the behavior and appearance of the city's cabbies. Some of these rules, notably the bans on smoking and eating in taxis and injunctions that drivers avoid consuming pungent food before work (e.g. enough garlic to slay a vampire), mean more pleasant rides for passengers. Others, such as those banning male drivers from having shaved heads or long hair, and those preventing female drivers from dyeing their hair or wearing big earrings, have met with derision.

As the Olympic Games approach, the city's taxi cab brigades will be upgraded. Most of the older cabs will be replaced with new car models – conforming to higher emission standards and equipped with GPS – so that even a first day driver from the nether regions of Fangshan District will be able to figure out how to reach your destination.

Despite their impressive numbers, cabs seem increasingly hard to find during rush hour or at the first sign of rain, snow or sand. It will be even more arduous if, as announced, the cab numbers are reduced. Luckily, you rarely need to worry about your physical safety in a taxi, since Beijing's endless traffic jams keep the most "impulsive" drivers in check. And in case you just arrived from Mars, make sure the photo on the dashboard license matches the face of your driver and that s/he engages the meter (*da biao*). Tips are not expected, but passengers are responsible for paying toll fees – generally the driver will pay the toll and add it to the bill when you reach your destination. If you're good at losing your stuff, get a receipt (*tapiao*, which lists the car's ID number and company phone number), and you'll be able to track it down.

Beijing Taxi Dispatching Center They can't directly send a driver to your house, but will alert all taxis with GPS in the vicinity of your exact location about your request for a taxi. (6837 3399)

Bejiing Yinjian Taxi Company The biggest taxi company in Beijing, owning 18 percent of all Beijing cabs. Dial their hotline and they will try to notify their drivers of your thirst to be transported. (96103)

Complaints

The Beijing Bureau of Communications Takes complaints concerning taxis, minibuses or other vehicles. No operator, but an English recording that gives instructions for faxing your complaint – which of course will mitigate your anger right away. (6835 1150, fax 6831 5960)

Chauffeured Cars

If you wish to travel like Yao Ming, you can hire a chauffeured car from one of the following companies.

ASM Chauffeur and Tour Services Pre-arranges transportation in cars or buses driven by English-speaking drivers. Airport pick-up and delivery service, chauffeur service (hire by the day) and personal guide service available. Pricing on website.
1003, CITIC Building, Jianguomenwai Dajie, Chaoyang District. (5166 1575) www.chauffeurasia.com 亚商公司，朝阳区建国门外大街国际大厦1003

Continues on p516

Obi Wan of *Er Huan*
Swami Ding and his mysterious oriental wisdom
by Matt P. Jager

Some of Beijing's cabbies can't read *pinyin*. Many haven't finished middle school. A handful of younger drivers are free-spirited university graduates who don't like working in offices. They are all, with few exceptions, Beijingers, and chatting with them offers a window into the lives and minds of the human engines of our beloved city. You never know – you might just learn something from them, too.

Ding Chunchang lives on the south side. He speaks in a deliberate Beijing drawl, swallowing whole syllables and peppering his speech with street talk that he knows I won't understand. His wife runs a courtyard inn hidden in the Xuanwu alleys, where people still live and communities still thrive – despite encroaching destruction. Ding rarely drinks because he is a driver and takes his profession seriously, but from time to time, he and his wife invite me to their inn for home-style *zhajiangmian*.

Ding is the wisest man in Beijing. He applies Zen teachings to stay calm during rush hour and soothes irritable passengers with Buddhist parables.

He taught me how to mix noodles. The greasy fare in *lao* Beijing restaurants can never hold a candle to home-cooked *zhajiangmian*. I arrived at the inn to a spread of purple radish, cucumber, bean sprouts, garlic and vinegar and other nutritious condiments. The noodles came, thick and white. I dumped them into my bowl and scooped sauce on top. Ding watched me carefully as I churned my chopsticks to slather the noodles in the *jiang*. "You must mix the noodles from the bottom with so much sauce," he said. "Watch me." Taking my bowl, he dug the chopsticks to the bottom of the noodles, and with a gentle turn of his wrist, upturned the mass of them, allowing the dark sauce to filter through. It was almost like time filtering through thick strands of traffic.

"I'm *laobaixing*," Ding said as we were eating. "I am a common man, and I wouldn't want to be powerful or famous. Do you know why?" I didn't, but I wanted to. "That George Bush – if he has a stomachache or wants to sleep late, his secretary will run into the White House and shout, 'Wake up, Mr. Bush! Today you must take care of this and that matter!' And that is the most powerful man in the world. Do you know what I do when I wake up with a stomachache? I roll over and go back to sleep."

Ding's wife carried in several bottles of beer. "Do you want more noodles?" she asked. "We can boil some more." Ding, however, had more earthy wisdom to impart. "If you have a stomachache," he said, "you must eat raw white radish. Your belly will fill up with air, and you will fart the pain out."

"And also," he said, pointing to the booze, "you should never eat too much when you want to drink with your friends. Eat noodles until you are 80 percent full, and then if you are still hungry, drink the broth. That way you will feel full, but still have room for beer."

A bowl of broth later, I was content, but not stuffed. Ding chatted with us while we started into the beer. "Everyone needs a hobby. I love calligraphy. I have never studied, but it centers me." I leaned over to clink bottles with his wife and knocked a beer over. "No problem," he said as we laid newspapers over the spill.

Ding contemplated the floor. "You know," he murmured thoughtfully, "wet newspaper has the perfect texture for practicing calligraphy. Honey, bring my ink and brush. I will paint while you drink." And so we chatted and toasted away the evening, as Ding's thick brush smeared over yesterday's headlines.

Lesson 36: Use Zen teachings to stay calm during rush hour

TRANSPORTATION

Beijing Limo Call Beijing Limo for airport pick-up, corporate events or sightseeing. Choose from stretch limos, buses and vans, all with bilingual drivers. Over 80% of the company's clients are expatriates or foreign visitors.
18 Jianguo Lu, Chaoyang District. (6546 1688, 139 1113 5613) www.beijinglimo.com/english/index.htm 朝阳区建国路18号

Transportation Smartcards

In May 2006, Beijing improved the lives of millions of commuters by unveiling prepaid transportation IC cards (市政交通一卡通 *shizheng jiaotong yikatong*). These smartcards can be used to pay for bus, subway and sometimes taxi rides. The cards can be purchased and topped up at all subway stations and many bus stations, including the big ones listed below – go to the window marked 市政交通一卡通. Travelers must pay an RMB 20 deposit for the card and can put as much as RMB 1,000 on it. The fare is deducted automatically with a simple swipe of the card over a machine.

Magic Bus: No Cause to Fuss

Creaky, crowded and extensive, Beijing's bus network is currently undergoing a major overhaul. The city is currently planning to replace some 40 percent of its 17,500 buses with new, fancier and cleaner models. These replacements, which will be completed by you-know-when, are expected to include 5,000 natural gas-powered buses. By 2010, planners vow, Beijingers will never have to walk more than eight minutes to find a bus station downtown.

Most buses numbered between 1 and 100 operate within the Third Ring Road. Buses numbered 200-212 provide only night service. Those in the 300s prowl the suburbs, those in the 400s travel from the center out to the suburbs, while those in the 600s and 700s snake through residential areas. The 800s are heated in the winter and most are air conditioned in the summer. Buses in the 900s are long-distance. The past year welcomed several routes numbered in the 500s to the Beijing streets. Buses run from 5.30am; about half of them stop around 8.30pm and the rest operate until 11pm. Night buses run from 10pm or 11pm to 5am.

Every bus stop has the number of the bus or buses, each stop on their route, the direction they travel and the times of the first and last buses. Bus routes are available at any newspaper stand in the Chinese language city map (RMB 3-5) or as a mini-booklet (RMB 5). In addition, the following English language website has an excellent map that will display each of Beijing's bus routes (see www.bjbus.com/english/default.htm).

When paying with cash, the flat rate for ordinary buses is a whopping RMB 1, but the rate increases incrementally for long-distance trips. Night and air-conditioned buses empty your wallet at RMB 2-6. Wielding your smartcard yields big discounts – 60 percent off the original ticket price for buses 1-899, and 20 percent off the price of long-distance buses. Student monthly cards get an even more impressive discount – 80 percent off all buses but the 900s.

Major bus terminals:

Chaoyang: Dongdaqiao bus terminal

Dongcheng: Andingmen bus terminal

Haidian: Dongwuyuan (zoo) bus terminal

Xicheng: Gangwashi bus terminal

Chongwen: Tianqiao bus terminal

Xuanwu: Guang'anmen bus terminal

Long-distance bus stations:

Chaoyang: Bawangfen Terminal (Xidawang Lu)

Dongcheng: Dongzhimen Terminal (Dongzhimenwai Xiejie)

Xicheng: Beijiao Terminal (Deshengmenwai)

Chongwen: Majuan Terminal (Guangqumen)

Fengtai: Lizeqiao Terminal (Lizeqiao); Muxiyuan Terminal (Haihutun)

Emission Statement
The steamy bus to a cleaner future
by Reid Barrett

Next stop: Utopia

From belching smokestacks to mounds of coal cakes, the agents of Beijing's air pollution are easy to spot. The city's initiatives to reduce emissions are, conversely, easily missed. But they exist, and if you want to witness one of the most ambitious, head to Zhongguancun Beidajie, north of Renmin University, and find a bus stop for the 801. Wait for a gray Mercedes-Benz bus with "No Emission" and "Fuel Cell" emblazoned on its sides, and a spout on its roof emitting steam.

This is no diesel belcher: It's a fourth-generation hydrogen bus, one of three in Beijing, that is being tested here and in dozens of European cities by Daimler-Benz and its Canadian partner Ballard Power Systems. The technology, on which Daimler-Benz has been working since the 60s, is the stuff of green dreams. Hydrogen stored in a tank on the roof is pushed down into a steel fuel cell crate where electrons are siphoned off hydrogen atoms as they pass through semi-permeable membrane sheets. The electron and the proton then race down parallel tracks to meet again at the engine, where they recombine with oxygen to make water while giving off a teensy bit of energy to the engine. When this happens millions of times a second, the reaction is powerful enough to move a 13-ton bus, which emits nothing into the atmosphere but water vapor – like a giant teakettle.

So why isn't every city in the world converting their dirty hydrocarbon fleets to clean hydrogen ones? Well, for one thing, Daimler-Benz's hydrogen bus costs about USD 1.2 million, compared to about USD 250,000 for a diesel version. Mass production would slash per unit cost, but local project engineer Jason Cox reveals that much more testing is needed before this can happen. Hydrogen buses also have limited range, so hydrogen filling stations would be needed along bus routes. This is not a simple matter of installing a few pumps: hydrogen needs to either be compressed in large, strong tanks or liquefied at extremely low temperatures. Another concern is that producing hydrogen is difficult. You either have to extract it from water, which takes a lot of electricity, or from methane, which leaves behind … greenhouse gases!

These technical hurdles can be overcome, but it will take time. Fortunately, Daimler-Benz is not alone: Beijing's Tsinghua University is developing its own version of hydrogen buses. Cox is also comforted by the results of the Beijing experiment, which, among other things, proved that hydrogen buses can run in tough conditions – Beijing's poor air quality so lowered the efficiency of the buses that they had to be readjusted with more powerful filters. "Everyone involved thought, 'I hope these things run,'" says Cox. "But they've exceeded [people's] expectations, myself included."

Subways

Fast, reliable, cheap, intimate – what's not to like about Beijing's subway system? In October 2007, the city unfurled an exhilarating new ticket price strategy: Rides cost a flat fee of RMB 2 regardless of number of transfers, distance, time of day or duration of travel. However, this benediction is rumored to be temporary, encouraging us to open our hearts to the sexy new Line 5.

Swipe a smartcard (see p516) or buy same-day tickets in the station. The first trains are at 5am (metro rail) and 6am (light rail), while last trains are at 10.30pm and 11pm, respectively.

Behold the future

The map of Beijing's subway systems was once gratifyingly tidy – a nice straight line (Line 1) strung through a neat little O (Line 2). Then came Line 13, disturbing not only because of its geometric irregularity but also the mysterious progression from Line 1 to 2 to the Western world's least lucky number (see Beijing Subway Network, p702).

Zhou Liying at the Beijing General Municipal Engineering Design and Research Institute has a secret diagram, which she keeps in her desk, detailing the future locations of lines 3 through 11. We've seen it ("You can't have this," she warns), and it's not pretty. It looks a lot more like London or New York than it does a minimalist abstract painting, and while that may be bad for map aesthetics, it's going to be good for public transportation.

Beijing construction projects are generally categorized as either "Pre-Olympic" or "Post-Olympic." Pre-Olympic subway lines include Four and Five, running north-south through Xicheng and Dongcheng Districts, respectively (construction of the stations has already begun). There's also Line 10, which meanders down from central Haidian until it butts into Line 5. A straight shot from Dongzhimen to the airport will obviate 80 *kuai* cab rides, but also bring Dongzhimen's traffic load a step closer to critical mass. Dongzhimen will also be adding a new lounge for airline travelers to complete pre-boarding procedures and check in their luggage.

Post-Olympics, things get a little crazy. "Don't put these on the map," Zhou says, "none

Notes from underground: Line 5 has arrived

PHOTO: ALEX PASTERNACK

of these lines are settled." Line 9 will go south from the Summer Palace, bringing Haidian the love it so richly deserves. Lines 6 and 7 will slash horizontally across the map, one through the Ping'an Dajie area, the other going through the south end of town. Line 8 ("We're really not sure about this one") goes down the middle, dog-legging the Forbidden City. Lines 11 and 12 pick up where 4 and 5 leave off, heading south, while 15 heads up via light rail to Shunyi. All this and a Huangcun route, too? You betcha!

While these blueprints are finalized, improvements are being made to Lines 1 and 2. Every night between 12.30 and 4am, workers are replacing tracks, trains (with air conditioning!), signals communication systems and power supply. Sixty trains will be replaced and 84 added by the Olympics to reduce the average interval between trains from three minutes to two.

Trains

Tibet, here we come! You've perhaps chanced upon news reports of the July 2006 opening of the Qinghai-Tibet Railway, which, according to CCTV, is just about the greatest thing since the Great Wall. These tracks connect Tibet to the rest of China like never before. Beijingers can hop the T27 from Beijing's West Railway Station, with stops in Shijiazhuang (Hebei), Xi'an (Shaanxi), Lanzhou (Gansu), Xining and Golmud (Qinghai) and Nagqu (Tibet). It takes 48 hours to complete the 4,064km journey, and ticket prices range from RMB 389 to RMB 2,540.

Closer to home, work is well underway on the 115-kilometer high-speed railway between Beijing and Tianjin. When it starts operations in early 2008, the elevated train (think *The Jetsons*) will link the new Beijing South Railway Station and Tianjin in about half an hour, with departures every three minutes during rush hour. Line 4 and Line 14 of the Beijing subway, now under construction, will have stops at the station, allowing metro commuters to board the train without exiting the station. Each train will be able to hold more than 100 passengers. The project is designed to facilitate regional integration, so that the Beijing-Tianjin area can become more like the Pearl River Delta region (Hong Kong-Shenzhen-Guangzhou-Macau).

Even cooler, plans are in the works for a high-speed rail link between Beijing and Shanghai, which is planned for completion by 2010. The railway, which boosters claim will reach speeds of 350km/h, will be built alongside the current route, but will cut travel time between the two cities from 12 hours to five.

In the meantime, you can ride the "Iron Rooster" to discover all the wonders of China. Speed increases are taking place throughout the rail network – velocities along major lines were raised from 160 to 200km/h in October of 2006.

Going from the capital's two main train stations (Beijing West Railway Station and Beijing Station) will also become easier, as a direct underground shuttle is expected to be finished by – well, you know when. The original South Railway station was demolished in 2006 – the replacement under construction will serve as the terminus for the Beijing-Tianjin and Beijing-Shanghai express trains. Construction of the new Beijing South Railway Station is scheduled to be finished in August 2008.

Tickets go on sale 10 days in advance at train stations and at ticket agencies around town. They can also be purchased online (www.51piao.com/train) for pick-up at one of their many locations or delivery for an additional 10 *kuai* within the Fourth Ring Road. Round-trip tickets for trains starting from and terminating in Beijing can now be purchased 12 days before the return date.

Ticket Center Hotline Call 9510 5105 to book your ticket up to ten days in advance and pick up and pay for your ticket at your local agent no more than four days in advance of departure. You'll be advised of the location nearest you.

Stations

Beijing Station (Beijing Huochezhan) *Beijing Zhan Jie, Dongcheng District. (5182 1114)* 北京站，东城区北京站街

Beijing West Railway Station (Beijing Xikezhan) *Lianhuachi Donglu (east of Xisanhuan Lu), Fengtai District. (5182 6253)* 北京西站，丰台区莲花池东路

Beijing North Station (Beijing Beizhan) *Xizhimen, Xicheng District. (5186 6223)* 北京北站，西城区西直门

Braving the Iron Rooster
Riding the rails from sea to Xizang
by Michael Arnold

Discover China's vast panoramas – and freak snowstorms – by train

When it comes down to it, traveling through China by train is still the most romantic way to see the country. Beijing is conveniently connected to every major city in China by rail – services to the provincial capital of Tibet having been added at last in 2006 – and modern railway speeds being as they are, few places are much farther than an overnight trip away from the capital. As a much cheaper alternative to domestic flights, the Chinese railway system remains an ideal method of transport – at least, it should be.

The fact is that the train ticketing system is controlled by a computer program that looks like something out of Microsoft's DOS archives, making the booking of good tickets a nightmare. No matter how far a traveler is going, the system will book their ticket for the entire journey, meaning that many vacancies are unable to be made available to other passengers by the booking system.

"Good tickets" usually means hard sleeper class accommodations. Soft sleeper tickets – semi-private bunks in lockable rooms of four beds each – are far more expensive, but much easier to book thanks to low demand. Doing an overnight on a Chinese train in either hard or soft seat class can be unthinkably awful – the seats make sleep improbable, the surrounding noise, fog-thick cigarette smoke, constant visitations of snack merchants, hot lights and crowds of seatless fellow passengers who cram the aisles make it damn near impossible. God forbid that you be reduced to a standing class ticket. For those on a budget, however, keep in mind that a seat class ticket coupled with a cheap bottle of *baijiu* will still be significantly cheaper than a sleeper ticket.

Seat carriage toilets – squatting holes over the naked tracks – clog and stink up fast. The hard sleepers are usually more than adequate – bathrooms are often good, lights go out at ten and although there's not that much room between bunks, sleep is possible, perhaps even comfortable, with the rhythm of the wheels striking up their tender lullaby.

Sleeper tickets in both classes can be booked up to ten days prior to departure, but are available to travel agents and pay-per-minute hotline sales a day earlier, meaning that hard berths are often sold out in advance. The agencies themselves are all over town – almost every row of shops has one – and so it's unnecessary to go all the way to the train station to buy tickets. Most agencies have an RMB 5 booking fee.

If the service you're wanting is full, there's little option but the horror of a standing ticket, and to try to upgrade to a bed on the train – try to be amongst the first passengers to rush on (you'll have ruthless competitors) and get to the carriage with the booking office to register your name. You'll be given the option to buy a sleeper ticket as beds become available. Otherwise, hawkers outside the railway station may approach you with much sought-after tickets – beware that some of them are counterfeit and others are stolen.

Another option is to arrive at the station on the morning of your intended departure – there's a booth outside Beijing Railway Station that onsells tickets which have been returned, of which there are often many. If you have language difficulties, the station has a window for foreigners – window number 1 inside the main ticket hall.

Some additional tips for your journey:
• Make booking your return ticket your first priority as soon as you get to your destination.
• Choose a middle bunk – top bunks are cramped and other passengers sit on the lower bunks.
• If you're in seat class and you really, really need to lie down, you can sleep under the seats if you're prepared to wipe off the phlegm and sunflower shells in the morning, or you can try climbing up on the baggage rack and spread out on the packs – it's been done, successfully, before. Pack a good pillow.
• Don't ride on slow trains with four-digit numbers – they're cheap, but often have no air conditioning. Choose K (fast), T (especially fast), Z (no stops and lightning fast) or D (bullet) trains.
• If you're told there are no tickets to where you're going, ask other people – even the guards at the door can sometimes organize legal tickets that the counter sellers are unable to issue.
• Avoid traveling during national holiday weeks – but if you must, trains are lightly booked on those nights when good Chinese people should already be home with their families (such as the night of Spring Festival).

Spring Festival, when Chinese travel in the hundreds of millions, is not the best time to ride the rooster

Cars, Cars, Cars

Licensed to ill

Not enough stress in your life? Want to contribute to Beijing's pollution and traffic jams – or escape to the countryside? Knowing how to drive doesn't appear to be a prerequisite to getting behind the wheel in Beijing, but having a Chinese license is.

Obtaining a license

To get a Chinese driver's license, a foreign applicant aged 18-70 must possess a valid foreign driver's license and have a valid visa and residence registration certificate (from the applicant's local PSB bureau). He or she must undergo a brief eye exam at an approved public hospital, among which are the China-Japan Friendship Hospital and Peking Union Medical College Hospital (see Health & Beauty p476 and p477 for addresses). The applicant must translate his or her foreign license into Chinese, pass a computerized test of the rules of the road, sub-

"She's a beauty, mate, but how much petrol does she consume?"

mit a completed application form (in Chinese) with several passport-sized photos, and pay fees. The computerized test involves true/false and multiple-choice questions and can be taken in English, French, German, Spanish, Korean and Japanese. You must score 90 percent or better on the challenging 100-question test to pass. Applicants with valid foreign licenses do not need to pass a road test.

Though they can complete all these steps on their own, many foreigners opt instead to engage companies like Beijing Easy or FESCO to help them with the formalities for a fee of about RMB 800. Both of these companies supply clients with English-language versions of China's Road Traffic Safety Rules and Regulations.

If you want to do it on your own, bring your documents to the Foreign Affairs Branch of the Automobile Administrative Office. There, you'll be provided with an application form, told to have your foreign/international license translated, asked to undergo the eye exam and invited to make an appointment for the test. After you pass the test, file your completed application along with all your documents and the RMB 10 fee. Then get ready for road rage.

Automobile Administrative Office This is where the computer test is administered and licenses are issued.
Foreign Affairs Branch, Public Security and Traffic Administrative Bureau, 18 Nansihuan Donglu, Chaoyang District. (8762 5155) 北京市交管局外事处，朝阳区南四环东路18号

Beijing Easy Provides all-in-one service that includes translating your home license, booking your road test, arranging the eye exam, preparing your application, supplying an English language version of China's Road Traffic Safety Rules and Regulations and paying all fees. They'll even take you to and from the test center.
803 8/F, Huashang Building, 2 Yanjing Xili, Chaoyang District. (5128 0322) www.beijing-easy.com 北京易在，朝阳区延静西里2号华商大厦8层803

FESCO Provides all-in-one service for RMB 800. Includes translating your home license, giving you a medical check-up, preparing your application, providing you with a road test manual and paying all fees. Services can be purchased individually: medical test (RMB 80); license translation (same day: RMB 120, 3-day: RMB 90, 5-day: RMB 60). Sells English version of the test preparation manual (RMB 150). For an extra fee you can even take the written test at FESCO.
14 Chaoyangmen Nandajie (near Yabao Lu), Chaoyang District. (8561 6663) www.fescochina.com 外企服务公司，朝阳区朝阳门南大街14号

12 points

Congratulations: your Chinese license is valid for six years, but must be re-registered periodically throughout that time. It's based on a 12-point system, with points deducted for traffic violations. If you lose all your points within a one-year period, you must take a remedial class to "relearn the rules" and pass a traffic rules exam again. If you get stopped for drunk driving, you'll lose six points if mildly intoxicated and all 12 points if wasted. You'll also pay a fine ranging from RMB 200 to 2,000 and have your license suspended for at least three months. You could also be arrested and put in jail for up to 15 days. Less drastic violations include ignoring a red or yellow light (three points), exceeding the speed limit (three points) and driving without a seatbelt (one or two points).

Parking tickets

Now that you've got your new license and you're buzzing around Beijing, what do you do if you get a parking ticket? Depending on the mood of the meter man/maid, you'll be fined RMB 200 and possibly docked penalty points as well. The address of the place to pay the fine is usually printed in red on the ticket. Show the ticket and your new Chinese driving license to the nice lady sitting at the computer: after she deducts your points for you (if directed), you'll get a small ticket, with which you can pay the fine at any branch of ICBC. If you're unlucky enough to have your car towed, call the number on the yellow towing sign to find out where to pay the RMB 200 fine.

Separated at Birth?

by Jackie Yu

Chevrolet Spark

Chery QQ

BMW X5

Shanghuan CEO

Daimler Chrysler Smart

Shanghuan Noble

Toyota Land Cruiser

Beijing Automobile Luba

Doh, doh, doh, doh, doh

Accidents

May what follows be of purely academic interest to you, oh driver. But ... forewarned is forearmed.

Down by law

A new law on the responsibilities of drivers involved in accidents came into effect on July 1, 2007. It is designed to speed up the accident-resolution process to prevent fender benders from causing enormous traffic jams. Here's what it stipulates:

After a minor accident, stop your car immediately in the position of the accident, turn on your hazard lights, and jot down the other driver's license plate number, license number, insurance policy number and contact information (name, phone number, ID or passport card number). Call the police immediately (110) if the other driver appears to have been drinking alcohol, or lacks either a license or license plate.

The law suggests that you mark the scene with chalk (show the positions of all the wheels of both cars) – starting from July 1, all insurance companies are obligated to distribute free chalk to their customers – and take photographs from different angles. After that, you and the other driver must decide whether you agree about respective responsibilities for the crash. If you can't reach an agreement, call the police – when they arrive, officers will assign responsibility based on the evidence at the site and the testimony of bystanders and will provide and help fill out accident claim forms. They can assess fines on the spot and call tow trucks if needed.

Alternatively, if you can agree on culpability, cut out the constabulary middleman and file the claim yourselves. The first thing to do after documenting the accident is to move your car to the side of the road – unless it no longer runs. If you fail to do so, the police will fine you RMB 200 and may strip two points from your license.

Filing a claim

You should then call your insurance company within 48 hours and obtain an accident report number. The insurance company can also send a representative to the accident site and help fill out a report. But you may have to wait several hours for the insurance rep to arrive. If you want to save time, you and the other driver can fill out

TRANSPORTATION

A new law allows police to fine drivers who fail to move their vehicles out of traffic after a minor fender bender

claim forms by yourselves. If you don't have the proper forms on hand, you'll have to agree to meet up later to fill them out – if the other driver doesn't show up, you should report him/her to the police. But with a little foresight, you have printed insurance claim forms in your glove compartment – they are available for download from the Beijing Traffic Management Bureau website (www.bjjtgl.gov.cn/uploadfile/20070614xys.doc) and thus complete the formalities on the spot.

Comprehensible culpability

In the past, the contingencies for collision liability were fairly complex: besides full and 50/50 liability, 60/40 and 70/30 splits were legal possibilities. But the new law provides only for full and half/shared liability, which aims to reduce the amount of time drivers spend haggling over who was at fault. Shared blame situations which would previously have resulted in long negotiations of whose transgression was more serious is now a simple matter – if both drivers broke traffic rules, they share responsibility evenly.

Fixing the damage

If the insurance rep has visited the site and estimated the cost of repairs, you can take your car directly to a garage to have it repaired. If you've prepared the claim on your own, you'll have to visit the insurance company to get a damage estimate before you can take it to a garage. The insurance company can repair the car in its own garage – if you go to an outside garage, you'll have to pay for the repairs and apply for a reimbursement up to the total of the estimate. Make sure to provide all the necessary documents: driver's license, identification, vehicle license numbers, an insurance receipt, a reimbursement application letter, photos of both cars (if you have them) and a receipt for the repairs.

On the other hand ...

After a minor accident, many Beijingers will promptly negotiate a cash settlement rather than involve the authorities and insurance companies and risk losing points and/or paying a fine – taxi drivers are especially amenable to such an arrangement. The most prudent course is to let the other driver make the opening bid and then negotiate the payment based on respective responsibilities. If you select this route, consider not revealing your mobile phone and license numbers lest the other party should later decide to file a claim or contact the police. Further note that such informal settlements will invalidate any insurance claim you later might decide to make.

Buying a set of wheels

There are many roads to car ownership. You can buy a car from an auto market or dealer, or delegate the process to a car broker or your company. You could also import a new or used car from overseas, but know that most older models will fail China's emissions test, and that the process is expensive and involves a fair bit of red tape. Finally, you could buy a friend of a friend's car. Many foreigners, especially diplomats, buy used cars from fellow *laowai* because it's easier to transfer ownership between expatriates (the black plates, or red-and-black plates in the case of diplomats, need not be changed).

You don't need to be a Beijing resident to buy a car. Nor do you need to show a driving license, which may help explain Beijing's current traffic situation. To register the car, you must have a passport or ID card, temporary residence certificate, vehicle purchase invoice, and other documents. The dealer or market will supply their documents to transfer ownership. If buying from a private seller, you will need an ID card or passport and the seller will need the bill of sale, Certificate of Title and Certificate of Registration. (All these forms must be accompanied by one photocopy.) All outstanding parking tickets must be paid before the ownership title can be transferred.

Auto markets and dealers

Many of Beijing's dealers are clustered in vast markets, making comparative shopping easy. There are also individual dealerships. Besides selling you a car, the dealer will get you on the road by helping you pay the various taxes, register the car, obtain your license plates and apply for insurance.

Beijing International Car-Trading Service Garden Lot is filled with locally made and imported new and used vehicles.
63 Gucheng Xilu, Shijingshan District. (8892 7346) www.bjicg.com.cn 北京国际汽车贸易服务园，石景山区古城西路63号

The auto industry is booming here, but what would happen if car-ownership rates in China reached US levels?

Beijing North Vehicle Distributing Market One of the biggest car markets in China.
A1 Fengguan Lu (East area, 300m north of Fengyi Qiao; West area, 100m west of Fengyi Qiao), Fengtai District. (6382 4466) www.beifang-auto.com 北京北方汽车交易市场，丰台区丰管路甲1号（东区，丰益桥北300米；西区，丰益桥西100米）

Beijing Norinco Motors Market Sells models by Shanghai and FAW Volkswagen, Citroen, Nissan, Suzuki and more.
1) West 1, Yangqiao, Fengtai District. (6753 8063) ; 2) Southeast of Huaxiang Qiao, Nansihuan Lu, Fengtai District. (6379 5555) 北方车辆大世界，1）丰台区洋桥西1号；2）丰台区南四环路花乡桥东南侧

Beijing Used Car Trading Market Beijing's largest used car market has over 200 used car dealers.
1) 123 Nansihuan Xilu, Fengtai District, 2) Southeast corner of Majialou Qiao, Nansihuan Lu, Fengtai District. (5111 8888, 5111 8899) www.2sc.com.cn 北京旧机动车交易市场，1）丰台区南四环西路123号；2）丰台区南四环路马家楼桥东南角

Beijing Yayuncun Car Market The only car market in Beijing supervised by the Beijing Municipal Government, this new and used car market has just moved to an enormous area north of the Fifth Ring Road.
Beiqijia Zhen on Litang Lu (north of Beiwuhuan Lu), Changping District. (6176 6699) www.beiyacheshi.com 北京亚运村汽车市场，昌平区北五环外立汤路北七家镇

Northern Star (Shanghai) Automobile Mercedes-Benz's authorized regional distributor. All Mercedes are imported at present, but Daimler is in talks with the Chinese government about manufacturing cars in China.
1/F Pacific Century Place, A2 Gongti Beilu, Chaoyang District. (6539 1710) 奔驰北星公司展厅，朝阳区工体北路甲2号盈科中心1层

Oriental Enterprise International Auto Plaza Four stories filled with just about any kind of car you can imagine. Car accessories and maintenance training also available, as well as car insurance and license plate purchase. This may be the only place in Beijing where you can purchase a Lotus Elise.
A1 Yaojiayuan Lu, Chaoyang District. (5119 3111) 东方基业国际汽车城，朝阳区姚家园路甲1号

Car brokers

Beijing Car Solution Run by expat Bob Foday, BCS will bring new or used vehicles to your home or office for a test drive. Bob and his minions will have the car inspected, handle the registration and help you buy insurance.
Rm. 1142 Greenlake Office Building, 9 Chaoyang Gongyuan Xilu, Chaoyang District. (1350 138 0047) www.car-solution.com 朝阳区朝阳公园西路9号碧湖居写字楼1142

Car accessories

Xijiao Auto Accessory Market Located in a sprawling 50,000-square meter lot, this market has more than 700 stalls selling accessories from engine systems, to car alarms, to seat covers and decorations. Also, several on-site car showrooms display imported and domestic cars.
Daily 9am-6pm (summer), 9am-5.30pm (winter). Northeast corner of Sijiqing Qiao, Xisihuan Lu, Haidian District. (8843 7888) 西郊汽配城，海淀区西四环路四季青桥东北角

Siyuanqiao Auto Accessory City Includes more than 600 stalls as well as on-site car repair services.
Daily 8.30am-7.30pm. Liu Gongzhufen village (near Siyuan Qiao), Chaoyang District. (5190 7777) 四元桥汽配城，朝阳区六公主坟村

Registration and taxes

Most new and used cars must pass a safety and emissions test that is administered at an Official Inspection Point (see below). The test is waived for some new, locally made cars. All cars must pass the test in each subsequent year, and the sticker you receive must be affixed on the windshield. The entire procedure costs under RMB 200. If there's anything wrong with the car, you will have to make the necessary repairs and take the test again.

Next, apply for the car's license and number plates at an Automotive Administrative Office (see below). Bring your passport, residence permit, completed registration form, safety certificate and proof of ownership (bill of sale) to an Automobile Administrative Office. The number plates cost RMB 145, the car's license costs RMB 20, and you'll also have to pay RMB 20 for photos of your car.

Finally, pay various taxes. The purchase tax on a new made-in-China car is around 8 percent of the price of the vehicle. The purchase tax on

Many of Beijing's 3 million drivers are new to the skill

imported cars is calculated at 10 percent of the value of the car in China (which includes any import duties paid). There's no purchase tax on a used car: instead, the buyer pays a title transfer fee, between RMB 200 and 900, depending on the car type, registration date and engine size. Appraisals can be done at used car markets.

You must pay a Road Tax (usually RMB 110 per month, payable at the Automobile Administrative Office or district collection point) and a User Tax (RMB 480, payable at the local tax bureau – contact the Foreign Section of the Beijing Tax Bureau, see below).

Automobile Administrative Office Foreign Affairs Branch, Public Security and Traffic Administrative Bureau, 18 Nansihuan Donglu, Chaoyang District. (6839 9114) 北京交管局车辆管理所，朝阳区南四环东路18号

Beijing Tax Bureau Foreign Section (Chaoyang Office, Foreign Department of Chaoyang Local Taxation Bureau.)

40 Guangqu Donglu, Chaoyang District. (6779 9245/6) 朝阳区地税局涉外所，朝阳区广渠东路40号

Insurance

At bare minimum, you are required to purchase third-party liability coverage, which costs over RMB 1,000 per year for a very modest car. Most people pay more – between RMB 2,000 and RMB 5,000 per annum – for a policy that covers vehicle damage, robbery, theft and other rosy potentialities. Since 2006, the government has instituted a mandatory insurance named SALI (交强险), which sets car owners back a standard rate of RMB 1,050/year, adjusted depending on accident history.

PICC (The People's Insurance Company of China) 69 Dongheyan Jie, Xuanwu District. (6315 6688) www.piccnet.com.cn 中国人民财产保险公司，宣武区东河沿街69号

China Pacific Property Insurance 6/F Ocean Plaza, 158 Fuxingmennei Dajie, Xicheng District. (95500, 6642 8888 ext 3643) www.cpicbj. com 中国太平洋财产保险公司，西城区复兴门内大街158号远洋大厦6层

Rentals or leasing

Do you suffer from fear of commitment? Many firms can help arrange for you to rent a locally made car with a driver who speaks some English for USD 850 to USD 1,100 per month. Also look for ads placed in laowai haunts like Jenny Lou's or in that's Beijing (www.thatsbj.com). The last, most expensive option is to rent a car (chauffeured or self-driven) from an agency, but renting a self-drive car requires a Chinese driver's license, a valid passport, a Beijing Residence Permit and a cash deposit.

Avis (Anji Car Rental and Leasing) Beijing has one location of Avis and rents models such as the Shanghai GM Sail (RMB 218 per day) to VW Passats (RMB 550+). Cars come with daily mileage limits (usually 150 to 200km) and there is an additional fee per kilometer. Foreigners need a Chinese driver's license, a credit card and a passport with any visa designation except "L" (tourist).
16 Dongzhimennei Dajie, Dongcheng District. (8406 3343, 8406 3342) www.avischina.com 安飞士汽车租赁，东城区东直门内大街16号

Cycle China (Van Rental) A rental includes extra legroom, AC and a driver, and vans can hold ten people or six people and six bikes. RMB 600/day (up to 8 hours, 150km), RMB 350/half day (4 hours, 50km) or RMB 50/hour. RMB 2.5/km over limit.
12 Jingshan Dongjie, Dongcheng District. (8402 4147) www.cyclechina.com 非常之旅，东城区景山东街12号

Beijing Beiqi Taxi Beiqi offers short- and long-term leases on locally made cars. A VW Jetta costs RMB 400 per day with a driver and RMB 5,500 per month without, while an Audi A6 is RMB 12,000 monthly. Surcharges apply if you drive more than 3,600 kilometers per month. Discounts on year-long leases. You must pay a deposit in cash and may need a guarantor.
Daily 8.30am-5pm. 1) 28 Xizhimen Nandajie, Xicheng District. (8661 1062); 2) 4/F, Yuanyang Hotel, 15 Dongsanhuan Nanlu, Chaoyang District. (8766 5998 ext 8053) www.beiqitaxi.com.cn 北汽出租汽车公司，1）西城区西直门南大街28号；2）朝阳区东三环南路15号远洋宾馆4层

Beijing Century New Concept Car Rental Popular brands to choose from, like VW Polo, Citroen Fukang and VW Jetta. You can rent a Fukang for RMB 320 per day or RMB 5,700 per month with a RMB 5,000 deposit.
1/F Yuexiu Market, Chaoyangmenwai Dajie, Chaoyang District. (800 810 9001) 北京世纪新概念汽车租赁，朝阳区朝外大街岳秀市场1层

Beijing TOP-A Car Service Co., Ltd. Rents a range of new and second-hand car models – with or without driver – including Audi A6, Buick GL8, VW Passat, Toyota Crown and Hyundai Elantra. Prices range: RMB 5,000-25,000 per month with a deposit of RMB 5,000-50,000. Daily 24 hours.
Rm 6F-2/3, Ambassador Mansion, B21, Jiuxianqiao Lu, Chaoyang District. (6438 1634, 139 1008 2709) www.expatslife.com 北京途安汽车租赁有限责任公司，朝阳区酒仙桥路乙21号国宾大厦6F-2/3室

Longtan Wenyuan This RV rental place usually services Beijing's movie industry, but 6-12-seater RVs (6-8 people sleeping) with driver can be yours for RMB 1,200-1,400 per 24-hour period. You also pay for the driver's meals, tolls and gas (which is a lot for these gas-guzzling imports). Bonus – everyone will think you're a movie star.
Daily 8am-8pm. 8-A Beijing Movie Studio, 77 Beisanhuan Zhonglu, Haidian District. (8204 2517) 龙潭文苑，海淀区北三环中路77号北京电影制片场A区8号

Shouqi Car Rental Beijing's largest car rental chain offers a large variety of models, though availability is spotty. At the low end, a domestically-made Suzuki compact goes for RMB 120-150 per day or RMB 3,000 per month; one can splurge on an Audi A6 (RMB 1,500-2,000 per day or RMB 17,000 a month). In the mid-range are Hyundais (RMB 250-950 per day) and Hondas (RMB 400-850). Models come with limited miles, typically 180km per day, and extra mileage is charged steeply (RMB 2 per kilometer). RMB 5,000 to RMB 15,000 is also required as deposit, a Chinese driver's license is a must, and those without a Beijing resident's card (hukou) must find a city resident to be the guarantor for the rental.
Various locations throughout the city. (800 810 9090, 6232 8701) http://www.sqzl.com.cn 首汽租赁公司

TRANSPORTATION

White-Knuckle Motoring
One commuter on driving in Beijing – and Shunyi
by Ann Mah

Driving in Beijing is not for the faint of heart

I've been driving for 17 years – which I figure is about 17 times longer than most people in this town – but nothing could have prepared me for driving in Beijing. From the minute I took my first spin down Guanghua Lu, terror has characterized every single one of my behind-the-wheel experiences. Is it the drivers who don't look before they change lanes? The games of chicken when headed down narrow streets? Motorists who throw their car in reverse on the Airport Expressway? The constant fear of being suddenly cut off? Yes. It's everything.

Don't get me wrong. On the days when I have bags of groceries to ferry home from Jenny Lou's, a pile of Ikea shelving units to return, or a wall of framed pictures to pick up, nothing could be more convenient than my hoopty. I've learned to spot the bicyclists who whiz from behind parked cars and have become adept at driving with one hand on the wheel, one hand on the horn – and one foot hovering continuously over the brake.

Despite these skills, I live in fear of the dreaded invitation issued by well-meaning friends: "Why don't you come out to our place in Shunyi?"

It's not just the pastel Stepford homes and soulless strip malls that deter me. Nor is it the 30-kilometer drive (which any Shunyi-burbanite will assure you takes only twenty minutes without traffic, never mind that traffic is omnipresent). It's not even the fact that, late one night heading back into town, my worst driving fears were realized when a two-ton dump truck slammed into the side of our sedan, causing us to spin across three lanes of traffic. (Some higher power was watching over us; the car was crushed but we walked away with a mere scratch.)

No, it all comes down to crap. Literally. As in the oceans of sewage that flooded Jingshun Lu when a pipe burst minutes before my four wheels drove through the puddle, drenching my car. It took me weeks to get rid of the stench; in fact, if I close my eyes, I can still smell it. I know these things can happen anywhere, but there's something about the Potemkin atmosphere of Shunyi that seems to proliferate steaming piles of... Anyway, I digress.

After 17 years of behind-the-wheel experience, I didn't think I had much more to learn about driving. But as it turns out, driving in Beijing – much like living in Beijing – has changed me. I now expect my fellow motorists to careen in front of me with only millimeters to spare. Signaling? What's that? Flashing your brights is an indication that you want to – nay, must – pass. You don't need your sideview mirror – it only impedes you from zooming down narrow streets. And as for that old-fashioned adage that pedestrians have the right of way... Well, excuse me while I emit a mirthless chuckle.

Of course, my lessons from Beijing's motorways haven't been all gloom and doom. A few weeks ago, my husband and I rented a car in Washington, DC. As I sped along the Beltway (D.C.'s answer to the Third Ring Road), my husband cautioned me about local drivers. "People say they're the worst in the country," he told me. One glance at their politely blinking signals and I knew I had nothing to fear. Bad driving? They ain't seen nothing yet.

Road hazards include overloaded bikes, oblivious pedestrians and, in Shunyi, oceans of sewage

TRANSPORTATION

To My Yongjiu (Forever)

Whither has thou gone?
by Eric Abrahamsen

Object of desire

You were my trusty steed, and carried me wherever I wanted to go. From midnight trips to the QuikMart to marathon voyages to Xiangshan, you uttered no more complaint than your customary gee-jee gee-jee squeak, so pleasing to the ear.

Chosen out of practicality (you were the largest domestic model available), I came to appreciate you for your particular charms – your capacious basket, and your steel-trap rack on the back upon which many a lissome lass perched (in blissful violation of traffic law), arm lightly about my waist, only to dismount a half-hour later with numbed and frozen bottom. Thank you for the opportunity to warm that bottom.

Beijing contained no surface which you could not navigate. Your single gear – that circle of totality, that Ring Road in parvo – encompassed the lazy Sunday cycle as well as the hell-for-leather race to get to work, and even allowed for a little late-night drag racing on Ping'an Dajie. You laughed at traffic, sniffed at pedestrians; the glare of cabbies slid cleanly from your classy black paint job.

I loved you because you were what I wanted to be – unattractive but reliable, with a quiet, humble strength. Apparently constructed of pig iron, your solidity translated into pure exhilaration on the straight aways, with the wind in my hair and your inertia hinting at perpetual motion. No flimsy kick-stand for you – you stood tall on a complicated locking stand that withstood my drunken stumbles and the roaring winds of May. Your bell took ten foot-pounds of pressure to sound, but when it sounded … birds and pedestrians alike took flight.

Now you're gone, like two other Yongjiu (Forever) 28-inch bicycles before you, and I hope the bolt-cutter-wielding knaves have treated you well. I wish I could say I'll never buy another bike, but if I get another just like you, I'll never know the difference.

PHOTO: LUNA ZHANG

Two and Three Wheels

Mopeds, motorcycles, scooters and sidecars

While the appeal of scooters and motorcycles is clear in this congested town, the laws that govern them can seem opaque. Some people say that you can drive such vehicles without a license. Others aver that police officers ignore infractions by foreign drivers. Don't believe it.

You must have a Chinese E-class motorcycle license to legally operate a motorcycle, scooter or moped over 50cc. If you wish to drive a mo-

They call him "The Cruiser"

TRANSPORTATION

Befriend your neighborhood bike whisperer

torcycle with a sidecar ("*kuazi*"), you'll need a D-class license (which also, incidentally, entitles you to drive E-class vehicles). You cannot use your C-class automobile license, or B-class minibus license, to drive a motorcycle.

To obtain such a D- or E-class license, you must have a valid foreign motorcycle license (e.g. an M-class license in the United States) and "convert" it into a Chinese one. Doing so involves passing a computerized test on China's traffic rules – you need to score at least 90 out of 100 to pass. You or your representative must go to the exam center to book a test date – the standard delay is around three weeks. You must also undergo a brief health exam. To get a license, you'll also need some passport-style photos, a valid passport and a temporary residence certificate. Several companies will handle all the paperwork and test booking for you, notably Beijing Easy and FESCO (see p523). Your foreign license must have two-wheel or three-wheel vehicle authorization to be converted into a D-class Chinese license.

All motorcycles and scooters must have license plates. To drive inside the Fourth Ring Road, you need 'Jing A' (京A) plates. Foreigners must have black plates; Chinese nationals have yellow ones – yellow plates can be exchanged for black ones. The Beijing government stopped issuing new plates for motorcycles in 1998 – to limit accidents and pollution – so you'll have to buy old plates taken from a scrapped bike by your dealer. These plates are expensive, costing around RMB 8,000-10,000. Some dealers will try to sell you Jing B (京B) or Hebei Province (冀) plates. While these plates are cheaper (RMB 2,000) and may be legal, you cannot use them to drive inside the Fourth Ring Road. Fake plates are also available for around RMB 300.

The only restrictions for Jing A plate holders is that they cannot drive on the elevated lanes of the Second, Third and Fourth Ring Roads or cruise Chang'an Jie. Besides helping you obtain plates, the dealer can help you pay the road tax, get insurance and inspection certificates, and complete the registration procedures.

Some motorcycle owners take a cavalier approach to the law, but do so at considerable risk. Drivers involved in an accident who lack either proper plates or a driver's license are held liable for the accident; they are fined and their vehicle is usually confiscated. Moreover, the police conduct spot checks around town, and students in Wudaokou have had their wheels impounded.

More on *kuazi*

The *kuazi*. The name itself commands respect. Also known as the Changjiang "CJ" 750, it consists of a Chinese-made motorcycle and sidecar, built to strict 1938 specifications. Faster than a bike, the *kuazi* can easily squeeze through the most enticing alleys, without allowing for the suicidal speeds of a racing bike. Safe? Arguably. Watch the quick right turns, and try to avoid sudden turns while reversing – as your bike may flip. But cool? Depends who's riding.

The *kuazi* ranges from RMB 3,500 to RMB 30,000, though a bike in good condition should be available for RMB 10,000-18,000, and should come with your choice of new paint jobs (as long as you like black).

New bikes also require a license plate, road tax and insurance, which your mechanic should be able to arrange. You also need to pass the D-class driving test, which consists of a hellish 100-question test and two simple practical tests, usually taking several months in all.

Essential to owning a CJ is a good mechanic, preferably one dedicated enough to drive to you when you break down. While the *kuazi* develop individual personalities after a number of years, they sadly develop health problems to match. You know what they say – keep your friends close and your mechanic closer.

Kuazi dealers: Mr. Zhang (136 5120 1816, Chinese) and Bill (130 3119 5542, English) www.cj750.com. Luke (133 1131 8301) does custom paint jobs and is known to offer good, if fairly expensive, service in Shunyi.

Electric bikes

Electric bikes also require a license plate, though operators do not need a driver's license. The plate costs RMB 10 and is available from a district registration office – bring your passport or ID card, purchase receipt and the quality certificate that came with the bike when you bought it. Bring one photocopy of each document as well for their records. You can find your district's registration office on this website: http://www.bjjtgl.gov.cn/fwzn/dh/ddzxc.htm (Chinese only)

Bicycles

Cycling through old Beijing on a clear fall day is many people's idea of perfection. Bicycles are available in nearly every permutation and size in the city, but our sentimental favorite is the classic Flying Pigeon. Thieves have taken some of the fun out of cycling: the problem is so pervasive that many cyclists purchase cheap used bikes which they can afford to "lose." Reduce the chances of theft by investing in a good lock and parking your steed in designated zones monitored by an attendant. Bike shops are listed in the Shopping chapter, p389. You can also rent a bicycle from one of these shops. Note that most hotels and hostels can also arrange rentals, as can a few department stores.

Bicycle Rental Rents bikes for RMB 30 per day. Tandem and three-person bikes are also available, starting at RMB 20 per hour, with discounts offered on half- and full-day rentals. *9am-8.30pm. Behind Di'anmen Department Store, Xicheng District. (6404 1336 ext 2414)* 地百租车处，西城区地百后面

Bicycle Kingdom Rents a variety of bikes and helmets. Prices range from RMB 60-120 for a single day and from RMB 35-57 per day for a week or longer, depending on the bike rented. Reservation recommended and deposits vary. *North Garden office B402-5, Oriental Plaza, Wangfujing, Dongcheng District (8549 4541, 133 8140 0738) www.bicyclekingdom.com* 自行车王国，东城区王府井大街东方广场北花园写字楼B402-5

Shuangren Yizhan Chain of bike rental shops charging RMB 10 per hour for a one-seater, RMB 20 per hour for a tandem. Requires leaving an ID card/passport or cash deposit (RMB 100-200). *Daily 6am-11pm. 1) Qianhai Nanyan, near Han Cang, Xicheng District; 2) across from Di'anmen Department Store, Xicheng District; 3) Houhai Nanyan, near the amusement park, Xicheng District. (130 7013 5600, 6089 1616)* 双人驿站，1)西城区前海南沿汉仓旁；2)西城区地安门商场对面；3)后海南沿儿童乐园旁

Beijing at your fingertips ...

Discover Beijing with this series of area guides to the city's most exciting neighborhoods. Practical, light, and extremely user-friendly – each area guide features a large map in English showing the precise location of hundreds of bars, restaurants, hotels, boutiques, sightseeing spots and much more!

Collect 'em all!

CBD · Chaoyang-Lido · Haidian · Houhai · Sanlitun · Shunyi · and more!

Find the maps in the latest issue of *that's Beijing* or to order a copy, please e-mail distribution@immersionguides.com

www.immersionguides.com

EXCURSIONS

PHOTO: JANEK ZDZARSKI JR

tbjkids

Beijing's first & only monthly magazine for families

It's a Monthly!

Look for **tbjkids** in over 300 Beijing schools and family-friendly venues on the first Monday of every month

Got a story idea?
Want to see your family or school in the magazine?
Contact our editor at 5820 7100 ext. 802 or editor@tbjkids.com

Want to subscribe or get extra copies?
Contact our distribution department at 5820 7101 or distribution@tbjkids.com

Want to advertise?
Contact our sales department at 5820 7885 or sales@tbjkids.com

www.tbjkids.com

Find tranquility just beyond the Fifth Ring, at Tanzhesi

Escape!
Spiritual replenishment is close at hand
by Michael Arnold

The business of reinventing this city takes its toll on us all, and the worker's will is not unfaltering: For both true-born Beijingers and for your average expat who's made an elegant escape from the rat race of home and come to this alarming metropolis of oriental shades – where whorls of incense smoke drift about with the smuts of coal, where a million cellphones toss their soundless reverberations through solid temple walls – the pace of the information age and the weight of the centuries can be wearing on the spirit. It's fortunate that the tonic for the taxing effects of Beijing's velocity is close at hand – just outside the city limits.

PHOTO: NATALIE BEHRING

EXCURSIONS

Take your anger out on a piece of paper; inner peace is within range

Municipal Beijing and the clusters of cities just beyond its reach are dignified old places rich in the trinkets of history and spectacular landscapes – studded with temples and tombs that have secreted away the ages in the shadows of mountains; with towers and barricades and great gates that remain after the heroes who built them were felled by foreign sword; with peaks and wonders of nature that have stood for millennia, impassively observing the Chinese civilization gather and rise.

Foreigners staying in the capital are living in an unprecedented age with the liberty and means to share these treasures of Chinese heritage. The distance of a few hours' drive or a short journey by bus or train holds much of interest to soothe any beleaguered soul; an overnight or weekend away in a historic coastal town or under the bright streetlights of a modern city can refresh and re-energize anyone having second thoughts about their existence in Beijing. Adventuring in the mountains or circling ancient lands by bike can work those muscles weakened from hours of sitting in Beijing's languid traffic.

Of course, there's more to excursions outside the city than mere renewal; genuine Beijing fans will be seeking something more intimate – to further consummate their relationship with this fascinating place. One's affair with Beijing is kindled with increasing familiarity, and to travel more broadly at her extremities is to bring more of her within; put more plainly, it is to make more of a home of this old soil. For what is travel if it is not to make a map of strange places within the mind and make it all one's own familiar territory?

Beijing is a punishing mistress – those who are here by choice often tire of her charms and begin to doubt their reasons for staying. If that's where you are – if the connections between your days are beginning to become indistinct and the hazy skies are making ill of your sunsets, then browse the following pages and try to take some initiative in this relationship. Pack a spare pair of underwear and socks, twist your water supply tap tight off and double lock your apartment door – then make a weekend out of a loving investigation of Beijing's most delightful and difficult-to-reach places.

PHOTO: GWYNN GUILFORD

Daytrips

Dying to get out of the city for a day? Whether you like communing with the elements, temple touring, fruit picking, swimming, biking, spelunking or just looking for a down-home country-cooked meal – there are options aplenty. Note that several excursion destinations such as the Great Wall, Ming and Qing Tombs, and Fragrant Hills are covered in the Sightseeing chapter (see p227). The following destinations are divided by district and include directions by public transportation and car.

Changping District

China North International Shooting Range Located on the grounds of a weapons research institute about an hour out of town, the China North International Shooting Range offers a selection of four handguns and five rifles for fixed target practice, as well as a double-barreled shotgun for shooting flying discs (aka skeet or clay pigeons). Priced by the bullet, the firing can quickly get expensive, particularly if you are a skeet-shooting aficionado (RMB 200 per session) or really like guns and want to try them all. The facility features a paintball area where you can satisfy your thirst to wage safe but exhilarating war against a thinking, breathing adversary (minimum RMB 80 per person per pellet charge). Bring your passport.
Daily 8.30am-4.30pm. RMB 3-8 per bullet. Nankou Town, Changping District. (6977 1368 ext 3103) 北京国际射击场，昌平区南口镇
Approx. distance: 40km
Bus: Take long distance bus 919 from Deshengmen to Nankou (1.5 hours), then take minibus 11 (RMB 1) or taxi (RMB 10). The bus runs from 6am until 6pm, about every 15 minutes. RMB 10 for air-conditioned buses, RMB 4 for non-A/C.
Car: Take the Badaling/Changping Expressway to Nankou and follow the signs.

Silver Mountain Pagoda Forest (Yinshantalin) Five Jin dynasty towers make this park a worthy visit. Here lie the ruins of the once great Fahua Temple, upon which the five towers were built, known at the time of their construction as the Da Yan Sheng Temple, an eminent place of Buddhist learning. Silver Mountain itself makes for a good hour's climb for the fit and enthusiastic, and provides good views of the pagoda forest and surrounding areas.
Daily dawn to dusk. RMB 15 (Nov 1-Mar 31); RMB 20 (Apr 1-Oct 31). (8972 6426, 8972 6425) 银山塔林，昌平区
Approx. distance: 60km
Bus: The fastest bus route is the 845 express (RMB 9) from Xizhimen (the stop is between Xizhimen and Chegongzhuang subway stations on Xizhimen Nan Dajie) north to Changping Dongguan – a taxi from there should cost RMB 100-200, or a bumpy 50 minute ride on the 31 minibus is RMB 4 (bus stops are unmarked, but wait at the stop where you get off the 845 and go in the same direction). Route 31 takes you to Xihu Village (西湖村) from where it's a 10 minute walk straight up the main road to the park gate. Be waiting for the last bus back to Changping by 4.30pm.
Car: Take Anli Lu (安立路) from Anhui Qiao (安惠桥) on North Fourth Ring Road to Lishui Qiao (立水桥) and eventually merge onto Litang Lu (立汤路) heading north. Pass through Daliushu Roundabout (大柳树环岛) in Xingshouzhen (兴寿镇), following the sign to Silver Mountain Pagoda Forest (银山塔林). Parking is RMB 5 for cars and RMB 10 for larger vehicles.

Fangshan District

Shangfang Mountain and Yunshui Caves Southwest of the city center, Shangfang Mountain has long attracted Buddhists seeking to escape the world. It is dotted with shrines, temples, tombs and monasteries, though only a third of the latter remain open. Hiking around and up the 800-meter mountain is a chance to discover its waterfalls and varied plant and animal life – keep an eye out for monkeys! Located on the side of Shangfang Mountain, the Yunshui Caves are home to a mix of neon-lit Buddhas and Buddhist scenes set amongst a hundred millennia's worth of geological formations. Watch out for lifelike rock shapes, such as ones resembling mushrooms and tigers, as well as 18 naturally formed "monks." One cave is notable for sculptures laid out to depict the 18 layers of Buddhist hell in a Dantesque snapshot.
Shangfang Mountain: Daily 8am-5pm. RMB 40. Shengshuiyu Village, Hancunhe Town, Fangshan District. (6131 5542) 上方山，房山区圣水峪村韩村河镇
Approx. distance: 60km
Yunshui Caves: Daily 8am-4pm. RMB 40, RMB 28 (students). Shangfang Mountain, Yuegezhuang, Fangshan District. (6131 5542) 云水洞，房山区岳各庄上方山
Approx. distance: 75km
Bus: Take bus 917 from Tianqiao (near Tiantan Park) to Fangshan Bus Station, then switch to a minibus to Shangfang Shan (上方山).
Car: Take Jingshi Expressway to the Yancun Exit (阎村出口) where you'll turn onto Jingzhou Road (京周公路). Follow signs past Zhoukoudian (周口店) and towards Yunju Temple (云居寺). Turn north at the sign for Yunshui Caves (云水洞) or Shangfang Shan (上方山).

Silver Fox Cave (Yin Hu Dong) Supposedly 4,500m in length, this cave is named after the unique crystalline formation deep within it that looks like a fox hanging upside down. Visitors descend a steep staircase 80m below ground to a large cavern. Discovered by coal miners in 1991, the cave is over 100m deep and has an average temperature of 13 degrees Celsius year round – great to visit during the torrid summer months. Guided boat rides (RMB 20) on the underground streams are available.
Daily 8am-5.30pm. RMB 43. Xiayingshui Village, Fozizhuang Town, Fangshan District. (6036 3236) 银狐洞，房山区佛子庄乡下英水村
Approx. distance: 55km
Bus: The 917支 Tianqiao-Yinhudong Zhixian Bus goes directly from Tianqiao to the cave. Be careful, as the regular 917 only goes to Fangshan. From there it is still 30km to the cave by minibus. To get to the cave from the Peking Man site, return to Fangshan expressway exit and follow the above directions.
Car: Take Jingyuan Lu (京原路) from Yamenkou Qiao (衙门口桥) on West Fifth Ring Road (10km west of Lianhua Qiao (莲花桥) on West Third Ring Road) to Shimenying (石门营) Roundabout. Turn left at the roundabout, following signs past Jietai Temple (戒台

EXCURSIONS

寺) and Tanzhe Temple (潭柘寺) where you'll pick up signs for Silver Fox Cave.

Ten Crossings (Shidu) Located on a particularly twisty stretch of the Juma River in the shadow of tall karsts, Shidu has reasonable claim to the title "Guilin of the North." It is a fully developed tourist destination with a bungee jump, horseback riding, rock climbing, fishing, boating, hiking trails and plenty of restaurants. The bungee jump (RMB 205) is one of Shidu's claims to fame – don't worry, the equipment is imported from New Zealand and the staff is professionally trained. Shidu also is one of the municipality's best rock climbing sites. If you get far enough away from the main strip, Shidu is very pleasant indeed. See listing for Gushanzhai Village, below.
Shidu, Fangshan District. (6134 9009) 十渡旅游风景区，房山区十渡
Approx. distance: 100km
*Bus: Catch 917 bus from Tianqiao. Shidu is the last stop.
Train: Regular trains depart from Beijing's West Railway Station.
Car: Take Jingshi Expressway to Liulihe (琉璃河) Exit. After exiting the highway follow the sign toward Hancunhe (韩村河). Turn left, following the sign to Shidu at Fangyi Intersection (房易路口), and continue until you reach Changgou Middle School Intersection (长沟中学路口), where you turn right, again following the Shidu sign. Then keep driving until you reach Nanquanhe Bridge (南泉河桥) T-junction, where you turn right toward Yunju Temple (云居寺). Continue for some 10km to the "Shidu 28km" sign, leading you to turn left. After 8km, turn right at the Shidu 20km sign and follow the road to Shidu.*

Gushanzhai Village at Qidu, Shidu Scenic Area Shidu Scenic Area consists of ten villages, one at each of the Juma River ferry crossings between Zhangfang and Shidu. Western tourists flock to Shidu Village for the bungee jumping, but for a more authentic experience, head to Gushanzhai, "Lonely Mountain Village," at Qidu (the seventh crossing). There's a ten-kilometer loop through the valley, starting with a swaying 200m suspension bridge (RMB 20) followed by a winding dirt path (horses are available for rent, but the scenery is best absorbed on foot). The valley around Gushanzhai spent part of prehistory underwater, and the resulting rock formations are fascinating, particularly the mountaintop formation Quanshoutianmen (Dog Guarding Heavenly Door). Later on, the trail passes by a series of small waterfalls before reaching Erchipu (two foot falls), where visitors can take pictures from behind the waterfall. Heading back, one can take the fork up the steep stairs – it's worth the climb for the view and a chance to pass through Yixiantian (One Line of Sky), a fantastically narrow trail through the canyon. The entire loop takes a few hours and is perfect for an afternoon out of the city.
Daily May 1-Sep 11 8am-6pm, other times of the year, 8am-5pm. RMB 60. Qidu Village, Zhangfang Town, Fangshan District. (6134 8888/0078) 孤山寨，房山区张坊镇七渡
Approx. distance: 100km
*Bus: Take bus 917 from Tianqiao (near Tiantan) to Shidu, then get off at Qidu.
Car: Take Jingshi Expressway to Liulihe Exit, and then drive past Hancunhe and Zhangfang. Follow the signs to Qidu (seventh crossing).*

Zhoukoudian Peking Man Museum While the history and controversy surrounding Peking Man is intriguing (see Sidebar, p545), the museum at Zhoukoudian is rather flat and non-interactive. However, basic material and exhibits do have clear English labels, and the most interesting feature of the museum, a Chinese language video featuring graphic recreations of Homo erectus pekinensis, shows how much more could be done to breathe life into Peking Man. The scientifically disinclined may enjoy hiking around the neighboring rolling hills and mountains, known as Dragon Bone Hill ('Long Gu Shan'), an allusion to local folklore about the bone fragments uncovered long ago.
Daily 8.30am-4.30pm. RMB 30. Fangshan District. (6930 1278) 周口店北京猿人遗址博物馆，周口店房山区
Approx. distance: 50km
*Bus: Take bus 917 from Tianqiao near Tiantan Park goes to Zhoukoudian.
Car: Take the Jingshi Expressway to Yancun (闫村) Exit, turn onto Jingzhou Road (京周公路) and follow the signs.*

Fengtai District

Marco Polo Bridge and the Lugouqiao Anti-Japanese War Memorial Hall First constructed in 1189, the bridge left a strong impression on Marco Polo 700 years ago, when he praised it as "a very fine stone bridge, so fine indeed, that it has very few equals in the world." Although the bridge was most recently restored about 20 years ago, the Ministry of Cultural Relics tastefully left a patch of smoothly worn, undulating original stones along the center of the bridge. A total of 501 distinctive stone lions line the bridge. Adjacent to the bridge is the city of Wanping, home of the Anti-Japanese War Memorial Hall. The memorial hall offers a grave, artistic and informative lesson on the Anti-Japanese War. Highlights are a few IMAX-type war exhibits and a really cool hologram display.
Marco Polo Bridge:
Daily 7am-7pm. RMB 20, RMB 10 (students). Wanpingcheng (15km SW of Beijing), Fengtai District. (8389 2521) 卢沟桥，丰台区宛平城
Lugouqiao Anti-Japanese War Memorial Hall *Tue-Sun 9am-4pm. RMB 15, RMB 8 (students). 101 Wanpingcheng, Lugou Qiao, Fengtai District. (8389 2355)* 卢沟桥抗日战争纪念馆，丰台区宛平城卢沟桥
Approx. distance: 16.5km
*Bus: Take bus 309 from Wanzi (near Beijing West Railway station), 339 from Liuli Qiao (on West Third Ring Road) or 748 from Yuxin Xiaoqu (near Tsinghua). You can also take 624 from Gongzhufen or 964 from Fuxingmen.
Car: Take the Jingshi Expressway southwest from Liuli Qiao to Lugou Qiao Exit.*

Haidian District

Fenghuang Mountain and Dragon Spring Temple Each of Fenghuang's three hiking routes is reasonably challenging. The 1,000-year-old temple's unpretentious aura is charming, as are the local legends inscribed on signs by the gate and the ritual connected with the venerable local maidenhair trees, which, according to tradition, people feel compelled to hug.
Daily 6am-6pm. RMB 25, RMB 13 (students). Inside Xishan Nanchang, Haidian District. (6245 5933) 凤凰岭风景区，海淀区西山农场内
Approx. distance: 33km
Bus: Take bus 346 from the Summer Palace directly to Fenghuangling.

The Mystery of Peking Man
Hunting for hominids in Zhoukoudian
By Martin Adams and Kaiser Kuo

Peking Man: pensive and provocative

The discovery in 1929 of an almost complete skull cap of "Peking Man" at Zhoukoudian near Beijing seemed to offer crucial proof of man's development from apes. Here, said scientists, was another species of Homo erectus: a tool-using, organized, creative, fire-controlling type who hunted big animals and was just 300cc of brain space and a Norse saga or two away from us – Homo sapiens.

Coming a few years after the famous Scopes trial, when Darwin's Theory of Evolution was being attacked by creationists and biblical literalists, the Zhoukoudian discovery clinched the hypothesis that a direct line of human evolution stretched back to common African origins. This still left the problem of how the next evolutionary step – from erectus to modern man – occurred. One theory is that the crucial transformation took place independently in various parts of the world.

Life for Peking Man, according to convention, was a challenging round of deer-hunting, tool-using and running away from the local giant hyenas.

A different picture emerges from *Dragon Bone Hill*, a recent book by two American paleoanthropologists who offer a fresh take on the Zhoukoudian discovery. Peking Man, they say, was a scavenger and occasional cannibal who raided hyena caves for scraps, but as often as not ended up as dinner for the outsize carnivores. The authors reject the notion that evolution from erectus to sapiens occurred independently in separate locations. Instead, they propose a theory of "clinal replacement": geographically linked populations of erectus formed a sort of transcontinental "gene sea" across which genetic change gradually spread.

But aside from the controversy about Peking Man and his relation to modern humans, the findings at Zhoukoudian are embroiled in a more recent historical controversy: all the Peking Man skulls, teeth and bone fragments went missing in World War II, and have never been recovered. They were handed over to the US army in 1941 for transport to America to prevent them from falling into Japanese hands, but when Pearl Harbor was bombed, US personnel in China were taken into custody, and along with them, the remains. At some point after this, the bones went missing.

One popular theory places Peking Man in a watery grave. After the Japanese took the bones, goes this version, they sent them off to Japan aboard the Japanese vessel Awa Maru in 1945. En route, however, the Awa Maru was sunk by an American submarine in the Taiwan Straits. Supposedly, the bones remain there today, despite a Chinese salvage attempt in 1977.

Or was Peking Man buried beneath a tree in Ritan Park? In 1966 a Japanese army veteran divulged with almost his last breath that he, in fact, took the bones under orders and buried them beneath a specially marked pine tree in Beijing's Ritan Park at the end of the war. Subsequent investigations found the tree, but no trace of Peking Man. The search continues today.

A fearsome gauntlet of uniquely carved stone lions titivate Marco Polo Bridge

Car: Take Badaling Expressway from Madian Qiao on Third Ring Road to Beiqinglu Exit by the tollbooths. Exit and head west on Beiqing Lu until the end. Make a right and follow signs, eventually turning left to Fenghuang Mountain.

Dajue Temple In the shadow of the Yangtai mountains, where the hamlet of Beianhe drowses amid lush groves of peach and cherry trees, a sparkling, bright stream rushes down from the peaks – only to be captured within this charming temple. The stream flows to a deep central pond where worshippers of the Buddha come each year to release goldfish and turtles to demonstrate compassion and receive blessings. The original "Magic Spring Temple," was built on this site during the Liao dynasty (907-1125 AD). Since then, it's been continuously restored – right up until the present day when it has been unceremoniously revised as a site for a snazzy restaurant and pretty teahouse. The rest of the Ming complex, designed as a series of increasingly grand halls, is a lovely little place rife with historical treats. The largest hall is set with an inscription in the hand of Qianlong, and more imperial calligraphy adorns the fourth building – once a library of sacred texts and currently a museum – left by the First Prince Chun, whose tomb can be found nearby. Behind this hall, you'll find yourself in the modest rear courtyard where you can sit awhile at the edge of the spring that inspired it all. Qi Wang Cemetery (七王坟) is just north of Dajue Temple.
Daily 8am-5pm (Apr 1-Oct 31). RMB 20. Beianhe Village, Haidian District. (6245 6103) 大觉寺，海淀区北安河乡
Approx. distance: 30km

Bus: Take route 633 direct or 346 from the Summer Palace to the last station and walk straight ahead for about 2km. Driving or hiring a taxi is recommended for seeing additional sites in the area not serviced by public bus routes. If you've not arrived by taxi, it may be difficult to find one in the area on weekdays.
Car: From Madian Qiao on North Third Ring Road, take Badaling Expressway to Beianhe Exit, turn west to Beiqing Lu, pass Sujiatuo Intersection and follow signs.

Jiufeng Forest Park Just 18 kilometers northwest of the Summer Palace, Jiufeng Forest Park doesn't pretend to be a wilderness experience. But this welcome retreat, with its rocky outcrops and forested hillsides, isn't a simple walk in the park, either. There are three or four hours of hiking to be done here, up and down the stone steps and well-trodden dirt trails. Some trails hug the greener, lower hills, pausing at small, simple pagodas and great impromptu picnic spots. Others are more ambitious, including a long, hot march up to 1,153m – a climb of more than 700m from the main ticket gate. There's no chairlift here, so the 360-degree views remain the preserve of those who earn them the hard way.
Daily 7am-5pm, peak season; 7.30am-5.30pm, off-peak. RMB 10 (adults); RMB 8 (students). 5 Xiufengsi Lu, Sujiatuo Town, Haidian District. (6245 5816) 鹫峰森林公园，海淀区苏家坨镇秀峰寺路5号
Approx. Distance: 30km
Bus: Catch bus 346 from Yiheyuan (the Summer Palace) bus station.
Car: Take the Badaling Expressway to Beianhe Exit. At Beianhe, turn left onto Beiqing Lu, keep driving along the road and follow the signs to Jiufeng.

All Together Now
Excursion groups and tour companies
by Haley Warden

When you're in good company, the future's bright

Beijing has a lot to offer the intrepid soul, but you don't have to be Jack Kerouac or Indiana Jones to get on the road. After a busy week, planning a hike and taking a public bus to some unfamiliar destination might just sound like too much of a hassle. Aside from the convenience and good company, group travel can allow participants access to locations and information that would be difficult to find without excellent Chinese, a lot of patience, and a car. Below is a partial list of organizations in the Beijing area.

Beijing Hikers Offers beautiful and often challenging hikes around Beijing, as well as some kid-friendly options. Informative website.
For more information, see Listing in Sports and Fitness chapter, p428

Chinese Culture Club / Beijing Amblers See Listing in Sports and Fitness, p430

CnAdventure See Listing in Transportation, p510

Cycle China Not just bicycles anymore, Cycle China organizes day-long and weekend hiking, rafting and horseback riding tours in Beijing and beyond, as well as cycling tours, including a hutong tour, a Summer Palace tour and a Great Wall tour, as well as weekend excursions to Inner Mongolia. All guides speak English. Also offers customized trips.
Price range: RMB 300 for trips around Beijing.
12 Jingshan East Street (East gate of Jingshan Park), Dongcheng District (6402 5653, 139 1188 6524)
www.cyclechina.com 非常之旅。东城区景山东路12号（景山公园东门对面）

Lüye A China-wide, web-based outdoor adventure club. Website users post trips for sign-up online (Chinese language only). 绿野 www.lvye.info, www.lvye.org

High Club In season, High Club organizes riding excursions near Kangxi Grasslands. RMB 270 per person includes two hours of riding, transportation, tolls, English tour guide and lunch.
Call Lucy (8580 5080) www.highclub.cn 海卡俱乐部

Mountain Bikers of Beijing (The MOB) See Listing in Sports and Fitness, p418

Nordic Ways One of the most developed groups organizing sporting events around Beijing, Nordic Ways promotes Nordic-friendly sports like cycling and cross-country skiing. Highlights include the September Great Wall Bike Festival, and the winter ski events like a qualifying race for the Cross-Country Sprint World Cup.
www.nordicways.com

Sanfo A Chinese outdoor equipment store that organizes weekend and week-long hiking, camping and horseback-riding trips. Their Chinese-only website has information about upcoming tours.
See Listing in Shopping / Sports Equipment, p410

WestChina This small tour company organizes original tours around Beijing and beyond, as well as custom tours (including winery and spa tours). Trip guides are knowledgeable and seek to provide less physical, fun tours for everyone. Contact Caroline (135 8168 2703) www.westchina.net.cn

WildChina Destinations all over China, but those near Beijing include birding in Shandong and sightseeing in Pingyao, Shanxi province.
See Listing in Transportation, p511

PHOTO: ADAM PILLSBURY

Yunmeng Shan's piquish peaks: eminently peekable

Huairou District

Cloud Covered Mountain (Yunmeng Shan) About 85km north of Beijing, the area's craggy peaks, topped by bonsai-ed cypresses and spilling over into lush summer growth, recall traditional ink paintings. The park, which boasts a dense forest offering more than 100 varieties of trees, also contains a wild botanical garden that overlooks the western shore of Miyun Reservoir. The mountain's highest peak, situated 1,414m above sea level, is accessible through a fairly easy hike that takes approximately five hours. On either side of the creek, the terrain rises to rocky outcrops – some with sheer drops, others contorted into sculptural forms. The park's camping site, which is available to visitors free of charge, consists of desolate barracks in a clearing in the middle of the forest.
Apr 1-Nov 15, 7.30am-7.30pm, closed winter. RMB 36 (adults), RMB 18 (kids). Liulimiao Town, Huairou District. (6162 2381) 云蒙山，怀柔区琉璃庙镇
Approx. distance: 82km
Bus: From Dongzhimen long distance bus station, bus 936 (only weekends) will take you directly there. Or take bus 916 (weekdays) from Dongzhimen to Huairou and change to a mini bus there.
Car: Take Jingshun Lu to Kuliushu Roundabout (枯柳树环岛 almost to the Sixth Ring Road). At the roundabout, follow signs to Huairou. In Huairou follow signs toward Fengning/Huairou (丰宁/怀柔) to the Yanqi Roundabout (雁栖环岛) on National Road 111. Continuing on 111, you'll see signs for Yougu Shentan (幽谷神潭) and finally Yunmengshan Mountain (云蒙山). Stay on 111 and follow the signs.

Red Conch Temple (Hongluo Si) Once one of the most sacrosanct locales under the Buddhist sky, Hongluo Si is the largest Buddhist center in northern China. Emperors used to prostrate themselves here. Nowadays, operated by a managing firm, Hongluo Temple is more of a Buddhist Disneyland. The temple's name originates from a legend about a pair of red-glowing snails that are said to be the incarnations of the two daughters of the Jade Emperor who protect the site from within their mountain spring.
Daily 8am-5.30pm (summer), 8am-4.30pm (winter). RMB 40, RMB 20 (children). Hongluo Mountain, Yanxi Town, Huairou District. (6068 1175) 红螺寺．北京市怀柔区雁栖镇红螺山下
Approx. distance: 55km
Bus: Take bus 916/936 (RMB 7 / RMB 12 with AC, 1.5 hours) from the Dongzhimen long distance bus station – leaving from bay 5. Some buses stop early at the Huairou Station – swap to route Xi 6 at Fuqian Dongjie Dongkou (府前东街东口) to complete the trip (RMB 2). Taxis from Huairou should cost around RMB 10.
Car: From Sanyuan Qiao on Third Ring Road, take Jingshun Lu, which turns into National Road 101, to

Huairou Qiao. Turn toward Huairou and follow signs to Qingchunlu Roundabout (青春路环岛) driving north for another 10 minutes.

Sky Pool Valley (Tianchi Xiagu) The big draw here is a kilometer-long pool inside the mountain, but there are also trickling waterfalls and a long cave. The views are stunning, and since there is a circular path around the mountain you don't have to retrace your steps.
Daily Mar-Nov, closed in winter. RMB 20, RMB 10 (students). Huangtuliang Village, Huaibei Town, Huairou District. (6162 2577/2078) 天池峡谷，怀柔区怀北镇黄土梁村
Approx. distance: 75km
Bus: Take bus 916 from Dongzhimen to Huairou, then change to the minibus going to Yunmengshan and get off at Huangtuliang.
Car: Take Jingshun Lu all the way to Kuliushu Roundabout (枯柳树环岛)almost to Sixth Ring Road). At the roundabout, follow signs to Huairou. In Huairou follow signs toward Fengning/Huairou (丰宁/怀柔) to Yanqi Roundabout (雁栖环岛) on National Road 111. Continuing on 111, you'll see signs for Sky Pool Valley (天池峡谷).

Small West Lake (Xiaoxihu) If Shanhaiguan is where the Great Wall meets the sea, Xiaoxihu, just over 60 kilometers northwest of Beijing, is where it tests the waters. What was once a forested valley is now a drowned landscape where only the highest hilltops survive and ruined sections of the Great Wall sink beneath its dammed waters, only to resurface again meters later.
Daily 7.30am-5pm, peak season; 8am-5pm off-peak. RMB 25, half price for students. Xishuiyu Village, Jiuduhe Town, Huairou District. (6165 1111) 小西湖，怀柔区九渡河镇西水峪村北
Approx. distance: 60km
Bus: Catch bus 916 from Dongzhimen long distance bus station to two stops before the main Huairou terminal, then take a minibus to the village of Xishuiyu.
Car: Take Jingshun Lu past the Sixth Ring Road and turn left, continuing to Xiaotangshan Roundabout. Turn right then follow the road into the mountains. Xiaoxihu is a few kilometers beyond the Huanghua section of the Great Wall.

Ziyunshan Mountain The mountain's name, which translates as "Purple Cloud Mountain," comes from the rainbows frequently spotted here that give the range a purple hue. Hikers can scale the peaks, the tallest of which is 900m above sea level, while swimmers will be drawn to the 30 stunning green pools that dot the range. During the warmer months, when the mean temperature ranges a comfortable 22-26°C, come here to swim, hike, fish, camp, barbecue, have campfires, pick wild fruit and, of course, *lu tian ge wu* (dance and sing under the sky).
Weekends only. RMB 15, half price for students. Duanshuling Village, Huaibei Town, Huairou District. (6162 2327) 紫云山，怀柔区怀北镇椴树岭村
Approx. distance: 75km
Bus: Take bus 936 from Dongzhimen.
Car: take Jingshun Lu all the way to Kuliushu Roundabout (枯柳树环岛) almost to the sixth ring road. At the roundabout, follow signs to Huairou. In Huairou follow signs toward Fengning/Huairou (丰宁/怀柔) to Yanqi Roundabout (雁栖环岛) on National Road 111. Continuing on 111, you'll see signs for Ziyunshan (紫云山).

Mentougou District

Ancient Ming Village (Cuandixia) This village offers a snapshot of history, as it has been preserved virtually unchanged since it was built by a single, extended family during the Ming dynasty. It contains some 70 courtyard homes, many of which have been converted into simple guesthouses. Villagers open their homes and hearts to city-slicker refugees. Nightly accommodation can be found in any home that has room enough and averages RMB 15-25. Not much to do there, but siestas and strolls are as complicated as your plans should get.
Daily 24 hours. RMB 20. Cuandixia Village, Zhaitang Town, Mentougou District (6981 9233) 爨底下，门头沟区斋堂镇
Approx. distance: 90km
Bus: From Pingguoyuan subway station take Bus 929 (支) (RMB 7, 2.5 hours) bus to Zhaitang Town. From there take a taxi (RMB 10-15, ten minutes) to the gate. Twice a day (7.30am and 12.30pm) 929 支 goes all the way to the gate.
Car: Go west from Hangtian Qiao on West Third Ring Road along Fushi Lu (阜石路) until it merges into Jinding Nanlu (金顶南路). Stay on this road until you reach Jin'an Qiao (金安桥). Turn right onto Jinding Xijie (金顶西街) and continue northwest for about 15 minutes – the road's name changes to National Road 109 (109国道) – until you reach a fork intersection. There, go left, following the sign toward Hebei (河北). Stay on this road for about 90 minutes until you reach the town of Zhaitang Zhen (斋堂镇), where you'll see signs for Cuandixia. Turn right and head northwest for another 5.5 km to Cuandixia.

Miaofeng Mountain Given the views of the hills, the fir trees dotted around, the sprinklings of pear blossom and the forthcoming rose blooms, one understands why Miaofeng was deemed a worthy home for goddesses. Venerated by Taoists as the spiritual abode of several divinities, Miaofeng was home to several temples by the Ming dynasty and became the object of an annual pilgrimage, in the fourth lunar month, by believers from all over northern China. The festival, held annually from April 1-14, is a widely advertised event that draws artists, soothsayers, craftsmen and merchants from far and wide – not to mention tourists.
Daily 8am-5pm. RMB 30, RMB 15 (students). Miaofengshan Scenic Area, Mentougou District. (6188 2935/6/7) 妙峰山风景区，门头沟区
Approx. distance: 55km
Bus: Take 929 zhixian (支线) from Pingguoyuan to Miaofeng.
Car: From Hangtian Qiao on West Third Ring Road, go west on Fushi Lu (阜石路), which merges into Jinding Nanlu (金顶南路) by Pingguoyuan Subway Station. Stay on this road until you reach Jin'an Qiao (金安桥), then turn right onto Jinding Xijie (金顶西街), and continue northwest for about 15 minutes – the road's name changes to National Road 109 (109国道) – until you reach a fork intersection. There, go left, following the sign toward Hebei (河北), continuing on until you reach Danli (担礼). At Danli turn off the highway, follow the Miaofeng Mountain (妙峰山) signs north for another 20 minutes until you arrive.

Ordination Terrace Temple (Jietaisi) Inside Jietai Temple, the hundreds of niches once filled by miniature Buddhas are empty. Over 1,300 years old, the temple

Continues on p554

Get Away to Your Getaway
Paths to your country home
by Adam Pillsbury

Take a left at the tree

Until recently, the only foreigners with country homes outside Beijing were *guanxi* masters. The property acquisitions typically involved creative negotiations and contracts of uncertain validity that neither party was eager to publicize – not least because foreigners cannot legally buy country properties but may only lease the land-use rights for fixed periods. Today, such contracts seem more secure and many foreigners are leasing cottages in Miyun and Huairou – with predictable results. Prices are rising, luxury properties are being developed, and at least one management firm offers busy Beijingers a complete country home service – from site search to renovations. So how does one acquire a country cabana? Here are two scenarios.

DIY *Nongjia*
In 2005, Laura and Dominic Johnson-Hill obtained a 75-year lease on a four-room farmer's home in a sleepy village with dramatic views of the Great Wall for only RMB 12,000. It featured a *kang* bed, an outdoor latrine, a well and, well, not much else. They spent an additional RMB 4,000 to pave the dirt floors, paint the interior, put in windows and light sockets, and build outdoor sinks. More recently, they added a patio, a spot of lawn, a vintage refrigerator, and a barbecue. The house is simplicity itself, but it's the perfect antidote to city living.

It took them a year and a half of exploration and assiduous courting to sign a lease. Their limited budget meant looking in an area that was three hours from Beijing in 2004, but they knew a new expressway would reduce the driving time by a third. They introduced themselves to the village's main businessman, and ate many boozy meals in his restaurant. "He is the ultimate *guanxi* guy: He's got money, knows the police and the local government, and is very kind," says Dominic. "The minute you find someone like that you know you're in business. He'll tell you who to talk to in the village and what brand of cigarette or *baijiu* they like."

The village leader was distrustful at first – no foreigners had ever lived in the village – but the Johnson-Hills kept showing up with their daughters and established that they were non-threatening and friendly. After 15 months, they got the green light and the right price, and a leasing contract giving them exclusive land use rights was drawn up, to which the Johnson-Hills, the local powerbrokers, and the property owner and his relatives affixed their thumbprints and signatures. Money was then exchanged for the deed, though the name on the deed could not be changed. "I don't know how long this contract will stand for, but it does feel quite secure because I have the right signatures and the people in the village accept it," says Dominic. Such acceptance has been fostered by the newcomers' policy of keeping an open door and sourcing food, furniture and labor locally. "We're dealing with good people and have built our standing by earning respect," says Dominic. "It sounds complicated but it isn't."

Outsourced Opulence

At the other end of the comfort, elegance and price spectrum is the magnificent country home owned by Jim Spear and Tang Liang. It is set among chestnut, peach and apple trees in the hills above the village of Mutianyu, only an hour's drive from the Fifth Ring Road, and offers sweeping Great Wall views from its two gardens, picture frame windows and even the shower. The sprawling home sits on the footprint of two *nongjia* (country homes), the first of which Spear and Tang leased in 1994 as a weekend retreat for their daughters. Spear spent 13 years designing and redesigning this home, which he calls his "classroom."

The import of this for flush Beijingers seeking a signature getaway is that Spear and Tang have leveraged their experience and relationships by opening Beijing ABC Management Consulting Co., which assists clients in finding, leasing, and renovating country properties in Mutianyu and a neighboring village called Yingbeigou. Separately, they have also invested in three local restaurants, including the Schoolhouse at Mutianyu (see also Grandma's Place, p553).

Beijing ABC introduces clients to a number of properties, conducts due diligence (e.g. to make sure the prospective lessor(s) has exclusive rights to the property), and helps them draft a comprehensive lease. The duration of the lease is negotiable, but a typical length is 30 years.

Jim Spear and Tang Liang's swanky scrub spot boasts a Great Wall vista

Then, Spear sits down with his clients and helps them convert simple farmhouses or other structures into year-round vacation homes that all boast Great Wall views and mod cons – heated floors, indoor plumbing with constant water pressure, full kitchens, sky windows and Wi-Fi. "We draw on the vernacular tradition using local building materials and labor combined with a contemporary flair." Roofs are raised, basements are dug, skylights and windows are pierced, and hearths and deck are built to create a unique compound that, in Spear's words, is "tailored to the aspirations of each client."

Of course, such tailoring comes at a price. Spear reveals that "the turnkey budget for projects we have worked on has ranged from about RMB 750,000 to more than ten times that amount, [which] includes paid up lease, all of our services, all construction costs, and a variety of miscellaneous costs such as payments for use of trees and increase in electric power consumption rating, and so on." If that seems a lot, just wait a year or so: Spear says prices are rising rapidly thanks to a limited supply of desirable sites and full knowledge among locals of market values. Spear's final words of advice? "Look before you leap."

Great Wall, Wi-Fi, courtyard garden, etc – simple as Beijing ABC

Champagne, scenery and cutting-edge architecture at Commune by the Great Wall

Cold feet?

Book a bucolic boutique bunk near the Wall

City-slickers unprepared to lease their own country home can enjoy comfortable rural idylls at the following hotels.

Grandma's Place When Jim Spear's mother is not visiting from the US, her handsomely restored country house in Mutianyu village is available for rent. Featuring a brick *kang* bed in the master bedroom, thick wood beams and a commodious green patio where guests can take in Great Wall views, Grandma's Place also offers modern amenities such as Wi-Fi, air conditioning, and high-quality toilets and shower. Many hiking trails lead off into hills and to the Great Wall. Rates include breakfast. Nearby dining options include the Schoolhouse at Mutianyu; picnic baskets can be ordered from the Country Store. Photos and directions available on the website. Chauffeur service from Beijing can be arranged. Rates: weekdays RMB 800, Fri & Sat RMB 1,200.
51 Mutianyu Village, Huairou District. (6162 6506) www.grandmasplaceatmutianyu.com 奶奶家，怀柔区慕田峪

Commune by The Great Wall Kempinski The recipient of a Special Prize for architecture at the 2002 Venice Biennale, the Commune by the Great Wall is a collection of 42 strikingly modern villas surrounded by verdant mountains and the Shuiguan section of the Great Wall. Once the exclusive preserve of high rollers and celebrities, The Commune became accessible to guests of less exalted status with the opening of Phase 2 in December '06. For while the Phase 1 villas may only be rented in full at considerable expense, individual rooms and suites are available in the Phase 2 buildings – visit the website to see the various options. The clubhouse boasts three separate dining facilities, a lounge, a swimming pool, function hall and an art gallery, and the function room can be leased for corporate functions. Before going on a long hike, parents can drop off their kids at Commune of the Children, a club with full- and half-day programs featuring swimming, storytelling, arts and crafts and more (RMB 150-290). The Commune is located just off the Badaling Expressway, a 60-90 minute drive from downtown Beijing. Chauffeur service from the city and airport available. Rack rates: Phase 1 (entire villa) RMB 12,500-23,380/night, Phase 2 RMB 2,340-3,200.
Daily 9.30am-4.30pm. The Shuiguan Great Wall exit on the Badaling Expressway, Yanqing County. (8118 1888 ext 5706) www.commune.com.cn 长城脚下的公社，延庆县八达岭高速路水关长城出口

Red Capital Ranch Nestled in the hinterlands of Huairou District within walking distance of the Great Wall, the Red Capital Ranch is a self-described "Manchurian Lodge" owned by Laurence J. Brahm, the entrepreneur behind Beijing's Red Capital Club, a restaurant, and Red Capital Residence, a boutique hotel. The ten distinctively decorated "villas" are more like standalone rooms equipped with stony bathrooms with high-pressure showers, as well as translucent canopy curtains, smart lighting and plump queen-sized beds – the most desirable villas have rooftop terraces. The ranch staff can help arrange picnic packs, while the Wall supplies thrills and satisfaction for climbs that are challenging, but not dangerous. The comfortable compound includes a handful of tranquil pavilions, a cigar bar and "Secret Tibetan Spa experience" (RMB 288 per hour), among other amenities. Intrepid Ranch dwellers can also rent mountain bikes (free of charge). Chauffeur service available from Beijing. Rates: USD 190-200.
28 Xiaguandi Village, Yanxi Town, Huairou District. (Reservations: 8401 8886, 6402 7150) www.redcapitalclub.com.cn 新红资避暑山庄 北京怀柔区雁栖镇下官地村28号

was never restored after Japanese soldiers destroyed it 70 years ago, though carved marble embellishments hint at the temple's former splendor. Initiation rituals for novice monks joining Jietaisi included fasting and burning marks onto their freshly tonsured heads. The temple dates back to before the Tang dynasty, though the current building was part of a Qing-era refurbishment. Several old pines on the premises date back over 800 years to the Liao and Jin Dynasties.
Daily 8am-5pm. RMB 35. Ma'an Shan, Mentougou District. (6980 2645/2232); Guesthouse (6980 5940) 戒台寺, 门头沟区马鞍山麓
Approx. distance: 40km
Getting there: See Tanzhesi below; follow the signs.

Temple of the Poor and the Wild Mulberry (Tanzhesi)
First built during the Jin (晋) dynasty (265-420 AD), Tanzhe Temple's age is implied by the country saying: "First there was Tanzhe, and after there was Youzhou." (Youzhou is an old name for Beijing.) While it doesn't depart from the three-courtyard layout of a classic temple, the scenery from the surrounding hills and forest is refreshing. Even today, monks come from all over Asia to study at Tanzhesi. Most visitors come to the Hall of Guanyin to see where the devout daughter of Kublai Khan prayed so ardently that she wore indentations into a rock. The majestic, ancient Emperor Tree still stands with incense placed at the base of its trunk. Don't miss the Stupa Park at the bottom of the hill that contains the graves of monks from the Liao and Jin dynasties.
Daily 8am-5pm. RMB 35. Tanzhe Shan, Mentougou District. (6086 1699) 潭柘寺, 门头沟区潭柘山下
Approx. distance: 40km
Subway/bus: Take the subway to Pingguoyuan, change to bus 931. From Fuchengmen, Tourist Bus 7 (6303 5066) makes a three-stop journey to Jietai Si, Shihuadong Caves, and Tanzhe Si. The tour costs RMB 38.
Car: Take Jingyuan Lu (京原路) from Yamenkou Qiao (衙门口桥) on West Fifth Ring Road (10km west of Lianhua Qiao (莲花桥) on West Third Ring Road) to Shimenying (石门营) Roundabout. Turn left at the roundabout, following signs to Jietai Temple (戒台寺) and Tanzhe Temple (潭柘寺).

Miyun County

Black Dragon Pool (Heilong Tan) Black Dragons are apparently swimming aficionados, as this is one of two "Black Dragon Pools" within the Beijing municipality. The eponymous pool is augmented by 18 smaller ones and several waterfalls. People swim here but the water quality can be suspect. In autumn, wild geese flock here.
Daily 8am-6pm. RMB 36. Shicheng Town, Miyun County. (6102 5028) 黑龙潭, 密云县石城镇
Approx. distance: 100km
Bus: Take bus 980 from Dongzhimen to Miyun Gulou, then change to a minibus going to Heilong Tan.
Car: Take Jingshun Lu to Kuliushu Roundabout (枯柳树环岛), follow signs to Miyun direction, from there turn onto Mixi Lu (密溪路), which will lead you to Black Dragon Pool.

Cloud Cave Valley (Yunxiugu) A little piece of heaven, this upland valley is carpeted in trees and endowed with large flat slabs of rocks (making it an easy hike), running streams, waterfalls, caves and a section of the Great Wall.
Daily 24 hours. RMB 31, RMB 16 (students).
Xinchengzi Town, Miyun County. (8102 2307) 云岫谷, 密云县新城子镇

Approx. distance: 100km
Bus: Take a long distance bus from Dongzhimen to Miyun (such as 980), then change to a minibus. Takes 2-3 hours.
Car: Take Jingmi Lu to Miyun, then follow Jingcheng Lu to Sangyuan Intersection, turn right and drive on for another 35km.

Cool Valley (Qingliang Gu) Cool Valley lives up to its name: Cut deep into the mountain and blanketed with green trees and tall grass, the hike up is cool but humid, and filled with a humming chorus of chirping cicadas. At the top, vendors sell hard tiger-shaped pillows filled with horsebeans (can dou) alongside a tea stand fitted with a small TV in anticipation of karaoke-loving customers. The valley, babbling with brooks and pools of progressively increasing clarity, sports the usual carved characters etched into the walls. A rusty series of iron stairs scales the rock face, and what once looked to be a series of deafening waterfalls has now been tamed with a rather dodgy-looking dam.
RMB 36, RMB 18 (students). Sihetang, Shicheng Town, Miyun County. (6901 5208) 清凉谷, 密云县石城镇四合堂
Approx. distance: 110km
Bus: Take bus 987 from Dongzhimen to Heilong Tan, then change to a minibus heading for Sihetang.
Car: Take Jingshun Lu to Kuliushu Roundabout (枯柳树环岛), follow signs to Miyun direction, from there turn onto Mixi Lu (密溪路), which leads to Cool Valley.

White River (Baihe) Miyun's Baihe River Valley is home to one of the most developed rock climbing areas near Beijing. There are as many as 45 established sport (bolted) and traditional routes. The main climbing area is adjacent to a sandy beach near the river, which makes it an ideal place for camping. In winter, there is an ice-climbing park with a man-made ice wall. One group that heads out to Baihe often is Longtan Lake Park Climbing Wall (6718 6358 ext 9031). You can call them for more information or to find out when they're going next. (Make sure you bring all your own gear.) Baihe River is about four kilometers in from the gate on fairly decent trails. There are camping spots on both sides of the river, but cross over to the far side for better views and more privacy. If camping is not your cup of tea, stay in local village guesthouses.
Baihe Climbing Area 白河, 怀柔区龙潭涧景区
Car: Take National Road 111 through Huairou to Miyun County City (about 1hr) and then turn north at Heilong Tan (黑龙潭). You will pass through three tunnels and then on the left there is a large stone marker for Baihe Valley. From there it is less than 30 minutes to the bottom of the valley and the main climbing area. Camping RMB 20.
Daily 8am-5pm. Longtan Jian Scenic Area, Huairou District. (6161 8140)
Baihe Trailhead 白河攀岩, 密云县黑龙潭方向
Approx. distance: 110km.
Bus: Take bus 916 (RMB 8, about 1hr) from Dongzhimen long distance bus station to Huairou Station (怀柔站). From there take minibus 10 (RMB 6, about 1hr) to Baichazi (柏查子). From there take a taxi (RMB 15-20, 10 minutes) to the entrance gate.
Car: Take Jingshun Lu to Jingmi Lu to Huairou. In Huairou go around the Yanxi Roundabout and take Huai Feng Road (怀丰路) to Baichazi and then to Yunmeng Xianjing. Take a right at the reception center and go straight.

The Buddha Tooth Pagoda at Badachu is a looming tusk of an edifice

Pinggu County

Jinhai Lake & Jinhai Lake Water Park Located two hours east of Beijing, the lush hills embracing Jinhai Lake are dotted with pavilions, rock formations, caves, historical spots and what is purported to be Asia's largest peach orchard. If you tire of hiking and chomping on peaches, you can fish, rent a boat, go swimming or visit the water park for water skiing and parasailing. Jinhai is very popular with native Beijingers.
Weekdays 8am-5pm, weekends 8am-5.30pm. RMB 18, RMB 9 (students). Haizi Reservoir, Pinggu District (East). (6999 1356) 金海湖水上公园，平谷区海子水库
Approx. distance: 90km
Bus: Take long distance bus 918支 from Dongzhimen. Bus departs Dongzhimen 7.25am, 8.30am, 9.05am and 2.32pm, but the last direct bus back to Beijing is around 11am. For the return trip, take the 5.15pm minibus to Pinggu where you can get on the 918 again. One-way takes about 2 hours.
Car: Take Jingshun Lu to Kuliushu Roundabout. Turn right and go straight to Yingbin Roundabout in Pinggu District and follow signs to Jinhai Lake.

Shijingshan District

Badachu This large, easily accessible park in Beijing's western hills has for centuries offered a heady fix to devout Buddhists, temple junkies, hiking enthusiasts and fresh air fiends. The eight temples and monasteries scattered around this site south of the Fragrant Hills include the Temple of Divine Light, the only temple at Badachu that still has resident monks. The temple is complemented by the reconstructed 13-story Buddha Tooth Pagoda, on a site which previously contained a sacred Buddha tooth. Badachu's other seven temples are not as striking, but some worthy of a visit are Fragrant World Temple (6th), the largest temple, and the Cave of Precious Pearls (7th), the temple perched highest up the mountain.
Daily 6am-7pm (summer), 6am-6pm (winter). RMB 10. Badachu Lu, Shijingshan District. (8896 4661) 八大处公园，石景山区八大处路
Approx. distance: 19km.
Bus: Take 972 from Pingguoyuan subway station, 347 from Xinjiekou, 389 from the Yuquan Lu subway station or 958 from Shijingshan Amusement Park (Bajiao Youleyuan subway station) to Badachu.
Car: Take West Fourth Ring Road and exit at Dinghui Beiqiao. Go west on Tiancun Lu past Xiwuhuan and turn north onto Badachu Lu. Or take Fushi Lu from Dinghui Qiao, turn right at Jinyuan Qiao and follow the sign onto Tiancun Lu, which leads to Badachu Lu.

Fahai Temple Tucked into the south side of the Cuiwei Mountains in western Beijing, Fahai Temple is the humble home of an amazing collection of Ming dynasty murals. With RMB 20 and a complimentary flashlight in hand, one can examine the five-century-old frescoes which depict a meeting of Buddhist deities. Commissioned and funded by eunuch Li Tong in honor of his emperor Zhengtong of the Ming dynasty (reigned from 1435-1449, 1457-1464 AD), this 236.7 square meter mural was made by two master painters and 13 artisans that worked from 1439-1443. Keep an eye out for the six-tusked elephant on the back wall whose long appendages each represent a quality that leads to en-

lightenment. Closed until spring 2008 for renovations. Tian Yi Eunuch Tomb (description below) is in the same location and is open for visitors.
Daily 9am-5pm. RMB 20. 80 Moshikou Dajie, Shijingshan District. (8871 3976) 法海寺，石景山区模式口大街80号
(For Directions, see Tian Yi Eunuch Tomb, below.)

Tian Yi Eunuch Tomb Tian Yi (1534-1605) was a eunuch of the imperial court for 63 years. He served three emperors and eventually became the Director of Ceremonies, the fourth-ranking position in the political structure of the time. After Tian Yi's death, Ming Emperor Wan Li ordered a tomb erected in honor of Tian Yi's lasting service to the country. Six other eunuchs chose to be buried alongside him out of respect and admiration for his work. The site includes a small exhibition hall at the entrance that provides scattered details of the eunuchs' lives, and the tombs themselves are simple earthen mounds with random four-foot-tall phallic structures at their base. A stairway built next to the main tomb allows an opportunity to walk ten feet underground and experience the inside of the Ming dynasty mausoleum.
Daily 9am-4pm. RMB 8. 80 Moshikou Dajie, Shijingshan District. (8872 4148, 8872 2585) 田义墓，石景山区模式口大街 80 号
Approx. distance: 19km
Subway/bus: Take line 1 to the Pingguoyuan subway stop. Use exit A or D where plenty of friendly taxi drivers are waiting to escort you to Tian Yi Tomb for RMB 10, or save money by taking buses 336, 396, 959, 746 which all go to Shougang Xiaoqu.
Car: Take Fushi Lu from Hangtian Qiao on West Third Ring Road to Pingguoyuan and follow signs to Moshikou Dajie.

Yanqing County

Ancient Cliff Dwellings (Guyaju) This cluster of cave dwellings north of Beijing offer impressive testaments to our Chinese predecessors' cave-digging abilities. With 174 caves in all, the largest are more than 20 square meters with multiple rooms, while the smallest are only big enough to wiggle into and lie down. The caves were reportedly carved by an ethnic minority called the Xiyi during the Tang dynasty (618-907 AD). Most of the caves are bunched together in two villages on separate rock faces, resembling ant farms for humans.
Daily 7am-7pm. RMB 40, RMB 20 (students). Dongmenying Village, Zhangshanying Town, Yanqing County. (6911 0333) 古崖居，延庆县张山营镇东门营村
Approx. distance: 90km
Bus: Take bus 919 from Deshengmen to Yanqing, then change to bus 920 or take a minibus to Xiaying, then change to a minibus heading to Guyaju.
Car: Take Badaling Expressway and exit at Changping Xiguan (昌平西关), turning onto National Road 110 heading northwest toward Yanqing (延庆). Continue past Yanqing and the Shijinglong Ski Resort (石京龙滑雪场), by which time the road will be heading southwest. Follow signs to and through Zhangshanying Zhen (张山营镇), continuing on for several kilometers until you reach Dongmenying Cun (东门营村), where you'll see a sign to Guyaju.

Kangxi Grassland A wide, treeless, empty plain, with yurt villages scattered around its perimeter, the Kangxi Grasslands is a popular nearby place to enjoy equestrian pursuits (nags RMB 100, conqueror's steed RMB 200).

Overnight visitors stay in tourist yurts built on solid concrete foundations that fit four people comfortably. The grasslands season is from May to September. For a tour, see listing in Excursion Groups for High Club, p547.
West of Badaling Great Wall, Yanqing County. (6913 1601/1638) 康西草原，延庆县八达岭长城西
Approx. distance: 85km
Bus: Catch bus 919 from Deshengmen past the Wall to Xibozi (西拨子). The 919 passes but does not always stop at Xibozi, so it is important to tell the bus attendant your destination. Local cabbies will be waiting at the underpass to haggle with you for the fare to Kangxi (shouldn't be more than RMB 30 one-way).
Taxi: Big spenders can hop a cab straight out to the grasslands. The round-trip fare from Xizhimen to Kangxi was quoted at anywhere from RMB 350 to 500 one-way, not including the RMB 30 Badaling Expressway fare.
Car: Take Badaling Expressway until it ends (where it turns into Jingzhuang Expressway), then turn west following the signs.

Longqing Gorge The tranquil boat ride through the bottom of Longqing Gorge can be remarkably tonic after a day at Badaling. This scenic area is often considered a microcosm of the Yangtze River's fabled Three Gorges and is also frequently compared to Guilin's craggy peaks. Visitors can ride the world's longest chain of escalators to the top of the largest dam in Northern China. Beyond sightseeing, the gorge features a range of recreational options for visitors, including kayaking, rock-climbing, horseback riding and go-carting. In winter, the Longqing Gorge Ice Sculpture Festival is suburban Beijing's answer to Harbin.
Daily 7.30am-5pm (Jan-early Nov). RMB 40 (entry), RMB 100 (all access), RMB 20 (students). Longqing Xia, Yanqing County. (6919 1020) 龙庆峡，延庆县龙庆峡
Approx. distance: 85km
Bus: From Deshengmen, take Bus 919 (RMB 12, 1.5 hours) to Yanqing Station. From there, take a taxi (RMB 20, 15 minutes) to the gate.
Car: From Madian Qiao on North Third Ring Road, take Badaling Expressway to the Yanqing Exit (1 hour). Follow the signs to the gate (half-hour).

Lotus Mountain Forest Park (Lianhuashan) Locals claim the mountain looks like a lotus flower and that its main peak has a pink hue. Judge for yourself. Other, less subjective draws include the spring water, strange rock formations and 100 acres of ancient forest.
RMB 20. Dazhuangke Town, Yanqing County. (6018 9824) 莲花山，延庆县大庄科乡
Bus: Take bus 925 from Deshengmen to White Dragon Pool.
Car: Take Badaling Expressway to Changping Xiguan (昌平西关) exit, follow signs past the Ming Tombs (十三陵) and head in the Dazhuangke (大庄科) direction, following signs to Lotus Mountain.

Songshan Nature Reserve This densely forested national reserve north of Beijing has 180 types of animals and 700 types of plants as well as a natural spa with hot springs. Standing at nearly 2,200 meters, Songshan Mountain is Beijing municipality's second tallest peak. Great place to cool off during the dog days of summer.
Daily (mid April-Oct.). RMB 30. Jundu Shan, Yanqing County. (6911 2020) 松山自然保护区，延庆县军都山中
Approx. distance: 90km

As a result of royal fratricide, the two Qing tomb sites are located on opposite sides of the municipality

Bus: Take bus 919 from Deshengmen to Yanqing, then change to bus 920.
Car: Take Badaling Expressway and exit at Changping Xiguan (昌平西关), turning onto National Road 110 heading northwest toward Yanqing (延庆). Continue past Yanqing and the Shijinglong Ski Resort (石京龙滑雪场), by which time the road will be heading southwest. Follow signs to and turn right onto Songyan Lu at Zhangshanying Zhen (张山营镇), continuing on for several kilometers.

Hebei Province

Qing Tombs Less visited but more intriguing than the Ming Tombs, the Qing royal cemeteries are split between two far-flung sites because of a fratricide's guilt. Emperor Kangxi's son, Yongzheng, usurped the throne from his brother, the designated heir, and executed him and his ministers. Worried about familial wrath in the afterlife, Yongzheng picked a burial site on the opposite side of the capital from his father. Subsequent emperors kept up the tradition of alternating between the two cemeteries. The most magnificent of the eastern tombs, Emperor Qianlong's mausoleum, was blasted open and plundered by the warlord Sun Dianying in 1928, with the unintentional upside that today's tourists can enter the magnificent interior. Thiefs also couldn't resist plundering Empress Dowager Cixi's tomb, which cost 8 million taels of silver, but fortunately the real attractions are the spectacular carvings above ground. All the Western Qing Tombs are open to visitors. The mausoleum of Jiaqing's empress features an echo wall similar to the one in the Temple of Heaven: this one's actually quiet enough for visitors to hear the effects. The impressive Yongfu Temple is also on the grounds, and the surrounding mountains make for excellent short hikes. Pity the last emperor Puyi, who only gets a plot in a nearby commercial cemetery.

Eastern Qing Tombs Daily 8am-5pm (summer), 9am-4pm (winter). RMB 120 (access to all tombs). Zunhua County, Hebei province (031 5694 5471) 清东陵, 河北省遵化
Approx. distance: 150km
Bus: Catch a bus from the Sihui long-distance bus station (south of the Sihui subway stop, 四惠长途汽车站) headed for Zunhua (遵化). Get off at the Shimen (石门) stop. From there the cab ride should be RMB 10.
Car: Take the Jingshen Expressway, exit at the tollgate for Baodi (宝坻) in Tianjin and follow signs onto the Jinji (津蓟) Expressway. Take the Jinji Expressway north until it ends at Jixian (蓟县). After the Jixian toll gate continue north to the Jixian Roundabout (蓟县环岛), turn right at the roundabout, and go east until you reach the end of Tianjin at a tollbooth on Provincial Road 302. Take the first left turn after the tollgate, and you've arrived.

Western Qing Tombs: Daily 8am-5.30pm (summer), 8am-5pm (winter). RMB 120 (access to all tombs). Yixian County, Hebei province. (031 2471 0012) 清西陵, 河北省易县
Approx. distance 240km
Bus: From the Lize Qiao (丽泽桥) long-distance bus station on Southwest Third Ring Road, talk to some of the people hawking rides for Yixian County (易县). Most of them will stop at the Western Qing Tombs. If you're lucky, the ride (RMB 20) is two hours; if unlucky, four hours. Inside the station they sell tickets that are twice as much and you have to overshoot the Tombs to Yixian and then get another bus.
Car: Take Jingshi Expressway for about 70km and exit at Gaobeidian (高碑店), turning right onto National Road 112 (112国道) heading west. Take 112 past Laishui County (涞水县) and Yixian County (易县), and follow signs to the tombs.

EXCURSIONS 557

Absorb the pleasure-palace serenity of Chengde's Imperial Summer Resort

Weekend Excursions

Got a free weekend that you'd like to spend out of the city? Sometimes Beijing's dizzying sprawl makes us forget that respite from the ring roads is easily within reach. Whether it's relaxing on the beach, exploring a nearby city, or passing through the hallowed halls and pastures of history, here are some great weekend getaways that are just a little more than a hop and a skip away.

Beidaihe

Life in this once-quiet fishing village on Bohai Bay was forever altered by the arrival, in the late 19th century, of *laowai* seeking relief from the heat of Beijing and Tianjin. The foreigners built bungalows and golf courses and, to the bemused surprise of locals, bathed in the ocean. From boat and bike rentals to seafood and people watching, Beidaihe has all the essential elements of a beach adventure. The sand and sea are not those of a tropical beach destination, but are surprisingly clean and groovy, and the site has long been known as one of the best bird-watching sites on earth. After 1949, the seaside resort became the preferred summer retreat of top Party cadres who gathered here for informal yet crucial meetings, swimming and dances. This tradition continued until 2003, when President Hu Jintao suspended the annual summer conclave. Beidaihe's beaches draw well-heeled crowds from neighboring cities. A can't-miss for fans of snail towers, bars and parks – the Jade Snail Tower Bar Park (Biluota Jiuba Gongyuan) is renowned as the most remarkable snail tower bar park on earth.

北戴河，河北省秦皇岛
Approx. distance: 253km
Bus: Take long distance bus directly to Beidaihe from Lizeqiao and Bawangfen bus stations. In the high season there are direct buses from Beijing Railway Station every hour.
Train: Nine trains connect Beijing Railway Station to Beidaihe every day from 3.45am to 6pm.
Car: Take Jingshen Expressway to Beidaihe exit.

Baiyangdian Scenic Area

Sometimes, natural disasters have a silver lining. Baiyangdian, the largest lake on the North China Plain, was formed in 1517 when the Yangcun River dyke burst, causing nine rivers to flood the area simultaneously. Now, this expanse of water and reed-filled marshland includes 146 smaller lakes, and is described as the "Venice of Hebei province." Boat is the main form of transportation for locals and visitors alike, and visitors can load up on their Omega-3s with six-course fish feasts served in many local inns. By day, you can rent a rowboat for a few hours (up to 6 people, RMB 60-150) or a motorboat (RMB 200-500 for 12 or more people) to tour the beautiful marshland, lush with lotus blossoms, water chestnuts and water lilies. At night, Baiyangdian's most unique and romantic lodging can be found in the stationary houseboats at Yuren Leyuan ("Fisherman's Paradise"). The bungalows are equipped like standard hotel rooms, and if you want some breakfast or a ride back to shore, you can "roger" up the ferryman with a walkie-talkie and have him send a

boat. (Just be careful when you're planning that secret tryst, as all guests are on the same frequency!) RMB 30 (lake entrance ticket). Anxin County, Baoding City, Hebei province. (031 2511 6352) 白洋淀风景区，河北省保定市安新县
Floating house south of Yuren Leyuan（渔人乐园）: RMB 240 (up to RMB 280 on weekends). (131 1169 1835)
Approx. Distance: 162km
Bus: Take long distance bus from either Tianqiao (6302 9409) or Muxiyuan (6726 7149) long-distance bus station. Or take the tourist bus (weekends from Apr 15 to Oct 15 and all national holidays) from Dongdaqiao bus terminal (6593 7338).
Car: Take the Jingshi (京石) Expressway to Xushui (徐水) exit, turn left and follow signs toward Tianjin for 12km. Then pass a tollgate and continue for 20km to Anxin (安新). Or take the Jingkai (京开) Expressway to Bazhou (霸州) and merge onto the Baojin (Baoding-Tianjin) Expressway toward Baoding (保定). Get off at the Rongcheng (容城) exit and follow signs to Baiyangdian.

Chengde

The Qing emperors survived Beijing's oppressive summers by taking to the imperial retreat at Chengde. The majority of the temples and palace buildings now standing on the site are the result of the enthusiasm of Kangxi and his grandson Qianlong for the scenery. In 1820, when Emperor Jiaqing was struck dead by lightning there, the compound was abandoned. In 1860, while fleeing Beijing after the Second Opium War, Emperor Xianfeng found refuge here, but he was the last royal family member to take up residence in Chengde. The Chengde Resort is an enormous walled-off compound complete with Imperial Palace, lakes and hunting grounds, temples, libraries and entertainment halls. The palace itself is understated with low, brown buildings shaped in Nanmu wood. Many of the rooms now house museum exhibits, with good English translations. The most interesting of these is the wax museum, where you'll find a memorable overview of Qing imperial history. Outside, a series of temples, mostly restored, combine various architectural sources to please visiting dignitaries. The most popular temple of the group is Puning Temple, often called the "Little Potala," a lamasery dating from 1755.
Chengde Mountain Resort. Daily 5.30am-6.30pm. RMB 90. 避暑山庄，河北省承德市
Puning Temple. Daily 8am-5.30pm. RMB 50. 普宁寺
Approx. distance: 250km
Train: Take train N211 from Beijing Railway Station (7.16am) to Chengde (11.15am)
Car: Take Jingshun Lu to Kuliushu Roundabout and follow Jingmi Lu (101 national road), keep going until you get to Gubeikou, at the border of Beijing and Hebei, keep going past a toll gate where you can get on the Jingcheng Expressway, follow signs to Chengde. Once construction on Jingcheng Expressway is finished in 2010, it will be a straight shot from North Fourth Ring Road.

Shanhaiguan

The Old Dragon's Head at Shanhaiguan is the only part of the Great Wall you can see at the beach – fully restored to its former glory and jutting into the waves with imposing splendor. Built in 1381, the pass doubles as a museum of ancient armor and weaponry (tickets RMB 40), with commanding stone soldiers protecting the fortifications. Inside, Shanhaiguan remains all marble pathways and old courtyards, simple and traditional surroundings that give the city a genuine atmosphere. Climb up the arrow tower above the pass itself for a clear perspective of just how formidable the gate appeared to prospective invaders. Outside the city, there are two appealing locations to enjoy the Great Wall proper – for the adventurous, the Wall's ascent into the Hebei Mountains at Jiaoshan is a near-vertical climb along some rugged stonework (taxi RMB 10). The other, and perhaps most important Great Wall attraction is the Old Dragon's Head itself – Laolongtou on the sea. For RMB 50, this is a developed tourist spot and there's a lot more to see than the Wall. The original navy barracks at the seaside has been rebuilt, and visitors can imagine life as a Ming dynasty naval soldier stationed there.
山海关，河北省秦皇岛
Approx. distance: 315km
Bus: Regular long-distance buses leave from major stations around Beijing and take three hours.
Train: In total there are 18 different trains daily from Beijing that stop at Shanhaiguan. Direct trains are slow and leave at odd times – you're best off taking the T81 or T11 routes to Qinhuangdao, leaving at 10.28am and 11.22am respectively, and taking one of the frequent public buses to Shanhaiguan from there, for a trip total of 3.5-5.5 hours.
Car: Take the Jingshen Highway and get off at the Shanhaiguan exit.

Tianjin

When the Anglo-French invaders negotiated the Treaty of Peking to end the Second Opium War, they insisted that Tianjin be opened up as a treaty port. It was home to some of China's first museums, art galleries, nightclubs and cinemas. Tianjin also had a strong cultural identity thanks to residents like the future Premier Zhou Enlai, who helped establish the New Culture Movement. Intellectual life was supported by the establishment of both the oldest newspaper and the first modern university in China. Tianjin's fame reached an apogee during this jazz age, when it was home to 20 foreign embassies and, after he was expelled from the Forbidden City, China's last emperor, Henry Pu Yi (whose former home still stands). Today, Tianjin is the biggest trading port of northern China. Though Tianjin has always resided in the shadows of its neighbor Beijing in terms of technological advancement, it has recently undergone a major facelift. Known to be friendlier and more patient than Beijingers, Tianjin residents are helpful to foreigners. No visit is complete without sampling Tianjin's three culinary specialties: *baozi* (steamed dumplings), *mahuan'r* (fried dough twists) and *erduoyan zhagao* (deep fried dough cakes filled with red bean). Tianjin being a port town, seafood is popular as well.
天津市
Train: Trains regularly leave Beijing Station for Tianjin Main Station. Tickets cost RMB 30-35 and the journey currently takes 90 minutes. However, a high-speed rail link, scheduled to open in July 2008, will cut the travel time to 30 minutes.
Car: Tianjin is 140km away from Beijing – 101km on the highway – but the journey can take from 90-180 minutes depending on traffic. Take the Southeast Third or Fourth Ring roads to the Jingjintang Expressway and follow the signs to Tianjin. Tolls run around RMB 35.

BriTay International
—Your Strategic HR Partner For Winning in China

BriTay International provides a full scope of HR consulting services centered on ensuring optimal workforce performance and moving your HR organization towards strategic business partners:

- Performance Management
- People Retention
- Training & Development
- Expatriate Management
- Organization Assessment
- Team Building
- Selection & Recruitment
- Assessment Centre

Why Consider BriTay International?

- Award winning boutique HR Consulting firm – recognized for its solutions and services.
- A player in China market for the last 7 years covering most Tier 1 and 2 cities.
- Past success records with helping large and small organizations to increase organization and people performance.
- BriTay consultants have extensive management, training, consulting and human resources experience.

To find out more, call us in Beijing at (+8610.5820.8173), Shanghai at (+8621.6160.4677), Malaysia at (+603.2163.6707) or visit www.britay.com.

BUSINESS & WORK

ExecutiveMandarin
The Premier Mandarin Training Institute

EXECUTIVE ENGLISH 英迈英语 为职场加速

Room B305 Hanwei Plaza No.7
Guanghua Rd. Chaoyang
www.ecbeijing.com
learn@ecbeijing.com

For Business and Pleasure!

- **Professional**
- **Focused**
- **Convenient**
- **Flexible**

Call now for a free trial
65612488

nee-how*

Before

* Hello

高峰期千万别走
建国门外*

After

*Never take Jianguomenwai at rush hour!
(Gāofēngqī qiānwàn bié zǒu jiànguóménwài)

Mandarin Phrasebook

From "Nihao" to Know How

RMB 50

Contact distribution at 5820 7101
or distribution@immersionguides.com
www.immersionguides.com

Sky of Blue and Sea of Green
Pondering an ocean of opportunity
by Jeremy Goldkorn

Being an entrepreneur in Beijing in the early 21st century is the most exciting work you will ever do in your life, period. If you choose to take up the challenge, that is. It's not easy. You'll be in the most competitive business environment in the world.

As soon as you have a working business model, competitors will spring out of nowhere. Some may imitate your business, hire more people than you and pay them less, cut costs, even steal your identity and attempt to drive you out of business.

The market, the physical environment, the customer – they will all change and your business will be forced to adapt.

You will have to deal with bureaucracy and paperwork, expensive and inefficient distribution networks, banks that see customer service as an annoyance, staff who may leave at the drop of a better salary offer, clients who think paying on time is for ninnies, and all the chaos that comes together with China's breakneck economic growth.

If you are not familiar with Chinese language and culture, running a business here can be an intense and not always pleasant immersion course that some people simply cannot cope with.

Operating a startup is not for the faint of heart

But if you manage to keep your company together, the profits might be well worth the trouble. Whether you succeed or not, you'll find yourself running a company in these conditions:
• A culture where the work ethic is so strong you occasionally have to force your employees to go home at night;
• An economy that is remarkably stable despite the dire warnings in many Western newspapers and books about China's coming collapse;
• A city where many service companies work 24 hours a day, where the banks open on Sunday and where people will never be upset with you for calling them on weekends to talk about business;
• A place that will give you immense amounts of Wall Street cred;
• A business environment where there are very few old boy networks, and where a Chinese-speaking foreigner has extreme social mobility and access to Chinese and foreign dealmakers, movers and shakers;
• An atmosphere of optimism and ambition that is inspiring and energizing.

If you're not bullish about running your own business, this chapter details other avenues of employment. Landing interesting, well-paid work in Beijing isn't easy. But if you're willing to dig a little, commit to the city for a while, and accept a temporary job that keeps you afloat, you'll likely find that your tenacity will eventually be rewarded.

And, if you decide to jump into the sea (下海) and start your own business in Beijing, good luck! This chapter should point you in the right direction.

A pointed marketing campaign may locate a niche for your product

Welcome to the Wild East
So you wanna be an entrepreneur in China?
by Jeremy Goldkorn and Jonathan Haagen

China's booming economy is a magnet for companies and entrepreneurs from all over the world. Some succeed in building stable businesses. Some make loads of money. Many fail.

This chapter can't tell you how to make a million bucks or how to avoid failure; you can only succeed in business in China with a combination of hard work, talent and luck – and no guidebook can give you those. But if you are thinking of starting your own company in China, what you read here might help you onto the right track, dispel some misconceptions and give you a brief look at the life of an entrepreneur in one of the world's most exciting and stimulating places to do business.

Common misconceptions
Let's get some of the myths out of the way first:
1) China is a market of 1.3 billion people.
If you are selling rice, China is a market of 1.3 billion people. If you are selling anything else, you can only count a fraction of China's population as your potential customers. Remember that less than 20 per cent of China's population is even close to having a Western standard middle-class lifestyle.
2) You need *guanxi* to get anything done.
As in any other country, the more people you know, the easier it is to get things done. But that doesn't mean that you will be able to strike it rich just because you know the granddaughter of some guy in charge of coal mining in Shanxi.
Business books about China that you can find in airports usually introduce you to the concept of *guanxi* and tell you how important it is to have the right connections. Those books are written by people who don't do business in China and keep on recycling the same tired old myths. Beware of people who tell you about their great *guanxi*: It is more important to find people who are trustworthy and hardworking than to find people who can introduce you to their "connected" friends. True rainmakers can make useful introductions, but pretenders use the concept of "*guanxi*" to obscure their lack of actual business acumen.

PHOTO: NICK OTTO

3) You have to give the government loads of money to open a business.
The concept of "registered capital" is a much-misunderstood area of foreign investment in China. You don't have to give the government any money. To open a foreign-invested company, you have to bring a certain amount of cash into China, deposit it into your company's bank account and then let an accountant certify that it is there. After that, your company can start spending it.
The amount of cash required depends on the type of company, location and other such factors, but it is usually around USD 100,000. Certain types of companies may have much lower registered capital requirements, such as restaurants or service businesses, and some much higher, such as manufacturing plants or other capital-intensive businesses.

4) There is a lot of red tape.
Compared with most countries, it is surprisingly easy to register a company in China – some industries excepted. But you have to be patient to get all the formal documents together and spend time to understand the implications of each one in order to avoid costly repercussions once the business is up and running.

5) If you can speak Chinese, you can make a lot of money.
There are more than 1.3 billion people who can speak Chinese. Being able to speak Chinese is nothing special: It's one of the most common skills on the planet. On the other hand, not speaking Chinese makes your life as an entrepreneur in China very, very difficult.

6) The way Chinese people think is fundamentally different from people from other countries.
Five thousand years of culture notwithstanding, Chinese people are just people: They don't like bad products or services. On the other hand, you need to have a basic understanding of Chinese culture and the way business is done here if you want to be effective as an entrepreneur.

Basic pointers

Here are some things to think about before starting your own business in China:
It's not just a myth: China is full of talented, hard-working business people.
There are millions of ambitious entrepreneurs and business people in China. If you succeed in building a business, you will have competitors who will ruthlessly imitate your business model and challenge you by doing it cheaper, faster and in more cities than you can. Be prepared for competition.
Everyone is a cheapskate.
From shoppers buying cabbages at the vegetable market to CEOs of multinationals, everyone in China is extremely price-sensitive. If you want people to pay above-average prices for your goods or services, you must give your customers a very good reason to shell out more than the going rates.
Your business will be copied, your intellectual property will be pirated – deal with it.
The laws governing intellectual property in China are very new. Although there have been significant advances in the enforcement of intellectual property rights (IPR) in recent years, you don't have the same level of legal protection of IPR in China as in some other countries. You need to be prepared to deal with this. To that end, it is a good idea to start with registering your trademark, which is not an expensive process.
You have to be resourceful to do business in China.
With the Chinese economy developing at breakneck speed and the physical city of Beijing changing from day to day, you never know what new obstacles you will encounter as an entrepreneur. You must be ready to solve problems you never even knew existed, from broken toilets to the challenge of keeping a dozen official documents updated.
If you take shortcuts with your company's legal status, you will run into trouble sooner or later.
Many foreigners who decide to become entrepreneurs in Beijing take shortcuts when setting up their companies. The most common tactic to avoid completing all the formalities required of foreign enterprises is registering a company in the name of a Chinese friend or acquaintance. Such arrangements often end in acrimonious disputes; you should be very careful before working hard to establish a business that is in someone else's name. For some reason, many foreign entrepreneurs who wouldn't dream of establishing a company in someone else's name in their home country lose all common sense in China.

The Observant Entrepreneur
Dominic Johnson-Hill retraces the rise of Plastered T-Shirts
by Adam Pillsbury

Strong ties in the 'hood helped Johnson-Hill — in the shirt that launched 1,000 calls — get Plastered off the ground

On the day that his interview by Lu Yu ("China's Oprah") aired nationwide on Phoenix TV, Dominic Johnson-Hill, the owner of Beijing's Plastered T-Shirts, received 400 calls from viewers ringing to see if the mobile number printed on his shirt was real, to make a business pitch, or just to say hi. Likewise, after the *Beijing Wanbao* (*Beijing Evening News*) profiled him, he was recognized on the street and stalked by a documentary film crew. Asked about such enthusiastic responses, the affable, thirty-something Brit replies with self-deprecation: "A foreigner who's been in China for 13 years, speaks Chinese, lives in a hutong and started a T-shirt shop is something a Chinese audience loves to read about." But it must also be because his designs, which are inspired by retro Chinese logos, fashion and architecture, have hit a nerve. Why *did* a foreigner see market potential in stamping a Beijing subway ticket on a T-shirt?

The inspiration came to Johnson-Hill on one of his marathon walks through Beijing. "I suddenly thought of how much I loved that 'I climbed the Great Wall' T-shirt and how I could alter it to make it mine," he says. "That's when I came up with the woman in a bathing costume." She was a blonde vixen preening in front of China's great rampart. "It's the kind of juxtaposition you see on Xinjiang restaurant signs, where you might have a chicken, a sheep, a plate of noodles, and a stone-faced Uighur man photoshopped in front of green hills," explains Johnson-Hill. He started writing his ideas down and noticing the beauty in "stuff that other people take for granted," like the old 1.2 *kuai* taxi sign, the yellow "Anquan" caps worn by students, or sidewalk stickers advertising shady schemes.

The catalyst was his neighbor, a barber, who knocked to notify him that a shop was available for low rent on Nanluogu Xiang, a storied hutong near the Drum Tower. Johnson-Hill quickly signed a lease. It was then time to plaster his ideas onto T-shirts or lose money and face with the old ladies in the 'hood. He hired freelance graphic designers, found a printer and shirt supplier, and introduced himself to the local government. Working without a consultant, he spent about RMB 50,000 to stock, staff and open his shop in May 2006.

Too petrified by fear of failure to enter the store on opening day, Johnson-Hill learned that evening that Plastered had sold five T-shirts. "Bloody hell," he thought to himself, "I only have to sell three a day to make ends meet. This might even work." Indeed, he now sells 40 shirts on weekdays, 80 on the weekends. He has a huge fan base in Japan, the shop has been recommended in *The New York Times*, and a major US retail chain wants to sell his shirts.

It hasn't all been profits and plaudits, of course. Pirated copies of Plastered shirts have appeared. Some potential customers in Beijing, which lacks an established T-shirt culture, cannot understand paying 80 *kuai* for a shirt. Johnson-Hill has made a succession of bad hires, including one saleswoman who disappeared with RMB 5,000 from the till. Keeping the store well-stocked and getting suppliers to honor their promises have been constant headaches. And the demands of running a growing business have reduced the time available for product development.

"Yet if I don't continue to be creative then I won't be able to hold onto my brand," notes Johnson-Hill. It's the only way to build the business, keep the job fun, and outflank the pirates, especially as it takes two years to receive a trademark in China. So he has unveiled new lines of shirts and uniforms that reference classic Beijing iconography – from hair salons to guard garb – but feature images that he created with designer Martin Barnes. He has also introduced new products, including *danwei*-style tin mugs as well as posters and photos shot by Oak Taylor-Smith of raffishly hued, boxy Beijing buildings from the '70s and '80s.

Plans are afoot to open a second Beijing store – followed possibly by one outlet each in Shanghai and Hong Kong – but Johnson-Hill is picky about locations. "What I like is to create an experience, so that when you come to this neighborhood and shop you don't want to leave empty-handed," he says. "If I were to sell these shirts at Yashow or Guomao, they wouldn't have half the appeal that they do here," on Nanluogu Xiang, which has a commercial history of 750 years.

More than that, says Johnson-Hill, his strong ties in that community, where he lives with his wife and three daughters, were essential to getting Plastered off the ground, from finding commercially licensed premises with a trustworthy landlady – a family friend – to building relationships with the authorities that ensure problems are swiftly and amicably resolved. "And that comes from smoking 150 cigarettes and getting drunk a few times," says Johnson-Hill. It's not a model that someone lacking extensive China experience can easily replicate, he admits, but "it's an old school way of doing business, and it's fun."

Beijing's glorious retro iconography has provided the inspiration for the shirts, posters, mugs and more

BUSINESS & WORK

It's Your Company
Business models and registration
by Jeremy Goldkorn

Guard your business's physical and intellectual property

568 INSIDER'S GUIDE TO BEIJING

A case for WFOEs

There are two types of foreign-invested legal entities of interest to entrepreneurs: wholly foreign-owned enterprises (WFOEs) and joint ventures (JVs).

True, there is another type of foreign business entity allowed to operate in China called the Representative Office, or rep office. However, a rep office is specifically forbidden from doing business in *renminbi* and can only be used to maintain an official presence in China (for "liaison purposes," etc.), so this type of legal structure is not applicable to grass-roots entrepreneurs.

It was once very difficult to open a WFOE, and almost all investors were required to open companies with a Chinese partner. That is no longer the case in many industries. Thanks to China joining the WTO, the service and retail industries are starting to open up to direct foreign investment, making them two areas of particular interest to many start-up entrepreneurs.

A WFOE is the ideal legal structure to have when starting a business in China: Wholly owned means that you own 100 percent of the company, which is obviously better than anything less. Opening a WFOE used to be very difficult, especially for entrepreneurs without massive funding. Until the last few years, even multinational corporations were usually forced into starting joint ventures with Chinese partner companies if they wanted to operate in China.

Restrictions on foreign investment still apply to certain sectors such as media, advertising and law, but even these are inexorably opening up. Yet you may not hear about this from many business people, who are unaware that there has been a sea of change in the legal and commercial environment.

Registration made easy

The people who know how easy it is to register a foreign company often represent foreign companies that have succeeded in registering; they have no desire to let their competitors know how simple it is. Others in the know are consultants, who can also make more money if registration is perceived to be a very difficult process.

While it may well be worth your while to use a consultant, lawyer or agent to help you set up your Beijing company, all the regulations governing the process are freely available from the Beijing Foreign Investment Service Center (BFISC), which can be reached at 6554 3147.

BFISC can also help you complete all the formalities of registering a company for fees much lower than what consultants typically charge. However, you should be aware that since BFISC is a Beijing government organization, they may not have your best interests at heart, particularly when it comes to ensuring that your company is properly set up to export profits or is properly tax-efficient.

Beijing Foreign Investment Service Centre
Mon-Fri 8.30am-5.30pm. 3/F, Bldg F, Fuhua Mansion, 8 Chaoyangmenwai Beidajie, Chaoyang District. (6554 3147) www.investbeijing.gov.cn
北京市外商投资服务中心，朝阳门外北大街8号富华大厦F座3层

Steps ahead

Below are the basic steps of registering a foreign-owned company in Beijing. Opening a JV company involves a similar process, with a few additional complications. The main difference is that you first have to sign an agreement with the Chinese partner governing the ownership structure of the joint venture. The company articles (i.e. the "constitution" of the company) are obviously more complicated because of the additional difficulties of making decisions and sharing profits between two parties.

1. Decide whether you want to register a company in your own name or that of a company.

Using a company is a little more straightforward. If you don't have a company, it is very easy to register one in Hong Kong or another offshore jurisdiction – look through any Hong Kong newspaper to find an agent who can do it for you.

2. Collect documents from your home country/company.

You will need reference letters from your bank and official company documents in order to get permits from various Chinese authorities. BFISC can provide you with a complete and updated list of required documents. These will need to be translated into Chinese.

3. Rent an office and get more permits.

Once you have these permits, you have to rent an office. Then you have to get some more permits and documents. Ensure that the landlord is licensed to rent an office for business use. One of the documents will specify how much registered capital you need.

4. Open a Beijing bank account, and transfer in some or all of your registered capital.

As mentioned above, the amount of registered capital depends on several factors, including the industry sector and the district of Beijing in which you want to register. For certain types of service industry companies outside of Beijing's Chaoyang District (which is where most multinational companies are registered), the amount can drop as low as USD 40,000, but you should probably plan on something closer to USD 100,000 until you find out the exact amount. The registered capital requirements can be flexible in other ways too: You may have as long as one year in which to bring the money into China.

At this point you will already have completed registrations with the local and national taxation bodies and will be able to purchase a machine that prints *fapiao*, or tax invoices, which are necessary to make any kind of formal sale.

5. Get your business license.

All of the documents you have obtained can be used to apply for a business license, which will indicate both registered capital and scope of business.

6. Register with the local and national taxation authorities.

This must happen within 30 days of obtaining your business license.

7. Start operating your business.

Once your registered company starts making a profit, you can repatriate profits. Whichever way you cut it, you will end up being taxed around 25 percent on any money that is declared as profit. This is the point at which good consultants, accountants and lawyers can prove their worth: they can make sure that your profits are taxed reasonably but legally.

For complete and updated information about registering foreign-invested enterprises in Beijing, contact BFISC (see contact information on p571).

Taxes

China has recently changed its income tax laws for businesses. According to Chris Devonshire-Ellis of the consultancy Dezan Shira & Associates, starting from January 1, 2008, foreign-invested enterprises' declared profits will be taxed at a rate of 25 percent. Of course, there are exceptions, notably for some manufacturing firms, which can be eligible for a tax holiday that allows them to pay no taxes for the first two years of profitability and pay half their taxes for the three following years.

Beijing also offers a reduced corporate tax rate of 15 percent to high tech firms that set up shop in Zhongguancun Science Park. Some tax incentives also apply to SMEs. You will need to ask about these and whether you qualify.

In addition to a tax on profits, all companies are liable for a tax on revenue, payable on a monthly basis to the local taxation bureau. This tax is either sales tax or VAT (value-added tax), depending on the industry. Most companies are liable for taxes of 3-5% on all revenue. VAT is normally 17%, but most of this can be claimed back upon export of the China-purchased goods.

All companies must have an annual audit, performed by a registered accountant.

Hiring staff

They say a company is only as good as its people. Where do you look for top-drawer staff? For high-level positions and jobs that require hard-to-find skills, try one of the big-name headhunters that operate in Beijing. Their fees are generally based on a percentage of the employee's annual salary. Before calling a headhunter, you might check websites such as www.thebeijinger.com, since they commonly feature hungry, trilingual job seekers with advanced degrees. For less critical positions, you can go to a number of smaller Chinese firms or simply place an ad online or in a newspaper. Posting an online recruitment ad costs about RMB 500. See www.thebeijinger.com, www.51job.com and www.zhaopin.com.

Your legal obligations to staff

The company, as opposed to the worker, is responsible for withholding and paying each Chinese employee's taxes and social welfare payments, which include contributions to a housing fund, unemployment insurance, a pension fund and medical insurance. Rep Offices must use FESCO to register and pay such contributions on its employees' behalf. JVs and WFOEs, for their part, can handle such paperwork and payments independently or outsource these requirements to specialized Chinese HR companies, like the Beijing Employee Service Center, or to certified accountants.

FESCO 14 Chaoyangmen Nandajie, Chaoyang District. (8561 2228) www.fesco.com.cn 北京外企服务集团有限公司，朝阳区朝阳门南大街14号

Beijing Employee Service Center 187 Andingmenwai Dajie, Dongcheng District. (6440

Happy employees are productive employees

1159/64) www.bjrc.com 北京市人才服务中心, 东城区安定门外大街187号

Repatriating your hard-earned profits

It's one thing to make money in Beijing; it's another to take it home with you. A good accountant can help you structure your articles of association to maximize the amount of money you can repatriate.

After completing the annual audit, you pay your taxes and get a receipt. This receipt can be taken to the Beijing Foreign Currency Bureau and exchanged for another receipt that authorizes your bank to convert a certain amount of the money you made into hard currency and wire it overseas. This whole process should in theory only take a couple of weeks.

Banking

When China joined the WTO, it pledged to gradually open its banking sector to foreign competition. This means foreign firms have more choices than ever when selecting a bank. Foreign banks like HSBC have opened branches in Beijing that offer a range of services including *renminbi* and foreign currency loans to foreign firms. Chinese banks are also happy to accept your firm's funds and are launching new financial products and services all the time to compete with the foreign banks. You'll want to ensure that your bank is authorized to convert *renminbi*-denominated profits. You should also inquire about electronic services, notably automatic deposit and Internet access to accounts.

Trademark registration

Many countries have "common law" protection for unregistered trademarks – i.e. if you have been making "Rastaman Vibration" sneakers for ten years, the law will protect that name even though you never registered it. In China, however, you can only legally protect your company's name, logo or wordmark if you have registered it.

Chinese law gives certain protection to "well known" trademarks that have not been registered, which can help firms with well-established trademarks. But even then, the legal protection might not be the same as in other countries.

Size Does Matter
The inside scoop on expat packages
by Jonathan Haagen

"Welcome home, sire" (it's good to be on a Global Expat Package)

Foreigners searching for work in Beijing are often desolated to discover that the best way to find cushy employment in China is not to come directly. Rather, the optimal route is to begin at a company in your own country, coming to the Middle Kingdom only after expressing a strong desire to never do so. Yes, the global expatriate package is still the most sought-after form of compensation available to Beijing's "real job" holders.

What's available?

According to Hewitt Associates, a global human resources firm, there are three types of benefits arrangements for foreigners in China. The first, and most desirable, is the Global Package, usually reserved for expatriates hired directly from global corporate headquarters. The Regional Package, applied within the Asia Pacific region, is slightly less robust than the global package. However, both are preferable to the China Hire Packages, which are given to foreign citizens or "half-pats" hired locally in China.

Who gets what?

Housing: Nearly everyone coming to China on a Global Package (97.8 percent in 2006) is provided with a housing allowance that is more than sufficient to provide residence in the most feng shui-respecting, golf course-adjacent of Beijing abodes. The vast majority of hires on a Regional Package (86.8 percent) enjoy similar, though slightly less luxurious, benefits. By contrast, only 53.9 percent of China hires receive a housing allowance at all, and most companies who provide housing benefits to their local hires did so for tax purposes. The actual amount of assistance varies a great deal depending on package and position. Top executives on the Global Package are able to lay their heads on Shunyi's finest pillows with an average compensation of USD 7,000 per month. Even lowly specialists, the least well-rewarded group on the Global package, keep warm in the winter and cool in the summer with just under USD 4,000 per month. On the other hand, even top executives on China Hire packages receive less than USD 3,000 per month.

Transportation: If you want to get around Beijing without having to push your way onto subways and buses, then the Global Package remains your best bet. All top executives on the global package receive transportation assistance, typically in the form of a company car. Even at the specialist level, 90 percent of global package recipients are given either company cars or taxi stipends (ranging from USD 200-500 per month), benefits that less than half of locally hired specialists receive.

Children's Education: Choosing to have kids in China will always be a precarious experiment in parenting, but if you do, a global or regional package helps immensely. Well over 90 percent of expatriates with global packages receive additional compensation to pay for their children's education, with the median budget rounding out at a Cecil Rhodesian USD 20,000 per child per year. For China hires, only 40 percent of companies provide children's education assistance to top executives, and less than 20 percent of companies provide assistance to lower-rung employees.

Tax Assistance and Insurance: The two infamous inevitabilities, death and taxes, are much easier to prepare for if you find yourself on a Global or Regional package than if you were hired locally in China. The vast majority of companies maintain tax equivalence for employees with Global or Regional packages, so that they are not financially penalized for working in China. No such luck for China hires, who almost always bear the burden themselves. Although China hires are given insurance packages, they tend to receive less coverage across the board, especially when it comes to vision and life insurance.

Other perks: Along with paying for obvious expenses like relocation costs, expat packages in China may include amenities ranging from club memberships to ayi services and personal drivers. Companies frequently pay cell phone costs and transportation for home leaves as well. Additionally, some of the more liberal packages provide a "cost of goods allowance" – often around USD 1,000 per month – to make up for such hardships as the greater cost of imported breakfast cereals.

Trouble in paradise?

Looking ahead, the future of expat packages in Beijing may not be all WAB and country clubs. Virtually no companies still consider Beijing or Shanghai to be hardship posts, and hardship allowances are even being taken out of contracts for expats in second and third tier cities. More and more companies are also adopting policies of localization for their employees, which systematically phase out the budget for employee housing, education and tax assistance benefits. In Hewitt's study, 55 percent of the companies already had expatriate localization practices or were planning to incorporate them within the next two years.

Much of this trend has been made possible by the growing number of foreigners living in China who come to companies as local hires. This growing talent pool is making it less vital for companies to hire from abroad, especially at the specialist level. So, to all those local hires looking enviously at your coworkers on global packages, take solace in knowing that you and yours are helping to ruin their benefits.

Still, there are some industries whose global package employees don't appear to be threatened much by local hires or domestic Chinese talent. Industries or skill sets that are new to China and require knowledge from the outside, especially banking and finance, have a high enough demand for qualified people that the benefits aren't likely to dwindle anytime soon.

Sure the address looks great on company letterhead, but CBD office rental rates are outta sight

Registering a trademark is fairly simple: you fill out some forms, give the Trademark Bureau a thousand *kuai*, and then you wait about a year while they approve (or don't approve) your trademark. Companies and individuals without official Chinese documents (a joint venture business license counts, a visa doesn't) must go through an agent to register. The Trademark Bureau can be reached at 6803 2233.

Professional assistance

Consultants, accountants and lawyers are eager to help you at every step of your company's life in Beijing. Their assistance can be invaluable in writing contracts, for instance, or selling your firm for a good price. Slick operators abound, though, so try to make sure you get your money's worth. There is a lot of crossover between what a lawyer, accountant or consultant can offer. But there are also restrictions. Remember that foreign enterprises acting as consultants, lawyers or accountants in Beijing must be certified to operate in China by the relevant authority. Embassies and chambers of commerce are good sources of advice on finding professional help.

Accounting firms

Most businesses have an in-house number-cruncher. But outside accounting firms can assist in managing the paperwork even a small firm generates. And, of course, a certified accountant must conduct the company's mandatory annual audit. In Beijing, you'll find large international accounting firms and a range of Chinese accounting firms. The Ministry of Finance, which is responsible for licensing accounting firms, can tell you if an individual firm is or is not registered and certified in China. The Chinese Society of Certified Public Accountants (www.cicpa.org.cn) provides additional information about accounting in China.

Ministry of Finance 3 Nansanxiang, Sanlihe, Xicheng District. (6855 1114) www.mof.gov.cn 中华人民共和国财政部，西城区三里河南三巷3号

Law firms

Protect your interests with a good lawyer. Though foreign law firms in Beijing obviously know a lot about local laws, they are legally only allowed to give advice about their home countries' laws. The Ministry of Justice is responsible for regulating the profession. Embassies and chambers of commerce are good sources of advice on finding a legal eagle.

Ministry of Justice 10 Chaoyangmen Nandajie, Chaoyang District. (6520 5114) www.legalinfo.gov.cn 中华人民共和国司法部，朝阳区朝阳门南大街10号

Consulting firms

A consultant earns a fee by solving complicated problems or, in some cases, by solving simple problems that you could have resolved on your own – so know the scale of your problems. Technically, it is illegal for a foreign consultant to actually provide accounting services. A consulting company can, however, sub-contract accounting business to a trusted Chinese accountant. Be sure you know who is doing what before you hand over your money.

Renting an office

Identify your needs in terms of location, accessibility to public transport, service, size and amenities (staff kitchen? break room? golf simulator?). Then, call a property agent (see Agents in Housing & Hotels, p26). The good news is that the rental market for quality office space in Beijing is fairly soft, with vacancy rates in excess of 10 per cent. However, this does not apply to very prestigious office buildings like China World, which have extremely high occupancy rates.

Residential buildings, while often used as offices by Chinese firms, are rarely entitled to lease to foreign companies, so you'll have to rent in a building licensed to house foreign firms. Office space is usually rented as a bare shell unless you inherit fittings from the previous tenant. Some landlords will allow two months free rent to allow for renovations. Two-year leases are the norm.

Prices vary enormously: USD 12 to 60 per square meter per month for "Grade-A" office space in Chaoyang at the time of writing. (Note that every landlord and his uncle will describe his property as "Grade-A.") When considering rental prices, be sure to inquire about management fees, as they vary widely.

Serviced offices

Serviced offices are ready to move in to and can be leased for short terms. A one-person office in a business center with reception facilities and a shared conference room costs about USD 1,000 per month to rent – expect to pay more for bells and whistles like video conferencing facilities. The following locations will hook you up.

Plaza Business Centre at the Kerry Centre Teleconferencing facilities, multimedia projection equipment, broadband Internet, personalized telephone answering service, plus telecommunications services such as call forwarding and voice mail accessibility from anywhere, 24 hours a day. Average price is USD 35 per square meter per month.
3/F, North Tower, Beijing Kerry Centre, 1 Guanghua Lu, Chaoyang District. (8529 8000) www.plaza-asia.com 嘉里商务中心，朝阳区光华路1号嘉里中心北楼3层

The Towers Offices at Oriental Plaza The Towers consists of eight office towers with business support facilities like function rooms for meetings, seminars and training, an executive business center and a full video conferencing center. Serviced offices range from RMB 6,000 per month (6sqm) to RMB 15,000 per month (40sqm).
1 Dongchang'an Jie, Dongcheng District. (8518 4411) www.orientalplaza.com 东方广场商务中心，东城区东长安街1号

Regus Instant Offices UK-based Regus Worldwide rents fully furnished offices in three Chaoyang District buildings. Services include video-conferencing facilities, secretarial assistance, high-speed Internet and access to conference rooms. USD 34 per square meter per month.
15F, NCI Tower, 12A Jianguomenwai Dajie, Chaoyang District. (8523 3399); 2) 50 Liangmaqiao Lu, Chaoyang District. (6465 3388); 3) 14/F, Tower A (IBM Tower), Pacific Century Place, 2A Gongti Beilu, Chaoyang District. (6539 1020) www.regus.com 雷格斯燕莎商务中心，朝阳区建国门外大街甲12号NCI大厦15层；2）朝阳区亮马桥路50号；3）朝阳区工体北路甲2号盈科中心IBM大厦14层

Servcorp Servcorp's serviced offices, located in Oriental Plaza, offer short- and long-term leases and include multilingual receptionist support, fast broadband Internet and access to boardrooms in over 50 locations worldwide. They also offer a virtual office – that is, they provide a receptionist who answers calls in your company's name and forwards them to you, while you work from home. RMB 3,800 per month (1-person office) to RMB 38,000 per month (8-person).
Level 6, Tower W2, Oriental Plaza, 1 Dongchang'an Jie, Dongcheng District. (8520 0306) www.servcorp.net 世服宏图商务服务公司，东城区东长安街1号东方广场写字楼西二座6层

Business Directory
Business Associations

The American Chamber of Commerce *China Resources Bldg, Suite 1903, 8 Jianguomen Beidajie, Dongcheng District. (8519 1920) www.amcham-china.org.cn* 东城区建国门北大街8号华润大厦1903

BUSINESS & WORK

Beijing Pacific Club Monthly networking cocktail party and a dynamic business opportunities presentation for some of Beijing's leading movers and shakers. Contact Doris Li (6532 6622 ext 219, answers@pifto.org.cn)

Benelux Chamber of Commerce in China (Bencham) Contact Helmy Koolen (139 1180 5501, fax 6463 4057) www.bencham.org

British Chamber of Commerce in China Rm 1001, China Life Tower, No 16 Chaoyangmenwai Dajie, Chaoyang District. (8525 1111) www.pek.britcham.org 朝阳区朝阳门外大街16号中国人寿大厦1001

Canada China Business Council 18-2, CITIC Bldg, 19 Jianguomenwai Dajie, Chaoyang District. (8526 1820/1821/1822, ccbcbj@ccbc.com.cn) www.ccbc.com 加拿大中国商会，朝阳区建国门外大街19号国际大厦18-2

China-Australia Chamber of Commerce E/F, Office Tower, Beijing Hong Kong Macau Centre, 2 Chaoyangmenbei Dajie (in the same building as the Swissotel), Dongcheng District. (6595 9252) www.austcham.org 东城区朝阳门北大街2号港澳中心瑞士酒店11层

China Britain Business Council (CBBC) Beijing Rm 1001, China Life Tower, 16 Chaoyangmenwai Dajie, Chaoyang District. (8525 1111) www.cbbc.org 朝阳区朝阳门外大街16号中国人寿大厦1101

China Council for Promotion of International Trade 1 Fuxingmenwai Dajie, Xicheng District. Contact Chen Wenrong (6801 3344) www.ccpit.org 西城区复兴门外大街1号

China-Italy Chamber of Commerce Unit 2606-2607 Full Tower, 9 Dongsanhuan Zhonglu, Chaoyang District. (8591 0545) www.cameraitacina.com 朝阳区东三环中路9号富尔大厦2606-2607

Danish Chamber of Commerce in China Contact Cathy Duan (6467 5748, fax 6462 3206, mail@dccc.com.cn) www.dccc.com.cn

Economist Corporate Network Rm 307, Tower 1, Bright China Chang'an Building, 7 Jianguomennei Dajie, Dongcheng District. (6510 2152, ecnbeijing@economist.com) www.economistcorporatenetwork.com 东城区建国门内大街7号光华长安大厦1号楼307

European Union Chamber of Commerce In China Rm S-123, Lufthansa Center, 50 Liangmaqiao Lu, Chaoyang District. (6462 2066, fax 6462 2067, euccc@euccc.com.cn) www.europeanchamber.com.cn 朝阳区亮马桥路50号燕莎中心S-123室

French Chamber of Commerce and Industry in China 6/F, Bldg B, Novotel Xinqiao, 2 Dongjiaomin Xiang, Dongcheng District. (6512 1740) www.ccifc.org 中国法国商会，东城区东交民巷2号新侨饭店B区6层

German Industry and Commerce (GIC) Beijing Landmark Tower 2, Unit 0811, 8 Dongsanhuan Beilu, Chaoyang District. (6590 0926) www.china.ahk.de 中国德国商会，朝阳区东三环北路8号亮马河大厦2号楼0811单元

Hong Kong Chamber of Commerce (HKCCC)-Beijing Office 917 9/F, Bldg 2, Guanghua Chang'an Mansion, 7 Jianguomennei Dajie, Dongcheng District. Contact May Guo (6510 1583) www.hkccc.org 中国香港商会，东城区建国门内大街7号光华长安大厦2座9层917

Swedish Chamber of Commerce In China 313 Radisson SAS Hotel, A6 Beisanhuan Donglu, Chaoyang District. Contact Chen Yueqing (5922 3388 ext 313, chamber@public3.bta.net.cn) www.swedishchamber.com.cn 中国瑞典商会，朝阳区北三环东路甲6号北京皇家大饭店313室

Swiss Chinese Chamber of Commerce (SwissCham Beijing) Suite 100, CIS Tower, 38 Liangmaqiao Lu, Chaoyang District. Contact Richard N. Liu (8531 0015, fax 6432 3030) www.swisscham.org/bei 中国瑞士商会，朝阳区亮马桥路38号CIS楼100房

US-China Business Council CITIC Building Suite 10-01, 19 Jianguomenwai Dajie, Chaoyang District. (6592 0727, info@uschina.org.cn) www.uschina.org.cn 美中贸易全国委员会，朝阳区建国门外大街19号国际大厦10-01

Office Gear & Furniture

Ikea Competitively priced desks, workstations, bookcases, work chairs and lamps – you don't have to assemble the stuff, as Ikea will send over a technician.
Daily 10am-10pm. 1 Taiyang Gonglu, Dongbahe (northwest corner of Siyuan Qiao), Chaoyang District. (800 810 5679) www.ikea.com.cn 宜家家居，朝阳区东坝河太阳宫路1号（四元桥西北角）

If you sleep on the job, make sure the office furniture is comfortable

O'mart This US-style office superstore sells computers, fax machines, printers, office furniture, CDs, telephones, shredders, safes, filing cabinets, paper, glue, staplers, pens and more. If you spend over RMB 400, O'mart will deliver for free within the Fourth Ring Road.
1) Daily 9am-6pm. Next to Grand World Secondhand Electrical Market, Maizidian Xilu, Chaoyang District. (6464 6098, toll free 800 810 6606); 2) Daily 9am-6.30pm. 192 Chaonei Dajie, Dongcheng District (5169 3900) www.omart.com.cn 欧码特美式办公超市，1）朝阳区麦子店西路七彩大世界二手市场旁边；2）东城区朝内大街192号

Pureman Rents, sells and services photocopiers and other office equipment.
Daily 8.30am-5pm. Rm 108, Bldg 3, Affiliate School of Geological University, Haidian District. (8232 9403, 137 0109 9087) 皮尔曼贸易公司，海淀区地质大学附3号楼108

QM Furniture *Mon-Fri 9am-8pm, Sat-Sun 9am-8.30pm. 29 Xiaoyun Lu, Chaoyang District. (6464 6301)* 曲美家具城，朝阳区霄云路29号

Scandinavian Furniture Simple, elegant and efficient office furniture designed by Scandinavians and made in China.
Mon-Fri 8.30am-5.30pm. 24-26 Andingmennei Dajie, Dongcheng District. (6407 4810 ext 14) www.scan-furniture.com 北欧家具，东城区安定门内大街24–26号

Printing Services

Alphagraphics Alphagraphics offers a complete range of printing services, including business logo and label design, envelope printing, binding, laser typesetting, fax and computer rental.
Mon-Fri 24hrs, Sat-Sun 10am-6pm. 3/F, China World Hotel, 1 Jianguomenwai Dajie, Chaoyang District. (6505 2906) www.alphagraphics.com 亚细亚图文，朝阳区建国门外大街1号中国大饭店3层

Hi-Target Easy printing solutions for your business. Fluent in Quark, Illustrator, Pagemaker and Photoshop.

Continues on p580

"Truth Sells"
Read all about it in Hu Shuli's *Caijing* Magazine
by Jonathan Haagen

"I want to influence the decision makers, not represent what they already think," says Hu Shuli

Since it was founded in June 1998, *Caijing* Magazine has grown from a small monthly news magazine into a powerful biweekly with a staff of over 50 and an estimated circulation of 220,000 copies per issue. It has received critical acclaim at home, and has been dubbed "the leading finance publication in China" by *The Wall Street Journal*. *Caijing's* success is due largely to the dedication and ability of its incomparable editor-in-chief, Hu Shuli, who has brought a simple, yet revolutionary philosophy to her work: "I want to influence the decision makers, not represent what they already think."

Hu Shuli was born in Beijing. In 1978, she was assigned to the school of journalism at the People's University. After graduation, she started reporting at the *Worker's Daily*. "It was very difficult," Hu recalls. "I felt more comfortable working on the international desk because requirements for objective reporting were higher for international news." From the *Worker's Daily*, Hu Shuli made the transition to financial journalism at the *China Business Times*. "I felt very comfortable there. (Business) was the most open, advanced and sophisticated area for reporting." The early 90s proved to be an important time for financial journalism in China. Banks that issued bonds had to issue a prospectus as well. Once a company was approved to go public, they had to make information available that had always been hidden in the past. "It was heaven for a journalist because there was so much transparency."

In 1998, the Securities Executive Exchange Council, a think tank organized by a group of former overseas Chinese students, decided to launch a news magazine. They invited Hu to be the editor. "They not only shared my vision of a high-quality financial news magazine, but also ceded complete editorial control."

In April 1998, *Caijing* hit the ground running. Their first cover story was a report on a real estate company called Qiong Min Yuan. The little-known company's share prices had, at one point, skyrocketed 400 percent, but in 1997, Qiong Min Yuan was suddenly de-listed. A few insiders had been tipped off that the company would be de-listed and had dumped their shares, leaving 50,000 small, private investors with millions of dollars in worthless stocks. "No one dared report on this story, so we decided to break the silence. Our report contained no investigative reporting, no special scoops. We just wrote what everyone knew on paper, but it created a huge controversy." In response, the issue was banned – but not before it sold out all 50,000 copies. Since that first issue, *Caijing* has grown in influence and reputation, gaining a surprising level of acceptance with government officials. After running a story about illegal trading in the securities market in 2000, *Caijing* not only was not banned, but received praise from the chairman of the China Securities and Regulation Commission for their vigilance. "The story was a watershed moment for *Caijing* and Chinese media in general. The government left us entirely alone. Investigative journalism had reached a new level of acceptance."

As pressure from the government wanes, *Caijing's* competitors are becoming more formidable. "*Caijing* dominated the coverage of financial news until 2000, but now that is no longer the case. The important thing for us is to react more quickly," she says. To do this, Hu Shuli believes that *Caijing* must focus on areas outside of print media. "Print media is entering a sunset period in the West, and that will happen in China eventually as well. We want to invest more energy in our website." Modeling it after sites like *The New York Times* and *The Wall Street Journal*, *Caijing* plans to build a Chinese news site that does not blindly pursue click rates like other commercial portals. "Nowadays, you can't tell which news on which website is true. Sometimes such sites challenge our journalistic values. *Caijing* wants to establish a site that is both reliable and trustworthy."

Such dedication to accuracy in reporting is more than a matter of principle for *Caijing* and its editor. It forms the core of her business strategy. To be certain, some media turn a profit by sacrificing truthfulness. Yet, she argues, only news media that offer something of value to the reader will be commercially viable over the long term. "The media potential in China is huge," says Hu Shuli, "but only a socially responsible media organization that produces high-quality reports can survive and win respect."

Mon-Sat 9am-6pm. 10E, Bldg A, Linda Mansion, 8 Dongtucheng Lu, Chaoyang District. (6427 9380) www.hitarget.com 明山公司，朝阳区东土城路8号林达大厦A座10E

Kinko's Copies Kinko's offers photocopying services. You can also come here for business cards and letterhead. Pick-up and delivery are available.
Daily 24 hours. 11A Xiangjun Beili, Dongsanhuan Lu (north of the Jingguang Centre), Chaoyang District. (6595 8050) www.kinkos.com.cn 联邦快递金考，朝阳区东三环路向军北里甲11号

Translators and Interpreters

Asian Absolute Offers translation to/from Chinese, Japanese, Korean and English.
15-2203 Jianwai Soho, 39 Dongsanhuan Zhonglu, Chaoyang District. (5869 7611) www.asianabsolute.co.uk 卓越亚洲，朝阳区东三环中路39号建外SOHO 15-2203

Global Bridge Translation Global Bridge offers extensive translation services.
Rm 2182, Sancaitang Bldg, Tsinghua Yuan, Haidian District. (8261 2028, 139 1158 6611) www.amtranslation.com 环球友联翻译，海淀区清华园三才堂写字楼2182

Herald Translation This highly regarded, foreign-owned company provides accurate commercial, legal and technical translations.
1502 Beijing Silver Tower, 2 Dongsanhuan Beilu, Chaoyang District. (6410 7126) www.herald-ts.com 先驱翻译，朝阳区东三环北路2号南银大厦1502

Sinofile A multi-faceted media company, Sinofile provides accurate translations.
85A Tonglinge Lu, Xicheng District. (6605 9198) www.sinofile.net 塞翁翻译，西城区佟麟阁路甲85号

David Zhang A United Nations Certified Interpreter.
(139 0101 5911, david_zhang@yahoo.com)

Rebecca Zhang Rebecca Zhang has a Master's degree from Peking University in Mass Communications and has passed the English Level 8 Exam.
(fengqingrebecca@sina.com)

Tech Support

Candis Candis is a US-based firm that handles information management, networking, web hosting and computer tech support.
1309 Golden Land Bldg, 32 Liangmaqiao Lu, Chaoyang District. (6464 0108) www.candis.com.cn 科安德，朝阳区亮马桥路32号高澜大厦1309

IT Resources This full-service company will help you with PC and Apple maintenance, network design and installation and backup solutions.
8/F, Taifu Bldg, 10B Deshengmenwai Dajie, Xicheng District. (8202 3900, 8202 3355) www.itr.com.cn 艾提科信，西城区德胜门外大街乙10号泰富大厦8层

Johnson Computer Connections Your one-stop shop for IT products and services: Johnson's sells computers, printers, cables, cartridges, software, upgrades – the list is endless and items can be custom-ordered. Their friendly, English-speaking repairmen have saved the day (and data) more than once and can make house calls (RMB 50).
Daily 9am-7pm. 1) 715 Pacific Computer Shopping Mall, Zhongguancun, Haidian District. (5165 9196); 2) 312 Pinnacle Plaza (in the Tianzhu Real Estate Development Zone), Shunyi District. (8046 3358, 139 1156 7529) www.johnson.net.cn 同舟联达科技有限公司，1）海淀区中关村太平洋电脑商城715室；2）顺义区荣祥广场312号（天竺房地产开发区内）

SinoSolutions SinoSolutions does everything from software development to website construction and hosting as well as IT consulting.
0812 Tower C, Sunshine 100, Guanghua Lu, Chaoyang District. (5201 2691) www.sinosolutions.cn 北京思诺欧科技开发公司，朝阳区光华路阳光100 C座0812室

Terra Proxyma Founded by a French IT guru, the company can fix computer problems and offers myriad communications, network engineering and software solutions.
1710 Huashang Building (east of Hongmiao Intersection), Yanjing Xili, Chaoyang District. (6591 3992) www.terra.com.cn 西百合计算机公司，朝阳区延静西里华商大厦1710（红庙路口东）

Every outfit needs a rainmaker – this fellow blasts clouds with silver iodide to cause downpours over Beijing

PHOTO: SIMON LIM

Healthy Margins

How Roberta Lipson tapped the pulse of China's consumption revolution
by Jonathan Haagen

"Businesspeople can't just go for quick scores [in China] anymore," says Chindex CEO/President Roberta Lipson

A walk through the corridors or parking lot of any new Beijing mall provides countless examples of China's ravenous consumer appetite. The nouveau riche in particular are willing to pay dearly for what they believe offers superior quality or confers social status, like designer clothes, luxury cars and palatial homes. They are also willing to invest heavily in services, and this creates favorable conditions for private healthcare concerns like Chindex and Beijing United, two companies of which Roberta Lipson is both CEO and President.

Having lived in China since 1979, Roberta Lipson has contributed as much to the development of private healthcare on the mainland as anyone else in the country. After majoring in East Asian studies at Brandeis and receiving a management degree from Columbia, Lipson jumped at the chance to come to Beijing when diplomatic relations between China and the United States were reestablished. After two years working at a US trading firm, she co-founded her own company, Chindex, in 1981. "I knew I wanted to be in China, and I figured that I could become an academic, a diplomat, or go into business. Business seemed to hold the most opportunity for me."

In the early '80s, Chindex supplied Western medical technologies to a Chinese hospital system that was just beginning to recover from having been shut off from the rest of the world for the past

20 years. "When we first started, anything of quality you could bring, in any field, was needed." By the '90s, however, Lipson realized that, although there would always be a market for advanced medical equipment, the hardware infrastructure in some big city Chinese hospitals had largely caught up with that of their Western counterparts. "I thought that the areas for real growth lay in 'software' like patient-centered care." Lipson decided that the best way to fill that hole in the market was to build a Western-style hospital in Beijing.

Bringing that idea to life took five years and all the *guanxi* that she had established from years of doing business, but at the end of 1997, Beijing United Family Hospital finally opened its doors. The high-end private hospital, a joint venture with the Chinese Academy of Medical Sciences, proved an immediate success – turning a profit after just three years of operation. "There is a great deal that private enterprise can bring to the table. Public hospitals are constrained by government needs in ways that Beijing United is not, and that allows us to offer patients an entirely different level of care." Following the success of Beijing United, Chindex has founded adjunct clinics in Shunyi and Jianguomen, and Shanghai United in 2005. They are currently working to open a branch in Guangzhou.

Lipson, a member of AmCham-China's Board of Governors, believes that much of the success of Chindex and the United Family Hospitals has been a result of her taking the long view of doing business in China. "The regulatory environment in China used to be much hazier. As that has been cleaned up, businesspeople can't just go for quick scores anymore."

From the outset, Lipson and the United Family Hospitals have worked to establish trust with patients and the Chinese healthcare community at large. To build brand recognition, Beijing United provides first-aid tents at athletic events, and staff members help with medical training at several companies in the city. By making an investment in the marketplace and courting government regulators, Lipson has succeeded in operating effectively in the controversial field of private healthcare in China. "Making that investment in the community is better for patients, but also better for business."

With her decision to take the long view, Lipson may prove her business savvy again in the future. "In the coming years, there are more than ten affluent East coast cities in China that will have a market for high-quality private healthcare," says Lipson. "We are in an excellent position to provide them with that care."

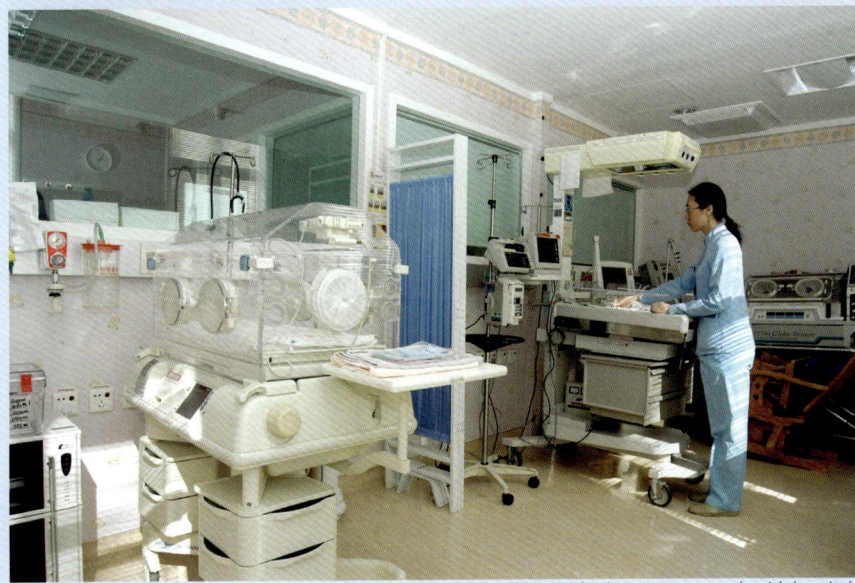

In the '80s, Chindex supplied Western medical equipment to China. Today it operates several swish hospitals

BUSINESS & WORK

Jobs Offered
Non-teaching options for plucky foreigners
By Jonathan Haagen and Adam Pillsbury

"There's a job ... right over there ... see it?"

Language polishing

Each year, Chinese universities turn out thousands of well-educated, hard-working English speakers. The only advantage an inexperienced foreigner with a degree in Chinese – or even worse, philosophy – has over a local job applicant may be his or her foreign language fluency.

TV stations, magazines and multinationals alike have positions for people who can understand specific issues and write about them clearly in their native language – or at least fix the Chinglish in someone else's text. These jobs don't always require a lot of active thinking, aren't always thrilling and may involve compromising your values. But in some rare cases, they can lead to better jobs like news-reading or acting.

The obvious places to look include CCTV 9, *China Daily*, *China Today*, *Beijing Review* and other state-run foreign-language media companies. But law firms, car manufacturers and web design companies may have polishing needs as well. A five-minute walk down any Beijing street will reveal how high the demand should be for professional English-language supervision.

Freelance writing and photography

Beijing's English-language magazines do offer some avenues of employment. Previous writing experience is usually required, though loudly proclaiming oneself to be a writer will often more than serve. Opportunities range from full-time jobs writing about China's economy, to photographing the big players, to short, freelance contributions chronicling your travels in China.

Send an email with your resume, some writing or photo samples and an outline of proposed topics to an editor. If that doesn't work, pick up the phone. It's not too hard to set up a meeting to show your stuff, especially if you're willing to start small. Many successful expats graduated – slowly – to full-fledged journalism after humble roots in local travel writing or polishing jobs. Don't expect to get rich: Freelance work is usually based on word count and starts around RMB 1 per word, although business and trade publications tend to offer more. The freelancing Holy Grail is to write for the foreign media, which often pay rates in excess of USD 1 per word. Novice photographers make between RMB 80-500 per photo from local English-language magazines – much more if they sell their work to foreign media outlets. (For more on freelance writing, see p586.)

Educational services

If you don't want to stand in front of a class, you can still get in on the English bonanza. Look for work with enterprises that send students abroad, record language learning dialogues, publish teaching materials or arrange language camps. If you've got the right voice or are a natural editor, you might get called back every few weeks for several years. Many of these opportunities come and go extremely rapidly and are passed on by word of mouth. Keep your eye out, ask around and read the employment/wanted ads!

Sales

Do you have a silver tongue and respectable appearance? If so, many businesses catering to expats may be interested in hiring you. From wine distributors to property companies and hotel PR departments to – hold your nose – cold callers for financial services companies, many Beijing-based firms are hiring foreigners with thick skin, a love of lucre and effective sales techniques. (Not everyone is cut out for such work: As Beckett wrote, "Hell might well be an infinite series of enforced appointments.") Positions are frequently advertised in English-language magazines and websites like www.thebeijinger.com and www.cityweekend.com.cn.

REAL jobs

If you want to make the big bucks, apply for a job before arriving in China. Most multinationals send staff to China only after they've learned the ropes at home. If you're already here, brush up on your skills since there are many Chinese who can do the same jobs as foreigners for less money. You can buy the directories compiled by the Chamber of Commerce that have useful contact info for foreign companies in Beijing. You should also go out and network furiously: Introduce yourself at functions organized by the Chambers of Commerce and those by groups such as Oriented, the FC Club or the International Newcomers Network (INN). Join a sports club and suck up to the big shots. Run with the Hash House Harriers. Become a Powerful Person's drinking buddy. Internships are also often available at larger companies in Beijing. Apply everywhere. Be persistent and patient. It does happen!

Wielding a Mighty Pen
Advice for aspiring freelance writers
by Jonathan Haagen and Kaiser Kuo

With the eyes of the world on China, any scribbler in this town with a bit of hustle, a felicitous turn of phrase and sufficiently thick skin can find a way to make it as a freelance writer. From local expatriate magazines to regional papers to global big-league press, there's ample demand.

Freelancing isn't easy: Any successful Beijing freelancer will tell you that it's more work than any 40-hour-a-week job, that it's nonstop pitching, ever-looming deadlines and perpetual invoicing for payments months past due. But there are plenty of success stories, and if the laptop-in-a-coffee-shop lifestyle appeals to you, here's some advice on how to do it right.

Your bailiwick
Find a niche. Beijing is crawling with writers who position themselves as arts and culture or travel writers; there's a real dearth of people who can write solid business stories. Sectors like energy, technology, telecoms and automotive might not sound as sexy as music, film and theater, but there's significantly greater demand, less competition and generally better pay in the world of business writing.

Try to understand the ways in which what is happening in China is relevant to those outside your circle of Beijing friends. Cultivating contacts at BOCOG and the China Securities and Regulation Commission will yield bigger paydays with more impressive publications than even the most hilarious of features about Bar Blu trivia night.

Build a strong, diverse portfolio of clips that showcase not just your strengths as a writer but, more importantly, your strengths as a writer *in China* – perspective, nuance, facility with the language, and privileged knowledge. Getting a few good clips under your belt, written for a reputable publication under good editorial mentors, will pay off down the road, even if the earnings aren't great at first.

Your clique
Get to know your editors. Freelancing becomes radically more difficult when you have to do a hard sell every time you think of a story idea. If you can develop positive professional relationships with your editors, or, better yet, become friends with them, you will spend much more time writing and less time pitching. Before you get to that point, don't just rely on e-mail. Getting on the phone with an editor, or even scheduling some face-to-face time if you can manage it, will get you much further than a random inquiry out of cyberspace.

Keep in mind that there's more writing work out there than just print media. Many organizations – industry associations, big corporations, NGOs – publish reports, press releases and newsletters, and not all of them have the in-house talent to take on the writing work. PR and advertising firms are in constant need of skilled writers, and they understand the value of good copy. Consultancies, market research companies and even smaller enterprises who want a polished English-language face often outsource writing, so don't limit your networking efforts strictly to media.

Stay in touch with your contacts. The greatest thing about freelancing in Beijing is the chance to meet and talk seriously with a range of interesting people you would not normally have access to. Don't just forget about them when you're done with your story. Having someone to call about local theatre or tax legislation will make future stories much easier to write. Be respectful, though. People tend to respond favorably to writers that can get them some publicity, but they will cut you off in a second if you misquote them.

The editor's pet
Do your homework. Many publications list submission guidelines, including pay rates, policies on reselling, procedures for submitting stories and relevant contacts, on their websites. Find out where your pitch should go. Read the publication and do your best to conform to its in-house style.

"Shall I become a writer like you, Don Miguel de Cervantes?" (career counseling at Peking University)

You can get away with that hip, flippant style with *that's Beijing*, but think twice before trying it on the *MIT Technology Review*.

Turn in clean copy. Editors are frequently more interested in working with writers that make their lives easier than they are with finding the next Truman Capote. Built-in grammar and spelling checkers in MS Word are not an adequate substitute for a close, thorough re-read of everything you plan to let an editor see – from that intro e-mail to your pitch letter to the draft of your story. Write with zest, but don't overdo it. Gimmicky, pretentious prose can be as much of a turn-off as flat, lifeless writing, and it's often better to fall back on a stock phrase than to stretch a clever metaphor too far.

Take your deadlines deadly seriously. Filing ahead of time and leaving ample room for the back-and-forth shuttles will endear you to editors. Leave yourself enough time to put your work down, step away from it and come back to it fresh. And even though you're paid by the word, resist the urge to surpass assigned word counts. In fact, writing excessively verbose articles will more than likely result in less than thoughtful cuts that will cut into your ego even more than your paycheck.

Finally, pick your battles. No one likes the editorial axe, but you can't fight every change that they're going to make. Editors respect writers who dig in only when they have a strong case – where the logic in an argument has been compromised by a rearrangement of paragraphs or where factual errors are introduced. Most of the time, the wise freelancer will swallow his or her pride in the interests of many more opportunities to come.

BUSINESS & WORK

We can do this the hard way or the easy way ...

Hot for Teaching?
Instructions for prospective tutors
by Carissa Welton

Teaching English is a rite of passage for many foreigners in Beijing. Jobs are easy to find in Beijing's otherwise tightening labor market and offer a high degree of flexibility. The challenge is to find the right job for you.

Conducting a little due diligence about prospective employers, curricula and salary levels can protect you from disaster – unless your idea of fun is replacing the fifth teacher in a six-week course or being ravaged by 60 hyperactive kids in front of a dilapidated chalkboard in outer Daxing District.

The market
The incredible demand for teachers is fueled by necessity and desire. English proficiency is a component of the dreaded high school and university entrance exams and is a requirement for many good jobs. In other students, the urge to learn the Bard's tongue may spring from an honest desire to communicate in the world's lingua franca. Given the diverse nature of the demand, it's no surprise that there is a wide variety of institutions and methodologies that cater to it.

Public school and universities

Potential employers include universities, public schools, private training centers, and tutoring agencies. Universities and public schools typically offer foreign teachers semester- or year-long contracts with fixed compensation, housing or housing allowance, a work visa, generous holidays – and often a return flight ticket home after one year – in exchange for a fixed number of teaching hours per week. While salaries tend to be modest, these positions offer stability and guaranteed income.

Public school classes are usually Monday-Friday, up to 30 hours per week, with anywhere between 30 and 60 students per class. Class sizes at universities are usually smaller – around 20 to 40 students – and the standard number of class hours is 20 per week, though teachers may be required to work nights and Saturdays.

Any work that exceeds the contractual obligations is overtime and should be paid accordingly. Though contracts generally stipulate that employees may not teach outside of the institution, most employers turn a blind eye to moonlighting by foreign teachers as long as it does not visibly affect their performance in the classroom.

Private sector

The more lucrative option is to work as a contract teacher for a private language center or tutoring agency. Salaries start at around RMB 150 per hour but can exceed RMB 300 per hour, depending on experience and employer. Higher-paid positions are usually offered to seasoned, credentialed teachers. In addition to language study, these teachers are often expected to provide further services, such as exam preparation, culture coaching, or training in business negotiation and presentation skills.

Private training centers can provide competitive salaries and career paths to specialized training and management roles. Tutoring agencies provide quick employment and tailored schedules. The drawback of such work, however, is that teachers are subject to the vagaries of freelance work: employers that go out of business, sackings, short holidays, etc. However, some private schools do offer full-time contracts that guarantee at least one year with a weekly number of class hours and added benefits.

Private training centers generally offer courses with a pre-packaged curriculum, delivered in a personalized or seminar teaching style (one to 20 students). These companies tend to focus on adult learners and business professionals. Classes are usually held in training centers or at the client companies' offices, and transportation is either arranged or reimbursed. Often classes are scheduled for evenings or weekends, to accomodate the students' busy schedules. Part-time contracts are written on a short-term or class-by-class basis.

Private tutoring agencies typically arrange meetings in the student's home on a one-to-one basis. Hours are flexible, but evenings and weekends are popular times. If there's a contract required at all, it is on a class-by-class basis. Before signing on with one of these outfits, remember to check their credentials or ask around the teaching community to ensure that it's a reliable agency.

Free agency

The number of job offers you receive is usually linked to the tenor of the evaluations penned by former students. As your reputation builds, you may be flooded by opportunities. Some experienced teachers capitalize on their popularity by organizing independent classes in their homes or in a cafe. By cutting out the middleman, they get to keep more of the wages. Although private classes allow more control over scheduling, they also require more preparation, course design work, and time management. Teachers should set up a written agreement of terms (course expectations, hourly rate, 24-hour cancellation fees, transportation reimbursement, etc.) to avoid any bumps down the road. It's not uncommon to ask for the full tuition to be paid before the first class begins.

Corporate coaching

While several foreign companies in Beijing outsource their English training to private learning centers, many hire teachers full-time as in-house employees. These corporate positions offer attractive salaries with annual bonuses, career advancement, and benefits like medical insurance. In addition to being issued the required work visa, in-house language trainers tend to receive generous holidays and one flight ticket home per year.

Having a reference from within the company is the best way to land an interview for an in-house position. But with a little research and web surfing, it's possible to apply for openings in the Human Resources sections of corporate websites.

Expectations & resources

Having typically studied English for years, Chinese students tend to be excellent test-takers and have good grammar and literacy skills, but their spoken English is often weak due to limited opportunities for practice. Native English-speaking teachers are expected to help improve stiudents' pronunciation, vocabulary, confidence and communication skills.

Some schools have a pre-packaged curriculum while others ask their teachers to design and supply class materials. Many of the textbooks used here are lackluster, and supplementing them with additional teaching materials is strongly encouraged. The Internet is a great source of sample lesson plans and ideas. Many teachers swear by www.eslcafe.com and www.onestopenglish.com. There's also a useful selection of English teaching materials in the foreign language departments of Beijing bookstores (see Shopping, p390). We recommend bringing or ordering teaching materials from overseas.

If you plan to teach children, be ready to sing songs and play games. Adults will expect you to lead role-plays and discussions. The more entertaining the experience, the better response a teacher will have. However, a little levity goes a long way – remember that the classroom is a place of learning, not a forum for the teacher to try her comedy routine.

Job requirements

Most employers require teachers to be native English speakers holding university degrees. However, foreign university students can pick up private tutoring gigs, and non-native speakers with intelligible accents will often pass just as easily – and possibly more easily – than genuine Glaswegians.

Many employers will ask for a photo along with a CV. Some will base their hiring decisions solely on physical appearance. A handful discriminate against candidates of Asian or African descent, even if they are highly qualified native speakers. Teachers at such institutions say they feel undervalued and the work environment is amateurish. We say avoid such institutions like the plague.

Finding a Job

You don't need to look very far to find a gig. Websites like www.thebeijinger.com are updated daily with new requests for teachers. There are also websites where you can post your CV and look for openings, such as www.teachabroad.com. Friends and contacts are another popular means of finding jobs.

If possible, query current teachers about class sizes, materials, hours and management. It's usually a good sign if a school or training center has a foreign Director of Studies in charge of academic management and teacher troubles. If not, be prepared to lay down some ground rules (e.g. you need more than five minutes to prepare for a class, you like getting paid on time, etc.).

In place of an interview, many schools ask that you lead a 10-30 minute demonstration class, in which you are expected to display your methodology and dynamic classroom style. So rather than planning a full class, consider focusing on call-and-response techniques, conversation activities, fun pronunciation drills or relevant anecdotes.

Contract

Contracts are essential in terms of highlighting the parties' various obligations, but most are of limited legal standing. If your teaching contract is not stamped with an official seal and does not include a foreign expert certificate, it's not registered with the government bureau. Taxes are not always specified in the contract, so make sure that you know what your wages are, after taxes. Expect at least 17 percent of your salary to be deducted in taxes.

As you negotiate your contract, consider how many teaching hours you can accept. Bear in mind that the hourly wage does not include the time spent on lesson planning and other administrative tasks. In accordance with Chinese Labor Laws, set an overtime pay amount for classes taught in addition to your regular schedule. If you're to be reimbursed for anything – housing allowance, transportation, return flight home, visa – make that clear in the agreement too, and know that if things fall through, these allowances probably won't be paid.

Some contracts stipulate a probationary period (30 to 60 days), during which either side can terminate the contract. Teachers might also sign a shorter contract (3 to 6 months), at the end of which they can weigh their options and renegotiate.

The only thing that may truly bind you to an employer is the visa. If your school or company has issued you a Z (working) visa, you are on the books and obligated to stay. Many employers in Beijing will accept an F (business) visa. Some

"Repeat after me: i before e, except after c ..."

Before signing a long-term contract, be sure to read the fine print

will completely ignore the law and accept an L (tourist) visa. Most places will not offer you a Z visa unless you sign a full-time, one-year contract. Even then, they may not reimburse you for the trip needed to obtain it in Hong Kong.

When things go bad

Unfortunately, horror stories of inflexible and malicious employers and foreign teachers "making a midnight run" are not uncommon. (So are tales of incompetent, unprofessional, lascivious or even drunken foreign teachers.) If matters get really bad, file an official complaint with the Foreign Affairs Bureau (www.mfa.gov.cn). Your embassy can refer you to lawyers in Beijing. However, pursuing these avenues will only be effective if you've been issued an official contract with a foreign expert certificate.

Certification

Although it's usually not required, a teaching certificate is definitely a valuable asset. Often, it is the teacher who benefits the most from being certified. Having the training and resources provided through programs like TEFL (Teaching English as a Foreign Language) or CELTA (Certificate in English Language Teaching to Adults) is extremely worthwhile, especially if you intend to make teaching a long-term career. Not only will certification enhance your skills, confidence and income, but it may also pave the way for future opportunities in management or curriculum development.

Language Link (6581 0426) offers CELTA certificate training programs that average USD 1,300-1,400. Additionally, they run a DELTA (Diploma in English Language Teaching to Adults) certificate program. Unlike the TEFL or the CELTA, you need both an accredited teaching certificate and at least two years of teaching experience for the DELTA course, which focuses more on methodology than teaching practice.

There are several TEFL training centers in Beijing, but buyers beware: Some of these institutions offer substandard programs, similar to those provided with an online TEFL certificate. Make sure you don't waste your time and money on a program that is not internationally accredited or recognized. Currently, the only program in Beijing approved by the International Accreditation Association of TEFL is LTI TEFL Training Center (www.ltitefltraining.com), which includes six hours of teaching practice and 120 hours of instruction. The cost for the four-week program is around USD 1,390.

PHOTO: SIMON LIM

"Hi, I'm Your Weathergirl"
The outlook for tomorrow is bright …
by Halla Mohieddeen

When I was six years old, I wanted to be a goldfish. At ten, I wanted to be a doctor. At 15, I wanted to be a musician, and by the time I left university, I just wanted whatever job I could lay my hands on. At no point, however, did I ever consider being a weathergirl, and yet when I came to Beijing, that's exactly what I ended up doing.

To be honest, I fell into it purely by chance. I was relaxing and watching CCTV 9 when an advert looking for weather forecasters appeared. One swift email to the relevant Hotmail address later, and I had an audition scheduled.

Most of my initial cockiness dissolved, however, when I arrived for the audition and saw the state-of-the-art studio and plush makeup rooms. Not least when I figured out how hard it actually was to point at imaginary objects on a blue screen or pinpoint on a map where Shijiazhuang is (let alone how to pronounce the damn thing).

Sure, I was a novice when I started and I had a few rather embarrassing attempts to muddle my way through, but with time that steep learning curve has leveled out. I've picked up the skills, and can recognize a lot of what I do in the broadcasts aired back home.

There are the occasional oddities though, which remind you that you're in China. The insistence on covering yesterday's weather can

Humidity's rising, barometer's getting lo-o-o-w …

be draining, Chinglishy scripts can be difficult to work into intelligible English, and the random assignments that pop up at the last minute – like being drafted in to sign autographs at a PR event I know nothing about – occur frightfully frequently.

Yes, it's easy to moan about working conditions here compared to other countries, but it's also easy to forget how unlikely these opportunities would be anywhere else. In the UK, BBC weather presenters are all trained meteorologists. When I started out, my only qualifications appeared to be my white face and ability to speak English. Yet the Chinese Meteorological Administration took a chance with me, and while they gain from my experience as a native speaker, I gain from their experience in broadcasting. Now, with the familiarity I've gained and the camera time I've clocked up, doors are open to me that would've remained resolutely shut earlier. Everyone's a winner.

True, it's difficult to take myself seriously (you're a weathergirl, are you kidding?!), but this job is a great one. And there's more to it that the mere ego-boost of being on TV. My family gets to see me every week, despite living 10,000km away, and getting pampered in hair and makeup before going on air is heavenly. The real pleasure though, comes from working a mental job, with unbelievably friendly people, and knowing that never in a million years would I have gotten the chance to wax lyrical about cloud patterns and the likelihood of rain on telly back home.

PHOTO: COURTESY OF HUAFENG

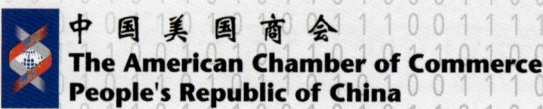

AmCham Daily
Your online China hand

www.amchamchinadaily.com

ADULT EDUCATION

LOOKING FOR THE BEST MANDARIN LANGUAGE TRAINING?

Enroll now at the Academy of Chinese Language Study, Beijing's premier Chinese Language School.

- 10 years of experience and a yearly intake of over 2,000 students
- Over 70 highly qualified and professional teachers with extensive teaching experience
- General Chinese, Business Chinese and Survival Chinese courses offered
- Start classes on any Monday
- All levels and durations available (4 weeks to one year)
- Small classes averaging 5-8 students for optimal teacher attention
- Modern & spacious facilities conveniently located in the CBD SOHO and Lido District
- Customized classes and private tutoring available
- Internationally recognized and accredited academy

8472 1920 / 40
info@acls.com.cn   www.acls.com.cn

Lido Campus
Lead International Building 4th Floor
No 2 A Wang Jing Zhong Huan Nan Lu,
Chao Yang District

丽都校区
朝阳区中环南路甲2号佳境天城A 4层

SOHO Campus
JianWai SOHO Building A 5th Floor
No 39 Dong San Huan Zhong Lu,
Chao Yang District

SOHO校区
朝阳区东三环中路39号建外SOHO A座5层

Achieving cultural fluency is often a matter of finding the right learning environment

Hanyu Fever
... is here to stay
by Haley Warden

The deluge of foreign *liuxuesheng* coming to the capital to learn Mandarin continues to flow on. As effervescent Beijing buzzes with Olympic anticipation, China's global significance is bolstered with each passing day. Some students are lured to the capital by the booming economy or China's rich cultural heritage, while others find cheap bottles of Yanjing to be an ideal intellectual lubricant. Whatever the reason, international students have come to form a significant number of the city's foreigners.

The source

Though China does offer non-language study opportunities, most students come to China in order to learn China's official spoken dialect – Mandarin Chinese (or *Putonghua*, literally "common speech"). Beijing is widely regarded as the best place in the world to learn *Putonghua*, and the city has responded to the demand with dozens of university and privately-run language programs.

So-called "Mandarin" Chinese was chosen by the PRC government in 1955 as an effort to bridge the linguistic gaps between the 1,500 dialects spoken throughout China. Despite the fact that, according to a government survey, only 53 percent of Chinese speak *Putonghua* (only eight percent as their native language), it is the lingua franca of China, and is drilled into elementary and middle school students across the country. *Putonghua* is based on the Beijing dialect, which was chosen in part because all the government officials had to learn it anyway in order to get along in the capital. More importantly, the Beijing dialect was relatively easier to learn, with only four tones - other major contenders, such as Cantonese, have many more.

ADULT EDUCATION

"Consider yourself lucky. When I was your age, there were ten tones!"

Thus, it's no wonder that students flock to Beijing to learn *Putonghua*, as it is the cradle of *Putonghua* development and standardization. Beijing has over 70 universities and countless private language centers. Yet the city's popularity with foreign students also presents a danger – namely, that students will fraternize mostly with their peers and won't practice their Chinese much outside the classroom. If you want full immersion, consider studying in a provincial town with a small population of *laowai* – or try a program whose students must pledge to speak *Putonghua* only.

Beyond the second tone

Sure, language immersion is a major part of what attracts students to Beijing, but in truth, Beijing also attracts foreigners to study everything from art to medicine. Note, however, that whereas informal, non-degree programs don't usually require Mandarin proficiency, universities such as the Central Academy of Fine Arts will only enroll students who have proven Chinese language ability in their undergraduate and graduate programs. In order to do this, students take the Hanyu Shuiping Kaoshi (HSK), a test which determines your Chinese level (More information on the HSK is available in this chapter, p616).

Additionally, there are several professional degree programs offered in English by Chinese universities, often in cooperation with well-known schools from abroad. MBA programs run by American universities are also gaining ground, particularly in Beijing and Shanghai. Typically using foreign teaching methods to investigate China-based case studies, some of these programs are beginning to garner significant international recognition.

The list hardly ends here. After mastering Mandarin, you can study anything from Accounting to Zoology at a Beijing university. And, of course, there are few better places to study Traditional Chinese Medicine than Beijing.

If enrolling at a university doesn't fit your schedule, look into the courses offered by private schools, culture clubs and community groups. Casual intellectuals too busy for regular commitment might consider finding a language partner, or attending a lecture at a community club or bookstore. Any university will be able to hook up foreign students with tai chi or calligraphy lessons.

Whatever your study plans, you'll find essential information to get you started in the pages that follow.

Get your study on at Tsinghua University, "the MIT of China"

Chinese Language

Chinese Language programs continue to account for the dragon's share of foreign study enrollment in Beijing. Weighing the amount of time, energy and money you can devote to your quest for lingual alacrity, you'll find many options to choose from.

The most popular way to learn Mandarin in Beijing is full-time enrollment in a Chinese university language program for a semester or longer. While these programs are relatively easy on the wallet, they are often less rigorous than other options. For a more intensive language-learning experience, quite often involving a "language pledge," one might consider paying the hefty fee for Western-trained teachers on a program run by a foreign university.

Alternatively, private language centers often design courses tailored to the needs of those industrious worker bees with only evenings and weekends to spare. Of course, any kind of program can be supplemented by a self-imposed language pledge, an informal language partner, or by living with a Chinese flatmate or a host family (see Housing and Hotels, p25 and There's No Place Like Home, p27).

Studying Chinese at a university

What's the difference between the different university programs? Do the foreign students at Peking and Tsinghua University magically become geniuses, due to their proximity to the most brilliant students in China? Are Mandarin students at UIBE infused with CBD-savvy Chinese language business skills? Do BLCU students find that beer chemically increases memory retention? According to interviews with foreign students enrolled at these schools and others, programs and teaching standards at the universities don't vary all that much. Across the board, students report that the teachers at these programs employ "very Chinese" teaching methods, often preferring rote learning, with plenty of memorization and recitation.

Mandarin language programs at these universities average 16-20 hours of class per week, focusing on listening, speaking, writing and reading. Generally, there are placement tests within the first one or two weeks, and a student should be able to switch levels if needed. Many programs

The lake on Peking University's charming campus

use the same books, which are predominantly published by Peking University, Tsinghua University and Beijing Language and Culture University. In fact, the big differences between these programs lie not so much in teaching style and quality as in the students who attend and the location of the school (see University Directory, p607).

If you're considering a program at a Beijing university, think about your goals and preferred level of intensity. Many students bemoan the temptation of falling back on their native language with their compatriots. So if you know you'll be tempted, choose a smaller program with fewer foreign students. Inquire about course flexibility – some schools are much more accommodating than others in matching your classes to your proficiency in different areas. Be sure to read materials from the universities and understand their requirements ahead of time.

Applying

If you're considering applying directly to a university in Beijing, the web is the place to start. All universities listed in this chapter have websites in English with information on how to apply and, often, a downloadable application form. Most Beijing universities administer all foreign student affairs – from admissions to housing – through an office called the "International Student Office" (*liuxuesheng bangongshi*). This office will be your principal point of contact with the university throughout your studies.

To apply, you'll have to fill out forms and provide academic transcripts and photocopies of your passport. Art students are also expected to include a portfolio in an appropriate format, such as slides or digital images. Universities also require proof that you have international medical insurance, unless you are on a scholarship that includes it. Medical insurance can be arranged in China, but your university may insist on seeing proof of coverage before you arrive. In addition to the forms and documents, you will likely have to pay an application fee of RMB 400-800. Usually, the application deadline is three months prior to the start of the semester.

Once admitted, unless already in Beijing, you will be sent a form (JW 202), which you should take to your local Chinese embassy or consulate to obtain a student visa (an F visa for a semester, or an X if you plan to study for a year or more). For the X visa, you'll also need to pass a general medical exam, which sometimes can be done after arrival in Beijing. If you decide you want to remain in China after completing your studies, you will have to get a new type of visa. Technically, you can only alter your visa status outside the Chinese mainland – a quick visa run to Hong Kong is usually sufficient – but word on the street is that Beijing's visa consulting companies can work wonders (see their ads in local English magazines or on websites like www.thebeijinger.com).

Ivory towers – what's the damage?

Studying Chinese at a Beijing university will set you back RMB 19,000-28,000 per year in tuition fees, but you may end up paying twice that for a subject other than Chinese. Some foreign students come to Beijing on study abroad programs headquartered in a Western country, which is far more expensive, often costing the equivalent of a semester of university at a private school in the USA. To be sure, students who want to avoid a US-style higher educational fleecing have many cheaper options available.

The average expenditure by foreigners for a year of university in Beijing is RMB 50,000, including accommodation, food and sundries. In addition to tuition fees, you will have to consider living arrangements. You are not required to live in international student dorms, but if you do, expect to pay anywhere from RMB 1,250 to 3,700 per month depending on your desired comfort level. Dorms run the gamut from drafty cinderblock buildings with communal bathrooms and no air conditioning to hotel-style suites with single rooms, private bathrooms and daily cleaning service.

Off-campus accommodations – especially shared ones, near campus – cost about the same as dorms. So which option is better for you? Living on campus usually means a shorter commute to an 8am class. It also eliminates the need to spend two weeks flat-hunting and dealing with a landlord. On the other hand, dorm rules can cramp your style: no guests allowed after 11pm and, in some cases, locked doors at midnight. Typically, a newcomer spends at least one semester on

Continues on p604

The ABCs of KTV
Booze cruise to fluency … in a box
by Lee Ambrozy

Forget about another night of character cramming! Get thee to a KTV hall. Anecdotal research proves that hollering into a microphone with Chinese friends through the wee hours of the morning is the most efficient way to improve your character recognition.

The following songs range from beginner ballads and situational standbys to a couple of rather cancerous canticles. Look up the lyrics of any of these songs on baidu.com to practice in advance.

Wiggle your giggle brush, 'cause "Women dou shi Zhongguoren!"

INSIDER'S GUIDE TO BEIJING

嘻刷刷 (Xi Shua Shua) Giggle Brush
Artist: 花儿乐队 Flower Band
Chinese boy bands might have nothing on the Backstreet Boys but spiky Japanime hair, but they will provide KTV novices with a song containing less than 100 unique characters, and providing lots of opportunities to ham it up. "*Xi Shua Shua*" is perhaps that flip-flop kind of love that makes little girls' hearts flutter.

甜蜜蜜 (Tianmimi) Sweethearts
Artist: 邓丽君 Teresa Teng
A classic hit from the '90s coveted by crooners of all ages, this is a song that waxes sweet on the tender closeness shared between fortunate lovers.

康定情歌 (Kang Ding Qingge) Kangding Love Song
Every Chinese person can sing this folk song – therefore you must sing it too. If you can sing it in a high falsetto you have true charisma … a great icebreaker for a really tough or traditional crowd.

朋友 (Pengyou) Friend
Artist: 周华健 Emil Zhou
This tune is a must for all *guoji youren* in China – and the quintessential drinking song! Great bond-making fodder for your taxi-driver types, and requires minimal sobriety to make it to the end.

老鼠爱大米 (Laoshu Ai Dami) Mice Love Rice
Artist: 杨臣刚 Yang Chengang
Who knew that mice loved rice? Maybe you always thought it was cheese they pined for … well, this love song is about as cheesy as it gets. People will generally hate you for ordering this song, so wield it with the utmost irony.

对面的女孩 (Duimian De Nühai) The Girl Across the Way
心太软 (Xin Tairuan) A Heart Too Soft
Artist: 任贤齐 Ritchie Ren
"The Girl Across the Way" mercilessly lives on in the repertoire of foreigners and other creepy people trying to impress the "girl across the way." Not recommended for big-nose male types. On the other hand, a "softhearted guy" is always going to make an impression on that special lady, in a register most guys can master!

我们都是中国人 (Women Dou Shi Zhongguo Ren) We Are All Chinese People
Artist: 刘德华 Andy Lau
National icon Andy Lau does it best, but use with caution: if you're not sporting "black hair, black eyes" and "dragon blood" your rendition might close a business deal, but it could just make you look strange.

十年 (Shi Nian) Ten Years
Artist: 陈奕迅 Eason Chen
If you must venture into pop songs but away from saccharine lyrics, try lovelorn agony. Here is your stepping-stone: a sappy lost-love number and dependable crowd pleaser. Even if you can't make it through some of the tougher verses, wailing noises will usually suffice till you make it to the chorus.

你快乐，所以我快乐 (Ni Kuaile, Suoyi Wo Kuaile) You're Happy, So I'm Happy
感情生活 (Ganqing Shenghuo) Emotional Life
催眠 (Cui Mian) Hypnosis
Artist: 王菲 Wang Fei
Wang Fei's enormous repertoire is sure to provide something for any female KTV queen, even if the titles sound wimpy. These few suggestions are a place to start – simple, slow, and easily mastered, even in traditional characters.

Ping Pong party — bring your own paddle

campus before considering moving out. (For more information on renting an apartment, see the Housing & Hotels chapter, p22).

As you decide on your accommodations, know that older, cheaper dorms and apartments can be fairly run down, which can be quite a culture shock if you've just arrived in China. The newest, most expensive "international" dorms, on the other hand, are more like hotel rooms than typical dorm rooms in Western universities.

Scholarships

The scholarship most commonly awarded to undergraduate and graduate foreign students in China is the one given by the China Scholarship Council (CSC), which is funded by the Ministry of Education and provided 10,000 scholarships in 2006. China has an educational exchange agreement with many countries, including most European nations. The China Scholarship Council offers one scholarship per 800,000 inhabitants in each of these countries. Applications for the scholarship are typically processed through the country's Ministry/Department of Education. Applying involves filling out forms, providing transcripts and, sometimes, writing an essay. While in some countries the process is quite competitive, in others, scholarships go unused. The CSC typically grants a monthly RMB 800 stipend to language students and offers round trip plane tickets. For more details, see www.csc.edu.cn. This website also provides good general information about studying in China.

According to *Beijing News*, the Beijing Municipal Government will be setting up a scholarship for foreign students in Beijing, the first of its kind in China. The fund has RMB 30 million prepared and will benefit some 1,500 foreign students studying in Beijing.

The Chinese Government also offers the HSK Winner Scholarships for top HSK Test scorers overseas. One scholarship is awarded per country where the test is held. (For more information about the Hanyu Shuiping Kaoshi, see p616).

Several foreign countries fund students for study in China. One of the more famous programs is Germany's DAAD (Deutscher Akademischer Austausch Dienst). For years on end, the program has brought 20 students from Germany to China annually, both for language study and one-year internships.

PHOTO: HAN XU

604 INSIDER'S GUIDE TO BEIJING

At BLCU, classmates from around the world will help you feel at home

And of course, various overseas universities offer study-in-China scholarships to their students.

College life

Chinese universities are closed campuses, meaning they have gates manned by uniformed security guards whose job is to prevent miscreants and ne'er-do-wells from entering. However, they rarely stop anyone from walking in.

These campuses are little cities of their own. They maintain vestiges of the old *danwei* ("work unit") system in that they often host an affiliated kindergarten and elementary school to which the faculty and staff, many of whom live on campus, send their kids. There is everything you need inside the university gates, or immediately outside, from supermarkets, restaurants, laundromats, bookstores and post offices, to printing and film development shops, bicycle repair shops and medical clinics. Most campuses have stadiums or outdoor sports complexes with basketball and tennis courts, a soccer pitch and aerobic machines. Such facilities will undoubtedly often be packed – welcome to China – so athletically inclined foreign students may prefer to join off-campus commercial gyms.

Chinese campuses tend to go to sleep around 11pm, but in the evening the streets invariably stream with people, as happy couples occupy park benches and classrooms swell with diligent students crouched over their books. On the weekends everybody is out and about. Students will sell their used books and CDs on the sidewalk while student organizations set up tables to market their causes and the student radio station broadcasts its programs. However, because the foreign student population is so transient, you will not find many international student organizations aside from an odd rugby or football (soccer) club (BLCU is the notable exception).

You'll find an array of student groups on campus, including sports clubs and groups with a social or humanitarian focus. There are sports groups ranging from backpacking to table tennis and squash, running the gamut from outdoor adventure to cozy winter walloping. Some social groups focus on activities like dancing and singing, while humanitarian groups include organizations working to promote environmental awareness or volunteering to improve rural education. These groups will often hand out flyers and recruit members at the beginning of each semester.

Zhongguancun's hustle-bustle technology malls keep Haidian humming

Chinese campuses are not "dry," so all self-respecting universities in Beijing will at least have one bar on campus that is often open late – even on school nights – and serves cheap beer. And if no one on campus has yet noticed the affinity students have for alcohol and the profit that can be made from it, someone off campus has certainly thought of opening a bar down the street.

University universes

While university campuses are sprinkled all over Beijing, most of the big names are clustered in Haidian, where Wudaokou is a hub of student social activity. Strategically located on burgeoning Chengfu Lu in between Tsinghua and BLCU, here is where students go for wireless and coffee shops, as well as to dine, drink, boogie and shop. The light rail Line 13 is an important transportation artery connecting uni-land to the greater city. As a result, fashion boutiques and entertainment venues sprawl out from the Wudaokou station. Korean restaurants, groceries, salons and karaoke dens are particularly well represented. The neighborhood is also home to several Japanese restaurants, plenty of bookstores and groovy hangouts like cafe-bar Lush and cafe-bakery Sculpting in Time. For more of what's in the area, see map, p698.

Southwest of Wudaokou is a neighborhood called Weigongcun, bounded by BFSU to the east, Minzu Daxue (Central University for Nationalities) to the south, and the Beijing Institute of Technology to the north. Weigongcun plays host to several nice restaurants and a few bars and clubs where students can unwind, and some of the most authentic ethnic minority cuisine in the city can be found in the area.

A great way to get a feeling for the different university neighborhoods and how they relate physically to one another is on a bike. Riding through the Xicheng and Haidian District campuses is a great way to spend a lazy spring or fall afternoon. You can pedal from campus to leafy campus between the Beijing Zoo and the Old Summer Palace, covering miles without having to suck much exhaust.

University Directory

Beijing Film Academy This is your best bet if you want to hook up with the future players in China's film industry, even if, as some critics complain, they are likely to make cheesy romances with little or no depth after graduation. Tuition RMB 45,000 for undergrads, RMB 54,000 for grads. Language program tuition is RMB 9,000 per semester.
4 Xitucheng Lu, Haidian District. (8204 5433) www.bfa.edu.cn 北京电影学院，海淀区西土城路4号

Beijing Foreign Studies University (BFSU or "Beiwai") Beiwai teaches over 30 different languages, as well as Chinese. In addition to several short-term programs, the university offers four-year BA and two-year MA degree courses in Chinese. While students report a dearth of motivated classmates, they appreciate the university's comfortable, laid back – even family-like – social environment. Adjacent to Weigongcun, the area is home to some great eats, too: cafe-bakery Sculpting in Time is close to campus, and Chuanleyuan Jiujia, one of Beijing's best Sichuan restaurants, is a ten-minute walk south. Tuition RMB 11,150 per semester, RMB 21,150 per year.
2 Xisanhuan Beilu, Haidian District. (8881 6438) www.bfsu.edu.cn 北京外国语大学，海淀区西三环北路2号

Beijing Institute of Technology BIT offers a mix of technical and engineering degrees, along with a range of full- and part-time evening classes. Correspondence courses available in subjects such as Financial Accounting and Decoration Design. Tuition USD 2,400-2,800. Language program tuition USD 2,000.
5 Zhongguancun Nandajie, Haidian District. (6891 3294), www.bit.edu.cn 北京理工大学，海淀区中关村南大街5号

Beijing Language and Culture University (BLCU or "Beiyu") BLCU welcomes 6,000 foreigners per annum – the largest crop of foreign students in the PRC. Foreign students outnumber Chinese students here by a large margin. Thus a cornucopia of international diversity, it offers short-term programs as well as BA, MA and PhD degree courses. You can take some of their courses online for credit. Beiyu is a very lively, social campus, with a party school reputation. The Bla Bla Bar, a raucous meat-market of a hangout, is right on campus, and BLCU's extracurricular splendors abound. With adjacent Wudaokou's clusters of nearby bars, cafes and restaurants, finding time to do homework may get a bit difficult, but there will be no problem making friends or finding language partners. Tuition is RMB 23,200 per year.
15 Xueyuan Lu, Haidian District. (8230 3951) www.blcu.edu.cn, www.eblcu.net 北京语言文化大学（北京语言学院），海淀区学院路15号

Beijing Normal University (BNU or "Beishida") Organized to train teachers, Beishida boasts a high level of instruction. The campus is not as beautiful as Beida or Tsinghua, but its central location offers easier access to the subway station and to cool spots like Houhai. Because short-term program students study alongside degree-seeking undergraduates, the combined motivation of the students is relatively high. Serious students appreciate the distance from Wudaokou, as they spend more time outside class interacting in Mandarin with lo-

Continues on p610

Emulate your Korean classmates: Study hard, be beautiful

ADULT EDUCATION

Paper or Plastic?
Dictionary druthers
by Chris Allen and Gabriel Monroe

Reference by radical doesn't always feel rad, but it's good for you

A galaxy of sophisticated, high-tech language learning tools is available to the current generation of Da Shan wannabes, from software, electronic dictionaries and websites to palm-sized smart phones and scratch-pad PDA tutors. Are rain-swollen, dog-eared paper dictionaries antiquated beyond efficacy?

Electronic dictionaries certainly have the potential to surpass paper dictionaries in utility as well as convenience, because there are no space restrictions, so there can be *pinyin* for everything, lots of examples and lots of obscure entries. Meanwhile, clever programs for your "electric brain" like Wenlin and Clavis Sinica can certainly help infuse an email exchange or a web search with commodious comprehension shortcuts. However, there are actually a handful of notable advantages to using paper dictionaries.

Tactile stimulation

Studies have shown that the tactile stimulus of paper books speeds the process of learning to read for babies. Analogously, paper dictionaries are good for beginning Chinese students. Having to use the radical index means you become more intimate with each character, and get to know each of its strokes. Repetitive tactile stimuli like radical searches and writing Chinese characters by hand is really the only way to retain long-term memory of the shapes and meanings. The fragrant finger massage of an inquisitive flip through the dictionary is an experience full of multi-sensory signifiers that aid memory retention.

Character building

Lots of people describe their dictionary as a "best friend" or "trusty steed," but then get upset when their friend betrays them by not having *pinyin* for an example sentence, or when it's hard to find a character by looking in the radical index. Learning Chinese is a tough journey and you can't expect to have someone there holding your hand, even at the beginning. Expect your Chinese dictionary to be more like a puppy. You have to learn how to get the best out of it. If you don't put the effort in, it will chew your shoes and pee on the floor. Sometimes it will delight you and other times it will infuriate you, but whatever you do, don't put blind faith in it.

Weather "resistance"

While not rain proof per se, a dictionary is certainly more weather resistant than an e-dictionary. If, heaven forbid, you get caught in a sandstorm or accidentally drop your dictionary in the loo as you study while you brush your teeth, your trusty paper dictionary will emerge barely fazed – if perhaps a little swollen or gritty – while a robotic tool would be thoroughly ruined.

Face

Dictionary bliss is eminently satisfying. A gigantic, hardcover cinderblock of a dictionary that's passed every cuss word test and never let you down – well, never mind that it's inconvenient to use! Even if you hurt your wrist every time you pick it up, the intimidation factor of having such an infallible tome on display will terrorize friends into abandoning bets before they are settled. They'd most likely prefer to shower you and your dictionary with cash, prayers and kisses, rather than be proved wrong again.

Electronic dictionaries

Clavis Sinica (www.clavisinica.com)

iCiba (www.iciba.com) The most famous software/website in China for online translation. Contains a simple edit box for you to input your text and get your translation.

PlecoDict (www.pleco.com/products.html) Provides a sophisticated range of services for your handheld device, including the third edition of the *Oxford Concise English & Chinese Dictionary*, containing approximately 38,000 entries. PDAs can be purchased in China for RMB 1,000 and up (see Zhongguancun, below).

Rikai.com Website lets you paste in a bunch of Chinese text, digitizes it, and shows a full range of translations for each character as you mouse over them.

Wenlin (www.wenlin.com) CD-ROM software combining a high-speed expandable Chinese dictionary, a full-featured text editor and flashcard system.

Zhongwen.com (www.zhongwen.com) A Chinese-English dictionary that includes a traditional Chinese character etymology feature. This traces Chinese characters to their roots using the individual parts of characters called radicals.

Zhongguancun (See Shopping p392 for details) This neighborhood, just south of Tsinghua and Peking Universities in the northeast, is the place to go for electronic everything. Besta (好意通) and Wen Qu Xing (文曲星) are well-respected dictionary brands, and Hao Ji Xing (好记星) is putting out faux-PDA dictionaries (RMB 400 and up) with very good hand-writing recognition. Prices run from around RMB 200 for a basic English-Chinese dictionary without *pinyin*, to RMB 500 or more for one with handwriting recognition and English menus, specialized vocabulary dictionaries, and other gadgets like a planner, calculator and encyclopedia. Bargaining is the norm, so check out pconline.com.cn (Chinese-only) to see the going price for dictionaries, and go to a few vendors before making a purchase.

Paper

Contemporary Chinese Dictionary (Xiandai Hanyu Cidian, 现代汉语词典) The must-have Chinese-Chinese dictionary for native Chinese speakers and non-native speakers who have learned Chinese. Published by the Institute of the Chinese Academy of Sciences.

New China Idiom Dictionary (Xinhua Chengyu Cidian, 新华成语词典) Contains 8,400 *chengyu* with *pinyin* transcription, modern equivalents of classical terms, the original source of the expression, and examples of common usage.

Langenscheidt Pocket Dictionary Chinese-English English-Chinese The Chinese-English section is somewhat abridged, but the English-Chinese half – modern, clear and always on the money – is the best of any pocket dictionary by a country mile.

Pocket Oxford Chinese Dictionary with Talking Chinese Dictionary and Instant Translator Move your mouse over a character in any electronic document and have the Instant Translator provide you with its translation.

ADULT EDUCATION

cals and Chinese students than their peers further north. Administrators at this school are said to be extremely friendly and helpful, and have the resources to answer almost any question a student could ask. Apart from Chinese, you can study everything from applied chemistry to statistics. Additional *fudao* (tutoring) classes are offered free of charge for help with class work. Tuition RMB 11,600 per semester, RMB 22,400 per year.
19 Xinjiekou Dajie, Xicheng District. (5880 7960) www. bnu.edu.cn 北京师范大学，西城区新街口大街19号

Capital Normal University Several bus stops down from most other major universities, most of Shoushida's Chinese teachers have overseas teaching experience. The 26 PhD and 60 MA programs are all open to foreign students. Tuition RMB 21,580 per year.
105 Xisanhuan Beilu, Haidian District. (6890 2651) www.cnu.edu.cn, www.ciecnu.edu 首都师范大学，海淀区西三环北路105号

Central Academy of Drama Centrally located on blossoming Nanluogu Xiang, one of Beijing's hippest hutongs, Gong Li and Zhang Ziyi's alma mater boasts a tradition of training celluloid vixens. Perhaps your *tongxue* will be the next huge movie megastar! With plenty of pleasant hangouts right around the corner, the location couldn't get any better. Tuition USD 3,200 per year for undergrads, USD 4,000 for masters, and USD 4,600 for PhDs. Language program tuition USD 1,100 for long term courses.
39 Dong Mianhua Hutong, Dongcheng District. (6403 5626) www.zhongxi.cn 中央戏剧学院，东城区东棉花胡同39号

Central Academy of Fine Arts Foreign students studying Chinese here tend to be happy with the quality of instruction and accommodations, though they complain other campus services can be underwhelming. Note that the full-year academic undergraduate and graduate programs (art, art history and theory, architecture and design) are only available to those with relatively high language proficiency (HSK Level 4 for undergrad, Level 9 for PhD). Tuition RMB 40,000 for undergrads, RMB 45,000 for masters, RMB 50,000 for PhDs. See also Art, Design, and Culture for summer program (p620).
8 Huajiadi Nanjie, Chaoyang District. (6477 1019) www.cafa.edu.cn 中央美术学院，朝阳区花家地南街8号

Central Conservatory of Music Home of the next generation of classical masters and often visited by the world's foremost musicians – among them Placido Domingo, Ravi Shankar and Yitzhak Perlman. Tuition RMB 33,000 for undergrads, RMB 38,000 for masters, RMB 42,000 for PhDs.
43 Baojiajie, Xicheng District. (6641 3202) www.ccom. edu.cn 中央音乐学院，西城区鲍家街43号

Peking University (Beida) Beida's striking campus, much of which was once part of the original Yuanmingyuan (see p237), is nearly as much of a draw as the phenomenally gifted student body. Often referred to as its "the Harvard of China," PKU is situated between the two imperial summer palaces, and the electronic goods super-mall paradise Zhongguancun. Nearly 4,000 foreign students – the second-largest group in the country – study there, mostly through programs affiliated with foreign universities. The language program has a heavy homework load and the very early enrollment deadline tends to bring in an internationally diverse group of dedicated students. Provides a sign-up-based tutor program for international students. Tuition RMB 26,000 per year for language programs.
1 Yiheyuan Lu, Haidian District. (6275 1230, 6275 1231) www.pku.edu.cn 北京大学，海淀区颐和园路1号

Renmin University of China (Renda) The third most prestigious university in town (after Tsinghua and Beida) has several short- and long-term study programs as well as one of Beijing's biggest English corners. Just outside the east gate are the UME International Cineplex and many options for mall carousing. Students frequent the comfy Mag cafe just outside the West Gate. The shortest program offered is a one-year course, and many students go on to attend Bachelor's or Master's programs. Due to a low foreign student to Chinese student ratio, opportunities to practice Mandarin are abundant. Students say that Renda feels like a "real university," with a very motivated core of foreign students. Tuition RMB 21,500 per year.
59 Zhongguancun Dajie, Haidian District. (6251 1588) www.ruc.edu.cn 中国人民大学，海淀区中关村大街59号

Tsinghua University Regarded as China's MIT – with an attitude to match – recent renovations brought Tsinghua squarely into the 21st century. Famous alums include Hu Jintao, Zhu Rongji and Nobel Prize-winning physicist Chen Ningyang. The verdant campus boasts proximity to Wudaokou as well as a couple of its very own neighboring hot spots. Haidian's two best live music venues, 13 Club and D-22, anchor a strip of nice restaurants along Chengfu Lu, directly across from the school's south gate. Aside from compelling environs, Tsinghua offers several Chinese language programs that include numerous electives. Tsinghua has exchange programs with several prestigious foreign universities. Language program tuition RMB 19,000 per year. Tuition RMB 20,000 for undergrads (RMB 26,000 for sciences), RMB 23,000 for masters (RMB 30,000 for sciences), RMB 30,000 for PhDs (RMB 40,000 for sciences).
Chengfu Lu, Haidian District. (6278 4857) www. tsinghua.edu.cn 清华大学，海淀区成府路

University of International Business and Economics (UIBE, "Jingmao" or "Duiwai") UIBE is a business-focused university in northern Chaoyang District that offers Mandarin language programs with the option of integrating a business component. Students say that the quality of the business classes is poor in comparison to the language program, of which students speak very highly. The school offers sports and other social activities aimed at giving foreign students a chance at integrating with Chinese students, but many students admit to spending a lot of time just hanging around the dorms, preferring to practice their Mandarin with other foreigners. Their classroom environment is described as "relaxed," but the school does make an effort to divide people speaking a common language between all classes, weakening students' urge to fall back on their mother tongue. There are also some non-traditional options for scholarly pursuits – particularly interesting are the Department of Evening University and Department for Correspondence Education. UIBE also boasts an Applied Economics degree taught in English. Tuition RMB 9,990 for the first semester, RMB 9,100 for subsequent semesters.
12 Huixin Dongjie, Chaoyang District. (6449 2001) www.uibe.edu.cn 对外经济贸易大学，朝阳区惠新东街12号

Homework help is just a bed away with a Chinese roommate

Studying Chinese with a foreign-run language program

While language programs run by foreign universities or study abroad specialists are comparatively expensive by a wide margin, they definitely have their advantages. Highlights include teachers trained in Western classroom methods, and more streamlined administration than that of most Chinese universities, as well as structured opportunities for language immersion. However, look carefully within yourself as you enthusiastically contemplate the idea of a language pledge. Unless you're willing to forego clubbing and plan on living with a Chinese student, the Chinese language pledge is usually more of a Chinglish language pledge, and even that may fall apart by the end of the semester.

These programs are hosted by Chinese universities, and participants usually live in foreign-student dorms on campus. Check program websites for application guidelines, which vary widely. Deadlines come several months before these programs start, so interested students are advised to plan ahead. Programs are generally reserved for current undergraduate or graduate students.

Associated Colleges in China (ACC) ACC is a summer, fall, and spring intensive Chinese language program administered by Hamilton College and hosted by Capital University of Economics and Business (CUEB) in Beijing. Curriculum focuses on studying the language through small group and individualized instruction, with a high level of participation and interaction. Full-time language pledge is "strictly enforced," but it's not uncommon for students to sneak off to nearby Sanlitun and give in to their Anglophonic urges. Tuition USD 4,990 for summer, USD 10,500 fall or spring.
Capital University of Economics and Business, Hong Miao, Chaoyang District. (6595 9258) www.acc-beijing.com.cn/ or www.hamilton.edu/academics/acc/index.html 美国各大学联合汉语中心，朝阳区朝外红庙首都经贸大学十二号楼

CET Academic Programs Formerly known as China Educational Tours, CET offers two programs in Beijing. The intensive Chinese Language program has a full-time language pledge and dorm rooms shared with local Chinese students. For even more intense immersion, CET also offers a well-respected intensive language program in Harbin, Heilongjiang province. The Chinese Studies program option, based in Capital Normal University (see p610), combines Chinese Language and Area Studies, emphasizing learning outside of the classroom and immersion into the local environment. Option to room with a local student. Tuition (Chinese language): January term USD 3,290, Spring or Fall USD 9,490, Summer USD 5,690.
1) Chinese Language program, Beijing Institute of Education, 2 Wenxing Jie, Xizhimenwai, Xicheng District. (6834 2428); 2) Chinese Studies program, Capital Normal University, 83 Xisanhuan Beilu, Haidian District. (6890 2796) www.cetacademicprograms.com 1）西城区西直门外文兴街2号北京教育学院西楼309室； 2）海淀区西三环北路83号首都师范大学一校区国际文化大厦722室

ADULT EDUCATION

Beauty and the Bike: A serene scene awaits CIEE students in autumn

CIEE While CIEE has many different programs for educational exchange, its Beijing study abroad program is reserved for current students at American universities. There is a language and "Ethnic Study" program for absolute beginners, and an intensive Mandarin program hosted at Peking University for beginner through advanced levels. In addition to the language offerings of the program, advanced students can take advantage of a large range of electives offered by the PKU Chinese department, and are allowed one course taught in English. Students generally live on campus, but a limited number elect to stay with a host family. Tuition USD 10,000 per semester, and USD 19,200 for the academic year.
For more information, including application instructions, see their website: www.ciee.org/program_search/program_detail.aspx?program_id=48

Harvard Beijing Academy The first program out there that has posed a serious challenge to Princeton's hegemony over intensive summer Mandarin study. Open to students from all colleges and countries, this two-month summer language program is designed for intermediate to advanced students of Chinese. Students spend the fifth week of the nine-week program conducting a social study in a choice of locations where they research some aspect of Chinese society that will form the basis for papers that may be published and presented at an academic conference. Tuition USD 5,000.
Beijing Language and Culture University, 15 Xueyuan Lu, Haidian District. www.summer.harvard.edu 哈佛北京学院, 北京语言文化大学 (北京语言学院), 海淀区学院路15号

Inter-University Program for Chinese Language Study at Tsinghua (IUP) IUP offers a 32-week Academic Year Program, a 16-week Semester Program, and an eight-week Summer Intensive Program, and boasts a teacher to student ratio of 1:2. All programs are located on the Tsing-hua University campus in Beijing, but IUP encourages students to live in apartments off-campus. Probably the best choice in Beijing for advanced-level students of Mandarin, a prerequisite is the equivalent of two years of college-level Mandarin by the application deadline. Tuition USD 13,000 for year program, USD 7,000 for semester program, and USD 4,000 for summer program, not including housing or textbooks. Wen Bei Lou 502, Tsinghua University, Chengfu Lu, Haidian District. (6277 1505) http://ieas.berkeley.edu/iup 清华IUP中文中心, 海淀区成府路清华大学文北楼502

Princeton in Beijing (PiB) Jokingly referred to as "Prison in Beijing" for its academic intensity and heavy study load, this eight-week summer program has maintained its popularity for years. Hosted at Beijing Normal University, the Chinese Language Program emphasizes total immersion through a language pledge and frequent contact with faculty at meals and in campus life. Prospective students should be aware that PiB exclusively uses Princeton University teaching materials and methods, mostly developed by program director Chih-p'ing Chou. Apply early, as the competition is hot and spaces fill up quickly. Tuition USD 4,500.
Beijing Normal University, 19 Xinjiekouwai Dajie, Haidian District. www.princeton.edu/~pib 北京师范大学, 海淀区新街口外大街19号

PHOTO: HAN XU

Private learning centers

Why study Chinese outside the hallowed halls of Beijing's universities? If you're employed full-time, you may not have a choice, since most universities offer classes only during weekdays. Though their hourly rates are far higher than universities, private language centers will happily plan classes around your schedule – even if that means Sunday morning at 7am. Another advantage is that they can tailor their curricula to your specific language needs.

Furthermore, private institutions are often more bureaucratically nimble than universities. They may embrace the latest teaching methods and textbooks, and hire extrovert teachers who are responsive to their students' needs; a welcome contrast to burned-out professors who simply repeat the content of the textbooks they co-authored 25 years ago. Nonetheless, some private language centers are fly-by-night operations whose standards are suspect.

Joe Livesey has no reservations about the quality of instruction at private language centers. Livesey studied at Beijing Language and Culture University (BLCU), Global Village (a private center) and with a tutor and observed "no real difference in the quality of teaching." Livesey warns that the university habit of starting classes at 8am every day "may have a negative effect on your studies" – or at least on your nightlife.

Where private language centers truly shine is in their ability to address specific Chinese language needs that cannot be met by a general university class. TLI student Sharon Ruwart was impressed by the fact that TLI tailor-made a class for a friend of hers who was already fluent in Chinese, but needed to learn technical words for a scientific conference. "The infinite flexibility is hard to find," notes Ruwart, "but it does come at a price." Indeed, you can expect to pay RMB 120 an hour for individual classes at TLI – and even more elsewhere. By comparison, a semester-long Chinese course at BLCU ends up costing about RMB 33 per hour.

The following is a partial list of private Chinese language schools in Beijing.

1 on 1 Offers semester, part-time, and summer programs. Standard semester is 15 hours a week for 19 weeks and costs RMB 18,810. For part-time students, one on one tutoring is available at RMB 110 per hour for 25 hours; discounts available if you sign up for more hours.

Don't despair – there's a class out there for you

Room 503, Bldg 7, Huaqing Jiayuan, Wudaokou, Haidian District. (8286 3272) www.1on1mandarin.com 海淀区五道口华清嘉园7号楼503

The Academy of Chinese Language Study (ACLS)
Boasting some 12,000 alumni, ACLS offers a wide range of Mandarin courses of varying length for children, teens and adults of all proficiency levels, including General Chinese, Business and Executive Chinese, as well as summer or winter holiday camps and a host of extra-curricular activities. Class sizes average 5-8 students, and customized courses and private tutoring are available. A 120-hour, four-week Intensive Mandarin course costs RMB 6,000, while Executive Chinese, offered before and after business hours, ranges RMB 230-260 per week (four hours each week).
1) B401, Lead International Building, 2A Wangjing Zhonghuan Nanlu (in the Lido area) Chaoyang Dis-

trict. (8472 1920/40); 2) Building A502 Jianwai Soho, 39 Dongsanhuan Nanlu,Chaoyang District. (5869 5425/26) www.acls.com.cn 丽都校区：1）朝阳区中环南路甲2号佳境天城A 4层；2）朝阳区东三环中路39号，建外SOHO A座5层

Chinese Horizon Offers intensive, group and individual classes and can arrange homestays. Minimum registration: 60 hours. Maximum number of students: six for group classes, 10 for intensive classes. Group classes meet on weekdays and cost RMB 6,500 for 100 hours. Individuals pay RMB 7,200 for 60 hours.
4B Bldg 7, Julong Garden (near Workers' Stadium West Gate), Chaoyang District. (6508 5358) www.chinesehorizon.com 朝阳区工体西路聚龙花园7号楼4B（工体西门附近）

Beijing Mandarin School Beginners and intermediate level students pay RMB 3,600 for 60 hours. Intensive lessons cost RMB 5,600 for 120 hours. Private lessons start at RMB 80 per hour. Also offer children's lessons, HSK lessons, and specialty classes focusing on character learning and business vocabulary.
Rm 904, 9/F, E-Tower, Guanghua Lu, Chaoyang District. (6508 1026) www.beijingmandarinschool.com 北京普通话学校，朝阳区光华路数码01大厦9层904

Berlitz Offers both one-on-one (RMB 150 per 45 minutes) and group lessons (RMB 50 per 45 minutes), after placement in one of ten levels. For one-on-one lessons, a tutor can be sent to a designated meeting place (student reimburses transportation cost). Check for available promotions.
Sunjoy Building Ste 801, 6 Ritan Lu, Chaoyang District. (6593-0478) www.berlitz.com 北京贝立兹语言培训有限公司，朝阳区日坛路6号新族大厦801

The Bridge School This well-established school offers group classes (3-10 students) in the mornings and evenings at RMB 3,950 for 72 hours. Intensive classes are offered for RMB 9,500 for 180 hours. Individual classes are offered anytime, anywhere (including home or office) and cost RMB 85-95 per hour, minimum two hours.
1) Rm 1308, 3/F, Guangming Hotel, Liangmaqiao Lu, Chaoyang District. (8451 7605) 2) Rm 903, 9/F, E-Tower, 12 Guanghua Lu, Chaoyang District.(6506 4409, 6467 8822) www.bridgeschoolchina.com 博瑞智文化培训学校，1）朝阳区亮马桥路光明饭店3层1308；2）朝阳区光华路12号数码01大厦9层903

The Capital Mandarin School Business, survival, and intensive Mandarin classes, as well as HSK prep, available for all levels. Customized lesson plans available for both private (RMB 60/hour) and small group lessons (RMB 2,730 for a two-month session).
Room 1601, E-Tower (across from the Kerry Center), C12 Guanghua Lu, Chaoyang District. (6592 5672) 首都汉语学校，朝阳区光华路丙12号数码01大厦（嘉里中心对面）1601室

Easy You Offers both one-on-one lessons (RMB 310/hour for short term) and small group lessons (RMB 195/hour for short term). Small groups have six students, minimum two weeks of class. Lower prices if you book more weeks in advance.
E1-1502 Lanchoumingzuo, 9 & 10 Jiqingli, Chaoyang District. (6553 1801/5) www.easyou.com.cn 易游，朝阳区吉庆里9.10号蓝筹名座E座1区1502

Executive Mandarin Offers corporate training lessons, private one-on-one sessions or small and regular group classes for three different levels. One-on-one tutoring is RMB 120/hour, small groups (2-4 students) are RMB 65/hour. Immersion packages cost RMB 3,120/48 hours for a small group class, RMB 5,760/48 hours for private class. Private tutoring can be conducted at your home, as well.
3B05 Hanwei Building, 7 Guanghua Lu, Chaoyang District. (6561 2486/7/8) www.ecbeijing.com 北京壹迈语言文化交流中心，朝阳区光华路7号汉威大厦3B05

Frontiers Offering classes from beginning to advanced levels, as well as business Chinese and HSK prep. Group classes are offered day and evening (RMB 2,000/44 hours). Individuals pay RMB 70-80 per hour depending on level of instruction.
3/F, Bldg 30, Dongzhong Jie, Dongzimenwai, Dongcheng District. (6413 1547) www.frontiers.com.cn 东城区东直门外东中街30号楼3层

Global Village With classes available from 7.20am-9.10pm Mon-Fri and from 9.30am-4.05pm Sat and Sun, this school not only has a flexible class schedule, but it is the best bang for your buck at RMB 240 per 15 hours. Class sizes range widely, so try several different ones.
West of Wudaokou light rail station, Haidian District. (6253 7737/ 8472 2432) 地球村学校，海淀区五道口轻轨站西侧

Jun Cheng Group classes meet from 10am-noon Mon-Fri and cost RMB 800 per month. Minimum of six students needed to start a new class. Individual classes cost RMB 90/hour on evening and weekends and RMB 80/hour on weekdays.
Beijingzhan Dongjie (opposite to Sanyuan Jin'an Hotel), Dongcheng District. (8511 4713) www.junchengedu.com 北京君诚语言学校，东城区北京站东街（三元金安大酒店对面）

Mandarin Avenue Offering group and individual classes (RMB 40/90 per hour respectively) as well as classes in Chinese knotting, cooking, painting and classical instruments (RMB 50-70 per hour for two-hour classes). In-home classes available in the Shunyi area.
Daily 8am-9pm. Opposite South Gate of Capital Paradise (near Piazza Cafe), Shunyi District. (8046 5311) 尚东，顺义区名都园南门对面（翰风餐厅旁边）

Mandarin House Provides Chinese programs for general interest, business and HSK preparation. Also offers a unique work-study program, where students are matched with unpaid internship positions to gain valuable Chinese workplace experience. Intensive courses cost RMB 1,500 per week. Combined courses that have group lessons in the morning and private lessons in the afternoon cost RMB 2,150 and up per week. Private tutoring costs RMB 170 per hour. Children's Chinese language program costs RMB 3,500 per semester.
Rm 807, Bldg A, Beijing Fortune Plaza, 7 Dongsanhuan Zhonglu, Chaoyang District. (6288 2308) www.mandarinhouse.cn 美和，朝阳区东三环中路7号北京财富中心A座807

Taipei Language Institute (TLI) Group (2-4 people) classes cost RMB 65/hour, whereas individual tutoring costs RMB 110/hour. Classes are taught at the TLI center and students must attend at times scheduled. Teachers use TLI textbooks and customized materials.
International Youth University, 40 Liangmaqiao Lu (near the 21st Century Hotel), Chaoyang District. (6461 2973) 台北语言学院，朝阳区亮马桥路40号（二十一世纪饭店附近）

The Dude System
... for suprasegmental phoneme mastery
by Kaiser Kuo

The tonal variances in Mandarin Chinese are notoriously difficult for foreign students to get a handle on. Unfortunately, they're also probably the most important aspect of Chinese pronunciation. With brutally maimed tones, even reciting 100 Tang poems would be guaranteed to elicit groans of pain rather than accolades or admiration. To achieve any level of fluency, the tones must be tamed.

As a grad student in the States many years ago, I worked as a teaching assistant for a lower division course called "Chinese Humanities." One of the early units was on the Chinese language, and the professor would spend a lot of time focusing on the peculiar properties of the spoken language. He explained to these young scholars how Chinese is "a phonemically poor language, augmented by the use of suprasegmental phonemes." What he meant was that there aren't a lot of basic sound units in Chinese until you add the tones. Those tones scare a lot of folks off of learning Chinese. Call them "suprasegmental phonemes" and you can scare 'em off a class on Chinese Humanities, too, which may have been the professor's intention anyway, since the course was overenrolled.

I reviewed this whole business of tones in the sections I taught, and came up with my own explanation – one closer to their hearts. I called it the Dude System:

Tone the First: Dude, the disapproving tone, as to the clumsy roommate who's just knocked

"Singing pitch for first tone: duuude."

over your Graphix and gotten bong water all over your Poli Sci 142 reader: "Dude, I can't believe you spilled my bong again!"

Tone the Second: Dude?, in the concerned but creeped-out way you might address the roommate you discover sitting naked and cross-legged in the dark, chanting "Nam myoho-renge-kyo" and sounding a little brass bell.

Tone the Third: Duude, scornfully, as if your roommate has asked to borrow 50 dollars so his sensei can align his chakras: "Yeah right, dude."

Tone the Fourth: Dude!, as if exclaiming in triumph to your roommate when coming home from class having gotten a date with mega-babe Elena from Macroeconomics.

It worked, I suppose, though I regretted having taught it that way when I'd get quizzes back with some version of my Dude System repeated under the question on suprasegmental phonemes. Yeah, tones are hard for lots of people. I've known plenty of Mandarin students who can't get them right unless they draw marks in the air with a finger as they speak, like some dim-witted conductor.

No shame in that, dude. As long as the system works.

The Test

Two years of partying will quickly go by, and then you will wake up one morning distressed by the realization that The Test, the raison d'etre for many Korean students, is in two weeks, and – because you are not Korean – you haven't even started to prepare.

The Test, of course, is the Hanyu Shuiping Kaoshi (HSK), or the Test of Chinese Language Level. The Chinese equivalent of the TOEFL (Test of English as a Foreign Language), the HSK test is designed to measure a non-native speaker's proficiency in Chinese. It was the only officially sanctioned test of Chinese language at the time of publishing. You will have to take the HSK test if you plan to enroll in a degree program at a Chinese university. Most schools require HSK Level 6.

Your score on the HSK test, although unnecessarily cloaked in letter and numerical codes, is essentially a number between 1 and 11, which represents your level of Chinese. Styled a bit like the long-gone Imperial Examinations, the HSK is not given as a single exam. Rather, it consists of three separate, aptitude-based tests: Basic (Levels 1-4), Elementary-Intermediate (Levels 5-8), and Advanced (Levels 9-11). A new, fourth test has been introduced, called HSK Threshold, and is for true beginners (defined by the HSK as less than 200 hours of study). Full-time foreign students generally master about three levels per year of study. The 135-minute Basic Test is comprised of 140 multiple-choice questions, while the Advanced Test includes, among other sections, a written composition and an oral interview over 180 minutes. All tests feature listening, grammar and reading sections.

A whole industry is emerging to help you pass the HSK, offering books, prep courses, flash cards, sample tests and more. Beijing Language and Culture University (BLCU), which is tasked with administering the HSK test, publishes several new HSK prep books annually. Their campus bookstore (next to the campus' East Gate, on Chengfu Lu) is well stocked with tomes on the subject, and BLCU bulletin boards are crowded with ads for evening HSK prep courses.

The exact test dates change every year, but the exam is always held on a Sunday morning. Note, however, that the tests have different dates: in 2007, the Basic test was held twice (April and November), the Elementary-Intermediate exam three times (April, June, November), the Advanced twice (April and October), and Threshold only once (August). Registration for each test date is open for about a week, a month in advance. There is online registration and payment available, although at the time of writing, some kinks remained with the website.

In 2007, the HSK prices were as follows:
Basic Test: RMB 200
Elementary-Intermediate Test: RMB 250
Advanced Test: RMB 400

Allow about a month for test results and certificates to be sent out.

The test is also given in many foreign countries. Email or call the HSK Centre, or check their website, for more information.

HSK Centre, Beijing Language and Culture University, 15 Xueyuan Lu, Haidian District. (8230 3672, service@blcu.edu.cn, HSK1@blcu.edu.cn) www.hsk.org.cn. 北京语言大学汉语水平考试中心,海淀区学院路15号

"If only this thing could take the test for me..."

They say French is the language of love ...

Non-Chinese Language

Learning other languages in Beijing

You may think you have most of the world covered once you've gotten down English and Mandarin. What about the other 4-5 billion people? Proficiency in multiple languages is not only useful, but darn fun too. Luckily, cosmopolitan Beijing has plenty of language centers to help you become multilingual beyond the phrase, "my friend will get the bill." Here's a rundown of schools outside of local universities that will help you on your way to membership in the polyglot pantheon.

Alliance Française de Pekin With upwards of 50 French and Chinese teachers, the Alliance Française offers preparation seminars for the TEF (French Evaluation Test), as well as oral and practical French classes at the basic, intermediate and advanced levels. Class size is limited to 20. Tuition is about RMB 20 per hour; the shortest course is 50 hours. The French Cultural Center (2nd location) also has a library, which is open to the public. Special classes for firms and embassies are available.
1) Rm 421, Block 2, Beijing Language and Culture University, 15 Xueyuanlu, Haidian District. (8230 3619); 2) French Cultural Center, 18 Gongtixilu, Chaoyang District. (6553 2678); 3) French School, Sanlitun Dongsanjie, Chaoyang District. (6553 2678) (there is English teaching in the third location for foreign students) www.alliancefrancaise.org.cn 北京法语培训中心. 1) 海淀区学院路15号北京语言学院教学2楼421; 2) 朝阳区工体西路18号; 3) 朝阳区三里屯东三街法国学校内

Beijing New Oriental School Provides various English courses – including GRE and TOEFL preparation classes – as well as German, French, Spanish, Korean and Japanese language classes.

ADULT EDUCATION

"Now that we have MBAs, we'll have no excuse ..."

Prices start at RMB 1,800 for approximately 90 hours, but classes are large (30-40 people). *Zhongguancun Plaza, Haidian District. (8261 1818) www.neworiental.org* 北京新东方学校，海淀区中关村广场

Berlitz The Berlitz Language Training Center offers language training in Spanish, Japanese, French, German, Dutch, Korean and even Bahasa Indonesian. Teachers are all native-speaking or fluent instructors, and the curriculum stresses practical usage: the first lessons cover the survival vocabulary needed by new arrivals in foreign lands. There are also specialized classes for commercial, financial and law-related language-acquisition. Private tutorials available at RMB 300 per hour.
Rm 801, Sunjoy Mansion, 6 Ritan Lu, Chaoyang District. (6508 0244) www.berlitz.com 贝立兹，朝阳区日坛路6号新族大厦801

FESCO FESCO offers one-on-one tutoring in English, Japanese, French, German, Spanish and more. Prices vary according to whether you want a Chinese teacher or a native speaker, and transportation fees for the tutor must be provided.
14 Chaoyangmen Nandajie, Chaoyang District. (8561 8287) www.fesco-training.com.cn/english 外企服务集团，朝阳区朝阳门南大街14号

The Goethe Institute This prestigious German organization has a teaching staff made up of native German speakers and professionally trained Chinese teachers. Weekend courses are designed to improve conversational German, while intensive courses prepare students for study abroad. Courses (RMB 1,800 for 80 hours) are divided into a range of basic and advanced levels. The Goethe Institute's library collection - free and open to the public - includes over 10,000 mostly German books that cover literature, history, art, music and travel in Germany. Classes begin every two months; students can also join mid-course.
17/F, Building B, Cyber Tower, 2 Zhongguancun Nandajie, Haidian District. (8251 2909) www.goethe.de/peking 歌德学院，海淀区中关村南大街2号数码大厦B座17层

Non-Language Programs

Say you're looking to get a doctorate in micromorphology at a Chinese university, or you need that MBA to advance your career. Perhaps you love hitting the books but your passion for language study has been duly sated. Not to worry. Beijing offers the curious scholar a solid selection of degree and non-degree programs in many subjects beyond "common speech."

Business & Law

Many of the following programs require an extensive application process that echoes that of applying to programs in the USA. For instance, they require an application form, official transcripts, a personal statement, a resume, letters of recommendation, sponsorship letters, as well as an application fee (USD 40-200) and a GMAT score. Interviews in English may be required. Applicants should hold a Bachelor's and have work experience (2-3 years for an MBA and 8 or more for an EMBA).

Beijing International MBA Program Graduates of the Beijing International MBA (BiMBA), a joint venture with Peking University, receive degrees from New York's Fordham University. An 18-month full time (tuition RMB 120,000), 28-month part time (tuition RMB 150,000) and two-year executive MBAs (tuition RMB 290,000) are offered in English, with two concentrations: general management and finance.
Rm 101, China Center for Economic Research, Peking University, Haidian District (6275 4800, 6275 4802, admissions@bimba.edu.cn) www.bimba.org/english 北大国际MBA，海淀区北京大学中国经济研究中心101

CEIBS EMBA Program The China Europe International Business School (CEIBS), which offers a full-time MBA program in Shanghai and a part-time Executive MBA program in Beijing, both in English and in *Putonghua*. Beginning each September, the two-year program is designed for managers with over five years' experience, and classes meet once a month, Friday through Monday. Tuition RMB 308,000.
3/F, Tower A, Raycom Info Tech Park, 2 Kexueyuan Nanlu, Zhongguancun, Haidian District. (8286 1677, 8286 1688, embabj@ceibs.edu) www.ceibs.edu/emba 中欧国际工商学院，海淀区中关村科学院南路2号融科咨讯中心A座3层

Cheung Kong Graduate School of Business Set up in 2002 by Hong Kong tycoon Li Ka-shing, the Cheung Kong Graduate School of Business offers a 20-month Executive MBA in Beijing as well as full-time one year MBA (tuition RMB 248,000) and PhD programs in Shanghai. In 2007, tuition for the EMBA was RMB 338,000. Merit based scholarships available.
3/F, Tower E3, Oriental Plaza, 1 Dong Chang'an Jie, Dongcheng District. (8518 1050) www.ckgsb.com/web2005/index-en.php 长江商学院，东城区东长安街1号东方广场东3座3层

Robert H. Smith Executive MBA Program Taught entirely in English, graduates receive an MBA degree from the University of Maryland's Robert H. Smith School of Business in 18 months. The Executive MBA program meets approximately once a month for four consecutive days, and is the same 54-credit program as the one granted at the University of Maryland. An added benefit is that students can take classes in any of the Smith locations worldwide, such as Shanghai, Zurich, and College Park, Maryland. Tuition is USD 39,750.
317A Tower 2, Bright China Chang An Bldg, 7 Jianguomennei Dajie, Dongcheng District. (6510 2600) www.rhsmith-umd.cn 马里兰大学史密斯商学院，东城区建国门内大街7号光华长安大厦2座317A

Rutgers EMBA Program Rutgers offers a fully accredited 14-month Executive MBA (EMBA) program designed for working professionals who want to remain on the job while obtaining a US MBA. Classes are taught in English once a month over nine-day periods, held all day on two consecutive Saturdays and Sundays, and three hours per night for two nights during the intervening week. The program's 18 courses are taught by Rutgers faculty flown in from the US, and can be completed between the Beijing and Shanghai classrooms if necessary. The student body is evenly split between PRC nationals and expatriates, who represent ten different nationalities. At the time of writing, tuition was USD 37,050.

Suite 2505A, CITIC Building, 19 Jianguomenwai Dajie, Chaoyang District. (8526 2528/29/13) www.rutgers.cn 新泽西州立大学，朝阳区建国门外大街19号国际大厦2505A

Tsinghua-INSEAD Dual Degree Executive MBA Programme INSEAD, hoping to become the "Business School for the World," with dual campuses in France and Singapore, partners up with Tsinghua University in a dual degree program aimed at training top-tier Asian executives. The program is administered at both the Singapore campus and at Tsinghua. This dual degree Executive MBA program takes 18 months, meeting over five days every six to seven weeks. Tuition costs USD 75,000.
North 311, Shunde Bldg, Tsinghua University, Haidian District. (6279 5662) www.insead.edu/tiemba 海淀区清华大学顺德楼北311号

Temple/Tsinghua Universities Master of Laws Program Philadelphia's Temple University runs a joint one-year Master of Laws program with Tsinghua University in Beijing that focuses on American and international business and financial law. Applicants must be either current law students, practicing lawyers or law degree holders. Graduates of the program are awarded a Master of Laws Degree from Temple University and a Certificate of International Business Legal Study from Tsinghua University. Classes are taught in English by US-trained faculty members from Temple, Tsinghua and New York University, as well as experienced American lawyers. Tuition for the 18-month program is RMB 170,000.
Office of Tsinghua/Temple Master of Laws Program, Tsinghua University School of Law, Mingli Building, Tsinghua University, Haidian District. (6279 4565, templels@dns.law.tsinghua.edu.cn) www.tsinghua.edu.cn/docsn/fxy/english/llmPrgm.htm 清华大学／美国天普大学法学硕士项目，海淀区清华大学法学院明理楼1层

Traditional Chinese Medicine

"TCM" encompasses a wide range of medical options, from pharmaceutical medicine to acupuncture to massage. The programs listed below are fairly well-established and accept foreign students, but new options are becoming available as Western interest in Chinese medicine increases.

Beijing University of Chinese Medicine More than 1,189 foreign students attended the university in 2005 to study Chinese in addition to Acupuncture and Moxibustion, Chinese Pharmaceutical Processing, Public Health Management and other disciplines. English undergraduate degree programs last as long as five years, require HSK Level 6 and cost RMB 45,000 per year. The program in Chinese costs considerably less, at RMB 35,000. Other short training programs last from one week to two months, require no Chinese ability (courses are taught in English or a translator is provided) and can cost as much as RMB 8,500 per month (RMB 6,800 in Chinese).
11 Beisanhuan Donglu, Chaoyang District. (6428 6322) www.bjucmp.edu.cn 北京中医药大学，朝阳区北三环东路11号

The China Academy of TCM Three-month courses for beginners or intermediates. Beginning courses cost USD 2,500 and run from August to October; intermediate courses begin in January, end in April, and cost USD 2,900. Classes are taught in Chinese and meet five days a week.
16 Dongzhimennei Nanxiaojie, Dongcheng District. (6401 4411) 中国中医科学院，东城区东直门内大街16号

Art, Design and Culture

Ever had designs to design the design of design itself? Fancy studying painting with China's most renowned art faculty? The following organizations offer formal or ongoing courses in the arts, and some provide one-on-one courses.

Beijing Central Art Gallery & Cultural Venue This art gallery is both an exhibition area for some of the best Chinese art by outstanding artists from China and overseas and a unique cultural venue for courses on pearls, jade, Chinese painting and calligraphy (RMB 150/person/lesson). A practical class on pearls gives valuable background information on the different types of pearls and how to buy from dealers (RMB 330/person). Likewise, a class on jade identification and maintenance is also offered (RMB 480/person).
02 Riverville Square, 1-1, Lilai Garden, Tianzhu Shunyi District. (6450 8483/8646) www.bjcagallery.com 硕华画廊，顺义区天竺丽来花园1区1号温榆广场02号

Whimsical statues testify to inspiring times at The Central Academy of Fine Arts

Central Academy of Fine Arts The Central Academy of Fine Arts has a three-week summer studio art program taught in English for pre-college to postgraduate artists. Program costs USD 2,900 with roundtrip airfare included.
8 Huajiadi Nanjie, Chaoyang District. (6477 1019, cafasummerschool@hotmail.com) www.cafa.edu.cn/asp/summer.htm or call the New York International Education Coordinator (+1 718 875 4060). 中国中央美术学院，朝阳区花家地8号

FESCO Training Center Over 300 full- and part-time teachers offer classes in tea ceremony, cooking, Beijing history and culture, tai chi, Traditional Chinese Medicine, Chinese painting and more. Prices are approximately RMB 200 per hour.
14 Chaoyangmen Nandajie, Chaoyang District. (8561 8287) www.fesco-training.com.cn/international-e/e-gaishu.htm 外企服务集团，朝阳区朝阳门南大街14号

The RAFFLES-BICT International College RAFFLES-BICT International College offers diploma programs in Fashion Design, Graphics Design, Interactive Media, Product Design, Interior Design and Business Administration. The three-year full-time courses (taught in English) are open enrollment. Tuition between RMB 13,000 (Business Administration) and RMB 20,000 (Fashion Design). Scholarships available.
Clothing Building Complex, 6 Huixin Nanli, Chaoyang District. (6427 7618) www.rafflesdesign-institute.com 北京莱佛士学院，朝阳区惠新南里6号院紫光大厦

The Midi School of Music trains the musical geniuses of tomorrow

Music

The mother of all music programs in Beijing is offered at the Central Conservatory, where budding musicians can study with some of China's greatest. Most musical instrument shops offer instruction in modern music. Aspiring rockers should keep in mind that many local musicians teach in their spare time, either privately or through schools, so it isn't necessarily bad form to approach them after a show. Expect to pay between RMB 40-75 per hour. (For more, see Musical Instruments, p405, and Music Practice Rooms, p657.)

Central Conservatory
See listing in Art & Culture p214.

Midi School of Music While the Midi School of Modern Music may not be the most conveniently located of Beijing's schools, its setting – in the shadows of Xiangshan – makes it just about the prettiest campus in town. Midi has a two-year full-time program – taught primarily in Chinese – and boasts teachers from Beijing and beyond who train the next generation of musicians in styles ranging from jazz and Latin to rock and blues. The school draws a host of talented international artists to host workshops and master classes. A new partnership with the North Melbourne Institute of TAFE means that Midi grads will also get Aussie certification. Tuition RMB 16,450.

12A Ruiwangfen (near Xiangshan), Haidian District. (6259 0101) www.midischool.com. cn 北京迷迪音乐学校，海淀区瑞王坟甲12号（香山附近）

Sheets and Giggles

Learning to play an instrument in Beijing
by Eric Mendel

To find the right music teacher, of course you must take into account your instrumental skill/experience level, as well as your financial and linguistic resources. Word of mouth is often the best way to find what you're looking for, and with tens of thousands of Beijing piano students, you can easily find your way to a few teachers.

Keep in mind that most teachers will charge more for house calls. Also, be conscious that midday siesta time (roughly 11:30am-2pm) is a strongly guarded tradition. You may be expected to turn off the amp, or you may find your otherwise supportive fan base of courtyard grannies suddenly united against you.

Even Yitzhak digs learning to play a new instrument

International schools
Many schools, such as ISB, maintain lists of teachers who give private lessons, mostly geared for children and English-language instruction. Dulwich College maintains a weekend lesson program through the school itself, making it easy for children and adults to start with half-hour lessons. Expect to pay no less than RMB 250/hour for beginners.

Conservatory students and professors
Many students – of widely varied instructing experience – moonlight as private lesson instructors; classes are sometimes formally arranged through the schools. Conservatory students usually charge at least RMB 100/hour. Finding an English-speaker is possible, but may cost more.

Another option is to try to track down a conservatory professor, but they are usually very busy and inundated with prospective students. Younger teachers might be willing to teach privately for as little as RMB 250/hour; but famous pedagogues cost up to RMB 2,000. See page 610 for conservatory listings.

Piano cities
Piano dealers, big and small, usually have connections with teachers, often on the premises, starting as low as RMB 40/lesson. Group lessons are often available. Many also rent upright and grand piano practice rooms, for about RMB 10-25/hour.

Traditional Chinese instruments
In addition to the conservatory and international school options listed above, Chinese instrument teachers can be found in the Peking Opera schools, or just by visiting a local park. Lai Jin Yu Xuan teahouse in Zhongshan Park has a specialized *guqin* studio (instruction in Chinese only).

Sheet music, CDs, and instruments
The stores near Central Conservatory and China Conservatory are great bets for printed materials. The retail branch of the Central Conservatory's publishing house – Tian Tian – is just inside the west gate. Huasheng, an independent store on the opposite side of the Second Ring Road, sells a slightly wider selection of scores and books, with a cafe to boot. A number of smaller specialty shops in the area sell instruments. For a wider selection, try Tom Lee or Parsons Music (see Shopping, p408 for details). Import brands like Baldwin, Bosendorfer, Steinway, and Yamaha can be found at branch outlets as well as larger retail outlets.

Community Learning Resources

In Beijing, non-intensive arts courses, lectures, trips and workshops on topics from calligraphy and history to *jiaozi*-making and rock music are here for the taking. An increasing number of organizations, including the following, will help expand your skills and horizons in Beijing. Also, the foreign student offices of all Beijing universities can help students find instructors of calligraphy, painting, tai chi and other disciplines.

Cultural Groups

Beijing International Society
This organization arranges various cultural activities and evening lectures by highly regarded scholars, journalists and artists. These are designed to help foreign residents learn more about Chinese art, religion, history and archeology. Typically, three to four events are organized per month. Become a member (RMB 250 per year; RMB 150 for students) to receive their monthly newsletter. Non-members can usually pay to attend specific events. *www.bisociety.com*

Chinese Culture Club Started in 2000, the CCC offers guided English tours, daytrips and weekend excursions. They also offer seminars and workshops on a variety of topics, such as film screenings, art and tai chi classes, and cooking. CCC also has a book club to discuss Chinese-themed literature. Sign up for their weekly online newsletter through the website to learn more about the CCC's events. Though non-members can attend most events, members enjoy discounts and can participate in exclusive outings. *Kent Center, Anjialou, 29 Liangmaqiao Lu, Chaoyang District. (6432 9341) www.chinesecultureclub.org* 中国文化俱乐部，朝阳区亮马桥路29号安家楼肯特中心院内

Neighborhood Chinese Club Provides a series of interactive and educational cultural activities. Learn how to cook Chinese food, perform a tea ceremony, paint your face Peking Opera-style, play Chinese musical instruments or improve your ping-pong skills. Language courses also offered. Yearly membership is only RMB 50. *(8450 1789) www.chineseneighbor.com/activities.htm*

Libraries

The Bookworm The Bookworm, Beijing's best English-language bookstore and lending library, also hosts a fabulous lecture series. Speakers have included Peter Hessler (author of *River Town*) and Rachel DeWoskin (*Foreign Babes in Beijing*). One-year membership costs RMB 300, half-year is RMB 200, or family membership is RMB 500. Membership extensions at a discount.
Daily 9am-2am. 2/F Building 4, Sanlitun Nanjie, Chaoyang District.(6503 2050) www.beijingbookworm.com 书虫，朝阳区三里屯南街4号楼2层

Capital Library While its range of foreign language books is not as impressive as the National Library's, it does offer foreigners the option of borrowing books. It costs RMB 10 to process a reader's card and, depending on the type of card you choose, a deposit ranging from RMB 100 to 500. Foreign-language newspapers and periodicals can also be accessed and regular lectures are organized on weekends.
Daily 9am-7.30pm. 88 Dongsanhuan Nanlu, Chaoyang District. (6735 8114) www.clcn.cn.net 首都图书馆，朝阳区东三环南路88号

National Library This national institution has a great range of English and other foreign language editions, including periodicals and academic titles. Foreigners can access the books only at the library and are not permitted to borrow, but the selection makes it well worth the trip. Their website has a searchable online database that is available in both Chinese and English. Reader's cards are available for RMB 5/month or RMB 20/year.
Daily 9am-9pm. 33 Zhongguancun Nandajie, Haidian District. (8854 5593/4089) www.nlc.gov.cn 国家图书馆，海淀区中关村南大街33号

L is for Learning

And ... look out!
by Shelley Jiang

Let them think what they want — you are a learning, growing, scabby machine!

I suspect that I have become the laughingstock of my apartment complex. Every day, the old men and women on the stoop see me awkwardly finagle my way onto my bike, wobble for a few seconds, then finally push off. Sometimes it takes more than one try. Sometimes I completely lose balance and drop everything, bike and all. But there are definitely stares, and sometimes they all fall silent.

It's embarrassing, but I couldn't ride a bike at the age of 22, and it hadn't occurred to me to learn until I arrived in Beijing. Here I was presumably inspired by the mayhem that passes for "traffic," and perversely lured by the notion that I could meet flying death at any moment on the street. What better to motivate me than pure and simple survival?

So I got a small bike that rattled fiercely – rather advantageous, I thought, so other people would have plenty of warning to get out of the way. A friend patiently taught me from the basics until I could trace lopsided circles in a clearing. Scratches, bruises and dirt made my legs start to look like the drawing board of a particularly bored and destructively-minded child.

Beijing is an intimidating biking instructor. I used to count the number of near-misses, but it got a little depressing. Apparently, most Beijing drivers don't seem to mind *that* much if you *lightly* hit and scratch their car. You're a girl? They may just sigh and send you off with an exasperated wave. Oddly enough, profuse apologies seem to make the situation worse.

Still, I surprised myself. I stopped denouncing all cars that came within five feet of me as dangerous and irresponsible. Eventually, I started trying to pass other bikers.

The key to learning anything as an adult – building new synapses between old neurons – is that you have to have a *hou lianpi'r* (厚脸皮儿). Literally "thick skin on your face," it means indifference to attention and public opinion. Fortunately, after countless spectacular tumbles in a city of experienced bikers, my skin has thickened up nicely. Once you're used to the stares and fear no shame, learning gets easy – brush off the dust and get up laughing, never mind that people think you're completely ridiculous. Which makes Beijing the perfect place to plunge into something new: You're already the center of attention anyway, so what difference do a couple more stares make? Fall on your face in traffic, bust a *yangge'r* move with senior citizens in the park, learn to squat or taste *baijiu* without making a face. It's these small, sometimes elusive achievements that make Beijing a little more like home.

The Bridge School

http://www.bridgeschoolchina.com

The Bridge School*

Having **15** years history of Chinese teaching,
Voted "The Best Chinese Language School" by the readers.
More than 100 teachers teach with books desighed by T.B.S,
make it easy for busy Westerners to learn Chinese.
Group lesson will be started every month.
One on one class starts anytime.

Guangming Hotel:
Office Building Room 0503,5/F
Tel: 8451 7605   Fax: 6468 0287

E-tower:
Room 903, 9/F
Tel: 6506 4409   Fax: 6504 6389

E-mail: info@bridgeschoolchina.com

USEFUL INFO

"Piotr, my dear, you look marvelous"

For Igor's Sake
A useful chapter
by Shelley Jiang

One Sunday evening in late spring you suddenly glance at your passport and realize it's about to expire in three days. Not only that, but you're also overcome by a powerful longing for your pet iguana, which you left in Norway. You decide to import him immediately. He'd be a good addition to your comedy routine – you volunteer weekly at an orphanage, and Igor'll make the kids laugh. And should dear Igor get lonely, well, you could always call up your old school chum to see if his lizard Piotr mightn't be interested in a little rendezvous. Maybe they'll hit it off really well, and soon perhaps you'd have to schedule a ceremony, and take your best suit to the dry cleaners, and mail out invitations... It'd all cost an awful lot, wouldn't it? You finger your empty wallet and start to have second thoughts about the whole enterprise. Fortunately, at this point a demand draft for RMB 272,000 falls out. You're not quite sure what a demand draft is, nor what to do with it, but you do know that the answer to this – and all your other random, pressing questions about the nuts and bolts of life in Beijing – is in the Useful Info chapter of the *Insider's Guide*. Thoughts of Igor dancing in your head, you flip through these pages and reach for the phone ...

USEFUL INFO

Community Directory
Alumni Groups

Graduates of foreign universities lead fast-paced lives that frequently cause them to move. If an alumnus listed below has left Beijing by the time you read this, check out the most recent issue of *that's Beijing* for up-to-date contact information.

All Universities Group
A consortium of a number of alumni groups, with regular social gatherings. Schools include Berkeley/Haas/Boalt, Yale, Cornell, Harvard/HBS, MIT/Sloan, Kellogg, Stanford/GSB, Cambridge, Oxford, Columbia, Chicago GSB, NYU, Brown, UPenn, Princeton, Cornell, Georgetown, U of Washington, UCLA, U of Texas, Thunderbird and INSEAD. Contact Rocky Lee (rockylee@gmail.com)

Brown Club of China
Michael C. Keefrider (mck@alumni.brown.edu)

Canadian Alumni Network (CAN)
Alumni from all Canadian universities, colleges and institutions in China. The CAN currently has 18 alumni representatives and over 1000 alumni in Beijing. (info@clubcanada.net)

Carolina Club
A club for graduates from North Carolina, especially UNC. Elyse Ribbons (chinesetarheels@gmail.com)

Colorado State University Alumni
Meets periodically with visitors from Fort Collins. (paulgillis@yahoo.com)

Columbia University Alumni Association of Beijing
Alex Whitworth (beijing@alumniclubs.columbia.edu)

Cornell Club of Beijing
Gary (grc3@cornell.edu)

Dartmouth Club of China
(dartmouthchinaclub@gmail.com)

Duke Alumni Club of Beijing
http://groups.google.com/group/duke-alumni-beijing

Fletcher Club of Beijing
Happy Hour on the second Wednesday of every month at 6.30pm at Frank's Place.
Mosud Mannan (mosudmannan@hotmail.com)

Georgetown University Alumni Club of Beijing
http://groups.yahoo.com/group/hoyasinbeijing

GGSB Grenoble Graduate School of Business Alumni
(6512 1740 ext 46, cjheyer@ars-mc.com)
www.mti-brothers.com

Harvard Alumni Club of Beijing
Charles Krabek (mgchina@public.bta.net.cn)

INSEAD Beijing Alumni
(inseadbeijing@gmail.com)

Johns Hopkins Alumni Club of Beijing
(nick.sheets@gmail.com) http://groups.yahoo.com/group/hopkinsbj/

London School of Economics Alumni of Beijing
Zuyu Tan (ztan@vip.sina.com)

MIT/Sloan Alumni Club of Beijing
Stephen Terry (stephenterry@alum.mit.edu)

The Oxford and Cambridge Club
www.occb.cn

Rutgers Alumni of Beijing
(8526 2528/29, rutgers@rutgers.cn)

Stanford Business School Alumni Association
Fred Yang (139 1029 5300, yangfred@mail.com)

Stanford University Alumni
(beijingstanfordalumni@yahoogroups.com)

UC Berkeley Alumni Association of Beijing
Rocky Lee (139 1188 4761, rockylee@gmail.com)

UCLA Beijing Club
David Wang (david_dw_wang@yahoo.com)

UCL (University College London) Alumni
Hiu Ng (uclchina@gmail.com)

University of Maryland/Robert H. Smith School of Business Alumni Association
Kelly Liu (6510 2600, kliu@rhsmith.umd.edu) www.rhsmith-umd.cn

University of Notre Dame Alumni Club
Jenn Hinkle (jennifer.hinkle.2000@alumni.nd.edu)

University of Pennsylvania Club of Beijing
(penn@cross-search.net)

University of Texas McCombs Business School Alumni Association
AJ Warner (warner88@gmail.com)

University of Toronto Alumni Group
(vincci.ching@utoronto.com.hk)

University of Virginia Club
Max Quillen (max.quillen@alumni.virginia.edu)

University of Washington Alumni
Su Cheng Harris-Simpson (sucheng@asia.com)

Wellesley College Alumni Association
Saeri Yuk Ziebart (saeri@ziebart.org)

Yale Club of Beijing
www.yaleclubbeijing.org

Chinese Culture Groups

Beijing International Society (BIS) Provides foreign residents with opportunities to learn about China from leaders in culture and the fine arts, religion, history and archaeology. Organizes evening lectures and outings to places of historical and cultural interest. Annual membership fee RMB 250, students enrolled in a Chinese university RMB 150.
For more info, see Adult Education, p624.

Chinese Culture Club (CCC) Dedicated to promoting Chinese culture through programs and events held in a small-group setting. Offerings include weekly film screenings and discussions, history lectures and hands-on courses on subjects such as calligraphy, painting, TCM and tai chi.
For more info, see Adult Education, p624.

Neighborhood Chinese Club Offers a variety of activities including culture, entertainment, art, fashion and more.
For more info, see Adult Education, p624.

Community Groups

Baroque Chamber Chorus of Beijing Founded in 1994, the Baroque Chamber Chorus has a repertoire ranging from Palestrina madrigals and Haydn masses to Stravinsky, Fauré, Gershwin and even Chinese works. They perform in the original language at the Beijing Concert Hall and other venues. Rehearsals every Sunday.
(6538 5368) www.beijingbaroque.com

Beijing #1 Toastmasters Club Monday meetings help members improve communication and leadership skills.
www.tmbj1.org

Beijing Actors Workshop A group for writers, actors and directors that organizes structured improvisation and scripted scene work in English and Chinese, method acting, exercises, theatre games and monthly public performances. Meetings every Wednesday at 8.30pm at The Playground.
(6407 6889) http://bjactorsworkshop.googlepages.com

Beijing Amateur Chess Club (BACC) Meets Wednesdays 8pm at the Stone Boat Cafe.
(6501 9986, mnario2004@yahoo.com)

Beijing Harmonica Society Classical and folk harmonica players and guitar players, other instrumentalists welcome. Two Sundays a month.
(mund@sohu.com)

Beijing Improv Weekly workshops Wednesday at 8pm at Jiangjinjiu Bar, as well as occasional shows.
www.beijingimprov.com

Beijing International Forum An international group of young professionals and students that holds weekly discussions on current affairs. Meetings (Sat 3-5pm) are free, and both Chinese people and foreigners are welcome.
Frank Yu (frankyu@gmail.com)

Beijing Linux User Group (BLUG) BLUG is an open-for-all non-profit organization promoting and supporting the Linux community. Meetings on the second Tuesday of every month are designed to appeal to users at all levels.
www.beijinglug.org

Beijing Macintosh User Group Multilingual group for users of Apple Macintosh computers.
www.beimac.com

Beijing Organic Consumers Association A Yahoo Group for Beijing residents interested in organic produce and consuming responsibly.
http://health.groups.yahoo.com/group/beijing_organic_consumers

Beijing Playhouse China's English-community theater presents contemporary semi-professional productions of shows like *The Sound of Music*, *A Christmas Carol*, and Neil Simon's comedy *The Odd Couple*, all with Chinese subtitles. They love new talent, and professional experience is not necessary, though ability to perform in English is required.

PHOTO: SIMON LIM

Having a ball in the community

38 Liangmaqiao Lu, Chaoyang District. (137 1890 8922) www.beijingplayhouse.com 北京剧场，朝阳区亮马桥路38号

Beijing Wine Club Regular wine events such as wine quiz nights, blind tastings, winery tours and parties.
www.beijingwineclub.com

The Capital Club Private club for the crème de la crème of the business community.
50/F, Capital Mansion, 6 Xinyuan Nanlu, Chaoyang District. (8486 2225 ext 260, member@thecapitalclub.com) 朝阳区新源南路6号京城大厦

China Capital Toastmasters Club Develop your public-speaking and leadership skills. Meetings (Thu 7-9pm) in the Zhaolong Hotel Training Room, in the Admin Bldg behind the hotel.
(6509 7771) www.cctmc.org

China Club Beijing Holds business and social networking events in a unique Chinese courtyard setting. Monthly activities include theme dinners, wine tastings and family gatherings.

Continues on p634

USEFUL INFO

Eight Books for '08
Literary rambles through Beijing's old and new
by Ann Mah

A pile of tomes! The perfect way to sate your Beijing curiosity

There's life in Beijing – and then there's *reading* about life in Beijing. If you've ever been curious about the daily life of a cultural revolution-era Beida exchange student, wanted to learn more about Chinese regional cuisine, or are simply waiting for Peter Hessler to write another excellent Sino-centric tome, dip into these books. From cooking to camping in an ancient temple, they're like a trip back in time – or simply across town.

Peking Picnic by Ann Bridge – Set in 1920s Beijing, this is a dreamy novel about the adventures of a group of expats during an overnight excursion to Jietai Temple. Ann Bridge was the *nom de plume* of Lady Mary Dolly Saunders O'Malley, the wife of the British envoy to China who lived in Beijing from 1925-27. Though the book does not lack off-color descriptions of locals, it is still a fascinating glimpse into life as an expat during the warlord era, sketched in an evocative and languorous fashion. We love Bridge's descriptions of sleeping in an ancient courtyard surrounded by blooming peach trees, their meals taken at a table "correctly spread with linen, glass and a profusion of silver."

Hand Grenade Practice in Old Peking by Frances Wood – Witty and charming, this is Wood's account of her time as a Peking University exchange student in 1975-76. Whisked from England to a Beijing dormitory, she encounters suspicious roommates, North Koreans with immovable helmet hair and an ever-changing curriculum. A must-read for all exchange students – former and current – who have ever complained about their living conditions. Woods bathed only once a week in a *communal* shower stall!

Peking Story by David Kidd – If you've ever wondered what life was like behind the courtyard spirit wall, dip into this detailed memoir. From 1946-50, Kidd lived in a grand mansion in the heart of Beijing, the ancestral home of his wife's family. Wealthy aristocrats, with a garden that stretched for acres, they were forced to give up their home in 1949. Though his young marriage didn't last, Kidd's narrative of life in a manicured courtyard house is evocative, the descriptions of his wife's family in later years heartbreaking.

Classic Food of China by Yan Kit-So – Including detailed descriptions of regional cuisine and meticulous recipes, this fascinating Chinese cookbook covers everything from culinary history to table manners. Use it to whip up your favorite dish, or as a primer on Chinese cuisine.

The Eye of Jade by Diana Wei Liang – With her snappy intelligence and sharp intuition, Liang's private investigator, Mei, could give Alexander McCall Smith's *No. 1 Ladies Detective Agency* a

Languorously traipse through 1920s rural Beijing

run for its money. Set in the shady world of antiquities, Mei's adventures take her to locales familiar to local or transplanted Beijingers: the Liulichang market, Old Summer Palace, Chaoyang's cheap and cheerful noodle bars and beyond. This lively mystery, the first in a series, provides a glimpse of modern China, both the bright sheen of economic growth and the corruption lying underneath.

Foreign Babes in Beijing by Rachel DeWoskin – It has its critics and admirers, but this memoir of life in 1990s Beijing certainly provides a different – and refreshing – point of view: a woman's. DeWoskin moves to Beijing to work for a public relations firm and soon finds herself the star of a hit Chinese soap opera of the same title. Many of her adventures will be familiar to seasoned Beijing-hands, but her wit and writing set her apart.

Chinese Lessons by John Pomfret – Fascinating yet flawed, this memoir traces the lives of Pomfret – a 1981 Nanda exchange student – and five of his Chinese classmates, who each follow very different paths. Though at times the conceit feels forced, Pomfret's insights about the New China are sharp. Perhaps, however, he should have edited out the accounts of his (many!) love affairs.

Moonbeams, Dumplings & Dragon Boats: A Treasury of Chinese Holiday Tales, Activities and Recipes by Nina Simonds, Leslie Swartz and the Boston Children's Museum – The perfect resource for culturally inquisitive kids – and their parents – this lovely, illustrated book is jam-packed with myths that explain local festivals, with recipes (including mooncakes, just in case you wanted make you own) and activity suggestions. A wonderful gift for families new to Beijing.

USEFUL INFO

51 Xirongxian Hutong, Xidan, Xicheng District. (6603 8855) www.thechinaclubbeijing.com 西城区西单西绒线胡同51号

ChocoJing The chocolate appreciation society of Beijing meets about once a month to hold tastings, explore different types of chocolates and their origins, and in general have an excuse to gorge themselves silly.
www.iheartbeijing.com/chocojing.html

Commonwealth Society of Beijing (CWS) A charitable non-profit that meets every second Tuesday of the month. Membership fees are RMB 100, which go toward organizing charity fundraisers.
(sisneo@hotmail.com or tpbm@hotmail.com)

DramaQueens Offers drama "therapy" courses for creative souls looking to improve spontaneity and self-expression and relieve stress. Four-week introductory and intermediate courses in English and Chinese are RMB 600.
Contact Angela (139 1161 6884, beijing.dramaqueens@gmail.com) for English and Xiaogang (1381 113 7034) for Chinese.

FESCO International Training Center Provides Mandarin training and classes on topics ranging from Chinese knot-making to massage to Buddhism. Also helps foreigners with such things as hiring Chinese staff and obtaining a driver's license.
For more info, refer to Business & Work on p570 or Transportation on p523.

Foreign Correspondents Club of China (FCCC) The club for accredited foreign journalists and select hangers-on. Hosts speaker events, social gatherings and other activities.
(8532 3807) www.fccchina.org

Global Communicators Toastmasters Club Meets Wednesdays to help develop communication and leadership skills.
www.toastmasters.org.cn

International Festival Chorus (IFC) With singers from over 23 countries, the IFC annually holds three concerts of large-scale choral works at the Forbidden City Concert Hall. The IFC, which has sung in over seven languages, seeks to promote Western classical choral music in Beijing. New members are always welcome. Also has a children's choir and a chamber choir.
www.beijingifc.org

International Newcomers' Network (INN) A non-profit organization set up in 1994 to help expatriates settle into Beijing. Meetings are held at 10am on the last Monday of each month except December and are followed by lunch. Topics change monthly. All foreign passport-holders welcome. RMB 40 includes coffee/tea and pastries.
Function Rm, 3/F Athletic Centre, Capital Mansion, 6 Xinyuan Nanlu, Chaoyang District. (8486 2225 ext 110) www.innbeijing.org 朝阳区新源南路6号京я大厦康乐中心3层

International Vegetarian Club of Beijing Vegetarian information and restaurant listings in Chinese.
www.ivu.org/ivcb

Montrose Wine Club Monthly get-togethers to learn more about wine and food pairings.
1) Daily 11am-7.30pm. B1/F, 37 Kerry Centre Shopping Mall, 1 Guanghua Lu, Chaoyang District.

(8529 9494); 2) Daily 9.30am-9.30pm. China World Shopping Mall, 1 Jianguomenwai Dajie, Chaoyang District. (6505 1328) www.montrosechina.com 1) 朝阳区光华路1号嘉里中心商场地下1层B-37; 2) 朝阳区建国门外大街1号国贸商场（华云超市旁边）

Rotary Club of Beijing A cross-section of local businesses and professional leaders who come together to build lifelong friendships, promote high ethical standards and provide volunteer service. Meets Tuesdays at the Kempinski Hotel.
(6581 3668, rotarybj@vip.sina.com)
www.rotary3450.org/beijing

Teacher Development Forum (TDF) This forum offers free idea sharing and support for all teachers of English in China. Meets on the first three Mondays of the month at The Bookworm.
(6506 5108) www.tdf-esl.com

Foreign Culture Groups

American Community Club (ACC) A membership organization for AmCham members, their families and American citizens and permanent residents in Beijing. ACC seeks to provide ongoing support, information and social activities while helping to serve the local community.
Rm 1903, China Resources Bldg, 8 Jianguomen Beidajie. (8519 2363) www.amcham-china.org.cn/acc 建国门北大街8号华润大厦1903室

Australia and New Zealand Association ANZA provides opportunities for social support and networking for Australians and New Zealanders in Beijing.
www.anzabeijing.com

AustCham Kooka Networking Connect with the Australian community in Beijing at their meetings every Thursday evening at 6:30pm.
www.austcham.org

Beijing American Club Private club for international business executives and their families. Business, social and recreational facilities and activities.
(8519 2888) www.americanclubbeijing.com

Black Beijing Founded by African-Americans, this informal organization aims to join together people throughout the African diaspora.
(african_americans_beijing@yahoo.com)

British Club of Beijing Coffee meetings on alternate Tuesdays from 10am to noon with interesting speakers. All foreign passport-holders welcome (coffee RMB 20 for members, RMB 40 otherwise). Membership RMB 100 per year. The Capital Club has a dress code of no jeans or sneakers.
50/F Capital Mansions, 6 Xinyuan Nanlu, Chaoyang District. www.britclubbj.org 朝阳区新源南路6号京城大厦

Canadians in China www.canadiansinchina.com

Caribbean Association in China This non-profit group provides a support network for the Caribbean community in China. Through island-flavored social events open to anyone interested in the Caribbean, the association fosters a stronger understanding and appreciation of the region's culture.
(caribbean.association.china@gmail.com)

A hot and spicy gent? Must be Canada Day in Beijing

Club Canada A Canadian social club that helps to ease the transition for new arrivals and organizes social and leisure events.
www.clubcanada.net

French Cultural Centre A public library, reading club, movie theater and cafe, the French Cultural Centre also offers French language classes. Library membership (RMB 200 per year) gives you unlimited access to over 20,000 French books, CDs and DVDs.
6 Gongti Xilu, Chaoyang District. (6553 2627) www.ccfpekin.org 法国文化中心，朝阳区工体西路16号

Goethe Institute This prestigious German organization, with a staff of native speakers and professionally trained Chinese teachers, holds German courses all week. Their library collection – free and open to the public – includes over 10,000 mostly German books and multimedia. A library card costs RMB 200 per year, students RMB 100.
17/F, Bldg B, Cyber (Shuma) Tower, 2 Zhongguancun Nandajie, Haidian District. (8251 2909) www.goethe.de/peking 歌德学院，海淀区中关村南大街2号数码大厦B座17层

Indonesians in China
(beijingsindonesiangroup@yahoo.com)

Instituto Cervantes Organizes Spanish language classes and cultural events.
1A Gongti Nanlu, Chaoyang District. (5879 9666) http://pekin.cervantes.es 北京塞万提斯学院，朝阳区工体南路甲1号

Irish Beijing Community Noticeboard
www.irishbeijing.org

Italian Women's Association A non-profit, non-denominational, non-political association. The group meets on the first Thursday of every month at 10.30am at the Cultural Institute of the Italian Embassy.
Contact the Italian Embassy for details.

Nederlandse Vereniging Peking Dutch-speaking community group that meets on the second Saturday of every month. Includes free Bitterballen.
www.dragondancers.com.cn/nvp.html

Nordic Club of China Social group for Danes, Icelanders, Finns, Norwegians and Swedes.
www.prc.nu/nordicclub

Overseas Chinese Network Welcomes people born or raised outside of mainland China and their friends and relatives.
www.ocnetwork.org

PHOTO: SIMON LIM

USEFUL INFO

Dreaming of blue skies for queer people

Polish Community Polish Happy Hours on the last Friday of the month, cultural exhibitions, receptions and more.
Renata and Iwona (139 0116 8244; renatainokomis@yahoo.com, wir_3@yahoo.com)

St. David's Society of Beijing Network for the Welsh and friends of Wales. Meets every last Friday of the month at The Pavillion and also hosts annual events like St. David's Day, a Christmas party and rugby games.
(8532 3088) www.stdavidschina.org

SWEA Beijing Organizes social activities for Swedish-speaking women in China.
www.swea.org

UFE-Union des Français de l'Etranger Welcomes newcomers to Beijing and organizes regular large events among the French community.
www.ufechine.com

Zhong Breizh A non-profit association of Bretons and friends dedicated to promoting Brittany in Beijing. They meet every two months and hold a Candlemass dinner and a Fest-Noz celebration.
(zhongbreizh@hotmail.com)
http://zhongbreizh.spaces.live.com

GLBTQ Resources

Beijing ain't a bad place to be gay, particularly as a *laowai*. Don't expect rainbow flags flying over Tian'anmen any time soon, but hateful homophobia is all but unheard of, and aside from the rare story about someone getting fleeced by a "money boy," the gay community itself is very friendly to outsiders. Incidentally, it's also one of the few places in the world where a same-sex couple can walk down the street, hand in hand, without turning heads.

Of course, traditional values persist, and many gay and lesbian Chinese stay closeted to all but a few: Non-discrimination law has yet to protect alternative sexualities, so most people choose not to come out to their employers. A large number of Chinese GLBTQ eventually marry to maintain a relationship with their parents. Most successful Chinese gay activist groups stay non-political, generally as public health and HIV/AIDS prevention organizations.

For queer Chinese and *laowai* alike who want to connect with the community beyond the clubs (p311), the Internet is the place to start. Proficient Chinese readers should check out the many gay- and lesbian-themed blogs, message boards, information and links listings – just do a search for any of the terms on p638. Several English-language email lists have up-to-date information about the gay scene in Beijing and Asia.

PHOTO: TOM CARTER

Aibai and ICCGL The Aibai Culture & Education Center (ACEC) and Los Angeles-based Information Clearinghouse for Chinese Gays and Lesbians (ICCGL) do extensive community service, mostly focused on AIDS/HIV awareness, civil rights and education about safe sex. Their website and forum have a vast collection of up-to-date news, information and resources.
Aibai: (6496 8273) www.aibai.cn, www.gaychinese. net **ICCGL:** *www.iccgl.org*

BGLAD (Beijing Gay, Lesbian and Allies Discussion) This should be a Beijing rookie's first stop for an intro to the local scene. Multicultural and multisexual, they aim to bring the queer community together in a supportive, friendly and fun safe space. Hosts a queer-friendly night every Sunday at Houhai Zoo and occasional queer movie and dinner meetings.
http://groups.yahoo.com/group/BGLAD

Common Language (Tongyu) Hosts a popular Saturday afternoon salon (2-6pm) for Chinese-speaking lesbians at Le Jazz, with a discussion or lecture beginning around 4pm. Tongyu runs a hotline (8618 1549, 8641 0745) and often joins forces with Aibai to provide legal and health information to the queer community and increase support for gay rights among the general public.
Tongyu: (8629 0507, tongyulala@gmail.com) www. lalabar.com **Lala Salon:** *Le Jazz, 4/F, FullLink Plaza, 18 Chaoyangmenwai Dajie. (135 0139 0576)* 同语拉拉沙龙，朝阳区朝阳门外大街18号丰联广场4层乐杰士酒吧

proMen A social network for "English-speaking gay professionals who are tired of weekend clubbing." Their Thursday happy hours at Zeta Bar, with drink specials until midnight, draw over one hundred attendees.
http://groups.yahoo.com/group/promen

Other resources

Beijing's Other Attractions Throws some queer-friendly events in town, including San Francisco Sundays (see BGLAD, above).
www.boaevents.com

Fridae A weekly e-newsletter with essays and newsbytes of interest to the gay and lesbian community in Asia.
www.fridae.com

Go Pink China Gay tour group service.
www.gopinkchina.com

Tongzhi Studies Academic research and exchange program working on gender and sexuality issues in Chinese-speaking communities around the world. Based in New York.
www.tongzhistudies.org

Utopia Asia Up-to-date info about gay and lesbian venues in many Asian cities, including Beijing.
www.utopia-asia.com

Environmental & Humanitarian Groups

Beijing Cultural Heritage Protection Center (CHP) This private non-profit aims to raise awareness, organization, strategy, education and skill levels of communities trying to protect ancient relics and sites. A project between CHP and *that's Beijing*, the Friends of Old Beijing program has volunteers who patrol neighborhoods slated for conservation.
Bailin Temple, 1 Xilou Hutong, Yonghegong Dajie, Dongcheng District. (6403 4932, heritage destruction hotline 6176 8040) www.bjchp.org 北京文化遗产保护中心，东城区雍和宫大街戏楼胡同1号（柏林寺内西长廊）

Beijing Horizon Educational Center (BHEC) BHEC seeks to promote fair development in education by providing resources and training for teachers in underprivileged areas and by teaching arts to children of migrant workers in Beijing.
(6348 0852, ty6962@sina.com)

Beijing Huiling A community-based non-profit, Huiling provides the mentally disabled a safe place to learn, grow, socialize and support themselves. Volunteers welcome. Visitors are welcome to visit Huiling's traditional courtyard.
31 Dashizuo Hutong, Jingshan Qianjie, Xicheng District. (6404 6631) www.huiling-bj.org 慧灵智障人士社区服务机构，西城区景山前街大石作胡同31号

Beijing Human and Animal Environmental Education Center (BHAEEC) This private shelter rescues mistreated animals and finds them new homes. Volunteers help take care of the animals and follow-up on adoptions, among other tasks.
West of the Aviation Museum in Xiaotangshan Town, Changping District. Xue Mei (5129 8676, English) or Mrs. Bai (133 8131 3120, Chinese) www.animalschina. org 北京人与动物环保科普中心，昌平区小汤山镇

Chi Heng Foundation CHF provides education and support for AIDS orphans in central China and promotes AIDS awareness across the country.
Rm 801, Bldg 6, Wanda Plaza, 93 Jianguo Lu, Chaoyang District. (5820 8559) www.chiheng.org 智行基金会，朝阳区建国路93号万达广场6楼801

China Charity Federation A network of non-governmental charity organizations working in China.
Xinlong Mansion, 33A Erlong Lu, Xicheng District. (6605 5845) www.chinacharity.cn 中华慈善总会，西城区二龙路甲33号新龙大厦

Children's Art Initiative (CAI) CAI aims to enrich the lives of the children of rural migrant laborers through a 10-day summer art camp. The organization is volunteer-run, comprised of professionals, artists, art teachers and university students, and is always looking for new volunteers.
Steve Hwang (139 1106 8400)
www.childrensartinitiative.org 儿童才艺行动

China Environment and Sustainable Development Reference and Research Center China's largest public-sector library and information center dedicated to environment and sustainable development. The center's mission is to make environmental knowledge accessible to the general public. They organize regular talks and movie screenings.
Rm 701, China-Japan Friendship Environmental Protection Center, 1 Yuhui Nanlu, Chaoyang District. (8465 0856) www.chinaeol.net/cesdrrc 中国环境与可持续发展资料研究中心，朝阳区育慧南路1号，中日友好环境保护中心701室

Chinese Association for NGO Cooperation (CANGO) Seeks to create a network of Chinese NGOs while serv-
Continues on p640

Let's Talk About (Same-Sex) Love
A Mandarin-Gaylese phrasebook
by Haley Warden

Ready to come out?

INSIDER'S GUIDE TO BEIJING

On the brink of a much more accepting era, China's queer folks are opening up new modes of expression, such as social groups, an online Beijing-based talk show and China's first gay-themed student group. Beijing is a remarkable place to see first-hand how China's gays and lesbians are finding their feet (and each other). But if you want to join in on the GLBTQ (socially moderate and entirely un-political) revolution, you'll have to brush up on your Gaylese.

A Gay Old Time

同性恋 **(tong2xing4lian4)**: "Same-sex love," a textbook word for homosexuality or a homosexual person. "Gay" and "les" are used in Chinese as well.

同志 **(tong2zhi4)**: "Comrade" or "same ambition/will" is used today as a colloquial term of address for all GLBTQ, but during the Communist period everyone was a dutiful comrade of the revolution.

酷儿**(ku'er)**: Literally "cool-er," this splendid transliteration of "queer" is a brand-new term.

拉拉 **(lala) and** 拉子**(lazi)**: A colloquial umbrella term for "women who love women," encompassing lesbians of all persuasions as well as bisexual women. There's debate about whether this comes from the nickname of the main character, Lazi, in a Taiwanese lesbian novel, *The Crocodile's Journal*, or if it's just a transliteration of "lesbian."

双性恋 **(shuang1xing4lian4)**: Bisexual

异性恋**(yi4xing4lian4)**: Straight, heterosexual

Rock and Role

"419" (si4yao1jiu3): Originally from the English "4 1 night," Chinese Internet slang for "have a one night stand."

"1" (yao1): For gay men, "top" or dominant role

"0" (ling2): For gay men, "bottom," receiving or non-dominant role

"P": Femme, or female role in a lesbian couple, from *po*, which means wife. (Gender roles are quite fixed in the Chinese lesbian community.) Generally very girly, the young ones often have super-permed '80s rocker hair and lots of makeup. "P" is a noun and "PP" is an adjective (e.g. "really femme/pretty" is "*hen* PP").

"T": Butch, from the English word "tomboy." The male-role counterpart to P, Ts almost exclusively have short hair and dress in men's clothing. Called *lao gong*, "husband," when in a committed relationship with a P. Some Ts identify with the male gender.

不分 **(bu4fen1)**: "Not divided," for those who don't assign themselves a defined "role." Chinese *lala*s usually expect that foreign women *bufen*, but they'll still ask.

Mars, Venus, and … Menus

跨性别者**(kua4xing4bie2zhe3)** Literally "one who straddles genders." Still a new concept in the Chinese queer community, this word indicates anyone who transcends traditional gender boundaries, e.g. transgender, transsexual, androgynous, transvestite, intersex, people who have changed their biological sex through surgery, and everyone else I'm forgetting, like that dude in *The L-word* who thinks he's a male lesbian.

反串**(fan3chuan4)** Transvestite

变装皇后／国王**(bian4zhuang1 huang2hou4/guo2wang2)** Drag Queen (King)

阴阳人 **yin1yang2ren2** Intersex (one born with a combination of male and female sex organs). Yin-yang, which Westerners recognize as the black and white circular swirl, represents a harmonious balance of masculine and feminine energy. Deep.

中性 **(zhong1xing4)** "Middle gender" or "neutral," a non-derogatory adjective that usually describes a tomboyish woman or a feminine man. The midpoint between feminine and masculine, *zhongxing* refers more to style and behavior and does not imply homosexual or transgendered identity.

ing as a bridge with foreign organizations working for poverty alleviation, environmental protection and social development.
Rm 601, Bldg C, Yonghe Dasha, 28 Andingmen Dongdajie, Dongcheng District. (6409 7888) www.cango.org 中国国际民间组织合作促进会，东城区安定门东大街28号，雍和大厦东楼C座601室

Chinese Juvenile Rights Protection Center Volunteer lawyers offer free legal aid to children around China, and the organization plays an active role in legislation regarding children.
4/F, Annex Bldg, 212 Zhouzhuangzi, Fengbei Lu, Fengtai District. (6381 3995) www.chinachild.org 中国青少年维权中心，丰台区丰北路周庄子212号附属楼4层

Compassion for Migrant Children (CMC) Provides educational and social assistance (such as counseling) to the children of migrant workers and their families. See website for volunteer and internship opportunities.
Office 233, Xintai Bldg, 8 Xiaguang Li, Chaoyang District. (6465 6100) www.cmc-china.org 打工子弟爱心会，朝阳区霞光里8号鑫泰大厦233室

The Culture Development Center for Rural Women Seeks to provide women information and skills to improve their chances of escaping poverty. The group runs the Practical Skills Training Center for Rural Women, which also draws attention to issues of gender and citizen awareness. Welcomes volunteers.
Rm 301, Bldg A, Jiali Mansion, 180 Beiyuan Lu, Chaoyang District. (6498 3764, njnbst@263.net) www.nongjianv.org 农家女文化发展中心，朝阳区北苑路180号加利大厦A座301室

Friends of Nature FON promotes environmental protection and sustainable development through education and advocacy, and welcomes volunteers.
Rm 368, Wanbo Bldg, 53 Ganyu Hutong, Dongcheng District. (6523 2040) www.fon.org.cn 自然之友，东城区甘雨胡同53号万博写字楼368室

Global Village Beijing Works to educate and raise awareness of environmental issues, sustainable development and eco-tourism. They also publish a newsletter and try to change behavior at a local level.
Rm 301, Bldg C, Huazhan International Apartments, 12 Yumin Lu, Chaoyang District. (8225 2046) www.gvbchina.org 北京地球村环境文化中心，朝阳区裕民路12号华展国际公寓C座301室

Hua Dan Project Works with migrant workers in participatory theater workshops that foster creativity and develop leadership skills and self-awareness. Hua Dan stages performances and holds performance workshops on Sunday evenings. Volunteers needed.
www.hua-dan.org 花旦

Jane Goodall Institute The institute's hands-on environmental and humanitarian education programs encourage students to organize and participate in community activities for conservation, sustainable development and animal protection.
Rm 1309, Beijing City International School, 77 Baiziwan Nanerlu, Chaoyang District. (6778 3115) www.jgichina.org 珍古道尔环境文化交流中心，朝阳区百子湾南二路77号北京乐成国际学校1309室

Lifeline Express Started by Hong Kong donors, Lifeline Express is a mobile eye hospital that provides free operations for people from poverty-stricken areas. Also runs training centers for local doctors and welcomes volunteers.
Rm A609, 6/F Nanxincang Business World, 22A Dongsi Shitiao, Dongcheng District. (5169 0999) www.lifeline-express.com 东城区东四十条甲22号南新仓国际大厦6层A609

Magic Hospital Designs and implements entertainment programs for sick, neglected, orphaned and abused children. They visit hospitals and orphanages to put on performances and organize games and activities to bring excitement and fun into the children's lives.
1402 Xingfuyuan Apartments, 6 Gongti Beilu, Chaoyang District. www.magichospital.org 妙妙乐园，朝阳区幸福一村西里16号幸福公寓1402室

Maple Women's Psychological Counseling Center This non-government organization aims to combat domestic violence, particularly among the poorer segments of society. Their hotline provides psychological, legal and social counseling to women in need. They also research women's issues.
Rm 104, Bldg 3, Wanboyuan, 72 You'anmen Neidajie, Xuanwu District. (8354 8050, hotline 6403 3383) www.maple.org.cn 红枫，宣武区右安门内大街72号万博苑小区3号楼104室

Operation Blessing Beijing This organization improves education, funds tuition, and provides surgeries and rehabilitation for orphans, disabled children, children of migrant laborers, and the elderly.
Rm 106, Golden Land Bldg, 32 Liangmaqiao Lu, Chaoyang District. (6466 9296) www.obchina.org 博恩组，朝阳区亮马桥路32号高斓大厦106室

Planet Finance Planet Finance is a French organization working on microfinance, farmer training and poverty alleviation in China.
Rm 2508, MOMA Bldg 5, Xiangheyuan Lu, Dongcheng District. (8440 8458) www.pfchina.org 沛丰，东城区香河园路当代万国城5号楼2508室

Prevention Through Education (PTE) This NGO develops local school-based HIV/AIDS education and prevention programs.
www.pte-china.org

Red Cross Society of China *8 Beixinqiao Santiao, Dongcheng District. (8402 5890) www.redcross.org.cn* 中国红十字会，东城区北新桥三条8号

Salvation Army The organization has been developing poverty alleviation projects in China since the early 1990s. Accepts volunteers and donations of used clothing.
Rm 102, Unit D, Shemao Apt. 2 Guanghuali, Chaoyang District. (6586 9331) www.salvation.org.hk 救世军，朝阳区光华里2号舍贸公寓D门102

Sun Village This NGO brings together children of prison inmates in a village where they live, play and grow up in a safe and healthy environment, receive care, therapy and education, and avoid social stigmatization.
Banqiao Village, Zhaoquanying, Shunyi District. Zhang Shuqin (6044 3757) www.sunvillage.com.cn 太阳村，顺义区赵泉营镇板桥村

UNICEF Works to support children's rights and the provision of basic services, such as health care, education, immunization, sanitation and hygiene and access to clean water.

Humanitarian groups like Compassion for Migrant Children help open up a world of knowledge

12 Sanlitun Lu, Chaoyang District. (6532 3131) www.unicef.org/china 联合国儿童基金会，朝阳区三里屯路12号

WWF One of the world's leading environmental organizations, the WWF (formerly known as the World Wildlife Fund) is working on projects to preserve and protect China's vast and diverse environmental resources and treasures. Sign up to volunteer online. *1609 Wenhua Gong (inside east gate of Beijing Working People's Culture Palace), Dongcheng District. (6522 7100 ext 3271) www.wwfchina.org* 世界自然基金会北京办事处，劳动人民文化宫东门内文华宫

Xiao Xiao Niao (Little Bird) This 24-hour helpline is run by migrant workers for migrant workers. This "mutual assistance" program also organizes forums and community outreach activities. New arrivals to the city can call for general advice and have their questions answered by trained migrant volunteers.

BA 318, Northern Jiayuan Hotel, 218-1 Wangfujing Dajie, Dongcheng District. (6851 5323, 139 1050 6125) www.xiaoxiaoniao.org.cn 小小鸟，东城区王府井大街218-1号北方佳苑饭店写字间BA318室

Religious Services
Buddhist

It's not easy being Buddhist. Any student of the dharma in search of a temple or a *sangha* will likely be confronted by throngs of tourists and counterfeit Fuwas outside the door. Still, for those willing to brave these trials, active temples exist, as well as many smaller temples off the tourist beat. The Lama Temple and Baita Temple are major Tibetan Buddhism sites, and Guanghua and Fayuan are Chinese Buddhist temples.

Within the gates of Niu Jie Mosque: the handsome road to heaven

Most temples hold major ceremonies on the first and fifteenth of each lunar month. For those annoyed at "spiritual" kitsch and noisy *youke*, just remember, that's dukka. Now get over it.

Guangji Temple Though somewhat overshadowed by neighboring Baita Temple, Guangji boasts some serious credentials as the headquarters of the Chinese Buddhist Association. In the two beautiful tree-filled courtyards, worshippers and monks kneel side-by-side in prayer. The relatively new temple halls, rebuilt after a huge fire in 1934, are closed to the public. Although there is a guest center, this active temple is comfortably free from tourists and maintains the austerity of a place of worship. Somber does not imply silent, though, as the sound of prayer bells, chanting and even faint street noise drifts through the air. Several friendly Buddhist shops next door sell incense, books, CDs and statues. *Daily 8am-4.30pm, guest center 9-11:30am and 2-3:50pm. Free. Xisi, Fuchengmennei Dajie, Xicheng District. (6616 0907)* 广济寺，西城区西四阜成门内大街 *For other listings and contact information, see the Sightseeing chapter.*

Jewish

Chabad Lubavitch of Beijing The Rohr Family Chabad Community Centre hosts all events (classes, activities, Bar and Bat Mitzvah lessons, youth activities, holiday programs and activities, etc.) and is home to a Hebrew school, the Ganeinu International School (ages 1.5-12), a Kosher store, a mikvah, and the Chabad offices. The Chabad House offers Orthodox Shabbat services and meals at sunset on Friday and 11am on Saturdays. The Chabad Yabaolu primarily serves the Russian community and downtown Beijing, hosting Shabbat services and meals.

1) Community Centre, 262 J, Grand Hills, Jingshun Lu, Chaoyang District. (8470 8239); 2) Chabad House, D5A Kings Garden Villa (Jingrun Shuishang Huayuan), 18 Xiaoyun Lu, Chaoyang District. (8470 8236, 139 1065 0642); 3) Chabad Yabaolu, Rm 906, 9/F, Asia Pacific Bldg, 8 Yabao Lu, Chaoyang District. (133 6670 1744) www.chabadbeijing.com 1) Community Centre, 朝阳区京顺路大湖山庄262 J号； 2) Chabad House, 朝阳区霄云路18号京润水上花园D5A号； 3) Chabad Yabaolu, 朝阳区雅宝路8号亚太大厦9层906室

Kehillat Beijing Members are predominantly Conservative, Reform or Reconstructionist, but this lay-led, egalitarian Jewish congregation welcomes all Jews to its services on Fridays at 7pm. RSVP for the community dinners afterwards at 8pm. Also runs weekly discussions. *3/F Ballroom, Capital Club Athletic Center, Capital Mansion, 6 Xinyuan Nanli, Chaoyang District. (6467 2225) www.sinogogue.org* 朝阳区新源南里6号京城大厦京城俱乐部健身中心3层宴会厅

Muslim

Non-Muslim visitors may have to make arrangements in advance and are usually not permitted to attend prayer and services. Call for exact prayer times, as they change with the times of sunrise and sunset.

Niujie Mosque The oldest and largest mosque in Beijing, this is also the most popular. *88 Niu Jie, Xuanwu District. (6353 2564)* 牛街清真寺，宣武区牛街88号

Dongsi Mosque The city's second largest mosque is the headquarters of the Beijing branch of the China Islamic

Association and houses valuable Islamic manuscripts in its library.
13 Dongsi Nandajie, Dongcheng District. (6525 7824) 东四清真寺，东城区东四南大街13号

Nan Douya Mosque Located in a beautiful Chinese-style building near the Chaoyangmen subway station.
4 Douban Hutong, Dongcheng District. (8406 8225) 南豆芽清真寺，东城区豆瓣胡同4号

Xiapo Mosque *129 Chaoyangmenwai Ertiao (about 1km south of FullLink Plaza), Chaoyang District.* **(8562 6316)** 下坡礼拜寺，朝阳区朝外二条129号（丰联广场向南1公里）

Christian
Catholic
Aside from the churches listed below, the British Embassy holds services Sunday at 10am and the Canadian Embassy holds services Saturday at 5.30pm. Note: Catholic churches in Beijing are officially independent from the Roman Catholic Church.

North Church (Xishiku) The largest and one of the most beautiful churches in Beijing, Xishiku is obscurely located on the bend of a small road north of Xi'anmen Dajie, west of Beihai Park. All services in Chinese.
Service hours: Mon-Sat 6, 7am; Sun 6, 7, 8, 10am, 6pm. 33 Xishiku Dajie, Xicheng District. (6617 5198) 西什库天主教堂，西城区西什库大街33号

St. Joseph's (East Church – Dongtang) Originally built in 1655, this centrally located cathedral offers services in Chinese and Latin for Chinese citizens and foreigners.
Service hours: Mon-Sat 6.30, 7am; Sun 6:15 (Latin), 7, 8am. 74 Wangfujing Dajie, Dongcheng District. (6524 0634) 东堂，东城区王府井大街74号

St. Michael's (Dongjiaomin Church) Built in 1902 as the French embassy church in the foreign Legation Quarter, St. Michael's now welcomes Chinese and foreigners to its Chinese-language service.
Service hours: Sun 7, 8am, 6pm. 13A Dongjiaomin Xiang, Dongcheng District. Contact Father Gao Yang (8511 5405, 137 0130 5933) 东交民巷天主教堂，东城区东交民巷甲13号

Xuanwumen Church (South Church – Nantang) Also known as the Cathedral of the Immaculate Conception, the oldest Catholic Church in Beijing is currently the Diocesan Cathedral.
Service hours: Sun 6, 7, 8.30, 10am (English), 4pm (English). 141 Qianmen Xidajie (at the Xuanwumen subway station), Xicheng District. (6602 6368) 宣武门教堂，西城区前门西大街141号

West Church (Xizhimen) Also known as the Church of Our Lady of Mt. Carmel, the newest and yet least well-kept of the four cardinally named churches.
Service hours: Sun 8am (Chinese). 130 Xizhimennei Dajie, Xicheng District. (6615 6319) 西堂，西城区西直门内大街130号

Mormon
The Church of Jesus Christ of Latter Day Saints Foreign passport-holders only. A separate branch for Chinese citizens meets in the afternoon.
Service hours: Sunday 9.30am-12.30pm. 4/F, Golden Tower (Jintai Dasha), Hepingli Beijie (near the Liu-fang light rail station), Chaoyang District. 朝阳区和平里北街金泰大厦4层

Orthodox
The Russian Embassy (p648) holds Orthodox services.

Protestant
Beijing Baptist Church Foreign passport holders only. Also holds a Sunday school at 10am.
Service hours: Sun 11am, 5.30pm. 3/F, CTS Plaza (Zhonglü Dasha), 2 Beisanhuan Donglu, Chaoyang District. Pastor Laterza (6474 1869) 北京浸礼会，朝阳区北三环东路2号中旅大厦3层

Chongwenmen Church (Ashbury Methodist) Originally built in 1870, the first American Methodist church and the largest existing Protestant church in Beijing holds services in Chinese with English translations.
Service hours: Sun 8, 10:30am. 2 Hougou Hutong, 4 Chongwenmen Neidajie (near Chongwenmen subway station), Dongcheng District. (6513 3549, 6522 9984) 亚斯立堂，东城区崇文门内大街4号后沟胡同丁2号

Beijing International Christian Fellowship Multicultural, Bible-centered, interdenominational gatherings for foreign passport-holders. Services translated from English into five languages. Offers Sunday services, classes, various ministries and a counseling center.
1) Services Sun 9.30am (bilingual), 11:30am (English). Rm 220, 21st Century Theatre, 40 Liangmaqiao Lu, Chaoyang District. (8454 3468, 139 0110 4943); 2) Services Sun 10am. 2/F, Tower 1, Alexander City Club Banquet Hall, 6 Chaowai Dajie, Chaoyang District. (159 0127 5352); 3) Services Sun 9, 11am. B/F auditorium, Raycom Bldg C, 2 Kexueyuan Nanlu, Zhongguancun, Haidian District. (8286 2813) www.bicf.org 1) 朝阳区亮马桥路40号二十一世纪剧场220室 2) 朝阳区朝外大街6号新城国际1座亚力山大会馆2层 3) 海淀区中关村科学院南路2号融科资讯中心C座地下

Capital Community Church A warm international and interdenominational church gathering for foreign passport-holders. Classes at 9.30am for all ages during the school year.
Service hours: Sun 10.45am. B/F, Yosemite Clubhouse, 4 Yuyang Lu, Houshayu Zhen, Shunyi District. (8046 4796, 136 1100 5842) 顺义区后沙峪镇榆阳路4号优山美地俱乐部

Congregation of the Good Shepherd Interdenominational congregation with traditional liturgical worship. Foreign passport-holders only.
Service hours: Sun 10am. 3/F Capital Mansions Athletic Center, 6 Xinyuan Nanlu, Chaoyang District. (8453 1139, 135 2200 1229) www.goodshepherdcongregation.com 朝阳区新源南路6号京城大厦俱乐部3层

The River of Grace A church emphasizing relationships, compassion and service. Has a Sunday school. Foreign passport-holders only.
Service hours: Sun 10am. 2/F, The Great Hotel, 1 Zuojiazhuang Lu (behind CTS Plaza at Sanyuan Qiao), Chaoyang District. (131 2690 5684, 6466 1680) www.theriverofgrace.com 朝阳区左家庄路1号贵国酒店2层（三元桥中旅大厦南边）

From cardboard boxes to unneeded money bags, your junk is always useful to someone

Support Groups

Alcoholics Anonymous Meetings in English morning and evening daily. Meetings in Chinese evenings Mon-Thu and Sat.
*Rm 1026, 10/F, Bldg A, 40 Dongzhong Jie, Dongcheng District. (hotline 139 1138 9275) www.aabeijing.com
东城区东中街40号A座10层1026室*

Beijing Hemophiliac Group Provides resources (some in English) and organizes occasional activities.
(6876 1757, 133 9181 9237) www.xueyou.org

Families with Children from China Network of foreign families who have adopted or seek to adopt orphans in China.
(fccbeijing@gmail.com, janeliedtke@yahoo.com)

Hongshulin China's first grassroots organization for those diagnosed with HIV, Hongshulin not only provides patients with resources and support but also works to increase understanding of AIDS and HIV in China. Subscribe to their private newsletter for meetings.
(6329 6183) www.chain.net.cn

La Leche League Support for breastfeeding mothers and babies. Meets on the fourth Friday of each month at 1pm in the Beijing United Family Hospital Yurt. French- and Chinese-speaking groups also available.
Serena Johnson (xiaohua68847@yahoo.com)

Our Chinese Daughters Foundation OCDF is a non-profit organization servicing families during and after the adoptive process. They also support orphanages and run language- and culture-focused tours to help adopted children connect with their native culture.
(8403 4979) www.ocdf.org

Selective Mutism Virtual Support Network (SMVSN) Does your child have difficulty talking in social settings or at school? Do they lack social skills? Do you consider them extremely shy? Your child may have an anxiety disorder called selective mutism. SMVSN offers professional contacts in China and abroad and provides resources to educate parents and teachers.
*(135 2199 1703)
www.selectivemutismchina.gmxhome.de*

Practical Information Directory
Donations

Visit www.npo.org.cn for a list of non-profit organizations that accept donations.

Badachu For the dharmically inclined, these temples in the Fragrant Hills will accept donations, including clothes.
See Excursions, p555, for contact information.

China Charity Federation
See Environmental and Humanitarian Groups, p637.

Moving Mountains Moving Mountains organizes charity events and sporadic donation drives. Contributions go toward improving the lives of young people and rural families, increasing and enhancing educational opportunities, assisting people with medical problems, protecting the environment and aiding disaster relief efforts.
www.thedonationcenter.org

Operation Blessing Beijing *See Environmental and Humanitarian Groups, p637.*

Red Cross Society of China *See Environmental and Humanitarian Groups, p637.*

Beijing Donation Centers
The city government runs a network of charitable donation centers, which accept everything from used clothing to old computers and cash. Goods are donated to disaster areas in Jiangxi and Inner Mongolia. (6356 2755, Chinese only) http://bjjz.bjmzj.gov.cn

Dongcheng District: 32 Dongsi Shisantiao. (6402 1629 or 6402 1638)
Xicheng District: 16 Gaojing Hutong, Xizhimen Neidajie. (6227 4355)
Chongwen District: 2 Peixinjie. (6716 2676)
Xuanwu District: 18 Chongxiao Hutong, Baiguang Lu. (6355 6360)
Chaoyang District: Aux. Bldg 6, Daojian Yuan. (6530 1151)
Haidian District: 15 Xiyuancaochang. (6262 5347)
Shunyi District: Xinshunyi Dajie. (6944 5221)

Dry Cleaning & Carpet Cleaning

Chemdry Specializes in carpet cleaning.
Mon-Fri 9am-6pm, Sat-Sun variable. 400A, Lido Commercial Bldg, Jiangtai Lu, Chaoyang District. (6436 2846) 肯洁干洗，朝阳区将台路丽都商务楼400A

Fornet For more outlets, visit www.fornet.com.cn
Daily 8am-8pm. Section A, Bldg H, Just Make Mansion, Xingfucun Zhonglu, Chaoyang District. (6417 7767) 福奈特，朝阳区幸福村中路杰作大厦H座A段

Ilsa Locations at Tuanjiehu, Shuangjing, Zhongguancun and more. See www.chinawashing.com/map
Daily 8.30am-9.30pm. Rm 109, Bldg C, Phoenix City, Sanyuan Qiao, Chaoyang District. 伊尔萨，朝阳区三元桥凤凰城C座109室

Pride The *laozihao* of dry cleaning, Pride opened in 1927 in Shanghai. See www.pld1927.com
Daily 8am-10pm. A101, Bldg 8, Dushi Xinyuan, Chongwen District. (6705 4816) 普兰德，崇文区都市馨园8号楼101室

Embassies

If your embassy has moved, or you can't find it in the list below, this website has an up-to-date list of all the embassies in Beijing: www.travelchinaguide.com/embassy/foreign/beijing

Australia *Mon-Fri 8.30am-4.55pm. 21 Dongzhimenwai Dajie, Chaoyang District. (5140 4111) www.austemb.org.cn* 澳大利亚大使馆，朝阳区东直门外大街21号

Austria *Mon-Fri 9am-5pm. 5 Xiushui Nanjie, Chaoyang District. (6532 2061) www.aussenministerium.at/peking* 奥地利大使馆，朝阳区秀水南街5号

Bangladesh *42 Guanghua Lu, Chaoyang District. (6532 2521) www.bangladeshembassy.com.cn/em* 孟加拉国大使馆，朝阳区光华路42号

Belgium *Embassy: Mon-Fri 8.30am-12.30pm and 2-5pm. 6 Sanlitun Lu, Chaoyang District. (6532 1736) Visa section: Mon-Fri 8.30am-2.30pm. Rm A-F, 10/F, Oriental Kenzo Plaza, 48 Dongzhimenwai Dajie, Dongcheng District. (8447 6235) www.diplomatie.be/beijing* 比利时大使馆，朝阳区三里屯路6号。比利时签证处，东城区东直门外大街48号东方银座10层A-F室

Canada *Embassy: Mon-Fri 8am-noon and 1-4.30pm. Consular section: Mon-Thu 9-11am and 1.30-3pm, Fri 9am-noon. Visa section: Mon-Thu 8.15-11am and 1-3pm. 19 Dongzhimenwai Dajie, Chaoyang District. (6532 3536) www.beijing.gc.ca* 加拿大大使馆，朝阳区东直门外大街19号

Czech Republic *Embassy: Mon-Fri 8am-4.30pm. Consular section: Mon-Thu 8.30-11am. 2 Ritan Lu, Chaoyang District. (8532 9500) www.mfa.cz/beijing* 捷克共和国大使馆，朝阳区日坛路2号

Denmark *Mon-Fri 9am-5pm. 1 Sanlitun Dongwu Jie, Chaoyang District. (8532 9900) www.ambbeijing.um.dk* 丹麦大使馆，朝阳区三里屯东五街1号

Finland *Embassy: Mon-Fri 8.30am-noon and 1-4.45pm. Visa section: Mon-Fri 9-11.30am. 26/F South Tower, Kerry Centre, 1 Guanghua Lu, Chaoyang District. (8519 8300) www.finland.cn* 芬兰大使馆，朝阳区光华路1号嘉里中心南楼26层

France *Mon-Fri 8.30am-noon, 2-5.45pm. 3 Sanlitun Dongsan Jie, Chaoyang District. (8532 8080) www.ambafrance-cn.org* 法国大使馆，朝阳区三里屯东三街3号

Germany *Mon 8am-noon, 1-5pm; Tue-Thu 8am-noon, 1-5.30pm; Fri 8am-noon, 12.30-5pm. 17 Dongzhimenwai Dajie, Chaoyang District. (8532 9000) www.deutschebotschaft-china.org* 德国大使馆，朝阳区东直门外大街17号

Continues on p648

USEFUL INFO

The Attack of the 50-Foot Megastar!!!
Beijing's ten most ubiquitous personalities
by Lee Ambrozy

You see them in countless roadside adverts, magazine covers, television interviews and on giant LCD screens around Beijing. You can feel their presence in the air, hear their voices everywhere. But who are they? Where do they come from? And what do they want!?

Ai Weiwei   Google Index: 121,000

Ai Weiwei's career took off on the mainland after a homecoming from a ten-year stint in NYC. He's regular fodder for art, architecture, fashion and even rock magazines and has a finger in every pie of the creative world. His defiant artwork makes him the lovable dissident, and his laid-back attitude and Santa Claus demeanor make him instantly approachable.

You'll cry, you'll laugh, you'll empathize, you'll learn on A Date with Luyu

Chen Luyu   Google Index: 191,000

The "Oprah of China" is much thinner than the real thing but doing her best to produce a meaty talk show for mainland audiences. On *A Date With Luyu* she meets with farmers and rock stars, and blends social issues like living with AIDS, the children of migrant laborers and drug addiction into her programs and greater Chinese society.

Hung Huang   Google Index: 158,000

This most savvy of media moguls is the CEO of CIMG media. Her expanding empire publishes Chinese versions of Beijing and Shanghai *Time Out*, as well as trendy, art-oriented *iLook* magazine. Hung Huang has more connections than Imelda Marcos has shoes, owing to the fact that her mother was an interpreter for the Chairman himself.

Liu Xiang   Google Index: 5,120,000

This 26-year-old cleaned up at the 110m hurdles at Athens 2004 with a gold medal and a new world record. Now, in the midst of Olympic fever he is cleaning up millions in endorsements. Mengniu Milk, Coca Cola, banks, and countless other products bear his sweaty figure, usually with arms raised in Olympic victory. This summer, Liu will defend his gold, and the hope and honor of the Chinese people – but will he choose a nice glass of milk, or cola before the big race?

Li Yong   Google Index: 1,100,000

Television host extraordinaire, this man makes glittery bolero jackets and ruffles look like habitual lounge wear. His Count Dracula style is the most sought after on all ten CCTV stations, where he hosts song and dance extravaganzas and talent shows. Li Yong's striking profile (did I mention Dracula?) and his chatty, glib routine have made him one of the most recognizable faces in China.

Pan Shiyi   Google Index: 1,550,000

The Donald Trump of China, and one of the most visible personalities shaping the face of Beijing. Pan Shiyi and his wife Zhang Yi are Soho China, responsible for the endless white cubes of Jianwai Soho; asymmetrical Soho Shangdu and Soho Chaowai are the latest to grace the skyline. Through the simple appropriation of these four letters, they gave the Chinese white-collar class a real estate-based lifestyle to aspire to: Small Office Home Office.

Pan's next move: Soho in the South Sanlitun badlands?

Shan Tianfang   Google Index: 164,000

Any taxi passenger will have fallen under the spell of his sandpaper voice. The ups and downs, emphatic elongation of words and edgy pauses are dramatic enough to keep any listener engaged, even if you can't make out a word. That is Shan Tianfang doing *pingshu* – story hour. You somehow intuitively know that Old Shan has big droopy jowls, and that he would be the coolest grandpa.

Zhang Yimou   Google Index: 2,950,000

This world-famous director is the Spielberg of Chinese film. Never far from debate and scandal, his films have bridged East and West for decades. His latest film, *Curse of the Golden Flower* (2006), may have been a debacle, but it put his name all over the news despite its public rejection. Locals are waiting in anticipation for his next mega-project: Zhang's directorial extravagance and vision will fill the "Bird's Nest" stadium as he directs the Olympic opening and closing ceremonies.

Zhou Jielun (Jay Chou)   Google Index: 7,340,000

Taiwanese pop divinity Zhou has liberated the mainland world with his cool, R&B-style easy listening and god-like ability to never change his facial expression. You can also spot Jay in alpha-male cinematic roles and prominent advertising campaigns around town. He plays a central role in most KTV romps as well: fans range from pre-teens to *nainais*. See the way his mouth hardly moves when singing? Effortless!

Zhou Xun   Google Index: 2,660,000

She's impish and sprightly – she's the trendy new "it" girl and semi-liberated sex symbol of contemporary film. Zhou Xun's quirky looks and "bad girl" roles give her an edge in a world saturated with virginal "good girls." Zhou Xun dares to be photographed smoking a cigarette, to plaster her sex kitten images all around the town, to leave a trail of boyfriends … and the public dares with her.

PHOTO: NICK OTTO

USEFUL INFO

Hungary Mon-Thu 9am-noon, 2-5pm, Fri 9am-noon, 2-3pm. 10 Dongzhimenwai Dajie, Chaoyang District. (6532 0665) www.huemb.org.cn 匈牙利大使馆，朝阳区东直门外大街10号

India Mon-Fri 9am-1pm, 2-5.30pm. 1 Ritan Donglu, Chaoyang District. (6532 1908) www.indianembassy.org.cn 印度大使馆，朝阳区日坛东路1号

Indonesia Mon-Fri 10am-noon and 2-5pm. 4 Dongzhimenwai Dajie, Chaoyang District. (6532 5486) 印度尼西亚大使馆，朝阳区东直门外大街4号

Ireland Mon-Fri 9am-12.30pm and 2-5pm. 3 Ritan Donglu, Chaoyang District. (6532 2691) www.embasyofireland.cn 爱尔兰大使馆，朝阳区日坛东路3号

Israel Mon-Fri 9am-5pm. 17 Tianze Lu, Chaoyang District. (8532 0500) http://beijing.mfa.gov.il 以色列大使馆，朝阳区天泽路17号

Italy Mon-Fri 9am-noon. 2 Sanlitun Dong'erjie, Chaoyang District. (8532 7600) www.ambitaba.sk/Ambasciata_Pechino 意大利大使馆，朝阳区三里屯东二街2号

Japan Mon-Fri 9am-noon, 1-5pm. 7 Ritan Lu, Jianguomenwai, Chaoyang District. (6532 2361) www.cn.emb-japan.go.jp 日本大使馆，朝阳区建国门外日坛路7号

Kazakhstan Mon, Wed, Fri 9am-1pm. 9 Sanlitun Dongliujie, Chaoyang District. (6532 6182) www.kazembchina.org 哈萨克斯坦大使馆，朝阳区三里东六街9号

Laos Mon-Fri 8.30-11.30am and 2-4.30pm. 11 Sanlitun Dongsijie, Chaoyang District. (6532 1224) 老挝大使馆，朝阳区三里屯东四街11号

Malaysia Mon-Fri 8.30am-5pm. 2 Liangmaqiao Beijie, Chaoyang District. (6532 2531) www.kln.gov.my/perwakilan/beijing 马来西亚大使馆，朝阳区亮马桥北街2号

Mongolia Mon-Fri 9am-1pm and 2-5pm. 2 Xiushui Beijie, Chaoyang District. (6532 1203) www.mongolembassychina.org 蒙古大使馆，朝阳区秀水北街2号

Myanmar Mon-Fri 8am-noon, 1-4.30pm. 6 Dongzhimenwai Dajie, Chaoyang District. (6532 0351) www.myanmarembassy.com 缅甸大使馆，朝阳区东直门外大街6号

Nepal Mon-Fri 10am-5pm. 1 Sanlitun Xiliujie, Chaoyang District. (6532 1795) www.nepalembassy.org.cn 尼泊尔大使馆，朝阳区三里屯西六街1号

Netherlands Mon-Fri 8.30am-12.30pm and 2-3pm; visas 9-11am. 4 Liangmahe Nanlu, Chaoyang District. (8532 0200) www.hollandinchina.org 荷兰大使馆，朝阳区亮马河南路4号

New Zealand Mon-Fri 8.30am-12.30pm, 1.30-5pm. 1 Ritan Lu Dong'erjie, Jianguomenwai, Chaoyang District. (6532 2731) www.nzembassy.com/china 新西兰大使馆，朝阳区日坛路东二街1号

Norway Mon-Fri 9am-noon, 1-5pm; visas 2-4pm. 1 Sanlitun Dongyijie, Chaoyang District. (6532 2261) www.norway.cn 挪威大使馆，朝阳区三里屯东一街1号

Pakistan Mon-Fri 8.30am-1pm, 2-5pm. 1 Dongzhimenwai Dajie, Chaoyang District. (6532 2504) www.embassyofpakistan-beijing.org.cn 巴基斯坦大使馆，朝阳区东直门外大街1号

Philippines Mon-Fri 8.30am-5pm. 23 Xiushui Beijie, Chaoyang District. (6532 1872) www.philembassy-china.org 菲律宾大使馆，朝阳区秀水北街23号

Russia Mon-Fri 9am-noon, 2-7pm. 4 Dongzhimen Beizhongjie, Dongcheng District. (6532 1381) www.russia.org.cn 俄罗斯大使馆，东城区东直门北中街4号

Singapore Mon-Fri 8.30am-noon and 1-5pm. 1 Xiushui Beijie, Chaoyang District. (6532 1115) www.mfa.gov.sg/beijing 新加坡大使馆，朝阳区秀水北街1号

South Africa Mon-Fri 8.30am-noon and 1-5pm. 5 Dongzhimenwai Dajie, Chaoyang District. (6532 0171, safrican@163bj.com) 南非大使馆，朝阳区东直门外大街5号

South Korea Mon-Fri 9am-noon and 1.30-5pm. 20 Dongfang Donglu, Chaoyang District. (8531 0700) www.koreaemb.org.cn 韩国大使馆，朝阳区东方东路20号

Spain Mon-Fri 8am-2pm. 9 Sanlitun Lu, Chaoyang District. (6532 1986) www.mae.es/embajadas/pekin 西班牙大使馆，朝阳区三里屯路9号

Sweden Mon-Fri 8.30am-12.30pm, 1.30-5.30pm; visas Mon-Fri 9am-noon. 3 Dongzhimenwai Dajie, Chaoyang District. (6532 9790) www.swedemb-cn.org 瑞典大使馆，朝阳区东直门外大街3号

Switzerland Mon-Fri 9am-noon. 3 Sanlitun Dongwujie, Chaoyang District. (8532 8888) www.eda.admin.ch/beijing 瑞士大使馆，朝阳区三里屯东五街3号

Thailand Embassy: Mon-Fri 9am-noon and 2-5.30pm. 40 Guanghua Lu, Chaoyang District. (6532 2151). Visa and consular section: Mon-Fri 9-11.30am. 1/F Huabin Int'l Bldg, 8 Yong'an Dongli, Jianguomenwai Dajie, Chaoyang District. (8528 8771) www.thaiembbeij.org 泰国大使馆，朝阳区光华路40号，泰国领事馆，朝阳区建国门外大街永安东里8号华标国际大厦1层

United Kingdom Embassy: Mon-Fri 8.30am-11.30am, 1-5pm. 11 Guanghua Lu, Chaoyang District. (5192 4000) Visa and Consular sections: Mon-Fri 9am-noon and 1.30-3.30pm. 21/F North Tower, Kerry Centre, 1 Guanghua Lu, Chaoyang District. (8529 6600) www.uk.cn 英国大使馆，朝阳区光华路11号，英国领事馆，朝阳区光华路1号嘉里中心北楼21层

United States of America Embassy: 3 Xiushui Beijie, Chaoyang District. (6532 3831) Visa section: Mon-Fri 8am-1pm, 2-5pm; citizen services: Mon-Fri 8.30am-noon and 2-4pm. 2 Xiushui Dongjie, Chaoyang District. http://beijing.usembassy-china.org.cn 美国大使馆，朝阳区秀水北街3号，美国领事处，朝阳区秀水东街2号

Vietnam Mon-Fri 9-11.30am and 2-4pm. 32 Guanghua Lu, Chaoyang District. (6532 1155) 越南大使馆，朝阳区光华路32号

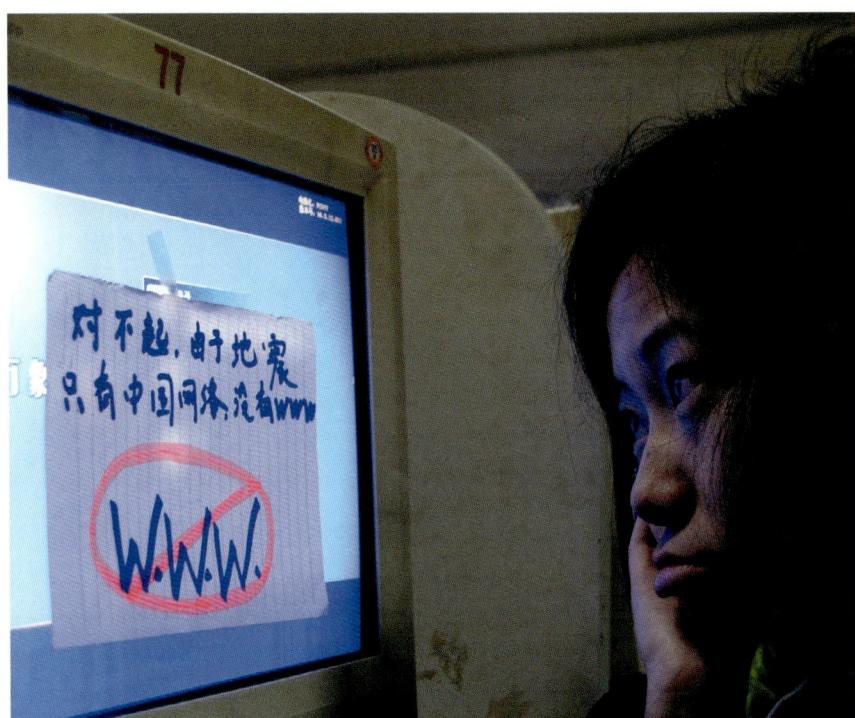
The earthquake that broke the Internet (in January '07) broke my heart

Government Departments

Visit www.ebeijing.gov.cn for a list of government organizations.

Mayor's Office Noodle stand rip you off? Well, you're takin' it straight to the mayor.
2 Zhengyi Lu, Dongcheng District. (12345)
市长办公室，东城区正义路2号

Holidays

Here are the major holidays and festivals observed in Beijing. Expect a week off during Spring Festival, Labor Day and National Day.

New Year: Jan 1
Spring Festival (Chinese New Year, Chunjie; 1st month 1st day): Feb 7, 2008 (Year of the Rat); Jan 26, 2009 (Year of the Ox)
Lantern Festival (Yuanxiao Jie; 1st month 15th day): Feb 21, 2008; Feb 9, 2009
International Women's Day: Mar 8
Tomb Sweeping Festival (Qingming Jie): Apr 4 or 5
International Labor Day: May 1
International Children's Day: Jun 1
Teachers' Day: Sep 10
Mid-Autumn Day (Moon Festival, Zhongqiu Jie; 8th month 15th day): Sep 14, 2008; Oct 3, 2009
National Day: Oct 1

Internet

Dial-up service

You can get dial-up modem access by using an Internet Service Provider (ISP). No sign-up needed: The charges will be tagged on to your phone bill. You pay both the phone company (RMB 1.2 per hour) and ISP provider.

Popular ISPs:
95963 (user name and password are both 263; RMB 0.07/min)
16900 (user name and password are both 169; RMB 0.05/min)
95933 (user name and password are both 18; RMB 0.07/min, for not more than RMB 48 per month)

ADSL

Registration and installation of ADSL service costs RMB 300 if you already have a phone line installed, and it can take a few weeks. Note that only the person who registered the phone account – i.e., your landlord – can register for ADSL. To do so, visit one of Beijing Telecom's service centers (with passport or *shenfenzheng*), apply online (www.bjtelecom.net – Chinese only) or call the

PHOTO: TOM CARTER

USEFUL INFO 649

One glaring moment later, the vows were exchanged

service number 10000 (no English service available). Fixed plans are about RMB 29 per 30 hours, and unlimited plans are available (e.g. RMB 120 for 512KB, RMB 150 for 1MB). The pay-as-you-go plan charges RMB 0.05 per minute (or 3 *kuai* per hour, comparable to prices at a *wangba*, which is also the average rate for set plans. Connection quality varies around town, ranging from passable to slow as a dead snail.

Internet cafes

If you need to get your World of Warcraft fix in the company of pasty chain smokers, follow sweat suited school kids to the local *wangba* (网吧). Prices vary depending on location and time of day, but are usually RMB 3-10 per hour. Internet cafes dot the Beijing landscape, but if you are desperate with not a *wangba* in sight, head to a big hotel, where you can find Internet access in the business centers at a steep premium – as much as RMB 20 for 10 minutes.

Wireless Internet (Wi-Fi)

There are many places around town that allow you to satisfy your Internet and coffee addiction at the same time. Many places will give you a login and password when you make a purchase, but some trusting cafe owners allow unfettered Wi-Fi access under the assumption that you will eventually buy something. For a list of Wi-Fi locations – other than Starbucks – check out: www.chinapulse.com/wifi

Another option for getting online wirelessly is to use the GPRS or CDMA 1X mobile phone networks, either through your cell phone or computer. These methods are 2-3 times faster than dial-up and are good anywhere there is mobile service. China Mobile charges RMB 0.03 per KB of data for GPRS; packages of RMB 5 and 15 include 10MB and 50MB of data every month, respectively. See p665-6 for more about mobile service plans.

Law Firms

Genesis Law Firm *7/F, Bldg C, International Investment Mansion, 6-9 Fuchengmen Beidajie, Xicheng District. (6621 2828, 6657 9966) www.genesislawfirm.com.cn* 建元律师事务所，西城区阜成门北大街6–9号国际投资大厦C座7层

King & Wood PRC Lawyers *31/F, Bldg A, Jianwai Soho, 39 Dongsanhuan Zhonglu, Chaoyang District. (5878 5588) www.kingandwood.com* 金杜律师事务所，朝阳区东三环中路39号建外Soho A座31层

Lehman, Lee & Xu *Dongwai Diplomatic Bldg, 22 Dongzhimenwai Dajie, Chaoyang District. (8532 1919) www.lehmanlaw.com* 朝阳区东直门外大街22号东外外交公寓

Tianyuan Law Firm Tianyuan has experience with home purchases, but limited English services. *11/F, Bldg C, International Enterprise Mansion, 35 Jinrong Jie, Xicheng District. (8809 2188)* 北京天元律师事务所，西城区金融街35号国际投资大厦C座11层

Marriage

For a marriage between a Chinese citizen and a foreigner, the Chinese party must be a Beijing resident. (If s/he lacks a Beijing *hukou*, the couple will have to marry wherever s/he has official residence.) Foreigners must bring their passports and residence permits to the Beijing

Municipal Civil Affairs Bureau, as well as a "Certificate of Marriageability" stating that they are single and thus eligible to marry. Embassies can provide the document, which must be translated into Chinese by an agency. Remember also to bring three 5x3.8cm photos.

Seeking to bask in the reflected glory of the Olympics, many couples are planning their banquets for 2008, with August 8th being the most popular date. On the other hand, a contending faction believes that 2008 is actually an unlucky year for marriage: Lichun (the start of spring) falls on February 4, before the Spring Festival on February 7. Thus, as a "year without a spring," 2008 is also the "year of widows," according to superstition.

Wanhonglongxiang Wedding Agency Take your ceremony to new heights – 600 meters in the air. Pledge your undying love in a hot air balloon while soaring above Beijing. The ride lasts an hour and offers a stunning bird's-eye view of the city. Reservations must be made at least one month in advance. The cost ranges from RMB 8,800 (hot-air balloon flight only) to RMB 13,000 (all inclusive package).
Rm 155, Bldg 2, Maihao Shidai, 47 Xizhimen Beidajie, Haidian District. (6226 3167) www.bjmarry.com 万红龙翔婚庆公司，海淀区西直门北大街47号院迈豪时代2号楼155室

Mail & Couriers

Domestic letters within Beijing costs RMB 0.80 for the first 100g and RMB 1.20 for each additional 100g; outside of Beijing, the base price is RMB 1.20 (RMB 2 per additional 100g). Postcards are RMB 0.80, and registered mail costs an additional RMB 3.

Airmail to other Asian countries starts at RMB 5; to Europe, North America, Australia and New Zealand–RMB 6, and to South America, the Caribbean, Africa and Oceania–RMB 7.

International shipping

You can send international mail and pick up some overseas parcels from some neighborhood post offices. When sending international parcels from such post offices, you are limited to the boxes they sell, the largest of which can hold about 30kg. Prices vary according to destination and delivery method – a 30kg box sent by ground mail to the US cost RMB 663.5 at the time of writing (RMB 757.7 to the UK) and takes 2-3 months. A 1kg box, the cheapest, cost RMB 83.5 to ship economy class. For faster delivery, one can send by airmail, which, for a 30kg box sent to the US, costs about RMB 3,000 at time of writing.

Do not seal your box before shipping, as you must fill out a declaration form and let the post office inspect your effects. Goods that are often pirated, like CDs, DVDs and clothes, will receive more scrutiny than other items and you may have to prove their authenticity. Even if you can prove authenticity, the post office may limit the amount you can send.

Parcels that are inspected by Chinese customs, or those upon which duties and/or taxes must be paid, can only be picked up at the Beijing International Post & Telecommunications Office. In addition, from this branch you can send articles that don't fit in regulation boxes.

Beijing International Post & Telecommunications Office *Daily 8am-6.30pm. Jianguomenwai Dajie, Yabao Lu (300m north of the Jianguomen overpass), Dongcheng District. (6512 8114) www.bipto.com.cn* 北京国际邮电局，东城区建国门外大街雅宝路（建国门桥向北200米）

Express mail providers

The following express mail providers (*kuaidi* in Chinese) have both drop-off centers and pick-up service. If you are staying in a hotel, the concierge or business center should be able to have your letter or small parcel shipped by domestic or international courier. Deliveries within Beijing by a local company will cost about RMB 10 for most items.

Beijing Zhaijisong Express Offers express delivery within China.
11/F, Zhaowei Tower, 14 Jiuxianqiao Lu, Chaoyang District. (400 678 9000) ww.zjs.com.cn 北京宅急送快运公司，朝阳区酒仙桥路14号兆维大厦11层

DHL This German delivery giant has express centers in the China World Trade Centre and COFCO Plaza.
45 Xinyuan Jie, Chaoyang District. (800 810 8000) www.cn.dhl.com DHL快运，朝阳区新源街45号

Express Mail Service (EMS) Run by the postal service, EMS is a cheaper alternative to private companies, especially for domestic deliveries, though their international service is not as speedy (about seven days to North America). They also offer special prices on next-day delivery service between cities in the Bohai Delta (including Beijing and Tianjin), the Pearl River Delta, the Yangtze River Delta, the Northeast and the Chengdu-Chongqing region. Check the website for international EMS rates and more information. Post offices have example EMS slips filled out in English and Chinese. *Available at most post offices. (11185) www.ems.com.cn*

FedEx FedEx also operates self-service counters in Kodak Express shops all over the city. Call for locations.
Rm 101, Tower C, Lonsdale Center, 5 Wanhong Lu, Chaoyang District. (400 889 1888) www.fedex.com/cn_english 联邦快运，朝阳区万红路5号蓝涛中心C座101

USEFUL INFO

Shunfeng Express Provides domestic courier service. 2 Shunhuang Lu, Xiaxinpu Village, Huanggang Town, Chaoyang District. (400 811 1111) www.sf-express.com 顺丰速运，朝阳区黄岚乡下辛堡村顺黄路2号院

STO Express Same service as most local *kuaidi* companies. Qingfengyuan, Fenzhongsi, Fengtai District. (8769 7913/15/16/17/18) www.sto.cn 申通快递，丰台区分钟寺清风苑

TNT Skypak International express delivery company. Airport Materials Circulation Base. 9 Bajie, Shunping Lu, Shunyi District. (6947 7060, 800 810 9868) www.tnt.com TNT块运，顺义区顺平路八街9号空港物流基地

UPS In addition to international deliveries, UPS plans to offer domestic service. 1818, Bldg 1, China World Trade Center, 1 Jianguomenwai Dajie, Chaoyang District. (800 820 8388) www.ups.com UPS快运，朝阳区建国门外大街1号国际贸易中心1座1818

Money & Banking

Opening an account

Foreigners can open a *renminbi* or foreign currency account by showing a passport and visa or certificate of residence. A basic *renminbi* savings account has a minimum requirement of RMB 1.

Major banks allow you to open foreign exchange accounts as well as foreign banknote accounts, and all major currencies are accepted. Bank of China offers saving deposit accounts as well as several types of time-deposit accounts. The simplest time-deposit account, with lengths of one month to two years, require only RMB 50 to open, but a seven-day notice account requires a minimum of RMB 5,000.

HSBC similarly offers savings and deposit accounts to non-PRC citizens, but with lower minimum requirements. Other banks offer similar products.

Only foreign residents employed in Beijing can open a checking account. The applicant generally needs a guarantor who has a Beijing *hukou* (residence permit) and has stable employment in Beijing. The guarantor must supply the bank with a photocopy of his or her ID card, while the applicant provides a copy of his passport and residence permit. In addition, the applicant's employer must affix the company's chop on the application. China Merchants Bank, however, requires only a passport, a letter from one's employer and a residency permit to open a checking account.

Major banks in Beijing

Banking hours and days vary from bank to bank. Most Chinese banks operate 9am-5pm and have branches that are open on Saturdays and Sundays. To find the branch nearest you, call the bank.

Agricultural Bank of China 31,000 locations and ATMs in urban and rural China – the most of any bank within China. Hotline: 95599. 23A Fuxing Lu, Haidian District. (6829 7532) www.abchina.com 农业银行，海淀区复兴路甲23号

Bank of Beijing Though you most likely won't have an account here, you may have to pay your electricity and gas bills here. Hotline: 96169. 17 Jinrong Jie, Xicheng District. (6622 6060) www.bankofbeijing.com.cn 北京银行，西城区金融街17号

Bank of China The second-largest bank in China after the Industrial and Commercial Bank, the BOC has 10,000 domestic and 600 overseas outlets. Hotline: 95566. Yatai Dasha, 8 Yabao Lu, Chaoyang District. (6519 9988) www.bj.bank-of-china.com 中国银行，朝阳区雅宝路8号亚太大厦

China Construction Bank Hotline: 95533. 25 Jinrong Jie, Xicheng District. (6759 7114) www.ccb.com 建设银行，西城区金融街25号

China Merchants Bank Hotline: 95555. 156 Fuxingmennei Dajie, Xicheng District. (6642 6969) http://english.cmbchina.com 招商银行，西城区复兴门内大街156号

Citibank Four branches in Beijing (Zhongguancun, Kerry Centre and Chaoyang). Hotline: 800 830 1880. 1/F, Tower 2, Bright China Chang'an Bldg, 7 Jianguomennei Dajie, Dongcheng District. (6510 2458) www.citibank.com 花旗银行，东城区建国门内大街7号光华长安大厦B座1层

HSBC Five branches and nine other ATMs, including at Zhongguancun, China World, the Lufthansa Centre and Pinnacle Plaza. Hotline: 800 820 8878. 1/F, Block A, COFCO Plaza, 8 Jianguomennei Dajie, Dongcheng District. (5999 8888) www.hsbc.com.cn 汇丰银行，东城区建国门内大街8号中粮广场A座1层

Industrial and Commercial Bank of China (ICBC) The ninth-largest bank in the world and the largest in China. 20,000 branches in China and 106 branches overseas, including in London, New York City, Frankfurt, and eight other major cities worldwide. Hotline: 95588. 55 Fuxingmennei Dajie, Xicheng District. (6610 8048) www.icbc.com.cn 工商银行，西城区复兴门内大街55号

ATMs

Most ATMs accept foreign bankcards connected to the Cirrus, Plus, AmEx, Visa and MasterCard networks. Some local banks charge transaction fees (RMB 25 for Bank of China) but many do not; your home country bank will probably slap on a fee for each withdrawal in Beijing. Custom-

Envision a sunny financial future in the reflective sphere at the Bank of China (Xidan Branch)

ers of Barclays, Bank of America, BNP Paribas, Deutsche Bank, Scotiabank or Westpac can use their bankcard free of charge at all ATMs of China Construction Bank, a member of the Global ATM Alliance. Maximum single-day withdrawal limits vary but range RMB 3,000-5,000, with a per session limit. For a list of ATMs, see www.moveandstay.com/beijing/guide_banks.asp.

All Chinese bankcards are on the UnionPay system, which has expanded its network to a growing number of merchants and ATMs in 22 countries. See their website (www.unionpay.com) for the latest info.

Credit cards

Most major banks, including the Bank of China, China Construction Bank, China Merchants Bank and ICBC, offer credit cards with Visa or MasterCard. These work like any other credit card and can be used internationally. Different banks have different requirements for foreign applicants, who must be employed in Beijing. Merchants Bank's requirements are relatively simple: a passport, residence permit, and employment and income certificate (with company chop affixed).

International money transfers

Before you consign your paycheck to a continent-crossing carrier pigeon, consider using your bank account (cheapest) or Western Union (fastest, convenient if you're on the road). Note that approval must be obtained from the State Administration of Foreign Exchange to transfer RMB sums over USD 10,000 in value.

If you have an account in a major bank (see p652), then you can directly transfer unlimited sums of money to or from your bank account in your home country. Telegraphic transfers via the SWIFT network usually take one to three working days, though it may be longer depending on the two banks' relationship. Or, if you are not in a hurry, you can have the Chinese bank issue a demand draft, which you then mail to or present directly at the home bank. The demand draft method incurs no flat fee, but is slower. If you are transferring between currencies, banks will apply the current exchange rate; there may also be a conversion fee, so check first. Bank of China will also process money transfers for cash, with an additional 1-3 percent fee for foreign currency notes.

			Bank account transfers	
		Western Union	Bank of China	ICBC
	Time	15 minutes	1-3 working days	1-3 working days
	Flat fee	USD 15-40 for the first USD 10,000; USD 20 for each additional USD 500	RMB 150 (for telegraphic only)	RMB 100 (for telegraphic only)
	Percent fee	-	0.1% (RMB 20-250)	0.08% (RMB 16-160)

USEFUL INFO

Even if you do unearth authenticity from the treasure heap, your loot may not be able to go home with you

Money transfers via Western Union arrive in just 15 minutes, but the steep fees make this option recommended only for stranded travelers who need money in a hurry or can't access their bank accounts. With counters at China Post and the Agricultural Bank, Western Union has the convenience of thousands of locations in China (including 549 in Beijing). Some branches of China Post can pay out money in US dollars – call for specific locations. China Post locations can send a max of USD 2,000 and receive a max of USD 10,000. Agricultural Bank limits receiving to USD 20,000 but has no maximum sending limit. Transfers to African countries operate on a different fee schedule (USD 13-85 for the first USD 2,500).

Western Union *(800 820 8668, China Post Beijing 6659 9111 ext 8459) www.westernunion.com*

Faster cash
American Express American Express members can cash personal checks for USD 2,000 to USD 3,000 over a 21-day period at the Bank of China. Credit card and passport required.
Rm 2313, Tower 1, Guomao Bldg, 1 Jianguomenwai Dajie, Chaoyang District. (6505 2228 ext 6601) 美国运通，朝阳区建国门外大街1号国贸大厦1座2101

Visa Certain banks, notably Bank of China and HSBC, can provide cash advances with a Visa card. Many ATMs allow Visa card-holders to withdraw money up to a daily limit (usually RMB 3,000).

Moving & Relocation
Sorry to see you go. Were you planning on taking that couch?

Homeward bound
To prevent commercial exporters from trying to avoid duties, China only allows foreigners with Z visas to ship a house full of personal effects. Other people can ship smaller amounts or use the mail service. If you believe that something in your shipment may violate regulations, you have two options: Declare everything and try to get an exemption, or hide the contraband and hope for the best.

The process for a full relocation takes about four to six weeks, but you may need up to six months or more to resolve issues involving pets or vehicles. Plan for about three months to leave China, twice that if moving with kids or pets. Also, keep in mind that summer is the busy season for moving, when relocation companies and the relevant government bureaus will be swamped with pleading foreigners just like you. Remember to start the relocation process as early as possible and keep every document you've ever been given.

Relics inspection
While a Chinese relics inspection is not required, it's a good idea for those exporting lots of antiques. Exports are regularly inspected, packing lists are translated, and if any of your articles are found in violation, your whole shipment will be subject to delays and extra charges. Anything that was made before 1949 is subject to customs inspection and fees. In addition, anything considered to be of museum quality

– Tibetan artifacts, Buddha statues, rare woods, etc. – or anything made before 1795 cannot be exported from China at all. If the piece you bought came with a relic certificate, a relics inspection is unnecessary. In addition, you are charged 10-20 percent duties by customs of your destination country, but if they suspect that you are bringing in a commercial shipment it could be much higher.

Friendship Store The store can conduct relics inspections on site (good for a few items). To schedule a relics inspector to conduct a home visit, contact a relocation company.
Mon and Fri 1.30-5pm. 17 Jianguomenwai Dajie, Chaoyang District. (6500 3311 ext 255) 友谊商店，朝阳区建国门外大街17号

Long-term storage

The following companies offer long-term storage in Beijing. Prices are usually dependent on volume, duration of storage, accessibility requirements during the storage period and, sometimes, the type of goods stored.

Move One Relocations Climate-controlled storage, with personal lockers available. Move One also offers document storage; they will deliver a document by email or by hand upon request.
See Relocation Firms (p656) for details.

OTTO Packing & Transport Co., Ltd. Provides professional document and personal item storage. Able to deliver specific documents to customers upon request. Shipping to client is free if storing above a certain amount.
See Relocation Firms (p656) for details.

Pets

Moving an animal in or out of a country is often the most difficult task that the average relocating family will face. Consult the relocation companies and relevant embassy at least four months in advance for your destination country's regulations on vaccinations and quarantine. The details on importing and exporting a companion animal can be found in Pets, p655.

Asian Express
See Relocation Firms (p655) for details.

Asian Tigers
See Relocation Firms (p655) for details.

Export-A-Pet Provides door-to-door service for shipment of pets, with service in over a dozen countries.
Shop B2, Marina Cove Shopping Centre, Sai Kung, NT, Hong Kong. (+852 2358 1774) www.export-a-pet.com

Move One Relocations
See Relocation Firms, below, for details.

World Care Pets *(6211 6185, 138 0110 2540) www.worldcarepet.com*

Vehicle

Moving a car out of China has gotten much easier in the past few years, but it still costs quite a bundle to ship and is still a load of paperwork. You need your passport, residence permit, your company's customs registration card, the invoice for the vehicle, vehicle information (make, model, year, engine and chassis numbers) and the relevant customs applications for your country of destination.

Relocation firms

The firms below offer international and domestic relocation services. International companies have well-trained employees and strict standards, but their prices are steep – almost USD 1,000 per cubic meter. Less experienced Chinese companies charge much, much cheaper rates: around RMB 2,000 per cubic meter.

AGS Four Winds *Rm 51, Unit 2, Bldg 5, Tayuan Compound, Chaoyang District. (6566 3405) www.agsfourwinds.com*
朝阳区塔院公寓5号楼2单元51号

Asian Express International Movers *Rm 1612, Tower D, Soho New Town, 88 Jianguo Lu, Chaoyang District. (8580 1471) www.aemovers.com.hk* 朝阳区建国路88号Soho 现代城D座1612

Asian Tigers K.C. Dat (China) Ltd. *Rm 302, Grand Rock Plaza, 13 Xinzhong Xili, Dongcheng District. (6415 1188) www.asiantigersgroup.com* 东城区新中西里13号巨石大厦302

BAL International Cargo Ltd. *B11, 16/F, Hanwei Plaza, 7 Guanghua Lu, Chaoyang District. (6561 4171/2/3/4) www.bim.com.hk* 朝阳区光华路7号汉威大厦16层B11

Beijing Belle Transport Co. Ltd. *Rm 409-410, One World Apartments, 16 Xinyuan Nanlu, Chaoyang District. (8453 1240, 8453 1027) www.bellepack.com* 朝阳区新源南路16号世芳豪庭409-410

Beijing Doda International Cargo Transportation Co. Ltd. *256 Nanyangzhuang Cun, Shibalidian Xiang, Chaoyang District. (6748 8828) www.doda.com.cn* 朝阳区十八里店乡南洋庄村256号

CIM Continental International Moving *Rm 201, Lugang Bldg, Chaoyang Port, 1A Dongsihuan Nanlu, Chaoyang District. (8762 5110) www.cimmover.com* 北京和乔百丽居货运代理有限公司，朝阳区东四环南路甲1号朝阳口岸综合楼201

Crown Worldwide Ltd. *Rm 201, West Tower, Golden Bridge Bldg, Jianguomenwai Dajie, Chaoyang District. (6585 0640) www.crownworldwide.com* 朝阳区建国门外大街甲1号金之桥大厦西楼201

Hiboo International Group *Rm 2502, Bldg 8, Wanda Plaza, 93 Jianguo Lu, Chaoyang District. (5820 6459) www.hiboo.com.cn* 朝阳区建国路93号万达广场8号楼2502室

Kerry EAS *Datong Mansion, 21 Xiaoyun Lu, Chaoyang District. (6461 8899)* 朝阳区霄云路21号大通大厦

Move One Relocations *Zhubang 2000 Bldg, 100 Balizhuang Xili, Chaoyang District. (6581 4046) www.moveone.info* 朝阳区八里庄西里100号住邦2000大厦

OTTO Packing & Transport Co., Ltd. *46 Xishuncheng Jie, Deshengmennei, Bei Erhuan, Xicheng District. (5260 8300) www.ottochina.com* 西城区北二环德胜门内西顺城街46号

Rhema *Rm 306, Shengsha Business Bldg, 16 Dongsanhuan Beilu, Chaoyang District. (6586 9115) www.rhemachina.com* 朝阳区东三环路16号盛厦商务楼306室

Santa Fe *8 Er Jie, Beijing Capital Airport Logistics Zone, Shunyi District. (6947 0688) www.santaferelo.com* 顺义区首都机场物流中心2街8号

Schenker DB Logistics *5 Tianwei Sijie, Tianzhu Airport Industrial Area A, Shunyi District. (8048 0126, 8048 0099) www.schenker.com* 顺义区天竺空港工业区A区天纬四街5号

Sirva Relocation *A812 The Spaces Shangdu International Center, 8 Dongdaqiao Lu, Chaoyang District. (5870 0866) www.sirvarelocation.com* 朝阳区东大桥路8号尚都国际中心A812

Moving within Beijing

Moving can be a hassle in any country. Rest assured, however, that there are plenty of inexpensive moving companies that can help you get your booty to that brand-new pad in no time. Some international firms will do local moves and provide high-quality, expensive service, while local companies can help you move quickly and cheaply. Prices vary by company and area; Haidian movers, for instance, typically cost around RMB 150 to 200 per move, while Chaoyang movers can get as expensive as RMB 400. Call at least one day in advance, and further ahead during the summer peak season for urban migrations.

You should also note that it usually takes a three- to five-man team of movers about three hours to move a 15 square meter roomful of stuff, but be sure to keep a sharp eye on the proceedings: While you'll undoubtedly be impressed by the mind-boggling loads these guys can carry up and down multiple flights of stairs (ever see a man hoist an entire refrigerator on his back?), they may not exactly be known for their finesse. It's always advisable to have someone watching your stuff being put into the truck in addition to the action upstairs.

On the plus side, moving companies usually won't tack on a "distance charge" if your new place is within 15km of your old location – but for every additional kilometer, they will add an additional RMB 4 to the final bill. But the buck doesn't just stop there: if your place does not have an elevator, the *louceng fei* is RMB 10-20 per floor. Unwieldy items like refrigerators exceeding a depth of 20cm will bump the cost up another RMB 30-50, and the *caizhuang fei* – a variable disassembly/reassembly fee for large furniture items that can't fit through tight doorways – around RMB 40 for an average armoire. Pianos are an even bigger issue – moving one will set you back an additional RMB 180-240, depending on the size.

Below are a few companies offering services at a reasonable cost, so relax – affordable moving companies are in no short supply. Now get packing!

Beiao Likang Moving Company For RMB 180 you get four guys, 13.5 cubic meters of truck space and 15km travel distance. A second trip costs the same. Extra charge for walkup.
180 Beiyuan Lu, Yayuncun, Chaoyang District. (6422 6688) 北奥利康搬家公司, 朝阳区亚运村北苑路180号

Chang'an Banjia RMB 150 buys you 15km travel distance. RMB 10 per floor (above ground) if no elevator.
38 Qianbajia, Shuangqinglu, Haidian District. (6292 8498) 长安搬家, 海淀区双清路前八家38号

Stone Moving Service They will ask you to specify any large or heavy pieces or any that need de-/re-installation so that there are no surprises in the bill. Prices range RMB 100-270 (depending on the truck size) and include four guys and 15km travel distance.
50 Dongwei Lu, Chaoyang District. (8431 2266) www.stbj.com.cn 四通搬家, 朝阳区东苇路50号

Interdean International Moving *1807, Bldg C, Heqiao Mansion, 8 Guanghua Lu, Chaoyang District. (6581 6950)* 朝阳区光华路8号和乔大厦C座1807

Yuming Banjia Gongsi RMB 180 per truck for 15km, RMB 10 per floor if no elevator. RMB 50 for large appliances (TV, refrigerator, etc.)
27 Dewai Xindejie, Xicheng District. (6203 3265) 裕民搬家公司, 西城区德外新德街27号

Selling your stuff

There comes a time in every Beijing expat's life when he or she decides to abandon the world of earthly possessions and lead the life of a spiritual renunciate – or when he or she decides to move – and that second king-sized bed quickly ceases to seem convenient.

When the day comes to liberate yourself from your stuff, know that Beijing has a number of companies specializing in buying back second-hand goods. Simply call them up, give them

Move your important artifacts with love and tender care

an address and schedule a time. Bear in mind that virtually all of these companies speak only Chinese, so get a friend to help if necessary. Depending on the quality, age and material of your furnishings, these companies will offer a sum of money – don't expect a huge payoff, mind, but there are far worse ways to have your apartment emptied out.

For those who prefer karmic payment to monetary, a number of organizations accept donations within Beijing. For info, see p637.

Beijing Gaojia Recycling Company *Outside the Fifth Ring Road, Chaoyang District. (6292 7146)* 北京中联二手物资回收公司，朝阳区五环外

Beijing Fangzhou Recycling Company *188 Siji Qingshe Chapeng, Haidian District. (8885 1670)* 北京方舟物资回收公司，海淀区四季青社茶棚188号

Music Practice Rooms

Rooms with a couple of amps and a drum kit abound in the rock capital but often are off-limits to all but a select few. The following list is far from extensive – ask your favorite band where they practice. Standard rooms are outfitted with two vocal mics, a guitar amp (possibly two), a bass amp, a drum kit, a couple of monitors and a mixer through which additional instruments might be routed. Most rooms – essentially all of them, except at Fierce – are victims of constant musical abuse, and equipment is regularly plagued with problems. Bring as much of your own gear as possible to ensure a trouble-free experience. Don't expect to borrow an instrument, but it may be possible to rent one.

Ao Yue Piano Not for bands – the three practice rooms (RMB 10 per hour) feature pianos, with a variety of Chinese musical instruments available upon request. *See Shopping, p405, for listing and address.*

Fierce Hard to find for the first time in the maze of the Gongzhufen flyover and roundabout, but well worth the trip: This is Beijing's best place to rehearse, bar none. High-end equipment – Pearl and Slingerland drums (and a Sabian cymbal sponsorship), Mesa Boogie and Marshall guitar amps, Warwick and SWR bass amps, Shure microphones – professional service and careful maintenance. Oh, and a monster room (RMB 400 per hour), featuring recording, a full percussion section (including congas), dozens of keyboards and several drum kits, where Black Panther rehearses. These guys rent gear to the big boys, so if you're lucky, you might get to play the snare that Norah Jones' drummer did. RMB 30, 50 and 400 per hour. Rooms open until midnight. *See Shopping, p426, for address. (6398 7610)*

Mao Dou Recording and Production Studio On the top floor of a housing complex, this completely soundproofed studio is sub-partitioned so that guitar, bass and vocals can all be recorded simultaneously, with drums being added in later. Ideal for anyone who doesn't want to deal with the hassle and expense of a large-scale professional studio. Recording RMB 150 per hour.
Daily 10am-midnight. 562, Bldg 9, Liangjing Mingju, Yile Zhongjie, Tongzhou District. (5801 3203) www.themaodou.com 毛豆录音制作室，通州区怡乐中街靓景明居9号楼562

Snake Pit Down a steep flight of stairs, past underground rooms with no windows and a communal shower/toilet, a spacious room welcomes rockers with shag-carpet, wall hangings and a decent sound system.

The dudes that run the place are into metal but are happy to accommodate all comers, and have actually purchased a timer for a trouble-free booking experience. RMB 20 per hour.
Daily 9am-midnight. B/F, Andelu, Bldg 14 (100 meters north of the Andingmen subway station, north side of the building with KFC, down the stairs west of the Quick shop), Dongcheng District. (8412 4753) 蛇穴，东城区安德路14号楼地下1层（安定门地铁站往北100米，肯德基的楼北侧快客便利店楼梯西则）

Tianyin In addition to renting gear to some of the city's larger-scale events, Tianyin boast four rooms of various sizes that host some surprisingly big names as well as some of the capital's starvingest artists. While all of your amp/drum/cable/mixing needs are fulfilled, equipment quality wavers between usable and fixable. The bar is stocked with juices and beer, a pool table provides welcome relief from the strains of rehearsals, and a small shop sells a range of equipment for every band member. Reserve early and reserve often, as the staff's scheduling skills haven't improved with Tianyin's growing popularity. RMB 60, 150, 300 per hour, depending on room size and equipment. Discounts for reserving more time.
Daily 24 hours. Tianhai Shangwu Dasha, 107 Dongsi Beidajie, Dongcheng District. (6402 0297) 天音，东城区东四北大街107号天海商务大厦

Xuan Zhuan The drums (Mapex) sound fantastic and the amps (two guitar, one bass) are good. Recording averages RMB 300 per hour.
See Shopping (p428) for listing and address.

Pets & Vets

In this dog-eat-dog world, dogs are no longer just for eating. Dragons and birds abound, and even fish are no longer restricted to the table or the *fengshui* corner.

Importing a pet

Only holders of Z-visas are allowed to import a pet, limited to one per passport. Before entering China, check your home country's policies toward animal export. Any animal can be imported into China, but anything other than a companion animal – a dog or a cat – is considered to be exotic and must undergo a special inspection upon entering China. Companion animals must have certification of up-to-date rabies vaccination status, an official export certificate from the source country and a health certificate from a qualified veterinarian.

Upon arrival, all companion animals are subject to a 30-day quarantine period, which takes place at a government-run facility and requires an initial deposit of RMB 1,000. The final cost, calculated afterwards, is usually about equal to the deposit. If you use an experienced relocation company, you may be able to reduce the length of quarantine to one week or even overnight. Officials rarely grant requests for home quarantine except for elderly pets or pets with difficult medical requirements. After quarantine, animals are taken to the Beijing Ornamental Animal Hospital for verification of the rabies vaccination.

The procedure for "exotic" animals is more complicated. Before arriving, the owner must contact the Entry-Exit Inspection and Quarantine Bureau to find a suitable quarantine site, which must then be inspected and granted a temporary quarantine permit by the Quarantine Bureau. The owner must then apply for an "Animal and Plant Inspection and Quarantine Permit" from the Beijing Quality Control Inspection Bureau. The animal will then be subject to a 45-day quarantine upon arrival, the exact fees for which are not known.

Most airlines allow small pets to be brought on board in soft-sided carriers if they fit underneath the passenger seat. Larger pets will go in the pressurized cargo hold. The cost of transportation depends on your departure point. It is your responsibility to point out small pet carriers, which may go unnoticed, to custom officials. A small litter box is a good idea for cats, as the plane flight can be long and pet-oriented facilities in the airport are nonexistent.

Dog rules

Living in Beijing with a pet can be a challenge, especially given the lack of wide-open spaces. Only dogs, however, are regulated, due to a rapid rise in the incidence of rabies. The Beijing government requires all dogs be registered at the nearest police station (*paichusuo*), with the goal of preventing unregistered and presumably unvaccinated dogs from running amok.

Restrictions vary depending on location, with one set of rules for urban Beijing (roughly within the Fifth Ring Road) and another for outer Beijing (e.g., Shunyi). In urban Beijing, only one dog is allowed per household and the dog can't be taller than 35cm at the shoulder, though guide dogs are an exception. Procedures differ slightly for diplomats living within an embassy – contact the Foreigners Management Office of the Beijing Municipal Police Security Bureau (8401 5327) for details.

To register within the city, you first need a dog-keeping permit from your neighborhood committee. Bring them a passport with a residence permit, a proof of residence (the deed or a rental contract) and, for imported

Gemen'r *of a feather travel together*

dogs, a quarantine certificate. Then take the dog-keeping permit, all documents above, and two passport-sized photos of the dog (head shot from the front) to the local police station. Some police stations may want to see the dog itself. The registration fee is RMB 1,000, reduced to RMB 500 for neutered or spayed dogs.

Fortunately, that hefty RMB 1,000 entitles you to a free check-up, including a rabies vaccine, at officially licensed animal hospitals. These official hospitals will then issue the Beijing Animal Health and Immunity Certificate (the red booklet), which is necessary to re-register your dog every year, to move to another city in China, and to bring it out of China. Annual registration renewal costs RMB 500.

Outside of city areas, one dog is allowed per passport holder. All that is needed in the 'burbs is a passport and two photos of the dog being registered, though it is recommended you obtain a rabies vaccine and Animal Health and Immunity Certificate. Registration in these areas costs a measly RMB 200. Residents of Shunyi villas may be able to register their dog directly at the villa office, bypassing the police station. If your heart is set on a large dog or own one already, it's best to check the policies of your residential compound before signing a contract.

If your dog is caught without registration, you will be fined RMB 2,000 in addition to the registration fee. If this is not paid, the animal will be kenneled and put up for adoption until accounts are settled. In most cases, however, it is sufficient to assure the security officer that you intend to register the dog very very soon.

Exporting a pet

The process of exporting a pet is like following a paper trail as you fumble from one form to another. A good rule of thumb is to keep every piece of paper used to bring the animal into China and every scrap related to something that was done to your pet while here. At least four months before departure, check the requirements for exporting a companion animal to your country, as well as the latest restrictions of the Entry-Exit Quarantine and Inspection Bureau.

Most countries require animal companions to be vaccinated between one and twelve months before entering from abroad. All dogs must be vaccinated for rabies. Legally licensed hospitals will update your Animal Health and Immunity Certificate (the red booklet) upon vaccinating a pet. This is the official proof of vaccination and is necessary to export your pet.

Next, pets will need an exit health examination at Beijing Ornamental Animal Hospital, the government's official facility. The exam must be done between seven and ten days before departure. Fees vary, but it's a good idea to bring at least RMB 800 in cash for each pet. Upon successful completion of the exam, you will receive the Beijing International Companion Animal Health Inspection Form. Take this and the red booklet to the Entry-Exit Quarantine and Inspection Bureau to receive the Animal Health Certificate, which is valid for two weeks. You'll need all three documents at the airport to bring your pet out.

Many countries, including those in the European Union, require testing for the rabies antibody titre for imported pets. To do this, a veterinarian can take a sample of your pet's blood one month after vaccination. You will then have to take this sample (in a sealed, refrigerated test tube) to the official laboratory in your destination country. Most countries also require dogs to be microchipped for import, and a few require the same for cats, as this is considered the most effective method for pet identification.

Inspection treaties for some animals, such as rabbits and fowl (can you say "bird flu"?), vary from country to country, so it is best to check with the Beijing Entry-Exit Inspection and Quarantine Bureau well in advance of departure. Note that all animals must be shipped in a carrier with ventilation on all four sides, and will not be shipped in extreme temperatures.

For listings of relocation companies that ship pets, see p655.

This section was updated with the help of the International Center for Veterinary Services (p664).

Beijing Entry-Exit Inspection and Quarantine Bureau
Mon-Fri 8.30-11.40am and 1-5pm. 6 Tianshuiyuan Jie, Chaoyang District. (5861 9881/ 9044) 北京出入境检验检疫局，朝阳区甜水园街6号

Beijing Ornamental Animal Hospital (Guanshang or Beijing Pet Hospital) See p664 for listing.

Finding a pet

If you decide to buy a dog or cat, take your time and consider asking a qualified vet to recommend a licensed breeder or a reliable rescue center. The International Center for Veterinary Services warns that most animals found in pet shops and especially animal markets are unhealthy. Such animals are often taken from their mothers at too young an age and may be bleached with harmful chemicals. What's more, they are usually unvaccinated. If you do buy from a breeder, ask to see his or her registration and licenses with the Agricultural Bureau, or seek out breeders for whom you have recommendations.

On the following pages are some suggestions for where to acquire a new pal. Small pets are the easiest to find, particularly traditional pets such as fish and birds. While a variety of dog breeds are available in Beijing, keep in mind the requirements of non-native species. A Siberian Husky, for example, may not flourish in the Beijing summer. Flower markets often sell fish, turtles, ducklings and birds and the requisite equipment. Many veterinary hospitals also offer pets for adoption.

Aisida Dog Market This one-stop market on the outskirts of the city has numerous dog and cat sellers, a pet clinic, a restaurant and a demonstration area where dogs can show off their tricks. All kinds of dogs, from regular terriers and larger collies to rare breeds such as hairless Chinese varieties are available. All canines are vaccinated and mostly kept in roomy cages.
Daily 8am-10pm. 8A Fatou, Wangsiying Town, Chaoyang District. (6736 6155) 艾斯达狗市，朝阳区王四营乡堡头甲8号

Carepets This website lists cats available for adoption. Rescued from difficult situations, the cats are all domesticated, have had shots and have been "fixed." Carepets also provides post-adoption support.
http://carepets.blog.com.cn

Cat Friends Established in 2001, Cat Friends has dozens of stray cats vaccinated, dewormed, spayed and waiting for adoption. Post-adoption medical support included. Also sells cat supplies and toys through their website, with all profits going to cat rescue.
Contact Scarlett (135 0131 5988) www.beijingcat.org

Dasenlin Flower Market Has an excellent selection of freshwater fish, aquatic plants and coral. Most of the saltwater fish vendors specialize in importing fish.
Mon-Fri 8.30am-6pm, Sat-Sun 8.30am-6.30pm. 5 Zaojunmiao, Haidian District. (6211 9255) 大森林花卉市场，海淀区皂君庙5号

Guanyuan Fish and Bird Market The usual suspects of googly-eyed goldfish share the stalls with scorpions, insects, loaches, spiky aquatic critters and more.
North of Fuchengmen (inside Xierhuan), Xicheng District. 官园鱼市场，西城阜成门北（西二环内）

Laitai Flower Market Enormous selection of fish, turtles, groovy fish tanks and tchotchkes. Bargain hard for a good price.
Mon-Thu 9am-6pm, Fri-Sun 9am-6.30 pm. 9 Maizidian Xilu, Chaoyang District. (6463 6145) 莱太花卉市场，朝阳区麦子店西路9号

Prime Pet Shop Focuses on matching you with the right dog, cat or rabbit. Also has pet grooming. Manager Stanley Kam speaks English.
Daily 10am-7pm. Rm 103, Bldg 304, Huizhong Beili, Yayuncun, Chaoyang District. (6485 5577) 赛狼，朝阳区亚运村惠忠北里304号楼103室

Qiqi Pets Sells cats, dogs, pet supplies and has animals available for adoption. Dr. Yuan speaks English.
Daily 9.30am-6pm. 8 Laiguangying Donglu (northwest corner of Capital Garden), Shunyi District. (8142 2927, 139 1090 0985) 奇奇，顺义区来广营东路8号（名都园西北角）

Warrior, Muse and Musician
A cricket of many talents
by Shelley Jiang

If your income isn't quite enough to fuel your high-flying Beijing lifestyle, it may be time for a new pet. A cricket, believe it or not, was once the surefire path to riches, eternal glory and even literary and artistic recognition.

Insignificant as these little guys may be in Western culture, crickets are heavyweights in China – especially when it comes to a good fight to the death. From emperors on down, people have loved dueling crickets since the Tang Dynasty, whether for the excitement alone or for considerable wagers of land and money. The stakes are no less high today: A 2004 raid on a Shanghai cricket gambling den uncovered more than RMB 1.8 million in bets.

The ideal fighting cricket has a black face and big jaws perfect for ripping off its opponent's head with one clean snap. Before matches, crickets are starved to provoke them into a foul frenzy. Still, these days even crickets are suspected of "doping" with stimulants or, ironically enough, bug repellant (to scare the other guy).

But crickets aren't kept solely for dueling. A brave fighter was also a good muse. Inspired by a valiant match, scholars might pen a poem or two to honor the scrappy insect, while artists would paint its victory portrait. Imperial concubines took crickets to bed to hear their singing. In fact, Ming emperor Xuande (r. 1426-35) even

Patient prodding inflames the cricket rage

established a cricket tax: Peasants had to give their best specimens to the imperial cricket-assessor – and disobedience was a capital offense. According to a Ming-dynasty history, one couple went as far as to kill themselves, after their prize cricket escaped, rather than face the tax collector empty-handed.

A fighter's life was often nasty, brutish and short, yet the lucky few that attained Mike Tyson status could live like kings. They feasted on fish, apples, water chestnuts and even ginseng, while their lesser counterparts had to subside on flour and mosquitoes. Doting owners might provide a harem of females and, upon death, a coffin and a funeral.

Musically gifted crickets could count on homes of exquisite bamboo, gold, or ivory cages or hollowed out gourds – now priceless works of art. In winter, lucky crickets might snuggle against their owner, so the body heat would keep them chirpy. You may wonder what's so appealing about non-stop buzzing against your skin, but to Chinese people, the singing was a sign of poignant sadness as summer turned to fall.

Interested in joining the cricket craze? The fiercest monsters cost up to RMB 10,000, but most are around a few *kuai*. From September to November, head to Panjiayuan, Taoranting, or Guanyuan Market to check out fights or pick up a little Tyson of your own.

A charming scene like this is only legal outside the Fifth Ring Road

Tian Yu Fish Market Get your fish here and everything you need to keep them swimming healthily.
Tuanjiehu Lu (just northeast of Tuanjiehu Park), Chaoyang District. 天宇鱼市，朝阳区团结湖路（团结湖公园东北）

Yiya Pet Store and Hospital A one-stop solution for all your canine supply needs, including grooming, hospital services and miscellaneous products. They have purebred puppies and kittens for sale.
Store and grooming: Daily 9am-7pm. Hospital: Daily 8.30am-9pm. 34 Gongti Beilu, Dongcheng District. (6552 6178, 6552 6177) 怡亚，东城区工体北路34号

Pet food, accessories and services

Major Western pet food brands are widely available in large supermarkets, while more specialized and imported pet foods can be bought at vets' clinics for higher prices. There are also good Chinese brands, but keep in mind the 2007 pet food scare in America. Beyond food, there are pet fashions to be considered. Didn't you always wonder what that sixth sense was?

Coolbaby The Chaoyang Park location features a dog park, store and restaurant spread over 40 acres. A fee of RMB 10 (per human) allows your dog to spend the day running, swimming, jumping through hoops, playing catch and enjoying a bit of freedom. The other two branches are stores only, selling dog and cat food, tearless shampoos (RMB 25-135), toys and more.
1) Daily 8.30am-8pm. Chaoyang Gongyuan Nanlu (inside the Chaoyang Park Tennis Center), Chaoyang District. (131 2111 1166); 2) Daily 10am-8pm. 52 Gulouwai Dajie, Dongcheng District. (8411 0547); 3) Rm 6, Bldg 14, Dongzhimennei Dajie, Dongcheng District. (8407 4198) 1）酷迪宠物餐厅，朝阳区朝阳公园南路1号朝阳公园网球中心内；2）酷迪宠物超市，东城区鼓楼外大街52号；3）东城区东直门内大街14号楼6号

Dongjiao Market Find a home for your creature companion, as long as it fits in a tank or a cage.
See Shopping, p400.

Fruits & Passion When your pet really needs that extra sparkle: high-end pampering products such as eau de toilette, shampoo, sprays for freshness and luster and deodorizer.
Daily 10am-9pm. NB146, China World Shopping Mall (near the ice rink), 1 Jianguomenwai Dajie. (6505 1538) 嘉贝诗爱犬热狗系列，建国门外大街1号国贸商城地下一层NB146商铺（冰场旁）

Guanyuan Fish and Bird Market Sells tanks for your fishy friends and cricket cages.
See p660 for address.

Taobao.com *See listing in Shopping, p408.*

Yiya Pet Store and Hospital Their grooming experts hail from Hong Kong, that locus of hair expertise, and will give your dog a wash, trim or even a dye job, with prices starting at RMB 200.
See listing on p662.

Finding a vet

The recent pet trend has triggered a huge demand for animal care providers, with over 120 veterinary hospitals in Beijing. Unfortunately, unlicensed clinics abound, some "vets" have received little formal training, and others have gained most of their experience working with large farm animals. Thus, it is recommended that you take your pets to legal, officially licensed veterinary hospitals: Only they are allowed to purchase and administer vaccines in Beijing. Moreover, they are required to buy high-quality imported vaccines from the Animal Husbandry Bureau, thus avoiding the dangers of fake or low-quality vaccines. Ask to see your vet's license and look for the bronze sign from the Beijing Agricultural Bureau (北京市农业局).

Aikang Veterinary Hospital Dr Liu Xi and Dr Zhang Zhihong speak English.

Useful Numbers
A handy telephone directory

Listen to your elders: Do it by the numbers

Emergency Numbers
Emergencies & Ambulance: 120
Fire: 119
Police: 110
Traffic accident: 122
Foreigners Section of the Beijing Public Security Bureau: 8402 0101
International SOS Assistance: 6462 9100

Clinics and Hospitals
Bayley & Jackson Medical Center: 8562 9998
Beijing International SOS Clinic: 6462 9112
Beijing United Family Hospital: 6433 3960
Beijing United Shunyi Clinic: 6433 3960
Beijing Vista Clinic: 8529 6618
Global Doctor Clinic: 8456 9191 (24 hours)
Hong Kong International Medical Clinic: 6553 2288 (24 hours)
International Medical Centre: 6465 1561 (24-hour ambulance)
Peking Union Medical Hospital: 6529 5284
Sino-Japanese Friendship Hospital: 6422 2952

Information
Local Telephone Directory: 114 (Chinese); 2689 0114 (English). To look up phone numbers in another city in China, dial 0 + area code + 114.
Time: 117
Weather: 12121
Beijing Railway Info: 6512 9525
Beijing Travel Taxi Company: 6515 8604/05
Beijing Capital Airport Info: 6512 8931
Consumer Complaint Line: 12315 (Chinese)
Immigration Bureau of Beijing: 6525 3102
Postal Service: 11185
MasterCard: 6510 1090/95
Tourist Info: 6513 0828
Visa Card: 6506 4371

Bank Hotlines
Agricultural Bank: 95599
Bank of Beijing: 96169
Bank of China: 95566
Bank of Communications: 95559
Citibank: 800 830 1880
CITIC Industrial Bank: 95558
Construction Bank: 95533
Guangda Bank: 95595
HSBC: 800 820 8878
Huaxia Bank: 95577
ICBC: 95588
Merchants Bank: 95555
Minsheng Bank: 95568
Pudong Development Bank: 95528
Shenzhen Development Bank: 95501
Standard Chartered: 6566 9888

Country Codes
Dial 00 and then the country code for international calls.
Country Code Directory: 95115

Australia: 61	**Malaysia:** 60
Austria: 43	**Mongolia:** 976
Belgium: 32	**Myanmar:** 95
Canada: 1	**Nepal:** 977
China: 86	**Netherlands:** 31
Czech Republic: 420	**New Zealand:** 64
Denmark: 45	**Norway:** 47
Finland: 358	**Pakistan:** 92
France: 33	**Philippines:** 63
Germany: 49	**Russia:** 7
Hungary: 36	**Singapore:** 65
India: 91	**South Korea:** 82
Indonesia: 62	**Spain:** 34
Ireland: 353	**Sweden:** 46
Israel: 972	**Switzerland:** 41
Italy: 39	**Thailand:** 66
Japan: 81	**United Kingdom:** 44
Kazakhstan: 7	**USA:** 1
Laos: 856	**Vietnam:** 84

PHOTO: TOM CARTER

USEFUL INFO

Daily 9am-10pm. 45 Tianshuiyuan Dongli (opposite the south gate of Tuanjiehu Park), Chaoyang District. (6504 2085) 爱康动物医院，朝阳区甜水园东里45号楼底商

Beijing Ornamental Animal Hospital (Guanshang / Beijing Pet Hospital) Run by the Health and Quarantine Station of China, this hospital provides the Beijing International Companion Animal Health Inspection Form needed to export your pet. After vaccinating your pet (RMB 60), they can give you the official red booklet for RMB 30. Veterinary acupuncture also available. Services available in Chinese, English (Dr. Tony Beck) and Japanese.
Daily 9am-6.30pm. 7 Beisanhuan Zhonglu, Xicheng District. (6204 9631, English 6202 3827, emergency 135 0103 0572) www.chinapet.com.cn 北京观赏动物医院，西城区北三环中路7号

Fangzhuang Banlü Veterinary Hospital Daily 8.30am-10pm. Bldg 20, Area 3, Fangxingyuan, 23 Nansanhuan Donglu (facing Sanhuan, 100m west of Fangzhuang Qiao), Fengtai District. (6760 5989) 方庄伴侣动物医院，丰台区方庄南三环东路方星园3区20号楼底商

International Center for Veterinary Services This full-service hospital has a team of local doctors working side-by-side with international specialists. International-standard facilities offer the full range of health care services, including immediate on-site blood testing, and a surgery, treatment and quarantine rooms, a kennel and a pet shop selling imported and certified safe pet foods. Boarding, day care, grooming and obedience training also available. All services in English and Mandarin.
Mon-Sat 9am-6pm (by appointment only). Kent Center, 29 Liangmaqiao Lu, Anjialou (in the same courtyard as Cherry Lane Movies), Chaoyang District. (8456 1939/1940/1941) www.icvsasia.com 北京新天地国际动物医院，朝阳区安家楼亮马桥路29号肯特中心

K.K. Animal Hospital Treatment, surgery, vaccinations and other veterinary services for your pets. Offers kenneling, grooming, obedience training and a wide range of pet care products.
Daily 9am-7.30pm. 801-802 Pinnacle Plaza, Shunyi District. (8046 2358, 133 1129 3008) 康康宠物医院，顺义区荣祥广场801-802

Pet Shop and Grooming Parlour This pet salon offers a wide range of pet products and grooming services. Veterinarian Dr. Tony Beck is in attendance on Wed and Sat.
Tue, Thu-Fri 9am-6pm; Wed, Sat 10am-4pm.118A Shunhuang Lu, Sunhe Xiang, Chaoyang District. (8459 3083) 朝阳区孙河乡顺黄路甲118号

Wa Wa Pet Hospital Specializes in rare dog breeds and miniature pigs for RMB 2,500 each. Veterinary care includes acupuncture for RMB 50-70 a session.
Daily 24 hours. Bldg 1, Nongguang Nanli (200m south of Jinsong Bridge), Chaoyang District. (8737 1999) 娃娃动物医院，朝阳区农光南里1号楼（劲松桥往南200米）

Wanghong Veterinary Hospital Daily 8am-10pm. 1/F, Bldg B3, Lianhuachi Donglu, Xicheng District. (6344 7717) 望虹动物医院，西城区莲花池东路乙3号楼1层

Wangjing Veterinary Hospital Daily 24 hours. 7A Huajiadi Nanjie, Chaoyang District. (6475 2626) 望京宠物医院，朝阳区花家地甲7号

Kennels

Leaving your pet in a kennel is never easy, especially in Beijing where standards vary widely. Check out the facility before you board Fifi there.

Dogs DayCare in Beijing Cindy will look after your dog in her home for daylong stays or longer. Includes walks and grooming for RMB 30-70 per day. Cage space is limited.
Daily 8am-8pm. Rm 511, Unit 5, Bldg 31, Hualong Compound, Longwangzhuang, Tongzhou District. (8377 8817) 托狗所，通州区龙王庄华龙小区31号楼5门511号

Qiqi Pets Animals apparently get lots of exercise here. Cost is RMB 60-90 per day, depending on the animal's size. Pick-up and delivery service available for a fee (RMB 50-100).
See listing on p660.

Sheerwood Beijing Equestrian Club The boarding fees of around RMB 500 per week are used to support a veterinary clinic for rescued pets.
East of Old Airport Road (south bank of Wenyu River), Shunyi District. (5188 4137, 135 0108 6611) 西坞马术俱乐部，顺义区温榆河南岸老机场路东边

Telephones
Mobile phones

The future has arrived, minus flying cars and aliens, making a cell phone a social necessity. If you want to become one of the over 508 million cell phone users in China, see Shopping, p405, for where to pick one up. New phones range from about RMB 300 to ridiculous, though a used phone can be picked up for as little as RMB 200.

Once you've picked a model, you'll need to choose a service provider and billing plan and purchase the corresponding SIM card (i.e. a telephone number). Don't lose the SIM card's punch-out casing: It comes with a password that you'll need in order to retain your phone number if your phone is lost or stolen. To start making calls, you'll have to either sign up for a telecom account or buy pre-paid phone cards, which are available in several denominations and widely sold in cell phone shops, convenience stores and newsstands.

But which plan is right for you?

While China Mobile tends to have better coverage in China, China Unicom's network is advancing rapidly. Base domestic long-distance rates for all plans add RMB 0.07 per six seconds to the local rates. Each network has IP numbers, which you dial before the phone number, for additional savings.

Nokia will connect you to plucky buddies, disgruntled landlords and feisty foes alike

China Mobile

Shenzhouxing is the cheapest overall, while Donggan Didai, with a monthly minimum fee of RMB 10, is ideal for those who send more than 120 text messages every month. The most expensive, Quanqiutong features international roaming. Text messages (SMS) are RMB 0.10-0.20 each.
(10086) www.china-mobile.com 中国移动

	Shenzhouxing (Easy-Own)	Donggan Didai (M-Zone)	Quanqiutong (GoTone)
Flat Fee	-	RMB 10-50 (includes 120-1,000 SMS)	RMB 50
Local	RMB 0.60 per min	RMB 0.12-0.25 per min	RMB 0.40 per min
Incoming	RMB 0.60 per min	RMB 0.12-0.25 per min	Free
Add-ons (Monthly fees; sign-up basis)	RMB 3 eliminates roaming fees. RMB 10 gets 500min of incoming calls. RMB 20 gets unlimited incoming calls and local rates of RMB 0.25 per min.	RMB 3 for RMB 0.50 per min roaming fees. RMB 15 for 500min of incoming calls and 10MB of GPRS.	Monthly packages of RMB 99-299 include local minutes, lower long-distance rates, and GPRS.
IP numbers	12593 (save RMB 0.40 per min on local calls and RMB 1.00 on domestic)	17591 (save RMB 0.60 per min on domestic)	17591 (save RMB 0.60 per min on domestic)

USEFUL INFO

China Unicom

China Unicom offers CDMA (Xin Shikong) as well as GSM (Shijie Feng, Up Xin Shili, Ruyi Tong) network service. The IP number 17911 grants savings on long-distance calls.
(10010) www.bj.chinaunicom.com 中国联通

	Xin Shikong (CDMA)	Shijie Feng (GSM/CDMA)	UP Xin Shili (GSM)	Ruyi Tong (GSM)
Flat fee	-	RMB 1.48 per day + RMB 10 per month	RMB 15-50 (includes 250-1,000 SMS)	Pay as you go; or RMB 80 or 200
Local	RMB 0.20-54 per min	RMB 0.40 per min	RMB 0.25 per min	400min (RMB 0.2/min) or 600min (RMB 0.13/min)
Note	-	Users can switch between CDMA and GSM	-	Pay as you go (with no flat fee): RMB 0.54 per min

Bringing a cell phone from home

Almost all GSM phones (those that use a SIM card) are useable in China. One notable exception is dual-band GSM phones from North America, where the GSM network operates on a different frequency than that of the rest of the world; thus, North American phones must be at least tri-band to work abroad.

You can, of course, pay expensive roaming charges, but a cheaper way is to unlock your cell phone so that it is no longer fixed to your home network and will accept SIM cards from local networks in any country. The process of unlocking differs from phone to phone, so check with your service provider for details. Nokia users can get a free code online (http://unlock.nokiafree.org), and other phones may require paying a fee to the home service provider, while third-party businesses can also do the trick. If you want the ability to read and write Chinese on your phone, a technician must install Chinese software; make sure the Chinese version also uses your native language and be sure to store your phonebook and data onto a SIM card beforehand.

Many large stores that fix cell phones can make these changes for you, usually for about RMB 100 to unlock and RMB 300 for software. Zoomflight (中复) is a reliable store, with branches all over the city, and another large mobile phone center, on the bottom floor of the Xidan mobile phone market, has representatives from most major mobile phone manufacturers. For more information on unlocking mobile phones, see www.thetravelinsider.info/roadwarriorcontent/unlockingfaq.htm.

Landlines

In order to get a phone line installed, you have to apply to Beijing Telecom (a branch of China Telecom) or to China Netcom. Remember to apply for international and long distance service or else you'll have to use IP cards.

Both Beijing Telecom and China Netcom charge the same monthly fee of RMB 21.6 for a landline or RMB 32.4 for an ISDN line. They also charge the same long-distance rates, but Beijing Telecom's discounted hours are longer than those of China Netcom (midnight-7am). Domestic long-distance calls are RMB 0.7 (discounted rate RMB 0.4) per min; to Hong Kong, Macau and Taiwan RMB 2 (Beijing Telecom discount RMB 1.5); and calls abroad are RMB 8 (discounted rate RMB 4.8).

For more billing info, see Housing, p32.

Beijing Telecom Installation of both regular landlines and ISDN lines costs RMB 200.
1 Chaoyangmen Beidajie, Dongcheng District. (10000, 5950 3000) www.bjtelecom.net 中国电信北京公司，东城区朝阳门北大街21号

China Netcom Regular landlines cost RMB 235 to install, and ISDN lines cost RMB 315. If you already have a regular phone line, then you can add an ISDN line for RMB 95.
Daily 8.30am-6pm. 65 Jianguomennei Dajie, Dongcheng District. (10060) www.bj.cnc.cn 中国网通北京公司，东城区建国门内大街65号

International calls

To make an international direct-dial (IDD) call from China, dial 00, the country code, then the domestic phone number. Note that a pre-paid IP card has significantly cheaper rates for international calls. If you wish to make a collect call or a credit card call, dial "108" and then the

"Good news and bad news. I've got two sacks full of cockroaches. The bad news is ..."

country code. This will connect you to an operator in the country that you are dialing. Note: for the US, dialing 108-888 connects you with AT&T, 108-712 with MCI, and 108-16 with Sprint.

Phone cards

IP cards can be used for your mobile or home phone to make domestic and international calls. Buy them from cell phone stores, newsstands and China Telecom outlets. Never pay the face value of an IP card – the going rate for a RMB 100 card was RMB 30-40 at time of writing. Different IP cards have different long-distance rates and call qualities for different countries, so it's best to check the back before buying. The 17930 card, for example, is rare, but is your best bet for calling the US or Canada: North American rates are RMB 2.40 per min, and other foreign countries RMB 3.20 (compared to the regular RMB 8). Some IP cards can be used at public telephones, while most will work only from a home or mobile phone, so inquire before purchasing.

IC cards are used for domestic calls at yellow payphones and come in a variety of values (and sell for face value).

Voice over Internet Protocol (VoIP)

In addition to phone cards, many people now use services that make cheap international phone calls over a broadband Internet connection. Services like Skype (www.skype.com) and Google Talk (www.google.com/talk) are straightforward and popular. With a microphone headset, these software programs allow you to make free computer-to-computer and cheap computer-to-telephone calls. Most people attest to reasonable call quality in Beijing on a home ADSL connection, and if you don't have broadband access at home, you can usually find these programs and headsets at Internet cafes around town. Alternately, if you make a large volume of international calls, stand-alone VoIP services such as BroadVoice (www.broadvoice.com), Lingo (www.lingo.com) or Vonage (www.vonage.com) offer cheaper and more reliable service. Unlimited monthly plans range from USD 25-35 (requires international credit card).

Tickets

A number of websites sell tickets for concerts, dance performances, sporting events, fashion shows, movies and other cultural events. Tickets can be paid for in cash, online, or through bank transfers, and they deliver within the Fourth Ring Road 24 hours after ordering. The websites listed below are in both Chinese and English:
www.228.com.cn *(800 810 1887, 8408 5551; delivery min. RMB 100)*
www.emma.cn *(6553 5699; delivery min. RMB 200)*
www.piao.com.cn *(800 810 3721, 6417 7845; delivery min. RMB 100, within Fifth Ring)*

USEFUL INFO

Visas

If you're a foreigner reading this in Beijing, chances are, you've got a Chinese visa. If not, you could be in a bit of trouble. Visa application and extension procedures can be time-consuming and are subject to change, due to the political climate or other factors. Keep in mind that in the months running up to the Olympics, Beijing police and visa officials are enforcing restrictions and tightening control of visa issuance policies. What follows is a bare-bones rundown on what you might need to know.

Visa basics and types

All visa-holders are required to register with the Public Security Bureau (PSB) in their neighborhood within 24 hours of arrival in Beijing or after moving. (Registration at a hotel counts as registration at the PSB.) It is important to take this requirement seriously: Local authorities run frequent checks in apartment compounds, especially in the time running up to the Olympics.

If you have a single-entry visa but want to take a quick jaunt abroad, you need to apply for a re-entry visa at the Exit & Entry Administration of the PSB (see below) – this won't extend the overall length of your original visa, however.

The fine for overstaying your visa is RMB 500 per day, with the total sum limited to a maximum of RMB 5,000.

For more information on visas, refer to www.bjgaj.gov.cn/epolice/qianzheng.htm

L (lüyou) – Tourist Visa
The L visa is issued for family visits, sightseeing, or "other private purposes." L visas usually grant a period of 90 days to enter China and are generally valid for 30 days, though one may request a longer stay (they've been known to grant up to 180 days). Double- or multiple-entry is available.

F (fangwen) – Business Visa
Officially, the F visa is designated for foreigners who are coming for a visit, an investigation or a lecture; to do business, scientific-technological and culture exchanges or short-term advanced studies; or to intern for a period of no more than six months. They are also issued to students studying for up to six months. As with the L visa, F visas usually grant you a period of 90 days to enter China and are then valid for 30 days, though a visa officer can, and usually will, grant a longer duration of stay. It is possible to get double- or multiple-entry visas for a stay of six or twelve months, for which one needs more documentation, such as a visa-issuance letter from a Chinese governmental organization or invitation letters from both a foreign company and its branch in China.

Z (jiuye) – Work Visa
The Z visa allows the bearer to work full-time in China with a Chinese or foreign company, school or other entity, and is also granted for accompanying family members. Applicants need a visa notification issued from the inviting organization and a work permit issued by the Chinese Labor Ministry or a Foreign Expert's License issued by the Chinese Foreign Expert Bureau. Family members need proof of kinship.

X (xuexi) – Student Visa
The X visa is intended for foreigners who come to China to study or intern for more than six months. Students need letters from their university.

G (guojing) – Transit Visa
Required for travelers staying in China for over 24 hours. Single- and double-entry visas are available. This visa grants a period of 90 days to enter China and is valid for 7-10 days per entry. Details for nationalities vary, so check with the Chinese embassy or consulate in your country first.

D (dingju) – Resident Visa
D visas are for foreigners who set up permanent residence in China. Apply through the local entry-exit department of the public security bureau in the city or county of planned residence.

J (jizhe) – Journalist Visa
J-1 visas are issued to journalists working in China for over one year. J-2 visas are issued to those on temporary assignments in China. Applicants need to submit a press card and official letter from the Department of News, a branch of the Ministry of Foreign Affairs.

C (chengwu) – Crew Visa
C visas are issued to crew members (and their accompanying family members) on international trains, airliners or water vessels.

Tourist Group Visa
For a group of at least five people entering and leaving China together.

Diplomatic or Service Visa
Issued to members of diplomatic missions, foreign governments, or the UN, traveling to China on official missions or for accreditation.

Residence permits

Z, X and J-1 visas only grant initial stays of 30 days. Before the 30 days are up, you must apply for residence permits at the Exit & Entry Administration of the Public Security Bureau. Each visa type requires slightly different documentation, which your company or university should supply, but all those planning to stay one year or longer must have health certification from the Exit & Entry Inspection & Quarantine Bureau. Residence permits replace the visa and grant unlimited exit and entry from China for the duration of its validity.

Residence permits issued for Z and J-1 visas are usually easily renewed, requiring only the same documentation with which you procured the permit, but students on an X visa will have to have a letter from the university – difficult for those on one-year programs who wish to stay longer.

Whether you come to Beijing by Boeing 777 or double-hump camel, you'll still need that pesky visa

Renewing or changing your visa

In most cases, visas can be extended fairly easily. L visas can generally be extended for an additional month with little hassle; F visas will require sponsorship letters from your employer or school/university. Applications for a visa extension should be submitted at least five business days before the original visa is to due to expire. Visa extensions are handled by the Exit & Entry Administration of the PSB.

It's much more difficult to change your visa from one type to another. In fact, it's impossible to change an X visa to any other without leaving China and procuring an entirely new visa. L visas can change to F and X visas, with supporting documents from the company or school. For all other unapproved visa changes, it may be necessary to leave the country or hire a visa agent.

Exit & Entry Administration of the Public Security Bureau *Mon-Sat 8.30am-4.30pm. 2 Andingmen Dongdajie (by Xiaojie Qiao), Dongcheng District. (8402 0101, 8401 5294)* 北京市公安局出入境管理处, 东城区安定门东大街2号

The Hong Kong run

Think of it as bureaucracy's way of making you take a vacation. Every now and then it's necessary to leave the country for a night to renew or extend your visa. If it's time for a night out, and you have too many issues for the mainland to handle, you have a good excuse to head to Hong Kong. (Not directly, though; save yourself some money by flying into Shenzhen, hopping bus 101, and then taking the Kowloon Canton Rail.) At the end of your pilgrimage, in the China Resources Building in Wan Chai, lies the Visa Office – otherwise known as the "Ministry of Doom" due to its intimidating facade.

You may be forgiven for imagining that the Visa Office of the People's Republic of China would not bother closing for Easter – forgiven, but wrong. Check the calendar before you head over, for the city shuts down for holidays such as Buddha's Birthday, Christmas, Chinese New Year and Hong Kong SAR Establishment Day. Obtaining a tourist visa requires only a passport and a photo, which can be taken while in line, but is rarely given for more than a month. If you're in a hurry, you can drop off your visa in the morning and pick it up in the afternoon for an express fee of HKD 250.

If this all seems like a bit much for you, Hong Kong travel agencies can arrange visas for mainland China. The China Travel Service (CTS) is best for L visas and for applications that have all requisite supporting documents. Otherwise, head to a visa agent, who can help with such things as obtaining L, X and F visas,

Hong Kong: the visa run gauntlet

changing single- or double-entry visas to multiple-entry ones, changing your visa type, obtaining invitation letters, and getting international and Chinese driving licenses.

Seen in another light, the visa run is also an excuse to head south to one of the world's most cosmopolitan cities. Try heading out to one of the outlying islands, such as Lantau or Cheung Chau for great hikes and beaches. While it's possible to find a visa dealer in Beijing with comparable prices, munching on fresh seafood and sipping a pint in the tropical sun is a remarkably satisfying way to prolong your stay on the Chinese mainland.

Visa Office of the Ministry of Foreign Affairs of the PRC Mon-Fri 9am-noon, 2-5pm. 7/F, Lower Block, China Resources Bldg, 26 Harbour Rd., Wan Chai, Hong Kong. (+852 3413 2424) 签证办公室，香港湾仔港湾道26号华润大厦7层

China Travel Service (HK) Ltd (CTS) With 43 locations. See website for details.
1/F, Alpha House, and 2/F, 27-33 Nathan Rd. (entrance on Peking Rd.), Tsim Sha Tsui, Kowloon, Hong Kong. (+852 2851 1700) www.ctshk.com 港中旅，香港九龙尖沙咀弥敦道27–33号良士大厦1层（北京路入口2层）

CITS Hong Kong Rm 604-606, 6/F, Tower 2, South Seas Centre, 75 Mody Rd., Tsim Sha Tsui, Kowloon, Hong Kong. (+852 2732 5888) www.cits.com.hk 香港国旅，香港九龙尖沙咀么地道75号南洋中心2座6层604–606

Shoestring Travel 4/F, Alpha House, 27-33 Nathan Rd., Tsim Sha Tsui, Kowloon, Hong Kong. (+852 2723 2306) www.shoestringtravel.com.hk 天星旅行社，香港九龙尖沙咀弥敦道27–33号良士大厦4层

Hong Kong prices, no Hong Kong

There are several "visa consulting" outfits operating in Beijing that can help with the kinds of services that the Hong Kong visa agents provide. They usually charge prices that are only slightly cheaper than the cost of going to Hong Kong and using an agent there. Many visa consultants advertise on www.thebeijinger.com

Green card

A Chinese Green Card, while difficult to obtain, provides a more permanent solution to residency difficulties. This off-white card is granted to foreigners of "extraordinary" ability. Applicants must have Chinese national family members, make large direct investments in China for three consecutive years, contribute significantly to China's development, or hold a high-level position in a company deemed to promote China's social, economic, business or scientific progress and have lived in China for three out of the past four years. The card is valid for five years for foreigners under 18, and ten years for those over 18. A Chinese Green Card may not be easy to obtain, but the reward is a renewable permanent residency card, which will allow you to enter and exit China as you please, visa free.

For more information on obtaining a Green Card, contact the Exit & Entry Administration of the PSB (p669).

Beijing 2009
Olympic hangover: a sci-fi fable
by Gabriel Monroe

This is Beijing in the year 2009. For two weeks last summer, the world witnessed a sort of pristine, harmonious, "new Beijing." The city they saw seemed too good to be true: clean air, no traffic, progressive green-mindedness, and indelibly – a fluent, effortlessly convenient blend of ancient and modern. It was a miraculous flattery of the city we thought we lived in. The strangest part of all was that after the torch blazed on to distant territories … the Olympic magic didn't end.

After promising the world a technologically, culturally and environmentally groundbreaking showcase, Beijing had no choice but to put up. Thanks to desperate eleventh-hour inspiration and zeal, Beijing delivered the goods. Today we've inherited fixtures like the Olympic Spirit Anti-Smog and Sandstorm Ultra-Wind System (OSASSUWS) of 50-meter tall propeller blowers outside the Fifth Ring Road, as well as a booming local market for double-nicotine fresh air ciggafilters (hollow, nicotine-enhanced atmosphere filtration cones).

Beijing 2009: hypertong hypertropolis

Of course, the most astounding breakthrough of all was the 6D "hypertong" central Beijing infrastructure system. Hyper-manifested hutongs, or hypertongs (超级胡同or 超同) – a long-awaited city planning compromise between conservationists and progressionists – extend hutong-ly, in every direction from every hutong surface, forming an unlimited, multidimensional web of quaint, historic alleyways. The conversion to hypertong technology created a significantly expanded quantity of inhabitable (yet eminently livable) downtown real estate. Amazingly, engendered by Beijing's ancient geomantic planning principles, the hypertongs' finitely bounded nexus of infinite matter generates an inexhaustible energy source – 100% green, 100% free. The fourth dimension is time; the fifth dimension is you.

Yet for some reason, now that traffic jams, dust storms, pollution and the profligate real estate boom are all fading memories – now that Beijing has become an efficient, modern city, while immaculately maintaining, even magnifying, its ancient charm – there has been an exodus of sorts. After briefly bobbing restlessly in the Olympic torch's wake, most of Beijing's foreigners have moved on to Mumbai – to continue surfing the global vanguard. In fact, *laowai* have become so rare, so suddenly, that they are now commonly greeted around town with a popular Chinglish pun of astonished curiosity: "Laowai! Lao-why? Why why why? Why you still here?"

An inquisitive bunch – with well-documented adventure streaks and competitive history fetishes – *laowhy* are a noble breed of immersionists. A typical Beijing 2009 afternoon finds them strolling the hypertongs, looking to bump into a *laotou* to *liaotian'r*, whiling away the afternoon over tea and friendly titters. Once in a while though, the *laowhy* unconsciously congregate in the retro-upmarket Neo-Sanlitun Majestic Pub Grotto and find themselves reminiscing wistfully in Chinglish about the *old* New Beijing, and sometimes, with a sniffle and a smile, hankering for the days when they'd dream for a month of a nice cheese.

USEFUL INFO

Back Through the Looking Glass
Now what?
by Ann Mah

After you leave, the party goes on without you, as exhilarating as ever

When I left Beijing, I knew I'd miss it. After all, my husband and I had made a home there, the first in our married life. For four years, we filled our lungs with the city's pea-soup pollution and experienced the highs (street food on demand!) and lows (er, street food, part 2) of expat life. Of course living in Beijing changed me – I never thought it wouldn't. But what I didn't expect, after all the congested traffic and upset tummies, bouts of homesickness and feeling like an outsider, was my affection for the northern capital. Yes, there is life after Beijing. It is tinged with a renewed appreciation for living in the States, and a bittersweet nostalgia for that other place we used to call home.

It comes in waves, the nostalgia, hitting me as powerfully as one of the cement mixers that trundle up and down Guanghua Lu. Sometimes I miss unexpected things – like the carefree exuberance of floral-on-floral outfits, or the twelve-hour time difference. It used to drive me crazy that I lived half-a-day ahead of my friends and family, that while I hurried to work on Monday morning, they were tucking into their Sunday supper and a new episode of *Big Love*. Now that I'm twelve hours behind, I miss being ahead of the game, reading *The New York Times* before everyone else and sending e-mails while they slept. I no longer have that extra cushion of time to remember birthdays or Mother's Day – or to cheat on my deadlines.

Occurring more often are my cravings for Beijing's food. Naturally I miss the salty, spicy, silky cubes of *mapo doufu* and bitter crunch of stir-fried *kugua* – but also Alameda's *pao*, crisp, chewy and cheesy. Or Sasha's Kiosk burger, served with a huge pile of fries and an even bigger smile. Or the savory chicken lula kebab at Rumi, with its accompanying heap of delicate, fragrant basmati rice. I miss going out to eat half the nights of the week, miss picking up a check and not flinching, miss paying the bill without wrinkling my brow to calculate a 15 percent gratuity. (On the plus side, I've lost five pounds since moving back.)

On the days when the bathroom needs scrubbing, the floors need mopping and the pile of ironing seems as vast as Everest, I miss our helpful *ayi*, Xiao Wang. But though it takes me twice as long to press a stack of shirts, I've learned a lot about our iron's steam function – and my own ability to adjust. And that's the other thing about Beijing: It's made me tough. If I can handle 24-hour construction sites, weeks of gray days, and working in another language, I can handle anything. I am a champion at sitting in traffic. My stomach is stronger than iron. And I will never again be afraid to go to a cocktail party alone. I found a sense of adventure I never knew I had, pushing myself in ways I didn't expect. Seeking lost temples with nothing more than a book from the 1930s and a friendly cab driver. Rand McNally and Google Maps are a delight, but they have removed the thrill from weekend outings. The signs to Mt. Vernon and Monticello are impossible to miss. No matter how many times I rehearsed Chinese vocabulary and phrases for interviews, my heart was in my throat from the first question to the last.

Of course I miss being an expat, being different and special, but now that I've left Beijing's small pond, I realize there's a danger in that, too. Here in the States, among so many people who are wittier, more articulate, and better educated, I often feel intimidated. And yet there is also a constant challenge – to work the extra hour (or five), shake off the complacency, to rise to the competition and improve myself in the process.

More than anything, I think I miss Beijing's bustle, that crackle of energy in the air, the anticipation, the feeling that anything is possible. Where else could a skyscraper mushroom practically overnight, or a block of hutongs be destroyed in a morning? I crave the frenetic pace, exhausting yet exhilarating, the nonstop blur of activity that makes the city feel new every single day. I miss knowing a place so intimately, having an encyclopedic knowledge of each restaurant, bar, shop and art gallery. In the months since I've left, restaurants have moved, bars have closed, malls have opened. I used to be an expert, but Beijing is not my city anymore.

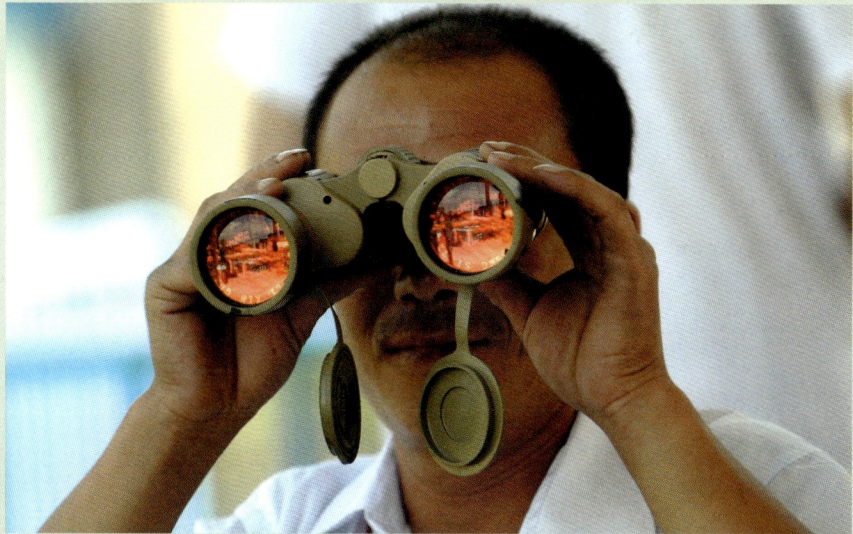

Life after Beijing looks rough

Immersion Guides

Guidebooks for Beijing and beyond

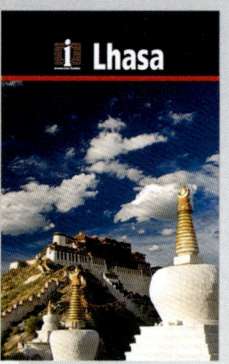
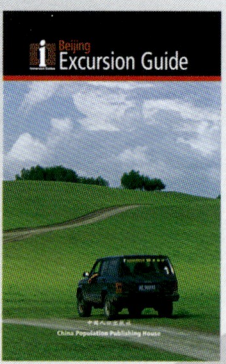

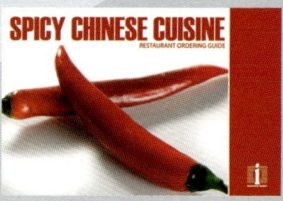

As Beijing's leading publisher of English-language guidebooks and maps, **Immersion Guides** brings China to visitors and residents alike. Transcending the scope of typical tourist guidebooks and written by long-term residents, **Immersion Guides** offers readers the resources they need to explore China in depth. Each title is regularly updated to keep pace with China's breakneck development.

Comprehensive, in-depth, and nuanced, **Immersion Guides'** books will make an insider out of anyone!

Available at bookstores around Beijing or to order a copy, please e-mail distribution@immersionguides.com

www.immersionguides.com

INDEX

+39 Italian Restaurant
 and Lounge 78
1 on 1 613
1001 Nights 82
13 Club 290, 296, **343**
15 Qianhai Beiyan 288, **296**
17 Miles KTV 322
180 degrees 290, **296**
2 Kolegas 292, 296, **343**
2008 Great Wall Marathon 269
2008 Olympic Games 14, 22, 209, 417,
 436, 437, **440-461**, 671
21 Cake 109
22 Film Studio 392
3.3 Shopping Center 396
3/4 Gallery 194
33 T Shirt 361
365 Inn 45
3818 Cool Gallery 194
3E International Kindergarten 138
66Show.net 432
6ixty 8ight 366
798 Art District. See Factory 798
77th Street 396
798 Photo Gallery 194
798 Space 194
798/Red Gate Gallery 194
99 Massage and Spa Center 495

A

A Helping Hand Adoption Agency 125
A Life as Film 398
A You Fashion 353
Aardvarks Rugby Club 431
ABC Music & Me Day Camps 148
Abstract art 178
Acanta Cigar Shop 412
accessories 353, 529
accidents. See cars (accidents)
accounting firms 574
ACLS 613
acrobatics 204
acupuncture. See Traditional Chinese
 Medicine
ADSL. See internet
ADULT EDUCATION 595-626
Adoption **124 -125**, 654
Aeroflot 509
Aesthetic beauty art (xingshi mei) 185
Afunti 99
Agatha 363
Agricultural Bank of China 652
Agrilandia 160
AGS Four Winds 655
Ai Jiang Shan 81
Ai Qing 184
Ai Weiwei **178**, 647
Aibai and ICCGL 637

Aibosen Blindman Massage 495
Aigle 353
Aika 374
Aikang Veterinary Hospital 664
Air Canada 509
Air China 509
Air France 509
air quality 441
airlines 509-510
airports 506-509, 516
Aisida Dog Market 660
Akers. Rich 293
Alameda **65**, 100, 101, 102
Alan Wong 279
Alba 64
Alcoholics Anonymous 644
Aldo 368
Alexander Creek Park **66**, 103
Alfa 284, 296, 318
Alien Street Market 154, **400**
All Nippon Airway 509
All Sages Bookstore 390
Alliance Française de Pekin 617
Alona Studio 439
Alphagraphics 577
alumni groups 630
Amazon.com 390
Amcare Women's and Children's
 Hospital 476
American Cafe, The **60**, 160
American Chamber of Commerce, The
 575
American Community Club (ACC) 634
American Cuisine 60
American Steak & Eggs **60**, 102, 160
American-Sino OB/GYN Service (ASOG)
 472, **477**
American-Standard &
 Moen Specialty Store 374
Amrita Fitness 424
amusement parks. See kids (fun places)
An Die An Niang 66
Anantara Spa 497
Ancient Cliff Dwellings (Guyaju) 556
Ancient Coin Museum 251
Ancient Ming Village (Cuandixia) 549
Ancient Music Center 254
Ancient Observatory 251
Ang Jianping 208
Angel 284, 293, **296**
Anglo-French Forces 237
Anglo-French Invasion 559
Annie's Cafe **78**, 98, 100, 102, 160
Antiques & "antiques"
 262, **385-389**, 654, 555
Ao Yue Piano **146**, 405, 657
apartments. See housing
Aperitivo 283, **296**, 316

APM 221
Apple Centre 392
Apple Experience Centre 392
April Gourmet 55, **105**, 106
aquariums. See kids (fun places)
Arario Beijing 194
archery 432
architecture (art) 191
architecture (sightseeing) 262
Area 292, **297**
Arena 291, **297**
Aria **68**, 101, 291, **297**, 317, 320
Arrow Tower 251
Arrows Made of Desire 333
ART & CULTURE 175-226
 art districts 206-208
 art galleries 194-197
 art history 178-183
 art museums 196-197
 art schools 620-621
 art supplies 389
 artists 184-187, 332-337
 kids 167
art hoods 177
Arthur M. Sackler Museum 264
artists (music) 332-337
Artist's Village Gallery 191, **194**
Asakura 491
ASC Fine Wines 111
Asian Absolute 580
Asian Express International Movers 655
Asian Games of 1990 14
Asian Star **87**, 99
Asian Tigers K.C. Dat (China) Ltd. 655
Asiana Airline 509
ASM Chauffeur and Tour Service 513
Assaggi **78**, 98
Associated Colleges in China (ACC) 611
Astor Grill, The **60**, 100
At Café 64
Athena 69
Athena Xu 363
ATMs 652-653
Aussie rules football 418
Aussino 381
AustCham Kooka Networking 634
Australia and New Zealand Association
 634
Australian International School of
 Beijing (AISB) 138
Austrian Airlines 509
Automobile Administrative Office
 523, 530
Avis (Anji Car Rental and Leasing) 531
Awfully Chocolate 109
ayis. See nannies
A-Z Kids 164
Azure Clouds Temple (Biyun Si) 259

B

B&Q 374
Ba Guo Bu Yi 86
Babyface 284, **297**
babysitters. *See* nannies
Bacchus 111
Bad News Bears Baseball Club 418
Badachu (excursions) 555
Badachu (donations) 654
Badaling Great Wall 269
Badaling Ski Resort 432
Badaling Wild Park 164
badminton 418
Baihe Climbing Area 554
Baihe Trailhead 554
baijiu 301
Bainaohui Computer Shopping Mall 392
Baiyangdian Scenic Area 558
Bajia Dazhaimen Restaurant 77
bakeries 104-109
BAL International Cargo Ltd. 655
Ball House 288, **297**, 321
balloons 155
Bamboo Garden Hotel 46
Bameede 353
Banana 291, **297**
Banana Leaf **88**, 99
Bang & Olufsen 377
Bangkok Nursing Home Hospital 479
Bank of Beijing 652
Bank of China 652
Bank, The 284, **297**
banking 571, **652**
Banner Travel Service 510
Baodao Optical 360
baozi (dumplings) 90
Bar & Club Directory 296-310
Bar Blu 279, 283, 286, **297**, 316
bargaining. *See* haggling
bars. *See* nightlife
Baroque Chamber Chorus of Beijing 631
baseball 418
basketball 418
bathhouses 496
Bayley & Jackson Medical Center 477
beaches 558
Beanstalk International Bilingual School (BIBS) and Beijing International Bilingual Kindergarten 138
Beanstalk International Kindergarten (BIK) 138
Beanstalk International Kindergarten Summer Camp 148
Bed Bar 278, 288, **297**, 317, 319, 320
Bed Top the Thing 382
Beer Mania 283
Beiao Likang Moving Company 656
Beidaihe 558
Beihai Park 259-261
Beijing #1 Toastmasters Club 631
Beijing 2008 Olympic Games. *See* 2008 Olympic Games

Beijing ABC Management Consulting Co 551
Beijing Actors Workshop 631
Beijing Administrative Bureau for Cultural Relics 269
Beijing Amateur Chess Club (BACC) 631
Beijing Amblers 428
Beijing American Club 634
Beijing Amusement Park 164
Beijing Ancient Coins Exhibition Hall 268
Beijing Aquarium 164
Beijing Art Now Gallery (BANG) 195
Beijing Ayi Housekeeping Service 128
Beijing Ballroom 420
Beijing Baptist Church 643
Beijing Beiqi Taxi 531
Beijing Belle Transport Co. Ltd. 655
Beijing Binfen Gardening & Landscaping 382
Beijing BISS International School 139
Beijing Black Tiger Academy 146, **430**
Beijing Capital International Airport 506
Beijing Car Solution 529
Beijing Central Art Gallery & Cultural Venue 195
education 620
Beijing Century New Concept Car Rental 531
Beijing Children's Hospital 476
Beijing City Archive, The 252
Beijing City International School 139
Beijing CJ750 Sidecar Club 421
Beijing Comic City 154
Beijing Commune 195
Beijing Concert Hall 214
Beijing Conference Center 202
Beijing Country Golf Club 423
Beijing cuisine 63
Beijing Cubic Art Center 195
Beijing Cultural Heritage Protection Center (CHP) 637
Beijing Curio City 385
Beijing Da Dong Roast Duck Restaurant 63
Beijing Dance Academy 216
Beijing Daxing Capital Golf Club 423
Beijing Devils Rugby Club 431
Beijing Doda International Cargo Transportation Co. Ltd. 655
Beijing Donation Centers 645
Beijing Easy 523
Beijing Emergency Medical Center 481
Beijing Employee Service Center 570
Beijing Entry-Exit Inspection and Quarantine Bureau 660
Beijing Exhibition Theater 202
Beijing Ex-pat Housemaid Service 128
Beijing Fangzhou Recycling Company 657
Beijing Film Academy 607
Beijing Fine Jewelers 363

Beijing Flying-man Club 422
Beijing Folk Arts Museum 249
Beijing Football Club 418
Beijing Foreign Investment Service Center 569
Beijing Foreign Studies University (BFSU or Beiwai) 607
Beijing Friendship Hospital 476
Beijing Fubang'emin Waterski Club 418
Beijing Gaelic Football Club 423
Beijing Gaojia Recycling Company 657
Beijing Gehua Baihua 389
Beijing General Municipal Engineering Design and Research Institute 518
Beijing Glasses City 360
Beijing Golden Light Exhibition Services 378
Beijing Golf Club 423
Beijing Golfer's Club 424
Beijing Green Equestrian Club 428
Beijing Harmonica Society 631
Beijing Hash House Harriers 431
Beijing Hemophiliac Group 644
Beijing Hikers **428**, 547
Beijing history 6-13, 235
Beijing Honma Golf Service Store 409
Beijing Horizon Educational Center (BHEC) 637
Beijing Hotels Travel Guide 44
Beijing Huijia Kindergarten 139
Beijing Huijia Private College 139
Beijing Huiling 637
Beijing Human and Animal Environmental Education Center (BHAEEC) 637
Beijing Improv 631
Beijing Institute of Technology 607
Beijing Intech Eye Hospital 482
Beijing International Badminton Club 418
Beijing International Car-Trading Service Garden 528
Beijing International Christian Fellowship 643
Beijing International Christian Fellowship (BICF) Counseling Center 480
Beijing International Dragon Boat Team 418
Beijing International Forum 631
Beijing International Golf Club 423
Beijing International Ice Hockey 428
Beijing International MBA Program 619
Beijing International Post & Telecommunications Office 651
Beijing International Society (BIS) 625, 630
Beijing International SOS Clinic 471, 477
Beijing International Tennis Centre 438
Beijing Jiancai Jingmao Dasha 374
Beijing Jiu-Jitsu Academy 430
Beijing Jockey Club 434
Beijing Kailong 409
Beijing Kendo Club 430

Beijing Ladies Golf Club 424
Beijing Language and Culture University (BLCU or Beiyu) 599, 607, **616**
Beijing LDTX Modern Dance Company Studios 216
Beijing Legend Holiday Golf Club 424
Beijing Limo 516
Beijing Links Golf Club 423
Beijing Linux User Group (BLUG) 631
Beijing Lizhi Gardening 385
Beijing Longteng Athletics Thing 409
Beijing Lu Xun Museum 265
Beijing Macintosh User Group 631
Beijing Mandarin School 614
Beijing Marriott West 47
Beijing Mayor's Office 649
Beijing Meisong Golf Club 424
Beijing Mengda Accessories Jewelers 363
Beijing Merry Home Consulting 128
Beijing Milun School of Traditional Kung Fu 430
Beijing MoCa 195
Beijing Modern Dance Company Theater 202, **215-216**
Beijing Modern Music Festival 211
Beijing Motorsports 421
Beijing Municipal Communication Commision 505
Beijing Museum of Natural History 164, **263**
Beijing Music Festival 208, **211**
Beijing National Security Bureau 24
Beijing New Art Projects 195
Beijing New Music Ensemble 212
Beijing New Oriental School 617
Beijing No. 1 Kindergarten Experimental Sister School 139
Beijing No. 55 Middle School and High School 139
Beijing Norinco Motors Market 529
Beijing Normal University (BNU or Beishida) 607
Beijing North Station (Beijing Beizhan) 519
Beijing North Theater 202
Beijing North Vehicle Distributing Market 529
Beijing Okhotsk Beer 292, **297**
Beijing Olympics. *See* 2008 Beijing Games
Beijing Organic Consumers Association 631
Beijing Organizing Committee for the Olympic Games (BOCOG) 440
Beijing Ornamental Animal Hospital (Guanshang or Beijing Pet Hospital) 660, **664**
Beijing Pacific Club 576
Beijing People's Art Theater (Beijing Renmin Yishu Juyuan) 200
Beijing Photographic Equipment City 392
Beijing Pine Valley International Golf Club 423

Beijing Planetarium 164, **263**
Beijing Planning Exhibition Hall 264
Beijing Playhouse 631
Beijing Police Museum 268
Beijing Rivers and Resort Golf Training Academy 424
Beijing roast duck 61, **63-64**
Beijing Seven-Color Light Children's Theater 202
Beijing Shougang Basketball Center 434
Beijing Softball League - "United Beijing" 434
Beijing Sound 208
Beijing South Railway Station (Nanzhan) 519
Beijing Sport University 422, 430
Beijing Star Kids Children's Bookstore 150
Beijing Station (Beijing Huochezhan) 519
Beijing Stone Carving Museum 245
Beijing Street Hockey 428
Beijing Suicide Research and Prevention Center 481
Beijing Sunhe Ethical Goods Market 400
Beijing Swing 420
Beijing Symphony Orchestra 208, **210**
Beijing Tap Water Museum 265
Beijing Tax Bureau Foreign Section 530
Beijing Taxi Dispatching Center 513
Beijing Telecom 666
Beijing Tennis Center 438
Beijing Tennis Club 438
Beijing Theater Area 222
Beijing Tokyo Art Projects 195
Beijing Tongrentang Traditional Chinese Medicine Clinic 486
Beijing TOP-A Car Service Co., Ltd. 531
Beijing Traditional Opera Theater 202
Beijing Ultimate Frisbee 439
Beijing United Family Dental Orthodontics & Implant Center 481
Beijing United Family Hospital & Clinics (BJU) 125, 128, 153, 472, **478**
Beijing University of Chinese Medicine 620
Beijing Used Car Trading Market 529
Beijing Vista Clinic – Kerry Center 478
Beijing West Railway Station (Beijing Xikezhan) 519
Beijing Windspeed Bike Shop 389
Beijing Wine Club 631
Beijing Winter Swim Club 435
Beijing World Youth Academy (WYA) 139
Beijing Xinbiaozhi Furniture Center 378
Beijing Xiyi Elementary School 139
Beijing Yaoshang Golf Club 424
Beijing Yayuncun Car Market 529
Beijing Yilun Piano Center 146, **405**
Bejing Yinjian Taxi Company 513
Beijing Yiquan Golf Club 424
Beijing YMCA Fitness Center 427
Beijing Yoga 439
Beijing Youth Palace 202

Beijing Youth Palace Cinema 222
Beijing YWT Interior Design Specializes 374
Beijing Zhaijisong Express 651
Beijing Zoo 164
Beijing Zoo (shopping) 401
Beijing's Other Attractions 637
Beisihuan Lighting Market 385
Beiwai. *See* Beijing Foreign Studies University
Beixin Jingfeng Fabric 399
Beiyu. *See* Beijing Language & Cultural University
Beking 378
Bell Tower 278
Bellagio **66**, 101, 284
Benelux Chamber of Commerce in China (BenCham) 576
Benetton 151
Berlitz 614, 618
BFISC 569
BGLAD (Beijing Gay, Lesbian and Allies Discussion) 637
Bhodi-Sake 88
Bianyifang Kaoyadian 61
Bibo **410**, 422
BICF Counseling Center 481
Bicycle Kingdom 537
bicycles 534. *See also* biking
  purchase 389-390
  rental 537
big & tall (clothing) 353
Big Bell Temple 254
Big Shoes 368
BigDog Balloon Party Shop 155
biking 418, 537, 547
Bikram Hot Yoga 439
Bioscor Beijing Clinic 482
birth control 483
Birth. *See* pregnancy
Biteapitta **82**, 96, 100, 160
Bixiulan 151
Bla Bla Bar 290, **297**
Black Beijing 634
Black Dragon Pool (Heilong Tan) 554
Black Skin Book (heipi shu) 180
Black Sun Bar 285, **297**
Blanc de Chine 356
Blissliving 382
Blockhouse 100
blood 467
Blue Goat Books & Cafe 390
Blue Zoo Beijing 165
Bo Concept 378
boating
  excursions 544, 558
  sightseeing 236
  sports 418-419
Bodhi Therapeutic Retreat 495
Bohai Bay 558
Boloni Home Decor (Beijing) Co. Ltd. Lifestyle Museum 374
BookMark, The 150

bookstores 390-392
   kids 150
Bookworm, The 150, 317, **390**, 624
Bose 377
Botanical Garden 258
Botao Haute Couture 353
Boucherie Michel **105**, 106
Bounceabout 154
Bower & Wilkins 377
bowling 419
Boxer Rebellion of 1900 245, 252
Boyu Lighting 385
Brain Failure **333**, 345, 347
Brasserie Flo **69**, 98, 160
Brazilian Churrascos 66
Brewery, The (Jiuchang) 177
Bridge of Love 124
Bridge School, The 614
Bridge, Ann 632
British Airways 509
British Chamber of
   Commerce in China 576
British Club of Beijing, The 139, **634**
Broadway Asia Theater Group 177
brokers 529
Bronze Bodies Tanning Club 493
Brother Pipe 412
Brown Club of China 630
Browns 318
BTG International Travel & Tour 510
Buddha Bar 288, **298**
Buddha Tooth Pagoda 555
Buddhism. *See* religious services
Bumrungrad International 479
bungee jumping **419-420**, 544
Bus Bar 298
buses 3, 506, **516-517**
   terminals 516
BUSINESS & WORK 561-594
   associations 575-577
   licenses 570
   MBA programs 619
   offices 575
   registration 569
   supplies 392
   taxes 570

C

C. de France 491
C.L. Ma Furniture 385
C5 Art 195
Cafe Cha 72
Cafe de la Poste **69**, 98
Cafe Europa **69**, 101
Cafe Sambal 71, **87**, 99
Cafe Taipan 96
cafes & teahouses 64-65
Cai Guoqiang 179
Cai Yunjian 94
Caijing 578-579
cameras 392
Camp Adventure 2007 148

camping **428**, 549, 554
Canada China Business Council 576
Canadian Alumni Network (CAN) 630
Canadian International School of Beijing
   139
Canadians in China 634
Candy Floss Cafe 289, **298**
Cantilever House 191
Cantonese cuisine 65
Cao Fei 185
Cao Xueqin Former Residence 240
Cao Yu 199
Caochangdi 177, 178, **190**
Caochangdi Arts Workstation 216
Capital Club, The 631
Capital Community Church 643
Capital Gymnasium 214, 434, 438
Capital Library 624
Capital Mandarin School, The 614
Capital Museum 263
Capital Normal University 211, **610**
Capital Theater 200, **202**
Capone's **78**, 291, **298**
Carepets 660
Cargo Club 284, **298**
Caribbean Association in China 634
Carolina Club 630
carpet cleaning 645
carpets **374**, 645
Carrefour **105**, 106, 153, 155
cars
   accessories 529
   accidents 525-526
   brokers 529
   buying 528-529
   driving license 522-523
   exporting 655
   insurance 530-531
   parking tickets 523
   registration 529-530
   renting and leasing 531
   taxes 529
Carsick Cars 333
Cartier 363
Casa De David 421
Casa Habana 291, **298**
Castle Interiors Home 375
Cat Friends 660
CAT Lifestyle Mall 396
Cat Shop 382
Cave Cafe 298
Cave of Precious Pearls 555
caves 543, 549, 554, 555, 556
CBD 291
CCTV 224-225
CD Jazz Club 292, **298**, 343
CDs 398
CEIBS EMBA Program 619
celebrities 646-647
Cellar Le Pinot 111
Cellar, The 292, **298**
CELTA (Certificate in English Language
   Teaching to Adults) 592

Central Academy of Arts and Design
   389
Central Academy of Drama 200, **610**
Central Academy of Drama Theater
   202
Central Academy of Fine Arts 598, 610,
   621
Central/South American cuisine 65-66
Central Conservatory of Music
   202, 207, 211, **214**, 610
Central Experimental Drama Theater
   202
Central Philharmonic 207
Centro 298
Century 21 26
Century Domestic Services 128
Century Star Skating Club 430
Century Theater 202
Cepe **78**, 98, 102
certification (teaching) 592
CET Academic Programs 611
Chabad Lubavitch of Beijing 642
Chaina 366
Chairman Mao Memorial Hall 231
Champion Rink 430
Chanel 356
Chang and Biörck 382
Chang'an Banjia 656
Chang'an Grand Theater 202
Changhong Cinema 222
Changling Tomb 268
Changping District (excursions) 543
Chaowai Furniture Warehouse 385
Chaoyang Eye Hospital Store 360
Chaoyang Kosaido Golf Club 424
Chaoyang Park **165**, 284
Chaoyang Tennis Club 438
Chaoyang Theater **202**, 204
Charcoal Bar 81
Charlie's Bar 291, **298**
Chaterhouse Booktrader 150, **390**
chauffeured cars 513
Cheers 283, **298**
cheese 105
Chemdry 645
Chen Chu 266-267
Chen Kaige 177, 219, 220
Chen Lingyang 182
Chen Luyu 647
Chen Xigang 208
Chen Yi 208
Chen Zhong 447
Chen, Jackie 280-281
Cheng Fei 444
Cheng Guang Hall 260
Chengde (excursions) 559
Chengwaicheng Furniture Mall 378
Cherry Lane Movies 222
Cheung Kong Graduate School of
   Business Set 619
Chi Heng Foundation 637
Chicco 151, 153, 155
Chief Chop Deals 382

678 INSIDER'S GUIDE TO BEIJING

Children's House Olympic Summer Camp, The 148
Children's Art Initiative (CAI) 637
Children's House Montessori Kindergarten, The 140
Children's Learning Center of Beijing (CLCB) 140
China Academy of TCM, The 620
China Acrobatic Troupe, The 204
China Art Archives and Warehouse 195
China Art Seasons 195
China Arts Bookstore 390
China Aviation Museum 165
China Blue Gallery 195
China Britain Business Council (CBBC) Beijing 576
China Buddhist Institute 244
China Buddhist Literature and Cultural Relics Museum 244
China Capital Toastmasters Club 631
China Center of Adoption Affair (CCAA) 124-125
China Charity Federation **637**, 645
China Children's Art Theater 202
China Cinema 222
China Club Beijing 634
China Conservatory 210
China Construction Bank 652
China Council for Promotion of International Trade 576
China Doll 279, 283, **298**, 316, 317, 319, 320
China Environment and Sustainable Development Reference and Research Center 637
China Film Archives 222
China Grand Theater 202
China hire packages 572
China Honey Bee Museum 265
China Merchants Bank 652
China Millennium Monument Art Museum 195
China National Film Museum 222
China National Symphony Orchestra and Chorus 208, **210**
China National Women's Volleyball Team 452
China Netcom 666
China North International Shooting Range 543
China Pacific Property Insurance 530
China Philharmonic Orchestra 208, **210**
China Ping Opera Theater 202
China Puppet Theater 165, **202**
China Red Sandalwood Museum 262
China Science and Technology Museum 165
China Southern Airlines 509
China Swan International Tours 510
China Travel Service (HK) Ltd (CTS) 670
China World Fitness Centre 427
China World Hotel **47**, 435
China World Trade Shopping Mall 396

China Youth Union 128
China-Australia Chamber of Commerce 576
China-Italy Chamber of Commerce 576
China-Japan Friendship Hospital 472, 476
Chindex 582-583
Chinese Association for NGO Cooperation (CANGO) 640
Chinese Contemporary Beijing 190, **195**
Chinese cuisine **66-68**, 84-85, 92-93
Chinese Culture Club (CCC) 430, 547, **624**, 630
Chinese culture groups 630-631
Chinese Horizon 614
Chinese Juvenile Rights Protection Center 640
Chinese Military History Museum, The 167, **265**
Chinese New Year. See holidays
Chinese Taoist Association, The 244
Ching Pavilion 72
ChocoJing 634
Chonggong Cinema 222
Chongqing Fandian 86
Chongwen Workers' Palace 202
Chongwenmen Church (Ashbury Methodist) 643
chopsticks 394
Christianity. See religious services
Christian Dior Couture 356
Chuan Ban **86**, 93
Chun Hui Yuan Warm Springs Resort 497
Chun Yu Ting 298
Chunliushe 199
churches. See religious services
Church of Jesus Christ of Latter Day Saints, The 643
CIEE 612
CIM Continental International Moving 655
Cinema Directory 221-223
Circular City (Tuan Cheng) 10
Citibank 652
CITS Hong Kong 670
city walls & gates 251-252
CJW 291, **299**
Clavis Sinica 609
climbing 420, 546, 554, 556, 559
clothing stores 353-356
    kids 151
Cloud Cave Valley (Yunxiugu) 554
Cloud Covered Mountain (Yunmeng Shan) 548
Cloud Nine Bar 299
clubbing 295. See also Bar & Club Directory
Club Canada 635
Club Les Fleurs 495
Club Taku 290, **299**
ClubFootball 145, **422**
ClubFootball Junior Courses 148
clubs. See Bars & Clubs Directory

CnAdventure 510
Coal Hill (Jingshan) 258
Cobra 338
Coco Banana 284, **299**
Coco Zen 322
Cold Blooded Animal 338
Colombini 378
colonial ruins 266-267
Colorado State University Alumni 630
Columbia University Alumni Association of Beijing 630
Come & Surprise Hair Studio 491
comedy clubs. See Beijing Improv
Comfortable Blind Massage 495
comic books 154
Common Language (Tongyu) 637
Commonwealth Society of Beijing (CWS) 634
Commune by the Great Wall 191
Commune by The Great Wall Kempinski **167**, 553
Communist Party 13, 207
Community Directory 630-637
community groups 631-634
Compassion for Migrant Children (CMC) 640
complaints (transportation) 513
Comptoirs de France 109
computers 392-393
concert halls 210, **214**
concubines 235
Confidant Medical Services 482
Confucius Temple and Guozijian 243
Congregation of the Good Shepherd 643
consulting firms 574
Continental Airlines 509
contracts (housing) 36
contracts (teaching) 590
Cool Jade Jewelry Studio 363
Cool Valley (Qingliang Gu) 554
Coolbaby 662
Copa Fashion 353
Cornell Club of Beijing 630
cosmetics 393, **396**, 482, 488-489
Cosmo 284, 299, 311
counseling 480-481
CourtYard Annex 190, 195
CourtYard Gallery 195
courtyards 23-24, 38-39
CourtYard, The **72**, 101
Crab Island
    kids 167
    sports 435
Creation Gallery 195
credit cards 653
Crescent Moon Muslim Restaurant 94
cricket (sport) 420
crickets 661
Crocs 368
Crossing Festival 216
Crown Worldwide Ltd. 655
Crowne Plaza Wuzhou 47

679

INDEX

Crystal Jade Palace Restaurant **65**, 100
CSI – Bally Total Fitness 427
Ctrip 44, **511**
Cuckoo Bookstore 390
Cui Jian 325, 338
Cui Xiuwen 182, 185
Cuiwei Mountains 555
Cuiyunshan Ski Resort 432
cultural groups 624
Cultural Revolution 14, 130, 178, 185, 200, 208, 231, 249
Culture Development Center for Rural Women, The 640
Cushman & Wakefield 26
Cycle China
    excursions 547
    sports 418
    transporation 531
cycling. See biking
Cynical Realism (wanshi xianshi zhuyi) 180, 185, 186

D

D-22 279, 290, 293, 318, 320, 326, 330, 331, **343**
Da Dong. See Beijing Da Dong Roast Duck Restaurant
Da Qinghua 66
Dadizheyang Outdoor Garden Furniture 378
Daguanlou Cinema 222
Dahua Cinema 223
Daisy's Beauty Salon 491
Dajue Temple 546
Dali Courtyard 71
Daming Optical 482
dancing
    art 177, 215-216
    kids 145
    sports 420-421
Dangdai International Arts Festival 211
Dangdang.com 408
Danieli's 78
Danish Chamber of Commerce in China 576
DanZ Centre 145, **421**
Dara 379
Dartmouth Club of China 630
Dasenlin Flower Market 660
Dashanzi Art District. See Factory 798
Dave's Custom Tailoring 369
David Zhang 580
Daxin Textiles Co. 399
day trips 543-557
Dazhong Arts & Accessories 246, **377**
DC Design 375
Decathlon 410
Decay 361
decorating companies 374-378
delis 68
Deluxe Restaurant, The 65
Demokratic Snowboard Skate Surf Shop 410

Den, The 284, **299**, 318
Deng Xiaoping 179
dentistry 481-482
Department of Fish and Animals 249
Department of Resurrection 249
department stores 396-398
Der Kindergarten 140
Desert Oasis Bar (Shanmulan) 289, **300**, 311
Deshengmen 251
design companies 41-42
designer clothes 356-360
Destination 284, **300**, 311
Deutsche Botschaftsschule Peking 140
DeWoskin, Rachel 633
DHL 651
DHY 435
Diamond Throne Pagoda 259
dictionaries 608-609
Die Kochmützen 73
Digao Audio 377
Dimensions Art Center 196
Din Tai Fung **83**, 99, 100, 160
Ding Ding Xiang **74**, 100, 160
Ding Xilin 199
Dingling Tomb 268
Dini's Kosher Restaurant 82
dinner parties 107
Disanji Bookstore 390
Ditan Ice Arena 430
Ditan Park 167
Ditan Swimming Pool 438
DIY Club 410, 418
Diyi Lou 66
Dizhi Cinema 223
Dkids Photography Studio 154
Do Link 379
doctors. See HEALTH & BEAUTY
dogs. See pets
Dogs DayCare in Beijing 664
Dolomite 410
donations 645
Dong Lai Shun 74
Dongbianmen Watchtower 251
Dongcheng (nightlife) 292
Dongchuang Cinema 223
Dongdan Indoor Swimming Pool 438
Dongdan PE Center 418
Dongfang Massage 495
Dongfang Qicai Dashijie 378
Donghuamen Night Market 160
Dongjiao Market **400**, 662
Dongsi Mosque 643
Dongsi Workers' Culture Theater 223
Dongtu Cinema 223
Dongwuyuan Wholesale Market 403
Dongyuan Theater 202
Dongyue Temple 249
dorms 601
Dou Wei 338
Dowager Cixi 234, 236, 260, 557
Dragon Air 509

Dragon Decoration & Engineering Co. Ltd 375
Dragon Fire Swim Team 146
Dragon Foot Club 495
Dragon House Jewelry 363
Dragonfly Therapeutic Retreat 495
DramaQueens 634
drinking games 304
Drive-in Cinema 223
driving (sport) 421-442
driving test. See cars
Drum and Bell 254, 278, 288, **300**
Drum Tower Youth Hostel 45
dry cleaning 645
Duke Alumni Club of Beijing 630
Dulwich College Beijing 140
Dulwich Community Programmes (DCP) Summer Sports Camps 148
dumplings 90
Dunhill 369
Durty Nellies 292, **300**
DVD Shop 398-399
DVDs 398
Dynasty Antique Furniture 385

E

East End Arts District 177
East Forever 418
East Gate Cinema 221
East Gate Plaza Fitness Center 418
East Ocean Seafood Restaurant **65**, 160
East Pioneer Theater 203
East Shore Live Jazz Café 288, **343**
East Village 181
Eastern Qing Tombs 557
Easy Home 375
Easy Spirit Shoes 368
Easy You 614
EasyExpats.com 408
eBay.com 408
Echo Wall, The 241
Economist Corporate Network 576
education (adults) 597-625
education (kids) 131-144
El Fogoncito 66
Elaine's Vegetarian Restaurant and Bar 88
electronics 377-378
Elephant, The **83**, 457
Elite Dental Clinic 481
Elong 511
embassies 645-648
embroidered shoes 151
emergencies 172-173, 466
emergency card 487
emission tests 528-529
Emperor Chongzhen 12
Emperor Wanli 12
Emperor Yongzheng 242
Emperor's Treasure Bar 300
environmentally friendly shopping 394-395

environmental & humanitarian groups 637-641
Equidorf 428
Equuleus International Riding Club 428
Eric Paris Salon & Hair Club 491
ERIC Paris/Kératase Institute 491
ES Lifestyle 491
Esprit Home 382
Essence Vale Spa 497
Ethan Allen (Markor Furnishings) 379
Ethnic Cultural Palace Theater 203
Eton Camp 148
Eton International Bilingual Academy 140
Eudora Station Bar and Restaurant 160
eunuchs 235, 249, 254, 556
European Union Chamber of Commerce In China 576
Eve's Temptation 366
Evolution Fitness Center 427
EXCURSIONS 539-560
    daytrips 543-557
    weekend trips 558-559
Executive Mandarin 614
exfoliation 498
ex-pat packages 572-573
Explorer 410
Export-A-Pet 655
Express Mail Service (EMS) 651
Exquisite Bakery **109**, 161
Exquisite Chinese Classical Furniture 379, 382
extracurriculars (kids) 145-149
Extreme Beyond 410
Extreme Experience 420
eye care 360, **482**
Eye on the Lake 288, **300**
exhibition halls 264

F

F2 gallery 190, **196**
fabrics 399-400
Face 279, 284, **300**, 317, 319
Factory 798 (Dashanzi) 190
Fahai Temple 555
Families with Children from China - Beijing Chapter 125, 644
Family Fu's Teahouse 634
Family Learning House, The 141
Family Tailor 369
Fang Lijun 179, 180, 191
Fangcaodi Primary School 141
Fangshan District (excursions) 543-544
Fangshan Restaurant 77
Fangzhuang Banlü Veterinary Hospital 664
Far East Int'l Youth Hostel 45
FedEx 651
Fei Fei 369
Feiteng Yuxiang **86**, 99
Felissimo 382
fencing 422
Feng Boyi 180

Feng Huo Lun Motorcycle 389
Feng Ling 353
Feng Xiaogang 177, 219
Fenghuang Mountain and Dragon Spring Temple 544
Fengshan Hot Spring Resort 499
Fengtai District (excursions) 544
Fengtai Sports Center 435
Fengyuxue Ritan Park Climbing Wall 420
Fenxing Fencing Club 422
Ferranini Kitchen Furniture Shop 375
FESCO International Training Center Business 570
    training 616, 621, 634
    transportation 523
festivals
    art 208, 211, 215, 216
    bike 547
    film 177
Fierce 405, 657
films 217-223
fines 527
First National Archives, The 252
Fish Nation **69**, 161, 289
Fisherman's Paradise 558
fishing (sport) **422**, 544, 549, 555
fitness clubs. *See* gyms
Five Colours Earth 353
Five Dragon Pavilions (Wu Long Ting) 261
Five Pagoda Temple (Wuta Si) 244
Fletcher Club of Beijing 630
Flexa 379
Flora Homeware 382
Flora Spa 499
Flower's Secret 366
flowers 400
flying 422
FM3 338
FOOD 51-116
Foot to Foot Reflexology 495
football **422**, 426
    kids 145
Forbidden City 12, 229, **231-234**, 249
Forbidden City Concert Hall 214
Foreign Correspondents Club of China (FCCC) 214
foreign culture groups 634-637
Foreign Language Bookstore 150, **390**
forests 543, 548, 556
Forever Bicycle Store (Min Lu Bicycle Store) 389
Fornet 645
Fragrant Hills Hotel 259
Fragrant Hills Park (Xiangshan) **259**, 555
framing 378
Francis Drake 279
Frangipani 492
Frangrant World Temple 555
Frank's Place 278, 292, **300**, 312
freelance writing 585-586

French Chamber of Commerce and Industry in China 576
French Connection 353
French Cultural Centre 222, **635**
French LEquipe 422
Fridae 637
Friedman, Karen MSW 124-125
Friends of Nature 640
Friendship Hotel Swimming Pool 438
Friendship Store 150, **391**, 396, 655
Friendship Supermarket 105
frisbee 439
Frontiers 614
Frost Nails 492
Fruits & Passion **393**, 662
Fu Jia Lou 63
Fu Ku **87**, 161
Fu Mingxia 446
Fuda 405
Fulite 380
Fundazzle 167
Furla 361
furniture 375, **378-381**, 382, 385, 576-577
Fusheng Record Shop 398
fusion cuisine 72-73
Fusion Fitness Center 427
Fusuijing Hutong 247

G

Gaelic rules football 423
Galatea Bridal 370
Galerie Urs Meile, Lucerne-Beijing 190, **196**
Galleria Continua 196
galleries. *See* art & culture
Ganges Indian Restaurant **77**, 98
Gao Brothers 181
Gao Xingjian 200
Gaobeidian Furniture Street 385
Gaojingzhong Kitchen Supplies 382
Gaon Korean Restaurant 81
Garden Court, The **72**, 100
Garden of Delights 66
Garden of Harmonious Virtue 236
gardens 258
Gary Lewis Salon 491
gays & lesbians 636-639
    NIGHTLIFE 275-348
Gege Fu 77
Gelipu 111
Genesis Law Firm 650
Geng Jianyi 179
Genghis Khan 10, 243
Georgetown University Alumni Club of Beijing 630
German cuisine 73-74
German Industry and Commerce (GIC) Beijing 576
Gezou 321
GGSB Grenoble Graduate School of Business Alumni 630
Giant Bicycles 389

Giordano 361
Gisa 78
GL Cafe 96
GladBuy.com 408
Glamorous Pharmacy 334
glasses 360-361
Global Bridge Translation 580
Global Communicators Toastmasters
    Club 634
Global Village 614
Global Village Beijing 640
go carting 556
Go Pink China 637
Go West 322
Gobi Gear 361
Goethe Institute 223, **635**
Gogo 288, **300**, 383
Gogo Fish 383
Gold Sailing 418
Golden Corolla 500
Golden Dancing Academy 421
Golden Elephant Medicine 409
Golden Five Stars Market 403
Golden Holiday 511
Golden Keys 26
Golden Lens Photography 392
Golden Peacock Dai Ethnic Flavor
    94
Goldenport Motor Park 421, 435
Goldfish Home 288, **300**
Goldsail Concert Hall 214
golf 423-424
golf groups & training schools 424
Golf Town 410
Gome 378
Gongti 100 419
Gongyi Meishu Fuwubu 389
Good Life Domestic Services 128
Goose 'n' Duck
    167, 285, 292, **300**, 318
gongti. See Workers' Stadium
Grand Hyatt 47
Grand View Garden 203
Grand World Secondhand Electrical
    Market 405
Grandma's Kitchen **60**, 100, 161
Grandma's Place 553
Grape Restaurant 94
grasslands 556
Great Hall of the People 14, 214, **230**
Great Wall 6, 8, 167, 191, **268- 273**, 547,
    549, 550, 552, 553, 554, 559
Great Wall Bike Festival 547
Great Wall Music Festival and School
    211
green cards 670
Green Leaf (Lüye) 547
Green T. House **72**, 101, 102, 284
grocery stores 104-105
Guang'anmen Cinema 223
Guanghua Temple 249
Guangji Temple 642
guanxi (relationships) 564

Guanyuan Fish and Bird Market
    660, 662
Guanyuan Market 247
Guo Jingjing 446
Guo Moruo's Former Residence 240
Guo Peiji 62
Guo Wenjing 208
Guo'an Theater 203
Guozijian Imperial College 243
Gushanzhai Village 544
Gustomenta **74**, 161
Guxiang 20 46
Gymboree Beijing 167
gyms 424-428

H

Haba Toys 155
haggling 402
Hai Bar 288, **300**
Haidhi Angkawijana 279
Haidian Book City 391
Haidian District 290, 606
    excursions 544-546
Haidian Hospital 477
Haidian Park 167
Haidian Theater 203
Haidilao Hot Pot 74
Hailong Shopping Mall 392
Hair Plus 491
Hair Rodeo 492
hair salons 491-492
Hair Show 492
Haitanghua Pyongyang Cold Noodle
    Restaurant 81
Hall of Clocks 234
Hall of Great Mercy 254
Hall of Guanyin 554
Hall of Jade Ripples 236
Hall of Jewelry 234
Hall of Prayer for Good Harvests 240-241
Hall of Supreme Harmony 234
Han Ci Horse Club 428
Han dynasty 8, 234
Han Na Shan **81**, 98
handbags & wallets 361
Hanggai 334
Hanyu Shuiping Kaoshi. See HSK
Haosha Fitness Center 427
Haowai Furniture Warehouse 385
Happy Eye 360
Happy Land Arts and Crafts Center 167
Happy Valley Amusement Park 167
Harley Davidson 390
Harrow International School Beijing 141
Hart Center of Arts **196**, 222
Harvard Alumni Club of Beijing 630
Harvard Beijing Academy 612
HA-Sports Fitness Center 427
Hatsune **80**, 98, 101, 102, 297
Havana Cafe 284
Hazara 77
He Yong 254

HEALTH & BEAUTY 463-502
health recipes 474-475
Hebei Mountains 559
Hebei Province (excursions) 557
Hebei Saibei Ski Resort 432
Hedgehog 333
Hejia Clothing 362
Helen Sun Bakery and Cake Shop 161
Helen's Interiors 377
Hengyun/Henry Music 408
Heping Massage Center 495
Herald Translation 580
Herbal Spring 500
Herrenhauser 288, **300**
Hezi Leisure and Health 495
Hiboo International Group 655
Hiersun 363
High Club 547
high street fashion 361-363
hiking **428**, 544, 546, 547, 548, 549,
    554, 555
hills 258, 259
Hilton 317
Hi-Target 577
Ho Ho Hang Antique Furniture 388
hockey 428
Holiday Inn Lido 47
holidays 158-159, **649**
holistic healing 480
home (buying) 33-41
home (country) 550-553
home (renting) 22-24, 28-34
home accessories 41-42, **374-385**
Home and Beyond 383
home appliances 377
home essentials 381, 382-385
Home Inn 46
homestay 25-27
Homexcel 380
Hong Kong 669-670
Hong Kong Boss Fitness Club 427
Hong Kong Chamber of Commerce
    (HKCCC)-Beijing Office 576
Hong Kong International Medical Clinic
    478
Honglingjin Park **168**, 432
Hongqiao Market 155, **403**
Hongshulin 644
Hongxia Cinema 223
Hongyun 398
Hope Bar 288, **300**
Horizon 161
horseback riding **428**, 544, 556
Hosa Skating Center 428
hospitals 468-469, **476-478**, 481
hostels 45-46
hot pot 74, 76
Hot Loft, The **74**, 100
Hot Station 362
Hotel Cote Cour 47
Hotel Equipment Corporation (HEC)
    376, **383**
hotels **44-48**, 259, 553

INSIDER'S GUIDE TO BEIJING

Houhai 168, 283, **288**
Houhai Sharks 334
Houhai Zoo 288, **302**
HOUSING & HOTELS 19-50
HSBC 652
HSK 616
Hu Shuli 578, 579
Hua Dan Project 640
Hua Jia Yi Yuan 63
Hua'an Feiniu 74
Huacheng Shoe Store 368
Huaibei International Ski Resort 432
Huairou District (excursions) 548-549, 553
Huajiadi 180
Huang Ting 65
Huang Yue Studio 369
Huanghuacheng Great Wall 271
Huaqing Hot Springs Hotel 500
Huaqing Jiayuan Pool/Gym 438
Hugo BOSS 357
Huguang Guild Hall (Huguang Huiguan) 203, 255
Hui 367
Hujialou Cinema 223
Hujingyuan Tailors 369
humanitarian groups 637-641
Hung Huang 647
Huns 8
Hutong Bar 288, **302**
Hutong Cuisine 146
Hutong Pizza 71, **82**, 100, 103
Hutong Ren 46
hutongs 10, 12, 55, 238, 239, 244, 245, 247, 248, 278
Huxley's 288, **302**

I

I Spa 500
i-Ultra Lounge 279, 285, **302**
ice cream 74, 77
ice skating 428, 430
iCiba 609
IEUM 196
Ifugao 383
Ignition Dance and Art Center 421
Iidea 399
Ikea 153, 155, **380**, 576
Il Casale 79
Illinois Home 380
Ilsa 645
Image Momentum 492
Imagine Gallery 196
Immendorf, Jorg 194
imperial cuisine 77
imperial exams 255
Imperial Vault of Heaven 241
imports 528
In 353
Incense Burner Peak 259
Indian cuisine 77-78
Indian Embassy School 141

Indian Kitchen **77**, 98
Indonesians in China 635
Industrial and Commercial Bank of China (ICBC) 652
in-line skating 432
Inner Mongolia 547
INSEAD Beijing Alumni 630
Instituto Cervantes 214, 223, 635
insurance (car) 530-531
insurance (health) 466, 470-471
IntelliFitness 427
Inter United Football Team 422
InterContinental Beijing Financial Street 48
Interdean International Moving 656
International Academy of Beijing 142
International Beer Town 290, **302**
International Center for Veterinary Services 664
International Festival Chorus (IFC) 634
International Medical Center (IMC) 478
international money transfers 653-654
International Montessori School of Beijing (MSB), The 142
International Newcomers' Network (INN) 634
International School of Beijing (ISB), The 142
International School of Collaborative Learning, The 142
international schools. See schools
International SOS. See Beijing International SOS Clinic
International Students Office 601
International Vegetarian Club of Beijing 634
internet 649-650
Inter-University Program for Chinese Language Study at Tsinghua (IUP) 612
Irish Beijing Community 635
Iron & Fish 288, **302**
Islam. See religious services
Isshin Japanese Restaurant 80
IT Resources 580
Italian cuisine 78-80
Italian Embassy Cultural Office 223
Italian Women's Association 635
Ivy Academy 143
Ivy Bilingual School 143
Ivy Chinese Culture Summer Program 148
Ivy Kids Book Club 150
IZ 335, 338

J

Jaan 72
Jacadi 151, 153
Jack & Jones 362
Jack Toys 155
Jade Garden **83**, 99
Jade Palace Hotel Bowling Center 419
Jade Rainbow Bridge 261

Jam House 278
Jane Goodall Institute 640
Japan Airline 509
Japanese cuisine 80-81
Japanese Occupation 13, 544
Jasmine 66
Java and Yangon 58, **87**
Jazz-Ya **80**, 283, **302**
J-Ballet School 145, **421**
Jeannie Fei 369
Jean-Paul Gaultier 357
Jenny Lou's 55, **105**, 106, 112
Jereme Leung 54
Jesuit missionaries 207, 237, 251, 272
jewelry 363-366
Ji Xian Tang 288, **302**
Jia 21 Hao 95
Jia Na Ma Ni Tibetan Carpets 374
Jia Xiang Tea Shop 412
Jia Zhangke 219, 220
Jiali Manicure 493
Jiangjinjiu Bar 288, **343**
Jianguomenwai (nightlife) 291
Jiayi Vogue Square 151, **403**
Jimmy and Tommy Foreign Trade Fashion Club 353
Jin Ding Xuan **65**, 100, 101
Jin dynasty 234, 259
Jindian Xintuo Shop 390
Jindinghu Ski Resort 432
Jing 72
Jing'an Entertainment Center 419
Jingetiema 380
Jinghua Wushu Association 146, **430**
Jingjusishi Fabric Market 399
Jingshan Park 258
Jinhai Lake & Jinhai Lake Water Park 555
Jinlandao Bowling Club 419
Jinshanling Great Wall 271
Jinsong Cinema 223
Jipin Tihui 494
Jiu Yuan 80
Jiufeng Forest Park 546
Jiuhua Spa and Resort 500
Jiumen Xiaochi **63**, 71, 96
jobs 584-593
  non-teaching 585-587
  teaching 588-591
Johns Hopkins Alumni Club of Beijing 630
Johnson Computer Connections 393, 580
Johnson-Hill, Dominic 566-567
Johnson-Hill, Dominic and Laura 550, 551
Jointek 111
joint ventures (JVs) 569
Joinway Dental Clinic 482
Jones Lang LaSalle Firm 22
Joyo.com 408
Joyside 333
Judaism. See religious services

judose 456
Jun Cheng 614
Jundushan Ski Resort 433
Junqin Hua 66
Justine's 72
Juyongguan Great Wall 271

K

K.K. Animal Hospital 664
Kagen **81**, 279
Kai Club 302
Kang Deco 380
Kangxi 234
Kangxi Grassland 556
Kaorou Ji 94
Kapok Hotel 47
karaoke. See KTV
Karolina Lehman 383
Kavenna Diamond 363
kayaking 556
Kehillat Beijing 642
Kempi Deli **68**, 105
Kempinski Hotel 48
Kerry Centre, The
　　Hotel 48
　　Kerry Sports 427, 438
　　Kerry Mall 396
Kerry EAS 656
Kerwin, Naomi 125
Kidd, David 633
KIDS 117-174
　　fun places 164-171
　　excursions 573
　　TV 225
Kids' Gallery 168
Kids' Gallery Summer Program 148
Kids Plus 155
Kindermusik Summer Camp 148
Kindermusik with Sarah 146
KindyROO International Early Childhood
　　Development 168
King & Wood PRC Lawyers 650
King Roast Duck 63
King's Dental 482
Kingdom Bike Rental 418
Kingdom Travel Beijing 511
Kingkow 151
Kinko's Copies 580
KinStar Bilingual School 143
Kiosk **68**, 96
Kishow Kids Club 168
KISS 291, **302**
Kitai 9
kites 157
KLM Royal Dutch Airline 509
Knight Frank 26
KNS 410, 434
Kokomo 279, 283, **302**, 316, 318, 320
Kong De Cai 152
Kong Yiji 67
Kookai 362
Korean Air 509

Korean Arario Gallery 190
Korean cuisine 81-82
Koryo Group Tour 510
Kro's Nest, The **82**, 103
KTV 322, 602-603
kuazi. See sidecars
Kublai Khan 10, 260
kung fu. See martial arts
Kunming Lake 236
Kuomintang 268
Kushinosato 81
Kynge, James 16-17

L

La Baie des Anges 71, **302**
La Casa Del Habano 412
La Leche League 644
La Mansarde 72
La Paleta 65
La Senza 366
La Taverne 72
La Vincci 370
lacrosse 430
Ladies' Street 283, 285
Lager, Chad 293
Lai, Leon 220
Lai Si Te Shoe Beauty Salon 367
Laitai Flower Market **400**, 660
Laitai Flower Market Basement 381
Laitai Xinda Ceramics 383
lakes 549, 555, 558
Lama Temple (Yonghegong)
　　229, **242-243**
Lan **87**, 101, 102, 291, **302**, 317, 318,
　　319
Lan Na Thai 88
landlords 29-31
language learning (Chinese) 599-616
language learning (other) 617-618
Lang Ken 353
Lang Lang 208
Lanyao 408
Lao Li 191
Lao She Teahouse **64**, 203
Laser 8000 322
Latinos 292, **302**, 319
Lau Pa Sak **87**, 99, 302
law firms 650
　　business 619
　　property 36-37
LCX Building 396
Le Bistrot Parisien **72**, 92
Le Cafe Igosso 72
Le Cool 430
Le Hugo 94
Le Petit Gourmand 391
Le Petit Paris 72
Learning Center of Beijing, The 143
Learning Center Summer Enrichment
　　Programs, The 148
leasing. See homes
Lee, Vivienne 356

Legation Quarter 232-233
Legend of the Wooden Lamp 385
Lego 155
Lehman, Lee & Xu 650
Lei Garden 65
Lemon Leaf **88**, 100
Len Len 81
Lenscrafters 360
Leo Hostel 45
Leon's Pipes Store 412
Leroy Merlin 377
Levi's 353
Leyou 153, 157
Li Jia Cai 77
Li Shan 179
Li Shaohong 220
Li Tong 555
Li Xianting 191
Li Xiaopeng 445
Li Yong 647
Li Yuan Theater 203
Li Zhenhua 187
Liangma Antique Market 388
Liangma Flower Market 400
Liangzi Sports and Fitness 495
Lianhuashan Ski Resort 433
licenses
　　driving 522-523
　　business 570
Lidai Diwang Temple 249
Lido Deli 105
Lido Hotel Pool 438
Liedtke, Jane Dr. 125
Life Shop 383, 388
Lifeline Express 640
lighting 385
Ligne Roset 381
Lihong 26
Lijia Baby 153
Lily's Antiques 388
Lily's Boutique 369
limousines 513
Lin Dan 451
Lin Zhaohua Drama Studio 201
Lin, Yang C. 212
Lindesay, William 269
Linfuxiang Fabric 399
lingerie 366
Link Step 367
Lion Mart 108
Lipson, Keith 212
Liqun Roast Duck Restaurant 63
Liquor Factory (Jiuchang) 178, **190**
libraries 624
Lisheng Sports Store 410
L'Isola 79
Little Felicio 152
Little Italy **80**, 162
Little Penang 99
Little Sheep **74**, 100
Little Suzhou Water Town 236
Little Western Heaven (Xiao Xi Tian) 261

Liu Sola 208
Liu Xiang **443**, 667
Liu Xiaodong 180, 185
Liu Yiming 347
Liuyin Park 168
Liuzheng Massage Clinic 486
Living Dance Studio 216
Lizhi Stocks 385
Loco 290, **303**
Loewe 361
Lohao City 108
Lomography 392
London School of Economics Alumni of Beijing 630
Lonely China Day 333
Long Corridor 236
Long Island Massage & Spa 497
Long Long Ago Courtyard 289, **303**
Long March 196
Long.com 368
Longevity Hill 236
Longfengshan Ski Resort 433
Longfusi Dajie 362
Longmen Children's Educational Toys 157
Longqing Gorge 556
Longqing Gorge Bungee 419
Longtan Lake Park Climbing Wall 554
Longtan Wenyuan 531
Longtanhu Climbing Center 420
Longtanhu Park 168, **432**
Longxi Wenquan Golf Club 424
Lotus in Moonlight **91**, 100
Lotus Mountain Forest Park (Lianhuashan) 556
Lotus Spa 497
Louis Vuitton 357
Loushiming Lamp Studio 385
Love Island 303
Lovely Nails 493
Lu Li 198
Lu Lu **86**, 99
Lü Shengzhong 179
Lu Xin Jiayuan 377
Lu Xun Museum 247
Luce Cafe 71, **80**
Lucheng Sports School 435
Lufthansa Airlines 510
Lufthansa Center 152, 154, 157, 396
Lugouqiao Anti-Japanese War Memorial Hall 544
Luna Lounge 278, 288, 293, **303**
Luo Zhongli 178
Lush 290, 293, **303**, 320
Lüsongyuan Hotel 47
Lycee Français de Pekin (The French School) 143
Lynx **60**, 162

M
M.A.C. 393
Ma Ke 220
Ma Liuming 181

Ma Music 338
Ma Zhongjun 200
Made in China **63**, 98
Made in China Outlet 362
Maggie's 287, 291, **303**, 457
Magic Hospital 640
Magic Rock 290, **303**
Magic Spring Temple 546
magicians 154
maids. See nannies
mail & couriers 651-652
Malls at Oriental Plaza, The 397
Mammolina Children's Home 143
man purse 355-356
Manchu Ministry of Public Works 252
Manchus 12
Mandarin 597, 598, 615
Mandarin Avenue 614
Mani's Body Combing 427
Manzo **81**, 103
Mao Dou Recording and Production Studio 657
Mao Dun's Former Residence 238
MAO Livehouse 289, 316, 318, **343**
Mao Zedong 13, 230, 231
Maple Women's Psychological Counseling Center 640
Marc Jacobs 357
Marco Polo Bridge 544
MARE 69
Marella Gallery 190, **196**
markets 400-405
Marni 357
marriage 650-651
martial arts
  kids 146
  sports 430
massage 491, 495-497, 498-499
Matsuko **81**, 98
maternity. See pregnancy
May Fourth Movement 13, 199, 230
Me To We Volunteer and Leadership Trip 149
Med, The 69
media 211
Medical Directory 476-486
medical supplies 409
medical tourism 479
Mei Lanfang 220
  residence 238
Mei Mansion 86
Mei's Lounge Professional Manicure and Pedicure 498
Meirenji 362
Melody 322
MEN Shopping Center 403
Meng Jinghui 179
Men's and Women's Lacrosse 430
mental health 480-481
Mentougou District (excursions) 549, 554
Merry Water World 168
Meshiya 81

metal music 346
Mexican Embassy Cultural Office 223
Mexican Kitchen, The **66**, 162
Mexican Wave **66**, 291
Miao Feng Zhou 497
Miao Ling 74
Miaofeng Mountain 549
Middle 8th Restaurant **95**, 99
Middle Eastern/Persian cuisine 82
Middle Way Chinese Medicine Clinic 486
Midi School of Music 622
MIkids' Multiple-Intelligence Summer Camp 149
Mikihouse 152
Milan Station 361
Mima 64
Min Jie Classical Furniture Art 389
Ming dynasty 10, 12, 61, 207, 249, 251, 254, 261, 271
Ming Dynasty City Wall Ruins Park 251
Ming Tombs 268
Ministry of Civil Affairs 124
Ministry of Finance 574
Mirch Masala 77
MIT/Sloan Alumni Club of Beijing 630
Mix 284, **303**
Miyun County (excursions) 554
MNG 356
mobile phones. See telephones
Model Operas 200, 208
modern dance 177
Modern European Design 381
Mondo Gelato Beijing 77
money 652-654
Mongols 10, 273
Monkey Business 511
Montrose Wines **111**, 643
Monument to the People's Heroes 231
Moon River Country Club Golf Club 424
Morel's **69**, 100
Mormon. See religious services
Moscow Restaurant 83
mosques 243, 643
motor sports 421
motorcycles
  buying 389
  licenses 535-537
Mou Sen 200
Mountain Bikers of Beijing (The MOB) 418, 547
Mountain Yoga 439
mountains 543, 548, 549, 554, 555, 556, 559
Move One Relocations 655, 656
movies 217-223
moving 654-656
  moving companies 655-656
  reselling 656
  storage 655
Moving Mountains 645
Mr. Magic 154
Mrs. Shanen's Bagels **68**, 108, 162

Mughal's Beijing 78
Muma 338
Muse Parisian Vietnamese Brasserie 94
Museum of Ancient Architecture 229, **262**
Museum of History 14
museums 262-268
    art 196-197
    excursions 544, 546, 559
    kids 164, 165
    pass 238
Mushi 357
music
    artists 332-337
    classical 207-214
    festivals 322. *See also* festivals
    kids 146
    metal 346
    musical instruments 405
    nightlife 279, 322-347
    practice rooms 657-658
    punk 325-326
    resources 210
    schools 622
    venues 342-344
Music Centre 398
Music Home 146
Musicacoustica 211
Muslim cuisine 94
Muslim. *See* religious services
Mustard Seed Garden 187
Mutianyu Great Wall 271
Mutianyu Village 551, 553
Muxiyuan Fabric Market 399
My Humble House 72
My Spa 500

N

Na Mu Zhuo Ma 389
Nail Plus 493
nails 492-493
Najia Xiaoguan 77
Nali Mall 403
Nam Nam 94
Nan Douya Mosque 643
Nan Mu Xiu 408
Nan Nan Nails 493
Nanjie 278, 283, 286, 287, **305**, 320
Nanluogu Xiang 289
nannies **126-130**, 473
Nanyuan Airport 509
Nanshan Ski Village 433
Nashville 285, **305**
National Art Museum of China 179, **196**
National Grand Theater 210
National Library 624
National Library Concert Hall 214
National Museum 230
National Museum of Modern Chinese Literature 265
National Theater of China, The 200
National Theater, The 260
Natural Beauty 491

nature reserves 556
Nature's Secret 381
Naxi Popo 389
NC. Style 360
Nederlandse Vereniging Peking 635
Neighborhood Chinese Club 624, **631**
Neighborhood Chinese's Happy Children Summer Camp 149
New Century International Children's Hospital 477
New China Children's Store 154, 157, 168
New Culture Movement 13, 559
New Generation Painting 180
New Get Lucky 285, **344**
New Pants 335, 338
New Trend Roller Skating World 169, **432**
New World Champion Skating Rink 430
Nightman 323
Nike Store 410
Nine West 368
Nine-Dragon Screen 261
Nirvana Fitness Center 427
Nirvana Yoga Center 410
Nirvana Yoga Global Trade Mansion Yoga 439
Nishimura 81
NIGHTLIFE 275-348
Niujie Mosque 243, 613
No Name Bar 288, 293, **305**
No Name Restaurant 71, **95**, 99
Noble Court 65
Nogabe **335**, 338
Noise 362
Noodle Loft 67
Nordic Club of China 636
Nordic Way 547
North Church (Xishiku) 643
Northern Star (Tianjin) Automobile 529
Northwest Airlines 510
NOVA Zhongguancun 397
NU2YU Baby Shop 154
Nuage 94
Nyonya Kitchen 88

O

O'mart 577
O2SUN Bookstore 391
Obelisco **66**, 292, 305
OCDF Adoption 125
Ocean Image Dive Club 432
Odds and Ends (7788) women's rugby team 422
offices (rentals) 575
Offroader 4x4 Club 421
Okaïdi 152
Old Dragon's Head 559
Old South Street 278, 280
Old Summer Palace (Yuanmingyuan) 12, 170, 234, **237**, 606
Olive, The 69
Olympic Sports Centre Paintball Strike Range 432

Olympic Sports Centre Stadium 434, 438
Olympics. *See* 2008 Beijing Games
OM Yoga 42 439
On Top 318
One East on Third 60
Onemoon 196
online shopping 408
Only 363
operas 208, 210
Operation Blessing Beijing 640
Opium War 237
optometry. *See* eye care
Orchard, The **69**, 100, 162
orchestras 177, 207, 208, **210-211**
Ordination Terrace Temple (Jietaisi) 549
organic groceries 104-105
Orient Home 377
Oriental Dragon Archery Club 432
Oriental Enterprise International Auto Plaza 529
Oriental Taipan Massage and Spa 497
Orthodox Christianity. *See* religious services
OTTO Packing & Transport Co., Ltd 655
Ou Ning 187
Our Chinese Daughters Foundation 125, **644**
OurLounge 162, 169
outdoors. *See* EXCURSIONS
Ouyang Yuqian 199
Overload 338
Overseas Chinese Network 636
Oxford and Cambridge Club, The 630
Oxford Baby Bilingual Kindergarten 143

P

Pacific Century Club 427
Pacific Century Place 154, 157, 397
paichusuo. *See* Public Security Bureau (PSB)
Pakistan Embassy College 143
Palace View Bar 292, **305**
Palette Vino **111**, 292, **305**
Palm Springs Spa 500
Pan Shiyi 647
Panino Teca **68**, 96
Panjiayuan Antique Market 389, 403
Paomo Guan 67
Papa John's 163
Paper 65
parasailing 555
Park Classic Toys 157
parks 165, 169, 170, 171, 256, **258-261**, 555
Partyworld 323
Pass By Bar 289, **306**
Pattaya Pleasures 500
Paulaner Brauhaus 73
Pavilion of Wonderful Images (Miao Xiang Ting) 261
Pavillion 284, **306**
Pazi Hot Pot City 74

Pearl Market 363
pearls 364-365
pedicab tours 239
Peekabook House 150
Pei, I.M. 259
Pekin Fine Arts 196
Peking Down Town Backpackers
    Accommodation 45
Peking Duck. See Beijing roast duck
Peking Man 545
Peking Opera Museum 255
Peking Uni International Hostel 45
Peking Union Medical College Hospital
    472, **477**
Peking University (Beida)
    200, 264, **610**
Peking University Hall **203**, 211, 214
Peking University Third Hospital 477
Peninsula Beijing 48
Peninsula Palace Beijing Shopping
    Arcade, The 397
People 8 72
People's Art Experimental Theater 203
People's Insurance Company of China
    (PICC) 530
People's Liberation Army 13
People's Theater 203
Pepper 285, 290, **306**
Perfect Vision Optometry 482
performance art 181
Peter's Tex-Mex Grill **60**, 163
pets 655, 658-664
Pet Shop and Grooming Parlour 664
Pettis, Michael 293
pharmacies 409
Phil's Pub 283, **306**
Philippe Starck 54
phones. See telephones
photocopies. See printing services
photography art 181
Phrik Thai 88
Pi'erman Maoyi 368
Piazza Cafe **73**, 163
pizza 82-83
picnics 546
Pili Pili 285, **306**
Piñatas by Mr. Zhang 154
Ping Xin Tang Clinic 486
Pinggu County (excursions) 555
Pink Loft **88**, 99
Pipe's 284, **306**, 412
Piv: 383
Pizza Buona 82
PK14 333
PLA Song and Dance Theater 203
Place, The 397
Planet Finance 640
planetariums 164
plants 400
Plastered T-shirts 152, **363**, 566-567
Platform China 196
Platform Gallery 190
playgrounds. See kids (fun places)

Plaza Business Centre at the Kerry
    Centre 575
PlecoDict 609
Poachers 457
Poachers Inn 283, **306**
Polish community 636
Political Pop (zhengzhi bopu) 180, 185
Poly Museum, The 262
Poly Theatre **203**, 210, 214
Pomegranate, The 292, **306**
Pomfret, John 633
pool (billiards) 418
pools. See swimming
Poplar Kids Republic Bookstore 150
Ports 360
Potato & Co 384
Potter's Wheel International Sports
    Center 146
Potter's Wheel International Sports
    Center Tennis Camp 149
Powerhouse Gym 428
Prada 360
pregnancy 472-473
Press Club Bar 291, **307**, 318
pressure points 465
Prevention Through Education (PTE) 640
Pride 645
Prime Pet Shop 660
Prince Chun 546
Prince Gong's Mansion 237
Princeton in Beijing (PiB) 612
printing services 577, 580
Private Kitchen No. 44 71
proMen 637
Propaganda 290, **307**, 321
property. See homes
Protestant. See religious services
Public Security Bureau (PSB) 32, 669
Pu Yi (Henry) 249, 559
Puning Temple 559
Punjabi Restaurant 78
Punk 492
punk music 325, 326
puppets 165
Pure Girl 279, 280, 281, 283, **307**, 457
Pure Lotus Vegetarian 91
Pureman 577
Purple Haze **88**, 99
Pyramid Glassware Stocks 384

Q

Q Bar 279, 283, 287, 293, **307**, 320
Qantas Airlines 510
Qi 67
Qian Cao Hua 356
Qianlong 234
Qianmen 251
Qianmen Carpet Co. 374
Qianmen Chang Gong 45
Qianxiangyi (Beijing Silk Store) 400
Qiaobo Ice and Snow World 434
Qidu 544
Qin dynasty 8, 12, 61, 207, 231, 234,

    242, 243, 244, 254
Qin Gallery 196
Qin Shihuang 8
Qinchao Fu 67
Qing Song Blind Doctor Massage 497
Qing Tombs 557
Qingnianhu Park 169
Qingqing's Stall 368
Qionghua Island 259
Qiqi Pets 660, 664
Qiseguang Baby Store 154
Qiu Ran Nail Salon 493
Qiu Xiaofei 182
QM Furniture **381**, 577
Qu Na'r 68
Qu Xiaosong 208
Quan Ju De **61**, 64
Quiksilver 356

R

Radiance 384
RAFFLES-BICT International College,
    The 621
Rainbow RC Hobby Club 422
Raj Indian Restaurant and Bar 78
real estate agencies 25-26
Recycle Band 335
Red Ball Football Club & Bar 422
Red Capital Club 77
Red Capital Club Residence 47
Red Capital Ranch 553
Red Club, The 307
Red Conch Temple (Hongluo Si) 548
Red Cross Society of China 640
Red Gate Gallery **196**, 251
Red Hero 356
Red Lantern House 45
Red Passion Folks Arts Gallery 378
Red Phoenix, The 360
Red Rain Dance Supplies 410
Red Rock Bar 290, **308**
Red Rose 99
Redmoon 292, **308**
Reflector 335
Reggio 290, **308**
registration
    business 569
    PSB 32
    cars 529
Regus Instant Offices 575
relics inspection 654-655
religious services 642-643
relocation firms 655-656
Renda Middle School and
    High School 144
Rendinghu Park 256
Renewal Spa Club 500
Renmin University of China (Renda)
    211, **610**
rental
    bikes 537
    cars 531
    home 22-24, 28-34

offices 575
Restaurant Directory 57-95
　family-friendly 160-164
Re-TROS 333
Rhema 656
Rhesus negative 467
Ricci, Matteo 207
Rickshaw, The 283, 286, 293, **308**, 316
Rikai.com 609
Ritan Hotel South Building 404
Ritan Office Building 404
Ritan School 144
Ritz-Carlton Beijing, Financial Street 48
Ritz-Carlton Spa 500
River of Grace Church, The 644
rivers 554
roast duck. See Beijing roast duck
Robert H. Smith Executive MBA
　Program 619
Roca 377
rock climbing 544
rock music 324
Rockland 398
roller skating 432
Rong Xin Tailor and Boutique 369
Rotary Club of Beijing 634
Rouge Baiser 384
Round Altar, The 241-242
Round City 260
Rousseau, Paul 369
Royal Furniture 381
rugby 431
Ruifuxiang 400
Ruins Band 335, 338
Rumi **82**, 163
running 431
Rutgers Alumni of Beijing 630
Rutgers EMBA Program 619
RVs 531

S

Sa Lang Bang 82
Saga Youth Hostel 45
sailing 418
Sakyamuni Buddha 260
salons 490-491
Salsa Caribe 283, **308**
Salud 289, **308**
Salvation Army 640
Sam Cinema 223
Samling/Tufenkian 374
Sampan Seafood 65
San Shi Zhai Kite Store 157
San Wei Bookstore 391
sandwich shops 68
Sandy Nailspa 493
Sanfo 410, 547
Sangria Bar 285, **308**
Sanlian Taofen Bookstore 391
Sanlitun Area 279, 283
Sanlitun Bar Strip 283, **308**
Sanlitun Kindergarten 144

Santa Fe 656
SAS 510
Saveurs de Coree **82**, 98
Scandinavian Furniture 577
Scar Art (shanghen yishu) 178
Schenker DB Logistics 656
Schiller's 73
Schindler's Anlegestelle 73
Schindler's German Food Center
　108, 321
scholarships 604
Scholl 368
schools
　Chinese 599-616
　kids 131-144
　non-lanugage 619-623
　other languages 617-618
　TCM 370
　universities 607-610
School House at Mutianyu, The 169
scooters 535-536
scuba diving 432
Sculpting in Time **64**, 163
SDM Dental 482
Sea of Mercy 91
Second Hand Rose 338
Second Opium War 559
secondhand clothing 366-367
Selective Mutism Virtual Support
　Network (SMVSN) 644
Senli & Mae 370
Senses **73**, 103, 163
Sephora 393
Sequoia Bakery and Cafe **64**, 96, 312
Serenity Spa 500
Servcorp 575
Serve the People **88**, 99
serviced apartments 22
Seven Colors 308
sex 483
Sex Store, The 366
SFI Luxury Boutique 360
SGA Junior Golf Coaching 145
Shanghai cuisine 83, 86-87
Shan Tianfang 647
Shang dynasty 234
Shang Gu City Classical Furniture and
　Arts Center 381
Shangfang Mountain and Yunshui Cave
　543
Shanghai Airline 510
Shanghai Symphony 207
Shanghai Tang 360
Shangmei Ice Skating 430
Shangri-La Hotel 48
Shanhaiguan 559
Shantung Silk 400
Shard Box 366
Sheerwood Beijing Equestrian Country
　Club **428**, 664
Shelcore Toys 157
Shenghua Universal Golf Advisors
　(SGA) 424

Shengli Cinema 223
Shengtangxuan 157
Shi Zhiyong 450
Shichahai Sports School 418
Shidu Ju Ma Fun Park 419
Shidu Scenic Area 544
Shijinglong Ski Resort 434
Shijingshan Amusement Park 170
Shijingshan District (excursions) 555
Shilihe Lighting Market 385
Shin Kong Place 397
shoes 368-368
Shoestring Travel 670
Shooters 279, 283, **308**, 320
shooting **432**, 543
shopping centers 396-398
SHOPPING 349-414
Shopping Directory 353-405
　kids 150-157
Shoudu Shidai Cinema 223
Shouqi Car Rental 531
shows. See ART & CULTURE
Shuang An Supermarket 108
Shuangren Yizhan 537
Shuangyushu Fashion Street 363
Shunfeng Express 652
Si Chou Lu 65
Sichuan Restaurant 237
Side Park 170
sidecars 535-537
Siegel, Frank and Jennifer 312-313
SIGHTSEEING 227-274
siheyuan. See courtyards
Sihui Jiancai Cheng 377
Silicon Valley Computer City 393
Silk Hair Studio 492
Silk Market 404
Silver Fox Cave (Yin Hu Dong) 543
Silver Jewelry 366
Silver Mountain Pagoda Forest
　(Yinshantalin) 543
Simatai Great Wall 271
Simba International Hair Dressing Salon
　492
Simonds, Nina 633
Singapore Airlines 510
Singaporean, Malaysian & Indonesian
　cuisine 87-88
Singing Dragon, The 384
Sino Bright School (Beijing No. 25
　Middle School) 144
Sino-Chu 292, **308**
Sinofile 580
Sino-Japanese Youth Center 438
SinoScuba 146, **432**
SinoSolutions 580
Sino-Swiss Hotel 48
Sirva Relocation 656
Six, Olivier 293
Siyuanqiao Auto Accessory City 529
skateboarding 432
ski clubs 434
skiing **432-434**, 547, 555

Sky Outdoors 411
Sky Pool Valley (Tianchi Xiagu) 549
SLD (Sulede) 290, **308**
Sleepy Inn 45
Small West Lake (Xiaoxihu) 549
Smallville 163
Smart Health Medical & Dental Center 482
smartcards (transportation) 516
Snake Pit 657
Snapline 333
Snow Favor 411, **434**
Snow World Ski Park 434
soccer. See football 422
softball 434
Sogo Department Store 154, 397
Soho New Town Cinema 222
Soka Art Centre/ Soka Modern 197
Solaris Tanning Studio 494
Song dynasty 9, 254
Song Kun 182
Soong Ching Ling's Former Residence 237
Song Tang Zhai Museum of Traditional Chinese Folk Carving 229, **262**
Songshan Nature Reserve 556
Songzhuang 177, 180, **190-191**
Sony ExploraScience 170
Sorabol **82**, 98
Souk **82**, 285, **308**
Sound of Universe 398
Source, The 87
South Beauty **87**, 99
South Gate Space 203, 214
South German Bakery, Cafe Konstanz and Bodenseestube 109
South Silk Road **95**, 99, 185
Soviet Realism 180
spas 496-497, 547
Spa Chi, The 497
Spa de Feng for Men Only 501
Spin Ceramics 384
Splash Recreation Club 170, **438**
SPORTS & FITNESS 415-462
    equipment 409
    kids 145-149
Sports 100 411
Sports Beijing 145
Sports Beijing Morning Tennis Camp 149
Sports Beijing Sports & Soccer Summer Camp 149
Sports Street 411
Spring Festival 158, **254**
squash 431
Squash Ladder Club 431
St. David's Society of Beijing 636
St. Joseph's (East Church – Dongtang) 643
St. Michael's (Dongjiaomin Church) 643
St. Regis Beijing, The **48**, 318
St. Regis Spa & Club 428, **438**, 501
Stanford Business School Alumni Association 630
Stanford University Alumni 630

Star City 221
Star Gallery 190, 197
Star Live, The 292, 321, **344**
Star Trooper Laser Tag 432
Stars, The 178
Steiff 157
Steinway and Sons 408
Stellar International Cineplex 221
Still Thoughts Vegetarian Restaurant 91
STO Express 652
Stone Boat Cafe 96, 291, 317, 318, **344**, 457
Stone Moving Service 656
storage 655
street food 90
students 599-406
Studio of the Tranquil Heart, The 261
Stupa Park 554
Su Yang 334
SUBS **333**, 336-337
subways 518-519
Sui dynasty 8, 244
suicide prevention 480-481
Sukhothai 88
summer camps 148-149
Summer Palace (Yiheyuan) 170, **234-236**, 547
Summergate Wines 111
Sun Village 641
Sun Yaoting 249
Sun Yat-sen 259
Sunniwell City Karting Club 422
Sunny Baby Kids' Clothing 152
Sunny Dental Care 482
Sunny Gold Street Market 404
Sunny Ray Dance Company 421
Sunplace Sports & Fitness 430, **439**
Sunset Grill 284, **308**
Sunshine Learning Center 144
Sunshine Nails 493
Sunstyle 381
Sunwind Outdoor 411
Super 8 Hotel 46
Super Bar Street 285
Super Bra 366
Super Moverz 146
Superwing Paragliding Club 422
Sure Save 108
Sureline Design & Construction 377, 400
Surface 356
Suzie Wong. See World of Suzie Wong Club, The
Swami Ding 514
Swarovski 366
Swartz, Leslie 633
SWEA Beijing 636
Swedish Chamber of Commerce In China 576
Swedish School Beijing 144
swimming
    excursions 549, 554, 555
    kids 146, 167, 168
sports 435-438

Swiss Air 510
Swiss Chinese Chamber of Commerce (SwissCham Beijing) 576
Swiss Road Hotel 47

T

T.O.T.S. 157
Tafi 73
Tag Team Records 340, 341
Tai Bo Tian Fu Shan Zhen 74
Tai Chi Workshop 431
tailoring 369-371
Taipei Language Institute (TLI) 614
Taj Pavilion, The **78**, 98
Tam, Vivienne 360
Tammy's Framing Shop 378
Tan Dun 208, 209
Tan, Allan 22
Tandoor, The 78
Tang Contemporary Gallery 197
Tang dynasty 8, 9, 244
Tang Dynasty (band) 325, 338, 347
Tango 284, 292, **308**, 323
TangoRen 421
Tangyun Tailor 370
tanning 493-494
Taobao.com 409
Taoism 249, 244
Taoranting Park 170
Tasty Taste 65
Tathagata Hall 248
tattoos 494
Tattoo Artist Alliance 494
taxes
    business 570
    car 529
    property 36
taxis 4, 513-515, 531
TCM. See Traditional Chinese Medicine
Tea Street 412
Teacher Development Forum (TDF) 634
teaching. See jobs
tea **114-115**, 412
technical support 580
TeeTime Golf 424
telephones 664-667
Temple of Divine Light 555
Temple of Heaven (Tiantan) 240
    park 170
Temple of the God of Taishan Mountain 249
Temple of the Origin of the Dharma (Fayuan Si) 244
Temple of the Poor and the Wild Mulberry (Tanzhesi) 554
Temple/Tsinghua Universities Master of Laws Program 620
temples 229, **240-249**, 259, 543, 548, 549, 554, 555, 559, 642
Ten Crossings (Shidu) 544
Ten Fu's Tea 412
tennis
    kids 146, 170

sports 438
Tennis Fans Club 438
Terra Proxyma 580
TGI Friday's 163
Thai cuisine 88
Thai International 510
Thailand 479
that's Beijing 2007 Reader Bar & Club Awards 315-321
that's Beijing's 2007 Reader Restaurant Awards 97-103
Theater Directory 199, **202-203**, 631
Things of the Jing 366
Thinking Hands 197
threads 399-400
Three Guizhou Men 68
Tiamo Italia 77
Tian Chi 94
Tian Shan Pai 94
Tian Yi Eunuch Tomb 556
Tian Yu Fish Market 662
Tian Zhuangzhuang 220
Tian'anmen Gate 230
Tian'anmen Square 14, **230**
Tianchu Miaoxiang 91
Tiandi Yijia 77
Tianhe Liangzi 497
Tianjin (excursions) 559
Tianjin Airport 508
Tianlang Hot Air Balloon Club 422
Tianqiao Acrobatics Theater **203**, 204, 214
Tiantan Park 170
Tianyi Kung Fu Club 431
Tianyin 658
Tianyu Market 157
Tianyuan Law Firm 650
Tibet Shop 389, 412
Tibetan 242, 244, 245
Tibetan (shopping) 412
tickets 519-521, **667**
Tiffany & Co. 366
Tiger Sports 411
Tigerway Golf & Fashion Store Chains 411
Time Cafe 69
Timezone 8 Bookstore 392
Tim's Texas Roadhouse 285, **309**
TNT Skypak 652
tobacco products 412
Today Art Museum 197
TEFL (Teaching English as a Foreign Language) 592
Together 291, **309**
Tom Lee Music 146, **408**
Tom's DVD Shop 398
Tom's Tailor Shop 370
tombs 258, 546, 556, 557
Tongjiao Temple 249
Tongren Hospital 477
Tongzhi Studies 637
Toni & Guy 492
Tony Studio 492

Top Cellar 111
Top Club – Yang Yuan Tang Foot Massage 497
Top Electronics City 378
TOPS Shoe Beauty Salon 367
Torana Gallery 374
Torres 111
Tot to Teen **153**, 157
Touch 288, **309**
Touch Spa 501
Tower for Observing the Moon 243
Towers Offices at Oriental Plaza, The 575
toys 154-157
trademarks (business) 571, 574
Traders Cafe 88
Traditional Chinese Medicine 469, 484-486, 598, 620
traffic 441, 505
trains 519-521
Traktirr Pushkin **83**, 163
translation services 580
TRANSPORTATION 503- 538
travel agents 510-511
Treasure House 366
Treaty of Peking 237
Tree, The **82**, 100, 101, 283, **309**, 316, 318, 319
Trek Bicycle 390, 412
TRIBEIJING 431
trick-biking 432
Tsinghua University 610
Tsinghua University Outdoor Swimming Pool 438
Tsinghua-INSEAD Dual Degree Executive MBA Programme 620
Tuanjiehu Park
 kids 170
 sports 432
Tuanjiehu Pool 438
TUI China Travel Co. Ltd. 511
TV 218-219, **224-225**

U

UC Berkeley Alumni Association of Beijing 630
UCLA Beijing Club 630
UFE-Union des Français de l'Etranger 636
UIBE 599
UME International Cineplex 221
UNC Alumni Club China 630
Underground City 265
UNICEF 641
United Airlines 510
Universal Studios 197
Universal Theater 203-204
University College London (UCL) Alumni 630
University Directory 607-610
University of International Business and Economics (UIBE, Jingmao or Duiwai) 610
University of Maryland/Robert H. Smith School of Business Alumni Association 630
University of Notre Dame Alumni Club 630
University of Pennsylvania Club of Beijing 630
University of Texas McCombs Business School Alumni Association 630
University of Toronto Alumni Group 630
University of Virginia Club 630
University of Washington Alumni 630
University Rock Climbing Hall 420
UPS 652
urban explorers 266-267
US-China Business Council 576
USEFUL INFO 627-674
utilities 32
Utopia Asia 637

V

V/A 338
V2 367
Vairocana Buddha 248
Vajra 492
valleys 549, 554
Vanilla Garden 91
vans 531
vegetarian cuisine 88-94
Verve Wellness Art 428
veterinarians 662-664
Vics 284, **309**, 317, 319
Victor's Place and Curry House 78
video art 181
Vietnam Airlines 510
Vietnamese cuisine 94
Villa Lifestyle 384
villages 544, 549, 551, 556
villas 23
Vincent Cafe/Creperie **72**, 163
Vineyard Cafe **69**, 71
Visa Office of the Ministry of Foreign Affairs of the PRC (Hong Kong) 670
visas 601, **668-670**
Vision Infinity 360
Vita 381
Viv International Medical Beauty Clinic 482
Voodoo Kungfu 347

W

W Dine & Wine 69
Wa Wa Pet Hospital 664
wallets 361
Wal-Mart 385
Wan Xiaoli 334
Wanda Cinema 221
Wande Photo Equipment 392
Wanfangting Park 170
Wang Bin 346
Wang Guangyi 180
Wang Liqin 448
Wang Qingsong 191

Wang Yue 344
Wangfujing Bookstore 392
Wangfujing Department Store 398
Wangfujing Foreign
    Languages Bookstore 392
    kids 150
Wangfujing Musical Instrument City 408
Wangfujing Pharmaceutical Store 409
Wangfujing Slingshot 420
Wangfujing Xinhua Bookstore 151
Wanghong Veterinary Hospital 664
Wangjing Veterinary Hospital 664
Wanlong Ski Resort 434
Wansha Cashmere Store 400
Wanyou Antique Furniture 389
Warehouse 190
Warlord Period 13
Warring States Period 8-9
water bottles 395
waterfalls 549, 554
Watson's 396, 409
Wawu **81**, 96
Wayne's 356
weddings 370
weekend excursions 558-559
Wei Liang, Diana 633
Wellesley College Alumni Association 630
Wen Hui 216
Wenjin Hotel 48
Wenlin 609
West Church (Xizhimen) 643
West Wing Bar 292, **309**, 311
WestChina 547
Westcoast Bathing Centre 501
Western Academy of Beijing 144
Westin Beijing Financial Street 48
WFOEs. *See* wholly foreign owned
    enterprises
Whale Baby Clothing 153
Whampoa Club 54, **63**, 71
What? Bar 292, **344**
White Cloud Temple (Baiyun Guan) 244
White Dagoba (Baita Si) 10
White Nights 83
White River (Baihe) 554
White Space 190, **197**
wholly foreign owned enterprises
    (WFOEs) 569
Wild Children 338
WildChina 511, 547
windsurfing 418
wineries 547
wines 106, 107, 110-112, 278, 305, 312
Wing Chun Kung Fu Class 431
Wins Arts and Framing 378
wireless internet. *See* internet
Wo Ai Wo Jia 26
Wonderful Electronic Shopping Mall 393
Wonderland 266
Woo, John 220
Wood, Frances 633
Workers' Gymnasium 214, **435**

Workers' Stadium
    art 203, 214
    nightlife 284
    sports 435, 438
Workstation Arts Center 216
World Care Pets 655
World Health Store 428
World of Suzie Wong Club, The 279,
    285-6, **310**, 316-320, 457
World Park 170
World War II 13
Writers Bar 292, **310**
writing. *See* jobs
Wu Guanzhong 178, 185
Wu Hao 336-337
Wu Tianming 219
Wu Xin Zhai Carpet Store 374
Wudaokou 283, 290
Wudaokou Clothing Market 404
Wudaokou Workers' Club Cinema 223
WWF 641

X

X'Change Bar 292, **310**
Xi Gongjiang Hutong 247
Xi'an Film Factory 219
Xiangjiang Mingcheng 74
Xiangyang Xiaozhu 91
Xiao Fu Xing 153
Xiao He 334
Xiao Lu 179
Xiao Rong 345
Xiao Shan Cheng 74
Xiao Wang Fu **63**, 163
Xiao Xiao Niao (Little Bird) 641
Xiapo Mosque 643
Xicheng
    nightlife 292
    sightseeing 246
Xicheng Workers' Culture Cinema 223
Xidan Books Building 392
Xidan Outdoor Market 404
Xidan Science & Technology Shopping
    Mall 405
Xidan Shopping Center 398
Xie Xingfang 451
Xihe Yaju 164
Xijiao Auto Accessory Market 529
Xin Bar 288, **310**
Xin Dong Cheng Space For
    Contemporary Art 197
Xin Rong Theater 203
Xin Yue Xing Cheng Massage Center 497
Xinde Chinese Clothing Shop 356
Xing Mu Handcraft 385
Xingfu Mama (Happy Mother) 154
Xinhua Post DVD Shop 399
Xinjiang & Muslim cuisine 94
Xinjiang Islam Restaurant 93, **94**, 99
Xinjiang Red Rose 94
Xinjiekou Cinema 223
Xinjishi 86

Xinmin Film Company in Shanghai 218
Xinxingguang Audio Shop 378
Xiushui 2 (east) 405
Xiushui 2 (west) 405
Xiushui Fuzhuang Shichang. *See* Silk
    Market
Xu Beihong 229
    Museum 262
Xu Bing 179
Xu Xiang Zhai Vegetarian Restaurant 94
Xu's Antique Carpets 374
Xuan Zhuan 408, 658
Xuancaotang 291, **310**
Xuanlong Pool Hall 418
Xuanwu Hospital Pain Treatment Center
    477
Xuanwumen Church (South Church –
    Nantang) 643
Xue Chen 453

Y

Yale Club of Beijing 630
Yan Club Art Centre 197
Yan Kit-So 633
Yandai Xiejie 363
Yang Quanren 61
Yang Shaobin 180, 191
Yangrou Hutong 366
Yanhuang TCM Clinic 486
Yanqing County (excursions)556-557
Yansha Outlets 405
yaogun. See rock & roll
Yard, The 88
Yashow 3066 370
Yashow Market 153, 368, **405**
Yashow Market Tailors 370
YCIS Summer Experience in China 149
Yen party organizers 294-295
Ye Shan Jun Wild Fungus House 74
Ye Xiaogang 208
Ye Zhi Feng 377
Yellow River Cantata 208
Yesasia.com 392
Yew Chung International School 144
Yi Bag 361
Yicitang 494
Yingbeigou Village 551
Yingxie Cinema 223
Yingxiong 412
Yishikang Eyeglass Company 361
Yiya Pet Store and Hospital 662
YMCA. *See* Beijing YMCA Fitness Center
yoga 439
Yoga Club 439
Yoga Yard 412, **439**
Yongfu Temple 557
Yonghegong. *See* Lama Temple
Yongle Emperor 10, 229
Yongzheng 557
Yotsuba **81**, 98
Young Choreographers Project 216
Youth Palace 323
Youyi Youth Hostel 46

INDEX 691

YSO Dance Studio 421
Yu Chen Hand Painting Store 356
Yu Hong 179, 182
Yu Long 210
Yu Xin 87
Yuan dynasty
    10, 236, 243, 244, 249, 259, 260
Yuan Dynasty Bar Street 278, **310**
Yuan Shikai 13
Yuanlin Golf Club 424
Yuanmingyuan Village 179
Yue Fu Zhai 381
Yue Minjun 180, 191
Yuebin Restaurant 62, **63**
Yuexiu Clothing Market 405
Yugong Yishan 279, 292, 318, **344**
Yuming Banjia 656
Yunfoshan Ski Resort 434
Yunnan cuisine 94-95
Yunnan Impression 95
Yunshui Caves 543
Yunshuige 356
Yunteng Shifu 93, **95**
Yuquanying Flower Market 400
Yuxiang Renjia **87**, 99
Yuyuantan Park 170
Yves Delorme 385

Z

Zang Han Zhai Carpet Gallery 374
Zara 356
Zemo Elysée 360
Zen Spa 501
Zeta Bar 292, **310**, 317
Zhang Chu 338
Zhang Dali 180, 186
Zhang Guozheng 450
Zhang Huan 181
Zhang, Rebecca 580
Zhang Shichuan 218
Zhang Xiaogang 180
Zhang Yimou 177, 219, 220, 647
Zhang Yining 449
Zhang Ziyi 220
Zhangwang Hutong 278
Zhao Bandi 181
Zhaoling Tomb 268
Zhaolong Hotel 48
Zhaolong Int'l Youth Hostel 46
Zhejiang Pearl Shop 366
Zheng Zhengqiu 218
Zhengren Shoe Shop 367
Zhengyici Theater 203
Zhihua Temple 245, 254
Zhiyin Wanli Instruments 408

Zhong Breizh 636
Zhong Wu 412
Zhongguancun 609
Zhongguancun Bookstore 392
Zhongguancun Mall 398
Zhonghai Computer Market 393
Zhongshan Park 171
Zhongshu Grand Forest Flower Trade Market 400
Zhongwen.com 609
Zhou dynasty 8, 234
Zhou Enlai 231, 237
Zhou Jielun 647
Zhou Long 208
Zhou Xun 647
Zhou, Andy 355
Zhoukoudian Peking Man Museum 544
Zhu Yuanzhang 10
Zi Yue 338
Ziguang Cinema 223
Ziran Dongli Wind/Kite Surfing School 419
Ziyo 335
Ziyunshan Mountain 549
Zizaoshe Design 381
Zizhuyuan Park 171
ZOOMFLIGHT 405
zoos. See kids (fun places)

LEGEND

Art Galleries

Bars & Clubs

Cafes & Teahouses

Cinemas & Theaters

For Kids

Grocery Stores

Hair Salons

Hospitals & Clinics

Hostels & Hotels

Massage & Spas

Other

Restaurants

Schools & Universities

Shops & Boutiques

Sightseeing Spots

Sports & Fitness

Villas

693 INDEX

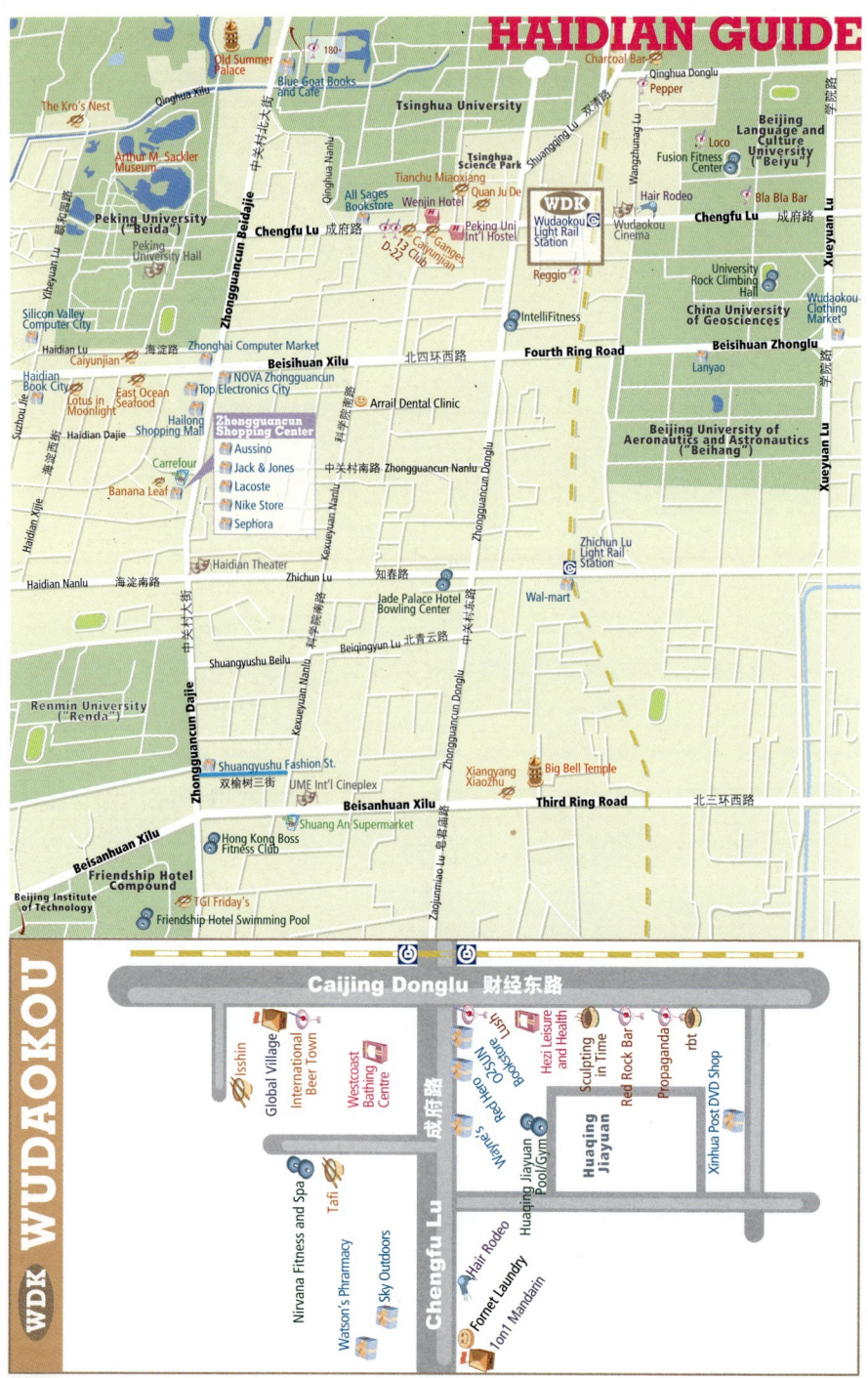

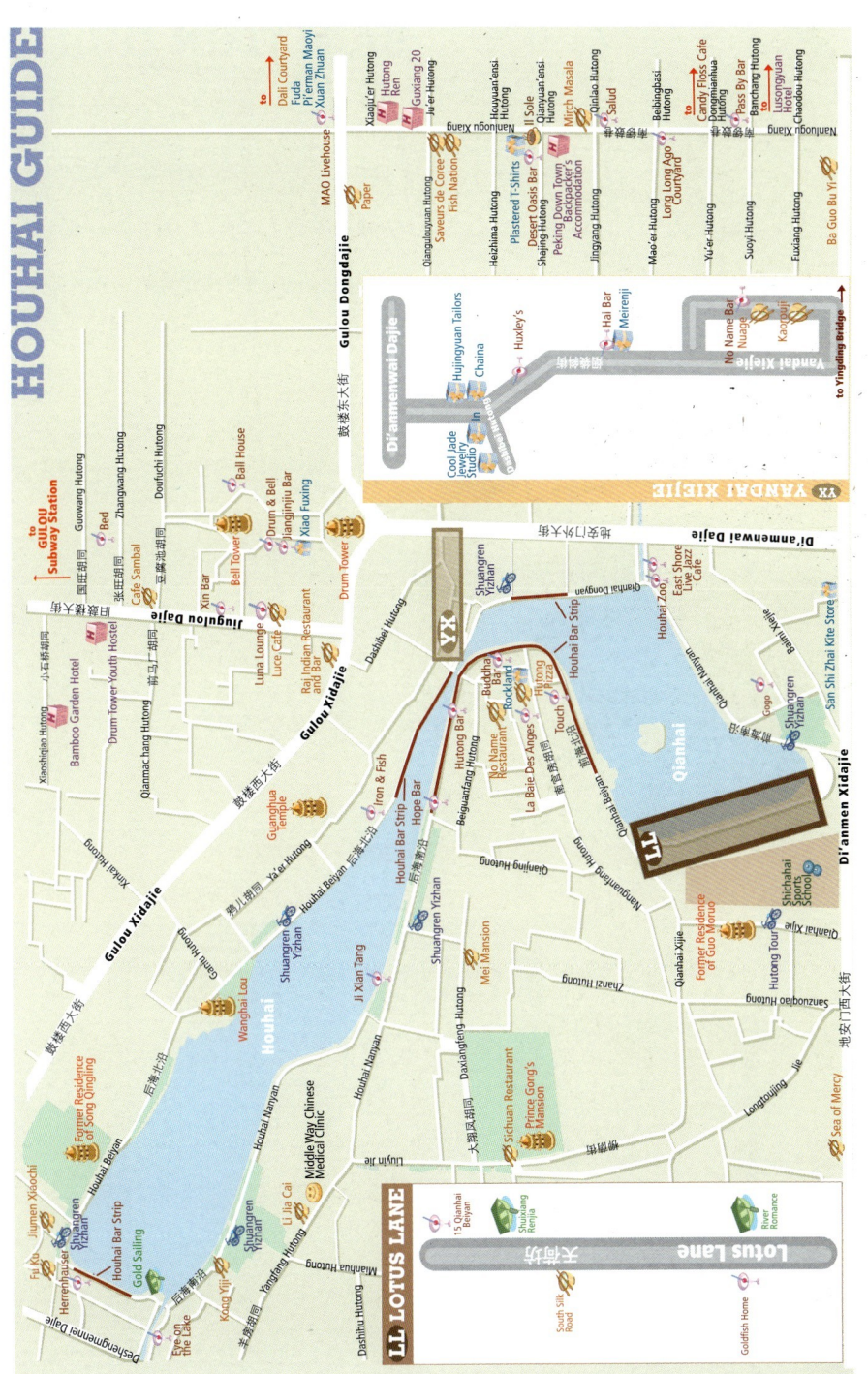

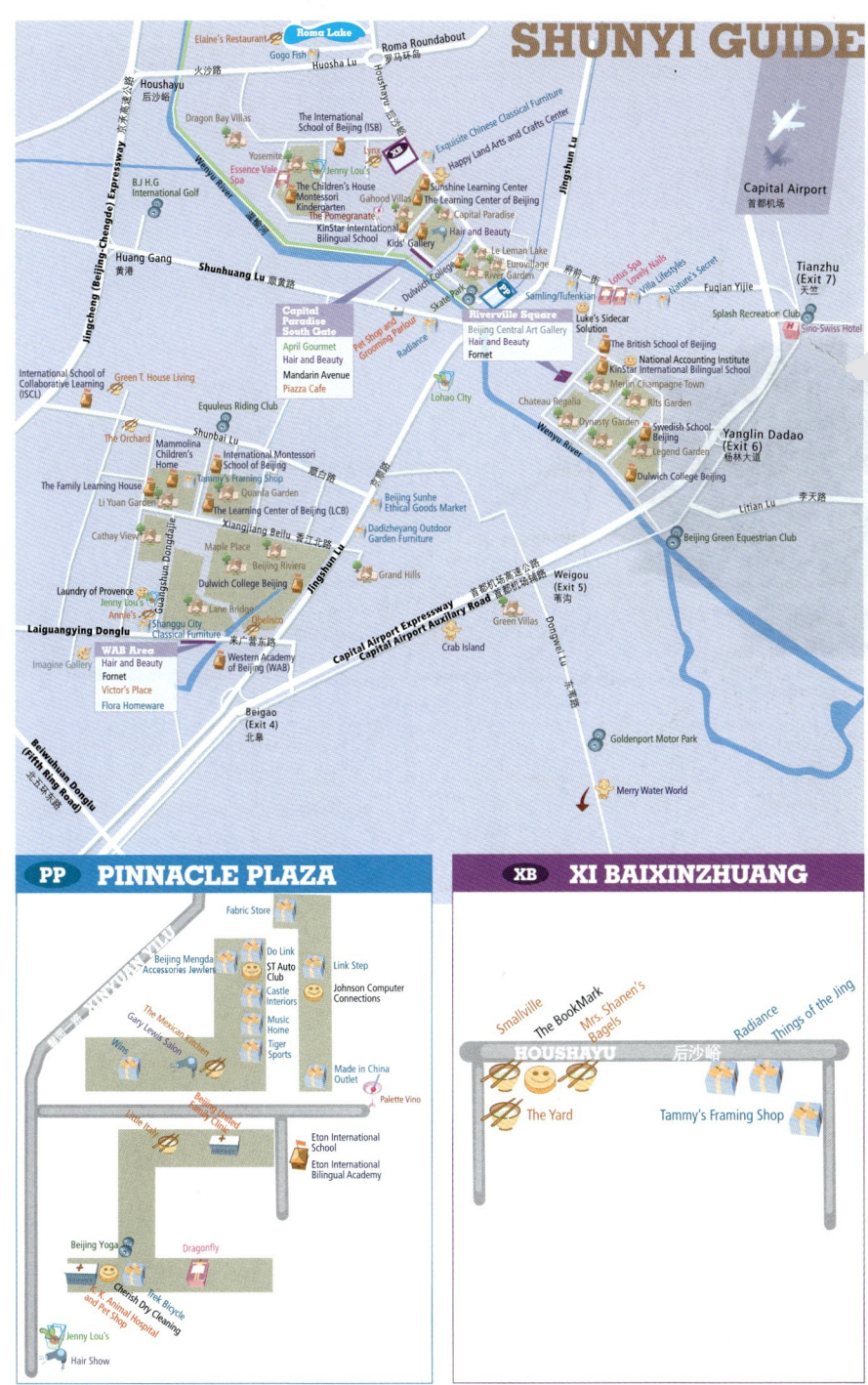